The Student Guide 2007

Published by Chambers and Partners Publishing
(a division of Orbach & Chambers Ltd)
23 Long Lane, London EC1A 9HL
Tel: (020) 7606 1300 Fax: (020) 7600 3191
email: info@ChambersandPartners.co.uk
www.ChambersandPartners.com
Our thanks to the many students, trainees, pupils,
solicitors, barristers and graduate recruitment personnel
who assisted us in our research. Also to Chambers and
Partners' recruitment team for their knowledge and
assistance and to the researchers of *Chambers UK 2007*
from which all firm rankings are drawn.

Publisher: Michael Chambers
Managing Editor: Fiona Boxall
Editor: Anna Williams
Deputy Editor: Michael Lovatt
Writers: Adam Betts, Angela Morris, Hannah McCarthy,
Helen Lyle, Ify Okoye, James Plummer, Joanna Mason,
Katie Cooke, Louise Carr, Rav Casely Gera, Russell Bramley
Editorial assistant: Joanne Grote
Database: Andrew Taylor
A-Z Co-ordinator: Francesca Parker
Production: John Osborne
Business Development Manager: Brad D. Sirott
Business Development Team: Neil Murphy,
Richard Ramsay
Proofreaders: Alison Woodhead, James Randall,
Jennifer Gallagher, John Bradley, John Quick,
Nicholas Widdows, Sally McGonigal, Sarah Weise
Printed by: William Clowes Ltd, Beccles, Suffolk

so you want to be a lawyer...

We've written this book to give you the information, tools and confidence to help you make a sound career decision.

The Student Guide is the only publication to offer these three key ingredients:

- The True Picture: an insight into the training schemes at 150 law firms, based on in-depth interviews with hundreds of trainees. The trainees were selected by us, not by their law firms, and they to us spoke freely and frankly under the protection of anonymity.

- Chambers Reports: a look at life inside more than 50 barristers chambers in London and the regions. These reports were written after visits to each of the sets and interviews with pupils, barristers and clerks.

- Ranking Tables: covering law firms and chambers in all parts of England and Wales and a wide spectrum of practice areas. These are reproduced with the permission of *Chambers UK*, the well-known guide to the legal profession.

All the books we publish have one thing in common – they are independent. In a market flooded with publications for law students we take great pride in this fact. No one can buy an editorial feature and no one's money influences what we say about them.

This book could be the most useful thing you read this year and we wish you great success for your future career.

The Student Guide team
September 2006

CONTENTS

first steps

a-z unis & law schools 55

solicitors

www.chambersandpartners.co.uk

the true picture

why do all law firm recruitment brochures look the same? the true picture is the antidote. it is the product of six months spent interviewing hundreds of trainees and newly qualified solicitors at 150 firms in england and wales. we asked them to tell us about their training contracts in their own words... and they did!

a-z solicitors   593

the phone numbers, addresses and e-mails you need to make your applications. plus loads of really useful facts and figures on the top law firms. all in simple, easy-to-follow a-z format

barristers

chambers reports   767

impeneterable, incomprehensible and in another world... it's too easy to stereotype the bar. we banged on the doors of 53 chambers across the country to have a nose around and quiz the inhabitants

a-z barristers   881

details of some of the leading pupillages

 **STUDENT GUIDE**

november
2006

1	**law fair:** university of sussex
	training contract deadline: wollastons (2008)
2	**law fair:** qmu, london
3	**law fair:** university of east anglia
6	**law fair:** university of leeds
7	**law fair:** university of leeds
8	**law fair:** cardiff university hull university
9	**law fair:** university of reading
10	**vacation scheme deadline:** lovells (christmas)
11	**law fair:** university of oxford
14	**law fair:** university of leicester
15	**law fair:** university of liverpool lse university of bristol queen's university, belfast
	vacation scheme deadline: herbert smith (christmas)
16	**law fair:** lse; university of southampton university of bristol
17	**vacation scheme deadline:** clifford chance (winter) cms cameron mckenna
20	**law fair:** university of newcastle-upon-tyne
21	**law fair:** university of durham university of warwick
22	**law fair:** university of birmingham
23	**law fair:** university of manchester
	vacation scheme deadline: bristows (christmas)
24	**vacation scheme deadline:** denton wilde sapte (christmas)
27	**law fair:** ucl
28	**law fair:** ucl
29	**law fair:** university of sheffield
30	**law fair:** university of cambridge (solicitors)

december
2006

31	**training contract deadline:** vertex law

Nadia Shahbazi
Trainee, Addleshaw Goddard, Manchester

"I thoroughly enjoyed the LPC. It prepared me for life in Commercial Law, with its emphasis on developing business acumen and focus on providing practical solutions.

BPP's Law School in Leeds was centrally located and offered an impressive range of facilities. The course was well structured and the professional, supportive tutors delivered a high standard of teaching.

Overall I felt that BPP offered a well-rounded package and gave a good grounding for my training contract."

LAW SCHOOL

CALENDAR OF EVENTS

january 2007

12
vacation scheme deadline:
skadden arps

17
law fair:
university of exeter

19
vacation scheme deadline:
freshfields · allen & overy
training contract deadline:
allen & overy (gdl)

23
law fair:
kings college, london

24
law fair:
kings college, london

26
vacation scheme deadline:
dundas & wilson · slaughter and may
pannone · dorsey & whitney

31
training contract deadline:
bristows (feb interviews)

vacation scheme deadline:
addleshaw goddard · lawrence graham
allen & overy · lewis silkin
ashurst · lovells
baker & mckenzie · manches
barlow lyde & gilbert · mcgrigors
berwin leighton paisner · norton rose
bird & bird · olswang
clifford chance · osborne clarke
clyde & co · pinsent masons
davenport lyons · reed smith/richards butler
dla piper · sj berwin
dmh stallard · simmons & simmons
eversheds · taylor wessing
farrer & co · tlt solicitors
field fisher waterhouse · travers smith
hammonds · white & case
herbert smith (summer) · withers
jones day (easter & summer) · wragge & co
latham & watkins

february 2007

1
law fair:
university of cambridge (barristers)

9
vacation scheme deadline:
capsticks · denton wilde sapte

10
vacation scheme deadline:
nabarro nathanson

11
vacation scheme application deadline:
hbj gateley wareing

14
vacation scheme deadline:
cleary gottlieb · ince & co
holman fenwick & willan · weil, gotshal & manges

15
vacation scheme deadline:
king

16
vacation scheme deadline:
cms cameron mckenna · stephenson harwood
speechly bircham

18
training contract deadline:
baker & mckenzie (non-law)

19
vacation scheme deadline:
dechert

23
vacation scheme deadline:
mccormicks · watson farley & williams

28
vacation scheme deadline:
bristows (easter and summer) · shadbolt & co
covington & burling · shoosmiths
dickinson dees · walker morris
kendall freeman · ward hadaway
macfarlanes · wedlake bell
reynolds porter chamberlain

march 2007

1	**vacation scheme deadline:**
	mills & reeve trowers & hamlins

15	**vacation scheme deadline:**
	forsters mishcon de reya

30	**vacation scheme deadline:**
	taylor walton

31	**vacation scheme deadline:**
	bevan brittan laytons
	coffin mew & clover lester aldridge
	foot anstey penningtons
	government legal service pricewaterhousecoopers
	halliwells thomas eggar
	hill dickinson

april 2007

27	**vacation scheme deadline:**
	pannone (summer) morgan cole

30	**vacation scheme deadline:**
	howes percival

june 2007

30	**training contract deadline:**
	bp collins ibb

> "BPP's Careers Service was invaluable and helped me secure a training contract before I even started the GDL"
>
> Ruth Stone,
> former GDL and LPC Student

Tel: 0845 070 2882
Email: lawadmissions@bpp.com
Web: www.bpp.com/law

july 2007

13	**training contract deadline:**
	blake lapthorn linnell hill dickinson
	cobbetts

15	**training contract deadline:**
	watson burton

27	**training contract deadline:**
	mccormicks trethowans

28	**training contract deadline:**
	sidley austin

30	**training contract deadline:**
	davenport lyons taylor walton
	finers stephen innocent

31	**training contract deadline:**

addleshaw goddard	foot anstey
asb law	forbes
ashurst	freeth cartwright
baker & mckenzie (law)	freshfields
barlow lyde & gilbert	gov. legal service
berwin leighton paisner	halliwells
bevan brittan	hammonds
bircham dyson bell	harbottle & lewis
bird & bird	hbj gateley wareing
boodle hatfield	henmans
brabners chaffe street	herbert smith
brachers	holman fenwick & willan
browne jacobson	howes percival
burges salmon	ince & co
capsticks	irwin mitchell
charles russell	kendall freeman
clarke willmott	king
cleary gottlieb	knight & sons
clyde & co	latham & watkins
cms cameron mckenna	lawrence graham
coffin mew & clover	leboeuf, lamb, green
covington & burling	lester aldridge
cripps harries hall	lewis silkin
dechert	lovells
denton wilde sapte	lupton fawcett
dickinson dees	mace & jones
dla piper	macfarlanes
dmh stallard	manches
dundas & wilson	martineau johnson
dwf	mayer, brown, rowe & maw
eversheds	mcdermott, will & emery
farrer & co	mcgrigors
field fisher waterhouse	mills & reeve

contacts

The Law Society
113 Chancery Lane,
London WC2A 1PL
Tel: 020 7242 1222
E-mail: info.services@lawsociety.org.uk
www.lawsociety.org.uk

Education and Training Department
Tel: 0870 606 2555
E-mail: legaled@lawsociety.org.uk
www.training.lawsociety.org.uk

Trainee Solicitors Group
The Law Society
113 Chancery Lane,
London WC2A 1PL
Helpline: 08000 856 131
E-mail: info@tsg.org
www.tsg.org

The Bar Council
289-293 High Holborn
London WC1V 7HZ
020 7242 0082
www.barcouncil.org.uk
For all other departments including the
Education and Training Department and the
Equality and Diversity Committee contact the
main switchboard.

Gray's Inn, Education Department
8 South Square, Gray's Inn,
London WC1R 5ET
Tel: 020 7458 7800
www.graysinn.org.uk

Inner Temple, Education & Training Department
Treasury Building, Inner Temple,
London EC4Y 7HL
Tel: 020 7797 8250
www.innertemple.org.uk

Lincoln's Inn, Students' Department
Treasury Office, Lincoln's Inn,
London WC2A 3TL
Tel: 020 7405 0138
www.lincolnsinn.org.uk.

Middle Temple, Students' Department
Treasury Office, Middle Temple Lane,
London EC4Y 9AT
Tel: 0207 427 4800
www.middletemple.org.uk

The Institute of Legal Executives
Kempston Manor, Kempston,
Bedfordshire MK42 7AB
Tel: 01234 841000
E-mail: info@ilex.org.uk
www.ilex.org.uk

Government Legal Service
Chancery House,
53-64 Chancery Lane,
London WC2A 1QS
Tel: 020 7649 6023
E-mail: glstrainees@tmp.com
www.gls.gov.uk

Crown Prosecution Service
50 Ludgate Hill,
London EC4M 7EX
Tel: 020 7796 8053
www.cps.gov.uk

The Law Commission
Conquest House, 37-38 John Street,
Theobalds Road,
London WC1N 2BQ
Tel: 020 7453 1220
E-mail:
communications@lawcommission.gsi.gov.uk
www.lawcom.gov.uk

Citizens Advice Bureaux
Head Office, Myddelton House,
115-123 Pentonville Road,
London N1 9LZ
Tel: 020 7833 2181
Volunteer Hotline: 08451 264264
www.citizensadvice.org.uk

Legal Services Commission
Head Office, 85 Gray's Inn Road,
London WC1X 8TX
Tel: 020 7759 0000
www.legalservices.gov.uk

Chartered Institute of Patent Agents
95 Chancery Lane,
London WC2A IDT
Tel: 020 7405 9450
E-mail: mail@cipa.org.uk
www.cipa.org.uk

Institute of Trade Mark Attorneys
Canterbury House, 2-6 Sydenham Road,
Croydon,
Surrey CR0 9XE
Tel: 020 8686 2052
www.itma.org.uk

**Institute of Chartered Secretaries
and Administrators:**
16 Park Crescent,
London W1B 1AH
Tel: 020 7580 4741
www.icsa.org.uk

The Law Centres Federation
Duchess House,
18-19 Warren Street,
London W1T 5LR
Tel: 020 7387 8570
E-mail: info@lawcentres.org.uk
www.lawcentres.org.uk

Free Representation Unit
6th Floor 289-293 High Holborn
London WC1V 7HZ
Tel: 0207 611 9555
Email: admin@freerepresentationunit.org.uk
www.freerepresentationunit.org.uk

The Bar Lesbian & Gay Group
Email: info@blagg.org
(BLAGG) www.blagg.org
Lesbian & Gay Lawyers Association
www.lagla.org.uk

The Society of Asian Lawyers
c/o Saima Hanif
4-5 St Gray's Inn Square
Gray's Inn
London WC1R 5AH
Email: info@societyofasianlawyers.com

Society of Black Lawyers
9 Winchester House, 11 Cranmer Road
Kennington Park Road
London SW9 6EJ
Tel: 020 7735 652

The Association of Muslim Lawyers
PO Box 148, High Wycombe
Bucks HP13 5WJ
Email: aml@aml.org.uk
www.aml.org.uk

The Association of Women Barristers
1 Pump Court Temple
London EC4Y 7AB
Email: janehoyal@aol.com
www.womenbarristers.co.uk

Group for Solicitors with Disabilities
c/o Judith McDermott
The Law Society, 113 Chancery Lane
London WC2A 1PL
Tel: 020 7320 5793
Email: secretary@gsdnet.org.uk
www.gsdnet.org.uk

LPC Central Applications Board
PO Box 84, Guildford,
Surrey GU3 1YX
Tel: 01483 301282
www.lawcabs.ac.uk

CPE Central Applications Board
PO Box 84, Guildford,
Surrey GU3 1YX
Tel: 01483 451080
www.lawcabs.ac.uk

Online Pupillage Application System
Technical Assistance
E-mail: pupillages@gtios.com
www.pupillages.com

Career Development Loans
Freepost, Warrington WA4 6FB
Tel: (freephone) 0800 585505
www.lifelonglearning.co.uk/cdl

Let's start with one of the most basic questions – Do you want to be a barrister or a solicitor? Here we give a simple description of each so you know where next in this book to turn.

barrister

Ask a solicitor about the key difference between the two sides of the profession and they will probably tell you it's the size of your average barrister's ego. At first sight the role of a barrister certainly looks a lot cooler than that of a solicitor. Even if you've only ever seen fictitious ones in TV dramas, you know the deal – it's all about striding into courtrooms, robes flowing; tense moments waiting for missing witnesses and razor-sharp cross-examinations. Glamorous? It's downright sexy! The truth is there's a great deal more to the job than looking good in a wig and gown…

Essentially barristers do three things:

- Appear in court to represent others
- Give specialised legal advice in person or in writing
- Draft court documents

How much of these a barrister does depends on the type of law they practise. Criminal barristers are in court most of the time, often with only an hour or two's notice of the details of their cases. By contrast, Chancery barristers spend most of their time in chambers writing tricky opinions and advising in conference on complicated legal points.

Barristers must display the skill and clarity to make complex or arcane legal arguments accessible to lay clients, juries and the judiciary. Their style of argument must be clear and persuasive, both in court and on paper. Of course, it has been some time since barristers have had exclusive rights of audience in the courts. Solicitors can, and some have, become accredited advocates in even the higher courts. This blurring of the distinction between the two halves of the profession hasn't been an utter disaster for the Bar, although solicitor-advocates are undertaking a lot more straightforward cases. With more complicated and lengthy matters barristers are still briefed to do the advocacy, not least because this is often the most cost-effective way of managing a case. As a point of interest, solicitor-advocates do not wear the wig and gown and are referred to as 'my friend' rather than 'my learned friend'.

Solicitors value barristers' detailed knowledge of the litigation process and, as a result, their ability to assess and advise on the merits and demerits of a case. A solicitor will pay good money for 'counsel's opinion'.

A barrister must understand the client's perspective – certainly in the area of commercial law – and use their legal knowledge to help construct a solution that makes business or common sense as well as legal sense. If you're hoping a career as a barrister will allow you to remain at the top of an ivory tower, you might wish to consider life as an academic.

Most barristers are self-employed. This is why you hear the expression 'the independent Bar'. A minority are employed by companies, public bodies or law firms and they make up 'the employed Bar'. To prevent independence from turning into isolation, barristers work in groups called sets, sharing premises and professional managers, etc. Barristers do not work for their sets, just at them, and as 'tenants' they contribute to the upkeep of their chambers and give a percentage of their earnings to their clerks and administrators. Unlike employed barristers and solicitors, those at the independent Bar get no sickness pay, holiday pay, maternity leave or monthly salary. What they do get is a good accountant!

To enter practice, LLB grads need to complete the Bar Vocational Course (BVC) before starting a much sought-after, year-long barristers' pupillage. At the end of that it's a case of finding a set that wants you to join them as a member of their chambers – this is called tenancy. Once you have that then the legal profession is your oyster.

Being a barrister is a great job, but the competition is fierce. If your appetite has been whetted you will find much more information in the final, orange section of this book, where we have detailed the recruitment process and laid bare some of the more obscure practices and terminology. We have also tried to give a fair assessment of some of the difficulties that young hopefuls may encounter. The **Chambers Reports** section gives an invaluable insight into the lives of pupils and junior barristers at some of the best sets.

The professional body regulating this side of the profession is The Bar Council.

solicitor

Most budding lawyers qualify as solicitors rather than as barristers. The role of a solicitor is to provide legal services directly to lay clients, who could be individuals, companies or public or other bodies. In short, clients come to solicitors for guidance on how to deal with their business or personal proposals and problems. These could be anything from drafting a will to defending a murder charge or buying a multibillion-pound business. The solicitor advises on the steps needed to proceed and then manages the case or the deal for the client until a conclusion has been reached. They will bring in a barrister if and when a second opinion or specialist advocacy is needed. The solicitor's role is much more like that of a project manager than the barrister's.

There are around over 100,000 solicitors in England and Wales with practising certificates issued by the Law Society (these need to be renewed annually), the majority of them in 'private practice'. In the last 30 years the number of practising solicitors has risen by an average of roughly 4% per year.

- 'Sole practitioners' account for nearly half of the 9,000 or so private practice firms in England and Wales.
- Less than 2% of firms have 26 or more partners, but these big firms employ more than a third of all private practitioners.
- Over a third of all solicitors practise in London.
- Just over 20% of practising solicitors are employed by businesses outside the legal profession, public sector organisations or charities.

If nothing else, these statistics should tell you that becoming a solicitor will not mean the same thing for everyone.

Most readers will be well aware that after their degree, law school awaits. Law grads need to take the Legal Practice Course (LPC). Non-law grads must first complete a law conversion course before being eligible for the LPC. After law school comes the training contract, which is presently two years in length and can be undertaken with a firm of solicitors, law centre, employed solicitor in industry or commerce or public body. You might be interested to know that there are proposals on the table to shorten the length of the training contract to 16 months, but given that changes to the training framework are discussed more often than the average solicitor changes their socks, we suggest no one gets too excited for the moment. Upon satisfactory completion of their contract, the trainee is signed off and is admitted to the roll. In plain English that means they qualify. There is an enrolment ceremony at the Law Society for anyone who wants to give mum and dad a day to remember and a new photo for the mantelpiece.

Exactly when you should apply for a training contract depends on the kind of firm you hope to join. If you are studying for a law degree and you

- There are more than 11,000 new law graduates each year, over half of them with Firsts or 2:1s.
- Almost 9,000 students sit the LPC exam each year. The pass rate is roughly 85%.
- The number of new traineeships in the year ending 31 July 2005 was 5,732.
- Over three-fifths of new trainees are women.
- Almost a fifth of new trainees are from ethnic minority groups.

want to work in a commercial firm, the crucial time for research and applications is your penultimate year at uni. If you are a non-law student intending to take a law conversion course before going to a commercial firm then you'll have to juggle exams and career considerations in your final year. Students wanting to enter high street practice usually don't need to worry about training contract applications quite so early. Unlike commercial firms, which generally offer contracts two years in advance of the start date, smaller firms do so closer to the start date.

Larger, commercial firms commonly offer their future trainees scholarships to cover law school fees and other basic expenses. Public sector organisations, eg the Government Legal Service, may also come up with some cash. Sadly, students hoping to practise in smaller firms soon learn that financial assistance is highly unlikely and this can make law school an uncertain and expensive time. Reading our Funding section on page 52 may help.

Needless to say, your choice of training contract will determine the path (and perhaps also location) of your future career. A firm's clients, its work and its reputation will determine not only the experience you gain, but probably also your future marketability as a lawyer. At Chambers and Partners, we've made it our business to know who does what, how well they do it and

what it might be like working at a particular firm. In the Practice Areas section of this book, you'll find the core results of the research carried out for our parent publication Chambers UK. Our league tables show which firms command greatest respect from clients and other professionals in different areas of practice. In the True Picture section of this book we've profiled 150 of the leading firms in England and Wales. This section of the book should help you understand what kind of firm might suit you and the kind of work you can expect to receive when you get there.

It will probably help you to envisage the scope of the legal market by grouping law firms into different categories.

magic circle

Traditionally defined as Allen & Overy, Clifford Chance, Freshfields Bruckhaus Deringer, Linklaters, and Slaughter and May. Seen by many as the elite, these mammoth firms pay big salaries to hardworking lawyers. Their business is very corporate and/or finance-oriented, much of it international. They have the pick of the best students and offer superb, mass-scale training. The large size and big-money deals of magic circle firms will definitely not appeal to all students, so if you think you'd fare better in a different environment then follow your instinct. For most niche practice areas, the magic circle is rarely the logical choice.

london: large commercial

The top ten City of London firms (including the magic circle) offer around 1,000 traineeships between them each year, representing approximately a fifth of all new training contracts registered with the Law Society. There's not such a huge difference between the magic circle and firms such as Herbert Smith, Lovells, CMS Cameron McKenna and a few others. The make-up of the chasing pack is constantly changing and next year we might mention different law firms.

The work in these big firms is almost entirely centred on business law and business clients. Salaries are essentially the same as paid by the magic circle and, generally speaking, the lawyers work equally hard much of the time, if not all of the time. As a trainee you can expect to assist on big, high-value deals and cases (though not always conducting particularly challenging duties). If you are working against a deadline then you will be expected to stay until it is finished. This can mean working through the night and coming in at weekends from time to time.

london: American firms

In the 1990s the number of American law firms setting up in business in London rose significantly. A decade on and many of these are now offering training contracts to students intending to qualify as English solicitors. At the risk of over generalising, these firms are characterised by international work (usually corporate or finance-led), smaller offices and rather long hours. On the other hand they usually give trainees a good amount of responsibility and pay phenomenally high salaries. Lawyers at the hotshot US firms frequently work opposite magic circle lawyers on deals; indeed many of them were magic circle and top-ten firm partners or associates before they joined a US firm. The arrival of the US firms has had a knock on effect on City law, not least on City salaries, which have soared in the past decade.

london: mid-sized commercial

Again, the work is almost entirely centred on business law and business clients. Salaries are slightly lower than at the big firms. While the hours are usually a little shorter, there will still be some late-night working. Arguably, the smaller deals and cases handled by these firms allow trainees to take more interesting roles. The work of these firms is likely to be more domestic than international and

so there is less chance of a trainee going to work overseas during their contract. The atmosphere in these firms is generally more intimate than at the giants of the City and there is more likelihood of working for partners directly.

london: small commercial

Commonly these firms will have certain areas of practice that play a big part in their business – eg real estate – or a specific clientele that has fuelled the firm's growth. The hours will tend towards those at the mid-sized firms, although the pay packet is likely to be lighter, but if you want to be a partner's right hand (wo)man or get stuck in with client relationships, this is your kind of firm.

niche firms

Particularly in London, there are scores of niche firms to choose from. Construction, entertainment, IP, insurance litigation, shipping, family... the list goes on. If you are absolutely certain that you want to specialise in a particular field – especially if you have already worked in a relevant industry – a niche firm is an excellent choice. Be aware that many firms described as niche practices actually offer other types of work. Be aware also that some niche firms do try to woo students by talking a little too much about their other areas of practice.

regional firms

The City of London may be the beating heart of blue-chip, international business, but there's more to life than an EC postcode. In the regions, there are some very fine firms acting for top-notch clients on cases and deals the City firms would snap up in a heartbeat. There is even a measure of international work going on. These firms' recruitment standards are as high as found in the City; indeed they are home to many lawyers who have escaped the City. Other, smaller firms prefer to focus on the needs of regional clients and would therefore suit anyone who wanted to become an integral part of their local business community. If you are applying to join a firm in Newcastle, for example, and have studied and lived in London all your life, be prepared to be asked why you want to move to the area. The last thing firms want is to spend a fortune training you, only to have to sign your leaving card when you swan off to the capital on qualification. Salaries are lower outside London, in some cases significantly so, but the cost of living is much more reasonable. You will hopefully benefit from less frenetic hours.

national and multi-site firms

There are several multi-site firms in the UK. For example, Eversheds has ten UK branches; DLA Piper has eight in the UK; Shoosmiths mostly operates in smaller cities and towns from the South Coast up to Nottingham. There are other examples of firms with several offices within a single region, all of them with differing approaches to recruitment and whether or not trainees move between offices during their contracts. Make sure you know the firm's policy or you could find yourself leaving your nan to look after your cat while you move to a new town for six months… or getting up at 5am to sit in traffic on the M62. The experience you gain in your training contract will undoubtedly be determined by which part of the firm's network you work in and whether or not the firm shunts work around its offices.

general practice/high street

These range from substantial, long-established firms in large town centres to sole practitioners working above shops in the suburbs. They act for legally aided clients, individuals funding themselves and local businesses. Staple work includes landlord and tenant problems, conveyancing, personal injury, employment, family, wills and probate, and crime. It's increasingly likely that firms have an additional specialism in small-ticket commercial work for local businesses. Be prepared to earn considerably less than your peers in commercial practice and don't expect there to be an abundance of amenities or resources in the office. Excessively long hours are unlikely unless you're on a rota for police station duty. If you want to grow up fast as a lawyer and see how the law actually affects individuals and the community in which you practise then this is the kind of firm to go for. Larger firms may take on four or five trainees a year; the smallest will recruit on an occasional basis.

Anyone thinking of entering this sector of the legal profession should be aware that there are likely to be major changes in the public funding of legal services. Lord Carter of Coles is presently undertaking a wide-ranging review and we have summarised the issue in a special feature called Get Carter.

Away from private practice there are many options for legal training.

law centres

From its roots in North Kensington in 1970, the network of UK Law Centres has grown to around 60 today, each set up as either a registered charity or a not-for-profit company and run by its own local management committee. Most Law Centres employ 10-15 lawyers. Advice is given to the public without charge, with funding coming from local government grants and the Legal Services Commission (LSC). The legal problems handled may vary from one Law Centre to another, but those who work in them can all be described as social welfare law specialists. Law Centres tend to take on cases with a wider social impact, say, a local authority's decision on rent arrears. Once legal needs within society have been identified, it's a case of using little matters to change the big

Get Carter

In July 2005 the DCA published a paper entitled 'A Fairer Deal for Legal Aid'. This set out the government's long-term strategy for the provision of legal aid. As a direct response to this, Lord Carter of Coles was instructed by the Secretary of State and Lord Chancellor, Lord Falconer, to review the present procedures and practices for the provision of legally aided services to the public and to devise new, more efficient models.

Why?

- In the last nine years the cost of legal aid has risen from £1.5 to £2.1 billion. This is a rise of 10% in real terms.
- Over half the budget goes on criminal defence. Apparently this is a bad thing.

Carter's review covers the provision of all legally aided services – criminal, civil and family. The review into the provision of criminal defence was the first interim report to be published and this came out in March 2006.

What Carter didn't like about the old system

- 75% of criminal legal aid expenditure is spent on payments made on the basis of hours worked by lawyers. This is believed to disincentivise efficient working practices. This is where new Carter contracts will come in.
- Much of the budget goes on time spent waiting in police stations and travelling to magistrates' courts. Some barristers think that attempts to address this complaint will increase localisation, ie nobody will travel out of circuit if they are not going to get paid for it.
- Currently there are around 2,500 suppliers of criminal defence services. Employing a diseconomy-of-scale argument, Carter presumes that this prevents them from structuring their work in a cost-effective way.
- The combination of several suppliers all getting paid for hours done has led to large administrative costs for suppliers and the

Legal Services Commission. Carter's answer is to issue fewer supplier contracts in a bid to force consolidation of suppliers. In other words fewer, larger firms.

Carter's final report in July 2006 included detailed proposals for not only criminal legal aid but also proposals for civil and family legal aid. The review has its own website where you can download the full report and see a very charming photo of Lord Carter: www.legalaid-procurementreview.gov.uk.

The proposals in relation to crime

- Introduce fixed fees for police station visits.
- Defence services in magistrates' courts and Crown Courts to be paid for under revised systems of graduated fees.
- Defence services in very high-cost cases to be paid for under individual case contracts with single defence teams working to strict cost and case management rules.
- These changes to be implemented in stages from January 2007.

The proposals in relation to civil and family

- Suppliers to concentrate on providing services to meet all civil legal aid needs of their communities.
- New supplier contracts to promote greater links between suppliers.
- New fixed fee schemes for areas such as housing and debt advice.
- New graduated fee scheme for private law family cases.
- New graduated fee scheme to replace hourly rates in court in child care cases.
- These changes to be implemented in stages from April 2007.

The reforms are likely to have knock on effects in the number and size of firms in this area of the profession, and will also affect barristers' earnings. It is worth keeping an eye open for news on Carter issues.

picture, perhaps by way of a test case that makes it to the House of Lords, the European Court of Justice and the broadsheets.

There are various routes to a career in this sector. Newly qualified solicitors with relevant experience in private practice are recruited, so too are people who have worked as paralegals for non-profit agencies and gained supervisor level status. A career may also begin at a Law Centre: every year the LSC funds 15-20 training contracts in 14 Law Centres. Mirroring a training contract in private practice, the trainee will experience different areas of law. At junior level salaries roughly match high street firms; at senior level the gap widens. What you gain is less hierarchy and terms and conditions that emulate those in local government. Flexible and part-time working is common. *An extended version of this feature appears on our website.*

working in-house for a company

A number of large companies and banks offer training contracts and/or pupillages. For information on in-house legal teams registered to take trainees check the Law Society's website and for pupillages, refer to the Bar Council.

We spoke to one recently qualified solicitor who trained in-house with an international bank. He had already built up experience of the financial sector through working as a transaction manager, and eventually asked the head of the legal department in the bank he worked at if they would be willing to fund him through part-time CPE and LPC courses. A training contract with the bank was the other vital piece of the jigsaw, and the bank agreed to this too. The proposal was feasible as the bank was already an accredited training provider and had a solicitor with sufficient experience (and interest) who was happy to take on the role of training supervisor. The only thing the bank couldn't provide was sufficient contentious training and so it arranged a secondment to one of the law firms on its legal panel.

Our source felt his training was as good as, if not better than, anything available in private practice. "*I was given my own work to manage and had a great deal more latitude than in a conventional training contract. I got responsibility earlier and a lot less grunt work to do.*" In-house trainees certainly develop very marketable skills because almost everything they do has a practical application and their sector knowledge is immense. Cold calling heads of legal at banks or companies you're interested in is not recommended. Usually a trainee will be recruited after having already worked within the organisation in some other capacity, and even then "*you have to exercise discretion in trying to obtain a contract.*" A softly-softly approach usually works best.

Most in-house lawyers started out in private practice, switching to the role some time after qualification. They do so because of a general perception that the rewards are good and the hours more manageable than in a law firm. In-house lawyers don't lose touch with private practice; indeed part of the job involves selecting and instructing law firms to provide specialist advice to the company. This part of the job ensures the in-house lawyer plenty of invites to parties, lunches and sporting events as the different law firms curry favour.

local government

Some 3,500 solicitors are employed in local authorities and there are hundreds of local authority legal departments in the UK. Some offer training contracts, but there's no central list of vacancies and no single recruitment office, so you must contact each legal department separately and keep an eye open for job ads in the local, legal and national press. The website www.lgcareers.com is the best place to start your research. There are opportunities for both vacation work experience and/or paralegalling but law school sponsorship is rare. The typical salary for a local authority solicitor is £29,700-£39,900.

Because the activities of local authorities are so varied, training contracts involve a real breadth of work. You're quite likely to undertake property, planning and environmental law; litigation and prosecution work; consumer protection, housing, education and childcare; employment, personal injury, administrative and commercial/contracts. Usually trainees follow the same seat system that prevails in private practice but for local authority trainees there is the added bonus of having rights of audience in civil and criminal courts and tribunals that outstrip those of peers in private practice. In all seats, your clients will be officers from different departments of the local authority.

For many, the real appeal is working for a public sector organisation that's concerned with the local environment and community. For others, it's the excellent working conditions and benefits; part-time working, flexi-time and job sharing are not uncommon. Most local government lawyers remain in the public sector, but the job is portable across the UK, and lawyers can also transfer to the GLS or CPS or private practice. Some local authorities operate their legal departments along commercial principles and all must adhere to the principle of 'Best Value'. If ever you doubt whether a career in local government can be high flying, you might wish to consider the fact that many current local authority chief executives trained as solicitors.

government legal service

Lately, between 20 and 30 trainee solicitors and pupil barristers have been recruited each year by the Government Legal Service (GLS) to work within different government departments and offices. At one end of the scale there are full-time litigators, and at the other, people drafting new legislation or advising ministers. We'd recommend anyone applying to the GLS to have a long think about the role government lawyers take, particularly considering how law and politics interact and the impact that they can have on life and society in the UK, whether this is by bringing about the prosecution of drugs smugglers or human traffickers, or drafting new sexual offences or employment legislation.

If the idea appeals, read our True Picture feature on GLS training contracts on page 346 and the pupillage feature on page 803 of the Chambers Reports.

crown prosecution service

If you have a passion for criminal law, and the idea of billable hours and contract drafting leaves you cold, the Crown Prosecution Service (CPS) may appeal. The CPS is the government department responsible for bringing prosecutions against people who have been charged with a criminal offence in England and Wales. All stages of the process are handled by the CPS, from advising the police on the possibility of prosecution to preparing the case for court and the final prosecution of the case in court. Prosecutors appear on a daily basis to conduct cases in the magistrates' courts and although most Crown court trials are conducted by barristers in private practice, the opportunities for in-house lawyers (known as Higher Courts Advocates) to deal with these cases are increasing significantly. The Director of Public Prosecutions, Ken Macdonald QC is keen to improve and modernise the service offered by the CPS. An essential part of that determination involves the development of in-house advocacy making the Service one that routinely conducts a large proportion of its own cases in all courts. The CPS is not the only authority that can institute criminal prosecutions: they can, for example, also be brought by the Serious Fraud Office and HM Revenue & Customs.

The CPS employs about 2,800 lawyers in England and Wales to handle more than 1.3 million cases in the magistrates' courts and about 115,000 in the Crown Courts.

CPS prosecutors review and prosecute criminal cases following investigation by the police. They also advise the police on matters of criminal and evidence law, some working from Criminal Justice Units, which have been established within police stations to combat the problem of failed prosecutions. Lawyers here advise the police on the appropriate charge for the crime, spending one day in the office preparing cases and the next in the magistrates' court, dealing with administrative matters relating to each case. Lawyers in the Trial Unit handle Crown Court cases, including murder, rape and robbery. Because Crown Court matters are usually dealt with in court by self-employed barristers, prosecutors are regularly responsible for instructing counsel, although increasingly they can become Higher Courts Advocates and conduct those trials themselves. While it may lack the grit and glamour of Law and Order, the work of the CPS can have its exciting moments.

Prosecutors can expect to come into contact with 30 or 40 cases each day, and although they don't have the same intense client contact as defence lawyers, they do interact with everyone from magistrates, clerks, solicitors, probation and police officers, to civilian and expert witnesses and even serving prisoners. They also liaise with racial equality and victim support agencies as well as victims and witnesses themselves. For example, where a prosecution is abandoned, the prosecutor will inform the victim of the reasons. It's easy to see why one prosecutor told us: *"You must be flexible and prepared for anything."* You must also be fairly *"bulletproof"* as the service sometimes gets flak for failed prosecutions. A qualified prosecutor's salary ranges from £25,648-£47,685 nationally and £26,954-£53,667 in London (pay award pending April 2007).

The CPS expects all trainees to have completed the LPC/BVC before taking up a post and is currently training around 47 solicitors and 16 pupils (although please note that this cannot be used as an accurate guide as to how many places will be available from year to year). A trainee's salary starts in the region of £18,425-£23,822 (p.a. pending) depending on location and is subject to annual review.

The traditional LLB to LPC/BVC route is by no means the preferred route into the CPS. Many CPS trainees have juggled work and part-time study; some have entered the service 'sideways', having left school with few academic qualifications. Inclined to grow its own lawyers, the CPS has fertiliser in the form of a 'Law Scholarship Scheme'. The funding pays for its recipients' full A-level, Law Degree (or equivalent), ILEX, LPC and BVC course fees and expenses, depending on what stage of education staff are at. In addition to this a national campaign for legal trainees is being launched in October 2006 for an October 2007 start; anyone who holds a BVC or LPC, or who will complete one in 2007, is welcome to apply. Details can be found on the CPS website .

CPS caseworkers are the beneficiaries of the service's eagerness to grow talent from within. This being so, perhaps becoming a caseworker is the way forward for future trainees. They assist prosecutors by researching cases and making recommendations on information required and charges to be brought. Beyond these duties, they liaise with advocates, witnesses, police and court staff; provide support to witnesses and victims and additionally attend court to assist counsel on a regular basis. London caseworkers will usually be able to do a three-month stint at the Old Bailey. Impressive organisational skills and an ability to relate to people are essential. Remuneration runs between £18,425 nationally and £19,441 in London (p.a. pending).

Theoretically you could start anywhere within the CPS and end up as a prosecuting lawyer. As CPS Training Principal Lesley Williams told us: *"If you see your career in the CPS, come aboard with us at any level and show a commitment to the service."*

For vacation placements and work experience your starting point should be www.cps.gov.uk.

other career options

legal executive

If you haven't found one of those elusive training contracts or are thinking about moving sideways into a legal career, you could consider the Institute of Legal Executives (ILEX) course. Those who complete the course become legal executives – qualified lawyers who are sometimes known as the 'third branch' of the legal profession. There are over 22,000 legal executives and trainee legal executives across the country. No prior legal training is required to enrol on the course, which makes it suitable for school leavers, new graduates or those already engaged in a career and looking to branch out. It can be taken on a part-time basis, giving trainees an opportunity to combine study with practical experience.

Trainees initially study for a Professional Diploma in Law, which takes about two years part-time. The course includes an introduction to key legal concepts as well as legal practice and procedure and can be examined either by the mixed Assessment route (a portfolio, case studies and one end of course examination) or the examination Route (four papers). Trainees then progress to the Professional Higher Diploma in Law, which allows specialisation in a particular area of practice, usually guided by the job the trainee is doing at the time. On completion, trainees become members of ILEX. To become a fully qualified ILEX fellow, it is necessary to gain five years of qualifying experience in a legal background (at least two after completing the exams) and be over the age of 25.

Law graduates are exempt from the academic part of the course and can take examinations solely in legal practice, enabling the qualification to be gained in a little over twelve months. For those without a law degree, the professional qualification will usually take three or four years to complete while in full-time employment. There is no set time to complete the examinations, so trainees can work at their own pace. ILEX graduates end up in employment across the full spectrum of legal services from private practice to government departments and the in-house legal departments of major corporations.

Some ILEX fellows continue studying and eventually become fully qualified solicitors. As they will already have been examined in some of the core subjects required by the Common Professional Exam Board, and the others can be taken as single subjects over another one or two years of part-time study, most fellows can seek exemption from the CPE and move straight on to the Legal Practice Course. ILEX fellows may also be exempted from the two-year training contract.

Although ILEX can provide a useful route to qualification as a solicitor, it is by no means the quickest. However, positions for trainee legal executives may be available when solicitors' training contracts are not and, crucially, the route does enable the student to earn whilst studying. A full list of colleges offering the course (including via distance learning) is available at www.ilex.org.uk.

paralegalling

If you have time to fill before starting your training contract or you are yet to be convinced you want to spend time and money on law school, paralegal work can provide a useful introduction to legal practice. Employers regard time spent paralegalling favourably as it demonstrates commitment to the profession and enables candidates to gain valuable experience and commercial or sector insight. Some firms and companies – though not all – offer traineeships to the most impressive of their own paralegals, but you should always keep in mind that the job is a valuable position in its own right. Guard against giving the impression that you will leave as soon as something better crops up. There is no single job description: some experienced paralegals may run their own cases; others with little to offer by way of experience may end up doing very dull document management tasks for months on end.

The paralegal market is competitive, so those with no legal qualifications or practical experience may find it harder to secure a position. Indeed, some top City firms require all paralegal applicants to have completed the LPC. The good news is that it is likely to be easier to find a paralegal position now than in the past couple of years as the transaction market is busier.

When starting out, it may be necessary to work a number of short-term contracts until one firm decides it wants you on a long-term basis.

This can be a career in its own right, and experienced paralegals with specialist skills can make a very decent living. For information on current vacancies, check the legal press or register with a specialist recruitment agency. You should also find out if your law school's careers office has contacts and regularly check the websites of any firms in your area. Some firms employ paralegals from among those who write to them on spec.

the serious organised crime agency (soca)

This agency is sponsored by, but operationally independent from, the Home Office. It was formed in 2006 when four bodies were swept together. These were the National Crime Squad, the National Criminal Intelligence Service, the part of HM Revenue & Customs that dealt with drug trafficking and associated criminal finance, and the part of UK Immigration that dealt with organised immigration crime. SOCA is an intelligence-led agency with law enforcement powers and a remit to reduce the damage caused to people and communities by serious organised crime. The agency has a small legal department that advises on operational and policy issues, but there is no training scheme of any kind. Any job vacancies with SOCA are advertised on its website: www.soca.gov.uk.

her majesty's court service

HM Court Service is the part of the Department for Constitutional Affairs that is responsible for the daily business of the court system. On 1 April 2005 the old court service and the magistrates' courts were swept together into this one body that is now aiming *"to ensure that access* [to justice] *is provided as quickly as possible and at the lowest cost consistent with open justice and that citizens have greater confidence in, and respect for, the system of justice."* As the statement suggests, this was no April Fool's joke, and HMCS is now responsible for:

- Administration of the civil, family and criminal courts in England and Wales – right up to the Court of Appeal.
- Providing ushers and dealing with timetabling.
- Modernising the physical appearance of courts.
- On a lighter note, making courts available as filming locations for any programme or film that needs a court. *Judge John Deed* has to be shot somewhere after all.

Most jobs are administrative in nature; however, the service recruits Judicial Assistants at various times throughout the year. JA appointments are temporary, and each lasts for a three-month term. There are usually ten positions at any one time, regularly filled by high-achieving types at the start of their careers, who are able to acquire a depth of understanding both of the law and of the appellate process. Appointments are sometimes renewed, but only for a maximum of twelve months. JAs assist the Lord Justices in the Civil Division of the Court of Appeal at the Royal Courts of Justice, including legal research, advice and providing assistance in drafting judgments.

JAs may also help define the shape and nature of appeals in less well-presented cases. Applicants for JA positions must:

- Be qualified lawyers who have completed pupillage or traineeship.
- Possess word processing skills.
- Be able to demonstrate intellectual ability (by way of a 2:1 degree).
- Have the ability to work under pressure as part of a team.

As and when they become available, positions are advertised in *The Times* weekly law supplement and the *Law Gazette* as well as on the HM Court Service website: www.hmcourts-service.gov.uk.

Those looking for a longer term career might consider the roles of administrative officer, bailiff, and county and Crown Court ushers or clerks.

Court clerks do not have a legal advisory role and do not need legal qualifications. The 91 Crown Courts and 218 county courts in which they work are presided over by members of the judiciary. Magistrates' clerks do give legal advice to lay magistrates and managers of the court. Approximately 381 magistrates' courts operate in England and Wales, and between them they handle the majority of the country's criminal proceedings. In a busy metropolitan court, as well as the usual TV licence and traffic offences, the clerks will encounter drug trafficking cases and other serious crimes on a reasonably regular basis. A rural court is likely to be quieter and crimes of violence less common.

All court clerks need to be able to:

- Think on their feet and deal confidently with people.
- Very occasionally exercise the power to order individuals into custody for contempt of court, although those we spoke to said that the vast majority of defendants treat them with respect.

Magistrates' clerks must additionally:

- Provide magistrates with reliably sound advice on issues like self-defence, identification of suspects, and inferences from the silence of defendants after arrest.

A shift in recruitment policy has seen the traditional route (by which those without degrees could train while studying for the Diploma in Magisterial Law) overtaken by the recruitment of LPC and BVC graduates as trainee court clerks. As the individual progresses through a structured training programme, the number and complexity of their court duties will increase until ultimately they are advising lay magistrates on points of law and procedure. Most courts operate nine or ten sessions a week and most clerks will be in court for the majority of these. The remaining time will be spent exercising powers delegated to them by the magistrates, such as issuing summonses. For more information about careers with the magistrates' courts or any other part of HMCS, refer to its website.

the law commission

Many laws are the product of political expediency and are drawn up at the will of the government of the day. However, the government is not always best placed to see where reforms could best be made. The Law Commission, which is an associated office of the Department of Constitutional Affairs, was set up by Parliament 40 years ago to keep the laws of England and Wales under review and propose reform where necessary.

Its key purpose is to ensure that the law is as fair, modern, simple and cost-effective as possible, and to do so the commission employs about 15 research assistants to help with the task. At any one time, it will be engaged in about 20 projects of law reform. As a researcher you could be dealing with both common law and statutes going back many centuries. You will analyse many different areas of law, identifying defects in the current system, examining foreign law models to see how they deal with similar problems, helping to draft consultation papers or preparing reports of recommendation for the Lord Chancellor. The commission also works on the consolidation of statutes and the repeal of obsolete statutory provisions. Recent papers were published on such diverse subjects as a partial defence to murder, violence against children and unfair terms in contracts.

The Law Commission recruits law graduates and postgraduates, those who have completed the LPC or BVC, and people who have spent some time in practice but are looking for a change. The job of research assistant involves some fascinating (and some less fascinating) subjects and is intellectually challenging. Candidates should have a First or high 2:1 at degree level plus a keen interest in current affairs and the workings of the law.

The job suits those with an analytical mind and a hatred of waffle; they have also got to love research because there's a lot of it. So far, more than two-thirds of the commission's recommendations have been implemented by the government – you can see what they are on the commission's website – so you will get the satisfaction of seeing your work put into practice. Another plus point is that if you go on to train as a solicitor or barrister, you will be streets ahead of your peers in terms of your research skills and knowledge of how statutes work. For further information on short and long-term careers at the Law Commission, check out www.law-com.gov.uk. The recruitment campaign for positions as a research assistant commencing September 2007 opens in January 2007.

legal services commission

This government body was created by the Access to Justice Act 1999 and replaced the Legal Aid Board in 2000. It employs nearly 1,700 staff and operates from London and 12 towns and cities across England and Wales. It manages the distribution of public funds for both civil legal services and criminal defence services. The work of the LSC is essentially broken down into two departments covering these areas: the Community Legal Service and the Criminal Defence Service.

- The large Community Legal Service (CLS) handles civil cases. Caseworkers assess the merits of applications for legal funding and means test applicants. They also assess and authorise claims for payment for legal services. The department also helps ensure that people can get information and advice about their legal rights and help with enforcing them through bringing together legal aid solicitors, Citizens Advice Bureaux, Law Centres, local authority services and other organisations in over 200 regional CLS partnerships.

- The Criminal Defence Service (CDS) organises the supply of legal advice to those accused of crime through the use of local solicitors who are accredited by the service. It also performs an audit role, dealing with the authorised providers of criminal legal advice. There are no financial or other limits as to who is entitled to claim free legal advice on criminal cases, so it is merely the lawyer's financial claims and the quality of their services that are scrutinised.

Part of the CDS' work is the Public Defender Service. Set up in 2001 with four offices, this has now increased to eight. The PDS offices are staffed by solicitors and accredited representatives who are directly employed by the Legal Services Commission (LSC) but provide independent advice. These offices employ their own lawyers to advise members of the public in what the LSC believes to be a more cost-effective and efficient way. The PDS is the subject of a four-year review so keep your eyes and ears open as to what happens next.

- The Contracting Sections of both departments audit claims for 'Legal Help', the funding used for preliminary and basic advice on how individuals might be represented.
- The Planning and Partnership Sections of both departments employ consultants and executives in order to better understand how the LSC should spend funds and place its resources, including initiatives such as electronic billing.

Jobs at the commission are advertised in local and/or national newspapers, as well as online. A first point of contact is www.legalservices.gov.uk. A few work experience placements crop up, usually in the CLS and tending to last about six weeks.

patent attorney
Patent attorneys can earn a bundle, but it's a long and arduous route to qualification. The profession in the UK numbers some 1,200 practitioners who are regulated by the Chartered Institute of Patent Attorneys (CIPA). Patent attorneys work either in private firms or are employed by large companies or government departments. It is their job to obtain, protect and enforce intellectual property rights for their owners. For more information about IP law see page 128.

The website www.cipa.org.uk has a useful careers section, but to summarise: it takes on average about four or five years to become a UK Chartered Patent Agent and/or a European Patent Attorney. All candidates must have a scientific or technical background (usually a relevant degree) and an appetite for learning the relevant law. Attention to detail, good drafting skills and a logical, analytical mind are essential and, increasingly, the ability to speak French or German is seen as key. The traditional route is to work and study for professional exams simultaneously. By taking the Certificate and Master's courses in intellectual property run by Queen Mary's College, University of London, Manchester University, Bournemouth University or Brunel University, a candidate can gain exemption from some of the professional examinations. Some employers may allow time off, and even funding, for these courses. Tracking down a graduate trainee position is made all the easier by Inside Careers' useful guide to the patent attorney's profession: www.insideinformation.com.

trade mark attorney
Trade mark attorneys advise clients on all aspects of trade mark registration, protection and exploitation in the UK and Europe, liaising with counterparts in other parts of the world whenever necessary. Good communication and drafting skills are required, although technically a degree is not. The road to qualification involves passing the exams set for the Institute of Trade Mark Agents (ITMA) and these comprise five foundation papers followed by three specialist papers. Candidates with certain degrees, such as law, may be exempt from some Foundation Papers.

Again, it is most common for aspiring practitioners to study while learning on the job as a trainee trade mark agent. With no central admissions procedure, students need to approach firms or in-house trade mark departments directly. www.itma.org.uk has a helpful careers page.

compliance officer or analyst
Banks and other financial services companies are eager to recruit law and non-law graduates into their compliance units. These units take on the vital role of advising senior management on how to comply with the applicable laws, regulations

and rules that govern the sector. They also ensure that the banks' own corporate procedures and policies are followed. Other functions relate to the handling of complex regulatory and internal investigations and examinations. Due to the proliferation of financial regulation in the past ten years the importance of compliance departments has grown enormously so that in larger banks they are often equivalent in size to in-house legal teams and offer equally solid career prospects.

Through compliance risk management banks improve their ability to control the risks of emerging issues, thus helping to protect the organisation's reputation. The role of compliance officer or analyst requires astute advice, clear guidance, reliable professional judgment and the ability to work in a team. Attention to detail and a determination to see the consistent application of compliance policies and practices are essential. The extent of reliance on compliance teams means regular exposure to senior management occurs much earlier for trainees in this area than for trainee solicitors at law firms. A minimum 2:1 degree is standard for successful applicants and salaries are typically comparable with other graduate trainees in the City. With compliance teams numbering up to a hundred staff, in the longer term there is plenty of scope for career development.

The compliance unit at UBS bank, for example, is organised into the following teams that reflect the make up of its business:

Product teams
- Equities
- Fixed Income, Rates and Currencies
- Investment Banking, Research and Private Equity

Specialist teams
- Money Laundering Prevention
- Risk Assessment, Logistics and Risk Control
- Education

Jurisdictional teams
- Switzerland
- Continental Europe, Middle East & Africa

UBS, like other banks, offers a two-year compliance analyst training scheme, over the course of which a trainee will gain a broad base of business knowledge and technical experience. UBS' scheme starts with a six-week period of formal classroom training to develop core skills and knowledge; this is undertaken alongside new graduate recruits into other parts of the bank. After this, there are three six-month placements in the London office and a short placement in an international office.

It is not usually necessary to have completed the GDL, LPC or even a law degree before undertaking a graduate scheme, although those with a mind to move across to an in-house legal role later in their career would need to find the time to qualify as a lawyer. Being legally qualified opens up the door to general counsel work and it is not uncommon for a bank's head of legal to also lead the compliance team.

are you hot or not?

It's rarely 'who you know' and mostly 'who you are' that secures you a job these days. Clearly there are some things you can't change about yourself – your age, roots, ethnicity, gender, a disability. There are other things you shouldn't have to change – your sexual orientation, personality, values. Having said that, you can't approach the world of work without making a few nips and tucks to your identity and addressing the content of your CV to see if it can be improved upon.

a matter of degrees

So you've not got a law degree. So what? From the top sets at the Bar to the little-known solicitors firms on the high street, non-law graduates are just as able to secure training positions as their LLB peers. In the few cases where employers prefer law grads they will specify this, so unless they hear differently, conversion route applicants may proceed with confidence. Indeed, many recruiters tell us just how highly they regard staff with language skills and scientific or technical degrees, particularly where their clients' businesses will benefit.

It's a fact of life that many solicitors firms and barristers chambers subscribe to the idea of a pecking order of universities. It's not quite as widespread as it once was, but it's still there. Go to some of the biggest firms in the City and around half the trainees will have attended Oxford or Cambridge University. A tour of the university law fairs – held over the autumn and spring terms – quickly shows which other universities are regarded as the richest pools for recruitment. Among the best attended by recruiters are Bristol, Nottingham and Durham. You can't change the identity of your university so if you perceive it may put you at relative disadvantage, make sure you get the best degree possible and work on enriching your CV in other ways.

Your degree result is perhaps the single thing on your CV that has most impact. Net a First and

you'll impress all and sundry (at least on paper); walk away with a 2:1 and your path to employment will be made smoother; end up with a 2:2 and you're going to have to perform some very fancy footwork to get a training offer. In exceptional circumstances, the effect of a poor degree result can be softened by a letter from your tutor stipulating the reason why you underachieved. Alas, it's rarely relevant that you just missed a 2:1 by a percentage point or two; however, if you were a star student who suffered a serious accident or illness as finals loomed, confirmation of this (perhaps also by way of a doctor's letter) should assist. Having spoken to a number of trainees and a couple of pupil barristers who left university with 2:2s, we would never presume to discourage anyone from applying for a training position, but these people all had other impressive qualities and/or CV-enhancing experiences. If you find yourself at the back of the queue in the job market, think hard about what you can do to overcome that 2:2 – a year or more in a relevant job, a further degree, a commitment to voluntary work perhaps.

Possibly unaware that they could be applying for training contracts and vacation schemes in their second year, many new undergraduates are lulled into a false sense of security concerning their academic performance in the first year. If the only marks you have to show recruiters are amazing thirds, you'll struggle to make headway. As boring as it may sound, work for good results throughout your degree. At the very least, doing so will maximise your chances of a great final result.

student daze

Don't become a dullard! Your first year away from home (or for some, full-time employment) is a time to explore new-found freedom and practically unlimited opportunities. Almost every university will have a wide range of societies, meeting groups and sports clubs. At the vast majority, if your leisure pursuit of choice is not on offer, they'll give you the cash to set it up, providing you can rustle up a handful of like-minded individuals and it's not illegal. Pursuing your interests will give an extra dimension to both your university experience and, crucially, your CV.

Sometimes the flood of info from university bodies such as the students' union and careers service can be so heavy that you feel you are drowning in e-mails, flyers and posters telling you of this job vacancy, that Amnesty meeting or the other CV workshop. Resist the temptation to let it all wash over you. Relevant work experience is vital to almost every successful job application, so keep your eyes open for suitable positions and use them to test your own ideas of what you would like to do. Many universities run law-specific career seminars in association with solicitors firms or barristers chambers. Be savvy, go along and find out as much as you can by talking to trainee solicitors and recruiters.

Do remember that only a minority of law firms and chambers throw drinks parties or sponsor libraries – the legal profession is not limited to the folk who've actually bought you a drink. Build up a decent understanding of the structure of the profession before deciding what kind of lawyer you want to be and which firm you want to work for. Just because your friends seem to know what they want doesn't make their choices right for you. Similarly, your tutors and family can only help you so far. Research, research and research some more until you are confident of your preferences. Demonstrating your understanding of what the work will entail and being able to explain honestly and realistically why you want to do it will be one of the most important things to get across to recruiters.

If you want to become a commercial lawyer, you'll need this thing they call commercial awareness. We're not suggesting you become an Alan Sugar, rather that you should gain a sense of what's going on in the commercial world: football clubs being bought and sold; the rise of China as an economic powerhouse; the dominance of the big supermarket chains; the convergence of media technologies; big issues in the oil and gas sector. If you have zero interest in all this stuff, what makes you think commercial law will interest you? Why not read the *Financial Times* now and again or find an Internet site that will give you headline bulletins in bite-sized chunks. Keep up to date in a way that suits you and make sure you're not oblivious to the events going on around you at national and international level.

Students looking to go into criminal or family law should similarly keep abreast of changes in these fields. Needless to say, anyone interested in human rights issues will have a full-time job keeping up to date will all the cases and developments arising out of the war in Iraq and anti-terror measures here in the UK.

travel broadens the mind

You know that, but will recruiters agree? In short, yes, so don't play down the time you've spent exploring the world – independent travel requires a good deal of organisational and problem-solving skills. If you've itchy feet and if you haven't already been out there for a look-see, what's stopping you? The career can wait.

grey matters

Older applicants often worry needlessly that they are at a disadvantage. Far from it – so long as you have something to show for your extra years, you may find it easier to impress recruiters. You already know how to work, your people/client-handling skills are doubtless better developed and you may even have relevant experience. We've chatted with successful barristers and solicitors who've done everything from secretarial work, pub management and film production to police work and PR. But when is old too old? If you're still in your 20s, get over yourself – you're still a baby. If you're in your 30s, ask what it is you can offer a law firm that would make your application stand out. And if you're older still? Never say never. We have run into a small number of 40-something trainees. Given that each year after qualification a certain percentage of the UK's lawyers move firms or even drop out of the profession for good, the argument that employers expect 30 years of service from all new recruits simply doesn't hold water. Of greater relevance is the adage concerning old dogs and new tricks, so if your coat is greying, consider carefully how you'd cope with being asked to revert to puppyhood. It is worth remembering, of course, that the UK labour market is about to see a new era in which anti-age discrimination legislation will bite. We await the outcome of any cases affecting the legal profession with great interest.

you're not from round here are you?

London attracts young professionals from all over the world, so you can skip this bit if you're a Brit intending to work in the capital. If you hold an EU passport or have a pre-existing right to live and work in the UK and you are following the appropriate path to qualification, you should also proceed with optimism. Applicants who tick none of these boxes may find doors are easier to push open if they apply to firms with business interests in the country or region from which they come. This is because law firms have to show sound reasons why an overseas applicant is worth employing over someone who needs no work permit. Generally, the people we encountered who were neither EU nationals nor had a permanent right to live and work in the UK were training in City firms with international business or with specialist shipping practices. Additionally, a number of barristers chambers will take pupils who intend to return to practice in their home jurisdiction. In all cases, excellent written and spoken English is essential and you will need a convincing reason why you have chosen to commence your career in Ol' Blighty.

Regional firms and sets are often most comfortable recruiting candidates with a local connection, be this through family or education. Quite simply, they want to know that whoever they take on will be committed to a long-term career with them. They are wary of having their brightest and best skip off to higher-paying jobs in London on qualification. The picture across the UK is a variable one: some firms clearly state their preferences for local lads and lasses; others tell us that most of their applicants do have links with the region, but that they are happy to consider anyone. Over the years we've found Irish trainees in Staffordshire, Londoners in Exeter and Scots in Birmingham, but we've also found that law firms in certain cities tend to pick people with strong ties – ever-popular Bristol is the most obvious example.

breaking down barriers

Despite the legal profession being more diverse than ever before, for students with mental or physical disabilities things are not straightforward. In the experience of the Group for Solicitors with Disabilities (GSD), many students with disabilities have great difficulty in securing work placements and training contracts. The good news is that there are sources of advice and assistance available and the GSD has been actively involved in approaching law firms to set up designated work placement schemes for disabled students. The group also provides a forum in which students and practitioners can meet in order to share experiences and provide one another with guidance and support. Would-be barristers should refer to the Equal Opportunities (Disability) Committee of the Bar Council.

single white male

An apt description of the legal profession 30 years ago maybe. In the course of our research around 150 firms provided us with lists identifying their trainees. In most firms the girls outnumber the boys, something which we would expect to see given that more women have gone into the profession than men for at least a decade. The names reflect a healthy spread of ethnic backgrounds. It is worth mentioning, however, that female and non-white trainees still have too few senior-level role models and there are always a small number of law firm sex or race discrimination claims going through the employment tribunals.

We know scores of gay and lesbian lawyers for whom sexual orientation is entirely a non-career matter, although sexuality sparked debate in mid-2006 when a Law Society report criticised law firms, and in particular City firms, for having non gay-friendly working environments. It's fair to say that the report was widely viewed as way off the mark and the weeks following its publication saw many gay and lesbian City lawyers refute the claims and question the sampling methods used.

> During the year from February 2005 to February 2006 a Law Society-commissioned study found that among first-year trainees:
> ○ 61.5% were women.
> ○ 17.6% were from minority ethnic groups
> ○ 47.5% were located in London
> ○ The average age of trainees was 27
> ○ 22.3% were over 27
> ○ 0.3% were over 50

A number of diversity-related organisations have sprung up and you may see evidence of them at your university. Without doubt anything that encourages genuine diversity in the workplace is to be commended, but before signing on the dotted line with any intermediary – especially if you are asked to hand over any money for their services – make sure you know you are dealing with a respected organisation. Ask if they are affiliated with particular law firms and if so how. Consider whether you actually need the services of these organisations at all. A cynic might argue that the big law firms are merely in competition with each other for the best students who just also happen to be non-white, and that those students need no special help from third parties.

If you know your university gets less attention from law firms than, say, Oxford or Bristol, then a diversity-related organisation may well be just what you need to get your foot in the door. Remember too that the topic of diversity covers more than just ethnicity; if you think your accent or upbringing or a disability could stand in your way then find out if there is anything these organisations can do for you.

balancing act

What with studying hard, reading the *FT*, helping out at the local CAB, captaining both the university rugby team and its netball team, debating, acting as student law society president, acting on stage and attending all the careers events that crop up throughout the year, you'll hardly have time for a pint, let alone the ten that students supposedly put away in between lectures. Your mum and dad may tell you your years at university are supposed to be a fun, carefree time, but frankly back in their day the job market was less competitive and no one built up a small mortgage in debt before the age of 21... well, only if they had a really wild time. Besides, what do the olds know? They were too busy listening to Bachman-Turner Overdrive and having sit-down protests.

Of course you must have fun, and you absolutely must develop your interests and friendships because these, in many cases, last far longer and can be more rewarding than any career. Ultimately, it all comes down to finding the right balance.

pro bono and volunteering

Even if your idea of a dream come true is handling mergers and acquisitions in a City firm, it's time to dig deep into the corners of your soul and find your inner altruist. Recruiters are always looking for candidates with practical experience in a legal environment. As Kara Irwin, Director of the BPP Pro Bono Centre, puts it: *"Lawyers always see this as the most interesting thing on a candidate's CV. As well as being something tangible that students can contribute to the community, it gives them the opportunity to really develop important legal skills."* Volunteering can often be the best way to gain such skills, and there are plenty of available options for students who are willing to give up some of their spare time.

Every little bit counts, whether it's a half-day a week helping out at your local CAB or six months overseas work as an intern on death row appeals. However, you should perhaps ask yourself – are you able to commit to the project you start? If you're just doing something to add a notch to your CV bedpost, it's going to look pretty obvious. We've spoken to some of the law schools and pro bono organisations to find out about the sort of things on offer. We've also put together a non-exhaustive list of other organisations involved in pro bono to get you started in your quest to save the world.

make the most of your law school

Most post-graduate law schools, and increasingly university law departments, now have pro bono initiatives in place. The College of Law in London, for example has an established service for leaseholders in dispute with their freeholders over service charges, major works or the appointment of a new managing agent. After receiving training, students can go on to represent members of the public before the Leasehold Valuation Tribunal and the Rent Assessment Committee. At some colleges, pro bono is not just an option; it's a compulsory element of the course. At the Student Law Office of Northumbria University, which has

achieved Legal Services Commission Quality Marks for its housing and employment advice, all LPC and BVC students advise real clients, from the initial interview through to advocacy before tribunals and the small claims courts.

Many law schools engage in outreach work in the local community. The College of Law's Streetlaw Plus programme for its London GDL students focuses on legal literacy, with students working directly with residents of the Clapham Park Estate in South London. BPP's Streetlaw activities have included presentations to schoolchildren and inmates of Pentonville Prison.

Pro bono is not necessarily just about providing advice to individuals; it can involve carrying out research for pressure groups and international organisations. At BPP's Pro Bono Centre students have set up an intellectual property group and recently helped to conduct research in association with a leading IP firm giving advice to the International Chamber of Commerce. Its Human Rights Unit provided research support to the International Bar Association's Human Rights Institute, Reprieve and Liberty.

For undergraduates, it can often be more difficult to find a centrally organised pro bono initiative at university. If this is the case where you are studying, use your initiative to seek out work of your own. If you're young and inexperienced, don't worry; providing administrative support to an overworked legal charity still looks great on your CV and may well lead on to other things later on.

the free representation unit (fru)

Becoming a ratified member of the FRU is a really good idea if you're thinking of going to the Bar, but it's an equally good idea if you are intending to be a solicitor specialising in any contentious area of law, because chances are you'll be doing at least some of the advocacy yourself.

FRU representatives offer free advice and representation to clients who are not eligible for legal aid, appearing on their behalf before employment and social security tribunals. There is also a limited amount of work in criminal injuries compensation appeals and some immigration matters. Law students can train to become a social security representative in the final year of an LLB, while non-law graduates can do this in their GDL year. The employment option is only open to LPC and BVC students, and it should also be noted that FRU only operates in and around London, though several of the regional BVC and LPC providers have advice clinics that allow students to gain experience of tribunal advocacy.

To qualify, you'll need to attend an induction day and satisfactorily complete a legal opinion exercise. Once that's done, you'll be able to take on a case after discussing it with one of the caseworkers. Once a case is yours, you must see it through from beginning to end. A pupil barrister with a series of employment tribunal wins behind her told us: *"As a rep you'll get experience in using a whole bundle of practical legal skills. You'll conference with your client, conduct legal research, draft submissions, negotiate with your opponent, and if the case doesn't settle, you'll make oral submissions to the tribunal and get to examine and cross-examine witnesses."* From time to time, seasoned FRU reps have been known to take cases to the Employment Appeal Tribunal or the Social Security Commissioners and it's not unheard of for their names to appear in the reported decision.

If we haven't sold it to you already, it might also be pointed out that a very high proportion of the pupils and junior barristers who we interviewed for our **Chambers Reports** had worked for FRU or another similar organisation at some time during their training. It could well be the thing that saves your application from the shredder.

the possibilities are endless…

Here's a sample of the many pro bono opportunities on offer for students.

www.probonouk.net

This very useful site will identify the advice organisations working in your area. It has a section devoted to students.

LawWorks

This organisation used to be called the Solicitors Pro Bono Group. Its website http://lawworks.org.uk is a good source of advice and information, including details of student membership.

The AIRE Centre

This organisation provides information and advice throughout Europe on international human rights law, including the rights of individuals under the provisions of European Community law. It also offers direct legal advice and assistance on a case-by-case basis to legal practitioners or advisers. Internships are available for students who have a good working knowledge of international human rights law and EU law. Students must be able to commit themselves to a minimum of one day per week. A second European language is an advantage. www.airecentre.org

Amicus

This charity provides assistance to US attorneys working on death row cases. It gives training and arranges internships in the USA for UK postgraduate students. As internships are unpaid (though a limited number of scholarships do exist), interested applicants should have a plan for funding the placement. www.amicus-alj.org

Bar Pro Bono Unit

Established in 1996 by Attorney-General Lord Goldsmith QC, the unit matches individuals in need of legal representation with barristers in private practice willing to undertake work on a pro bono basis. Opportunities are available for students to provide administrative support to the unit on a part-time basis. This could mean anything from envelope stuffing to allocating cases to members of the panel. www.barprobono.org.uk.

Citizens Advice Bureaux

The Citizens Advice service has over 22,000 volunteers in over 2,000 bureaux. Those with real commitment and enough time can train with the CAB on its Adviser Training Programme to gain a widely recognised qualification that may subsequently enable your law firm training contract to be reduced by up to six months. Not all volunteers have the time or the inclination to train as advisers, so if admin, IT or reception work is enough for you, why not request one of these roles or offer to help out with publicity and media activities. Debt, benefits, housing, employment, consumer issues, family matters and immigration are the most commonly raised problems, some six million of which are handled each year. www.citizensadvice.org.uk

Independent Custody Visiting

Independent custody visiting began in the wake of the Scarman Report following the Brixton riots of 1981. Independent custody visitors (ICVs) work in pairs, conducting regular unannounced checks on police stations in their area to monitor the welfare of the detainees. Anyone over the age of 18 can apply to become an ICV. The Independent Custody Visiting Association website contains full details. www.icva.org.uk

Law Centres

Law centres provide free and independent legal services to people who live or work in their catchment areas. Their work is typically in fields where legal aid is not available – eg employment and immigration law. Working at a law centre is very much a career in itself; however, many centres accept student volunteers to provide administrative support and assistance with casework. The website www.lawcentres.org.uk provides links to individual law centres across the UK.

Liberty

This is a well-established human rights organisation providing advice and representation to groups and individuals in relation to domestic law cases involving the Human Rights Act. Liberty has opportunities for a small number of students to provide general office assistance and help with casework. Students should be able to commit at least one day a week. www.liberty-human-rights.org.uk

Victim Support

The Victim Support Witness Service operates in every Crown Court across England and Wales, providing guidance and support to witnesses, victims and their families before, during and after court proceedings. Volunteers need to be able to commit at least two hours per week. www.victimsupport.org.uk

Refugee Council

The Refugee Council is largest refugee agency in the UK with offices in the East of England, West Midlands, London and Yorkshire and Humberside. It provides advice to asylum seekers and refugees on the asylum procedure, support and entitlement. Volunteers can offer their assistance in three areas: direct services, office-based and community-based. www.refugeecouncil.org

If you opted to spend your time at uni reading great books or hunched over a microscope, you can still come to the law via a one-year conversion course known as the Graduate Diploma in Law (GDL). You may also see the course referred to as the CPE (Common Professional Exam) or PgDL (Post-graduate Diploma in Law). The GDL will bring you up to a required standard in the seven core legal subjects that are typically taught in the first two years of an LLB. Because skills like textual analysis, research, logical argument, writing and presentation can be acquired in a whole range of disciplines from Classics to chemistry, legal employers tend not to make a distinction between applicants with an LLB and those with the GDL.

The standard requirement for admission is a degree from university in the UK or Republic of Ireland. It is possible for non-graduates to get on to a course if they've shown the requisite drive and have exceptional ability in some other field. Such candidates – and those with a degree from an overseas university – must obtain a Certificate of Academic Standing from the Bar Council or Law Society before enrolling on the GDL.

The course is no walk in the park. Taken full-time it lasts a minimum of 36 weeks, during which you'll be expected to undertake 45 hours of lectures, tutorials and private study each week. It is possible to take the course part-time over two years. Assessment tends to be by written exams, with regular coursework and an extended essay thrown in. Depending on the institution you attend, there will be more or less emphasis on academic essays, written problem questions or practical preparation of debates for the classroom. Because the institutions that offer the GDL vary in perceived quality, their approach and the composition of their student bodies, it is well worth doing your research before you apply. City University and Nottingham are renowned for offering more academic courses, often attracting a large number of students headed for the Bar. In London, BPP, for example, is packed with City types and there are reams of paper and manuals that need to be consigned to memory.

- There's a huge amount to take in so get into a good study routine early on.
- You'll be given reading lists, but never underestimate the value of a full set of *Nutshells* crib books.
- Attend classes!

On the GDL you will be given a grounding in the core principles and statutes and be exposed to the key case law in each area. Legal reasoning is, for the most part, an exacting discipline – there is not much room for posturing, even if the opinions of some esteemed judges may defy any conventional standards of logic. English Common Law is an intriguing amalgam of cold logic and a concern for justice to be done – a combination of metaphysics, logic and ethics, with a good bit of policy thrown in.

- **Land Law:** Well-defined rights over property are important for raising money, renting out properties, even – it has been argued – the flourishing of democracy and the entire capitalist system. Remember this when you are dealing with the arcane vocabulary needed to work out what kind of rights a divorced wife has over a matrimonial home bought by her husband; how someone can squat an abandoned house; and how to decide who, if anyone, owns wild animals or the treasure you dig up in your garden. More pressing concerns include how to not get screwed over if you buy a house with a friend; how to claim a right of light when a new building blocks out the sun from your garden; and how to prevent the bank foreclosing on your mortgage. Finding the answers involves some mind-numbing jargon, and it's safe to say that at times the subject feels drier than the Sahara. But for the technically and metaphysically minded, it's like getting under the bonnet of an antique car with a box of medieval tools. Words to try and work into dinner party conversation: incorporeal hereditament, chattel, lien, fee simple, restrictive covenant.

- **EU:** The law of the European Union is massively important since the European Court of Justice (ECJ) is effectively the highest court of appeal for all its member states. This course studies the institutions, sources and underlying principles of the EU system and substantive European law. Big subjects include the establishment of a free market, the free movement of workers, competition policy and the freedom of establishment as well as the incorporation of the European Convention on Human Rights into our national law. For Europhiles it is a fascinating mix of politics, history, economics and comparative jurisprudence. This is the stuff of competition law; an enduringly popular area of commercial practice, particularly for those with a love for Brussels.

- **Trusts and Equity:** The uninitiated (and fans of Dickens) would be forgiven for thinking that trusts are the preserve of tax-evading toffs. The truth of the matter is that the 'trust' (the legal arrangement whereby one person holds property for another) has a multiplicity of uses. It has applications in the worlds of high finance and charity as much as in providing a nest egg for a beloved grandchild. The trust is a key contribution made by 'equity' – a rather opaque term for a line of law that calls upon ideas of 'fairness' to remedy any injustices brought about by the strict application of black letter law. Top tip: If you haven't done your preparation for your trust tutorial – the cry 'it's unconscionable' will likely get you out of jail free. The course deals with how to set up a trust with its various formalities, quirks like how to set up trusts for illegitimate kids without your wife knowing, what happens in fiendishly complicated financial transactions

when someone tries to set up a trust to avoid tax (the name Vandervell will haunt you for years after) and how to establish a valid charity. You'll also look at the duties of trustees, remedies against them and how to recover money that has been misapplied. Trusts and equity are the bread and butter of Chancery law, which preoccupies some of the biggest brain boxes at the Bar. They also crop up in solicitors' practice through anything from complex financial transactions to advice to individuals.

- **Contract:** The law of contract governs when an agreement becomes legally binding and thus enforceable. The principles you learn here underpin any commercial agreement you'll have to draft, peruse or persuade someone to sign. You'll look at how to tell when a contract is formed, the required formalities, permissible terms and what happens if the seller has lied to you about the fact your house is built on a rubbish dump or is haunted. Interesting issues include what to do if you make a mistake in signing a document because you've forgotten your specs; whether displaying a flick knife in your shop window is an offer to sell it and what to do if your letter of acceptance of a job offer gets lost in the post. It will certainly make you think twice about signing on the dotted line, encourage you to actually read the small print and see the phrase 'self-induced frustration' in a whole new light.

- **Crime:** Some people think the law begins and ends at crime. Perhaps they watch too much *CSI*. In terms of human interest this subject reaches parts that the others don't even know exist. Whether your interest is in policy or in the gruesome things that people do to one another, the crime course should provide plenty to engage and surprise. The syllabus touches on all the usual suspects: sexual offences; theft; assault and homicide as well as more philosophical discussion of the elements of a crime, known as the

Actus Reus (the behavioural element) and the Mens Rea (the requisite state of mind). Also covered are the liability of secondary parties, as well as the inchoate offences – incitement, conspiracy, and attempted crimes. As well as being able to advise your underworld drinking buddies, by the end of the course you'll also be in a better position to explain why it's okay for a wife to consent to her husband branding his initials on her backside, but not for grown men to allow each other to whip their genitals with stinging nettles.

- **Tort:** The law of civil wrong covers anything from tripping on a wonky paving stone to keeping the neighbours up with your pirate radio station or publishing porkies on your website. To show that a tort has been committed you must prove the person suffering the loss was owed a 'duty of care', that there was a breach of that duty and that some kind of loss resulted from the breach. The big subjects here are negligence and nuisance, but also covered are a veritable ragbag of wrongs ranging from defamation, occupiers' liability and liability for fire and wild animals. The common thread is working out who is to blame for a chain of unfortunate incidents leading to some kind of injury – either physical or financial. The most famous case is Donoghue v Stevenson which involves a lady finding a snail in a bottle of ginger beer. Other gems include a dwarf who was trampled by a circus elephant and a war of words between columnist Julie Burchill and actor Steven Berkoff. Other intriguing problems are whether the fire brigade has a duty of care to answer an emergency call and what happens if you suffer some kind of nervous illness from witnessing a horrific accident or you slip on spilt yogurt in a supermarket. This is the field which fuels the so-called compensation culture and gives lawyers a bad name. If constitutional law is *The West Wing* and Trusts is *Bleak House,* Tort is more like *You've Been Framed* or maybe even *Jackass.*

- **Constitutional and Administrative:** On 'Con and Ad', as it is affectionately known, you'll be required to study and write thoughtful essays on the impact of the EU, human rights legislation, the process of judicial review and the functioning and evolution of the Houses of Lords and Commons. You'll also look at constitutional issues and big topics like the Royal prerogative, the rule of law and Parliamentary sovereignty. For ivory tower types this will be a welcome respite from talk about reasonable behaviour and old statutes. While the constitutional side of the course may be mostly academic, the administrative aspects underpin public law – an area which involves challenging the government and its agencies – something that should appeal to rebels and rabble-rousers.

how to apply

All GDL applications are made through the Central Applications Board (www.lawcabs.ac.uk). It's worth getting your application in as early as possible if you have your heart set on a particular institution. Applications for first-round 2007/08 applications must be made by 1 February 2007. The institutions will consider these and make offers between 1 February and early April. Applications made from 1 February until early April will be considered in early April. Later applications will be considered as and when they are received. In short, the later you apply the more flexible you may have to be about where you study. It's also worth bearing in mind that if you intend to go on and do an LPC or BVC at a very popular institution you might stand a better chance if you choose it for your GDL. The GDL is now offered at around 30 different universities and law schools in England and Wales. Our website has full details of course providers, fees and other useful information.

After the academic stage of training, the year-long LPC is akin to a finishing school for young professionals run by someone with shares in a paper mill. It can be taken part-time over two years, and some of those who do it this way combine it with a three-year training contract.

Be warned that this is not an academic course. If the LLB or CPE was cookery school – learning about new ingredients, trying new techniques, reading recipes – this year you're in the kitchen, scrubbing spuds, washing dishes and getting ticked off if you're late for class. The LPC is designed to provide prospective solicitors with the skills required for the world of work, so essays are replaced with letters of advice, mooting with advocacy and textbooks with manuals and precedents as students get to grips with the practical tasks they will face every day in the office. The course also introduces students to essential practical issues and procedural techniques that they are unlikely to have previously encountered, for example, professional conduct, accounts and tax.

Students straight from demanding university degrees may feel like they've stepped back to junior school with all the handouts, copious spoon-feeding and prosaic material to get through. There will be literally kilos of paper to file. Many students resign themselves early to the thought that the LPC year is to be endured rather than enjoyed.

The first part of the year is spent on certain compulsory elements. Students are taught and then assessed on legal skills such as interviewing, advocacy, drafting, letter writing and legal research. They also cover knowledge areas including civil and criminal litigation practice, conveyancing and business law. These are examined in February. The remaining months are devoted to three elective subjects that are examined in the summer. Commonly subjects like private acquisitions, debt and equity finance, commercial law and advanced property law are studied by those headed for City law firms. Family law, private client and personal injury/clinical negligence are typical choices of those who are avoiding commercial practice. The range of electives available to students varies from one course provider to another. For a full list of who offers what, refer to our website.

The LPC doesn't quite go so far as tell you how to unblock a photocopier or how to match your shirt and tie but here are some of the things you will learn:

- When to use 'Yours sincerely', how to conduct yourself in a meeting and the politest way to stop a chatty client mid-flow.
- What forms you need to submit to Companies House to register a new company or appoint a director.
- How much tax you need to pay on an old piece of equipment that you've had for five years and are selling on to your son.
- What procedure you need to follow when you're exchanging contracts to buy or sell a house over the telephone.
- When precisely you should post a claim form if it has to arrive on Tuesday and there's a Bank Holiday the day before.
- How to draft a witness statement.
- How many different bank accounts you'll need for your clients' money and why you can't switch funds between accounts willy nilly.
- Who you can act for and who you can't.
- Your duties to the court.

There is growing debate about whether much of the course couldn't be better learnt on the job rather than in the classroom. The key participants in the debate are the Law Society, the law firms and the law schools. The Law Society in particular has proposed sweeping changes in professional legal education, though its proposals are not always received well.

A Law Society recommendation to scrap the requirement for all trainee solicitors to take the LPC hit the buffers in the face of arguments that this proposal risked lowering standards. The society has not abandoned its aim to broaden access to the profession and is now proposing changes to the LPC to allow greater diversity between providers in the delivery of core course components. Among other things, these latest proposals consider the provision of more skills assessments and even the possibility that students could study elective subjects at different providers. Experience tells us that nothing coming out of the Law Society is ever simple – and certainly nothing related to legal training – so perhaps all readers need to know for now is that the LPC remains the route to training as a solicitor. As and when things become concrete the LPC providers are likely to be swift to take advantage and make their course offerings known to students.

- Overall LPC pass rate for 2005: 81.2% (6,527 students)
- Pass with Distinction: 21.3%
- Pass with Commendation: 35.9%
- Pass: 23.9%
- Refer/resit/defer/fail:18.8%
- Withdrawn: 2.9%

Figures published by the Law Society

The LPC table on our website will reveal that the cost of taking the course is substantial. This is of most concern to the many students who self-fund because there is no financial support from the type of law firm in which they intend to practise. Since the Access to Justice Act 1999, the government has promised to fill gaps in the coverage of legal services in the UK, yet less than 0.5% of public spending currently goes on these services. The number of students training to provide advice to legally aided clients is shrinking and so the Legal Services Commission (LSC) has

in the last few years set aside an annual figure of £3 million to help fund students who agree to go into legally aided practice for at least two years after qualification. Around 100 students benefit each year. The grants are awarded via law firms so don't think about applying to the LSC direct. If you want to know which law firms will have available funds, this information will be posted on the LSC website. To ensure good use of the funds, the LSC requires beneficiaries of the grant to take elective subjects that are pertinent to smaller and high street firms, law centres and local authority practice.

At the other end of the scale, those students signed up to train with the country's biggest and most profitable commercial law firms benefit from generous law school sponsorship packages. These rarely come without conditions; indeed with each passing year the conditions become more stringent. Ten years ago few firms cared which LPC provider you chose. Now, an increasing number of them tell you where to go. This development needs to be understood in the wider context of an increasingly competitive LPC provider market. The two front runners in the rapidly changing race for LPC supremacy are BPP Law School and COL. Each is busy signing deals with large law firms to provide either tailor-made electives or entire bespoke courses. For example, if you choose Linklaters for your training contract you must study a Linklaters LPC at the COL's new Moorgate branch. Choose Berwin Leighton Paisner and you must take the new LPC+ which contains elective subjects designed by the firm in collaboration with COL. Sign with Addleshaw Goddard and you must take a standard LPC course with commercial electives at one of BPP's three schools in Manchester, Leeds or London. Your classes will still be shared with students headed to other firms. Both BPP and COL have contracts with other law firms. We expect more to follow and for other LPC providers to climb into bed with commercial law firms.

Another product of the increasingly competitive LPC market is the introduction of MBA-style modules onto the course. Behind this is the idea that young lawyers need a greater awareness of the business context in which their clients operate. If you think that as a crime or family lawyer such knowledge will be superfluous, think again. As a partner in a law firm, you too may one day be running a business of your own.

how to apply

The Central Applications Board administers all applications for full-time LPCs. Its website is www.lawcabs.ac.uk . Applications for the 2007/08 full-time course that are received by 1 December 2006 will be processed between 1 December and late March. Applications received before the end of March will be processed at the end of March. Applications received any later will be processed as and when they are received. Later applicants' chances of securing a place popular providers are reduced but be aware that, nationwide, there are more validated places than enrolled students on both full and part-time courses. Applications for part-time courses should be made directly to the providers.

There are plenty of things to consider when choosing a law school, so be sure to arm yourself with as much information as possible. Request prospectuses, attend open days, chat to representatives visiting your university, talk to current students and ascertain your priorities.

- **career issues**: Your future employer (if you have one) may well specify where you go and at the very least they should be able to give you advice, based on the experiences of current trainees. If you don't yet have a training contract, look into the range of extra-curricular activities, clubs and societies on offer

that may help you improve your CV. Also think about the quality of careers advice available at each institution. Have they got a good record of getting students placements and training contracts?

- **electives**: Find out if your future employer wants you to take any particular electives. Otherwise, find out which course providers offer the electives best suited to the type of practice you want to move into. Some may have restrictions on elective combinations or run electives only when there is sufficient demand. For a full run-down on who offers what, see our website.

- **assessment grades and pass rates**: Pass rates are published on the Law Society's website each autumn, but be aware that direct comparisons are impossible as each institution examines and marks independently of the others. The Law Society visits and inspects each institution and then publishes a report. Once based on a simple grading system from excellent to satisfactory, the picture has been muddied by the Law Society's decision to revise its assessment grading. As the new system will take another two years to roll out to all LPC providers, direct comparisons between them will be difficult for a while.

- **teaching and assessment methods**: Most institutions timetable around 14 hours of classes per week, but there uniformity ends. If you have travel plans, you may want to check term dates, as these can vary between institutions by a good couple of weeks. Similarly, if you are going to have a long commute to classes, or are hoping to fit in part-time work, check the timetabling of classes. Some places will fix you up with neat morning or afternoon timetables and a day off mid-week; others will expect you to hang around between classes that are spread throughout the day. The latest thing is e-learning. Instead of large lectures, The College of Law is making 'i-tutorials' available online and on DVD. Examination and assessment methods vary too, with some schools expecting more coursework, others placing greater emphasis on exams. Whereas some institutions only permit a modest statute book and practitioner text to be taken into the exam room, others hold entirely open-book exams leading to students precariously balancing files and books Jenga-style on tiny exam desks.

○ **facilities:** For every school where students must shoehorn themselves into flip-up seats in vast lecture theatres, there is another where they can lounge on a swivel seat in their own mock office. Take the LPC course at a university and you'll belong to a proper law faculty (complete with Klix coffee machine and last week's *Independent*); elsewhere, orchids and acres of plate glass may convince you that you've strayed into the offices of a City firm. For some students, a large institution is nothing less than a giant speed-dating opportunity; for others it will offer desired anonymity. Conversely, the intimacy of smaller classes in a smaller school may appeal.

○ **tactics:** Some of the most popular institutions require you to put them as first choice on the LawCabs application form. We have included this type of information on the LPC providers table on our website. Check also whether your university, GDL provider or law firm has an agreement or relationship with a provider.

○ **money and fees:** Fees vary and so do the institutions' policies on the inclusion of the cost of textbooks and Law Society membership, etc. Even if you have sponsorship from a law firm, living expenses still need to be taken into account. The cost of living in London especially can be a nasty shock if you haven't lived there before.

○ **location:** Plenty of students find that tight finances restrict their choice of school. Living at home will save you a packet... if you can stand it. If you're lucky enough to be able to strike out on your own, it's worth considering what you like or don't like about your university or GDL provider and whether you want to prolong your undergraduate experience or escape it. Be aware that certain LPC providers are dominated by graduates of local universities.

○ **social mix and social life:** Would you prefer to be somewhere with students following a similar career path or mix it up with a wider cross-section of people? Studenty cities such as Nottingham and Bristol are always a lot of fun, but the bright lights of the capital may be irresistible. Experience tells us that compared to those in other cities, students in London tend to slink off the moment classes end.

lpc provider snapshots

In past editions we chose to write features on those LPC providers that were rated as 'Excellent' or 'Very Good' by the Law Society. The Society has now changed the way in which it grades providers and is no longer awarding a simple, single grade (from 'Excellent' down to 'Satisfactory').

The new grades will not be known for all providers for another two years, effectively leaving students looking at two different grading systems. We have decided not to use Law Society grades to identify the best providers for inclusion in this guide this year.

On our website you will find a table detailing all of the providers and allowing a comparison of their fees, student numbers, available option subjects and useful tips for applicants.

the lpc providers

- Anglia Ruskin University
- Bournemouth University
- BPP Law School, London
- BPP Law School, Manchester
- BPP Law School, Leeds
- Bristol Institute of Legal Practice at UWE
- Cardiff Law School
- College of Law at Birmingham
- College of Law at Chester
- College of Law at Guildford
- College of Law at London
- College of Law at York
- De Montfort University
- Inns of Court School of Law
- Leeds Metropolitan University
- Liverpool John Moores University
- London Metropolitan University
- Manchester Metropolitan University
- Nottingham Law School
- Oxford Institute of Legal Practice
- Staffordshire University
- Thames Valley University
- University of Central England in Birmingham
- University of Central Lancashire
- University of Glamorgan
- University of Hertfordshire (p/t)
- University of Huddersfield
- University of Northumbria
- University of Plymouth
- University of Sheffield
- University of Wales, Aberystwyth
- University of Wales, Swansea
- University of Westminster
- University of Wolverhampton

what trainees say

This year we have chosen to provide feedback on those LPC providers attended by trainees at the 150 firms featured in The True Picture. They have had time to reflect on the usefulness of the LPC course in practice. Where we received only limited feedback on providers we chose not to include them to avoid the problem of bias due to insufficient sample size.

The following comments are at times contradictory, yet this is not surprising given that trainees' views ranged from positive to negative with regard to the same institutions. We have taken care to ensure that the following spliced sound bites are a representative cross-section of what trainees thought of their time at the following law schools.

It should also be borne in mind that, because the LPC landscape is shifting so much, so too is the make-up of the student body at a number of providers. What former students may have seen as a bonus or a problem in this respect could have changed by the time you take your course in 2007/08 or 2008/09.

bpp law school

london: Very slick • amazing facilities • good central location • the student lifestyle ranks far below looking professional and getting results • I went into it expecting hard work, and I got it • heavy workload but very well structured • the teaching was very good and prepared you well for the exams • nice place but aimed at the major firms and the magic circle • it felt like most people were going to City firms • the LPC was very relevant for what I am doing now and I still refer to my notes • very professional, amazing facilities • I liked the way they structured things; you had to take responsibility • the tutors were commercially aware and really knew what they were doing • I made some really good friends there • they treat you like a businessman • things are taught very much with a view to going into corporate law

leeds: Staff good, quality of materials good • I was so pleased the BPP course was available in the North • I had a choice of providers in Leeds but knew it would be the best one to have on my CV • it felt a bit transitory; it hadn't yet got its own culture • I didn't have to go to London, so I could live at home

NB: Insufficient BPP Manchester feedback was available from trainees

cardiff law school

Excellent. I loved it. The course was so well taught and you were not anonymous. Time and effort was put in by each and every tutor • I though it was brilliant; it was well organised and all the tutors were fantastic – they were really on the students' level • a very sociable year • I went there because of their 'excellent' rating • good at trying to find you a training contract and provide you with career updates and talks • my tutor set me up on a vacancy list that led to me getting this training contract

college of law (all branches)

COL has so much experience • very good teaching • the practical focus of the course allowed you to see the relevance to what we were learning • there was a big discrepancy in workload over the terms; it should have been better structured • people need to realise that it's very time consuming… late nights, weekends – it really takes over • if you do what you're told you'll pass • almost spoon-fed, but I quite liked that • a pretty full year and then a lot of cramming. • it was intense and there was no time to get bored • I liked the open-book exams • it was a big shock to the system. When you go into practice then it makes sense • the right sort of atmosphere, though others criticised the policy of forcing people to sit at prescribed tables

• I felt a bit old for signing the register • really helpful careers service which I continued to use after I'd finished my LPC • a good mix of corporate and other pathways • I was quite wary at the start because of my age, but there were a number of mature students • split into mornings and afternoons, so I had every afternoon off • four afternoons a week: I liked the timetable • the course was a stepping stone to work: it's a bit more like a job with an actual physical workload • **london:** I went there because the COL was more diverse than BPP so the law felt broader for longer. I met people who would be high street solicitors • a nice pleasant atmosphere • it's very big so it's quite impersonal. You don't get to know the teaching staff so it's a bit like a conveyor belt, but I was lucky and made good friends • my boyfriend was at Westminster and he found there wasn't as much going on socially; I played girls' football • if I'd had a choice I wouldn't have gone there. London misses out on the social life that Nottingham has because everyone lives so far apart

guildford: It was hard work but I was well taught and I made good friends • very supportive teachers • superb, very well resourced • nice and leafy and great being close to London. Very good on the social side • I was glad to get out of the city – no tube, no commute. I liked all the villages and green fields surrounding the college • the location is spectacular • I am totally in love with Guildford • I was able to live locally with my parents • I got to play football regularly • laid back atmosphere and less competitive

chester: Such a lovely place and cheaper than Guildford or London • a lot of regional firms' students • people tend to be going to firms in the North West so you get none of the City types • it's not the biggest place so it can feel restrictive if you're there for two years • lots of resources • a good mile out of the city centre • I wasn't ready to make the change to the Big Smoke • a down-to-earth place • bloody hard work, not as much of a doddle as everyone thinks. I got a distinction though

birmingham: Very good, very professional; you have to work quite hard • provided with all the books and the packs – a lot to get through but the course is very organised • like a sixth-form college with friendly tutors and good pastoral care • I took all the commercial electives I could • seemed well taught, the majority of teachers were very good • incredibly well organised and efficient – they get the job done

york: One of the best places I've ever lived • York is great to go around and have a few beers • I had absolutely no problems but if I had I could have seen my personal tutor • there were always people to talk to • intense • lots of people knew each other • a lot of people going to northern firms. Having said that it's a bit depressing if you only get to know one kind of lawyer • it has lost some of the commuter students since BPP opened in Leeds • a closed environment • small and intimate • more personal than Cardiff • I found it hard to shift back into a rigid, structured, school system • it's based in an old school building • the tutors ranged from excellent to hopeless • I got my head down and treated it like a nine-to-five job so I got the results I wanted • a good background for starting work • focused on what you need to learn

inns of court school of law
(to be known as the city law school from 2008)

I couldn't recommend it more highly • not academic enough to be interesting and not practical enough to be interesting • it was a case of spoon-feeding. Having so many students packed onto the course necessitates that way of teaching • I chose it because there was more civil liberties-type options • nice buildings, history, trees • staff were helpful • a good learning-by-doing approach • a gruelling, boring course – it's a matter of getting through it • not intellectual but

rigorous in getting you ready for practice • excellent, really good staff and teaching • small, only 120 people, so you know everyone's name • the teachers are friendly; I would recommend it

northumbria university

I am very positive about my experiences • the Student Law Office is great. I did three cases and in one of them we won three grand for the guy. It's nice to have the experience before you start your training • the students were a mixed bag, not just northern • I did the LPC by way of the law exempting degree. As to how recruiters view the exempting degree, they are split into two camps – those who don't know and then have their eyes opened, and those who know all about it and really rate it • Newcastle is an awesome city

nottingham law school

I went for the quality of the teaching. What you learn stands you in good stead for starting work • it was a brilliant law school • the place to go for the LPC • the calibre of students around you pushes you on. There are times you think it might be easier to be at other institutions • no tutors were unconvincing; all seemed commercially aware • I was able to do commercial electives • the small group seminars work well • the tutors were good at giving feedback • a lot to remember in one year; it's not absolutely fascinating but really very well run • on the whole well taught and well structured, it set me up well for practice • very commercially focused • got you through what you needed to do • not the most exciting course but it got me thinking about law in a different way: from an academic way to a practical one • a lot of rote learning, handouts and learning straight off those • an intense year • the case studies were extremely useful • bit of a factory, but you can definitely tell they are good at it • they make it as pain-free as possible • pretty regimented and stuff, particularly as I had had some time out before • slightly boot campish, but good fun nonetheless • I couldn't hack the ridiculously long days • very big, so split into three cohorts • it was very much a City and commercial LPC as the magic circle was putting so much money into it, but it has changed again now • Nottingham is a brilliant place to be a student • I managed to get brand new accommodation right next to the law school • I didn't enjoy living in Nottingham. I grew up in a rough place but the level of street crime was a little too much in Nottingham • a decent provincial city – not as good as people made it out to be

oxford institute of legal practice

The course is a bit turgid but Oxford is a pretty good place to study. It's so easy; everything is within walking distance • great; I don't know why they've lost the City consortium students • the only people who failed were the ones who didn't do any work • I didn't enjoy it, not the place itself and not the LPC. I was with a lot of City trainees – people going to smaller firms were in the minority • the work itself was very different from university so it was quite a shock – no more essays and plenty of form filling • supportive • the classes were big but the tutors were better than those where I'd done my GDL • excellent facilities and a nice environment; I think it's partly a size thing • I liked it less than BPP • unbelievably boring and dragged out to the nth degree of tedium • looking back, I had a great year – no lectures, paid to be a student, went to the odd class • I was able to move back

home • It's nice and small so it is more intimate than the London providers • I tried to challenge tutors but they don't want you to answer in your own way. They want you to answer from the book and to stop thinking independently. It's the same at BPP. In a way it prepares you more than you realise for how firms want you to behave; you do have to conform to their standards

bristol institute of legal practice, university of the west of england

Very intensive and a lot of contact time • I enjoyed the skills subjects but was not so keen on the others • I went because they had advanced criminal litigation • really good course, the only negative was that, unlike the COL, at UWE it was a nine-to-five timetable that changed every week. For me it was harder to study and impossible to get a part-time job • the course instructors were brilliant • it was a shock to the system and fairly unforgiving; I was ill at a couple of stages • the work just doesn't ever stop • I went because it had a very good report from the assessors • one of the top-ranked courses • tutors were very good and I made a great group of friends • a lot of tutor contact and group work • many of the tutors were still practising as well as teaching • lots of one-on-one contact with tutors • very good preparation for being a trainee • UWE has not got great sports facilities • out on the edge of town • it can be a pain getting to the campus but Bristol is a fantastic place to live

the bar vocational course (bvc)

The BVC is the vocational stage of training for those intending to practise at the Bar in England and Wales. It additionally attracts international students keen to acquire the qualification before returning to practise in their own countries. The course lasts one academic year (two for part-time students) and is offered at nine law schools: three in London and six others in Bristol, Cardiff, Leeds, Manchester, Newcastle and Nottingham. Applications are made using the online system www.bvconline.co.uk; the first round for 2007 admissions opens on 17 October 2006 and closes in mid-January. A clearing process runs from March to July 2007.

make a considered decision

Before firing off a BVC application, it's worth taking a long hard look in the mirror and asking yourself whether the BVC is right for you. Have you really got what it takes to succeed at the Bar? Get sufficient experience and seek enough advice to make an informed decision about pursuing a career as a barrister. For a dose of harsh reality, look at the table on page 740 and note the yawning gulf between the numbers completing the BVC and those securing pupillage and tenancy. From 2008 only those who have completed pupillage will be 'called to the Bar', so there will no longer be a consolatory title for those who complete the BVC but don't progress to the next stage of training. If nothing else makes you think long and hard about whether a BVC is worth doing, the cost certainly should. Fees exceed £10,000 at all but a minority of the providers and living expenses come on top. Do the maths and explore the funding options, the main ones being scholarships from the Inns of Court, bank loans and, if you're lucky, the Bank of Mum & Dad.

It is the huge expense of the BVC year that led many of the students and barristers we have spoken with to advocate a tightening on entry requirements. The Bar Council does not support this view and has instead validated certain providers to take even more students. In 2006, for example, BPP was permitted to start a BVC course in Leeds, offering places to 48 full-time and 48 part-time students and other providers have added part-time courses. The Bar Council's stance is that access to the Bar must be more open. But at what cost? As more places are validated, collective BVC student debt rises because there is no corresponding increase in the number of pupillages.

If, after some honest conversations with yourself and others, you're 100% convinced the course is right for you, then go for it. Whatever happens at least you'll know you went into the BVC with your eyes wide open to the risks and challenges.

securing a place

When it comes to getting a place on the BVC, don't underestimate the competition. While meeting the Bar Council's criteria isn't onerous in itself – if you're a member of an Inn and have a 2:2 LLB or GDL pass under your belt you've made the grade – the real entry standards are slightly higher. High demand for places means academic grades do matter. BPP, for one, has upped the ante by formally requiring a 2:1, save in exceptional circumstances. The course directors we spoke to emphasised that they also want to see *"evidence of a commitment to the Bar,"* be it through mini-pupillages, paralegalling or pro bono experience. *"Plenty of public speaking,"* particularly in competitive arenas such as mooting and debating, also helps an application stand out. To make a well-targeted application you need to check out the application criteria on the course provider's website. It's also worth noting that providers focus on those who have listed them as first choice on the BVC online form. Nottingham for example has *"only looked at first-round, first-choice applicants for the last three years."*

High demand may make for competition at the application stage, but once on the course don't expect to find a full class of students who are destined to be stars of the Bar. The increasing number of BVC places combined with a lack of formal interview or assessment as part of the application means that at some institutions there are BVC students who are frankly not up to the job or who just seem ill-suited to the nature of practice at the Bar. And, while plenty of international students who gain places are highly capable, there are others whose English is not up to advocacy standard. Past BVC students tell us it can be particularly frustrating when you are pitted against a poor English speaker or overly nervous opponent in an advocacy class.

choosing a provider

Research thoroughly what the various institutions have to offer by reading prospectuses, attending open days and chatting to past and current students. Current Bar Council rules mean course content, class sizes and assessment vary little, but there are differences between schools that can make or break the year. Here are some things to think about when doing your homework:

- **Cost:** Some providers and locations are significantly cheaper than others. London is the priciest but there is variation even in the capital. If you're an international student, look out for the differential in price, and part-timers should note whether year-two fees are higher;
- **Location:** Out-of-London providers are the best option for those looking for pupillage on the circuits because of their strong links with local barristers, judges and other professionals. It does not, however, follow that London is the only place for a capital-bound pupil. Professionals do get involved with London BVC students but, in our assessment, such contact is a bigger thing in the regions. London students are closer

to the Inns of Court though regional students can easily maintain links with their Inns;
- **Size:** Smaller providers pride themselves on being more intimate and collegiate. Student feedback indicates this does matter;
- **Facilities:** By taking a BVC at a university, students can tap into a wider range of support services, sports and social activities than elsewhere. As for library and IT resources, naturally the level of dedicated BVC space and facilities varies from one institution to another, as does the level of hi-tech gadgetry used in teaching;
- **Options:** The available option subjects vary from one provider to another so read the small print. Although a popular choice, a judicial review course, for example, is not offered across the board. See our BVC providers table on www.chambersandpartners.co.uk/chambersstudent for a comparison of what's offered at the nine providers. The table also shows the fees charged at each and gives provider-specific application tips;
- **Pro bono:** Across the nine providers the organised opportunities range from minimal to superb.

what can you expect from the course?

The academic study of substantive law is not the focus of the BVC. Instead the spotlight is on developing the skills of advocacy, drafting, opinion writing, conferencing, negotiation, case analysis and legal research. Students are required to wade through civil and criminal litigation procedure and grapple with rules of evidence. Learning for the multiple-choice tests used to examine this 'knowledge' component is *"a very time-consuming part of the course,"* but in fact only counts for 15% of the final mark. It is only in the final term that students have some choice and pick two option subjects. These only give a taster of an area of practice but at least it's a start. Most teaching is delivered to groups of 12 people, with the rest tackled by way of classes of six for oral skills and some lectures. Methods vary slightly but learning is commonly by way of case studies – mock sets of papers that are followed through the litigation process. Written-skills classes often involve interactive drafting exercises, whereas role play and video-recording are used to improve oral and performance skills. The skills acquired are tested in over a dozen assessments that *"come thick and fast,"* especially in the second and third terms. Written skills are tested through a mix of unseen, seen and take-home tests (depending on where you study) while actors are drafted in to play all kinds of characters in oral assessments.

The course and assessments sound hectic and course directors tell us *"it is a tough course, so students do have to work hard,"* yet student opinion on this differs. Many tell us the BVC experience is *"not a particularly testing year,"* but by no means all. Students tend to fall into three groups: those who struggle; those who rest on their laurels a bit because they already have a pupillage offer; and those who throw themselves into the course to achieve high marks, sometimes because they still need to impress chambers' recruiters. As one course director conceded: *"There is a possibility that bright students with well-developed skills will find it frustrating"* after the demands of a challenging undergraduate law degree or an intensive conversion course. But even for them, the BVC does represent a chance to *"snap out of an academic mind-set and into a practical one."*

making the best of it

Many students complain that the course is overly long and frustratingly artificial; all believe it is too expensive. Reforms have been suggested over the years, but a recent Bar Council consultation paper put the prospect of imminent change to bed by concluding that a major review should wait until at least 2008. Don't hold your breath.

The best way to approach the BVC is as a transition from the ivory tower to the courtroom. Try to extract as much worthwhile experience from it as you can, whether or not you have pupillage. The BVC year is a great time for mooting and other advocacy competitions and most providers have pro bono units. One student *"found the BVC year gave me the chance to get really involved with the Inn and FRU."* The Inns run their own mooting and debating competitions and provide opportunities to socialise with barristers, judges and other students at dinners, lectures and advocacy training weekends. You will also have the time during holidays and reading weeks to squeeze in mini-pupillages or court marshalling to spruce up your CV.

the lowdown on the bvc providers

bpp law school, london
Number of places: 264 f/t, 96 p/t

As soon as you walk into BPP's steel and glass Holborn headquarters you'll be left in no doubt that BPP means business. Sign up and you become a client of this big, professional education company with a distinctly corporate feel. BPP spares no time, effort or resources in pushing its students hard. *"The feedback we get from students is that the course is rigorous,"* director of BVC programmes Richard Holt told us; *"a lot of students come here because of this."* Reflecting the fierce competition for places, BPP now requires *"a 2.1 minimum, save in exceptional circumstances,"* for its full-time course. The course content is much the same as that offered by rivals, but what you will get at BPP is an überorganised and tightly structured experience. You'll work in small groups of six for advocacy, negotiation and conferencing and can choose from a broad range of nine option subjects. A *"realistic setting"* is provided in numerous mock court rooms in the school, while classrooms come complete with interactive boards that allow tutors to scrawl over a student's piece of drafting in front of the whole class.

With regard to pro bono involvement, each student is required to complete five hours of activities; many participate to a far greater extent. Last year's cohort was very keen on mooting and a student-run competition culminated in a final at the Royal Courts of Justice before two Court of Appeal judges. BPP softens its corporate image by emphasising the *"approachability of its staff"* and the welcoming atmosphere of its BVC enclave (dedicated study rooms and common room). However, there's no disguising the fact that it has a more commercial edge than most of its rivals, or that this is something of which it is proud. If you're someone who wants an air of professionalism to their BVC year, BPP is ideal.

bpp law school, leeds
Number of places: 48 f/t, 48 p/t

BPP has jumped at the chance to exploit the northern market by opening a brand-new BVC programme in Leeds in September 2006. The BVC course may be new here but BPP is no newcomer to the city – following the company's Leeds launch in 2004, its GDL and LPC courses quickly became established. Expect BPP London's hallmark professional approach to be in evidence on the Leeds BVC as well as an almost identical course structure and similarly state-of-the-art facilities. With promised involvement from members of the Northern Circuit and fees coming in at a couple of grand lower than in London, this provider will no doubt be inundated with applications.

bristol institute of legal practice
Number of places: 120 f/t, 48 p/t

This provider is working hard to compete with its rivals. A couple of stats indicate that Bristol may not attract as many high-calibre students as it would wish: some 25–35% of students gain pupillage before, during or after the course and recent figures showed 40–50% of the cohort failing at least one assessment on the first attempt. However, a reshaped course, competitive fees and strong links to the active Western Circuit all make it well worth investigation. The proportion of teaching by way of lectures has been *"reduced dramatically"* such that students now work primarily in groups of 12 (six for oral skills). Each group has a base room equipped with computers and a mini-library of core reference texts, and everyone has a key to their room. New digital cameras allow students to record themselves onto DVD whenever the urge takes them. The base-room culture is designed to *"enhance peer learning and encourage constructive criticism."* To avoid everyone getting too pally and relaxed, a shuffle of base groups at Christmas aims to *"take students out of their comfort zone."* The institute has some tricks up its sleeve, such as a compulsory, two weeks of work-experience placements and, new this year, four advocacy master classes for each group, presided over by barristers from the Western Circuit. With about 40 former students now on the circuit this is bound to involve alumni. A decent range of option subjects is offered and students can get stuck into pro bono projects via the student union-based Free Legal Representation Service. Such activities can be arranged so that they fulfil the requirements of both options. Another new initiative enables students to attend inquests, represent juveniles at police stations and to go into prisons to advise on prisoners' rights. There's definitely a sense of renewed impetus at the institute. As members of the University of the West of England, students have access to wider student facilities. The campus location in the north of Bristol receives mixed reviews from students.

cardiff law school
Number of places: 60 f/t

A BVC year in Wales is an option for those looking for an intimate and affordable course in a well-established, university-based law school. Located on a campus that is *"green, pleasant and seconds away from the city centre,"* Cardiff Law School offers the BVC to a mere 60 students each year. The student body is *"small enough to make the difference,"* tutor Chris Humphries told us. *"All the staff and students know each other by name."* Compared to other providers, the school has a high proportion of international students, with around 25% coming from overseas. Domestic students come from across Wales and other parts of the UK and it is common for around 6-8 of them to secure pupillage while still on the course. Two placement weeks play their part in the job hunt, with these mini-pupillages and marshalling weeks at county and Crown courts

"all organised on students' behalf" by the school. As for the course itself, a decision to *"front-load the knowledge subjects"* means there is a lot of criminal and civil litigation and sentencing study to cram in the first term. The decision to do this is designed to equip students with the *"underpinning knowledge needed to deal with the skills* [tuition]." Cardiff is bulking up its extra-curricular offering and the 2006 starters will be able to undertake school-sourced pro bono work, including through the recently launched Innocence Project which enables students to work with prisoners and solicitors to investigate alleged wrongful convictions. Last but not least, a thumbs up for the atmosphere in Cardiff and for the way in which BVC students are able to involve themselves in the wider life of the school (it has many GDL and LPC students) and university, as well as developing contacts among the local employed Bar, independent Bar and judiciary.

the college of law, store street, London
Number of places: 240 f/t, 48 p/t

Situated just off Tottenham Court Road, the College of Law's Store Street branch offers a London BVC with a bit of a difference. The course *"integrates knowledge and skills while following the litigation process, meaning that the timetable is never the same from week to week,"* course director Jacqueline Cheltenham explained. There are no lectures; all classes are based in groups of 12 (fewer for some, but not all, oral skills sessions) that stick together until students choose from the wide range of option subjects in the final term. Now validated for 240 full-time students, the college can no longer claim to offer a significantly smaller BVC than its London rivals, but there undoubtedly remains a warm atmosphere among teaching staff and students. Given that the college as a whole is vast, this is quite an achievement and largely down to the efforts of staff and to keeping areas in the building dedicated to BVC students. "*A good pool of practitioners from various chambers*" visits the college to give students feedback on advocacy, judge competitions and preside over mock trials. Many students become heavily involved in the well-organised Tribunal Representation Service that provides opportunities to appear at the Leasehold Valuation Tribunal, just around the corner from the College. Opportunities are also there to handle small claims, social security and employment cases. The College of Law has thus far not displayed the same super-slick corporate feel of BPP, but the two are going head to head in the legal education market right now and one wonders what kind of influences will drift over from the LPC side, where the college has been getting into bed with some of the UK's biggest law firms.

the inns of court school of law
(to be known as the city law school from july 2008)
Number of places: 575 f/t, 75 p/t

As recently as a decade ago ICSL was the only BVC provider. The school developed the course and is still author of a series of manuals that are used by many students elsewhere and even those starting out in practice. Sited at the edge of Gray's Inn, the school has occupied a position in the heart of legal London for a very long time and, despite the undermining of its hegemony, ICSL still makes much of its longevity and traditional appeal. It still educates more full-time students than the other two London providers combined. Some question the school's ability to deliver the best course because of the sheer size of the student body, but ICSL points out that the majority of classes take place in groups of 12 (six for advocacy) and that students are split into four manageable cohorts, each with a course director. The course still includes some larger group sessions, albeit that these make full use of some pretty smart facilities in the interactive lecture theatre. Pro bono opportunities are plentiful as the school enjoys links with numerous organisations across the capital, including FRU (with which students can complete one of their two option subjects). Relationships with practising barristers and judges are strong, with practitioners visiting regularly for a variety of evening events. In a first for London providers, the 2006 intake will have the chance to tack an LLM in Professional Legal Practice onto their BVC.

manchester metropolitan university
Number of places: 108 f/t, plus some p/t

Close involvement with members of the Northern Circuit makes MMU a highly attractive choice for anyone wanting to break into the Bar in this region. The strength of the professional links enjoyed by MMU is undoubtedly one of the jewels in its BVC crown. Advocacy master classes see local barristers coming in on a regular basis to give students feedback, and professionals also get involved in MMU's practitioner-mentor scheme, offering useful careers and study advice. The BVC is taught at the university's four-year-old law faculty building, a space-age construction that comes complete with "*interactive white boards and plenty of aircon.*" MMU adopts a 'syndicate group' approach, organising its students into groups of 12 with their own rooms with IT facilities and core texts. Each is set up "*like a mini-chambers,*" course director Alan Gibb informed us, adding that working with the "*same people week in, week out, gives you a very supportive network.*" Recognising that the current lack of organised pro bono activities is "*a bit of a weakness,*" MMU has plans to open a unit in 2007. With FRU and plenty of advice centres in Manchester, it's not as if current students miss out on pro bono opportunities; they just have to be a bit more proactive. MMU's BVC students can take advantage of the wider university sports and social scene and are eligible to apply for student accommodation. All in all, competitive fees, great facilities and those all-important links to professionals make this provider a good choice up north.

university of northumbria, newcastle

Number of places: 128 f/t, 48 p/t
+ 40 on exempting LLB

In addition to its conventional BVC, Northumbria offers what no other provider can – an integrated LLB/BVC combined over four years. Students taking this 'exempting degree' can apply for a BVC place on this sought-after course during the second year of their undergraduate LLB. They then spend the following two years combining undergraduate options with the components of the BVC. A parallel LLB/LPC course is also run. Northumbria's model has proved popular with students and with the Bar Council, largely because there are some very practical benefits to combining the two courses. There is additionally a cost saving and those students receiving some form of state support are commonly able to do so for all four years.

Take the full-time BVC and you can bag an LLM if you complete a research project (in just about any area of law you can think of). Completing this may take a few extra months, but it is still possible to wrap up the BVC and LLM in a year. Another major plus for Northumbria is a nationally recognised Student Law Office which gives hands-on experience in advising members of the public. Involvement with the SLO is optional for ordinary BVC students but compulsory for those on the exempting degree. The latter are assessed on the handful of cases they deal with over the course of the final year. The BVC has a purpose-built home in central Newcastle, enabling students to get the most out of everything the city and university have to offer, including rubbing shoulders with practising professionals at guest lectures, moots and mock trials.

nottingham law school

Number of places: 120 f/t

Part of Nottingham Trent University, NLS offers a challenging BVC that competes well with its London rivals. It is refreshingly upfront about the fact that only those applicants with a fighting chance of pupillage will receive an offer of a BVC place. The tough recruitment criteria result in impressive statistics: over 60% of enrolling students from the 2004-5 intake had obtained pupillage when we checked in the summer of 2006. No wonder NLS makes great efforts to keep tabs on its BVC alumni. Bar students can tap into the social, sporting and other facilities offered by the university, but occupy their own dedicated building. This *"makes a huge difference,"* course director James Wakefield ventures. *"I know every student's name and they all know each other – there's a very collegiate feel."* Nevertheless, the NLS BVC year is judged by students to be a demanding one. James warns that *"this is not a drop in, drop out environment"* and students are expected to spend five full days a week on their studies. Skills and knowledge learning focuses on the seven briefs that are followed throughout the year. Criminal advocacy sessions are held in courtrooms at Nottingham's old Guildhall. A new full-time pro bono coordinator and a public-access advice clinic at NLS have enhanced the range of real-life experiences open to students, and there is no shortage of links with professionals in London and the Midlands. Barristers and judges present guest lectures on a regular basis, and there are sponsored plea-in-mitigation and mooting competitions plus a marshalling scheme. New from 2006 is a pupillage-interview training day and, to help students keep contact with their Inns in London, NLS organises coaches to Inn events. NLS is dangling a new carrot in front of prospective applicants: successful BVC students with a GDL will be automatically awarded an LLB.

funding

Training a lawyer is an expensive caper. Many of the students who secure training contracts or pupillages before commencing their studies will receive funding to cover their course fees and some living expenses. Full details of what solicitors are now offering their future trainees are given in the Salaries and Benefits table on page 84. Further information about the funding of pupillages is given in the Bar section at the back of this book

taken for granted

There's a super-slim chance your local education authority may come to the rescue with a grant or allowance if you make it past the rainforest of application forms. Funds are sometimes available to applicants with physical or other difficulties, carers or those with children. www.dfes.gov.uk/studentsupport

An organisation called the Educational Grants Advisory Service (EGAS) can carry out a charity and trust search on your behalf. Their really useful website is www.egas-online.org.uk. Also see www.support4learning.org.uk

The Law Society has various schemes and bursaries that are worth looking into. Read our website feature Funding news from the Law Society for further information.

bank loans

Already got a huge overdraft? No problem. You could still qualify for a special package from a high street bank. Interest rates are low and the repayment terms usually favourable, but sniff around to see what the different banks are offering. Many banks have graduate loan schemes tailored to the needs of the legal profession, and will, for example, regard pupillage as a formal part of the training when it comes to determining the time for repayment.

Scott Jago, manager of legal student services at the NatWest Legal Centre, advises students to arrange any required loan as soon as they have been accepted onto a course. *"Law students need to plan their expenditure carefully,"* he told us. Scott also recommends that students stick to a budget, drawing down against their loan on a monthly basis. *"If you want a manageable student debt when you start work, then monthly budgeting during your studies is essential."*

career development loans

Barclays Bank, The Co-operative Bank and RBS provide these on behalf of the DfES. Full details are at www.lifelonglearning.co.uk/cdl. You can borrow up to £8,000 to fund up to two years' study.

surf for a scholarship

Surf the Internet for scholarships and bursaries. Here are some of the funds we found:

- BPP Law School scholarships awarded by seven of the key staff; each set their own criteria, eg the applicant is the first lawyer in their family.
- The Law Society Bursary Scheme is open to GDL or LPC students.
- The Law Society Diversity Access Scheme supports talented people who face obstacles to qualification.
- Inderpal Rahal Memorial Trust supports women from an immigrant or refugee background.
- The Kalisher Scholarship and Kalisher Bursary are for BVC students who intend to practise at the criminal Bar.
- Loans from the Leonard Sainer Foundation.
- The Student Disability Assistance Fund – see www.bahshe.demon.co.uk.
- Universities and publicly funded colleges have discretionary college access funds available to assist especially hard-up students.

the inns of court

Pupil barristers and GDL and/or BVC students headed for the Bar can apply for a range of scholarships from the four Inns of Court and many base their choice of Inn on the likelihood of getting their hands on some of the £3 million plus that is paid out each year. Some awards are merit-based, others consider financial hardship. All pupillages come with a minimum chambers' award of £10,000. Some sets pay far more and allow students to draw on these awards while on the BVC.

part-timing and the four-letter word

If a decade of loan repayments doesn't appeal then you must do as fools and horses do – work. Full-time study and work are uncomfortable bedfellows so consider seriously whether you ought to be studying part-time. Doing so may allow you to work in a more rewarding job while also performing better at college. Part-time study may initially seem an affront to fresh undergraduates. You may have to mingle with mature students, men and women with wives, husbands, kids, mortgages... bald spots even. We say revel in the difference – it will be good practice for when you are a lawyer.

For LLB grads or students who have completed the GDL, paralegalling may be an option. Indeed, there are many options on the periphery of the profession, from commercial contracts negotiation and transaction management to social policy or other research. Whatever job you do, working while studying brings with it a commodity to be traded on – respect.

capital concerns

Newsflash: London streets aren't paved with gold – just concrete, pigeon droppings and chewing gum. Rent and living costs in cities like Sheffield, Nottingham and Cardiff are far lower. But don't assume that out of London means within your price range – Guildford, for example, is as pricey as it is pretty.

Before taking any further steps, sit down and add up what you think you'll need and then add some more. If you need to study for the GDL and LPC or BVC, and you do so at the most expensive places, course fees could cost you around £18,000 (GDL/BVC) or £15,000 (GDL/LPC). Do so at the least expensive schools and these figures could be reduced to around £10,000 and £8,000 respectively. It's worth thinking about if money is the main sticking point.

benefits, benefactors, begging...

Living at home while you study may not sound that appealing but sometimes needs must. Forget ideas of declaring bankruptcy to evade student debt; why not consider other creative ways to ease the debt burden.

- A student card will get you cheap travel, discount haircuts, cinema tickets and drinks in some places. If nothing else, you will be a cheap date.
- Law books are pricey so don't go on a spending spree before term starts. College libraries will have the core texts and we guarantee you'll find former students with books for sale. Check out noticeboards for second-hand tomes.
- A number of law schools, chambers and solicitors firms run competitions. Do a Google search.
- Market research focus groups will pay decent money for an hour or two of your time. Consider carefully any decision to become a human guinea pig in a medical trial. And gents, if you choose to make a 'special donation' remember that, come 2027, a stranger might well knock on your door and call you dad.

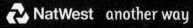

a-z universities and law schools

BPP Law School

68-70 Red Lion Street, London, WC1R 4NY
Tel: (0845) 070 2882
Email: lawadmissions@bpp.com
Website: www.bpp.com/law

college profile

BPP is the leading provider of professional legal education in the country with over 4,000 students based across four specially designed and highly equipped Law Schools. As the leading provider, they have the skills and resources to offer you the individual support needed to prepare you for the realities of legal practice. This is achieved using a unique mix of academic and practitioner lecturers, first rate facilities, award winning pro bono projects and an unrivalled careers service.

BPP's careers service comprises not only specialist careers advisors, but also careers tutors, who have worked in practice and sat on recruitment selection panels. This distinctive blend of knowledge and experience ensures you are fully equipped with the knowledge and support needed to secure a training contract or pupillage.

graduate diploma in law (full-time, part-time, and distance learning)

BPP's GDL is taught with a practical, student-centred approach to not only familiarise you with the basic principles of law, but to also introduce you to legal practice. You will be taught using a combination of large and small group sessions, allowing you to develop your knowledge and skills fully by receiving maximum support and individual feedback. Although competition for places at BPP is intense, graduates from BPP's GDL are guaranteed a place on the school's LPC and intending barristers can apply to join their BVC.

BPP's new Distinctive GDL offers the chance for you to add a specialist subject to your GDL by participating in an optional short-course in an area of law that interests you. If you are unsure whether a career in law is for you, BPP's popular taster course, the BPP Summer School, is available to give you an insight into the legal world.

legal practice course (full-time and part-time)

BPP's LPC is designed to prepare you for real life as a trainee solicitor, and the new MBA-style approach to the course offers business and financial training whilst working with sophisticated client portfolios and case & transaction simulations. Taught by experienced solicitors from a variety of practice backgrounds, you will benefit from a course designed in close collaboration with the top legal firms in the country and a wide range of electives ensuring you can study the area of legal practice most important to you.

bar vocational course (full-time and part-time)

BPP's BVC, run in Leeds and London, is highly regarded by the profession and is the only course in London to be unconditionally validated by the Bar Council for the full six-year term. Studying the BVC at BPP will allow you to concentrate on developing your essential barristerial skills of drafting, opinion writing, advocacy, conference and negotiation. These skills will be refined using groups as small as six students alongside practising barristers, who will become your opponents in mock trials and final assessments.

BPP Law School operates an exclusive scholarship programme for selected BPP students. Applications must be received by the beginning of August prior to you commencing your course. Please visit the website www.bpp.com/law for more information.

contact
Admissions Department

apply to:
full-time GDL and LPC
Central Applications Board

part-time GDL and LPC
Directly to BPP Law School

full-time and part-time BVC
www.bvconline.co.uk

summer school
Directly to BPP Law School

locations
Leeds, London (Holborn & Waterloo), Manchester

PROFESSIONAL EDUCATION®
LAW SCHOOL

Cardiff Law School

Cardiff Law School, Cardiff University, Museum Avenue, Cardiff CF10 3AX
Tel: (029) 2087 4941/4964 Fax: (029) 2087 4984
Email: law-lpc@cf.ac.uk or law-bvc@cf.ac.uk
Website: www.law.cardiff.ac.uk/cpls

contact

LPC: Byron Jones
Tel: (029) 2087 4941/6660
Email: law-lpc@cf.ac.uk

BVC: Lucy Burns
Tel: (029) 2087 4964
Email: law-bvc@cf.ac.uk

other postgraduate law courses:
The Postgraduate Office
Tel: (029) 2087 4351/4353

university profile

Cardiff Law School is one of the most successful law schools in the UK and enjoys an international reputation for its teaching and research. In the most recent assessment of research quality conducted by the Higher Education Funding Council, Cardiff achieved a grade 5 rating, placing it in the top law schools in the country. Cardiff offers opportunities for students to pursue postgraduate study by research leading to the degrees of M.Phil and Ph.D. In addition, taught Masters degrees in the areas of canon, commercial, European legal studies and medical law are offered in full and part-time mode.

legal practice course and bar vocational course

A part of the Law School, the Centre for Professional Legal Studies is the leading provider of legal training in Wales and is validated to offer both the Legal Practice Course and the Bar Vocational Course. Students are taught by experienced solicitors and barristers who have been specifically recruited for this purpose. The Centre prides itself on its friendly and supportive teaching environment and its strong links with the legal profession. Placements with solicitors' firms or sets of Chambers are available to students pursuing the vocational courses, while students studying the Bar Vocational Course additionally enjoy placements with Circuit and District Judges. In 2005 Cardiff's Legal Practice Course once again achieved the highest rating following the Law Society's assessment visit. The course has consistently been rated "Excellent" by the Law Society; one of the few providers of this course to hold the top ranking. The Law Society praised the challenging learning environment and stimulating range of activities.

facilities

The Law School has dedicated accommodation for the vocational courses which houses a practitioner library, courtroom facilities, fixed and moveable audio visual equipment for recording practitioner skills, inter-active teaching equipment and extensive computer facilities. In addition, the main law library contains one of the largest collections of primary and secondary material within the UK. The Law School is housed in its own building at the heart of the campus, itself located in one of the finest civic centres in Britain and only a short walk from the main shopping area. The University has its own postgraduate centre, together with a full range of sports and social facilities. Cardiff is a vibrant capital city with excellent cultural, sporting and leisure activities.

UCE Birmingham

School of Law, Franchise Street, Perry Barr, Birmingham B42 2SU
Tel: (0121) 331 6600 Fax: (0121) 331 6622

college profile

UCE Birmingham's School of Law has been a major centre for legal education and training in the city of Birmingham for over 30 years and is committed to providing a service that meets your needs – whether academic, professional or personal. Approachable and experienced staff are part of the extensive range of support provision and learning facilities, including a legal practice resource centre, dedicated IT workrooms, a mock courtroom and legal office. And, of course, students have all the additional benefits that you would expect to find in a large university.

postgraduate diploma in legal practice/lpc (full or part-time)

The LPC is recognised for the quality of its training for students who enter general and specialised practice in small and medium size firms, with distinctive electives for this sector. Training will develop the full range of practice skills, commercial awareness and self-sufficiency that a trainee solicitor needs. With its careers guidance and support, small class sizes and enthusiastic and committed staff, they ensure that individual study needs are met and students receive the support and encouragement to maximize their potential.

graduate diploma in law/gdl (full or part-time)

The GDL course is designed for non-law graduates wishing to enter the profession as solicitors or barristers. UCE Birmingham's GDL provides legal training, which although primarily academic in nature reflects the demands that legal practice will place on that academic knowledge. The GDL emphasises active and student-centred learning. A variety of teaching methods are employed in order to develop the legal skills which will form the basis of a successful career in law. A commitment to individual personal basis ensures students are given every possible advantage in their chosen career.

pgcert/pgdip/llm corporate and business law (full or part-time)

Explores relevant and topical legal issues relating to the corporate and business world.

pgdip/llm international human rights (full or part-time)

USA Pathway: Specialises in the conflict between the US Death Penalty and international standards. Students may undertake a semester's internship in the USA.
European Pathway: Studies the increasing importance of Human Rights in the UK and European law, including international environmental law and conflict, and refugees.

pgdip/ma criminal justice policy & practice (full or part-time)

Studies how criminal justice policy is formulated and how criminological theory relates to practice.

contact

Apply to:
full-time GDL and LPC courses
Central Applictions Board
part-time GDL and LPC courses
Direct to university
other courses
Direct to university

contact names
GDL　Dr Ewan Kirk
LPC　Martyn Packer

other postgraduate courses
The Faculty Office

Email: lhds@uce.ac.uk
Website: www.lhds.uce.ac.uk
Website: www.uce.ac.uk

UCE BIRMINGHAM
Faculty of Law, Humanities, Development and Society

City University

The City Law School, City University, Northampton Square, London, EC1V 0HB
Website: www.city.ac.uk/law

college profile

The City Law School is one of London's major law schools, offering an impressive range of academic and professional programmes. It is the first law school in London to educate students and practitioners at all stages of legal education. Law has been taught at City since 1977. The GDL course is one of the largest and most respected in the UK, with a strong reputation with the Bar and amongst City law firms. In addition to post-graduate legal training for both solicitors and barristers, The City Law School offers a well-established CPD programme which includes the PSC for trainee solicitors and Higher Rights training.

The School's vocational and professional programmes are delivered through the Inns of Court School of Law (ICSL became part of the City University in 2001), which for generations has been the leading educator of barristers in the country and is now also the only provider of the Legal Practice Course (for intending solicitors) in London that carries the Law Society's highest rating of "Excellent".

graduate diploma in law/cpe (full time)

Designed to enable non-law graduates to complete the first stage of professional training, this GDL is one of the largest and most respected GDL courses in the UK, with a long-standing reputation with the Bar and strong and growing reputation amongst City law firms.

bar vocational course (full or part-time)

A forward looking IT based course focusing on the needs of the modern bar, particularly advocacy. From 2006-07, there will be opportunities to enrol on the school's LLM in Professional Legal Practice, awarded on successful completion of the BVC and a supervised dissertation.

legal practice course (full time)

The ICSL LPC is the only provider in London that carries the Law Society's highest rating of "Excellent". The course has been devised to meet the needs of students in practice, with a heavy emphasis on the teaching of practitioner skills. Small group teaching is emphasised to give students the most effective environment for learning. A wide range of electives is offered.

graduate entry LLB (two years full time)

A well established broader conversion course for non-law graduates providing an opportunity to develop special interests.

LLM programme (full or part-time)

LLM International Law with opportunities to specialise in Human Rights Law or Environmental Law.
LLM International Commercial Law with opportunities to specialise in International Competition Law or Maritime Law.
LLM Criminal Litigation.

contact

GDL/CPE
(020) 7040 8301
cpe@city.ac.uk

BVC/LPC
(020) 7404 5787
lpc@city.ac.uk
bvc@city.ac.uk

LLM
(020) 7040 8167
llm-lawdept@city.ac.uk

LLM criminal litigation
(020) 7404 5787
llm-icsl@city.ac.uk

LLB (graduate entry)
(020) 7040 3309
law@city.ac.uk

The College of Law

Admissions, Braboeuf Manor, Portsmouth Road, Guildford GU3 1HA
Freephone: (0800) 328 0153 Overseas: +44 (0)1483 460382
Fax: (01483) 460460
Email: admissions@lawcol.co.uk
Website: www.college-of-law.co.uk/perfectforpractice

contact
Freephone:
(0800) 328 0153
If calling from overseas:
+44 (0)1483 460382
Email:
admissions@lawcol.co.uk
Website:
www.college-of-law.co.uk/
perfectforpractice

college profile
The College of Law is the UK's largest provider of postgraduate legal education, with six centres in five different cities: Birmingham, Chester, Guildford, London (two) and York. It combines an international reputation with long-standing success and educational innovation, and more course choices in more locations than any other provider. All College courses are taught by qualified lawyers and designed to reflect the challenges of life in practice, featuring cutting-edge learning methods, unrivalled resources and excellent student support. The College has established links to the legal profession and boasts an award-winning pro bono programme and the largest and best-resourced careers service in legal education. In May 2006, The College of Law made history by becoming the first independent institution to be granted full degree awarding powers. This means students who successfully study both their GDL and LPC or BVC at the College will be awarded an LLB law degree.

graduate diploma in law (GDL) full-time/part-time
Designed to build knowledge and skills that more than match a law degree – with a clear focus on preparing students for life in practice. Taught by lawyers with real practice experience. Students who successfully complete the course and go on to pass either the LPC or BVC at the College will be awarded an LLB law degree.

legal practice course (LPC) full-time/part-time
The College LPC is rigorous and practical, giving students the opportunity to develop the skills essential for practice. The course offers unrivalled flexibility, with four different study routes allowing students to specialise in their chosen field. Taught by lawyers, with over 90% of face-to-face training in small, student-centred workshops.

bar vocational course (BVC) full-time/part-time
Designed to resemble practice as closely as possible, the course is structured around case-work at the Bar, and students benefit from an outstanding programme of course-related activities, including an award-winning pro bono programme. The majority of teaching is in small groups, with tutors who have practised as barristers, solicitors, or even sat as judges. Study in London or Birmingham*.

open days
Find out more about The College of Law and its courses by attending an open day or arranging a centre visit. For more information and to book a place, visit www.college-of-law.co.uk/perfectforpractice.

*Subject to Bar Council approval.

Manchester Metropolitan University

School of Law, All Saints West, Lower Ormond Street, Manchester M15 6HB
Tel: (0161) 247 3050 Fax: (0161) 247 6309
Email: law@mmu.ac.uk

contact
CPE/GDL: Harriet Roche
LPC: Paul Duffy
BVC: Wanda Clarke

college profile

The School of Law is one of the largest providers of legal education in the UK, and enjoys an excellent reputation for the quality and range of its courses. It is one of only six providers that offer the full range of law courses LLB, GDipL, LPC and BVC. The School's courses are well designed and taught, combining rigorous academic standards with practical application. In September 2003, the School moved into a brand new, state of the art building, in the heart of Manchester.

bar vocational course (full-time)

This course provides the vocational stage of training for intending practising barristers. However, skills learnt on the course such as advocacy and drafting are transferable to other professions. The BVC is skills based and interactive with particular emphasis on advocacy which is taught in groups of six. The course adopts a syndicate (mini-chambers) approach. Students are allocated to a particular group which has its own base room which contains extensive practitioner legal resources both in hard copy and online form. Each room has the latest in IT and AV equipment. There is also a BVC court room and a separate BVC resource room. Excellent student support is provided including careers advice and an additional professional programme that is designed to bridge the gap between student and professional life. A particular feature of the course is the close links it enjoys with the Northern Circuit whose members are involved in Advocacy Master Classes, the teaching of professional conduct and in a student mentoring scheme.

legal practice course
(full-time or part-time: part-time = attendance on Thursdays over two years)

The legal practice course provides the vocational stage of training for those wishing to qualify as a solicitor. Offering a full range of private client and commercial electives, the school aims to cater to students who are looking to practice in specialised areas (eg entertainment law or advanced criminal litigation) as well as students who wish to develop a broad subject base. A mentor scheme operates to put students in touch with local practitioners. Consistently recommended for its state of the art resources, student support and careers guidance and staffed by approachable and knowledgeable teaching staff, the LPC at Manchester Metropolitan University will provide a sound foundation for your legal career.

graduate diploma in law/cpe
(full-time or part-time)

An increasing number of graduates enter the legal profession this way, with employers attracted by the applicant's maturity and transferable skills. The course places emphasis on the acquisition of legal research and other relevant legal skills. On completion students normally join the School's LPC or BVC Course. This means that if the full-time mode is followed a non-law graduate can become professionally qualified in two years. There is a guaranteed place for CPE students on the school's LPC course.

the
MANCHESTER
METROPOLITAN
UNIVERSITY

Nottingham Law School

Nottingham Law School, Belgrave Centre, Nottingham NG1 5LP
Tel: (0115) 848 6871 Fax: (0115) 848 6878
Email: nls.enquiries@ntu.ac.uk
Website: www.ntu.ac.uk/nls

contact

Nottingham Law School
Belgrave Centre
Nottingham NG1 5LP
Tel: (0115) 848 6871
Fax: (0115) 848 6878
Email: nls.enquiries@ntu.ac.uk
Website: www.ntu.ac.uk/nls

bar vocational course

Nottingham Law School has designed its BVC to develop to a high standard a range of core practical skills, and to equip students to succeed in the fast-changing environment of practice at the Bar. Particular emphasis is placed on the skill of advocacy. Advocacy sessions are conducted in groups of six and the School uses the Guildhall courtrooms for most sessions. The BVC is taught entirely by qualified practitioners, and utilises the same integrated and interactive teaching methods as all of the School's other professional courses. Essentially, students learn by doing and Nottingham Law School provides an environment in which students are encouraged to realise, through practice and feedback, their full potential.

legal practice course

The LPC is offered by full-time and part-time block study. This course has been designed to be challenging and stimulating for students and responsive to the needs of firms, varying from large commercial to smaller high street practices, and it still carries the endorsement of a large cross section of firms from major corporate through to high street.

Nottingham Law School's LPC features: integration of the transactions and skills, so that each advances the other, whilst ensuring the transferability of skills between different subject areas. Carefully structured interactive group work which develops an ability to handle skills and legal transactions effectively, and in an integrated way. A rigorous assessment process that nevertheless avoids 'assessment overload', to maintain a teaching and learning emphasis to the course. A professionally qualified team, retaining substantial links with practice. An excellent rating from The Law Society's Assessment Panel in every year of its operation.

the graduate diploma in law (full-time)

The Nottingham Law School GDL is a one year conversion course designed for any non-law graduate who intends to become a solicitor or barrister in the UK. The intensive course effectively covers the seven core subjects of an undergraduate law degree in one go. It is the stepping stone to the LPC or the BVC, and a legal career thereafter. It is a graduate Diploma (Dip Law) in its own right and operates on a similar basis to the LPC (see above), though inevitably it has a more academic basis.

From September 2006, students who complete their GDL with Nottingham Law School and then embark on the school's excellent rated LPC or BVC will be eligible for a full LLB on successful completion of that professional course.

NOTTINGHAM
LAW SCHOOL

University of Wolverhampton

School of Legal Studies, Molineux Street, Wolverhampton WV1 1SB
Tel: (01902) 321633   Fax: (01902) 323569

contact
Admissions Assistant
Tel: (01902) 321633
Fax: (01902) 323569
Email:
sls-enquiries@wlv.ac.uk
website:
www.wlv.ac.uk/sls

college profile

Based in Wolverhampton and offers courses for students intending to follow a variety of careers within the legal profession. The law school has been offering these courses for over 30 years. Its LPC programme has had consistently good ratings. The lecturers are drawn from experienced solicitors, barristers, academics and individuals from business and industry. There are excellent IT facilities, a well-stocked library, bookshop and a sports centre. The School also offers an LLM in International Corporate and Financial Law, which draws together a number of legal issues with an international dimension such as the regulation of financial services and financial crime. It also deals with matters such as international banking law and international corporate finance. The School also offers an MA in Practice Management, a course developed in connection with the management section of the Law Society. It is taught on a flexible, part-time, block-delivery basis and is designed to provide an outlet to complex managerial and organisational issues facing practice managers.

legal practice course (full/part-time)

The vocational training course for those intending to practise as solicitors, the University's LPC offers a sound basis for a professional career. The core subjects of Business, Litigation and Conveyancing are taught, together with a range of commercial and private client options. Professional skills courses, practical workshops and seminars are all part of the training. Additional benefits include close links with local practitioners, mentoring, CV distribution and group social activities. The Legal Practice Course is housed in modern, purpose-built, dedicated accommodation which includes LPC Resources room and video suites. The course is taught by experienced professionally-qualified staff with close links with the local profession. It has active personal tutor support, in-house and guest practitioners, a Practitioner Liaison Committee and a careers tutor.

common professional examination (full/part-time)

The academic stage of training for non-law graduates wishing to become solicitors or barristers. A full programme of lectures and tutorials is offered on this demanding course. Students are taught by experienced practitioners. Places on the LPC are guaranteed for successful students. Teaching methods on the CPE are varied and include lectures, group-led discussion and debate, workshops, oral presentations and independent research. The course includes an intensive induction programme involving use of library, methodology and an introduction to IT. The course benefits from its own dedicated teaching space within the school and also involves study skills sessions including advocacy, interview skills and drafting. The course as a whole is designed to provide the essential skills necessary for a successful career in law.

UNIVERSITY OF
WOLVERHAMPTON

www.chambersandpartners.co.uk

solicitors

solicitors timetable

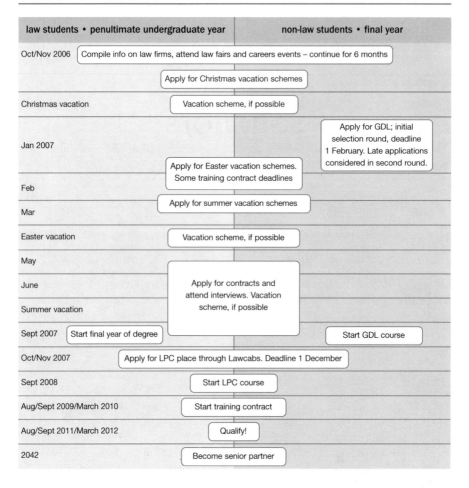

law students • penultimate undergraduate year	non-law students • final year
Oct/Nov 2006	Compile info on law firms, attend law fairs and careers events – continue for 6 months
	Apply for Christmas vacation schemes
Christmas vacation	Vacation scheme, if possible
Jan 2007	Apply for GDL; initial selection round, deadline 1 February. Late applications considered in second round.
	Apply for Easter vacation schemes. Some training contract deadlines
Feb	
Mar	Apply for summer vacation schemes
Easter vacation	Vacation scheme, if possible
May	
June	Apply for contracts and attend interviews. Vacation scheme, if possible
Summer vacation	
Sept 2007	Start final year of degree	Start GDL course
Oct/Nov 2007	Apply for LPC place through Lawcabs. Deadline 1 December
Sept 2008	Start LPC course
Aug/Sept 2009/March 2010	Start training contract
Aug/Sept 2011/March 2012	Qualify!
2042	Become senior partner

Notes

1   *It is important to check application closing dates for each firm as these will vary.*

2   *Some firms will only accept applications for vacation schemes from penultimate-year students, whether law or non-law. See A-Z pages for further information.*

3   *Some firms require very early applications from non-law graduates. See A-Z pages for further information.*

4   *The timetable refers primarily to those firms that recruit two years in advance. Smaller firms often recruit just one year in advance or for immediate vacancies.*

www.chambersandpartners.co.uk

vacation schemes: i know what you did last summer

So you want to be a lawyer, but do you know why? Do you know how a solicitor spends their time and what goes on inside the offices of a law firm? If you are not too sure what's in store after law school then you may have problems convincing recruiters that you are committed to a career in law. And, deep down, even you may have doubts that you are on the right path. Vacation schemes are an ideal solution to several problems: lack of knowledge, lack of certainty and lack of CV material. Spending one, two or more weeks in a law firm gives you a taste of life as a solicitor and a chance to quiz trainees about their experiences. Even if you are not sold on a particular type of practice by the end of the experience, you'll know why and be able to look at firms of a different size or orientation.

welcome to the real world

Maybe you have already decided which type of training contract you want. Perhaps you even know exactly which firm you want to work for. If so, can you be sure your assumptions about it are correct? You wouldn't spend good money on clothes without trying them on, so why assume that you and an employer will be a good fit? You can pick up a lot about a firm at interview and on assessment days, but do remember that these are often conducted in stylish client suites that give little away about a firm's true character. Even the interviewers may be putting on an act, be it good cop, bad cop or yeah-I've-got-that-on-my-iPod-too cop. Spend an extended period of time in a place and you will see the reality of working there. All around you, deals will blow, people will stress, crises will be averted and people will bitch. Believe us, a lawyer is not going to postpone a rant or a resignation just because a student is in the office and might hear about it. Watching how lawyers interact with clients, with each other and with support staff, seeing how work is distributed and handled, even observing who makes the tea can be pretty enlightening.

playing your part

Reading about a law firms' latest work on websites and perhaps even the national press makes it all sound rather exciting. How are these big deals and cases actually conducted? Attending a vacation scheme can be a useful way of understanding how court battles and M&A deals are broken down into component stages as you are likely to be given files to read through. Do your best to understand the key steps and any major problems within a file as you will probably be asked for your opinion and possibly asked to prepare a note on a particular aspect of the file. Another typical vac scheme exercise is to conduct research that will better inform the solicitors on a particular topic. Vac schemers are likely to be invited along to meetings, both internal and with clients, and court visits are also possible at some firms, either to watch an application on an actual case or for an arranged tour. In short, the tasks you will be given may contribute in some small way to live files, but you can't expect to do anything too significant.

bad manners

Aside from such exercises and other watch-and-learn type activities, the graduate recruitment team will commonly arrange talks about the firm's key departments and how its training contract is organised. There are also plenty of social events, partly to leave you with good memories of a fun working environment and partly to look at your social skills. While buying the rounds, recruiters and trainees will also be looking out for vaccies who revert to student union bar mode once the beer starts flowing. Best behaviour is advised at all times; bad-mouthing the firm, flirting with the HR assistant and throwing up on the pavement are not. And while we are on the subject of vac scheme etiquette, even if you are given your own Outlook account, we recommend you resist sending e-mail funnies or bitchy banter across the intranet. Staff are unlikely to have the time or inclination to monitor your e-mail traffic. That's not to say they won't notice someone spending a lot of time mailing. We also recommend that you switch off your mobile phone when in the office. Your boss will use theirs but is unlikely to want to hear your crazy frog/Nikki from BB/Little Britain ring tone.

under pressure

If a vacation scheme confirms that you have found the firm of your dreams, you'll be happy to hear that your time there can act as a useful foot in the door. Just don't overestimate the size of your shoe. Even though many firms have a fast-track application process for those who have attended a vacation scheme, a training contract interview – never mind a job offer – is not guaranteed. Some firms do place their vacation schemes at the heart of the recruitment process, taking the lion's share of their trainees from the scheme. Does this make a placement a fortnight-long interview? Effectively, yes. It will serve you well to go in with the attitude that your actions will be scrutinised at all times and by anyone, including current trainees and secretaries. Don't get paranoid; just be yourself. The impression you want to leave people with is that you're polite, willing to put effort into whatever tasks you're asked to perform and confident enough to approach people in the office. Take your lead from how trainees interact with more-senior colleagues but don't get cocky. Any familiar behaviour you witness is likely to have developed after a period of assimilation into a team.

it's a numbers game

Having sold vacation schemes to you as a jolly good idea, it is only fair to point out that it's not always easy to get your hands on one. The strongest candidates always manage to secure a clutch of vac scheme offers and a few become serial schemers, perhaps incentivised by the good money on offer. Don't feel too disheartened if you don't manage to secure a place on an organised programme; it doesn't mean you'll never get a training contract. After all, those serial schemers can only accept one training contract. Do try to build up your CV in other ways. Firms look favourably on candidates who have broadened their horizons and gained other types of experience – perhaps in another legal or commercial environment or with a voluntary organisation. Improving your CV in this way may be the step you need to take to secure a vac scheme at a later stage.

Another thing to bear in mind is the timing of your application. Schemes are frequently targeted at penultimate-year law grads and final-year non-law grads, which can leave other students frustrated. The simple fact is that law firms most want to see those people who are ready to apply for training contracts. The law firms' literature should make it clear if applications are being sought from a particular group of students. It is interesting to see that one or two law firms (eg Nabarro Nathanson) are now also considering pre-vac scheme schemes for first-year law students.

Take care with application forms and prepare for interviews as thoroughly as for a training contract. For tips on how to prepare refer to How to **Make Applications and Get Selected** on page 73.

vacation schemes

firm name	number of places	duration	remuneration	deadline
Addleshaw Goddard	75	1-2 weeks	Not known	31 January 2007
Allen & Overy	20 at Christmas 75 in summer	Christmas: 10 days summer: 3 weeks	£250 p.w.	31 October 06 (Christmas) 19 January 07 (summer)
Ashurst	Easter (grads & final year non-law); summer (penult year law)	Easter: 2 weeks summer: 3 weeks	£250 p.w.	31 January 2007
Baker & McKenzie	London: 30 international: 3-5	London: 3 weeks Lon/o'seas: 12 weeks	£270 p.w.	31 January 2007
Barlow Lyde & Gilbert	Yes, plus open days and drop-in days	Not known	Not known	31 January 2007
Beachcroft	Yes in summer	Not known	Paid	Not known
Berwin Leighton Paisner	50	2 weeks	Not known	31 January 2007
Bevan Brittan	50	Not known	Not known	31 March 2007
Bird & Bird	20	3 weeks	£260 p.w.	31 January 2007
Boodle Hatfield	10	2 weeks	Not known	1 January 2007
Bristows	Yes	Christmas/Easter: 1 week summer: 2 weeks	£200 p.w.	Christmas: 23 Nov 06 Easter/summer: 28 Feb 07
Burges Salmon	40	2 weeks	£250 p.w.	Not known
Capsticks	Yes	2 weeks	Not known	9 February 2007
Cleary Gottlieb Steen & Hamilton	Easter and summer	Easter: 2 weeks summer: 3 weeks	Not known	14 February 2007
Clifford Chance	Christmas, Easter and summer (some overseas)	Christmas: 2 days others: 2-4 weeks	£270 p.w.	Christmas: 17 Nov 06 Easter/summer: 31 Jan 07
Clyde & Co	20	2 weeks	Not known	31 January 2007
CMS Cameron McKenna	55	2 weeks	£250 p.w.	Christmas: 17 Nov 06 Easter/summer 16 Feb 07
Coffin Mew & Clover	Open week in July	Not known	Not known	31 March 2007
Covington & Burling	16	Not known	Not known	28 February 2007
Davenport Lyons	Yes	Not known	£200 p.w.	31 January 2007
Dechert	Easter and summer aimed at penult year law	Not known	Not known	19 February 2007
Denton Wilde Sapte	Open days in December and summer scheme	Not known	Not known	24 November 2006 9 February 2007
Dickinson Dees	40	1 week	£125 p.w.	28 February 2007
DLA Piper	200	2 weeks	£230 p.w (Lon) £170 p.w (Ors)	31 January 2007
DMH Stallard	Yes	1 week	Unpaid	31 January 2007

vacation schemes

firm name	number of places	duration	remuneration	deadline
Dundas & Wilson	Yes	4 weeks	Not known	26 January 2007
DWF	20	1 week	Paid	Not known
Eversheds	250	1 or 2 weeks	£225 p.w. London £175 p.w. regions	31 January 2007
Farrer & Co	40: Easter and summer	2 weeks	£250 p.w.	31 January 2007
Field Fisher Waterhouse	Yes: July	2 weeks	Not known	31 January 2007
Foot Anstey	Yes	Not known	Not known	31 March 2007
Forsters	10	Not known	£250 p.w.	15 March 2007
Freshfields Bruckhaus Deringer	100	2 weeks	£550 total	19 January 2006
Government Legal Service	60	2-3 weeks	£200-250 p.w.	30 March 2007
Halliwells	63	2 weeks	£170 p.w.	31 March 2007
Hammonds	64	2 weeks	£230 p.w. (Lon) £180 p.w. (Ors)	31 January 2007
HBJ Gateley	Yes	2 weeks	Not known	11 February 2007
Herbert Smith	115: some o/seas (winter: non-law)	Not known	Not known	winter: 15 Nov 06 spring/summer: 31 Jan 07
Hewitsons	Yes	1 week	Not known	Not known
Hill Dickinson	Yes	1 week	Not known	31 March 2007
Holman Fenwick & Willan	Yes	2 weeks	£250 p.w.	14 February 2007
Howes Percival	Yes: summer	Not known	Not known	30 April 2007
Ince & Co	15	2 weeks	£250 p.w.	14 February 2007
Irwin Mitchell	Yes	Not known	Not known	Not known
Jones Day	20 at Christmas: non-law 10 at Easter: non-law 40 in summer: law	2 weeks	£400 p.w.	Christmas: 31 Oct 06 Easter/summer: 31 Jan 07
Kaim Todner	Yes	Not known	Not known	Not known
Kendall Freeman	Yes + work experience for first-year undergrads	Not known	Not known	Not known
Kirkpatrick & Lockhart Nicholson Graham	Yes: July	Not known	Not known	15 February 2007
Latham & Watkins	Yes: August	2 weeks	£300 p.w.	31 January 2007
Lawrence Graham	32: Easter and summer	2 weeks	£220 p.w.	31 January 2007
Laytons	6	1 week	Not known	31 March 2007
Lester Aldridge	8	2 weeks	£75 p.w.	31 March 2007
Lewis Silkin	16	1 or 2 weeks	Not known	31 January 2007

www.chambersandpartners.co.uk

vacation schemes

firm name	number of places	duration	remuneration	deadline
Linklaters	30: Christmas (non-law, 80: in summer (law), some o/seas	Christmas: 2 weeks Summer: 2 or 4 weeks	Not known	Not known
Lovells	90: Christmas, Easter and summer	2 or 3 weeks	£300 p.w.	Christmas: 10 Nov 06 Easter/summer 31 January 2007
Macfarlanes	54	2 weeks	£250 p.w.	28 February 2007
Manches	24	1 week	Not known	31 January 2007
Mayer, Brown, Rowe & Maw	32: Easter and summer	2 weeks	Not known	Not known
McCormicks	Yes: summer	Not known	Not known	23 February 2007
Mills & Reeve	Yes: summer	2 weeks	Not known	1 March 2007
Mishcon de Reya	15	2 weeks	£250 p.w.	15 March 2007
Morgan Cole	Yes	Not known	Not known	30 April 2007
Nabarro Nathanson	60: summer	3 weeks	Not known	9 February 2007
Norton Rose	15 at Christmas 30 in summer plus open days	Christmas: 2 weeks summer: 4 weeks	£250 p.w.	31 October 2006/07 31 January 2007
Olswang	Yes: summer	2 weeks	£250 p.w.	31 January 2007
Osborne Clarke	Yes: Easter and summer	1 week	Not known	31 January 2007
Pannone	50: Easter and summer	1 week	None	Easter: 26 Jan 07 summer: 27 April 07
Penningtons Solicitors	Yes plus information days	Not known	Not known	31 March 2007
Pinsent Masons	130	2 weeks	Not known	31 January 2007
PricewaterhouseCoopers Legal	Yes: summer	2 weeks	Not known	Not known
Reed Smith Richards Butler	30	2 weeks	£250 p.w.	31 January 2007
Reynolds Porter Chamberlain	20	2 weeks	£250 p.w.	28 February 2007
Shadbolt & Co	6	2 weeks	£200 p.w.	28 February 2007
Shoosmiths	35	2 weeks	£230 p.w.	28 February 2007
Simmons & Simmons	Yes	Not known	Not known	Not known
SJ Berwin	60	2 weeks	£270 p.w.	31 January 2007
Skadden	Yes: Easter and summer	2 weeks	Paid	12 January 2007
Slaughter and May	60 (penult year of degree)	2 weeks	£275 p.w.	26 January 2007

vacation schemes

firm name	number of places	duration	remuneration	deadline
Speechly Bircham	16	3 weeks	£250 p.w.	16 February 2007
Stephenson Harwood	18	2 weeks	£250 p.w.	16 February 2007
Taylor Walton	8	Up to 3 weeks	£183 p.w.	30 March 2007
Taylor Wessing	38	2 weeks	£250 p.w.	31 January 2007
Teacher Stern Selby	20	Not known	Not known	Not known
Thomas Eggar	Yes	1 week	Travel expenses	31 March 2007
TLT Solicitors	36	1 week	Paid	31 January 2007
Travers Smith	Christmas: 15 Summer: 45	2 weeks	£250	31 January 2007
Trowers & Hamlins	25-30	2 weeks	£225 p.w.	1 March 2007
Walker Morris	45	1 week	£180 p.w.	28 February 2007
Ward Hadaway	Yes	1 week	Not known	28 February 2007
Watson, Farley & Williams	30	2 weeks	£250 p.w.	23 February 2007
Wedlake Bell	8: July	3 weeks	£200 p.w.	28 February 2007
Weil, Gotshal & Manges	20: Easter and summer	Not known	Not known	14 February 2007
White & Case	Easter: 20 Summer: 40	Easter: 1 week Summer: 2 weeks	£300 p.w.	31 January 2006
Withers	Yes: Easter and summer + Milan opportunites	2 weeks	Not known	31 January 2007
Wragge & Co	Yes: Easter and summer	Not known	Not known	31 January 2007

www.chambersandpartners.co.uk

how to make applications and get selected

Firms can afford to be choosy so don't assume that a CV filled with any old guff and a half-hearted appraisal-day showing will secure you a training contract.

www.

Who? Why? What? Narrowing down the list of the firms you'd like to work for, assessing whether the firm's a good cultural match for you and making sure they do the kind of work you want are good starting points.

- The **Practice Areas** section of this book summarises the main types of work and ranks the best firms in those fields.
- Look at firm's own websites and those of the legal press – *The Lawyer* (www.lawyer.com), *Legal Week* (www.legalweek.com) and *The Law Gazette* (www.lawgazette.co.uk).
- The **True Picture** will give you a sense of a firm's culture, the specifics of what work current trainees have experienced and how easy they found it to get the seats they wanted.
- Better still, take a vac scheme and sample the work yourself.

Once you've narrowed the field, remember to do a quick idiot check:

- Do your qualifications and experiences fit what the firm wants?
- When is the application deadline? Most commercial firms recruit two years in advance. A few of the big City firms have even earlier application deadlines. Smaller firms recruit one year in advance, sometimes even closer to the start of the contract. Some firms may offer a paralegal position for a trial period before a training contract is discussed.
- Are you applying at the right time? See the **Solicitors Timetable** on page 66.

mailshotshy

Word and mailmerge may enable you to fire off 100 applications in a day but it's not the best approach.

Targeted and carefully reasoned CVs, letters and application forms stand out. Here are a few tips:

- Don't put anything in your CV unless you can expand on it at interview.
- Avoid chronological gaps in your experience: if you've taken time off, put it down and be prepared to explain why.
- CVs are a chance to make your achievements shine: keep them to two, possibly three, pages max and make the most of your strengths by effective use of headings, bullets and bold text.
- Covering letter: Unless stated otherwise, always include one with your CV. It's a chance to expand on why you want to work for a firm and what experience/interests fit you for it, as well as giving the reader a more personal insight into your qualities. One page should do.
- No gimmicks: Avoid photos, bizarre fonts or lurid colours, bribes or jokey applications.
- Spellcheck: thers nothing moor distratcing ad unprofesional than mistakes.

good form

If firms don't ask for a CV they'll want you to complete a dreaded application form. Remember:

- Forms take time: start early and get them in on time. We've heard of online applications submitted just two minutes past a deadline being rejected. Construct a table of the firm's you are applying to, their deadlines and where you are with your application to each.
- Practice makes perfect: photocopy any form that needs to be handwritten and prepare a rough draft. Tipp-ex and different colours of ink look shabby.
- Read the questions: make sure you're answering the question posed, not the question you want to answer. Plan each response carefully, making sure that however little you have to say, you fill much of the box available. Acres of white space look bad.

- On the other hand: make sure you use the questions to cover your whole range of skills and attributes.
- Include a covering letter: unless asked not to. Your letter should highlight the best aspects of your application and relevant experience is fine.
- Keep a copy: weeks later you may struggle to remember what you wrote.

show me what ya got

Qualifications, gap year conservation work, 17 A*s at A-level, endless vac schemes: applicants must show high levels of academic and personal achievement. The top applicants will always reap a sheaf of offers, but care and attention can go a long way.

- Applications should demonstrate teamwork and problem-solving skills as well as commercial outlook/commitment to high street practice.
- Get work experience or vac schemes and try to speak to lawyers wherever you can; it all helps you understand the reality of practice.

interphew!

Having secured an interview, make sure you prepare, prepare, prepare. After all, you wouldn't qualify for the Olympics, then laze around eating cheeseburgers until the day of the race. Remember:

- Detailed preparation helps boost confidence and gives weight to your answers. No one likes a bluffer.
- Be up to date with legal news and current affairs: the law doesn't exist in a vacuum. *The Lawyer, Legal Week, The Law Gazette* and Tuesday's law supplement in *The Times* are good ports of call.
- Study the firm's own literature just prior to interview. If you know which partner will be interviewing you, research him/her.
- Practise answering questions, even the most obvious ones. Can you actually justify why you want to be a lawyer? Don't find out that the answer is 'no' in your interview.

the big day

Here are some general tips:

- Arrive early: If you arrive late, in a rush or pouring with sweat, you're liable to flummox yourself, make a bad impression, keep partners waiting and undo all that hard prep. Arriving early to sit in a nearby cafe and review your application is a much better way to go. Keep the firm's number on you in case you are genuinely delayed.
- Dress appropriately: Casual dress won't convey the right message, nor will anything too racy or alternative. Even if you hate the idea, suits for men and something equally formal for women is the safest choice.
- Be polite to everyone you meet: don't take your nerves out on the receptionist and be careful what you say to those friendly trainees you meet. Bad impressions travel fast.
- Interviews are a two way process: remember the experience is also a chance to assess the firm, its people, atmosphere and whether you'd like to work there. You must avoid appearing arrogant, but you have every reason to be confident not awestruck.
- If more than one person interviews you: try to speak to everyone on the panel.
- Listen carefully and think clearly before answering questions.
- Body language: don't fidget; maintain eye contact as far as possible without scaring anyone.
- Expect to be tested: if your answers are challenged, don't get defensive or aggressive.
- Interviewers want you to shine, not trip you up: difficult questions are designed to test your reactions so try not to freeze.
- Any questions? Prepare a couple of sensible questions for the end of the interview.

testing times

Many firms put candidates to the test via written tests, negotiation exercises and group tasks. These sessions tend to be firm specific and can change year-on-year but your LPC or GDL provider may have a back catalogue of student feedback on different firms' assessment days.

- Reasoning tests can be hard to prepare for, because the companies who supply firms with papers guard their secrets carefully. Some law firms will post sample papers out in advance and your careers service may have a back catalogue.
- The Watson Glaser and HSL tests are the two most commonly used. These tend to feature multiple-choice, reasoning-based questions centred on snippets of commercial information. They test business awareness and intellectual rigour. Some tests need to be completed in a given time; others assess speed by having too many questions. Make sure you know which kind you're sitting.
- You may be asked to write a letter or summarise a piece of research. Such tasks should be equally accessible to law and non-law students.

- Group exercises determine how well you work in a team. Don't simply jockey for position: listen to others, pick up on what they're saying and make your own comments on their suggestions.
- Don't forget to ask around: a friend who attended the same assessment day can brief you on what to expect. Don't hang all your hopes on insider tips as firms may vary their assignments.
- Don't relax too much if there's a social event.

the hardest word to say…

No one likes being rejected but, if things don't work out and you just can't understand why, bite the bullet and phone up to ask.

- However hard it is to hear, finding out your strengths and weaknesses will help you.
- Should you reapply to a firm that has rejected you? It may work for some candidates, especially if they got through to a later stage of the process, however many firms will not want to revisit your application.

Case Study: A typical Linklaters' Assessment Day

8.45am: Arrive
- Current trainees are on hand to involve you and roughly 17 other candidates in general chat and help calm nerves.

9.15am: One-hour written test
- 10 mins to explain the process then 50 to answer 80 multiple-choice, commercially focused questions. Linklaters uses the Watson Glaser test, aiming *"not to catch people out but test their intellectual rigour and suitability to be commercial lawyers."*

10.15am: 45-minute first interview
- A lawyer (likely a managing associate) takes you off for initial interview. This focuses on you, your abilities, experiences, leadership qualities, etc… essentially *"all the soft skills that would suit your work as part of a team in a major organisation."*

11.00am: 30-minute break
- A trainee escorts you back to the main group for a coffee, mini-tour of the building. HR assures us that *"trainees are not there to interrogate and report back on candidates,"* but watch what you say.

11.30am: 30-minutes of interview preparation
- Time to prepare responses to a commercial case study. The exercise is presented as a brief in which the candidate is a trainee who is asked to research a company or organisation and report back to a partner. There will be several pages of information to read and process before deciding how to present your thoughts. No flip charts or PowerPoint presentations are involved.

12.00am: 45-minute second interview
- A partner takes you to the second interview. The first 15-20 minutes are spent presenting and discussing your research findings. Discussion moves on to broader commercial matters. Finally there are questions *"to test a candidate's ability to think speedily and dexterously on the spot."*

12.45pm: Leave
- The partner will escort you to the door. You stagger off down Silk Street to await a decision within days. Meanwhile, Linklaters' staff gather *"to discuss every stage of the assessment together."*

applications and selection

firm name	method of application	selection process	degree class	number of contracts	number of applications
Addleshaw Goddard	See website	Interview + assessment centre	2:1	45-50	1,500
Allen & Overy	Online	Interview	2:1	120	2,700
asb law	Application form	2 interviews + written exercise	2:1	5	1,000
Ashurst	Online	2 interviews	2:1	50	2,500
Baker & McKenzie	Online	Oral presentation + interview	2:1	38	2,000
Barlow Lyde & Gilbert	Online	Interview day	Not known	16-18	2,000
Beachcroft	Online	Interview + assessments	2:1 preferred	40	Not known
Berwin Leighton Paisner	Online	Assessment day + interview	2:1	40	2,000
Bevan Brittan	Online	Not known	Not known	Not known	Not known
Bircham Dyson Bell	See website	2 interviews	2:1 preferred	8	450
Bird & Bird	Online	Assessment day	2:1	18	900
Blake Lapthorn Linnell	Online	Interviews & assessment day	2:1	8-10	300
Boodle Hatfield	Online	Interviews + assessment	2:1	6-8	Not known
BP Collins	Handwritten letter & CV	Interview + selection day	2:1	Not known	Not known
Brabners Chaffe Street	Application form	Interview + assessment day	2:1 or postgrad	7	Not known
Brachers	Online	Interviews	2:1	2	400
Bristows	Application form	2 interviews	2.1 preferred	Up to 10	3,500
Browne Jacobson	Online or CV & covering letter	Telephone interview + assessment centre or open day	2:1	12	600
Burges Salmon	Application form	Not known	2:1	20-25	1,500
Capsticks	Application form	Summer placement + interview	2:1 or above	4-5	150
Charles Russell	Online	Assessment day	2:1	17	1,500
Clarke Willmott	Application form	Interview	2:1 preferred	12	500
Cleary Gottlieb Steen & Hamilton	CV & covering letter	2 interviews	High 2:1	6	2,250
Clifford Chance	Online	Assessment day	2:1	130	2,000
Clyde & Co	Online	Interview + assessments	2:1	22	1,000+
CMS Cameron McKenna	Online	Interview + assessment centre	2:1	60	1,500
Cobbetts	Online	Assessment day	2:1	25	1,000

applications and selection

firm name	method of application	selection process	degree class	number of contracts	number of applications
Coffin Mew & Clover	CV & covering letter	Interview	2:1 (usually)	5	400+
Covington & Burling	Online	2 interviews	2:1	4	Not known
Cripps Harries Hall	Application form	Interview	2.1	7	Up to 750
Davenport Lyons	Online	Interviews	2:1	7	2,000
Davies Arnold Cooper	Application form	Not known	2:1 (usually)	5	Not known
Dechert	Online	Interview + assessments	2:1	Up to 15	1,500
Denton Wilde Sapte	Application form	Interviews + assessments.	2:1	30	1,500
Dickinson Dees	Online	Interview + assessments	2:1	Up to 18	800
DLA Piper	Online	Interviews + assessments	2:1	90+	2,500
DMH Stallard	Online	Interviews + assessments	2:1	10	218
Dorsey & Whitney	CV & Letter	Not known	2:1	4	Not known
Dundas & Wilson	Online	Assessment day	2:1 preferred	26	200
DWF	Online	2 interviews	2:1	10	700
Eversheds	Online	Assessment day	2:1	80	4,000
Farrer & Co	Online	Interviews	2:1	8-10	800
Field Fisher Waterhouse	Online	Interviews + written assessment	2:1	17	1,200
Finers Stephens Innocent	CV & covering letter	2 interviews	2:1	5	800
Foot Anstey	Letter & CV or online	Assessment day	2:1 preferred	12	Not known
Forbes	Handwritten letter & CV	Interview	2:1	4	350+
Ford & Warren	CV & letter	Interviews + exercise	2:1	6	500
Forsters	Online	2 interviews	Not known	Not known	Not known
Freeth Cartwright	Online	Interview + selection day	Not known	Not known	Not known
Freshfields Bruckhaus Deringer	Online	2 interviews + written test	2:1	100	2,000
Government Legal Service	Online	Assessment day	2:1	22-30	1,200+
Halliwells	Online	Group exercise, presentation + interview	2:1	38	1,500
Hammonds	Online	Assessment + interview	2:1	40	1,300
Harbottle & Lewis	CV & letter	Interview	2:1	4	800

applications and selection

firm name	method of application	selection process	degree class	number of contracts	number of applications
HBJ Gateley Wareing	See website	Not known	2:1	Not known	Not known
Henmans	Application form	Assessment day	Not known	3	450
Herbert Smith	Online	Case study + interview	2:1	Up to 100	2,000
Hewitsons	Application form	Interview	2:1	10	850
Higgs & Sons	Online or letter & CV	Interview	2:1 usually preferred	4	250+
Hill Dickinson	Online	Assessment day	Not known	Not known	Not known
Hodge Jones & Alien	Application form	Interview	2:1	6-7	500
Holman Fenwick & Willan	Online	2 interviews + written exercise	2:1	8	1,000
Howes Percival	Online	Assessment day	2:1	8	300
IBB Solicitors	Online	Assessment day	2:1	6	400
Ince & Co	Letter & CV	2 interviews + written test	2:1	8-10	1,500
Irwin Mitchell	Online	Assessment centre + interview	None specified	20-25	1,200
Jones Day	CV & letter	2 interviews	2:1	15-20	1,500
Kaim Todner	CV & letter or online	Interview	2:2	7	400
Kendall Freeman	Online	Interview + assessement	2:1	7	Not known
Kirkpatrick & Lockhart Nicholson Graham	Online	Interview + assessment	2:1	Up to 15	1,000
Knight & Sons	Online or paper application	Interviews + presentation	Not known	3	200
Latham & Watkins	CV & letter	3 interviews	2:1	10-15	Not known
Lawrence Graham	Application form	Interview	2:1	20-25	800
Laytons	Application form	2 interviews	1 or 2:1	8	2,000
LeBoeuf, Lamb, Greene & MacRae	CV & letter	Not known	2:1	10	950
Lester Aldridge	Letter, CV & application form	Interview	2:1	10	300
Lewis Silkin	Online	Assessment day	2:1	5	800
Linklaters	Application form	2 interviews + assessments	2:1	130	3,500
Lovells	Online	Assessment day	2:1	90	2,500
Lupton Fawcett	Online	Interview + assessment day	2:1 preferred	2-3	300

applications and selection

firm name	method of application	selection process	degree class	number of contracts	number of applications
Mace & Jones	Online	Interview	2:1	4-5	250
Macfarlanes	Online	Assessment day	2:1	30	900
Manches	Online	2 interviews	2:1	10	900
Martineau Johnson	Online	Half-day assessment centre	2:1	10-12	500
Mayer, Brown, Rowe & Maw	Online	Interview + assessments	2:1	25-30	1,000+
McCormicks	Application form	Assessments day + interview	2:1	4	350
McDermott, Will & Emery	CV & covering letter	2 interviews + written exercise	Not known	Not known	Not known
McGrigors	Online	Half-day assessment centre	2:1	10-15	Not known
Mills & Reeve	Online	Assessment centre	2:1	20	600
Mishcon de Reya	Online	Not known	2:1	8	1,000+
Morgan Cole	Online	Assessment centre + interview	2:1 preferred	Not known	Not known
Nabarro Nathanson	Online	Assessment day	2:1	25	1,500
Norton Rose	Online	Interview + group exercise	2:1	60	2,500+
Olswang	Online	Interview + assessments	2:1	20	2,000
Orrick, Herrington & Sutcliffe	Letter & CV	2 interviews	2:1	6	Not known
Osborne Clarke	Online	Assessment day	2:1	20	1,000
Pannone	Online	2 interviews	2:1	14	1,200
Payne Hicks Beach	Letter & CV	Interview	2:1	3	1,000
Penningtons	Online	Not known	2:1	14	1,000
Pinsent Masons	Online	Assessment day	2:1	55	2,000+
Prettys	Letter & CV	Not known	2:1 preferred	5	Not known
PricewaterhouseCoopers Legal	Online	Not known	2:1	Not known	Not known
Pritchard Englefield	Application form	Interview	Generally 2:1	3	300-400
Reed Smith Richards Butler	Online	Interview + assessment	2:1	30	1,500
Reynolds Porter Chamberlain	Online	Assessment day	2.1	15	900
Salans	Handwritten letter & CV	Interviews + workshop	2:1	3-4	500+
Shadbolt & Co	Online	Interview + assessment	Usually 2:1	4	100

applications and selection

firm name	method of application	selection process	degree class	number of contracts	number of applications
Shearman & Sterling	Online	Interviews	2:1	15	Not known
Shoosmiths	Application form	Full-day selection centre	2:1	14	1,000
Sidley Austin	Application form	Interview(s)	2:1	15	500
Simmons & Simmons	Online	Assessment day	2:1	50	2,500
SJ Berwin	Online	2 interviews	2:1	45	2,000
Skadden	Online	Interview + exercise	2:1	8	700
Slaughter and May	Online or covering letter & CV	Interview	2:1	85-95	2,000+
Speechly Bircham	Application form	Interview	2:1	7	500
Stephenson Harwood	Online	Assessment centre	2:1	12	Not known
Stevens & Bolton	Online	2 interviews + assessments	2:1	4	200
Tarlo Lyons	Application form	2 interviews	2:1	3	200
Taylor Walton	CV & covering letter	2 interviews	2:1	Not known	Not known
Taylor Wessing	Online	2 interviews + psychometric test	2:1	22	1,195
Teacher Stern Selby	Online	2 interviews	2:1 (not absolute)	3-6	500
Thomas Eggar	Letter & CV	Assessment centre + interview	2:1	Not known	Not known
Thomson Snell & Passmore	Letter & application form	Assessment interview	2:1	4	500
TLT Solicitors	Online	Assessment centre	2:1 preferred	8	500+
Travers Smith	CV & covering letter	2 interviews	2:1	Up to 25	2,000
Trethowans	Letter & application form	Interview + assessment day	2:1	3-4	250+
Trowers & Hamlins	Online	Interviews + assessments	2:1	20	1,600
Vertex Law	Online	Assessment day + interviews	Usually 2:1	2	Not known
Walker Morris	Online	Interviews	2:1	18	Approx 800
Ward Hadaway	Application form & letter	Assessment centre + interview	2:1	10	400+
Watson Burton	Application form & letter	Not known	2:1	7	1,000
Watson, Farley & Williams	Online	Assessment centre + interview	2:1	12	1,000
Wedlake Bell	Application form	2 interviews	2:1	7	Not known
Weightmans	Online	Not known	Not known	Up to 12	Not known

applications and selection

firm name	method of application	selection process	degree class	number of contracts	number of applications
Weil, Gotshal & Manges	Online	Not known	2:1	12	Not known
White & Case	Online	Interview	2:1	25-30	1,600
Wiggin	Online	2-day selection	2:1	3	500
Withers	Application form	2 interviews + exercises	2:1	14	1,000
Wollastons	CV & application form	3-stage interview	2:1	2	500
Wragge & Co	Online	Telephone discussion + assessment day	2:1	30	1,000

deal or no deal: the art of managing offers

After all the hard work involved in securing a training contract offer, you'll need to know what to do when you actually land one. The Law Society publishes its 'Voluntary Code to Good Practice in the Recruitment of Trainee Solicitors' at www.lawsociety.org.uk/becomingasolicitor/training.law#9 and we recommend you read through these guidelines if, at any stage, you are in doubt as to what you should do. The guidelines address the conduct of both recruiters and students.

On offers the guidelines say:

- If you're still an undergrad, an offer of a training contract can only be made on or after 1 September in your final undergraduate year. If you've impressed the firm during a vacation scheme or period of work experience, the firm must wait until this date before making you an offer.
- At an interview, you will be told if there is a further stage to the selection process. You should also be told within two weeks of reaching the end of the process whether or not you have been successful.
- Offers should be made in writing. If you receive an offer by phone you don't need to say yes or no: you can ask the firm to send a formal offer in writing for you to consider.

On deadlines, the guidelines say:

- No deadline should expire earlier than four weeks from the date of the offer. If you need more time to consider an offer, firms are supposed to consider your request 'sympathetically' provided you have a good reason. No definition of 'good reason' is given in the guidelines.
- If a firm is going to pay your law school fees, it should set out the terms and conditions of the arrangement in the training contract offer letter. The firm's willingness to provide financial assistance should not affect the time limit for accepting the contract.
- If you feel you need more time you will have to enter into diplomatic discussions with the law firm, telling them how much longer you need. Make sure you get written confirmation of any extension to the deadline as simply asking for it won't be enough.

You may want to hang on to an offer from one firm while you pursue applications with others. This is okay, but you must bear in mind the following:

- You should not hold more than two (as yet unaccepted or declined) offers at any one time.
- Students are supposed to respond promptly to a firm that's made an offer, either by accepting or rejecting it. The word 'promptly' is not defined in the code.
- Because offers can and will be made with time limits for acceptance, do guard against allowing a deadline to elapse. The stupidity tax you may otherwise pay doesn't bear thinking about.
- Once your preferred offer has been accepted in writing, you must then confirm to everyone else that you are withdrawing your application. This is only fair to busy recruiters and other applicants who may suffer if you clog up a shortlist.

The guidelines are silent on the issue of what happens if a student changes their mind after accepting an offer. It's a rare firm that will be particularly sympathetic to a post-acceptance withdrawal but, on occasions, these things do happen. We can give no general advice on this subject, as each individual case will have its own merits. What we can say is that the whole trainee recruitment market relies on all parties playing by the above 'rules'. So what if a law firm puts pressure on you to accept an offer earlier than the guidelines say they should? Again, there is no simple answer as the Law Society's code of conduct is voluntary. If this situation arises you will have to enter into delicate negotiations with the law firm. We also recommend that you report the problem to your university or college careers adviser and ask if they can recommend a course of action.

a quick look at the markets

It's party time in training contract central. Get those applications mailed off and just sit back and wait for the big-money offers to roll in. Are we joking? Yes and no. For a segment of our readership, snagging a training contract in 2007 will be easy business because the market is in very good health. Not only are commercial firms going to offer more traineeships to 2009 starters, a good number of them have found extra places for people hoping to start earlier.

If you're aiming for the City or a big regional firm it's good news on job offers and good news on money. The *Student Guide* salary-o-meter went bananas over the summer of 2006 when law firms began announcing their latest pay and sponsorship rates. With the cost of training now higher than ever, perhaps it's only a matter of time before we see a trend for more law firms to link law school sponsorship to a minimum term of post-qualification employment.

Pay Cheques in the City

The most handsome law school packages now approach £30,000 for those taking both the GDL and the LPC. New trainees in major City firms now typically start somewhere between £28,000 and £31,000 pa, with American firms frequently paying more. There's an amazing £35,000 for a first-year trainee at Cleary Gottlieb Steen & Hamilton. When it comes to NQ salaries the news is even better, with the UK-firm benchmark now set at £55,000 for one-year PQEs and certain American firms paying astonishing rates. The firm making the headlines on NQ salaries 2006 is Latham & Watkins, which has recently initiated a training scheme. Its NQ salary is £88,000. Not far behind is Cleary with a hefty £84,000 for the first year post-qualification and LeBoeuf, Lamb, Greene & MacRae which added a £15,000 bonus to its £75,000 NQ salary in 2006.

With commercial trainee salaries higher than they have ever been, it leaves us wondering how another segment of our readership will feel when they learn that the Law Society proposes to do away with requirements for a minimum trainee salary. The last figures published by the society required that trainees receive no less than £17,110 pa in central London or £15,332 pa elsewhere. The idea behind removing the salary safety net is to encourage more firms to offer traineeships, albeit lower-paid ones. It's impossible to predict what effect the change will have, but you can bet your parents' mortgage that any additional training contracts arising as a result will not be accompanied by law school funding. Though it's hardly a return to the days when aspiring lawyers actually paid firms to train them, we could be facing a two-tier legal profession in which a generation of debt-ridden, extremely poorly paid lawyers co-exist with the fat cats. Some would argue that we have this already.

Undeniably there are plenty of people who would welcome a training contract at any price simply because the number of student hopefuls outstrips the number of training opportunities. In 2005 there were 8,649 LPC students and approximately 5,700 training contracts. The Law Society takes the view that limiting the number of LPC places is not the answer and, indeed, has authorised law schools to take more students than ever.

While the factors affecting the number of training positions are many, all stem from the financial considerations facing the law firms. The buoyant market for trainees and NQs at commercial firms results from a thriving economy that is providing plenty of work. In stark contrast, those law firms offering services to publicly funded clients face uncertain times, not least because of the changes to be made following Lord Carter's review of legal aid. Find out more by reading **Get Carter** on page 17.

salaries and benefits

firm name	1st year salary	2nd year salary	sponsorship/ awards	other benefits	qualification salary
Addleshaw Goddard	£21,500 (Manch/Leeds) £30,000 (London)	£24,000 (Manch/Leeds) £33,000 (London)	GDL & LPC: fees + £7,000 (London) or £4,500 (elsewhere)	Corporate gym m'ship, STL, subsd restaurant, pension, pte healthcare	£35,000 (Manch/Leeds) £53,000 (London)
Allen & Overy	£31,000	£35,000	LPC: fees + £7,000 GDL: fees + £6,000 (London), £5,000 (elsewhere)	Pte healthcare, PMI, STL, subsd restaurant, gym m'ship, 6 weeks unpaid leave on qual	£55,000
asb law	£18,500	Not known	LPC: interest-free loan	Not known	Not known
Ashurst	£30,000	£33,500	GDL & LPC: fees + £7,500, £500 for first-class degree or LPC distinction, language bursaries	PHI, pension, life ass, STL, gym m'ship	£55,000
Baker & McKenzie	£31,500 + £3,000 'joining bonus'	£34,000	LPC: fees + £8,000 GDL: fees + £6,000	PHI, life ins, PMI, pension, subsd gym m'ship, STL, subsd restaurant	£55,000
Barlow Lyde & Gilbert	£29,000	£31,000	GDL & LPC: fees + maintenance	Not known	£50,000
Beachcroft	£29,000 (London) £21,000 (regions)	£31,000 (London) £23,000 (regions)	GDL & LPC: fees + £3,500	Flexible scheme inc holiday, pension, pte healthcare, EAP	Not known
Berwin Leighton Paisner	£30,000 + £2,500 golden hello	£33,000	GDL & LPC: fees + £7,200	Flexible package inc PHI, PMI, subsd gym m'ship	£53,000
Bevan Brittan	Not known	Not known	GDL & LPC: fees + bursary	Not known	Not known
Bircham Dyson Bell	£29,000	£31,000	GDL & LPC: fees	Pte healthcare, life ass, PHI, pension	£46,000
Bird & Bird	£28,000	£30,000	GDL & LPC: fees + £5,500	BUPA, STL, subsd sports club m'ship, life cover, PHI, pension, childcare and eyecare vouchers	£50,000
Blake Lapthorn Linnell	£18,000	£19,500	LPC: fees + maintenance	Pte helathcare, life ass, pension, childcare vouchers	£32,000
Boodle Hatfield	£27,500	£29,500	GDL & LPC: fees + maintenance	Pte healthcare, life ass, STL, pension, PHI, conveyancing grant	£46,000
BP Collins	£19,000	£20,000	Not known	Not known	Not known
Brabners Chaffe Street	£20,000	Not known	LPC: assistance available	Not known	Not known
Brachers	£17,400	£19,500	GDL/LPC: £6,000 discretionary award	Not known	£31,000

Notes: PHI = Permanent Health Insurance; STL = Season Travel Ticket Loan; PMI = Private Medical Insurance EAP = Employee Assistance Programme

www.chambersandpartners.co.uk

salaries and benefits

firm name	1st year salary	2nd year salary	sponsorship/ awards	other benefits	qualification salary
Bristows	£30,000	£32,000	GDL & LPC: fees + £7,000	Pension, life ass & health ins	£45,000
Browne Jacobson	£22,500	£25,000	GDL & LPC: fees + £5,000	Not known	Market rate
Burges Salmon	£24,000	£25,000	GDL & LPC: fees + £6,000	Bonus, pension, pte healthcare, mobile phone, gym m'ship, Xmas gift	£37,000
Capsticks	Not known	Not known	GDL & LPC: scholarship contributions	Bonus, pension, PHI, death-in-service-cover, STL	Not known
Charles Russell	£28,000	£30,500	GDL & LPC: fees + grant £5,000 (London) £4,500 (Guildford) £3,500 (Cheltenham)	BUPA, PHI, life ass, pension, STL	£48,000
Clarke Willmott	£20,000	£21,500	LPC: fees	Life ass, pension, gym m'ship, bonus	£34,500
Cleary Gottlieb Steen & Hamilton	£35,000	£40,000	LPC: fees + £8,000	Pension, PHI, disability ins, health club m'ship	£84,000
Clifford Chance	£31,000	£34,000	LPC: fees + £7,000 GDL: fees + £6,000 (Lon) or £5,000 (elsewhere), prizes for first-class degree & top LPC performers	Interest-free loan, pte healthcare, subsd restaurant, fitness centre, life ass, occupational health service, PHI	£55,000
Clyde & Co	£29,000	£32,000	GDL & LPC: fees + £6,000 (Lon/Guild) £5,500 (elsewhere)	Interest-free loan on joining, pension, life ass, PMI, subsd gym m'ship, STL	£50,000
CMS Cameron McKenna	£30,000	£33,500	GDL & LPC: fees + £7,500 (Lon/Guild/Oxf), £5,000 (elsewhere)	Bonus, gym m'ship, life ass, pension, pte healthcare, STL, counselling, subs'd rest, buy-holiday scheme	£54,000
Cobbetts	£21,000	£22,000	GDL & LPC: fees + £4,000	BUPA, gym m'ship, pension, STL, death-in-service cover, counselling	£33,000
Coffin Mew & Clover	Competitive	Competitive	LPC: discussed with candidates	Not known	Competitive
Covington & Burling	£35,000	£37,000	GDL & LPC: fees + £7,250	Pension, PHI, pte healthcare, life ass, STL	Not known
Cripps Harries Hall	£17,500	£20,000	LPC fees: 50% interest-free loan, 50% bursary	Not known	£31,500
Davenport Lyons	£28,000-£28,666	£29,332-£30,000	No	STL, client intro bonus, subsd gym m'ship, discretionary bonus, life ass	Not known
Davies Arnold Cooper	£27,000	Not known	GDL & LPC: fees + maintenance	PMI, STL	Not known

Notes: PHI = Permanent Health Insurance; STL = Season Travel Ticket Loan; PMI = Private Medical Insurance EAP = Employee Assistance Programme

salaries and benefits

firm name	1st year salary	2nd year salary	sponsorship/ awards	other benefits	qualification salary
Dechert	£35,000	£40,000	LPC: fees + £7,000	PHI, life ass, subsd gym m'ship, STL	£56,000-£66,000
Denton Wilde Sapte	£30,000 + £1,000 joining bonus	£32,000	GDL & LPC: fees + £5,500 (£6,000 in London)	Flexible benefit scheme, STL	£53,000
Dickinson Dees	£19,000	£20,000	GDL & LPC: fees + financial assistance	Not known	£34,000
DLA Piper	£31,000 (London) £22,000 (other English)	£34,000 (London) £24,000 (other English)	GDL & LPC: fees + maintenance	Pension, pte healthcare, life ass, PHI	£53,000 (London) £35,000 (other English)
DMH Stallard	£20,000 (Brighton & Crawley) £25,000 (London)	£22,000 (Brighton & Crawley) £27,000 (London)	Not known	Not known	Not known
Dorsey & Whitney	£29,000	£33,000	Not known	Pension, health ins, life ass	£55,000
Dundas & Wilson	£30,000 (London)	£33,500 (London)	GDL & LPC: fees + maintenance	Life ass, PHI, pension, STL, holiday-purchase scheme	£52,000
DWF	£21,000	Not known	LPC: fees	Flexible scheme	Not known
Eversheds	£29,000 (London)	£32,000 (London)	GDL & LPC: fees + maintenance	Regional variations	£50,000 (London)
Farrer & Co	£28,000	£30,500	GDL & LPC: fees + £5,000	Health & life ins, subsd gym m'ship, STL	£44,000
Field Fisher Waterhouse	£29,000	£32,000	GDL: fees + £5,500 LPC: fees + £6,000	STL, medical ins, life ass, pension, GP service	£50,000
Finers Stephens Innocent	Highly competitive	Highly competitive	GDL & LPC: fees	Pension, PMI, life ins, long-term disability ins, STL	Highly competitive
Foot Anstey	£17,500	£20,000	LPC: £9,600	Pension	£30,500
Forbes	Not known	£17,720	Not known	Not known	Highly competitive
Forsters	£28,500	£30,500	GDL & LPC: sponsorship available	STL, PHI, life ins, subsd gym m'ship, pension, EAP, pte healthcare	£47,500
Freeth Cartwright	£19,000	Not known	Not known	Not known	Not known
Freshfields Bruckhaus Deringer	£31,000	£35,000	GDL: fees + £6,250 LPC: fees + £7,250	Life ass, PHI, pension, interest-free loan, STL, PMI, subsd staff restaurant, gym	£55,000
Government Legal Service	Over £20,000 (London)	Not known	LPC: fees + £5,000-£7,000 GDL: possibly	Pension, subsd canteen	See website

Notes: PHI = Permanent Health Insurance; STL = Season Travel Ticket Loan; PMI = Private Medical Insurance EAP = Employee Assistance Programme

www.chambersandpartners.co.uk

salaries and benefits

firm name	1st year salary	2nd year salary	sponsorship/ awards	other benefits	qualification salary
Halliwells	£22,145	£23,175	GDL & LPC: fees + £4,500	Pension, subsd gym m'ship	£34,000
Hammonds	£27,000 (London) £20,500 (other)	£30,000 (London) £23,000 (other)	GDL & LPC: fees + £4,500	Pension, life ass, subsd gym m'ship, STL + others	£48,000 (London) £34,000 (other)
Harbottle & Lewis	£27,000	£28,000	LPC: fees + interest-free loan	Lunch, STL	£46,000
HBJ Gateley Wareing	£20,000	£22,000	LPC: fees + £4,000 GDL: fees	Not known	£34,000
Henmans	£18,600	£20,400	Not known	Not known	£31,000
Herbert Smith	£31,000	£35,000	GDL & LPC: fees + up to £7,000	Bonus, PHI, PMI, STL, life ass, subsd gym m'ship accident ins, interest-free loan, pension	£55,000
Hewitsons	£18,000	£19,000	None	Not known	£31,500
Higgs & Sons	£17,000	£18,500	Not known	PMI, life ass	£26,000
Hill Dickinson	£20,500 (+ Lon weighting)	£22,000 (+ Lon weighting)	LPC: sponsorship available	Not known	Not known
Hodge Jones & Allen	£20,000	Not known	Not known	Pension, life ass, disability ins	£27,000
Holman Fenwick & Willan	£28,000	£30,000	GDL & LPC: fees + £5,000	PMI, PHI, accident ins, subsd gym m'ship, STL	£50,000
Howes Percival	See website	See website	GDL & LPC: funding + maintenance grant	Pension, PHI	Not known
IBB Solicitors	£20,000	£22,000	Not known	Life ass, pension, PMI, subsd gym m'ship	Not known
Ince & Co	£28,500	£31,500	LPC: fees + £6,000 (London), £5,500 (elsewhere)	STL, PMI, PHI, pension	£48,500
Irwin Mitchell	£18,540 (outside London)	£20,600 (outside London)	GDL & LPC: fees + £3,000	Healthcare, pension, sub'd gym m'ship	Not known
Jones Day	£39,000	£45,000	GDL & LPC: fees + £8,000	Pte healthcare, sports club m'ship, group life cover, STL	£60,000
Kaim Todner	£17,150	£17,500	Possibly LSC sponsorship	Not known	£24,000
Kendall Freeman	£29,500	£33,000	GDL & LPC: fees + £6,500 (London) or £6,000 (elsewhere)	Not known	£52,000
Kirkpatrick & Lockhart Nicholson Graham	£30,000	£33,000	GDL: fees + £5,000 LPC: fees + £7,000	PHI, life ass, STL, subsd gym m'ship, pension, pte healthcare	£53,000
Knight & Sons	Not known	Not known	Interest-free loans may be available	Subsd restaurant, parking, subsd healthcare	Not known

Notes: PHI = Permanent Health Insurance; STL = Season Travel Ticket Loan; PMI = Private Medical Insurance EAP = Employee Assistance Programme

salaries and benefits

firm name	1st year salary	2nd year salary	sponsorship/ awards	other benefits	qualification salary
Latham & Watkins	£35,000-£35,500	£36,000-£36,500	GDL & LPC: fees + £8,000	Healthcare & dental scheme, pension, life ass	£88,000
Lawrence Graham	£28,000	£32,000	GDL & LPC: fees + £5,000 (London) £4,500 (elsewhere)	STL, on-site gym, life ass	£53,000
Laytons	Market rate	Market rate	GDL & LPC: funding considered	Not known	Market rate
LeBoeuf, Lamb, Greene & MacRae	£36,000	£39,000	GDL & LPC: fees + £7,000	Health, life & disability insurance contribs, STL, bonus	£75,000 + bonus
Lester Aldridge	£16,500-£17,000	£17,500-£18,000	LPC: funding available	Life ass, pension, flexible benefits	£31,000
Lewis Silkin	£30,000	£32,000	GDL: fees LPC: fees + £4,500	Life ass, critical illness cover, health ins, STL, pension, subsd gym m'ship, bonus	£46,000
Linklaters	£31,300	Not known	GDL & LPC: fees + maintenance	Bonus, life ass, PMI, PHI, pension, gym/health club m'ship, travel ins, STL, and others	£55,100 + bonus
Lovells	£31,000 + £1,000 joining bonus + £1,000 salary advance	£35,000	GDL & LPC: fees + £7,450 or £6,450 for GDL o/s London, £500 prize for first-class degree and £500 for top Lovells LPC, STL	PMI, life ass, PHI, STL, in-house gym, staff rest, in-house dentist, doctor & physio, local retail discounts	£53,000
Lupton Fawcett	Competitive	Competitive	LPC: funding is negotiable	Health ins, STL	Competitive
Mace & Jones	£17,000	£17,500	Not known	Not known	Negotiable
Macfarlanes	£31,000	£34,000	GDL & LPC: fees + £7,000, prizes for LPC distinction or commendation	Comprehensive package	£55,000
Manches	£28,000 (London)	£31,000 (London)	GDL & LPC: fees + £5,000	STL, PHI, PMI, pension, life ass	£50,000 (London)
Martineau Johnson	£20,000	£21,500	Not known	Not known	£34,000
Mayer, Brown, Rowe & Maw	£31,000	£33,500	GDL & LPC: + £7,000 (Lon/Guild) £6,500 (elsewhere)	STL, sports club m'ship, pte healthcare	£55,000
McCormicks	Highly competitive	Highly competitive	Not known	Not known	Highly competitive
McDermott, Will & Emery	£31,500	£35,000	GDL & LPC: fees + maintenance	PMI, dential ins, life ass, EAP, PHI, STL, subsd gym m'ship	£60,000

Notes: PHI = Permanent Health Insurance; STL = Season Travel Ticket Loan; PMI = Private Medical Insurance EAP = Employee Assistance Programme

www.chambersandpartners.co.uk

salaries and benefits

firm name	1st year salary	2nd year salary	sponsorship/ awards	other benefits	qualification salary
McGrigors	£29,000 (London)	£33,000 (London)	GDL & LPC: fees + £4,500	PMI, STL, Life ass, pension, lunch allowance, income protection	£52,000 (London)
Mills & Reeve	£22,500	£23,500	GDL & LPC: fees + maintenance	Life ass, pension, bonus, subsd gym & rest, STL, PMI	Not known
Mishcon de Reya	£29,000	£31,000	GDL & LPC: fees + maintenance	PMI, travel ins, subsd gym m'ship, STL, PHI, life ass, pension, doctor, EAP	Not known
Morgan Cole	Competitive	Competitive	GDL & LPC: fees + maintenance	Not known	Not known
Nabarro Nathanson	£30,000 (London) £22,000 (Sheffield)	£33,000 (London) £24,000 (Sheffield)	GDL: fees + £6,000 (London) or £5,000 (elsewhere) LPC: fees + £7,000 (London) or £6,000 (elsewhere)	PMI, pension, STL, subsd restaurant, subsd gym m'ship	£53,000 (London) £34,000 (Sheffield)
Norton Rose	£31,000	£35,000	GDL: fees + £6,000 LPC: fees + £7,000 £1,000 travel scholarship	£800 loan on arrival, life ass, pte health ins, STL, subsd gym m'ship, four weeks unpaid leave on qual	Not known
Olswang	£30,000	£34,000	GDL & LPC: fees + £7,00, (London) or £6,500 (elsewhere)	Pension, PMI, life cover, dental scheme, STL, subsd gym m'ship and staff restaurant, PHI	£53,000
Orrick, Herrington & Sutcliffe	£28,000	£32,000	GDL & LPC: fees + £4,000	Pension, PHI, subsd gym m'ship, STL, PMI, dental care, childcare vouchers	Not known
Osborne Clarke	£30,500 (London/TV) £24,000 (Bristol)	£31,500 (London/TV) £25,000 (Bristol)	GDL & LPC: fees + maintenance	Pension PMI, STL, PHI, life ass bonus	£51,000 (London) £43,000 (TV) £36,000 (Bristol)
Pannone	£21,500	£23,500	LPC: fees	Not known	£33,000
Payne Hicks Beach	£28,500	£30,500	GDL & LPC: fees	STL, life ass, PHI, pension	Not known
Penningtons Solicitors	£28,000 (London)	£30,000 (London)	LPC: fees + £4,000	Pension, life ass, PMI, STL, critical illness cover	Not known
Pinsent Masons	£30,000 (London)	£33,000 (London)	GDL & LPC: fees + maintenance	Not known	£53,000 (London)
PricewaterhouseCoopers Legal	£28,000	£32,000	GDL & LPC: fees + maintenance	Not known	Not known
Pritchard Englefield	£22,250	Not known	LPC: fees	Subsd training, luncheon vouchers, PMI, STL	£42,000
Reed Smith Richards Butler	£29,000 (London)	£32,000 (London)	GDL: fees + £6,000 LPC: fees + £7,000	BUPA, STL, life ass, pension, bonus, staff conveyancing	£50,000 + bonus (London)

Notes: PHI = Permanent Health Insurance; STL = Season Travel Ticket Loan; PMI = Private Medical Insurance EAP = Employee Assistance Programme

salaries and benefits

firm name	1st year salary	2nd year salary	sponsorship/ awards	other benefits	qualification salary
Reynolds Porter Chamberlain	£29,000	£33,000	GDL & LPC: fees + £6,000	Bonus, PMI, income protection, STL, subsd gym m'ship, pension	£50,000
Salans	£27,000	£29,000	LPC: fees	Private healthcare, pension, STL, critical illness cover	Variable
Shadbolt & Co	£26,000	£30,000	LPC: fee refund when TC starts	Private healthcare, PHI, life ass, paid study leave, STL, bonus, prof m'ships + subs	£46,000
Shearman & Sterling	£36,500	£39,500	GDL & LPC: fees + £7,000	Not known	£72,000
Shoosmiths	Market rate	Market rate	LPC: £13,000	Life ass, pension, staff discounts, Christmas bonus	Market rate
Sidley Austin	£29,000	£33,000	GDL & LPC: fees + £7,000	PMI, life ass, contrib to gym m'ship, STL, income protection, pension, subsd restaurant	Not known
Simmons & Simmons	£31,000	£34,000	LPC: fees + up to £7,500	Not known	£55,000
SJ Berwin	£31,000	£35,000	GDL & LPC: fees + £5,000-£7,000	Not known	£55,000
Skadden Arps, Slate, Meagher & Flom (UK)	£35,000	£40,000	GDL & LPC: fees + £7,500	Life ass, PMI, PHI, travel ins, subsd gym m'ship and resturant, pension, technology allowance, EAP	Not known
Slaughter and May	£31,000	£34,500	GDL & LPC: fees + maintenance	BUPA, STL, pension, subsd health club m'ship, 24-hour accident cover	£54,000
Speechly Bircham	£28,000-£29,000	£30,000-£31,000	GDL & LPC: fees + maintenance	STL, PMI, life ass	£48,000
Stephenson Harwood	£28,000	£32,000	GDL & LPC: fees + maintenance	Subsd health club m'ship, PHI, BUPA, STL	£52,000
Stevens & Bolton	£24,000	£26,000	GDL & LPC: fees + £4,000	PMI, life ass, pension, STL, PHI	£41,250
Tarlo Lyons	£28,000 (on average)	£30,000 (on average)	LPC: fees	Bonus, PHI, subsd gym m'ship, STL	£44,000
Taylor Walton	Not known	Not known	LPC: full sponsorship	Not known	Not known
Taylor Wessing	£30,000	£34,000	GDL & LPC: fees + £7,000	PMI, PHI, STL, subsd staff restaurant, pension	£53,000
Teacher Stern Selby	£29,000	Not known	Considered	Not known	£41,000
Thomas Eggar	Competitive	Competitive	LPC: 50% grant, 50% loan	Not known	Not known
Thomson Snell & Passmore	Competitive	Competitive	LPC: grant + interest-free loan	Not known	Not known

Notes: PHI = Permanent Health Insurance; STL = Season Travel Ticket Loan; PMI = Private Medical Insurance EAP = Employee Assistance Programme

www.chambersandpartners.co.uk

salaries and benefits

firm name	1st year salary	2nd year salary	sponsorship/ awards	other benefits	qualification salary
TLT Solicitors	£22,000	£23,000	GDL & LPC: fees + maintenance	Pension, PMI, subsd sports & health club m'ship, life ass	Market rate
Travers Smith	£31,000	£35,000	GDL & LPC: fees + £7,000 (London) or £6,500 (elsewhere)	PHI, PMI, life ass, STL, subsd bistro, health club m'ship	£55,000
Trethowans	Not known	Not known	LPC: fees	Pension, death-in-service cover, PHI, bonus, car parking & insurance scheme and others	Market rate
Trowers & Hamlins	£28,000	£30,000	GDL & LPC: fees + £6,000 (London) or £5,500 (elsewhere)	Bonus, pension, healthcare, life ass, STL, subsd staff restaurant	£50,000
Vertex Law	£21,000	£23,000	LPC: fees (50% paid + 50% int-free loan)	PMI, life ass, prof m'ships + subs	Not known
Walker Morris	£20,000	£22,000	GDL & LPC: fees + £5,000	Not known	£34,000
Ward Hadaway	£18,500	£19,500	GDL & LPC: fees + £2,000 int-free loan	Death-in-service cover, pension, flexible holiday scheme	£33,750
Watson Burton	£16,750 (+ Leeds weighting)	£18,250 (+ Leeds weighting)	LPC: fees	Not known	£34,000
Watson, Farley & Williams	£29,000	£33,500	GDL & LPC: fees + £6,500 (London) or £5,500 (elsewhere)	Life ass, PHI, BUPA, STL, pension, subsd gym m'ship	£50,000
Wedlake Bell	£27,000	£29,000	GDL & LPC: fees + £2,500	Pension, STL, subsd gym m'ship, life ass, PHI	Not known
Weightmans	Competitive	Competitive	GDL & LPC: fees	Pension, PHI, life ass	Not known
Weil, Gotshal & Manges	£37,500	Not known	Not known	Not known	Not known
White & Case	£36,000-£37,000	£38,000-£39,000	GDL & LPC: fees + £7,500 prize for LPC commendation or distinction	PMI, dental ins, income protection, life ass, pension, critical illness cover, travel ins, gym m'ship, retail vouchers	£67,500
Wiggin	£26,500	£31,500	GDL & LPC: fees + £3,500	Life ass, pte health cover, pension, PHI, subsd gym m'ship	£44,000
Withers	£28,750	£30,000	GDL & LPC: fees + £5,000, prize for GDL/LPC distinction	STL, PMI, life ass, bonus, subsd cafe, dental plan, pension, PC purchase plan	£48,000
Wollastons	£22,000	£23,000	LPC: fees	Not known	Not known
Wragge & Co	£22,000 (Birmingham)	£25,000 (Birmingham)	GDL & LPC: fees + £7,000 (London) £5.500 (elsewhere) prizes for LPC distinction or first-class degree	£1,000 int-free loan, pension, life ass, PHI, travel schemes, PMI, sports & social club, indep fin advice, subsd gym m'ship, Christmas gift	£36,000 (Birmingham) £51,000 (London)

Notes: PHI = Permanent Health Insurance; STL = Season Travel Ticket Loan; PMI = Private Medical Insurance EAP = Employee Assistance Programme

want any help with your homework?

You can never be too informed about the law firms to which you are applying and you can never be over prepared for an interview. By doing your homework you can also save yourself time by eliminating from your shortlist the law firms that just don't suit you. What recruiters most dislike is applications from people who have no idea about the nature of their firm's business – the bullets, if you like, from a scattergun aimed indiscriminately at the profession at large. If you want to be a personal injury lawyer, why would you apply to Clifford Chance. If you want to be a capital markets lawyer why would you apply to Anthony Gold. You think people don't make these mistakes? Think again.

Of course, we know **you** would never make such a basic error; nonetheless we think we can help. The following **Solicitors Practice Areas** section of the book contains scores of ranking tables drawn from our parent publication *Chambers UK* and these will give you a good sense of how well each law firm is regarded in a particular area of practice. Take, for example, the East Anglian corporate market where *Chambers UK* singles out Mills & Reeve as the best in the business and also identifies the other lead players. You can use the *Student Guide* as your first port of call for information on law firms across England and Wales, in legal areas stretching from human rights and family law to derivatives deals and telecommunications law.

Having ascertained which law firms interest you, it is open to you to look more closely at the reasons why each firm is successful in its chosen fields. The editorial that accompanies the ranking tables in *Chambers UK* gives details of team composition, important clients and highlight work. This editorial is too long to be reprinted in the *Student Guide*, so you'll need to look at *Chambers UK* itself. This weighty tome is a bit pricey for students but you may find a reference copy in your law library or careers service. It is also available to read online – for free – on our website. There, you will also find other Chambers and Partners legal guides: *Chambers Global*, *Chambers USA* and, soon, *Chambers Europe*.

How does Chambers and Partners arrive at its findings? After a lot of hard graft, that's how. Every year our team of around 90 researchers and editors carries out thousands of in-depth interviews with lawyers and clients in order to assess the reputations and expertise of legal professionals in 175 countries across the world. The tally for interviews for our 2006 UK guide, for example, topped 12,000. We're delighted to say that Chambers' rankings and editorials are referred to extensively by general counsel and other purchasers of legal services who look to our recommendations when choosing their lawyers.

The only danger is information overload at a time when you are already stretched. If you feel that comprehensive use of our publications is becoming too onerous then stick to the *Student Guide* until you are prepping for an actual interview. At that stage, you may find that a partner with whom you are due to meet is not only one of the lawyers we rank but has also submitted a biography revealing an unusual weekend hobby. Forewarned is forearmed, we say.

solicitors
specialist practice areas

banking & finance

put simply

Banking and finance lawyers inhabit a world of their own and speak a language that can leave the layperson bamboozled. The following specialist areas all have one thing in common – they relate to borrowing money or managing a financial position. It is the lawyer's job to advise on the legality of the investment (or borrowing) proposition, to document the parties' contractual relationship, to negotiate with the other party and to discuss potential outcomes should problems arise. The lawyer is also sometimes involved in "due diligence" on behalf of the lender. This involves review or drafting of an information memorandum or prospectus that describes the borrower's business.

Straightforward bank lending – where a bank lends money to a borrower on documented repayment terms.

Acquisition finance – where a bank lends money to a corporate borrower or private equity sponsor in order to fund its acquisition of another company (refer to our corporate law section on page 107).

Property finance – where a loan is made to enable (usually) a property acquisition or development. It will commonly be backed by the security of a mortgage deed binding property assets but could also involve other types of security.

Project finance – the money required to allow a project (eg a road or a hospital) to be started, continued or completed. Could be backed by mortgages on property or other assets, by rights over company shares or other types of security.

Asset finance – allows the purchase or leasing of things such as ships, aeroplanes and machinery. The lender would normally take security over the assets in question.

Capital markets – the borrower issues bonds to investors. Bonds are listed, traded debt instruments. Unlike loans they are actively traded on a market, similar to the way shares are issued and traded.

Securitisation – essentially this is where a lender wants to sell its loans. It does so by selling them to a shell company which then issues bonds to the markets. Bond investors get paid from the interest and principal on the loans owned by the shell company.

Islamic finance – many borrowers, lenders and investors in Muslim countries only participate in transactions if they are Shari'a compliant. This usually involves specific structuring; for example, payment of interest is not permitted under Shari'a law. Usually a Shari'a scholar must confirm that the product is Shari'a complaint before it is sent to investors.

Derivatives – at its most basic, this product lets a company or bank deal with a mismatch between incomings and outgoings. For example, if a UK company sells most of its products to French customers, its income will be in euros but most of its expenditure will be in sterling. A derivative will allow it enter into a swap with a bank to fix the euro/sterling exchange rate for the year so that it does not lose out if the value of the euro goes down against the pound. Derivatives can be used to hedge against, or bet on, almost anything, from foreign exchange and interest rates to the weather.

who does what

The work of the banking and finance lawyer is mostly transactional. The following are the key functions.

- Meeting with clients to establish the commercial context of a deal and to understand the specific requirements of the client.
- Negotiating with other lawyers and their clients to agree the terms of the deal; ensuring that they are recorded accurately in the loan documentation and any documents giving security. Lenders' lawyers usually produce initial documents. In many cases deals follow a well-worn path, never veering far from standard-form documentation. Borrowers'

lawyers try to negotiate more favourable terms for their clients. Both types of lawyer must understand when they can compromise and when they must hold out on a point – they will be guided by their clients and by a good understanding of market standards.

- On complicated or ground-breaking financings, lawyers actually assist with the structuring of the deal, as well as ensuring compliance with all relevant laws.

- Carrying out due diligence – an investigation exercise to verify the accuracy of information passed from the borrower to the lender or from the company raising finance to all parties investing in the deal. If financial instruments, such as bonds, are being offered to investors, the report will take the form of a prospectus and must comply with the requirements of the EU prospectus directive and rules in other countries where the bonds are sold. This can involve on-site meetings for a few days with management of the company – you will learn how their businesses work.

- Gathering all parties for the completion of the transaction, ensuring all agreed terms are covered in the written documents and that all documents have been properly signed and sealed. Just as in corporate deals, many decisions need to be made at properly convened board meetings and recorded in written resolutions.

- Finalising all post-completion registrations and procedures.

the realities of the job

- City firms act for international banks whereas the work of regional firms is generally simpler and domestic in nature, usually for UK banks and building societies or the companies they lend to. If you want to be a hotshot in international finance then it's the City for you. And if you want international travel you're likely to be able to find a job that caters to your wanderlust, even if you'll have little time for exploration on short business trips.

- Lawyers need an understanding of where the client wants to be and the legal risks involved in getting there. This may involve the movement of money across borders and through different currencies and financial products. International deals have an additional layer of difficulty: political changes in a country can render a previously sound investment risky – just ask anyone involved in Russian deals or derivatives.

- Clients can be demanding and the hours can be long. On the plus side, your clients will be dynamic and just as smart as you. It is perfectly possible to build up long-term relationships with investment bank clients, even when you're still quite junior. Working on deals can also be exciting – the team (the lawyers, the client, and any other advisers) plus the other side are all working to a common goal, often under significant time and other pressures. It might sound geeky but there are adrenalin highs on deals and tremendous satisfaction – and occasionally champagne – when a successful deal is closed.

- Banking and finance law requires hard work and teamwork. There are peaks and troughs as the deal flow depends on the buoyancy of the economy at large.

- You need to become absorbed into the finance world. The best way to get a taster while still a student is to read the City pages in your daily newspaper.

current issues

- The buoyant economy has led to an increased level of liquidity in the market (ie assets can be turned into cash quite easily). Because the capacity for debt volume has reached record levels, deals are larger than ever and debt structures have never been so complex.

- With so much high-quality work on offer, the

London banking market is more competitive than ever. Once-loyal relationships between clients and their lawyers can no longer be depended upon.

- Acquisition finance is really big right now and transactions often need to be completed quickly. Too much point-scoring by lawyers in the negotiation process can be a waste of precious time, so solicitors need to understand when it is time to stop talking and to get the deal done.
- In big City firms you'll become specialised early on. This may or may not appeal to you,

and if it doesn't then a smaller or regional firm may be a better choice.

- Secondments to banks are available, even for trainees. Subsequent moves in-house are common, especially for capital markets work or compliance roles to ensure that banks do not fall foul of financial services regulations. Banking law is also an ideal platform for a career in the financial markets; however, if you already know you want to become a banker, don't waste time training as a lawyer.

leading firms from Chambers UK 2007

Banking & Finance: General Bank Lending **Best of the UK**
[1] **Allen & Overy LLP**
Clifford Chance LLP
[2] **Linklaters**
[3] **Freshfields Bruckhaus Deringer**
White & Case LLP
[4] **Ashurst**
Baker & McKenzie LLP
Cleary Gottlieb Steen & Hamilton
Denton Wilde Sapte
Herbert Smith LLP
Lovells
Norton Rose
Slaughter and May
[5] **Addleshaw Goddard LLP**
Berwin Leighton Paisner LLP
CMS Cameron McKenna LLP
DLA Piper UK LLP
Eversheds LLP
Simmons & Simmons
[6] **Bird & Bird**
Burges Salmon LLP
Dechert LLP
Jones Day
Osborne Clarke
SJ Berwin LLP
Stephenson Harwood
Taylor Wessing
Wragge & Co LLP

Banking & Finance: High-end Acquisition Finance **London**
[1] **Allen & Overy LLP**
Clifford Chance LLP
[2] **Ashurst**
Linklaters
[3] **Freshfields Bruckhaus Deringer**
Shearman & Sterling LLP
Simpson Thacher & Bartlett LLP
White & Case LLP
[4] **Cleary Gottlieb Steen & Hamilton**
Kirkland & Ellis International LLP
Latham & Watkins LLP
Lovells
Skadden, Arps, Slate, Meagher
Slaughter and May
[5] **Baker & McKenzie LLP**
Debevoise & Plimpton LLP
Denton Wilde Sapte
DLA Piper UK LLP
Herbert Smith LLP
Macfarlanes
Simmons & Simmons
Travers Smith
Weil, Gotshal & Manges LLP
[6] **Addleshaw Goddard LLP**
Berwin Leighton Paisner LLP
CMS Cameron McKenna LLP

Banking & Finance: Trade Finance **London**
[1] **Denton Wilde Sapte**

Banking & Finance: Islamic Finance **London**
[1] **Norton Rose**
[2] **Allen & Overy LLP**
Clifford Chance LLP
Denton Wilde Sapte
[3] **Linklaters**
Taylor Wessing
Trowers & Hamlins
[4] **King & Spalding International LLP**
Stephenson Harwood
White & Case LLP

Banking & Finance
Thames Valley
1. **Osborne Clarke** *Reading*
2. **Boyes Turner** *Reading*
   Howes Percival *Milton Keynes*
   Shoosmiths *Reading*
3. **EMW Law** *Milton Keynes*
   Morgan Cole *Oxford*
   Pitmans *Reading*

Banking & Finance
The South
1. **Blake Lapthorn Linnell** *Southampton*
   Bond Pearce LLP *Southampton*
2. **asb law** *Crawley*
   Shoosmiths *Fareham*
   Stevens & Bolton LLP *Guildford*
3. **Clarke Willmott** *Southampton*
   Lester Aldridge *Southampton*
   Paris Smith & Randall *Southampton*

Banking & Finance
South West
1. **Burges Salmon LLP** *Bristol*
   Osborne Clarke *Bristol*
2. **Bond Pearce LLP** *Bristol*
3. **Charles Russell LLP** *Cheltenham*
   Clarke Willmott *Bristol*
   TLT Solicitors *Bristol*
   Veale Wasbrough Lawyers *Bristol*
4. **Ashfords** *Bristol*
   Bevan Brittan LLP *Bristol*
   Rickerbys *Cheltenham*
   Stephens & Scown *Exeter*

Banking & Finance
Midlands
1. **DLA Piper UK LLP** *Birmingham*
   Eversheds LLP *Birmingham*
   Wragge & Co LLP *Birmingham*
2. **HBJ Gateley Wareing** *Birmingham*
   Martineau Johnson *Birmingham*
   Pinsent Masons *Birmingham*
3. **Browne Jacobson LLP** *Nottingham*
   Freeth Cartwright LLP *Birmingham*
   Hammonds *Birmingham*

Banking & Finance
Wales
1. **Eversheds LLP** *Cardiff*
   Morgan Cole *Cardiff*
2. **Geldards LLP** *Cardiff*
3. **Berry Smith Solicitors** *Cardiff*

Banking & Finance
East Anglia
1. **Mills & Reeve** *Norwich*
2. **Birketts** *Ipswich*
   Eversheds LLP *Cambridge*
3. **Taylor Vinters** *Cambridge*
   Wollastons *Chelmsford*

Banking & Finance
Yorkshire
1. **Addleshaw Goddard LLP** *Leeds*
   DLA Piper UK LLP *Leeds*
2. **Eversheds LLP** *Leeds*
   Walker Morris *Leeds*
3. **Hammonds** *Leeds*
   Pinsent Masons *Leeds*

Banking & Finance
North East
1. **Dickinson Dees** *Newcastle upon Tyne*
2. **Eversheds LLP** *Newcastle upon Tyne*
   Ward Hadaway *Newcastle upon Tyne*
3. **Robert Muckle** *Newcastle upon Tyne*
   Watson Burton *Newcastle upon Tyne*

Banking & Finance
North West
1. **Addleshaw Goddard** *Manchester*
   DLA Piper UK LLP *Manchester*
2. **Eversheds LLP** *Manchester*
   Halliwells LLP *Manchester*
3. **Cobbetts LLP** *Manchester*
   DWF *Manchester*
   Hammonds *Manchester*
   Kuit Steinart Levy *Manchester*
4. **Brabners Chaffe Street** *Liverpool*
   Hill Dickinson LLP *Liverpool*
   Pannone LLP *Manchester*
   Pinsent Masons *Manchester*

banking & finance (continued)

Capital Markets: Debt
London

1. Allen & Overy LLP
   Clifford Chance LLP
   Linklaters
2. Cleary Gottlieb Steen & Hamilton
   Freshfields Bruckhaus Deringer
   White & Case LLP
3. Gide Loyrette Nouel
   Latham & Watkins LLP
   Lovells
   Shearman & Sterling LLP
   Simmons & Simmons
   Slaughter and May
4. Ashurst
   Baker & McKenzie LLP
   CMS Cameron McKenna LLP
   Davis Polk & Wardwell
   Denton Wilde Sapte
   Herbert Smith LLP
   Sidley Austin
   Skadden, Arps, Slate, Meagher
   Sullivan & Cromwell LLP

Capital Markets: High-Yield Products
London

1. Latham & Watkins LLP
2. Cravath, Swaine & Moore LLP
   Shearman & Sterling LLP
   Simpson Thacher & Bartlett LLP
3. Milbank, Tweed, Hadley & McCloy
   Skadden, Arps, Slate, Meagher
   Weil, Gotshal & Manges LLP
   White & Case LLP
4. Cahill Gordon & Reindel LLP
   Cleary Gottlieb Steen & Hamilton
   Clifford Chance LLP
   Freshfields Bruckhaus Deringer
   Linklaters
5. Allen & Overy LLP
   Debevoise & Plimpton LLP

Capital Markets: Equity
London

1. Freshfields Bruckhaus Deringer
   Linklaters
2. Allen & Overy LLP
   Cleary Gottlieb Steen & Hamilton
   Clifford Chance LLP
   Davis Polk & Wardwell
   Herbert Smith LLP
   Latham & Watkins LLP
   Shearman & Sterling LLP
   Skadden, Arps, Slate, Meagher
   Slaughter and May
   Sullivan & Cromwell LLP
3. Ashurst
   Baker & McKenzie LLP
   Lovells
   Simmons & Simmons
   Weil, Gotshal & Manges LLP
   White & Case LLP
4. Debevoise & Plimpton LLP
   Gide Loyrette Nouel
   LeBoeuf, Lamb, Greene & MacRae
   McDermott Will & Emery UK LLP
   Norton Rose

Capital Markets: Securitisation
London

1. Allen & Overy LLP
   Clifford Chance LLP
   Freshfields Bruckhaus Deringer
2. Linklaters
   Sidley Austin
3. Baker & McKenzie LLP
   Mayer, Brown, Rowe & Maw LLP
   Slaughter and May
   White & Case LLP
4. Berwin Leighton Paisner LLP
   Gide Loyrette Nouel
   Herbert Smith LLP
   Lovells
   Shearman & Sterling LLP
   Simmons & Simmons
   Weil, Gotshal & Manges LLP

Capital Markets: Structured Finance
London

1. Clifford Chance LLP
   Linklaters
2. Allen & Overy LLP
   Ashurst
   Freshfields Bruckhaus Deringer
   Simmons & Simmons
   White & Case LLP
3. Cadwalader, Wickersham & Taft
   Lovells
   Milbank, Tweed, Hadley & McCloy
   Sidley Austin
   Slaughter and May
4. Baker & McKenzie LLP
   Gide Loyrette Nouel
   Herbert Smith LLP
   Shearman & Sterling LLP
   Weil, Gotshal & Manges LLP

Capital Markets: Derivatives
London

1. Allen & Overy LLP
2. Clifford Chance LLP
   Linklaters
3. Freshfields Bruckhaus Deringer
   Sidley Austin
   Slaughter and May
   White & Case LLP
4. Ashurst
   Baker & McKenzie LLP
   Field Fisher Waterhouse LLP
   Simmons & Simmons

competition and antitrust law

put simply

It is the job of the UK and EU regulatory authorities to ensure that markets function effectively on the basis of fair and open competition. The competition rules in the UK and EU are substantially similar, but the UK bodies concentrate on those rules that have their greatest effect domestically, while the EU authorities deal with matters where the rules affect more than one member state. In the UK, the regulators are the Office of Fair Trade (OFT) or the Competition Commission; on matters also affecting other EU countries, it is the European Commission. Additionally, there are industry-specific regulatory bodies, such as Ofcom for the media and telecoms industry.

Competition authorities have extensive investigation powers – including the ability to carry out dawn raids – and can impose hefty fines. There were fines for the producers of herbicides when they were judged to have formed a Europe-wide cartel, and for companies involved in the price-fixing of football strips. In another example, the domestic authorities found a group of English public schools had formed a cartel for the purposes of setting fee levels. More recently, following a request from the Federation of Small Businesses, the OFT has persuaded the Competition Commission to investigate the activities of the UK's 'big four' supermarkets – Tesco, Asda, Sainsbury's and Morrisons.

who does what

The work of a competition lawyer can be divided into the following areas:

- Negotiating clearance for acquisitions, mergers and joint ventures
- Advising on the structure of commercial or co-operation agreements to ensure they withstand a competition challenge.
- Dealing with investigations by the regulators into the way a client conducts business.
- Bringing or defending claims in the Competition Appeals Tribunal
- Advising on cross-border trade or anti-dumping measures (preventing companies exporting a product at a lower price than it normally charges in its home market).

working for a regulator you would:

- Investigate companies and bring prosecutions.
- Advise on the application of new laws and regulations.

the realities of the job

- You won't get much independence; even junior lawyers work under the close supervision of experienced partners. In the early days the job involves a great deal of research into particular markets and how the authorities have approached different types of agreements in the past. You also need a genuine interest in economics and politics.
- The work demands serious academic thought, more so than in standard corporate transactional work. Even so, you can't just be a dry legal brain, you'll need to develop commercial acumen and really understand how clients run their businesses.
- This is a massively popular area of practice and hard to break into. You can enhance your prospects by knuckling down to some competition-specific studies; a master's degree will help.
- Advocacy is a relatively small part of the job, though in time you could end up appearing in the High Court or Competition Appeal Tribunal. Advocacy skills can also be honed on paper, and there will be ample opportunity to do this.
- In international law firms, you will get to travel abroad and may even work in an overseas office for a while. A great deal of business is done in Brussels. Unsurprisingly, fluency in another language can be a useful.

current issues

- On 1 May 2004, when 10 new member states were admitted to the EU, antitrust enforcement ceased to be the monopoly of the EC Commission and European Court. An EC Modernization Regulation effectively handed more power back to member states with respect to the enforcement of Articles 81 and 82 of the Treaty of Rome. Domestic authorities are definitely upping their game.

- The remit of the Competition Commission Appeal Tribunals has been widened to allow claims for damages brought by third parties. Private Enforcement can be a useful tool for competitor businesses and consumer groups, but thus far has not been extensively utilised, perhaps due to concerns over the cost of proceedings.

- Regulators now have the power to impose criminal sanctions. This has forced solicitors firms to consider how they will advise clients on the 'white collar crime' element of competition law. A few have started to employ specialists; others have formed close ties with boutique white-collar crime firms.

- There are increased opportunities to work for the regulatory authorities; the OFT, for example, employs many more investigators than before. There is also a trend for lawyers to switch between private practice and working for the regulators.

leading firms from Chambers UK 2007

Competition/European Law
London

[1] Freshfields Bruckhaus Deringer
Herbert Smith LLP
Linklaters
Slaughter and May
[2] Allen & Overy LLP
Ashurst
Clifford Chance LLP
Lovells
Simmons & Simmons
SJ Berwin LLP
[3] Addleshaw Goddard LLP
Baker & McKenzie LLP
CMS Cameron McKenna LLP
Eversheds LLP
Macfarlanes
Mayer, Brown, Rowe & Maw LLP
[4] Berwin Leighton Paisner LLP
Bird & Bird
Bristows
Denton Wilde Sapte
DLA Piper UK LLP
Field Fisher Waterhouse LLP
Latham & Watkins LLP
McDermott Will & Emery UK LLP
Norton Rose
Richards Butler LLP
Shearman & Sterling LLP
Wilmer Cutler Pickering Hale

Competition/European Law
The South

[1] Burges Salmon LLP *Bristol*
[2] Bond Pearce LLP *Plymouth*
Osborne Clarke *Bristol*
TLT Solicitors *Bristol*

Competition/European Law
Wales

[1] Eversheds LLP *Cardiff*
[2] Morgan Cole *Cardiff*

Competition/European Law
Midlands

[1] Pinsent Masons *Birmingham*
[2] Eversheds LLP *Birmingham*
Martineau Johnson *Birmingham*
Shoosmiths *Nottingham*
Wragge & Co LLP *Birmingham*

Competition/European Law
The North

[1] Addleshaw Goddard LLP *Manchester*
Eversheds LLP *Leeds*
[2] Dickinson Dees *Newcastle upon Tyne*
[3] Cobbetts LLP *Manchester*
Pinsent Masons *Leeds*

put simply

Construction law can broadly be divided into non-contentious and contentious work. The first involves lawyers helping clients at the procurement stage, pulling together all the contractual relationships prior to building work; the second sees them resolving disputes when things go wrong during or after the build. Because the amount of money at stake is relatively high, over the years many people have been tempted to take their disputes all the way to court in order to test a contractual or tortious point of law. Industry insiders also admit that it had become the norm for developers to recoup certain construction costs through litigation. As a result, construction cases litter English case law like chip wrappers on a high street on a windy Sunday morning.

About ten years ago a new trend began to take hold, and now people are increasingly working with each other when things go wrong. For example, most new contracts contain a mandatory arbitration procedure to be adopted in case of dispute and adjudication of disputes has become the industry norm. The process follows a 28-day timetable; far swifter than old-style litigation which frequently ran on for years. Since the Technology and Construction Court introduced its Pre-Action Protocol, many more disputes have been resolved through mediation and this, in turn, has changed the way lawyers must operate. All these developments have had a knock-on effect at the contract drafting stage. Some disputes are simply so complex, however, that the parties do still choose to slug it out in court.

projects

From an oil pipeline in Azerbaijan to a new prison in Bridgend in South Wales, specialist construction lawyers work hand in hand with finance and corporate lawyers to enable projects to come to fruition. A few City firms and the largest US practices dominate the biggest international projects, but there's work for lawyers countrywide. In the UK, the Private Finance Initiative (PFI), a part of the Public Private Partnerships (PPP), is an important source of work. PFI introduces private funding and management into areas that were previously the domain of government. So, for example, the new prison in Bridgend is being built by Costain working with Securicor, and for the first 25 years of its life these private companies will have a contract to run the prison.

Some law firms consistently act for the project company, usually a 'special purpose vehicle' (SPV) established to build, own and operate the prison or power station or whatever it may be. Often the project company is a joint venture between several 'sponsors' who contribute equity to part-fund the project. Project sponsors could include the manufacturer of the gas turbines installed in a power station, the construction company that will erect the plant, and the power company that will buy the electricity. The company could also be partially owned by a government body or banks. Other firms consistently act for the project promoters, the organisations that commission projects – for example an NHS trust that wants a new hospital, or a foreign government that wants a privately financed motorway. Then there are the firms that act purely on the finance side for banks, guarantors, export credit agencies, governments and international funding agencies. Other categories of client include the contractors, operators and so on. Each party requires its own legal representation.

Projects run for years, and so can the legal work. After the initial tender process, in which bids are built up over a couple of years, the successful bidder is selected to manage the project. It then secures finance and all necessary planning permissions and agrees construction, service and employment contracts. Lawyers drafting these contracts must understand the big picture because changing one contractual term can have knock-on effects throughout the entire transaction. It's a real challenge putting together something so complicated, so the only thing to do is to put in deadlines for the different stages. Anyone considering projects work must enjoy the challenge of creating a complex scheme and figuring out all its possibilities and pitfalls. They also need the ability to work with a team of people including colleagues, clients, other lawyers and professionals, funders and subcontractors.

who does what

To describe the work of all the different breeds of projects lawyers would take forever, so here we'll simply say that the field has specialists with excellent drafting and organisational skills in the areas of funding, construction, real estate, planning, energy, telecoms and all aspects of the public sector, including health, education and housing.

construction lawyers working at the procurement stage:

○ Lawyers negotiate and draft contracts – often based on standard-form JCT (Joint Contracts Tribunal) contracts – for programmes of building works, be these new builds or redevelopments. In any building programme there will be a multitude of parties; the contract stage is rather like creating a spider's web of relationships between landowners, main contractors, subcontractors, engineers, architects and others. A number of these relationships are documented by way of warranties.

○ If the client has invested in the land as well as undertaking the building project, you will work in conjunction with property lawyers. Between you, you will have to seek and obtain all the necessary planning consents as well as local authority certifications. If your builder client is not the owner of the land, expect to liaise regularly with the owner's solicitors over things such as stage payments, architects' certificates and other measures of performance.

○ Site visits will be likely at various stages of the development.

when a construction dispute arises:

○ Assess the client's position and gather all related paperwork and evidence. There can be a huge volume of documentation, some of it very technical. You don't have to read it all, but you do have to identify what is important and home in on the detail of that. This evidence will be vital in proving the client's case, whether through mediation, arbitration or litigation.

○ Follow the resolution methods set out in the contracts between the parties; the TCC Pre-Action Protocol leads to negotiations at an early stage.

○ Where a settlement is not possible, issue, prepare for and attend proceedings with the client, usually having instructed a barrister to advocate on the client's behalf.

the realities of the job

○ Good drafting skills require attention to detail and careful thought. Plus you need to keep up to date with industry trends and standards, and you really need to know contract law and tort.

○ People skills are fundamental. On the one hand you'll encounter contractors and subcontractors who have been schooled at the University of Life; on the other you'll be dealing with structural engineers whose world is one of complicated technical reports. On top of this there will also be corporate types and in-house lawyers with whom you must speak on a sophisticated level.

○ Is the construction world still a male-dominated environment? It's a point worth debating. Yes, some clients might see a visit to a lap dancing club as part and parcel of a good night out with business associates and advisers, but readers also need to know that there are many successful female construction lawyers (and architects and engineers, etc) in the business and they don't have to get caught up in this kind of activity. It's probably safe to say that any residual imbalance in the culture of the construction sector is rarely down to the law firms. It's also worth noting that this kind of behaviour does appear in other business sectors too.

- Most lawyers have a natural bias for either contentious or non-contentious work, and some firms like their construction lawyers to handle both aspects, so pick your firm carefully if you want to concentrate on one rather than the other.

- If you're looking to break into this area of law, a background in construction or engineering is a major bonus because you'll already have industry contacts and chances are you'll be able to combine legal know-how with practical advice – you'll know how the client thinks.

- Anyone considering projects work must enjoy the challenge of creating a complex scheme and figuring out all its possibilities and pitfalls. They also need the ability to work with a team of people including colleagues, clients, other lawyers and professionals, funders and subcontractors.

current issues

- The health sector has seen investment on a massive scale in recent times. It is not unusual to find complex hospital projects running into hundreds of millions of pounds. Schools are no less magnetic in terms of the investment of public funds. Charged by central government with upgrading and rebuilding the education infrastructure, many local authorities are choosing to shop locally for their legal services. Urban regeneration is dominating the work of many firms up and down the country.

- A new edition of one of the market's most widely used standard form contract – the JCT

– was published in 2005. The latest version has been commended for its greater simplicity and inclusion of third-party rights, something intended to reduce the need for collateral warranties from subcontractors and other parties.

- No other project has captured media attention like the troubled Wembley Stadium development. Following a litany of difficulties, including an increase in the price of steel, subcontractor disputes and delays in turfing the pitch and fitting the toilets, the contractor Multiplex has had a challenging year, not least because a clause in the initial contract obliges it to pay Wembley National Stadium for overrun costs. Indeed, Multiplex has ended up in disputes with a number of different parties.

- Lawyers are already gearing up for the slew of work, both contentious and non-contentious, that will emanate from the construction of the 2012 Olympic Village, the modification of rail links and general infrastructure redevelopment. It will be interesting to see the effect of EU procurement directives on the tendering process, and the economic consequences of the anticipated migration of qualified professionals to London from the regions. Projects such as Wembley Stadium will be salutary lesson on the need for caution.

- Nearly all international construction and engineering projects are governed to some extent by English or New York law, so experience in this field is internationally marketable. American law firms, in particular, are recruiting experienced English lawyers, which has forced up salaries to make international projects one of the highest-paid specialisms around. Top-level arbitration lawyers can expect to be able to work in places such as Singapore and Hong Kong. There are also ample opportunities to work in-house for large construction companies.

leading firms from Chambers UK 2007

Construction: Supplier-led
Best of the UK

1. Pinsent Masons
2. CMS Cameron McKenna LLP   Fenwick Elliott LLP
   Mayer, Brown, Rowe & Maw LLP   Shadbolt & Co LLP
   Wragge & Co LLP
3. Campbell Hooper LLP   Clifford Chance LLP
   Davies Arnold Cooper   Kennedys
   Kirkpatrick & Lockhart Nicholson   Reynolds Porter Chamberlain LLP
4. Barlow Lyde & Gilbert   Beachcroft LLP
   Berrymans Lace Mawer   Bevan Brittan LLP
   Burges Salmon LLP   Dundas & Wilson
   Glovers   Lane & Partners LLP
   Osborne Clarke   Speechly Bircham
5. Beale and Company Solicitors LLP   Corbett & Co
   Kingsley Napley   Winward Fearon

Construction: Purchaser-led
Best of the UK

1. Allen & Overy LLP   Berwin Leighton Paisner LLP
   Clifford Chance LLP   Freshfields Bruckhaus Deringer
   Linklaters
2. Ashurst   Eversheds LLP
   Herbert Smith LLP   Lovells
   Pinsent Masons   Trowers & Hamlins
3. Addleshaw Goddard LLP   Baker & McKenzie LLP
   CMS Cameron McKenna LLP   Denton Wilde Sapte
   Kirkpatrick & Lockhart Nicholson   Macfarlanes
   Mayer, Brown, Rowe & Maw LLP   Nabarro Nathanson
   Norton Rose   Taylor Wessing
4. Clyde & Co   DLA Piper UK LLP
   Field Fisher Waterhouse LLP   Hammonds
   Simmons & Simmons   Slaughter and May
   Wedlake Bell
5. Fladgate Fielder   Lawrence Graham LLP
   Lewis Silkin LLP   SJ Berwin LLP

Construction
Thames Valley

1. Blake Lapthorn Linnell Oxford
   Clarkslegal LLP Reading
   Denton Wilde Sapte Milton Keynes
   Morgan Cole Reading
2. Boyes Turner Reading
   Henmans Oxford

Construction
East Anglia

1. Mills & Reeve Cambridge
2. Eversheds LLP Cambridge, Ipswich
   Hewitsons Cambridge
3. Greenwoods Solicitors Peterborough
   Prettys Ipswich
   Taylor Vinters Cambridge

Construction
The South

1. Shadbolt & Co LLP Reigate
2. Blake Lapthorn Linnell Southampton
   Charles Russell LLP Guildford
   Cripps Harries Hall Tunbridge Wells
   Lester Aldridge Bournemouth
3. DMH Stallard Brighton
   Thomas Eggar Reigate

Construction
South West

1. Bevan Brittan LLP Bristol
   Burges Salmon LLP Bristol
   Osborne Clarke Bristol
2. Ashfords London
   Beachcroft LLP Bristol
   Pinsent Masons Bristol
3. Clarke Willmott Bristol
   TLT Solicitors Bristol
   Veale Wasbrough Lawyers Bristol
4. Bond Pearce LLP Plymouth
   Withy King Bath

Construction
Wales

1. Eversheds LLP Cardiff
2. Hugh James Cardiff
   Morgan Cole Cardiff

Construction
North West

1. Pinsent Masons Manchester
2. Addleshaw Goddard Manchester
   Eversheds LLP Manchester
   Halliwells LLP Manchester
   Hammonds Manchester
   Hill Dickinson LLP Liverpool
3. Beachcroft LLP Manchester
   Cobbetts LLP Manchester
   DLA Piper UK LLP Liverpool
   DWF Manchester
   Mace & Jones Manchester
   Pannone LLP Manchester

Construction
Midlands

[1] **Wragge & Co LLP** *Birmingham*
[2] **Eversheds LLP** *Birmingham*
Freeth Cartwright LLP *Nottingham*
HBJ Gateley Wareing *Birmingham*
Pinsent Masons *Birmingham*
[3] **Beachcroft LLP** *Birmingham*
Cobbetts LLP *Birmingham*
DLA Piper UK LLP *Birmingham*
Hammonds *Birmingham*
Martineau Johnson *Birmingham*
[4] **Browne Jacobson LLP** *Nottingham*
Geldards LLP *Derby*
Mills & Reeve *Birmingham*
Nelsons *Derby*
Shoosmiths *Northampton*
Wright Hassall *Leamington Spa*

Construction
Yorkshire

[1] **Addleshaw Goddard LLP** *Leeds*
Pinsent Masons *Leeds*
[2] **DLA Piper UK LLP** *Leeds*
Eversheds LLP *Leeds*
Walker Morris *Leeds*
[3] **Beachcroft LLP** *Leeds*
Denison Till *York*
Nabarro Nathanson *Sheffield*
The Hawkswell Kilvington *Wakefield*
Watson Burton LLP *Leeds*

Construction
North East

[1] **Dickinson Dees** *Newcastle upon Tyne*
Watson Burton *Newcastle upon Tyne*
[2] **Eversheds LLP** *Newcastle upon Tyne*
Ward Hadaway *Newcastle upon Tyne*
[3] **Hay & Kilner** *Newcastle upon Tyne*

Projects: Energy
London

[1] **Allen & Overy LLP**
Clifford Chance LLP
Linklaters
Milbank, Tweed, Hadley & McCloy
Shearman & Sterling LLP
White & Case LLP
[2] **Freshfields Bruckhaus Deringer**
Latham & Watkins LLP
Norton Rose
[3] **Denton Wilde Sapte**
Sullivan & Cromwell LLP
Trowers & Hamlins
[4] **Ashurst**
Baker & McKenzie LLP
Berwin Leighton Paisner LLP
Chadbourne & Parke
Herbert Smith LLP
LeBoeuf, Lamb, Greene & MacRae
Slaughter and May
Vinson & Elkins LLP

Projects: International Infrastructure
London

[1] **Allen & Overy LLP**
Clifford Chance LLP
CMS Cameron McKenna LLP
Freshfields Bruckhaus Deringer
Linklaters
[2] **Ashurst**
Baker & McKenzie LLP
Berwin Leighton Paisner LLP
Debevoise & Plimpton LLP
Dewey Ballantine
Lovells
Norton Rose

PFI/PPP
Best of the UK

[1] **Allen & Overy LLP**
Ashurst
Clifford Chance LLP
CMS Cameron McKenna LLP
Freshfields Bruckhaus Deringer
Linklaters
[2] **Addleshaw Goddard LLP**
Bevan Brittan LLP
DLA Piper UK LLP
Lovells
Norton Rose
Simmons & Simmons
[3] **Berwin Leighton Paisner LLP**
Denton Wilde Sapte
Eversheds LLP
Herbert Smith LLP
Pinsent Masons
Wragge & Co LLP
[4] **Beachcroft LLP**
Bird & Bird
Burges Salmon LLP
Dickinson Dees
Mills & Reeve
[5] **Dundas & Wilson**
McGrigors
Nabarro Nathanson
Osborne Clarke
Shadbolt & Co LLP
Trowers & Hamlins

corporate law

put simply

The life of the corporate lawyer is characterised by big money, big deals and long hours. Their work relates to the buying and selling of businesses, business assets and business equity. You'll often hear the umbrella term 'corporate finance'. Here are some of the other terms you'll encounter:

Mergers and acquisitions (M&A) are deals involving one company buying or joining with another. Depending on the relative sizes of the businesses it might be seen as a takeover (acquisition) or a fusion of the two businesses (merger).

Corporate restructuring involves changes to the composition of the businesses in a company's portfolio or the disposal of certain assets a company no longer requires. Perhaps it wants to concentrate on more profitable parts of its business; perhaps certain activities are no longer seen as acceptable to the general public or will fall foul of regulations.

Stock exchanges play an important role in corporate law. On the London Stock Exchange we have the Financial Times (FTSE) list, the Alternative Investment Market (AIM) and others. In New York they have the Dow Jones and NASDAQ lists among others, and there are many other exchanges and lists around the world. As a corporate lawyer, your work could involve exchanges anywhere in the world.

Rather than going straight to a bank for a loan, when businesses need money they are increasingly turning to private equity funds and venture capitalists. Familiar names in this sector include Blackstone Capital Partners, Apax Partners, 3i and Alchemy Partners. But what is private equity? Essentially it refers to the holding of stock in unlisted companies, ie those not listed on a stock exchange. The work of the PE lawyer takes in different forms of financing – eg when money is needed for a new business 'start-up', the expansion of operations, or when a company is bought.

It also covers management buyout (MBO) financing, say for a group of employees/managers who decide they want to buy, own and run the company they work for.

Private equity companies usually manage several different funds and have investment in numerous businesses at a time. Sometimes a number of private equity companies will compete to invest in the same business, as was the case with Canary Wharf Group, which eventually went to the highest PE bidder at nearly £5.3 billion. Other well-known businesses that have turned to private equity investment include DIY retailer Wickes, Legoland Parks, the AA and the shoe people Jimmy Choo. A surprising proportion of the UK workforce is employed by businesses that are under the control of private equity companies, sometimes without even knowing it!

On a smaller scale, venture capitalists are individuals or companies looking for a good return from an injection of money into a fledgling or growing business. If you've ever watched the BBC2 show *Dragon's Den*, you'll be familiar with the idea. As well as owning a stake in the business, it is common for the investors to have a big hand in its management.

who does what

The work of a corporate lawyer is mainly transactional, and whatever the type of deal, there are certain key phases:

- Negotiating and drafting the agreements – this will be done in conjunction with the client, the business that is being bought or sold, other advisers (eg accountants) and any financiers.
- Carrying out 'due diligence' – this is an investigation to verify the accuracy of information passed from the seller to the buyer, or from the company raising money to the funder. The ambit of the exercise is broad and will estab-

lish: the outright ownership of all assets; the status of employees; whether there are outstanding debts or other claims against the company; any environmental or other liabilities that could reduce the value of the business in the future, etc. If shares or bonds are being offered to the public, the report will take the form of a prospectus and must comply with statutory regulations.

- Arranging financing – this could come from banks or other types of investor; they will wish to have some kind of security for their investment, eg owning shares or bonds, taking out a mortgage over property or other assets.
- Gathering all parties for the completion of the transaction, ensuring all assets have been properly covered by the written documents and that all these have been properly signed and sealed. Company law requires that decisions are made at properly convened board meetings and recorded in written resolutions.
- Finalising all post-completion registrations and procedures.

the realities of the job

- Large companies listed on major stock exchanges tend to use the services of large City firms and the American firms in London. These firms will also take a large share of the international deals and compete with smaller City and regional firms for companies listed on AIM and privately owned companies.
- Your experiences will be affected by the type of client your firm acts for. Publicly listed companies, major private equity houses and the investment banks that underwrite deals have different demands and attitudes to risk than say rich entrepreneurs, owner-managed businesses and small to medium-sized enterprises (SMEs).

- Corporate lawyers need to be conversant in a variety of legal disciplines, and know when to refer matters to a specialist in, say, merger control, employment, property or tax.
- This is a very practical area of law, so commercial acumen is a must. Yet, the work is largely paper-based so you need to be well organised and have good drafting skills.
- Long hours arise through client demand, and their expectations have risen even further with instant communication via mobile phones, e-mail and BlackBerrys. Being surrounded by busy, intelligent, high-achieving people is half of the appeal.
- Corporate lawyers work in teams; indeed at times team spirit and adrenaline will be the only things that get you through yet another 20-hour day. It takes time to learn your craft, however, and in the beginning being the most junior member of a deal team can mean boring or unrewarding tasks. The banes of the corporate trainee's life are data room management (putting together and caretaking all the factual information on which a deal relies) and 'bibling' – the creation of files containing copies of all the agreed documents and information.
- A robust and confident manner is typical; stamina is a must. You have to keep pushing yourself because the deals wait for no one.
- The fortunes and schedules of corporate lawyers are tied to the general economy. Corporate lawyers are more likely to experience feast or famine than a steady flow of deals year after year; it is not unheard of for them to experience burnout after a few years.
- You need to become absorbed in the corporate world. The best way to get a taster while still a student is to read the City pages in your daily newspaper. If after six months you haven't developed a real interest then pick another area of practice.

current issues

- After Enron, the dotcom crash and various scandals involving City analysts, the role of the legal adviser in business transactions and corporate affairs has never been more important. UK lawyers confirm the rise of US working practices, particularly the increased emphasis on due diligence.
- Deals are increasingly regulated in an attempt to avoid shareholder litigation.
- After four or five quieter years, we now see a revival of confidence and activity in the M&A market. Private equity is an active and dominant force, and AIM is attracting attention from businesses around the world. All these factors mean that corporate lawyers are once again very busy.
- Right now the hot markets are China and the Middle East.
- A sound grounding in corporate finance makes an excellent springboard for working in industry. Lawyers move in-house to major companies, tempted by decent hours and salaries. Some go to banks, usually as in-house lawyers, occasionally as corporate finance execs or analysts. Company secretarial positions suit lawyers with a taste for internal management and compliance issues.

leading firms from Chambers UK 2007

Corporate Finance: High-end International Capability **London**	Corporate Finance: High-end Domestic Capability **London**	Corporate Finance **Thames Valley**
[1] **Clifford Chance LLP** **Freshfields Bruckhaus Deringer** **Linklaters**	[1] **Freshfields Bruckhaus Deringer** **Linklaters** **Slaughter and May**	[1] **Osborne Clarke** Reading
[2] **Allen & Overy LLP** **Skadden, Arps, Slate, Meagher** **Slaughter and May**	[2] **Allen & Overy LLP** **Clifford Chance LLP** **Herbert Smith LLP**	[2] **Boyes Turner** Reading **Manches LLP** Oxford **Shoosmiths** Reading
[3] **Ashurst** **CMS Cameron McKenna LLP** **Herbert Smith LLP** **Lovells** **Mayer, Brown, Rowe & Maw LLP** **Shearman & Sterling LLP** **Weil, Gotshal & Manges LLP**	[3] **Ashurst** **Macfarlanes**	[3] **Blake Lapthorn Linnell** Oxford **Clarkslegal LLP** Reading **Darbys** Oxford **EMW Law** Milton Keynes **Field Seymour Parkes** Reading **Howes Percival** Milton Keynes **Kimbells LLP** Milton Keynes **Morgan Cole** Reading **Pitmans** Reading **Wilmer Cutler Pickering Hale** Oxford
	[4] **Lovells** **Norton Rose** **Travers Smith**	
[4] **Baker & McKenzie LLP** **Cleary Gottlieb Steen & Hamilton** **Jones Day** **Norton Rose** **Simmons & Simmons** **Sullivan & Cromwell LLP** **White & Case LLP**	[5] **Berwin Leighton Paisner LLP** **CMS Cameron McKenna LLP** **Denton Wilde Sapte** **Jones Day** **Mayer, Brown, Rowe & Maw LLP** **Simmons & Simmons** **SJ Berwin LLP**	[4] **Blandy & Blandy** Reading **Matthew Arnold & Baldwin** Watford **Moorcrofts LLP** Marlow **Olswang Thames Valley** Reading

Corporate Finance: Mid-Market
Best of the UK

1. **Addleshaw Goddard LLP**
   Ashurst
   Berwin Leighton Paisner LLP
   DLA Piper UK LLP
   Eversheds LLP
   Jones Day
   Macfarlanes
   Travers Smith

2. **Burges Salmon LLP**
   CMS Cameron McKenna LLP
   Denton Wilde Sapte
   Kirkpatrick & Lockhart Nicholson
   Lawrence Graham LLP
   Nabarro Nathanson
   Pinsent Masons
   SJ Berwin LLP
   Taylor Wessing
   Wragge & Co LLP

3. **Baker & McKenzie LLP**
   Bird & Bird
   Charles Russell LLP
   Clyde & Co
   Cobbetts LLP
   Covington & Burling
   Dechert LLP
   Dickinson Dees
   Field Fisher Waterhouse LLP
   Hammonds
   Olswang
   Osborne Clarke
   Pannone LLP
   Stephenson Harwood

Corporate Finance
The South: Kent & Sussex

1. **asb law** *Crawley*
   Rawlison Butler *Crawley*
   Thomas Eggar *Worthing*
   Vertex Law LLP *West Malling*

2. **Clarkson Wright & Jakes** *Orpington*
   DMH Stallard *Crawley*
   Thomson Snell *Tunbridge Wells*

Corporate Finance: Lower Mid-Market
London

1. **Barlow Lyde & Gilbert**
   Lewis Silkin LLP
   Osborne Clarke
   Reed Smith
   Richards Butler LLP

2. **Beachcroft LLP**
   Dundas & Wilson
   Fox Williams
   Harbottle & Lewis LLP
   Marriott Harrison
   Morrison & Foerster MNP
   Reynolds Porter Chamberlain LLP
   Watson, Farley & Williams
   Withers LLP

3. **Bates Wells & Braithwaite**
   Bristows
   Davenport Lyons
   Davies Arnold Cooper
   Farrer & Co
   Finers Stephens Innocent
   Fladgate Fielder
   Holman Fenwick & Willan
   Howard Kennedy
   Kemp Little LLP
   Maclay Murray & Spens LLP
   Manches LLP
   Mishcon de Reya
   Salans
   Trowers & Hamlins

Corporate Finance
East Anglia

1. **Mills & Reeve** *Norwich*
2. **Birketts** *Ipswich*
   Eversheds LLP *Cambridge*
3. **Hewitsons** *Cambridge*
   Taylor Vinters *Cambridge*
   Taylor Wessing *Cambridge*
4. **Howes Percival** *Norwich*
5. **Greene & Greene** *Bury St Edmunds*
   Greenwoods Solicitors *Peterborough*
   Prettys *Ipswich*
6. **Kester Cunningham John** *Thetford*
   Steeles (Law) LLP *Norwich*

Corporate Finance: AIM
Best of the UK

1. **Berwin Leighton Paisner LLP**
   DLA Piper UK LLP
   Field Fisher Waterhouse LLP
   Lawrence Graham LLP
   Norton Rose
   Travers Smith

2. **Addleshaw Goddard LLP**
   Ashurst
   Charles Russell LLP
   Cobbetts LLP
   Eversheds LLP
   Faegre & Benson LLP
   Halliwells LLP
   Hammonds
   Jones Day
   Kirkpatrick & Lockhart Nicholson
   Marriott Harrison
   McDermott Will & Emery UK LLP
   Memery Crystal
   Nabarro Nathanson
   Olswang
   Pinsent Masons
   Simmons & Simmons
   Taylor Wessing

3. **Bird & Bird**
   Finers Stephens Innocent
   Fladgate Fielder
   Howard Kennedy
   Hunton & Williams
   Maclay Murray & Spens LLP
   Mayer, Brown, Rowe & Maw LLP
   McGrigors
   Mishcon de Reya
   Osborne Clarke
   Richards Butler LLP
   Rosenblatt
   Shepherd and Wedderburn
   Shoosmiths
   SJ Berwin LLP
   Trowers & Hamlins
   Wallace LLP
   Watson, Farley & Williams
   Wragge & Co LLP

Corporate Finance
The South: Surrey, Hampshire & Dorset
[1] **Stevens & Bolton LLP** *Guildford*
[2] **Blake Lapthorn Linnell** *Portsmouth*
Bond Pearce LLP *Southampton*
Clyde & Co *Guildford*
Paris Smith & Randall *Southampton*
Shoosmiths *Fareham*
[3] **Lamport Bassitt** *Southampton*
Lester Aldridge *Southampton*
Penningtons Solicitors *Basingstoke*
Shadbolt & Co LLP *Reigate*
[4] **Charles Russell LLP** *Guildford*
Clarke Willmott *Southampton*
Coffin Mew & Clover *Southampton*
Moore & Blatch *Southampton*

Corporate Finance
South West: Bristol & Surround
[1] **Burges Salmon LLP** *Bristol*
Osborne Clarke *Bristol*
[2] **TLT Solicitors** *Bristol*
[3] **Bond Pearce LLP** *Bristol*
Charles Russell LLP *Cheltenham*
Clark Holt *Swindon*
Roxburgh and Milkins LLP *Bristol*
[4] **BPE Solicitors** *Cheltenham*
Rickerbys *Cheltenham*
Veale Wasbrough Lawyers *Bristol*
[5] **Ashfords** *Bristol*
Bevan Brittan LLP *Bristol*
Clarke Willmott *Bristol*
Lyons Davidson *Bristol*
Thring Townsend *Bath*
Wilsons *Salisbury*
Withy King *Bath*

Corporate Finance
South West: Devon & Cornwall
[1] **Ashfords** *Exeter*
Bond Pearce LLP *Exeter*
[2] **Foot Anstey** *Plymouth*
[3] **Michelmores** *Exeter*
Stephens & Scown *St Austell*

Corporate Finance
West Midlands
[1] **DLA Piper UK LLP** *Birmingham*
Wragge & Co LLP *Birmingham*
[2] **Eversheds LLP** *Birmingham*
Hammonds *Birmingham*
HBJ Gateley Wareing *Birmingham*
Pinsent Masons *Birmingham*
[3] **Browne Jacobson LLP** *Birmingham*
Cobbetts LLP *Birmingham*
Martineau Johnson *Birmingham*
[4] **George Green** *Cradley Heath*

Corporate Finance
East Midlands
[1] **Browne Jacobson LLP** *Nottingham*
Eversheds LLP *Nottingham*
[2] **Freeth Cartwright LLP** *Nottingham*
Geldards LLP *Derby*
HBJ Gateley Wareing *Nottingham*
Hewitsons *Northampton*
Howes Percival *Leicester*
Shoosmiths *Nottingham*

Corporate Finance
North West
[1] **Addleshaw Goddard LLP** *Manchester*
DLA Piper UK LLP *Manchester*
Eversheds LLP *Manchester*
[2] **Halliwells LLP** *Manchester*
Hammonds *Manchester*
[3] **Brabners Chaffe Street** *Liverpool*
Cobbetts LLP *Manchester*
DWF *Liverpool*
Kuit Steinart Levy *Manchester*
Pannone LLP *Manchester*
[4] **Beachcroft LLP** *Manchester*
[5] **Hill Dickinson LLP** *Liverpool*
Mace & Jones *Liverpool*
Nexus Solicitors *Manchester*

Corporate Finance
Wales
[1] **Eversheds LLP** *Cardiff*
Geldards LLP *Cardiff*
M & A Solicitors LLP *Cardiff*
[2] **Berry Smith Solicitors** *Cardiff*
Morgan Cole *Cardiff*
[3] **Capital Law Commercial** *Cardiff Bay*

Corporate Finance
Yorkshire
[1] **Addleshaw Goddard LLP** *Leeds*
DLA Piper UK LLP *Leeds*
Eversheds LLP *Leeds*
[2] **Hammonds** *Leeds*
Pinsent Masons *Leeds*
Walker Morris *Leeds*
[3] **Cobbetts LLP** *Leeds*
Gordons *Bradford*
[4] **Irwin Mitchell** *Leeds*
Keeble Hawson *Sheffield*
Lee & Priestley *Leeds*
Lupton Fawcett LLP *Leeds*
McCormicks *Leeds*
Rollits *Hull*
[5] **Andrew M Jackson** *Hull*
Denison Till *York*
Gosschalks *Hull*
Langleys *York*
Schofield Sweeney *Bradford*

Corporate Finance
North East
[1] **Dickinson Dees** *Newcastle upon Tyne*
[2] **Ward Hadaway** *Newcastle upon Tyne*
[3] **Eversheds LLP** *Newcastle upon Tyne*
Robert Muckle *Newcastle upon Tyne*
[4] **Hay & Kilner** *Newcastle upon Tyne*
Watson Burton *Newcastle upon Tyne*

crime

put simply

Criminal solicitors represent defendants in cases brought before the UK's criminal courts. Lesser offences are usually dealt with exclusively by solicitors in the magistrates' courts; more serious charges go to the Crown Courts, which are essentially still the domain of barristers, not least because most defendants still prefer this. In the year ending September 2005 there were 905,587 convictions in magistrates' courts and 71,099 in the Crown Court.

'Everyday crime' is the staple for most solicitors – theft, assault, drugs and driving offences. Fraud is the preserve of a more limited number of firms. Fraud cases aren't all as long-winded and complicated as the infamous Guinness fraud trial, but they do require a different approach from, say, crimes of violence.

A summary of the work of the Crown Prosecution Service is given on page 19. Details of the Public Defender Service are given on page 24.

who does what

Most days are busy; the others are frantic. A hectic schedule of visits to police stations, prisons and magistrates' courts, plenty of face-to-face client meetings and advocacy mean this is definitely not a desk job. The solicitor's work sees them:

- Attend police stations to interview and advise people in police custody.
- Visit prisons to see clients on remand.
- Prepare the client's defence, liaising with witnesses, medical and social workers' reports, probation officers, the CPS and others.
- Attend 'conferences with counsel', ie barristers
- Represent defendants at trial or brief barristers to do so.
- Represent clients at sentencing hearings, to explain any mitigating facts.

for fraud solicitors:

- There is a considerable volume of paperwork and financial analysis; a head for business is vital.
- For trainees, the early years will provide minimal advocacy and masses of trawling through warehouses full of documents. The caseload will be smaller but cases can run for years.

the realities of the job

- The hours are long and can disrupt your personal life. Lawyers who are accredited to work as Duty Solicitors will be on a rota and can be called to a police station at any time of the day or night while on duty.
- Confidence is essential. Without it you're doomed.
- In general crime you'll have a large caseload with a fast turnaround, but this means plenty of advocacy.
- The work is driven by the procedural rules and timetable of the court. Even so, recent figures show that almost a quarter of trials do not proceed on the appointed day, either because defendants or witnesses are absent, or at the request of the CPS.
- Your efforts can mean the difference between a person's liberty and their incarceration. You have to be detail-conscious and constantly vigilant.
- You'll encounter some pretty horrible situations and some difficult and distressed people. Murderers, rapists, drug dealers, conmen, football hooligans, paedophiles. If you have the ability to look beyond the labels and see these people as clients who are deserving of your best efforts then you've picked the right job. Some will have drug or alcohol problems, others will be mentally ill, others just children.
- It can be disheartening to see clients repeat the same poor choices, returning to court again and again.

the criminal courts of england and wales

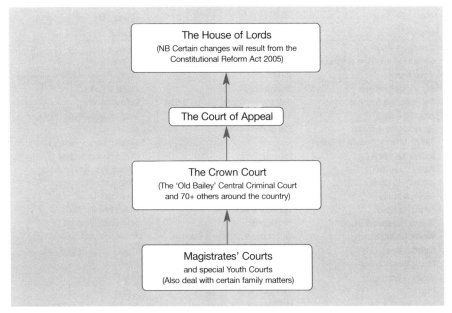

The House of Lords
(NB Certain changes will result from the Constitutional Reform Act 2005)

The Court of Appeal

The Crown Court
(The 'Old Bailey' Central Criminal Court and 70+ others around the country)

Magistrates' Courts
and special Youth Courts
(Also deal with certain family matters)

NB Certain military matters are deal with by Courts-Martial

○ Public funding of criminal defence means there's a good helping of bureaucracy. It also means you'll never be a millionaire.

current issues

○ Vast changes in legal aid funding have caused cold shivers and clammy hands among lawyers. If you want to spook yourself, read Get Carter on page 17.

○ Britain's FBI – the Serious Organised Crime Agency (SOCA) – has been launched. Promising elite staff and advanced technology, it aims to uncover and bring to justice the biggest and baddest crime bosses.

○ A subtle trend of placing greater importance on the victims of crime has been detected. In the past victims have been seen as merely witnesses. Not so since the introduction of the Victim's Personal Statement (VPS) and Tony Blair's prediction that SOCA will shift the focus from criminals to victims. A new 'victims' advocate' scheme has been piloted in the Old Bailey and Crown Courts in Birmingham, Cardiff, Manchester and Winchester. Perhaps these are the first indications of a leaning towards a more inquisitorial system rather than our well-established adversarial system.

○ The Criminal Justice Act contains provisions concerning the possible abolition of juries for serious fraud cases. Not yet engaged, the proposal was forced onto the back burner as it was met with huge resistance from practitioners, though it will no doubt rear its head again.

○ Check out www.clsa.co.uk for other news and discussion on major developments in criminal practice.

leading firms from Chambers UK 2007

Crime
London

[1] **Bindman & Partners**
Edward Fail Bradshaw & Waterson
Taylor Nichol
Birnberg Peirce & Partners
Kingsley Napley
Tuckers

[2] **BCL Burton Copeland**
Corker Binning Solicitors
Hickman & Rose
Russell Jones & Walker
TNT Solicitors (Thanki Novy Taube)
Birds Solicitors
Hallinan, Blackburn, Gittings & Nott
Hodge Jones & Allen
Stokoe Partnership

[3] **Andrew Keenan & Co**
Fisher Meredith
Iliffes Booth Bennett (IBB)
Meldrum Young
Russell-Cooke
Simons Muirhead & Burton
Venters Solicitors
Edwards Duthie
Henry Milner & Co
Kaim Todner
Powell Spencer & Partners
Saunders Solicitors LLP
TV Edwards
Victor Lissack, Roscoe & Coleman

[4] **Christian Khan**
Claude Hornby & Cox
Galbraith Branley
Hughmans
Lewis Nedas & Co
Reynolds Dawson
Christmas & Sheehan
Daniel Berman & Co
Goldkorns
J D Spicer & Co
McCormacks

Crime
Thames Valley

[1] **Blake Lapthorn Linnell** *Oxford*
Darbys *Oxford*
Macnab Clarke *Abingdon*
Morgan Cole *Oxford*

Crime
The South

[1] **Clarke Kiernan** *Tunbridge Wells*
Coffin Mew & Clover *Fareham*
Knights *Tunbridge Wells*

[2] **Bishop & Light** *Hove*
Blake Lapthorn Linnell *Portsmouth*
Hamnett Osborne *Haywards Heath*

Crime
South West

[1] **Bobbetts Mackan** *Bristol*
Douglas & Partners *Bristol*
Kelcey & Hall *Bristol*
Sansbury Campbell *Bristol*

[2] **Bay Advocates** *Torquay*
Nunn Rickard Solicitor *Exeter*
Russell Jones & Walker *Bristol*
St James Solicitors *Exeter*
Stone King LLP *Bath*
Walker Lahive *Plymouth*

[3] **Aidan Woods & Co** *Bristol*
Allen & Partners *Bristol*
Ashfords *Tiverton*
Dunn & Baker *Exeter*
Foot Anstey *Plymouth*
Stones *Exeter*
WBW Solicitors *Newton Abbot*

Crime
Wales

[1] **Gamlins** *Rhyl*
Huttons *Cardiff*
Martyn Prowel Solicitors *Cardiff*

[2] **Clarke & Hartland** *Cardiff*
Colin Jones *Barry*
Douglas-Jones Mercer *Swansea*
Goldstones *Swansea*
Graham Evans & Partners *Swansea*
Harding Evans *Newport*
Howe & Spender *Port Talbot*
Hugh James *Blackwood*
Robertsons *Cardiff*
Savery Pennington *Cardiff*
Spiro Grech McSorley *Cardiff*
Wilson Devonald *Swansea*

Crime
West Midlands

[1] **Glaisyers** *Birmingham*
Jonas Roy Bloom *Birmingham*

[2] **Bowcock Cuerden LLP** *Nantwich*
Carvers Solicitors *Birmingham*
Purcell Parker *Birmingham*
Tuckers *Birmingham*
Tyndallwoods *Birmingham*

Crime
East Midlands

[1] **Cartwright King** *Nottingham*
The Johnson Partnership *Nottingham*

[2] **Fletchers** *Nottingham*
Kieran Clarke Solicitors *Chesterfield*
The Smith Partnership *Derby*

[3] **Banner Jones Middleton** *Chesterfield*
Elliot Mather *Matlock*
Varley Hadley Siddall *Nottingham*
Ward & Griffiths *Nottingham*
Woodford-Robinson *Northampton*

Crime
East Anglia

1. **Belmores** *Norwich*
   BTMK Solicitors *Southend-on-Sea*
   Hatch Brenner *Norwich*
2. **David Charnley & Co** *Romford*
   hc solicitors LLP *Peterborough*
   Lucas & Wyllys *Great Yarmouth*
   Norton Peskett *Lowestoft*
   TNT Solicitors *Harlow*
3. **Cole Bentley & Co** *Great Yarmouth*
   Copleys *Huntingdon*
   Fosters *Norwich*
   Gepp & Sons *Chelmsford*
   Hegarty LLP Solicitors *Peterborough*

Crime
North West

1. **Brian Koffman & Co** *Manchester*
   Burton Copeland *Manchester*
   Draycott Browne *Manchester*
   JMW Solicitors *Manchester*
   Tuckers *Manchester*
2. **Cunninghams** *Manchester*
   Farleys *Blackburn*
   Forbes *Blackburn*
   Maidments *Manchester*
   Pearson Fielding Polson *Liverpool*
3. **Cobleys LLP** *Liverpool*
   Cuttle & Co *Manchester*
   Olliers *Manchester*
   RM Broudie & Co *Liverpool*
   Rowlands *Manchester*
   Russell & Russell *Bolton*

Crime
North East

1. **David Gray** *Newcastle upon Tyne*
   Howells LLP *Sheffield*
   Irwin Mitchell *Sheffield*
   McCormicks *Leeds*
2. **Grahame Stowe Bateson** *Leeds*
   Hay & Kilner *Newcastle upon Tyne*
   Henry Hyams *Leeds*
   Lester Morrill *Leeds*
   Sugaré & Co *Leeds*
   The Max Gold Partnership *Hull*
   Williamsons Solicitors *Hull*

Fraud: Criminal
Best of the UK

1. **BCL Burton Copeland**
   Kingsley Napley
   Peters & Peters
2. **Byrne and Partners**
   Corker Binning Solicitors
   Russell Jones & Walker
3. **Cooper Kenyon Burrows**
   Irwin Mitchell
   Pannone LLP
4. **Bankside Law**
   Bark & Co
   Bindman & Partners
   Cartwright King
   David Hanman Associates
   David Phillips & Partners
   Garstangs
   Hugh James
   McCormicks
   Simons Muirhead & Burton
   Tuckers
   Victor Lissack, Roscoe & Coleman
5. **Farleys**
   Hill Dickinson LLP

employment law

put simply

Employment lawyers guide their clients through the ever-growing area of workplace-related legislation, and in so doing they become intimately involved in the relationship between employers and employees. The divide between employers' and employees' lawyers is usually clear-cut, although some firms do act for both types of client. A few firms are known for their union connections. Always remember that the nature of a firm's clientele determines on which side of the fence its lawyers end up. Usually the job includes both advisory work and litigation, but when choosing a training contract you may wish to check that this is the case, or if the two roles are split.

Disputes are almost always resolved at an Employment Tribunal, or before reaching one. Tribunals are far less formal than a court, so for example barristers do not wear wigs or robes and modify their performance. Oftentimes individuals will be unrepresented. In these situations the tribunal panel usually forgives their inexperience, and may expect the employers' representatives to do so too.

The grievances leading to litigation fall into the following broad categories: redundancy, unlawful dismissal, breach of contract, harassment and discrimination. This latter category can be brought on the grounds of race, religious or philosophical belief, gender, sexual orientation, disability and age. Newspapers regularly report the detail of high-profile cases, so it's easy to familiarise yourself with the area. Such reports also give you a flavour of the human drama involved in the job.

who does what

employees' solicitors

- Advise clients on whether they have suffered unlawful or unfair treatment at work and establish the amount to be claimed. This will either be capped, or in the case of discrimina-

tion, can include additional elements to cover loss of earnings, injury to feelings and aggravated damages.
- Gather evidence and witnesses to support the claim.
- Try to negotiate a payment from the employer or take the matter to tribunal. If there is a breach of contract element to the claim, it might be heard in a court rather than a tribunal.
- If the matter does reach tribunal, the solicitor may conduct the advocacy themselves.

employers' solicitors

As well as defending or settling the above claims, employers' lawyers give general advice on:

- Negotiating employment contracts or exit packages for senior staff.
- Negotiating with unions to avoid or resolve industrial disputes.
- Formulating HR policies, and providing training on how to avoid workplace problems.
- Helping out on corporate deals by investigating and summarising the employment law issues affecting the businesses concerned.

the realities of the job

- You quickly develop an understanding of human foibles. By their very nature employment cases are filled with high drama.
- Clients may assume your role is to provide emotional support as well as legal advice. You need to take care to define your role appropriately.
- If acting for employers, you won't always like what you hear, but you still need to protect the clients' interests. Soon enough you'll see the advantage of preventative counselling and training programmes.
- This is a job for solicitors who want to do their own advocacy, although barristers are commonly used for high-stakes or complicated hearings and trials.

www.chambersandpartners.co.uk

- The work is driven by the procedural rules and timetable of the tribunals and courts.
- The law is extensive and changes frequently. You'll read more than your fair share of EU directives.

current issues

- In October 2006 the Employment Equality (Age) Regulations came into force and will undoubtedly prove significant, and not just for the 'stale, pale males' who will finally have a chance to bring a legitimate grievance. Looking at other countries where similar legislation has already been introduced, for example Ireland, claims are common and awards of damages can be high. Businesses will have to review their employment policies to ensure compliance, especially in the areas of performance management, training, benefits, retirement and redundancy. One particular area of concern will be recruitment, where job descriptions should not indirectly discriminate. Looking for an 'energetic graduate' for a 'funky, young firm' implies that older candidates need not apply, while requiring a 'mature person with gravitas and ten years' experience' rules out younger applicants. Proving that ten years' experience is strictly necessary for the job may be difficult. Likewise, rejecting a candidate for being overqualified could be discriminatory.

- The value of discrimination and harassment claims rises with no sign of abatement. Headline-grabbing cases abound, not least the Stephanie Villalba/Merrill Lynch equal pay and sex discrimination case, which rumbles on; HSBC's tribunal over the first-ever sexual-orientation discrimination claim to be filed, and HBOS being hit with an £11 million sex discrimination claim brought by Claire Bright. These cases carry substantial risk to the banks' reputations and illustrate the decision taken by a significant number of companies to fight claims. Investment banks are bulking up their in-house capabilities due to the rash of discrimination claims.
- The growth of in-house legal teams in large organisations means employer-led law firms need to specialise and offer added value to their clients. Many companies believe solicitors are too expensive and, privately, some solicitors acknowledge that they are indeed losing work to in-house teams.
- There is huge competition amongst trainees for employment seats, and even more for NQ-level jobs. Consider applying to train at specialist or employment-heavy firms if this is your intended area for specialisation. In many mainstream firms, gaining exposure to employment work can be a lottery.

employment law (continued)

leading firms from Chambers UK 2007

Employment: Mainly Respondent
Best of the UK

1
Allen & Overy LLP | Baker & McKenzie LLP
Herbert Smith LLP | Lewis Silkin LLP
Simmons & Simmons

2
Clifford Chance LLP | DLA Piper UK LLP
Eversheds LLP | Freshfields Bruckhaus Deringer
Linklaters | Lovells
Mayer, Brown, Rowe & Maw LLP | McDermott Will & Emery UK LLP

3
Addleshaw Goddard LLP | Beachcroft LLP
CMS Cameron McKenna LLP | Dechert LLP
Fox Williams | Hammonds
Macfarlanes | Nabarro Nathanson
Olswang | Pinsent Masons
Slaughter and May | Travers Smith

4
Ashurst | Bird & Bird
Charles Russell LLP | Farrer & Co
Norton Rose | Taylor Wessing
Withers LLP | Wragge & Co LLP

5
Barlow Lyde & Gilbert | Berwin Leighton Paisner LLP
Bevan Brittan LLP | Burges Salmon LLP
Denton Wilde Sapte | Mishcon de Reya
Osborne Clarke | Salans
SJ Berwin LLP | Speechly Bircham
Stephenson Harwood

6
Archon | Bates Wells & Braithwaite
Doyle Clayton | Finers Stephens Innocent
Harbottle & Lewis LLP | Kemp Little LLP
Lawrence Graham LLP | Manches LLP
Reynolds Porter Chamberlain LLP | Richards Butler LLP
Tarlo Lyons | Watson, Farley & Williams

Employment: Union/Applicant
Best of the UK

1
Russell Jones & Walker

2
Pattinson & Brewer
Rowley Ashworth
Thompsons

3
Bindman & Partners
Irwin Mitchell
Simpson Millar
Webster Dixon

Employment
Wales

1
Eversheds LLP Cardiff

2
Capital Law Commercial Cardiff Bay
Geldards LLP Cardiff
Hugh James Cardiff
Morgan Cole Cardiff

3
Dolmans Cardiff

Employment: Union/Applicant
Wales

1
Russell Jones & Walker Cardiff

Employment: International
Best of the UK

1
Allen & Overy LLP
Baker & McKenzie LLP
Herbert Smith LLP
Lewis Silkin LLP
McDermott Will & Emery UK LLP
Simmons & Simmons

2
Clifford Chance LLP
DLA Piper UK LLP
Eversheds LLP
Freshfields Bruckhaus Deringer
Linklaters
Lovells
Mayer, Brown, Rowe & Maw LLP
Slaughter and May

3
Ashurst
Bird & Bird
Dechert LLP
Fox Williams
Hammonds
Latham & Watkins LLP
Norton Rose
Taylor Wessing
Travers Smith
White & Case LLP
Wilmer Cutler Pickering Hale

Employment
Thames Valley

1
Clarkslegal LLP Reading
Olswang Thames Valley Reading
Osborne Clarke Reading

2
Boyes Turner Reading
Shoosmiths Reading

3
Cater Leydon Millard Abingdon
Henmans Oxford
Lewis Silkin LLP Oxford
Manches LLP Oxford
Pitmans Reading

4
B P Collins Gerrards Cross
Blake Lapthorn Linnell Oxford
Doyle Clayton Reading
Matthew Arnold & Baldwin Watford
Morgan Cole Reading
Penningtons Solicitors LLP Newbury

www.chambersandpartners.co.uk

Employment
The South

[1] **Blake Lapthorn Linnell** *Fareham*
Bond Pearce LLP *Southampton*
Clyde & Co *Guildford*
DMH Stallard *Crawley*

[2] **asb law** *Crawley*
Charles Russell LLP *Guildford*
Clarkson Wright & Jakes *Orpington*
Cripps Harries Hall *Tunbridge Wells*
Paris Smith & Randall *Southampton*
Sherrards *Haywards Heath*
Stevens & Bolton LLP *Guildford*
Thomson Snell *Tunbridge Wells*

[3] **Brachers** *Maidstone*
Coffin Mew & Clover *Southampton*
Lamport Bassitt *Southampton*
Lester Aldridge *Southampton*
Moore & Blatch *Southampton*
Rawlison Butler *Crawley*
Thomas Eggar *Chichester*

[4] **Furley Page LLP** *Canterbury*
Mundays LLP *Cobham*

Employment
South West

[1] **Bevan Brittan LLP** *Bristol*
Burges Salmon LLP *Bristol*
Osborne Clarke *Bristol*

[2] **Ashfords** *Exeter*
Beachcroft LLP *Bristol*
Bond Pearce LLP *Plymouth*
Clarke Willmott *Bristol*
TLT Solicitors *Bristol*
Veale Wasbrough Lawyers *Bristol*

[3] **BPE Solicitors** *Cheltenham*
Foot Anstey *Plymouth*
Michelmores *Exeter*
Rickerbys *Cheltenham*
Stephens & Scown *Exeter*
Withy King *Bath*

[4] **Bevans** *Bristol*
Charles Russell LLP *Cheltenham*
Lyons Davidson *Bristol*
Thring Townsend *Bath*

Employment:
Union/Applicant
South West

[1] **Burroughs Day** *Bristol*

[2] **Thompsons** *Bristol*

Employment
Midlands

[1] **Wragge & Co LLP** *Birmingham*

[2] **DLA Piper UK LLP** *Birmingham*
Eversheds LLP *Birmingham*
Hammonds *Birmingham*
Pinsent Masons *Birmingham*

[3] **Bevan Brittan LLP** *Birmingham*
Browne Jacobson LLP *Nottingham*
Cobbetts LLP *Birmingham*
HBJ Gateley Wareing *Birmingham*
Howes Percival *Leicester*
Martineau Johnson *Birmingham*
Mills & Reeve *Birmingham*

[4] **Freeth Cartwright LLP** *Nottingham*
Geldards LLP *Nottingham*
Irwin Mitchell *Birmingham*
Shakespeares *Birmingham*

[5] **Anthony Collins** *Birmingham*
BPE Solicitors *Birmingham*
George Green *Halesowen*
Higgs & Sons *Brierley Hill*
KJD *Stoke-on-Trent*
Lanyon Bowdler Solicitors *Telford*

Employment:
Union/Applicant
Midlands

[1] **Averta Employment Lawyers** *Solihull*

Employment:
Union/Applicant
North West

[1] **Thompsons** *Manchester*

[2] **Russell Jones & Walker** *Manchester*
Whittles *Manchester*

Employment
East Anglia

[1] **Eversheds LLP** *Cambridge*
Mills & Reeve *Cambridge*

[2] **Greenwoods Solicitors** *Peterborough*
Hewitsons *Cambridge*
Taylor Vinters *Cambridge*

[3] **Ashton Graham** *Ipswich*
Birketts *Ipswich*
Hegarty LLP Solicitors *Peterborough*
Prettys *Ipswich*
Steeles (Law) LLP *Norwich*

[4] **Gotelee & Goldsmith** *Ipswich*
Hatch Brenner *Norwich*
Howes Percival *Norwich*
Leathes Prior *Norwich*
Quantrills *Ipswich*
Wilkin Chapman *Lincoln*
Wollastons *Chelmsford*

Employment
North West

[1] **Addleshaw Goddard LLP** *Manchester*
DLA Piper UK LLP *Manchester*
Eversheds LLP *Manchester*

[2] **Cobbetts LLP** *Manchester*
DWF *Manchester*
Halliwells LLP *Manchester*
Hammonds *Manchester*
Mace & Jones *Manchester*
Pannone LLP *Manchester*

[3] **Beachcroft LLP** *Manchester*
Brabners Chaffe Street *Manchester*
Hill Dickinson LLP *Liverpool*
Weightmans *Liverpool*

[4] **Aaron & Partners LLP** *Chester*
Baines Wilson *Carlisle*
Berg Legal *Manchester*
Burnetts *Carlisle*
Keoghs *Bolton*
Kuit Steinart Levy *Manchester*
Ricksons *Manchester*

employment law (continued)

Employment
Yorkshire

[1] **DLA Piper UK LLP** *Leeds*
Eversheds LLP *Leeds*
Pinsent Masons *Leeds*

[2] **Addleshaw Goddard LLP** *Leeds*
Cobbetts LLP *Leeds*
Hammonds *Leeds*

[3] **Beachcroft LLP** *Leeds*
Ford & Warren *Leeds*
Irwin Mitchell *Sheffield*
Walker Morris *Leeds*

[4] **Gordons** *Leeds*
Hempsons *Harrogate*
Lupton Fawcett LLP *Leeds*
McCormicks *Leeds*
Nabarro Nathanson *Sheffield*
Rollits *Hull*
Watson Burton LLP *Leeds*

Employment:
Union/Applicant
Yorkshire

[1] **Thompsons** *Leeds*

[2] **Morrish & Co** *Leeds*
Rowley Ashworth *Leeds*

Employment
North East

[1] **Dickinson Dees** *Newcastle upon Tyne*
Eversheds LLP *Newcastle upon Tyne*
Ward Hadaway *Newcastle upon Tyne*

[2] **Jacksons Comm'l** *Stockton on Tees*
Robert Muckle *Newcastle upon Tyne*
Samuel Phillips *Newcastle upon Tyne*
Short Richardson *Newcastle upon Tyne*
Watson Burton *Newcastle upon Tyne*

[3] **Archers Law** *Stockton on Tees*
Crutes Law Firm *Newcastle upon Tyne*
Hay & Kilner *Newcastle upon Tyne*
Sintons *Newcastle upon Tyne*

Employment:
Union/Applicant
North East

[1] **Stefan Cross** *Newcastle upon Tyne*
Thompsons *Newcastle upon Tyne*

www.chambersandpartners.co.uk

environmental law

put simply

Advice to corporate clients on damage limitation, pre-emptive advice and defence from prosecution is the stock-in-trade of the environmental lawyer. The majority of those in private practice are working for, rather than sticking it to, big business; roles on the saintly side of this area of law are scarce. Opportunities do exist to work in-house for organisations like Greenpeace and Friends of the Earth or for niche public interest firms but these jobs are highly sought after.

Local authorities, government departments such as the Department for Environment, Food and Rural Affairs (Defra) and regulatory bodies like the Environment Agency are all employers of lawyers working in the environmental field and worth looking into if commercial environmental law doesn't sound appealing.

Environment law overlaps with other disciplines such as property, criminal law, corporate or EU law. The small size of most law firm environmental teams, and the need for practitioners to keep extra strings to their bow, means there are relatively few pure environmental lawyers around. On the one hand this makes for a very competitive area, but on the other the breadth of the discipline ensures a diverse and stimulating career.

who does what

Generally speaking the work of private practitioners breaks down into three areas:

- Advice on the potential environmental consequences of corporate, property and projects transactions – due diligence, you might call it. Will your client's new housing development destroy a colony of rare newts? Does the manufacturing business your client is buying have a history of environmental problems? How much waste is it discharging into rivers? Environmental issues can be deal-breakers.
- Compliance and regulatory advice – helping clients avoid investigation or even prosecution by the Environment Agency by ensuring their businesses keep within the regulations controlling how they operate.
- Defending clients when they get into trouble over water or air pollution, waste disposal, emission levels or health and safety. Such cases can involve criminal or civil disputes, judicial reviews and even statutory appeals, and can be the subject of damaging media coverage. Remember the recent case of a firm prosecuted and fined £250,000 for transporting radioactive material while a missing safety plug allowed a beam of radiation 1,000 times above safe levels to be emitted along the 130-mile route?

work in local authority legal departments:

- Here lawyers have a massive variety of work covering regulatory and planning issues plus waste management and air pollution prosecutions. They must also advise the authority on its own potential liability.

work for defra:

- DEFRA employs over 80 lawyers including trainees on GLS-funded schemes. Broadly it aims to promote sustainable development without compromising the quality of life of future generations. Two examples of its varied mandates are access to and the protection of the countryside, and the maintenance of good water quality and water environments.
- The lawyers' duties include litigation, drafting of subordinate legislation, advisory work and contract drafting.

work for the Environment Agency (EA):

- The EA has lawyers in Bristol and eight regional bases and is responsible for protecting and enhancing the environment and the regulation of corporate activities that have the capacity to pollute. As such the scope of work is vast: from waste management to flood defence, from air quality to environmental impact assessment, from contaminated land to climate change.

- As the prosecuting body for environmental crimes, there is plenty of prosecution work requiring the lawyers to gather evidence, prepare cases and brief barristers.

- Co-operation with government lawyers on the drafting and implementation of legislation.

the realities of the job

- The way in which environmental law spans disciplines means strong commercial nous and understanding of corporate structures are vital. All-round skills are best complemented by a genuine interest in a specific area (say renewable energy, conservation or water pollution) in this competitive and exacting field.

- Excellent academics are a must to help wade through, extrapolate from and present research and complex legislation; so too are sound judgement, pragmatism and a sense of improvisation in offering clients the most practical solutions.

- A basic grasp of science certainly helps.

- If you want to change environmental law, or crusade for a better planet, then nail your colours to the public mast; trying to get a company off the hook for having accidentally discharged three tonnes of mercury into a river may not be for you.

- Client contact is a big feature of this work and can endure over many years. Environmental risks can be inherently difficult to quantify and clients will rely on your gut instincts and powers of lateral thinking.

- What with visits to waste dumps or drying reservoirs, and a workload that can span health and safety matters, corporate transaction and regulatory advice all in one day, this is neither a desk-bound nor a quiet discipline.

- Research constantly advances and legislation is always changing in this field, so you'll spend a lot of time keeping up to date.

- An interest in European law is increasingly useful as more and more EU directives prescribe the boundaries of environmental law in the UK.

current issues

- Changes in environmental law are coming thick and fast; keep on top of them via websites like www.endsreport.com. You should enhance your CV and prime yourself by joining organisations such as the Environmental Law Foundation (ELF) and the UK Environmental Law Association (www.ukela.org). Most environmental lawyers are members of UKELA and students are welcome to attend events across the country. Look out for UKELA's annual essay and mooting competitions. The charity ELF (www.elflaw.org) provides a referral service for members of the public with environmental problems, organises lectures in London and produces regular newsletters for its members.

- Swathes of new EU Directives are impacting the UK. The not-so-snappily titled Waste Electrical and Electronic Equipment (WEEE) Directive is keeping lawyers busy at the moment.

- The Contaminated Land Regime, introduced in England and Wales six years ago, means clients acquiring sites can be liable for historic pollution. Now local authorities have woken up to the idea of taking action, the effects of the regime are starting to bite.

- Climate change isn't just for academics any more. Businesses need advice on how to navigate the EU Emissions Trading Scheme and the mechanisms for reducing emissions provided for under the Kyoto Protocol. Environmental lawyers in the top-flight firms are encountering this type of work more and more often. International issues in general are coming to the fore with initiatives like the Equator Principles and Corporate Social Responsibility prominent.

○ Finally, energy. We all need it and there isn't going to be enough of it. Scores of renewable energy projects have led to environmental lawyers working alongside planning and project finance colleagues. Oil and gas schemes continue unabated and the prospect of new nuclear installations is also hot.

leading firms from Chambers UK 2007

Environment
Best of the UK

1. Freshfields Bruckhaus Deringer
2. Allen & Overy LLP
   Burges Salmon LLP
   Clifford Chance LLP
   CMS Cameron McKenna LLP
3. Ashurst
   Berwin Leighton Paisner LLP
   Denton Wilde Sapte
   Eversheds LLP
   Linklaters
   Lovells
   Mayer, Brown, Rowe & Maw LLP
   Simmons & Simmons
   Slaughter and May
4. Addleshaw Goddard LLP
   Barlow Lyde & Gilbert
   Bond Pearce LLP
   Hammonds
   Herbert Smith LLP
   Jones Day
   Macfarlanes
   Nabarro Nathanson
   Trowers & Hamlins
5. Baker & McKenzie LLP
   DLA Piper UK LLP
   Kirkpatrick & Lockhart Nicholson
   Pinsent Masons
   SJ Berwin LLP
   Wragge & Co LLP
6. Dundas & Wilson
   Norton Rose
   Osborne Clarke
   Semple Fraser LLP
   Stephenson Harwood
   Taylor Wessing

Environment: Claimant
Best of the UK

1. Leigh Day & Co
   Richard Buxton
2. Public Interest Lawyers
3. Irwin Mitchell

Environment
The South

1. Blake Lapthorn Linnell *Southampton*
   Bond Pearce LLP *Southampton*
2. Clarkslegal LLP *Reading*
   DMH Stallard *Brighton*
   Manches LLP *Oxford*
   Stevens & Bolton LLP *Guildford*
3. B P Collins *Gerrards Cross*
   Brachers *Maidstone*

Environment
South West

1. Burges Salmon LLP *Bristol*
2. Bond Pearce LLP *Plymouth*
   Osborne Clarke *Bristol*
3. Ashfords *Exeter*
   Clarke Willmott *Bristol*
4. Bevan Brittan LLP *Bristol*
   Thring Townsend *Bath*
   Veale Wasbrough Lawyers *Bristol*

Environment
Midlands

1. Eversheds LLP *Nottingham*
   Wragge & Co LLP *Birmingham*
2. Pinsent Masons *Birmingham*
3. Browne Jacobson LLP *Nottingham*
   Hammonds *Birmingham*

Environment
East Anglia

1. Mills & Reeve *Cambridge*
2. Eversheds LLP *Norwich*
   Hewitsons *Cambridge*
   Taylor Vinters *Cambridge*

Environment
The North

1. Eversheds LLP *Manchester*
   Nabarro Nathanson *Sheffield*
2. Addleshaw Goddard LLP *Manchester*
   DLA Piper UK LLP *Sheffield*
   Pinsent Masons *Leeds*
3. Cobbetts LLP *Manchester*
   Dickinson Dees *Newcastle upon Tyne*
   Hammonds *Manchester*
4. Aaron & Partners LLP *Chester*
   Halliwells LLP *Manchester*
   Walker Morris *Leeds*

Environment
Wales

1. Eversheds LLP *Cardiff*
2. Geldards LLP *Cardiff*
   Hugh James *Cardiff*
   Morgan Cole *Cardiff*
3. Clarkslegal LLP *Cardif*

family law

put simply

Family lawyers deal with all the legal mechanics and complications relating to the process of marrying, having children, getting divorced, accessing children post-divorce, dividing shared assets, securing maintenance, and family disputes concerning passing on your assets after death. Pretty much the only part of family life they don't actually take part in is the moment of conception itself... except in the case of their own families of course.

Day-to-day matters include divorce, disputes between cohabitants, inheritance disputes between family members, prenuptial and cohabitation agreements, all matters relating to children and issues arising from registration of same-sex-marriages under Civil Partnership legislation. Whether working in the family department of a general high street practice with a high-volume caseload of legally aided work, or for a specialist practice dealing with high-value divorces and complex child or international matters, family solicitors are on their feet in court a good deal and fully occupied back in the office.

who does what

There is effectively a division within family practice between child law and matrimonial law, with some practitioners devoting themselves exclusively to one or other side of the fence and others planting a foot on either side.

matrimonial law tasks

- Interviewing and advising clients on prenuptial agreements, cohabitation arrangements, divorce and the financial implications of divorce. If this sounds narrow in scope don't be deceived – such cases can include issues over inheritance and wills, conveyancing, welfare benefits, company law, tax and trusts, pensions and even judicial review (particularly when it comes to public funding issues).

- Preparing the client's case for divorce and settlement hearings, including dealing with witnesses, and providing summaries of assets/finances. As such, accountants, financial and pensions advisers, and family lawyers from overseas jurisdictions are familiar faces.

- Attending 'conferences with counsel' – ie meetings with barristers.

- Representing clients in hearings or briefing barristers to do so.

- Negotiating settlements and associated financial terms.

child law tasks

- In private cases – interviewing and advising clients (husbands, wives or cohabitants) on the implications of divorce with regard to child contact and residence. In many instances this will result in court action. Dealing with disputes between parents or other family members over the residence of, and contact with, children.

- In public cases – representing local authorities, parents, children's guardians or children themselves on matters such as child care proceedings or abuse in care claims. Here social workers, probation officers, psychologists and medical professionals will also be involved in cases.

the realities of the job

- When it comes to relationships and families, no two sets of circumstances will ever be the same. You'll have a large and varied caseload with a fast turnaround, but this means huge scope for advocacy.

- You will encounter a real mix of clients, some at a joyful moment in their lives, many facing deeply traumatic and personal problems. A good family law practitioner combines the sensitivity, trustworthiness and capacity for empathy of a counsellor, with the clarity of thought, commercial acumen and communication skills of a hard-nosed lawyer. Your client may treat you as a shoulder to cry on, but you need to retain the detachment to achieve the result they need.

- Tough negotiating skills and a strong nerve are must-haves because, like criminal practice, your work has immediate and practical consequences. How often your client gets to see their children, what happens to their home, their family or their livelihood are all in your hands. The prospect of telling a client that they've lost a custody battle does much to sharpen the mind.
- A pragmatic and real-world outlook is useful, but you'll also need to spend time keeping abreast of legal developments. The Human Rights Act opened up new legal ground, while action groups like Fathers4Justice have intensified the scrutiny on child residence and contact issues. Even matrimonial cases are continually push at the boundaries, such as the recent ruling that ex-Arsenal footballer Ray Parlour must pay his former wife a percentage of all future earnings because of her part in establishing his career.
- On publicly funded matters you'll face your share of bureaucracy and you'll never earn mega-bucks.

current issues

- In the light of recent high-profile divorces such as those of Colin Montgomerie and Ray Parlour, London is arguably becoming the divorce capital of Europe. In such cases the wealth and assets involved far outstrip the reasonable needs of the parties and lawyers are looking for precedents. The House of Lords recently obliged with its decisions in Miller, where the issue is how to deal with a short marriage, and McFarlane, where the wife had given up a career to raise a family.
- Cases such as these help explain increased interest in prenuptial agreements. Everyone's heard of a 'pre-nup', but since the arrival in 2005 of same-sex 'marriage' through the Civil Partnerships Act there is also the 'pre-cip'. Lawyers are interested to see how the courts will handle the division of assets following the breakdown of a civil partnership.
- Collaborative law is a new buzzword. For some lawyers it is the way forward for family disputes; others say they've seen it all before with mediation. It doesn't suit every case, and if it doesn't work, the parties must change to new solicitors if they subsequently litigate. The take up of collaborative law is strong in places such as Cambridge and Bath, but negligible further north.
- A bill is currently going through Parliament regarding contact in private child law cases.
- These are challenging times for the publicly funded lawyer. Many firms are feeling the squeeze and some are choosing to limit, or even stop, legally aided work altogether. Lawyers are waiting for news on how the Carter Review will treat the public funding of care proceedings.

family law (continued)

leading firms from Chambers UK 2007

Family: Matrimonial Finance & Private Children
London

1. **Manches LLP**
   Withers LLP
2. **Alexiou Fisher Philipps**
   Charles Russell LLP
   Clintons
   Farrer & Co
   Hughes Fowler Carruthers
   Levison Meltzer Pigott
   Miles Preston & Co
   Payne Hicks Beach
   Sears Tooth
3. **Collyer Bristow LLP**
   Kingsley Napley
   Mishcon de Reya
4. **Anthony Gold**
   CKFT
   Dawson Cornwell
   Dawsons Solicitors
   Family Law In Partnership
   Forsters LLP
   Gordon Dadds
   Harcus Sinclair
   International Family Law Chambers
5. **Bindman & Partners**
   Bross Bennett
   Fisher Meredith
   Hodge Jones & Allen
   Osbornes
   Reynolds Porter Chamberlain LLP
   Rooks Rider
   Russell-Cooke

Family: Public Law Child & Child Abduction
London

1. **Bindman & Partners**
   Goodman Ray
2. **Dawson Cornwell**
   Reynolds Porter Chamberlain LLP
3. **Kingsley Napley**
   Russell-Cooke
4. **Fisher Meredith**
   Hodge Jones & Allen
   Osbornes

Family
Thames Valley

1. **Blandy & Blandy** *Reading*
   Boodle Hatfield *Oxford*
   Manches LLP *Oxford*
2. **Darbys** *Oxford*
   Morgan Cole *Oxford*
3. **Blake Lapthorn Linnell** *Oxford*
   Bower & Bailey *Oxford*
   Henmans *Oxford*
   Horsey Lightly Fynn *Newbury*
   Iliffes Booth Bennett (IBB) *Uxbridge*

Family
The South

1. **Lester Aldridge** *Bournemouth*
2. **Brachers** *Maidstone*
   Charles Russell LLP *Guildford*
   Paris Smith & Randall *Southampton*
   Thomson Snell *Tunbridge Wells*
3. **Blake Lapthorn Linnell** *Fareham*
   Coffin Mew & Clover *Portsmouth*
   Cripps Harries Hall *Tunbridge Wells*
   Ellis Jones *Bournemouth*
   Max Barford & Co *Tunbridge Wells*
   Scott Bailey & Co *Lymington*
   Watson Nevill Solicitors *Maidstone*
   Williams Thompson *Christchurch*

Family
Wales

1. **Harding Evans** *Newport*
   Hugh James *Cardiff*
   Larby Williams with Gwyn *Cardiff*
   Nicol Denvir & Purnell *Cardiff*
   Wendy Hopkins Family Law *Cardiff*
2. **Avery Naylor** *Swansea*
   Howells *Cardiff*
   Leo Abse & Cohen *Cardiff*
   Martyn Prowel Solicitors *Cardiff*
   Robertsons *Cardiff*

Family
South West

1. **Burges Salmon LLP** *Bristol*
   Clarke Willmott *Bristol*
   Foot Anstey *Plymouth*
   Stephens & Scown *Exeter*
   TLT Solicitors *Bristol*
   Tozers *Exeter*
2. **Act Family Law Practice** *Plymouth*
   Gill Akaster *Plymouth*
   Hartnell Chanot & Partners *Exeter*
   Wolferstans *Plymouth*
3. **Ford Simey** *Exeter*
   Rickerbys *Cheltenham*
   Stone King LLP *Bath*
   Stones *Exeter*
   Thring Townsend *Bath*
   WBW Solicitors *Torquay*
   Withy King *Bath*

solicitors

Family
Midlands

1. **Blair Allison** *Birmingham*
   Challinors *Birmingham, West Bromwich*
2. **Anthony Collins** *Birmingham*
   Divorce and Family Law *Birmingham*
   Rupert Bear Murray *Nottingham*
3. **Benussi & Co** *Birmingham*
   Freeth Cartwright LLP *Nottingham*
   Hadens *Walsall*
   Harrison Clark *Worcester*
   Irwin Mitchell *Birmingham*
   Lanyon Bowdler *Shrewsbury*
   Mills & Reeve *Birmingham*
   Nelsons *Nottingham*
   Osborne & Co *Birmingham*
   Turnbull Garrard *Shrewsbury*
   Tyndallwoods *Birmingham*
   Wace Morgan *Shrewsbury*
   Young & Lee *Birmingham*

Family
East Anglia

1. **Mills & Reeve** *Cambridge, Norwich*
2. **Buckles** *Peterborough*
   hc solicitors LLP *Peterborough*
   Silver Fitzgerald *Cambridge*
   Taylor Vinters *Cambridge*
3. **Cozens-Hardy & Jewson** *Norwich*
   Gotelee & Goldsmith *Ipswich*
   Hansells *Norwich*
   Hatch Brenner *Norwich*
   Kester Cunningham John *Cambridge*
   Leonard Gray *Chelmsford*
   Marchant-Daisley *Cambridge*
   Overburys *Norwich*
   Prettys *Ipswich*
   Rudlings & Wakelam *Thetford*

Family
North West

1. **Pannone LLP** *Manchester*
2. **Addleshaw Goddard LLP** *Manchester*
   Cobbetts LLP *Manchester*
   Green & Co *Manchester*
   Halliwells LLP *Liverpool, Manchester*
   Mace & Jones *Liverpool, Knutsford*
   Morecrofts *Liverpool*
3. **Brabners Chaffe Street** *Liverpool*
   Hill Dickinson LLP *Liverpool*
   JMW Solicitors *Manchester*
   Laytons *Manchester*
   Stephensons *Leigh, Manchester*

Family
Yorkshire

1. **Addleshaw Goddard LLP** *Leeds*
2. **Andrew M Jackson** *Hull*
   Grahame Stowe Bateson *Harrogate*
   Irwin Mitchell *Sheffield*
   Jones Myers Partnership *Leeds*
3. **Gordons** *Bradford*
   Lupton Fawcett LLP *Leeds*
   Zermansky & Partners *Leeds*

Family
North East

1. **Dickinson Dees** *Newcastle upon Tyne*
2. **David Gray** *Newcastle upon Tyne*
   Hay & Kilner *Newcastle upon Tyne*
   Mincoffs *Newcastle upon Tyne*
   Samuel Phillips *Newcastle upon Tyne*
   Sintons *Newcastle upon Tyne*
   Ward Hadaway *Newcastle upon Tyne*
   Watson *Newcastle upon Tyne, Leeds*

intellectual property

put simply

Intellectual property can be protected in several ways. A patent provides the proprietor of a new, industrially applicable invention or process with the exclusive right to work it for a certain period. A trade mark provides its owner with a limited monopoly to use the mark on certain goods or services, and a registered design provides the exclusive right to use the design. Copyright is slightly different in the sense that it exists as soon as material is created, without the need for any registration. Things that are copyrightable include music, paintings and drawings, works of literature or reference, databases and web pages. So, for example, Chambers and Partners has copyright in this book and no part of it can be reproduced by anyone else without our permission.

Intellectual property can be extremely valuable; sometimes the most valuable asset a person or business owns. Admittedly, the average five-year-old's paintings will have no commercial value, but imagine the money that can be made by selling or exploiting a revolutionary idea for, say, a cyclone-effect vacuum cleaner. Think about the commercial value in the distinctive shape of the glass Coca-Cola bottle or Jif's plastic lemon.

Increasingly the work of IP lawyers is crossing over with other disciplines, not simply IT and life sciences but also areas such as competition law and employment law.

who does what

The IP lawyer's role can involve the following:

- Searching domestic, European and international registers of patents, trade marks and registered designs to establish ownership of existing rights or the potential to register new rights.
- Taking all steps to protect clients' interests by securing patents, trade marks and registered designs; appealing unfavourable decisions; attacking decisions that benefit others but harm the lawyer's own client.
- Writing letters to require that third parties desist from carrying out infringing activities or risk litigation for damages and an injunction.
- Issuing court proceedings and preparing cases for trial, including taking witness statements, examining scientific or technical reports and commissioning experiments and tests. In the world of brand protection, junior lawyers may find themselves conducting consumer surveys and going on covert shopping expeditions.
- Instructing and consulting with barristers. Solicitor advocates can appear in the Patents County Court, but usually recognise the advantages of having a specialist IP barrister for higher court hearings.
- Drafting commercial agreements between owners of IP rights and those who want to use the protected invention, design or artistic work. The most common documents will either transfer ownership of the right to another party or grant a licence for them to use it.
- Working as part of a multidisciplinary team on corporate transactions, verifying ownership of IP rights and drafting documents enabling their transfer.

the realities of the job

- Lawyers must be able to handle everyone from sophisticated or pushy company directors to mad inventors and quirky artistic types. Clients come from manufacturing, hi-tech, engineering, pharmaceuticals, agrochemicals, universities and scientific institutions, media organisations and the arts.
- A degree in a relevant subject is common among patent lawyers. Brand and trade mark lawyers need a curiosity for all things creative

and must keep up with consumer trends. Both types of IP lawyer need to have a good sense for commercial strategy.

- Attention to detail, precision and accuracy: words are important and you must be meticulous in their use, particularly when drafting.
- In patent and trade mark filing, everything has a time limit. You will live by deadlines.
- The volume of paperwork involved can be huge on patent matters, though on the upside you'll visit research labs or factories to learn about production processes, etc.
- You'll learn that the development of new drugs and inventions is motivated more often by profit than philanthropy. Success or failure in litigation can dramatically affect a company's share price.

current issues

- The systems for procuring international IP rights are becoming more harmonised. The Office for Harmonization in the Internal Market (OHIM), in Alicante, Spain, grants Community trade marks and designs. The European Patent Office in Munich grants European patents. Through the Patent Cooperation Treaty, which has been signed by most countries and is administered by the World Intellectual Property Organization (WIPO), patent applicants in one country can preserve their options for patent protection in others around the world. The number of patent filings continues to increase year on year.

- There has been a noticeable rise in the level of interest in IP from government. At the last G8 summit counterfeiting was raised as one of the eight key points for discussion, primarily because of a need to get China to respect IP rights. The UK government is listening to lobbyists and has put in place the Gower Review of IP.

- The Thames Valley has a concentration of IT companies; Cambridge's Silicon Fen is the product of hi-tech and biotech university spin-out companies; London is always busy.

- Manufacturing, pharmaceutical and research companies employ patent specialists and there are in-house legal teams at all the large pharmaceutical companies. In the media, major publishers and television companies have in-house IP lawyers.

- European patent attorneys and trade mark agents work as a parallel profession. You can find out more about what they do on page 25. There are early signs of convergence between the legal profession and these other professions. Some law firms provide in-house trade mark and patent-filing services, allowing clients to sidestep patent and trade mark attorneys. This is an increasing trend and one that many clients favour, even if patent and trade mark attorneys do not.

leading firms from Chambers UK 2007

Intellectual Property **Thames Valley**	Intellectual Property **The South**	Intellectual Property **East Anglia**
[1] Olswang Thames Valley *Reading*	[1] Blake Lapthorn Linnell *Portsmouth*	[1] Mills & Reeve *Norwich, Cambridge*
Shoosmiths *Milton Keynes*	[2] DMH Stallard *Crawley*	Taylor Vinters *Cambridge*
Willoughby/Rouse Legal *Oxford*	[3] Bond Pearce LLP *Southampton*	[2] Hewitsons *Cambridge*
[2] Manches LLP *Oxford*	Shadbolt & Co LLP *Reigate*	Taylor Wessing *Cambridge*
Osborne Clarke *Reading*		[3] Greenwoods Solicitors *Peterborough*
[3] Matthew Arnold & Baldwin *Watford*		
NetworkLaw Limited *Wokingham*		

Intellectual Property: Patent Litigation
London

1. Bird & Bird
   Bristows
   Taylor Wessing
2. Simmons & Simmons
   Wragge & Co LLP
3. Herbert Smith LLP
   Linklaters
   Lovells
4. Baker & McKenzie LLP
   DLA Piper UK LLP
   Freshfields Bruckhaus Deringer
   Olswang
   Roiter Zucker
5. Clifford Chance LLP
   Field Fisher Waterhouse LLP
   Howrey LLP
   Marks & Clerk solicitors
   McDermott Will & Emery UK LLP
   Milbank, Tweed, Hadley & McCloy
   Stringer Saul LLP

Intellectual Property
North West

1. Addleshaw Goddard Manchester
2. DLA Piper UK LLP Manchester
   Eversheds LLP Manchester
   Halliwells LLP Manchester
   Hill Dickinson LLP Liverpool
3. Cobbetts LLP Manchester
   Hammonds Manchester
   Kuit Steinart Levy Manchester
4. Pannone LLP Manchester
   Taylors Blackburn

Intellectual Property
Midlands

1. Wragge & Co LLP Birmingham
2. Browne Jacobson LLP Nottingham
   Eversheds LLP Nottingham
3. Cobbetts LLP Birmingham
   DLA Piper UK LLP Birmingham
   Freeth Cartwright LLP Nottingham
   Martineau Johnson Birmingham
   Pinsent Masons Birmingham

Intellectual Property: General
London

1. Bird & Bird
   Bristows
2. Baker & McKenzie LLP
   Herbert Smith LLP
   Lovells
   Simmons & Simmons
   Taylor Wessing
   Willoughby & Partners/Rouse Legal
   Wragge & Co LLP
3. Ashurst
   DLA Piper UK LLP
   Field Fisher Waterhouse LLP
   Freshfields Bruckhaus Deringer
   Linklaters
   Olswang
4. Addleshaw Goddard LLP
   Allen & Overy LLP
   Arnold & Porter (UK) LLP
   Clifford Chance LLP
   Harbottle & Lewis LLP
   Lewis Silkin LLP
   Marks & Clerk Solicitors
   Richards Butler LLP
   Roiter Zucker
   SJ Berwin LLP
   Slaughter and May
   White & Case LLP
5. Briffa
   Collyer Bristow LLP
   Dechert LLP
   Eversheds LLP
   Finers Stephens Innocent
   Howrey LLP
   Jones Day
   Kilpatrick Stockton
   Mayer, Brown, Rowe & Maw LLP
   McDermott Will & Emery UK LLP
   Mishcon de Reya
   Orchard
   Redd
   Wedlake Bell
   Withers LLP

Intellectual Property
South West

1. Bevan Brittan LLP Bristol
   Osborne Clarke Bristol
2. Bond Pearce LLP Plymouth, Bristol
   Burges Salmon LLP Bristol
3. Ashfords Bristol
   Beachcroft LLP Bristol
4. Humphreys & Co Solicitors Bristol
   TLT Solicitors Bristol

Intellectual Property
Wales

1. Geldards LLP Cardiff
2. Eversheds LLP Cardiff
   Morgan Cole Cardiff

Intellectual Property
Yorkshire

1. Addleshaw Goddard LLP Leeds
2. DLA Piper UK LLP Leeds
3. Pinsent Masons Leeds
   Walker Morris Leeds
4. Eversheds LLP Leeds
   Hammonds Leeds
   Irwin Mitchell Leeds
   Lupton Fawcett LLP Leeds
   Sanderson Lumber Leeds

Intellectual Property
North East

1. Dickinson Dees Newcastle upon Tyne
2. Ward Hadaway Newcastle upon Tyne

litigation/dispute resolution

put simply

If you are an avid viewer of legal dramas on TV you could be forgiven for thinking that the average litigation solicitor is always in trial. Actually, this is far from accurate as the majority of disputes are resolved long before they reach the court steps. Less exciting maybe, but the law doesn't exist primarily to provide litigators with an adrenaline-charged career. Clients, especially commercial ones, usually want to finalise a settlement as quickly, cheaply and unobtrusively as possible.

Commercial disputes range from unpaid bills or unfulfilled contract terms to problems between landlords and tenants, infringement of IP rights, construction-related claims, the liabilities of insurers, shipping cases, defective products cases, media and entertainment industry wrangles – the list is long. To confuse matters a little, there are two divisions of the High Court – the Chancery Division and the Queen's Bench Division – and each hears different types of case. The following diagram shows the court system in England and Wales, and the Bar section of this guide summaries of the differences between the QBD and Chancery Divisions.

Unless settled by initial correspondence, disputes are concluded either by court litigation or some alternative form of dispute resolution. The most common of these other methods are arbitration and mediation, the former often being stipulated as the preferred method in commercial contracts, the latter commonly achieved through structured negotiations between the parties, overseen by an independent mediator. The increased use of such alternative methods is the reason why some law firms have renamed their litigation departments as dispute resolution departments. Even alternative methods of resolution have their problems: mediation is not necessarily adequate for complex matters, and there is a perception that it can be used by opponents as a means of 'bleeding' money or a covert form of interrogation.

As a trainee your workload will largely depend on the type of firm you go to and the type of clients it represents. The very biggest City firms are unlikely to give new recruits free rein on the latest international banking dispute, and it is quite possible that they may never go to court during their training contract, but they will be able to make a small contribution to major international cases that create newspaper headlines. Some of the biggest, longest-running disputes have been related to financial matters: the Equitable Life and BCCI litigations are good examples.

At firms handling much smaller claims trainees can usually deal with all aspects of a case, from drafting correspondence and interim court applications to meetings with clients and settlement negotiations. There are a number of litigation-led law firms that handle cases of all sizes and these represent the best opportunities for a litigation-heavy training.

who does what

claimants' solicitors

- Advise clients on whether they have a valid claim.
- Gather evidence and witnesses to support the claim.
- If correspondence with the prospective defendant does not produce a satisfactory result, issue court proceedings or embark on a process of alternative dispute resolution.
- Represent clients at pre-trial hearings and case management conferences.
- Attend 'conferences with counsel' (ie barristers) and brief barristers to conduct advocacy in hearings and trials.
- Attend trials with clients; provide assistance to barristers.

defendants' solicitors

- Advise on the validity of a claim brought against a client, making recommendations as to whether to settle or fight.
- Prepare defences, including gathering all evidence and witness statements.
- Represent clients at pre-trial hearings and case management conferences.
- Attend conferences with counsel and brief barristers to conduct advocacy in hearings, trials and arbitrations.
- Attend trials, arbitrations and mediations with clients; provide assistance to barristers when they are being used.

the realities of the job

- The work is driven by the procedural rules and timetable of the courts. This requires the solicitor to learn the rules and keep to deadlines. Good litigators understand how best to operate within the system, while also developing winning case strategies.
- A phenomenal amount of paperwork is generated and, certainly in the early years, litigators spend much of their time sifting through documents, scheduling and copying them in order to provide the court and all other parties with an agreed bundle of evidence.
- Litigators need to express themselves both concisely and precisely, especially when a high degree of legal analysis is involved.
- Unless the value of a claim is small, the solicitor's job is more about case preparation than court performance. Solicitor advocates are gaining ground, and once properly qualified they can appear in the higher courts; however, barristers still dominate court advocacy.
- Although there's a good deal of posturing required, only a bad lawyer will adopt a victory-at-all-costs approach. A good lawyer will understand the context in which the case is set and how the client's interests will be best served.

current issues

- The Law Society requires all trainee solicitors to gain some contentious experience, and they tend to discover early on whether they are suited to this kind of work. An increasing number of City firms find that they have more trainees than openings in their litigation departments and they get around this by sending some of them on a litigation crash course instead.
- The competition for litigation jobs at NQ level in big City firms is fierce. For most of them, it's simply not a mainstream activity in the way that corporate or finance is. Consider litigation-led firms if you are certain of your preference for this type of work.
- Herbert Smith made news in 2004 by opening an advocacy unit which now has more than 50 advocates. Denton Wilde Sapte also runs a unit, and many other firms have solicitor advocates within their ranks. While some people applaud this one-stop shop approach, sceptics point to the fact that for bet-the-company litigation, clients will invariably turn to barristers for their expertise and gravitas. In reality, solicitors rarely get enough exposure to become as good as the best QCs and junior barristers they encounter. Only time will tell if solicitor advocacy is the way forward or a passing phase in the development of commercial litigation. As a general rule, students who are passionate about becoming advocates in the area of commercial litigation should still consider their prospects at the Bar. If determined to become both a solicitor and an advocate, certain areas of practice have more scope for advocacy – ie family, crime and lower-value civil litigation to name three.
- It's worth knowing about the fallout from two gargantuan lawsuits that have concluded recently – BCCI and Equitable Life. We've summarised the story of each overleaf.

- In general there is now less domestic litigation, but more international litigation and arbitration. Commentators speak of the rise of Eastern Europe, primarily Russia, as a locus for disputes involving investors with burnt fingers.
- Banking/finance and regulatory litigation is expected to increase as a consequence of an agreement between the Securities & Exchange Commission (SEC) and the Financial Services Authority (FSA). Also starting to bite are the corporate governance provisions contained in the Financial Services and Markets Act 2000, which acts in much the same way as the Sarbanes-Oxley legislation in the USA. Both of these pieces of legislation are designed to counteract corporate skulduggery of the likes that led to Enron.

As the dust settles following the ignominious endings of the BCCI and Equitable Life disputes, the London legal market has engaged in a process of reflection and consolidation. Practitioners anticipate a dearth of major cases in the short term, as potential claims are channelled into mediation, arbitration and other forms of alternative dispute resolution. As well as a general reluctance to become embroiled in high-cost speculative litigation, this direction has been set by what clients and solicitors agree has been the escalating cost of disputes in general.

BCCI

After hearing evidence in this gargantuan case the judge, Mr Justice Tomlinson, turned to the then Lord Chief Justice, Lord Woolf, to express his reservations about the allegations of dishonesty and negligence brought against the Bank of England by the English liquidators of Bank of Credit and Commerce International SA (BCCI). The case, prosecuted by Lovells and defended by Freshfields Bruckhaus Deringer, collapsed spectacularly in 2005 after 12 years of litigation. Commentators immediately seized on the myriad contradictions, confusions and misdirections that dogged its progress, seeing them as endemic to a case unchecked by early intervention. There were also allegations that the courtroom conduct of the claimants' legal representatives was repellant and unnecessarily confrontational. It was as if the Civil Procedure Rules, aka the Woolf Reforms, designed to speed, smooth and minimise costs in litigation, had never happened...

Equitable Life

When Equitable Life, the world's oldest mutual insurer, dropped its long-running court action against Ernst & Young at the end of 2005, the auditors' barrister described it as "the biggest climbdown in English legal history." Barlow Lyde & Gilbert won praise for its representation of Ernst & Young and Allen & Overy attracted accolades for its performance on behalf of Equitable's six former non-executive directors, who were being personally sued by the Equitable. The case is viewed as the final nail in the coffin for multi million-pound speculative claims. While most commentators avoided the temptation of schadenfreude when discussing Herbert Smith's representation of Equitable – pointing out that, ultimately, a firm can only do as it is instructed – there was a general consensus that similar situations should be treated with greater circumspection in the future. The European Parliament has announced that it will investigate whether the British government did enough to protect Equitable Life policyholders, so we have yet to read the final chapter of this story.

litigation/dispute resolution (continued)

leading firms from Chambers UK 2007

Litigation: General Commercial (High Value)
London

[1] Clifford Chance LLP
Freshfields Bruckhaus Deringer
Herbert Smith LLP

[2] Lovells

[3] Allen & Overy LLP
Ashurst
Linklaters
Slaughter and May

[4] Baker & McKenzie LLP
Barlow Lyde & Gilbert
Norton Rose
Simmons & Simmons

[5] Clyde & Co
CMS Cameron McKenna LLP
Denton Wilde Sapte
Eversheds LLP
Mayer, Brown, Rowe & Maw LLP
Richards Butler LLP
SJ Berwin LLP

[6] Dechert LLP
Howrey LLP
Jones Day
Macfarlanes
Morgan Lewis
White & Case LLP

Litigation: General Commercial
Thames Valley

[1] Clarkslegal LLP Reading

[2] Boyes Turner Reading
Olswang Thames Valley Reading
Pitmans Reading
Shoosmiths Reading

[3] B P Collins Gerrards Cross
Iliffes Booth Bennett (IBB) Uxbridge
Matthew Arnold & Baldwin Watford

[4] Henmans Oxford
Manches LLP Oxford
Morgan Cole Oxford

Litigation: General Commercial (Mid-Market)
London

[1] Berwin Leighton Paisner LLP
Reynolds Porter Chamberlain LLP
Stephenson Harwood
Taylor Wessing

[2] Addleshaw Goddard LLP
DLA Piper UK LLP
Ince & Co
Kendall Freeman
Kirkpatrick & Lockhart Nicholson
Morgan Lewis
Nabarro Nathanson
Olswang
Pinsent Masons
Travers Smith

[3] Bird & Bird
Charles Russell LLP
Davies Arnold Cooper
Hammonds
Holman Fenwick & Willan
Lawrence Graham LLP
Lewis Silkin LLP
McDermott Will & Emery UK LLP
Memery Crystal
Mishcon de Reya
Salans
Watson, Farley & Williams

Litigation: General Commercial
The South: Kent & Sussex

[1] Cripps Harries Hall Tunbridge Wells

[2] asb law Crawley
DMH Stallard Brighton
Rawlison Butler Crawley
Thomas Eggar Crawley
Thomson Snell Tunbridge Wells

[3] Brachers Maidstone

Litigation: General Comm'l
The South: Surrey, Hampshire & Dorset

[1] Blake Lapthorn Linnell Portsmouth
Bond Pearce LLP Southampton
Clyde & Co Guildford

[2] Lester Aldridge Southampton
Stevens & Bolton LLP Guildford

[3] Charles Russell LLP Guildford
Shadbolt & Co LLP Reigate
Shoosmiths Fareham

[4] Clarke Willmott Southampton
Moore & Blatch Southampton
Paris Smith & Randall Southampton
Penningtons Solicitors Basingstoke

[5] Barlow Robbins Solicitors Guildford
Lamport Bassitt Southampton
Mundays LLP Cobham

Litigation: General Comm'l
South West: Bristol & Surround

[1] Burges Salmon LLP Bristol
Osborne Clarke Bristol

[2] Beachcroft LLP Bristol
Bevan Brittan LLP Bristol
Bond Pearce LLP Bristol
TLT Solicitors Bristol

[3] Charles Russell LLP Cheltenham
Clarke Willmott Bristol
Veale Wasbrough Lawyers Bristol

[4] Bevans Bristol
BPE Solicitors Cheltenham
Rickerbys Cheltenham

Litigation: General Comm'l
South West: Devon & Cornwall

[1] Ashfords Exeter
Bond Pearce LLP Exeter
Foot Anstey Exeter
Michelmores Exeter
Stephens & Scown Exeter

Litigation: General Commercial
Wales

1. **Eversheds LLP** *Cardiff*
   Geldards LLP *Cardiff*
   Hugh James *Cardiff*
2. **Morgan Cole** *Cardiff*
3. **Capital Law Commercial** *Cardiff Bay*

Litigation: General Commercial
West Midlands

1. **Wragge & Co LLP** *Birmingham*
2. **DLA Piper UK LLP** *Birmingham*
   Eversheds LLP *Birmingham*
   Pinsent Masons *Birmingham*
3. **Cobbetts LLP** *Birmingham*
   Hammonds *Birmingham*
   HBJ Gateley Wareing *Birmingham*
   Martineau Johnson *Birmingham*
4. **Anthony Collins** *Birmingham*
   Challinors *West Bromwich*
   George Green *Cradley Heath*
   KJD *Stoke-on-Trent*
   Moran & Co *Tamworth*
   Shakespeares *Birmingham*
5. **Clarke Willmott** *Birmingham*
   Sullivan & Co *Malvern*

Litigation: General Commercial
East Midlands

1. **Browne Jacobson LLP** *Nottingham*
   Eversheds LLP *Nottingham*
2. **Freeth Cartwright LLP** *Nottingham*
   Hewitsons *Northampton*
   Shoosmiths *Northampton*

Litigation: General Commercial
East Anglia

1. **Birketts** *Ipswich*
   Mills & Reeve *Cambridge*
2. **Eversheds LLP** *Cambridge*
   Hewitsons *Cambridge*
   Howes Percival *Norwich*
   Taylor Vinters *Cambridge*
3. **Ashton Graham** *Ipswich*
   Greenwoods Solicitors *Peterborough*
   Kester Cunningham John *Thetford*
   Prettys *Ipswich*
   Steeles (Law) LLP *Norwich*
   Wollastons *Chelmsford*

Litigation: General Commercial
North West

1. **Addleshaw Goddard LLP** *Manchester*
   DLA Piper UK LLP *Manchester*
   Halliwells LLP *Manchester*
   Pannone LLP *Manchester*
2. **Brabners Chaffe Street** *Liverpool*
   Cobbetts LLP *Manchester*
   DWF *Manchester*
   Eversheds LLP *Manchester*
   Hill Dickinson LLP *Liverpool*
3. **Beachcroft LLP** *Manchester*
   Hammonds *Manchester*
4. **Berg Legal** *Manchester*
   Keoghs *Bolton*
   Kuit Steinart Levy *Manchester*
   Mace & Jones *Manchester*
   Weightmans *Liverpool*

Insurance: Volume Claims
Best of the UK

1. **Beachcroft LLP**
   Berrymans Lace Mawer
2. **Davies Arnold Cooper**
   Fox Hartley
   Hill Dickinson LLP
   Keoghs
   Maclay Murray & Spens LLP
   Ricksons
   Wragge & Co LLP
3. **Brechin Tindal Oatts**
   Davies Lavery
   Eversheds LLP
   Halliwells LLP
   Hugh James
   Morgan Cole
   Robin Simon
   Weightmans

Insurance: General Claims
London

1. **Barlow Lyde & Gilbert** — Clyde & Co
2. **Allen & Overy LLP** — CMS Cameron McKenna LLP
   Freshfields Bruckhaus Deringer — Herbert Smith LLP
   Ince & Co — Reynolds Porter Chamberlain LLP
3. **Holman Fenwick & Willan** — Kendall Freeman
   Kennedys — Lovells
   Mayer, Brown, Rowe & Maw LLP — Simmons & Simmons
4. **Clifford Chance LLP** — Davies Arnold Cooper
   Norton Rose — Slaughter and May
5. **Beachcroft LLP** — Chadbourne & Parke
   Charles Russell LLP — Elborne Mitchell
   Eversheds LLP — Lawrence Graham LLP
   LeBoeuf, Lamb, Greene & MacRae — Pinsent Masons
   Steptoe & Johnson

Bet the company litigation

Herbert Smith
Barlow, Lyde & Gilbert
Cameron McKenna
Simmons & Simmons
Clifford Chance
Freshfields, Bruckhaus, Deringer

the civil courts of england and wales

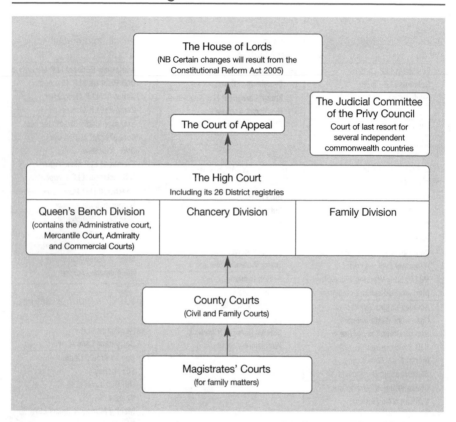

The House of Lords
(NB Certain changes will result from the
Constitutional Reform Act 2005)

The Court of Appeal

**The Judicial Committee
of the Privy Council**
Court of last resort for
several independent
commonwealth countries

The High Court
Including its 26 District registries

Queen's Bench Division	Chancery Division	Family Division
(contains the Administrative court, Mercantile Court, Admiralty and Commercial Courts)		

County Courts
(Civil and Family Courts)

Magistrates' Courts
(for family matters)

Other Specialist Courts

Employment Tribunals

Lands Tribunals

Leasehold Valuation Tribunals

VAT and Duties Tribunals

General and Special Commissioners (Tax)

Asylum & Immigration Tribunals

Europe

ECJ: Any UK court can refer a point of law for determination if it relates to EU law. The decision will be referred back to the court where the case originated.

European Court of Human Rights: Hears complaints regarding breaches of human rights.

www.chambersandpartners.co.uk

personal injury and clinical negligence

put simply

Personal injury and clinical negligence lawyers resolve claims brought by people who have been injured, either as a result of an accident or through flawed medical treatment. Injuries can be as simple as a broken wrist resulting from tripping over a paving stone, or as serious as a fatal illness caused by exposure to dangerous materials.

Clinical negligence cases could result from a failure to treat or diagnose a patient, or treatment going wrong. From bad boob jobs to the heartbreaking tragedy of brain-damaged babies, this can be an emotive area.

The claimant lawyer will usually act for one individual, but sometimes a claim may be brought by a group of people – this is called a class action or multiparty claim. The defendant lawyers will represent the party alleged to be responsible for the illness or injury. In most PI cases the claim against the defendant will be taken over by the defendant's insurance company who will then become the solicitor's client. Local authorities are common defendants for slips and trips, and employers end up on the hook for accidents in the workplace. In a majority of clinical negligence cases the defendant will be the NHS, although private medical practitioners or healthcare organisations are also sued.

who does what

claimant solicitors

- Determine the veracity of their client's claim and establish what they have suffered, including how much income they have lost and any expenses incurred.
- Examine medical records and piece together all the facts. Commission further medical reports.
- If the defendant doesn't make an acceptable offer of compensation, issue court proceedings.

defendant solicitors

- Try and avoid liability for their client and, if and when this looks unachievable, resolve the claim for as little as possible.
- Put all aspects of the case to the test. Perhaps the victim of a road traffic accident (RTA) wasn't wearing a seatbelt; perhaps the claimant has been malingering.

both solicitors

- Manage the progress of the case over a period of months, even years, following an established set of procedural rules.
- Attempt to settle the claim before trial.
- If a case goes to trial, brief a barrister and shepherd the client through the proceedings.

the realities of the job

- You can't be squeamish and must deal with medical issues and records.
- Claimant lawyers have face-to-face contact with large numbers of clients. Good people skills are needed.
- Defendant lawyers build long-term relationships with insurance companies.
- A large caseload, especially when dealing with lower-value claims.
- There is some scope for advocacy, although barristers are used for high-stakes or complicated hearings and trials. Solicitors appear at preliminary hearings and case management conferences.
- The work is driven by the procedural rules and timetable of the court.
- There is a mountain of paperwork to manage and produce, including witness statements and bundles of evidentiary material.

current issues

- Conditional Fee Agreements (CFAs) – commonly known as no-win, no-fee agreements – continue to be hotly debated. There were some changes made to the law in 2005 in an effort to simplify CFAs and make them more transparent, but these changes seem to have had little or no impact on claimants. Many solicitors dislike working on a no-win, no-fee basis because of the risk of not getting paid for work done, and they can find it hard to elicit appropriate payment agreements from insurance companies.

- You may have seen claims management companies – sometimes derided as claims farmers – advertising on the TV. They cause concern to lawyers because they are unregulated and often adopt unscrupulous tactics to win clients and claims. There continues to be a push for the regulation of such businesses, as illustrated by the Compensation Bill. The practice of claims farmers selling cases on to solicitors is under intense scrutiny.

- A number of claimant law firms, including several of the most well-known in the field, have come under fire for their part in the distribution of a £7 billion government-backed compensation scheme to sick miners. At least 45 solicitors have been referred to the Solicitors Disciplinary Tribunal.

- If companies such as Tesco and Sainsbury's enter the market for legal services they are likely to have a big impact.

- Opinion is split as to whether there is a growing compensation culture in Britain. Those who recognise one say CFAs must shoulder much of the blame; those who don't say that increased difficulties in securing legal aid have led to a reduction in the number of claims brought.

- Clin neg lawyers are concerned about the likely effects of the NHS Redress Bill. If it comes into force it will introduce a scheme allowing lower-value claims to be handled by the NHS without going to court. Obviously this would cut away some of the lawyers' bread-and-butter work.

leading firms from Chambers UK 2007

Personal Injury: Mainly Claimant
London

1. **Field Fisher Waterhouse LLP**
   Irwin Mitchell
   Leigh Day & Co
   Stewarts
2. **Anthony Gold**
   Rowley Ashworth
   Russell Jones & Walker
   Thompsons
3. **Hodge Jones & Allen**
   Iliffes Booth Bennett (IBB)
   O.H. Parsons & Partners
   Pattinson & Brewer
   Russell-Cooke
4. **Bindman & Partners**
   Bolt Burdon Kemp
   Levenes
   Prince Evans

Personal Injury: Mainly Defendant
London

1. **Barlow Lyde & Gilbert**
   Beachcroft LLP
   Berrymans Lace Mawer
2. **Greenwoods**
   Kennedys
3. **Davies Arnold Cooper**
   Davies Lavery
   Hextalls LLP
   Plexus Law
   Vizards Wyeth
4. **Badhams Law**
   Norton Rose
   Reynolds Porter Chamberlain LLP
   Watmores
   Weightmans

Personal Injury: Mainly Claimant
Thames Valley

1. **Boyes Turner** *Reading*
   Harris Cartier LLP *Slough*
   Henmans *Oxford*
   Osborne Morris *Leighton Buzzard*
   Thring Townsend *Swindon*
2. **Blake Lapthorn Linnell** *Oxford*
   Field Seymour Parkes *Reading*
   Pictons Solicitors LLP *Luton*

Personal Injury: Mainly Defendant
Thames Valley

1. **Henmans** *Oxford*
   Morgan Cole *Oxford*
2. **Eldridge & Co** *Oxford*
   Pitmans *Reading*
   Thring Townsend *Swindon*

Personal Injury: Mainly Claimant
The South

1. **Blake Lapthorn Linnell** *Southampton*
   George Ide, Phillips *Chichester*
   Lamport Bassitt *Southampton*
   Moore & Blatch *Southampton*
   Shoosmiths *Basingstoke*
2. **Coffin Mew & Clover** *Southampton*
   Colemans-ctts *Kingston-upon-Thames*
   DMH Stallard *Brighton*
   Penningtons Solicitors *Godalming*
   Thomson Snell *Tunbridge Wells*

Personal Injury: Mainly Defendant
The South

1. **Beachcroft LLP** *Winchester*
   Berrymans Lace *Southampton*
   Davies Lavery *Maidstone*
   Vizards Wyeth *Dartford*
2. **Bond Pearce LLP** *Southampton*
   Clarke Willmott *Southampton*
3. **Capital Law Insurance** *Fareham*
   Lamport Bassitt *Southampton*

Personal Injury: Mainly Claimant
South West

1. **Augustines Injury Law** *Bristol*
   Bond Pearce LLP *Plymouth*
   BPE Solicitors *Cheltenham*
   Clarke Willmott *Bristol*
   Lyons Davidson *Bristol*
   Thompsons *Bristol*
2. **Burroughs Day** *Bristol*
   David Gist Solicitors *Bristol*
   Rowley Ashworth *Exeter*
   Veitch Penny *Exeter*
   Withy King *Bath*

Personal Injury: Mainly Defendant
South West

1. **Beachcroft LLP** *Bristol*
2. **Bond Pearce LLP** *Bristol*
   CIP Solicitors *Bristol*
   Lyons Davidson *Bristol*
   Veitch Penny *Exeter*
3. **Bevan Brittan LLP** *Bristol*
   Morris Orman & Hearle *Cheltenham*
   Wansbroughs *Devizes*
4. **Foot Anstey** *Plymouth*
   Stephens & Scown *Exeter*

personal injury and clinical negligence (continued)

Personal Injury:
Mainly Claimant
Wales

1 **Hugh James** *Cardiff*

2 **John Collins & Partners** *Swansea*
Leo Abse & Cohen *Cardiff*
Russell Jones & Walker *Cardiff*
Thompsons *Cardiff*

3 **Loosemores** *Cardiff*
MLM *Cardiff*

Personal Injury:
Mainly Defendant
Wales

1 **Dolmans** *Cardiff*
Douglas-Jones Mercer *Swansea*
Hugh James *Cardiff*
Morgan Cole *Cardiff*

2 **Capital Law Insurance** *Cardiff Bay*
Cartwright Black Solicitors *Cardiff*
Eversheds LLP *Cardiff*

Personal Injury:
Mainly Claimant
Midlands

1 **Irwin Mitchell** *Birmingham*

2 **Barratt, Goff & Tomlinson** *Nottingham*
Freeth Cartwright LLP *Nottingham*
Rowley Ashworth *Birmingham*
Russell Jones & Walker *Birmingham*
Thompsons *Birmingham*

3 **Anthony Collins** *Birmingham*
Flint, Bishop & Barnett *Derby*
Higgs & Sons *Stourbridge*

Personal Injury:
Mainly Defendant
Midlands

1 **Beachcroft LLP** *Birmingham*
Berrymans Lace Mawer *Birmingham*
Browne Jacobson LLP *Nottingham*
Buller Jeffries *Birmingham*

2 **Davies Lavery** *Birmingham*
DLA Piper UK LLP *Birmingham*
Everatt & Company *Evesham*
Weightmans *Birmingham*

3 **Keoghs** *Coventry*
Wragge & Co LLP *Birmingham*

Personal Injury:
Mainly Claimant
East Anglia

1 **Kester Cunningham John** *Thetford*
Taylor Vinters *Cambridge*

2 **Ashton Graham** *Ipswich*
Edwards Duthie *Ilford*
Morgan Jones & Pett *Norwich*

Personal Injury:
Mainly Defendant
East Anglia

1 **Edwards Duthie** *Ilford*
Eversheds LLP *Ipswich*
Kennedys *Chelmsford*
Mills & Reeve *Norwich*
Prettys *Ipswich*

Personal Injury:
Mainly Claimant
North West

1 **Pannone LLP** *Manchester*

2 **Colemans-ctts** *Manchester*
Linder Myers *Manchester*
Mace & Jones *Liverpool*
McCool Patterson Hemsi *Manchester*
Potter Rees *Manchester*
Russell Jones & Walker *Manchester*
Thompsons *Liverpool*

Personal Injury:
Mainly Defendant
North West

1 **Beachcroft LLP** *Manchester*
Berrymans Lace Mawer *Liverpool*
Halliwells LLP *Manchester*

2 **DWF** *Liverpool*
Hill Dickinson LLP *Liverpool*
Horwich Farrelly *Manchester*
Keoghs *Bolton*
Ricksons *Manchester*
Weightmans *Liverpool*

Personal Injury:
Mainly Claimant
Yorkshire

1 **Irwin Mitchell** *Sheffield, Leeds*

2 **Keeble Hawson** *Sheffield*
Morrish & Co *Leeds*
Stewarts *Leeds*

3 **Ashton Morton Slack** *Sheffield*
Bridge McFarland Solicitors *Grimsby*
Langleys *York*
Pattinson & Brewer *York*
Rowley Ashworth *Leeds*
Russell Jones & Walker *Sheffield*
Walker Morris *Leeds*

Personal Injury:
Mainly Defendant
Yorkshire

[1] **Beachcroft LLP** *Leeds*
Berrymans Lace Mawer *Leeds*
DLA Piper UK LLP *Sheffield*
Irwin Mitchell *Sheffield*
Nabarro Nathanson *Sheffield*
[2] **Ford & Warren** *Leeds*
Halliwells LLP *Sheffield*
Langleys *York*
Praxis Partners *Leeds*

Personal Injury:
Mainly Claimant
North East

[1] **Thompsons** *Newcastle upon Tyne*
[2] **Browell Smith** *Newcastle upon Tyne*
Irwin Mitchell *Newcastle upon Tyne*
Marrons *Newcastle upon Tyne*
Sintons *Newcastle upon Tyne*
[3] **Gorman** *Newcastle upon Tyne*
Hay & Kilner *Newcastle upon Tyne*
Russell Jones *Newcastle upon Tyne*

Personal Injury:
Mainly Defendant
North East

[1] **Berrymans Lace** *Stockton on Tees*
Eversheds LLP *Newcastle upon Tyne*
Sintons *Newcastle upon Tyne*
[2] **Crutes Law Firm** *Newcastle upon Tyne*
Hay & Kilner *Newcastle upon Tyne*

Clinical Negligence:
Mainly Defendant
Best of the UK

[1] **Barlow Lyde & Gilbert**
Capsticks
Hempsons
[2] **Bevan Brittan LLP**
Eversheds LLP
Hill Dickinson LLP
Kennedys
Weightmans
[3] **Beachcroft LLP**
Berrymans Lace Mawer
Browne Jacobson LLP
Mills & Reeve
RadcliffesLeBrasseur
Trowers & Hamlins
Ward Hadaway
[4] **Brachers**
DLA Piper UK LLP
Reynolds Porter Chamberlain

Clinical Negligence:
Mainly Claimant
London

[1] **Field Fisher Waterhouse LLP**
Irwin Mitchell
Leigh Day & Co
[2] **Charles Russell LLP**
Kingsley Napley
Parlett Kent
Russell-Cooke
Stewarts
[3] **Anthony Gold**
Bindman & Partners
McMillan Williams
Pattinson & Brewer

Clinical Negligence:
Mainly Claimant
Thames Valley

[1] **Boyes Turner** *Reading*
Harris Cartier LLP *Slough*
[2] **Henmans** *Oxford*
Osborne Morris *Leighton Buzzard*

Clinical Negligence:
Mainly Claimant
The South

[1] **Blake Lapthorn Linnell** *Portsmouth*
Penningtons *Godalming, Basingstoke*
Thomson Snell *Tunbridge Wells*
[2] **Coffin Mew & Clover** *Fareham*
George Ide, Phillips *Chichester*
Moore & Blatch *Southampton*
Wynne Baxter *Brighton*

Clinical Negligence:
Mainly Claimant
South West

[1] **Barcan Woodward** *Bristol*
Parlett Kent *Exeter*
[2] **Bond Pearce LLP** *Bristol*
Clarke Willmott *Bristol*
Foot Anstey *Plymouth*
John Hodge *Weston-super-Mare*
Michelmores *Exeter*
Russell Jones & Walker *Bristol*
Withy King *Bath*

Clinical Negligence:
Mainly Claimant
Wales

[1] **Harding Evans** *Newport*
Hugh James *Cardiff*
Huttons *Cardiff*
John Collins & Partners *Swansea*

personal injury and clinical negligence (continued)

Clinical Negligence:
Mainly Claimant
Midlands

[1] **Anthony Collins** *Birmingham*
Challinors *Birmingham*
Freeth Cartwright LLP *Nottingham*
Irwin Mitchell *Birmingham*
[2] **Brindley Twist Tafft** *Coventry*

Clinical Negligence:
Mainly Claimant
East Anglia

[1] **Gadsby Wicks** *Chelmsford*
Kester Cunningham John *Thetford*
[2] **Attwater & Liell** *Harlow*
Morgan Jones & Pett *Norwich*
Scrivenger Seabrook *St Neots*

Clinical Negligence:
Mainly Claimant
North West

[1] **Irwin Mitchell** *Manchester*
Pannone LLP *Manchester*
[2] **EAD Solicitors** *Liverpool*
JMW Solicitors *Manchester*
McCool Patterson Hemsi *Manchester*
[3] **Donns Solicitors** *Manchester*
Lees & Partners *Birkenhead*
Linder Myers *Manchester*
Maxwell Gillott *Lancaster*
Walker Smith Way Solicitors *Chester*

Clinical Negligence:
Mainly Claimant
Yorkshire

[1] **Irwin Mitchell** *Sheffield*
[2] **Heptonstalls LLP** *Goole*
Lester Morrill *Leeds*

Clinical Negligence:
Mainly Claimant
North East

[1] **Ben Hoare Bell** *Sunderland*
Hay & Kilner *Newcastle upon Tyne*
Irwin Mitchell *Newcastle upon Tyne*
Peter Maughan & Co *Gateshead*
Samuel Phillips *Newcastle upon Tyne*

private client & charities

put simply

You have money. Perhaps a mountain of cash or maybe a carefully accumulated nest-egg, but either way you need to know how best to control it, store it and pass it on: enter the private client lawyer. Solicitors in this field advise individuals, families and trusts on wealth management; whilst some offer additional matrimonial and small-scale commercial capability, others focus exclusively on highly specialised tax and trusts, or wills and probate.

Whether it's for a multinational organisation such as the Red Cross, or for a slightly more local concern such as The Whitley Bay Fund for Disadvantaged Minors, specialised charities lawyers advise on all aspects of a not-for-profit organisation's activities.

who does what

private client lawyers

○ Draft wills in consultation with clients and expedite the implementation of wills after death. Probate involves the appointment of an executor and the settling of an estate. Organising a house clearance or even a funeral is not beyond the scope of a lawyer's duties.

○ Advise clients on the most tax-efficient and appropriate structure for holding money. If trusts are held in an offshore jurisdiction, lawyers must ensure their clients understand the foreign law implications.

○ Advise overseas clients interested in investing in the UK, and banks whose overseas clients have UK interests.

○ Assist clients with the very specific licensing, sales arrangement and tax planning issues related to ownership of heritage chattels (individual items or collections of cultural value or significance).

charities lawyers

○ Advise charities on registration, reorganisation, regulatory compliance (such as Charities Commission investigations) and the implications of new legislation.

○ Offer specialist trusts and investment expertise.

○ Advise on quasi-corporate and mainstream commercial matters; negotiate and draft contracts for sponsorship and the development of trading subsidiaries; manage property issues and handle IP concerns.

○ Charities law still conjures up images of sleepy local fundraising efforts or, alternatively, working on a trendy project for wealthy benefactors. In the wide middle ground you could be working with a local authority, a local library and four schools to establish an after-school homework programme, or you could rewrite the constitution of a 300-year-old church school to admit female pupils. Widespread international trust in British charity law means that you could also establish a study programme in Britain for a US university, or negotiate the formation of a zebra conservation charity in Tanzania.

the realities of the job

○ An interest in other people's affairs is helpful. A capacity for empathy, coupled with impartiality and absolute discretion are the hallmarks of a good private client lawyer. Whether it's little old ladies with their savings in a stocking, well-heeled, excessively moneyed City gents, or fabulously flash celebrities, you'll need to be able to relate to and earn the trust of your clients.

○ Despite not being as helter-skelter as some fields, the technical demands of private client work can be exacting and an academic streak certainly goes a long way, especially when it comes to tax and accounts matters.

○ An eye for detail and a rigorous approach will

help you see through the mire of black letter law (and regular new legislation) so as to spot the loopholes and clever solutions that will save your clients most money.

- The 'green wellies, two smelly Labradors and a 1950s Land Rover' stereotype of the typical client is far from accurate: lottery wins, property portfolios, massive City salaries and successful businesses all feed the demand for legal advice.

- The combination of practical, technical and social skills means it is a testing discipline. If you are wavering between private clients and commercial clients, charities law might offer a nice balance.

current issues

- HMRC is clamping down on tax avoidance and the role trusts can play in inheritance tax planning. Ever-increasing property values mean that, on death, more and more little old ladies' assets are getting caught in a net really intended to catch bad guys. Many firms are now preparing to review their will banks, a huge job for those that are holding thousands of them.

- A Charities Bill is currently held up in the House of Commons, following its successful trip through the Lords in 2005. Charity lawyers are frustrated at the delay, but are for the most part anticipating a Bill that will clarify and simplify the registrations and incorporations of new charities.

- A new trend in charities law is the increasing involvement of charities and social enterprise groups in non-core local public services like leisure, community transport and childcare provision. In July 2005 the Community Interest Company was established to bridge the gap and enable these joint venture projects.

- Firms right across the country bemoan a dearth of young lawyers who can claim to be true private client specialists. It looks like a good time to put your hand up and be counted!

leading firms from Chambers UK 2007

Trusts & Personal Tax
London
1. Macfarlanes
   Withers LLP
2. Allen & Overy LLP
   Baker & McKenzie LLP
   Boodle Hatfield
   Charles Russell LLP
   Forsters LLP
   Lawrence Graham LLP
   Speechly Bircham
   Taylor Wessing
3. Berwin Leighton Paisner LLP
   Bircham Dyson Bell
   Currey & Co
   Farrer & Co
   Harcus Sinclair
   Hunters
   Payne Hicks Beach
4. Collyer Bristow LLP
   Herbert Smith LLP
   Howard Kennedy
   Lee & Pembertons
   Linklaters
   Penningtons Solicitors LLP
   RadcliffesLeBrasseur
   Trowers & Hamlins
   Wedlake Bell
5. Davenport Lyons
   Dawsons Solicitors
   Harbottle & Lewis LLP
   Smyth Barkham

Trusts & Personal Tax:
Contentious
London
1. Allen & Overy LLP
   Baker & McKenzie LLP
   Herbert Smith LLP
   Withers LLP
2. Berwin Leighton Paisner LLP
   Boodle Hatfield
   Charles Russell LLP
   Harcus Sinclair
   Lawrence Graham LLP
   Macfarlanes
   Speechly Bircham
3. Clifford Chance LLP
   Laytons
   Taylor Wessing
4. Norton Rose

Trusts & Personal Tax
Thames Valley
1. B P Collins *Gerrards Cross*
   Boodle Hatfield *Oxford*
   Henmans *Oxford*
   Penningtons Solicitors *Newbury*
2. Blandy & Blandy *Reading*
   Boyes Turner *Reading*
3. Clarkslegal LLP *Reading*
   Field Seymour Parkes *Reading*
   Iliffes Booth Bennett (IBB) *Uxbridge*
   Matthew Arnold & Baldwin *Watford*

Trusts & Personal Tax
The South
1. Cripps Harries Hall *Tunbridge Wells*
   Thomas Eggar *Chichester, Crawley*
2. Adams & Remers *Lewes*
   Blake Lapthorn Linnell *Winchester*
   Charles Russell LLP *Guildford*
   Lester Aldridge *Bournemouth*
   Penningtons Solicitors *Godalming*
   Stevens & Bolton LLP *Guildford*
   Thomson Snell *Tunbridge Wells*
3. Brachers *Maidstone*
   DMH Stallard *Brighton*
   Godwins *Winchester*
   Lamport Bassitt *Southampton*
   Moore & Blatch *Lymington*
   Mundays LLP *Cobham*
   Paris Smith & Randall *Southampton*
   Rawlison Butler *Horsham*
   Whitehead Monckton *Maidstone*

Trusts & Personal Tax
South West
1. Burges Salmon LLP *Bristol*
   Wilsons *Salisbury*
2. Charles Russell LLP *Cheltenham*
   Clarke Willmott *Bristol*
   Michelmores *Exeter*
   Osborne Clarke *Bristol*
   Wiggin Osborne *Cheltenham*
3. Ashfords *Exeter*
   Coodes *St Austell*
   Foot Anstey *Plymouth*
   Hooper & Wollen *Torquay*
   Rickerbys *Cheltenham*
   Thring Townsend *Bristol*
   Veale Wasbrough Lawyers *Bristol*
4. TLT Solicitors *Bristol*

private client & charities (continued)

Trusts & Personal Tax
Wales

[1] **Geldards LLP** *Cardiff*
Hugh James *Cardiff*
[2] **Margraves** *Llandrindod Wells*

Trusts & Personal Tax
Midlands

[1] **Browne Jacobson LLP** *Nottingham*
Hewitsons *Northampton*
Martineau Johnson *Birmingham*
[2] **Higgs & Sons** *Brierley Hill*
Lodders *Stratford-upon-Avon*
Mills & Reeve *Birmingham*
[3] **Cobbetts LLP** *Birmingham*
Freeth Cartwright LLP *Nottingham*
[4] **Geldards LLP** *Derby*
Hallmarks *Worcester*
HBJ Gateley Wareing *Birmingham*
Pinsent Masons *Birmingham*
Shakespeares *Birmingham*

Trusts & Personal Tax
East Anglia

[1] **Hewitsons** *Cambridge*
Mills & Reeve *Norwich*
Taylor Vinters *Cambridge*
[2] **Birketts** *Ipswich*
Greene & Greene *Bury St Edmunds*
Howes Percival *Norwich*
[3] **Barker Gotelee** *Ipswich*
hc solicitors llp *Peterborough*
Roythornes *Spalding*
Willcox & Lewis *Norwich*
[4] **Ashton Graham** *Ipswich*
Cozens-Hardy & Jewson *Norwich*
Hansells *Norwich*
Hood Vores & Allwood *Dereham*
Kester Cunningham John *Cambridge*
Prettys *Ipswich*
Stanley Tee *Bishop's Stortford*
Wollastons *Chelmsford*

Trusts & Personal Tax
North West

[1] **Addleshaw Goddard** *Manchester*
[2] **Birch Cullimore** *Chester*
Brabners Chaffe Street *Liverpool*
Cobbetts LLP *Manchester*
Halliwells LLP *Manchester*
Hill Dickinson LLP *Liverpool*
Pannone LLP *Manchester*

Trusts & Personal Tax
North East

[1] **Dickinson Dees** *Newcastle upon Tyne*
Wrigleys *Leeds*
[2] **Addleshaw Goddard LLP** *Leeds*
Andrew M Jackson *Hull*
Gordons *Leeds*
Rollits *Hull, York*
[3] **Grays** *York*
Irwin Mitchell *Sheffield*
Lupton Fawcett LLP *Leeds*
McCormicks *Leeds*
Ward Hadaway *Newcastle upon Tyne*
Watson Burton *Newcastle upon Tyne*

Charities
Best of the UK
[1] **Bates Wells & Braithwaite**
Farrer & Co
Stone King LLP
[2] **Bircham Dyson Bell**
Withers LLP
[3] **Blake Lapthorn Linnell**
Charles Russell LLP
Russell-Cooke
Wilsons
[4] **Allen & Overy LLP**
Berwin Leighton Paisner LLP
Dickinson Dees
Harbottle & Lewis LLP
Hempsons
Herbert Smith LLP
Lawrence Graham LLP
RadcliffesLeBrasseur
Speechly Bircham
Trowers & Hamlins
Wrigleys
[5] **Addleshaw Goddard LLP**
Devonshires
Gordon Dadds
Howard Kennedy
Macfarlanes
Mills & Reeve
Winckworth Sherwood

Charities
Thames Valley
[1] **Blake Lapthorn Linnell** *Oxford*
Henmans *Oxford*
[2] **B P Collins** *Gerrards Cross*
BrookStreet Des Roches LLP *Witney*
Iliffes Booth Bennett *Ingatestone*
Manches LLP *Oxford*
Morgan Cole *Oxford*
Winckworth Sherwood *Oxford*

Charities
The South
[1] **Blake Lapthorn Linnell** *Fareham*
[2] **Cripps Harries Hall** *Tunbridge Wells*
Griffith Smith *Brighton*
Lester Aldridge *Bournemouth*
Thomas Eggar *Chichester*
[3] **DMH Stallard** *Brighton*
Thomson Snell *Tunbridge Wells*

Charities
Midlands
[1] **Anthony Collins** *Birmingham*
Martineau Johnson *Birmingham*
[2] **Band Hatton** *Coventry*
Cobbetts LLP *Birmingham*
Mills & Reeve *Birmingham*
[3] **Pinsent Masons** *Birmingham*

Charities
East Anglia
[1] **Hewitsons** *Cambridge*
Mills & Reeve *Norwich*
Taylor Vinters *Cambridge*
[2] **Hegarty LLP Solicitors** *Peterborough*

Charities
North West
[1] **Addleshaw Goddard LLP** *Manchester*
Lane-Smith & Shindler *Manchester*
[2] **Birch Cullimore** *Chester*
Blackhurst Swainson *Preston*
Brabners Chaffe Street *Liverpool*
Bremners Solicitors *Liverpool*
Cobbetts LLP *Manchester*
Kuit Steinart Levy *Manchester*

Charities
North East
[1] **Dickinson Dees** *Newcastle upon Tyne*
Wrigleys *Leeds*
[2] **Addleshaw Goddard LLP** *Leeds*
McCormicks *Leeds*
Rollits *York*
[3] **Irwin Mitchell** *Sheffield*
Robert Muckle *Newcastle upon Tyne*
Ward Hadaway *Newcastle upon Tyne*
Watson Burton *Newcastle upon Tyne*

property/real estate

put simply

Students often tell us that land law lectures bore them, confuse them and provoke a deep-seated loathing for the subject. Many new trainees would rather stick pins in their eyes than take a seat in real estate, but thankfully it's a different story once they've experienced it in practice...

Property lawyers are essentially transactional lawyers whose jobs are fairly similar to those of their corporate law colleagues. The only real difference is that real estate deals require an extra layer of specialist legal and procedural knowledge. At university and law school you learn a lot about the law but little about what it's like to do a deal. That tangible nature of the subject matter is hard to envisage from the lecture theatre, but immediately evident from the first day in the office. The work centres on actual buildings and land – cinemas, supermarkets, churches, million-pound mansions, farms, factories – imagine Cribs meets Restoration with a load of paperwork. Even the most oblique legal concepts have a bricks-and-mortar or human basis to them; for example, you can physically see and touch a right of way or a flying freehold.

It is common for lawyers to develop a specialism – residential conveyancing, mortgage lending and property finance, development projects, retail or office leasing, social housing, agricultural land, and the leisure and hotels sector are some examples. Most firms have a property department, and the larger the department the more likely the lawyers are to specialise.

If you're wondering what the difference between 'property' and 'real estate' is, don't trouble yourself any further. Real estate is just a newer name that's migrated over here from the USA, and it doesn't matter which term a firm adopts.

who does what

The busy schedule of a property lawyer will include the following activities:

- Negotiating sales, purchases and leases of land and buildings, and advising on the structure of deals. Recording the terms of an agreement in legal documents.
- Gathering and analysing factual information about properties from the owners, surveyors, local authorities and the Land Registry.
- Preparing reports for buyers and anyone lending money.
- Managing the transfer of money and the handover of properties to new owners or occupiers.
- Taking the appropriate steps to register new owners and protect the interests of lenders or investors.
- Advising clients on their responsibilities in leasehold relationships, and how to take action if problems arise, eg non-payment of rent or disrepair.
- Helping developers get all the necessary permissions to build, alter or change the permitted use of properties.

the realities of the job

- Real estate lawyers have to multi-task. A single deal could involve many hundreds of properties; a filing cabinet could contain many hundreds of files, all of them at a different stage in the process.
- Because the work is so paper-based you must be well organised.
- Good drafting skills require attention to detail and careful thought. Plus you need to keep up to date with industry trends and standards, and you really need to know the law.
- Some clients get stressed and frustrated; you have to be able to explain legal problems in lay terms.
- There will be site visits, but this is a desk job with a lot of time spent on the phone to other solicitors, estate agents, civil servants and technical consultants.

- Most instances of solicitor negligence occur in this area of practice. There is so much that can go wrong.
- Your days will be busy, but generally the hours are predictable; you'll rarely be called into a meeting in the wee hours.
- If you want to write threatening letters – forget it! Property transactions require a collaborative approach from all concerned.

current issues

- The increasing sophistication of real estate in the UK means more deals involve complex funds or joint ventures. It is not uncommon for high-value deals to be structured as corporate transactions, so that a buyer can acquire a company that owns property rather than the property itself.
- A lack of UK property for investors (domestic and overseas) to target has encouraged the development of more sites for resale at a profit. While there is definitely more interest in investment and development, investors are getting bored of paying silly money for UK property when they could get a better deal elsewhere, say in Germany, France or the Eastern Bloc.
- The domestic and European hotels and leisure sector has witnessed an increasing amount of consolidation, and there is a lot of money chasing the best-performing assets. Some of the largest deals of the past year have been in this sector, including the sale of Inter-Continental Hotels' Holiday Inn portfolio and the acquisition of Whitbread's UK hotel portfolio by a Whitbread/Marriott joint venture company.
- Urban regeneration projects feature high on the agenda, as do Olympic preparations.
- New on the scene are Real Estate Investment Trusts (REITs), originally developed in the USA and useful as a means of channelling investment into real estate.
- Law firms have experienced growth in income from real estate and many are undergoing recruitment drives as a result.
- Procedures are becoming increasingly streamlined and managed electronically.

property/real estate (continued)

leading firms from Chambers UK 2007

Real Estate: Big-Ticket
London

[1] Berwin Leighton Paisner LLP
Clifford Chance LLP
Linklaters

[2] Ashurst
Herbert Smith LLP
Lovells
Nabarro Nathanson
SJ Berwin LLP

[3] CMS Cameron McKenna LLP
Freshfields Bruckhaus Deringer
Macfarlanes
Slaughter and May

[4] Allen & Overy LLP
DLA Piper UK LLP
Lawrence Graham LLP
Olswang

[5] Dechert LLP
Denton Wilde Sapte
Eversheds LLP
Jones Day
Mayer, Brown, Rowe & Maw LLP
Norton Rose
Simmons & Simmons

[6] Addleshaw Goddard LLP
Forsters LLP
Travers Smith

Real Estate
West Midlands

[1] Eversheds LLP *Birmingham*
Wragge & Co LLP *Birmingham*

[2] DLA Piper UK LLP *Birmingham*
Hammonds *Birmingham*
Pinsent Masons *Birmingham*

[3] Cobbetts LLP *Birmingham*
HBJ Gateley Wareing *Birmingham*
Shoosmiths *Northampton*

[4] Higgs & Sons *Brierley Hill*
Knight & Sons *Newcastle-under-Lyme*
Martineau Johnson *Birmingham*
Reed Smith *Coventry*
Wright Hassall *Leamington Spa*

Real Estate:
Mainly Mid-Market
London

[1] Addleshaw Goddard LLP
Eversheds LLP
Forsters LLP
Taylor Wessing
Travers Smith

[2] Boodle Hatfield
Clyde & Co
Field Fisher Waterhouse LLP
Maxwell Batley
Richards Butler LLP
Speechly Bircham
Wragge & Co LLP ·

[3] Davies Arnold Cooper
Farrer & Co
Finers Stephens Innocent
Fladgate Fielder
Howard Kennedy
Kirkpatrick & Lockhart Nicholson
Lewis Silkin LLP
Manches LLP
Mishcon de Reya
Osborne Clarke

[4] Bird & Bird
Hammonds
Harbottle & Lewis LLP
Penningtons Solicitors LLP
Reed Smith
Trowers & Hamlins

[5] Dundas & Wilson
Halliwells LLP
Jeffrey Green Russell
McGrigors
Salans
Shepherd and Wedderburn
Stephenson Harwood
Wallace LLP
Wedlake Bell

Real Estate: Hotels & Leisure
London

[1] Berwin Leighton Paisner LLP
Clifford Chance LLP

[2] CMS Cameron McKenna LLP
Freshfields Bruckhaus Deringer
SJ Berwin LLP

[3] Allen & Overy LLP
Davies Arnold Cooper
Denton Wilde Sapte
Field Fisher Waterhouse LLP
Fladgate Fielder
Linklaters
Lovells
Richards Butler LLP

[4] Davenport Lyons
DLA Piper UK LLP
Douglas Wignall & Co
Gibson, Dunn & Crutcher LLP
Herbert Smith LLP
Paul, Hastings, Janofsky & Walker
Stephenson Harwood
Taylor Wessing
Wragge & Co LLP

Real Estate
East Midlands

[1] Browne Jacobson LLP *Nottingham*
Eversheds LLP *Nottingham*
Freeth Cartwright LLP *Nottingham*

[2] Geldards LLP *Derby*
Harvey Ingram LLP *Leicester*
Shoosmiths *Nottingham*

[3] Berryman *Nottingham*

Real Estate
North East

[1] Dickinson Dees *Newcastle upon Tyne*

[2] Eversheds LLP *Newcastle upon Tyne*

[3] Robert Muckle *Newcastle upon Tyne*
Ward Hadaway *Newcastle upon Tyne*
Watson Burton *Newcastle upon Tyne*

[4] Hay & Kilner *Newcastle upon Tyne*
Sintons *Newcastle upon Tyne*

www.chambersandpartners.co.uk

solicitors

Real Estate
The South

[1] **Blake Lapthorn Linnell** *Portsmouth*
Bond Pearce LLP *Southampton*
Clyde & Co *Guildford*
Cripps Harries Hall *Tunbridge Wells*
[2] **DMH Stallard** *Crawley*
Paris Smith & Randall *Southampton*
Shoosmiths *Fareham*
Stevens & Bolton LLP *Guildford*
Thomas Eggar *Chichester*
[3] **Charles Russell LLP** *Guildford*
Clarke Willmott *Southampton*
Mundays LLP *Cobham*
Rawlison Butler *Crawley*
Thomson Snell *Tunbridge Wells*
[4] **asb law** *Crawley*
Brachers *Maidstone*
Coffin Mew & Clover *Southampton*
GCL Solicitors *Guildford*
Lamport Bassitt *Southampton*
Lester Aldridge *Bournemouth*
Penningtons Solicitors *Basingstoke*
[5] **Clarkson Wright & Jakes** *Orpington*
Laytons *Guildford*
Moore & Blatch *Southampton*
Shadbolt & Co LLP *Reigate*
Steele Raymond *Bournemouth*

Real Estate
North West

[1] **Addleshaw Goddard LLP** *Manchester*
DLA Piper UK *Liverpool, Manchester*
Eversheds LLP *Manchester*
[2] **Cobbetts LLP** *Manchester*
Halliwells LLP *Liverpool, Manchester*
Hammonds *Manchester*
Hill Dickinson LLP *Liverpool*
[3] **Beachcroft LLP** *Manchester*
Brabners Chaffe Street *Liverpool*
DWF *Liverpool, Manchester*
Land Law *Altrincham*
Mace & Jones *Manchester*
Pannone LLP *Manchester*
[4] **JMW Solicitors** *Manchester*
Pinsent Masons *Manchester*

Real Estate
South West

[1] **Burges Salmon LLP** *Bristol*
[2] **Beachcroft LLP** *Bristol*
Bevan Brittan LLP *Bristol*
Bond Pearce LLP *Plymouth*
Clarke Willmott *Bristol*
Davitt Jones Bould *Taunton*
Michelmores *Exeter*
Osborne Clarke *Bristol*
TLT Solicitors *Bristol*
[3] **Ashfords** *Exeter*
BPE Solicitors *Cheltenham*
Charles Russell LLP *Cheltenham*
Foot Anstey *Plymouth*
Rickerbys *Cheltenham*
Stephens & Scown *Exeter*
Veale Wasbrough Lawyers *Bristol*
[4] **Davies and Partners** *Gloucester*
Thring Townsend *Swindon*
Withy King *Bath*

Real Estate
Yorkshire

[1] **Addleshaw Goddard LLP** *Leeds*
DLA Piper UK LLP *Leeds, Sheffield*
Walker Morris *Leeds*
[2] **Eversheds LLP** *Leeds*
Pinsent Masons *Leeds*
[3] **Cobbetts LLP** *Leeds*
Hammonds *Leeds*
Nabarro Nathanson *Sheffield*
[4] **Andrew M Jackson** *Hull*
Gordons *Leeds*
[5] **Beachcroft LLP** *Leeds*
Gosschalks *Hull*
Irwin Mitchell *Sheffield*
Keeble Hawson *Sheffield*
Lupton Fawcett LLP *Leeds*
Rollits *Hull*
Shulmans *Leeds*
[6] **Denison Till** *York*
Langleys *York*
McCormicks *Leeds*
Wake Smith *Sheffield*

Real Estate
Wales

[1] **Eversheds LLP** *Cardiff*
Geldards LLP *Cardiff*
[2] **Berry Smith Solicitors** *Cardiff*
M & A Solicitors LLP *Cardiff*
Morgan Cole *Cardiff*
[3] **Hugh James** *Cardiff*
Morgan LaRoche Ltd *Swansea*
[4] **Capital Law Commercial** *Cardiff Bay*
Dolmans *Cardiff*
Harding Evans *Newport*

Real Estate
East Anglia

[1] **Birketts** *Ipswich*
Eversheds LLP *Cambridge*
Hewitsons *Cambridge*
Mills & Reeve *Cambridge*
Taylor Vinters *Cambridge*
[2] **Ashton Graham** *Bury St Edmunds*
Greene & Greene *Bury St Edmunds*
Greenwoods Solicitors *Peterborough*
Kester Cunningham John *Cambridge*
Prettys *Ipswich*
[3] **Leathes Prior** *Norwich*
Thomson Webb *Cambridge*

Real Estate
Thames Valley

[1] **Pitmans** *Reading*
[2] **Blake Lapthorn Linnell** *Oxford*
Boyes Turner *Reading*
BrookStreet Des Roches LLP *Witney*
Denton Wilde Sapte *Milton Keynes*
[3] **Clarkslegal LLP** *Reading*
Field Seymour Parkes *Reading*
Harold Benjamin *Harrow*
Iliffes Booth Bennett (IBB) *Uxbridge*
Manches LLP *Oxford*
Matthew Arnold & Baldwin *Watford*
Olswang Thames Valley *Reading*
Penningtons Solicitors LLP *Newbury*
Shoosmiths *Reading*
[4] **B P Collins** *Gerrards Cross*
Blandy & Blandy *Reading*
Owen White *Slough*
Pictons Solicitors LLP *Luton*

human rights put simply

You know the kind of film where a crack team of secret operatives unites to save the world from government conspiracy or alien invasion, while average Joe Public carries on his everyday life blissfully unaware of any danger? Traditionally lawyers in this field are not dissimilar: they work long and unsociable hours to protest injustice enshrined in law and to fight for principle where most of us would offer little more than a pragmatic sigh, if we noticed a problem at all.

That said, events of the past few years have projected public interest issues to the forefront of national consciousness and brought concepts such as freedom of speech or movement to the top of the political agenda: the war in Iraq and its fallout; the War on Terror; extraordinary renditions; Guantánamo Bay; evidence gathered under torture; bombings in London; persecution of ethnic or religious minorities; ID cards; new arrest and detention laws; cartoons defaming religious figures and counter-protests inciting religious hatred. All these have put the relationship between the state and the individual under the magnifying glass, divided public opinion and had major implications in terms of legal challenges to new legislation and its impact on human rights.

Human rights cases invariably relate in some way to the UK's ratification of the European Convention on Human Rights through the Human Rights Act 1998 (HRA). Cases crop up in criminal and civil contexts, often through the medium of judicial review, a key tool by which decisions of public bodies can be questioned. Civil contexts could include claims regarding the right to education or community care under the Mental Health Act, cases of discrimination at work or, because the Act enshrines in law the right to family life, even family issues. Criminal contexts could relate to complaints against the police, prisoners' issues, public order convictions arising out of demonstrations, or perhaps extradition on terror charges. The raft of recent legislation spanning terrorism, security, religious tolerance and antisocial behaviour has intersected with the HRA and the Public Order Acts to create a whole new range of cases and issues. In one prominent case brought by Liberty in late 2005, the House of Lords ruled that evidence gained through torture in other jurisdictions is inadmissible in UK courts. Another instance saw the government and several police forces threatened with judicial review unless they investigated UK involvement in CIA extraordinary rendition flights via airports including Biggin Hill and Brize Norton.

immigration law put simply

This is an area that arouses considerable public and political interest. Lawyers deal with both business and personal immigration matters, the former having been embraced by the present government in its quest to manage economic migration. In this more lucrative area, lawyers assist highly skilled migrants obtain residency or leave to remain in the UK, and help non-nationals to secure visas for travel abroad. They also work with companies that need to bring in employees from overseas.

With issues of asylum and people seeking permission to stay in the UK on human rights grounds never out of the tabloid newspapers, this side of the immigration field is a hot potato. Lawyers represent individuals who have fled persecution in their country of origin, and for whom return could mean death or torture; they also take on cases for people whose right to stay in the UK is under threat or indeed entirely absent. Because changes in the public funding of such cases have left the area uneconomical to practise, there has been a reduction in the number of firms offering such services.

who does what

human rights lawyers:

- Advise clients (predominantly individuals but sometimes groups in class actions) on how to appeal a decision made or action taken by a public body, whether an institution such as the police, a local authority, a court, or a branch of government.
- Collect evidence, take witness statements, prepare cases and instruct barristers.
- Pursue cases through the procedural stages necessary to achieve the desired result. The final port of call for some human rights cases is the European Court of Justice (ECJ) so lawyers need to be fully conversant with both UK law and European law.

business immigration lawyers:

- Advise and assist businesses or their employees on work permits and visas. They need to be fully conversant with all current schemes such as those for highly skilled migrants and investors.
- Prepare for, attend and advocate at tribunals or court hearings, where necessary instructing a barrister to do so.

personal immigration lawyers:

- Advise clients on their status and rights within the UK, ascertaining which is the most advantageous line of argument for their client to run.
- Secure evidence of a client's identity, medical reports and witness statements and prepare cases for court hearings or appeals. Represent clients at these hearings or instruct a barrister to do so.
- Handle an immense amount of unremunerated form filling and legal aid paperwork.

the realities of the job

- Vocation, vocation, vocation: a commitment to and belief in the values you're fighting for are essential because salaries in this field are considerably lower than in most other areas of law. Working in the voluntary sector for orgnisations such as the Refugee Council, or taking on important cases pro bono, can provide the greatest satisfaction.
- Sensitivity, empathy and sympathy are absolutely essential qualities because you'll often be dealing with highly emotional people, those with mental health issues or those who simply don't appreciate the full extent of their legal predicament. Whether it's an immigration case involving flight from an oppressive regime or an abuse in police custody matter, you'll need a keen eye for the truth, shrewd judgement and the facility for getting the right information from clients who may not be the most reliable or stable sources.
- Strong analytical skills are required to pick out the legal issues you can change from the socio-economic ones beyond your control. You need to be able to manage a client's expectations and your own idealism; pragmatic and sensible advice, even knowing when to quit, is important.
- In the battle against red tape, bureaucracy and institutional indifference, organisational skills and a vast store of patience are valuable assets.
- Opportunities for advocacy are abundant, which means that knowledge of court and tribunal procedure is a fundamental requirement. Often cases must pass through every possible stage of appeal before they can be referred to judicial review or the ECJ.

current issues

○ The number of people looking for training contracts in the field far exceeds the number of available positions so you must evidence your commitment. A CV referencing voluntary work at a law centre or specialist voluntary organisation (eg the Howard League for Penal Reform), or membership of Liberty or Justice will help. A healthy interest in current affairs and the latest cases in the news will also assist.

○ Because much of the work is legally aided, the firms who specialise in these areas of work generally can't offer attractive trainee salaries or sponsorship through law school.

○ In immigration law there have been many modifications of late, among them changes affecting people applying for leave to remain or settle in the UK. Another example is the rule that migrant applications now need to be submitted to and dealt with at diplomatic posts overseas. This is causing concern amongst lawyers who feel that a move away from a centralised system will lead to loss of efficiency and poorer supervision. There is also much criticism of the abolition of various appeal rights and the substitution of an administrative review procedure.

○ It looks as if there is more change to come. In March 2006 the Home Office published a paper on proposals for the UK immigration system called 'Controlling our borders: Making migration work for Britain – Five Year Strategy for asylum and immigration'.

○ Lawyers dealing with business immigration increasingly need to help clients with more than just domestic inward bound work permits. With large companies now shunting employees around various countries on placements, they are being asked to arrange multi-jurisdictional work permits.

leading firms from Chambers UK 2007

Immigration: Personal **London**	Immigration: Business **London**	Immigration **Midlands**
[1] Bindman & Partners	[1] CMS Cameron McKenna LLP	[1] The Rights Partnership *Birmingham*
Wesley Gryk Solicitors LLP	Kingsley Napley	[2] Tyndallwoods *Birmingham*
Wilson & Co	Laura Devine Solicitors	
[2] Bates Wells & Braithwaite	Magrath & Co	Immigration **East Anglia**
Birnberg Peirce & Partners	[2] Bates Wells & Braithwaite	[1] Gross & Co *Bury St Edmunds*
Deighton Guedalla	Penningtons Solicitors LLP	Wollastons *Chelmsford*
Glazer Delmar	[3] Baker & McKenzie LLP	
Luqmani Thompson & Partners	Gherson & Co	Immigration **The North**
[3] Bartram & Co	H2O Law LLP	[1] A S Law *Liverpool*
DJ Webb & Co	Reed Smith	David Gray *Newcastle upon Tyne*
Elder Rahimi	Sturtivant & Co	Harrison Bundey *Leeds*
Fisher Meredith	[4] DJ Webb & Co	[2] Browell Smith *Newcastle upon Tyne*
	Fox Williams	Henry Hyams *Leeds*
Immigration **Thames Valley**	Harbottle & Lewis LLP	Howells LLP *Sheffield*
[1] Darbys *Oxford*	Lewis Silkin LLP	Jackson & Canter *Liverpool*
Turpin Miller & Higgins *Oxford*	Mishcon de Reya	Parker Rhodes *Rotherham*
	Taylor Wessing	

Human Rights
Best of the UK
[1] Bindman & Partners
[2] Bhatt Murphy
Birnberg Peirce & Partners
Christian Khan
Hickman & Rose
Leigh Day & Co
Public Interest Lawyers
[3] Deighton Guedalla
Harrison Bundey
Hodge Jones & Allen
Irwin Mitchell
Palmer Wade
Public Law Solicitors
Scott-Moncrieff, Harbour & Sinclair
Simons Muirhead & Burton
[4] A S Law
Ben Hoare Bell
Howells LLP

Education: Schools
Best of the UK
[1] Farrer & Co
[2] Reynolds Porter Chamberlain LLP
Rickerbys
Veale Wasbrough Lawyers
[3] Stone King LLP
Winckworth Sherwood
[4] Blake Lapthorn Linnell
Browne Jacobson LLP
DLA Piper UK LLP
Irwin Mitchell
Morgan Cole

Education: Individuals
Best of the UK
[1] Levenes
Teacher Stern Selby
[2] Douglas Silas Solicitors
Fisher Meredith
Maxwell Gillott
Russell Jones & Walker
[3] John Ford Solicitors
Langley Wellington
Ormerods
[4] Bennett Wilkins
Match Solicitors

Administrative & Public Law: Public Sector Law & Governance
Best of the UK
[1] Clifford Chance LLP
Eversheds LLP
Field Fisher Waterhouse LLP
Herbert Smith LLP
Mayer, Brown, Rowe & Maw LLP
Sharpe Pritchard
[2] Allen & Overy LLP
Beachcroft LLP
Bevan Brittan LLP
Capsticks
Pinsent Masons
[3] Baker & McKenzie LLP
Bates Wells & Braithwaite
Bircham Dyson Bell
Denton Wilde Sapte
Geldards LLP
Hempsons
Morgan Cole
Norton Rose
Trowers & Hamlins
Wragge & Co LLP
[4] Kingsley Napley
Payne Hicks Beach

Education: Universities
Best of the UK
[1] Eversheds LLP
[2] Beachcroft LLP
Farrer & Co
Martineau Johnson
Mills & Reeve
Pinsent Masons
Reynolds Porter Chamberlain LLP
Rickerbys
Veale Wasbrough Lawyers
[3] Berrymans Lace Mawer
Blake Lapthorn Linnell
Bond Pearce LLP
Dickinson Dees
Finers Stephens Innocent
Nabarro Nathanson

Administrative & Public Law: Commercial & Regulated Industries
Best of the UK
[1] Clifford Chance LLP
Herbert Smith LLP
[2] Allen & Overy LLP
Baker & McKenzie LLP
Freshfields Bruckhaus Deringer
Lovells
[3] Addleshaw Goddard LLP
Arnold & Porter (UK) LLP
Bird & Bird
Denton Wilde Sapte
DLA Piper UK LLP
Olswang
Simmons & Simmons
Slaughter and May
Wragge & Co LLP
[4] Bates Wells & Braithwaite
Field Fisher Waterhouse LLP
Kendall Freeman
Mayer, Brown, Rowe & Maw LLP
Norton Rose

Administrative & Public Law: Traditional Claimant
Best of the UK
[1] Bindman & Partners
[2] Bhatt Murphy
Christian Khan
Leigh Day & Co
Public Interest Lawyers
Richard Buxton
[3] Hickman & Rose
Irwin Mitchell
Levenes
Mackintosh Duncan
Public Law Solicitors
[4] Birnberg Peirce & Partners
Community Law Partnership
Howells LLP
Ormerods
South West Law Limited
Teacher Stern Selby

shipping

put simply

Essentially shipping law concerns the carriage of goods or people by sea, plus any and every matter related to the financing, construction, use, insurance and decommissioning of the ships that carry them (or sink carrying them, or are arrested carrying them or are salvaged carrying them). Despite being relatively self-contained and centred around specialist firms, or practices within firms, this is a varied discipline offering challenges for different breeds of lawyer.

who does what

Contentious lawyers' work is divided between:

- Wet or 'Admiralty' matters – broadly speaking tortious, concerning disputes arising from accidents or misadventure at sea anywhere in the world. Among other things it covers collision, salvage, total loss and modern day piracy, and requires swift, decisive action to protect a client's interests and minimise any loss.
- Dry matters – disputes and subsequent litigation relating to contracts made on dry land such as charter parties, bills of lading, ship construction or refitting, and sale of goods agreements. Like wet work it can require action in pretty much any jurisdiction in the world.
- Both wet and dry lawyers are involved in court and arbitration appearances, conferences with counsel, client meetings, taking witness statements and advising clients on the merits of and strategy for cases.

non-contentious lawyers:

- Are primarily engaged in contracts for ship finance and shipbuilding, crew employment contracts, sale and purchase agreements, affreightment contracts, and the registration and re-flagging of ships.
- May specialise in more niche areas such as yachts or fishing, an area in which regulatory issues feature prominently.
- Are less likely than their contentious colleagues to jet off around the world at the drop of a hat.

the realities of the job

- Wet work offers the excitement of international assignments and clients, reacting coolly to sudden emergencies and travelling to far-flung places to offer practical and pragmatic analysis and advice.
- Despite the perils and pleasures of dealing with clients and instructions on the other side of the world, back in the office shipping law has little of the all-night culture about it; hours are likely to be steady beyond those 'international rescue' moments.
- Non-contentious work touches on the intricacies of international trade, so it's as important to keep up with sector knowledge as legal developments.
- Dealing with a mixed clientele from all points on the social compass, you'll need to be just as comfortable extracting a comprehensible statement from a Norwegian merchant seaman as conducting negotiations with major financers. Shipowners, operators, traders and charterers, P&I clubs and hull underwriters will all come within your daily ken.
- Contentious cases are driven by the procedural rules and timetable of the court or arbitration forum to which the matter has been referred. A solid grasp of procedure is as important as a strong foundation in tort and contract law.
- Some shipping lawyers do come from a naval background or are ex-mariners, but you won't be becalmed if the closest comparable experience you've had is steering Tommy Tugboat in the bath, as long as you evince a credible interest in the discipline.

- Though not quite 'no place for a lady', parts of the shipping world are still male dominated. Women lawyers and clients are more commonly found on the dry side of business.
- If you decide to move away from shipping law, non-contentious experience should allow a transition into asset or more general finance. A few years of contentious shipping law should leave you with a solid grounding in commercial litigation.
- In the UK, shipping law is centred around London and a few other port cities. Major international centres include Pireaus in Greece, Hong Kong and Singapore. Some trainees even get to work in these locations.

current issues

- Increasingly there is a crossover between shipping, energy and international trade.

Liquefied natural gas (LNG) is a big driver, with Floating Production, Storage and Offshore Loading (FPSO) taking much of the limelight. FPSO installations are big news in the Caspian Sea, the Middle East, West Africa and the Far East. One knock-on effect is the extent to which UK firms are now working with lawyers in these regions, and sending their own lawyers to work overseas.

- The rise of China as an economic power is impacting on the cargo market, on ship building and on financing.
- Increased bank lending has led to the involvement of law firms that were not previously associated with the sector.
- Super yachts! We've never been on one, but we'd not turn Mr Abramovitch down if he offered us a cruise on his 377ft gin palace. The yacht market is hot right now.

leading firms from Chambers UK 2007

Shipping London	
[1] Holman Fenwick & Willan	Ince & Co
[2] Clyde & Co	
[3] Richards Butler LLP	
[4] Barlow Lyde & Gilbert	Bentleys, Stokes & Lowless
Hill Taylor Dickinson	Jackson Parton
Norton Rose	Stephenson Harwood
Thomas Cooper & Stibbard	Waltons & Morse
Watson, Farley & Williams	
[5] Clifford Chance LLP	Curtis Davis Garrard
Fishers	Hill Dickinson LLP
Lawrence Graham LLP	Mays Brown, Solicitors
MFB	Middleton Potts
Shaw and Croft	Waterson Hicks
Winter Scott	

Shipping: Finance London
[1] Norton Rose
Watson, Farley & Williams
[2] Clifford Chance LLP
Stephenson Harwood
[3] Denton Wilde Sapte
Holman Fenwick & Willan
Ince & Co

Shipping The Regions
[1] Eversheds LLP *Newcastle upon Tyne*
Mills & Co *Newcastle upon Tyne*
Rayfield Mills *Newcastle upon Tyne*
[2] Andrew M Jackson *Hull*
Davies, Johnson & Co *Plymouth*
Hill Dickinson LLP *Liverpool*
[3] Dale Stevens LLP *Felixstowe*
Foot Anstey *Plymouth*
John Weston & Co *Felixstowe*
Prettys *Ipswich*

sports, media and entertainment law

put simply

The bright lights, the red carpets, the reflected glory of stars of stage, screen and pitch… Is this a true reflection of legal practice in what we'll broadly call sports, media and entertainment law? So long as you know you'll always be a lawyer first and foremost, we are prepared to concede that this is one of the more exciting parts of the legal profession. In this area of the profession there's a niche for almost any kind of media tart or sports obsessive.

advertising and marketing law – put simply

Work encompasses pure advertising law advice – ensuring a client's products or advertisements are compliant with industry standards – plus general advice on anything from contracts between clients, media and suppliers, to employment law, corporate transactions and litigation.

the role involves:
- Copy clearance to ensure advertising campaigns comply with legislation such as the Consumer Protection Act (CPA) or regulatory codes controlled by the Advertising Standards Agency or Ofcom.
- Advice on comparative advertising, unauthorised references to living persons, potential trade mark or other intellectual property infringements.
- Defending clients against allegations that their work has infringed regulations or the rights of third parties, and bringing complaints against competitors' advertising.

the realities of the job
- Lawyers must have a good knowledge of advertising regulations, defamation and intellectual property law.
- The work is 'real world' and fast paced – a campaign that comes out today might need to be pulled tomorrow for legal reasons. Clients expect pragmatic advice that minimises the risks to which they are exposed.
- Clients are creative, lively and demanding. The issues thrown up can be fascinating and must be dealt with creatively.
- Many disputes will be settled via regulatory bodies but some, particularly IP infringements, end in litigation.

reputation management – put simply

These specialists advise clients on how best to protect their own 'brand'. Whether it's a footballer alleged to have been involved in rape, a newspaper that has made claims it can't back up, or a TV star snapped with a telephoto lens at a funeral, the client may require swift and decisive action be taken.

claimants' solicitors:
- Advise individuals – commonly celebrities, politicians or high-profile businessmen – on the nature of any potential libel action or breach of privacy claim, usually against broadcasters or publishers.
- A matter can be settled by way of an apology or retraction of published material, or it may go all the way to court. The lawyer must always consider whether allowing a case to reach trial is the best solution for the client, who may be averse to any further intrusion into their private affairs.

defendants' solicitors:
- Typically advise broadcasters and newspapers or other publishers on libel claims brought against them. With the burden of proof on the defendant, the lawyer's job is to help prove that what was published caused no loss to the claimant or was not in fact libellous. This requires an investigative approach and strategic thinking.

- Help clients stay out of trouble by giving pre-publication advice to authors, editors or production companies.

the realities of the job

- A comprehensive understanding of libel laws and a willingness to think laterally are essential.
- Individual claimants will be stressed and upset, so people skills, patience and resourcefulness are much needed.
- Solicitors prepare cases but barristers almost always get the glory attached to presenting cases in court.
- It's important to have a keen interest in current affairs, popular media and (whisper it quietly) keeping more than half an eye on the tabloids and gossip rags. If you combine that with ardent belief in freedom of speech and right to privacy, then so much the better.
- Tempting as it is, you just can't spill the beans on your latest case when you're out with friends... even if you do know more than popbitch.

entertainment law put simply

The film, broadcasting, music, theatre and publishing industries share a common need for commercial legal advice on contract, employment litigation and intellectual property law, among other things.

TV and film lawyers:

- Offer production companies advice on every stage of the creation of programmes and films, from research and development, to production and marketing, sponsorship and tie-ins.
- Film lawyers are closely involved with the complicated banking and secured lending transactions that ensure financing for a film. A trend for lending institutions to insure their loans to film production companies has led to a raft of related litigation.

- TV lawyers tend to be drafted in for specific purposes relating to the making of a programme: engaging performers; negotiating contracts; negotiating distribution and worldwide rights issues and defamation claims. As such, they need knowledge of compliance, defamation, privacy, confidence and finance law.

music lawyers

- Advise the three key components of the music industry: major recording companies, independent labels and talent (including record producers and songwriters as well as artists).
- Advise on contracts, such as those between labels and bands, or between labels and third parties, eg websites selling downloads and ringtones. The frequent breakdown of relationships, say when a band splits, together with the subsequent disputes over royalty payments and ownership of music copyright mean that litigation is not uncommon.
- Offer contentious and non-contentious copyright and trade mark advice relating to music, image rights and merchandising. Ensure correct crediting and royalty payments when other artists sample songs.
- Offer criminal advice when the things get truly rock n' roll. Imagine being Pete Doherty's lawyer...

theatre and publishing lawyers

- A small but select group of predominantly London lawyers advises theatre and opera companies, producers, agents and actors on contracts, funding and sponsorship/merchandising.
- Publishing companies and newspapers without an in-house legal team seek advice on contractual, licensing, copyright and libel matters.

the realities of the job

- Complete immersion in the chosen media allied to a good grasp of copyright and contract law are the basics, although a creative attitude to problem solving and a steady disposition help when faced with all those nervous artistic types.

- Fighting your way past the massive competition for a job in the entertainment sector may leave you feeling like the winner of Pop Idol, but it's important to remember that you're not. Keep your inner Simon Cowell on standby, to remind you that you are a lawyer and clients look to you for a rigour and discipline they may rarely exercise themselves.

- This is a sector where who you know makes a big difference, so expect to put in serious time getting your face known. And maybe dress more snappily than your colleagues in the tax department.

sports law put simply

Strictly speaking an industry sector rather than a specific legal discipline. Many firms boasting a sports law capability draw on the expertise of lawyers from several practice groups; relatively few have dedicated teams. But given the massive amounts of money floating around football, rugby, tennis, darts and most sports you care to mention, the desire to join the sports party is understandable. Whether representing a club, individual sportsperson, governing body, or company interested in offering sponsorship or funding, or working in-house at a sports broadcaster, a sports lawyer's workload encompasses regulatory matters, advice on media, advertising and image rights, plus general corporate and commercial advice.

sports lawyers' work involves:

- Contract negotiations, be they between clubs and sportspeople, agents and players, sporting institutions and sponsors, broadcasters and sports governing bodies.

- All manner of employment law issues. In the average football club, for example, there are contract renegotiations, transfers and player loans, player registration, work permits to be secured, internal disciplinary matters and defence of disciplinary matters at a governing body level, as well as all the employment issues associated with running a large institution with a large and varied workforce.

- Corporate and commercial work in the form of takeovers or public offerings (think Malcolm Glazer's aggressive and successful bid for Manchester United), debt restructuring and bankruptcy, and the securing and structuring of credit to finance stadium redevelopments.

- Intellectual property matters in a world in which official merchandise is a major part of sports teams' income. Litigation may be necessary to protect those income sources. Likewise, individual sportspeople's image rights have become increasingly valuable and require protection, often taking a central role in contractual negotiations.

- A variety of issues relating to the friction between sports regulations and EU or national law. In the field of competition law, the authorities ruled that Sky's football coverage in the UK constitutes an unfair monopoly and have forced wider broadcasting. Meanwhile, the UK government is considering returning cricket to the status of sporting national treasure, which would require coverage via domestic broadcasters. Then there's regulatory compliance within a sport, be it financial regulations or drugs policies, which can all easily lead to courtroom action or governing body hearings.

- Reputation management and criminal advice. The combination of young sportspeople, massive salaries and celebrity status is a heady one with sometimes unfortunate consequences. Whether it's combatting kiss and tell allegations, an invasion of privacy, or defending clients against more serious allegations of rape or affray, a sports lawyer can be kept very busy.

the realities of the job

- Sports lawyers need to be proactive, passionate and creative and have bags of commercial nous. It is sometimes said that a sports lawyer operates as a consultant, not a solicitor.
- Excellent interpersonal skills are essential, as is a capacity to see both sides of an argument. In transfers in any sport, lawyers can be dealing with several clubs, the clubs' lawyers, a player and multiple agents, all determined to secure the best deal possible.
- In multimillion-pound sporting industries, mistakes or loopholes will be ruthlessly exploited. Witness the current £150 million litigation by The Football League against Hammonds for allegedly failing to protect its interests during negotiations with ONdigital (now ITV Digital).
- You need to be able to deal with people involved at all levels of all sports, some of whom may be deeply conservative, structurally opaque and suspicious of outsiders.

current issues

- There have been developments in libel law. The 'qualified privilege' defence previously established in 2001 in Reynolds v Times Newspapers was re-examined when George Galloway MP sued The Daily Telegraph, and again in the case of Henry v BBC. The trend away from jury trials and towards trial by judge continues.
- The courts are now dealing with cases of ISPs being sued for publishing material sent by third parties through their servers or for hosting material on their websites.
- The courts have continued to develop the law of privacy.
- The popularity among claimants of no-win, no-fee Conditional Fee Agreements has led to an increase in the number of privacy and defamation claims brought.
- In the world of sport, the 2012 Olympics are already keeping lawyers busy.
- In the music industry Apple the iPod people triumphed over The Beatles' record label Apple when it was sued for breaching a prior agreement to say they would not use the Apple brand in relation to a music product.

sports, media and entertainment law (continued)

leading firms from Chambers UK 2007

Media & Entertainment: Broadcasting
Best of the UK

[1] DLA Piper UK LLP
Olswang

[2] Goodman Derrick
Herbert Smith LLP
Lovells
Richards Butler LLP
Wiggin LLP

[3] Clifford Chance LLP
Field Fisher Waterhouse LLP
SJ Berwin LLP
Taylor Wessing

Media & Entertainment: Computer Games
Best of the UK

[1] Harbottle & Lewis LLP
Osborne Clarke

[2] Ashurst
Bird & Bird
Briffa
Bristows
Lovells

Media & Entertainment: Music
Best of the UK

[1] Russells

[2] Clintons
Forbes Anderson Free
Lee & Thompson
Sheridans

[3] Bray & Krais Solicitors
Eversheds LLP
Hamlins LLP

[4] Harbottle & Lewis LLP
Michael Simkins LLP
Olswang

[5] Davenport Lyons
Engel Monjack
Spraggon Stennett Brabyn
Swan Turton
Wiggin LLP

Media & Entertainment: Theatre
Best of the UK

[1] Clintons

[2] Bates Wells & Braithwaite
Harbottle & Lewis LLP
Michael Simkins LLP
Swan Turton

Defamation/Reputation Management
Best of the UK

[1] Carter-Ruck
Davenport Lyons
David Price Solicitors & Advocates
Farrer & Co
Reynolds Porter Chamberlain LLP
Schillings

[2] Addleshaw Goddard LLP
Olswang
Wiggin LLP

[3] Charles Russell LLP
Simons Muirhead & Burton

[4] Bindman & Partners
Finers Stephens Innocent
Foot Anstey
Harbottle & Lewis LLP
Russell Jones & Walker
Taylor Wessing

[5] Clifford Chance LLP
Dechert LLP
DLA Piper UK LLP
Goodman Derrick
Lee & Thompson
Lewis Silkin LLP
Mishcon de Reya
Richards Butler LLP

[6] Brabners Chaffe Street
Cobbetts LLP
Eversheds LLP
Howard Kennedy
M Law
McCormicks
Pannone LLP
Teacher Stern Selby

Media & Entertainment: Film & TV, Finance & Production
London

[1] Olswang
Richards Butler LLP
SJ Berwin LLP

[2] Davenport Lyons
Harbottle & Lewis LLP
Lee & Thompson
Wiggin LLP

[3] DLA Piper UK LLP

[4] Bird & Bird
Charles Russell LLP
Howard Kennedy
Michael Simkins LLP
Sheridans
Simons Muirhead & Burton

Advertising & Marketing
Best of the UK

[1] Lewis Silkin LLP
Osborne Clarke

[2] Addleshaw Goddard LLP
Hammonds
Macfarlanes
Taylor Wessing
Wragge & Co LLP

[3] Lawrence Graham LLP
Mayer, Brown, Rowe & Maw LLP
Olswang
Swan Turton

[4] Baker & McKenzie LLP
Clarke Willmott
CMS Cameron McKenna LLP
DLA Piper UK LLP
Field Fisher Waterhouse LLP
Harbottle & Lewis LLP
Kaye Scholer LLP
Lovells
Reynolds Porter Chamberlain LLP

www.chambersandpartners.co.uk

Sport
London

1. **Bird & Bird**
   DLA Piper UK LLP
2. **Couchman Harrington Associates**
   Farrer & Co
   Hammonds
3. **Charles Russell LLP**
   Kirkpatrick & Lockhart Nicholson
   Olswang
   Teacher Stern Selby
4. **athletes1 Legal**
   Collyer Bristow LLP
   Denton Wilde Sapte
   Field Fisher Waterhouse LLP
   Freshfields Bruckhaus Deringer
   Harbottle & Lewis LLP
   Macfarlanes
   Max Bitel Greene
5. **Addleshaw Goddard LLP**
   Clintons
   Fladgate Fielder
   Herbert Smith LLP
   Michael Simkins LLP
   Onside Law LLP
   Simmons & Simmons
   Slaughter and May

Sport
The Regions

1. **Brabners Chaffe Street** *Manchester*
2. **Addleshaw** *Leeds, Manchester*
   Clarke Willmott *Southampton, Bristol*
   George Davies *Manchester*
   McCormicks *Leeds*
3. **Cramer Richards** *Leeds*
   Halliwells LLP *Manchester*
   Hill Dickinson LLP *Liverpool*
   Osborne Clarke *Bristol*
   Walker Morris *Leeds*

Sport
Wales

1. **Hugh James** *Cardiff*
2. **Loosemores** *Cardiff*

Sport: Horse Racing & Equestrian
The Regions

1. **Ashfords** *Exeter*
   Edmondson Hall *Newmarket*
   Taylor Vinters *Cambridge*
   Whatley Lane *Newmarket*
   Withy King *Marlborough*

tax law

put simply

Good tax advice saves money, and clients are happy to pay for it. The solicitor's job is to know the law inside out – no small task given that the Chancellor amends the tax regime every Budget day – and to ensure that clients structure their business deals or day-to-day operations such that they take advantage of breaks and loopholes while staying on the right side of the law.

On occasion matters veer into the territory of litigation. A case brought by Marks & Spencer against the Revenue in late 2005 earned the retailer's lawyers considerable kudos. The case found that UK tax legislation does not comply with European law, and that the Revenue could be liable for millions of pounds of repayments. Other companies swiftly cottoned on and are now seeking similar recompense in the form of copycat claims, spawning an influx of work for lawyers.

who does what

Private practitioners' work divides into four main headings:

- Tax planning – making sure that clients understand the tax ramifications of the purchase, ownership and disposal of their assets, including advice on structuring corporate portfolios in the most tax-efficient way.
- Transactional advice – working with corporate and other transactional lawyers on the structure of, say, an M&A deal, a joint venture or the acquisition of a large property portfolio. The tax lawyer's advice may determine not only how the deal moves forwards, but also whether it does at all.
- Ad hoc advice – colleagues from across the firm will ring up with quick queries on everything from VAT to their own income tax returns.
- Litigation and investigations – when a company is being investigated or prosecuted by

HM Revenue & Customs for not paying enough tax. Perhaps the company believes it has been charged too much and wants to appeal. Litigation is always conducted against or brought by the government, so you could say that all private practice tax litigators have a common enemy.

working for HM Revenue & Customs:

- Investigating companies and bringing prosecutions.
- Advising on how new laws apply to different situations.
- Defending cases brought against the government.

the realities of the job

- This is an intellectually rigorous area of law and ideally suited to brainiacs, which is probably why tax lawyers have an anoraky image. Despite being (for the most part) inaccurate, it remains unlikely that announcing yourself as a tax lawyer will impress anyone at parties.
- Corporate tax lawyers are highly paid, treated well by their colleagues and find intellectual stimulation in their work.
- There can be an element of drama on the litigation side; elsewhere it is rarely cut and thrust. That said, clients are now demanding of their lawyers not only the ability to translate and implement complex tax legislation but also a savvy awareness of how to structure deals in a legitimate and tax-efficient way that bypasses trouble from the Revenue. To some extent this encroaches on what was traditionally accountancy firm territory, to the consternation of many an accountant. However, it is the combination of bean-countery know-how and legal expertise that clients are increasingly calling for.
- Frequent changes in the law mean you'll never stop learning. Put another way, your briefcase will always contain homework.

- If you don't already wear specs, you will after a couple of years of poring over all that black letter law.
- Extra qualifications, such as the Chartered Tax Adviser exams, will be useful.
- It is not uncommon for lawyers to switch between government jobs and private practice. A number of tax barristers were once solicitors.

current issues

- The recent merger between the Inland Revenue and HM Customs & Excise (forming HMRC) has led to speculation about a more aggressive attitude to clamping down on tax avoidance. Many expect that, in time, HMRC will bring about more litigation, and firms that were once strictly transactional will need to build their litigation capabilities.

- Gordon Brown's tenth (and what many speculate will be his last) Budget held few surprises for the corporate tax community. However, it left the way open for the formation of Real Estate Investment Trusts (REITs), which will allow property portfolios to be invested in trusts to, among other things, avoid capital gains tax. A popular mechanism already in the USA, it is estimated that the REIT market could be worth as much as £10 billion within a year of its inception.
- London is becoming the nerve centre for the structuring of global tax transactions. A buoyant M&A market is generating big-ticket work, and corporate finance and capital markets transactions with a tax backbone are in plentiful supply. Tax structuring work in private equity and securitisation is similarly abundant.

tax law (continued)

leading firms from Chambers UK 2007

Tax
Best of the UK

[1] Freshfields Bruckhaus Deringer
Linklaters
Slaughter and May
[2] Allen & Overy LLP
Clifford Chance LLP
[3] Ashurst
Herbert Smith LLP
Macfarlanes
Simmons & Simmons
SJ Berwin LLP
[4] Berwin Leighton Paisner LLP
CMS Cameron McKenna LLP
Lovells
Nabarro Nathanson
Norton Rose
Travers Smith
[5] Addleshaw Goddard LLP
Cleary Gottlieb Steen & Hamilton
Clyde & Co
Denton Wilde Sapte
DLA Piper UK LLP
Field Fisher Waterhouse LLP
Fried, Frank, Harris, Shriver
Olswang
Pinsent Masons
Shearman & Sterling LLP
Skadden, Arps, Slate, Meagher
Weil, Gotshal & Manges LLP
Wragge & Co LLP
[6] Dechert LLP
Dorsey & Whitney
Eversheds LLP
Kirkland & Ellis International LLP
McDermott Will & Emery UK LLP
McGrigors
Osborne Clarke
Taylor Wessing
Watson, Farley & Williams

Tax
The South

[1] Osborne Clarke *Bristol*
[2] Burges Salmon LLP *Bristol*
[3] Blake Lapthorn Linnell *Portsmouth*
Bond Pearce LLP *Plymouth*

Tax
Midlands

[1] Pinsent Masons *Birmingham*
Wragge & Co LLP *Birmingham*
[2] DLA Piper UK LLP *Birmingham*
Eversheds LLP *Nottingham*
Hammonds *Birmingham*
[3] Bevan Brittan LLP *Birmingham*
Browne Jacobson LLP *Nottingham*
HBJ Gateley Wareing *Birmingham*
Mills & Reeve *Cambridge*

Tax
The North

[1] Addleshaw Goddard LLP *Leeds*
Eversheds LLP *Leeds*
Pinsent Masons *Leeds*
[2] Hammonds *Leeds*
[3] Dickinson Dees *Newcastle upon Tyne*
Halliwells LLP *Manchester*
Walker Morris *Leeds*

technology, telecoms & outsourcing

put simply

Technology lawyers differentiate themselves from more general commercial advisers by their specific industry know-how. They have to combine a keen understanding of the latest developments and advances in various technologies with a thorough knowledge of the ever-changing law that regulates, protects and licenses them. As forms of media and new technologies converge (think movies via cable, TV news to your mobile phone, record companies selling songs on the Internet), clients rely on Technology lawyers' skills of innovation and imagination in offering rigorous legal solutions to maximise and protect income and ideas.

As the dotcom crash fades in the memory, Technology law is once again a thriving and hectic sector. The majority of the top fifty firms possess dedicated groups of lawyers, there are specialists within the corporate/commercial groups of many more medium-sized firms, and there are numerous smaller specialist outfits. In short, there are plenty of job opportunities in this appetising and sexy area of law, in both the contentious and non-contentious spheres.

who does what

Technology lawyers:

- Advise on commercial transactions and draft the requisite documents to implement them. For example, a large public body or a multinational company might be outsourcing its IT functions or procuring a new system. There is a heavy emphasis on risk management advice, such as advising on the way in which a software agreement can prevent potential litigation in the future.
- Assist in the resolution of disputes. Clients in the technology sector (as in most others) tend to want to avoid the cost and effort involved with lengthy, protracted litigation. In addition, technology suppliers commonly have long-term working relationships with their customers, and realise that a heated punch-up in court would be detrimental to future business. Consequently, much of the litigator's work involves arbitration or other settlement procedures. Many disputes tend to be in relation to software or hardware that doesn't do exactly what it says on the tin, or simply doesn't work at all.
- Help clients police their IT and web-based reputation and assets. Cyber-squatting, ownership of database information and the Data Protection Act are common topics.
- Give clients mainstream commercial, corporate and finance advice.

the realities of the job

- You need to be familiar with the latest regulations and their potential impact on your client's business. How do you make the purchase of a ringtone by text a legally binding contract? Does a website need a disclaimer? What measures should your client take to protect data about individuals gathered from a website? Do sports highlights shown on mobile phones conflict with other broadcasting agreements or governing body regulations?
- You need a good grasp of the jargon of your chosen industry, firstly to write contracts, but also so you can understand your clients' instructions. You have to know your WLAN from LAN, your 3G from GPRS and your ISPs from your SMSs. Read trade journals or magazines like Media Lawyer and Wired, or magazines such as Computer Weekly or New Scientist.
- The ability to think laterally and creatively is a must, especially when the application of a client's technology or content throws up entirely new issues.
- Putting yourself about and being seen is important in a fast-changing industry with quick turnover, where law firms are forever merging or being founded.

○ In this 'frontier' world, gut instinct matters. The in-house lawyer who was laughed out of BT six years ago when he joined little-known Internet auction site eBbay is the one smiling now. He recently moved to head up the legal team of eBay's broadband-based phone service Skype, a perfect example of the convergence of Internet and telephone technology that is forcing traditional telecoms companies like BT to rethink their strategies.

current issues

○ Investor confidence in the technology sector has returned after the damaging dot.comedy years, and IT budgets, particularly in the private sector, have increased. Companies find it necessary to invest in the latest technology to gain or maintain a competitive edge. All this means work for lawyers.

○ Legislation and regulations, such as those upholding the freedom of information regime and the waste electronic and electrical equipment disposal regime, are also creating work.

○ Now that every player in the top 100 offers some form of TMT, the onus is on law firms to ascertain what will make them most competitive in a crowded market. They are refining or reshaping their practices, and their long-term strategies, well aware that a lot of firms piled into technology work in the late 90s, only to come a cropper soon after. This time round law firms tend to be thinking smarter.

○ As early as the late 1980s companies began outsourcing their IT functions. Having tested the waters with 'ITO' agreements, many leading companies have now become sufficiently emboldened to pass more of their business process functions to third-party service providers in business process outsourcings (BPOs) covering functions such as human resources, finance and accounting. In recent times there has been a great deal of activity in relation to UK public-sector procurement and the financial services sector. Multi-jurisdictional outsourcings are also on the rise.

○ Outsourcing lawyers represent customers and suppliers in the negotiation and drafting of outsourcing agreements. Customer clients range from government departments and local authorities to owner-managed businesses and large corporates. On the supplier side, key outsourcing service providers include the likes of Accenture, EDS and Capgemini. A distinction needs to be drawn between the work done in the private sector and that done in the public sector. High-end private sector work involves complex, high-value, often groundbreaking and increasingly multi-jurisdictional outsourcings, deals most often done by magic circle firms or large US outfits with London offices. Outsourcings in the public sector involve representing UK government departments, local authorities or suppliers of services to those entities. This work can be more commoditised than private-sector work, with the value of the deals often much lower. National firms such as DLA Piper, Addleshaw Goddard and Eversheds have cornered the market in public sector outsourcings, partly due to the fact that they can offer more competitive rates. Having said that, the national firms also advise on a significant number of private-sector outsourcings, especially domestic deals.

○ The long-term success of outsourcing agreements is aided by the involvement of experienced specialists in negotiations, rather than general corporate or commercial lawyers. If outsourcing negotiations are approached in an adversarial, point-scoring way, this can cause rifts in the relationships between parties, which in turn increases the likelihood of an agreement needing to be renegotiated before the expiry of its initial term. In a worst-case scenario a breakdown could lead to actual dispute.

leading firms from Chambers UK 2007

Information Technology
London

[1] Baker & McKenzie LLP
Bird & Bird
DLA Piper UK LLP
Field Fisher Waterhouse LLP
Linklaters

[2] Allen & Overy LLP
Clifford Chance LLP
Herbert Smith LLP
Kemp Little LLP
Lovells
Milbank, Tweed, Hadley & McCloy
Osborne Clarke
Pinsent Masons
Simmons & Simmons

[3] Barlow Lyde & Gilbert
Denton Wilde Sapte
Freshfields Bruckhaus Deringer
Latham & Watkins LLP
Mayer, Brown, Rowe & Maw LLP
Morrison & Foerster MNP
Norton Rose
Olswang
Slaughter and May
Taylor Wessing

[4] Addleshaw Goddard LLP
Berwin Leighton Paisner LLP
Eversheds LLP
Kirkpatrick & Lockhart Nicholson
Nabarro Nathanson
Pillsbury Winthrop Shaw Pittman

[5] Bristows
Harbottle & Lewis LLP
Tarlo Lyons
Technology Law Alliance

Information Technology
The South

[1] Blake Lapthorn Linnell *Southampton*
Bond Pearce LLP *Southampton*
DMH Stallard *Crawley*

[2] Clyde & Co *Guildford*
Shadbolt & Co LLP *Reigate*

Information Technology
Thames Valley

[1] Boyes Turner *Reading*
Clark Holt *Swindon*
Manches LLP *Oxford*
Moorcrofts LLP *Marlow*
NetworkLaw Limited *Wokingham*
Osborne Clarke *Reading*

[2] Olswang Thames Valley *Reading*
Shoosmiths *Northampton*
Willoughby/Rouse Legal *Oxford*

Information Technology
South West

[1] Beachcroft LLP *Bristol*
Burges Salmon LLP *Bristol*
Osborne Clarke *Bristol*

[2] Ashfords *Bristol*
Foot Anstey *Exeter*
Foot Anstey *Plymouth*

[3] Bevan Brittan LLP *Bristol*
Rickerbys *Cheltenham*

Information Technology
Wales

[1] Eversheds LLP *Cardiff*
Geldards LLP *Cardiff*
Morgan Cole *Cardiff*

[2] Hugh James *Cardiff*

Information Technology
Midlands

[1] Wragge & Co LLP *Birmingham*

[2] Eversheds LLP *Nottingham*
Technology Law Alliance *Birmingham*

[3] Martineau Johnson *Birmingham*
Mills & Reeve *Birmingham*
Pinsent Masons *Birmingham*

Information Technology
The North

[1] Addleshaw Goddard LLP *Leeds*

[2] DLA Piper UK LLP *Leeds*
Eversheds LLP *Leeds*
Halliwells LLP *Manchester*
Pinsent Masons *Manchester*
Pinsent Masons *Leeds*

[3] Irwin Mitchell *Leeds*
Nabarro Nathanson *Sheffield*

Telecommunications
Best of the UK

1. Allen & Overy LLP
   Baker & McKenzie LLP
   Bird & Bird
   Linklaters
2. Clifford Chance LLP
   Field Fisher Waterhouse LLP
   Freshfields Bruckhaus Deringer
   Herbert Smith LLP
   Mayer, Brown, Rowe & Maw LLP
   Olswang
3. Addleshaw Goddard LLP
   Ashurst
   Charles Russell LLP
   Denton Wilde Sapte
   DLA Piper UK LLP
   Eversheds LLP
   Kemp Little LLP
   Simmons & Simmons
   Taylor Wessing
   White & Case LLP
4. Dechert LLP
   Kirkpatrick & Lockhart Nicholson
   Lovells
   Norton Rose
   Osborne Clarke
   Preiskel & Co LLP
   Slaughter and May
   Towerhouse Consulting
   Wragge & Co LLP

Business Process Outsourcing
Best of the UK

1. Baker & McKenzie LLP
   Latham & Watkins LLP
   Milbank, Tweed, Hadley & McCloy
2. Addleshaw Goddard LLP
   Bird & Bird
   DLA Piper UK LLP
   Mayer, Brown, Rowe & Maw LLP
   Morrison & Foerster MNP
   Simmons & Simmons
3. Allen & Overy LLP
   Clifford Chance LLP
   Freshfields Bruckhaus Deringer
   Linklaters
   Lovells
   Norton Rose
   Pillsbury Winthrop Shaw Pittman
   Slaughter and May
4. Barlow Lyde & Gilbert
   Field Fisher Waterhouse LLP
   Pinsent Masons
   Taylor Wessing
   Wragge & Co LLP
5. Beachcroft LLP
   Berwin Leighton Paisner LLP
   Charles Russell
   Eversheds LLP
   Morgan Lewis
   Tarlo Lyons

international opportunities

The idea of the international law firm is far from new: UK law firms have ventured overseas since the 19th century. What has changed in recent times is the number of firms with offices overseas and the desire on the part of the largest firms to plant flags all over the globe. The Brits weren't the first in the game but they've certainly made up for lost time. The largest firm worldwide is our very own Clifford Chance, though it still has some way to go to catch up with Baker & McKenzie for the prize for most offices in most countries.

There are so many UK and US firms with overseas networks that students are spoilt for choice and keeping track of which firms are opening or closing offices in different countries is almost a full-time occupation. Wherever possible, we have mentioned the main changes from the past year in our **True Picture** reports. What we can never predict is exactly who is going to merge with whom.

The last five years have been characterised by European mergers and alliances as well as transatlantic tie-ups. Among the firms that have completed US-UK tie-ups in the past decade are Clifford Chance, Mayer Brown Rowe & Maw, Kilpatrick & Lockhart, Nicholson Graham, Jones Day, Dechert and DLA Piper. The spotlight is currently on Richards Butler, which is about to merge with Reed Smith.

The Americans have had a major influence on UK law firms in London since a wave of them came over to our capital in the mid-1990s. In response to this new competition, the UK firms have had to increase salaries, which in turn has led to a trend for raising lawyers' billing targets. At partner level, too, the UK firms have had to sharpen up. A drift of hotshot London partners from UK firms to American firms can, again, be explained by the higher remuneration on offer from the Americans.

The big UK and American firms are canny operators. They understand that to survive in a competitive legal market it is necessary to have a network of offices (or relationships with overseas law firms) in those parts of the world where the economies are active and/or growing. China is of real interest, as is the Middle East and the oil and gas-rich parts of Eastern Europe and Central Asia.

What all this means for trainees is simple: international work in London and overseas seat opportunities. The following table summarises where the seat opportunities lie and which firms send trainees to each location. As for international work back in London, the exact nature of a firm's clientele and worldwide office footprint will determine what trainees see from day to day. At White & Case, for example, there is a considerable amount of project finance work conducted in conjunction with Eastern European and Central Asian offices. CMS Cameron McKenna's superb energy practice brings similar work to London. At LeBoeuf, Lamb, Greene & MacRae there are many African LNG deals because of the firm's strong energy clientele. Trowers & Hamlins' dominance in the Middle East brings work back to our shores, as does Wiggin's relationship with the five major film studios in Los Angeles and Lawrence Graham's relationships with Indian businesses. These firms' international interests are certainly not limited to these sectors, but the above examples usefully illustrate the point.

If international work interests you then consider whether you would want to remain at home in the UK during your training or have the guarantee of an overseas seat. If it is the latter then pick a firm where you can be certain of securing a foreign posting. The competition at some firms is tough, while at others everyone who wants to go does. The **True Picture** reports should help you here. One other thing to bear in mind is your ability to speak another language. If you are fluent in Russian, for example, you may be collared for

Moscow instead of the New York opening you've got your eye on. It also follows that, where language skills would be useful – say in Italy – those who possess them will prove to be more-attractive candidates.

Although time abroad gives you experience of working in another jurisdiction, you'll not normally practise foreign law. An overseas seat is without doubt a very rewarding and challenging experience. It will usually be taken in an office that is smaller than your firm's UK office, and you will normally have greater responsibility. The trick to securing the most popular overseas seats is to wage an effective campaign of self-promotion and to get the prerequisite experience in the UK office before you go. The exact nature of this experience will depend on the type of seat taken abroad.

On arrival in a new country you don't need to worry about feeling too isolated. The local lawyers and staff will invariably be very happy to see you and welcome you into their office and probably also their homes. In some cities with a large influx of UK trainees there is a ready-made social scene and it's likely that the first thing to pop into your inbox will be an invite to meet the others. In Singapore, trainees make the most of the region by jetting off for group weekends on Malaysian or Indonesian islands. In Brussels they hook into the social scene attached to the vast EU machine. Another big plus is the free accommodation provided by the law firms. Usually, trainees are housed in their own apartments in smart areas close to a city's centre. It may be some time before they can afford such plush digs – and domestic help – back home.

overseas seats – who goes there?

location	firm
Abu Dhabi	Clyde & Co, Reed Smith Richards Butler, Shearman & Sterling, Simmons & Simmons, Trowers & Hamlins
Amsterdam	Allen & Overy, Baker & McKenzie, Clifford Chance, Freshfields Bruckhaus Deringer, Linklaters, Norton Rose, Slaughter and May
Athens	Norton Rose
Australia	Baker & McKenzie, Holman Fenwick & Willan
Bahrain	Norton Rose, Trowers & Hamlins
Bangkok	Allen & Overy, Herbert Smith, Watson Farley & Williams
Beijing	Allen & Overy, Bird & Bird, Clifford Chance, Freshfields Bruckhaus Deringer, Herbert Smith, Linklaters
Berlin	Hammonds, SJ Berwin, Slaughter and May
Boston	Dechert
Bratislava (Slovakia)	Allen & Overy
Brussels	Allen & Overy, Ashurst, Baker & McKenzie, Berwin Leighton Paisner, Bird & Bird, Cleary Gottlieb Steen & Hamilton, CMS Cameron McKenna, Clifford Chance, Cobbetts, Dechert, Dickinson Dees, Eversheds, Freshfields Bruckhaus Deringer, Hammonds, Herbert Smith, LeBoeuf Lamb Greene & MacRae, Linklaters, Lovells, Mayer Brown Rowe & Maw, McGrigors, Nabarro Nathanson, Norton Rose, Olswang, Shadbolt & Co, Shearman & Sterling, Simmons & Simmons, SJ Berwin, Slaughter and May, Taylor Vinters, White & Case
Bucharest	Linklaters
Budapest	Allen & Overy, CMS Cameron McKenna, Linklaters
California	Osborne Clarke, Weil Gotshal & Manges
Chicago	Baker & McKenzie, Mayer Brown Rowe & Maw

location	firm
Cologne	Freshfields Bruckhaus Deringer, Osborne Clarke
Copenhagen	Slaughter and May
Dubai	Allen & Overy, Clifford Chance, Clyde & Co, Denton Wilde Sapte, Freshfields Bruckhaus Deringer, Holman Fenwick & Willan, Linklaters, Norton Rose, Trowers & Hamlins
Düsseldorf	Bird & Bird, Slaughter and May
Frankfurt	Allen & Overy, Ashurst, Bird & Bird, Clifford Chance, Freshfields Bruckhaus Deringer, Linklaters, Lovells, Norton Rose, SJ Berwin, Slaughter and May, Weil Gotshal & Manges, White & Case
Geneva	Slaughter and May
The Hague	Bird & Bird
Hamburg	Taylor Wessing
Helsinki	Slaughter and May
Hong Kong	Addleshaw Goddard, Allen & Overy, Barlow Lyde & Gilbert, Baker & McKenzie, Bird & Bird, Clifford Chance, Clyde & Co, CMS Cameron McKenna, Freshfields Bruckhaus Deringer, Hammonds, Herbert Smith, Holman Fenwick & Willan, Linklaters, Lovells, Norton Rose, Simmons & Simmons, Skadden, Slaughter and May, Stephenson Harwood, White & Case
Johannesburg	White & Case
Lille	Brachers
Luxembourg	Allen & Overy, Linklaters, Slaughter and May
Madrid	Allen & Overy, Ashurst, Clifford Chance, Denton Wilde Sapte, Freshfields Bruckhaus Deringer, Hammonds, Linklaters, SJ Berwin, Simmons & Simmons, Slaughter and May

solicitors

location	firm
Milan	Allen & Overy, Ashurst, Bird & Bird, Clifford Chance, Freshfields Bruckhaus Deringer, Linklaters, Lovells, Norton Rose, Simmons & Simmons, SJ Berwin, Slaughter and May, White & Case, Withers
Moscow	Allen & Overy, Baker & McKenzie, Clifford Chance, CMS Cameron McKenna, Denton Wilde Sapte, Freshfields Bruckhaus Deringer, Herbert Smith, LeBoeuf Lamb Greene & MacRae, Linklaters, Lovells, Norton Rose, White & Case
Munich	Ashurst, Bird & Bird, Clifford Chance, Dechert, Linklaters, Norton Rose, Osborne Clarke, SJ Berwin, Weil Gotshal & Manges
New York	Allen & Overy, Baker & McKenzie, Cleary Gottlieb Steen & Hamilton, Clifford Chance, Dechert, Freshfields Bruckhaus Deringer, Linklaters, Lovells, Shearman & Sterling, Slaughter and May, Weil Gotshal & Manges
Oman	Trowers & Hamlins
Oslo	Slaughter and May
Paris	Allen & Overy, Ashurst, Bird & Bird, Clifford Chance, CMS Cameron McKenna, Denton Wilde Sapte, Eversheds, Freshfields Bruckhaus Deringer, Hammonds, Herbert Smith, Holman Fenwick & Willan, LeBoeuf Lamb Greene & McRae, Linklaters, Lovells, Norton Rose, Reed Smith Richards Butler, Shadbolt & Co, Shearman & Sterling, Simmons & Simmons, Slaughter and May, SJ Berwin, Taylor Wessing, Travers Smith, Watson Farley & Williams, Weil Gotshal & Manges, White & Case
Philadelphia	Dechert
Piraeus	Clyde & Co, Holman Fenwick & Willan, Ince & Co, Norton Rose, Reed Smith Richards Butler, Watson Farley & Williams

location	firm
Prague	Allen & Overy, Baker & McKenzie, Clifford Chance, CMS Cameron McKenna, Linklaters, Norton Rose, Slaughter and May, Weil Gotshal & Manges, White & Case
Rome	Allen & Overy, Bird & Bird, Clifford Chance, Denton Wilde Sapte, Linklaters
Rotterdam	Denton Wilde Sapte
São Paulo	Clifford Chance, Linklaters
Shanghai	Clifford Chance, Clyde & Co, Freshfields Bruckhaus Deringer, Herbert Smith, Holman Fenwick & Willan, Linklaters
Singapore	Allen & Overy, Baker & McKenzie, Clifford Chance, Clyde & Co, Herbert Smith, Linklaters, Lovells, Norton Rose, Shearman & Sterling, Stephenson Harwood, Watson Farley & Williams, White & Case
Stockholm	Bird & Bird, Slaughter and May, White & Case
Toronto	Ford & Warren
Tokyo	Allen & Overy, Clifford Chance, Freshfields Bruckhaus Deringer, Herbert Smith, Linklaters, Lovells, Simmons & Simmons, Slaughter and May, White & Case
Turin	Hammonds, SJ Berwin
Vienna	Freshfields Bruckhaus Deringer
Warsaw	Allen & Overy, Clifford Chance, CMS Cameron McKenna, Linklaters, Weil Gotshal & Manges
Washington	Baker & McKenzie, Dechert, Freshfields Bruckhaus Deringer
Wellington New Zealand	Slaugther and May

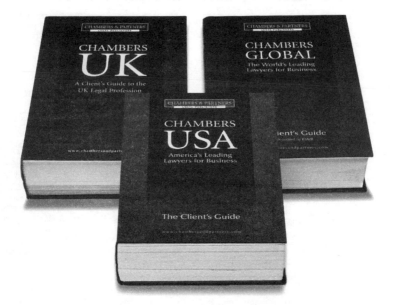

Chambers and Partners publishes a suite of legal guides that you should find helpful in your search for a training contract or pupillage.

- **Chambers UK** is the product of over 12,000 interviews with solicitors, barristers and their clients. It identifies the leading firms, sets and players across the full sweep of legal practice in the UK.

- **Chambers Global** sets out the results of our research into legal jurisdictions worldwide from Australia to Zambia. If you are considering a training contract with an international law firm, it's a must-read book.

- **Chambers USA** provides a more detailed analysis of the performance of the best firms across all US states.

These guides can all be read online:
www.chambersandpartners.com.

the true picture

the true picture

The True Picture reports on 150 firms in England and Wales, ranging from the international giants to small regional practices. Most handle commercial law, although many also offer private client experience. Others are 'general practice' firms.

how we do our research

The 150 firms all agree to provide complete lists of their trainees. After checking the lists are complete, we randomly select a sample of individuals for telephone interviews. Our sources are guaranteed anonymity to give them the confidence to say exactly what they want. The True Picture is not shown to the law firms prior to publication; they see it for the first time when this book is published.

Trainees tell us why they chose their firm and why others might want to. We talk about seat allocation and the character and work of different departments. We ask about the hours and the after-hours fun, and we ascertain what happens to people on qualification. We look for the things trainees agree upon, and if they do not agree we present both sides of the argument.

We're bored by the tired lines used in many recruitment brochures. You know the ones that tell you Smashing, Great & Partners is a standout firm because of its friendly culture in which everybody is down to earth and where approachable partners operate an open-door policy. These traits are not the preserve of a few firms. What we try to focus on instead is the detail of what builds a firm's character.

our findings

A couple of years ago the NQ job market was in dire health and many trainees were eternally grateful to have any job on qualification. This year a vastly improved job market encouraged qualifiers to be pickier about the area of law in which they specialised after training and we believe this accounts for lower retention rates at many firms. With the deals market buzzing, corporate departments have been run off their feet and the hours worked by corporate and finance lawyers are long. As a result, there has been a resurgence of interest in non-transactional departments for qualification, though unfortunately there were not enough of these jobs to satisfy demand. If you intend to use retention rates as a determining factor in your choice of firm, do be wary of the statistics being bandied around. Law firms make their own rules on how to calculate retention rates – you may not be getting a full picture from them. For this reason we collect our own statistics and include them in each law firm feature. We have collated statistics since 2000 and publish them on our website.

We try not to concentrate too much on current market conditions when writing the True Picture, as we recognise that things may have changed by the time our readers start their training. However, we also recognise that the climate of 2006 affects the fortunes and market positions of law firms, and this in turn may have a bearing on what firms will be like in 2009 and beyond. The other things we just can't predict are law firm mergers or closures. Thankfully, the latter are rare, but the mergers are a regular thing in the profession these days. When firms merge, trainees' contracts are honoured, though of course it does mean that new recruits find themselves in a different firm to the one they signed up to.

across the board:

- Some seats are more popular than others. The perfect example is employment law.
- Levels of responsibility vary between departments. In property you might have your own small files. In corporate you will generally work in a very junior capacity as part of a team.
- The experience in litigation depends entirely on the type of cases your firm handles; usually a trainee's responsibility is inversely proportionate to the value and complexity of a case. If your firm handles personal injury claims,

you may have conduct of matters yourself. If your firm goes in for long-running financial services litigation or multi-jurisdictional matters, you could be stuck for months on document management jobs.

- In times of plenty, corporate and finance seats mean long hours, commonly climaxing in all-nighters. Again, the size and complexity of a deal will determine your role, but corporate and finance usually require the most teamwork.
- Most firms offer four six-month seats; some offer six four-month seats and others operate their own unique systems. Trainees switch departments and supervisors for each seat. Most share a room and work with a partner or senior assistant; others sit open-plan, either with the rest of the team or with other trainees. Occasionally a trainee will even have their own room.
- All firms conduct appraisals, a minimum of one at the conclusion of each seat, and usually halfway through as well.
- Client secondments, where offered, are a great way to find out how to be a better lawyer by learning to understand a client's needs. They can be the highlight of a training contract.
- The Law Society requires all trainees to gain experience of both contentious and non-contentious work. Additionally, most firms have certain seats they require or prefer trainees to try. Some firms are very prescriptive, others flexible. Remember, a training contract is a time to explore legal practice to see what you're best at and most enjoy. You may surprise yourself.

jargonbusting
- agency work – making a court appearance for another firm that can't get to court
- all-nighter – working through the night
- cmc – case management conference
- coco – company-commercial department/work
- dispute resolution – litigation, mediation, arbitration, etc

- grunt work – also known as donkey work, monkey work or even document jockeying. Administrative (and boring) yet essential tasks including photocopying, paginating, compiling court bundles and scheduling documents, bibling (putting together sets of all the relevant documents for a transaction), data room duty (supervising visitors to rooms full of important documents, helping them find things and making sure they don't steal them) and proof-reading or checking that documents are intact.
- high net worth individuals – rich people
- infant approvals – court authorisation for a settlement involving a minor
- mentor partner – a partner who will guide you and buy you lunch
- NQ – a newly-qualified solicitor
- PQE – post-qualification experience
- training partner – the partner who oversees the training scheme
- trainee partner – a trainee who acts like a partner

what kind of firm do I choose?
Your choice of firm will be based on location, size and the practice areas available... then it's a matter of chemistry. Some firms are stuffier; some are more industrious and some are very brand-aware and involve trainees heavily in marketing. Some work in modern open-plan offices; others occupy buildings long past their sell-by date. Some focus on international business; others are at the heart of their local business communities. Some concentrate on contentious work, others transactional. The combinations of these variables are endless.

and finally...
We hope the True Picture will help you decide on the firms you want to target. No matter how hard or how easy securing a training contract is for you, you'll want to end up with the right one.

the true picture firms

	Firm name		City	Total trainees	Page
1	Government Legal Service		London	50	346
2	Eversheds LLP		London*	173	313
3	Clifford Chance LLP		London	250	267
4	Allen & Overy LLP		London	237	186
5	DLA Piper LLP		London*	165	297
6	Linklaters		London	268	418
7	Pinsent Masons		London*	115	483
8	Freshfields Bruckhaus Deringer		London	198	342
9	Addleshaw Goddard LLP		London*	88	183
10	Herbert Smith LLP		London	153	363
11	Slaughter and May		London	175	526
12	CMS Cameron McKenna LLP		London*	120	274
13	Lovells		London	148	422
14	Berwin Leighton Paisner LLP		London	80	217
15	Beachcroft LLP		London*	70	214
16	Ashurst		London	95	205
17	Mills & Reeve		Cambridge*	42	450
18	Hammonds		London*	79	352
19	Norton Rose		London	105	461
20	Denton Wilde Sapte		London*	63	290
21	SJ Berwin LLP		London	80	520
22	Simmons & Simmons		London	94	517
23	Nabarro Nathanson		London*	52	458
24	Hill Dickinson		Liverpool*	28	369
25	Halliwells LLP		Manchester*	76	349
26	Blake Lapthorn Linnell		Fareham*	21	230
27	Irwin Mitchell		Sheffield*	51	387
28	Baker & McKenzie LLP		London	60	208
29	McGrigors		London*	27	448
30	Wragge & Co LLP		Brirmingham*	55	588
31	Richards Butler	*These two firms*	London*	51**	491
32	Reed Smith LLP	*are merging*			
33	Clyde & Co		London*	45	271
34	Osborne Clarke		Bristol*	41	470
35	Barlow Lyde & Gilbert		London	35	211
36	Charles Russell LLP		London*	15	262
37	Mayer, Brown, Rowe & Maw LLP		London	59	440
38	Taylor Wessing		London*	46	540
39	Browne Jacobson LLP		Nottingham*	20	248
40=	Burges Salmon LLP		Bristol	39	253
40=	Dundas & Wilson		London*	6	305
40=	Reynolds Porter Chamberlain		London*	26	494
43	Cobbetts		Manchester*	52	277
44	Olswang		London*	41	465
45	Bevan Brittan LLP		Bristol*	36	220
46	White & Case LLP		London	52	578
47	Field Fisher Waterhouse LLP		London	34	319
48	Trowers & Hamlins		London*	33	557
49=	Lawrence Graham LLP		London	38	402
49=	Travers Smith		London	40	551

*Firms are listed in order of size as measured by partner and assistant figures provided to Chambers UK. * Head or primary UK office. ** Combined figures*

www.chambersandpartners.co.uk

	Firm name	City	Total trainees	Page
51	Macfarlanes	London	49	430
52	DWF	Liverpool*	18	308
53=	Penningtons Solicitors LLP	London*	28	480
53=	Ward Hadaway	Newcastle*	20	565
55	Pannone LLP	Manchester	29	457
56	Dickinson Dees	Newcastle*	28	294
57	Brabners Chaffe Street	Liverpool*	18	240
58	HBJ Gateley Wareing LLP	Birmingham*	14	358
59	Bird & Bird	London	26	226
60	Shoosmiths	Northampton*	32	512
61	Morgan Cole	Cardiff*	20	456
62	Stephenson Harwood	London	27	534
63	Speechly Bircham	London	11	529
64	Freeth Cartwright LLP	Nottingham*	13	340
65	Walker Morris	Leeds	30	562
66	Holman Fenwick & Willan	London	18	374
67	TLT Solicititors	Bristol*	14	548
68	Withers LLP	London	26	585
69	Shearman & Sterling LLP	London	17	509
70	Pitmans	Reading*	6	486
71	Bircham Dyson Bell	London	15	223
72=	Andrew M Jackson	Hull	13	190
72=	Dechert	London	20	288
74	Jones Day	London	42	390
75	Martineau Johnson	Birmingham*	19	437
76	Ashfords	Exeter*	24	200
77	Manches LLP	London*	23	432
78	Kirkpatrick & Lockhart Nicholson Graham LLP	London	21	397
79	Mishcon de Reya	London	15	453
80	Ince & Co	London	18	384
81	Hugh James	Cardiff*	19	379
82=	Farrer & Co	London	17	316
82=	Russell-Cooke	London	15	499
84=	Foot Anstey	Exeter*	16	327
84=	Lewis Silkin LLP	London*	12	415
86	Watson, Farley & Williams LLP	London	24	570
87	Sidley Austin LLP	London	10	515
88	Veale Wasbrough	Bristol	12	560
89	Lester Aldridge	Bournemouth*	14	412
90	asb law	Crawley*	9	197
91	DMH Stallard	Brighton*	17	300
92	Weil, Gotshal & Manges	London	19	575
93=	Cripps Harries Hall	Tunbridge Wells	7	285
93=	Wedlake Bell	London	14	572
95	Mace & Jones	Liverpool*	11	427
96	Thomas Eggar	Chichester*	16	546
97	Forsters LLP	London	8	335
98=	Anthony Collins	Birmingham	14	192
98=	Capsticks	London	9	256
100	Forbes	Blackburn*	15	330

*Firms are listed in order of size as measured by partner and assistant figures provided to Chambers UK. * Head or primary UK office.*

www.chambersandpartners.co.uk

the true picture firms (continued)

	Firm name	City	Total trainees	Page
101	Bristows	London	13	245
102	Skadden, Arps, Slate, Meagher & Flom (UK) LLP	London	6	523
103	LeBoeuf, Lamb, Greene & MacRae LLP	London	12	407
104	Stevens & Bolton LLP	Guildford	6	537
105	Boodle Hatfield	London*	10	235
106	iBB	Uxbridge*	11	382
107	Finers Stephens Innocent	London	10	322
108	Challinors	West Bromwich*	12	259
109=	BP Collins	Gerrard's Cross	6	238
109=	Howes Percival	Northampton*	16	376
109=	Trethowans	Salisbury*	6	555
112	McDermott Will & Emery LLP	London	4	445
113	Cleary Gotlieb Steen & Hamilton LLP	London	9	264
114	Laytons	London*	20	405
115	Harbottle & Lewis LLP	London	9	355
116	Robert Muckle LLP	Newcastle	8	497
117=	Coffin Mew & Clover	Southampton*	11	280
117=	Hodge Jones & Allen	London	13	371
119	Ford & Warren	Leeds	7	332
120	Henmans LLP	Oxford	6	361
121	Collyer-Bristow	London	6	282
122	Stephens & Scown	Exeter*	11	532
123=	Salans	London	7	502
123=	Shadbolt & Co LLP	Reigate*	9	506
125	Fisher Meredith	London	15	325
126	Kendall Freeman	London	17	393
127=	Payne Hicks Beach	London	6	478
127=	Warner Goodman & Streat	Southampton*	8	567
129=	Birkett Long	Colchester*	5	228
129=	Teacher Stern Selby	London	10	543
131=	BTMK LLP	Southend*	5	251
131=	Knight & Sons	Newcastle-Under-Lyme	5	400
133=	Lupton Fawcett LLP	Leeds	5	425
133=	Prettys	Ipswich	10	488
135	McCormicks	Leeds*	11	443
136=	Fox Williams	London	8	337
136=	Orrick, Herrington & Sutcliffe	London	13	468
138	Blandy & Blandy	Reading	6	233
139	Wiggin LLP	Cheltenham*	6	582
140	Hextalls	London	9	366
141	Ashton Morton Slack	Sheffield*	5	203
142=	Dorsey & Whitney LLP	London	8	303
142=	Kimbells LLP	Milton Keynes	4	395
144	Lee & Priestley	Leeds	6	410
145=	Anthony Gold	London	12	195
145=	Brachers	Maidstone	8	243
147	Palmers Solicitors	Basildon	4	473
148	Samuel Phillips & Co	Newcastle	3	504
149	Maples Teesdale	London	6	435
150	The Endeavour Partnership	Stockton-on-Tees	4	311

*Firms are listed in order of size as measured by partner and assistant figures provided to Chambers UK. * Head or primary UK office.*

www.chambersandpartners.co.uk

Addleshaw Goddard LLP

the facts

Location: Manchester, Leeds, London
Number of UK partners/solicitors: 179/528
Total number of trainees: 88
Seats: 4x6 months
Alternative seats: Hong Kong, secondments
Extras: Pro bono – Manchester Uni and Springfields legal advice centres

In 2003 a merger between striding northerner Addleshaw Booth and flagging City outfit Theodore Goddard resulted in catchy-named Addleshaw Goddard. Three years on and the "*ambitious and growing*" firm has impressed as much as it has proved unafraid to shake a few of the trees in its own back yard.

the right way

If you want to know exactly what the firm now seeks to achieve, read the senior partner's statement on its website. To summarise, the mission is to be consistent in the services provided from all three offices; to win business from many more FTSE 350 companies; and to be regarded as a credible alternative to magic circle firms. At the management's disposal is a large army of nearly 700 lawyers and a capability to move work around the offices. So far, so successful for AG. Sneak a look at the firm's recent track record and it's easy to see why it has earned glowing reports from the marketplace and new client mandates. News of a turnover exceeding £160 million for 2005/06 must have been as pleasing as the arrival of key lateral hires at partner level. While it's not all been traffic coming in through its doors, no one doubts that the overall picture is positive indeed.

Internally, the firm has adopted a culture-and-values programme called The AG Way, and apparently partners take it very seriously. This makes us all the sorrier to break the news that most trainee comments on the initiative were lukewarm at best. Although some felt "*immersed in the strategy of the firm*" and "*do adopt The AG Way,*" others said: "*It's not like it has a profound influence on me or impacts on my day.*" Some were less diplomatic: "*It's just marketing babble rammed down our throats.*" Whether you place much stock in this kind of thing or not, something is bearing fruit, as these comments evidence. "*Everyone seems to enjoy working together and that makes a massive difference,*" and "*AG is a young pretender; we all have these objectives and we are fighting hard to get somewhere.*" It's not only trainees who rate the firm's culture: AG snuck in at number 94 on *The Sunday Times*' most recent '100 Best Companies To Work For' survey.

When asked to describe the typical trainee our interviewees struggled to put their fingers on any defining features, but we found common threads easily. Quite simply, these guys are driven, so heed the warning that "*if you want to sit back and let things pass you by, then AG is not for you.*" We learned, "*you have to be proactive in developing your own training contract,*" and by all accounts supervisors have grown used to trainees being a bit pushy and asking for challenging work. In short, bright, communicative and confident but not cocky just about covers it. From 2007 all recruits will study their LPC at BPP in Leeds, Manchester or London. Another interesting pre-contract development is a voluntary week-long overseas trip to help build homes with the charity Habitat for Humanity.

corporate whaling

The firm is split into four divisions: contentious and commercial; finance and projects; corporate; and real estate. Trainees can if they wish see all four of these corners of the firm, and must take seats in real estate, something from the main transactional departments and something contentious.

A seat in corporate is highly likely to feature at some point. One corporate-averse character had greeted the news that they were to spend six months in the department with an anxious, "*Oh, bugger!*" They needn't have worried, as they quickly changed their tune. "*It was great; I had a really good run of deals and was very much on a level with everyone.*" Their experience was by no means unique. Another trainee suggested: "*If you show you are interested, you are allowed more of a free rein.*" Sounds perfect, though we sense that the work-shy would not fare well. The trainee who had "*a whale of a time working late*" – let's call him Ishmael – must either have had some kind of perverse fixation with after-hours grafting or maybe there really is "*a great team atmosphere.*" Perhaps it's the quality of the deals that keeps trainees keen; "*it's great to read about stuff in the newspaper and think, 'I was involved in that'.*" The Leeds team for example acted for investor 3i on the £200 million merger between travel companies Wallace Arnold and Shearings, undoubtedly one of the biggest deals in the region for 2005. A good example of cross-office working was the £52 million Travelodge sale of Little Chef roadside restaurants, which brought some 70 people from different departments together.

If banking appears in your seat schedule, you might be surprised at the level of autonomy available. "*Sometimes it is a bit scary as you are often looked to to keep the deal moving,*" but this pressure means "*you can learn more in two weeks here than in the whole of another seat.*" Clearly a department for the kind of person who will "*run with it, rather than buckle.*" A real estate posting brings the opportunity to work with "*a growing team nationally and a diverse range of clients.*" Again, trainees experienced "*a steep learning curve,*" but for these troopers that's okay – "*it's why we're in the job!*" The great thing about property is "*you learn on your feet very quickly*" and "*gain the confidence to deal with anyone and anything.*"

Reassuringly, none of the file-juggling trainees we spoke to ever felt "*hung out to dry.*"

The commercial group incorporates the IP, sport, defamation, IT, and brands and designs groups. The media and entertainment practice also sits under this umbrella, although it has been weakened by the departure of the London film and music practice to another firm, Michael Simkins LLP. Of late AG lawyers have represented the Barclay brothers on various libel and privacy matters, including issues arising from their purchase of *The Spectator* and other Telegraph titles. The Football Association has also sought similar advice, which leads us on to another strength – sports law. Clients in this area include the FA Premier League, the British Horseracing Board, World Snooker and the Rugby Football League.

three become one

Secondments to clients (eg The FA, adidas, Barclays, Astra Zeneca, Dixons) are worth watching out for – "*occasionally an e-mail comes round from HR asking who wants to go.*" Time spent with a client's legal team invariably turns out to be "*a brilliant experience to take a step outside of the normal working environment and realise just how unimportant the law is to clients.*" We presume this is a reference to the fact that clients often view legal issues as simply a distraction from the normal running of their operations. For the record, there is only one overseas seat (with a firm called Johnson Stokes & Master in Hong Kong), which could be seen as a reflection of the relatively low priority the firm has (thus far) placed on the international market.

It could be said that there are strings on the London office that are pulled from the North. Sure, there is noticeable movement of work and personnel (including trainees, if this appeals) between offices, and the "*one firm/three hub*" model is clearly being pursued, but AG cannot shake its northern roots. This is by no means a bad thing, of course, and perhaps London just needs more time to work out which muscles to flex. The three-office set-up in the capital is not ideal, but there are plans to consolidate when current lease commitments allow. In the meantime, the larger office – previously described as "*a bit brown*" – has been duly subjected to "*a tidy up to tide things over until the lease runs out.*" We're told "*they have really gone to town on the client suites,*" however the rest is "*still not the most glamorous place to work.*" For completeness, we should praise the shinier northern offices, where marble, glass, water features and airy atriums are the order of the day. Still, the Leeds office may boast a café and Starbucks outlet for fighting mid-afternoon lulls, but "*the canteen food is definitely better in London.*"

choirs, kickarounds and karting

Maintaining a work/life balance is always a battle for lawyers, but the trainees we spoke to were at least aware of the importance of addressing these conflicting demands. "*In places like corporate there are peaks and troughs, and we are encouraged to take advantage of the troughs. If you've just done a two-day long completion, then you will get time off in lieu. They don't want zombies working here.*" The average day is hard to pinpoint, but suffice to say we heard neither constant moans nor tales of an easy life.

What of the social side of AG? "*At first, trainees tend to move in packs, but then they get involved in their own departmental scene.*" It sounds like pulling rank is not the AG way, since "*relative seniority is not an issue – a partner might walk in at 5.30pm and say, 'Come on, let's go to the pub'.*" Sounds great, particularly as "*you don't have to talk about work.*" There is, perhaps understandably, something of a north/south divide amongst trainees. The Leeds and Manchester groups meet up for trans-Pennine socials, but those in the capital largely make do with their own company since there's a perception that "*London's a bit far.*"

Once in a while, departmental events bring everyone together, and a trainee conference is held in the autumn of each year, allowing recruits from all offices to "*meet in a hotel somewhere for talks and stuff during the day, and a piss-up at night.*" When back home, after-work and weekend drinks are often arranged between trainees and other junior lawyers. The Manchester crowd, for example, can usually be found in various pubs and bars around town. The infamous 'Didsbury Dozen' pub crawl apparently clocks up a month's worth of excess in one hit. We are unsure how many survivors there were after a recent, bank holiday, 12-venue crawl in the Chiltern area of Manchester. The 1pm kick-off time suggests there may have been few.

When we rang them, trainees were looking forward to the end-of-financial-year party. "*It's a thank you from the firm for doing so well,*" so we imagine that mutual backslapping and bevvies all round are the order of the day. Previous "*really-quite-decent events*" have included go-karting and a trip to Alton Towers. "*It's a good reflection on them,*" said an appreciative trainee; "*we're busy and we work pretty hard, so they try to reward us.*" Sportsfolk are well catered for during the netball and cricket seasons, when inter-office matches are a good way to show who's really the daddy, and the AG footie team managed to wangle a trip to Germany earlier in 2006. If you fancy working out your vocal chords instead of your metatarsals, join the AG choir. When we called, members of the 40-strong ensemble were practising for a performance in St Ann's Church in Manchester, where "*a last-night-of-the-proms atmosphere with lots of flag waving*" was expected. Better still, the choir's annual Christmas tour takes in gigs at all three offices... so rock 'n' roll!

In September 2006, some 30 of the 36 qualifiers took jobs with the firm. All stayed in Leeds, one left from Manchester and five left from London.

and finally...

If you have that *"can-do attitude"* and can match the firm's ambition, then maybe the right way is The AG Way. To the trainee who said *"we're all a bunch of keenos really – don't quote me on that,"* we hope you've learned a valuable lesson.

Allen & Overy LLP

the facts

Location: London
Number of partners/assistants: 206/754
Total number of trainees: 237
Seats: 4x6 months (some split seats)
Alternative seats: Overseas seats, secondments
Extras: Pro bono – Liberty, Battersea Legal Advice Centre; death row appeals; language training

For several years the magic circle firm Allen & Overy's graduate recruitment literature has used the slogan 'Start at the top... and work up'. If the quality of the brands you buy matter a great deal to you then chances are you'll value this one. *"It's like playing for one of the Premier League football clubs,"* a trainee told us.

branded product

The trainees we interviewed stated that their primary reason for applying to A&O was *"reputation – obviously."* How can this reputation be quantified? *"Large transactions, large clients, international work and a friendly atmosphere."* Here at Chambers we would also go so far as to add the words 'somewhat understated'. Think Liberty of London or Fortnum & Mason: quality brands with a fine English heritage yet known around the world. The firm was established in 1930 and advised Edward VIII on his abdication from the throne, but don't be fooled into thinking it is stuck in the past. A&O will soon move into a state-of-the-art building on the ancient site of Spitalfields in the City of London.

Since inventing the eurobond in the 1960s, Allen & Overy lawyers have enjoyed phenomenal success at the forefront of all things financial. Over half of its 2,500 lawyers worldwide devote their energies to banking and international capital markets, and the firm counts Merrill Lynch, Société Générale, HSBC and BNP Paribas among its clients. During 2005 it advised on 14 lending finance transactions that amounted to a total value of over £62.5 billion. In acquisition finance, the firm acted for sponsors KKR, Bain Capital and Vornado on the European financings of the $6 billion acquisition of Toys R Us as well as JPMorgan, Citigroup and Bank of America on the financing supporting Blackstone and Lion Capital's €1.846 billion acquisition of Cadbury Schweppes European Beverages. Deals of this size are commonplace and all add up to a reputation as one of the City's two pre-eminent finance practices. If the firm with which it shares that honour – Clifford Chance – wrestles for the best deals, we'd say A&O is more likely to issue a challenge for a duel, quietly confident that it has the skill and tenacity to win out. This is a firm that likes to play by the rules and subscribes completely to its motto of 'excellence in everything.' As one trainee put it: *"We all want to push ourselves to be the best we can. Everything we do has to be bang on the money."*

There's no avoiding A&O's core finance departments. If that fazes you then turn the page now. Yes, you will get a chance to influence the path your training contract is going to take right from the word go – even as early as your LPC year you will be asked if you have a preference for your first seat – but there are some rules. Everyone does at least 12 months of transactional work, either in international capital markets (ICM), corporate or banking. Four six-month seats are typical, although there is also the option to take some three-month seats, and many trainees do two three-monthers. You are less likely to qualify into a department where you have had only 12 weeks' experience but the short seats do at least provide variety to the training contract. Certain seats, currently private client, competition and environment, are only available for three months.

You are also promised time in your absolutely-must-have department, but be careful how much store you place on this promise because the most popular niche departments – employment and IP, for example – have limited space for trainees and qualifiers. It is also worth remembering that much of the work in such departments supports the banking and corporate teams rather than being 'stand-alone'. It should be stressed however that the work of A&O's non-core departments is exceptionally good across the board, and it is into a lot of different stuff. All we're saying is that you must recognise their relative size, and therefore the smaller number of opportunities, in these departments. Its litigators, for example, came out of the recent Equitable Life litigation with their reputations much enhanced. At A&O litigation seats seem to be like Marmite – trainees either love them or hate them – but as a contentious seat is compulsory for at least three months, it's *"something you have to do eventually."*

clueless?

So what exactly is ICM? Well, your seat here will introduce you to such delights as derivatives, general securities and structured finance. If even these terms leave you feeling a little uneasy, you are not alone. When we asked current trainees what they thought when they were told they would be sitting in ICM, they confessed that they felt *"completely daunted,"* one recalling thinking: *"'Oh my god, what is that?' – I didn't have a clue."* It seems the seat is not as overwhelming as it sounds, owing to the fact that *"you are heavily supervised and can always ask questions."* Of the derivatives team, trainees said: *"Although it is incredibly complicated, this is a very, very sexy area where all the big money is. Derivatives are known as the financial world's nuclear weapon."* As if that wasn't enough: *"You are working with the very best derivatives experts in the world. These guys wrote the book back in the 1980s – I can't big up enough how important they are."* As a result, even as a trainee you are likely to secure *"great exposure to top-quality work"* and *"the more confident you become, the more you have a free rein."*

Anyone planning to qualify in this department might wish to know that *"the negotiating is fairly aggressive; it's basically a bunch of lawyers shouting at one another down the telephone so you have to be able to hold your own if you want to do well."* However, working in derivatives is not all about verbal skills: *"this is also one of the most difficult areas of black-letter law I have ever come across,"* one trainee admitted. *"Some of the contracts are incredibly esoteric and it takes a big brain to get your head around it all."* In ICM, we heard that for trainees there is a great deal of drafting, following of precedents and document management to ensure that all parties have the right information. According to one interviewee: *"The benefits of a capital markets seat is that a transaction can be quite short and based on a lot of precedents, which means you can have quite a lot of responsibility."*

making the headlines

To capital market enthusiasts a corporate seat, in contrast, equates to *"huge transactions, bloody long hours and not a lot of responsibility."* One trainee explained how *"there are plenty of straightforward things for trainees to do, as we all learned this stuff at law school... there is only so much to know and the emphasis is on how quickly you can get a deal done."* This firm covers the kind of deals you read about *"even if you open the Metro, never mind the Financial Times."* To give you an example, lawyers have recently advised Alliance UniChem on its £7 billion merger with Boots. Being a part of these big-name deals is why *"some people absolutely love corporate."* As a case in point, one source declared: *"I even enjoyed the weekend I worked; it was really interesting. We were in meetings with the clients who were really high-profile figures that you read about in the press all the time. It didn't seem that painful to be there from Saturday until Monday."* If you are already itching to purchase your *"red braces and pinstripe suits"* this could be you one day. Do such 'fat cat' stereotypes actually exist in the corporate department, we wondered? *"Not everyone is a white, middle-class, overweight, Oxbridge-educated male, although there is plenty of that,"* a source chuckled, quickly adding that *"there are also a lot of ladies at the top of the tree who are excellent, as well as loads of people from international offices."*

chalking up top marks

As we indicated earlier, this firm is a formidable force in the finance arena. A trainee in the banking seat can expect *"quality work"* and *"a bit more time to work through documents than you get in corporate."* Trainee tasks are mainly of the drafting variety and document management often equates to chasing clients for their paperwork. Despite the myth that the bigger the machine that trainees belong to, the smaller the trainee cog and the more mundane their tasks, our sources were pleased with the level of client contact and responsibility that they were awarded. Said one: *"At no part of my training contract have I been relegated to the photocopier."*

Current trainees emphasise that many partners are *"great teachers as well as great lawyers."* Like the very clever university lecturers who you were not afraid to ask for help, trainees told us that working with such people boosted their confidence. However, we also heard about some *"old-school"* supervisors who bark at trainees and leave them to flounder with the *"huge responsibility"* they sometimes get landed with, *"usually by default, as everyone is so busy."* Character building, perhaps, but also *"incredibly stressful."*

Trainees also told us about their *"phenomenal experience"* on client secondments with investment banks. One told us: *"they gave me an office to myself and left me alone, it was like running my own practice, which was truly terrifying."* Typical tasks range from receiving confidentiality agreements and getting them negotiated to putting together pricing documents and term sheets. How do you know if such an experience is for you? *"The skill set required is to be very, very organised – you need to be a self-starter, otherwise you could end up sitting there as the work crashes around your ears."* There are secondments to financial institutions such as Goldman Sachs, Barclays Capital and Credit Suisse, companies such as Cable & Wireless and TUI, and even the human rights organisation Liberty.

If you would prefer time away from the office further from home, A&O's international network is there waiting. Secondments to New York and Hong Kong are *"by far the most popular,"* sources told us. You may find somewhere else that appeals by looking at the overseas seats table on page 174.

summit for the weekend?

Is there a typical A&O trainee? The way our interviewees see it: *"Most of the trainees are generally relaxed, unpretentious individuals who are extremely intelligent..."* but *"as everyone is clever no one feels the need to go round bragging about it."* If bragging is out of the question, what do trainees get up to in their spare time? Trips to the theatre and Wimbledon, water skiing and the NDCS Three Peaks Challenge are some of the highlights. Departmental socials range from Friday cakes in the office to summer parties and clay pigeon shooting at partners' houses. The trainees also choose to spend part of their annual budget on a ball, an event that guarantees *"lots of drinking and dancing and general studenty behaviour."* Every possible sport is available from football, cricket, netball and hockey to basketball and quorfball.

However, before you volunteer as captain, remember that this is a City law firm not a freshers' fair. *"There are loads of us on the e-mail list, but when it comes to arranging a match it is impossible to get a team together because so many people have to work late,"* one sporting source confided.

If it sounds like we are describing a top boarding school rather than a law firm, imagine our interviewees as the house captains and prefects. They emphasise how much you can learn and what fun you can have here, but also point out the pitfalls and pressures of belonging to such a highly acclaimed academy. *"Be under no illusions; you will get great training here but you will work hard for it."* Expect very long hours, often for prolonged periods – *"I regularly had to work until midnight and when it got really busy I would be there until 4am."* We wondered if our sources felt valued. *"After working really hard for months I was only given one day off, but I was invited to the closing dinner,"* recalled one. Another admitted: *"People do say thanks when you work excessively hard. They were grateful when I did a couple of all-nighters, but you don't get thanks for an 11pm finish; that is just expected of you."*

With all we have said, you could be forgiven for thinking that your background is important to the recruiters here. The firm's website claims that it doesn't matter where you went to university or what school you attended, if you are bright, enthusiastic and committed to a career in law. The stats bear this out: A&O visits 39 universities and last year recruited from this same number. The Oxbridge quotient (averaged over the past four years) is 39%. On further inspection we feel moved to say that diversity looks to be something the firm takes seriously and, at 20%, the proportion of female partners is quite good when compared to most City firms. Latest stats show that some 17% of the current trainee population is black or minority ethnic.

Staying on the subject of stats, in 2006, 102 of the 122 qualifiers took jobs at the firm, eight people didn't request a position, eight requested but were not offered, and four were offered but took jobs elsewhere. With regard to the nature of the jobs available, as the largest departments, corporate, banking and ICM offered the most positions.

any questions?

If you read the legal press you may be aware that A&O's overall achievements have been put under the microscope lately. To summarise: there is some debate as to why the firm has not pulled off the same supersonic post-Millennial financial performance as other magic circle players. Further stories discuss a perceived dissonance between the finance and corporate limbs of the firm, the former being a far stronger performer than the latter. A third story, which was likely to have been the most uncomfortable for staff to read, related to a supposed merger approach by A&O to Freshfields. What to make of it all? For prospective trainees, we'd suggest these things have relatively little relevance. Of more interest is how A&O moves its business forward and what this means for those who will start their training in the next two or three years. The crucial questions seem to be these: how will A&O move forward with its overseas network of offices, especially New York (will it merge there or reinforce?), and what kind of strategy does it want to follow (become more finance-focused or keep pushing to achieve greater corporate glory?).

and finally…

While you don't need to understand too much about high finance before you step through A&O's door for the first time, if you have an enthusiasm to learn from world experts, this is an excellent choice. Take it from one seasoned source: *"In terms of time spent at work you should not underestimate how little your life is your own in this job, but it's worth it. A&O is definitely a brand that opens doors."*

Andrew M Jackson

the facts
Location: Hull
Number of UK partners/solicitors: 30/94
Total number of trainees: 13
Seats: 4x6 months
Alternative seats: None

With its top-of-the-tree roost unshaken, it's little wonder that Hull-bound, commercially minded students usually have AMJ at the top of their list.

expanding horizons
An excellent client roster including MFI, Northern Foods, Express Dairies, the Road Haulage Association, Associated British Ports, AXA Insurance, Seven Seas and Carpetright has enabled AMJ to ride out the decline of the local fishing and shipping industries. But the firm wants to add to this list and is intent on developing a cross-Yorkshire presence. According to the trainees, it is *"looking outwards more."* One explained the plan: *"We are looking to Leeds for work. We want to be seen as competitors there, but not as pricey."* To push its reputation beyond Hull's city limits, *"the PR side is being examined, they've instructed an agency and are doing plenty of things to market more."* Behind the push is managing partner Rob Penrose, who is *"trying to take the firm to the next level... he seems driven to do this and it is having the effect of making the firm more driven."* We also learned of *"a group of younger partners who are trying to move the firm into the 21st century."* That's not to say there's a full-blown revolution underway. In the opinion of one source: *"There's a lot of history and tradition at AMJ and those traditional values are still important."*

age before beauty
Secure a contract here and you may encounter the traditional side of the firm earlier than you think, via an unexpected first six months in tax and trusts. A strong private client practice still has its place in this predominantly commercial firm, and far from being a wasted experience, the skills acquired in this seat are useful anywhere. Said one trainee: *"There was lots of client contact, and it was really good to watch one or two of the partners at work and get a feel for it."* Trainees meet plenty of old folk, most needing a will drafted and some wealthier individuals also looking for inheritance tax advice. One of our sources recalled a day when a client fell silent during their meeting. *"At first I was worried they'd died, but they were just asleep."*

Around 25 lawyers strong and twice the size of the litigation or corporate groups, commercial property is *"by far the biggest department."* According to our sources *"they are looking to expand even further into construction and real estate litigation,"* particularly since hiring a hot-shot construction solicitor from magic circle firm Freshfields. The property client list includes major names in food production, national retailers and care home developers. The latter may not operate the most glamorous of businesses but as one trainee rightly pointed out: *"We have an aging population in the UK so it's a huge sector right now."* AMJ is unquestionably smart to make a name for itself in old folks' homes; one of its most recent deals for HICA involved the acquisition and funding of a site for a new retirement village in Lancashire, but the work is certainly not limited to the North. Trainees in property assist on all aspects of leasehold deals, freehold acquisitions and development schemes, though *"it will vary as to what level you get involved at."* At the root of this is the *"tendency for some people to give trainees a longer leash than others."* By all accounts property has a few big personalities, most of whom our sources had enjoyed working with. *"There are some real characters in the department,"* said one, *"and I think it's good for trainees to learn how to get on with all types."*

you are what you eat

A seat that always goes down well is shipping and transportation. Once, the team focused purely on maritime cases; now road haulage disputes are coming to the fore and there is a stream of work for the insurance company AXA. Shedding light on AMJ's international activities, one trainee told us: "*A fair amount of the haulage stuff is coming from Holland and Belgium, and so fee earners regularly pop over. On the shipping side it used to be all fishing and trawlermen, now we are getting contractual disputes via instructions from London P&I clubs. There is still fishing work – EC regulations and incidents relating to the casting of nets – such as the entire Hull and Whitby fishing fleet being prosecuted by DEFRA.*" The appeal of the seat is the immense variety and unpredictability of the work. "*One moment it is a slip-and-trip from an insurance company* [sailors or ferry passengers], *the next a multimillion-pound dispute from London, the next talking to a trawlerman who is at risk of losing his livelihood.*" For responsibility it is one of the best departments because "*once they have gauged whether you like the work, you get a lot... I even went to interview a captain on board a ship.*" If you're happy to be pulled in all directions by a busy team this could be the high point of your contract.

In the dispute resolution department there are two seats: general litigation with a bit of PI and landlord and tenant, the other with a more commercial slant. "*I tended to do a lot of civil cases,*" recalled one trainee, "*and probate litigation, which is growing by the day. There are also insurance-based claims, debt recovery cases and Foods Standards Agency work – even cases from down south, both prosecuting and defending. We've always acted for Northern Foods and now we also have Arla Foods and Express Dairies.*" Corporate seats mean contact with these same clients plus smaller local businesses. In 2005 the team completed 15 deals, each worth over £1 million with an aggregate value in excess of £65 million. Additionally they acted for banks on some £40 million worth of financings. It may not be front-page-*FT* stuff but it is decent regional work.

for medicinal purposes only

Each new arrival is allocated a training contact partner or 'TCP' to act as mentor. "*It does depend on who you get, of course – luckily I get on really well with mine,*" said one source. The only real unresolved issue for most people was "*not knowing enough about the jobs situation at the very end of the contract.*" To summarise trainees' thoughts, although seats are allocated fairly well "*the job offers on qualification are a little less transparent... in the past there was no set date for making offers, and nods and indications were not always to be relied upon.*" The only thing we'd say here is that the overall retention rate at AMJ is decent: in September 2006 six of the seven qualifiers stayed on, with one other moving to Ireland.

Those who stayed have something to look forward to – a change of address in 2008. Having bemoaned their location above a job centre in a 1960s office block, staff have now "*let out a collective sigh of relief*" following the recent announcement concerning new premises. "*It will be an exciting time because our current building is long past its sell-by date and it will do the firm's image good to move into our own purpose-built building.*"

a marvellous idea

To promote communication internally there is a monthly newsletter named after the famous 17th century local poet Andrew Marvell. "*The Marvell can be of use and it's one of the attempts to build a family atmosphere in the firm,*" thought a source. These days trainees are just as likely to have come to Hull for the job as to have been born and bred locally. Nevertheless, the fact that so many people have family and friends in the area still has a dampening effect on AMJ's social scene. There was one ray of hope: *"Some people are really trying now, and that's to do with certain of the partners."* As well as departmental gatherings (litigation lunch together once a week), there are usually people in nearby Jaz or The George at the end of the week. Each summer there's a barbecue at a riverside hotel, and the firm is happy to throw money at the Hull TSG ball. *"Our firm takes the approach that it wants a lot of the junior fee earners to go, not just the trainees, so it pays for their tickets. The idea is to try and build up the legal community. It's a good event; last time it had an all-singing, all-dancing Casino Royale theme."* Sadly Daniel Craig was a no-show.

Though the hours are generally fine, trainees hint that in commercial seats they work longer than their peers in other Hull firms. *"In shipping, particularly, you have to stay back if you've got the work, and commercial property like to be the last ones there, but there's certainly no slave driving. In fact there's a really sensible approach by the majority of departments."* The ease of the journey home will usually more than compensate for staying later, and there's every chance that even before your training contract is up you could get yourself on the housing ladder. Hull may be bashed by the national media and top all manner of 'worst place for' surveys (*"Thanks a lot Phil and Kirsty"*), but speak to those who live and work here and they are genuinely upbeat. Said one chipper source: *"A lot of money is being thrown at Hull... and look what happened when Leeds had money thrown at it."* We heard about the £500 million being spent near the railway station, and *"half as much again out by the A63."* With plenty of really pleasant areas to live in, including new inner-city developments to compete with the established suburbs and surrounding villages, we reckon Phil and Kirsty might just want to look elsewhere for their next worst-place special.

and finally...

Andrew M Jackson is a high-quality firm offering a solid commercial training with the fascinating added extra of shipping and transportation. Add a sampler of private client work and it should appeal to anyone with a genuine desire to forge a serious legal career in the Humber area.

Anthony Collins LLP

the facts

Location: Birmingham
Number of UK partners/solicitors: 20/66
Total number of trainees: 14
Seats: 4x6 months
Alternative seats: None
Extras: Pro Bono – St Basils (Legal Advice)

Founded in the early 70s by the eponymous Mr Collins, this firm found initial success with licensing law. These days its praises are justly sung for social housing, charities, urban regeneration, family law and property dispute resolution. The firm has at its heart an ethical approach to business, and many staff and partners are happy to put their Christian values to the fore.

transformers: lawyers in disguise

What began as a one-man show has transformed itself over the course of four decades into a neat and tidy one-site operation of over 100 staff bringing in a healthy £10 million in 2006. Having recently put the seal on a referral alliance with East Midlands outfit Freeth Cartwright, and moved to glam, open-plan offices in the heart of Birmingham, AC clearly isn't letting the changing world pass it by. Mr Collins retired from the partnership recently (though he remains a consultant) but his ethical business template is a fine legacy.

The firm's work is based around three distinct areas: commercial services, private client and the grandly titled transformation group. The commercial services group incorporates coco, dispute resolution, commercial property and employment as well as the traditionally strong licensing practice. It represents a raft of Midlands-based and national companies including restaurant chains Frankie & Bennys, La Tasca, Bank and Chiquito. Wander around the Mailbox or Brindleyplace and the firm will have had involvement with many of the outlets. The private client group includes family lawyers, wills and probate specialists, and one of the region's best clinical negligence teams, best known for its mainly claimant representation in cases of brain-damaged children and other birth, orthopaedic and psychiatric injuries.

The transformation grouping, we're sad to say, doesn't have any lawyers capable of morphing into fully functional battle stations complete with real laser sounds and plastic projectiles. What it does have is an holistic view on urban regeneration, made possible through the collective efforts of property litigation/housing management specialists, charity law specialists and property and social housing development experts. The transformation group has a policy of encouraging staff to pursue areas of work close to their hearts, and this has resulted in a team with a genuine and impressive commitment to the social housing movement. They work for charities such as Mind and Tearfund; for social landlords such as Knowsley Housing Trust and Anchor Trust; and for various community and residents' associations, advising on the strategic planning of regeneration schemes. The group also has close connections with local authorities, and its best value projects (BVP) team handles a number of PFI, PPP and construction projects linked to EU and local authority attempts to improving standards of housing in the UK.

choices 'r' us

Our sources were drawn to the firm for *"its size, range of clients and variety of work."* In fact, the *"breadth on offer from corporate/commercial seats to high-value private client work"* moved one trainee to describe the firm as *"like Toys 'R' Us – we've got everything under one roof."* In the past, trainees have largely confined themselves to one grouping; this is no longer the case and it has become much more common for seats to be taken across transformation, private client and commercial services. *"Everyone tends to be fairly satisfied come rotation time,"* noted one; another chipped in with: *"Even if you can't be accommodated, they'll do all they can. I wanted construction, got BVP, but it's been construction focused."*

Moving between departments does bring a varying experience of levels of responsibility and freedom to work under your own steam, not least based on *"whether you hit at a busy time or not."* Giving a cross-section through groupings, while BVP involves *"huge projects that you just couldn't run yourself as a trainee"* and *"lots of research into particular clauses and drafting,"* commercial property means *"you get your own files to run for leases or smaller-scale transactions"* and *"lots of face-to-face or phone client contact."* Social housing sees trainees *"cross over between contentious and non-contentious work"* so that they might be doing their own advocacy, drafting witness statements or attending court, or on the other hand *"handling right-to-buy transactions for clients."* More *"desk-bound"* seats such as coco or regeneration can apparently involve *"great variety, even if the work is methodical,"* and *"interesting projects,"* but several interviewees had experienced them *"at a lull, so it was a lot of company law and all."* Those who had taken on private client seats enthused that *"they're the best place for training."* Family was described as *"manic and down to earth, lots of responsibility and stress and a varied clientele"* while a *"busy"* seat in clin neg gives trainees *"lots of client contact, attending confer-ences," "meeting counsel and medical experts"* and *"drafting instructions."*

the ac code

Regardless of the seat, trainees benefit from the firm's excellent paralegals who *"pick up a lot of the photocopying and more-boring work"* and from the *"generally fantastic supervisors"* who were praised for dishing out responsibility appropri-ately where possible. If there are issues to be raised, recently introduced regular 'best practice lunches' allow trainees to discuss the finer points of training with the firm, whilst the rigorous appraisal system leaves little to chance. Three-month-in sessions with one of the willing *"neutral third-party solicitors who have agreed to help out HR"* are followed up by end-of-seat feed-back meetings where supervisor and trainee *"comment on each other"* in the presence of the firm's training partner.

Aware that many in the firm have a strong Christian ethic, we asked trainees to what extent religion manifests itself in day-to-day AC life. Said one: *"Well, I'm a devout atheist myself, and I look at it objectively. If you want it, it is there but, not being Christian, I haven't and I haven't suffered as a result."* In fact, the majority of our interviewees did not consider themselves religious and com-mented that *"it was strange to begin with but it isn't pushed on you; sure, there are e-mails sometimes about prayer meetings and at firm-wide events there might be a prayer, but that's it."* If the thought of seeing a Bible on your supervisor's desk fills you with dread, think carefully about making an application, but if you have an open mind you might find it even *"makes you more tolerant."*

Tellingly, our sources found that the most prominent sign of the firm's broad religious ori-entation was the fact that *"the people are nicer, both courteous and considerate in a way you might not expect from a business. It's just a great place to*

work." Admittedly some teams (*"particularly those in transformation"*) are more noticeably Christian, and the charities team for example works for faith-based organisations like the Bible Society and Baptist Union. Overall, whether reli-gious or not, everyone we spoke to was respectful of *"the ethos that means you treat clients and col-leagues very well,"* and several spoke with conviction about the firm's permissive, inclusive atmosphere. *"You won't lose yourself here; every kind of personality is tolerated and encouraged, and that's very different to some of my contemporaries' experiences elsewhere."*

on a higher plane

Since the firm's recent move to a tall building on Edward Street in central Brum, trainees have been able to *"look down on Wragges... literally at least."* The *"fantastically equipped client floors, great open-plan working environment"* and *"beau-tiful ninth-floor balcony"* are welcome features after the *"cramped offices pre-move."* Even though they love working in the new building, trainees assure us that *"everyone really leaves at 5.15pm every day. When they told us this during the induc-tion we thought, 'yeah, right', but they really do."* On the rare occasions when late working is required *"you get time off in lieu."* Working decent hours means there is plenty of time for socialis-ing, and with the bars of Broad Street a few minutes away trainees are *"definitely good at keep-ing in touch as a group."* Digress is a popular choice for post-work drinks, and the Bull Ring's gazillions of shops can test the most ardent spendthrift. Even so, it was the events organised by the firm that most caught the imagination of our interviewees. *"We had a wonderful party for the move, including a massive paella and a choco-late fountain on the ninth-floor balcony,"* enthused one source. The annual minded trainee away-day normally includes good works of some kind, and last year involved *"wrapping Christmas pressies for* a charity." Trainees also enjoy *"monthly themed lunches when departments take it in turn to provide food for everyone."*

In this diverse and tolerant firm trainees fill the 20-30 age bracket and come from various parts of the country; indeed, in the assessment of one, *"only about 50% are from the Midlands."* At interview some sources observed *"an emphasis on whether you'd done charity or pro bono work,"* but confirm that there's no need for your CV to read like a hagiography. Still, we'd like to see the application form that requests the applicant to 'describe a miracle you have performed recently, how it affected others and how it shows your leadership qualities'. Assuming you make it to AC, after two years of training there's a good chance you'll stay on as an NQ; in September 2006 three of the four qualifiers did just that.

and finally...

Anthony Collins offers a broad training in a solid mid-ranked Midlands firm with a little bit extra. There's a chance to make a real difference to communities through the specialist work here.

Anthony Gold

the facts

Location: London
Number of UK partners/solicitors: 14/22
Total number of trainees: 12
Seats: Commonly 2x6 +1x12 months
Alternative seats: None

Combining the grit of the high street with the glamour of the City, Anthony Gold is equally at home helping out the man on the street or the multimillion-pound corporation. When it comes to family, personal injury, clinical negligence and housing law, the firm sparkles like the proverbial gold paving the streets of London.

three-ring circus

To understand what makes AG tick you need to get to grips with its geography, so dig out an *A to Z* if your knowledge of south London is a little shaky. The head office is a *"snazzy"* affair at London Bridge where staff gaze out over St Paul's Cathedral and Southwark when they don't have their heads down. AG HQ is both the firm's commercial hub and home to bustling PI and clin neg departments. It also has a particular niche in professional indemnity litigation, commonly for claimants seeking recompense against firms of architects, solicitors and surveyors that have provided negligent advice. London Bridge is where many firms would start and end, but Anthony Gold stretches to satellites in Streatham and Elephant & Castle, offices which are home to the *"more community-based"* end of things. Its *"more high-street"* identity is demonstrated quite literally by the fact the Streatham operation is located above the local Lloyds TSB. This branch mixes up housing and family cases with a steady stream of wills, probate and conveyancing. Meanwhile lawyers over in Elephant have a bit more legroom since AG swallowed up its upstairs neighbours, a small housing law practice. This merger means the Elephant-based solicitors have their hands fuller than ever with human rights and tenant-focused landlord and tenant cases.

The trio of locations makes for a varied working environment for the eager trainee. At London Bridge they *"sit together at the centre of an open-plan office"* which some say *"makes for a nicer working environment."* Translation: they don't have a boss breathing down their necks and can pick fellow trainees' brains when in a tight spot. Out in the satellites they might sit with a partner, potentially a more daunting prospect but great when they realise they can develop an *"interactive"* relationship that leaves a feeling that *"your opinion is valued as much as everyone else's."*

finding your seat

It is not just AG's office set-up that's intricate. New trainees must get to grips with a *"quite strange"* seat arrangement that's a more advanced formula than your traditional six-by-four rotation. The firm will *"try and establish your preferences well before you start,"* and then allow you to get stuck into what you've chosen over a single 12-month seat and a couple of shorter ones. Two seats chosen from family, housing and PI are obligatory for all, and then trainees can add a third chosen from employment, civil litigation and commercial law. This approach won't suit anyone hoping a game of legal musical chairs will reveal where their interests lie, and instead demands a more than a modicum of forethought on the part of the new recruit. Whatever your vintage – and AG takes on a fair few who are aging nicely – when you turn up for interview the firm *"wants to see some commitment to their main areas, such as PI, housing or family."* A quick survey of the current trainees revealed *"the vast majority"* have some sort of legal work behind them, and in such circumstances the firm is happy to consider a reduction in the length of the training contract.

If we had a penny for every time trainees uttered the words *"hands-on"* to describe their experiences, we'd be rich beyond our wildest dreams. To give you a flavour, day-to-day life in the reputed family department is *"a very hands-on experience"* with trainees making frequent *"trips to court and cons with counsel"* (in plain English, meetings with barristers). This is no run-of-the-mill family team, and, over the seat, trainees will encounter all manner of disputes involving children, same-sex couples and religious issues as well as more-routine divorce proceedings.

getting personal

If there is anything approaching a compulsory seat then it is PI, and in anticipation of this the firm expects trainees to study the PI elective on the LPC.

AG's notable PI team handles *"anything from fast-track trips a nd slips to quite substantial multi-track serious injuries or deaths."* In one sad case, lawyers sued the London Borough of Southwark on behalf of a nine-year-old girl who suffered catastrophic brain injury when falling from the window of her parents' council flat. This claim was settled for millions, and the firm is well known for high-value claims, preferring to leave bulk work for trade unions or legal expenses insurers to others. Where it does take referrals these come from organisations such as the London Cycling Campaign, Headway and the Spinal Injuries Association. Trainees are *"often the first point of call,"* so there's *"lots of direct client contact."*

Throw yourself into housing and you certainly won't be taking your own home sweet home for granted after dealing with disrepair claims against social landlords, representing clients faced with eviction or mortgage repossession, and getting to grips with the rights of residential and commercial leaseholders. *"Challenging but satisfying,"* there are certainly no concerns about lack of client contact during a housing seat. And, surprise surprise, there's that *"hands-on approach"* again. All this getting your hands dirty means only one thing: AG is not for the faint hearted. While your ego may be massaged by being *"treated more or less like a fee earner right from the start,"* working here won't be anything like your experiences on the LPC. The summary of one source was this: *"If you want to be spoon fed, it won't suit you."* Yet while this is undeniably *"a hard-working firm,"* there are few complaints about the length of the working day as people *"generally keep to office hours."* By their own reckoning, these trainees are *"more interested in working for people and getting a work-life balance than racking up billable hours."*

Whoever said combining business and pleasure isn't a good idea? Certainly not the Elephant lawyers who hold many of their team meetings *"over lunch in a local pub or café."* When it comes to pure pleasure, however, AG isn't over-indulgent. With staff scattered and no social committee, organised fun is sporadic. One source shared their deepest thoughts on the ad hoc, *"playing it by ear"* approach to post-work fun and said: *"To be honest, there could be more drinking."* Not to do AG down, everyone is invited over to London Bridge for monthly drinks in the boardroom, and funkier locations are found for special occasions such as last year's Christmas bash at London's Fashion & Textile Museum. It sounds as if some of the staff are pretty healthy – they'd already completed three charity runs by the time we went to press.

duty calls
AG set up in business in 1963 and has maintained a commitment to its original values. AG views itself as an ethical business, and its website tells us it is seeking "justice for all, irrespective of their means... We want to help people solve their legal problems: we're not just in it for the money." Continuing this theme, trainees spoke of the reputation for being *"very open and welcoming to people of all nationalities and backgrounds, with strong links to the gay community."* By all accounts the firm has thrown itself behind the pink pound and actively markets to gay businesses and individuals. Working in south London means exposure to an incredibly diverse clientele, and at times some incredibly complicated cases. One knotty probate involved a deceased man with considerable assets in Africa, plus five wives and almost 40 children.

Another side to AG's culture is a history of involvement with professional bodies. Managing partner David Marshall is a past president of the Association of Personal Injury Lawyers, the profession's largest practitioner group. Family department head Kim Beatson has chaired the profession's second-largest practitioner group, the Family Law Association, as well as the organisation Resolve; and partner Andrew Brooks is chairman of the Housing Law Practitioners Association. These appointments reflect a level of commitment to legal professional life above and beyond the call of duty. If you join AG you join a group of lawyers for whom commitment is the name of the game and even as a trainee you'll be encouraged to write articles for publication. In September 2006 three of the five qualifiers stayed with the firm.

and finally...
In terms of hard cash, Anthony Gold offers more than your average high street firm though less than City firms proper. We reckon that if you're motivated by things other a fat salary, this firm has the edge over most.

asb law

the facts
Location: Crawley, Brighton, Maidstone, Horsham, Croydon
Number of UK partners/solicitors: 43/51
Total number of trainees: 9
Seats: 4x6 months
Alternative seats: None

Cast your mind back to 1999! The Euro became the official currency everywhere on the planet except the UK, a teenage Britney Spears was unleashed on an unsuspecting public (oh, life before Kevin!) and we were all preoccupied with the prospect of a Y2K disaster. Undeterred by these troubling issues, the partners at asb *law* were busy hatching a plan to create a new firm through a three-way merger of some of the South East's most-established practices.

the sky's the limit
The fusion of Maidstone firm Argles & Court, Croydon's Stonehams and Burstows, with offices in Brighton, Horsham and Crawley, has resulted

in a firm with over 40 partners and 300 staff. It has increasingly taken a sectoral approach to business, targeting areas such as aviation, technology, e-commerce and computers (TeC), insurance, charities, education and the not-for-profit sector. The firm has an outstanding reputation in insolvency and recently retained its place on the panel of the Insolvency Service for England and Wales in the face of stiff competition from over 50 firms.

Asb also has a sterling reputation in corporate finance. In 2005 alone it was involved in transactions with a total deal value of £255 million, and banking instructions come from well-known lenders such as RBS, HBoS, Lloyds TSB and Bank of Ireland. The firm is a big hitter when it comes to employment and commercial litigation, recently representing the claimant in an £800,000 professional negligence case against a major firm of accountants and a major public school in relation to the Office of Fair Trading's investigation into a potential school fees cartel. A superb travel law practice has emerged from the pooled resources of the commercial litigation, employment, corporate finance, commercial and liability insurance groups at asb. The travel lawyers represent a host of operators – First Choice, Virgin Holidays and Thomas Cook/JMC – airlines, liability insurers and agents, as well as holidaymakers. They recently went to the Court of Appeal for First Choice following the successful defence of an injury claim after a swimming pool accident. Debt recovery is another strong area, as is real estate, where it advises on land acquisitions for house builders, office leases in central London and residential conveyancing for thousands of individuals across the region. The London Borough of Wandsworth turns to asb for planning, highways and general commercial advice and the firm has kept many thousands of racegoers happy by ensuring that Epsom, Sandown Park and Kempton Park racecourses completed the liquor licensing applications required by new regulations.

tough love

Although still *"a very young firm,"* asb has already had its share of knocks. In 2005 some jobs were cut after a review of staffing levels and a three-partner family and private client team defected from Croydon. *"Low morale"* was widespread in the affected offices. Some trainees believe that staff are *"now upbeat;"* others concede that *"the atmosphere still needs to go a long way,"* but feel that *"it's improving"* since the departure of the chief executive and a change in the management structure.

New trainees soon learn that, while there are no strictly compulsory seats (a point the firm wished to reiterate), *"many people do residential conveyancing due to the volume of work we turn over in that area."* They also discover that certain seats can only be taken in certain locations. For example, at the moment, conveyancing is offered in Maidstone; corporate and commercial litigation is *"only available at Crawley."* Tax, trusts and probate is a Brighton seat, as is insolvency. Family seats are mostly taken in Brighton, although *"there are people who do family in Maidstone and Horsham."* It's a complex matrix and trainees *"can't always necessarily determine the location"* they go to. What they can do is log the reasons why they wouldn't want to move to a particular office. Because *"relocation can be a bit of a pain,"* the firm provides a travel allowance (presently £1,200 per seat) to those who live 25 miles or more from the office in which they work.

Trainees say the firm doesn't feel like it is *"divided into offices; it's all interlinked,"* which brings us back to the sector approach we mentioned. By all accounts there *"isn't much sense of competition between departments or offices."* Marketing and staff events also help bring the offices together.

crawley and brighton

Crawley is *"the commercial hub"* of asb and *"the main office for trainees."* Described in turn as both *"the most modern office"* and the one where *"everyone takes themselves seriously,"* it is known for its strong corporate and commercial litigation teams and the absence of any private client services. Seats are also available in the general commercial law team and in the commercial property group. An open-plan office layout means there is *"always a buzz in the air."* The town of Crawley is unlikely to ever win any awards – at least none that it would want – but it can justifiably claim to be an excellent location for any law firm looking to capture business in the Gatwick Diamond, the region stretching from London down to Brighton and from Horsham over to East Grinstead.

Much as they do in other Crawley firms, trainees say this office is not particularly great for after-work socialising as *"everyone drives there."* When they do go out, The Brewery Shades and the Old Punch Bowl are the two main pubs. Lunchtimes are improved by *"a nice sandwich shop that delivers to the office,"* and to do their bit the comlit team *"have beers in the office every Friday afternoon."*

If Crawley is the commercial hub, then Brighton is definitely asb's *"social hub."* West Street is just *"full of bars,"* leaving trainees *"spoilt for choice"* when they're up for a night out. The beach is also just a stone's throw away from the office; ideal for the beach volleyball players on staff. Although *"a lot more relaxed than in Crawley,"* people still *"work hard"* and the family department *"has a good reputation for investing time and effort"* in their trainees. The group is currently representing a wife in financial proceedings in which her the husband has $50 million-worth of trust assets in the USA.

maidstone, horsham and croydon

The Maidstone office offers seats in residential and commercial property plus family and employment. In 2006 staff relocated to the Eclipse Business Park close to junction 7 of the M20, a move that brought together the occupants of four separate high street buildings. Speaking to us just prior to the move, one trainee said: *"I don't think it's within walking distance from town"* so *"you can't do your shopping during lunchtime."* On the upside, the new, *"comfortable,"* open-plan office has much more parking. A trainee's social circle is often broadened by membership of the local Young Professionals Group, through which *"you can meet with people in accountancy and other firms."*

As it's a smaller office, it's unsurprising that *"everyone knows everyone"* in Horsham. It is dedicated to private clients, and the trainees who visit here do so for residential conveyancing experience. One interviewee described a *"family atmosphere"* while another mentioned office outings to Glorious Goodwood and for group meals. Finally, the Croydon office has a good reputation for property litigation, but has not recently taken trainees.

speak your mind

"Training on the whole is very good," our sources said. The level of responsibility does vary from department to department and the general commercial team gets a rap on the knuckles for being *"guilty of not giving trainees enough demanding tasks to do."* There are other commercial seats where it can be *"a struggle getting work,"* but *"once you've proved that you're good enough to get involved, then you'll get stuff."* Either way, be prepared *"to do the rubbish stuff,"* such as opening the post in the mornings and paginating bundles, *"as well as the good stuff."* One trainee spoke of having *"my own caseload and being able to get on with it, talking with clients on a daily basis and taking instructions over the phone."* Others had negotiated commercial leases or done their own advocacy on *"straightforward"* small claims while working in the debt recovery team.

If you want to raise issues, the time to do so is during quarterly meetings between *"all the trainees, the lady from HR and the training part-*

ner." Some interviewees said *"you can be quite frank"* during these sessions; others conceded that *"at times, it can be a bit of a talking shop."* Given the many variables of the training scheme it sounds as if you need to speak up and make your interests known. This is not a *"quiet, stuffy firm,"* so if you're shy and retiring you'll not find it so easy. At the same time if *"you go in with a prima donna attitude saying 'I'm not going to... [open] the post [in the morning]', it won't wash."* Indeed, our sources felt that the selection of trainees is *"very personality driven"* and that those who succeed do so as much *"because of soft skills"* as their legal or academic ability. In September 2006 both qualifiers were winners.

and finally...

If you're up for exploring the South East for two years, asb law's diverse practice and quality clientele should appeal, especially if you've not yet decided what kind of lawyer you want to be.

Ashfords

the facts

Location: Exeter, Plymouth, Bristol, Tiverton, Taunton
Number of UK partners/solicitors: 49/72
Total number of trainees: 24
Seats: 4x6 months
Alternative seats: Secondments
Extras: Pro bono – eg Tiverton Saturday Surgery

Ah, the West Country... the English Riviera, cream teas, fishing villages, lots of places ending in 'combe'. Spanning this earthly paradise, like King Arthur astride his mighty steed Hengroen, is Ashfords.

devon knows how...

Ashfords has an unusual recent history. Until 2004 it was part of a strange half-merger with the firm now known as Bevan Brittan. Since the two broke

up, Ashfords has embraced its liberty and pursued an expansive track. A Bristol operation – opened on the day of the demerger – now sits on the notepaper with offices in Exeter, Tiverton, Taunton and Plymouth, where a new corporate team has recently been established. Since 2004 profits have increased and the client base grown. According to a survey in 2005 in *The Western Morning Mail*, the firm was lead adviser on more corporate deals than any of its West-Country rivals. Among the regional M&A and financings handled by Ashfords was the sale of Devon travel agent Let's Go Travel by Australian Stock exchange-listed Harvey World Travel. But it's not all West Country work: the firm is involved in all manner of things from the financing of prime City of London real estate to PFI waste management contracts in Manchester. Ashfords is proud to have built a clientele that includes Bank of Scotland, venture capital fund Eden Ventures and American oilfield-technology giant Schlumberger.

Lawyers in Exeter and Plymouth have a good handle on Devon and Cornwall's property scene. They helped the Exeter Chiefs rugby club with its new ground and worked on the redevelopment of St Austell town centre. Other clients include Devon County Council, South Devon Healthcare NHS Trust and South West of England Regional Development Agency. The property lawyers too have sought work beyond the region, recently winning instructions from London Borough of Wandsworth.

hunting the saboteur

Property is as good a place as any to start an examination of the four-seat training contract. True, time in the department isn't strictly compulsory, but it's very likely you'll get it, particularly in either Plymouth or Exeter. The seat is said to be *"a baptism of fire"* because there are high levels of responsibility from day one. Aside from *"a fair bit of time on bibling"* (compiling portfolios of copy documents), there will be *"tons of drafting practice"* and *"quite a bit of client contact."* One trainee even ran a conference call with the London lawyers on the other side of a deal. After that, running a few small deals yourself, say the sales of small industrial units, should be a doddle. Trainees find the experience of near full control on files *"invaluable,"* as it allows them to *"track a deal all the way from the initial client contact to conclusion."*

The Exeter office is also the centre for Ashfords' comlit, IP, PI and employment practices, and there's a secondment on offer from the office – six months with one of the firm's client's, Exeter University. Back in the office, the employment team gives trainees access to a juicy caseload and *"lots of tribunal time,"* sometimes unsupervised. You'll either find the *"personal focus"* of the work hugely appealing or you'll be *"shocked at how emotional it can be."* One particularly dramatic case saw the employment lawyers leap into action to obtain an injunction against a client's employee. The employee had installed a delayed disabling bug in a customer software package with the intention of crashing the customer's IT system.

Ashfords' commercially-driven offices in Exeter (285 staff), Plymouth (20 staff) and now Bristol (15 staff) are rather different to the branches in Tiverton (65 staff) and Taunton (50 staff), which are primarily occupied with private client, family law and crime. Take a private client seat in one or other and you'll experience a combination of *"trusts work with interesting legal issues"* and *"great client contact on the wills and probate side."* The department usually hands a trainee the first new file that comes in after they've joined the department. *"It's a buzz,"* one source admitted; *"of course, there are people you can go and ask about it."* The firm's family lawyers specialise in divorce and child-contact issues, primarily for privately paying individuals. Working with them, trainees get *"a decent amount of court time."*

taking a gambol

Your choice of office will affect your experience as much as your choice of seats. Having applied to the firm as a whole, successful candidates are then asked to nominate a preferred office. Large in size and offering a full range of departments, Exeter is often oversubscribed. Even if they'd originally asked for Exeter, some trainees told us they ended up preferring the smaller offices as *"you can get much more responsibility there."* The Taunton and Tiverton offices resemble high street firms in many ways; *"people just wander in with queries and it's usually a trainee's job to go and see them and get the details of what they need."* In Taunton and Tiverton, *"everyone really does know everyone,"* and if you live and breathe countryside these picturesque locations are definitely your best bet. The *Student Guide* will admit to a pang of jealousy when a trainee at Tiverton spoke of lambs gambolling on the hills outside their window.

The 1970s office building in Plymouth is a lamb-free zone, but there are compensations. The entire team sits on one open-plan floor *"so collaboration between departments just means walking across the room."* It's also one of the firm's most informal offices. *"I don't wear a tie,"* a trainee admitted, *"although I always have one with me in case a client turns up."* In Exeter you'll feel the benefits, and the disadvantages, of working in a brand-new, out-of-town office near to junction 29 of the M25. *"It's open plan with the bigwigs nestling among the rest of us,"* said one trainee. *"Everyone knows everyone, from the office manager to the secretarial support."* The building has a gym plus a café and break-out areas; however, *"it's right by the main road"* and, by all accounts, not much else.

Something of a corporate outpost, the Bristol office is hoping to secure big business for Ashfords. It can't yet offer four different seats, so the trainees who pick it as their home office need to visit elsewhere; nevertheless it is one of the most popular choices for applicants. A move to new offices in October 2006 should allow the head-count to rise and, indeed, the firm's chief exec has signalled that it could rise substantially. *"They've really involved the trainees in the move; taking us to have a look round and so on,"* a source reported. Despite being the firm's new corporate-standard bearer, distance from the Exeter head office does seem to have engendered a relaxed atmosphere in the Bristol branch, and *"someone usually does a bacon-butty run in the mornings."*

charlie don't surf (much)

Don't stress if you don't receive your first choice of location. *"They're really good about letting people do seats in other offices."* And *"if you're based in Plymouth, Tiverton or Taunton you're really encouraged to do one Exeter seat."* Although it is possible to get everywhere by train, this is really a firm for motorists. Actually, we can't imagine anyone living in the West Country without wheels. Oh, and if you've noticed that Ashfords lists a London office on its website, don't get too excited. It is reserved for client meetings and has no staff.

The West Country doesn't have a reputation for fast-paced, late-night deal-making. *"People come here from the City to regain a bit of work-life balance,"* trainees explained, quickly adding: *"But we're not surfing all the time; we do work hard."* The typical day runs from 9am to 6pm with many trainees coming in early so they can leave earlier. The schedule is more demanding in certain departments: in IP, for example, *"you might do one or two seven o'clocks in a week, or take occasional bits home."* Corporate and commercial property are the other culprits. In corporate, especially, you can have *"a few weeks with lots of 9pms towards the end of a deal."*

The work-related social scene differs from one location to another. Exeter and Plymouth celebrate the start of the weekend with drinks in the office. *"It's really nice as you get to meet people you*

don't sit near." In Plymouth, a hard core *"usually falls into the Ha! Ha! next door, and occasionally a partner puts a card behind the bar."* The Exeter office also hosts bimonthly events for trainees and solicitors, combining a presentation with *"a wine tasting or something like that."* The scene in the Tiverton and Taunton offices is quieter, although *"occasionally there will be drinks for someone's birthday."* Trainees compensate by arranging cross-office get-togethers, *"mostly in Exeter."* Plymouth trainees traditionally make the trip to Exeter for its black-tie Christmas party, while the Tiverton and Taunton offices generally also share a party. In Bristol, the quayside area is bursting with bars and restaurants and, when we spoke to them, trainees were looking forward to the move to the district. Should they ever feel isolated from the rest of the trainees, there's a six-monthly get together of all trainees.

showing your credentials

Of course, the real advantages of living in the West Country have nothing to do with bars and restaurants. *"All kinds of activities are organised by people at the firm, like kayaking in Plymouth Sound. It's one of the times you get partners and secretaries really having fun together."* This healthy, outdoorsy attitude must be catching as, in 2005, six plucky members of the firm – including the head of the Bristol office – tackled the famously tricky Royal Marines Commando Challenge assault course in aid of a Bristol charity.

So what sort of person would Ashfords be interested in? *"A link to the area is important,"* trainees noted. Despite the City background of some of the partners, it's clear that for its new intake the firm is looking for people who know this part of the world, and in practice this means a huge reliance on Exeter University – indeed, *all* the trainees we spoke to this year had spent some time there. If you are studying elsewhere then, even if you grew up in the area, *"you'll need to convince the firm you see your future here."* Otherwise, the trainee group is the usual mix of law and non-law grads, some with previous career experience and/or time spent abroad. A self-confessed *"outgoing, lively bunch,"* our sources confirmed that the firm is *"looking for people who can interact with clients"* and who are *"team-oriented."* Their mood was certainly high in 2006: all 12 qualifiers stayed on at the firm.

and finally...

Ashford's clients and work are sufficiently diverse to give most people all the choice they could wish for in their training. In a part of the world still with relatively limited career opportunities across the board, this is a gem.

Ashton Morton Slack

the facts

Location: Sheffield
Number of UK partners/solicitors: 18/18
Total number of trainees: 5
Seats: usually 4x6 months
Alternative seats: None

Sheffield has given us the Arctic Monkeys and a shed load of cutlery but, given that you've got your nose in this book, the city's legal opportunities are probably of more interest to you right now. Ashton Morton Slack is one of the major law firms in South Yorkshire and can claim to be the largest, non-national law firm in Sheffield. With client services running from asbestos-related disease claims to international trade and finance, it's fair to say there's something for everyone.

chasing success

Ashton Morton Slack came on the local scene over 100 years ago. Fast forward to 2005 and the firm underwent a major rebranding and restructuring exercise. It had for five years been operating as AMS Law following Ashton Morton Slack's merger with The Law Partnership in May 2000. However, it reverted to its previous moniker as this was a more recognisable name locally. The effects of the review of 2005 had filtered down to the trainees we spoke to; they felt their firm was *"becoming more client and staff-focused."* Management aspires to be listed in *The Sunday Times'* 100 Best Places to Work survey and is intent on *"developing things so that it is an attractive place to work."* More than this, the firm *"has modernised a lot"* in recent years, bringing in an updated IT system and hiring a dedicated HR team. Trainees rave about how the firm has *"improved its internal and external training."* Speakers come in to give talks and staff are encouraged to go on external courses and lectures. The only proviso is that *"when we get back, we have to do a presentation to the firm about what we have learned."* No pressure then! This investment in its staff also extends to the loan of money for driving lessons. No wonder the firm won the training and development gong at the 2005 Sheffield Business Awards. Perhaps this inspired it to increase the size of its trainee group (from three to five) in September 2006.

Following the restructuring, Ashton Morton Slack is now organised into three divisions: PI, private client and a business division that handles licensing, business crime and serious fraud, M&A and commercial property. A recent example of the business division's work was Sheffield-based GR Industries' acquisition of cosmetics company Harmer Personal Care of Bradford. The deal boosted GR Industries' turnover from £45 million to £60 million.

The firm may well be an *"all-rounder"* these days but let's be clear: PI work still accounts for over 50% of its revenue. The PI practice covers everything from trips and slips, RTAs, clinical negligence and miners' claims for industrial disease compensation. Claimant clients come from far beyond Sheffield and the firm additionally acts for well-known insurance companies and individuals referred by trade unions including Usdaw, the shop workers' union.

legal paral-eagles

Training seats are available in coco, commercial and civil litigation, probate and administration (which *"isn't all about drafting wills for old ladies"*), family, serious fraud, PI, commercial property and conveyancing, and an employment seat may soon become available. None of these options is compulsory and the firm is said to be *"flexible"* in its attitude to allocations. Litigation and coco were popular with those we spoke to, with the *"tremendous"* litigation department allowing trainees to *"get right in there"* on cases. One day you could be drafting affidavits, the next, going to London to the High Court. Advocacy starts *"pretty much from the first week,"* when you might be off to an interim application or a mortgage repossession hearing. *"If you're confident, they won't hold you back."* Another key aspect of this department is that *"you can have a laugh while getting on with your work."*

In terms of the type of candidate who will be made an offer, our sources said: *"It works in your favour to have ties to the area"* as *"the firm will try to recruit people who will stay long-term."* In addition, *"personality is very important to this firm"* and it looks for people who will be good at *"building strong relationships with our clients."* You actually don't need to be an external candidate to get a training contract. Ashton Morton Slack had a reputation for taking most of its trainees from among the ranks of its own paralegals, yet, our sources told us: *"This year they changed that."* The firm still awards traineeships to a mixture of internal and external candidates, but if you're thinking it's easier for internals, our sources reliably inform us: *"it is not."* In 2006 three of the four qualifiers stayed with the firm.

Still undecided? Ashton Morton Slack has *"the right balance of conservative values and a modern approach to expansion and development."* The modern side has already been highlighted above, but perhaps the conservative side shines through in terms of the firm's dress code. *"For litigation you have to wear dark colours and a suit. Elsewhere you need to be smart. For example, skirts not above the knee. No straps or midriffs showing in the summer."* Heaven forbid! Moreover, the firm is also *"strict about time recording and knowing your where-abouts."* The office building itself is more reflective of the modern side to the firm and whether or not trainees share a room with their training principal depends on the layout of the department.

question everything

The broad consensus is that although *"you have to do the photocopying when it's urgent and no one else is around,"* you are also exposed to *"difficult"* and *"challenging"* work. This can vary from VAT fraud to taking on the city council in its refusal to grant planning permission to your client. Work doesn't just come from your training principal, although *"the principals always try not to overload us... they co-ordinate things so that deadlines aren't missed."* The interaction between trainees and the lawyers supervising them is illustrated by this interviewee's comment: *"They tell us that, as a trainee, it is better to ask questions, no matter how stupid."* Moreover, mid- and end-of-seat appraisals work well as a time for *"taking stock of where you are."* Generally, our interviewees felt that throughout the firm they are, *"on the whole,"* listened to... so long as those listening *"think you know what you're talking about."* One subject that was discussed with us was salaries and benefits – whether they are enough and how they are calculated. On this point, the firm has just signed up to a new benefits scheme called 'You at Work' which, among other things, offers employees retail and childcare vouchers.

With office hours a welcome 9am to 5pm there's plenty of time for after-work fun, but trainees say the majority of events *"are aimed at marketing the firm"* and hinted that more could be done to promote staff socialising. There are occasional pub quizzes and trips to the theatre, but these are more down to *"individuals getting themselves into gear"* to organise things. If it's just a quiet drink you're after, pop to the Wig and Pen, one of the oldest pubs in the area and a favourite with lawyers and judges due to its proximity to the law courts. All Bar One or Boho are alternatives for when you just don't feel olde worlde, and if you want to mix it up with your peers at other South Yorkshire firms, the local Trainee Solicitors Group organises events.

and finally...

Now much more than a PI firm, Ashton Morton Slack is looking forward to a future that increasingly incorporates commercial practice. If your tastes veer that way and you want to work for a substantial, single-site legal employer in Sheffield, this is your firm.

Ashurst

the facts

Location: London
Number of UK partners/solicitors: 119/289
Total number of trainees: 95
Seats: 4x6 months
Alternative seats: Overseas seats, secondments
Extras: Pro bono – Islington and Toynbee Hall legal advice centres; Disability Rights Commission, Business in the Community, death row appeals; language bursaries

A healthy £214 million turnover, a broad range of seats and a defined *"people culture;"* Ashurst is a well-established City firm chosen by ambitious trainees wishing to avoid the magic circle.

a sense of pride

Most of our interviewees had pitched up at Ashurst after its recent rebranding but had applied to the firm before the image change. The Ashurst Morris Crisp of times past was known as a gentlemanly and traditional place, so they were delighted with *"the modern and fresh feeling"* they encountered. *"Brightly coloured carpets, lots of new artwork and logos everywhere"* were to trainees *"signs of a challenge to that fuddy-duddy image."* More significantly, they believed that *"the rebranding has had a major impact,"* telling us: *"All that superficial stuff seems to have filtered down; it is mirrored in people's attitudes... there's such a fresh, exciting atmosphere."* Genuine change takes time of course, but if trainees' noses do still detect the occasional whiff of *"old-school elements,"* the strong scent of the new is permanently in the air. *"We're constantly being asked for feedback and suggestions about the way the firm is run,"* commented one; another emphasising how *"continual efforts to improve the working environment, work-life balance and training"* is illustrative of *"a determination to keep moving forward."* Speaking of movement, the Ashurst-branded taxis you may see touring the streets of London are another signal of intent, albeit one that has sometimes been misread. *"When one of the white and rainbow cabs was in Soho recently, it apparently got mistaken for a Gay Pride taxi."*

a-list

Given its relatively (and we do mean relatively) small size, Ashurst performs excellently in the cut and thrust of City law. Its fantastic corporate department allows it to walk the red carpet, head held high, alongside bigger firms, and on many occasions it is the equal (and sometimes even the envy) of the magic circle. Why so? Well, the firm represents over 115 FTSE-listed clients and recent new instructions have come from Abbey, African Copper, Biofusion and Reuters. Not only does

Ashurst have a knack of profiting when bigger firms have conflicts of interests, it can also lay claim to being first-choice adviser on many an impressive mandate. It recently steered Electra Partners Europe through its £144 million acquisition of Travelsphere Holdings and Motorola through its £103 million offer for a 3G-software company. In 2006 long-term client Apax Partners handed the firm a place alongside Freshfields and Norton Rose on its £2.2 billion corporate acquisition of General Healthcare Group, while finance teams were busy advising Barclays Capital on the £1.85 billion leveraged re-capitalisation of The AA, and Merrill Lynch as arranger of separate £452 million and £659 million collateralised loan obligations.

Ashurst's recent performance has been stellar. It has beefed up its real estate group by snaffling CMS Cameron McKenna's non-contentious construction team head and elbowed aside Dechert to take the advisory role on Oceancrest's bid for the £1.5 billion Elephant & Castle regeneration, whilst simultaneously working on similar projects in east London in Stratford and Silvertown. Ashurst's management has also been paying attention to the European outposts, perhaps a result of an internal survey that revealed concerns about cohesion across the offices. Projects/project finance has been identified as a growth area that will help raise Ashurst's profile and profitability internationally. In Milan, for example, a five-partner projects team, including A&O's project finance expert in the city, has already been hired.

a-rresting development

Even if in the past Ashurst has never been widely perceived as a particularly international firm, there is a clear sense that it now recognises the importance of a good overseas network of offices. As well as London, Dubai and New York there are seven additional offices in Europe (Milan, Paris, Frankfurt, Madrid, Munich and Brussels) and Asia (India, Japan, Singapore).

Before you start planning to visit each office during your training, here's how the seat system works. Following a recent change, all trainees take four six-month seats, adhering to "*the rule that a corporate and an internal finance seat are compulsory.*" This comes as no real shock when you consider the firm's position in the corporate and finance league tables, though we sensed slight disappointment in trainees' voices when speaking on this matter. Perhaps they worried that the firm could lose its reputation as one of the best places for variety during a City training contract. We suspect they have little to worry about given that there are ample seats on offer in real estate, competition, tax, litigation, technology and commercial, IP, employment, incentives and pensions, and finally, energy, trade and infrastructure (including project finance and environment). Add in European postings and secondments to banks and corporate clients (eg Abbey, IBM, City Group, Lehman Brothers, Reuters and Fidelity Investment Services) and we'd say Ashurst still offers great choice. Requiring trainees to take corporate or finance seats makes sense, especially as this year across the City such departments have been experiencing problems come qualification time. As one trainee pointed out: "*Even if you don't want those departments long term, it does introduce you to the centre of the firm and a whole load of people.*"

Another development is the introduction of a two-week litigation course for those with no appetite for a full contentious seat. "*It lets the people who are really transactionally minded go their way and [by easing congestion] the litigators – or those with other interests – have what they want.*" Trainees asked us to commend the dedicated grad recruitment team, and in particular Gemma Baker, whose "*amazing memory*" and "*dedication to learning about you and what you want"* means that *"almost everyone gets the seats they ask for, even if it's not always in exactly the order they want."*

a-team

All the rebranding in the world won't change a firm's innate character and we think there are certain aspects of the old Ashurst Morris Crisp's persona that will, and should, endure. Trainees say the firm combines *"ambition and a relaxed outlook,"* praising the *"sociable atmosphere that lacks overly obvious hierarchy."* Several matter-of-fact interviewees acknowledged that *"obviously there are limits... in any law firm of course there's some hierarchy,"* but *"this firm seems to take suggestion very well. At away-days you're encouraged to be open and frank, and people are."* A strong *"team ethos"* means trainees are actively *"encouraged to attend client meetings and socials,"* and year-round dress down (*"suits for meetings, of course"*) creates *"a casual working environment, even if you do work hard."* Perhaps not everyone ends up like one of our sources, *"being good friends with a previous supervisor,"* but the majority do benefit in their work from *"a culture of constructive criticism and praise where praise is due."* Mid-seat and end-of-seat appraisals are the formal moments in generally easy day-to-day working relationships. If we did hear from some that *"depending on a department's workload you're not always stretched to the top of your capabilities"* and *"it's better to work for a partner than an associate,"* we were also told by others that *"I've found myself with almost too much responsibility."*

Quite how hard trainees graft depends on the department. Seats in international finance or corporate frequently involve *"very, very long hours for stretches."* The saving grace is *"the teamwork and a really welcoming atmosphere."* It is different again in smaller teams like tax or competition. They feature *"strong personalities – down-to-earth and very intelligent lawyers"* and the role of the trainee tends to revolve more around *"individual supervisors and working on their tasks."* The niche departments tend to offer *"a research-based role for trainees,"* spiced up by *"a lot of open discussion of issues."* Real estate is unusual for a larger department in that *"trainees get to manage their own files and clients from day one."* Just watch out for *"data-room work"* on the largest transactions, especially if the seat is construction-slanted. Litigation fans say their preferred department offers the greatest variety of work. *"Litigation trainees are on court duty every two weeks, so you get any applications that need doing and you pick up filing."* Young litigators also find themselves *"sitting in on arbitrations," "taking notes at client meetings"* and *"picking up the details of cases very quickly... because you have to."* Overall, trainees say they are *"used hard"* across the firm, yet beyond their time in corporate or finance their hours tend towards an even 9am to 7pm.

a-typical

Ashurst resides in two buildings close to Liverpool Street. One is *"very gaudily decorated"* and the other is *"modern, light, neutral and open plan."* Neither is *"what you could call, 'wow, amazing'."* Nevertheless, with a *"floor-by-floor redecoration"* seeing the older premises rejuvenated, daily life is pleasant enough, notwithstanding *"the tasteless corporate art on the client floor; it has hideous little aliens in black and white which are rather revolting."*

Aesthetics aside, what trainees like is *"working with people who are almost entirely people you like and whose company you enjoy."* Beyond acknowledging that the firm *"explicitly looks for a certain outgoing quality above and beyond simply academics,"* trainees couldn't pin down what makes a typical Ashurster. *"Everyone has interests outside work,"* they noted, also picking up on an increasing trend for *"fewer people from Oxbridge and more universities being represented"* in recent intakes.

There is a sprinkling of recruits from overseas and a number of second-careerers. The current trainee population included a former vet, a former doctor and former musician, so if you have a cool former existance or even just time spent working in a different career, the firm could well be interested. The only negative point we'd make on the subject of recruitment is that until Ashurst makes its diversity stats freely available it will be hard to counter any remaining allegations that there is still a streak of old-school tie.

If, as trainees say, the "*blonde-haired girls and sporty guys*" image doesn't hold true any longer, that doesn't mean Ashurst's fabled appetite for sport is diminished. The firm can put out able teams in anything from girl's football to dragon boat racing and rugby sevens to golf or broom ball. Apparently "*it's like ice hockey but with bigger sticks, a big ball and you play in trainers on ice.*" The trainees are "*a relatively sociable bunch,*" albeit that some intakes are more cohesive than others. There are parties to greet each new intake or show vac-schemers a good time, and firm-wide events such as the summer party at the Honourable Artillery Company are always well received. And yet there's nothing trainees like more than "*heading out together with friends from your intake after work.*" A tolerant, laid-back atmosphere among trainees appears to survive even the nerve-fraying run-up to qualification. Said one source: "*We've just been through it and there was none of the competitiveness or nightmare back-stabbing that some of my friends endured elsewhere.*" In September 2006 36 of the 41 qualifiers took jobs with the firm.

and finally...

The Ashurst brand stands for excellence in the City, good manners in its people and satisfaction for its trainees. A highly recommended choice for the discerning City applicant.

Baker & McKenzie LLP

the facts

Location: London
Number of UK partners/solicitors: 85/212
Total number of trainees: 60
Seats: 4x6 months
Alternative seats: Overseas seats, secondments
Extras: Pro bono – Waterloo Legal Advice Centre, UN High Commission for Refugees, death row appeals; language training

There are self-styled global firms, there are firms with overseas branches or foreign alliances and then there's Baker & McKenzie. Over 65 offices across 40 countries and three continents make B&M the granddaddy of international law firms. Remarkably, in what is the founder of an elite club of US-originated firms boasting revenue above $1 billion, each office has its own story to tell, and none more so than London.

pioneer story

On the firm's website you'll find an engaging history of B&M and its characterful founder Russell Baker, who paid his way through law school in 1920s Chicago by prize fighting at county fairs. Better still, buy the book from Amazon: at 327 pages Pioneering a Global Vision: The Story of Baker & McKenzie is quite a read, but it does sound like a page-turner. We won't pretend we've studied it, but as the title suggests one of the most significant parts of that history is the fact that B&M was opening overseas offices when most modern law firms were still in short pants. Venezuela in 1955; Brussels in 1957; Zurich in 1958 and London in 1961 – we won't list them all. Suffice to say the organisational principle of this steady and constant expansion required that each new branch should enjoy autonomy, equality and the opportunity to develop in its own way.

This almost franchise approach led to the firm being branded 'McLaw' in certain quarters, the suggestion being that some offices offered services reflecting the bog standardness of a fast-food joint. Several prominent economists, and even a US Secretary of State, have referred seriously to the Golden Arch Theory, which states that no two countries with a chain of McDonald's have ever gone to war with each other. Excluding civil wars, we reckon the same can be said of countries with B&M offices (readers are welcome to point out any conflicts we've missed). Hence, we propose Baker & McKenzie Theory. Silliness aside, just like McDonald's, the firm is quick to scent the moment when developing socio-economic and political stability means moving into a new market makes sound business sense. To harmonise the offices, a 'Visual Identity Programme' sets standards for documentation, prescribes fresh universal corporate values and gives new assessment criteria which see "*trainees in London appraised in exactly the same way as solicitors in Saudi Arabia.*"

the big smoke

The 45-year-old London operation is a perfect example of B&M's particular brand of expansion paying dividends. Steady growth was crowned last year with a monumental 35% profit rise that left the New Bridge Building in EC4 "*buzzing*" and staff feeling "*very much an autonomous office, in fact we're the biggest office internationally.*" Giving weight to the claim that London is a real success story, the office acts for some of the world's biggest multinationals, including Sony, Fujitsu, Cisco Systems, Hewlett-Packard, Pfizer, L'Oreal, Levi Strauss and Shell.

Well-developed employment, IT, IP, competition/trade and pensions teams hold their own alongside strong corporate and banking departments, even if trainees have observed "*an increasingly heavy focus on the corporate and finance side of work.*" Confirming the trend, last year the firm swiped four securitisation partners from Norton Rose, a BLP private banking expert and an acquisition finance ace from Linklaters. The strengthened finance team recently acted for One Equity on the €135 million refinancing of a major acquisition, and for the Turkish underwriters on Istanbul-based Bank Asya's £423 million IPO. Corporate is equally prominent, with lawyers working for companies such as BP, United Business Media, ING, France Télécom and Development Bank of Singapore.

the internationalists

We've long heard from trainees that the international aspect of the firm is attractive, but we wanted to learn about the day-to-day reality of working at a global firm. Opinions varied from the flippant ("*well, we've got a documentation centre in Manila so you e-mail stuff there*") to the bald ("*the international slant doesn't make a lot of difference; there are foreign lawyers at the end of a phone if you need specific advice*") to the beaming ("*I've been to Warsaw, Geneva, Milan, Luxembourg and Prague for work, talked to clients and counsel all over the world, and got to know people face-to-face at some of our European conferences – it's fantastic*"). It is fair to conclude that quite how global your work feels is down to a mixture of luck, personal preference and how excited you get when speaking to clients at the end of a phone line in Bangkok instead of Milton Keynes.

An established secondment programme allows qualified solicitors to spend several years overseas, and there are oodles of potential foreign seats to be sampled by trainees. People have previously visited Chicago, Sydney, New York, Hong Kong, Tokyo, Madrid, Moscow, Brussels, Prague, Toronto and Brazil. A couple of caveats before you click onto the most accessible cheap flight website: first, specific locations may also involve specific seats with attendant complications (employment in Sydney is a mite competitive), and second, not all locations are available all the time. There is an increasingly frequent requirement for trainees *"to present a case for an overseas seat and find partners to support you. Basically treat it like a business proposal."* We spoke to those who had benefited from this trend, and to those who'd had their fingers burned by *"a last-minute cancellation"* or felt *"the firm overplayed the secondment possibilities in the recruitment literature."* By contrast, in some instances B&M had allowed trainees to take seats overseas in practice areas not previously offered in the location. In short, you mustn't expect carte blanche to travel whither you will, and must be prepared for competition. For students already chomping at the bit, a summer programme offers foreign placements. Full details online.

nichely does it

The four-seat training programme offers such regulation choices as corporate, commercial, banking and property, and then there are more niche seats in employment, IP and IT, pensions, tax, dispute resolution, and competition/trade. On close inspection we'd say B&M trainees genuinely do have readier access to good-quality niche areas than many of their City contemporaries, even if qualification into niches is still a competitive business. Trainees must complete at least one of their two compulsory contentious and corporate seats in the first year, a practice that reflects B&M's *"slightly more corporate slant these days,"* as well as a tendency for niche-hungry trainees to try to defer transactional experience until the end of the contract. The attraction of specialist seats is understandable at a firm where niche isn't a synonym for corporate support. IP and IT seats are popular because they involve *"a huge range of work across all types of IP patents and trade marks;"* employment is equally so for its *"exciting tribunal cases and glamorous clients."*

Most trainees recognise the importance of gaining corporate experience: *"It gives you a sense of what the firm's really about on a global level"* and *"exposes you to lots of people across the firm."* Seats are available in corporate east (public deals), corporate south (private acquisitions) and corporate west (*"everything else"*). More than this *"you are asked to look around for diversity and the teams are encouraged to give you work – you can even switch between groups."*

the elves and the lawyermakers

Our sources found flexibility and responsiveness major features of their training contracts, whether it was *"dealing with small claims telecoms matters myself"* in dispute resolution, *"getting lots of client contact"* in property, or *"more of my own work, feeling as though I'm progressing to junior associate level"* in corporate tax. Barring the odd rule-proving exception, good supervisors are at the heart of a culture in which *"if you prove you are willing and able they'll give you as much responsibility and client contact as you can handle."* As another commented: *"That brings pressure, but it's what you want and it's what makes you improve."*

"Trainee breakfasts" and ample *"induction training in each seat"* complement more casual *"advice and direction from your supervisor when you need it."* Several sources had been able to develop *"light bantery relationships with supervisors"* and the majority agreed the firm had achieved *"good communications between work providers, trainers and trainees."* Defining how that atmosphere is created, trainees were quick to praise the *"fantastic contribution"* of *"very good people who by and large actually want to be supervisors. They see it as in their interests to produce good-quality NQs."* Equally, trainees were impressed with administrative staff, telling us: *"A lot of the foot soldier stuff is done for us," "it never ceases to amaze me how people work to sort your life*

out and make it easier." We rather liked this trainee's once upon a time: *"I was in until 2am one night, and came in the next morning for a meeting. The room was perfectly laid out, all my bundles were photocopied, the librarians had done research packs for everyone attending... it was like elves had done it."*

the (not so) full monty

Late-night working isn't required all the time: hours of *"9am to 6.30 or 7pm are fairly normal."* When they are there *"until 2.30 or 4am or some ungodly hour,"* little things like taxis home and dinner render the experience more pleasant. As do modern offices on the edge of the City, close to St Paul's. These have *"stunning views of the river and the cathedral,"* a subsidised canteen and a Starbucks downstairs.

The after-work social scene is pretty standard: local pubs, sports fixtures, that sort of thing. And then there's the annual, trainee-penned Christmas pantomime, a piece of satiric tomfoolery in which few partners are spared. Last year's Legally Blonde/Lord of the Rings show followed a young trainee journeying to the eighth-floor office of the London senior partner, battling her way past *"bundling in the corporate department"* and the terrifying *"blonde-haired, oxbridge employment team."* In previous years the event has climaxed with *"a group of boys doing The Full Monty routine,"* but *"last year they wore thongs and this year we didn't have it at all."* Maybe those employment lawyers have had a word...

Of B&M's recruitment policy a collective finger is put on *"a slightly quirky, little-bit-different quality that marks the firm out"* and results in a *"slightly older,"* *"more rounded"* group of trainees than the norm for the City. *"Everyone is ambitious in life, but no one is cut-throat,"* said one source; *"we attract people who are hard-working, intelligent and down to earth."* In 2006, 26 out of 32 qualifying trainees showed their loyalty to the firm by staying on.

and finally...

Baker & McKenzie guarantees a solid City training with an international element and a welcome breadth of practice areas to suit more varied tastes. Throw in an attractive list of overseas seats and post-qualification placements and you've got the measure of the place.

Barlow Lyde & Gilbert

the facts

Location: London
Number of UK partners/solicitors: 83/195
Total number of trainees: 35
Seats: 4x6 months
Alternative seats: Possibly Hong Kong, secondments
Extras: Pro bono – Toynbee Hall Legal Advice Centre

A leader in the insurance world, Barlow Lyde & Gilbert is building on major successes in general commercial litigation to reposition itself as a top-flight dispute resolution firm.

fire in the hold

BLG's insurance expertise covers everything from marine, aerospace and transport through to property and financial risk. It is even involved in insurance issues surrounding the cancellation of concert tours. It defends accountants and solicitors, architects, surveyors and other professional advisers in negligence cases. With additional expertise in clinical negligence, BLG is also on the NHS Litigation Authority defence panel. A large PI team works for insurers and local authorities. Those insurance clients include a succession of big names including AXA, Zurich, Direct Line and Norwich Union.

One consequence of the variety in the size and complexity of BLG's work is that trainees can have hugely different experiences: from managing the defence of injury claims worth just a few thousand pounds to making a small contribution to mega-litigation such as the Equitable Life case against Ernst & Young in which BLG saw off a whacking £2.6 billion claim by the troubled financial institution against its accountants. From Hurricane Katrina to the explosion at the Buncefield oil depot, wherever there is a disaster you'll often find BLG in the background.

And what of the firm's non-contentious business? There's no denying that some parts of the operation have had a turbulent few years characterised by partner and assistant departures, internal reorganisations and even the closure of its technology-sector venture in Oxford. Encompassing corporate, employment, commercial and technology departments, the firm's non-contentious division does a lot of work for the firm's insurance clients, but also boasts standalone clients such as UPS, Dixons and IBM.

a game of two halves

The various professional liability teams are grouped together with the general commercial litigation team into the enormous PLCL division where nearly half of all trainees sit at any one time. PLCL is as close to a compulsory seat as BLG comes and don't be surprised if you actually get two seats here. The good news is that work is incredibly varied and even two-timers report completely different experiences.

In the professional liability segments of the department, when assisting on smaller cases you'll typically encounter "*a lot of research, drafting reports to insurers and instructions to counsel and liaising with clients on the telephone.*" "*You're in at the deep end, but in a good way.*" Trainees working on major pieces of litigation, whether in the PL or CL part, find themselves "*doing a lot of admin*" (bundling, scheduling, liaising with clerks and paralegals). "*On a big case you're a small cog in the machine,*" but there are compensations in the form of "*access to high-level, interesting*

meetings," and if a case moves into the trial phase during your tenure you could get some quality court time. Even if your role is small, "*you feel very much part of the team,*" and when a good result comes "*you're proud to have been involved.*" Of course, it helps if the case interests you. One "*football mad*" trainee spent six months on the firm's high-profile defence of Hammonds against a £140 million negligence suit brought by the Football League. One of his colleagues told us: "*He lapped up the documents, spent time in court... he had a great time.*"

brains on call

Put PLCL behind you and you could wind up in any one of the other insurance departments, including marine, aerospace, transport and trade. There's also a growing casualty and commercial risk practice dealing with property and PI claims – for example, advising an insurer on whether damage to a policyholder's property is insured, and on how they might recover some cost by pursuing a claim against those responsible for the fire. "*I'd asked for some real hands-on work,*" said one trainee, "*and I got it.*" "*I'd look through a file,*" said another, "*discuss my thoughts with a partner and draft a letter of claim.*" While trainees have a reasonable level of control, they are well supervised, which "*takes the pressure off.*"

If you really want to delve into the nitty-gritty of insurance law then try the reinsurance team. Essentially, reinsurance is the process of insurers insuring their own risks by paying another company to take on part of the liability. If an insurer agrees to pay out on a policy but its reinsurer doesn't agree to pay them back, disputes occur. Such disputes are big, complex and secretive, frequently involving major incidents such as sinking oil platforms or disasters such as 9/11 and often being resolved through arbitration. Reinsurance can strike the novice as an impenetrable area; indeed, one trainee admitted that after six

www.chambersandpartners.co.uk

months "*I still don't know anything about it.*" The firm provides support ranging from a software program that allows you to learn basics at your own pace, to plenty of supervisor input. Two in-house know-how lawyers are backed up by sage advice from Professor Merkin of Southampton University who is "*happy to answer queries and is always quick and really helpful.*"

The structure of the training contract reflects the firm's emphasis on litigation. Yes, it is possible to secure two non-contentious seats, but only if most of your peers are satisfied with just the one. Express your interest early and be consistent. While the commercial and technology seat is popular, most people encounter non-contentious work in the corporate department. One litigation-mad trainee found that they enjoyed it more than they thought: "*It gives you the real basics, an understanding of how businesses work, their structure, and so on.*" Believe it or not, "*some people come here to be litigators and then fall in love with corporate.*"

own goal

In most seats you'll share an office with your supervisor. "*You're asked for your opinions a lot and you learn a lot by osmosis, overhearing the telephone conversations and so on.*" The exception to this is the set-up in casualty and commercial risk where trainees sit together in an open-plan section of the office. If the walls of the London office start to close in around you, there are avenues of escape. "*A steady flow*" of trainees go on client secondments where they discover that "*it really builds confidence to have in-depth client contact and to understand the client's ways of working.*" At the time of going to press two trainees were beavering away in BLG's Hong Kong office but this has not always been the case, so don't apply to BLG if you are insistent on having time abroad.

Generally, trainees found seat allocation "*fairly transparent,*" noting that "*more people get what they want than not*" and there is "*relatively little behind-the-scenes politicking.*" Yes, "*partners do have favourites,*" so it doesn't hurt to impress those you're eager to work with at NQ level. However, approaches to a partner regarding trainee seats were deemed less appropriate. In September 2006, 13 of the 17 qualifiers stayed on at the firm.

The firm's post-Equitable Life drive to rebrand itself as a top general commercial litigation firm got off to a bad start with an own goal on the PR front. The firm placed a succession of high-profile press advertisements in the summer of 2006. "*It was surprising to see the firm in the press,*" admitted one trainee, "*but there was a concensus that we needed to put ourselves about a bit more.*" The first ad in the series reproduced the names of scores of general counsel at FTSE-listed companies, with the strap line "If you'd like your name kept out of the legal pages, you'd better remember ours." The result was general disdain from publicity-shy GCs, with at least one reportedly severing ties with the firm as a result. "*I try not to think about it,*" said one trainee, while another noted stoically: "*We're waiting to see what the results are before we come to any conclusions.*" In early September the Advertising Standards Authority upheld several complaints. Nevertheless, with the Equitable Life result in the bag, there is a sense that the firm is "*now playing at the top of the field*" in litigation.

booze, laughs & graft

"*People think of Barlows as quite old fashioned and staid,*" said one source, "*but it feels laid back.*" Although City dress is de rigueur, "*ties do come off when it's hot.*" Of partners, trainees say: "*You can ask a question any time, although of course they do sometimes ask you to come back later.*" One felt "*it can be hard to see who the partners are – many of them are quite young.*" Like many litigation-led firms, hours are reasonable by City standards with 9am to 6.30pm fairly normal. Of course, trials and corporate closings bring late nights, but one soon-to-be NQ noted: "*I can count my midnights on one hand and I've only ever done two Saturdays.*"

BLG is one of the more sociable firms in the City: "*One of its big selling points is that it's a Friday-night-in-the-pub kind of place.*" The beneficiary of the firm's fondness for a tipple is the local Slug and Lettuce. "*It's only because it's over the road,*" explained a shamefaced source. The firm splashes out on Christmas and summer events, and there are various barbecues and socials throughout the year to which "*partners do actually come.*" Working in the insurance world is all about developing relationships; it is a very face-to-face business and as such trainees are dragged along to many meet-n-greets. Paralegals are often invited to socials too, and trainees agreed that "*it's nice to get to know them better.*"

BLG recruits a good proportion of non-law grads and a number with previous commercial experience. Trainees identified a BLG personality type – "*approachable, outgoing and intelligent,*" "*confident but not arrogant, and up for having fun.*" Usually at least half of the new recruits are women, though this shrinks to around 15% among UK partners. Not spectacular, but not bad by insurance-firm standards. What's more, one of BLG's best-known partners is a woman – Equitable Life victor Claire Canning. The vac scheme produces a high number of recruits, so it's just as well veterans of the scheme called it "*challenging and well organised.*" Serial schemers ranked it as one of the best in the City. Although two weeks in a single department wasn't to everyone's taste (daily talks on the rest of the firm fill in the gaps), it offers "*real work,*" including drafting and reporting tasks.

and finally...

BLG *is* litigation, now perhaps more than ever. If you think that's your thing, or you have an affinity with the insurance sector, you'll get a thorough training here and you'll probably have a good time in the process.

Beachcroft LLP

the facts

Location: Birmingham, Bristol, Leeds, London, Manchester, Winchester
Number of UK partners/solicitors: 147/311
Total number of trainees: 70
Seats: 4x6 months
Alternative seats: None

Newly rebranded Beachcroft is a big beast with territory extending from the north of England to the south and some 1,250 lawyers and staff in six cities. Shedding the cumbersome Wansbroughs bit of its name – "*it was always a bit of a mouthful*" – is not the only thing that's changed though.

onwards and upwards

Trainees were flattered to have been involved in Beachcroft's recent makeover, telling us: "*Historically the firm's representation at student law fairs has been pretty poor, so they got some trainees down from all the offices to meet an agency to talk about some new ideas.*" The result: "*Finally we have cups and T-shirts and all that shebang with our new logo on.*" Such changes sound superficial, and were the Beachcroft makeover limited to such fripperies we might be scornful, but it comes at a watershed time for the firm. A management reshuffle has created a seven-partner corporate-style board, with a new senior partner, a new managing partner and various non-executive directors. An LLP conversion was a unanimous decision, and one that must have focused partners' minds on many aspects of the business, including its revenue streams and profitability. In 2005/06 revenue was just shy of £100 million, and management has ambitiously projected £112 million for 2006/7. So how will they get there? On the Beachcroft website, new senior partner Simon Hodson explains: "The move to LLP status is the catalyst for Beachcroft to become a more commercial and transparent organisation by matching the business environment in which our clients are operating..." In other words, everyone from top to bottom adopting a more commercial attitude.

Bristol is home to around 30% of the firm's lawyers, who between them handle much of the firm's massive portfolio of public sector work. In London there are two offices, a larger one in Fetter Lane near the Royal Courts and a smaller one in Eastcheap, in the heart of the City's insurance community. The London headcount roughly equals that in Bristol and these lawyers handle corporate and commercial work, as well as insurance matters. The Leeds, Birmingham and Manchester offices account for 12, 13 and 14% of staff respectively and cover mainly litigation, insurance and public sector matters. The Winchester office is a tiddler and off the radar for almost all trainees. If you are applying to the firm with specific legal practice areas in mind, you should ascertain whether your preferred office location can give you the seats you want. It is rare for trainees to move between offices, so you have to make the right choice at the outset.

bristol's healthy options

Bristol trainees choose from a good list of contentious and non-contentious seats, among them personal injury, clinical negligence, professional indemnity, projects, construction, insolvency, employment and technology. The office has also opened up a corporate department, in line with a firm-wide drive in this area. However, most notable in Bristol is the celebrated healthcare team which acts for a swathe of public and private sector clients, including the mammoth NHS Litigation Authority. As well as defending clinical negligence claims against healthcare professionals and their employers, lawyers are adept at dealing with tricky issues of patient consent, declarations for withdrawal of life-sustaining medical treatment, and the application of mental health, children's and the human rights legislation. Last year it mediated a novel judicial review and human rights challenge, and advised a primary care trust on the first High Court declaration allowing a prisoner to refuse nutrition and medical care.

Trainees encounter the NHS in several of their seats, as the Service's needs extend in all directions from IT and employment advice to PFI projects, construction and property. According to trainees, the Bristol IT and IP team is growing, and for one trainee it turned into their busiest seat – "*hard work but enjoyable.*" One client is the Welsh Assembly, which Beachcroft advises on the IT aspects of its 'Informing Healthcare' programme. Construction and employment seats are popular, although both have "*relatively long hours and a demanding workload.*" In employment, one trainee had done masses of work for the NHS, which is hardly surprising as it is Europe's largest employer. Construction law was the highlight for another source for three reasons: the superb supervisor, the generally "*professional and well-run*" department and its full programme of social and marketing events with clients.

london life

The London offices attract people who are less drawn to the public sector. It looks to be an ideal place for anyone who wants to "*have a go at most things,*" as it offers employment, technology and commerce, construction, projects, corporate, financial services, property and masses of litigation. The employment team recently represented a fire authority in a case brought on behalf of some 1,600 part-time firefighters, the largest single test case heard by an Employment Tribunal. Litigators represented McAfee Inc and the Federation Against Software Theft in proceedings seeking injunctive relief against ten ISPs. An insurance litigation seat in the Eastcheap office is "*quite research-based, but you get good exposure to*" *things like fraud investigatory work, pre-litigation advice and commercial risk management."* Beachcroft has a formidable reputation in this sector and is on the legal panels of many leading insurers and reinsurers. In the past year its lawyers have advised insurers on issues such as the London terrorist incidents on 7 July 2005, the collision of a barge with Battersea Bridge, claims arising out of the Admiral Duncan pub bomb blast and the Asian tsunami. *"The firm's enormous clout with its insurance clients"* results in a regular stream of commercial instructions as well as litigation.

In the corporate seat trainees encounter clients in other sectors, for example last year lawyers advised Mean Fiddler Group plc, operators of musical festivals such as Glastonbury, in its takeover by US and Irish co-investors. As recently as 2005 trainees had told us: *"The firm is never going to be known for corporate and commercial work,"* but there are signs that it wishes to make deeper inroads into these activities. *"There's definitely a massive push,"* concluded one source. *"London has a big corporate department and they want one in Manchester too. Clients want us to offer all the services they need."* Interestingly trainees think that this heightened attention on corporate work *"might be reflected in the kind of person they recruit."* But let's not get too carried away: in the grand scheme of things it would take a drastic change of direction to detach Beachcroft from the insurance and public sector work for which it is so well known.

An added bonus, and *"almost the Holy Grail"* of a London training contract, is a secondment to client Unilever. Those who had been lucky enough to secure the Walton-on-Thames-based assignment judged it to be *"incredible – a phenomenal opportunity."* No wonder *"everyone scrambles for it."*

northern exposure

The Leeds office handles a significant amount of insurance litigation and public sector work, with healthcare again on the agenda. Attendance at inquests can be one of the most interesting ways a trainee can spend their time, and if it appeals to you then head for the health and social care department, which offers national coverage to clients on everything from GP regulatory problems, serious adverse events, complex employment tribunals, and projects and funding of hospitals. Some of the work is ideally suited to those with a medical background (or leanings) as they will sit in on interviews under caution with doctors accused of gross negligence or even manslaughter.

The professional indemnity seat brings trainees into contact with the firm's insurance clients. Trainees are drafted into all aspects of trial preparation, a role that led one to report: *"I really enjoyed the litigation seat as I could apply the fundamentals of what I'd learned at law school."* In personal injury seats, trainees find they can slot into the department quickly. *"There's always lots to do and you never feel like you're imposing,"* one remarked. Regular attendances at employers' liability inquests and court provide exciting breaks from desk-bound activities. Reassuringly, *"they don't expect you to know the law backwards and there are always hundreds of people to answer questions."*

The Manchester office is well known for its insurance litigation for the likes of Allianz Cornhill and Zurich. On the agenda here are catastrophic injury claims and group litigation. Trainees also get to try commercial litigation, which brings *"lots of court action"* though usually just *"watching colleagues in action."* Trainees found the seat *"fast-paced... things always need doing yesterday."* If Beachcroft's grand plans for the future of the firm reach fruition, trainees say we will see more corporate transactions handled in Manchester. *"It's exciting, and it's good to be here at a stage like this,"* commented one transaction-minded trainee.

pride in your work

In such a large firm it can be difficult to bring lawyers together from across the network. One rare occasion was a recent team-bonding day in Birmingham that strangely involved painting and playing in a salsa band. *"Then a South African lion tracker came on and drew the analogy between working together at the firm and how lions work together, which was absolutely fascinating."* Individual departments sometimes organise foreign gadabouts to places such as Barcelona, Nice and Amsterdam, but it is the trainees who try hardest to bond. Each year they have a small budget to do with as they wish: *"Last year we did a school sports day with an egg and spoon race, and this year we're doing crazy golf."* Genius.

Manchester trainees boast that their social life is the envy of their peers across the country. *"It's the party office, definitely, and there's a great sense of camaraderie."* One told us: *"There's always so much going on, and there'll always be a massive night out that comes from nowhere, usually involving us ending up on Curry Mile."* Regular hangouts include posh old pub Mr Thomas's Chop House, and vodka bar Revolution. The last office Christmas party was held at Manchester City's football stadium, where *"we had a good old singsong, and a dance and all kinds of embarrassing things."*

Perhaps inspired by the lion tracker, the Bristol office also has a novel approach to partying. *"This summer we're having a James Bond-themed ball at Bristol Zoo,"* confirmed one trainee. The Londoners have their summer party on board a Thames river cruiser, but most of the time it's left up to the trainees to organise their own fun – *"We do things like ice-skating and going for curries."* Someone told us about a breakfast at Smiths of Smithfield, opposite London's meat market, but whether this was after a big night out or after a good night's sleep, we're not certain. Meanwhile up in Leeds, there's plenty of fun to be had as *"we're a minute from Greek Street"* which is awash with good bars.

In September 2006, 25 of the 26 qualifiers took jobs with the firm.

and finally...

By not bragging loudly about its achievements Beachcroft has acquired an enigmatic reputation. Whether trainees will in the future still bemoan the fact that *"people haven't heard about us,"* or whether it'll be T-shirts and mugs all round, remains to be seen.

Berwin Leighton Paisner LLP

the facts

Location: London
Number of partners/assistants: 167/336
Total number of trainees: 80
Seats: 4x6 months
Alternative seats: Brussels, secondments

This is a firm brimming with confidence. It is little wonder that morale is high and there are smiles all round at Berwin Leighton Paisner.

on a roll

The two words most often associated with BLP are 'real estate'. Long before the current surge in the firm's all-round reputation, its real estate practice was known as just about the best on the block. Real estate remains terribly important to the firm, and it is still consistently top-rated. If anything, commentators agree that it is getting better and better at a time when the property market is increasingly defined by more-complicated deal structures and international transactions. But to understand why BLP is now so fêted, so often, you have to look beyond its giant real estate division. Patience has proved to be an important virtue for the corporate and commercial lawyers at the firm. It has become increasingly clear that the 2001 merger between smaller corporate firm Paisner & Co and the already sizeable Berwin Leighton has paid dividends. The BLP lawyers not only gained new clients in previously non-core practice areas, but also acquired expertise that allowed them to keep pace with the trend for the 'corporatisation' of real estate transactions.

Success beyond the confines of the traditional real estate practice generated a good deal of confidence in the firm. BLP's management has been both brave and considered in its decision-making, and a string of very capable lawyers have been drawn in from other law firms. Most notable perhaps is Robert McGregor from Clifford Chance, who now heads up the real estate division. Other notable hires include two securitisation partners, one of them from Lovells, and a French Slaughter and May corporate finance partner. The firm is now moving into a phase when it is exploring the world outside the UK. Having decided to pursue a 'good friends' policy it's not about to open any foreign offices, but that's not to say it doesn't want a piece of the European action.

The chunky real estate department (which is also home to planning and construction lawyers) is divided into three sections, each of which welcomes in trainees. A seat in real estate is *"technically not compulsory, but all trainees go through the department"* at some stage. Of late, lawyers have been advising on the regeneration of Liverpool city centre in time for 2008, when the northern jewel becomes the European Capital of Culture. They have also advised the consortium behind the construction of the Shard of Glass office tower at London Bridge. In the related discipline of planning, BLP also kicks considerable butt. For trophy client Tesco, one of the many projects it is working on is the proposal to develop a new 120,000 sq ft store in Dartford. In the associated areas of construction, real estate finance and property litigation, BLP also performs very well. Trainees' experiences of the real

estate divisions are positive, but when it comes as a first seat some can find the prospect a little intimidating. To ease their nerves, the department makes great effort with supervision. *"I loved real estate because of my supervisor,"* recalled one trainee; *"she always made time for me no matter how busy she was."*

arabian nights

We told you BLP's activities had broadened out in recent times, so here's what this means for trainees. Asset finance, corporate finance, project finance, insurance and reinsurance, licensing and product liability are all coming on apace, and the good news is that the firm offers seats in all these areas. Recent expansion in project finance, for instance, is indicative of the firm's vision for the future. The department's clientele is international and the firm works on high-profile matters for the likes of the Sultanate of Oman, the Ministry of Defence and the Saudi Arabian government. Seats here prove popular with trainees, who rather like the idea of being instrumental in improving a country's infrastructure. Sometimes there's even the chance of an overseas trip: *"As this department's grown so much you could find yourself in Dubai working on an energy contract for the Middle East."* Stay at home and there are still challenges to be met. Telling us about their role on a PFI deal, one trainee said: *"At first I was petrified, but in the end I was doing things on my own and taking instructions directly from clients."*

In the commercial litigation seat it's common for trainees to get involved in sizeable cases. *"I got onto one major fraud action, doing freezing orders, which I really enjoyed as it touched on the criminal side,"* said a source. In the corporate recovery (insolvency) seat there is plenty of *"tricky technical stuff"* to get your head around, but luckily the supervisors are *"very accommodating."* Trainees are given a few of their own small cases which, despite some comments about *"coming pretty close to feeling out of my depth,"* is generally seen as a *"really rewarding"* feature of the seat.

It is likely that all trainees will visit the busy corporate finance department where their work includes *"low-profile attendance at client meetings"* and *"helping to draft things like investment agreements."* Some of our sources had assisted with the all-important *"verification exercises on AIM IPOs"* and naturally there are also more administrative duties. The hours can be *"knackering"* at times and some trainees reported that they had done *"three all-nighters and a lot of 1am and 2ams in a row."* This is symptomatic of the fact that BLP is making its mark in London's mid-sized deals market. Long hours can leave trainees disoriented. One who'd grafted rather hard in their first six months admitted to some soul searching over their choice of firm. *"You do think, 'Crikey, have I done the right thing?' but when you're quaffing champagne at 5am at the end of a deal you think, 'It can't be that appalling.'"*

every little helps

It has not escaped our notice that, as the fortunes of the international retail giant have grown, so too have BLP's. Barely a week goes by without some news item about just how many pounds the average Briton parts with in the store and which part of the world the Tesco Empire has just conquered. The news story that broke shortly after our interviews related to Tesco's referral to the Competition Commission over its land purchase and sale programme. You can Google it if you want the nub of the story and to see where BLP fits in.

Trainees were keen to point out that although Tesco is clearly the firm's biggest client, BLP doesn't feel Tesco-centric. *"It is possible to go through the whole of your training contract without coming into contact with Tesco much,"* said one, while another stressed that *"having Tesco as a client is great, but we want to maintain and improve our relationships with other clients too."* The firm offers trainee secondments to the supermarket's HQ in Hertfordshire, as well as to clients like Schroders and London Underground. There is also a new overseas seat option in Brussels.

shaky hands

Trainees insisted we emphasise that partners are approachable, so much so that *"they often approach you. If you pass a partner you haven't met in a corridor he'll shake your hand and ask your name and background information – it's really nice."* With the firm expanding at such a pace, presumably this means partners must sometimes feel like shaky-hands man. Maybe it's their way of guarding against losing the BLP culture as the firm expands. On this subject, trainees say: *"They're really careful about incorporating people and having them adopt the BLP attitude of maintaining an open culture. It really does want to be seen as the most attractive place to work."*

There are regular drinks dos in the office and every Friday a gang of trainees troops off to The Fine Line near the office. Our sources had also been on a fair few departmental jollies including day trips to Paris. Last year there was a charity bike ride led by the senior partner. We were expecting to hear about a leisurely pedal around Hyde Park, but the event had more of the Tour de France about it as it involved cycling from Paris to Reims. All the stops were pulled out for last year's Christmas party, a masquerade ball in the Royal Courts of Justice. *"It was a really amazing event in a huge room with vaulted ceilings, a trapeze artist, a gospel choir and a casino – it was awesome."*

So do trainees have any gripes at all? Well, we finally unearthed some grievances, albeit relatively trivial ones. *"They could shorten the name,"* thought one interviewee. Another said: *"The lifts are too slow."* A third suggested that BLP's two adjacent office buildings should be connected by *"some kind of underground tunnel."* We doubt anyone's losing sleep over these issues.

q&a

Here are a few questions some readers might be pondering on. There's a firm called SJ Berwin, is there a link? Yes, Stanley Berwin set up SJB after a successful career at Berwin Leighton. Is BLP a Jewish firm? The firm's founders were Jewish and BLP still maintains strong links with the Jewish community, although it does not describe itself as a Jewish firm. It's a great choice whatever your religion, or lack of one. If I accept a TC with BLP will I have to go to London for my LPC? Yes, from 2006 all recruits will study the BLP LPC+ at the new Moorgate branch of The College of Law. The course will include electives that have been tailor-made for the firm; other classes will be taken with students going to different law firms. Should I apply to BLP even if I don't want to do property work? It would be wise to see the inner workings of this core practice, even if you then qualify in something else. What are my chances of staying on after qualification? Right now, excellent. In the summer and autumn of 2006, BLP had numerous vacancies for assistant solicitors in transactional teams and had even been recruiting staff from Australian firms. In September 2006, 24 of the 28 qualifiers stayed on with the firm, with the real estate, construction, business technology services and planning departments all popular destinations.

and finally...

It would be easy for a firm in BLP's position to be nauseatingly self-congratulatory but you really don't get the sense that people here are sitting back on their collective laurels. It was a genuine pleasure to speak to trainees at a time when their mood was so high; they spoke about the firm with a degree of admiration that was truly encouraging.

Bevan Brittan LLP

the facts

Location: Bristol, Birmingham, London
Number of UK partners/solicitors: 67/173
Total number of trainees: 36
Seats: 4x6 months
Alternative seats: Secondments

Rooted in Bristol with expanding offices in London and Birmingham, Bevan Brittan is a leader in public sector work and, in particular, healthcare. In recent times it has swung more towards the private sector and become a firm of choice for public-private partnerships.

public service, private passions

At the heart of Bevan Brittan's long love affair with the public sector is its close relationship with the NHS, especially the NHS Litigation Authority, which is the service's centralised clinical negligence claims handler. One of just a dozen firms supplying the authority's considerable needs, BB tackles some highly complex and emotive issues; for example, *"you might be defending a claim that's been entered on behalf of a child who's developed cerebral palsy, allegedly because its mother didn't have a caesarean in time."* Following a reduction in NHS clin neg instructions the firm is now targeting more private healthcare providers. Aside from clin neg work, the employment, property and coco departments also have strong relationships with the NHS, representing numerous hospital trusts and primary care trusts.

Some of BB's most interesting work has come out of its burgeoning projects practice. An expert in public-private partnerships, the firm has advised many NHS trusts, education authorities and private sector developers on major schemes under the private finance initiative (PFI). Last year it advised on the £320 million rebuild of two hospitals in Nottinghamshire. Even the government itself uses BB;

it has a key role in the mammoth project to rebuild/refurbish every school in Britain. Success in the UK has enabled the firm to develop its reputation overseas, and it recently advised on the first PPP hospital project in Canada.

BB's plan to extend beyond its traditional client base exploits its lawyers' enormous experience of operating "*at the forefront of the interface between the public and private sectors.*" In addition to expanding the PFI practice, BB aims to increase the volume of private-sector work coming into all other departments. The corporate team, for example, has lately been dealing with everyone from private healthcare providers to pub chains. But change happens slowly and, for now at least, trainees say that public sector expertise remains "*very much its heart.*"

It wasn't clear from our interviewees that there is any real difference between working for the public and private sectors. "*Public sector clients are just nicer,*" said one. "*They're not necessarily nicer,*" said another. "*You have to be much more aware of budget; because it's taxpayers' money, you have to ensure you're adding value,*" one explained. "*Public sector clients have no idea of budgets,*" declared another. "*With company directors it's their money at stake, but with public sector clients you're dealing with someone far removed from the money source.*" We'll let you make your own mind up; but suffice to say, you don't have to have taken a solemn vow of non-cooperation with capitalism to work here. In fact, you probably couldn't if you had.

no sniggering at the back

There are no compulsory seats, but you are likely to spend time in the projects and medical law departments. In the latter trainees' tasks begin with "*sorting piles and piles of medical records and obtaining documents.*" Don't worry, "*as you progress through the seat you'll get much more responsibility,*" eventually drafting witness statements, attending hearings or case management conferences and briefing barristers. In addition, as the NHSLA requires six-monthly reports on the progress of each case, a key trainee job is to prepare these reports, which gives them "*an excellent understanding of the nuts and bolts of litigation.*" More than this, "*you have to be a doctor as well as a lawyer.*" Said one trainee: "*I'm forever looking things up in medical dictionaries.*" Another added: "*It's a shame it's only a six-month seat; by the time I know what I'm talking about it'll be time to leave.*" We wondered whether the trainees ever found the work too gruesome or tragic, but on this point they were surprisingly sanguine. "*You just have to step away from it,*" said one; "*objectify it a little.*" And it's not all gore: "*You have to learn not to giggle, too, with words like 'penile' and 'discharge.'*" The seat also carries with it the immense burden of "*deciphering doctors' handwriting.*"

In the projects team you'll "*probably be surprised with the amount with which you're entrusted.*" Projects work is notoriously document-heavy, and PFI even more so. As such, you'll be "*up to your ears in 300-page documents.*" Rather than treating trainees as glorified secretaries, supervisors often hand over responsibility for document management, leaving them to "*draft, check for consistent use of language or liaise with clients to obtain documents.*" One told us: "*Having responsibility for the documents for a certain project meant it was really my baby. I felt very much involved.*" Because projects "*can take years to set up*" you won't see the whole lifespan of one in your time in the department. However, because the firm gets you involved on more than one matter, "*you do get to see beginnings, middles and ends.*"

In commercial litigation you'll usually be given a couple of small cases to manage; in property you'll look after at least one residential file from start to finish; and in employment, one trainee we spoke to had even attended an employment tribunal without supervision. "*You think, gosh, I've got all this responsibility, but you're* not on your own; you think of all the options and talk it through with people and see what they think." The firm seems to have engendered a culture of using trainees well. "There's an emphasis on training you for qualification, not just using you as cheap labour," concluded one. In practice they work more closely with associates than their supervising partner, an arrangement trainees actually prefer as "associates can be much easier to approach." Essentially, "partners do the high-level stuff while associates are in a much better position to actually give you work." Mid and end-of-seat appraisals and monthly informal assessments ensure steady feedback.

initial wobbles

Mostly, trainees seemed happy with seat allocation. "It's very much done through the official processes," said one. "I've never heard of anyone having a quiet word in a partner's ear." As in any firm, there are fads and fashions. For now "employment is the new black." The HR team runs an extensive training programme commencing with an induction for all held in Bristol. "You meet the other trainees, NQs, partners, department heads... it's very hectic but really useful." Slightly scarier is the trainee away-day, where recruits are whisked off to a secluded country house for team-building exercises led by two former SAS personnel. "You have to get a pot of jelly out of a circle of rope with another circle of rope," explained one trainee, still quivering from the experience. "The people with the rope are blindfolded and the others all shout instructions." This may all sound a bit Lord of the Flies but trainees confirm that the slap-up dinner that comes afterwards doesn't include a pig's head on a stake.

Although it is possible to take seats in different offices, trainees apply to, and are based at, just one. The Birmingham office doesn't offer the same extensive seat list the others do, but is the only office for tax and pensions seats. Similarly,

London alone offers a banking option and Bristol alone offers PI. BB is on an expansion drive, however, so at interview you should probably check what your preferred office can offer. After the initial induction, videoconferencing facilities and e-mail bear the brunt of inter-office trainee relations. And of course, there's always the telephone: "I do call trainees in other offices if they're on the same seat as me, to compare notes and ask for advice," confirmed one interviewee.

yeah but, no but

By the time you read this all three offices will be ensconced in swish, new, open-plan buildings. The open-plan layout seems to neatly symbolise the firm's tone – "open," "democratic" and "friendly" were the words trainees used. "People from other firms always comment on how nice and open people here are," bragged one Birmingham trainee. There is, however, a sense that the firm's new interest in commercial clients could alter the mood. "When I arrived," said one soon-to-qualify trainee, "I'd have described the mood as relaxed. It's still informal, but perhaps more determined now."

To give you some background: in 2004, Bevan Brittan emerged from a reasonably long, but relatively fruitless, combination with West Country firm Ashfords. If you ever hear people mention Bevan Ashford, that's what they're talking about. Don't start imagining BB as some trauma-scarred shell of a firm; the demerger was something that suited both firms and it has freed BB to push for greater national prominence in its target sectors. BB's management has used the demerger as an opportunity to launch a barrage of new initiatives, new client care standards, pro bono opportunities and 'development tracks'. We won't bore you with the details of these; suffice to say they suggest that BB has taken a leaf from the books of larger firms. Any organisational shift can lead to a certain amount of tension. "Some of the partners are a bit cynical about the new branding and stuff," admitted one trainee, but under the corporate gloss and management-speak, the core values of the firm appear intact. "*It doesn't feel like the public sector work is less important,*" one trainee assured us, reiterating that the firm is "*very much positioning itself with reference to both sets of expertise.*"

BB is a 9.30am to 6.30pm kind of place, with projects and some other commercial departments at times proving the exception. The new Bristol office is on the city's redeveloped waterfront which will eventually teem with bars and restaurants. In London there's already a "*fantastic*" social scene and the Birmingham trainees also have their favourite after-work hang-outs. Each office has a summer party and a Christmas ball, and the *Student Guide* award for best after-dinner entertainment goes to the Bristol office. "*The trainees and partners work together on a short film... this year's was 'Bevan Little Britain',*" a ten-minute short featuring, among other gems, the chief executive in a flouncy dress wailing, "*I'm a laydee!*"

and finally...

Be it the public sector focus, the atmosphere or the transvestite cinema projects, Bevan Brittan inspires a majority of its qualifiers to stay at the firm. In 2006 16 of the 18 took jobs across the three offices.

Bircham Dyson Bell

the facts

Location: London, Cardiff, Edinburgh
Number of UK partners/solicitors: 43/87
Total number of trainees: 15
Seats: 4x6 months
Alternative seats: Secondments

Venerable Westminster outfit Bircham Dyson Bell has set itself the lofty ambition of breaking into the top 50 within the next five years. Posting a 22% increase in half-yearly turnover is

definitely a step in the right direction, but striding forward doesn't mean leaving the past behind.

the aims afoot

There was a buzz about our interviews with Birchamites this year. Words like "*growing,*" "*dynamic*" and "*going somewhere*" were thick in the air and the scent of anticipation hung heavy. "*You feel like part of something,*" they told us. "*There's a plan afoot!*" In its simplest terms that plan is to reach the top 50 as soon as possible, but our sources were quick to refine upon its everyday implications. "*It means a drive to market and get the firm's profile out there,*" opined one, "*but we're not looking to grow massively, rather at our own pace.*" Publicly the firm has committed itself to the sort of growth characterised by last year's lateral hires and merger with niche social housing practice Jenkins & Hand (albeit that a shard has already splintered off). In essence the firm is enhancing existing strengths rather than embarking on wholesale revolution. "*Sure the marketing director is out there a lot and we're going to law fairs, which never used to happen, but it hasn't suddenly transformed into a super-sleek, ultra-modern firm, not by any stretch of the imagination.*"

Hastily embracing anything would be a paradigm shift for a firm that has long been regarded as conservative with a small 'c'. Indeed a typical description would paint Birchams as quintessentially traditional, gentlemanly, and with working practices that occasionally impinge on an evening, but never on a weekend. Trainees readily admit that the balancing act between its established character and its new sense of ambition "*might become more difficult in the long term,*" but were happy to report that these elements are "*co-existing happily*" at present.

the house, doctor

Co-existing doesn't necessarily mean seamlessly integrated. In our capacity as legal physician, all the symptoms we observed point to a clear diagnosis of bipolar disorder. Symptom one: the office. Birchams resides across four floors of a beautiful Georgian building on Broadway, close to St James's Park and in the heart of Westminster. Behind the period façade, the interior has been modernised as befits a 21st century law firm. It's definitely a neat metaphor for the Birchams of today, but perhaps senior partner Ian McCulloch's lyrical prose on the website takes it a tad too far. "Our office reflects the personality of our firm: built from stone to outlast us all, yet contemporary and technologically up-to-date on the inside... a modern classic." In fact, trainees observed a somewhat higgledy-piggledy logic in a layout that incorporates a *"hotchpotch of open-plan spaces, private offices and work-bench things"* and speaks of the different characters of departments.

Birchams is one of the few firms involved in parliamentary matters, and its parliamentary, public law & planning department (PPP) is, along with real estate, at the heart of the firm's current expansion. For the uninitiated, the Parliamentary lawyers primarily work on the promotion of and opposition to legislation, being heavily involved in some of the largest projects in the UK from Crossrail to Docklands Light Railway extensions, from the £1.4 billion London Gateway container port to the Merseytram scheme in Liverpool. The real estate department is also thriving on a steady diet of work associated with such projects (for example, property aspects of the Merseytram project) as well as possessing a strong client list of its own that includes Exxon-Mobile, Esso, Marks & Spencer, Fred Perry and HSBC. The recently bolted-on social housing team has widened the department's remit and brought in a fantastic range of local authority and housing association clients. Trainees say there's a *"young, driven, buzzing"* atmosphere in the open-plan space occupied by these departments.

This atmosphere is shared by a *"half-open-plan"* coco team, which is coming along very

nicely by all accounts. Advising Falkland Islands Holdings on a hostile bid for the Portsmouth Harbour Ferry Company is illustrative of the sort of work the team handles for a variety of financial institutions and mid-rank companies. The department's work also overlaps substantially with a well-developed charities law team. In stark contrast, the private client department occupies nearly an entire floor of private offices and *"feels like a different world."* "Dusty antique clocks on the wall" and a hushed atmosphere epitomise what is still perceived by outsiders to be Birchams' heartland. Even if in reality its influence within the firm is on the wane, the recent hire of a former head of capital taxes at HM Revenue & Customs should put paid to notions that the firm no longer values this side of its business. We've no doubt Birchams will be advising wealthy private individuals and helping companies to structure tax-avoiding trusts for many years to come.

Of course plenty of firms have unusual office layouts, but here it was the suite of client meeting rooms that really clinched our diagnosis of institutionalised duality. Some were styled according to a *"clean lines, hi-tech, modern"* vision during the latest office refit, others have retained *"a traditional, sober décor, antique-lined feel."* It doesn't take a genius to work out which clients are taken where.

ask and ye shall receive

When it comes to seat rotation and their own professional development, trainees benefit from a decidedly responsive attitude within the firm. The four-seat training structure has no compulsory elements, and seats are on offer in all parts of the firm. There's even a client secondment to Esso. Despite talk of a litigation bottleneck last year, we were told *"everyone generally gets what they want."* The same seems to be true when it comes to getting good quality tasks, even if the specific nature of a department's work can impinge on the level of autonomy. So while real estate is renowned as *"a place where you hit the ground running with 50 files and the phone ringing from day one,"* PPP often means *"a lot of prep work and research on huge projects that you don't see through to the end."* That said, *"drafting petitions for objectors to Crossrail when it's their house at stake"* or *"working out the intricacies of legislation drafted in the 1800s"* has its rewards. Private client, incidentally, is seen as *"a more academic and complex environment,"* where *"trainees are less capable of doing the work because it's so complicated."* In spite of this *"a real attempt is made to get you involved on the larger trusts"* and there is plenty of *"probate and power of attorney matters to get your teeth into."*

"Conscientious" supervisors help to keep things on an even keel via chatty mid-seat and more formal end-of-seat appraisals. *"Mine normally intervenes when she can't see me for files!"* chuckled one trainee. Birchams seems determined to keep trainees in the loop in other ways too. *"With all the changes, there have been lots of meetings to keep us up to date and ask our opinions. You feel like everyone has a say."* To prove this point, one source explained how, after a request for guidelines on how trainees should behave at client events, Birchams organised a training day culminating in a drinks event *"where we practised our newly acquired networking skills on the partners."* We're guessing 'How much do you earn?' wasn't a popular icebreaker.

share and cher-alike

Trainees here are united in their level-headedness and, though the current batch isn't quite as mature as their predecessors, most have *"a year or two of other experience in the wider world."* Recent example of Birchams trainees' exploits include recruitment, lobbying, travel, aid work and professional trumpeting. Few of them have law degrees. They characterise themselves as *"people who can get down to the job and hit the ground running but still have fun."*

One consequence of a marginally younger trainee population is a newly energised social scene centring around the pubs of St James's, more specifically the Old Star, which has the great distinction of being *"about two steps away from the office."* A more sophisticated bar, Zander, has a cocktail list *"to die for,"* however its prices make it *"a payday venue only."* Other attractions are summer picnics in the park, a Christmas Carol Service at St Margaret's church next to Westminster Abbey and a rowing regatta on the Thames that will hopefully become a regular fixture. Crack teams of four from each department trained for several weeks before the day of the race. Alas, none could beat the litigation crew whose *"adversarial nature won out."*

Entirely less pleasant to contemplate was news of last year's Christmas party that saw the managing partner and a young trainee sing a duet together. Having mobilised themselves to storm the entertainment committee and vote out the tradition of a trainee-led comedy revue, we wouldn't normally have much sympathy for those Birchams youngsters forced to endure the karaoke cacophony that replaced it. But, our hearts melted when we learned the song that MP and young trainee crooner chose: *"It was 'I Got You Babe' and it was as embarrassing as it sounds."* Less Sonny and Cher, more Pitchy and Sharp, it seems.

Only three of the seven qualifiers accepted NQ positions at the firm in 2006. It's a low figure for a firm that clearly has expansion on its mind, but we'd add that offers were made to six trainees and some secured jobs elsewhere before discovering that their hoped-for departments were in fact available.

and finally...

Bircham Dyson Bell is a distinguished London firm with some very distinctive work that would suit the discerning candidate.

Bird & Bird

the facts

Location: London
Number of UK partners/solicitors: 54/116
Total number of trainees: 26
Seats: 4x6 months
Alternative seats: Overseas seats, secondments
Extras: Language training

London mid-sizer Bird & Bird is doing well. An ambitious European expansion drive has most recently added offices in Lyon, Madrid, Frankfurt and Rome, and revenue was up by 20% to nearly £100 million in 2005/06.

clever birds

Behind the Birds' success is a business plan that has turned a one-office technology and IP specialist into a pan-European IP/IT-heavy, general commercial firm. Now with 14 offices, the firm's business has a distinctly European flavour, and trainees quickly discover that in the London office many clients come from beyond UK shores. Last year, for example, it secured a House of Lords victory for Dutch pharmaceuticals client Synthon over GlaxoSmithKline concerning the antidepressant drug Seroxat. Proving that it's two-way traffic, recently the French Birds won a victory in the Paris Court of First Instance after its pharmaceutical client Allergan sued beauty product manufacturer Klein Becker, which was running a comparative advertising campaign claiming one of its products was "Better than Botox".

While pharmaceuticals companies are classic Bird & Bird clients, the firm's long track record in IP practice takes in product developers from almost every sector you could name. In this digital age, telecommunications and information technology companies are important, and here the firm works for multinational giants of the likes of Nokia, Eriksson, Cisco and Intel. It's not hard to see the wisdom of the firm's pan-European business strategy is it?

intellectual pursuits

Here's how a Bird & Bird training contract breaks down. No seat is strictly compulsory but trainees must take assignments in four of the following departments: corporate, commercial, dispute resolution, real estate, employment, banking, IP and tax.

For anyone not entirely at ease in a sharp suit and brogues, "*IP is less corporate than the other departments. The people are intellectual and down to earth and they really push the law on groundbreaking cases.*" As well as being legally qualified, a good number of the partners and fee earners here are scientifically qualified, a fact not lost on those trainees who have also come to the firm after more years studying the periodic table than tables of cases. From hardcore patent litigation to disputes over trade marks and copyright, many of the matters on lawyers' desks are worth millions in potential revenue; winning or losing a case can have a big impact on the client's share value and income.

The commercial seats – Comm 1 and Comm 2 – are always popular, the latter so much so that it is frequently oversubscribed. Comm 2 lawyers dispense advice to telecoms and other private sector companies, so for example a trainee had spent time researching communications satellites, and others reported work relating to the Internet and new technologies. Someone else told us they were "*working on projects to do with ridiculous things, things I didn't even know were possible.*" The department's clientele could be behind its popularity. "*Some of my work was for clients in film and sports,*" one source gleefully told us. Very specific in their interests, they told us: "*I came here because I was interested in media work and liked the sector focus. You really get the chance to get involved in one type of industry.*"

Comm 1 is not as sexy, though it does have "*a nice mix of different types of work – big-scale project work, work for public sector clients, for which I was doing lots of document management and some data protection... it was mainly smaller self-contained projects for some interesting, quirky clients.*" The NHS, HM Prison Service, the Department for Work and Pensions, and the Department of Constitutional Affairs all use the group's services on some pretty major projects, commonly outsourcing deals worth hundreds of millions of pounds. One trainee had become totally absorbed in "*cross-European data protection work, liaising with offices across Europe and working on IT contracts and general procurement issues.*"

nestworking opportunities

Though you must wait until after qualification before there are any guarantees of time abroad, a programme of placements for trainees is emerging. The placements range from a few weeks to three months and recently trainees have visited Beijing, Paris and Brussels. Technically a seat could be taken in any one of the firm's 14 offices, though this is at the discretion of the foreign offices. Even if you're not one of the lucky few who get to go abroad, you could work your way into a UK-based client secondment. A little Bird revealed that "*someone is doing a litigation seat with* [a well-known online company] *and someone got to go to glamorous Luton to work for AstraZeneca.*" The icing on the cake for this source was the fact that "*someone else got to go to Wembley.*" We hope their office was fully built before they arrived.

Trainees tell us the firm has diversified its activities and "*made a bit of a push to get a broader image, so we're not just seen as an IP and telecoms firm.*" Certainly they get to spend seats in non-core departments and clearly appreciated the opportunity to sample other types of work. Slightly disappointed, one trainee had found employment "*really quiet, so I was just doing some work permits*

and it was a bit of a waste of time," but it was the corporate seat that turned out to be universally less popular. There's nothing suspicious to report; it's just that corporate isn't high on the typical trainee's agenda at this firm. The firm is trying its best to inspire interest in the department, but when asked why trainees had chosen Bird & Bird in the first place, one said they'd looked deep into their soul and realised: "*I just wasn't interested in banking and M&A work.*" More positive reports from the dispute resolution department, where one trainee was gainfully employed "*drafting applications to court and dealing with disputes over small amounts of money. There was also the predictable management of vast bundles and some legal research on court procedures.*" Those who visited the competition law team found plenty of "*good intellectual work;*" similarly, the tax team offered "*lots of research and advising international companies on investing in the UK and abroad. It was challenging and tough going, complicated stuff.*"

Trainees say the atmosphere varies between departments: "*Corporate is more serious because of the work. Litigation is very buzzing – the people are much more energetic and lively.*" Unlike some of the firms we've researched, it was nice to hear that "*there's a lot of crossover between departments with drinks, talks and seminars.*" More than this, "*they are keen to get you to call someone from another department if you need advice and most people are very patient with your silly questions. Some of the people here are real experts in their field and they are enthusiastic about sharing their knowledge.*" It's also good to learn that "*you are judged by the work you do, and on how you fit into the team culture*" – which effectively means the experience is what you make it.

high kicks

Despite the appeal to scientist types and "*IP geeks,*" this firm has gone for "*a weird combination of people who have done other things first.*" The result being *"a good mix of ages from 22 through to people of 30 who have worked in pharmaceuticals for a few years before."* All our interviewees agreed on *"a decided lack of massive egos,"* instead concluding, *"there are lots of strong characters and individuals. People are ambitious, but no one's trying to succeed on the back of others. There's a real team feel."* We thank the trainee who gave us the following mental image: *"We've been known to describe ourselves as funky – I don't see it myself. Everyone is quite conservative and traditional. It's not like people are wearing cut-off jumpers and diesel jeans halfway down their arse and smoking weed in the hallways."*

Trainees pick up a massive amount of information from supervisors and colleagues on a daily basis and thought formal training sessions were generally well handled and well planned. That said, one revealed that *"we've also had some pretty odd training sessions. One on speed-reading was pretty useless. We took on a very Victor Meldrew mentality – told how to look at a page and take in bits and bobs. What Rubbish!"* The 2006 qualification round was a far less contentious subject. This year 11 of the 14 September qualifiers took jobs at the firm, going into the commercial, IP, dispute resolution, real estate and employment teams.

The firm has outgrown its various nests along Fetter Lane such that Comm 1, for example, is *"in a separate building, sandwiched between ten floors of Charles Russell."* As if this wasn't enough, it has recently had to adjust to the arrival of a burlesque club in the basement of one of its buildings. *"There used to be a bar in the basement called Walkers where they did £1 pints. The new place has caused a storm because it was supposed to be a strip bar! In fact it's a cabaret bar full of 1920s women, called Volupté."* Despite the convenience of getting everyone down there for a few can-can dances, the firm instead chose to hold its most recent *"lavish"* annual summer party at the Westminster Boat Club. There are also 'partners drinks' for all staff three times a year, and trainees get together for nights out bowling,

playing pool and summer performances at Regents Park's outdoor theatre. The young birds have even organised weekend getaways, recently taking in the delights of Budapest and the Isle of Wight. Play footie and foreign junkets await you. The firm's London squad did their best at a recent pan-European Bird & Bird tournament held in Brussels, but unfortunately lost to Germany on penalties. *"They had cheerleaders, which put them at an advantage."* Maybe the Brits should have taken a few of the Volupté girls along.

and finally...

We can't fault the summary of the trainee who told us: *"Bird & Bird has found a particular sector and is incredibly good at it."* For students the question is whether this sector is one you want to become absorbed in.

Birkett Long

the facts

Location: Colchester, Chelmsford
Number of UK partners/solicitors: 19/30
Total number of trainees: 5
Seats: 4x6 months
Alternative seats: None

One of Essex's finest, Birkett Long's combination of commercial and private client expertise gives its trainees a head start in regional practice.

moving out, moving on

All change at Birkett Long. We were all set to talk about the firm's triangle of offices in Colchester, Chelmsford and Halstead but then found out it's now more of a straight line. Halstead, the first office to put Birkett Long on the map way back in 1821, has closed. All business and personnel have shifted to the existing office in Colchester and to the firm's shiny new premises in Chelmsford.

From these two offices the firm caters for private and public companies along with local authorities, charities, educational establishments and individuals. Some examples from this assortment include Chelmsford company e2v technologies, which supplies sensor and thermal imaging technology for such projects as the Hubble space telescope, and Partnership Health Group, which operates treatment centres on behalf of the NHS. Trainees say the firm's diverse clientele makes getting a decent selection of seats pretty straightforward and *"because there are only a few trainees you will be able to do the things you are keen on, unless there is a business reason to say otherwise."* The only caveat is that *"you should take the initiative as HR aren't mind readers."*

Mystic Meg may not have a desk at Birkett Long but some aspects of the training contract can be predicted. *"They try to put you in residential or tax and trusts to start with so you can get to grips with the way things are done."* Residential conveyancing in particular gave our interviewees the chance to *"learn the Birkett Long way."* Skills gained in this department can then be used in commercial property, where the firm works for a variety of local business owners, retailers and individuals with investments. It needn't be this way though: *"I was down for six months in residential and six months in commercial property,"* said one trainee, *"but I felt that was too much. I discussed it with HR and they agreed to change it to three months in each. They are quite flexible like that."*

Tax, trusts and probate work involves more client contact than one source had envisaged was possible. Setting up trusts and drafting wills, as well as advising on aspects of income tax and capital taxes, *"I ran some of my own files under supervision,"* they explained. And this isn't the only department to offer so much hands-on experience; another trainee told us that *"the level of responsibility I have enjoyed across my seats has been a real high point."* A stint in commercial litigation *"may not be for everyone"* but offers trainees a bird's-eye view of county court and High Court proceedings. *"All the members of the large team have been asked to take me to any court hearings they have, so I'm getting a lot of experience that way,"* reported a source. Equally, corporate seats mean *"a lot of drafting and a lot of good experience."* The team advised Colchester-based Healthcare Homes when it bought The Pri-Med Group and became the largest care home provider in the region. There are further seat options in employment, IP & IT, family and personal injury. It would be easy to say that the two sides of the business – private client and commercial – allow trainees to choose between two set paths, but their advice is simple: *"You shouldn't write off any areas of the law until you have experienced them. And, similarly, don't assume that what you want to do is set in stone."*

mud, mud, glorious mud

A good example of the potential to combine different types of practice is the respected rural business department – *"It's a bit private client, but at the same time it is commercially based."* The group gives specialist advice to farmers and landowners throughout the area, its work encompassing farm sales and purchases, diversification into other businesses and dealings with EU regulations, planning law and rights-of-way issues. A seat here is *"fantastic for making client contact and learning about agricultural law and the farming way of life."* Just make sure your wellies are in the back of the car for the many farm visits.

Whether you're wading through mud to inspect an outbuilding or sitting behind your desk drafting documents, it seems there are few nasty surprises at Birkett Long. *"I got a really good feel for the place at my interview,"* recalled one trainee. *"I figured everyone was friendly and it turns out my first impression was right."* Another of our interviewees was certain that whatever seats you took, as one of only five trainees you would feel valued: "*They are investing in you, not using you for two years.*" Evidencing this, in September 2006 both qualifiers took jobs with the firm, as did one of their predecessors the year before.

driving the market

Aware of the firm's long history one source noted: "*The firm's ethos is not old fashioned but a lot of the values are very traditional. There is emphasis on face-to-face client contact, the need to maintain the client relationship and to keep the environment open and transparent.*" This combination of classic and contemporary is good news for the trainee: "*They are thinking like a big firm and really considering how to make the training contract more uniform and successful.*" "*It is always trying to look forward,*" agreed another.

As well as fulfilling their training and fee-earning duties, our sources had been drawn into various Birkett Long marketing initiatives. As a result they were clued up on the importance of "*networking, meeting clients and putting out a strong presence.*" The firm recently organised an event called 'Businesswomen with Drive', a golf and spa day set up to showcase both the firm and the driving talents of the female participants. If you're keener on socialising than sport you'll be pleased to hear that the firm's social committee organises regular barbecues, quiz nights, trips to the theatre in London and a summer party described this year as "*a lovely affair.*" There's also plenty of informal socialising at a local bar, Roberto's – "*it's all very inclusive,*" trainees reported.

Reflecting on its position in the legal market, the firm recruits trainees two years in advance of the contract start date. In general, those attracted to the firm "*are not completely money-motivated, but they like the idea of getting the best of both worlds at a medium-sized firm – somewhere where you get the quality work and the work-life balance.*" Inspired by the redevelopment of former army garrisons and the quayside area, local websites proclaim the renaissance of Colchester. London is just a manageable train ride away, learning and culture are catered for at nearby Essex University and the pleasures of the countryside and coast are close at hand. If you're thinking of applying to Birkett Long it's likely you'll already know all this. Most trainees do have a connection with the area, and it's not hard to explain: "*the firm has an excellent reputation in the region and local people will apply because they already know the work we do.*" Yet the firm is not unwilling to consider applications from beyond the region, as this trainee explained: "*The area where I did my training contract wasn't an issue as I have lived all over the country. I just knew I didn't want to work for a massive firm.*"

and finally....

It may not be massive, but Birkett Long is definitely eyeing up the opportunities for growth. Its new location in Chelmsford is three times the size of the old office and it "*wants to attract the right kind of trainees to help the firm get to where it is going.*" Specifically, its plan is to develop more commercial business from the region and to try to lure clients away from London firms.

Blake Lapthorn Linnell

the facts

Location: Fareham, Portsmouth, Southampton, London, Oxford, Winchester
Number of UK partners/solicitors: 92/208
Total number of trainees: 21
Seats: 4x6 months
Alternative seats: Secondments

Writing a feature on Hampshire, Oxford and London firm Blake Lapthorn Linnell is a challenge. As soon as you think its geographical coordinates are fixed there are murmurings of change. We reckon this expanding, south of England firm has a few more moves to show yet.

long distance love

Back in 2003 Oxford nonagenarian Linnells hopped into bed with roving-eyed South Coast firm Blake Lapthorn. Three years later and the merged firm found another law firm to join in its quest for regional prominence. In May 2006, White & Bowker of Winchester and Chandlers Ford (minus its employment department) came on board, bringing the grand total to nearly 300 lawyers.

At the time of writing BLL had four offices in Hampshire, though plans were already afoot to relocate many people to a large building in Chandlers Ford. The Hampshire group has seats in banking, commercial property, residential conveyancing, insolvency, commercial, pensions, commercial litigation, 'fitness to practice' (professional disciplinary matters), property litigation, charities law, personal injury and clinical negligence, probate, tax and trusts, employment and family law. The Oxford office is a "*brand new, huge and lovely*" building located adjacent to the ring road and towards Botley. Its lawyers work in both commercial and non-commercial fields and provide seats in commercial property, residential conveyancing, IP/IT, employment, corporate, construction, personal injury and clinical negligence, commercial litigation, private client and family law. The London office is small and can provide a trainee with a seat in insolvency.

Trainees join the firm knowing they may be required to work in any of the offices, switching between the two counties and/or London as and when required. At each seat rotation one person may be asked to travel as far as Manchester for a particular client secondment. Though the options are plentiful, particular seats only become available when departments need trainees, and they continually assess their workloads and staffing levels.

just a secondment of your time

In the four-seat scheme, trainees are steered towards property, litigation and a commercial area of practice. Many will also go on secondment to clients such as ICI, Capgemini, National Air Traffic Systems, First Choice or the Nursing & Midwifery Council (NMC). Wherever they go, trainees find they have access to good work for good clients. Among the firm's top deals of 2005 was the £92 million recommended bid for Hampshire's oldest independent brewery, George Gale & Co, by London's Fuller, Smith and Turner, which increased Fuller's pub portfolio to over 360. Away from pubs, one of BLL's most important clients is telecommunications giant Alcatel. Last year the finance and projects team advised this client in connection with the UK Highways Agency's National Roads Telecommunications Services Project, for which Alcatel will provide a high-speed digital telecommunications network capable of carrying CCTV footage, emergency telephony and electronic signage. The contract is thought to be worth over £90 million to Alcatel. Things have not been entirely smooth on the corporate front however, and two of the firm's top corporate partners (behind certain of the above deals) recently defected to rival firm Shoosmiths. Their replacements are a partner and a senior solicitor from Lester Aldridge, so it looks as if there's been some shuffling around down on the South Coast.

a most convenient marriage

BLL has recruited quite a few new senior figures lately: the former head of Penningtons' travel law unit; the former head of aviation at Clyde & Co; a transport project finance expert from London's Watson, Farley & Williams; the former head of technology law at Cambridge firm Taylor Vinters; an ex-Ashurst corporate lawyer; and a former in-house legal counsel for a technology-based manufacturer. It's all about *"bringing in the right people to give us the foundations to take us to the next level."* If you sense that BLL is pushing its commercial practice areas, then you're right.

Trainees kindly summed up the firm's strategic business plan for the coming five years. *"What they want to do is consolidate on the South Coast and develop in the Thames Valley and London."* So how exactly does a merger with White & Bowker, with its strong private client focus, fit in with this goal? Our sources accepted this was an interesting question, and offered theories about the motive for the merger. *"About a year ago they made it public that they wanted to move to Chandlers Ford and had found a building,"* they told us. It was a building which was too large for BLL to fill. *"The idea seemed to go off the boil for a while... and now we're merging with White & Bowker, which has lawyers in Chandlers Ford."*

So let's recap. The firm wants more commercial work. The firm merges with a Hampshire rival with a reputation for excellence in local matters and private clients. Confused? So were some trainees. *"There's a limit to what we can achieve if we stick to the regions,"* thought one. *"In a sense the firm is being pulled in two directions. On the one hand merging with this smaller firm brings in private client and family, etc. On the other they've been trying to get rid of some of the old family work and massively trying to expand corporate and increase in London. I'm not sure they've got the game plan completely sorted."* Some people had clear views on the wisdom of growing in London, and they as much as told us that a merger in the capital, though *"not discussed openly,"* was *"on the cards."* How right they were. When we went to press the firm was in negotiations with a well-known London outfit called Tarlo Lyons.

Looking at it from a different angle, White & Bowker coming on board reassures trainees that the firm won't become commercially focused to the extent that the private client side suffers. The good folk of Hampshire and Oxfordshire contribute a notable portion of the firm's annual turnover, so nurturing this business makes sense. BLL assists private individuals in many ways – protecting their wealth through trusts, buying and selling houses, and seeking recompense for injuries caused by accidents or through negligent medical treatment. Publicly funded work, however, is not a part of the plan. Just prior to its merger, White & Bowker jettisoned its criminal team.

a most inconvenient journey

We reckon the job of allocating seats at BLL is only marginally easier than completing a Chinese puzzle wearing a blindfold and boxing gloves. We did hear of *"a few tensions"* about late notification (*"probably because heads of departments were procrastinating"*) and a period when trainees' e-mails seemed to disappear into the ether, yet our sources were the first to acknowledge the *"challenging"* nature of the task HR must perform. In fact they experienced the difficulties first hand: *"Last week we met up with the White & Bowker trainees,"* explained a South Coast source, *"but no one from the Oxford office could come down."* That's not to say Oxford trainees don't make the effort to go south. *"Our training days are usually in the Fareham office and it takes ages to get down there,"* one of them told us. Improving communication across the network has become a priority, with all parties keen to see increased integration. A 'trainee community' page on the intranet and a dedicated 'trainee day' in Newbury are steps in the right direction.

Though local ties will still always go down well with the firm, the trainee group now includes people with only loose affiliations to BLL's heartlands. As the firm's patch has extended, it has had to think carefully about the kind of recruit who will be prepared to relocate during their training contract. As a first-year explained: *"Some people end up moving house and others settle for commuting."* The latter isn't easy, as the journey between the South Coast and Oxford is a good hour and twenty minutes by car, and nigh impossible by public transport.

because you're worth it

Overall, the trainees' reports on their seats were positive. *"You get a good level of responsibility and a good level of exposure to work if you show enthusiasm,"* said one. Another had valued their time in private client, despite not being drawn to the work. *"I found it a good learning experience and was happy with the clear guidance I was given... I became very involved in my supervisor's work."* A third told us: *"One of the best things about being at a regional firm is getting your hands on work that gives you really good experience. You get to meet clients, and although at first you're observing and taking notes, pretty soon you're drafting proceedings and getting your own files."* All agreed with the trainee who told us: *"I was immediately made to feel part of the team and encouraged to get involved. My opinions were valued... I was not on a conveyor belt, not anonymous."*

The range of seats enables trainees to learn so much about what a legal career can offer. In residential conveyancing they appreciate the importance of developing good relationships with local estate agents; in commercial property how housing developments come together; in litigation that there is no need to panic before a first court appearance; and in the burgeoning area of professional disciplinary law, exactly what happens when lawyers, accountants, teachers and health professionals mess up. The firm recently won a contract to act for the Law Society in this regard, having already snared the NMC, the General Teaching Council, the Chartered Institute of Public Finance Accountancy and the General Optical Council. In short, no one has any complaints about the scope of the training at BLL.

The firm makes a loan of £10,000 to help with LPC costs, to be repaid after qualification only if an NQ job offer is made but declined by the trainee. In September 2006, 13 of the 15 qualifiers did stay on. Trainee salaries are reasonable for the South Coast but not as high as Oxford trainees would like. There's one more financial consideration for trainees – the purchase of a car, essential not only for inter-office commutes but also to get to work everyday. Study the firm's office addresses and you'll notice a penchant for out-of-town business parks. Unfortunately, driving to work doesn't aid the socialising, which according to our sources is already *"fragmented because of the geographical differences."* Trainees do meet up as a group from time to time, and each year there's either a lively firm-wide Christmas party or a summer event. In terms of hours, life is pretty good – somewhere around 9am until sixish being the norm.

and finally...

Blake Lapthorn Linnell has manoeuvred itself into a position as the largest regional firm in the south of England, and we must now wait to see what it does with this new status. Remember, the big picture is important because it will determine what the seat menu looks like in future years and the kind of opportunities that become available to future trainees.

Blandy & Blandy

the facts
Location: Reading
Number of UK partners/solicitors: 17/23
Total number of trainees: 6
Seats: 4x6 months
Alternative seats: None

Some clever person at Blandy & Blandy has worked out that the firm is the 25th oldest law firm in the country, and the oldest in Reading. Having been in existence since 1733 it's no wild claim.

blandy by name...

Blandy & Blandy is a part of the fabric of the town. The office on Friar Street has always been its home, and the upper floors were for many years the residence of members of the Blandy clan. Until the recent retirement of a seventh-generation Blandy lawyer, there was always at least one member of the founding family in situ, and charmingly, a lawyer from the firm has held the position of Under Sheriff of Berkshire since 1837. Goodness, there's even an office ghost.

To stay in business for nigh on 275 years you need a loyal client base, and in Blandys' case this has been the rich folk of Reading, owners of large Berkshire estates, and various charitable foundations. Its traditional side is epitomised by the Maiwand Lion emblem on its website homepage. (If you want to find him, the lion has his own statue behind the office in Forbury Gardens.) Modern graphics also feature to publicise the commercial side of Blandys' business, and trainees think this dual imagery sums things up perfectly. "*Blandys was until a few years ago primarily a private client firm, and there's been a drive to build up the commercial side. It's now a firm with a 50:50 split.*"

As to how well the two sides coexist, "*you don't really feel the division as so many of our clients cross the divide. Being in Berkshire we attract a lot of wealthy clients who also have businesses.*" So presumably the ideal client is a rich company director who wants to lease a new factory unit to allow his business to expand, once he's tied up a merger with his one-time rival, divorced his wife, sold his house and made future provision for his children and favourite cat charity.

...not so blandy by nature

Trainees are welcome in all seven departments: corporate, employment, commercial property, dispute resolution, probate tax and trusts, family law and residential conveyancing. First-years commonly go into the seats left over after second-years have taken their pick. "*HR may try and persuade you to try your hand at something, and sometimes people do split seats, but as much as possible they try to give you your choices.*"

Our colleagues on *Chambers UK* rate Blandys' private client teams very highly, and working with them can be "*rewarding*" if you enjoy probing into the affairs of others. The probate seat involves taking notes at client meetings, drafting letters and wills, and maybe even organising the occasional funeral or house clearance, which admittedly can be "*bizarre.*" In family, "*as well as drafting court forms you're also preparing chronologies of cases, letters and instructions to counsel.*" If the touchy-feelies gives you the heebie-jeebies, seek refuge in the tax and research elements of probate and the financial forensics involved in family. In both departments clients are the kind who pay their own bills, with some of them being very wealthy indeed.

In commercial property "*a standard job would be to produce a first draft of a lease or rent deposit deed, or to produce a note of the contents of a lease so a senior lawyer can see at a glance what it contains.*" The integration of planning lawyers into the department is a real bonus. One trainee got to help out on a compulsory purchase order inquiry relating to the upgrade of Junction 11 of the M4 motorway for one of its local authority clients.

rights of passage

The dispute resolution seat is characterised by a stream of advocacy, most of it over the road in Reading County Court, and often with the trainee acting as agent for a law firm some distance away. Known to be the place where "*you really get your hands dirty,*" rarely a week goes by when the trainee isn't in court for a mortgage repossession. Just as there are highs, so there are lows. Photocopying and paginating bundles are "*all part and parcel of the job,*" but at least "*fee earners join in as well. I've even seen partners pagi-*

nating... not happily, but doing it." The work centres on high-value personal injury, landlord and tenant matters, probate disputes and general contract and commercial claims. In one interesting case the firm represented a landowner when the Ramblers' Association applied for a judicial review of a decision concerning a right of way. It progressed all the way to the Court of Appeal.

After the excitement of litigation, some trainees find it "*difficult to rein yourself back in*" for the more administrative elements of the coco experience. Company secretarial duties are described as "*the bread and butter,*" though trainees also provide assistance on transactions and can sit in on the meetings and negotiations leading up to completion. "*You work incredibly closely with your supervisor*" and "*they talk you through all the basic stuff.*" Individual appraisals are scheduled two months before end of each seat, and everyone gets to say what they think in a relatively informal setting. "*I can't think of any partner I am too nervous to approach,*" reported one source.

where the heart is

Local connections frequently influence trainee recruitment, and on the whole staff are "*Reading people who have been here for quite a while.*" "*Nine to six gives a nice work-life balance,*" then "*people generally go off and enjoy their personal lives away from the office.*"

Despite the efforts of staff who ran the Reading Half Marathon last year (and lured a Meridian TV crew to the office to film them), we detected some disappointment at the firm's lack of sporting prowess. If all you're after is a drink or two, Friar Street has the usual chain bars and old-man pubs, and "*there's a fair amount of mingling with other younger solicitors in Reading through the YSG.*" Trainees know their peers at the indigenous Reading firms, but are less familiar with their peers at Osborne Clarke and Olswang,

whose main offices are in London. "*Blandys is not a very corporate firm,*" they told us, "*it's not attempting to be London style.*"

Paintings of Blandys' past decorate the office walls, suggesting a certain "*element of the olde worlde.*" Trainees accept the firm is "*quite traditional*" and "*in many respects cautious,*" but baulk at calling it out of date. "*We are looking to expand and to take on clients of increasing size, because the firm has realised that it must do so to survive,*" confirmed one. Another agreed, though didn't expect sweeping changes: "*They're looking to grow, but they're not looking to do it in a rush. They'll not move out of the area or merge.*" Blandys' Friar Street office has been extended once already, and the question now must surely be, would the firm ever leave for more modern premises? At the moment trainees say not.

The retention figure in 2006 was a disappointing zero out of three, but the year previously all three qualifiers had stayed.

and finally...

Though it has bags of it, the decision to pick Blandys shouldn't rest on character and history alone. More important is what it intends to do in the years leading to its 300th birthday. And that is a question only Blandys can answer.

Boodle Hatfield

the facts

Location: London, Oxford
Number of UK partners/solicitors: 29/49
Total number of trainees: 10
Seats: 4x6 months
Alternative seats: None

Boodle Hatfield is as much a Mayfair institution as the Royal Academy or Claridges and older than both of them.

top hat or boot?

As any Monopoly player knows, Mayfair is one of the most coveted areas of real estate in the world. As early as the mid-18th century the area was developed at the instigation of the Duke of Westminster's Grosvenor Estate which, even today, continues to own vast swathes of properties there. As you can imagine, any firm that has an in with the Estate has a fair old chance of doing well, and this has effectively been the basic business strategy of Boodles since the day it set up shop 280 years ago. Luckily the Grosvenor Estate has evolved, so making Boodles' role far more than stewarding a dusty portfolio of old houses in W1. Grosvenor now owns property all over the UK and is active in many major developments, including the £920 million Paradise Street project in Liverpool and redevelopment of Crawley town centre. Naturally the firm has picked up a few more clients over the last three centuries, some of the latest being furniture store ILVA (Denmark's answer to IKEA) and the IBM Pension Fund.

If you're after a firm that offers a terrific array of seats then look elsewhere. Boodles puts trainees through a standard four-seat programme, with the basic template covering property, tax and financial planning (TFP), corporate and litigation. Within these four there is a certain amount of variety as to how you will spend your days: for example, the property seats are commercial development, construction, estate lease work and residential conveyancing, and the litigation seat can be taken in matrimonial, commercial lit, property lit, or the affiliated employment team.

"*Everyone is keen to get the property experience early on as there is huge exposure to the work*," and "*you use everything that you did on the induction course, which perhaps isn't true for the other seats.*" In this seat they can expect quite a bit of responsibility and their own files, although "*all outward correspondence goes through the supervisor.*" For one source the seat meant "*some small management files that I could manage on my own, and lots of helping the supervisors. I was kept in the loop and involved in everything.*" For another it was "*40% Grosvenor work and 60% everything else.*" Everyone had "*lots of client contact, going along to meetings with the estates.*" If you should develop a deep attachment, take heart, as it is perfectly possible, and indeed common, for trainees to do a couple of different property seats, ditching another option to make time. The wealth of work available means "*you don't have to fight for things to do, they keep you very busy,*" and there are endless opportunities to "*go to important meetings and meet some influential people.*" Views on how interested you have to be in property for Boodles to be a good choice of firm differ. One trainee was emphatic that "*you don't need to be a massively property-minded person;*" another, perhaps more realistically, argued that "*it helps to be interested in it.*" Even if it doesn't turn out to be your chosen qualification area "*you can use that seat to get broad legal skills under your belt.*"

a dogs' life

Despite the enormous importance of property (it represents over 40% of all Boodles' work), there are other departments to try. Understand who some of the clients are and it's easy to see why a trainee would suggest that "*tax and trusts is almost as big as property here.*" Actually it represents around a quarter of the firm's work, but you get their meaning. The quality of instructions that come from the raft of wealthy private clients is certainly impressive: we're talking about old money, landed estates and "*new entrepreneurial types who've made a lot of money and want to know what to do with it.*" Dealing with complicated foreign investments or "*arranging some more extraordinary gifts*" (eg a lady dog-owner, keen to know it would be cared for when she joined the choir invisible) prove to be interesting distractions from "*bread-and-butter wills and trusts.*" And should you become obsessed with wealthy folk, you can ask for a stint in the firm's Worcester Street office in Oxford, where the team also has a notable matrimonial practice.

Some trainees loved *"the squabbles"* of a litigation seat in Boodles' broad disputes department. Recently it has acted for a sports-marketing business in a case against a former partner alleged to have breached restrictive covenants in the partnership agreement, and influenced the Food Standards Agency's shellfish-testing methods through an action for the cockle industry's Kershaw's Quality Foods. Through a range of smaller disputes, trainees get solo court time which is unanimously viewed as *"great experience."* The litigation department accounts for around 20% of the firm's business, leaving a final 15% for the small corporate department, thus offering trainees a blend of company and commercial law, property finance and work on other lending facilities. *"It was a great seat,"* recalled one source. *"I went to meetings, got involved in deals and drafted some things that made me feel important at the time."*

good cheer

Whatever the department, *"you'll be integrated into the team from the off,"* if only because the firm has *"been careful to make sure the supervisors are really good and supportive."* The size of the firm and its trainee population means *"everyone knows each other,"* and trainees frequently work closely with senior figures, often sitting in their room. This arrangement is useful for *"getting your face known,"* and means you're never far from an expert – *"the partners always answered my problems and sorted me out."* The general mood is positive: *"Everyone seems to be really cheery, there's a real family and team atmosphere from the secretaries upward. They really look after you."* Best of all: *"We don't have the nightmare stories of eight-hour photocopying sessions; we don't get treated as cannon fodder."*

Trainees are recruited from traditionally well-respected universities, and their reasons for choosing the firm are easy to understand. One said: *"It was more to do with clout than size really; it's been around a long time and is very well known."* They see it as *"a really classy firm"* where *"you are looked after and will get a good bite of the cherry,"* and speak of *"a definite feeling of loyalty."*

Try as they might to assure us of the firm's modernity and *"dynamism,"* the overriding feeling one gets is of traditionalism and an *"old English style."* This permeates even the firm's new offices at 89 New Bond Street, where *"old paintings of the founding partners"* are said to contrast with *"new, trendy, studded-leather walls."* As if the firm's website didn't give big enough clues, trainees reminded us that *"the firm is old and we are proud of that."* Not that it's a museum piece; *"we're aware that we can't be stuck in the past; we know we need to move on to survive."* We hear that one way is by working on the balance between *"those who have been in the firm for a number of years and those who have joined in the last five years, made partner early and have a more exciting entrepreneurial attitude."* And speaking of the partnership, we are delighted to report that the firm flies in the face of established convention in that there are slightly more female than male senior figures. If you want to find out more check the firm's website. (Well done Boodles!)

In terms of hours, a 6.30pm finish is common (occasionally later in corporate), reflecting a place that *"doesn't work late but works hard."* The trainees *"gel really well"* and frequently catch up over drinks and lunch, sometimes *"socialising with Forsters' and Gordon Dadds' trainees."* These firms share not only the neighbourhood and a certain 'Mayfair feel' but also some training arrangements. Come Thursday or Friday evening you might find *"20 or 30 people ranging from the reprographics guys through to partners"* having a drink or two in Bonds, a recently revamped pub. Actually, our interviewees thought there should be more pubs in the vicinity: *"I wish they would open a few more round here; it's mainly restaurants, which is great for the clients, but we'd definitely like more pubs."* Keen shoppers will have already noticed Boodles' location puts it within a credit card's throw of some amazing shopping. This is all well and good, but we sense that it doesn't take too long before you end up muttering something along the lines of *"it would be nice if the shops weren't so close."* There are sports teams for football and netball, and each summer dragon boat crews compete with teams from Grosvenor. The two also battle it out at pub-games nights, which in previous years have usually been won by Grosvenor's representatives. This year Boodles pulled off a notable victory. A fantastic result on the NQ retention front, too, in 2006. *"All five of us are staying: three going to commercial property, one to private client and one to corporate,"* said a September qualifier of a score that maybe says all you need to know about the firm's orientation. For the record one more trainee who qualified earlier in the year also stayed on.

and finally...

If you want a premier property and private client practice in a grand London neighbourhood, Boodle Hatfield is a super choice. Established and Establishment as it may be, there's a certain gentility to the culture that should go down a treat with students trying to avoid the testosterone of the City.

BP Collins

the facts

Location: Gerrard's Cross
Number of UK partners/solicitors: 20/48
Total number of trainees: 6
Seats: 4x6 months
Alternative seats: None

About 25 minutes north along the Chiltern line from London Marylebone you reach Gerrards Cross, a quaint one-main-street town that is home to such diverse luminaries as Ozzy Osborne, Cilla Black, Gary Lineker and a solid mid-sized regional firm called BP Collins.

sharp and juicy

If you're wondering quite what a 20-partner outfit with well-regarded charities, employment, environment, litigation and tax & trusts teams is doing in relatively rural Buckinghamshire, then you're more inquisitive than the trainees we interviewed. None would have had much to say on the subject, except that a recent 40th-anniversary celebration had involved a presentation from firm founder and early partners, including a potted history of the firm. *"Apparently, it started off as ten little high-street practices set up by Brian Collins, with the first office above a butcher's shop,"* they remembered with some effort. Not that we're judging them for it; we rather got the sense that BP Collins isn't a place where the past weighs heavily on anyone's mind.

These days the private client and family teams serve rich commuters, and the corporate, employment, property and commercial litigation teams are at the heart of a *"five-year plan for growth."* One trainee summed up their employer as a *"West End firm in the regions... it's compact but ambitious with great-quality work."* Another judged it to be *"trying to generate the same quality of work and expectations as a smaller City practice."* This is easily explained when you learn that *"most of the partners made a life decision to move here"* but did not plan on losing out on *"big, multinational and London-based clients, AIM work and deals in the double-figure millions."* They still work on deals for buzzy media companies, assist telecoms clients in tax disputes and receive regular instructions from 1927 Limited (distributors of Juicy Couture), disposable razor and biro company BIC, Continental Tyre Group, Pinewood Shepperton Studios and pasta sauce company Sacla. Such work gives substance to the suggestion that BP Collins is not only squaring up to regional rivals like IBB, but can hold its own against many a London firm. Trainees perceive that, in particular, "*the Heathrow area and Thames Valley business and retail parks are what we're targeting.*"

Yet, trainees take wry pleasure in the idiosyncrasies of the firm's evolution. "*Sometimes I think we could change our slogan* [from 'enlightened thinking: inspired solutions'] *to 'chaotic and dynamic',*" chuckled one trainee, while another noted that "*practice groups can work in entirely different ways, even though they're just down the corridor from each other.*" Undoubtedly, "*time will iron out those differences*" and for the moment the "*excitement of growth and of future potential*" was highlighted by all. "*Everyone loves the idea of working at a place that's getting better and better; it generates enthusiasm,*" reflected one source. Proving this point, all three of the qualifiers accepted NQ jobs in September 2006.

forfar five east fife four

The traineeship takes a slightly unusual and tongue-twisting form – "*four seats of five months then a fifth of four months in the area you'd like to qualify in.*" The straightforward choice of seats in private client, litigation, family, employment, property and coco at least makes seat selection easy, not least because you will be aided and abetted by the estimable Christine Russell, "*who does her best to make rotation painless*" and "*guarantees you your two preference areas before the fifth seat.*" Some seats are acknowledged to be "*tougher than others,*" sources admitted, directing this comment at "*coco and litigation.*" The former is a "*very busy*" department that recently saw one lucky trainee "*advising a client on purchase of a business – an associate-level piece of work – it just absorbed my life for two months.*" True, not everyone is quite so fortunate, but the majority encounter "*little poor work and plenty of first drafts*" and leave the department

with a sense that no effort has been wasted. Just as demanding is litigation, where "*there's a wide spectrum of work*" from "*lower-end debt recovery for individuals*" or "*any number of disputes around the one-grand mark*" to "*larger-scale commercial breach-of-contract matters*" and fairly regular "*multimillion-pound Chancery Division cases.*"

"*Important to the firm's turnover,*" the property department is "*bigger and not as intimate*" as the others but still scores highly with trainees. It's probably got something to do with "*the huge amount of client contact*" and a varied workload incorporating "*normal landlord and tenant stuff, big transactions and housing legislation.*" There's relatively little residential conveyancing but "*the firm likes to try and give you one standard home sale to handle from start to finish.*" Elsewhere, employment is "*a great seat because everyone in the team is really passionate*" and "*they're happy to let you get involved.*" Trainees find themselves "*regularly going to the employment appeals tribunal,*" handling research points or drafting, and sometimes "*really getting stuck into more complex cases*" such as "*a disability discrimination claim complete with NHS mediation.*" Perhaps unsurprisingly, the private side of the firm's practice "*feels slightly more traditional with an older clientele.*" Family is "*a fun seat*" involving oodles of "*high-value ancillary relief*" matters for the good (divorcing) folk of Gerrards Cross. "*It's complicated financial settlements so you're not saving the world and there's no children work,*" explained sources. Meanwhile, trainees in private client savour "*the much slower pace of work*" that results from "*complex tax planning and probate.*" "*Research skills*" and an easy ability "*to deal with a lot of elderly clients*" come in handy here, with office days enlivened by "*off-site visits with your supervisor to witness wills.*"

Overall, "*there's massive individual responsibility: you get files, run with them and there's decent support if you do drop the ball.*" Not that they're in the habit of doing so, but with "*a training partner in each department who you meet once a month for 5-15 minutes to run through any problems*" it would be hard to let the ball get anywhere near the floor. Work is fired in at trainees "*from everyone*" and being the only trainee in a department means you "*really are a communal resource.*" Equally communal, if not quite so welcome, trainees have the dubious pleasure of "*opening the post, which means we've got to be in for 8.30am every day.*" At least, in the busier departments, more mundane photocopying or bundling work tends to be "*taken away by paralegals.*"

every little helps

Rising with the lark to open the post focuses the mind on commuting issues. Amost all trainees live outside "*affluent, very pricey*" Gerrards Cross and in nearby High Wycombe or Banbury. Some even drive in from south London. Whether by car or train, "*no one commutes for more than about 40 minutes,*" at least they didn't until a new Tesco megastore over the main railway line collapsed while still under construction. If news reports on that particular engineering cock-up are the only time you've heard mention of this "*diddy, Bucks outpost,*" you aren't alone. Several of the trainees had no prior connection to the firm before starting their traineeships and it's easy to see why they remain amused by the contradiction of "*a very profitable law firm getting all this great business from a side street in a tiny town entirely geared to moneyed, middle-aged couples.*"

The firm's various offices in town are "*jumbled*" and in "*various states of repair.*" Apparently refits are planned and there is also the prospect of new space being rented to allow departments to work more closely with each other. Thankfully, the presence of on-site kitchens spares trainees from the exorbitant prices in the local shops (£8.50 for a hand-stitched Cornish pasty? Just wait 'til that Tesco does finally open...), but the relative paucity of local bars and typical journey times mean that "*although we get on well, we're not always out on a Friday.*" "*It's a problem of opportunity, not inclination,*" stressed one source. Firm-organised social events ("*every three months or so there'll be dinner and drinks*") or a carefully planned "*nights in The French Horn playing pool*" are usually grabbed with enthusiasm.

"*Mostly you can get away at 6pm,*" interviewees told us, "*but if a case or a transaction is at a significant point, you won't leave until 8pm.*" For one hardy soul, a particularly testing time in a contentious seat had "*absorbed my life from 8.30am until 9.30pm for two months in a row.*" Nevertheless, with excellent academics from good universities and an appetite for "*really high standards of commercial practice,*" those we spoke to were "*robust*" and "*socially adept*" enough to "*handle whatever is thrown our way – that's what gets you ahead here.*"

and finally...

BP Collins offers an impressive all-round training and looks to have ambitious plans for the years ahead. So what if it means decamping to Gerrards Cross? If it's good enough for the Prince of Darkness...

Brabners Chaffe Street

the facts

Location: Liverpool, Manchester, Preston
Number of UK partners/solicitors: 60/120
Total number of trainees: 18
Seats: 4x6 months
Alternative seats: Secondments

This North West firm is into its second century yet remains fast on its feet. Its growing squad tackles the needs of mainly commercial clients and provides a fertile training ground.

football crazy

The year 2006 has proved to be a big one for Brabners. The *"down-to-earth, no-nonsense"* firm recently extended hospitality to those affectionately known as the *"James Chapman gang."* Not some music-hall act, the JCG were the commercial and sports law teams of the recently disbanded Manchester firm James Chapman & Co. The JCG pitched up at Brabners after their litigation colleagues joined weighty rival Halliwells. If Halliwells got more people out of the deal, Brabners got the sexy bits of the old firm. Football is the mainstay of the JCG sports lawyers, and even though Malcolm Glazer's takeover of Manchester United loosened their traditional ties with the club, as one interviewee rightly pointed out: *"They've got a massive number of sports clients and we can now act for these clients in a greater capacity than Chapman could on its own."*

Trainees saw the JCG acquisition as one of many plusses for the firm. *"As time goes by we become stronger and stronger; we have a broad base in so many areas now,"* said one. They could be right; Brabners is pushing up the league tables with growing profits (turnover rose by 20% last year) and a strong client base largely driven by its busy corporate and commercial property teams. The Manchester, Liverpool and Preston offices play in a solid formation and, according to our interviewees, *"you certainly get the feeling that the firm is keen for new business and clients. It is very proactive and, as trainees, we are encouraged to play a part in its growth."*

The coco group was on the ball when one of Liverpool's leading family businesses sold its car dealership group in an £18 million deal, and outside the region it acted for HBOS to finance the redevelopment of Penrith town centre (which, appropriately enough, included a new football club). Like others in the increasingly busy North-West legal market, Brabners has benefited from a boom in property development. Its lawyers lately completed a number of residential sites in Manchester for Merseyside Developments, and, further afield, sorted out the lease for a large, new Pickfords warehouse in Gateshead and the sale and leaseback of Sainsbury's distribution centre in Rotherham.

you decide

Trainees choose an office on the understanding that it is where they will almost certainly spend their entire training contract. Liverpool and Manchester currently have eight trainees each and Preston, the smallest office, has two. The seat options are property, corporate, commercial, sports, litigation, private client and family law, with sports only available in Manchester. Bear in mind that you may not actually want to do four different seats, and that if you find an area that hits the spot there's scope to do a further six months in the department.

In Liverpool's commercial property department we found a fast-paced environment with plenty of work to keep trainees on their toes. Pesky admin tasks like dealing with the Land Registry *"become your bread and butter, but you also have a good involvement in other, more interesting matters."* Most important to trainees was the chance to run their own files. A litigation seat also offers some autonomy and is a good place to get a look-in on novel cases. One source did a lot of charity-related litigation while another represented several registered social landlords. IP issues and media fall-outs also feature from time to time, alongside shareholder disputes and competition law wrangles.

Compared to these seats *"the pace in private client is slower"* and so trainees singled it out as a good place to start. *"Everything was very carefully checked, but I didn't just sit there and listen. I saw files through from beginning to end and got a lot of direct client contact,"* recalled one. While there is *"less pressure on billing than in commercial or property,"* there is a corporate element to the work: *"We deal with a lot of business succession issues, where shares are passed down through families. I have planned and drafted trusts with tax implications,"* one interviewee reported with a measure of pride. Liverpool trainees additionally have the opportunity to go and work in the offices of one of the firm's most important clients, Mersey Docks.

it could be you

Corporate in Manchester means *"working with a lot of different people, all with different personalities and styles."* Far from creating conflict, these dynamics seem to suit the trainees, who say they are *"immediately made to feel part of the team and given a lot of responsibility." "I have hardly ever done any photocopying,"* a source boasted. One trainee was involved in *"about five really big deals"* for medium-to-large businesses. The firm also assists banks and leading retailers as well as some companies with international business. Mention litigation to a Manchester trainee and likely as not they'll quote *"drafting experience"* right back at you. *"I've written some really long letters in response to contentious matters,"* said one. Advocacy also crops up, with one interviewee having been to *"four trials and the Court of Appeal – I didn't have to beg; the partner asked me to come along."*

In Preston you'll find Brabners' most northerly office. It has a good commercial litigation department with niche expertise in contentious environmental work (think protestors up trees) and there are also teams dealing with corporate, employment, real estate and agriculture and rural affairs. In the private client realm, the Preston office, together with Liverpool, has been appointed by Camelot to advise lottery winners. Let's hope trainees hit the jackpot (sorry!) when their numbers come up to take a seat in this department.

you've got mail

There are plenty of winners across the firm, according to trainees. They impressed us with tales of *"Easter eggs with our names on, ice creams every day over the summer, and the managing partner thanking us all for working so hard in the hot weather."* Not only do *"little things like that make you feel part of a family,"* they also helped place the firm at number 90 in *The Sunday Times'* 'Best Companies to Work For' survey in 2006. Or maybe it's the office premises themselves. In Manchester, Brabners has moved to a flash new home that really pushed the button for one trainee. *"The new offices? Oh my God, they're so beautiful. There's some really cool artwork and some beautiful chairs from Italy in the reception. There's even one of those big American fridges in the kitchen and we have a plasma screen telly. The conference rooms are really plush too."* Before the Liverpudlians get too jealous (*"what can I say, it's just an office"*), they too are moving in 2007. Not to be outdone, Preston has also been spruced up.

Before settling into life in their own offices, trainees spend the first week of their training contract together on the Liverpool-based induction course. They congregate again at the annual AGM, held at a country house hotel in Cheshire. Last year *"we started off with a chat about the firm then got sent out into the grounds and split into teams. Each one had to assemble a go-kart and we had races at the end."* Blimey, lawyering's tough these days...

If you're into sport you'll be well catered for at Brabners. Naturally, football is on the agenda, as is cricket and a few other things. We won't dwell on the details of the post-work bar scene as planned office moves may mean the trainees have entirely different tastes in bars by the time you get there. Suffice to say, they are a sociable lot. Indeed, social events attract people from all levels of the firm. No bad thing, say trainees, as *"it's a lot easier if you have spoken to someone over a few beers to knock on their door and ask for advice. It breaks* down the barriers." Here's the drill: "*When we get to Friday, someone sends out a group e-mail and then we grovel to the partners for money.*" And, bless them, those smashing partners regularly provide. "*I never expected a law firm to be so generous,*" said one trainee before legging it to the bar.

as mischievous as ever

Last year we reported that a trainee's mischief gene is inhibited in the open-plan environment of the office. We're told we're wrong on that one. "*There are some big personalities here and it's an outgoing firm. We all get on really well and there is always time for a laugh in the office,*" said one source. Another recounted their interview experience: "*They slagged off my tie; that is typical Brabners... in a nice way, of course.*" So who would this open, outgoing, up-for-a-laugh firm like to meet? "*They don't want someone loud with green hair necessarily, but someone approachable who is equally able to get on with partners. It's not much fun for a partner to sit with someone they get no response from. I believe 'socially capable' is the term.*" And don't forget responsible. "*They leave it to you to judge when it's time to speed up, put the foot down and get the work out. But it is not uncommon when you complete [a deal] for partners, trainees and assistants to go out for a drink and let their hair down.*" One trainee who clearly felt very much at home at the firm told us: "*It's all fresh, all exciting; I really look forward to coming to work in the morning. Is that sad?*" Even if we'd been mean enough to say yes, we doubt they'd have minded. In September 2006, four of the seven qualifiers stayed, others moving on for jobs in specific practice areas.

and finally...

Fall for Brabners' straightforward charms and you'll find yourself with a training contract you can rely on. There are no surprises here, just a solid grounding for anyone wanting to build a career in the North West and have some fun along the way.

Brachers

the facts

Location: Maidstone
Number of UK partners/solicitors: 19/27
Total number of trainees: 8
Seats: 4x6 months
Alternative seats: Lille
Extras: Pro bono – Maidstone CAB

This old Kentish firm is well known in the South East. It advises everyone from farmers to pharmaceutical companies and could be a canny choice for students looking for a broad, good-quality training outside London.

a farmer's life

"*Don't think you need to have Kent on your CV to get a job here,*" say our sources at Brachers. Maybe so, but we think you should do your homework on the economy in Kent and the South East generally. The Maidstone firm is positioned on the southern edge of a key region that's set to see an influx in investment in the years to come. We're referring to the Thames Gateway, an area stretching 40 miles eastwards from London on both sides of the River Thames and the Thames Estuary. A proposed expansion of the international rail terminal at Ashford, minutes down the M20 from Maidstone, is also attracting interest. Ideally positioned is not always something that could be said of Brachers, but things are now definitely looking promising.

Brachers is one of those firms that has evolved slowly from a traditional market town practice with strong links to the local farming community, to a more modern commercial entity. Those connections with the rural economy still matter to the firm and a number of its best deals are in this sector. Last year the Brachers property team acted for the Secretary of State for Health on the sale of a large, former dairy farm for £3 million. Lawyers also advise many farmers on issues such as milk quotas, contamination problems and agricultural occupancies. Perhaps better described as scientists than farmers, the trustees of the East Malling horticultural research station turned to the firm for help on the reorganisation of substantial property holdings which comprised labs, light industrial units, housing and land used for crop research.

working with children and animals

Did someone mention health? In this sector Brachers has an enviable clientele comprising the NHS Litigation Authority and around 50 NHS trusts. For the former it defends clinical negligence actions, thus providing a popular way for trainees to spend six months of their contract. The NHS trusts that come knocking on Brachers' door seek advice on everything from employment and HR problems, pensions, data protection to corporate and clinical governance questions and property transactions.

The presence of private client and family law departments, as well as a close affiliation with specialist financial investment services organisation, Ashcourt Asset Management, gives a clue to the presence of wealthy individuals and families in the region. Trainees get to meet just as many of these private clients as they do commercial ones. There's "*a lot of will drafting*" to get stuck into and the private client lawyers are no strangers to administering multimillion-pound estates and undertaking seriously complicated tax and trusts work. At least they're not dog walking; we're told that Holly, the Jack Russell belonging to the head of the department, has not been seen around the office for a while.

Rich landowners, individuals with inherited wealth and those who have made money in business ventures all use the services of the firm's family lawyers. This "*interesting*" seat involves "*a lot of client contact*" and will suit anyone with a fascination for human, and animal, drama. You might expect a family law seat to teach you how to draft a divorce petition; you probably realise that you'll spend time attending to the oh-so-important task of preparing court bundles for hearings, but you'd never normally expect to be caught up in RSPCA prosecutions. If you believe you should never work with animals or children, then steer well clear of family law at Brachers. Apparently the odd combination of work arises because of one of the family law partners' passion for animal welfare.

knock, knock. who's there?

A good bedside manner may not always be the best approach in all areas of Brachers' work. It claims to have the single largest debt recovery unit in the South – it is certainly highly rated – and acts for a major credit card company (lips remain sealed as to which one). The firm's commercial side is growing generally and it now represents a number of major companies in transportation, education, recruitment and commercial services. The corporate department has a "*fairly young and energetic*" feel to it and involves trainees on deals from the start. Their tasks range from straightforward minute-taking and form-filling to liaising directly with clients. Their message on hours is that, even in this transactional department, the standard 9am to 5.30pm won't be dented too much. "*There are no nightmare stories about staying until midnight for a completion,*" confirmed one source.

No seat is compulsory and trainees can elect to take only commercial options, should they wish. The list of potential seats currently reads like this: employment, private client, family, litigation, PI, clin neg, healthcare, property (residential and commercial) and coco. A few trainees are also given the opportunity to go and work in France for three months as part of an exchange with a law firm in Lille. At the end of their two-year package of seats, two of the three qualifying trainees stayed on at the firm in September 2006.

kentish town

Although Brachers has a small outpost in London, our interviewees seemed quite happy with their lot in Kent and weren't at all eager to get on a commuter train to the capital. They saw the firm as a whole as *"fairly progressive"* given its long history. A couple of sources rather liked the fact that there was something a little quirky about the place. Maybe they were referring to the ghost that supposedly haunts the office... not that anyone's seen it. Trainees commonly have their own offices, and when they do have to share, it tends to be with a fellow trainee rather than a supervisor (or a ghost).

Anyone relocating to the Maidstone area, or who simply hasn't sorted out their accommodation in time, might be interested in renting a room in the two-bedroom cottage owned by the firm. *"As good as any student house"* (tasteful 1960s decor) and located within spitting distance of the office (*"you can see through the windows of the cottage from the office"*), it is available to trainees at *"a modest rent"* (so says the firm's website). They may not be able to pull sickies, but at least the trainees who occupy the cottage can avoid the hellish commute into work every morning. Apparently the local traffic can be nightmarish: *"It can take you 40 minutes just to get two miles"* as *"the office is on one of the main roads from the M20 to Maidstone"* and there are also *"about four schools on the road."*

let's blow the budget

Trainees admitted that their social life can be a bit muted, suggesting that this is because people don't tend to live close by and everyone drives to work. Nevertheless, they make the most of an annual trainee social budget of £1,500. Trainee entertainment includes lunches, Orange Wednesdays at the cinema and drinks as a group once a month. The trainees are also allowed to make full use of the firm's season tickets for Charlton Athletic. Other freebies come via the firm's membership of Law South, a group of firms in the South East with resources for training purposes. Our sources mentioned that Law South has put together a package that gives members various discounts.

If they want to spend time with other colleagues, trainees can do so at the occasional quiz nights and seasonal parties or on the firm's annual day out to France in June. The last French voyage took everyone to Calais. Every Thursday there's a buffet lunch for fee earners and staff who are spread across four separate buildings to bond over the sausage rolls. Perhaps connected, *"lots of people go to the gym"* after work rather than to the pub.

and finally...

The trainees we spoke to urged readers to view this full-service firm as somewhere to get a sound training in a supportive environment where *"people want to help you to learn."* Make no mistake, the capital may only be about 30 miles away but there's actually a world of difference.

Bristows

the facts

Location: London
Number of UK partners/solicitors: 26/57
Total number of trainees: 13
Seats: 4x6 months
Alternative seats: Secondments
Extras: Language training

With 160 years of IP practice under its belt it is no surprise that Bristows leads the way in patents, trade mark and copyright matters. It may not be the biggest firm around but its client portfolio is enough to leave your mouth gaping. If you're tired of your lab coat but reluctant to "*let the technical knowledge go to rot*" then Bristows may be your firm.

the appliance of science

Some of the biggest players in the biotechnology, pharmaceutical, telecommunications, media and software industries, as well as a selection of the most famous commercial brands, all flock to Bristows' door. They know that here their intellectual property needs will be served by lawyers who are experts in their field and amply qualified beyond the law. But can you be of use without a science degree?

True, many trainees can list half the alphabet after their names, but Bristows is "*by no means a closed shop*" to non-techies, albeit those with arts, humanities, languages, or indeed law, backgrounds are usually in the minority. We get the impression that the science community's loss is the legal profession's gain, as the trainees' combined brainpower would be enough to keep the kettle boiling in the *Student Guide* office until deadline day. However, even though a BSc, MSc or PhD can give you "*a head start on the terminology or background of a case, or at least how to understand and apply the science,*" the firm wants to hear from "*sharp intellects*" irrespective of their owner's familiarity with the business end of the periodic table. This is because Bristows' work stretches beyond IP law into corporate, commercial property, tax and employment. So, in a slight adaptation of that classic workplace motto, "*you don't have to be a scientist to work here, but it helps.*"

fcuk that

When trainees say they are dealing with the "*best work in the field,*" they're not wrong. Our parent publication *Chambers UK* has consistently ranked Bristows top for IP. The engine room of the firm, its IP litigation department is commonly "*the main reason why people come here,*" and a seat of at least six months is compulsory for all trainees. This big-brained team tackles contentious trade mark, copyright, design and, of course, patent matters, and for the record around 80% of them have technical backgrounds across the physical and life sciences, nine of them being PhDs. Bulging scrapbooks of past publications suggest a group that is really operating at the sharp end, and a number of the partners teach patent litigation on the Bristol University Diploma in IP Law and Practice course.

The client list reads like a who's who of Tottenham Court Road's finest, with such names as Hitachi, Canon, Sony, Toshiba and Fujitsu instructing on the defence and enforcement of the IP attached to their innovations. The reach of the patent practice stretches things even farther, with the loyalty of clients in pharmaceuticals and healthcare products being particularly important. Access to breast cancer drug Herceptin was all over the news in 2005 in relation to 'postcode lottery' dispensing, and the media attention is unlikely to let up in light of its manufacturer Chiron's upcoming defence in the UK Patents Court of an action brought by rival Roche. Drug giant Novartis has also sought counsel in connection with the enforcement of the patent for transplant surgery immunosuppressant drug cyclosporine, trade name NEORAL, against the generics company IVAX Pharmaceuticals. These drugs sit at the leading edge in medical science, and enforcing and challenging rights over their patents is serious business. With share prices closely linked to the outcome of such disputes, you are just as likely to be reading headlines in the *FT* as *Chemist & Druggist Weekly*. Just as "*intellectual input in the thinking around the case*" is actively encouraged in trainees, so too is an understanding of the commercial context.

Copyright, trade mark and design disputes come from the fashion, software, consumer products and media sectors. We're sorry to report that we have Bristows to thank for its sterling animal rights work on a recent copyright dispute over the Crazy Frog music. The lawyers are putting their mark on our wardrobes too, with their work for French Connection in the successful defence of its famous FCUK trade mark from revocation proceedings alleging invalidity on the grounds of public policy and accepted principles of morality.

(sky)diving in at the deep end

A seat in the non-contentious commercial IP department is sure to figure. Well-known client brands will be all too familiar to those of you making the most of university life because Bristows' client portfolio covers a multitude of vices, and is no doubt responsible for making a hefty dent in that student loan. Brands indispensable to scholarly existence such as Diageo (owners of Guinness, Smirnoff and Baileys), Cadbury Schweppes, Tetley, MTV and Sony Computer Entertainment regularly instruct on licensing, merchandising and brand strategy. Again, there is a strong showing in the hi-tech arena. Non-contentious advice is in relation to R&D, licensing and other transactions to do with the protection and exploitation of new technologies.

Expect six more months to be taken up with either corporate or property law; however, beyond this seat rotation is thought to be "*pretty flexible*" with the option of three or six-month layovers in other departments. The potential to discover the workings of the firm in multiple shorter seats, as opposed to the classic four-seat set-up, is seen as a positive thing. The nature of the work and levels of responsibility vary from seat to seat, but trainees seem content that the firm "*really takes it seriously that it is a training contract*" and that "*it is all about you learning.*" Whichever department they found themselves in our sources were able to "*pester*

people for advice and support: it is easy to ask questions, and you get the right amount of supervision for the piece of work.*" If this all sounds too good to be true, then perhaps it should be noted that although trainees "*are not dogsbodies,*" some of the more mundane tasks do necessarily fall to them. One second-year claimed "*familiarity with the workings of a photocopier,*" and with pre-trial documentation that won't bundle itself, as well as "*elements of proof-reading,*" trainees are certainly expected to pitch in with the administrative legwork. "*Up-front, constructive and painless*" appraisals at the end of each seat elicit formal comments on performance, although ongoing informal feedback means you're rarely left in the dark until form-filling time.

Pretty much every trainee can sample life on the other side of the fence when "*parachuted*" in to a client's in-house legal team. This is usually undertaken in the second year, commonly after the stint in commercial IP. Much more than "*three or more months away from the beady eyes of the partners,*" client secondments mean greater freedom and masses of responsibility. One source was delighted to report that "*any contract worth less than £100K would be chucked at me.*" Trainees return to Lincoln's Inn a little older, a little wiser and filled with a newfound appreciation of "*what clients are really after.*"

what not to wear

Bristows' quaint Lincoln's Inn location oozes character, and trainees seem to welcome the distinction from the "*power tripping*" offices of some of their more "*sterile*" City rivals. "*Our place is not shiny and new, but that simply wouldn't go with the character of the firm.*" A base in the heart of legal London really comes into its own during the summer months, when "*lounging around on the grass*" at lunchtime is the order of the day. Indeed, perhaps the traditional and historic location has parallels with the general Bristows culture.

"Image is clearly important," and an outwardly professional approach finds form in a strict dress code. Apparently the office fashion police have itchy trigger fingers when it comes to dishing out cautions, as one trainee grumbled: *"I have been told off a few times about the clothes I wear."* That said, our interviewees were quick to stress that *"behind the scenes this is a fun place to work"* and *"never boring."*

If there was one feature that united the trainees we spoke to, it was their keen commitment to maintaining *"a happy trade-off"* on the work-life balance tip. *"There is no culture of staying late just to stay late. Once the work is done you can head off without being made to feel guilty... and people enjoy being here because of that."* Without the *"horrific"* hours thought to be the norm amongst their (more extravagantly paid) contemporaries in the City, it is left for trainees to sum things up thus: *"You know you won't have to absolutely flog yourself;"* however, there is certainly no room to *"relax or slack off because Bristows is a serious player with big clients who expect a good product."* In September 2006, six of the seven qualifiers took jobs at the firm, three of them becoming IP litigators.

People looking for a *"raging"* social life built around the firm should look elsewhere. Thursday or Friday drinks are always on the cards for those who make the short trip to the Seven Stars at the back of the Royal Courts. Here the lawyers are on first-name terms with the staff, and mutual insults are traded across the bar. More formal events are peppered throughout the calendar, with a spring ball being the highlight. Pub quizzes, a winter party, departmental Christmas dos, and other *"random free-drink events"* are further evidence of *"a relaxed and non-hierarchical"* approach to socialising. Sporting wants are catered for with football, netball and cricket teams for *"basically anybody who wants to play,"* irrespective of ability.

and finally...

Potential applicants be warned: Bristows' *"wonderful and charming"* graduate recruitment team also happens to be amongst the most efficient in the City, and has a reputation for processing applications at lightning speed. Many trainees we spoke to had already bagged their training contracts long before the first buds of spring, and could rest assured that a law school funding cheque would be winging its way from the firm's accounts department. So, if you suspect you're right for Bristows, it might just pay to start that to-do list at the Bs.

Browne Jacobson LLP

the facts

Location: Nottingham, Birmingham, London
Number of UK partners/solicitors: 60/200
Total number of trainees: 20
Seats: 4x6 months
Alternative seats: None
Extras: Pro bono – CAB, ProHelp, Prince's Trust, Criminal Injuries and Compensation Scheme

This one-time Nottingham litigation firm with heavy public sector leanings has stretched out in several directions. Now a serious Midlands-wide player, Browne Jacobson is breathing down the necks of even the most stalwart of transactional heavyweights.

risky business

The classic BJ training used to mean lots of litigation for public authorities (known in the firm as IPR – insurance and public risk), and lots of insurance litigation (BPR – business and professional risk). As the firm's other practice groups have grown, trainees have been spending more time in the 'business services' half of the firm, which covers commercial litigation, corporate and property transactions, as well as other specialist areas such as tax and employment.

The healthcare work for which BJ is so well known comes from its relationship with various health authorities and trusts as well as the giant NHS Litigation Authority. After trying a seat in this area one trainee said: "*I enjoyed it, especially the advice to trusts.*" As you might expect, "*this type of litigation is not to all tastes. The NHSLA is a particular and demanding client and there are very set procedures you have to follow. I enjoyed the academic parts though, and you end up giving advice in all sorts of interesting scenarios. One involved a hunger striker in a hospital; it was at the cutting edge of the law. With these very immediate situations you just get thrown into things and work for however long it takes... there's a lot of adrenaline.*" If you follow the news you'll be aware of a number of tricky conflicts between patients' relatives and clinical staff, sometimes when proposed treatment is deemed too invasive or media sensitive for doctors to proceed without a court order. "*If there is legal doubt in a trust's mind they will contact their solicitors. Some of the senior partners here are those who they naturally turn to.*" Much of a healthcare trainee's time is taken up with large clinical negligence cases where patients or their families are suing after an error in treatment. The claims are frequently worth a lot of money but are slow running, which makes it impossible for trainees to take a lead role. Commonly, they end up buying a medical dictionary for this seat and, whether it be from the gruesome pages of the dictionary or their supervisors, they "*learn all sorts of stuff about medical practice you would never know otherwise.*"

Commercial lit seats are less about anatomy and more about autonomy. The opportunity to advocate in various bankruptcy or interim hearings led one delighted source to tell us: "*The variety has been fantastic and I have been so busy.*" A seat in employers' and public liability brings slip-and-trip cases, "*defending large public bodies from people suing them for thousands for things like a broken thumb.*" These small cases are ideal for new lawyers: "*You might have a caseload of 30 files, all fast-track and small claims, which are appropriate and good to learn on.*" The seat allows trainees to "*walk the line between support and responsibility... at the end you are ten times as confident as at the beginning.*"

In the environmental and regulatory law department trainees get to work on criminal prosecutions prompted by public bodies such as English Nature and the Countryside Council for Wales. "*It's quite nice to think you are saving habitats and not acting for the bad guy... in fact that's one of the nice things about the firm acting for so many of these big public bodies; you are acting for benevolent organisations.*" And this is not the only seat with such specialised public sector work. Aside from the sometimes-unique clinical issues that land on partners' desks, there are also cases relating to abuse in children's homes and coroners' inquests; rare work available in only a limited number of firms.

special deliveries

The business services group has been working hard to raise its profile, completing 110 deals with a total value of around £1 billion in 2005. Many of them were for Midlands-based owner-managed businesses and for clients in the firm's particular areas of interest – the retail, healthcare/pharma and transport sectors. Last year it advised on the £23 million management buyout of Interflora, which involved 1,800 individual florists and a big equity investment from 3i. Lawyers also advised Centres For Assisted Reproduction on a collaboration agreement with an American company to provide genetic screening analysis for IVF services in the UK and Europe. The considered view of one trainee was that "*if you really want to learn about the process of corpo-*

rate deals, this firm is a good choice. There are some very good corporate lawyers here, but there are deals that are too big for a firm like BJ, and only suited to the magic circle. In those sorts of firms, as a trainee you are lucky if you get to do the photocopying. In that respect it's not such a bad thing to be in a smaller firm, as you really get involved." The advice from another was to "push hard for responsibility. You start each six months with a pretty low level, and it can be frustrating to have to go back to square one, but do the simple things right and you will be given better work." Apparently a corporate seat can be "a lot of fun, mainly because of the people in the department." One of our sources had been given a role in client meetings, which meant "it was possible to develop quite a good relationship with clients, and I even did some small deal completions on my own." Whatever the seat, trainees conclude that "it never feels too stressful." "Trepidation is the most I can say I experienced," mused one trainee. "Of course you worry you will do something wrong, but you learn through experience and you do have support. If you had all the responsibility and no support, that would be dangerous, but even the partners don't mind if you knock on their door and ask for advice."

go west

If Nottingham is the firm's heart then Birmingham and London must also be regarded as vital organs, and Birmingham in particular is the office to watch. Now seven years old, its revenues rose by 50% last year and this helped the firm increase its income to over £30 million for the first time. The Brum office offers seats in corporate, construction, employment and medical negligence, plus insurance litigation, with the chance of more to come in the future. The firm has grand plans for the West Midlands, as this trainee explained: "Browne Jacobson is no longer just a Nottingham firm: it's a Midlands firm. In a few years time it will have two pretty much equal-sized offices. The market is saturated in Nottingham, although not entirely and not in relation to some relatively new practices, but the established practices are as big as they are going to get here." Someone with an eye on the future concluded: "It's at the back of a lot of people's minds: would I want to move there, and would it be a good career move to go to Birmingham?"

London, the smallest office, is the one least visited by trainees. Just a few go to the capital for six months of professional indemnity litigation spiced up with bits and pieces for other teams. One person who'd done a stint down south reported on a wealth of advocacy opportunities: "Any kind of small hearing before masters... you're in court all the time here." For most people, however, London remains a mystery.

To reflect the growing number of seats across the three offices there have been some changes to the way in which they are allocated. "They have tried to do a lot in the last year to formalise the system; it no longer requires 'having a word'. Just recently we were given a list of the seats available, whereas before it used to be an informal process – not well organised or transparent. Now you sit down with the managing partner and discuss it. He decided to take over the role of training partner when the last one left." As one person saw it: "They do now seem to listen to people. I don't know if people always get what they want, but I don't know if you can always predict what you are going to like."

child's play

Ignore the three-city thing and BJ is arguably still a firm of two halves. "The insurance litigation side doesn't have much crossover with the business services side. It's not like two separate firms, but you do have people who aren't aware on a daily level of the other side. Trainees can be the link between the departments; they end up knowing everybody."

There are attempts to meld the two halves, even little things such as a pool tournament at Number 44, the firm's new Nottingham office deli/cafe, and the managing partner's weekly 'Good News Email', detailing achievements from around the firm. Certainly, everyone was pleased by the news that the firm had secured a place in *The Sunday Times*' '100 Best Companies to Work For' survey in 2006. As one trainee put it: *"Everyone talks a lot about the firm's culture, and I never really know what that means, but there's a kind of family feel to the place, which is a bit odd given the size of the firm. I hope it will remain – people are certainly very aware that it needs to be preserved."*

Doing its bit, a sports and social committee organises activities such as an annual pub crawl/treasure hunt. *"It's one of those things that they think about changing every year and then people are up in arms at the idea."* We suspect they'd also be up in arms if the partners tried to back out of their traditional on-stage entertainment at the firm-wide January party. Another enduring fact of BJ life is the firm's allegiance to the pub next door to its Nottingham office, The Royal Children (also known as The Kids). *"You can go to the pub and have a drink with the managing partner and it would not be that odd."* Long may it continue, we say. In September 2006, eight of the ten qualifiers took jobs with the firm.

and finally...

There are several good reasons for choosing Browne Jacobson. Bigger than most in Nottingham, the firm has prestigious clients, accomplished lawyers and it is actually run from Nottingham (*"unlike Eversheds, which is run from Cardiff"*). Consider also the inroads into the Birmingham market, where many of the firm's hopes for the future are likely to be realised. If it can achieve in Birmingham what it has in Nottingham, it will be great news for future trainees.

BTMK Solicitors LLP

the facts

Location: Southend-on-Sea, Chelmsford
Number of UK partners/solicitors: 15/33
Total number of trainees: 5
Seats: Varying in length
Alternative seats: None
Extras: Pro bono – CAB

The product of a merger between crime and family specialists TMK and the more commercially oriented Bates Travell, BTMK is an Essex champ with a knockout reputation in community law and a nice line in business services for local enterprises.

life is a roller coaster

BTMK offers a staple diet of crime, family and civil litigation seats, and can also cater for the commercial palate should a trainee acquire one. Most trainees work in County Chambers and Baryta House in Southend and the firm is willing to tailor the training contract to the individual, so *"if you show a particular interest, most departments will cater to it."*

You know that old cliché, 'it's a steep learning curve'. Well, sit tight and hang on because the curve here is as steep as the rollercoaster at Southend's Adventure Island. The firm knows its stellar in-house training programme can only take trainees so far and has adopted an ethos of learning by doing – *"you are thrown in at the deep end, and you just get on with it."* Trainees are kept on the right track with endless checklists and fortnightly appraisals in their first year, ensuring there is always someone watching over them, making sure they don't go off the rails.

Trainees encounter clients from day one, taking speculative calls, assessing their needs and booking them in for appointments with solicitors. One reported seeing his first client on his second day... solo! The key message is don't expect to hide in the office performing a support role or taking on endless admin tasks. Generally *"people are reluctant to just dump admin work on you as they know it's not the best use of your time and you're not learning."* If advocacy is your thing, there's plenty on offer, from summary judgment applications and case management conferences to magistrates' court appearances. We hear that nobody is pushed into it but, as one interviewee pointed out, *"anyone who doesn't like advocacy may want to question if they really want to do the areas of law on offer here; they're all heavily advocacy-based."*

In the second year, trainees are gradually weaned off intensive supervision and encouraged to prepare to fly the nest by spending 12 months in the same department. As one trainee commented, *"the level of responsibility and experiences offered have been amazing. I run my own files, I go to court on my own cases, and I feel really experienced and confident because I basically do the work of a solicitor."* Sounds ideal, so let's take a closer look at exactly what this means in each seat.

if you're not on the list...

Embarking upon an all-consuming crime seat is a *"lifestyle choice."* Fast-paced and unpredictable days introduce the trainee to the full spectrum of crazy characters caught up in shady deals, sex, drugs, and blood and guts, as well as white-collar fraudsters for whom a paper cut is the nearest they get to violence. In crime circles the firm is known for its interesting mix of serious fraud and everyday crime. Particular expertise in asset confiscation has led to some international cases, requiring co-operation with lawyers overseas. However, if you are drawn to the excitement of money laundering, drugs and complex fraud, it's probably worth bearing in mind that in the early days *"the day-to-day work can be mundane... and it'll be a good few years before you get any of the really good stuff."* Our sources had been able to

learn from *"fantastic lawyers,"* some of whom have attained higher rights of audience allowing them to advocate in the Crown Court. Those opting for crime in their second year are encouraged to participate in the Police Station Accreditation Scheme, which gets them on the rota for police station duties – in other words the usual round of low-level theft, outside-the-club, drink-induced scuffles and minor drugs offences. The firm is very fair when it comes to dishing out unsociable evening and weekend work, allowing trainees to have Saturday night adventures of their own. One of the biggest lessons when adapting to criminal practice is coming to terms with *"things being done on the hop with not much time to prepare."*

The family department suits multi-taskers. A seat here offers substantial amounts of advocacy, including urgent non-molestation applications to protect clients from domestic violence. Trainees also get to see experienced barristers in action when they attend court to take notes of more complex hearings in divorce and childcare cases. A significant number of the clients are legally aided and can be anyone from a grandparent to a young child, as well as the *"stereotypical single mum with five kids."* By all accounts *"child cases are the most difficult to deal with, so you have to be adaptable."* Especially when they're crying in your office!

The civil litigation seat is a hotchpotch of landlord and tenant matters, commercial cases, debt matters, personal injury, employment and *"anything else that walks through the door."* The atmosphere is less frenetic than in crime or family but remains interactive. *"It's not too stuffy and people have a laugh but you do need to be on the ball and get the work done."* Once again, advocacy is core to the seat, so the sooner you take your first faltering steps the better. One of our sources had made a fairly significant application in front of a district judge in the county court within her first two weeks. *"It's good to get the experience, get used to the formalities and demystify it all,"* she told us.

sold to the highest bidder

From a beautiful Victorian conversion complete with garden, to an open-plan, glass-fronted office building, BTMK's different locations couldn't be more different. In each, trainees are expected to be punctual, smart (no midriffs in the summer, ladies) and respectful. Rather like the kids on TV's *That'll Teach 'Em* who went back in time to sit O-levels, they learn the timeless value of precision and good manners, though their tutors aren't so strict, and modern-day contraband isn't confiscated by matron. All up, trainees think BTMK has pitched the balance of high standards and office banter just right. In 2006, three of the four qualifiers stayed on at the firm.

The social calendar is packed with charity fun runs, barbecues and get-togethers in Southend's pubs and clubs. At last year's Christmas party partners auctioned off their non-legal skills for charity. One lucky bidder was wined and dined over lunch; another employed a partner as a home chef for an evening. Let's hope his language was more Ainsley Harriott than Gordon Ramsay.

pearls of wisdom

The word 'thorough' doesn't even begin to describe the recruitment process. Although it is currently under review, all – yes all – applicants attend a five-minute interview at either the Law Society or Anglia Ruskin University – just a quick chat to weed out ill-matches. After that, the firm will consider CVs and then the real fun begins. Those who make the cut attend an infamous recruitment day which, be warned, is tough, tiring and jam-packed. Expect to be bombarded with advocacy tasks, spelling and maths tests, group discussions and interviews. Our sources had a few pearls of wisdom for surviving the day. One: "*Follow your brief: if you are asked to do a three-minute presentation that means three minutes. A lot of people ran over, but the point was to see if you could articulate an idea well in three min-*

utes." Two: "*How you carry yourself is a big factor. Carry yourself in a professional manner and it will make a lasting impression.*" Three: don't worry about your academic credentials. If you have made it this far you have everything to play for. Finally: those who make it tend to be dynamic, positive types who offer something extra. As one trainee observed: "*They seem to go for the independent, not overly academic people who are willing to muck in and get their hands dirty.*"

and finally...

If you share our view that the real lessons in law only start with the training contract, rest assured that BTMK takes its role as educator very seriously.

Burges Salmon LLP

the facts

Location: Bristol
Number of UK partners/solicitors: 65/190
Total number of trainees: 39
Seats: 6x4 months
Alternative seats: Secondments
Extras: Pro bono – Bristol University Law Clinic, Bristol Neurological Unit, Drug Addiction & Recovery Agency, Bristol & Avon Enterprise Agency

(To the tune of *The Quartermaster's Stores*)
It's big. And it's pink. Far more national than you'd think.
Burges Salmon. (Burges Salmon)
Burges Salmon. (Burges Salmon)
Just one site. That's all right. Great profits, future's looking bright
Burges Salmon in Bristol.

sing when you're winning

If we choose to open with an upbeat musical number, it's because there seems no more fitting reflection of the feel-good story we hear about

Burges Salmon each year. The firm with the pink writing paper is relentlessly chipper, and although the corn may not be as high as an elephant's eye in Bristol all the signs are that BS continues to be a harmonious ensemble.

Decidedly in and of the South West, this firm has pursued a highly successful strategy of sticking resolutely to a one-site policy while challenging for national work and meeting City law firms head-on. A 300% increase in income over the past decade, and the fact that more than 75% of the firm's work arrives from outside the region, leaves no doubt that the Salmon are where they want to be. Trainees certainly think so, chorusing in unison (although without the jazz hands and sparkly, ostrich feather costumes) *"success has been based on doing very high-quality work at a lower price than London firms. It's not rocket science but it is a very effective strategy so why change it?"* Why indeed.

deal us in

BS sees itself as the elite firm outside London. Its client roster is plump with major names and multinationals: BAE Systems, Virgin, the Association of Train Operating Companies, Ofgem, Reuters, CompuServe, Coca-Cola, Orange, Honda, First Group, MoD, EMI... Such established relationships helped the firm to score some notable instructions lately. Commercial and transport lawyers advised FirstGroup on its successful bids to operate the Greater Western and Thameslink/Great Northern rail franchises (combined value £2 billion), making it the UK's largest rail company. Meanwhile, corporate bods advised Coca-Cola on the establishment of £1.38 billion medium term notes, projects partners helped the MoD on the restructuring of the £2.5 billion Skynet PFI military satellite contract, and the southwest agriculture-dominated real estate team won appointments from the Crown Estate on two major London portfolios, including many addresses in ultra-smart St James's.

Impressive but let's not get carried away. Fact: BS cannot compete day by day, like for like, with the magic circle. Nevertheless it is a nimble, alert and more-than-capable adversary. Witness the corporate instruction from FTSE100 construction giant Wolseley in relation to its £140 million buyout of insulator distributor Encon. BS fought off Wolseley's regular corporate advisers Eversheds and Freshfields to secure the deal. Similarly, property finance lawyers worked on the establishment of an innovative Shari'a-compliant Islamic finance tool for Bristol & West Property Finance and broker Gamble & Spencer. Traditionally this area has been the preserve of large London firms.

Beyond eye-catching work, what defines BS is its breadth of practice. Our parent guide *Chambers UK* ranks the firm in over 30 practice areas, putting them in the top tier for more than half of these. Covering private and commercial practice, the firm is adept in disciplines as varied as environment, tax and trusts, banking and finance, family law, partnership law and rail transportation.

six of the very best

Trainees explore the firm's activities through a six by four-month seat system. The first four seats are effectively set: one – corporate and financial institutions or commercial; two – property; three – commercial disputes and construction or agriculture; four – tax and trusts or employment, pensions and incentives (EPI). The fifth seat is a free choice, either used *"to go back strategically to a department you want for qualification"* or *"to broaden your experience in a related field."* The sixth seat returns them to the department in which they hope to qualify. With the bewildering range of departments on offer a little structure is probably quite helpful, but even more choice comes through the option of client secondments to Babcock, Nirex, Nationwide and GMAC. After qualification, more secondments are available to the MoD (no uniform required), Orange, Ofgem, Nationwide and US firm Thompson Hine.

All are in agreement that the advantages of six seats far outweigh the downsides. Making a mark in each new seat requires "*hard work*" and "*no time to tread water,*" but few want to shirk the challenge, recognising that the repeated experience of engaging with a new discipline has its own rewards. "*I came back to the same area for my fifth seat that had been my first and you realise how useless you were back then! I was doing the same tasks with ease, taking on higher level work and a lot more client contact.*" Job done.

some compromise

This brings us to another salient point: BS trainees work really quite hard. Despite a recruitment strategy that has focused on the work-life balance attainable in Bristol, readers would do well to remember that "*getting City-level work does mean longer days and later nights,*" not least because of the influence of an influx of City lawyers looking to reorder their work-life priorities without necessarily doing the career equivalent of stringing up a hammock for 40 winks. To give you an example, the firm recently snaffled DLA's head of IP Jeremy Dickerson, notably a new father. As trainees rightly observed: "*These people come in and they've gained a slightly more relaxed lifestyle, but they import their work ethic and want to kick on and do very well.*" Our sources had found "*that attitude can rub off, and some do feel the pressure to keep up and work longer.*"

While you're not out the door at the dot of half five what you get at BS is a decent compromise between "*quality of work and quality of life – everyone is dedicated but no-one wants to flog themselves.*" The true advantages of Bristol are attractive surroundings, decent housing at an affordable price, and ready access to the coast and countryside at weekends, or even in the evenings.

"*A 20-minute walk down the river to work clears the mind...*" How many people can say that?

Obviously, with so many departments on offer the exact nature of work varies enormously and anatomising each area is beyond our means here, suffice it to say BS lawyers do genuinely benefit from a quality of work that lives up to the hype. Whether it's "*handling small-scale trusts, interacting with government departments and assisting on big schemes*" in the "*quieter*" pensions team; "*attending meetings, health and safety interviews and court hearings for train companies*" in the fast-paced disputes team; or "*working for lawyers on property and acquisition finance deals, and popping champagne with clients at completion*" in banking, trainees seemed happy. As were those who'd spent time on "*cerebral research, putting together schemes to minimise tax exposure based on very fine points of interpretation*" in the "*definitely more old-school*" tax and trusts team; or "*litigating against a local farmer and going head to head with him in court myself*" in property litigation; or "*working closely with local authorities on tangible projects where you see the results of what you've done*" in planning.

Many of those we spoke to traced their commitment to the firm back to "*the effort and time put into recruitment from day one.*" More than this, "*it's to do with the way we treat clients, the way we approach work, the way the firm treats its employees. There's a broad holistic approach that puts quality at the core.*" In the past we've made a connection between such proud standards and the firm's more conservative side, but this year's trainees say their experiences confounded that expectation. "*It was less conservative than I thought and very open to new ideas. If something isn't working they'll change, whether it's a supervisor who isn't very good or a way of doing something.*" Nonetheless, we sense that there is still a whiff of the old in certain departments with "*older school partners.*"

stretching the definition of fun

When, during interviews, one source responded to our question with: *"Hmm, I could answer the question better if it was phrased this way,"* then proceeded to do so, we smiled and carried on typing. Experience has taught us that these trainees are forthright, articulate, no-nonsense and lots of fun. They come via the most reputable redbrick and Oxbridge, and many (though not all) possess some direct or indirect connection to the South West. In September 2006, the firm did not match its usual near-perfect NQ retention result: only 14 of the 18 qualifiers stayed, the others either moving away from Bristol or simply not offered a job with the firm.

Secure a job here and you'll have to work just as hard to keep up socially, because BS offers a full selection of pastimes. There is mountain biking, sailing, football, netball, rugby, touch rugby, running, dragon boat racing, golf, squash and a bushel more, although you can participate as much or as little as you like. Said one more sedentary type: *"At lunchtime you see all the serious runners lycraed-up in the lobby doing stretches. I just about manage to make it to Boots for a meal deal."* Bristol's bars, particularly those on the waterfront adjacent to the office, mean *"trainees have a fabulous social life"* and varied nightlife opportunities. By paying a mere *"two or three quid a month"* membership of the firm's social club showers staff with *"weekend trips to London and Manchester,"* cinema, theatre and concert discounts and other cultural goodies. Work-life balance? We're surprised anyone has the time to bill a penny.

and finally...

A top training in Bristol with all the lifestyle benefits that choice implies, for breadth, depth and quality of experience you'd struggle to do better than Burges Salmon. Are we convinced? Entirely.

Capsticks

the facts

Location: London
Number of UK partners/solicitors: 31/55
Total number of trainees: 9
Seats: 4x6 months
Alternative seats: Secondments
Extras: Pro bono – Putney Law Centre

Life at Capsticks is rather different from when, 25 years ago, Brian Capstick opened the doors on his new, niche, clinical negligence firm in Putney. It has remained faithful to its old neighbourhood but a lot else has changed. *"We used to fill one floor of an eight-floor building; now we fill all eight."*

when the only business was clin neg

Capsticks may exist in a relatively sedate part of London but its name is known throughout the country as a top legal adviser to the NHS and an increasing number of private healthcare providers. Apparently, in the old days when the only business was clin neg, *"everyone finished by 5.30pm and went to the pub."* These days it's a harder-working place and the firm has expanded into other areas of law from employment to property. Its evolution mirrors the ever-growing needs of the health sector, be this in relation to policy advice, new hospital building programmes within the context of public-private partnerships, EU legislation, commercial contracts with suppliers or claims brought by patients. Most recently, *"the property and commercial sides of the firm have certainly got bigger"* and trainees say that, in these areas, *"we're up against big City firms."*

"Basically there are five departments and most trainees do seats in four out of the five." Generally, second-years get their preferred seats with first-years slotting in around them. Seat allocation also takes into account the needs of the firm, so *"occa-*

sionally when there's a big inquiry – such as the Victoria Climbié inquiry – basically one person gets taken out of the equation."

when you want justice

Traditionally trainees have always taken a clinical seat ("*it's classic Capsticks work*"), often going on part-time or short-term secondment to hospital clients to help in their claims departments and get a feel for things from the NHS's point of view. The clinical department, split over two floors, is still the largest in the firm and includes a clinical negligence group and an advisory group. The clients are the NHS Litigation Authority, primary care trusts, health authorities, NHS trusts and private sector healthcare providers. As in any seat, with clin neg "*it takes a little time to adjust to the work,*" but before long you'll be attending conferences with barristers, and going along to court hearings. Sometimes the advocacy will fall to the trainee: "*Going to make an application in front of a High Court master – say for an extension of time – is a really good experience,*" confirmed one source. The trainee usually has few of their own files in this seat as the claims being defended are both sensitive and high in value. Common scenarios involve brain-damaged babies or other injuries caused by surgical error, failure to diagnose and that ever-present problem of patients contracting MRSA following surgical procedures. In the space of six months "*you can get to see a good spread of cases, but it's maybe not so good for getting a sense of how a single case runs.*" For some the most striking thing about the experience is the idea that "*we're defending a public body so we're on the side of the angels. There are a lot of human issues, a lot of high-profile, gritty, cutting-edge issues – life support machines, consent, babies dying...*"

There are two parts to the dispute resolution department. The standard commercial litigation team covers "*various disputes between health bodies and contractors.*" It is "*a sweeping-up department in many ways as it handles so many different things.*" The other side to the department's work is professional regulatory issues, including a good deal of prosecution for the General Dental Council and The General Chiropractic Council. Everyone who had experienced this type of work agreed that "*you feel like you're doing something for justice when you're bringing to account badly performing dentists who are doing bad things to patients.*"

when the nhs needs a new hospital

Take a seat in the commercial department and you'll be exposed to "*a small amount of standard contract law dealing with hospital cleaners, car park owners, etc*" and plenty of big LIFT and PFI projects. "*There were three large LIFT projects coming to a close when I was there; the hours tended to be long coming up to the close of a project but the team was supportive and thanked you for the work you did.*" Don't be too surprised if you leave as late as 8pm or 9pm, very occasionally 10pm or 11pm. "*No one clock-watches, it's just that if there's work to do you have to get it done. At least there are good take-aways nearby.*" For a trainee the seat is characterised by "*a fair number of people popping in to discuss things,*" quite a lot of document management ("*issuing updated drafts*") and reasonable amount of client contact when documents need to be signed.

The NHS owns an enormous amount of land and "*because of political changes in the health service it's always changing. We have a lot of big, complicated, new transactions and projects – building new hospitals, regenerating health sector properties.*" "*It's way beyond simple conveyancing...*" Given the way public sector budgets work, come the end of the financial year things get really busy, though for the most part "*there's a strong emphasis on work-life balance – I was regularly out by 6pm.*" One trainee commended the quality of interaction with their supervisor: "*I was asked for comments and questions on cases all the time. It was a really productive atmosphere to work in.*"

The employment department has a ton of work as the health sector employs so many people. "*Basically the NHS is the biggest employer in the world after the Chinese army and the Indonesian railways or something daft like that.*" Much of it is contentious and this is perfect for anyone who hopes to attend a tribunal and do a spot of advocacy. Among the interesting redundancy, unfair dismissal, race and sex discrimination cases our sources had spotted was one involving "*a male student nurse who sued for sex discrimination because he wasn't allowed to do ECGs on female patients.*" Trainees often like the seat because they can get their hands on short projects and "*see something through from start to finish.*" There can be some travel in order to collect witness statements or give presentations to NHS trusts, and trainees generally liked the interaction with employer clients as they tend to be "*very personable and used to interacting with lawyers.*"

Each department has its own series of training events to which all trainees go along, so "*in effect there are always things to go to*" and "*quite a few outsiders coming in to speak.*"

when doctors get angry

Trainees almost always have good academics and then something extra. "*Most of us had taken a few years out before coming here and got other experience. That's not completely universal, but on the whole it's true. Trainees here tend to be more mature and experienced... that could have been a factor in why they chose us or it could just be coincidence.*" If you have some kind of health sector experience we suspect the firm will inspect you closely. Said one source: "*I set out to find a firm that specialised in medical law and I think they chose me because of my background. I had insight into the nuts and bolts of medicine and how the NHS works. I understood the needs of the profession.*" On the whole, trainees were adamant that a background in medicine is not required – "*one trainee was a surgeon before and one had studied medical legal issues at postgraduate level;*" as for the rest – they had nothing.

The process of recruitment at Capsticks is a thorough one. The firm finds most of its trainees from among those who complete its vac scheme. At the two-partner interview applicants will be asked questions on simple scenarios such as 'What would you do if a client wanted instant advice on a subject?' or 'What would you do if a doctor phoned you up with a claim against him and was angry?' "*It didn't feel like bright lights in the eyes or anything like that, but the questioning was fairly wide ranging.*" If an offer is made and a student accepts, Capsticks likes them to come back to spend a little more time at the firm.

when you just need a beer

"*If people want to be genuinely engaged with and motivated by their work,*" trainees say Capsticks is an ideal choice. "*For me,*" said one, "*what's really come across is the high quality and interesting nature of the work,*" explained a trainee when we asked about the firm's appeal. Having started their contracts and been able to compare their working lives to those of their peers further east in the Square Mile, our sources came to value the ability to "*maintain a sense of proportion.*" They also enjoyed working with "*people from different backgrounds, different academic institutions, different countries... it's genuinely a nice place to work.*" In September 2006, two of the three qualifying trainees took jobs with the firm, going into the dispute resolution and commercial teams.

Capsticks' office is a "*functional*" 1970s block that, despite any flaws ("*pigeons everywhere, noise from the trains*"), is "*a lot better than most buildings in the NHS.*" Virtually all solicitors have their own office and the view goes all the way to the arch of

Wembley Stadium. Located in the heart of Putney, the neighbourhood is a busy one with plenty of restaurants and bars. "*You'll often find everyone over the road in a bar called Putney Station – secretaries, partners, trainees...*" and as many people live reasonably locally (some trainees told us they walked to work) it's no problem if a Friday night out goes on later than expected. Capsticks' social committee organises bowling nights, a Christmas pantomime, comedy nights, picnics and jazz evenings, cricket and rugby. For the firm's 25th anniversary there was a black-tie celebration at the Mandarin Oriental hotel in Knightsbridge at which "*everyone entered into the spirit of things.*" Apparently a good number of the staff have been at the firm "*since the beginning, since the 1980s, so it's still a bit like a family in some ways. Everyone knows everyone and there's no real hierarchy.*"

and finally...

Three cheers for the Capsticks training scheme. This is a brilliant place for anyone who gives a damn about the health sector, whether or not they've worked in it before and whether or not they want to work on clinical or commercial issues. One final pearl of wisdom: "*Do the summer placement! Without exception it is the best way in.*"

Challinors

the facts
Location: West Bromwich, Birmingham
Number of UK partners/solicitors: 33/37
Total number of trainees: 12
Seats: 4x6 months
Alternative seats: None

From its early days in the 1930s Black Country to its present expansionist phase, Challinors has been a West Midlands firm through and through.

labor omnia vincit

Briefly, the story goes like this: in 1996 two established firms joined forces to dominate the legal scene in West Bromwich and hopefully conquer the lucrative Birmingham market. Named Challinors Lyon Clark, the firm dropped its excess baggage (a Smethwick office and the last two bits of its name) and recently merged with a smaller but similarly well-established Birmingham law firm called Cartwright & Lewis. Size -wise, Challinors is now nearing 250 staff and partners, with trainees enthusing that this growth, coupled with an increased emphasis on its Brum office, make for exciting times.

Even if the immediate future is all about increased involvement with regional business clients, Challinors doesn't appear to have plans to prune back its private client or publicly funded work. Put simply, it is a firm pursuing many interests from several offices. From the Birmingham suburbs of Edgbaston and Harborne to the city's centre and West Bromwich, lawyers serve clients ranging from the man who tripped on a cracked pavement and then saw an advert on the telly, to local businesses, building societies and national charities. As a trainee there's no need to nail your colours to the mast too early; some happily plump for one or other side of practice while the rest split their time evenly between law for private individuals and law for commercial clients.

Trainees all spend time in the West Brom HQ and visit Edmund House just behind Colmore Row, aka Brum's Lawyer Central. West Brom offers seats in most of the firm's key areas, and an extra floor of space in Edmund House now means that commercial dispute resolution, company/commercial, employment, family, clinical negligence, licensing and construction seats are all available in the city centre. The two smaller offices in Harborne and Edgbaston take one or two visitors each.

that'll teach 'em

It's odds on you'll get property as your non-contentious seat. Whether this is purely residential conveyancing or a commercial/residential mixture depends on office and personal preference. Some undoubtedly find it *"a stifling seat,"* referring to the department as *"a battery farm,"* but there are highlights, for example when buying and selling houses at auction. The classic case is a client who makes a successful bid and then struggles to pay the deposit. *"They'll say 'Oh no! I've not brought my cheque book' and try and pay with a debit card, not realising you can't put £20K on a card."* The other options for non-contentious work are trusts and probate or company/commercial in Edmund House. Here trainees may work with the widely admired partner Malford Harris, many of whose clients come from the not-for-profit sector. One of his biggest recent deals involved the merger of National Governors' Council and the National Association of School Governors into a single body representing some 350,000 English school governors.

The range of contentious departments is broad to say the least: civil litigation, personal injury, clinical negligence, family, crime, commercial dispute resolution and construction law are all available. This last area of practice benefits from a rather unique legal-surveying hybrid called Challinors Blizzard. Here trainees work alongside lawyers and the brilliantly named Keith Blizzard, a surveyor who regularly acts as an expert witness in construction trials, mediations and arbitrations. *"It's great – you see litigation from an expert's point of view,"* said one trainee. Drafting, preparation of expert reports, plenty of client meetings and first-hand experience of mediations are the other bonuses.

Front-line experience is a defining characteristic of other seats too. In commercial dispute resolution (including insurance, professional negligence and property disputes) trainees work as part of a team sampling different kinds of cases and working styles. *"They also let you run cases that perhaps wouldn't be taken on because they are too small."* Once in charge of such a file, the trainee gets to interview their own client, take witness statements, draft statements of claim or defence, set aside applications and attend hearings. *"And when any of the fee earners had a trial on their cases I went along and sat behind counsel,"* a source recalled with pride.

the doctor will see you now

Challinors is part of a seven-strong consortium of firms called the Midlands Accident Lawyers, which seeks work on local television and radio. However, the merger with Cartwright & Lewis brought in defendant insurance company clients, meaning trainees can now experience both perspectives of PI work. If you like PI then claimant clinical negligence should be right up your street too... but only if you're hardy, as *"cases can be quite sad when you get clients who aren't going to be around in a couple of months time."* It's worth knowing that claims for things like birth defects or non-diagnoses of cancer are frequently high in value and can run for years, making it impossible for a trainee to take the lead. Instead, they mainly observe and support, although accompanying fee earners to conferences (often in London) with top barristers and doctors offers excitement.

Trips to the capital can mean long days, particularly as medical conferences often start at 5.30pm, after surgery hours. While such trips are not the only reason for long days, hours at Challinors are generally pretty good. Coming in at eight-something in the morning and leaving the office before 6pm is normal. Most trainees work in an open-plan setting, sharing space with paralegals and other junior fee earners; the odd seat will involve sharing a room. The office buildings are all different, and the route to work governed by office location, so while at Edmund House it's the train or bus, in West Brom people tend to drive.

brummies and brommies

There are many larger, better-known outfits in Birmingham, but our sources *"didn't want to work at those big firms."* Instead they chose Challinors because *"I wanted to have Birmingham and Black Country clients and really know the people I worked with."* Suggesting that Eversheds and Wragges are no longer so regionally focused, they see major competition coming in the form of Shakespeares, Higgs & Sons or Putsmans. However, the comparison that really excited them was to liken Challinors of 2006 with Gateley Wareing several years ago. *"We're a firm on the up... and that means opportunities for me as a trainee... in five years we'd definitely like to be competing against Gateley Wareing."* Now there's enthusiasm for you.

One thing which distinguishes the firm from competitors is its dominance in the West Brom market. *"The Black Country represents the bread and butter of Challinors. That's where the firm is from and the chief exec and the deputy senior partner are still based there."* Nevertheless, everyone understands that *"the emphasis will be on Birmingham in terms of growth, because the firm is looking to expand the commercial side and other non-commercial areas have probably expanded as much as they can. Birmingham is the natural place for growth."* Unsurprisingly, local applicants always appeal. All our sources were brought up in the West Midlands and had done their LPC at the Birmingham branch of the College of Law. Each year some of the new starters will have already spent time working at the firm as paralegals. You definitely get a sense that trainees feel a part of the organisation. Said one: *"I don't know many other firms where you can openly go up to the sen-*ior partner and give him your views."* In September 2006, both of the qualifiers took jobs with the firm.

ticket to ride

We wondered if we had been unfair in describing West Brom as a social vacuum last year. We needn't have. In stark contrast, when working in Birmingham city centre, trainees hit the jackpot: *"It's got so much to offer. You can meet friends at other firms for lunch. In the evenings you can go to any number of wine bars and there's a lot of young professional people in Birmingham... you just step out of the office into the hubbub."*

A particularly active organisation, the Birmingham Trainee Solicitors' Society runs social, sporting and professional events. The firm also does its bit. Departmental training plugs gaps in legal knowledge; departmental and firm-wide seasonal parties are a good opportunity to mix with colleagues. Every Christmas the AGM is followed by a knees-up (complete with Tom Jones impersonator in 2005), and there's also a day out, last time in Liverpool, which meant a ferry on the Mersey, the Beatles museum and shopping, followed by a slap-up meal and drinks. Back in Brum, the trainees frequent bars such as Utopia, Metro and Bar One Ten, with those in West Brom needing to hop on the tram for the 15-minute ride into the city.

and finally...

Challinors' greatest selling point is that tastes leaning towards publicly funded work, private clients or commercial ventures can all be accommodated. Twinned with this is a philosophy that allows even the newest recruit to get stuck in and show their worth on a file. If you're wondering about the Latin words at the head of this feature, we think they might be worth learning. They form the West Bromwich town motto and mean 'work conquers all'.

Charles Russell LLP

the facts
Location: London, Guildford, Cheltenham, Oxford
Number of UK partners/solicitors: 93/117
Total number of trainees: 15
Seats: 4x6 months
Alternative seats: Secondments
Extras: Pro bono – Bethnal Green Law Centre, Young Enterprise; language training

More than 200 years old, this mid-sized London and regional firm has a superb track record in private client matters and performs excellently in commercial work. Its flagship London office is complemented by established branches in Guildford and Cheltenham, and new offices in Oxford and Geneva.

you say you want an evolution
The Charles Russell brand was once dominated by its prestigious private capital and family practices. With 70% of business now sourced in the commercial sector, and lawyers making inroads in media, telecommunications, corporate and sports law, it's clear that the firm has undergone something of a transformation over the past two decades. Yet something prevents it from letting go of the past: indeed why would it when it has a reputation as one of the best places in the country for private client and family law? Fittingly, in May 2006 the firm elected a new senior partner, Patrick Russell, a descendant of the very same Russells that give the firm its name. Trainees sense that this attachment to the past ensures *"the family feeling has stayed with the firm through the years."*

The majority of the firm's trainees are based in London, where they are presented with the classic four-seat rotation. Their training allows them to sample very different seats in four of the following groups: coco, real estate, litigation and dispute resolution, employment/pensions, private client and family. Something for everyone, you might say.

the coach, the cash and his lawyers
It's onwards and upwards for CR's *"ever-expanding"* coco team. The group reported a 153% increase in the value of M&A deals handled in 05/06, and a resurgent AIM market has brought a flood of work. Advice given to Cable & Wireless on its €162 million acquisition of a majority shareholding in Monaco Telecom from Vivendi Universal is considered a high point. Naturally on such deals trainees have a minor role, and give them their due they fully understand they *"can't be let loose on the £100 million stuff."* Compensations are to be found on smaller deals, where *"decent work can fly in from anywhere for you to have a stab at."* Some of our interviewees had been tasked with *"drafting documents from the off,"* meaning they were happy to oblige with *"the odd bit of photocopying"* at other times. Corporate trainees were keen to remind us that a busy department equates to *"harder work and considerably longer hours"* than in other seats. They were also keen that potential applicants appreciate just how fundamental the push in the corporate department is to the firm, so don't say you weren't warned...

A seat in the property department demands a proactive outlook and good organisational skills. The nature of the work means *"you're never going to do everything in one day,"* so if you are a stickler for clearing your desk before leaving the office of an evening you'll just have to get over it. *"Lots of responsibility"* extends as far as running and completing your own small transaction files, in addition to performing more administrative chores on bigger deals run by your seniors. The trainees' verdict is that if you *"step up to the challenge, there's a massive benefit as you can take skills on to other departments."*

www.chambersandpartners.co.uk

CR's celebrated IP, technology, media, and sports capability is a major draw for some trainees who know that the lawyers here work on subjects that prompt water-cooler tête-à-têtes up and down the country. When Sven Göran-Eriksson was stung by the *News of the World's* fake sheikh, he used CR's defamation and reputation management unit to bring a breach of confidence action. These lawyers also offer pre-publication advice to the likes of ITN, provider of news content to ITV and Channel 4 news, and bring a touch of Hollywood glamour to the firm with their work on feature films such as Al Pacino's recent flick 'The Merchant of Venice' and Universal Pictures' League of Gentlemen movie 'Royston Vasey'. If Edward and Tubbs don't do it for you then the work of the IP team might be more alluring. It recently advised a client entering into a licensing agreement with Elle 'The Body' MacPherson, in relation to her Intimates lingerie range.

back to the old skool

If what you really fancy is some time away from the commercial arena, go for the private client or family departments. Wealthy trusts and landed gentry typify the *"old-school"* element of the clientele, though the firm also represents a sizeable quota of entrepreneurs, new-money folk and celebrities. Trainees say the seat is *"quite interesting if you like snooping into rich people's financial affairs"* and suggest you hold your horses on the ritual destruction of those LPC notes since *"the trust and tax side is pretty difficult and they can come in useful."* They report *"a high level of responsibility and leeway to get on with things,"* even if this comes at the expense of client contact. *"The matters are often very personal and the clients may not be too sure about a trainee sitting in and learning about their miserable lives."* A rich variety of clients and *"lots of crossover"* with the commercial side of the firm led one trainee to proffer the suggestion that *"the old stuff is now becoming the trendy stuff."*

As in many firms of this size, trainees tell us their workload is a matter of *"quality and not quantity."* Though naturally there are busy periods, the workload and hours lead trainees to conclude they are *"never left to feel completely stressed out."* Informal feedback and encouragement is readily available, and *"you are given a heads-up if there are issues to address or gaps to plug."* Overall they gave a big thumbs-up to the training programme, with one interviewee asserting: *"I can't fault the training I've had here, I get the feeling I'm more advanced than I would have been elsewhere."*

The smaller Guildford and Cheltenham training programmes have fewer seat options but greater flexibility as to the number, order and length of seats. Cheltenham trainees will normally experience litigation, property, coco and private client, while the Guildford programme also throws an additional family option into the mix. It is true that CR boasts a 'one firm' ethos, however on joining some non-London trainees felt that it was *"only natural to have concerns about being isolated, as there is a danger that London might be seen as the centre of the universe."* Such fears turned out to have been largely unfounded as trainees and management *"work hard to keep everyone integrated and foster links."* Across all three offices the current crop of trainees has buddied up to such an extent that they are hanging out at weekends, and the out-of-towners also go up to London for training days and meetings. In 2006, eight of the 11 London qualifiers took jobs with the firm. All three Guildford qualifiers also stayed, but the single Cheltenham qualifier did not.

beach volleyball anyone?

In CR's New Fetter Lane HQ, just a short dash from the Royal Courts, *"space and clean lines"* mark out the reception and client areas. By contrast, the nooks and crannies left unseen by the public are described as *"a little bit cramped."*

Still, the eighth-floor meeting rooms afford attractive views of the sun setting over the London skyline, though contemplative moments would certainly be interrupted if the helipad on the floor above were ever to be brought out of retirement. The building once belonged to kindly Robert Maxwell, former owner of Mirror Group Newspapers and presumably at least one helicopter.

The social and sporting side of CR is "*a great way to get involved and build your place in the firm.*" The last out-of-hours trainee event began with a civilised lunch in the West End and then became something of a blur with some hazy recollections of a Baywatch-themed night in one of Chelsea's cheesiest venues. "*Everyone is welcome to rock up and have a go*" at cricket, tennis, netball, softball and sailing, and football is played to "*medium standard,*" except "*when you're playing against clients no one wants to see you flying in with sliding tackles and leg breakers.*" The main exception to the all-comers welcome policy seems to lie with rugby, where "*you wouldn't turn up if you were useless.*" One of the jobs of the all-office social committee is to organise the "*infamous*" sports dinner held in January. "*Basically a big piss-up,*" all trainees are invited regardless of whether or not they play any sport. When we called, our interviewees were looking forward to the firm's annual summer ball, an event to which future trainees are invited. At least one trainee was aiming to "*test out how much leeway there is the next morning,*" so we're guessing that Friday's Outlook probably didn't include any high-powered breakfast meetings.

Since the academic requirements for trainees are both "*stringent*" and "*a given,*" the recruitment process at CR aims to delve deeper by "*choosing personalities.*" Our hearts sink when interviewees preface any comment with the phrase "*I know it sounds cheesy but...*" however we were pretty close to welling up when one first-year gushed: "*When we all turned up on day one, I thought that the rest of the group were the type of people I would have been mates with anyway.*" It's always hard to type people, but the view that "*you will shine here as an all-rounder*" is perhaps understandable given the diversity of work on offer.

and finally...

If you are undecided about the exact nature of your legal tendencies, but you know you're looking for a prestigious and good-natured firm with interesting work, Charles Russell would certainly fit the bill. Those hoping to get a foot in the door must get their thinking caps on though because the current online application form asks for their thoughts on the greatest ever invention and, bizarrely, which animal their friends would most liken them to. One trainee suggests you "*don't go for anything too obvious like a lion or a tiger.*" We're not entirely sure why.

Cleary Gottlieb Steen & Hamilton LLP

the facts

Location: London
Number of UK partners/solicitors: 16/50
Total number of trainees: 9
Seats: 4x6 months
Alternative seats: Overseas seats, secondments
Extras: Pro bono – LawWorks, Liberty, Devon & Exeter Racial Equality Council

The UK office of this international giant is just one of 12 located in the world's major financial and commercial centres. The establishment of a City of London foothold in 1971 put Cleary ahead of the game, as many other US firms didn't reach UK shores for another 25 years.

don't fence me in

The London office, like the firm as a whole, operates non-departmentally, and from a trainee's perspective this is great if you want to simultaneously work on a variety of matters across practice areas and international borders. The department-free structure leads to an *"organic and very fluid"* atmosphere that is *"open and quite collegey."* Even with no departments, trainees get a change of scenery every six months as they move between willing supervisors. The trainee and supervisor are not joined at the hip and *"you can ask around for jobs"* on the understanding that *"you will control your own workload."* In practice, since the office is so busy *"work comes your way without you needing to do anything."* Although you can influence the kind of things you get involved in, don't plan on being too picky – when it's all hands to the pump you may be used as *"an extra pair of hands"* by anyone in the office. Continuity is highlighted as a key strength of doing things the Cleary way – *"You don't just offload something after six months."* This cuts both ways: you don't get chucked off a great deal when you switch departments but if you're working on a lemon *"you can never get away from it."*

The benefits keep coming, as Cleary's lawyers are encouraged to postpone decisions on specialisation until a few years after their training. This certainly makes qualification a more relaxed prospect than the cut-throat scramble for the most desirable positions that is common in the City. The firm has an excellent NQ retention record and in September 2006 both qualifiers took jobs.

where everybody knows your name

If Cleary's US ancestry influences the London office, it doesn't do so to the extent that London doesn't have its own identity. The office is roughly *"half American and half British, so it is difficult to identify a generic type of person. Everyone seems quite different and works differently,"* explained trainees. It adds up to *"an amazing breadth of experience, as people have worked all over the world."* Digging a little deeper we did find certain common characteristics – people seem assertive, confident and determined, and yet manage to remain *"incredibly good-natured."*

Many of the English-qualified lawyers take the New York Bar exam in order to become 'proper' American attorneys later in their careers. The firm has moved away from encouraging trainees to do this, so for now you will have to ditch your *Ally McBeal* fantasies and settle for something a little more *This Life.*

There is no room to hide at this firm: *"People know who you are – everybody knows your name."* Our sources genuinely believed that the small trainee intake, expanded to five in 2006, allows a more intimate, personalised experience with a large dose of responsibility. And logically this has to be true. The firm handles heavyweight deals usually associated with the magic circle, but does so without an army of junior staff – ergo the few trainees in the office get their hands on decent tasks.

This message must be out there to students because, if recent years are anything to go by, your application form will sit in a pile with another 2,000. Better make it a good one to avoid it being filed under B for bin. *"Grades are obviously important,"* acknowledged our interviewees, and applicants also need to show *"attention to detail – all the classics really."* What you may not realise is that *"since the office is small they place a large onus on how other juniors take to you."* In the view of one source this makes a *"try before you commit"* vacation placement an absolute must. *"It is quite a big call to make that jump [to a US practice],"* so *"never accept anyone else's comments on what the firm is like."*

stepping up to the plate

Landing a job here may mend a few fences with your long-suffering bank manager, but what of the stories concerning the long hours that come with pledging allegiance to the star-spangled banner? *"US firms are renowned for working you harder"* and by all accounts these ideas *"don't arise without reason."* Said one candid source: *"As a rule the demands and pressure are higher here."* Some chalk this up to the more compact teams working on transactions; others point to the lower ratio of trainees to lawyers at Cleary. So whereas *"friends at magic circle firms work equally as hard"* on occasions, Cleary's trainees sense that they do so more of the time and that periods of downtime are shorter. As such, *"weekends are not sacred by any stretch of the imagination and you may be asked to drop holidays."* If this sounds relentless, be assured that *"when we have downtime they are flexible, so if you work late you can stroll in a little bit late."* We ended up concluding that although *"the money is great"* you might end up throwing a chunk of it in the direction of a personal shopper and the nice men from Ocado.

"Maybe the biggest difference [between this and bigger firms] *is the level of responsibility,"* one trainee pondered. *"You have to be able to take responsibility on your own shoulders; you need the confidence to put things into effect without worrying about making a mistake because you cannot afford to have someone talk you through every little thing."* Weekly training sessions were highlighted as a great way to get to grips with growing up as a City lawyer. *"Trainees take it in turns to give a presentation on a recent business or legal issue in front of the whole of the English practice."* Naturally this is quite a nerve-wracking experience. Having said all this, trainees must also accept *"dogsbody work at the lower level"* now and again. As one source put it: *"You still do some desperately dull stuff like the admin support on the bigger deals, but this is the same with any training contract."*

tongue-twisting transactions

The London practice is anchored in international finance and corporate transactions, and when trainees tell us it is *"thrilling and buzzy to be involved in the big deals,"* we kind of believe them. The London office recently assisted global company Mittal Steel with a $3.2 billion term and revolving credit facility agreement arranged by a selection of the biggest banks on the planet. In another matter Russian state bank Vnesheconombank (VEB) used the lawyers on a $500 million syndicated term loan agreement with a consortium of 40 international banks. And Cleary's London, Rome and Washington offices together advised Italian aerospace and defence company Finmeccanica on its £1.01 billion acquisition of GKN plc's 50% stake in helicopter builder AgustaWestland. Never mind your brain, if you can get your tongue around all that lot perhaps this is the place for you. In any mammoth deal the tax aspects are crucially important so the US and UK tax lawyers in London are *"involved in almost everything."* As such the discipline is considered an important element of the training.

International travel is another defining feature of Cleary life. There will be no need to pack a bum bag and camera because *"when you are away you are working pretty hard."* When looking through the roll call of recent transactions we noticed a decidedly Russian flavour, as US investors move into this market. This type of work is described as *"entertaining"* at times and will quite likely involve jetting off to Moscow for short trips. In 2006, all four of Cleary's qualifying trainees took NQ positions, passports at the ready for whatever lay ahead.

give a man a fish...

One of our interviewees claimed they had *"worked for a supervisor who couldn't be more accommodating,"* and it soon became clear that this experience was by no means a one-off. *"It is very easy to ask questions;"* and although the view is that giving you the answers directly *"defeats the object,"* the partners and associates will offer *"helpful hints."* A well-equipped library affords all the electronic resources a trainee could ask for and *"we all have BlackBerrys and laptops to make things as easy as possible."*

Out-of-hours shenanigans are a little bit thin on the ground it must be said, so don't come here thinking you'll be hanging out with work mates all the time. *"In the grand scheme of things the social scene is a small part of life here,"* confirmed a source. *"It is nice when it happens, but it is not that significant."* *"When people do finish their work they go home; you are working too hard to be going out drinking a lot... you are generally too tired."* It's not that people are antisocial; *"I have certainly made friends here,"* stressed one interviewee. Each summer, UK associates get to widen their circle of friends when they fly over to America to visit their New York cousins. The trip is by no means office-based and includes plenty of social events.

and finally...

We were given a lot of guidance from our interviewees before putting together this report. They definitely wanted us to stress that *"it would be unwise to say that people don't work hard here,"* but also that the rewards are huge – and not just financially. Consider Cleary Gottlieb if you think you'll get a kick out of being involved in some of the heftiest deals around – and we do mean involved – or if you've a particular interest in becoming dual qualified at some stage.

Clifford Chance LLP

the facts

Location: London
Number of UK partners/solicitors: 237/717
Total number of trainees: 250
Seats: 4x6 months
Alternative seats: Overseas seats, secondments
Extras: Pro bono – various law centres and charities, death row appeals; language training

So, what do you know about the biggest law firm on the planet? Huge and impersonal, right? Ultra-serious with a competitive atmosphere. We had a nose around to see if we could confirm or refute these and a few other common preconceptions.

legal machinery

Pretty much everyone we spoke to understood that CC is *"seen as a big machine,"* with its trainees being the proverbial *"small cogs."* They too had shared this idea before arriving. *"For some reason, I thought it would be like an exam hall – a huge room with two and a half thousand desks stretching into the distance,"* recalled one. Indeed CC has crowed loudly about its gargantuan proportions and what these mean for geographical coverage and revenue. Here's what trainees say about working for such a vast organisation: *"It would be nice and warm and fluffy if you knew everyone here, but you can't."* Instead, each separate practice group forms a more *"intimate"* working community such that *"it doesn't feel like I am coming to work at CC the firm, it feels like I'm coming to work in whatever department I'm in at the time."*

Assuming the magic circle flicks your switch – and it certainly doesn't do it for everyone – why choose CC over the other four players? Trainees with useful inside knowledge of the others argued that *"the atmosphere here is quite different, people are more diverse."* They may have a point here; after studying lists of recruits we reckon that CC and Linklaters come top of the ethnic diversity stakes and CC scores high on its recruitment from a reasonably big pool of UK universities. What CC doesn't have is a particularly traditional set of attitudes; after all, in this United Nations of a law firm, which tradition would you preserve? Chatting about the type of people who work at the firm, one trainee told us: "*I thought everyone would be quite staid and boring, but they are normal and down to earth.*" The "*broad church*" that is the CC trainee pool comprises "*all types.*" Naturally "*academic ability is important for understanding those tricky concepts,*" but beyond this "*the focus is on personality*" and being a "*team player.*" Another source went so far so to say: "*They don't want you to conform, so I don't have to tone myself down – I can be who I want to be.*"

For all new arrivals, a two-week induction kicks off proceedings. This is complemented by practice-area-specific orientation at the start of each seat and "*quite a lot of scheduled ongoing training.*" Additionally there is useful, but optional, online training. All very impressive, but even so, trainees still believe "*your colleagues are your best resource,*" which we suppose is an endorsement of the overall quality of supervisor-trainee relationships. The proverbial "*steep learning curve*" is in evidence, and the "*pace of work can be quite hard so you don't always get the chance to consolidate – sometimes you have to stop your supervisor and take a moment to orient yourself.*" One trainee summed things up by describing the training as "*like being on a roller coaster but knowing you have the safety bar down.*"

With around 250 demanding trainees and a huge degree of choice, seat allocation is something of "*a jigsaw puzzle*" for the HR team. The comment that "*you will not get the sexy seats all the time*" is true of most of the firms, and here as much as anywhere, being "*a little bit realistic*" is probably the best way forward. One other piece of advice is that if you've a burning desire for a particular seat you should "*make it clear that you want one thing, and keep the message going.*"

easymoney

Seen by many as the powerhouse that drives the firm as a whole, the massive international finance and capital markets divisions are phenomenally successful all around the world. It would be highly unusual to go through a full training contract without sampling at least one of the specialist financial units. A seat within the "*huuuuge*" banking group affords "*the thrill of being a part of the biggest deals around.*" Trainees readily admit that it is simply "*part of the game*" that, as more transactions veer towards the $billion value mark, the trainee's role becomes "*smaller and smaller.*" In other words, the volume of "*rubbish and not very taxing*" work increases. Nevertheless, they say they are "*still involved and following what's going on.*"

The asset finance group specialises in leasing and financing involving corporate assets and infrastructure. "*We were working on a deal which made the front page of the papers every day,*" recalled a past occupant of the seat. On one deal the London, New York and Hong Kong offices worked together on a $750 million securitisation of a fleet of ships. In another, lawyers advised BNP Paribas on the first Japanese Operating Lease (JOL) for two easyJet A320s. We're guessing the trainee who told us that completing a big piece of research was "*like being back at uni*" wasn't suggesting it was done feet up in front of an afternoon soap. "*Cutting-edge*" derivatives work will push you beyond your "*previous knowledge based on* [80s Eddie Murphy classic] '*Trading Places',*" or maybe time in debt and equity capital markets, securitisation, structured finance or energy and infrastructure finance will provide your requisite experience.

As well as finance, corporate is well worth checking out since its lawyers handle some of the world's beefiest M&A and equity offerings. Note the "*Oh crap!*" response of a trainee who walked straight into one of the biggest deals of the year, "*working a 4am and a Sunday within the first week."* Ultimately they came to view the deal as *"kind of like my baby, so I didn't worry about the late nights."* Periods of downtime and vague 'Internet research' are a thing of the past across the City although even as recently as 2005 they could have given some CC trainees their first contact with client eBay, which instructed the firm on its $2.6 billion cash and stock offer for Skype. Lawyers also recently advised Spain's Telefónica on certain aspects of its £17.6 billion recommended takeover of O$_2$, and HJ Heinz on its £470 million acquisition of HP Foods. All very impressive, but due to the scale of these transactions trainees can't expect to run the show. Their role on a deal team is generally limited to *"transaction management,"* in other words *"taking client calls"* and *"shitty jobs"* like *"searches and bibling."* Trainees' advice is to take it as an opportunity to *"prove yourself"* and hopefully earn more challenging work. In short, *"a lot of the classic trainee tasks are necessary evils... you have just got to get them out of the way."*

flights of fancy

Throw a dart at a world map and, provided you avoid the blue bits, chances are CC will have an office wherever it lands. To be precise, there are 29 offices in 20 countries. Some of the foreign seats are fearsomely competitive, so if you like the sound of Moscow, for example, best start brushing up on the Russian vocab, as the firm takes language skills into account. A full list of the options appears on page 174, and anyone who wants to go abroad can. Back in London other options include a range of client secondments, plus seats in things like communications media and technology, competition, construction, planning and environment, tax, pensions and employment, real estate and dispute resolution. The firm handles major disputes ranging across such areas as administrative and public law, competition, employment, IP, maritime and

international trade, insurance and real estate; and with CC being CC there is of course a massive focus on banking/finance and securities litigation. It also does rather well on construction disputes, and was recently successful in the High Court for Multiplex in its spat with Cleveland Bridge over a north west London football stadium project which apparently suffered a couple of minor snags.

Some trainees see the requirement for contentious experience as a bit of a bind. For these die-hard transactional types with no interest in law beyond the cut and thrust of corporate or finance, a whole six months in litigation strikes them as *"a waste of time."* They can opt for time spent volunteering at a legal advice clinic every few weeks, because the CC induction programme covers litigation elements sufficiently comprehensively to allow participants to tick off Law Society requirements. One trainee who was two thirds of the way through a three-finance-seat plan concluded pragmatically: *"It meant my litigation spot could be taken up by someone else who is more into it."* Another thought *"meeting real people face to face"* was *"nice because most of our clients are big banks"* and *"it really does make you feel like a lawyer."*

hard day's night

On the subject of hours, trainees spoke candidly. *"Yes, people work hard, and I have been caned at times,"* said one; *"sometimes I leave at six, other times it's nine or eleven."* The only thing we'll add is that there is a certain degree of inconsistency between supervisors as to how busy things become. If you end up sitting with a senior associate who is gunning for partnership, you may find there's no let up. One trainee who was taking a pounding when we rang had experienced just this problem. *"I am sitting with a senior lawyer who works very hard, and as a consequence I have to work very hard."* Fortunately, trainees have a degree of influence on who they sit with, since CC's seat selection process allows them to specify a preferred area of practice and preferred individual. You are recommend to *"pick brains"* in your target departments to find out about the type and volume of work and the supervisors' personalities. Undoubtedly, those trainees who *"go for the big-name practice areas and big-deal buzz are going for a lifestyle choice as well."* Witness the person who said: *"Some people talk about working long hours as if it is a bad thing. I enjoy my work, so I am spending a bit longer doing something I enjoy. What is so bad about that?"* No matter where you sit in the firm, *"if you are a self-starter you can really put your face around, make your own opportunities and go for it."* Alternatively, you can *"go to a department and keep your head down and be unwilling to take on any extra work. The net result is that you will do a lot less work than those who really want it. It's up to you."*

eye of the tiger

CC's *"skyscraping"* offices in Canary Wharf are filled with *"facilities without compare,"* including an *"awesome"* gym. One trainee took inspiration from the gym's pumped-up atmosphere without even breaking sweat. *"Sometimes I like to just walk through after lunch. There is something about the Rocky-type music and people in Lycra which gets you fired up before going back to your desk."* If the 20-metre swimming pool, aerobics studio and squash courts make this place sound like a leisure centre, then the pool tables, Playstations and table football in the games room conjure up images of a youth club. Restaurants, coffee shops and dry cleaners are all well used; however, some of our sources were unconvinced about the hairdressers, with one trainee voicing *"fundamental objections to getting your hair done at work."* All up, the Docklands des-res is as flash as it comes, and when you're taking a battering on the hours front *"the building makes you feel a bit better about your-*

self. *If you were working late and you were in a craphole you would hate it."*

Socially there's a lot going on. If you're in a seat when the department has its annual retreat then you'll be whisked off to somewhere like Nice or Lisbon. These trips (*"free booze and a good time"*) help trainees integrate into their teams. Even when back at Canary Wharf *"the rewards can be great,"* especially when you are *"taken to good restaurants for closing dinners and cocktail parties in the West End."* Naturally the vast trainee group has its own social scene, which starts on a high in the first few weeks when *"everyone goes out and gets lashed."* (Is this sounding like uni to anyone else?) However, the pace tends to *"let up"* after a while. The trainee balls each winter and summer are highlights, even if the term 'ball' is used fairly loosely since the idea is to *"turn up, drink as much free booze as you can and fall over."* No need to feel out on a limb if drinking isn't your thing; in such a large firm you'll always find like-minded people, and staff are often able to get to cultural events through *"free tickets to art exhibitions, private viewings and discounted opera and theatre tickets."* Sports-wise, pretty much every interest is catered for – some CC lawyers recently trekked from the 89th parallel to plant the firm's flag at the North Pole, raising an ice-cap-sized chunk of money for children's charities in the process.

For details of the new Clifford Chance LPC at the College of Law in London, see the firm's website.

and finally...

As in all the magic circle firms, the majority of trainees stay with the firm on qualification. Some 112 of the 122 qualifiers did in September 2006, the majority going into finance, capital markets and corporate jobs. NQs then have the option to stay long term and gun for partnership, or use the Clifford Chance brand as a springboard to an in-house position or smaller firm. Either way the training is a fantastic start to a legal career.

Clyde & Co

the facts

Location: London, Guildford
Number of UK partners/solicitors: 110/174
Total number of trainees: 45
Seats: 4x6 months
Alternative seats: Overseas seats, secondments
Extras: Pro bono – RCJ CAB, Lambeth Law Centre, Guildford CAB; language training

Clyde & Co's traditional strengths in shipping, international trade and insurance have left it with a worldwide footprint made up of 18 offices stretching from Caracas to Hong Kong. Its most recent flag-planting exercises have taken it to Moscow, Los Angeles, New York and Shanghai.

the best a seaman can get

Clydeworld looks pretty darn interesting from where we're sitting, and should you be attracted to any of its strong suits we reckon you'll see it the same way. In marine, transport, aviation, commodities and energy work it would be no exaggeration to say that wherever and however goods are moved around the world Clydes' lawyers are involved in some way. The firm has also built on its insurance litigation skills to become a Trojan of the Commercial Court, acting in many of the biggest litigations of recent years. In 2005 it was in the Commercial Court seeking freezing orders worth $106 million in a spat between Ukrainian and Russian oligarchs over control of a Ukrainian power company privatised following the Orange Revolution. The dispute itself was to be determined by the London Court of International Arbitration. Another matter saw litigators successful in their defence of the UK government when over 48,000 angry Railtrack shareholders sued over the decision to allow the company to go into administration.

Though there are no strictly compulsory seats for trainees, most people find their contract reflects the firm's overall orientation. Roughly translated this means time in marine, trade and energy and/or insurance practice groups. Rather like electric shavers, marine work can be 'wet' or 'dry'. Put very simply, if everything goes well and cargo arrives after its voyage, it's a dry shipping matter, perhaps a problem has arisen over payment or late delivery and so on. If the ship has a collision or sinks, then it's a wet shipping matter. If you're working on dry matters, you're likely to get a degree of control over relatively small cases. *"We act for one small shipping insurer which refers three or four cases a week,"* a trainee elaborated. *"The partner comes in, hands me a claim file; I refer and organise the file, set out what I think the advice should be, discuss it with the partner, and draft the advice."* By contrast wet disputes are commonly much larger and as a result you might find yourself *"stuck on slightly dull jobs"* as the files navigate their way through a drawn-out litigation process. Whether you go wet or dry you'll benefit from the department's *"friendly"* atmosphere. One trainee looked back fondly on their time in the department, describing it as the social hub of the London office: *"There was a department outing to the pub at least once a week."* The fact that the pub is named The Ship surely can't be a coincidence.

twisted sisters

Given that a person can insure against almost any event from war threatening their Middle Eastern investments to laryngitis threatening their multi-platinum recording career it's no wonder the insurance/reinsurance team at Clydes is so busy. Again putting it simply, trainees encounter disputes over the interpretation and application of insurance policies. Reinsurance, in case you're wondering, is insurance for insurers. Clydes works for some of the enormous companies that effectively underwrite the whole insurance industry, enabling it to sustain itself through major natural and man-made disasters. If you fancy working with the hurricane sisters Katrina, Rita and Wilma, this is the place to come.

The disputes handled in Clydes' insurance division tend to be *"mega-mega-litigation: international, worth hundreds of millions of pounds, and lasting years."* Obviously a trainee can't run these files solo and, just as in wet shipping, must take on more administrative tasks. However, the issues themselves are *"really interesting,"* and further compensation comes in the form of research points and a *"snazzy"* annual party at the Royal Courts of Justice, where you're *"encouraged to mingle with the clients."* If the thought of schmoozing with insurers fills you with horror, you'll be pleased to hear that *"after a long day at Lloyd's they want to talk about anything but insurance."*

not open all hours

Yes, the firm is heavily litigation-focused, but don't think non-contentious work is sidelined. With around half of all seats transactional, those who wish to do two non-contentious seats are usually accommodated (though *"it's best to make your wishes known pretty early to be sure"*). There are seats available in smaller departments such as IP/IT and employment, as well as two larger departments – coco and property. We learned that *"people tend to see property as the short straw"* but once they begin they're usually intrigued. The *"young, energetic"* team serves a range of top high street names (eg Carphone Warehouse, Zara, Jigsaw), getting trainees to help with *"arranging and negotiating transactions, chasing missing documents and solving problems."* With some of their own smaller matters to handle some reported feeling *"a bit in at the deep end"* until they'd got the hang of things.

More than one trainee told us: *"You really get out of your seats what you put in"* and *"they'll present you with a lot of opportunities but it's up to you to seize*

them." Furthermore, *"you need to decide what you want to do and push for it; if you're indecisive, you won't thrive."* Though hours vary between departments they are deemed reasonable. In coco you might be in from 9am until 8 or 9pm, and trainees reported *"the occasional midnight,"* not ideal, but a walk in the park compared to some firms. In litigation and property seats you'll generally be out by 7.30pm. One trainee told us of a colleague who, flushed with enthusiasm in their first seat, stayed until 1pm catching up on paperwork: *"The partners were horrified when they found out."*

where dubai 'em...

But what if you don't know what seats to push for? After all not every trainee comes to the firm with an understanding of shipping or insurance. Clydes responds by giving all new trainees a week of training and meet-n-greet sessions – *"They made a good effort to introduce us to everyone, right up to the senior partner."* The first week of any new seat is also dotted with talks introducing the relevant industry and issues, and throughout the year you'll have *"lunchtime lectures coming out of your ears."*

Each six months there are foreign placements, most often in Clydes' Dubai and Piraeus offices. Dubai in particular offers *"far more responsibility than in London,"* with trainees dealing directly with clients on relatively important matters. They are supplied with accommodation and car hire or taxi money, and it's not the social desert you might expect. *"Lots of law firms are opening up there now,"* said one returnee, *"so there are lots of other trainees to go out with."* As yet there are no seats in the recently opened NY and LA offices (initially opened to develop the aviation practice), though some trainees already speak of these as *"exciting prospects."*

In all seats trainees are supervised by a partner or senior assistant; and most enjoyed sharing office space with them. *"They're not dragons,"* said one, *"you can make the odd personal call."* Supervisors were generally viewed as *"pretty helpful"* and willing participants in the mid and end-of-seat reviews. The subject of seat allocation, however, produced some of the strongest comments in our interviews. Trainees understood that "*business needs are paramount*," but felt somewhat uncomfortable with the opaqueness of the system and their inability to influence decisions beyond specifying their preferences. One veteran of the system went so far as to call the process "*Machiavellian.*"

...guildford actually

Sign up to a training contract at Clydes and you get a two-for-one deal. The firm operates from separate offices in London and Guildford, and trainees are required to spend at least one seat in each. While "*a lot of trainees find this annoying,*" others rather liked the chance to do "*top-class London work but with the niceties of the countryside, especially in summer.*" For many trainees, their non-contentious seat will also be their Guildford seat. Some opt to find accommodation there; otherwise it's a "*manageable*" commute from Waterloo or Clapham Junction. After all, "*in summer, better 40 minutes on a train than 20 on a tube.*"

Guildford compensates for the commute with a modern, open-plan office with great facilities – there's even subsidised Starbucks coffee and snacks. Anyone wishing to spend more than one seat in Guildford can, and every year several trainees opt to qualify there. If you're looking for an office romance, however, you might want to note that Guildford "*tends to attract married staff, especially those with kids.*"

let them eat cake

Clydes' global interests mean "*there are often e-mails flying around from international people asking for advice,*" and fittingly, the firm is full of trainees from international backgrounds and linguists. We also spotted a number of people with commercial experience gained prior to their training contract, and were told that the average

trainee was slightly older than the norm for the City. And yet our sources indicated that the most recent intake was "*less distinctive*" and "*more academic*" than those who've gone before. On another point, despite recruiting at least as many female trainees as males, the firm still boasts a low ratio of female partners in the UK. "*I try not to think about it,*" admitted one female source, while others expressed confidence that "*the management are eager to make up more women partners.*" In 2006, only one UK senior associate was promoted to the partnership, and he was a he. Plenty of ladies among the 14 September NQs (out of 21) in 2006.

One trainee described their colleagues as "*the people who weren't quite cool at school but were really intelligent and very friendly.*" Others suggested the mood changes from floor to floor: so while insurance is "*quite buttoned-up and serious,*" the mood in shipping is more genial. At least in all departments lawyers make time to browse the snack trolley that trundles around the London office several times a day dispensing cakes and sandwiches.

In London much of the socialising is on a departmental basis, while in Guildford there is "*more socialising between departments,*" mostly in the nearby Guildford Tup. Each office has a summer party, waiting until Christmas to come together for a firm-wide do. The firm provides a budget for trainees to organise their own events, which have recently included go-karting and that old staple, ten-pin bowling.

and finally...

International expansion and growth in non-contentious areas of work are allowing Clyde & Co to broaden the scope of its already high-quality training. Even so, shipping and insurance litigation should still be regarded as the firm's bread and butter, and hence central to the training experience. Remember also that time in Guildford is part of the package.

CMS Cameron McKenna

the facts
Location: London, Bristol, Aberdeen, Edinburgh
Number of UK partners/solicitors: 111/413
Total number of trainees: 120
Seats: 4x6 months
Alternative seats: Overseas seats, secondments
Extras: Pro bono – Islington Law Centre; travel bursaries; cultural/language training

Hard core it ain't, but that doesn't make CMS Cameron McKenna a soft option. With its corporate and banking expertise, stellar energy work and a network of overseas offices, this firm can give you a classic City training.

going nuclear
When speaking to the trainees at this top-20 firm we got the impression that the appeal of Cameron McKenna has nothing to do with being the biggest, or offering the most areas of practice, or shouting about your credentials. Its approach is simply to get down to business without fuss.

While it may not be as corporate-driven as some of its City neighbours, this firm does have a good hold on the corporate finance market. It acts for a number of FTSE companies – two of them in the FTSE 100 – and has acted in some impressive recent deals, such as a capital markets bond issue to raise £550 million for Wellcome Trust, the world's largest medical research charity. This deal was a landmark in the sense that it was the first corporate-style bond issue by a not-for-profit organisation in the UK. The firm also assisted publishing company Informa on a number of deals including its $1.4 billion acquisition of conference organiser IIR. If you ever eat at the Italian restaurant Carluccio's, you can thank the firm for helping it gain admission to AIM.

Straight corporate aside, the range of opportunities in diverse departments such as pensions, projects, employment and immigration is a big draw for trainees. The area where Cameron McKenna really puts the boot into rivals, however, is energy and national resources. Here its top-notch regulatory practice advises National Grid on BETTA (new electricity trading and transmission arrangements for Great Britain) and leading off from this is the All Island Project, through which the firm is helping to implement a single electricity market in Ireland. In relation to oil and gas, lawyers advised BP on its disposal of three oil fields in Trinidad and Tobago. Also out of the UK, they have extended their expertise to Saudi Arabia where they have been drafting new electricity legislation. Other energy clients include ExxonMobil, Talisman Energy and Cairn Energy. Sealing off the practice, and of increasing prominence, is its nuclear expertise. The firm advises the United Kingdom Atomic Energy Authority on its current and future decommissioning activities, both for plants in the UK and others in Central and Eastern Europe.

well-oiled
It was this energy expertise that sparked Cameron's initial interest and now almost wholesale encroachment into Central and Eastern Europe. It has offices in Bulgaria, the Czech Republic, Hungary, Poland, Romania, Russia and Slovakia and a hand in deals right across this loosely shaped region. In 2005 lawyers busied themselves on the sale of Slovak electricity generating company, Slovenské elektrárne, one of the largest M&A deals in Central Europe that year. Evidencing the fact that work in this part of the world has moved beyond just that in the energy sector, the firm acted on the financing of the first major PPP in Poland, the A1 toll road.

CMS Cameron McKenna is justifiably proud of its projects practice. Aligned with the energy practice, it provides "*a constant supply of very good deals*" for the enthusiastic trainee to assist on. The Channel Tunnel and its rail link scheme is a biggie (the group advises the Department for Transport) and further clients include Metronet and John Laing. London lawyers also get to work in conjunction with colleagues in Central and Eatern Europe, where the firm advised on the Warsaw National'Stadium, gave specialist input into the first-ever wind farm project in the Czech Republic and advised on a gas-fired power plant transaction in Poland. We're also pleased to advise readers of the lawyers' involvement in transport projects in Canada at the Okanagan lake crossing, Kicking Horse Canyon and Golden Ears Bridge. Admittedly, the Richmond Airport – Vancouver rapid rail transport project in British Columbia has a higher value but it also has a far less interesting name. Day-to-day trainee life in this department means either a small role on a large transaction or "*running a very small project*" yourself. All in all, one trainee "*found the whole experience very interesting. I was in dialogue from day one with clients, including directors.*"

Projects work crosses over into construction law, especially when parties fall into dispute, and there is additionally a linked seat in project finance. This last department is said to be "*pretty intense as the hours are quite tough.*" As an example, one trainee "*worked on a large transaction for a private company, financing the building and improvements to a railway line. I was involved in making sure the bank had all the information it needed in order to loan the money.*" Trainees had good things to say about the banking sector in general. Apparently, "*you do get to play an important role in transactions. You are organising, albeit minor, documents and drafting. It's exciting being involved in things and going to completion meetings.*" Tax seats, too, provide a dose of responsibility, although not always sweet to the taste. "*A trainee going into that seat without any tax experience would find it horrendous, I reckon,*" said one former occupant. Another agreed that "*it was horrific but, looking back it was a good experience and the team is excellent.*"

exploration

With all this meaty work on offer, how does a trainee pick their way around it all? To summarise, the firm looks for trainees to spend time in three of the main practice groups: corporate; banking; property; energy, projects and construction; commercial and insurance. Apart from this, there are no real compulsories. It's true that seat rotation can get a little fraught, though most trainees recognised HR had "*a thankless task.*" One told us: "*It is a very hot topic because it is so important to trainees. Sometimes people can be disappointed.*" Others questioned the transparency of the process but concluded that "*perhaps this is as transparent as it gets at any firm.*" When it can be made smoother by splitting seats, the firm is usually happy to allow trainees to do this, and sometimes business needs will dictate a split. The end result is that not everyone does four straight seats of six months and some people return for more of a seat that really interested them.

Many trainees take the opportunity to complete a seat abroad in one of the firm's offices or within the CMS alliance of law firms. Seats in Eastern Europe can certainly be an eye-opener: "*Being a lawyer there is a really respected profession,*" one trainee said before hastily adding: "*Not that it isn't here, but you know what I mean. You have to be quite deferential to superiors.*" Another trainee told us: "*In my intake 30 people out of 35 left Mitre House, but not necessarily abroad – some went to Bristol.*" The Bristol seats are in commercial and banking litigation and Aberdeen is also an option. You could even find yourself on secondment to an oil client up in Scotland. And speaking of client secondments, our sources "*would definitely recommend one. A lot of lawyers don't understand how clients' businesses work and you need to know this in order to give a really good service to them.*" At present, there are several openings with banks and corporates.

time flies

Is there any chance of coming off the rails under the weight of all that responsibility? Trainees said: "*It's tough sometimes because of tight timescales but partners and other staff bend over backwards to help you and they understand when you need supervision.*" And what of the firm's reputation as a half-way house between the rigours of the magic circle and the supposedly easier training options available at mid-sized firms? Late-night and weekend working is inevitably more common in certain departments, so for example real estate is reputedly a busy department, "*but only between nine and five-thirty,*" while corporate often works "*silly hours.*" One trainee told us: "*The hours were long at one point, but they recognised the effort everyone had put in and a lull period was arranged to let people recover.*" Another trainee finished an intense project on a Wednesday and was told they could take the rest of the week off. Perhaps this trainee's comments sum things up best: "*It's not a hotbed of ambition and stress like the magic circle. It's not so intense; it's a friendlier environment, with interesting work and niche departments.*" In the ultimate test of the firm's popularity with its trainees, it retained 30 of its 35 qualifiers in September 2006.

Cameron McKenna is one of a growing number of City law firms to sign students up to a particular law school for the LPC and has made the decision to send future trainees to BPP in London. But this dictatorial approach is not typical of training generally. "*They wanted to listen to where I thought I could fit into the firm, as opposed to being told, 'you're a trainee, you'll fit in anywhere we want you to',*" said one source. It got us thinking about what type of person would fit in, or if there was a 'type' at all. Someone who likes a few drinks at the end of the working week? Someone who enjoys hitting a ball round the field with clients on a summer evening? Someone who "*shows enthusiasm and shows willing?*" Cameron seems to cater for all those people and a few more besides. The most common trait among trainees seems to be their eagerness to please and keenness to be treated fairly. The firm recruits from many universities worldwide.

The high spots on the trainees' social calendar are a trainee ball to which future joiners are invited and an annual firm-wide ball. There were stories circulating of a spot of overindulgence at the last trainee bash, and our sources were clearly of the 'no publicity is bad publicity' school of thought, proudly telling us: "*It shows we are a sociable bunch and we do let our hair down.*" They also mentioned that partners from the overseas offices are being flown in for the 2006 Christmas party, "*which is great; it's good to meet the people we don't often see in person. There is quite a lot of money spent on entertaining the troops, which makes for a great atmosphere.*" This, and a reasonably relaxed dress code, helps to keep morale high.

and finally...

To test the water at CMS Cameron McKenna you can apply for a two-week vacation placement over the Christmas, Easter or summer breaks. This will allow you sufficient time to find out if the firm's practice specialsims, including energy, projects and Eastern and Central European work, are things you'll enjoy sampling during your contract.

Cobbetts

the facts
Location: Manchester, Birmingham, Leeds
Number of UK partners/solicitors: 136/117
Total number of trainees: 52
Seats: 4x6 months
Alternative seats: Brussels, secondments
Extras: Pro bono – ProHelp

Cobbetts is well known for its heavy emphasis on property and related areas of practice and it has famously enjoyed a reputation for staff satisfaction. The past five years have been characterised by a major expansion programme that has transformed Cobbetts' business.

acquiring minds
Early in the new millennium Manchester-based Cobbetts set itself the ambitious target of becoming the leading firm operating outside London. In terms of its strategy, there was one word written in bold, double underlined capitals at the top of the page – mergers. In the space of 36 months the firm underwent five and expanded from a one-site operator to a three-city player at lightning-quick pace. A Leeds operation was established by swallowing the firm Read Hind Stewart, followed by housing specialists Walker Charlesworth & Forster and then planning boutique Wilbraham & Co. Cobbetts also moved into the Birmingham market through its merger with established commercial firm Lee Crowder, and in the meantime had bagged Fox Brooks Marshall in Manchester to give the firm a second office in its home city. This seems to have marked the end of the Cobbetts' crusade, at least for now. These days it's all about *"bedding down the mergers."*

As we've already mentioned, Cobbetts was always known for its property strength and the firm continues to act for major names including Whitbread Group, Matalan, Sports World, H3G, De Vere Group, Peel Holdings and Bruntwood Estates. Chunky commercial property deals are two-a-penny for the Cobbetteers, a recent example being Harrison Development's £90 million town centre project in Lichfield. Advising banks such as RBS on their substantial property portfolios keeps property lawyers busy and there are also plenty of public sector clients on the books, a number of them using the firm on regeneration projects.

With property the *"bedrock of the firm,"* you'd be forgiven for thinking that a seat working on bricks and mortar would be compulsory. Officially, a property seat is not compulsory but in practice go to the Manchester office for your training and it's more than likely that your first or second seat will be property practice in one of its various guises. Such is the myriad of opportunities in this sector that *"if it's your bag you can have your fill."* One interesting option is property litigation where recent tricky cases have included clearing two halls of residence at the University of East London in readiness to sell them off. With numerous stubborn students less than keen to depart, Cobbetts' lawyers were kept busy with a flurry of possession proceedings. Other property-related experiences include social housing, licensing work, planning and specialist telecoms advice helping Orange and other mobile phone operators spread their tentacles across the nation by siting masts.

the possibilities are endless
So it's all property then, right? Wrong. Cobbetts' trainees get to explore a whole world of legal practice through seats in commercial litigation, banking, corporate/commercial, employment and even private client. Unsurprisingly, the Manchester head office offers the widest range of options, but recruits to the

Leeds and Birmingham offices are given all the basics, with the Midlands office also providing a chance to try out charities law. A range of client secondments (eg RBS and Orange) can satisfy those *"keen for more commercial awareness"* by allowing them to work in-house for up to six months and an affiliated law firm in Brussels called McDermott, Will & Emery Stanbrook & Hoper also takes a few Cobbetteers under its wing.

To illustrate the quality of trainees' experiences, we've selected some of the things they told us about contentious seats, where all reported ample client contact, court attendance and advocacy experience. Commercial litigation brings with it a certain weight of responsibility: *"Even the menial tasks carry a great degree of importance and you're in for the high jump if a trial bundle isn't in on time."* Social housing litigation is a *"great but misunderstood"* trainee seat that spans ASBO and employment litigation as well as governance issues and property development problems. In banking litigation, client contact takes on a whole new dimension as trainees are invited to schmooze at *"lunches, wine tastings and days at the races."* With plenty of large banks turning to Cobbetts, the nitty-gritty work in this department involves *"mainly claims against guarantors"* and sees trainees *"issuing proceedings, writing letters and attending court a lot."*

the f-word

Cobbetts isn't one of those firms that will force you around its network. You pick an office and see out your two years of training there. This one-city experience means a local connection *"in some way, shape or form"* is a factor for Cobbetts when it takes its pick of applicants. Yet, look for a Cobbetts type and it's hard to pin one down: the firm's *"policy of recruiting people with various strings to their bow"* leads to plenty of variety when it comes to trainee age and life experience.

Where you will find common ground is in the collective culture that has been embraced by staff. Unquestionably, niceness pervades Cobbetts from top to bottom and our sources were more than aware of the firm's reputation as the nauseatingly nice guys. *"You'll hear this all the time and it'll make you sick, but Cobbetts really is a very, very friendly firm,"* one source explained. For trainees, this warm culture engenders *"first-class"* training because *"the focus is on supervision and people take the time to train you fully."* As well as *"more formal"* mid and end-of seat reviews, there are monthly chats with training officer Janet Toombs, known for having *"a really good relationship with trainees."* Some might feel *"coddled"* by all this help but the vast majority of those who spoke to us were well and truly sold on Cobbetts Culture. We listened with interest about *"a major emphasis"* placed on the life aspect of work-life balance and several of our sources were more than happy to boast about a lack of long hours when compared with some rival firms. Most truly believed this to be a firm where you can get the best of both worlds: *"If you want to do good-quality work for well-known clients but don't want to kill yourself by working every hour of the day, then Cobbetts is a good place to come."*

making the right moves

In past years we'd have stopped there, convinced that Cobbetts is great for combining great work with great hours and a generally relaxed atmosphere. This year we have to temper our enthusiasm with a few cautionary words. The firm's 2004/05 financials make less than impressive reading and debate is underway in the legal press as to whether the rapid expansion strategy has paid off. There is no doubt that, at £190,000 per equity partner (PEP), profitability has taken a dip and it is by far the lowest of the top 50 firms. On top of this, the rate of increase in turnover does not match those of other rapidly growing regional firms. Our sources believe the recent announcement that 20 salaried and equity partners are to be let go *"is inevitable because PEP is so poor,"* partly a function of the firm being *"too partner-heavy after the mergers."* But irrespective of top-heavy numbers, there's no disguising that income isn't what it could be. All this begs the question: is the relaxed Cobbetts Culture compatible with getting the firm to the top of the leader boards? *"The hours are almost too good to get the targets the firm wants,"* one trainee told us, while another put it more bluntly: *"Cobbetts has itself to blame – it brands itself as laid-back with flexible hours but the work has to get done. The people at the front line of the firm need to be putting the hours in to generate the fees."*

A cultural shift at Cobbetts may be necessary if it wants to really make a big impact in the market; those who don't want to pull in that direction may find this is not the firm for them. Current trainees certainly believe this is one factor behind the partner cuts, one telling us that *"the unofficial line is there was a hit list of people they wanted to get rid of."* All said and done, the majority of those we spoke to weren't concerned about their own future at Cobbetts as they had received *"lots of assurance that only the partner level is affected."* On the contrary, a number of those we spoke to seemed to back the *"hard-nosed business decisions"* and *"strong leadership"* that may be necessary to secure the future Cobbetts is striving for. It might just be that future trainees will see a slightly tougher work-life balance defining the Cobbetts Culture. Through all of this, Cobbetts is determined to live the dream of *"competing with the big boys"* by investing heavily in swanky new premises. *"Branding is important"* and the firm wants the image to match its grand ideas. The Leeds lawyers now occupy *"a beautiful riverside office"* and the Manchester contingent only has to wait until mid-2007 to move under one newly refurbished roof.

With change in the air, all manner of issues are being re-examined; right down to how trainees are best recruited, trained, supervised and rotated. The firm has instituted a trainee-led review of its current scheme, so changes could be in place by the next round of recruitment.

cobbetteers: all bar one...

Moving on to the social scene, with each office being slap bang in the centre of a city there's no shortage of watering holes to keep Cobbetters amused of an evening. In Leeds on Friday *"it's always dead in the office by 5pm,"* at which point *"there's a mass exodus to Greek Street."* Manchester has *"its own Ally McBeal bar"* (an All Bar One across the road) and in Birmingham many people tend to go out on a Thursday, either to All Bar One or Digress. The Cobbetts' Young Professionals group *"has really blossomed this year"* and trainees across the firm have organised regular networking events at swish locations such as Malmaison and Harvey Nicks in Birmingham. If this still leaves anyone unsatisfied they can tap into plenty of organised fun by paying a subscription of a measly £2 per month to the Cobbetts Social Club.

Most trainees stay with the firm after qualification. In 2006, 17 of the 24 did so, with Leeds managing full retention. A number of those who left had wanted corporate or employment positions but there simply weren't enough available.

and finally...

Over the years, trainees have consistently spoken of their satisfaction with life at Cobbetts. It's unlikely that any changes the firm makes will erode the firm's culture to such an extent that the best elements are lost entirely. What does seem fairly certain is that, for now, the merger phase is over.

Coffin Mew & Clover

the facts

Location: Southampton, Fareham, Gosport, Portsmouth
Number of UK partners/solicitors: 19/42
Total number of trainees: 11
Seats: 6x4 months
Alternative seats: None

This solid South Coast firm has an attractive mix of commercial and private client work in which trainees can bury themselves.

perpetual motion

CMC's roots go back to the 1800s and its longevity has ensured it a decent position within the regional legal market. "*With private clients, word of mouth always helps,*" said one trainee, referring to the firm's success in this area of practice: "*People give a good account of us.*" As a result, this side of the firm's business is as thriving as it was when horses pulled carts through the cobbled streets of Southampton. Of course, there have been many changes over the years and the firm has adapted to meet them. It has consolidated its sprawling network of neighbourhood offices into four sites, refreshed its paintwork a few times, installed air-con and grown in size. It has also sprouted a commercial limb, which is now sufficiently bulky to create a "*clear 50/50 balance*" between the two areas. In today's CMC, trainees are as likely to experience the rush of a deal closing as the detail of a local dignitary's will. The trainees' views on this were overwhelmingly positive. "*I love the balance between commercial and individual interests – it's why I chose the firm,*" enthused one.

CMC's diverse interests make the firm an ideal training ground for someone with similarly catholic tastes. The six-seat scheme allows trainees to range freely across the firm. "*I like the fact that I will experience two more departments than my friends*" said one, while others appreci-ated the chance to "*test out different areas if you're unsure.*" It may even lead to a personal revelation; for one trainee "*it changed everything I thought I would enjoy – I presumed I would qualify into a private client seat, but then I found corporate.*" The set-up is not entirely ideal as "*you don't get to work on something from beginning to end,*" but at least "*you see bits of many things to make up for it.*" While there are no hard and fast rules for seat selection, trainees are "*definitely encouraged*" to tackle both commercial and private client seats. Such perpetual motion means the allocation is a bit like "*musical chairs;*" however, people were quick to point out that the firm is "*very good at trying to fit you in with what you really want,*" particularly in the second year. And besides, "*they won't employ five trainees who are all the same, so all training contracts will be different.*"

Trainees usually get to check out the wallpaper inside three of the four offices (Gosport – "*one road in, one road out*" – is a high street branch and has no trainees). A full range of legal services is offered in Portsmouth, Southampton and Fareham, and trainees gauged that the same amount of elbow grease was required in each. The hours are "*quite civilised*" (8.30am until 5pm is fairly typical) and "*the quality of work is always impressive,*" said one source, "*and you're expected to be a part of that.*"

doctors and houses

"*If you are commercially minded you will do very well here, as this area is growing.*" Trainees in Southampton's corporate department were glad they sharpened their pencils to step up to an "*intense and complicated area of the law.*" They told us: "*You're very involved from beginning to end on matters, albeit at a low level,*" which trans-lates into a lot of due diligence and the filling in and filing of documents. What clinched it for one source was "*the great variety of work, from advising very small businesses to deals in the millions.*"

Last year the department completed £200 million worth of transactions, including assisting the University of Southampton when it embarked on a £92 million development and refinancing programme. Lawyers also helped a client with contractual, marketing and advertising advice when it launched a new alcoholic product. In keeping with the firm's location, contracts for large yacht and super-yacht refits also abound.

Trainees tend to take a commercial property seat at some point in their two years. Being appealing not only on its own, this work is seen as "*a useful addition to corporate, because it allows you to understand better the property aspects of corporate work.*" The property seat is as varied as corporate and trainees start by spending two weeks with the residential conveyancing team, building their knowledge from the ground up. The department recently worked on the sale, financing and leases of a group of surgeries in Hampshire and Sussex. Refreshment comes in the form of deals relating to restaurants, pubs, marinas and clubs in the expanding Portsmouth social scene.

Our parent publication *Chambers UK* makes a fuss of CMC's top-ranked social housing practice. Trainees who do a seat in this department work for numerous registered social landlords, including Housing for Women, First Wessex Housing Group and Signpost Housing Group. In the Southampton employment seat, meanwhile, they "*cover an awful lot of law,*" with this smaller department providing an intensive learning experience.

urning your stripes

Just because the commercial seats are "*buzzing*" does not mean that private client is the wallflower at the school disco. "*Probate is probably the most hands-on seat of all of them,*" observed one trainee, wiping their brow. "*There are a lot of home visits and leg work, and it's great for a first seat as you immediately get client contact.*" Often dealing with "*nice but mad old ladies,*" you will run your own files, draft powers of attorney, take will instructions and generally "*get a great deal of satisfaction from helping people.*" The amount of responsibility is generally seen as a very good thing, not least because "*you don't have time to worry about things.*" It seems you just can't get away from the ideas conjured up by CMC's name. "*Winter is busier here in private client, we're working with a lot of old people and they tend to die more in the winter. It's nice and steady in the summer.*"

Other experiences include the "*form filling and billing*" of PI, with added clinical negligence claims to spice things up, and the "*absolutely superb*" family seat. One trainee credited much of the enjoyment of the seat to Pauline Johnson, head of the department with over 25 years experience in the field. "*She's a top-notch family lawyer who only handles matters over a million. All her cases are interesting and you do shadow her a lot.*" The department's clients are a mix of business people and wealthy individuals, including those whose fortunes have been generated over several generations. There are also clients resident abroad, including a number in sunny Spain and even sunnier Bahrain. The department sees a lot of divorces, financial disputes and cohabitation problems, and has a growing reputation in pre-nuptial agreements.

clover-hoofed

"*We are reasonably conservative,*" said some of our sources, although this is not to say that there isn't a culture of openness across the firm. "*There is never a problem asking questions,*" said one, "*and you don't always need to go to your supervisor, sometimes you can go to a secretary or an associate.*" It may be good to talk in the office but it's even better out of it. The trainee intake is almost always "*a close group who like to spend time together.*" Their pub of choice in Southampton is the Varsity, which is "*always heaving*" on a Friday night. More active pursuits include summer rounders and trips to the dogs, plus regular quiz nights to exercise the old grey matter and possibly impress colleagues with your in-depth knowledge of 80s pop. In the mornings, Southampton trainees muck in by *"doing the post;"* far from being the dullest chore of the day, it's a great way to catch up on any gossip from the night before.

You know that view some people have of lawyers – distant, straightlaced, cloven-hoofed? *"We are not like that"* declared the trainees, *"we are approachable and we like to think we are part of the community."* Which sounds like a reminder that this is a distinctively South Coast business, unlike several of the firm's local rivals that have offices elsewhere in the UK. In September 2006, four of the firm's five qualifiers took jobs.

and finally...

If you want to sample the CMC community early on, the best way is to attend an open week. Effectively three days long, there's half a day of talks about the firm followed by a series of half days in different departments, shadowing partners and meeting trainees. Ample time to size up this particular Coffin.

Collyer Bristow LLP

the facts

Location: London
Number of partners/assistants: 32/18
Total number of trainees: 6
Seats: 4x6 months
Alternative seats: None
Extras: Pro Bono – CAB.

"When I applied I knew that this was meant to be a quirky, even odd little firm and so it has proved." This was one trainee's affectionate portrait of a place that is rich with interesting work and interesting characters.

on that note...

Dominated by its hefty litigation department. CB handles cases relating to employment, property, construction, insolvency, IP, media and pretty much anything else you could dream up. The team acted for the League Against Cruel Sports in a challenge brought by the Countryside Alliance against the Hunting Act 2004 and successfully represented a co-defendant in the case brought by the President of Equatorial Guinea against a group (including Mark Thatcher) alleged to have fomented a military coup in the country. Meanwhile litigious types have also been busy helping Stelios and his easyGroup's orange-themed easyMobile venture. The new phone company needed to fight off a claim brought by Orange on various more or less obvious grounds. Lawyers have advised the family of Sergeant Gordon Gentle (who was killed by a roadside bomb in Iraq) as it fought for the right to be represented at the subsequent inquest.

CB is no stranger to the music industry, where is represents predominantly artists, with a few small, independent labels and publishers thrown in for good measure. Damien Rice, Purple Haze Records, Deep Purple and Jane McDonald are all fans of the firm. Its lawyers recently advised an individual in a court case concerning her role as a singer on Pink Floyd's 'Dark Side of the Moon' and have been helping Status Quo in a dispute involving former band members.

going for gold

If all that doesn't move you, it's worth remembering that music and related media clients also provide a fair whack of the coco department's work. Yes, the firm has clients from start-ups to established companies in entirely glamour-free industry sectors, but those celebs do pop up again and again. Commercial lawyers have this year advised Damien Rice on film soundtrack deals, negotiated a book-publishing deal for Katie Price, advised MOBO on its tenth-anniversary awards and Mercury Music Prize on sponsorship matters. Sports instructions also come in for the coco lawyers – they advised the insurance company Allianz on sponsorship agreements with the Williams Formula 1 team, helped extreme sports company Sports Vision on a range of commercial agreements for the 2005 Boardmasters Newquay Surf Festival, and Sport England on everything from the unification of English karate governing bodies to the implementation of the £6 million Talented Athlete Scholarship Scheme. Individuals like double-gold Olympian Ben Ainslie and golfer Ernie Els also turn to CB.

In 2004 a Geneva office was opened to serve existing Swiss-based multinational clients like Philip Morris International and to target sports corporates such as UEFA, Formula 1, the IOC, FIFA and the FIA. The Geneva office also works in tandem with the London private client practice which, along with the family team, represents "high-profile and high-net-worth clients, judges, solicitors, media people, City business people, that sort of thing..." To give you a clue as to just how prestigious the family team is, we'll tell you that it was involved in the ground-breaking Miller and McFarlane cases. Last but not least, the property team handles commercial work for developers like Cadugan Developments and Crest Nicholson, as well as residential conveyancing for that varied private clientele.

stone throwing and diplomacy

Training involves one compulsory litigious seat and three selected from the four remaining departments. The details of seat rotation are "more or less left to us trainees to sit down and talk out," but when the "annual tight spot over corporate seats came up" this year, CB was willing "to let all of us do a seat of four months as a solution." Within individual seats it is "very much up to the individual to pursue the kind of work they're inter-

ested in." As such our sources had successfully pitched for "employment matters in litigation" or "a fair amount of IP in corporate." Private client duties have even seen some trainees assist consultant Clive Woolf, who represents Carribbean death row prisoners.

Trainees are not assigned a supervisor for each seat and instead share an office with "a departmental caretaker who keeps an eye on your progress." Being "more loosely attached to the department as a whole" means that "work will come from all directions," but it definitely requires "courage" and "an awareness that to get the most out of it you need to pipe up and ask for stuff." When your desk becomes overloaded, "diplomacy" is a most useful skill: "It's hard to say no as a trainee, but you learn to say, 'I've got x, y and z to do in a certain time for this person; I'll do the work if you can clear it with them'."

An important factor in the training here is "the absolute plethora of people who are interested in teaching and sharing their knowledge." A top-heavy structure at CB ("if you throw a stone two feet you'll always hit a partner") means that "trainees often get work that associates might get elsewhere." Our sources in litigation had "done lots of advocacy," "discussed strategy with clients" and "attended tribunals regularly." In coco "you will occasionally get statutory books and annual returns to complete, but you also help draft complex documentation." Family and private client seats allow "more space and time to air thoughts and ideas, bouncing them off partners and really seeing top cases," while a seat with the "younger, more assistant-heavy" property team requires "juggling lots of files at the same time, pushing them through to conclusion" and "a lot more paperwork."

In some ways, both the training and the firm's structure are redolent of times past; certainly trainees told us "there are fewer well-defined HR processes than at other firms," adding as an afterthought: "If you want to know how you are doing every single day, and exactly where you stand, it might not suit you." Perhaps to address this issue, trainee appraisals have recently been scheduled for every three months instead of six.

fontastic

CB's Bedford Row offices are in the heart of legal London ("the Family Court just behind, barristers' chambers all around") and it has occupied them for around 180 years. Young Collyer Bristow types do identify an old-school or more traditional element to the firm, but say that certain clients "pretty much demand we're like that – you can't be too wacky if you're working for a judge." Importantly, they see it as an integral part of the firm's character, one telling us: "I wouldn't change anything – it's a complex bit of machinery that's evolved organically and I wouldn't go tampering." It's not as if nothing changes: the office has been renovated, a Swiss office opened and in 2006 the firm went for a rebrand of its logo and website, etc. "Er, the Collyer's sort of purple and old school and the Bristow is grey and in a new font. It's all about diversity and being the best of both worlds." Even more dramatic was the introduction of a more relaxed dress code, albeit accompanied by "several pages of rules about what constitutes business casual."

In truth, trainees are in no hurry for the firm they joined to morph into another City clone. Most had chosen CB precisely because it offered "an alternative to the Magic Circle in work and atmosphere." Standard hours of 9am to 5.30pm may sometimes extend, but following the office refurbishment, "in the new sections the air con and systems switch themselves off at 7pm. You can put them back on, but they go off again at 9pm." As trainees observed, "even the building doesn't want you to do standard City hours." A good thing too because it sounds as if everyone has a full life away from the office. Among partners there are novelists, writers of radio comedy, art lovers and

musicians. "The firm is incredibly tolerant about supporting your interests," confirmed a source. The trainees are no less alternative and recent intakes have included an ex-journalist, a former surgeon, an ex-RAF bod, and a one-time researcher. We heard about one ex-history student who'd started a well-attended history club complete with newsletter giving interesting details about the locale. (Sample fact: Oliver Cromwell reputedly haunts nearby Red Lion Square). CB also generously supported the trainees when they completed the Three Peaks Challenge this year in aid of charity. "24 hours non-stop in a car together or climbing taught us that we definitely like each other," laughed one footsore source.

Ad hoc evenings in local pub, The Enterprise, or lunches in shady Grays Inn Gardens are buttressed by end-of-month drinks "where partners take it in turns to put their card behind the bar." There are also football matches and other sports, and on the day we called several people were planning to take a Jack the Ripper walking tour after work. The Christmas party, meanwhile, gives trainees a chance to lampoon colleagues with "rewritten Christmas carols taking the piss out of the firm." And there's just one more thing to mention – the Collyer Bristow Gallery, "an independently run art gallery which occupies our meeting rooms." Regularly changing exhibitions keep trainees alert and each year they take on the role of sales desk personnel at the annual "Christmas sale of 250 pieces of art at £250 each with proceeds going to charity."

and finally...

The only real downside of training at Collyer Bristow – and similarly oriented firms – is that "you can't necessarily rely on getting a job in the area you want at the end of the contract." In 2006 one of the three qualifiers stayed on in an NQ position, although two had the previous year.

Cripps Harries Hall LLP

the facts
Location: Tunbridge Wells, London
Number of UK partners/solicitors: 40/50
Total number of trainees: 7
Seats: Commonly six of varying length
Alternative seats: None

Located in one of the country's most genteel towns, Cripps Harries Hall has established a fine name over the last 175 years. After a reorganisation of its business in 2005, turnover and profits have been given a boost.

once upon a time...
This firm was founded in 1852 by a certain Mr Cripps, gentleman lawyer and registrar at Tunbridge Wells County Court. Some 70 years on and Mr Harries joined the practice; then in 1933 Mr Hall got his name above the door and went on to produce a son, who eventually became the firm's senior partner in the early 1990s. Over the years, the firm developed a reputation as the place for the well-to-do of Tunbridge Wells to go for legal advice. Private clients are still hugely important: even now around a quarter of Cripps' income is generated by its private client department. Allied to this practice group is a charities law team that advises such familiar organisations as the Royal Geographical Society and Macmillan Cancer Relief.

Over the past two decades, Cripps' commercial departments have grown to the extent that they now dominate. Then, in 2005, the firm undertook a review of its commercial practice groups and adopted the concept of 'business streams' to better cater to the needs of clients. It now targets organisations in specific sectors, among them hotels and leisure, transportation, house-building and property development, each of which are important in the South East.

A healthy public sector practice has emerged, too. For example, Cripps has had extensive involvement with the Channel Tunnel Rail Link, and was appointed to the government's 'L-Cat' (legal category) panel, which allows it to advise central government departments. Cripps lawyers additionally represent local authorities and other public sector bodies, such as the Crown Prosecution Service (albeit on non-criminal matters).

The beauty of a Cripps training is that you can dip in and out of diverse activities and work for all manner of clients. Generally trainees do six seats, following a pattern devised for them at the start of the training. No need to worry if you develop a burning interest for something that's not on your schedule: "*Nothing's set in stone, so if it fits in with the firm's business needs it is usually feasible to change a seat.*" It turns out that most of our sources had shortened a seat here or extended one there, and they thought the flexibility in the system "*brilliant.*" All seats are taken in Tunbridge Wells as the firm's London address is used primarily for client meetings.

A common seat pattern incorporates property (residential, commercial or both), dispute resolution (commercial, private client or property disputes) and private client (wills and probate or trusts and tax planning). Other options include employment, corporate, planning and family. Some trainees veer more towards private client matters; others choose to stay on the commercial side. Whichever tack they take, "*it's all about learning vital skills, picking them up from partners on the telephone, learning different drafting styles.*"

poncho-ing above its weight
No trainee avoids property, which has emerged as the big daddy of the commercial departments. The lawyers here handle everything from residential conveyancing and the construction of new

housing developments, to high-value commercial transactions and urban regeneration projects. A few years ago the firm got a massive boost when it was selected by City law firm Lovells to pioneer something called the Mexican Wave. Through this arrangement, Lovells sends Cripps smaller-scale work for one of its most valued clients, Prudential's property investment arm PruPIM. The Mexican Wave is both a great source of revenue and superb publicity for Cripps, helping it to win new work of its own.

Property seats bring all the usual tasks – "*rooting around for deeds, helping to negotiate and draft leases... buying and selling residential properties and preparing reports on title.*" Here, and right across the firm, "*the supervisors are all different, and they work in different ways. The work you get depends on how busy they are and how much time they can give to supervising you. But there's always an emphasis on getting you to do things that are useful and trying to make you the main contact on files.*" A trainee who had taken a planning seat had been amazed by the work: "*I sat in on council meetings when they were debating the local plan – it was interesting and really relevant. The partner takes you to absolutely everything and you get real hands-on exposure to how the developments get negotiated... it's a whole other world!*"

In dispute resolution, trainees try their hand at advocacy in small-scale preliminary hearings. Luckily the local county court is conveniently located just five minutes' away, close enough that the jitters don't build up too much before you stutter your request to the district judge. Less nerve-wracking, and even more plentiful, are invitations from colleagues to accompany them to court appointments. Trainees usually run simple debt collection files solo, while assisting on much larger, and sometimes international, disputes. We even heard of trainees making trips to Belgium and Italy for evidence collection.

where there's a will

If things French are your baguette, then ask for a corporate seat, where you might be able to assist the firm's French-qualified lawyer on inward investment deals for our Gallic cousins. Kent is full of French-owned businesses, and the firm has wisely spotted an opening in this particular market. The employment department is a halfway house in terms of the clients it represents and trainees get used to dealing with both employers and employees. Given the popularity of this seat, its occupants are limited to just three months, but they make the most of it, helping out on discrimination and harassment cases, and learning how to negotiate redundancies and the whacking great pay-offs that are commonly made to departing execs.

Of course we mustn't forget the private client work that has made Cripps what it is today. In this department there's a great deal of client contact, be this with little old ladies planning what to do with all their worldly goods when they die, or wealthy businessmen who want to keep their fortunes safe from the taxman. Sometimes the job will take a trainee to a frail client's home for the signing of a will, sometimes it will mean poring over statutes or dusting down ancient trust deeds. Across the board trainees felt well supported in their day-to-day work, and knew that in return their best efforts were required at all times. "*The quality of work and the standards expected of you are very high,*" one told us. Low-key monthly chats with supervisors, and longer meetings at the end of each seat, followed by meetings with the head of HR and the managing partner, all add up to a pretty comprehensive appraisal system.

risqué management

If you know Tunbridge Wells then you'll be aware of its lovely Georgian architecture, its rich history and its conservative reputation. As to whether the latter is reflected in the firm's character is a good question without a simple answer. Trainees tell us that Cripps is not old-fashioned, but the environment within which it operates is sometimes restrictive. We heard tell of a mail-out on the Civil Partnerships Act being returned by one client who was upset about the firm advising on same-sex marriages, and recently the trainees concluded that a Moulin Rouge-themed summer party would be too risqué for the town. In certain departments, partners have conservative views on what constitutes acceptable office dress. It's not that the firm is inherently stuffy; it's more that the traditional tastes of some clients are respected.

There are several examples of the firm's modernity. In 2005 it became an LLP and hived off its successful personal financial management arm into a separate company. It has invested substantially in IT, and devised a new initiative focusing on client care called 'Extra Mile'. The partnership has also gone a little further with regard to employees, as this trainee explains: "*One of my criticisms used to be that they listened to staff but didn't always act. More recently they have become aware of the importance of consultation as a way to show they care about our views. We've now got a consultation committee with a fee earner and member of the support staff from each area.*"

wells' belles

Our sources had deliberately avoided London training contracts, because they didn't fancy the commute and the hours. Yet there are days when the hoped-for benefits of working in Tunbridge Wells do not materialise. For some people the daily commute means a leisurely walk into work; for others a short drive can take up to 40 minutes when the traffic is backed up. The town is not a cheap place to live either, especially when you have a big student debt

(including the repayment of Cripps' loan for LPC fees).

The view from our interviewees was that "*if you have geographical links to the area, it helps your application.*" That said, only a minority were truly local, with broad southern connections being the hook for most. Should you arrive in town without a friend in the world, the easiest way to make some is at end-of-month drinks or evenings spent over a bottle of wine in Sankey's wine bar. Some of the younger, unattached trainees hinted that the social scene was not as lively as they had hoped, but as this trainee explained: "*A lot of the people who work here are quite settled and there aren't loads of single people to go out with.*" The obvious solution is to take up a hobby, maybe join the netball team. Lingering in the fourth division not so long ago, the Cripps ladies are now securely in the second. They recently beat off a challenge from a team of Cripps boys, though we suspect the lads' ignorance as to the rules of the game may have hindered them.

As to what explains the repeated imbalance between male and female trainees at the firm is more complicated. Each year Cripps only manages to recruit one or two lads onto the seven-strong intake, so it sounds as if it's time for the boys to raise their game in the application stakes. In September 2006, all seven of the qualifying trainees accepted positions at the firm.

and finally...

The appeal of Cripps Harries Hall boils down to excellent quality clients and varied work; "*individual attention from people who know who you are;*" and the level of professionalism that one comes to expect of a 175-year-old firm.

Dechert

the facts

Location: London

Number of UK partners/solicitors: 42/82

Total number of trainees: 20

Seats: 6x4 months

Alternative seats: Overseas seats, secondments

Extras: Pro bono – North Kensington Law Centre

In Anglo-American Dechert we have proof that the old adage about leopards not being able to change their spots is just plain wrong.

getting hitched

In the 1990s Titmuss Sainer Dechert and its counterpart across the pond, Dechert Price & Rhoads, were separate law firms, albeit that they were 'going steady'. Their alliance – an engagement almost – led to a full merger in 2000, at which point the English lawyers braced themselves for cultural change. They were pleasantly surprised to receive a gentle nudge rather than a nasty jolt. Six years on and the mid-sized City player *"in general feels more American than it used to,"* with the American influence having been persistent but not negative. As far as our sources were concerned, *"the firm has been building on areas where it can interact with the US but also still caters for UK-based clients."* They also felt *"the London office has maintained its own culture, so for example there is less of a formal hierarchy over here."*

Lest they forget the importance of the other side of the Atlantic, in their first week trainees are sent out to Philadelphia to visit *"the engine room of the firm"* and to meet the new recruits stateside. Our interviewees were enthusiastic about the trip: *"It was great to meet people I now speak to regularly on the phone"* said one seasoned source. Others highlighted its opportune timing for the London intake to *"gel."* Trainees soon find this *"group bonding"* is put to good use on their return

to the UK. The new intake is tasked with deciding among themselves who goes where for the first seat – *"It was surprisingly democratic,"* one source told us. Year in year out, interviewees commend the flexibility of the training scheme at Dechert, putting much of this down to a popular six-seat system. *"It's a great opportunity to experience all aspects of the firm,"* said one. *"I am a real fan,"* another concurred; *"it is a luxury to return to the seats you enjoy."* Dechert trainees have considerable input in the *"tailoring"* of their training contracts. *"I knew where I wanted to qualify so went to seats where I could gain the experience I needed,"* we heard from one, while another explained: *"I had no idea where I would end up so I wanted my training to be as broad as possible."* Training manager (and former College of Law head honcho) Bernard George is *"a bit of a legend"* and is praised for helping trainees *"think about where we are going and understand the firm's business needs."*

hedging your bets

The business needs of this firm are something we ought to stop and consider. More specifically, where does Dechert see itself heading? In the past most trainees applied for the breadth of practice areas open to them. In the heady days of the courtship with all-American Dechert, London trainees received greater exposure to transactional work but niche areas were still perceived as a real strength. Now, financial and corporate seats are becoming less of an exception and more of a rule, with many of the niche departments existing as support functions. *"In the long term this firm sees itself doing far more big-ticket transactions,"* one perceptive source concluded. *"If you look at where they are taking on partners it is clear that corporate and financial services are the departments which are set to grow."*

You may be scratching your head wondering what 'financial services' actually means. Essentially the firm provides general regulatory and structuring advice to investment funds and commodities clients, and specifically advises UK funds on regulatory issues surrounding their US operations. Slightly baffled? We don't blame you. Investment funds aren't part of the syllabus at law school and consequently, like one interviewee, you may find this seat *"very, very scary at first."* However, if you are prepared to embark upon its *"steep learning curve"* you can expect good guidance. *"I had a great supervisor who talked things through and got me very involved,"* confirmed one old hand. Tasks like redrafting an existing prospectus or proofreading an entire document are typical; apparently doing them *"helps you to internalise the information when just reading it might be boring."* Understanding tax issues is key to this work so you may also be advised to do a tax seat if you are interested in qualifying in financial services. Still reading? If so, the phrase 'horses for courses' may spring to mind..

If you are prepared to do give financial services your best shot you could be acting on groundbreaking investments of the future. Dechert is known for its hedge fund expertise and, as these things go, hedge funds are pretty exciting at the moment. In addition to the business pages, hedge funds have also made the headlines on the sports pages lately. Remember all that hype over the bid for Manchester United? Hedge funds were part of the financial structure that enabled Malcolm Glaser to move in on the club. They were also considered in talks to buy out Newcastle United. It's not all football transactions though, and we doubt you'll end up with a complimentary season ticket.

sweet deals

Take it as read that you'll do a corporate seat; no bad thing given that Dechert has tucked some pretty decent deals under its belt. Working hand-in-hand with colleagues in Philadelphia, Paris and Brussels, London corporate lawyers recently represented Philadelphia-based packaging giant Crown Holdings in its $2.4 billion refinancing. There is some decent action going on in real estate too. You may be aware that in the past Dechert London was a big name in the property stakes, particularly in the retail sector. Real estate work hasn't disappeared in the shift towards finance and corporate; many of our sources had done seats in this department where the client list includes Tate & Lyle, Bhs Group, Frogmore Estates and a whole host of property finance lenders.

As Dechert has offices in the US and Europe *"a lot of the work is internationally focused,"* and in addition to the Philadelphia trip, trainees are offered secondments to Belgium and Germany (if they sprechen Deutsch). *"People know that the work in the Brussels office will be EU-focused but going to Munich is more of an unknown quantity."* After a little investigation it turned out to be *"private equity and financial services"* – the result of the office having a not dissimilar orientation to London. Short secondments may also be available to US offices.

If UK litigation is more up your street, how about working in the High Court as an assistant to a judge? A few lucky secondees are given the chance to *"observe all kind of cases and to learn loads in the process."* Trainees who opt for this seat need to be able to speak up for themselves: *"Having a High Court judge ask you what you thought of a case is a bit intimidating at first but you get used to it – they really want you to understand what it is all about."* In the past trainees have also been sent to human rights organisation Liberty, although this has now apparently been *"scrapped,"* doubtless as a result of the firm's steady shift towards transactional work.

In September 2006, eight of the 13 qualifying trainees took jobs at the firm. *"People do stay on here because they feel comfortable,"* asserted one trainee; however, it looks clear to us that if transactional work with a US bent isn't your cup of tea, you might not feel quite so comfortable.

rodent-free zone

As if to drive home the firm's new intentions, Dechert's working environment has also been improved. The firm left its old "tacky" offices near Fleet Street to move opposite Blackfriars Bridge into a shiny new building with *"a very modern design and lots of glass."* True, some trainees reminisced fondly about their old home – *"you could be putting together a data room and suddenly a cute little mouse would appear"* – but overall the new site has won over hearts and minds. *"It's beautiful..."* one interviewee sighed, *"and it has air conditioning."* At the risk of sounding a bit too feng shui, we would even go so far as to say that intra-firm relations appear to have improved as a result of the move. *"Everything is more open than it used to be; we are all on two floors rather than five and you see people wandering around a lot more."* When we pressed this last point further, it transpired that *"the loos are on the other side of the corporate department so you can't help but walk through there."*

To quote Dechert's website, after hours *"you will be encouraged to participate in the firm's many sports and social events. There is something to suit all tastes so no excuses allowed!"* If you had read this and dreaded partaking in compulsory softball tournaments, you'll be relieved to hear that *"there is plenty on offer but no huge pressure to get involved; you are free to do what you want."* Another source agreed: *"There are some sporty people here but it is not an overwhelming culture."* For those more interested in a plain-old pint after work, *"there are plenty of visits to the pub: trainees go for drinks together most Fridays and some of the departments have regular get-togethers."* An annual firm-wide summer party is the social highlight; the last one being held on a Thames riverboat.

When asked what sums up trainees at this firm, our sources replied: *"We are a mixed bunch: some of us are chatty and bubbly whilst others are* more stereotypically English in their reserve." Nothing out of the ordinary then. We'll add here that Dechert has always struck us as a very reasonable employer where staff benefit from an environment where *"there is no strong hierarchy."* *"I can just wander into a partner's room and start chatting,"* one interviewee enthused; *"sometimes I will even put my feet on their desk or perch on a filing cabinet."* Whether or not this is commonplace we can't say, but just in case it's not, can we suggest you save clambering on the furniture until you've found the lie of the land.

and finally...

Perhaps there is no better evidence of the London office's evolution into a US-style operation than a recent announcement about salaries. Trainee pay is climbing, as are NQ pay cheques. Interestingly, those qualifying into the financial services group will receive £10,000 more in their first year than their contemporaries in other groups.

Denton Wilde Sapte

the facts
Location: London, Milton Keynes
Number of UK partners/solicitors: 132/262
Total number of trainees: 63
Seats: 4x6 months
Alternative seats: Overseas seats, secondments
Extras: Pro bono – RCJ CAB, The Prince's Youth Business Trust; language training

Denton Wilde Sapte came into being through the 2000 merger of energy, media and real estate specialists Denton Hall and banking outfit Wilde Sapte. It's since gone from *"traditional blue to funky orange"* in its rebranding and offers trainees a quality City training with an emphasis on finance, energy and real estate.

newly streamlined

Management has been working hard to get this firm back on track after what has been a difficult few years. Troubled Dentons saw a host of partner and staff losses including the biggest ever team walkout – the resignation of 40 media and IP lawyers in 2004 to go to DLA Piper. In early 2005 the current chief exec Howard Morris took the reins, promising to make the changes needed to become more focused and financially robust. The idea was to streamline the firm into sector specialisms and redefine the international footprint. To this end, the firm is now structured into four key industry-facing groups: financial institutions; real estate and retail; energy, transport and infrastructure; and technology, media and telecommunications (TMT).

TMT is rebuilding after its losses and this is most visible on a global scale; Dentons' Dubai office has a new head of TMT and his department accounts for a large percentage of the revenue generated from the Middle East practice. The Dubai and London teams worked together for the investors in Emirates Integrated Telecommunication Company (a vehicle of the Dubai royal family, no less) and lawyers from the global TMT network also advised a consortium bidding for Nigeria's second-largest mobile network. In the UK, Virgin, Nokia, the Office of the Deputy Prime Minister and the Highways Agency continue to keep lawyers busy, and they recently finished a $4 billion IT outsourcing project for the MoD.

A formidable energy practice acts for EDF Energy, RWE, npower and British Energy and is doing well in the renewables, nuclear power and energy-trading sectors. In transport, the firm advised Virgin and Stagecoach on rail franchise bids. In real estate finance, headline deals include the £355 million RBS financing of an investor's acquisition of 91 nursing homes, and the planning, retail and development sections within the real estate division also have much to trumpet.

under african skies

Financial institutions are at the heart of Dentons business and it acts for a number of leading UK, European and global players: Barclays; Citibank; HBoS and National Australia Bank to name but a few. It is respected for its acquisition finance capabilities, plus its expertise in trade finance, asset finance and Islamic finance. In asset finance, the group acted for Barclays Capital on the acquisition of a portfolio of 25 aircraft from Airbus Financial Services, valued at around $900 million. And in social housing finance, lawyers advised Royal Bank of Canada when Local Space and Newham Council formed a partnership to meet homeless and temporary housing needs in London. Over in the corporate department, teams in London and Paris worked together to advise Total when it strategically acquired ExxonMobil's downstream oil and gas assets in 14 African countries.

Which brings us to the firm's international footprint (a detail the trainees mentioned often). Prominent links in the Middle East allow Dentons to take full advantage of the boom in energy and infrastructure work there. The firm has certainly invested heavily in Africa in recent times, securing formal associations with local firms in Botswana, Ghana, Tanzania, Uganda and Zambia. Business from Africa and the Middle East, together with work coming out of the CIS (Russia, Kazakhstan, Uzbekistan), has become extremely important to the firm, particularly since the closure of its Asian and European network.

None of this has escaped the notice of trainees. The assessment of one clever cookie was this: *"The biggest areas of the firm are banking and finance, property and energy. It's a lot more of a focused firm now since all the bad press."* Another went so far as to say: *"We're a banking firm now, we are no longer a media firm."* Others agreed with this synopsis: *"It's different from when people came here for the media work;" "we're strong in technology and telecoms but not really in media anymore."* A trainee's comment that *"it's moving away from what made Dentons different from the rest"* did ring true with others we questioned. One concluded: *"It has become a lot more like the other firms I was looking at. It has lost a bit of its distinction and doesn't have the flexibility you would have had when the TMT work was strong."* A third countered with the comment that *"it's a healthy shift to banking work, and it's very timely."*

While trainees had mixed feelings about the shift in emphasis, they all knew one thing – *"virtually every trainee will do a seat in either real estate or banking or both, as they are the biggest departments and need the most trainee bodies."*

choc full of options

Although the number of trainees has reduced in recent years, seat allocation is still complex. Negotiations sometimes end in a compromise by both trainee and firm (*"which sweetens the blow a bit"*) and there is an opportunity to split some seats. Trainees recommend making the most of whatever seat you find yourself in, pointing out that banking, for example, can take any number of forms. *"There are five different sub-groups,"* one trainee informed us before rattling off the list: asset finance; trade and project finance; corporate lending and reconstruction; financial markets and regulation; and structured finance. In any of these the hours can be taxing and unpredictable, but individual supervisors sound like they are sympathetic. Typical trainee tasks include quite a bit of drafting and sitting in on client meetings, and some of our sources spoke of contributing in an important way to film finance deals and Islamic law-compliant bonds. One trainee's experience of trade finance was *"cocoa beans and*

bizarre jurisdictions I've never heard of;" another drafted post-completion documents for aviation financing. *"There's no faffing about,"* was one trainee's honest assessment.

For real estate, you're going to need to utilise all the people skills you can muster as *"you are really expected to build up a rapport with clients."* This seat enables trainees to work on many smaller matters, which is reportedly *"good for improving client skills and time management." "It's a really good seat to do as a trainee"* summed up one interviewee. The department acts for retailers, developers, house builders, investors, banks and PFI contractors and one of its top deals in the past year was a £365 million sale and leaseback of a portfolio of 91 nursing homes across England, Scotland and Ireland for London & Regional. Recalling time in corporate also brought back happy memories for some of our sources. *"There is a lot of camaraderie with everyone working together and you are an essential part of any transaction,"* said one. But *"you've got to be enthusiastic; if you don't jump in there someone else will and you'll miss out."*

The other seat options are energy and infrastructure; employment and pensions; tax; competition; TMT and dispute resolution.

lunch date

One trainee who was coming up to qualification told us: *"When I started at Dentons there were lots of international opportunities. Then the European network drifted, Asia fell apart..."* This led to disappointment among those trainees who'd chosen the firm for its overseas opportunities. All is not lost though; even with the closure of many of its international offices, *"you do still get opportunities to go abroad,"* be this to one of Dentons' own outposts in Paris, Moscow or Dubai or to an allied firm. *"I've heard a Holland placement is really fun, either in Rotterdam or Amsterdam,"* said one source. Another had spent time in the *"fantasti-*

cally busy" Dubai office tackling mainly projects work. Sadly, African placements don't appear on any trainee itinerary and interested parties for the European and Middle Eastern experiences should be prepared for *"quite a bit of competition."* If overseas isn't for you, there are UK secondments to the offices of energy and banking clients.

We hear that across the firm formal training is *"intense with a lot of material to get through."* Department-specific sessions at the start of each seat are a real help. There were no complaints about the standard (*"they seem to have a large training budget"*), although some people baulked at the sheer amount of training – *"we miss a lot of lunchtimes."*

rumour has it

As a result of the merger in 2000, the firm had been operating out of two offices, one on Chancery Lane and the other in nearby Fleet Place. In 2006 it off-loaded the Chancery Lane premises to fellow orange-branded firm Lewis Silkin. Outsiders assume that this must have been an emotional step to take – Dentons had occupied the office for many years – but our sources only saw the positives of having almost everyone together in Fleet Place. Inside, each department has its own vibe and partners and supervisors are a healthy mixture of *"the old-school and the progressive."* There is reportedly *"no fear factor, no yelling or shouting."*

While the firm *"tends to attract gregarious trainees,"* our sources did not believe the firm looked for a set type. Yet, as the firm steps further into its new plan for the future, we'd suggest that applicants will need to show at least a passing interest in finance and/or real estate or energy. Which brings us on to a less positive story: Dentons has been plagued by relatively low retention rates on qualification in the last couple of years and, after speaking to many trainees whose future careers lay elsewhere, we can tell you that 2006 did not herald a massive turnaround. In the September of 2006, 23 out of 37 qualifiers took jobs at the firm. Of the 37, 32 people applied for jobs and 26 were made offers. It looks as if many of the departees moved elsewhere in order to get jobs in areas they really wanted; even some of those who stayed made compromises about choice of department. One trainee who relatively reluctantly accepted a job in banking said that *"the majority of jobs that came up are in that department and not a lot of trainees fancied doing banking."* Actually we have the full breakdown of where NQs went – banking and finance 34%; corporate 14%; real estate 16%; tax 7%, employment and pensions 7%, dispute resolution 7%; energy and infrastructure 5%; TMT 5%; international 2%.

Socially, *"there's no excuse not to know the people you are working with"* due to an abundance of local bars and some good, firm-wide parties. It's not all boozing and dancing though, *"I just did a 5k run,"* said one trainee, plus there are all the regular sports teams, a choir and *"lots of random things like dragon boat racing and quiz nights."* And don't forget the drama group, recently resurrected, which hired a theatre to put on a performance of Neil Simon's 'Rumours', raising money for charity in the process. Apparently, *"if you want to start a society you only have to ask."*

and finally...

Denton Wilde Sapte has had its problems but with new focus, new business and a growing optimism it is beginning to make its own (good) fortune once again. Put it on the list if you're after broad City training with a balance between overseas and domestic work, but do remember the emphasis on certain types of practice.

Dickinson Dees

the facts
Location: Newcastle-upon-Tyne, Stockton-on-Tees
Number of UK partners/solicitors: 72/123
Total number of trainees: 28
Seats: 4x6 months
Alternative seats: Brussels, secondments

As Northumbrian as small pipes and little laddies dancing for their daddies, Newcastle's Dickinson Dees effortlessly marries two hundred years of history in the region with a very modern ability to mix it on a national level. London law firms don't underestimate this premium regional, so why should you?

it's a stitch up
Dickie Dees doesn't so much have the legal market in the North East sewn up, as nail-gunned to the floor. The sheer weight and breadth of its expertise casts a heavy blanket over pretty much everything from agriculture to corporate finance, employment to charities, energy and natural resources to intellectual property. Indeed, our colleagues on *Chambers UK* rank it in 25 practice areas and pin first-place rosette on 12 departments. However, trainees say: *"There's never any complacency; we take care to be competitive in terms of what we can offer and prices,"* a watchfulness that is wise in a market where *"some of the smaller local firms have been gearing up."* The firm must also guard against bigger rivals: Eversheds' recent theft of its food manufacturing client Kavli after a competitive tender, and a rare senior departure to a Midlands concern, Martineau Johnson, are cases in point. As they say, you win some, you lose some, but at least when it wins, Dickie Dees tends to win quite big. Witness the public sector team securing a role on the £120 million North East schools regeneration programme, or the way the projects group this year beat a plethora of top London and national firms to instructions from Nexus on the £500 million Tyne & Wear Metro upgrade. Bar the odd dropped stitch, it's hard to see the firm losing its pre-eminent position locally, unless it entirely takes its eye off the North East market in a push for work from further afield.

national service
Regional stability has given Dickie Dees the perfect base from which to mount an assault on the national firms and the legal stronghold of London. Armed with the compelling weapon of *"regional fees, but City-standard advice,"* the firm has enlisted big-ticket clients like Sainsbury's, English Partnerships and US chemical group Huntsman, as well as developing longer-term relationships with the likes of transportation giant Arriva, Parkdean Holidays and old friend, car dealer Reg Vardy. Its size allows the firm to operate in several theatres of battle at once, and it continues to thrive in the transport field, this year advising public transport megalith Go-Ahead Group on a successful bid for a £585 franchise to run South East UK railway services. Thameslink Rail, Govia, the London Central Bus Company, Merseyrail Electrics Limited and London General Transport Service also turn to the firm, as do a cavalcade of public sector clients.

The projects team is working closely with Darlington Borough Council as it builds the UK's first 'Education Village' and recently won instructions from a London education authority on its £180 million Building Schools for the Future programme. It also took its first PFI instruction from Barclays Bank on the Bolden Schools project. In short, all the signs are that Dickie Dees is thriving in the long march to national success, trading *"on equal terms with firms like Trowers, Eversheds or Addleshaws."*

Aware of this success, our sources were sufficiently perceptive to note: "*At some point we're going to hit the wall where the 'low regional fees' angle won't be enough anymore.*" Although there are no signs of that happening any time soon, the prospect of "*maybe one day having a permanent London presence,*" together with potential "*implications for our regional-national balance,*" continue to give trainees cause for thought.

car-toon antics

Like a Geordie Wile E. Coyote confronted with the 'Ingenious Bird-Torture Devices' section of the new ACME catalogue, the average Dickie Dees trainee is virtually a-drool at the choice of work on offer to them. Take a deep breath: seats can be taken in any of the 38 practice areas including agriculture and rural affairs, banking and finance, charities, competition law, construction, corporate finance, education, employment, energy, family, financial services, IT, IP, insolvency, licensing, litigation, local government, pensions, planning, private client, real estate, social housing, tax and transport. There are also secondments to clients such as Durham City Council. It's enough to make a trainee mheep-mheep for sheer joy. There is a caveat: trainees are required to take three of their four seats within the coco, litigation and property groupings, each of which is wide in scope.

Some are fortunate enough to make the overnight crossing to Belgium, where a three-month placement with an allied Brussels firm provides an up-close-and-personal experience of EU competition law. Others are blessed with six months in Middlesbrough in the Teesside office (family, commercial litigation, property or corporate seats), which despite not being hotly contested, has its compensations. In this smaller office trainees enjoy "*getting involved with marketing and business development*" as well as the greater responsibility afforded to

them. What's more, the sweetener of a petrol allowance or "*a very plush lease car*" makes the daily 50-minute commute from Tyneside to Wearside more bearable. We hear the firm intends to start recruiting directly into the office in the near future.

toonful harmony

If you're reading this down south and are now giving the frozen north greater consideration than you might previously have thought possible, we salute your intelligence but you'll have to get in line. Several of the current trainees had made the move to Newcastle without knowing much about the place; understandably most recruits have a family or study connection. The advice is this: "*The firm wants trainees who will enjoy their time here and stay on, so you have to be able to see yourself settling in the region.*"

There are parallels to be drawn between this firm and Bristol big daddy Burges Salmon, which has a similar history and a similar strategy for the future. Internally, trainees at each of these successful, established players praise their firm's culture, they find it to be welcoming and believe it is possible to "*shine as an individual.*" It is only when you speak to people on the outside that you hear criticisms of conservatism, starchiness or impersonality. Invariably such criticisms come from those who have opted for smaller, less established firms, sometimes having sampled these larger firms. Perhaps all we need do is remind readers that choosing a law firm has a lot to do with personal preferences, and what's right for one person is wrong for another. The view from within at Dickie Dees is that "*senior members of the firm have retained a personal touch,*" and trainees speak with pride of the contributions they are able to make.

The exact nature of these contributions depends on the character and the specific workload of each department. For example, "*the *stereotypically chest-beating"* corporate department is distinct from *"the more relaxed and informal"* environs of real estate. Most departments allow *"client interviewing and autonomy on smaller jobs"* plus *"learning to think on your feet and research things for yourself so you are prepared to respond to a huge range of queries."* Whether it's *"drafting documents on a £5 million loan facility"* in banking, engaging with *"complex, tax-based problems"* in private client, *"attending tribunals and client development seminars"* in employment, or getting immersed in a niche area like IP, there is plenty of responsibility to be had. What's more, appraisals every three months, combined with continual in-house training, ensure *"you always know how you're doing."* We sense that when trainees reach the end of their contracts they are very aware of the strides they have made. As one put it: *"Getting to the point where something happens, and you know what to do and how to react, has been the biggest high."*

sorted for cheese and fizz

Dickie Dees' main St Anne's office occupies a beautiful spot right on the banks of the Tyne, but it is the firm's newer Trinity Gardens building that had trainees talking this year. Close to Newcastle's law courts, it hosts private client, financial planning and property lawyers and features the standard roof terrace, glass atrium and *"pretty dodgy corporate art"* that are de rigueur for any self-respecting new build. *"The lovely café and excellent staffroom on the top floor"* is both a source of happiness to those now resident in Trinity Gardens and a source of envy to those in St Anne's. In our yearly update to the ongoing saga of the bad coffee in St Anne's we can exclusively reveal that *"the horrible glowing orange machines"* continue to be a poor substitute for kettles and kitchens. We sense this one may run and run.

Which is exactly what the hardy types who signed up to the 'corporate decathlon' have been doing. This endurance test is just one of the many sporting activities it is possible to get involved with: beyond football, cricket or the usual suspects, the *"sponsored walk over Hadrian's Wall with the grad recruitment team, existing and future trainees"* says a lot about the way the firm operates. If your preferred method of kicking back has more to do with boozers than boots there's an ample selection of bars in Newcastle city centre, at the Baltic Mills, or on the waterfront. If the smell of greasepaint does it for you, the social committee always comes up trumps. For a number of years it's organised a Stars in Their Eyes-style talent contest with half a dozen acts and three judges, *"a good cop, a bad cop and a funny one."* Tickets for the event sell out fast, not least because the night encourages *"lots of rude comments and heckling, it was great!"* Last year's winner, Jarvis Cocker, *"was so convincing he performed again at the annual dinner dance!"* Said event is another high point and sees the entire firm packed into St James' Park, *"the only place that will fit us all in."*

With eight of the 11 qualifiers accepting jobs at the firm in September 2006, Dickie Dees isn't getting any smaller. At least two of those who left did so for love beyond the region.

and finally...

A Dickinson Dees training will undoubtedly take you far in the legal profession, but with so much increasingly important work coming in – romance aside – it's generally not the sort of place you move on from. If what you want is a life in the North East, and a sizeable employer with impeccable credentials, this is still your firm.

DLA Piper (UK) LLP

the facts

Location: Birmingham, Leeds, Liverpool, London, Manchester, Sheffield, Scotland

Number of UK partners/solicitors: 324/502

Total number of trainees: 165 (in England)

Seats: 4x6 months

Alternative seats: UK-based secondments

Extras: Pro bono – The Prince's Trust and other regional schemes

DLA Piper may have effectively shed the Rudnick Gray Cary bit of its post US merger name, but little else about the firm is dropping off. International expansion, increased profits, sky-high ambition; can anything stop this legal empire builder?

how to make friends & influence people

Possessed of the resolve of a rottweiler after a bone and the dewy idealism of a young bush baby, DLA Piper got where it is today by gazing with wide-eyed enthusiasm towards a vision of the future no one else could quite credit. *"It certainly doesn't lack ambition,"* one trainee told us in what may qualify as the understatement of the century. Just to fill you in: when most of our interviewees applied four or five years ago, DLA was a national firm with a no-nonsense, can-do attitude reflecting its Sheffield roots. In the interim it has *"become a global organisation,"* expanding via merger and acquisition so that today over 3,100 lawyers located in 22 countries across 59 offices throughout Asia, Europe and the USA are branded with the firm's blue square logo.

Few would have thought such a transformation possible, but DLA's management did. And the DLA Piper blitzkrieg shows no sign of abating. With the US merger maturing nicely, the last year has seen the firm swipe 80 lawyers from Ernst & Young Law's CIS network, giving it offices in St Petersburg, Tbilisi and Kiev while also significantly enhancing its Moscow presence. In Germany it poached a banking and finance team from Luther Menold as part of a plan to swell its 20-strong department to 50 within three years. In Italy a six-lawyer Milan-based public law team joined from Orrick Herrington & Sutcliffe and a TMT partner hopped on board, while across the border in France an M&A specialist signed up in Paris. Having recently snared Denton Wilde Sapte's African practice head and seriously entertaining thoughts of an Australian partner firm, there really does seem no limit to the firm's international ambition. What's more, results say the strategy makes business sense: the Europe, Middle East and Asia corporate group recorded an amazing 70% revenue jump to £83.8 million during the past year and clients like InBev – the world's largest brewer with a presence in 32 countries – recognised DLA Piper's reach by appointing it as one of only two global employment advisers.

In good old blighty things are also looking hot. Luring 40 lawyers from Denton Wilde Sapte's TMT team with the carrot of that international network and the prospect of mining the American connection appears to have borne fruit early. The firm won instruction to The Premier League on its £1.7 billion auction of broadcasting rights in 2006 and assisted a major US communications company in outsourcing all its field operation services across 13 European countries. Having enjoyed a faintly staggering 82% rise in average M&A deal size from £35.5 million to £66 million in 2006, the ambitious London corporate team is reaching for upper mid-tier market work with deals like the recent advice to Alternative Hotel Group on its £745.5 million bid for health club operator De Vere Group. However, the team has yet bigger fish to fry. Aiming its sights firmly on tackling deals around the £2 billion mark in

London, the firm has consequently upped the size of M&A deals it will farm out to other UK offices. All in all it's good news for everyone, not least trainees in the regions.

zeal or no zeal

So, DLA Piper has rampaged across the globe conquering swathes of foreign territories like a latter day legal Attila, but it is widely perceived that the firm has created a series of international associations rather than fully integrated mergers. We put this to trainees. *"That's utterly correct,"* said one, *"... sitting in London or Leeds you don't feel like part of a massive organisation."* It's a forthright perspective, but others agreed that *"there's no real difference in our day-to-day experience... maybe a little involvement with some European offices, but none with the US."* By contrast there were those who drew attention to *"efforts to encourage integration across offices,"* pointing out *"yes, at our lowly trainee level less so, but for partners and associates it's definitely more integrated; there are joint conferences and American lawyers are around a lot."* Some were even more bullish, mentioning *"handling bits of work for US colleagues,"* *"seeing referrals from the States"* and referencing *"the accent factor – you walk past any pod on any floor and you'll hear American voices on the speaker phones."*

Only time will tell which viewpoint is correct. In the meantime, we do get the impression that links between the various DLA Piper strands – certainly dealings with the USA – are developing. The amusingly titled 'Project Unify' is bringing systems into line and the firm is apparently considering moving to a single global accounting model. The ubiquitous DLA Piper branding and its trade mark 'Visions' and 'DLA Way' are being exported as well. Long known as a firm with big ideas and an almost religious fervour for its way of working, trainees are happy to laugh about *"the cult of DLA – it's the best description – it's probably the most vision-oriented firm I can imagine."*

If *"thinking big defines the firm"* then it is an attitude that has a lot to do with CEO Nigel Knowles who, as a driving force behind the firm's rampage, wins universal praise for an ability to *"sweep you along with his energy and charisma."* Knowles has always preached the DLA Way with missionary fervour and has *"been around to all regional offices reinforcing the global brand idea and explaining the plans for the future."* Attend the trainee induction and he'll pop up there too. But for all his vigour, perhaps it is inevitable that, as the firm enlarges and shifts in its focuses, the defined, 'cult-like' and truly distinctive atmosphere of DLA Piper should experience some dilution. Certainly, we observed a strain of disgruntlement that seemed to relate to the growing pains of reaching for bigger and better. *"The firm's aiming for more big work and bigger transactions,"* trainees reflected, *"so people are working longer and longer hours, but the remuneration hasn't gone up."* Others pointed out, with some reason, that *"the angle on choosing DLA Piper used to be 'magic-circle work without magic-circle hours', but that's not so true any more."* One concluded: *"If you came to the regions for a better life, but you've got lower salary and City hours, why wouldn't you go to the City?"* As seemed likely, by the time we went to print the firm had raised its regional and London trainee salaries to compete with (or better) regional and big City rivals, which should calm such monetary anxieties. However, it's also timely to reflect that cultural changes never sit easily with those who have experienced the pre-existing culture.

underneath the arches

Everything we heard in interviews this year reaffirmed the idea that each of DLA Piper's UK offices possesses an individual identity and offers specific experiences. This, coupled with the fact that an international network doesn't currently equate to overseas seats, means for the most part trainees are rooted firmly in one location. Hence, deciding where to go and why is a sensible starting point for any applicant.

In the UK, London "*differs most from the general DLA feel*" and it's not hard to understand why. As one source observed: "*The regional offices have more-defined profiles in their regional business communities and are big fish taking on the best work, whereas we're a smaller fish in the London market.*" Relishing the "*prime location*" of the firm's London Wall offices, the experiences of our sources in the capital were predominantly transactional, although the firm's strong national insolvency practice also makes for "*great restructuring work for major retail banks and insolvency practitioners*" and employment is a popular seat for its "*tribunal work, non-contentious corporate support and heavy client involvement.*" Among their peers elsewhere, the London trainees have a reputation for being "*less personable and cohesive as a group,*" although slightly longer working hours and the demands of London living offer some explanation. Certainly, with regular "*trips to the bars around Smithfields*" meaning that "*sometimes life is too sociable for the good of your liver,*" we won't rush to paint them as hermits.

crane sailing

One of the strongest common features across the offices is a glut of urban regeneration projects. The cities of Liverpool, Leeds, Manchester, Birmingham and Sheffield have all come in for, or are undergoing, hefty makeovers and barely an interview passed without reference to "*cranes everywhere on the horizon*" or "*a real buzz to the city; everything's changing.*" It also goes some way to explaining why the construction, real estate and projects/PFI teams have been performing so well of late, racking up some 29% of domestic income in the past year. Trainees in the Birmingham office told us that it was in these areas – replete with "*set systems and national objectives*" – that they were

most likely to find themselves "*working remotely for associates elsewhere.*" In Brum DLA Piper is located in the heart of "*the transformed city centre*" in a "*fantastic building that is vintage town house from the front and extended in modern fashion to the rear.*" Apparently, Birmingham has forged the "*closest links with London.*"

Geography dictates that "*the northern offices are a bit more cohesive as a group,*" not to mention closer to the firm's origins. As the birthplace of DLA, Sheffield is the "*root and mothership,*" and for trainees everywhere this office "*epitomises the strategy of being regionally strong, concentrating on core business locally and then looking further afield.*" A March 2006 move to "*state-of-the-art*" premises at Peace Gardens has not diluted the "*tell-it-like-it-is personality*" that defines the office, but neither is it immune to the themes of "*progression and development going on in the centre.*" The office has fine healthcare litigation (part of the insurance team) and environmental abilities, and projects, comlit and insolvency seats are all popular, the latter offering "*huge variety, from personal bankruptcy you handle yourself to attending meetings on major cases.*"

The short hop by train means "*Leeds trainees will often go to Sheffield for a joint night out,*" but they're definitely not visiting to gaze in awe at the new building. That's because "*our office in Leeds is by far the most prestigious,*" "*a beautiful glass building right next to the canal behind the railway station.*" Opportunities for socialising and shopping couldn't be better, but DLA Piper trainees aren't exactly taking things easy. Working "*hours of 9am to 7pm, and much longer when busy,*" the payoff comes with what they see as "*work for big well-known clients and the best quality DLA work outside London.*" The trainee who observed how "*the office in Leeds has become more corporatised and lost some of the familial feel of the smaller offices over my two years*" was relishing the change.

north by northwest

Although it *"works very closely"* with the smaller *"more laid-back"* Liverpool office, Manchester DLA Piper shares Leeds' appetite for hard work. The trainees spending time in banking, litigation, real estate and insolvency can expect long hours, though according to one source *"never past 1am."* The lack of all-nighters was perhaps what led sources to describe the office as *"a more-user-friendly version of London; you get to do the good work without the hellish hours."* The banking and corporate departments see *"a lot of flow between the North West offices,"* but life in Liverpool is undoubtedly *"more relaxed."* Generally, trainees work regular hours from 9am to 6pm unless caught up in a deal closure or other pressured activity. With recent deals including advice to Merseytravel on its concession to operate the £32 million Liverpool South Parkway interchange, the office has clearly been busy. The *"clean lines and glass walls"* of its open-plan India Quay premises ensure that *"everyone knows everyone else and there's a lot of banter."*

The number of offices in the UK means generalising is difficult, but trainees agree that *"training is very variable"* and *"depends entirely on who you're sitting with."* Whether they were based north, south, east, west or somewhere in the middle, some of our interviewees had experienced *"pretty poor supervisors and the depressing experience of not being taught,"* as well as supervisors who *"thoroughly go to work on you and give you a great training."* For the most part, formal training sessions make the grade and trainees are glad of the opportunity to meet up as a whole group for PSC elements early in the two years. They readily admit that the appraisal system *"could do with a bit of refinement."* Trainees have no doubt made these points with their office 'trainee co-ordinator', one of their peers whose job it is to *"take problems from us to a meeting every few months with grad recruitment, partners and all the co-ordinators from other offices."*

stick or twist?

What kind of recruit is DLA Piper looking for? Here's what the current trainees think: *"self-starters"* who are *"thick-skinned and self-reliant,"* with the capacity *"to accept you make mistakes at the beginning and learn from them."* The regional offices tend to recruit *"people with strong local connections, whether family or university links,"* but beyond this it's simply a case that *"you shine here if you are ambitious,"* *"outgoing and willing to get involved."* Having lived through interesting times over their two years of training, many of the qualifiers of September 2006 were faced with a difficult decision – take one of the many jobs available or go looking for a position in exactly the right practice area in their preferred city? This year only 52 of the 72 English DLA qualifiers stayed on, a lower proportion than in previous years, reflecting a buoyant NQ market and perhaps also the increasing appeal of the DLA training stamp on their CVs.

and finally...

Unafraid to dream the impossible, DLA Piper offers a robust training and the chance to go places at an expansively minded outfit. Just make sure you can hack the pace and pick the right office.

DMH Stallard

the facts

Location: Brighton, Crawley, London
Number of UK partners/solicitors: 46/48
Total number of trainees: 17
Seats: 4x6 months
Alternative seats: None

In the last 30 years, DMH has transformed itself from a Brighton high street firm to a commercial contender. This is the second largest firm in the South East by turnover (it hit £21.2 million in 2006) with territory extending from the flashing arcade games on Brighton Pier over the illuminated landing strips of Gatwick to the bright lights of London.

want blue chips with that?

DMH started life back in the 1970s when a trio of Sussex firms merged to form Donne Mileham & Haddock. Come the 1990s, the South Coast fish found its pool of clients rather too small and so opened an office in Crawley, near to Gatwick Airport, filleting its name to DMH to signal the start of a new era. Soon finding that business was more plentiful in the heart of what some call the Gatwick Diamond, the firm broadened the scope of its commercial law services and grew in size.

The noughties brought more change. In 2001 DMH merged with a small property and PI firm called Fairbairn Morris and then really cemented its London connections by merging with Stallard Solicitors in 2005. The area most bolstered by this second merger was corporate finance, and since then the DMH Stallard name has grown in stature. For instance, the firm landed the lead role on the £130 million sale of Cinque Ports Leisure to Graphite Capital Management early in 2006, one of the firm's biggest ever deals. With magic circle firm Linklaters on the opposite side, this deal was proof positive of DMH Stallard's ability to swim with the big boys. It has also racked up several placings on the Alternative Investment Market (AIM), which you might regard as the London Stock Exchange's little brother.

capital growth

The DMH-Stallard merger propelled the combined firm into the top 100 UK law firms, as measured by turnover. Behind this success is a wealth of new instructions; for example a coveted place on Southwark Council's panel for employment, general litigation and housing litigation matters at a time when the London borough is going through a multibillion-pound regeneration scheme. The firm also represented objectors to the London Development Agency's compulsory purchase of land in the Lower Lea Valley on the site of the proposed 2012 Olympic Village.

With a third London merger not ruled out, it's fair to ask – is DMH Stallard suffering from an identity crisis? Is it now a regional South East firm with an office in London or a London firm with a presence in the South East? This conundrum occupies trainees' minds to an extent. Some feel that "*the thrust for commercial work is now in London*" and "*there is more of a London emphasis since I joined.*" Others believe "*we are still Brighton-based and are proud of being a regional firm. The merger hasn't changed who we are.*" In short, we conclude that Brighton remains important, partly due to DMH's historical links with the town, partly because it is home to the bulk of the firm's private client work and partly because it still retains certain HQ functions. What Brighton can no longer claim to be is the major earner in the trio of locations, nor the future of the firm.

fender benders and art attacks

DMH Stallard's services can be broken down into six core areas: residential conveyancing and PI; private client; real estate; corporate; dispute resolution and employment. Trainees don't usually have a choice for their first seats but can mix and match pretty much what they want afterwards. The firm is "*very good at slotting you in where they can,*" and while there are no compulsory seats, trainees say you should expect a stint in commercial property. Most trainees move around the offices during their training contract. Having nominated a base office ("*the one closest to your address*") they are paid travel expenses when they work elsewhere. If that office happens to be London they also get a small London weighting.

What's popular then? For starters, "*any seat in Brighton*" as "*they provide a good regional experience in a friendly office.*" Proximity to the beach and the general fabulousness of the town have nothing to do with it (apparently). As well as services for private clients (which extend beyond tax, trusts and probate to include private defence in criminal matters, family law and conveyancing) the Brighton office is a hub for commercial property, property litigation and planning work. For example, last year lawyers helped win planning permission for Brighton & Hove Albion FC's new stadium. Brighton is described as "*the fun office*" where people "*generally do a nine-to-five day, have a good time at lunch and go out for drinks on a regular basis.*" It hosts art evenings for staff, running classes, talks by local artists and gallery trips. Believe it or not, the firm actually has professionally-managed art galleries in both its Brighton and Crawley offices. Then again, so does our illustrious leader, Mr Chambers, so maybe it's not that unusual.

While Brighton offers a whole moon crater of things to do after work, the same, unfortunately, cannot be said of the Crawley office. Work wise it focuses on coco, commercial property, commercial litigation and employment, and two of the most popular seats for trainees – IP and media/technology – are based here. The IP department works for such household names as Fender Musical Instruments and the £1 billion-turnover insurer Amlin Underwriting. Crawley has a very "*hard working*" feel to it and is viewed by some as "*the most efficient office of the firm.*" Trainees tell us they aim for a 9am-5pm day and "*get their heads down and work*" to achieve it. We could be cruel and suggest that this is to escape Crawley at the earliest opportunity. Actually, we will suggest exactly that because several interviewees told us in no uncertain terms that "*people don't like Crawley.*" "*Even the senior partner in the Crawley office doesn't even live in Crawley,*" offered one. Even without much of a social scene after work, the office itself is "*extremely friendly.*"

you decide

Like Crawley, the London office has a strong commercial focus with seats offered in coco, commercial litigation, commercial property and employment. We're told that London "*has a different identity*" to the other offices, but this isn't surprising given the recent merger and its location. The hours on a good day stretch from 9am to 6pm and, unlike in the other two open-plan offices, "*most people tend to share rooms.*" London is also smaller than the other two offices ("*about 50-60 people work there*") and so "*people tend to stick together and go out a lot.*" And when they go out, "*everyone goes out – partners, secretaries and fee earners.*" The venues of choice are "*the Corney & Barrow next door*" and "*quite a few bars in The Minories.*" Unsurprisingly, London postings are quite popular with trainees.

At DMH Stallard "*quite a lot is demanded of you,*" but you are surrounded by supportive colleagues. With the increasing commercial focus of the firm comes the "*expectation that we deliver the same level of service as London firms. We are meant to match their service levels, which can involve working long hours at times.*" Trainees say "*the work we're given is of a high standard*" and that they are "*involved in real files from the off.*" More than this, most claim it is "*a place where you can pitch your ideas as a trainee,*" even if some feel management "*doesn't always listen.*"

Every February there's an AGM, usually held in Brighton. Team-building activities during the day are rounded off with "*a posh meal and dancing in the evening.*" Appreciated by most as an "*opportunity for the management committee to brief you on how the firm has done and what is to come,*" the odd cynic viewed the AGM as "*a promotional tool.*" Well, as they say, you can't please all of the people all of the time, an aphorism which neatly sums up what happened in September 2006 when "*there were jobs for everyone but some people did not get their first choice.*" Consequently, only three of seven qualifiers stayed on. And yet we suspect that DMH Stallard is a firm that tries to please as many people as possible as often as possible. Certainly each year it asks all staff to vote on the nature of the summer party. The voting options in 2006 included a day at the races, a country and western evening and a James Bond themed night in a London bar. For sporty types there are a number of firm-wide and office-centred activities – cricket, football, rowing and more. Additionally, staff are no strangers to charity events, taking part in dragon boat racing and Cancer Research UK's Race for Life.

DMH Stallard tends to attract those who wouldn't say no to the money offered by London firms, but would say no to long City hours. The subject of salaries repeatedly cropped up in our interviews, with trainees telling us they were "*a bit too low for the regions and plain too low for London.*" Maybe they feel this way because they have seen the firm growing in stature with each passing year. In fairness to the firm, many trainees across the Southern Home Counties have issues over pay.

and finally...

Trainees note that the firm "*used to like to recruit people who came from the South East, just to make sure they stay on after they qualify.*" We hear that, as the firm expands, this is becoming a thing of the past, so their message is this: don't let your background stop you from applying.

Dorsey & Whitney LLP

the facts
Location: London, Cambridge
Number of UK partners/solicitors: 12/38
Total number of trainees: 8
Seats: 4x6 months
Alternative seats: Secondments

Pick Dorsey & Whitney and its network of offices spanning North America, Asia and Europe and you may not receive a ticket to the USA but you will get top-quality work across several practice areas and the benefits of a big firm behind you.

coalition of the billing
Where America leads, the UK follows. Think cable TV, Starbucks and the BK Stacker Quad. London may now be overflowing with soy lattes and SUVs, but at Dorsey's Liverpool Street office the accents are (mainly) British and much of the legal business home grown. "*We are definitely seen as part of the US firm but we are slightly separate,*" confirmed one source. The set-up is simple: London lawyers work on both UK business and, together with their counterparts in the USA and elsewhere, cross-border matters. The corporate team (which includes US-trained attorneys) recently worked on the UK aspects of the sale of the $1 billion parts and accessories arm of Dana Corporation, an Ohio-based supplier of vehicle technology. Another transaction requiring their input was the acquisition of Polaroid by Petters Group Worldwide, a Minnesota entity with a strong record in corporate acquisitions and investments.

Perhaps seeking to improve cross-cultural exchange, Dorsey sent US trials group leader Paul Klaas over in 2005 to manage the London office and strengthen the bridge between the countries. Trainees reported "*a bit more American culture creeping in*" (the firm offers training on 'how to sell yourself' and one source mentioned that "*we often call each other attorneys, not lawyers*"), but emphasised that "*ours is very much a UK style of working.*" And socialising too: "*The guys from the US ask us why we go for drinks so often and why we have to go outside the office for birthday celebrations or leaving dos.*"

hot wheels and hi-tech
So what's the draw of a modest-sized US outfit that's been in London since 1981? "*I didn't come to Dorsey because it was a US firm. I just liked them at interview,*" said one trainee. Another told us:

"I'd heard a lot of good things about them and worked opposite them when I was a paralegal at another firm." To give you a quick snapshot, the London office has a good reputation in domestic and cross-border capital markets, M&A and real estate transactions as well as IP, tax and general commercial litigation. More latterly, Indian capital markets work has flourished. Essentially, the office has a nice broad practice profile that is not overly weighted to any one sector and the training contract reflects this. Four six-month seats can be taken in any one of the litigation, corporate, real estate, tax and IP teams plus there's the odd client secondment on offer.

"IP was a big thing for me, and Dorsey is very good in that area," said one source. The firm revs the engine of many a car manufacturer and its IP lawyers advise luxury wheel-spinner Daimler-Chrylser in relation to all trade mark infringements. One trainee did a bit of hands-on research when they *"had to go on a recce to a rival garage to take photos."* It's not just motors; another *"helped to organise a client's affairs over seven or eight jurisdictions. I had daily dealings with overseas attorneys from Europe to Hong Kong."* The IP department also works out of a small Cambridge office, picking up clients from the so-called Silicon Fen hi-tech and biotech business communities. Another source *"preferred property... because it allowed a lot more responsibility."* Here, trainees help negotiate new leases, transfer existing leases, get to grips with different types of leases... *"For me it was pretty much leases, leases, leases really. Plus I had a lot of contact with the Land Registry and local authorities."* The work handled by the team is a combination of pure real estate and assistance to the corporate department on deals such as the Dana matter.

how to outmanoeuvre the tax man

Last year the tax litigation team won a ground-breaking case for Marks & Spencer against the Inland Revenue in the European Court of Justice, finding that UK tax law does not comply with EU regulations. But just as the champagne corks were popping and the implications of the win broadcast, DLA Piper rudely gatecrashed the party by taking four of the seven-strong team that worked on it. *"There was a funny atmosphere around the place... but it didn't really affect trainees too much. I think there is now more of a focus on general commercial litigation,"* one source revealed. The hiring of Taylor Wessing's head of UK commercial disputes to broaden the contentious offering certainly backs up this view. The firm then swiped a Slaughter and May litigation team of three senior associates to redress the balance. We won't say it was a revenge strike, but Dorsey also took a corporate partner from DLA Piper. The increased focus on general commercial litigation, even if born out of necessity, suited one trainee down to the ground: *"I learned about tax and I learnt that I didn't like tax."* They added: *"Actually the firm is good at taking notice of what you like and don't like; they know you will work better at something you are interested in."*

Trainees told us that *"as the office is growing we are looking to put more-formal training structures in place,"* yet wondered whether this was a good thing. In some ways the entire scheme is becoming more regimented: uniform start dates and a more formalised (*"and more scary, I reckon"*) interview process for applicants. In others it is not: feedback is mostly still delivered informally and there is genuine freedom in seat selection. Whether any changes will result in a different kind of Dorsey trainee remains to be seen. Those we spoke to this year fitted well with the firm's permissive ethos: all free-thinking individuals, quite driven, rather pragmatic. They agreed with this assessment, telling us: *"You have to be fairly independent... You are not spoon-fed."* We rather like the sound of the office environment – hard working but loosely regulated. For example: *"You need to find your own way of working; you need to decide whether you like* music on in the background, things like that." They admit the learning curve is steep, one telling us: "*I was talking to a friend at another firm about what I'd done and they asked, 'Did you do that on your own? Not with an associate?' They didn't believe me when I said I'd handled it myself.*"

back to the drawing board

A bit like the star cheerleader having a squad of people to catch them after an aerial somersault, "*all the trainees are willing to jump in and help out if you have a lot of work and they don't.*" There is also support from partners and supervisors: "*The guy I'm sharing an office with is fantastic; he'll answer any questions and he has a big whiteboard he draws diagrams on for me.*" Whether you share an office depends on the department. Said one interviewee: "*I have my own office now which is nice, but you learn more if you are in with some-one.*" There was a clear consensus that the small size of the office is a big plus for a trainee. "*If you do your work well news quickly gets round. You can build up a good reputation and when you move departments you are not suddenly going to people you have never seen before.*" Furthermore, "*a lot of people don't see you as a trainee, they see you as a junior lawyer and they use you as such.*" Trainees are also allowed to participate in important client marketing activities.

In 2006 the trainee group certainly had varied backgrounds: different ages, further study, work experience, life experience and all things in between. Perhaps because of this, their social life does not follow the usual twenty-something, bars-and-beers routine found at some of the bigger firms. "*People do things together, but it is not necessarily the case that everyone goes to the same pub every Friday night.*" The trainees are not standoffish as such, just more self-contained, happy to do their own thing. "*We get on with each other without feeling the pressure to be always out with each other,*" explained one.

The only negative point to make about the Dorsey experience is connected with the idea that a number of US firms have been slow to promote English-qualified partners in London. It is suggested that this, in turn, has been the cause of associate losses. Our trainee sources were not unduly fazed by the issue, telling us: "*It could be years away when partnership happens, and by then the climate may have changed dra-matically.*" "*Things are looking up at Dorsey. There's a good chance if I stay here and make the grade I could be made up to partner. They've brought a lot of new people in, so they'll have to do it sometime.*" Ready to test the theory, in 2006, three of the four qualifying trainees accepted positions at the firm.

and finally...

Trainees at Dorsey & Whitney seem like self-reliant sorts who take pleasure in their relative independence. Not a firm for anyone who needs handholding, this lesser-known choice is defi-nitely an interesting one for students seeking an out-of-crowd experience.

Dundas & Wilson

the facts

Location: London, Edinburgh, Glasgow
Number of UK partners/solicitors: 74/181
Total number of trainees: 6 (in London)
Seats: 4x6 months
Alternative seats: Edinburgh, Glasgow

Dundas & Wilson dominates Scotland's premier league of law firms and wipes the floor with almost all rivals across almost all areas of com-mercial practice north of the border. Not so long ago it famously beat magic circle firm Freshfields to a major instruction on a £630 million property trust.

london calling

No one pretends that D&W's London office, which has been open since 2002, is anywhere near as successful as its operations in Glasgow and Edinburgh. What is true is that as the Scots lawyers' work has become more national – and international – the importance of a good London office has become crucial. What we now see in London is a strengthening of capacity in key areas such as construction and projects, private equity and employment through a hiring spree. In the past couple of years senior lawyers and partners have been drafted in from the likes of Hammonds, Pinsent Masons, SJ Berwin and CMS Cameron McKenna. *"When I first started we were on one floor of Bush House on the Aldwych; now we are on three,"* confirmed one trainee. Another referred to D&W as *"an appealing prospect for a junior lawyer in London – there is a real buzz here."* Trainees predict further developments as the firm's *"strong desire for growth"* is *"not cooling off."* One declared: *"We are not going for world domination but there is no end in sight."* Expansion in the capital has certainly contributed to healthy financial results in the last year, with both revenue and partner profits jumping by an impressive 20%.

cooking on gas

Most of the trainees we spoke to had undertaken a seat in property, which is one of D&W's several strong suits. Time spent in this *"very young department"* is deemed *"good for you"* because, not to beat about the bush, it is *"bloody hard work."* Trainees take on *"a huge workload and a huge amount of responsibility,"* dealing with clients directly and juggling their own caseloads. This means *"lease drafting, licences, research, replies to enquiries"* and ample opportunities to *"get involved in the negotiations."* Expect more of a support role on large matters; this is when *"you realise the importance of being organised as your own deadlines have to fall in line with those of the*

bigger deals." Among the £10 billion worth of transactions completed by the London real estate lawyers are National Grid's sale of the 75-acre Southall gas works site and its proposed development of the 50-acre Beckton gas works in the Thames Gateway area. If you tackle property before any other seat then *"after that, everything seems quite easy."*

In a construction seat you will *"really get your teeth into things;"* drafting collateral warranties and appointment agreements for private developments as well as PFI/PPP projects, many of which will involve working hand in hand with the Scottish lawyers. One trainee who had formed negative opinions in advance of the seat was forced to address their prejudices after a *"pleasant surprise."* *"It was interesting"* and the *"people you work with are great fun,"* they admitted. Much of their satisfaction came from *"feeling part of a team, working well together and going out together."* Invites to swanky client events *"show they are proud of their trainees,"* and trainees soon learn that holding your own at these gigs is a skill in itself. The team's flagship work has included the recent redevelopment of 55 Baker Street, the former Marks & Spencer HQ and a dispute relating to the Dublin Port Tunnel, the largest infrastructure project ever undertaken in Ireland. All up, trainees get to *"dabble in all sorts of things, getting an idea of real-life problems and issues."*

Corporate cats are catered for with *"AIM listings and big share acquisitions."* While trainees are typically to be found carrying out due diligence, data room management and company secretarial duties, as the team interacts with all other departments, corporate seats do at least allow them to gain insight into how the firm works as a whole. If you like corporate, the banking practice may also appeal. *"Growing very quickly,"* it is staffed by *"a fresh team with drive, enthusiasm and lots of ideas."* The developing employment practice is also recommended by trainees. Across the seats, *"the official line is that trainees shouldn't be doing crap admin-type work..." "that said, there are elements of proof-reading and other things that are a pain."*

difference is good

Some words of warning for readers of a contentious disposition: *"If you want to do heavyweight litigation then don't go to D&W in London."* There certainly are contentious experiences available in the construction, employment and property litigation seats but, as things stand, D&W's London office has clear transactional and advisory leanings. Of course, current growth plans could change this.

We detected no long-hours culture, and this had come as a pleasant surprise to trainees who told us that *"if you are around at past half-six or 7pm it is considered to be quite a late night."* Indeed, there's a general feeling that trainees are well looked after, with extra days holiday, a bonus and pension payments being introduced in recent times. Our sources spoke of a support environment where *"everyone makes time for you"* and *"offers to chat through"* any issues as they arise. *"Training is taken very seriously,"* we were told, and *"we are always invited to sessions."* Away from the seminar room, *"we are an integral part of the team, known by everyone and relied upon heavily."* It sounds like you shouldn't have much to complain about but if you did want to voice some thoughts on how your contract is progressing then regular performance reviews are the perfect forum. Competency is assessed under various headings and addresses all the usual things such as communication, analytical skills and legal drafting. Although *"done well,"* the thoroughness of the assessments can be *"a bit of a pain as they take time and are another layer of admin."*

Apart from good academics, *"there is no checklist"* for recruits, and people are *"respected for being themselves – difference is good."* We're told this approach has ensured the presence of *"some*

characters," though not along the lines of *The Fast Show's* office joker Colin Hunt. Overall the London office is *"slightly more laid back"* than its Scottish parent, and this comes across in little things like the dress code, for example – in the summer *"no ties for the boys"* and *"flip flops for the girls"* are quite acceptable. Similarly, our sources confirmed that the open-plan working environment is *"not highly regimented or formal"* and that it is perfectly possible for a trainee to sit right next to a senior-level partner.

highland flings

That D&W subscribes to the 'three offices, one firm' view is clear from the exchange of personnel between London, Glasgow and Edinburgh. The entire trainee intake is treated to an induction course in Edinburgh and Glasgow, which allows the London recruits *"to see the firm as a whole and liaise with people in Scotland."* The London trainees then get to work with their Scottish counterparts when they come down to the big smoke for six-month secondments in the capital. London trainees are also encouraged to spend time in either Edinburgh or Glasgow, and those who take up the offer find that things couldn't be made any easier. The firm sorts out some digs, pays your rent and council tax and bungs in a £500 travel kitty. Keep it for yourself if you fancy flying business class; share it with your friends and family if you're happy to slum it on National Express. Best of all you'll still be paid your London salary, so you'll be one of the most flush trainee solicitors north of the border.

Out of hours, D&W *"makes a real effort to get everybody together."* Expect *"drinks do's every week"* in aid of... well, *"any excuse for drinks."* Every year the entire firm is invited to a May ball, which means the whole of the London office jets up to either Edinburgh or Glasgow and is *"put up in a nice hotel for the knees up."* Trainees were bowled over by the venues the firm has chosen in the past – The Prestonfield Hotel in Edinburgh, for example, has been described in the national press as "beyond swank" – and the firm pulls out all the stops... "*black tie, string quartet,*" that kind of thing. The London office has a pretty full-on Christmas party at which trainees put on a show with sketches "*sending up the firm and the idiosyncrasies of its main characters.*" Some people "*get terribly worried and nervous about it but there is always raucous laughter,*" though our sources "*weren't sure whether they were laughing with us or at us.*" We say, who cares? On a more regular basis, after-work fun includes treasure hunts around nearby Covent Garden, pub quizzes, boat trips, barbecues and bowling nights; all courtesy of a social committee that takes its job very seriously.

and finally...

Eager to attach themselves to an organisation that describes itself as "*a forward-thinking and vibrant firm,*" in 2006 the three September qualifiers all accepted job offers from D&W. It is the 'forward-thinking' bit of this label that is key, because the task ahead for D&W is to make an impact in the London market and become more than a supporting limb for the Scottish offices. Its success will depend on who it manages to recruit at senior level and how well it can use its sterling reputation in Scotland to develop new business in the capital.

DWF

the facts

Location: Liverpool, Manchester
Number of UK partners/solicitors: 69/135
Total number of trainees: 21
Seats: 4x4 + 1x8 months
Alternative seats: None

Twenty-one-year-old DWF is one of the North West's strongest commercial firms. Having doubled in size since the new millennium, it has come

a long way from its insurance litigation roots and now offers a broad training in its Liverpool and Manchester offices.

all brand new

DWF celebrated its coming of age in 2005 by launching a brand new image. Cue a trendy logo, snappy strap line, new values and a revamped website. For trainees it's all "*just a bit trendier and seems a bit more professional.*" As for the firm's new values, one source confessed sheepishly: "*I couldn't tell you what the values are off the top of my head but I know I should.*" The rebrand was quickly followed a restructuring at the top and the appointment of new managing partner Andrew Leaitherland, described by one source as "*a 36-year-old whizz kid.*" He has already impressed trainees with monthly reports that make "*a really good read*" as they contain "*stuff you might not otherwise know as a trainee.*" Whatever else these changes mean, at least the football team is happy: "*Improving the firm's profile in the North West is part of a whole change in business development, so we've got new, branded kit.*"

musical chairs

Here's how the scheme works: trainees apply to either Manchester or Liverpool as there is no tradition of moving between the two, probably because the same seat options are available at each. The firm's make-up ensures a high probability of seats in insurance litigation, corporate, commercial property and commercial litigation, with other possibilities including banking and asset finance, health and safety, IP, employment, construction, pensions, planning and insolvency and business recovery.

The seat pattern is a slightly unusual four seats of four months followed by an eight-month running jump into the trainee's intended qualification department. The early short seats are popular for the usual reasons: they are "*long enough to give you a flavour"* but over in good time if the department is not for you. It can be frustrating to move on when *"you've just got to grips"* with it all but at least there's a chance to return for your final seat. That's the theory; in practice things don't necessarily go so smoothly and we heard mixed reports about seat allocation from our sources. Trainees understand that the eight-month seat in the second year has a knock-on effect for the allocation of other seats; because *"there's not much space for movement"* some first years are left *"less than overwhelmed"* with their lot. Top of the grumbles list are short notice before switching departments and repeated disappointment following a failure to get a preferred seat. So how does the firm respond to these moans? Well it seems HR has been listening and we're told the system has recently *"really improved"* to the extent that even first years believe *"our requests don't go ignored."*

Having started out as an insurance litigation firm, DWF has not bitten the hand that has fed it for more than two decades. This insurance division still generates a lot of revenue and no one is likely to emerge from their training without spending at least four months there. Defending insurers on personal injury claims is the main activity of the teams in both Manchester and Liverpool, but interestingly the firm has also grown a claimant division where the work is *"nearly all car accidents and some debt recovery."* A professional indemnity team in the main deals with solicitors' botches. PI seats require trainees to get their heads down for *"lots of process work"* and *"wading through medical reports."* These activities are balanced out by the many opportunities to attend court hearings, especially when sitting with the claimant team. The Manchester office's in-house barrister has a strong fan base among trainees whose ears prick up when he tours the offices announcing: *"I've got a hearing in half and hour, who wants to come?"* With the courts just across

the road, it's easy enough to take him up on the offer. Trainees can also expect to make a few simple court appearances solo. From what we can gather, with insurance litigation *"people come down on very definite sides of the fence:"* they either love it or they hate it. Admittedly none of our sources were wildly enthusiastic about insurance lit, telling us they were put off by *"the whole idea of a claims culture"* and the sometimes *"monotonous"* nature of the work. Maybe their heads were turned by the other seats on offer...

from cooking oil to motor oil

Commercial property provides *"lots of client contact combined with plenty of legal research."* *"It's always busy"* and trainees can make a rapid progression from *"scheduling and registering deeds"* to handling smaller deals such as lease assignments. The growing team is now breaking into residential development and is involved in chunky regional work for major names like St Modwen Properties. A seat in corporate can entail some long hours (*"I had one all-nighter for a completion"*) but also allows the trainee to get stuck into M&A transactions, partnership issues and IPOs. Princes is one of several food producers on the firm's books and the corporate team recently helped this client acquire Unilever Best Food's edible oil business. As for other big-bucks deals, they advised on the £30 million sale of car dealer Smith Knight Fay to European Motor Holdings.

Banking and asset finance seats attracted plenty of praise from our sources, one saying it's a seat where trainees can *"grab responsibility"* from the start. Well-known lenders (Bank of Scotland, RBS, Lloyds TSB, Yorkshire Bank, Skipton Building Society) are the main clients and an average day will involve liaising with one or more of them. A commercial seat in Liverpool will expose the trainee to a smattering of competition law and IP in addition to bread-and-butter contractual advice to clients on terms and conditions or other ongoing business issues. Much of this seat's popularity can be laid at the door of supervising partner Laurence Pritchard who *"handles a bit of everything."* Recent IP highlights include advising Burton Foods on the Jammie Dodger trade mark, so think about that next time you're dunking one in your tea. Land in employment and there will be plenty of opportunity to mix contentious and non-contentious experiences. Education, food and automotive clients account for much of the business but 20% of DWF's employment work derives from its place on the panels of DAS and Allianz Cornhill, two large legal expenses insurers. *"Drafting contracts, amending precedents and finding out what clients want"* is all in a day's work, with the real excitement coming from attending tribunals and *"negotiating damages with the other side."*

not so puzzling

If our interviewees are to be believed, *"DWF people are DWF people regardless of which office they are in."* So what is the DWF type? The recruitment brochure shows a faceless man slotting his head into a jigsaw piece, presumably to convey the idea that DWF wants trainees who will 'fit'. Frankly we can't imagine anyone finding this image particularly helpful, and interestingly our interviewees indicated that the trainee population comprised *"very different personalities."* There does seem to be some things holding them together though – a *"sociable"* nature and *"a lack of arrogance"* for starters. Furthermore, all but a few trainees are *"from Manchester, Liverpool or somewhere in between"* and had *"family, university or work-related"* links to the region before starting at the firm.

We note less cross-office interaction at trainee level than at some regional rivals. After a joint induction and a bit of bonding on the PSC, communication between the recruits at the two

offices dwindles to *"sending quick e-mails to people in the same seat as you at the other office."* In short, *"everyone gets too busy"* and arranging joint socials is just too much like hard work. Choosing between Manchester and Liverpool isn't just about deciding between rival cities, accents or football teams; it's about picking very different offices. In contrast to Manchester's recently refurbished open-plan set-up, Liverpool staff occupy an older building that *"feels like a labyrinth in the first few weeks."* What it does have is *"character,"* and the separate rooms *"work well for trainees because you can sit with your supervisor."* This may be a moot point as we hear rumours of a move to new open-plan premises.

Each year almost all qualifying trainees stay with the firm and in September 2006, six of the seven did so. *"The fact retention rates are high shows that the firm wants to invest in you,"* we were told. Unsurprisingly, there is an element of jostling for the most sought-after NQ positions, and in such circumstances this may prompt a transfer between offices. Whatever the problem, our sources have faith that the training principal *"will go out to bat"* for them.

picked for the team

It's hard to pin down the Manchester trainees on a Friday night as they have so many watering holes to choose from. Over in Liverpool trainees' habits are more predictable: wander into The Living Room and they will be there. Liverpool also seems to have the edge when it comes to DWF events as an active social committee organises an endless stream of things from wine tasting to trips to Chester Zoo and the dog track. Drinks in the boardroom never fail to please and are organised for even the most spurious of reasons. In both offices we heard a fair amount about the efforts of the Young Professionals groups whose mission is to help DWF youngsters mix with clients and other young professionals. The things they organise provide a welcome contrast to the *"grown-up events where partners and associates already know each other."*

In two of the most football-crazy cities in the country it was only right that we asked about sport, and we're glad we did. Trainees told us that the firm's recent rebranding has given a new lease of life to the sporting side of the firm and that new strips and funding for training and tournaments means DWF is back on the *"footy and sports radar"* after years of *"no support from above for that sort of thing."* Glad to hear it. Come on you reds... and blues.

and finally...

If you have a genuine commitment to this part of the country and you want to develop a commercial career at a firm that's intent on securing a bigger share of the increasingly heated North West legal market, it's a good firm to try for. It is neither weighed down by history nor managed from outside the region, and for many readers these factors alone will steer them in DWF's direction.

The Endeavour Partnership

the facts
Location: Stockton-on-Tees
Number of UK partners/solicitors: 9/7
Total number of trainees: 4
Seats: 4x6 months
Alternative seats: None

The Endeavour Partnership turns out small but perfectly formed deals for a raft of regional clients. Trainees with an interest in a career on Teesside should give this niche firm close inspection.

teesside: the comeback kid
From its heyday in heavy industry, through massive job losses and decline, the North East is bouncing back. Teesside has been renamed as the Tees Valley and even Middlesbrough FC, which fell to Division Three and liquidation in the 1980s, has returned to the Premiership. No one doubts there is still a way to go (in football as well as business – the team was on the wrong side of a 4-0 thrashing in the UEFA Cup this year), but it is on the right track. Further north, Newcastle has seen the good times roll for a few years now and has a number of strong law firms. There are fewer concentrating primarily on the Tees Valley, hence The Endeavour Partnership's decision to set up in business. It was founded in 1999 by four partners from Middlesbrough firm Punch Robson. Two more joined from Eversheds after that firm closed its Teesside office. Endeavour now has nine partners, with the most recent addition pitching up in 2006. It is not alone, however; Newcastle giant Dickinson Dees also chose to open an office in Stockton-on-Tees.

The Tees Valley pioneers are now neighbours on the Teesdale Business Park. This regenerated space was the site of Margaret Thatcher's 'walk in the wilderness' in 1987 when, after around 10,000 job losses in the area and the site just an abandoned wasteland, the Iron Lady thought it was time to put something back. The park's businesses now employ more people and contribute more to the economy than in the days when a vast engineering works dominated the site. It is home to some household name businesses, among them Abbey, Barclaycard and Churchill Insurance. Call centres, you ask? Sounds like it.

Endeavour's main concern is the representation of businesses based in the Tees Valley, although it doesn't turn its nose up at clients from Newcastle, Gateshead or further afield. As an example, the firm played a key role in securing the future of the £53 million ship Resolution, a Teesside-based vessel and the only one in the world developed to build offshore wind farms. The ship was owned by a Middlesbrough company and the team pulled off some nifty manoeuvres to allow it to sign a joint venture with a Dutch shipping group. When a courier failed to arrive on time, trainees and other staff got to experience the eleventh-hour drama first hand, helping to fly documents from Holland to Manchester and the Isle of Man. The deal involved aspects of shipping law, tax and commercial contracts and was indicative of the firm's preferred style of working – drawing together expertise from across its departments.

foursquare

If like our sources you have an aversion to high street practice and want your training to be purely commercial, you'll be pleased to learn that there's not a private client to be found on the firm's books. *"I knew the area so had a good idea of their business, and they're the biggest firm around here. I knew I wanted to work there,"* explained one source. The seat rotation is simple: *"You can't request things; it is all mapped out at the start."* Working to a fixed plan isn't necessarily a bad thing: *"You get a really good idea of what the firm and each department is like by the end and the structure helps your progression. It's very straightforward."* Trainees start in employment or litigation and then move on to property and coco, ending up in whichever seat they didn't do at the beginning.

Litigation encompasses a variety of work ranging from contractual claims to more complex commercial matters and construction disputes. *"You start off assisting on quite small tasks for partners and assistants, then move on to drafting skeleton arguments and get more involved in matters."* Employment means a bit of executive severance, a soupçon of restrictive covenants, some discrimination and a few redundancies. One trainee *"started off with a lot of contract work then became more active on disputes,"* ending up with a couple of unfair dismissal and constructive dismissal claims to look after by themselves.

Of course, property is the best seat for having your own files. *"The big difference in this seat was*

the level of responsibility," concluded one interviewee. Sometimes you will be working alongside the commercial team, at other points working for large companies undergoing a restructuring. There are also some residential matters to deal with as the firm represents some developers. *"There is a large development in Scarborough going on at the moment,"* one trainee told us. *"Development is pretty strong across the region generally."*

With four partners and three solicitors, coco is the biggest department in the firm and is understandably seen as the *"premier group."* It handles all the usual acquisitions and disposals, MBOs and joint ventures, and often works on transactions supported by venture capital. The recruitment of a partner specialising in IP/IT work looks to be an interesting development for the firm. In terms of hours, one source told us: *"I was warned to say goodbye to my social life, but for the most part it was okay."*

Trainees firmly believed that *"in general, the structure of the training is very good."* In most departments there are meetings every week to review their progress and work out what supervisors can give next. Two appraisals per seat ensure that *"if there are issues we can easily sort them out."* The open-plan office is ideally suited to trainees – *"If I have a quick query I just turn around and ask."* We hear the firm is thinking of getting wi-fi to cut out the need for phones and computer cables. *"They're not necessarily at the edge of technology, but they like to keep near enough to the edge,"* said one trainee.

handy locals

Trainees looking at this region will know the benefits of locating here. You may not be able to buy a whole street for £35K and have change left over for a bag of chips anymore, but the cost of living is very reasonable. Other advantages to arriving at Endeavour's door were revealed by trainees keen to emphasise that *"because it is a small firm and everyone knows each other you get to the stage where you can be yourself with people. You don't* have to go around impressing people for the sake of it." Our sources indicate that though staff work hard, "come 5.30pm, you realise the office is half empty, apart from a few partners."

As people generally drive to and from work, the social scene is a little less boozy than in city centre firms. That doesn't mean it's all work, work, work. "The firm encourages people to get to know each other outside the office, and there is a handy local. If people are going you'll get word of it and be included." A Christmas party and summer barbecue plus informal joining/leaving/birthday celebrations all serve to bring the staff together. The firm also displays a healthy sense of civic responsibility and a couple of years back struck a deal with the NSPCC to donate funds out of its profits. Staff get involved in all sorts of charitable activities, among them a sponsored weight loss challenge that raised money for the Asian tsunami appeal. Imagine the collective guilt at elevenses.

On the small matter of qualification and trainee retention, 2006 was a bad year for Endeavour as the two qualifiers both returned to their respective home regions at the end of their contracts. In light of this we wondered about the firm's attitude to candidates from outside the region. The view of trainees was that "generally the firm prefers to take on people in the locality for more security after the training contract." The firm as much as said this, but it also knows that it has recruited some good trainees from outside the area. Beyond the right accent and local knowledge other preferred qualities include "a sense of humour, willingness and enthusiasm."

and finally...
With its unstinting graft for regional clients and a supportive training environment, The Endeavour Partnership provides a compact base for a small number of commercially minded trainees. The plan is to grow the firm slowly, so expect to hear more from the Tees Valley in the future.

Eversheds LLP

the facts
Location: Leeds, Manchester, Newcastle, Birmingham, Nottingham, Cardiff, London, Cambridge, Ipswich, Norwich
Number of UK partners/solicitors: 318/911
Total number of trainees: 173
Seats: 4x6 months
Alternative seats: Overseas seats, secondments
Extras: Pro bono – various projects, eg Mary Ward Centre; language training

With ten offices in the UK and a name that is increasingly heard beyond these shores, Eversheds packs the whole kit and caboodle into one of the country's largest private practices.

variety as standard
Eversheds has forged its own path since the 1980s when it spied the benefits of an integrated legal network and set out to build one. It identified strong regional firms from Cardiff to Newcastle and brought them into the Eversheds fold. With around 60 first-tier rankings from our parent publication Chambers UK, it must be judged a resounding success. The firm has a knack of mixing stand-alone legal advice with volume-based services to mid-tier and major corporates, public sector organisations and leading financial institutions.

While Eversheds trainees were at pains to point out "we are not all identical and we are not all clones," it is fair to say the music the firm makes is more 'one voice' than experimental. Each office is physically separate, with the idea being that each contributes to the success of national practice groups. The country is sliced into Eversheds North, which contains Leeds, Manchester and Newcastle; Eversheds Central made up of Birmingham, Nottingham and Cardiff; and Eversheds London and South East, a group that brings together Cambridge, Ipswich and Norwich with the capital.

Despite standardisation, it shouldn't be assumed that there is an off-the-peg Eversheds experience to be picked up at each office. Modest but significant differences arise from the firm's strategy not to offer a full service out of every single office. The 'centres of excellence' approach has also meant many offices no longer service a predominantly regional client base, although in places local clients are still important to the firm and trainees had good experiences dealing with them. Big clients come to Eversheds knowing their needs will be taken care of from wherever is most appropriate and cost-effective.

The legal goliath knows a thing or two about keeping its trainees happy. Right from the start of their dealings with the firm, students were impressed by Eversheds' lively presentations; *"the recruiters seemed more open to being questioned, more willing to give information."* The typical trainee seeks out the firm for its status in the region they are interested in, while Londoners spoke of *"just feeling right about the place."* In all cases, notions of work-life balance are a deciding factor; however, *"given the size of the firm and the size of the clients, there are times when you are expected to work really hard. But we all chip in and get it sorted and then there'll be a bit of a breather where we can recharge our batteries."* The key message here is that: *"Eversheds is not a soft touch."* In the North, one trainee nodded in agreement: *"This is Eversheds; you are never going to be walking out of the door at 5pm."* We didn't expect to have to take them quite so literally, but we have since found out the contracted hours are 9am to 5.05pm, apart from Friday, when the official end of the working week is 4.40pm. Do the maths and you'll see what those extra five minutes are for...

eversheds4u

Up in Leeds, Manchester and Newcastle, training contracts now follow the standard four six-month seats on offer everywhere else in the network. A property seat, a commercial or corporate seat and a litigation seat are on the cards for all, *"so when it comes down to it, you only have the chance to choose one seat outright for yourself. Some people are a little frustrated by that, but I guess it does let you experience a spread of areas."* Trainees should also expect to receive work from a wide range of people in whatever department they sit.

One place where trainees take on a great deal of responsibility is the real estate department, not just in the North but across the network. This area is *"expanding fast and furious"* and is a haven of quality work. Work comes in from all over the country; key deals including the mixed-use redevelopment of Lewisham town centre, the acquisition of the ITN building in London and over two million sq ft of retail development throughout England and Wales. Contrary to a prevalent trainee view that property *"is never the most popular seat,"* on the whole Eversheds trainees loved it. Looking at another core area, the Manchester office has been *"aiming at the bigger fish,"* leading its corporate team to hit the headlines after being selected to advise on the auction of mobile phone retailer The Caudwell Group. This is, trainees told us, the *"largest deal outside the Square Mile, ever,"* as billionaire owner John Caudwell is to sell the entire business, which includes high street chain Phones4U. Due to the high value of many of the deals, much of a trainee's work in the corporate department relates to document management but our sources confirmed that they were also able to push for more autonomous roles on smaller deals.

The Newcastle office is a good example of a 'centre of excellence' in that here there is a large team defending clinical negligence claims for the NHS Litigation Authority. Over in Leeds there is a crack planning team, which has been appointed to work on the Olympic site in London. Trainees sitting here handle a lot of compulsory purchase orders.

the middle ground

The close-knit Nottingham and Birmingham offices have a lot of time for each other and operate almost as one unit. The Midlands trainees are used to spending time in each other's offices, completing one-off tasks or secondments, but with Cardiff *"it's a question of geography. Birmingham and Nottingham get on so well together, we are often the forgotten office."* It was interesting to hear this because Eversheds Cardiff is a very successful office that easily recruits ambitious, talented trainees. Said one Welsh source: *"We are absolutely the best place to be if you are in Wales or have connections to the region. We are seen as the best law firm in Wales by far."* In Cardiff, as well as major work in such fields as banking and finance, employment, construction and energy, there is a Legal Systems Group handling volume claims management for insurers and financial institutions. Although a seat in this last group is not always seen as especially interesting, it does allow trainees to measure their own progression. *"I started off doing claims handling,"* explained one source, *"but that was swiftly put to one side as I developed the litigation side of the work."*

Midlands litigation is on the up, according to trainees who had spent time in these seats, and work often gets referred there from London. In all areas of practice *"we're a good centre, geographically, to handle national matters for national clients."* Trainees said the arrangement between the firm and several FTSE 100 companies was a stroke of luck for them and that things were busy. *"If the work is there, the hours are there, and the work is definitely there,"* reported one source.

capital building

In East Anglia, the famed big skies have been a little dark of late. In Norwich the corporate team moved en masse to local rival Mills & Reeve and the Cambridge office recently waved goodbye to its IP team. In Ipswich, work is limited to projects and construction. The net effect of the absence of core departments from all offices is that recruits in East Anglia move around offices during their training. The three offices have, like others, made a play for national work. As one source explained: *"We still have some clients that are regional but this is increasingly less common. Most clients are from London or round that area; however, we want to retain the regional ones too – we want to have a mix."*

Trainees signing on in this part of the country can *"say initially what seat you would like and where you want to be. You won't always get it, though most of my year got the location they wanted."* Cambridge looks to be the dominant office offering the widest range of seats. Our sources reported spending a fair amount of time in London, which brings us on to the capital and its relationship to the East Anglian offices. The London office is expanding, especially in corporate and banking, which is all to the good, trainees said, but *"people in the East Anglia offices get a bit fed up hearing about it all the time. We came here to be in regional offices and after we lost the Norwich corporate team we wanted to hear more about how we are going to expand in East Anglia."* One wonders if they will be disappointed.

Eversheds London is aiming for a meaty 100% increase in turnover in the next five years, and is presently ramping up in the private equity, banking, media and real estate sectors as it aims to compete at a higher level. One London trainee's opinion was simply this: *"If we grow our profile in London, we will grow it everywhere."* The capital certainly has some interesting work for trainees to get their teeth into. Eversheds has recently faced Freshfields on an IP dispute between Apple Computer and The Beatles' record label (Eversheds' client) over the right to use an apple logo to sell music. IP is just one of the many seats on offer in this office, and those fortunate enough to secure it are drawn into the heady world of fashion, brands and media. Corporate and property seats also feature highly on trainees' wish lists.

split vision

This round-up of Eversheds around the country should prove that the firm is as diverse as it is large, but does it gel together as well as its 'one firm' philosophy suggests? A trainee in Cardiff concluded that *"work is beginning to be shared a lot more; it isn't selfishly held onto but farmed out instead."* A trainee in the Midlands added: *"It is a work in progress to get us excited about 'us as a region'. It's a relatively new concept and will evolve over time."* That may be so, but on a trainee level many we spoke to didn't have a huge amount of contact with their counterparts in other offices, telling us: *"It's a shame, and something the firm could do better."* It stands to reason that you are likely to feel more a part of your office than of the firm as a whole, but most people agreed that *"there's a big bonus to working in a large firm. There is a huge amount of back-up and knowledge. If you're trying to tackle a particular issue, someone out there will have had experience of it and you're able to tap into knowledge."* Anyone passionate about spending time abroad can apply for a seat in Paris or Brussels. Strangely, *"sometimes they are completely oversubscribed; sometimes they are begging people to go there."*

The classic *"normal"* and *"down-to-earth"* Eversheds trainee steps into a *"straightforward culture where people are not overly aggressive and there's an overall can-do, practical mentality."* *"It's a touch cheesy,"* said one trainee of the firm's well-publicised 'vision and values'. One boiled it down to mean *"high-quality work, putting the client first and employing people who are nice in the office."* The communication of these messages is taken seriously and 'Have Your Say' sessions are run on a regular basis to allow staff to quiz partners. *"Inevitably there will be different attitudes across offices as each has different work. And it will always be different to work in Leeds rather than London. That is no bad thing,"* summed up one trainee. *"The overarching vision of the firm relates to attitude and quality*

of work, and how hard you work." Such vision and values must mean something as the firm always retains a majority of its qualifying trainees. In september 2006 the overall results showed 58 of the 74 qualifiers took jobs across the network.

There's barely room left to mention the trainees' social lives; suffice to say that, as many of Eversheds' recruits are straight out of education, they are as full of enthusiasm for informal nights out in local hostelries as they are for larger, firm-organised events. You won't go short of parties or friends here.

and finally...

For students who know Eversheds is the place for them, *"the vacation scheme is definitely the way to go"* as the firm hires many trainees off the back of these two-week placements. If you're still wondering what Eversheds might be able to offer you, let's recap by saying that the national giant is looking to increase its international activities and the value of its transactional work at home. With a move away from servicing purely local needs, the opportunities for trainees are great but the experience will be quite different to working at a big, regional independent.

Farrer & Co

the facts

Location: London
Number of UK partners/solicitors: 60/135
Total number of trainees: 17
Seats: 6x4 months
Alternative seats: Secondments

Standing on the legal hallowed ground of Lincoln's Inn Fields, Farrer & Co has seen many a fad come and go in the last 300 years. But while its prestigious history does inform the present it is not the only defining feature of this distinctive firm.

sporting life

If those three centuries of practice have piqued your interest, you'll enjoy the facts, fun and frolics on Farrers' website, learning along the way that its long history is inextricably linked with some of the legal profession's and London's most interesting personalities and events. We won't dwell on such matters here because we know, like the firm's trainees, that an affection for Farrers' past can overshadow its modern-day achievements. "*The firm has really moved on in the last five years,*" they told us; "*younger partners are coming through, becoming team leaders and shaping the way the firm is run.*" In their eyes "*the collaboration between sports, media, IP, corporate and disputes*" is very much "*where it's at*" right now. And the evidence suggests they have a point.

Work on the London Olympic Games and Paralympic Games Bill has seen Farrers represent the British Olympic and Paralympic Associations, and in 2006 lawyers also won appointment to the Rugby League's governing body to advise on sponsorship, IP, disciplinary and anti-doping matters. UK Athletics and the All England Netball Team are also clients. At the same time corporate lawyers have been busy for multinational clothing retailer Pepe Jeans on the £14 million acquisition of high-end fashion business Hackett, and gold-mining company Serabi Mining plc used them on its £31 million admission to AIM. Exploiting strong connections with media and publishing companies, Farrers' corporate instructions frequently fall in this sphere. For example, last year it advised long-standing client Emap on an £18 million acquisition of political news service website De Havilland Information Services. Strength in this sector also breeds defamation and disputes work, with Farrers' litigators heavily involved in cases for newspapers such as The Sun and the News of the World. Here, believe it or not, they're pretty au fait with footballers and gay sex orgy photos.

None of this work is exactly hung heavy with dust or cobwebs, so we decided we would happily let our sources accentuate the modern. However, this being Farrer & Co, trainees were far too level-headed not to acknowledge the influence of the firm's phenomenal private client practice. "*The private client and estates work is still very important, not least revenue-wise,*" they explained, stressing that the recent hire of a Manches family law partner underlines the firm's ongoing commitment. We hear that "*the strategic head of private client is quite young and aiming to modernise this part of the business.*" Not too much, we hope, because frankly we rather like the sound of "*eccentric characters who don't realise how much money they've got or are about to get,*" or the historical detective work of sifting through "*tin boxes with the family crests on in gold to establish chain of title in property.*" And yet our delight in this aspect of private client practice leaves trainees uneasy: they worried about our understanding of the balance between old and new, fearing that we might resort to easy, yet harmful, stereotypes when describing the firm. "*You always mention tweed. It's not tweed and weekend duck-hunting!*" laughed one. "*Please, whatever you do, don't mention tweed.*" Okay.

the not-so-great divide

In past editions we've tended to use the structure of Farrers' office to highlight the inherent duality of the firm. On one side stunning period premises with impressive facade and high-vaulted ceilings; on the other "*a bog-standard modern office.*" A recent "*fusion-decor*" interior makeover ("*new square lamps, same beautiful painted ceilings*") has refreshed "*the flagship meeting rooms,*" such that the difference between the two parts of the building has lessened. However, it has not disappeared entirely, according to the trainee who split the firm as follows: "*Private client is letter-writing and signing things with fountain pens. The corporate side is everything e-mailed and tracking changes."* Given that trainees can experience both, perhaps these differences matter less than the *"character difference from the run-of-the-mill City law firms"* that distances Farrers from *"faceless, bland, corporate-London life."*

bring out the donuts

Farrers' trainees get a variety of training that is second to none, with six four-month seats being taken across the different practice groups. One seat must be selected from each of the following four groupings: property (commercial and private/estates options); charities or private client; litigation (family, media or general disputes); and corporate (including banking and employment). After these comes a wild-card choice (*"either to try a new area or broaden your experience of the area you want to qualify into"*), and finally a seat back in the trainee's intended qualification department. Some trainees take advantage of short client secondments, with one lucky so-and-so even spending time at the Lawn Tennis Association. Others include a national museum, a FTSE 100 company, an Olympic sporting body and a leading business school. This relatively rigid structure can occasionally throw up a less-desired seat, and this is the cue for training co-ordinator Donna Davies' *"coffee, donuts and sort-it-out sessions."* Apparently, *"she'll bend over backwards to accommodate you and sit you with someone who'll make the experience more interesting."*

As befits a firm with plenty of private clients, Farrers has a deft touch when it comes to personal relationships. A thorough appraisal system gives trainees formal feedback twice per seat, plus an additional session with the *"excellent"* training partner who is *"very serious about what he does."* Best of all, *"when you get good feedback via a partner on work you've done for a client, that's a high."* Our sources were impressed by *"the amount of responsibility you get, despite the odd mundane task,"* but

more significantly rejoiced at *"the way you're really trusted to be an ambassador for the firm."*

Among the ambassadorial moments are those first faltering steps in the world of litigation. *"I went to court with counsel by myself quite often, and I did get a last-minute chance to do some advocacy,"* recalled one trainee. *"I went in front of a master who looked like he'd been there for a hundred years. I had only 15 minutes to prepare the application, and there were several minutes of nerve-wracking silence when I finished, but it was successful thankfully!"* Private client seats involve a lot of direct contact with clients. Trainees *"run the lower-end probate files"* and may find themselves *"talking to clients, picking up expensive paintings for valuation or having a client bring in all their jewellery."* Tax and trusts advice, often for individuals domiciled abroad, can throw up *"interesting research points,"* and estates and private property (EPP) demands careful client-management skills when handling multiple private house purchases. *"There's a constant barrage of phone calls from clients wanting to know what stage their purchase is at; you really have to keep on top of everything."* Similarly, the family seat requires empathy and sensitivity when *"clients ring up to discuss their woes,"* but the satisfaction in gaining a favourable child custody or divorce settlement is *"a major highlight."*

censor sensibility

One interesting detail of Farrers' history is that it assisted several clients in obtaining money owed by the dramatist Sheridan as a result of failed stage productions. No stranger to controversy, Sheridan was once forced to make substantial changes overnight to his play 'The Rivals' after the opening-night audience found the sexual innuendo too racy. No such censorious attitudes hold sway when it comes to the annual trainee-penned Christmas revue, which *"can be quite risqué and is definitely not bland."* In the best tradition of good authorship, a boozy weekend away inspired the second-years of 2005/06 to write last year's scurrilous sketches and skits, a *Big Brother*-themed piece performed by both years that included (in no specific order) David Hasselhoff, a full-sized badger outfit, a Terminator character, partners running around killing mice, the grim reaper and a mad cricketer. The mind boggles. Despite comments that *"it was a bit tame this year,"* the no-holds barred, scattershot satire on staff members' peccadillos, habits and foibles is rumoured to have seen *"one partner leave."*

We're sure he or she was actually just leaving to honour another engagement, because if there's one thing which characterises Farrers' social life, it's a permissive, *"take it as you find it"* sensibility. Well-attended sports events like the rugby sevens or a regular cricket fixture against the *News of the World* are widely enjoyed, and departmental away-days or drinks at the nearby All Bar One are not uncommon, but the scene is not all-encompassing. *"On a Friday we'll go out for drinks for a few hours, but then people go on to do other stuff or meet other friends. Everyone has an outside life and interests, and that's healthy."* The hours people work is a factor in making an outside life possible, with 9am to 6.30pm an average day, and *"only occasional stints of staying to 8pm or 9pm."*

Farrers trainees call themselves *"naturally outgoing and confident, but not cocky."* They see themselves as *"bright young things with a bit of depth."* Many come from non-law backgrounds and from a broader range of universities than might be expected, given the firm's heritage. Year after year we notice a maturity of outlook from trainees with broad interests outside work. Just to give a sample, there are people who help run youth groups or charities, those who are heavily immersed in sports, and those who are already on the baby track. Traditionally strong retention rates (all seven in 2005, seven out of eight in 2006) and *"a genuine attachment to the firm and its culture"* give trainees the confidence to make plans for the future. Summing theirs up, one trainee told us: *"It seems like if you stay six years you could make partnership, and there are not many places you could say that. I'd only leave if I wanted to get out of London."*

and finally...

A quirky, characterful firm with a broad practice, Farrer & Co enjoys a mutually rewarding relationship with those distinctive candidates who match its permissive and balanced culture. While Macfarlanes, Withers and Charles Russell are all realistic alternatives, you'll probably get a strong gut feeling if this unique legal environment is the one for you.

Field Fisher Waterhouse LLP

the facts
Location: London
Number of UK partners/solicitors: 91/140
Total number of trainees: 34
Seats: 6x4 months
Alternative seats: Secondments

Mixing classic City practice with an array of niche specialisms, this mid-tier player has carved out a reputation as a jack-of-all-trades, and absolute master of some.

getting the message

The Field Fisher Waterhouse trainees we spoke to seem to be obsessed with size. They had wanted to join a firm of *"medium-size but with an international outlook,"* a firm *"big enough to get really decent work, but small enough to be recognised and valued."* That said, FFW is part way through an ambitious development plan, so its size is subject to change. And is the plan bearing fruit? It seems so. In the last financial year, turnover increased by 15% to a chunky £60 million, and there are specific and ambitious goals in mind for key parts of the practice. All in all, it is an exciting phase for the firm and a good point in time for those just starting out. *"We feel like we're in the right place at the right time,"* trainees told us; *"there is a real buzz."* Strategic plans are openly discussed with the trainee group, as evidenced by newly appointed managing partner Moira Gilmour's presentation on how she will take the firm forward. Indeed, our sources said they were kept in the loop on everything from *"the latest tender won, to who is running a marathon."*

All this is something of a turnaround for a firm which, say three years ago, looked a little directionless. Its many and varied successes just didn't hang together that well... or at least not obviously so. How things change. The good news for trainees is that there is still *"so much choice, depth and diversity"* in the work on offer. A *"brilliant"* six-seat rotation is the most sensible way of exploring the firm, and it has the added advantage of allowing trips to niche departments as well as mainstream ones. All recruits must gain experience of coco and then it's a case of suck it and see. Often trainees choose to return to their preferred qualification team for the final four months, and there are ad hoc and short client secondments for those who fancy a change of scenery.

holy merchandise, batman

FFW's famed IP department can be experienced through contentious or non-contentious seats. In the former, timing is everything and the type of work falling to trainees very much depends on what is coming to a head at any given moment. Timely trainees had done *"some really cool – if that is possible – legal work;" "lots of drafting, meetings and conferences with counsel."* Others had a harder time of it, enduring late-night bundling and admin sessions, albeit in the knowledge that *"the work you do has some importance to it."* Few other departments can boast such a star-studded client portfolio, and it is viewed as *"a novel and fun place to be."* Enforcement work for Apple Computer concerning its trade marks, designs and copyright meant *"there were iPods lying all over the place."* The group also acted for Warner Bros. in relation to the protection of the rights used in the merchandising for the 'Charlie and the Chocolate Factory' movie. Even the caped crusader himself needed help to protect the 'Batman Begins' device of DC Comics.

A stint in the *"brilliant"* (there's that word again) real estate department is a classic first-year posting. *"It's a bit of a baptism of fire"* as it is *"quite heavy going"* in terms of responsibility, but great for getting to grips with *"what it is really like to be a lawyer."* Amidst all the *"hustle and bustle"* you can run your own files, draft leases and have direct contact with clients and other law firms. Although *"daunting at first,"* trainees aren't flying by the seat of their pants as ample support is available and *"they do look after you."*

Corporate training is split into two imaginatively named seats – corporate 1 and corporate 2. The first has a public sector and corporate finance leaning, the second a more *"sexy"* M&A and capital markets feel. Whichever you're in, expect *"a little less responsibility." "You are not necessarily given a matter to run with,"* but *"they do really focus on your training, and they want to involve you in everything."* With *"hard work and a few late nights"* on the cards, it's a good thing *"you're happy to stay later with fun people and good banter."* Recent trainees have been able to assist with the BBC's £166 million disposal of BBC Broadcast to Macquarie Bank following an auction process. BP Oil UK also came to the firm on a £100 million exit from a retail joint venture with a major UK supermarket group.

niche work if you can get it

For the eggheads there's a seat in the *"trophy"* technology practice, which is viewed as a leading-edge and "*massively growing*" department. A spate of work has recently arrived from the public sector, with lawyers appointed as external legal adviser to the Home Office and the UK Passport Service. Headline-grabbing work for the latter has focused on the kind of gadgets James Bond's mate Q would be proud of – technology dealing with the recording and verification of facial recognition, and iris and fingerprint biometrics. All up, "*this is a really exciting environment because of the top work and the calibre of the people working here.*"

The professional regulatory team is hugely popular with trainees looking beyond common-or-garden commercial work. It advises professional regulatory bodies such as the General Medical Council on the legal implications of policy issues, the defence of judicial review proceedings and the prosecution of cases before disciplinary and performance committees. FFW represented the GMC in the recent appeal by controversial expert witness, paediatrician Sir Roy Meadows. Other favoured destinations include the somewhat "*unusual for a City firm*" personal injury and claimant clinical negligence practices. Areas of expertise here include asbestos diseases, road traffic and industrial accidents, and major transport disasters.

swings and roundabouts

Across the seats the level of responsibility is variable and depends very much on the department and the amount of decent work it has floating around. You could find yourself "*having a go at drafting from scratch and then making the amendments – by the end you have drafted the whole thing, albeit with some help and supervision.*" At other times "*you might be doing some big admin jobs like photocopying.*" Sometimes a bit of monkey work is a welcome relief, for example "*if you have a hangover…*" Either way, trainees seem happy enough with the swings

and roundabouts, and advocate that "*the size of the firm brings exposure to better work more quickly.*"

The trainee-review system is good for "*seeing how everything is going, setting challenges and planning how to broaden experience.*" It's a two-way process that allows the trainee to shape things. Witness the trainee who said: "*Within a week of mentioning my concerns about the potential imbalance in the seat so far, the issue was addressed.*" Bags of ad hoc advice and feedback are available from a web of supervisors and mentors who seem happy to answer those "*stupid*" and (we're sure) not so stupid questions. Formal training is complemented by internal and external lecture and seminar programmes. As an added bonus, "*we generally pop down for a free lunch and it's a good chance to catch up with the other trainees.*"

The offices are "*not beautiful but are being renovated.*" New client areas make "*FFW look smarter, more up to date and more marketable,*" trainees concluded. Apparently the website is also due an overhaul – "*thank goodness,*" one trainee heaved a sight of relief, "*it's so 1990s!*" If the trainees had their way you could expect to see "*some whizzy graphics and branding,*" so as to bring it in line with the firm's reputation as an IP and technology leader.

sneaking off home

Social and sporting life is handled by a committee made up of people from every layer from "*high-level partners down to a couple of trainees.*" Football, softball, hockey and netball are all played and there's also talk of a squash tournament in the future. It shouldn't be that hard to organise as the office building has its own courts in the basement. The trainees have a social budget which is theirs to manage as they wish. We asked how far the money stretched, and learned that "*quantity normally wins out over* quality." In a nice touch, it is left to first-year trainees to organise the annual qualification dinner for the second-years. At the time we conducted our research the identity of the venue was still under wraps, but the criteria were simple: "We want to find somewhere where we can cram everything into the evening – have dinner, a drink and a dance." Impromptu after-work drinks are centred on the nearby Emperor, described neatly as "a regular haunt for the usual suspects." If you're of an antisocial, or teetotal, disposition may we recommend stealth when departing the office of a summer evening: "If the weather's nice everyone's outside, so you may get dragged in whether you like it or not."

The phrase "lifestyle firm" came up repeatedly during the research process. Sounded like marketing spiel to us, so we dug a little deeper and this is what we got: "The firm really cares about its employees and how they fit in. It prides itself on its diversity and on being a different kind of place to work." If you want the facts on staff diversity then look on the FFW website and you'll see loads of stats on gender and ethnicity. They're respectable by City law firm standards, but what does that actually prove? So if not diversity of staff, maybe diversity of work is the factor we should re-emphasise. That, and one other claim which genuinely warms the cockles of our hearts – "You really get the respect of partners, your ideas are listened to, and that gives you confidence." In September 2006, 11 of the 12 qualifiers took jobs with the firm.

and finally...

Trainees are proud of their firm and grateful for the opportunity to "work with, learn from and be inspired by people who are recognised leaders in their respective fields." It could be said that this firm has something for everyone, whether they're a classic corporate cat or have a nose for the niche.

Finers Stephens Innocent

the facts

Location: London
Number of UK partners/solicitors: 34/37
Total number of trainees: 10
Seats: 4x6 months
Alternative seats: None

Finers Stephens Innocent is a commercial outfit with a weighty property department and an interesting line in media law. Its website features a lady checking her e-mails in the bathtub and a guy running across a field wearing batwings. It also tells us "There are two approaches to the law: the literal and the creative. The former applies the law as a rigid set of regulations. The latter uses skill and ingenuity to achieve a solution." Intrigued, we felt compelled to find out which approach has been adopted at Finers.

kooky or kookai?

The firm arranges itself around seven core practices: commercial property, litigation, coco, media & defamation/IP, private client, family and employment. Trainees do four six-month seats, in which the only compulsory is property. So far, so regular, so where does the creativity come into play? The answer is simple – through the people who work there.

One of our interviewees said: "I think the firm values individuality and creativity. The firm is very much a collection of individuals – everyone you work with is different and there's room for eccentric types." Without attempting to place him anywhere on the eccentricity scale, one of the best-known characters at Finers is Mark Stephens, who you are very likely to have heard on radio or TV, commenting on media law issues. Helping on one of the media cases was a high point for one trainee: "We were defending the Sunday Times against Harrods, which was suing for *breach of confidence after an article criticised Harrods' employment practices. It went to the Court of Appeal and it was me, the partner and counsel working together. While that was on I was loving coming to work – my friends thought I was mad!"* Such cases are not unusual for Finers: lawyers have lately defended Bloomberg on an Ofcom complaint raised by the Conservative Party over equal treatment at the last general election, and in what must be one heck of a case, they have assisted Sacha Baron Cohen following threats by the State of Kazakhstan to sue him over the antics of one of his alter egos, Borat. One trainee who had worked with the team put their finger on it when they told us that media law can be *"Ally McBeal-like with lots of random cases."* On a regular basis *"you look at the work and think, 'Is this a goer or is it just too weird?'"*

Some cases are more off the peg than off the wall. The firm has represented Monsoon/Accessorize on copyright, design right and criminal enforcement claims against various high street stores including Marks & Spencer, Primark, Next and New Look, which it claims have copied their product lines. For client Kookai it successfully defended two separate design right claims by Mulberry and Chloe in relation to handbags. Explaining the immense appeal of the IP and media work, one trainee told us: *"Within the department there is lots of contentious and non-contentious work and interesting IP stuff. The department is home to real experts, be this in defamation or publishing law."* Media/IP is clearly popular and trainees are right to stress that *"you are not guaranteed a place here."*

the villagers' voice

Maybe Finers is the ideal law firm for shopaholics. It acts for various stores and clothing labels, including BoxFresh and LK Bennett, commonly on matters relating to their retail outlets. Left peckish by shopping? How about business lease renewals and rent reviews for the likes of Pizza Hut? One of the most interesting things to have occupied Finers' property lawyers of late has been the uprooting of some 300 businesses from the proposed multibillion-pound site where the 2012 Olympic Village will be built. On behalf of the businesses, Finers negotiated with the London Development Agency over the terms of their departure.

Property provides a major chunk of Finers' income and so a property seat is *"a fact of life for trainees – you won't be able to avoid it."* Perhaps no one should, because it's where they get most responsibility. *"I was running my own files,"* recalled a trainee; *"you just go to the partner to approve letters and all the post comes to you."* The seat is designed to give trainees a good grasp of the legal issues and what it feels like to control a deal. *"They try and get trainees to do a sale and a purchase of a residential property so that you can see the whole transaction through."* One trainee's seat was *"50/50 commercial and residential,"* which had led to *"lots of research into easements and unregistered title, as well as drafting leases and licences, and some adverse possession."* The whole shebang by the sounds of it.

If you enjoy taking responsibility, but property doesn't do it for you, commercial litigation is a good place to be. Here trainees run small files, maybe even getting up in front of a High Court master on low-level applications. Another dispute-heavy seat is employment, where one source had divided their time between *"reviewing clients' employment policies"* and *"helping with an eight-day hearing at an Employment Tribunal."* The hours in corporate can be either *"hideous"* or *"quiet as a mouse."* It's not one of Finers' best-known areas of practice, and trainees were quite candid on this point. *"Don't come here if you're interested in massive corporate deals. We don't work on huge transactions, we work on AIM stuff."* That said, *"the variety here keeps it exciting, whereas my friends at big firms get lost in the drudgery of big deals."* Just in case you were wondering, corporate is not the only seat where longer hours can crop up. During a particularly hectic period in litigation one trainee stayed in the office from "*8.30am to midnight most days.*"

The West End is stuffed with firms that combine commercial practice with family law and private client advice. Finers is no different, and it even has some rich and famous clients. Recalling their time in private client, one trainee said: "*I mostly did will drafting, trusts and admin work. I had lots of client contact and there were lots of matters going on at once... though it was less manic than property because it was non-transactional.*" The family team deals with top-end cases involving "*not your run-of-the-mill individuals but high net worth.*" But as we always say, people are people whether they have money or not and working on divorces you begin to learn a lot about human foibles and how a lawyer can best deal with emotional clients.

a proud day

The private client and family departments occupy a separate building from the main commercial departments, which are in the main building on Great Portland Street. There's plenty of interesting artwork in the office; "*modern, avant-garde kind of stuff.*" However, the place is bursting at the seams, which means "*the firm can't expand because there's literally no room!*" On the plus side, "*it's nice being close to Marylebone High Street and Regents Park.*" Indeed, one trainee told us: "*Working in a West End firm is so different to the City. It's really conducive to going out, it's less formal, and it's smaller so it's much more personal.*" A drop-in breakfast every Monday morning, a monthly staff lunch, and wine and nibbles on the last Thursday of each month help staff mingle, and Friday is dress-down day.

One thoughtful trainee said: "*This is not a place where you feel too old, too female, or not clever enough. It's a very inclusive place.*" Another said of the recruitment process, "*Finers was one of the few firms that was looking past A-levels and your first degree; they were looking at you as a person.*" Several trainees have had a life before law, and we discovered a surveyor, an investment banker and "*a fossil person*" (we're guessing palaeontologist not OAP). For those with busy lives outside work, breathe easy – "*there's no pressure to go out drinking.*"

A new appraisal system is suitably "*soul-searching,*" but one fact of life at Finers is that NQ retention has traditionally not been high. Trainees had some views on this point, and interestingly said: "*There is a gearing problem – in lots of departments you have highly qualified people doing work that they're too expensive for. It's top heavy.*" Yet trainees stress that the firm is non-hierarchical, and given the following anecdote, perhaps they were right to do so. "*The department I was in was recruiting externally and asked me, as a trainee, to go along to the interview with the partner to give a second opinion.*" Turning the NQ-retention issue on its head, in 2006 all five of the qualifiers were offered and accepted jobs. After learning this, tales of "*a Be Proud Day with lots of balloons and champagne*" came as no shock. Asked to "*be proud of the firm and of ourselves,*" staff made up a brochure of the firm's and the clients' achievements and feedback, and put together an entirely uncensored newsletter. Despite our best efforts we couldn't persuade anyone to send us a copy. Pride seems to be a hot topic at Finers right now. "*There's a new marketing team that has been brought in to raise the profile of other non-Mark Stephens stuff – like the AIM work and private client. They want to show that the other departments are doing interesting things and that there is unity.*"

and finally...

After weighing everything up we're inclined to accept Finers' claim to bring creativity to the law, and we suspect they're quite specific about who they'll invite to train with them as a result. Nice work if you can get it.

Fisher Meredith

the facts
Location: London
Number of UK partners/solicitors: 14/42
Total number of trainees: 15
Seats: 4x6 months
Alternative seats: None

Fisher Meredith is a leading community law firm in south London. Just as it was at its inception in 1975, the firm is staffed by lawyers with a genuine desire to protect the rights of the individual and provide access to legal advice irrespective of the ability to pay for it. A number of the firm's key figures have law in their blood, not least senior partner Eileen Pembridge, renowned family law practitioner and Law Society member for south London.

a life of crime
Sounds perfect, but remember there's usually a but. The current state of legal aid funding makes life increasingly hard for firms whose clients are reliant on the public purse to pay the bills. Lawyers' rates of pay under legal aid have been cut, and this has created an environment of unease and uncertainty for the future. Ever the strategist, FM has developed a commercial limb to help plug the gap and fill the coffers; this has generally been welcomed as a positive move by trainees, though there are naturally a few purists for whom commercial work is anathema. FM now has trainee seats in crime, family, employment, housing, police and prison law, public services law, immigration and asylum, as well as in the business unit.

Usually trainees must take a seat in either the crime or family departments. The former is fast-paced with a high turnover of cases, and because *"the time from arrest to court is usually very short, there are things that simply have to get done*

quickly." As a trainee your days will be spent analysing evidence, writing letters, instructing experts and barristers, and generally chasing your tail. The department is organised into small teams consisting of a senior solicitor or partner, a junior solicitor and a trainee. The trainee cuts their teeth on magistrates' court matters and police station visits, but will also get the chance to help out with *"really meaty and interesting Crown Court work."* One trainee was sent to Pentonville prison to take instructions from a defendant charged with seven offences relating to firearms, armed robbery, false imprisonment and kidnapping – a lengthy process that took a painstaking five visits with an interpreter. If you can handle the *"million-miles-an-hour pace,"* the requirement to *"liaise with forensic experts in a fairly gruesome capacity,"* the lengthy hours and some less than savoury characters (recently one accused of *"necrophiliac pornography"* and sex with minors), a crime seat may turn out to be even more exciting than you dreamed it would be. And let's not forget that the lawyers here have reputations so strong that they are instructed by defendants in some of the most high-profile criminal matters, including the Damilola Taylor trial and the defence of individuals accused of involvement in the terrorist attacks in London in 2005.

doing it for the kids
Above all else, excellent people skills are needed in the family seat to cope with the disparate clientele that use the firm. Lawyers work for both privately and publicly funded individuals, advising on divorce and ancillary relief, child maintenance, contact and residence, and all issues resulting from family breakdown. Trainees gain advocacy experience at domestic violence injunctions, directions hearings and interim applications, and this is half the appeal of the work. Be prepared to have your heartstrings tugged though: *"I'll never forget one young boy who had been brought up in*

the most awful circumstances," revealed one source. On the plus side, there's a supportive *"collegiate atmosphere"* and with hours more regular than in crime *"the department tends to empty at about 5.30pm or 6pm."* Unsurprisingly, *"child abduction cases are the exception to that; here all the stops are pulled out."* A separate children's law seat has been spun off from the standard family law experience and it, too, provides plenty of advocacy for the trainee. In this seat, one trainee had come to understand the true nature of their calling: *"Moments like getting a child relocated with their family after being in care – that's why you do it."*

Some of our interviewees found the police and prison law seat *"really exciting and cutting edge."* This team's cases cover false imprisonment, assault and malicious prosecution issues. *"It's not something I'd considered, but it rolls on so nicely from crime, you hit the ground running,"* reported one past occupant of the seat. If you're looking for considerable responsibility and relative independence, choosing the immigration and asylum seat makes a lot of sense. Described as *"human rights heavy"* and inspiring, the hours can sometimes be long because *"life and liberty"* are at stake in some cases.

abusive process

Many students are looking for a career with a civil liberties focus, and when you also consider how highly recommended FM comes, it should be obvious that winning a training contract here is no cakewalk. Trainees are cherry-picked for their staggering achievements and demonstrated commitment to the cause. The trainee group of 2006 includes people who have worked for international aid charity Concern, Amnesty and the European Commission. *"There are no cardboard cut-outs, but generally successful applicants have some kind of altruistic quality"* plus strong academics. Our sources reminded us that the nature

of the firm's clientele requires determined and confident individuals. As one put it: *"We're based in Lambeth so you will serve a diverse community and you need to be a bit streetwise."* One interviewee recalled a client *"who kept calling me babes and patting me on the knee,"* and another *"who screamed at me, calling me a fag-whore when I said hello."* All in a day's work...

Trainees recommended that we alert potential applicants to the nature and amount of client contact involved in the job. One told us: *"It actually surprised me how much contact there was"* and *"I quickly realised some repeat clients had more knowledge than me."* Some can be demanding and unpredictable, perhaps because they have drug, alcohol or mental health problems, yet trainees meet all new clients, providing a triage-type service to match them with the right lawyer in the firm. It soon becomes apparent that legal aid work is not as glamorous as certain TV shows will have you believe, nor is it well paid like commercial law. Trainees are expected to muck in and take their turn on admin chores. At FM such things are shared out through the dreaded *"trainee-of-the-day rota,"* which involves delivering papers to court and other dogsbody duties.

we're not in kansas anymore, toto

Smart and still fairly new offices in Kennington may not quite match the beautiful rolling landscape depicted on the firm's website, but are certainly a vast improvement on FM's previous scruffy Stockwell home. The firm's investment in the building signals a certain confidence in the future, despite all the difficulties posed by legal aid cutbacks. The open-plan layout makes for effective *"learning by osmosis,"* and the careful placement of trainees next to supervisors allows *"a cascading of information – things fly back and forth all day."* At FM people's attitudes are pretty liberal and, much to the delight of one trainee, the dress code is sufficiently relaxed that *"you can wear red shoes!"* The workforce is *"richly diverse with openly gay people and a full ethnic mix... though I don't think a Daily Mail reader would be very comfortable here."* In 2006, four of the seven qualifiers took jobs at the firm.

The firm has a good social life, with football matches, yoga and team curry nights in Kennington all regular occurrences. In the office, morale is boosted by small but thoughtful gestures, such as hot cross buns at Easter or ice creams on a sunny day. There are also grander gestures, such as a recent office trip to Brighton. Despite the firm organising a coach to take everyone home at the end of the night, we're told *"not a single person made it, and some even woke up on the beach the next morning beside empty beer bottles."* Must have been some night out!

and finally...

If you're dedicated to the cause but worried about the future of legal aid firms, we reckon Fisher Meredith offers more security than most. Having built up a pretty fantastic reputation and developed its business unit, it has got what it takes to remain a strong player in the market. Our best advice is to get some work experience under your belt, harbour no illusions about what will be required of you, and get ready to roll up your sleeves.

Foot Anstey

the facts

Location: Plymouth, Exeter, Taunton
Number of UK partners/solicitors: 30/80
Total number of trainees: 16
Seats: 4x6 months
Alternative seats: None

South West firm Foot Anstey's ambitious plan for wider regional dominance has got more legs than a Dartmoor pony. A commitment to legal aid and private client work, plus success in litigation, commercial transactions and media law mean the firm is galloping ahead. Could you hack the pace?

premier foot forward

When we say ambitious plans, we do mean ambitious. After steering Foot Anstey through its merger with Somerset's Alms & Young in mid-2005, managing partner Jane Lister was to be heard vigorously outlining a five-year strategy aimed at doubling the firm's turnover and significantly increasing its size. Reaching for £22 million turnover by 2010 is some stretch, but at least the arrival of all those Somerset lawyers last year has the firm well on its way. With the new Taunton office *"completely bedded in,"* the firm was further boosted by the arrival of both Clarke Wilmott's new homes and bulk conveyancing team and its five-lawyer family law unit. Does it stop there? Of course not. Foot Anstey's roving eye is scouring the South West for possible new branches and looks to be particularly enamoured of Cornwall's scenic delights. *"It definitely wants to be the best in the West,"* stated one typically chipper trainee, before evidently realising an error. *"Oh, no, wait, we're not meant to say that, hang on...* [*Student Guide* researcher hears sound of a mouse clicking onto intranet] *...it wants to be the premier firm in the South West."*

Recognising that one of the most attractive features for prospective trainees is *"the firm's breadth of practice, from commercial work to legal aid,"* our interviewees spoke at length on this topic. *"The firm prides itself on having big business clients, regional private clients and legal aid clients; that's what differentiates us from rivals like Ashfords or Michelmores."* In practical terms, this allows trainees to sample seats as diverse as clinical negligence or planning, media/defamation or marine litigation, family or insolvency. This is especially handy for anyone *"still deciding where they fit in the legal spectrum."* In strategic terms:

"We want to offer the best service available across the widest practice area, covering the widest geographical area we can without going into Bristol."

very moving

To give substance to what might, after all, be a load of hype, we went looking for evidence of Foot Anstey's achievements. Across its three offices the firm had plenty to show us: big name clients such as Wrigley, NatWest, Trinity Mirror, Associated Newspapers and the Beer Seller, not to mention regional loyalty from Plymouth Marine Laboratory, The Arts Council England (South West), the University of Plymouth, Cornwall County Council and Cornwall Farmers Co-operative. The newspaper clients have come to rely on the firm's media/defamation expertise which has seen it involved in numerous actions for regional titles across the UK plus a few beyond. In one notable case, the lawyers represented a Jamaican national newspaper in an appeal heard by the Privy Council. Add in private client work and a determination to maintain a legal aid practice and the picture is complete.

When it comes to the four-by-six month training, trainees are able to choose not only from a plethora of seat options but also the three offices. Their training is characterised by *"a lot of flexibility from the firm about where you go and when."* Seats can be taken in coco, commercial property, crime, employment, private client, IP, family, planning, media, property litigation, marine litigation, personal injury and clinical negligence, although the specific business needs of the firm may mean not all seats are available in all offices all of the time. If trainees do move offices, it will ultimately be their decision, and we're told the firm is *"really good about travel expenses."* Many trainees return to a favoured department for their pre-qualification seat, a feature made possible by *"the diversity of*

personalities and tastes" among them. *"There's just such a mixed bag – some touchy-feely types who graduate towards the private client or legal aid work, and more commercially oriented people."*

coming away with sweet fa

Spanning fresh-faced law graduates and more seasoned second-careerers, the variety in the trainee population was something of a surprise to those who had undergone the firm's rigorous application process. *"Given the number of psychometric tests and interviews they do it's amazing we're not all identical,"* exclaimed one survivor of a Pop-Idolesque interview day which sees those who don't make the grade ejected at lunchtime. It's cruel but fair, and apparently effective. Trainees say they are *"all the kind of people who are keen to get on; studious and hard working but relaxed as well, definitely not too intense."*

Those earning the sweet reward of a training contract find themselves working closely with supervisors who are *"brilliant in giving you day-to-day supervision"* and *"do their level best to assign you interesting work."* The corporate/commercial and litigation teams are those where trainees can most commonly expect a back-seat role, with commercial property and family seats the place where *"you get to run your own smaller files."* A trainee's work is primarily filtered through supervisors, meaning firstly that *"feedback is generally a day-by-day occurrence,"* but they also get *"a sense of progression in each seat."* One satisfied source commented: *"They are great at pushing you so you're constantly working at the margins of your capabilities."* If corporate seats mean *"little client contact but a lot of drafting,"* the consolation is *"working incredibly closely with your supervisor on deals."* Whatever the seat, *"the good work far outweighs the grunt work."* In insolvency this would be *"endless variety from local individuals to national practitioners"* and *"small court appearances;"* in clin neg *"masses of client contact, instructing coun-*

sel and court attendance;" and in private client it is *"running probate files of your own."*

smile for the camera

The firm's aim is to *"boost cross-office cohesion,"* and the trainees are doing their bit by making an effort to keep in touch by e-mail and by catching up at trainee lunches every couple of months. Aside from the different departments, the other main differences between three office locations are in the premises themselves. FA Plymouth is based in an old TV studio which is still more than serviceable but *"beginning to feel a bit tired and run down."* A little bird told us that *"plans for new premises are in hand,"* so long as this doesn't compromise *"the commitment to legal aid clients who need to walk in off the street, not travel to a business park."* As *"the base for the management team,"* Plymouth has *"a more formal feel than Exeter,"* but there are other reasons for trainees in the cathedral city to feel smug. FA Exeter's Senate House is *"a new, spacious, glass-fronted office with views across town,"* also boasting *"a nice staff room with a Playstation and table football"* to make up for the *"slight airport lounge feel"* of the meeting rooms. FA Taunton has also benefited from a move to modern buildings that are *"a mini-version of Exeter."* Although staff are now further from the town centre, they've welcomed having more space. *"In the old place there were four people working in what was supposed to be the kitchen... open plan is bliss."* The new accommodation has also allowed the various Alms & Young, Foot Anstey and Clarke Wilmott teams to *"begin to pull together as one office."*

Everyone from senior partner to post boy meets up at the FA Christmas party in a plush hotel in Torquay. This is a much-anticipated event *"when people really let their hair down."* Darnit, our sources remained tight lipped concerning the last party: *"I couldn't tell you half of what happened... the IT team take lots of photos*

and it's safe to say a fair bit of editing goes on before anyone sees them." Otherwise, the socialising at each office is usually team-based, with *"trainees actively encouraged to get involved at marketing events."* When they're not smiling and doing the meet-and-greet thing, Plymouth trainees enjoy drinks in Revolution or *"going to the Barbican in the sun and looking out at the sea."* Exeter trainees mostly visit the local wine bar, with *"splinter groups going to the White Hart or Wetherspoons."* In Taunton, where there is a smaller trainee population and fewer younger staff, we're told there is room for *"a bit more socialising, maybe weekly or monthly drinks instead of six-monthly."*

It would have been remiss of trainees not to talk about the charms of the South West and its wealth of leisure opportunities. Most have *"a strong connection to the region"* and a quest to achieve *"the perfect work-life balance."* For them, the 9am to 5.30pm routine is achievable, though none are afraid to work harder, occasionally *"until 6 or 7pm if you really need to in a corporate seat."* Such equilibrium seems to promote a sunny disposition throughout the firm, with *"a lot of smiling people who always encourage and help you."* One source reflected: *"We were out on a bingo night recently for a secretary's birthday and I looked around and saw partners, support staff, trainees and associates. It was a good feeling."*

and finally...

It is said that the family that plays together stays together, and this year's NQ retention figures certainly prove this: all ten 2006 qualifiers were offered jobs (*"before Christmas [2005], which was a fantastic present"*). Full retention is good news in anyone's book, but trainees were also keenly aware of their place in the expansion plans: *"We're really included in everything the firm is doing; it's an exciting time and that's why I'd recommend it to anyone."* Can't you just feel the satisfaction from here?

Forbes

the facts

Location: Blackburn, Preston, Accrington, Chorley, Manchester, Leeds
Number of UK partners/solicitors: 27/58
Total number of trainees: 15
Seats: 4x6 months
Alternative seats: Secondments
Extras: Pro bono – Saturday drop-in clinic

A stalwart on the Lancashire legal scene for over a century, Forbes is now expanding (note the recent opening of a Manchester office) and forging its way into the commercial arena. However, throughout, it remains true to its roots in the provision of legal advice to individuals.

from mbo to rta

With over 170 fee earners, Forbes is one of the largest firms in the North West and operates from nine offices in Accrington, Blackburn, Chorley, Leeds, Manchester and Preston. Bar a small merger 15 years ago, Forbes has grown organically. Trainees have picked up on a sense that management now wants *"all areas of the firms to expand,"* with a particular push desired in relation to commercial work. And why not when you've got some interesting clients on your books. One source mentioned that the *"commercial departments deal with some of the big football clubs."* For the record these include Burnley FC and Blackburn Rovers FC. The firm is pretty comfortable dealing with transactions pushing into the millions of pounds, among them MBOs and group restructurings.

In the contentious realm the firm attracts a good deal of insurance work, largely advising local authorities. For example, lawyers represented Bolton Metropolitan Borough Council in the High Court in its claim against Municipal Mutual Insurance and Commercial Union. The case was widely reported in the insurance and legal press and dealt

with the issue of conflicting insurance policy wordings associated with exposure to asbestos. The firm has a dedicated public sector group that acts for over 40 such clients in the north of England. These include LEAs, housing associations, the emergency services and universities. Having said all this, our interviewees agreed that Forbes is best known for its criminal practice. The firm acts for both legal aid and privately funded clients and was one of the initial 25 preferred suppliers for the Legal Services Commission. It is also strong in family law and claimant PI.

The seats available for trainees include PI (predominantly claimant work); defendant insurer (dealing with insurance companies in PI work and the like); crime (magistrates' or Crown Court); coco; commercial property; conveyancing; commercial litigation; wills, trusts and probate; employment and family. Some trainees get the chance to go on a client secondment to the Co-operative Bank or an insurance company. No seat is compulsory.

Different departments obviously have different working styles and atmospheres, yet trainees agree that all offer quality work. For example, if you do a stint in the family department you do *"a spread of everything"* from divorce and finance work to childcare matters. The range of advocacy experience *"depends on your choice of seat,"* but in any litigious department there will be some. Before you start panicking, early attempts at advocacy are *"nothing complicated."* For Crown Court work – and for crime in general – *"you have to be very thick skinned."* *"You are always supervised,"* especially when assisting on *"serious offences such as rape and murder."* The crime department is split into teams, *"each with their own specialities."* The work can be quite last-minute as you may be phoned by a court saying that a case is listed in two days' time. On magistrates' court work the firm *"throws you in at the deep end; they don't mess around."* Trainees *"do everything"* from seeing clients before the court hearing to conducting research and case preparation. If the idea of swimming in such deep water fills you with dread, fear not. As one trainee explained: "*In the past, people said there wasn't enough support... Now we have mentors – who tend to be assistant solicitors or NQs – to go to if we don't want to ask our supervisor something.*"

If a crime caseload of up to 25 files sounds demanding then bear in mind that in a PI seat this can extend to upwards of 50 files. Road traffic accidents are the norm, with bigger accident claims and some clinical negligence cases also thrown into the mix. Sources tell us that the "*training is fantastic and hands-on*" and that they are "*constantly guided.*"

preston to service

It's unusual for trainees to do all their four seats in the one office as certain seats are only available at certain locations. Without a travel allowance at their disposal, trainees often prefer to work at the location most convenient for them to reach. In fact, a quick survey reveals that most trainees "*tend to be spread between the Blackburn and Preston offices.*" HR "*do ask you for your seat preferences but if they can't accommodate you, they can't accommodate you.*" It "*depends on where the space is.*" Rather than begrudge the process, most interviewees felt that Forbes benefited from "*open dialogue*" between trainees and HR/training principals. For example, every six months there are two training reviews with the two training partners, "*one at the beginning and one six weeks towards the end,*" while your supervisor tends to "*review things with you every few days.*"

Forbes attracts a mixed bag of trainees – everyone from redbrick graduates straight out of law school to those who have worked or paralegaled at the firm first, earning their stripes and partners' respect, perhaps while also studying for their LPC. To clarify, both full-time and part-time training contracts are offered, with the part-time

trainees taking four seats over three years. When it came to balancing work with study, one source confirmed that "*there was and there wasn't sympathy*" from the firm; "*it was a case of getting on with it.*" In fairness, Forbes does provide additional study leave for those taking exams and it tries not to move those who are studying around too much in the first 18 months of the contract. When internal candidates for traineeships apply they encounter "*a different process... It's not as rigid and there is less of an administrative process to go through.*" However, paralegals interested in applying for a training contract and then taking a crime seat are expected to complete the Police Station Representatives Accreditation Scheme.

Our interviewees concurred that whether candidates are internal or external, Forbes ideally looks for people who have links to the North West and want to work there permanently. Perhaps this no-nonsense approach explains why the firm "*normally has a good retention rate on qualification.*" In 2006 the results were somewhat mixed: four of the five internally recruited trainees but none of the four externally recruited trainees stayed on qualification.

heading for the 19th hole

Regardless of the office and department, the hours seem pretty standard. "*No one expects you to work after 5pm*" and "*there's no pressure to stay behind.*" With time on your hands you may feel inclined to take part in some of the firm's voluntary activities, such as the Saturday drop-in clinic in the Northgate office in Blackburn, where "*people can come in off the street with any problem.*" This isn't a "*pretentious firm;*" it's "*down-to-earth and very work-focused.*"

The jury is still out as to just how much interaction there is between the firm's different offices. Some interviewees felt the geographical separation impacted heavily on firm life; others pointed out that different offices "*work closely*" with each other on cases. For example, "*PI has monthly meetings by*" video link" and there are "some weekends away to try to get departments in different areas together." A bi-monthly staff newsletter keeps everyone in the loop as to where the firm is going and "what's going on in all the offices." Moreover, in the past year, a committee made up of employee representatives from each office has formed. This provides a bridge to management and a forum where issues can be raised and information shared. If all else fails, there are always inter-office football matches and the big dates on the social calendar.

The firm-wide Christmas party is apparently "a bit of a riot." Staff descend en masse on Ewood Park (Blackburn Rovers' ground) where the luxuries of a hired suite await. A hot buffet, free bar and disco keep everyone happy till around 8pm when people are free to do their own thing and continue partying in Blackburn or Preston as they so choose. In addition, the trainees get their own events throughout the year, with HR organising "drinks and canapés just before you move seats in September and March." The idea is "to give you an opportunity to check out who you're working for" in your next seat as the event is also attended by supervisors. Save for the Christmas party and certain charity events, other social activities arise as and when "people organise things themselves," such as "the odd trip to the races." On the sports front, football and cricket have been the games of choice since the netball team went into retirement. The firm also holds an annual golf day for clients to which "some employees are invited to go along." Better get practising your swing if you want to be in with a chance.

and finally...

Regardless of where you've started on the legal ladder, if you're partial to life in the North West, Forbes is a solid choice. If you want a taster, the firm runs a paid two-week vacation scheme in its Blackburn and Preston offices. Apply early as it gets over 120 applications for just six places.

Ford & Warren

the facts

Location: Leeds
Number of UK partners/solicitors: 20/40
Total number of trainees: 12
Seats: 4x6 months
Alternative seats: Canada

Leeds has been transformed in the last ten years. Built on coal mining, manufacturing, mullets and a bunch of other things that went out in the 80s, Leeds has pulled itself up by its bootstraps and now faces a future of designer clothes, gourmet dining and high finance. Holding back this rising tide of change, like some latter-day King Canute, is Ford & Warren..

keep on truckin'

Take a look at F&W's decidedly under-designed website and you'll be in no doubt as to which side of the flat cap/Harvey Nicks divide to find it. "We could commandeer corporate boxes at Lords," it declares. "We don't. We never have, because we've never needed to." Instead, the firm "has expanded solely through client recommendation," and the website is pretty much their only marketing effort.

The firm's practice focus reflects this retro approach. Its core work is in the transport sector, particularly road and rail, and it's damned good at it. Our parent publication, Chambers UK, ranks F&W number one in the UK for road transport regulatory advice. Anyone who drives on major motorways regularly will be familiar with Eddie Stobart's fleet of lorries; well, F&W recently stepped in to successfully appeal the removal of the company's licence in eastern England. The firm also saved the licence of another, slower fleet of industrial vehicles – the substantial milk float army of Express Dairies.

Another core area is employment law, where

F&W is at the forefront in the field of industrial relations, by which we mean it advises employers on union recognition and strike action, that kind of thing. The firm was the only one in the country to obtain an injunction against the RMT in 2005's rash of rail strikes. It also boasts growing public sector expertise, advising local NHS trusts and strategic health authorities on employment policy issues and litigation.

So how has Ford & Warren fared with its back-to-basics approach? In the past ten years, five of Leeds' 'big six' law firms have transformed themselves from regional independents to Yorkshire branches of national firms. They have a lot of muscle and a lot of resources. Surely firms like F&W are being squeezed out of the picture. Not a bit of it. In fact, the firm has expanded to fill an entire seven-floor office in just a few years.

towing the line

Although transport law is the firm's forte, the employment department is one of the most likely destinations for a trainee. The seat offers them *"little tasters"* of all the work undertaken, but there's a focus on the tribunal side of things. They usually observe several of these, which is *"useful for seeing the different styles of fee earners and how legal knowledge is used in practice."* They also regularly attend meetings with witnesses to collect evidence. Mostly this is a seat for honing drafting skills, which are then applied to *"everything from witness statements to advice on maternity pay and policies."* Research also figures pretty highly. It's been known for trainees to take a couple of smaller files to run under supervision which *"give you a really good grounding in how employment disputes work. It's much more structured than regular litigation."*

Don't worry, there is plenty of 'regular litigation' experience too. Again, the work of the com lit and insurance liability teams reflects the firm's transport client base; for example, there's a good deal of vehicle hire repossessions. *"You're repossessing a car or van,"* one trainee explained. *"You go to court to get an order which gives the defendant a set time to deliver it back. If that happens you either make an arrangement with them to allow them to keep it or you call agents to go and get it."* This apparently plain dish comes with a big dollop of responsibility. *"You'll deal with clients on the phone and in person, and with the other side's solicitors. You'll present applications in the district court as well,"* noted one trainee. *"You'll even deal directly with the defendants. Being yelled at can be a bit intimidating, but you get used to it."* Insurance litigation offers a similar combination of less-inspiring tasks (*"large-scale, future-loss calculations for quadriplegia in miners"*) and a high level of responsibility on smaller matters.

maple sauce with that?

Non-contentious training could come to you via the firm's corporate or commercial property teams. Both offer *"quite a lot of paperwork"* but also *"quite a few hands-on experiences"* from drafting board minutes to preparing licensing applications for pubs. Overall, most trainees appeared to have seen the usual benefits of a smaller firm in terms of enhanced responsibility in their seats. *"They won't give you acres of bundling unless they think you'll gain something from it,"* said one; *"there are office juniors for that."* We suspect this might be as much to do with the firm's determination to keep fees down as its concern for trainees, but the effects are the same. *"They're quite flexible,"* noted another recruit. *"If they think you're up to going to court they'll send you there, and if there's something you think you can help with, you can suggest it."* Generally partners supervise in their own special way. *"Some will have daily meetings with you to see what you're working on and how you're getting on,"* explained a source. *"Others will just tell you to 'come and ask if you need anything'."*

Would you believe it? F&W offers a foreign secondment. Spend six months with Canadian associate firm Gary Gilman and you'll be helping Canuck businesses to plan their move into the UK market. If Toronto appeals, be sure to push for corporate seats early on to get yourself prepared.

A trainee's fourth seat is usually spent in the department where they plan to qualify, meaning that some trainees spend their whole second year in one department. No trainee expressed any objection to this, nor to the allocation they'd received. We couldn't tell if that's because it all works so well or because trainees didn't have strong feelings about the areas they wanted to experience. The majority of trainees talked about ties to Leeds as the main reason for choosing the firm, rather than any special interest in its key areas of work. Retention rates have fluctuated wildly in the past few years but recent expansion has seen them go high, with all four September 2006 qualifiers staying with the firm.

no nonsense

Given that the firm's slogan is 'excellence through endeavour', it won't be a massive shock that *"you're expected to work hard."* When asked what sort of person would suit the firm, trainees replied: *"Someone who's not afraid to roll up their sleeves and get stuck in."* The open-plan layout means *"there's no chance of playing solitaire for three hours,"* and as a rule *"you come in, do your work and go home."* Like many northern firms F&W has an early-riser culture, with most trainees coming in at around 8.15am and usually leaving around 6.15pm. *"When you're busy there are some exceptionally long days,"* noted one trainee. *"I've been in until 10pm a few times."* Despite a *"subdued,"* hard-working atmosphere, trainees assert that *"you can have a laugh with anyone from the secretary up to the partners."* Most notably, they spoke of *"a real sense of team spirit"* in each department. Nevertheless, the details of

the firm's policies reinforce the work-first culture; personal e-mail use is discouraged and anyone tempted to flaunt that rule should know that all trainees and assistants' e-mail is copied to their secretary and supervisor. *"It's not spying,"* one trainee assured us. *"It's just so your secretary can schedule appointments."* Hmmm. Ford & Warren is a buttoned-up place in the sense that *"dress-down Friday hasn't filtered through from London yet."* We doubt it will any time soon.

In recent years F&W has taken roughly even numbers of male and female trainees, but a glance at that website shows just two women in the 20-strong partnership. Interestingly, female trainees leapt to the firm's defence. *"There are more women coming in all the time,"* one said, *"and there are a few higher up."* Does the firm's road-n-rail background put women off? *"I don't think so,"* said one. *"There's a female assistant in the transport department who can certainly hold her own."*

F&W trainees are *"very close"* and can often be found out together on a Friday night with *"a bunch of younger assistants and associates."* The office Christmas party is *"a real knees-up, but people are very conscious of the senior partners until they go home."* Overall, it's a good firm for those with a full life outside the office. *"The managing partner once told me he doesn't want to monopolise people's time,"* one trainee explained. In fact, trainees have a habit of quoting the management's philosophy. *"Integrity never goes out of fashion,"* one told us.

and finally...

Ford & Warren is justly proud of the reputation it has carved in its core areas, and of its particular approach. This isn't a firm willing to be anyone's booby prize; it's looking for a commitment to Leeds, to its areas of work and to its distinct approach. If you can tick those boxes you'll get a shot at an in-depth, challenging and unique training here.

Forsters LLP

the facts
Location: London
Number of UK partners/solicitors: 27/60
Total number of trainees: 8
Seats: 6x4 months
Alternative seats: None

You could be forgiven for thinking that Forsters is older than it really is. Formed as recently as 1998 it has become ingrained into the fabric of Mayfair, specialising in that most West End of legal disciplines: property. If you are tempted by real estate and fancy joining one of the younger kids on a rather old block, pull up a chair.

the breakaway
When Frere Cholmeley Bischoff resolved to become the London branch of Eversheds back in 1998 (which, FYI, is when Eversheds was effectively still a franchise operation), a core group of its property lawyers concluded that they would be better off setting up on their own. The ten solicitors moved into an office in the West End of London and set up under the name of Forsters, in memory of Frere Cholmeley's founder, John Forster. It is fair to say that they have never looked back and, eight years on, the firm now has 29 partners and a handsome reputation for real estate. The clientele comprises public bodies, private developers and large-scale property investors and includes familiar names such as Chester City Council, McDonald's, Knight Frank, British Airways Pension Trustees and Reed Elsevier. In addition the private client team represents a mix of old and new money, taking in 30 different landed estates.

estates of the nation
Trainees rate Forsters' six-seat programme, saying: "*It's great to move around and get variety.*" Crucially it allows them to sample "*five seats*" before you actually have to make your mind up about where you might want to qualify." Usually the last four months is spent in their intended qualification department. Even with the flexibility afforded by the scheme, the main message is that "*you would be hard pushed to avoid the property department.*" Property operates across the three primary sectors of public, investor/developer and retail. In public sector matters the firm has recently advised the Royal National Orthopaedic Hospital NHS Trust on the outline planning application for a £122 million redevelopment of its site at Stanmore in Middlesex. The £23 million purchase of a new warehouse (pre-let to Pirelli) in Staffordshire is typical of the work conducted on behalf of investors, as is the sale of a £155 million property portfolio for long-term client Clerical Medical, and the City-challenging retail team acted for Frogmore Estates in its acquisition of a £42.23 million shopping centre in Hull. Trainees frequently play a role in major transactions, for example "*doing little bits on sales of large retail units*" as well as getting their own files. A trainee's own portfolio will typically include "*a couple of leases, licences to assign, licences to underlet, that sort of thing.*" In this department "*you won't be treated like a spectator.*" That's not to say that any other department will be a free ride, "*it's just that in commercial property there's a bit more work to do.*" Perhaps it is the sheer volume of business being handled that led one trainee to suggest it was "*the most highly strung department, which means the training isn't as ordered as it is in other seats.*"

Property litigation trainees are exposed to both commercial and residential property disputes and note "*lots of opportunities for advocacy experience.*" Whether working on their own possession proceedings, taking witness statements, preparing documents or going to case-management conferences with the clients, "*you just have* to throw yourself into it." One source assured us: "I never felt out of my depth as the team prepares you well before you go to court," and anyway, "the really tricky stuff" is sent to junior barristers. Trainees also play a role on larger cases, one good example being the representation of a tenant in the recently reported case The Bishopsgate Foundation v Curtis, which is now the leading authority on the definition of a 'live/work' unit in the context of leasehold enfranchisement.

Trainees who can't get enough of property can try the construction department, which is becoming a player of some importance and is presently advising McDonald's on framework agreements to be used for the ongoing refurbishment/rebranding scheme for its existing restaurants throughout the UK. A seat in construction provides "a steep learning curve" on drafting warranties, liaising with contractors and architects, making amendments to building contracts and appointing professional teams. Those we interviewed had enjoyed the mixture of property and contract law that construction offers and were able to cross-refer the knowledge and experience gained in each seat.

private thoughts

Away from the firm's real estate core there are commercial litigators plus coco, employment, family and private client specialists. The firm's private client expertise was for some trainees as big a draw as real estate. In this department they "work much more closely with clients on personal things and communicate with them much more." In addition to standard wills and trusts work it is likely that a trainee will get some of their own probate files as well as witnessing that the private client lawyer's remit can also extend to commercial and property matters. Thinking ahead, one source told us the seat was good for giving you "ideas about what to do with your own money." The other advantage is that the hours in this seat

are "nine to six" more often than in the others.

Despite the comments of the person who suggested "we don't have a corporate department here really," the company and commercial seat introduces trainees to smaller-scale deals and some AIM listings. On these matters trainees become embroiled in the verification process prior to the public offering of shares, and attend "hours and hours" of meetings. During leaner times there is always company secretarial work, which is "great as you get to apply stuff from the LPC." This seat can demand occasional late-night working; "I had maybe a week of leaving at 11pm," recalled one source.

Halfway through each seat trainees have an informal meeting with their supervisor to "talk about the way things are going and flag things up that you each want improved." After a spot of form filling, the end-of-seat review is an ideal forum for "valuable, constructive criticism." A mentoring system ensures there is always someone neutral to go to for "an off-the-record chat" that won't go any further. This is not a firm for wallflowers, as it deals out responsibility to people as soon as it thinks they are ready and gives people every opportunity to speak up if they want a little bit more.

rock 'n' roulade

Forsters occupies a "lovely" building on Hill Street. The renovated 18th-century townhouse was built by the renowned writer and prominent figure of polite society Elizabeth Montagu. The style and location of its home is one explanation for why Forsters appears to have been around a lot longer than eight short years. Another is its association with traditional old establishments, not least its 330-year-old bank, C Hoare & Co, to which new recruits are taken during their induction week. And yet our interviewees suggested the firm was perhaps a little more "flexible and open to new ideas" than some of its peers. Come here and you'll be able to make such comparisons for yourself as you'll meet your contemporaries at Boodle Hatfield and Bircham Dyson Bell on shared PSC training sessions.

One thing we noted about our sources was their well-developed understanding of their employer and its plans. Trainees seemed to have spotted a shift in the language used by partners *"from that of expansion to consolidation."* They told us the firm shows *"no desire to grow and grow"* and that ultimately it *"wants to rely on its strengths"* in property, private client and the practice areas that feed off each. In September 2006, just one of the four qualifiers stayed on, taking a job in commercial property.

Many staff dive into the local Red Lion at the end of the week, although it is also full of *"American tourists eating traditional English pub fare"* and you have to beware of *"taxi drivers aiming for you in the street."* Trainees meet up for occasional drinks during the week and in summer they get involved in weekly softball matches against *"other property law firms and agents."* There's also the occasional cricket or football match against Serle Court, a set of barristers with which the firm works closely. If you aren't too bothered about playing sport but have, as one trainee put it, *"other qualities,"* then you might be drawn to the firm's book club. The club meets once a month and, at the time of our interviews, was discussing *Beyond Black* by Hilary Mantel. It allows everyone *"from the senior partners to the secretaries"* to get together and share their ideas, perhaps enjoying this most *"civilised"* of affairs with wine and strawberries under a canopy on the firm's roof terrace. *"Last time the librarian made a roulade."* There is a *"fantastic"* summer party each year, last time held at the Lansdowne Club *"with Pimm's in the courtyard and a meal"* followed by dancing to Any Swing Goes, a band whose conductor and vocalist is one of Forsters' property partners.

and finally...

It may appear to be one of the grand old dames of Mayfair property law but in truth Forsters is still just an excitable young outfit that happens to have a catalogue of Establishment clients. If you choose to come here you're more likely to witness the steady increase of successful teams than a dramatic transformation.

Fox Williams

the facts
Location: London
Number of UK partners/solicitors: 15/26
Total number of trainees: 8
Seats: 5x21 weeks
Alternative seats: None

In 2006 Fox Williams was rated as one of *The Sunday Times'* '100 Best Companies To Work For', a fitting time for the fantastic Mr Ronnie Fox to pass the baton to new senior partner Tina Williams and move on to pastures new. We had a chat with trainees to see what, if anything, was changing.

your employment prospects
Formed 17 years ago by fugitives from big City law, FW has expanded to become a fun-size commercial firm with renowned strength in employment and partnership matters. It sees itself as something of a mild-mannered pioneer in the profession: look at its website and you'll see links aplenty to innovative online services targeted specifically at HR professionals, the fashion industry and foreign investors looking to make money in the UK or bring in employees from overseas. In the firm's own words – "We think outside the box and are constantly developing innovative ways to mould and shape our service offering." Could this be the time to arm yourself

with some consultancy spiel to complement your legal jargon?

FW has a five-seat training scheme, with the typical trainee going through corporate, property, litigation and employment and then taking on some cross-departmental work with, say, the comm/tech team. These seats highlight the several strings to FW's bow, but be aware: "*If you're not keen on employment, don't come here.*" Employment is "*the beating heart*" of the organisation, and the general view of our sources on the subject is that "*it's a real pleasure to work with experts and become involved in important dismissals and contract reviews, etc.*" It's not just about laying off surplus workers with minimum fuss; "*we also have high-earning individuals and expensive executives coming to us for advice. I think they perceive us as being smaller and therefore more independent.*" Evidence of the employment lawyers' achievements is everywhere. They acted for long-standing client Caledonia Investments in an important equal pay ruling; assisted Donaldsons, a nationwide property consultant, on its successful integration of two teams of specialists who had moved across from an arch-rival; defended a claim for race discrimination for Sainsbury's Bank; and advised two big-name shareholder activists on their departure from Hermes Asset Management, a story that made it to the front page of the *FT*.

a nose for fashion

To give you some flavour of the other seats, in dispute resolution one trainee reported "*close involvement in two fairly big trials, which meant lots of bundling and disclosure and some time in court.*" Another was more specific and told us of "*high-profile work for* [former executive directors of] *Equitable Life. I was really getting my hands dirty – it wasn't just research.*" Among the companies that use the firm for litigation are ICI, RWE

npower and insurance and reinsurance broker Heath Lambert Group. One trainee reported a satisfying time assisting on "*a big case defending npower against a group of sales agents.*" As in any firm with meaty commercial cases, "*it wasn't much fun sorting out bundles until 2am, but the next day we won the case.*"

Despite the comparatively small size of the corporate team, trainees found themselves up against well-known mid-sized players on deals, and noted how "*corporate has an international flavour.*" Much of the time "*you're acting for entrepreneurial individuals*" rather than faceless corporations – for example, advising on the sale of Neal's Yard Remedies to entrepreneur and publisher Peter Kindersley (of Dorling Kindersley fame). All up it's an interesting seat though we did hear a few grumbles about how "*corporate work tends to be very cyclical,*" so "*if you transfer in a slow period you won't get the chance to perform.*" In the realm of partnership law the firm has thrown the weight of its experience behind a number of LLP conversions of English and American law firms, one of them being the recently merged transatlantic legal partnership of Kirkpatrick & Lockhart Nicholson Graham LLP.

A seat in property could mean "*working on development deals and portfolio reorganisations. I was running my own files and had lots of contact with the other side.*" There is likely to be overlap with the corporate team when property assets form part of a company sale or reorganisation. Comm/tech, meanwhile, is a catch-all "*mix of commercial contracts, IP and competition law,*" and it's where you'll be most likely to encounter FW's most fashionable lawyers. The likes of Mambo, Firetrap and Karen Millen use the firm, and it has developed a good reputation in the industry.

Trainees were keen to explain one of the most persuasive arguments for choosing FW, telling us:

"*It's a unique selling point that most matters are partner-driven – lots of clients like dealing with a partner. There are also short chains of command, so if something is delegated to you, you are likely to be reporting direct to the partner. Direct contact means that you get direct feedback.*" The firm has a formal appraisal system based on comprehensive monthly meetings, but in reality "*if something's wrong you'll hear about it sooner rather than later.*" Trainees also say that in a small environment "*you can really shine... Never underestimate the impact you can have as a trainee.*" Their advice is "*take the initiative because it's always gratifying when you have a good idea that works – however minor it is.*" Of course there are downsides, which the trainees summarise thus: "*It's a small firm which expects a lot. It's a tight ship and there aren't so many support staff so trainees have to work hard.*" Even so, the hours are "*pretty painless,*" typically "*in by 9.30am and out by 6pm.*" Training seminars can extend the day, but overall trainees allude to "*a relaxed work ethic.*"

marks and sparkle

Trainees describe FW as "*wacky*" with "*lots of quirks and lots of personalities – it's not all grey suiters.*" They agree that "*everyone is very nice and there's plenty of personal chemistry and interaction; people are laid-back and not overly aggressive.*" Indeed, during their induction week our sources were told an anecdote about a senior assistant who was sacked for being rude to a secretary, the message being "*whether you're a rainmaker or not, everyone has to fit into the team.*"

Apparently the firm is "*catholic*" in its recruitment. "*We come from all over and range from people straight out of university to those who are 30 and married,*" reported an unofficial census taker. Each week a newsletter from the HR department lets everyone know if someone's had a baby or passed their driving test. Spotting the potential for pranks, "*on April Fool's Day someone put that you could only go to the toilet twice in a day or pay a fine for charity*" and "*some of the partners fell for it.*" If you're the type who doesn't like joining in you should be aware that "*it's a bit like Cheers. Everyone partakes and you may feel alienated if you don't want to.*" The social scene is good, and trainees told us about a recent quiz night with the head of accounts as a "*silent, brooding*" quizmaster. Trainees get together for a half-yearly dinner and regularly visit their locals, the Red Lion or Bangers wine bar, on Fridays. The fact that the annual trainee revue at the Christmas party (when newer members of the firm were encouraged to lampoon their seniors) never materialised last year was variously considered "*a relief*" or "*a shame.*" We hear it was scheduled to go ahead at the Christmas 2006 party.

FW's "*sharp, not super posh*" office backs onto Marks & Spencer in Moorgate and is decorated with the firm's logo of "*five blue squares representing the five different practice areas.*" In keeping with its burgeoning fashion practice, there are photos of models on the walls, but we have learned that "*an M&S suit is de rigueur for trainees.*" Sadly NQ retention rates are not always as positive as trainees would wish: "*Only one of three were kept on last time and the others were sad to go.*" At least they will have been pleased with the improved figure for September 2006, when three of the five qualifiers stayed on.

and finally...

Fox Williams is a breath of fresh air, particularly when you consider how many trainees don't get to sample employment law at bigger firms. If you have employment law leanings, or a passion for fashion, this close-knit firm would be a good place to get an all-round commercial training.

Freeth Cartwright LLP

the facts

Location: Nottingham, Derby, Leicester, Manchester
Number of UK partners/solicitors: 63/93
Total number of trainees: 13
Seats: 4x6 months
Alternative seats: None
Extras: Pro bono – Nottingham Law Centre

Along with Melton Mowbray pork pies, Adrian Mole and Robert Kilroy-Silk, the East Midlands can lay claim to being the home of regional heavyweight Freeth Cartwright.

spread the word

Freeths' reputation once rested on its work for individuals, not least civil litigation, where it gained a high profile for multiparty product liability cases such as those concerning infant MMR vaccine and the Trilucent and 3M breast implants. Although still strong in this area, and in claimant clinical negligence, latterly Freeths has emerged, phoenix-like, as a commercial hotshot. On the banking side, it is appointed by the likes of RBS on a range of deals; other key clients include Experian, for whom it undertakes a variety of corporate work. Our interviewees made it abundantly clear that with the firm wanting to be seen as a commercial player, "*training contracts are more likely to go to people who can show that this is what they're interested in.*" And it seems the message has filtered through to students because "*trainees now join with the expectation that it's a commercial rather than private client firm. You'd go elsewhere if private client stuff was your thing.*"

The message has certainly reached potential clients; for example in April 2006 Freeths secured a place in the elite EM Law Share legal group set up by in-house lawyers at 18 local authorities and four law firms in the East Midlands. Hailed as the UK's largest ever public/private legal partnership, the venture is likely to bring in litigation, planning and commercial work. Big-name commercial clients include Coors Brewers, HMV, Waterstone's, Paul Smith, The Tanning Shop, Arriva and ntl.

hot property

These days property is where it's at, and for many trainees it's the main reason for applying to the firm. Freeths claims the biggest commercial property department in the region and in 2005 worked on deals with a cumulative value of £1 billion. Don't be surprised then if the firm "*prefers you to do a commercial property seat.*" The feedback on the department is positive – "*they make you feel really at home*" – so much so that even those initially reluctant can be swayed. "*Although it wasn't my first choice of seat, I ended up loving it,*" one source confessed. Impressive new clients include a major retailer we'd love to name but can't, bicycle manufacturer Raleigh and Metropolitan Housing Association. They now accompany such illustrious names as Barratt Homes and Bellway Homes, outdoor equipment retailer Blacks, Multiyork Furniture and Nottingham Trent University.

Certain other seats, while in lower demand, nonetheless offer a good base for trainees, particularly as first seat placements. "*In planning I was quite mollycoddled, but this was okay as I was a newbie,*" said one source; another had a similar experience in the private client group, "*an absolutely lovely department to do your first seat in.*" We hope all concerned will take this the right way, but apparently "*the secretaries are a bit like your grandma, they really want to look after you. Little things you didn't realise you needed help with they will be more than happy to help on – stuff like drafting a letter.*" Sweet.

Autonomy and initiative come with time, as this trainee explained: "*When I first started I was a gibbering wreck, wondering how I'd be able to man-*

age my workload. But now I've found myself asking for more." Sounds like they're ripe for a stint in litigation, which has a reputation for putting trainees in the eye of the storm on contract, professional negligence and insurance disputes. "*You're really chucked in at the deep end, and the first couple of months are rather daunting, but the support is there and after a while it becomes really enjoyable.*" Given a relatively free rein on smaller matters, "*you have to use your initiative on how you conduct yourself and your cases.*" As well as considerable client contact, the seat requires trainees to make small applications in court, which is naturally "*a bit scary, but good experience.*"

Though it offers less autonomy for trainees, the corporate seat is a popular choice. "*As the deals involve quite a few million quid, you can understand why trainees don't get much responsibility,*" explained a source. Perhaps fitting for a law firm in a city with such a vibrant nightlife, Freeths' corporate lawyers have worked on a string of deals relating to pubs. Most recently they advised Heritage Pub Company's shareholders on its £79 million sale to Globe Pub Company. This was the third deal in less than three years for Heritage's entrepreneurial owners. They had previously sold 55 pubs to Pubmaster for £19 million and then bought 240 more pubs for £43 million. Hardly small beer.

the sun always shines on fc

If you get to the firm and you haven't made up your mind which seats you want to try, it's not a problem. In fact, "*sometimes it helps to have an open mind... after you've sampled everything you can then make an informed decision.*" If, however, you arrive wanting to specialise in a specific area, the firm is willing to accommodate your wishes. Last year it created a tax seat where one hadn't existed before, solely on the basis of one trainee's hankering for revenue experience.

Trainees are appraised at the end of each six-

month seat and can ask for a mid-seat review if they wish. "*The penny starts to drop after three months and you find yourself starting to understand things,*" they told us. Supervisors seem good at keeping track of your workload and will delegate matters if you're at full capacity. Clients, too, may recognise when you've had to pull a late one or apply extra elbow grease: "*I had to stay till 10.30 last Friday night to finish up some work for a client, but they took me out for a curry afterwards which I really appreciated.*" We should stress this is the exception and overall trainees described their hours as relatively civilised with weekends in the office a rarity.

Trainees sense the firm values transparency wherever possible: "*We're always informed about decisions at the top level and have a good intranet that updates us every day.*" On Freeths' recently overhauled website the sun is always shining, presumably to imply a bright disposition and the notion of clarity. Trainees say this imagery is indeed reflective of the firm's mindset, but is perhaps not an accurate representation of the East Midlands, where in actual fact "*it's hardly ever sunny.*" Whether this assessment of the region's climate is accurate we cannot say. What is beyond question is that for Freeths' trainees a major part of the firm's appeal is the very fact it isn't in London. As amazing as it may be to those of us who live and work in the capital, there are people who prefer their air cleaner and their beer cheaper.

In May 2006 word reached us of a new two-partner Freeths office in Manchester and a work referral relationship with Birmingham firm Anthony Collins. We've a hunch the two firms will get on well.

in the lap of luxury

For now there are no strict rules concerning which of Freeths' offices trainees will visit. Manchester is too new and too small an operation to feature at all in the training and so for the purposes of this feature we will ignore it. The majority of trainees stay in Nottingham, taking all four seats from the wide selection available; a few also spend time in Derby or Leicester. Complete with in-house Starbucks, plasma TVs and state-of-the-art gadgetry, the plush Nottingham office is definitely the hub of the firm. *"It's very modern, all glass-fronted, nice lifts and open-plan."* The *"small and busy"* office in Leicester has seats in commercial litigation, insolvency, employment and clinical negligence, and trainees say: *"It's got a good atmosphere and you get to know everyone quickly."* Derby offers seats in commercial, property and litigation and is described as a miniature version of the snazzy Nottingham HQ. We did hear suggestions that moving away from Nottingham can leave you feeling a bit out of the loop, in which case the best advice is to *"get involved in things so you don't feel like you're missing out."*

In all three offices lawyers work open plan, something which trainees like as they find it easier to approach partners with any queries. The set-up helps trainees in more ways than one: *"I wasn't sure about open plan when I first started as I thought people could hear everything I was saying on the phone, but it's actually fantastic and a real bonus getting to listen and learn."*

partners in their boxer shorts

Trainees form an integral part of the firm's social scene and most get involved with the Nottinghamshire TSG, which provides a veritable smorgasbord of opportunities to network with trainees at other firms in the region. As fun as TSG dog track nights and go-karting may be, nothing can eclipse Freeths' annual Christmas pantomime, which is always organised by trainees. Last year it included the mind-boggling spectacle of *"partners doing the Full Monty, right down to their Freeth Cartwright boxer shorts."* Six months' recovery period is probably considered long enough before the

summer party comes around. A marquee is put up, the barbecue goes on, and trainees serve the drinks until *"everyone gets so drunk they just help themselves."* During the rest of the year, staff can be found at the firm's regular Nottingham hangout The Castle. Although the media portray the streets of Nottingham as drug and gun-ridden with more ASBOs per head of population than anywhere else, our sample of Freeths trainees portrayed a sophisticated café culture more akin to the Left Bank in Paris than the West Bank in Palestine.

and finally...

Nottingham has one of the country's highest graduate retention rates across the board, and its law school produces many prospective trainees with a strong desire to stay in the city. Within the East Midlands legal market Freeths is a big name and it can afford to recruit wisely, taking on only those who look to be in it for the long haul. In September 2006, four of the seven qualifying trainees stayed on with the firm.

Freshfields Bruckhaus Deringer

the facts

Location: London
Number of UK partners/solicitors: 177/539
Total number of trainees: 198
Seats: 3 or 6 months long
Alternative seats: Overseas seats, secondments
Extras: Pro bono – RCJ CAB, Tower Hamlets Law Centre, Liberty, death row appeals; language training

The efforts of some 2,400 lawyers in 27 offices ensure Freshfields Bruckhaus Deringer a reputation as one of the world's finest and most successful law firms. So what is it that makes picking this magic circle player over the others a smart decision?

corporate class

One word: corporate. The worldwide public and private M&A practice is undoubtedly the engine room of the firm. In 2005 in the UK alone it advised on 108 deals worth more than £72.7 billion. Spend some time in the corporate division – which you undoubtedly will – and you'll be digging into a choice selection of the most high-profile deals around. We're talking about the ones you read about in newspapers – and not just the *FT*. The £12 billion takeover of UK airport operator BAA by a Spanish-led consortium is one of the most sought-after instructions in the City for years; Freshfields has it. Mobile phone giant O_2's £17.7 billion takeover by Spain's Telefónica; Freshfields has it. Advice to Manchester United on the £800 million contested takeover bid by the Glazer family; Freshfields gave it. Incidentally one effect of this deal was the de-listing of the football club's shares from the London Stock Exchange, which, as another Freshfields client, looked to the firm for corporate advice on the much-publicised unsolicited public offer by Australia's Macquarie Bank.

With big deals like these powering the firm you shouldn't expect to be skipping home from work in time for a cuppa and a gander at *Deal or No Deal*. We suggest you listen to some friendly advice from current trainees who readily admit that "*you will be under the cosh in corporate*" and "*it is still quite an alpha environment, so you cannot be that delicate.*" It seems you might be so busy that the most suitable unit with which to measure your time will not be hours or days, but whole seasons. "*One IPO took my spring from me,*" reported one source. An extreme case, perhaps, but "*loads of all-nighters*" will be on the cards.

All that hard graft is worth it, we're told, as it is "*such great experience to have on your CV.*" Plus you get the opportunity to make those deals happen with an "*awesome bunch of people.*" Admittedly, responsibility levels seem to vary between trainees.

Some of our interviewees worked to "*short timetables*" as members of small deal teams ("*I was shocked at the level of responsibility;*" "*huge banks calling me up, not really realising I was not qualified*"), others remained firmly in the proverbial "*small cog in a large wheel*" role tackling "*menial*" but "*vaguely important*" tasks. It stands to reason that trainees get the "*grim*" grunt work because documents won't proof-read themselves and there's always a "*non-air-conditioned basement data-room*" that needs manning.

high flying

A finance seat is another of the compulsory elements to the Freshfields training, and trainees say a "*technical and intellectual*" atmosphere makes finance seats a little different to those taken in corporate. Trainees can work in any one of four sub-specialties, namely: structured and asset finance, banking, energy and infrastructure and, last but not least, restructuring and insolvency. Lawyers in the asset finance team have their heads in the clouds, commonly dealing with complex, cross-border aircraft financings plus the odd train, boat or oil rig thrown in for good measure. These guys have got the market wrapped up to such an extent that on occasion teams are assigned to both sides of a deal with a hastily constructed 'Chinese Wall' between them. This happened on Airbus Financial Services' signing of a $900 million loan refinancing deal with the UAE's Oasis International Leasing in relation to 25 aircraft leased to a number of worldwide airlines. Looking at the different working patterns of the teams, trainees conclude that structured finance, in particular, is "*more of a constant slog, churning through so many deals.*" The tricky nature of the subject matter plus notoriously "*harsh hours*" means you should expect a "*baptism of fire*" at the start. Duties range from "*proof-reading, checking amendments, document management and general admin tasks on these big deals*" to "*drafting agreements and e-mailing clients.*"

day 256

"One particular benefit of the Freshfields training programme is the three-month seat option that allows people to see a broader range of work." Steady on – there are some rules. Corporate and finance are compulsory. Your first seat must be six months in length and in one of these compulsory practice areas. Beyond that, you can mix and match to your heart's content, selecting three or six-month seats throughout the rest of your training contract. No one we interviewed had any serious problems with the seat selection process and, apart from high demand for the IP and antitrust/competition options in particular, the *"interests tend to even out over the trainee pool."*

It used to be the case that the dispute resolution department would want you to make an appearance for at least three months. From 2006, any die-hard transactionalists who choose to can get the Law Society off their backs with regard to their contentious training by attending a two-week litigation course and undertaking some pro bono work. Those who do want to bang heads together on big disputes have plenty to get them interested. The firm performed well on the Bank of England's defence of the highly unusual misfeasance in a public office action bought by the liquidators of BCCI. This dispute was successfully resolved – over a decade after the original writ was issued – when BCCI's liquidators withdrew their claim part way through the trial. They took their time though: after 256 days in court it had already become one of the longest trials on record.

The clients are served well, but how about the trainees? Some *"lucky"* sources had *"a smooth ride"* with *"no late hours, no filing"* and *"very little bundling."* For others, *"nasty document review"* was more common. On balance, *"the hours are friendlier and more forgiving"* than in transactional seats as *"the deadlines are longer; in corporate, it's always ASAP."*

it's business and it's personal

As tax considerations float above almost everything Freshfields touches, a stint in this department gives a great overview of the firm as a whole. The work is *"very technical,"* of course, so best suited to those who have *"a love of the law."* No matter how keen you are, you might find yourself in a position where you *"don't understand anything."* If so, don't worry as this seat is all about the learning, with *"lots of thinking, no faffing around"* and *"not a lot of responsibility."*

Freshfields' real estate lawyers have a stellar client base that ensures a stream of big deals. Lately they advised Brascan, the Canadian real estate, power and asset management giant, on its £337.5 million purchase of a 999-year lease of the 555,000 sq ft building at 20 Canada Square, Canary Wharf, currently let to BP and McGraw-Hill. We hear that this deal was closed in under four weeks, so if you are assigned to transactions like this *"there can be times when you are working unbelievably hard."* Even so, trainees say that *"if you want to make a lifestyle decision, pick here, as the working hours are shorter."*

The *"small, young"* and *"absolutely fantastic"* EPB (employment, pensions and benefits) team was flagged up by some trainees as their favourite seat because the work was *"far more interesting, with more responsibility and more client contact."* A matter of opinion, naturally, but when you end up *"preparing the rest of the department for changes in the law – leading training sessions,"* job satisfaction is surely likely. The nature of the work means you can chalk up experience on both the contentious and non-contentious side, often dealing with clients on a *"much more personal level."*

hands across the water

It is widely known that new joint senior partner Guy Morton is keeping his eyes peeled for a suitable American firm to hook up with. How such a merger would affect future trainees remains to be seen but, whatever happens, a certain degree of out-of-office action is likely to feature in the training contract. The international opportunities for trainees are legion – Tokyo, Hong Kong, Shanghai, Dubai, Paris and several other offices take secondees, as do a number of clients, some overseas. Recently trainees have been to the likes of IBM, Morgan Stanley, ExxonMobil and human rights group Liberty.

The firm's own graduate bumph lists the qualities it looks for in trainees: academic achievement, analytical skills, creativity, teamworking, interpersonal skills, etc. So far, so predictable, but who is it actually recruiting? Unsurprisingly, "*language skills are valued very highly*" and "*everyone is very keen.*" Apparently "*you need to have the confidence to back your own judgement*" and "*it's important to be outgoing, but not brash.*" Although no mention is made of schooling or university background in the literature, Freshfields is still viewed with suspicion by many who don't have the Oxbridge stamp on their CVs. The question is, should they? It is true that around half of the firm's trainees come from Oxbridge colleges. It is also true that some 50 universities worldwide are represented, as are some 20 nationalities.

style counsel

A thorough induction awaits all new trainees to show them the ropes and allow them to feel more confident about starting their first seat. Freshfields takes preparing recruits for life in the City further than most other firms in that it brings in a style consultant to "*give us a lecture on what we should be wearing.*" Luckily the constructive comments of the professional fashion bod are less acerbic than those offered by Trinny and Susannah: "*she is not mean*" and there is "*no naming and shaming.*"

Once their threads are in order, recruits move onto a thorough programme of trainee-specific,

departmental and firm-wide sessions. This is supplemented with more informal teaching from supervisors, who can be either an experienced associate or a partner. Trainees imply that relationships with supervisors can be a bit hit and miss. "*Much of your enjoyment depends on your supervisor,*" they told us; "*they may be really interested in training or you could be sitting with someone who thinks you are a secretary.*" One trainee was particularly unimpressed with the level of consistency, using us as an outlet for their gripes: "*It really is a waste of time if they are not serious about training you. We should be allowed to give feedback on our supervisors, but people don't want to be known as someone who makes a fuss.*" Still, the majority who had positive experiences could not have been keener to give credit where it was due, telling us: "*The type of supervision you get depends on your own confidence and own experience*" and "*an effort is made to make you feel welcome. People were friendly and encouraging.*"

The wider support systems were seen as "*exceptional.*" Nocturnal secretaries will have your rambling dictations "*typed overnight and on your desk the next morning*" and "*paralegals make many tasks much easier.*" IT support was also praised. If you don't have a PhD in PowerPoint "*you can scribble something on ten bits of paper and give it to someone else who will turn it into an excellent-looking presentation.*"

you are what you eat

So, that complicated question – why Freshfields in preference to its magic circle rivals? Trainees offer these answers: "*a collegiate atmosphere;*" "*Freshfields is a lot more fun;*" "*it is more work hard, play hard.*" And the best answer of all – "*free fruit… friends at other magic circle firms get unhealthy cakes and biscuits.*" We do wonder how these ideas (not the fruit) tie in with the "*traditional set of values at senior level*" and notions that this is "*quite a conservative place.*" One trainee even spoke of their *"impression that Freshfields follows the pack rather than leads it. Everyone is always looking at the other firms – on things like salary rises they always claim 'we were going to do it anyway' – well why not announce it then?"*

One area where the firm has been quick off the mark is in relation to the tailoring of an LPC course to suit the particular needs of its future trainees. Since September 2006, all have been attending BPP in London, where they continue to share most classes with other students. They do have some separate Freshfields-only electives classes and also spend eight or nine days training within the firm's offices.

At any of the big City firms the route to partnership can be long and convoluted, so it comes as little surprise that some trainees don't see themselves staying until retirement. *"Very few people admit to wanting to become a partner,"* some told us. Fortunately we did speak to a few who fancied sticking around for a crack at the top jobs, or at least to *"see how far I can go."* Starting off on the long road, some 45 of the 52 qualifiers stayed with the firm in August 2006, around half of them going into corporate or finance teams.

After the *"social maelstrom"* of the induction, the next thing everyone mentioned was the *"pretty amazing"* (and, according to the firm, massively subsidised) trainee summer ball. Although some people moaned about the *"cheeky 40 quid"* ticket price, the majority thought it well worth the investment, as *"they really push the boat out."* If 2005's Alice in Wonderland ball was anything to go by, then the 2006 Arabian Nights extravaganza was sure to have impressed the partygoers. Beyond that, the firm is *"good about giving trainees a budget for drinks evenings every so often."* Departmental and firm activities are also dotted throughout the year and trainees can expect to be invited to *"completion dinners or parties at some of the top restaurants in London."* A short stroll from the plush Fleet Street offices is

the Witness Box, which is arguably the backbone of the trainees' social scene. If you're into sport, the usual teams will be after your signature on the sign-up board and there are a few more unconventional offerings like dragon boat racing in London's Docklands.

You may be trying to understand the significance of the recent resignation of 30 partners. It sounds alarming but it's actually not. Changes to the firm's retirement plan made resignation financially prudent for many of the older partners, most of whom (but not all) remain at the firm in the role of consultant. One other news story you may have read concerns the idea of a lunch-date merger offer made to the firm by A&O. Sounds crazy – it's not going to happen, by the way – and naturally no one at the firm cared to even confirm whether the story was true. Oh to have been a hovering waiter...

and finally...

If you fancy the idea of sitting back with a morning smoothie to read about the fruits of your labours in the *FT*, then Freshfields may just be the firm for you. Just don't expect the smoothie moment to last much past 9am...

Government Legal Service

the facts

Location: London
Number of UK lawyers: 1,900
Total number of trainees: 50
Seats: 4x6 months
Alternative seats: Brussels
Extras: Language training

The GLS is the UK's biggest legal employer. Around 1,900 lawyers (as its solicitors and barristers are collectively known) work across some 30 government departments handling everything from the Mubarek Inquiry to goats trespassing on the motorway. It may have just one client – Her Majesty's Government – but training here is a vigorous and diverse experience offering significant responsibility. As the GLS says: "We don't just advise on the law – we advise on what the law should be."

dft, hmrc, bfg, lol

If a career in the GLS isn't near the top of the average law student's wish list, perhaps it should be because interesting opportunities abound within the service, whether in Whitehall, The Strand or Holborn. Government departments, it seems, are scattered about London like dandelion seeds. Don't worry about staring at the same office wall and drab government officials for four decades. Once qualified you'll be urged to pursue a diverse career by switching departments every two to three years and the GLS encourages personal development and on-going education. You could even find yourself undertaking a fully sponsored part-time MBA.

Life as a civil servant involves a welter of acronyms and abbreviations that are "*really annoying until you find yourself using them in ordinary conversation.*" For ease, the seven main trainee hubs are: the Department for Constitutional Affairs (DCA), the Department for Transport (DfT), Her Majesty's Revenue & Customs (HMRC), the Department for Community and Local Government (DCLG), the Department for Trade and Industry (DTI), the Department for Work & Pensions/Health (DWP/H) and the Treasury Solicitors department (TSol). Quite a mouthful, but it's only the tip of a departmental iceberg fully elucidated at www.gls.gov.uk. We'd suggest reading up on those other departments before making an application, not least to determine whether they take trainees, pupils, both or neither. By way of example, the Home Office is one of the most popular choices for applicants, but it only takes pupils.

Once installed as GLS lawyers, trainees usually spend three of their four seats in their 'home' department. Additionally, one litigation or Crown Prosecution Service seat and a policy or advisory seat are compulsory, although most trainees end up taking two of each. Regular mid-seat and end-seat appraisals keep trainee and supervisor abreast of which 'trainee objectives' have been achieved and help ensure that seat allocation takes account of individuals' interests. Flexibility seems to be the order of training and beyond, and recruits who hadn't been placed in a first choice of home department told us they had found themselves in a good position to negotiate over future seats. We also noted that trainees seem to be encouraged to take seats that reflected their academic or work experience strengths. Even if qualification doesn't bring the hoped-for area, NQs are happy in the knowledge that they can move in the future.

Supervision and feedback varies greatly from department to department, but in each seat all trainees have an individual supervisor as well as a line manager (often these are the same person). Other team members also have a hand in training: "*My supervisor would vet cases for me before they arrived on my desk, but team members regularly checked my work before it went out,*" remembered one trainee. Another concurred: "*As time went on in each department, people would approach me directly with work. I felt like a colleague, not a trainee.*" Responsibility comes early and there is "*little sense of being spoon-fed. Although you get support, you manage your own work.*" Only one of the trainees we interviewed had done any major photocopying; all had encountered "*high-level work from the very start,*" having been handed whole cases or discrete tasks on larger matters. They concluded that being part of such a vast, "*well-regulated and controlled*" organisation means "*you feel less exposed or pressured.*" At the end of the training "*it's*" highly unlikely that you won't be offered a position" and, knowing this, trainees work with the attitude that "it's all about meeting a standard, not beating others."

generalist attorneys

In the spirit of intra-governmental co-operation and to breed an expectation of the diversity that will define their later careers, trainees spend one seat away from their home department. Most relish the move, be it to the MoD, Defra or wherever. One trainee arrived in the Attorney General's office to find "brilliant work – my supervisor specialised in diversity and equality issues, so there was a lot of special advocacy and advisory work."

As the economic and legal heart of the GLS, TSol takes on the largest number of trainees every year, and because it handles most of the government's litigation (departments like Defra and the DWP/H do also have litigation teams), recruits based elsewhere will fulfil their litigation requirement here too. In TSol the scope of the GLS is most apparent: trainees had worked on immigration cases, defended judicial review challenges on behalf of secretaries of state and tackled Home Office PI cases including prison deaths. There are also Ministry of Defence matters and more-standard commercial and company law to be experienced.

Advisory seats can range from tax in HMRC – where one pupil had worked on the 12.5% drop in condom taxes – to assisting with bylaws, council tax and parish issues in the DCLG (formerly the Office of the Deputy Prime Minister). Another pupil had spent a seat in DfES assisting with the trust school aspects of the Education Bill. "It made me realise I loved advisory work," they told us. If you arrive in a department during a lull (think the VAT advisory group post-Budget), you might well be farmed out. One source who had encountered this told us: "I did work for the Postal Services Commission and I've also made legal presentations on powers for police officers."

yes minister

Working for the government is less about being ardently politicised than it is about understanding how legislation affects the public. "You do have to be interested in current affairs, but holding strong political persuasions is considered a disadvantage," explained one trainee. Essentially, the GLS is an employer like any other, and if you end up representing a (currently) Labour government-run Prison Service in a public enquiry, you do it without regard to the colour of your client's rosette on polling day. It's no different to representing a multinational corporate in the private sector or a stranger who walks in off the street needing a divorce.

Sure, the civil service is commonly portrayed as slow, overly bureaucratic and grey, so does it deserve such bad press, we asked. Generally our sources thought not. "It's so well organised," said one trainee, "but also very egalitarian. If I have difficulties I can voice them and they will be heard." Other advantages are to be found in the GLS's maternity leave and flexible working policies, which are "generous and unproblematic." One area where the public sector can't match the private sector is, of course, salaries. No one denies that the GLS lawyers pay "isn't exactly on par with the City;" that said, "no one's in dire straits" either. At least former private practitioners who have transferred to the service commonly find themselves becoming more enthusiastic about the law. "Within five months I was twice the lawyer I had been before," said one City refugee. "True, I did take a cut in salary, but it was fascinating work of real importance."

All lawyers and trainees have the luxury of a regulated 40-hour week ("we don't arse around here – straight in, straight out by 6pm) and see the work-life balance as a "highly underrated" advantage of the GLS. Working beyond 7pm is "rare" and working at weekends "unheard of." After-hours activities are organised by a host of committees; most departments arrange their own events and the trainees we spoke to had all attended Legal Training Network-organised activities such as wine tasting, ice skating and that old favourite – going down the pub.

sign me up

Applications for a GLS training contract should be submitted two years in advance of the start date. Those who meet the eligibility criteria sit an online reasoning test and then short-listed candidates are invite to an assessment centre. There they will complete a written exercise, do group exercises and have an individual interview. At the interview candidates will be asked to argue on a pre-selected current (usually legal) topic. They will also be asked to indicate two preferred 'home' departments, should they be successful in securing a position. This process applies equally to prospective solicitors and barristers.

Having previously specified that applicants only have a minimum of a 2:2 at degree level, the GLS has raised the bar to a 2:1 in 2006. The nature of its application form has changed and asks fewer general questions and a far more searching question that requires a well-analysed answer. The aim has been to weed out half-hearted applicants and early signs show that it may have done just that. From a massive 1,400 applicants in 2005, the figure went down to 700 or so in 2006. Applicants complete for between 21-25 places (the majority of them for trainee solicitors). Among current trainees there are plenty of non-law grads, second-careerers and people with young families. LPC fees and a maintenance grant are available to those who need them and trainees indicate that in exceptional circumstances the GLS has been known to provide financial support for GDL students.

Because the GLS training experiences of pupil barristers are so similar, you might also want to read our GLS pupillage feature on page 803.

and finally…

Unless you have your heart set on a silk-upholstered corner office and a retirement palace in Mauritius, you should look hard at what the GLS has to offer. Job security, work-life balance and a chance to work with policy and legislation in a huge range of areas at the highest level – no wonder our lasting impression is of lawyers who see their work as being *"fascinating, challenging, intense and important."*

Halliwells LLP

the facts

Location: Manchester, Liverpool, London, Sheffield
Number of UK partners/solicitors: 115/190
Total number of trainees: 76
Seats: 5x21 weeks
Alternative seats: Secondments
Extras: Pro bono – Manchester Uni Advice Centre

Is there any stopping Halliwells? In the last few years it has gobbled up rivals, sucked in competitors' partners and hiked its profit levels. As this northern juggernaut picks up pace, can it offer trainees a smooth ride?

on the road

The story of Halliwell's expansion is well known, but here's a quick recap. Already a highly profitable Manchester corporate firm with London and Sheffield outposts, it screeched, wheels smoking, into Liverpool in 2004 by taking over property boutique Cuff Roberts. It has since beefed up that office with a series of raids on local competitors. Most recently Halliwells has absorbed the bulk of insurance-heavy Manc firm James Chapman & Co. There are many statistics we could quote to illustrate the scale of Halliwells' expansion, but we've chosen the one that really matters to you. From hosting just 27 trainees in 2003 the firm now has a whopping 76. And it's not over yet: as the managing partner has announced his intention to move Halliwells into the UK's top 25, London is the next office tipped for major expansion.

Halliwells has a great reputation in everything from corporate and insolvency to transport and insurance litigation. This ensures a wide range of seats for trainees, albeit that Manchester offers the greatest number. The firm employs a five-seat system, with the specific aim that it should be *"easy to get back into your chosen department for your final seat."* These days, trainees are also encouraged to try a seat in another office to the one they regard as their base.

striking the balance

Despite there being no compulsory seats, trainees are likely to do dispute resolution, corporate and real estate seats. The insurance department focuses on the three Ps – personal injury, public liability and prof neg – and boasts clients ranging from AXA and Zurich to the Metropolitan Police. It offers a litigation baptism of fire as trainees get a portfolio of their own cases from day one. *"You don't have complete control over files, but you manage their day-to-day running, conducting hearings, meeting clients, discussing on the phone, drafting witness statements."* Granted, trainee responsibility is highest on smaller matters, where *"if you make a mistake it's not the end of the world,"* but on all cases, *"the more you do, the more responsibility you get. You're encouraged to think of ideas to move the case forward, and if they're approved, to go ahead and do them."*

A seat in the commercial litigation department exposes trainees to more-valuable matters: everything from defamation to a quarrel over the sale of Wrexham Football Club. One trainee who'd spent days slogging through files in search of evidence said: *"It all paid off when I was having a detailed discussion about the evidence with counsel."* One of the best aspects of the seat is the

steady supply of agency work that sees trainees providing local advocacy services for law firms in other areas. *"You get the papers and a day or two later you're off to the hearing... the first one's really nerve-wracking but you soon get the hang of it."*

from dawn till dusk

The corporate team's reputation rests on M&A and AIM flotations. There's no escaping the *"donkey work"* – everything from *"putting together bibles"* to *"drafting board minutes and filling in Companies House forms"* – but even on such tasks *"you can earn a great deal of trust."* Other duties include due diligence, verification and research; basically *"anything the assistants don't have time to do."* Indeed, with the department heavy on partners and trainees and light on assistants, *"you do get a lot to do and it can be quite stressful."* The hours, too, can be nasty, especially in the build-up to a deal completion. *"On my very first day we had a completion on and I was on the phone all night to the other side checking they had all the documents, page number by page number,"* explained one trainee. *"Eight to eight is basically normal throughout the seat,"* explained another veteran.

Real estate provides a less intense experience. *"I was dreading it as it seemed so boring at law school,"* admitted a source, *"but I really liked it. It's different when you see the business side."* With major matters such as a £32 million redevelopment in Merseyside, *"you're obviously not let loose on the negotiations"* and there is *"a fair bit of form filling,"* but when it comes to inspecting titles and researching potential obstacles to development, *"you get to be a bit of a detective, poring over maps and so on."* There's also a fair bit of contract drafting and, better still, trainees are usually given a residential or small commercial matter to run under supervision. These matters offer *"lots of client contact."*

The firm's other seat options include private client, family, environmental/regulatory, marine/shipping, corporate recovery, banking, construction, IP, tax and employment. In addition, the firm has a range of established and occasional client secondments, including to Tesco and the brewer InBev.

go-getters

With high levels of responsibility in all seats and the firm's reputation for assertiveness, it's no surprise that Halliwell's trainees are an ambitious bunch. *"You have to be able to stand up for yourself,"* one told us, with another adding that *"increasingly we're getting people who consider themselves on a par with magic circle trainees."* Not that the firm is only interested in academic high fliers: it has a long-standing policy of offering training contracts to talented paralegals who can prove their worth.

Even the super-confident trainees at Halliwells need good supervision and, generally, the partners seem up to the job. It's *"a mixture of red ink and sit-down feedback,"* as one source summed up the approach their supervisors had taken. Either way, *"you're never left wondering why changes have been made."* Though help is available, *"you're expected to be bright and show initiative... you can ask questions, but not every five minutes."* A minority of partners were deemed *"a bit hard to get hold of"* and a few *"characters who are tricky to handle"* were identified in corporate, but in such cases assistants step in and are *"always helpful."*

The appraisal system looks great on paper. Initial 'objectives meetings' at the start of a seat are followed up with a formal mid-seat appraisal with HR and then a relaxed, end-of-seat review. Is this ambitious timetable adhered to? *"Some supervisors think it's a waste of time,"* trainees confessed. *"The initials and mid-seats get done because HR is involved, but you still have to nag."* One source had *"never had an end-of-seat review,"* others reported a full complement of appraisals.

The five-seat system and the ability to have input into the choice of first seat won a thumbs-up from trainees, yet we still heard some complaints about the actual allocations. A few trainees said they had missed out on seats they'd asked for repeatedly or had been sent back into a department for their last seat when they would have preferred something new. Certain key departments – notably IP and employment – were dubbed the hardest to get into. *"You have to be political, speak to the partners,"* confirmed one old hand. Furthermore, the long-standing problem of late notification of seats hasn't gone away. Still, we've heard of far worse elsewhere and everyone we spoke to seemed to have had at least one or two of their favourite seats.

At qualification time *"there's a system in place – you give in your CV, have an interview, and so on,"* but according to some people *"it's a complete formality; the partners know who they want."* Is this a bad thing? Maybe so, at some firms. Here? Who knows – the classic Halliwells trainee is an assertive, confident individual, more than capable of impressing and networking their way into a job. In September 2006, all of the 21 qualifiers managed it.

work hard; play harder

In Manchester plans are afoot for a move in 2007 to the city's up-and-coming financial district, Spinningfields. Trainees confirmed that the atmosphere is *"hard-working and focused."* *"People aren't laid back about work, but they do have a sense of humour. You can stop for a chat, but people are busy."* When it comes to hours, you're looking at some of the longest in the North. Outside corporate, most departments see 8am to 6pm or 9am to 7pm as standard. Corporate walks to the beat of its own drum. Out of the office there are always something going on, not least because there is an active Trainee Solicitors' Group in the city. On Fridays, trainees can be found propping up the bar at a range of local nightspots. *"Spinningfields will have loads of new bars,"* one source gleefully reported. Make no mistake, while the firm works its people hard, it also rewards them – it pays for tickets to the TSG ball and the biannual 'office rallies' consist of *"a little bit of indoctrination and a lot of free booze."*

Although migrating Manchester staff and external hires have seen the Liverpool branch grow, it remains the more relaxed baby brother to Manchester's high achiever. *"There's more pressure for billing and raising business now,"* one ex-Cuff Roberts trainee told us, *"but in other ways they've adapted to us, not the other way round."* With all staff on one floor, *"everyone knows everyone; it's very much a place you can chat, if you have time."* The hours are closer to 9am to 5.30pm and, here too, the local TSG is central to the trainee social scene. The office also aims for a monthly night out for all trainees and associates, usually at Andersons or the White Bar. *"People do get pissed and enjoy themselves,"* trainees confirmed. *"One lad from accounts loves to get his bum out."* Said derrière is described as *"not bad."*

The Sheffield office is also said to be *"a lot more relaxed"* than Manchester. Here, the original insurance litigation focus has broadened out and seats are now available in real estate, construction, employment and corporate recovery. Takapuna is the venue for monthly office drinks. In London the vibe varies by floor: *"Corporate is very pressurised but dispute resolution is all loose ties and long lunches."* After-work fun is found in the local Corney & Barrow. Unusually for a firm of its size, Halliwells still brings all staff together for summer and Christmas parties in Manchester. *"People really let their hair down – even partners."*

and finally...

The people we encounter at Halliwells are ambitious, intelligent and demanding, so if you badly want to succeed and you're willing to work hard to do so, this could be one of the best options north of Watford Gap. As for London where hardcore firms are two a penny, the choice is a less obvious one but we'd still say it could be a smart one.

Hammonds

the facts

Location: Birmingham, Leeds, London, Manchester
Number of UK partners/solicitors: 140/264
Total number of trainees: 79
Seats: 6x4 months
Alternative seats: Overseas seats, secondments
Extras: Pro bono – various legal advice schemes; language training

Hammonds has experienced turbulent times of late and a brief Google session will reveal the legal press's downbeat opinions on the national firm's travails. Yet there's no doubting the quality of its training scheme or the upbeat optimism of its trainees.

rise, fall and rise again

Massive expansion over the past 15 years – in part through mergers with niche outfits and larger firms both at home and overseas – saw the Hammonds bubble inflate impressively. Then in 2004 and 2005 profit levels tumbled, arousing internal criticism of the firm's management. A multimillion-pound 'hole' was discovered in the accounts and the small matter of a £25 million overdraft became public knowledge. Partners deserted in some numbers, while emergency cost-cutting measures included a redundancy programme that affected 60 staff. The remaining equity partners agreed to be bound into a 14-month lock-in agreement designed to steady the ship and allow confidence to return. When it ended in mid 2006 further partner departures followed. It's not hard to see why some commentators have predicted bleak prospects for the firm.

But have they been fair? Recent financial figures showing a 61% profit increase have been a ray of sunshine, even if turnover only increased by 4% in 2005/06. New partners have arrived and, as the firm is right to point out, no law firm is immune from annual partner losses. The new management is serious about steering the firm on a sensible course. A recently completed strategy review has led to a new three-year plan based on streamlining management structures and integrating the domestic and international offices by reshuffling the firm's practice groups into four international departments. What's more, the overdraft has been reduced, all of which is grounds for cautious confidence. Even if time will be the best judge of how Hammonds deals with the years to come, what we can report with authority are the refreshingly frank opinions of trainees.

page 39 news

Those approaching qualification had, to put it mildly, *"seen the low times,"* but suggested taking Nostradamus-like press reports with a pinch of salt. *"Every business has its weak points, but fundamentally this is a good place to be. There is no reason to dwell on those sort of articles because as soon as you are off the front page, there will be someone else there."* Plenty of stiff-upper-lip action then, but trainees were keenly aware that bad news sells: *"If there was anything positive to say about us then it would be in small print on page 39. It has got to the stage where we are laughing at it."* Despite such resolute perspectives, most of our sources admitted to being *"disillusioned at times"* and that consolation in such low moments was found in spirit-of-the-Blitz optimism. *"You had faith because others were positive. It's kind of catching."*

Apparently, these difficulties of the recent past led Hammonds to *"really listen to clients and people within the firm, not just plan abstractly."* The top brass regularly tour the offices *"to keep us updated"* and beyond this charm/communication offensive there's been *"a tightening of the belt on costs."* Some perceive this element of tougher management as *"quite niggly"* – *"you don't get tea*

and coffee in internal meetings now" plus *"there are controls on stationery."* But others said they'd lost *"nothing you can't live without"* and that when needs must, results count – *"it actually looks to have worked."* When asked to consider the future, there was broad agreement on a sense that *"things are looking up"* because *"the firm has got a grip on strategy and is back on track."* In that positive context we mention less certain comments – for example, *"I am not convinced the problems have been resolved for good"* – because it's worth remembering that the firm has work to do. Thirty out of 40 trainees stayed on with the firm in 2006, including several who were aware of their value in the buoyant NQ market. *"I've got a strong CV and I would not have taken a qualification job if I wasn't 100% sure,"* said one. By contrast, at the time of going to press Hammonds was in talks to prevent three partners from leaving its Brussels competition team, other summer resignations included the national head of real estate, the Manchester head of corporate and the heads of sports and environment teams. In that sense the picture is both good and poor at the same time.

one size fits all

Hammonds has made significant effort to promote a one-firm mentality across its four UK offices (non-geographical '0870' numbers are standard), but after a period of so-called location-rotation training contracts that saw trainees move around three offices, new arrivals are now recruited into a single office. Three compulsory areas must be covered during a two-year, six-seat training: a corporate option (which can include finance or tax); real estate (including construction) and a contentious seat. Fitting these around your must-see departments makes seat selection something of a tactical affair, by all accounts not unlike *"playing chess."* Those with wanderlust can make a clear play for an overseas secondment or, if training in the regions, a London seat. Proud of its international network of offices, Hammonds can offer seats in Brussels (two places), Turin, Madrid, Berlin, Hong Kong and Paris.

Trainees told us that *"the balance of your workload is heavily tipped towards things you are proud to do – it's great to read about stuff* [you are working on] *in headlines."* They were also pleased to tell us that *"everyone's been really busy for the last nine months."* Little chance of idling or wasting away by the photocopier: *"You will be given work that stretches you, but is not beyond you."* After a period in a seat *"you're actually asked for your opinion."* Comprehensive formal training is delivered through *"regular sessions and ongoing weekly departmental meetings."*

corporate's a breeze

No matter which office a trainee is in, the corporate department's status as Hammonds' engine room means a seat here is highly likely. Top deals include Rensburg's £185 million acquisition of Carr Sheppards Crosthwaite from Investec (including the re-listing of Rensburg and the successful defence of Rathbone Brothers' £144 million hostile approach). And flexing international muscles, Hammonds' UK and European offices joined together to advise Anglo Asian Mining on its £76 million AIM listing. Unsurprisingly in the current full-bore corporate market, a corporate seat is *"dreaded"* by some trainees. Even those who loved it admitted that *"really hard-core hours"* are par for the course, but *"it's all hands to the pump... they get you really, really involved."* Trainees typically handle *"preparation of due diligence reports," "take care of conditions precedent"* and *"draft board resolutions and verification documents for AIM admissions."* They take pride in the fact that *"although you know there are safety nets there, the buck does stop with you on a lot of stuff."* In similar vein, the big deals in banking dictate long hours and the odd *"absolute stinker."* But, as in corporate seats, the redeeming feature is that

"even when pressure is on, everyone is still having a laugh – it's a really fun place." Our interviewees were particularly keen for us to highlight a growing energy practice straddling the corporate and finance teams. This team recently worked on the £165 million acquisition of four wind farms and a £300 million loan refinancing for British company Beaufort Wind.

you lookin' at me?

A real estate seat means maximum responsibility, perhaps *"managing 35-40 files."* This can lead to *"stressful times,"* but for the most part is viewed as *"enormous fun."* Confident that *"support is always available, you'll never be out of your depth,"* trainees also help out on bigger transactions and projects, of which the firm has many. Lawyers were recently instructed to advise Sheffield City Council in the regeneration of Park Hill, a 1960s residential block in the city centre which is grade II listed and the largest listed building in the UK. Other clients of the real estate group include Waitrose, the brewery Scottish & Newcastle and a fast-growing retailer called American Golf.

If clients ever find themselves in tricky situations the property litigation team steers them through. This department relies heavily on trainees, granting them a *"high level of trust."* Common trainee tasks here are *"briefing and instructing counsel, structuring arguments and plenty of research."*

In a general commercial dispute resolution seat, making an application in court shouldn't faze you too much because it happens frequently. One trainee gleefully remembered *"preparing a skeleton argument side by side with a senior figure who would have jumped in if needed. We did a role-play in advance, then I went home and practised in the mirror. I was briefed on everything so it ran according to plan."* Naturally litigation seats do also involve a good deal of document management tasks, but that comes as standard anywhere.

The construction team has seen some departures but remains a powerful force. It covers a decent array of top work that includes advice to the London Development Agency on projects relating to the 2012 Olympic Games. For a trainee, construction is a "*drafting-heavy seat*" where warranties and construction contracts figure prominently. "*If you hit the seat at a busy time it can be a shock to the system,*" explained one source. Meanwhile, a stint in employment means "*hands-on work*" in a group that recently snatched the role of employment adviser to Tesco from national rival DLA Piper. The chart-topping sports law practice is equally successful, with instructions coming from governing bodies, footie clubs (Chelsea, Arsenal, Fulham and Aston Villa) and sponsors like Nike, Carlsberg and Gillette.

Other trainee experiences include "*high-level research and drafting agreements from scratch*" in the commercial and IP seats, or stints in the environment, competition, pensions and international projects and finance groups. Sports and international projects and finance are only available in London. Last but not least we should mention that there are secondments to clients (eg Live Nation, formerly part of Clear Channel), for which trainees at any office can apply.

cliché police, arrest this man....

Despite Hammonds presenting itself as a single entity, prospective trainees need to make office-specific applications. As with any national firm, we'd recommend thoroughly researching where your chosen office fits with the regional competition and remember that you can't go into an international firm with a view to servicing the needs of the local small-business community. Most trainees say there is "*no particular type*" among their number, although some suggested that "*bookish people or wallflowers*" wouldn't flourish in an environment that requires an ability "*to connect with clients and work well in social situations.*" Oodles of "*energy and enthusiasm*" also help. "*We are all driven, directional and self-sufficient – we want to be successful... we are also a lot of fun.*" On that note, our sources say Hammonds has a (call the cliché police) "*work-hard, play-hard ethos,*" adding that "*you make friends pretty quickly here.*" A "*lively*" social scene reaches its zenith at the summer and Christmas parties. Hammonds also "*values its sports teams,*" and its achievements on the football pitch were especially fêted.

and finally...

Our sources are adamant that "*from a trainee perspective Hammonds is a brilliant place to learn,*" so if you're considering an application we suggest keeping an eye on the news but also taking any opportunity you have to speak with the firm's trainees throughout 2006/07.

Harbottle & Lewis

the facts

Location: London
Number of UK partners/solicitors: 23/40
Total number of trainees: 9
Seats: 4x6 months
Alternative seats: Secondments

The year 1955 was a good one for celebrity births: Bruce Willis, Whoopi Goldberg, Bill Gates, Eddie Van Halen... It also saw the creation of the law firm of choice for many in the world of entertainment: Harbottle & Lewis.

battle of the simons

We live in a time of integrated entertainment. The book, the play, the movie, the soundtrack album, the ring tones. At every step in the process there are funding and licensing issues. In film, Harbottles' financing expertise has impacted on 'Confetti' and 'Basic Instinct 2'. In TV, the firm recently helped make Sean Bean's latest Sharpe series possible, as well as Richard Curtis' heart-of-gold, Live8-inspired drama 'The Girl In The Café'. Keeping theatre-goers happy, they've advised on 'Billy Elliot', 'We Will Rock You' and the WW1 drama 'Journey's End', as well as helping regional theatres from Sheffield to Scarborough. In music, the firm advises Annie Lennox, Starsailor and, um, Shakin' Stevens. And let's not forget the increasingly lucrative world of computer games – PSP addicts will be pleased to hear the firm's been helping publishers negotiate deals with Sony to produce titles for the console.

When media clients do something out of the ordinary – perhaps a spot of M&A or maybe falling out with business associates – Harbottles' lawyers are again on hand to see them through. They recently helped secure a TV marriage, advising on the takeover of the producers of *Bad Girls* by the producers of *Supernanny*. And on the litigation front they stepped in when those reality-TV titans, Simon Fuller and Simon Cowell, went toe-to-toe over *The X Factor*'s alleged infringement of Fuller's copyright of the *Pop Idol* format.

Beyond all this the firm boasts employment, immigration and property practices, all reflecting its media focus – be it helping a well-known singer secure British passports for her family to helping Andrew Lloyd Webber sell four of his Really Useful West End theatres. It additionally works on general branding and contractual issues for a range of major companies including Sony Ericsson, Philip Morris and a little-known British firm called Virgin Group.

x-citing times

Harbottle's seat selection process is unusual in that there isn't one. You're given a list of all four of your seats when you arrive and there's a fairly standard pattern. *"Everyone gets litigation, coco, either IP/music (IPM) or film, television and theatre (FTT), and then either property or employment."* At least there's scope for negotiation (*"If you speak up early, they'll try to accommodate you"*)

and the firm will consider splitting seats or allowing trainees to sneak in work for other departments. The downside is that those with shared seats can be *"hellishly busy."*

Life in FTT isn't non-stop glamour. In fact, it's *"highly transactional – there's a lot of sale-and-leaseback work* [that's film finance btw] *and lots of contract stuff for TV writers."* In IPM the work is more contentious: *"I did a lot of minor trade mark infringements,"* said one trainee. Small-scale matters like this allow trainees to run files: *"You'll get a very sparse file and do the initial research. Then you might appoint an investigator and draft a letter of claim."* In time you may even *"go to court on your own."* Large cases are passed to the dedicated litigators and when sitting with them a trainee's experience depends entirely on what's going on in the department. Stumble into something as large as the *X Factor* dispute, for example, and it'll be *"pretty intense – they need confident, efficient people who will just step in and get on with it."* In such situations, giving you a wide range of activities might not be the team's top priority and *"if somebody says, 'make a bundle,' you just do it."* If a large matter goes to trial while you're there, you'll get some quality court time. One trainee who'd worked on a major defamation case concerning a very major celebrity spent *"a lot of time in court handling documents. I also got to attend conferences in chambers, which was pretty exciting."*

A common source of trainee work is the firm's debt practice, where you could find yourself alone before a judge applying for a default judgment to be set aside. *"The judge was very nice but very sympathetic to the other side,"* said one veteran. *"We got what we wanted, but he slapped me down when I tried to apply for costs."* With such responsibility it's just as well supervising partners are *"really positive and happy to sit down and answer questions."* It helps that *"with only a few trainees in the firm it's not like there's a constant stream of us knocking on their door, asking silly questions."*

virgin territory

As the coco team's work is quite varied, trainees find *"getting the work you really want rests on luck and skill."* The possibilities range from M&A to charity law advice, where you'll be handling constitutional requirements and drafting contracts. One trainee had even set up a tsunami charity in record time. There's also a client secondment to key client Virgin Atlantic Airways. The bad news is that this means schlepping to Gatwick every morning. *"Bus, train, bus, walk, bus"* was the journey summary of one former secondee. The good news is that once there you'll be rewarded with truly impressive levels of responsibility. *"You could be negotiating software contracts, reviewing supply arrangements before they go out or advising on employment issues,"* and the good people of Virgin aren't the only ones you get to meet. *"When there are meetings with potential suppliers, you're there as Virgin's legal representative,"* explained a past secondee. *"When people have flown in from Dallas and you're brought in to meet them, that's pretty scary."* Fortunately, trainees seem to get into the swing of it quickly. *"You realise that, as long as you ask about the major things, you really can handle small-scale negotiations yourself,"* one trainee noted, *"and the lines of supervision are clear."* In past years no free tickets have been available to secondees, but we hear that this may have changed. *"One of the top executives shared a train carriage with a trainee,"* explained a source. *"He was horrified to find they didn't get the same perks as employees and made a phone call."*

a touch of frost

You'll have noticed that life at Harbottles is not, in fact, one long stream of celebrity encounters. In fairness, the firm does its best to give trainees a sense of glamour: at induction, founding partner *"Laurence Harbottle gives you a talk and tells you an old story about some film star."* But it's the annual client party that offers new trainees a real introduction to the stars – previous new starters have held the door open for the likes of Janet Street Porter and Sir David Frost. OK, that's not that impressive, but in the right seat the star spotting is impressive. One trainee went to Monaco to handle release forms at a fashion event and rubbed shoulders with Giorgio Armani and Kelly Osbourne. (Hmmm... we practically tripped over the little imp in London's K West hotel bar a few months ago.) For the most part, though, it's the behind-the-scenes media clients, not the stars, who you'll be working with. Fortunately, they got the thumbs-up from trainees. *"Media clients are creative and at the cutting edge of new ideas,"* said one, *"and they're usually fun to work with."*

Harbottles combines crisp, modern interior decor with an olde-worlde location in Soho's Hanover Square. Trainees queued up around the block to praise the firm's culture, telling us: *"Everyone gets on; there's no division between the ranks."* At lunchtime the whole firm *"from the managing partner to the secretaries"* can eat together for free in the canteen. Best of all, *"there's a policy of not talking about work."* What's the topic of conversation, then? *"Big Brother at the moment,"* admitted one square-eyed recruit. *"It basically is a firm of telly addicts."*

Despite the pleasant atmosphere Harbottles isn't an easy ride. *"You do work hard,"* trainees assured us; *"you're always being challenged."* The hours bear this out: on average a healthy 9.30am until 6.30pm. *"You do get a fair few late nights and even the odd all-nighter in corporate."* Even so, *"you never feel it's a chore; it's a buzz with the whole team in."* This sums the firm up – you'll work hard but you'll do it in good company. *"People want to go far,"* explained one trainee, *"but it's not deeply competitive the way some firms are."* The tantrum-throwing tendencies of the average modern celebrity don't seem to have infected the firm and *"there's no room for big egos – people are just incredibly normal."* Socially *"there are odd drinks events and things but it's taken as read that people have their own lives and friends outside work."* As such, don't expect *"an all-pile-in-the-pub culture."* Be assured that when it does party, Harbottles *"does it well."* A *"swanky"* Christmas bash is always held somewhere like Claridge's.

Every year the firm receives over 800 applications for four training places, so who makes the grade? *"Someone whose life isn't just about law,"* trainees respond. *"They're looking for people with flair, with a life outside the office."* A quick peek at the intake bears this out – a high proportion of non-law grads and a few people with previous media experience. Harbottles is aware it might seem like a cushy backup option for those who are also targeting big City firms, *"and they'll try to spot that at interview."* In September 2006, both qualifiers took jobs with the firm.

and finally...

If you've a real interest in the complex issues surrounding the media and you're looking for a respected, mid-sized firm with a supportive atmosphere, this is a great bet. All we'll say is make sure your reasons for picking the firm are convincing, because parts in this show are few in number and there's a long queue for the auditions.

HBJ Gateley Wareing LLP

the facts

Location: Birmingham, Leicester, Nottingham, Edinburgh
Number of UK partners/solicitors: 63/113
Total number of trainees: 14 (in England)
Seats: 4x6 months
Alternative seats: None

In January 2006 Midlands commercial player Gateley Wareing merged with Edinburgh firm Henderson Boyd Jackson (hence the HBJ in the name). English-Scottish mergers are relatively rare, particularly where there is no London element, so we had plenty to ask our interviewees.

straight from the horse's mouth

What we find most interesting about the recent tie-up is why it happened at all. Unaware that either firm had been touting for a partner, we spoke with Midlands senior partner Mike Ward who explained that the merger was originally mooted by a shared client, RBS, after someone at the bank identified similarities between the two firms. When we asked Mike if this was the start of something big for the firm, he told us: *"Financially what it did was make us think about the way the market was going; we're getting asked to have a one-stop service across the UK."* As for more merger plans, *"planning is probably putting too strong a suggestion there. We don't rule anything out, but everything has to stack up and make sense. We're a bit light in the South but it would have to be a like-minded firm and it would have to be well run and have a similarity of culture."*

Gateleys now qualifies as one of the UK's top 60 firms by revenue. Its first set of financial results after merger showed a combined turnover of £31 million, nearly £20 million of it coming from the English offices. Though the merger is highly significant it has not cast a tartan shadow over Gateleys in the Midlands, and the everyday experience of working there has not really changed. At this stage, for example, there are no plans for trainees to take seats north of the border. For now, their training contracts keep them in Birmingham, Nottingham and Leicester, with most trainees settling on an office at the start of the contract. Though Birmingham is the biggest office, the other two have a good range of all the main commercial options.

In the Midlands Gateleys is a big cheese in banking and construction, where it jostles for position with the likes of Eversheds, Wragges and DLA. Recent highlights include advice to Bank of Scotland and Barclays on the funding of the acquisition of the Warwickshire-based FTSE-250 company Mayflower Vehicle Systems, which designs and manufactures automotive bodies. The firm's construction lawyers work for major building companies on housing and commercial developments nationwide. Gateleys also has a very good profile in corporate finance, employment, litigation, corporate recovery and tax. Some recent press reports paint a rather bleak picture of the corporate market in the Midlands, citing partner moves from the Birmingham offices of the biggest firms to London. These are said to be a response to the decision of corporate clients, such as private equity houses 3i and Bridgepoint, to quit Birmingham. But just because big firms are feeling the squeeze it doesn't always follow that the firms in the tier below must. Gateleys has long found good work in the section of the market that larger rivals have ignored, and as a result Gateleys' corporate department appears to be in rude health. All up, people are feeling pretty positive, not least because of interest from new clients such as BT.

seats of learning

Corporate seats are especially popular with trainees. Recalling their time in the department, one told us: *"You do hear horror stories, but the hours weren't too bad – the latest I ever worked was 11pm."* As the transactions are fairly involved it's likely that you'll only be given a selection of smaller tasks, rather than a deal to call your own. Pleased with the level of responsibility they shoulder, trainees confirm *"the support is there and the supervision really is second to none… There's a good spread of people you can go and ask stupid questions."* The corporate recovery seat has a strong insolvency theme and blends contentious and non-contentious work, giving

trainees the opportunity to go to court for bankruptcy hearings. One past occupant of the seat said: *"It really helped put the skills that I got from the LPC into action – things like negotiation, client care, marketing and advocacy."* Because *"real one-on-one"* client contact is such a strong feature of the seat, *"it made me realise actually what it would be like to be a solicitor."*

The construction department is known as an *"energetic small team, with some great characters."* Construction law *"can be quite technical, which is a bit intimidating to start with, but once you get beyond all the terminology it's similar to any other non-contentious drafting seat."* Also popular, the property seat is *"really good for client contact as you get to speak to them on a daily basis."* Trainees get their own work, albeit closely supervised, and appreciate the level of responsibility this gives them: *"I was the main point of contact for clients, which was a bit scary initially, but it's good to feel that you own some files."*

Whereas most seats are based in a single office, the employment seat is split over all three, requiring trainees to divide their time between Birmingham, Nottingham and Leicester. Despite this, the seat gets positive reviews, and *"even though there's a hierarchy, being a trainee doesn't mean you do all the rubbish jobs."* Instead our sources had been treated *"pretty much as a newly-qualified."*

opportunity knocks

In most departments, trainees are taken to their supervisors' client meetings, and it's not uncommon for them to be *"primed on something beforehand"* to help them look good. Maybe it makes clients feel they're getting their money's worth, particularly if a trainee is doing a lot of work for them. We're pleased to report that clients are not backwards in coming forwards when it comes to thanking the trainees for their hard work. One source told us: *"A client wrote me a really nice thank you letter after a big piece of work I'd done."*

There are no overseas seats or secondments per se, but when we rang, one trainee was on a Law Society secondment in Brussels, helping with lobbying work and monitoring EU legislation. The firm had supported her application for the post, believing the skills she would pick up would be beneficial not only to her but also to the business. Examples such as this lead trainees to conclude that the firm is receptive to their ideas. *"To their credit,"* one said, *"you can approach the partners about anything and they'll think about it as they're always open to looking at new opportunities."* Trainees also feel the partners are *"free from arrogance, and you never get the hint of any backstabbing going on."* Perhaps because so many trained at the firm themselves, they seem keen to nurture each new intake. *"They even tell us that one day we'll be able to buy them out of their partnership when they retire!"* Even before they start their contracts, a buddy system gives future trainees *"someone to get an honest opinion from on what to expect."* And if there are problems after the training contract has started, the HR people traverse the firm's three Midlands offices every week, so everyone gets the chance to see them face to face. Perhaps this care and attention contributed to the retention of all seven English qualifiers in September 2006.

ode to a haggis

Gateleys' website implies a strong work ethic coupled with an emphasis on the personalities of its lawyers. Described by trainees as *"just normal people who do a bloody good job and know that quality is expected,"* the partners' profiles reveal secret passions for Joy Division, iPods, Halle Berry, Nigella Lawson, Kylie and, er, Jeremy Clarkson. Dubious celebrity crushes aside, our trainees inform us that these men, and women – albeit that there are noticeably fewer of them –

can be relied upon to *"always be first on the dance floor"* at the Christmas party.

The Birmingham HQ occupies the city's former ear, nose and throat hospital, a fine redbrick example of Victoriana on the outside, a slick, modern workspace on the inside. Partners sit in glass-fronted offices, which helps achieve the air of openness the firm seems so keen to promote. Right next door to the Birmingham office is a bar. This establishment, Bushwackers, is unsurprisingly the scene of many a fun-filled Friday night. Trainees are certainly no strangers to end-of-the-week pints, and can often be found scoffing pizza on Friday lunchtimes in preparation. *"People genuinely like spending time together outside work,"* they told us. At other times staff enjoy each other's company at comedy clubs and casino nights, or even venture onto the sports field. However, there's a small bone of contention when it comes to sport: one female trainee was adamant *"they should let girls go on the golf day."* And maybe they should, but she then confessed that the ladies do have events of their own: *"We have spa days, which the boys get a bit jealous of."*

The offices in Nottingham and Leicester are smaller but equally sociable. In Leicester, the firm has been known to lay on drinks evenings when *"they turn the ground floor into a pub and even have a draft beer with the firm logo on it."* Little things such as this confirm what we already knew about Gateleys – it never does anything halfheartedly. To give you another example, when the new Edinburgh office was welcomed into the fold last winter, the Midlanders chartered a plane and flew up to celebrate with them. Sure enough there was a ceilidh and ritual haggis eating.

and finally...

Medium-sized HBJ Gateley Wareing has a down-to-earth outlook and general air of mateyness that sometimes masks an appetite for hard slog. This is one for glass-half-full types, we'd say.

Henmans LLP

the facts
Location: Oxford, Woodstock
Number of UK partners/solicitors: 23/35
Total number of trainees: 6
Seats: 4x6 months
Alternative seats: None
Extras: Pro bono – CAB

This Thames Valley firm shares its name with personal injury lawyer Anthony Henman (Tim's dad, by the way), who was its senior partner for 28 years before slipping into the role of consultant. Around half the firm's work is in professional negligence and personal injury litigation, with property and private client also featuring large. Henmans has doubled in size in the past eight years, and continues to bolster its prof neg and commercial litigation practices in particular.

centred on court
So why did trainees ignore the big commercial firms to which many students gravitate and plump for Henmans? *"Most of my friends went to City firms, but I realised I just wasn't interested in finance and corporate work. This is a very different kind of work, a totally different kettle of fish,"* concluded one source. Everyone we spoke to believed they were onto a good thing: *"The quality of work and training is very high here, and there's also a really good breadth of work."* Apparently, *"you just need to have a good think about what areas of practice you're interested in."* The most sought-after areas here turn out to be family and personal injury, with litigation also perennially popular.

The firm's commercial litigators handle a broad sweep of work, recently representing the architects in the multimillion-pound construction and professional negligence case of Tesco v Costain & Ors. *"My litigation seat was split between professional indemnity and commercial litigation,"* explained

one source. *"I wasn't pigeon-holed – the jobs ranged from drafting to legal research, doing attendance notes at meetings, and finding information on companies the lawyers were going along to see."* Best of all, *"I got to go to court on a four-day trial."*

Staying with the litigation theme, the PI department works for both defendants and claimants. PI gets trainees interviewing witnesses and drafting their statements, researching injuries and likely awards from court, plus briefing counsel and attending court hearings. One recent case involved the death of an Oxford student who was thrown from a 'human catapult'. The team also encounters many cycling claims, which is unsurprising given the number of bicycles on Oxford's roads. Clin neg work is a good follow-on from PI. *"We handle cases with values into millions of pounds, things like misdiagnoses of cancer and brain-damaged children."* Recent case examples include a wrongful insemination during IVF treatment, and a high-value claim over failure to diagnose hypertension resulting in brain damage. Summarising this part of their training, one trainee said: *"PI and clin neg gave me a lot of experience. I attended conferences with counsel in London and went to an inquest as the firm's representative to look after the clients... it is top-end work."*

going to the dogs
A family seat brings masses of client contact, and because it's just a three-person team, the trainee effectively becomes the assistant, *"helping to draft matrimonial documents and doing more technical stuff as time goes on."* For the record, the family team and the private client team are geared towards the needs of *"high net worth individuals – we don't do publicly funded work."* In a private client seat the trainee helps on probate files and comes into contact with well-known charities. Confirmation of the firm's prominence in this field, Henmans was recently ranked in the top ten firms in the country for charity law by a leading

charities directory. Its client list features some of the biggest and most well-known names in the country: for example, Save the Children, RSPCA, Cancer Research UK and Oxfam. In a recent case, lawyers won a Court of Appeal victory for Guide Dogs for the Blind which had been bequeathed a significant sum of money in a will. It was your classic case of disappointed children contesting the will. *"Wills are a big feature of the seat,"* confirmed a trainee, adding: *"The team were keen to give me a good idea of what the work was about. There's also a lot of tax planning, but that's an area where trainees don't have such a valuable input."*

Property law is the usual whirl of activity: *"Lots of research and drafting, exchanging contracts and completions."* The deals on which the trainees work relate to residential, commercial and agricultural premises, which means that no two days need be the same. At this point we should alert readers to the fact that *"at the moment you can't do a seat in corporate, which is something that's under review. It's a very small department so there's no justification for a trainee."* Probably worth checking if you get to interview.

Only the first seat is chosen for the trainee, and it is sometimes possible to do two seats in a hoped-for qualification department. Again, readers may wish to note that if you want to maximise your chances of staying on after training *"the larger departments – PI and prof neg – always accommodate people."* The difficulty can be *"whether you as a trainee want the job that's going – it depends what areas they want to expand in."* In September 2006 two of the three qualifiers stayed on.

random acts of kindness

Henmans' two offices are quite distinct: Woodstock, smaller with only two departments, is *"like a little house, it's a lot quieter and laid back than Oxford."* Sitting in the shadow of Blenheim Palace, the lawyers here mostly handle private client and property work. True, you won't get the buzz of the city, but you can pop into the palace grounds for lunch, and there are good pubs nearby. The scope of activity in Oxford is more extensive, and for now the office is right opposite Christ Church College; it's a fantastic location but the building is *"far from modern."* Henmans is hoping to move both offices under one roof in 2007, most likely to a business park on the Oxford ringroad. As convenient as this will be in many respects, we suspect many charms will inevitably be lost in the move. When asked to sum the place up, trainees told us: *"Henmans is somewhere between a high street practice and a larger commercial firm."* The feel of the place is *"traditional without being unduly stuffy. The dress code is suits and ties, but the ties come off in the summer; it's quite informal."* Another fact worth mentioning is that some ten of its 21 partners are women – always good to see in a profession that still has too few women on the top rungs.

On the social front there are summer and Christmas celebrations, and the eponymous Mr Henman hosts a tennis tournament at his house each year. The last summer party was held at a local golf club and followed the tried-and-tested formula of cocktails, dinner and dancing. Some social events double up as charity fundraisers; for example a boys v girls netball match (*"both sides wore skirts"*), occasional dress-down days, an auction to drum up cash for Children in Need and an art exhibition to raise funds for tsunami relief. In Woodstock everyone lunches together on Fridays in the Kings Arms or the Crown, and when the troops are rallied for after-work drinks in Oxford it's usually the All Bar One on the High Street. However, certain of our sources wondered if the social scene could be perked up. Keen to point out that *"it's not the firm's fault – there are only five other trainees and it's not a particularly young firm,"* they concluded: *"It would be nice if there were more informal, spontaneous drinks."* At least the firm scores well for getting trainees involved in client marketing. One spoke of being invited to London to help out with a litigation department event, telling us: "*It's useful to learn how to balance a glass of wine and hold a conversation!*" Maybe such forays into the capital will become more regular because "*they've got a new marketing person in from a City firm to push things forward a bit.*"

If you're sizing Henmans up for a training contract, the assessment day sounds as exacting as a Wimbledon final. It involves an interview, a presentation, a verbal reasoning test and drafting and team exercises. Even if you perform well there is still another hurdle: "*You must demonstrate an interest in Oxford and a commitment to the area.*" Someone who shows more commitment than most is Mr Henman himself: "*He's been here for many years and he's quite a character!*" Apparently "*he's still supervising trainees and he's well liked.*"

and finally...

Despite some well-heeled clients and picturesque locations, this is anything but an olde worlde law firm. There's a sense of confidence about the place, which we assume comes from the fact that the lawyers here are winning the kind of clients and work that make Henmans a credible alternative to London law firms.

Herbert Smith LLP

the facts

Location: London
Number of UK partners/solicitors: 171/423
Total number of trainees: 153
Seats: 4x6 months
Alternative seats: Overseas seats, secondments
Extras: Pro bono – RCJ CAB, death row cases, FRU and others

A training contract at this top-ten City heavyweight places you in Europe's biggest and best litigation firm. But there's more, much more. Herbert Smith has muscled its way into contention on the transactional front too. With its strategic assault on the corporate and finance markets well under way, we reckon Herbies is a place for trainees who fancy some action.

hooking up

Herbert Smith's "*pre-eminent, all-singing, all-dancing*" litigation practice has always attracted students who like the sound of a legal punch-up. Even current trainees claim "*you'd be silly to come here not wanting to at least try litigation.*" It's just that we have noticed a shift in the last year or two. Gone are the days when our interviewees were interested in anything so long as it was litigation. Enthusiasm for the corporate and finance departments is running high, and there is a cache of niche practice areas to try. The trick these days is working out how to get the most out of your two years.

Right from the moment you receive your training contract offer, a password hooks you up to the future joiners section of Herbies' website. You can contact your peers, advertise for flat shares and find out about functions and get-togethers. When you arrive at the firm your first seat has been picked for you, although "*you can specify the areas you would prefer*" and "*they look at whom or what you are likely to get on with.*" After this, the rest of Herbert Smith, and some of its clients (eg BP and Coca-Cola) are your oyster. The intranet once again comes into its own, offering detailed profiles of seats as well as the names of current occupants for you to "*get the lowdown on what they involve.*" It's also a good place to find out more about the international secondments available throughout Herbert Smith's own network and in the offices of allied foreign firms. It's not quite a free-for-all at seat rotation time; everyone is required to do a contentious option and a corporate option.

cruise missile

Everyone knows about the *"mega"* litigation practice and its fearsome reputation; it's a first port of call for major clients in sticky situations. For example, litigators successfully represented British American Tobacco and its Formula 1 outfit, British American Racing, in the dispute with a joint venture partner concerning ownership of the team. Another case saw United International Pictures turn to Herbies after the London premiere of 'War of the Worlds', when a comedian allegedly assaulted Tom Cruise by squirting water in his face. UIP was advised on possible courses of action against the joker, the production company he was working for and the commissioning network, Channel 4, to prevent them from benefiting as a result of the incident. At the other end of the scale the firm is involved in many of the biggest, most complex, long-running commercial cases around. It famously represented Equitable Life in the huge claim against its former auditors Ernst & Young, which ultimately turned out poorly for Equitable.

On bet-the-company disputes or those attracting intense media interest, trainees have precious little autonomy. *"Everything is checked; it's the way it has to be."* Plus, as one self-deprecating source pointed out, if a dispute has progressed all the way to litigation then *"getting some trainee to muck it up is probably not the best way forward."* The seat has its highlights, of course: going to court to observe hearings, research (*"rewarding because your case or authority can end up in a submission, skeleton or particulars"*) and getting a *"first shot"* at drafting court documents. Naturally it also has its low points: a fair share of *"boring jobs"* and shuffling paper (*"irritating because you don't learn anything"*). Yet even the *"classic thankless task"* of bundling documents for court can be, well, not so thankless. If your skills are exemplary then *"judges will say, 'These are particularly well-prepared bundles'."* Be thankful that paralegal assistance is available when court deadlines are fast approaching, and that you can always *"go to your supervisor and ask for more varied work."* Another bonus is that working to court deadlines ensure more predictable hours for trainees. *"In corporate you always get the feeling that the client might phone up at six o'clock saying, 'I want this.' It happens less in litigation, so you can plan your late nights in advance."*

You may be aware of Herbies' old hard-man reputation: its litigators were never afraid to flex their muscles or wear down smaller opponents. Some trainees had even heard stories about *"partners being kept in a cage, fed meat and only unleashed on the other side on special occasions, when required to tear a few people to shreds."* The truth? According to trainees, *"any sort of barracuda image about Herbert Smith is undeserved."* While we doubt the litigators have gone soft, they are clearly aware that a super-combative approach to litigation is unsuited to the post-Woolf era, and it is only natural that trainees are attuned to newer attitudes.

A litigation seat can take many forms. Under the umbrella of commercial litigation, there are sub-specialisms in administrative and public law, banking, insurance and reinsurance, IT, energy and corporate fraud, investigations and asset recovery. Additionally, certain disputes are handled by an international arbitration group, and there are lawyers specialising in mediation and other methods of resolution. As an aside we should tell you that Herbies was the first UK law firm to set up an in-house advocacy unit with two QCs on the full-time staff. Although training to be a solicitor-advocate is encouraged, whether this results in as much advocacy as most litigators would like, we can't say.

monkey business

If deals and money flick your switch then you'll welcome *"the real pressures of working in the cor-*

porate field," be this in equity capital markets, M&A, private equity or US securities. Be warned: timing is everything when it comes to the volume and quality of work, and "some people will spend six months on one enormous transaction" working as "a deal monkey." The luckless simian's "irritating" duties will include proof-reading and data room management, lots of it. The thing to remember is that today's red-lined documents are tomorrow's headlined deals, and beyond the headline-grabbers there are "lots of smaller deals with a bit more responsibility for trainees." We know you like the front-page stuff though, so here's a sample of those big deals. BAA, the world's leading airport operator, used the firm in relation to the recommended £10.1 billion takeover offer from a Spanish consortium; NM Rothschild & Sons sought its counsel on the Glazer family's bid for Manchester United; and new client Fortune Brands used the firm and its German 'best friend' firm, Gleiss Lutz, on Fortune's role in Pernod Ricard's £7.4 billion takeover of drinks giant Allied Domecq.

A stint in one of the finance teams will place you right at the sharp end of where the firm wants to go. The top brass is aiming to establish a leading-five London finance practice within five years; as one trainee put it: "They're really kicking it up a notch." The powerful projects-related finance group is a good starting point, and all eyes are now on acquisition finance, property finance, securitisation and structured finance. Lawyers have already acted for RBS on a $245 million secured borrowing base facility for AIM and Toronto-listed Oilexco and Oilexco North Sea, and Goldman Sachs sent instructions in relation to the $120 million convertible bond offering for Winbond Electronics, a leading Taiwanese electronics company. With client wins like these, we weren't surprised to hear about the "entrepreneurial spirit and cool buzz" in finance. One trainee even told us the growth strategy could be "a victim of its own success," since, during their seat, "deals were rolling in one after the other." In finance you can expect a fair degree of responsibility, working on matters of all sizes; this in turn is "quite stressful" but "fun and such a great learning experience." There's just one downside – don't be surprised if you are "pretty tired by the end of the seat."

The "really cool" real estate department has its fans too. They tell us "the stuff they do here is a cut above," so the work seems "more like a corporate transaction than a conveyance." As a result, "gone are the days when you can head off at 5.30pm." A good example of the work is Anschutz Entertainment's £2.5 billion redevelopment of the Millennium Dome and 40 acres of land on the Greenwich Peninsula. The thrill of working on such huge matters is tempered by all the "moving paper around," yet "you've got to do the admin and get the basics right as a way of developing your attention to detail – and that's something no one has when they arrive." At least trainees can also get stuck into smaller files, drafting small documents, letter writing and generally "keeping the file going."

inclusion zone

Our sources agreed that "Herbert Smith is very good with supervision and risk management," so even if you start off on day one "floundering around as a new trainee, you soon get the idea as the individual training is so good." There is a decent balance between classic (ie dull) trainee jobs, carried out "in the context of something really rather exciting," and "times when partners have a lot on their plates and you are the front line on smaller deals." Another thing they value is the ongoing formal group training. "It is absolutely amazing, one of the firm's biggest selling points – they should push it more," thought one. In terms of appraisals, there's "a fair and constructive" system which is well executed.

In light of the firm's recent appointment of an 'inclusivity manager', we thought it only right to ask if there was a Herbert Smith type. The view on Trainee Street is that *"everyone has different styles of working and different personalities, which makes for an interesting place to train."* In past years we have heard about 'big characters' in some departments; this year our interviewees had less to say on this point, preferring to focus more on people's *"passion for the law"* and commercial attitudes. We still sense that quiet, passive types should look elsewhere, and one trainee clearly agreed. *"There is a danger in an environment where there are lots of terribly bright and competitive people that you might be left behind slightly. You have to grab* [your training contract] *by the horns."*

When the i's have been dotted and the t's crossed, trainees are usually invited to the completion dinners or celebrations that mark the end of a period of frenetic working. They like it when partners and clients *"recognise your hard work"* with *"champagne and good times;"* after all, weren't they a part of the team too? Once a month or so a drinks trolley trundles round each department at 5.30pm, and those with an even bigger appetite for winding down with colleagues can take advantage of *"tons of opportunities for drinks and social stuff."* One trainee told us they preferred the more *"intimate ad hoc things"* to the *"big balls and key events of the year,"* but each to their own, we say; either way *"you'll get to know many more people than you thought."* Herbies is a big firm and, as you would expect, there are *"quite enthusiastic sports teams,"* including hockey, football, netball and cricket.

In September 2006, 36 of the 41 qualifiers stayed on in NQ positions.

and finally...

Herbert Smith is in an ambitious phase and we suspect there's more to come from this rising City star. If you are attracted by litigation then of course you must apply, but be prepared to have your head turned by transactional work as the corporate and finance practices grow in stature. This has clearly been the case with the current trainees and frankly we think more of them are happier as a result.

Hextalls

the facts

Location: London
Number of UK partners/solicitors: 23/14
Total number of trainees: 9
Seats: 4x6 months
Alternative seats: Occasional secondments

Hextalls is based in Aldgate, the area of London where the City meets the East End. To one side are the gleaming towers of big business and to the other the thriving curry houses of Brick Lane and the high-rise flats of Tower Hamlets. Professionally, Hextalls is edging its way into a broader range of City work after years as a respected but relatively specialised insurance firm.

insuring the future

Because almost anything can be insured, from a ship's cargo to a film's profits, insurance firms handle a greater variety of work than you might think. Hextalls helps its insurance clients to defend their policyholders in professional negligence cases and personal injury suits. It also investigates shipping and travel insurance claims and advises on complex coverage disputes with policyholders and reinsurers, the mega-companies that underwrite the insurance market. Despite its relatively small size, Hextalls acts for some of the big names in the sector, including US giant CNA, Italy's Generali, and Germany's Gerling. Sometimes the firm advises policyholders directly, among them Sainsbury's and Peugeot-Citroën.

Over the last few years, the insurance industry has tightened its belt, and London firms have felt the pressure of competition from regional law firms with lower charges. Although it's not abandoning its core practice, Hextalls has announced its determination to beef up the non-insurance parts of its business in pursuit of a 50/50 split of work. The key areas of growth are employment, corporate and IT/technology. Change is never easy, however, and Hextalls' new direction has prompted some complaints. The firm's senior partner upped sticks in February to form his own insurance boutique, taking two partners with him, including the sole partner in the firm's New York office. This has prompted speculation that the new management team is hunting for a US merger partner.

bigsmall

Until now, Hextalls' seating plan saw every trainee spend six months in personal injury, employment, insurance/commercial litigation and corporate. With the firm's expansion, things have opened up a little and options in shipping and transport, travel and leisure, commercial property, professional negligence and the unusual combination of sports, insolvency and technology have joined the list. It's now possible for a trainee to do two non-contentious seats, should they wish to.

Personal injury remains one of the largest teams, and here trainees tackle cases ranging from accidents at work to slips and trips in shopping centres. "*You could be working with anybody,*" said one trainee, "*from a telecoms company to a public authority.*" The seat allows trainees to get their teeth into all aspects of the litigation process – "*attending court hearings, mediations and case management conferences, and drafting witness statements and instructions to counsel.*" Trainees usually get one smaller matter to run solo, under supervision. "*That made me a little nervous,*"

admitted one source, "*but everyone was really helpful.*"

As shipping and transport law is quite a specialised area ("*on the LPC you do shipping for about an hour*") trainees don't get quite the same level of responsibility ("*there was some bundling, arranging hotels for clients and so on*") but compensation comes in the form of interesting case scenarios such as "*a contract dispute about a turbine generator being transported across Iran.*" Commercial litigation, too, sees trainees helping out with the bundling tasks on higher-value cases but, again, they also have the chance to do more exciting things like make applications in the High Court before a master. The litigation handled by the sports and leisure team covers everything from sports professionals' injury insurance to accidents in hotels. The seat unfortunately "*doesn't mean flying off to Mexico*" or anywhere else exotic for that matter; it does, however, mean "*lots of speaking to clients and hotels, investigating foreign laws and quite a bit of advocacy.*" In short, all Hextalls' litigation seats seem to offer the right balance between assisting on larger matters and having control over smaller ones.

gainfully employed

It's a similar story with the non-contentious seats. Corporate offers "*a chance to really sharpen your drafting skills.*" The team "*likes to throw you in at the deep end – on my first day I was drafting a business sale-and-purchase agreement.*" Get that out of the way and there's still "*board minutes, resolutions, procedural stuff*" to get through. The department's supervisors were praised for "*providing plenty of feedback and mini lessons.*" In commercial property you can expect "*lots and lots of research*" but you'll also develop your organisational skills. "*It's a big change from some litigation departments where you'll have three or four cases,*" explained one source. "*Here you'll have a role on lots of files, arranging completions, exchanging documents and so on.*" One trainee reported being left to complete a complex four-way deal that involved liaising with three other sets of solicitors and clients. It's not all high stakes and sweaty palms; you're likely to get a small residential matter to handle yourself from start to finish. A few natural-born litigators find their non-contentious seat a nice surprise. "*I enjoyed it much more than I thought I would,*" admitted one such character after a spell with the property team.

The employment team is, as at most firms, "*really popular.*" It is set to expand, and with its former head now the firm's chairman it's unlikely to get overshadowed by other departments. This seat was identified as one that offers "*loads of responsibility,*" for which reason "*they generally like fourth-seaters.*" Hextalls provides a helpline service to various employer clients and trainees field many of the queries that come in; hence "*you do a lot random research.*" Drafting practice comes in the form of contracts, witness statements and instructions to counsel for tribunals. One trainee reported running a sex discrimination and unfair dismissal claim themselves, while another had conducted a case management conference. "*It was nerve-wracking,*" they admitted, "*but really good experience.*"

Trainees sit in an office with their supervisor, often a partner. "*I thought it'd be scary but it's really useful having constant supervision,*" said one. All drafted material is checked before it wings its way out of the building. "*I have had things come back with red ink all over them,*" admitted one trainee, "*but they'll talk you through it and give you constructive feedback.*" And if your supervisor isn't around, "*other team members are really approachable.*" "*You can ask them anything – as long as you've thought it through.*" With a small number of trainees, ensuring everyone gets the seats they want is not too tricky. "*It's not guaranteed,*" one trainee explained, "*but they try their best and I've got every seat I wanted.*"

nookie at the xmas party

Describing the atmosphere at Hextalls, one trainee said: "*It's not particularly formal. I mean it's smart business dress but it's not stuffy. Everyone knows me.*" The firm prides itself on "*family friendly*" hours, meaning 9am to 5.30pm much of the time, although we suspect as the non-contentious side of the firm expands, hours may be harder to control. Despite the firm's desire to expand, only one of the three September 2006 qualifiers stayed on with the firm. We understand that it might have achieved a better result had one trainee received their offer a little earlier.

Our sources were hopeful that expansion plans might involve a move – basically they gave Aldgate a general thumbs-down. "*It's just not that pleasant, especially at night – it has an effect on clients,*" thought one. We asked the firm and they said that a move may indeed be on the cards. At present, departments are split across six floors with the result that "*you only really see people from the department you're in. You can feel isolated from the other trainees.*" They make up for it by lunching together often, and there's a steady flow of social events for the whole firm to enjoy. "*There was a comedy night last week,*" one trainee explained, "*and the chairman came, which was nice.*" Other events have included a boat party on the Thames in the summer and a snazzy Christmas party in a Regent Street hotel, where the entertainment was provided by Roger de Courcy and his friend Nookie Bear. If you don't know of this legendary pairing, ask your mum.

and finally...

As Hextalls rises to the challenges of a shifting insurance market and redirects its operations "*there's a sense the period of flux isn't over yet.*" As one source put it: "*There's still an atmosphere of 'what's going to happen next?'*" Far from making them anxious, trainees see the change as positive, bringing increased opportunities for anyone joining at the junior end.

Hill Dickinson

the facts
Location: Liverpool, Manchester, Chester, London
Number of UK partners/solicitors: 141/179
Total number of trainees: 28
Seats: 4 x 6 months
Alternative seats: Occasional secondments

Hill Dickinson started out in early 19th-century Liverpool when the port city was riding high on shipping. Since then it's come a long way.

friends reunited
Our subject firm has a long and illustrious history and is intricately linked to the nation's shipping industry. In 1911, the firm's then senior partner narrowly avoided sailing on the Titanic's maiden, and only, voyage. Being spared, he then represented the owners in the claims and inquiry that followed. Even today, *"pictures of ships all over the walls"* remind trainees of the firm's shiptastic past. Over the years Hill Dicks has broadened its business interests; first through involvement in insurance litigation, then spreading out into general commercial practice.

Just as Merseybeat gave way to Madchester, so Hill Dickinson made the leap across the M62 with its merger with Manchester's Gorna & Co in 2002. It has also expanded into new areas of practice, with its property department further strengthened by a merger with Liverpool's Bullivant Jones in 2004. Since then, both the Liverpool and Manchester offices have expanded rapidly, with key partner hires in construction, professional indemnity, fraud, environment and clinical negligence. Until just a few months ago we would have told you that smaller offices in Chester and London complete the picture, but just before going to press the firm made a big announcement about its business in the capital.

After 17 years apart, Hill Dicks has chosen to reunite with former partners at London shipping specialist practice Hill Taylor Dickinson. The two had gone their separate ways when the HTD partners decided their international marine law interests no longer sat so well with the northern partners' desire to diversify into other areas of domestic work. The merger became effective on 1 November 2006 and the combined firm's revenue is anticipated to reach £63 million in the first year post merger. The trainee who told us: *"It's a very optimistic firm right now"* clearly now has even more to feel positive about.

northern exposure
One of the things the firm is most proud of is its appointment as official lawyers for the European Capital of Culture, Liverpool 2008. The majority of trainees are recruited into this office, although they stressed that, up north, *"you join the firm rather than any particular office."* In practice, most spend two or three seats in Liverpool, with one or two in Manchester and possibly Chester. The firm does not have any compulsory seats and, overall, the trainees we spoke to were happy with what they'd been allocated. *"You don't get much choice in the first year,"* admitted one, *"but you don't know what you want then anyway. In the second year if there's something you particularly want, you'll normally get it, especially if you speak up."*

A likely destination is the professional services department. *"No, it's nothing to do with ladies of the night,"* we were hastily reassured. The work centres on professional negligence claims, most in relation to solicitors but there are additional cases against against architects, accountants and, more unusually, veterinary surgeons. *"We had one claim against a vet for not shoeing a horse properly,"* recalled one trainee. When trainees are co-opted onto large, sensitive matters they don't usually have much responsibility (*"I spent two weeks Tippexing out markings and filing documents in chronological order*"), but it's a different story on smaller claims. "*I was lucky, and got to handle a small matter through pre-trial and trial,*" noted one satisfied customer. "*Your letters are always checked, but as you progress you spend more and more time on the phone, where it's just down to you.*"

In professional services, a lucky few trainees could become part of the glamorous sounding 'interventions team' set up to help the Law Society deal with miscreant or clueless solicitors. In a nutshell, the team bursts into a law firm, commandeers files and shuts the business down. The next part of the job is to take control of clients' files until new solicitors can be found. How exciting is that? Actually, not very. "*It's not that nice telling secretaries they're fired,*" noted one past practitioner of the art of intervention.

berths and deaths

The general insurance department has considerable experience of defending industrial disease claims. "*There's a lot of vibration white finger and a lot of asbestos-related disease,*" confirmed one trainee. "*You do a lot of investigative work. Sometimes the exposure was 60 or more years ago, so you've got to dig through the records to see how much they were exposed to, where else they might have been exposed, who the insurer was, and so on.*" Although interesting, thumbing through records is a major undertaking: "*At least they give you all the time you need and talk you through anything you don't understand.*" The best part of the seat is the advocacy, which includes running CMCs and making small applications in court. "*The only thing I don't do is make major decisions,*" confirmed a source.

Shipping seats combine contentious and non-contentious work, from the mundane (berthing agreements) to the dramatic (investigating deaths on the high seas). While it's not uncommon for a senior lawyer or partner to board a ship in the early hours to investigate something, the only trainees to whom this honour is extended tend to be those with previous maritime experience. For the rest the seat brings "*a lot of research*" and some drafting.

staff reunited

The recent past has seen a rise in the number of non-contentious seats in the training programme. Trainees hankering after coco, property, construction or IP/IT can be accommodated, and we're told that "*it's theoretically possible to do three non-contentious seats now.*" Perhaps this is why trainees say: "*It doesn't feel like a litigation firm any more.*"

Most of our interviewees praised their "*brilliant, really helpful*" supervisors; however, some acknowledged that "*a few are a bit ogre-ish*" and that "*you just learn to avoid them.*" One source had been allocated to an "*incredibly critical*" supervisor and told us: "*It is tough never getting any encouragement.*" Fortunately, in such (rare) situations trainees find that "*really helpful*" assistant solicitors are more than happy to step in. Furthermore, the firm's training committee meets every month with the trainee group. "*They really listen,*" said one source, "*and they're responsive to suggestions you make. I'm sure if there was a really serious problem they would tackle it.*"

In Liverpool, staff are spread across four offices ranging from the "*nice, bright, airy*" Corn Exchange to the "*vile*" State House. Thankfully the firm has secured space in a new development in the city centre and plans to move all staff there at the end of 2007. One trainee summed up the firm's development when they said: "*It's still a small enough firm that you smile at people in the corridor, but it's large enough that you don't always know who the people you're smiling at are.*" Manchester is said to be "*a bit more heads-down*" than Liverpool. "*Perhaps we feel we've got something to prove,*" mused one source. Chester, with around 50 staff, is "*a completely different ball game to Liverpool.*" Trainees who'd worked in the office told us: "*The partners have been there forever and it's very comfortable,*" although "*you do miss the buzz of the city offices.*"

looking ahead

We spoke to London trainees before the merger with Hill Taylor Dickinson, so much of what they told us about the London office's independence and a certain sense of isolation from the northern hub will not be especially helpful to readers. What we can say is that any applicant who specifies a preference for London is interviewed by that office and commonly spends their whole two years there. Staff at the small Hill Dicks office (which has been dominated by professional services and shipping work) are moving into Hill Taylor Dickinson's premises near Aldgate. HTD brings some 19 partners and a large staff to the equation, most of whom focus on shipping work. It would be unwise of us to second guess the exact nature of training in the new set-up, but we can report that there will be an annual intake of five recruits. The accounts of the Hill Dicks trainees we spoke to were positive and they had been responsible for many interesting tasks. "*I ran client seminars and social events,*" said a source, "*as well as doing lots of applications before High Court masters. The first one was a bit scary, but fortunately I had a very kindly master who told me what to do.*"

hippy hippy shake

In 2006, when we rang, all in the Manchester/Liverpool/Chester part of the firm had North West backgrounds, many being graduates of Liverpool's universities. Most have come to the firm within a few years of graduating, although one recent qualifier joined after ten years in the merchant navy. Standing between prospective trainees and a contract is a "*friendly, but quite testing*" assessment day. In addition to the usual interview and exercises, trainees are asked to make a short presentation. "*I did mine on belly dancing,*" admitted one recruit – "*I didn't demonstrate.*" For those who succeed, the prize – given at induction – comes in the form of a shiny Hill Dickinson umbrella. "*Mine broke in the first gust*

of wind," grumbled one recent starter. We're not sure if they get a replacement when they qualify, but in 2006, seven of the nine who completed their training contracts stayed on with the firm.

Up north, quitting time is generally around 6pm or 6.30 pm in most departments. After work "*there are loads of different bars people go to,*" noted a Liverpudlian. Christmas parties come in both department and firm-sized packages, and the firm's social committee also organises events throughout the year, including a riverboat party on – you guessed it – a ferry across the Mersey. "*This year there's going to be karaoke,*" lamented one trainee. "*I'm going to get out of singing by getting really pissed and hiding in the corner.*" It's a technique that never works...

and finally...

Hill Dickinson has proved itself capable of adapting to the changing face of the North West legal market and the merger in London is a very important development for all those working in the capital. Train here and you'll be able to get all the basics under your belt as well as a solid brand on your CV.

Hodge Jones & Allen

the facts

Location: London
Number of UK partners/solicitors: 20/41
Total number of trainees: 13
Seats: 4x6 months
Alternative seats: None

HJA's story is a classic. Back in 1977 three young solicitors met for a drink in a pub in Camden Town. Over two pints of Directors, Henry Hodge, Peter Jones and Patrick Allen hatched a plan to start their own firm to champion the concept of justice and legal advice for all in the community.

police, camden, action

The three friends found office space in Camden High Street above a small finance company that offered 'Loans From A Fiver'. Henry Hodge was dispatched on his motorbike to buy a telephone and the young lawyers' bank manager sent them their first client. Nearly 30 years later, Mr Justice Hodge is one of the first solicitors to have become a High Court Judge and was more recently made president of the Asylum and Immigration Tribunal; Peter Jones became Dean of Nottingham Law School and then Senior Pro Vice-Chancellor; and Patrick Allen, now senior partner at HJA, is one of the UK's best-known multiparty claimant lawyers.

Camden Town is as infamous for its drunks, drug addicts and dealers as it is for its bohemian attitudes and musical heroes. In the years since the passing of antisocial behaviour legislation it has acquired a reputation as the nation's ASBO capital, though this could all change following the last town hall elections. HJA's thriving crime department promises an *"absolutely dynamic, fast-moving and pressurised seat,"* where as a trainee you'll certainly work hard *"visiting dodgy corners of London, clerking big trials," "attending court hearings and briefing counsel."* You'll need to sharpen up to cope with *"the mix of riff-raff, street robbers and genuinely needy people."* And be prepared for the seat to take its toll emotionally, as one source explained. *"You find you're often dealing with prolific drug users, who can be aggressive. Sometimes it can be sad – you get people who have lost their way and their lives have just spiralled into crime."* One trainee recounted their first impressions of the firm: *"The reception room was full of a gaggle of screaming kids and strange characters and I thought to myself, 'God, what is this place?'"* Land in the crime department for your first seat and you might not know what has hit you: *"It's the most nerve-wracking experience in the world but you learn so quickly; there's no spoon-feeding... they push you to get the best out of you."*

HJA encourages its crime trainees to gain accreditation as a police station adviser. The drawback is that you will then be on call overnight and at weekends when it's your turn on the rota. Even if just staying back a bit later in the office to catch up on your work, the hours in crime tend to be longer, so be warned you may find *"the cleaners hovering around your ankles."* Of course the benefits of being on the police station rota are overtime pay to boost your salary and invaluable front-line experience to boost your confidence. The scope of the 16-lawyer department's activities take in murder, rape and violent crime, including gangland matters, plus serious fraud and cases brought under Operation Ore, targeted at Internet paedophiles. The firm advised a defendant in the recent QPR blackmail trial and represents members of So Solid Crew. If crime appeals then it's well worth considering complementary seats in prison law and civil actions against the police, and with the increasingly popular civil liberties team, which acted for 11 of the 13 families represented in the second New Cross fire inquest, the longest inquest in British coronial history.

Equally challenging, the small mental health team offers a seat with masses of advocacy. Trainees are given their own caseload, which they progress while assisting solicitors on more complex judicial reviews. Most of the team's clients are detained under the Mental Health Act, and trainees are frequently sent out to take their instructions or conduct tribunal appeals in the institutions where they are held. It is not a job for the travel-adverse or socially awkward. *"In some acute cases, it can be difficult to get any sense out of your client, especially if they become agitated or aggressive. You need sensitivity. It can also be frustrating as often you'll sit for long periods of time without getting very far because of the long pauses."*

Without wishing to be insensitive, if these seats prove to be too much like madness, personal

www.chambersandpartners.co.uk

injury may be a better option. In this area the firm has earned an exceptional reputation through involvement in much-publicised group actions, including MMR and Gulf War Syndrome. The department's bread-and-butter work of road traffic cases and accidents at work cases is what mostly occupies trainees. Completing the picture are seats in housing and welfare law, family, and property, wills and probate.

getting your priorities right

Because of HJA's dedication to *"justice for all – regardless of ability to pay"* it comes as no surprise that those trainee applicants who are selected share common experiences in a public service context. The cohort from which we sampled included people who had previously worked in a CAB and the NHS. Be prepared to evidence your commitment to the cause as well as common sense, computer skills, people skills and academic strength. This last requirement is tested at interview with a problem scenario, something along the lines of giving advice at a police station or a family law dispute. *"It's not terribly difficult, it just tests the basic knowledge that you should have accrued on the LPC,"* one trainee assured us. During the contract, ongoing training *"can be a little haphazard: in mental health law there is no specific programme, in crime there are a number of structured talks on various aspects of what we do, but it's a logistical nightmare to get everyone together in the office at the same time."*

Unless justice ranks higher on your list of priorities than money, steer clear of HJA because it is a firm full of people who are passionate about *"providing legal services for those most in need."* This places it in a sector of the profession where salaries are markedly lower by virtue of the paucity of the public purse. Having said this, HJA actually sits at the higher end of the pay scale for trainees in this sector and as such trainees are better off than the majority of their high street peers.

The firm's size, skill base and reputation also render it one of the best bets in an uncertain legally aided world. In the words of one trainee: *"We will survive because we are bigger – economies of scale mean we are more efficient... the firm has its head screwed on in a financial way."* Such optimism is likely to have played a part in the retention of the three of the four qualifiers who stayed on in September 2006.

cross words

This is a place where everyone mucks in and nobody has any airs and graces. Largely the thinking is left of centre, and interestingly certain of the partners have built careers in local politics. Both crime partners, Raj Chada was until recently the Labour leader of Camden Council and Greg Foxsmith was elected as a Lib Dem councillor in Islington this year. We're not sure how much political talk there is in the pub after work, but anyone interested in finding out should head for The Old Eagle or trendy bars such as Grand Union or The Camden Arms. Lately four of the firm's lawyers started training for a charity white-collar boxing event. They managed to get boxing legend John Conteh in to help them. Fewer bruises are likely at the annual game of rounders and picnic in Regent's Park. Sneak down to the basement of the office and you'll find photos of all the picnics over the years.

For now HJA's no-frills office is sandwiched between the Silverlink train station and British Transport Police HQ on Camden Road. However, a move about a mile south to Euston is in the offing for spring 2007. This represents a watershed for the firm, placing it in a part of London that is undergoing radical change. With the opening of the Channel Tunnel Rail Link at King's Cross-St Pancras in 2007, and Europe's largest inner-city redevelopment set to transform the adjacent derelict railway land into a vast business and residential district, the possibilities for the firm would appear to be limitless. If you want a hint at the scale of the plans go on the developer's website at www.argentkingscross.co.uk . Or you could catch Jude Law's new movie 'Breaking and Entering', which depicts pre-development King's Cross, and was partly filmed in streets near to HJA's office.

and finally...

It looks as if change is in the offing for this much-admired firm. Its size and resources, scope of work and reputation make it one of the most desirable firms to train with in this part of the legal profession.

Holman Fenwick & Willan

the facts

Location: London
Number of UK partners/solicitors: 64/89
Total number of trainees: 18
Seats: 4x6 months
Alternative seats: Overseas seats, secondments
Extras: Pro bono – Battersea Law Centre

In 1883, Britannia ruled the waves and our shipping industry was central to the success of our empire. How things have changed. And yet one name endures – Holman Fenwick & Willan. It is as much a key player in the sector as it ever was.

sorting the wheat from the chaff

You might think that shipping isn't as important as it was in the 19th century; in fact, it still carries 90% of the world's traded goods. Technological advances have made ships much safer but, even so, an awful lot can still go wrong. As a result, HFW is so often involved in litigation that it is among those most frequently before the Commercial Court. Whether it's a cargo ship that ran aground off the coast of Yemen or a gigantic oil spill in China's Yangtze River, the lawyers in HFW's Admiralty department are ready to fly off to an obscure part of the world to inspect the damage and advise their clients (usually the ship's owner and their insurer) on what action to take to salvage ships and/or cargo.

Actually, the majority of shipping litigation has nothing to do with collisions or sinkings. You know that old trick conmen use in movies when they have to hand over an attaché case of money. The case is always filled with bundles of plain paper, with just a single layer of real notes on show. Well, it seems this old trick has a shipping counterpart. "*A consignment of wheat is expected at a port and when it arrives it's mostly chaff, with a thin layer of wheat on top,*" explained one trainee. "*That was an interesting case.*" In fact, 'dry shipping' litigation – concerning cargoes and contractual matters – make up a good chunk of the work of the shipping and transport group at HFW. The firm's other key pillar is its trade and energy group, a broad collection of lawyers dealing with everything from commodities disputes to mining contracts. Recently HMS Holman has been navigating the muddy waters churned up by the collapse of Enron.

Lately the firm has sought to broaden its expertise so as not to be so reliant on its core strengths. Whereas trainees were once restricted to a single non-contentious seat, now it is usually possible to undertake two and "*last year someone wangled three.*" So what is trainee life like aboard the good ship Holman? This is not a simple question as trainees' experiences vary wildly, even within the same department. Take trade and energy litigation for example; one trainee described working on "*litigation at the pointy end – running to court and back, managing documents for a case in the Court of Appeal, doing pre-trial reviews and small hearings... you see all the different stages of litigation and you get a lot of court time.*" But listen to the experiences of another: "*I got caught up in a major case and basically hardly left the office for three weeks. It was the real trainee slog – filing correspondence chronologically in 12 lever-arch files, that sort of thing."* It's the same story in dry shipping. *"You do loads of really interesting research into strange and wonderful things,"* gushed one source. *"For trainees it's mostly photocopying,"* said another. Similarly conflicting views emerged from almost all departments.

fifty ways to leave your bundle

So what's going on? To a certain extent, of course, *"the experience you have of a seat depends on what's going on in the department. If there's a big matter on you'll always have a lot of paperwork to do."* But there's another factor, as evidenced by one person's observation that *"Holman's is really a hundred firms in one."* At HFW, it seems, the partner is king. *"The words 'house style' will get a laugh,"* said one interviewee. *"You'll learn to make a bundle with the index at the back, and then the next partner you work for will say, 'Who taught you to do that?'"* Surprisingly, trainees seemed nonchalant on this issue. *"You quickly learn the way each one does things and then there's no problem,"* said one. When we checked with the firm it told us that new house styles were to be introduced.

The same inconsistency is evident in the level of supervision in each seat; some trainees accused the firm of *"micro-managing"* their work while others noted that they'd been *"very much left to get on with things."* Fortunately, you're usually not limited to a single partner-supervisor, so if you think you're getting a raw deal you can seek gainful employment from elsewhere in the department. This is a firm that rewards an entrepreneurial approach.

Inconsistency crops up again in relation to seat selection. While there is no compulsory seat, no trainee would make it through their contract without visiting either shipping litigation or trade litigation. The firm is adept at putting trainees' particular skills to good advantage, and so anyone with experience or knowledge of shipping will be particularly rewarded with a high-responsibility shipping litigation seat. Those with clear preferences for a given department or supervisor are usually accommodated: *"With only eight trainees you're going to get what you want,"* mused one. Anyone interested in spending six months in one of the firm's offices in Paris, Dubai, Hong Kong, Shanghai or the Greek port of Piraeus can apply to be interviewed for the seat.

dubai it or steal it?

From its Victorian heritage to the old-fashioned fonts on its website, HFW is unquestionably traditional. Although the higher echelons of the firm contain *"a few real characters"* – the Admiralty department's marine consultants are actual ship's captains – our interviewees sensed that more modern brands of quirkiness wouldn't go down well. *"If you turned up for interview wearing crazy coloured clothes, it would raise eyebrows,"* suggested one. Nevertheless, it's *"very friendly and not at all stuffy."* Women can opt for tops rather than shirts, and while it's suits and ties for most men, not only do the swarthy seamen of Admiralty eschew ties, *"there's even a bit of a competition as to who can get away with the most buttons undone."* Despite a clear understanding that partners rule the roost, HFW's atmosphere was thought to be democratic. *"You feel you can rely on your colleagues,"* said one trainee. *"You can ask a partner you don't know a question and they'll take the time to go through it in detail."*

As the firm grows, its City office feels like it is *"bursting at the seams."* Although everyone still has space, our sources admitted: *"It's a bit tricky finding chairs for vac schemers"* and trainees occasionally have to share offices with each other instead of a supervisor. Again, when we checked with the firm we learned that a reorganisation was set to relieve the pressure.

As well as beefing up the non-contentious teams in London, the firm has opened a new Dubai office, snatching it, pirate-style, from the clutches of smaller shipping rival Hill Taylor Dickinson, and a new office in Melbourne. Both are expected to offer seats soon. The trainees we spoke to declared themselves to be "*pretty excited*" at the firm's expansion. "*It's really going great guns.*" Indeed it is – the firm posted a 30% increase in profits early in 2006.

Like many litigation-led firms, HFW keeps reasonable hours, with trainees working 9.30am to 6.30pm. In Admiralty, on a regular day when they're not running around averting disaster, "*the partners are gone by 5.30pm.*" When their work is done, the different departments like to socialise and the prize for the most fun-loving must go to the shipping lawyers. Twice a year HFW has a proper get-together: one year there's a big Christmas ball and small-scale summer drinks party, the following year this pattern is reversed.

playing politics

The key to a successful and rewarding training contract at HFW is playing the game and being a little political when necessary. Anyone too headstrong or arrogant might find the partner-first ethos stifling, especially when forced to adjust repeatedly to new ways of doing things. The meek will struggle to win the partner interest that is required to get the most interesting work. "*The firm is very good at massaging trainees into the shape they want,*" explained one source. "*But if you're careful you can massage them back to make a shape that suits you.*" What's clear is that those who have the necessary skill and nous to play the system are rewarded with top-class work, particularly in litigation. "*Going to the Royal Courts of Justice feels like playing at Wembley,*" gushed one veteran.

The other point trainees made was that "*it does help to be a bit of a brain.*" There's usually a

strong showing of Oxbridge graduates, a few who have worked before turning to the law and some people who've lived overseas. "*Every year there's someone a bit shippy,*" ie someone with maritime experience or a master's in shipping law. Men and women are recruited in equal numbers, although when you look at the list of partners and partner equivalents in the London office you'll see just six women among the 72 people profiled. At least the firm does quite well at selecting the right applicants: in September 2006, seven of the eight qualifiers were piped aboard as full crew members, and proving that not everyone becomes a shipping lawyer here, several entered the reinsurance and trade and energy teams.

and finally...

Training here isn't an easy option; you'll need both the confidence to manoeuvre yourself into a strong position and the humility to operate within the partner-is-king philosophy. For those willing to play the game, HFW offers litigation experience like few others.

Howes Percival

the facts

Location: Northampton, Leicester, Milton Keynes, Norwich
Number of UK partners/solicitors: 33/35
Total number of trainees: 16
Seats: 4x6 months
Alternative seats: Possible secondments

Howes Percival tends to attract those with a connection to the East Midlands or East Anglia who want a respected commercial firm to take control of their training. As one trainee put it: "*I wanted to work for a firm doing London-quality work but without the hours.*"

hp sorcery

Corporate and commercial work is what drives HP. It recently acted for the buyers in the £2 million disposal of Oxford United FC and advised on the sale of Leicester-based advertising and marketing agency Big Communications. The agency may not be a household name but its clients – Virgin Cola, Alliance & Leicester and Morphy Richards – certainly are. HP also boasts a solid reputation in commercial litigation, commercial property, insolvency, employment and liquor licensing. It handles UK and European property matters for American document management company Iron Mountain and assists the Dean and Chapter of Norwich Cathedral with their property concerns.

HP sells itself to clients as a firm offering a City-standard service at anything but City prices. Trainees say it is "*big on marketing and building client relationships*" and "*big on getting us involved in the marketing side.*" The opportunity to go on six-month client secondments is "*invaluable*" in terms of the first-hand commercial experience and learning how to develop client skills. Previously East Midlands trainees have spent time with DaimlerChrysler and tyre people ATS Euromaster, although the list of clients offering these opportunities is not set in stone. Back in the firm's offices, the range of seats on offer to trainees reflects the particular business successes of each office.

east-west relations

HP has four offices – Northampton, Leicester, Milton Keynes and Norwich – and certainly from a trainee's perspective there is a divide between the first three and the last. Applicants for training contracts can opt for an East Midlands deal or a Norwich one. Although some work is shared across the firm, trainees say: "*All the offices work quite independently*" with a "*separate client base and workload.*" Some people even considered there to be "*healthy competition*" between the offices.

HP used to be keen on trainees spending seats in different offices so that they could get a taste of what the other sites had to offer. Trainees now report that it isn't strictly enforcing this rule and that it is possible to spend your training contract in just one office. This could be a mercy if you find the cost and hassle of commuting (or moving to a different town) off-putting. It's not as if trainees never spend time as a group: "*There is always some type of communal training or seminar*" so you can "*get to meet everyone outside your office.*" Another way to get to know colleagues elsewhere is by attending the various firm-wide socials organised each year. The trainee summer party, for example, does exactly what it says on the tin: it's a party for the trainees of all four offices to welcome the next batch of recruits to the firm. The AGM is an opportunity for everyone from secretaries and trainees to the big guns to spend some quality time together. The last one was held in Bedfordshire and started with a trip to a water sports centre for jet skiing and "*team building exercises such as an obstacle course.*" A formal meeting to discuss the firm's progress was then followed by a fancy-dress party with a free bar.

It isn't all fun and games at HP though. Our sources were honest enough to admit that the sometimes-long hours wouldn't suit everyone and "*the office locations aren't exactly glamorous.*" When we asked for comments on the fact that only three out of the 33 partners were women, our sources assured us that "*there are more and more women coming through the lower levels*" and that "*as time goes on things will change.*" For now, here's a slice of life in each of the four offices.

northampton, mk and leicester

Northampton is HP's main and oldest office. The last Mr Percival, the great-great-great-grandson of the original Percival who co-founded the firm, retired from here last year, but not all the trappings of the past have disappeared from this *"slightly more traditional"* office. Above the boardroom table hangs an enormous chandelier, a fitting perfectly in keeping with the building's *"lovely 18th-century frontage"* but less so with the *"square, modern extension tacked onto the back."* Spread over three floors, the office houses tax, private client, residential conveyancing, employment and commercial departments. Trainees' hours run from around 8.45am to 6pm with *"not that many late nights"* unless you're in coco. The social life is generally *"good"* though not as crazy as some of the other offices (ahem, Leicester). Sources mentioned that *"the Northampton office feels slower"* than the others, maybe because the *"average age of lawyers is higher."*

The office in Milton Keynes is *"lively"* and fast growing, with perhaps slightly longer hours than in Northampton. No one seems to be complaining; instead trainees spoke about what the office had to offer them by way of experience. HP MK is best known for its coco work and, in the last year, together with corporate colleagues from Northampton and Leicester, the team concluded approximately 95 deals with a total value of approximately £780 million. Not bad going. The litigation department also packs a mean punch and is one of the biggest teams in the office. Recent cases have included a PFI-related claim against the British Museum and a £51 million insurance fraud claim. This may not come as a huge shock for some readers, but there *"isn't much of a social scene"* after work, as MK is *"a place where everyone drives."* The current batch of trainees tend to *"hang out and go to lunch together,"* with three of them even living together. If being so close with your peers isn't your cup of tea, you could always get involved in the various sports teams that play against clients.

Milton Keynes shares a reputation for being *"more vibrant"* with Leicester, HP's smallest office. Leicester has a real sense of *"dynamism,"* according to our sources and is particularly known for its strong employment team. Come Friday night, a band of regulars high-tail it to The Quay or another bar, often courtesy of the *"managing partner in property who pays for the drinks."* There's good cheer in the office too: *"If you have done a good deal there might be champagne"* or *"if the boss is feeling particularly happy, he might take you out for a drink."* A great sense of *"camaraderie between people"* could result from the fact that *"most of the associates have trained together and so are friends as well as work colleagues. Even the managing partner trained here."* The trainees tend *"to stick close to each other,"* but this is no great surprise given that there are only four of them. On the sports front there is cricket in the summer and five-a-side football, *"mainly against clients."*

norwich

Norwich is not exactly the black sheep of the family, but rather another breed of sheep that is pretty much left to do its own thing. *"They have a separate profit pool,"* explained one source. Norwich now accounts for approximately a third of the firm's total income and has over 120 staff, so whatever the arrangement it looks to be working well. This branch is strong in insolvency and has been appointed to act for both the Insolvency Service and HM Revenue & Customs, a big coup for a regional firm. The office also has an enviable reputation in licensing work, cornering the local market and acting for clients such as Number Ten Group, St Giles House hotel and Orgasmic outlets in York, Lincoln and Norwich. A large land-owning community leads to a good volume of private client work and commercial litigation is also a strong suit.

does what it says on the tin

Choosing seats is a pretty straightforward exercise in each office. *"Coco tends to be the flagship department of every office"* and as such will feature at some stage of your training. Add commercial property and commercial litigation and these are *"the three standards"* in the HP training contract. Tax and employment are not available as a seat in every office, while private client work does not feature at all in the East Midlands training. Across the seats and the offices, trainees were pleased with the quality of work they were given; some spoke of running their own small files at the end of a seat. Said one: *"I did a possession case completely on my own."* One or two sources remarked that cornering a supervisor could be tricky at busy times, saying: *"Although you tend to share with a partner or a senior fee earner, it does not necessarily mean you can go to them if they've got a heavy work commitment."* The good news is that trainees feel management does listen to them and that they could be *"fairly honest"* in what they said at quarterly meetings between trainees, HR and partners. Some sources told us they thought they were working longer hours compared to peers at other local firms, but they did say they *"reaped the rewards"* of choosing HP. We suspect the £22,000 starting salary (£24,00 for second-years, £37,000 for NQs) and LPC sponsorship was uppermost in their minds. On the whole, we'd conclude that trainees are pretty happy with their lot, an idea supported by the fact that four of the six qualifiers stayed on with the firm in September 2006.

and finally...

If you're looking for a training contract here, according to current trainees, getting onto the vacation scheme is a clever way to go about it. That way, if you impress during the scheme you can *"skip the assessment day and just go straight for the interview."*

Hugh James

the facts

Location: Cardiff, Merthyr Tydfil, Blackwood
Number of UK partners/solicitors: 47/67
Total number of trainees: 19
Seats: Notionally 4x6 months
Alternative seats: None

Hugh James is one of the biggest and best-known law firms in Wales. Its three offices in Cardiff, Merthyr Tydfil and Blackwood each cater for a different type of client, which means that trainees here encounter a real diversity of work.

a firm of two halves

HJ has four main groups: claimant PI; publicly funded law; business litigation and business services. *"It is almost as if the firm has two personalities: the branch office mentality and the Cardiff office one. The branch offices are more idiosyncratic and individualistic in their approach, whereas the Cardiff office is much more corporate and feels more like a discrete unit."* In brief, Merthyr and Blackwood are, at heart, grown-up, high street operations, albeit extremely sophisticated ones, dealing with PI, clinical negligence and other civil matters. Cardiff houses the corporate and commercial departments plus the family law team and an up-market asset management unit. It is all but guaranteed that trainees will work in Cardiff plus at least one of the other two offices.

While property litigation in Cardiff is one of the most intense seats, it can also be one of the most rewarding in terms of the variety of work undertaken and the depth of involvement. One trainee gave us a good summary: *"I did everything from boundary and tenancy disputes to obtaining ASBOs for a local housing association. I was gathering witness statements and dealing with the appropriate authorities including social workers and the police."* Clients include the local authorities of Cardiff and Blaenau Gwent, Welsh Water, The Environment Agency, Barratt Homes and the Welsh Rugby Union. The *"partner-heavy"* commercial property department in Cardiff offers involvement in a range of commercial transactions. *"Most of what you do here is leases, although I was involved in the large-scale first registration for a small town,"* recalled one source. Another had been responsible for reviewing a huge land contract: *"I had to compare it to an earlier version, pick out the differences and go through them with a partner – very scary as it was so important and I had to find everything."* On the down side, it's rare to take a file from start to finish and *"rather than having your own caseload you do a lot of post-completion work or work on deals pre-completion."* Despite being paper-based the seat is surprisingly challenging: *"In some ways it is a tough one because you get work coming in from all directions and every fee earner expects it to be done now."*

in the eye of the beholder

Clin neg in Merthyr was described as *"a wonderful department to work in. There is such a mish-mash of work – drafting instructions to counsel, dealing with medical experts, quantum research and researching generally on medical issues."* Beyond straight clinical claims the department has handled *"quite a big Consumer Protection Act case concerning faulty cataract lenses. You have ongoing contact with the clients and they tell you about their eyes... you go through their medical records and pick up quite quickly how to read them. It's very interesting so long as you're not a hypochondriac. We're also dealing with the E. coli breakout in south Wales, representing the families."*

Based in Blackwood, a PI seat is an excellent choice for anyone who wants to try their hand at advocacy or look after their own clients. *"I really enjoyed having my own caseload and being left to my own devices,"* explained one source. *"Help was there if I needed it, and I did feel like part of a team,*

but I certainly owned my work." However, *"the seat name is a bit of a misnomer actually; although it is down as PI it turned out to encompass a broad range of litigation. I undertook agency work on boundary disputes, small commercial matters and debt recovery as well as PI. But it was excellent experience and I found myself in court five or six times a week."*

taming the beast

Defendant fast-track litigation is one of the least popular seats, at least until trainees actually try it. Largely dealing with road traffic accidents, employment liability and property liability cases, the unit is reckoned to be *"quite pressurised"* and *"a bit of a beast, where you turn over work as quickly as possible."* Trainees undertake everything from the receipt of the initial letter of claim all the way through to recouping costs, sometimes having 60 or more of their own files. The clients who use this service include Royal Mail, Norwich Union and other insurance companies plus various local authorities. The lender services team is another fast-track type operation. *"We've just got a really big contract for HBoS to do remortgages... it's a very good seat for someone who hasn't worked in an office before. It's a young department with lots of support and you learn basic telephone and legal research skills – it really set me up well as the skills were transferable."*

Sit in wills and probate in Merthyr and you'll see clients every day; you may also be asked to spend time over in the Blackwood office. *"It's quite a big department in Merthyr because of the miners' compensation scheme; there's a lot of work arising from that... and when miners have died and we need to get grants of probate."*

The private client team in Cardiff, which generally looks after clients with more money, is referred to as the asset management team and its lawyers also handle trusts and probate disputes. The family team in Cardiff mainly acts for privately paying clients and its work is a combination of divorce and child care. Lawyers here are renowned for psychiatric cases and adoption and HJ is one of just two firms in Wales specialising in international abductions. We should also mention that although none of our sources had undertaken a crime seat, HJ also has the largest general crime practice in the South Wales valleys. It deals with a large amount of violent crime (often featuring weapons) and has a particular specialism in psychiatric murder.

huge aims

As different as the branch offices are, there have been efforts to harmonise their appearance with that of the Cardiff HQ; this, trainees say, reflects a general modernisation of the firm as a whole. One told us: *"When I applied here it was quite an old-school firm and then, in the time between getting my contract and starting my training, there was a massive transformation. I much prefer this firm to the one I applied to – we have just three offices now and there is a lot of interaction between them – more than I expected. And it's a lot more commercial; the firm has really progressed since I applied and they're even paying for the LPC now."* A different source detected a slight whiff of tension between the old and the new: *"The firm has aspirations to be more modern yet it also has its traditions. It has its own ways of going about things, like recruitment, man-management and seat allocation, that could do with being conducted in a more transparent way."* Certainly, some of our sources found the allocation of seats hard to understand. *"I have no idea how the decisions are made,"* mused one trainee. *"In the last couple of years some of us have asked for specific seats and not got them."* Yet others are aware that management must take into account big-picture issues: *"In our appraisal we are told that seat allocation depends on the commercial needs of the firm at that time. It would be a waste of everybody's time to stick us in a department where all that needed to be done was administration."* One was convinced the powers that be think carefully about seat allocation, telling us: *"I'm quite sure they consider your character and wouldn't send someone who is clearly a contentious lawyer to probate, for example."*

The firm scores highly when it comes to awarding NQ jobs – seven out of nine stayed in 2006. Not only are announcements made early in the year but it is quite common for second-years to migrate to their qualification department in the months running up to The Big Q. Indeed, right the way through the contract, management isn't that hung up about sticking to the four-by-six-month system. *"Other firms are rigid as to the number of seats you do and for how long. Here not many of us do four seats of six months, which can mean you spend more time doing things you enjoy."*

made in wales

At Hugh James, trainees are usually Welsh by birth or have become almost Welsh after time at a Welsh university. Girls commonly outnumber boys by some margin. Most become exposed to the firm on a vacation placement or a few days work experience while at uni or law school. Our researchers know them to be big talkers. Who knows, perhaps it's part of their training. Said one: *"The partners are always prepared to give you a hearing; it's not a draconian firm;"* another added: *"Everybody works hard here but it's not a stiff and formal firm; it's quite sociable."* Those of you who like the idea of winding down with colleagues after work should note that office locations do affect the social life. For instance, *"it can be hard to go for a drink with people in the Merthyr office because everybody commutes, but you don't have that problem in Cardiff."* What the branches may not have by way of a post-work scene they make up for in seasonal parties. Each office enjoys a string of shindigs, with a grand gathering of all staff once a year in Cardiff. We probably shouldn't repeat this but *"it's quite funny seeing partners wasted."*

One of the most useful questions we asked trainees was why choose Hugh James over any other firm in Wales? One of the best – and longest – answers we got was this: *"If you are looking for a diverse training contract there is no better place. You get very broad experience from working within dedicated teams where you do some very advanced stuff. You also get the opportunity to be involved in cutting-edge, newsworthy areas of law such as judicial reviews. But if this isn't what you are about you can also undertake low-profile work here; there is just a huge variety of it and so this may be a good place to go to if you don't have a fully formed idea of what you want to do yet."* Further insight came from trainees at the other major firms, who described Hugh James as more locally focused than their own employers. The other thing to factor in is the firm's success in contentious work: *"We're known as a litigation firm with an exceptional reputation in civil lit, and that attracts a lot of people to it."*

and finally...

Hugh James is ideal if you want to integrate yourself with the local business and residential communities and have one of the most impressive 'Made in Wales' stamps on your CV.

IBB

the facts

Location: Uxbridge, Chesham, Ingatestone
Number of UK partners/solicitors: 29/45
Total number of trainees: 11
Seats: 4x6 months
Alternative seats: None

Secure in the northern territories of London's broad commuter belt, IBB has one eye on the action in the capital and views itself as a competitor to London firms. Its decision to steamroll ahead with an expansion plan has resulted in turnover increasing by around 50% in the last five years, and it now has ambitions to break into the UK top 100 firms by revenue.

the notorious b-i-g

IBB services a broad clientele of businesses – mostly local – company directors, professionals and ordinary everyday folk in need of assistance with house moves, divorces or speedy exits from police cells. For IBB trainees this means a rounded contract incorporating commercial, private client and community legal services. Just in case you were concerned by all that talk of steamrollers and City law firms, trainees wish to assure readers that private client and criminal law will remain central to the firm's business plan because *"its reputation is so strong in these areas."*

IBB's four branches each have their own character, based on history, workload, atmosphere and, most importantly, clientele. Lovell House in Uxbridge is home to the firm's community legal services centre, where trainees can take crime, childcare and personal injury seats. The crime department offers two seats at a time: one dealing with general crime and one working with the specialist business investigations and governance team, aka BIG. In the general crime seat, the open-plan office is consistently in a state of alert as people dart in and out of courts, police stations and prisons, *"constantly on their mobiles as that's the only way they can be reached."* From early on trainees meet clients to take instructions, prepare cases for trial, liaise with barristers and undertake advocacy of their own in the form of case management hearings and pre-trial reviews. The seat demands flexibility as well as *"the ability to think quickly on your feet so that you can answer your client's questions."* The payoff is an experience that *"can be really quite confidence-boosting – the clients really trust you."*

The BIG team defends company directors and professionals, including accountants, dentists, doctors and airline pilots, when they land in hot water. The recent merger of the Inland Revenue service with Customs & Excise to form HMRC has resulted in a surge of prosecutions for tax fraud, meaning even more defence work for the BIG. As well as representing run-of-the-mill tax dodgers, the BIGsters have worked on some key conspiracy to defraud cases, such as a £60 million fraud concerning Microsoft's copyrights and trade marks, which was investigated by the UK's National Crime Squad and the FBI in the USA. That case led to a nine-month trial. Another case involved a £30 million time-share fraud. Serious organised crime is another specialism, and here the lawyers provided defence representation in the £90 million conspiracy to rob Swissport Heathrow of gold bullion, foreign currency and diamonds. Even with such major cases in the department, the BIG team offers plenty of client contact and is notorious for *"not being afraid to drop trainees in at the deep end and watch them learn to swim."*

In stark contrast, the personal injury seat is more of a marathon than a sprint. The progress of civil cases is generally more measured and methodical – okay slower – and as a consequence trainees are unlikely to see a matter through from start to finish. They encounter slips-and-trips, road traffic accidents and the firm's specialism, head injuries. If your key interest is advocacy, this seat probably won't suit you so well, but at least you can subject yourself to nerves and sweaty palms at the end of the seat when trainees make a small presentation to the rest of the team.

coco-cabana

The commercial team occupies brand new premises at Capital Court in Uxbridge. Proudly standing four storeys high, with the latest furnishings, plasma screens and air conditioning, it exudes a corporate feel that is suited to its clientele. The only negative is *"the awful fake palm trees."* Some of our interviewees admitted to cul-

ture shock when they arrived after a stint in Lovell House, describing it as *"like moving from one firm to another."* Apparently the first thing to learn is *"to fight the temptation to talk loudly"* because the atmosphere here is less hectic and more heads-down. *"It's a desk job really, very professional and hard working"* and the *"balance of work and play is very much on the work side."* Several seats are offered: company/commercial, commercial litigation and three property options – property litigation, landlord and tenant, and property finance. If you were wondering if the firm had any big recognisable clients, how about Coca-Cola, Slush Puppie and Hasbro, each of which give the firm employment work.

Be sure to choose your seats wisely as the level of responsibility and client contact seems largely dependent on the nature of the work and the nature of the supervisor. The burgeoning coco team demands trainees who are keen to take on plenty of responsibility. One coco trainee reported feeling *"not at all sheltered"* and was regularly encouraged to talk to clients directly. Another trainee felt the level of client contact and responsibility was far lower in the commercial property team due to the scale and value of the deals and the calibre of the clients. Here the firm acts for several residential developers, including the likes of Bellway Homes, and was recently asked by Dolce & Gabbana to help acquire new showroom premises.

herd mentality

The Chesham branch occupies an old manor house set against a backdrop of beautiful views. The way trainees described the location (swan-filled lake, frolicking deer, rabbits, etc) you'd think they were working on the set of the Bambi movie before the big fire sequence. The Chesham branch is entirely dedicated to private clients – high-stakes divorces, wills and probate, that kind of thing. Because of the sensitive nature of the work, trainees are eased into their seats gently, at first attending client meetings with a supervisor, eventually being given their own files. *"The more you express the desire to get into the meatier stuff, the more likely you are to get it."* The message from Chesham is don't be deceived by the idyllic surroundings outside: the office is an industrious and highly professional environment that demands the best efforts of trainees at all times. This doesn't translate into longer hours; as one commentator put it: *"In a sense you are master of your own ship. If you want to work late you can, but it's certainly not expected of you."*

The smallest branch, in Ingatestone in Essex, is somewhat of a mystery to trainees as no seats are offered there. We did a little digging and discovered that it is home to a charity practice and a property team.

let the games begin

The application process sounds pretty thorough. As well as the standard CV and letter trainees are asked to answer questions, such as: What do you consider to be the biggest challenges facing the legal profession today? Stage two is a relatively painless interview, ideally leading on to the assessment day. Make sure you are tucked up in bed nice and early the night before, because the day will leave you *"absolutely knackered, so drink a lot of coffee and eat a lot of the free mint imperials."* After hours of probing, things takes a heart-thumping turn when, in true *X Factor* style, each candidate is called out and told there and then if they've made it. Just as in the *X Factor*, *"IBB aren't blinkered: they do appreciate people who might be a bit older."* The key qualities inherent in successful applicants were a measured approach and an ability to listen as well as talk. *"It boiled down to having a certain level of confidence,"* one trainee concluded, adding a caveat along the lines of *"the ones who launch into a leadership tirade"* are given a miss.

The training contract begins with a week-long induction during which time expectations are made clear. Every seat has its own tailor-made skill set checklist, and three-monthly appraisals allow supervisors and trainees to sit down and assess whether those skills have been developed. Regular meetings between trainees, HR and training supervisors highlight possible improvements, spark debate and allow an exchange of information generally. As one trainee observed: *"They're always looking for ways to improve the supervision and feedback."*

The social side is not forgotten at IBB. Sports teams for football, netball and cricket encourage staff from the different branches to mingle, and the trainees describe themselves as *"a close-knit bunch"* who regularly go out to lunch together. They can often be found in the Three Tuns, the cheapest pub in Uxbridge. IBB's last Christmas party at The Grove hotel in Watford gave them a chance to put on their finery for a slap-up meal, disco and casino games.

and finally...

IBB has much to offer trainees. There aren't many firms where you could shake the hand of a local retailer one day and the mastermind that of a major heist the next. In September 2006, three of the four qualifiers took jobs with the firm.

Ince & Co

the facts

Location: London
Number of UK partners/solicitors: 48/67
Total number of trainees: 18
Seats: 4x6 months
Alternative seats: None
Extras: Language training

Alongside a chart-topping shipping practice, Ince & Co fields experts in the areas of insurance litigation, aviation and energy. Trainees come here because they want their work to be *"big and complicated with an international element,"* and from what we hear, Ince delivers.

don't take a seat

If you reckon that all training contracts are the same, think again. Train here, and you'll learn your trade within an unusual non-departmental model. Although allocated to a partner for four six-month stints, you will sniff out work from all corners of the firm for yourself. There are committees to ensure that work is distributed evenly and no one gets swamped, but the approach does leave you *"reliant on your own reputation for good work, so the onus is on you to build your place in the firm."* A daunting prospect, maybe, but one that offers a degree of flexibility and freedom that is lacking in the 'classic' seat-based training. *"You can pitch your efforts towards certain practice areas or target certain people to get the type of work you want."* One trainee, already thinking ahead, told us: *"At some stage in your career you are going to have to market yourself, so you may as well start early."* In this system work follows you around for the duration of your training contract, and beyond if need be, and trainees value that. *"You would never get the full story if you had to hand stuff over and didn't keep cases."* They believe they *"do a better job"* because of it. Those who thrive under the regime manage to hit the ground running. *"Not easy when you start somewhere new and you know nothing,"* but the harsh reality is that *"you are a fee earner"* and *"you have to be up to scratch."* At least effort is appreciated and *"people do notice."*

A no-nonsense summary then from a typically no-nonsense trainee: *"You do as well as you deserve to do."*

grow your own

Supervision and support has to be a bit more fluid than the norm. *"You can sit with a partner without ever actually doing any work with or for them,"* and in such cases *"they know what you are doing but just don't tend to interfere."* In this respect their role may be more pastoral than anything else, and again, the onus is on the trainee to seek direct assistance from the most appropriate lawyer. We're assured there are enough *"checks and balances,"* including formal six-monthly appraisals, and if ever there is any question over gaps in a trainees' experience or knowledge, *"the wheels start turning"* so that issues are quickly addressed.

The benefits of a firm without departments can be seen at qualification. At many other firms the summer scramble to bag a job in a preferred department can be a cut-throat business, bringing tears and tantrums as well as compromise and disappointment. Ince does things differently, and the nearly newly qualifieds we spoke to were relaxed about their futures. *"The joy is that we did not have to make the decision as to where we wanted to qualify;"* *"I am still in the 'Ince & Co department' and am not being forced to specialise too early."* It can be some years before a specialism emerges, and even then there is room for a few stubborn generalists. We sense that flexibility and variety keep Ince lawyers content: *"You do look at the firm and realise that a lot of partners trained here – many people are lifers, as it were."* In 2006, six of the eight qualifiers stayed on.

prestigious

The firm's 135-year pedigree and market-leading reputation as a pre-eminent force in shipping have led to involvement in possibly the archetypal shipping case of modern times, the sinking of the Prestige, which touches on many aspects of international and shipping law, including the obligation of a state to provide a port of refuge and rights of passage of ships. The shedding of some 77,000 tons of fuel oil resulting in major pollution to the Spanish and French coasts has also raised the prospect of a complete European ban on 'single skin' tankers. It's big stuff.

A 24-hour, 365 days per year, emergency response service handles disasters and crises around the globe. We've no idea what happens when someone presses the big red button on Ince's website, as no one here quite has the nerve, but all the same it reminds us a bit of the Batphone so we like it. This high-level work is not hoarded by high-level fee earners. Trainees may actually be involved "*at the sharp end,*" attending casualties and assisting in the taking of witness statements. Shipping brilliance ("*it's the foundation of the firm*") notwithstanding, trainees were at pains to point out that there is more variety of work here than many would imagine. "*Yes we have an excellent reputation for shipping, but there is also the insurance litigation as well.*" Of course, and didn't we also mention aviation and energy?

Ince's crack aviation lawyers have assisted on logistics aspects of the production process of Airbus' new flagship 555-seat double-deck jetliner, the A380. Instructions have also come in from the international airlines trade body, IATA, in relation to the renegotiation of international aviation treaties concerned with liability for war and terrorism. The firm's energy lawyers deal with work from oil majors and some of the largest contracting firms in the energy sector, and have particular expertise in relation to offshore oil and gas facilities. Lawyers recently provided advice to leading Italian contractor Saipem in connection with the Blue Stream pipeline project from the former Soviet Union to Turkey along the seabed of the Black Sea at depths of 2,150 metres. Greener types will no doubt appreciate a growing involvement in renewable energy, particularly wind-sourced.

Ince's reputation management function, which has arisen after years of handling the sort of serious maritime, energy and aviation incidents that predictably pique public interest, means that when things go horribly wrong for clients they can get help on media and public statements and press releases. Other unexpected work a trainee might encounter includes employment law and personal injury litigation, both areas in which Ince's clients need regular advice. Yet another activity for us to mention is corporate finance, because although trainees admit "*this is the place to come if you want to be a litigator rather than a transactional lawyer,*" there is transactional work going on here, including AIM listings and other smaller deals.

arrested development

The range and quality of work these trainees handle is impressive. They assist in the arrest of ships when an owner or charterer defaults on their obligations, a "*very exciting and stressful experience*" we are told. "*We had been watching a ship for five years to see if she came into a friendly jurisdiction.*" It seems that sod's law takes no account of international maritime law, so "*it happened on a Friday night and we ended up negotiating with the other side all weekend to get the debts paid.*" One trainee was certainly in good company when up against a partner from a prestigious City rival involved on an interim application. Another ran a whole property damage case in the county court. "*It was very much my case. I drafted all the submissions, did all the work and stood up and made the application. It was very challenging and great fun.*" Trainees can expect a lot of client contact, a lot of negotiations with other lawyers and "*quite a lot of legal research into the cerebral shipping area.*" The inevitable downside of training at such a litigation-heavy firm is that "*there are occasional periods of bundling.*"

When help is needed, "*there is an incredible amount of support*" from all quarters. "*The first port of call* [their pun, not ours] *is your fellow trainees. Chances are they have seen the issue before, or can recommend where to go to find the answer.*" Failing that, "*you can walk into any partner's office to pick their brain.*" "*A lot of faith is shown in you and the firm is genuinely interested in your development as a lawyer.*"

in the dock

"Absolutely fantastic" new digs on the top two floors of the recently refurbished International House in St Katharine Docks are an *"enormous improvement over the old office."* Fewer amenities in the area make it harder to pop out for a quick sandwich at lunchtime, but maybe this is the price you pay for *"air conditioning that works"* and balcony views over London and the Thames. We are told the move is absolutely in keeping with the general strategy of the firm, and that *"by modernising whilst remaining in a historical place we are continuing to build on our history."*

Trainees had much to say of Ince's culture. When one said it was *"almost a family firm"* they were referring to *"both the good things and bad things about a family."* Take from that what you will, but we think we know what trainees mean when they say *"the firm is kind of organic; it doesn't function in a corporate way."* The culture seems to have practical benefits – no billing targets and *"less petty admin – it is nice not having a form to fill in for every single thing."* *"You cannot slack off,"* but *"the hours relative to the pay are pretty good here."*

Out of work time, monthly 'Ince drinks' attract somewhat *"patchy"* attendance, though the Christmas party and May ball are *"usually quite drunken."* The former involves *"heading down to a local bar after work for a buffet and free bar all night. The hardcore then head off to a nightclub in the City."* The latter is a black-tie affair which opens with an *"obscure"* Latin grace, followed by a sit-down meal. *"After the speeches, there is dancing and further drinking. The hardcore then head off to a nightclub in the City."* Sound familiar? Sporting activities include five-a-side football, rugby, golf, go-karting, paintballing and, of course, sailing. The form for cricket matches, often against clients, is *"heading off to Dulwich for 20 overs each side, a good slogathon, followed by drinks and a barbecue."* How very civilised.

and finally...

Ince & Co allows access all areas in some classy shipping, insurance and energy sector work. For a liberating yet undoubtedly *"tough"* training environment, confident, brainy, outgoing types should look no further.

Irwin Mitchell

the facts

Location: Altrincham, Birmingham, Leeds, London, Newcastle, Sheffield, Solihull
Number of UK partners/solicitors: 113/215
Total number of trainees: 51
Seats: 4x6 months
Alternative seats: None

Now ranked among the top 25 UK law firms by turnover, Irwin Mitchell has a distinctive place on the legal map. Commercial and private clients flock to the firm for many things, not least its commanding PI and clinical negligence practice.

gang law fayre

Irwin Mitchell has come a long way since its somewhat gritty roots as a criminal firm representing rival factions during the villainous Sheffield gang wars of the 1920s. It now boasts an impressive presence on a national scale and a trainee population that has swelled to keep pace. Most recently, a merger with personal injury and clinical negligence firm Alexander Harris took effect on 1 May 2006, further cementing the firm's dominance in this sector. It also added smaller Solihull and Altrincham branches to an empire of four established UK offices, plus outposts in Madrid and Marbella.

Personal injury is the jewel in the IM crown. Its leading lawyers take on heavyweight multi-track claims and an army of legal execs and case handlers process a high volume of low-value fast-track cases. The subject matter of the work ranges from simple broken bones caused by RTAs and pavement slips and trips, to neurotrauma, occupational health issues, asbestos-related diseases and child abuse. With this work such a major part of the firm's business, trainees usually spend at least some portion of their contract here. This is rarely a problem for anyone, although we sense some forget just how successful the firm is at attracting juicy cases. "You can get a bit blasé about the quality work you are doing," confessed one; "in reality trainees here are really lucky." There have been many high-profile cases over the years, including group actions relating to vCJD, miners' illnesses and injuries and Equitable Life (though we appreciate that's not PI). IM lawyers recently established liability against the MoD on behalf of cousins Muhamet and Skënder Bici, in relation to a shooting incident in July 1999 in the Kosovan capital, Pristina. On such high-level stuff, trainees can't expect to take the lead and must be happy carrying out "the smaller tasks that make a huge difference."

PI trainees are given a taste of low-value work to experience what life must be like for the paralegals and legal execs who make up such a large part of the workforce. These smaller claims aren't worth very much in financial terms, but they represent a trainee's very own caseload and provide an invaluable grounding in such things as client management, drafting, quantification of claims, civil procedure and court advocacy. Trainees are expected to go before masters as IM's sole representative at small applications and case management conferences, so before they get anywhere near a court they're given "really good guidance and support, including a mock thing with the boss." And those awkward LPC role-play exercises may just turn out to be useful after all, as further duties include negotiating settlements with often more senior lawyers. Overall, the level of responsibility dished out to trainees is exceptional. Said one: "My supervisor set me very

challenging work. I covered every aspect of the case, and had a really great sense of achievement knowing that I was being relied upon."

faulty towers

The top-rated international travel team (hence the Spanish offices) is renowned for its skill on all aspects of PI, illness and serious injury abroad. Matters handled range from gastric illness ("puking, etc") and swimming pool accidents to gunshot wounds and air crashes. A seat in the equally well-regarded clinical negligence department brings exposure to some very topical issues. The representation of the family of a 69-year-old woman who died after taking part in a clinical trial of cannabis-based drug Sativex stands as a prime example. The seat demands greater patience, as trainees are subject to "a tighter rein early on," which ultimately gives way to the prospect of "getting stuck in with clients."

The feeling amongst trainees is that "the firm tries to make out like it is a fully rounded firm," but although "the commercial side is growing, it is less well developed" than the PI and clin neg sides. In light of the immense strength of the PI practice, this is not so damning, and no one is claiming that the services offered to business clients are undeveloped. The coco unit, for example, represented Schawk in its multimillion-pound acquisition of the creative services division of Nestlé UK. The employment team now represents both employers and employees, with a recent highlight being the successful defence of Sheffield Wednesday FC in a breach of contract claim that included issues relating to bonus payments.

The training programme also includes some fascinating specialist seats dealing with court of protection matters, human rights, charities law, police and public law, and business crime. The latter has lately offered work relating to Iraqi arms procurement, money laundering and criminal fraud.

like a rolling stone

If you're a homebody you'll need to think carefully before firing off an application, because IM can require trainees to up sticks and head off to any of its UK offices. Sadly Spain is off limits for now, so don't expect to be able to schedule a 3pm siesta into your Outlook without getting your collar felt by supervisors. Trainees told us they were happy to make the move between cities; however, *"it would be nice to get more notice."* Six to eight weeks' advance warning seemed to be the norm. The firm helps out with the train fare, removal costs and a bond on the new pad, but there is a sense that *"they don't quite realise the stress of it all"* and could do a little more to smooth the transition. London looks to be a particularly difficult move because, although bolstered by a London weighting, the pay cheque *"just doesn't cut it"* in the capital, especially when many trainees have already *"skinted"* themselves studying the LPC. When we asked the firm, it said it was addressing this issue.

With so much choice, it can be difficult to pick a path through the seat options and we sense that a flexible attitude serves trainees best. With *"'business need' being the most popular phrase at IM,"* the number and nature of the seats on offer in different departments change from one rotation to the next. On this point, one sceptical trainee believed HR was *"just looking out for the firm,"* but in fairness the majority took the view that there was no point wasting talent by having trainees left counting paperclips in slower departments. Previous complaints regarding a lack of contact from the firm prior to the commencement of the training contract have now been addressed, and future trainees are now provided with each other's contact details and those of current trainees who are willing to answer questions. The policy surrounding payment, or otherwise, of LPC fees, however, remains *"a bone of contention."* To clarify, the firm does pay GDL and LPC fees plus a £3,000 maintenance grant to those who are about to study. It does not pay fees retrospectively.

bunch of big heads

One thing shared by all our interviewees was a keen interest in protecting the quality of their life away from work. One put it this way: *"We work hard during regular hours, but if you are not busy, you leave."* The different departments do make efforts to organise group activities, and we were amused to hear about last year's PI division away day which brought together staff from all offices for an It's a Knockout-style bonding exercise. In an ironic twist, the day had its very own personal injury situation after a trip over a bale of hay. We can just imagine the organisers, suffering heart palpitations no doubt, handing over the first-aid kit to some of the finest personal injury bods in the country. Traditional firm-wide celebrations have been pushed off the calendar as a result of the firm's vigorous growth in the last few years, simply because *"there isn't a venue large enough"* to house the almost 2,000-strong staff.

The vastness of the IM empire means it's only natural that the offices have developed separate identities. As the original, and the largest office, *"Sheffield is clearly the hub,"* but there is plenty going on for trainees in all locations. On the sports front they can join teams for cricket, netball, rounders and football, and those able to show off even fancier footwork can have a go at salsa dancing. Monthly firm-financed drinks are always well attended, so don't be surprised if you happen to experience the pleasure of *"seeing a stickler of a partner in a new light when they are out drunk."* At the time of our research, we heard rumblings of a *"loosening of the purse strings"* after a *"hard-fought"* campaign for a separate trainee social budget. Alton Towers, paintballing, bowling and barbecues were already being planned.

It sounds to us like IM offers a *"down-to-earth"* and *"non-snooty"* working environment; we even heard that with some partners, "*it's just like working for your dad*," though as everywhere there are the odd few grumps who "*grunt to say hello.*" Up in IM's home city, Sheffield, it recently moved into "*pleasant, roomier and lighter*" open-plan offices with "*posh client areas with riverside views.*" "*Not even the partners have their own rooms now,*" reported one trainee, before sneakily revealing that some had pulled rank by calling dibs on "*the best spots in the corners.*" This move, we think, is reflective of the current buoyancy and profitability of the firm, and its confidence for the years ahead. In 2006, 17 of the 23 qualifiers stayed on.

and finally...

If you are looking for a big-name firm that puts individual clients as high on its list of priorities as corporate clients, IM could be the place for you. The only caveat is that you must be certain of your willingness to move between cities, and you must like the idea of fitting in with the machinery in what is effectively one of the biggest suppliers of legal services around.

Jones Day

the facts

Location: London
Number of UK partners/solicitors: 40/83
Total number of trainees: 42
Seats: Non-rotational
Alternative seats: None
Extras: Pro bono – Waterloo Legal Advice Centre

Day one at Jones Day London:
"*Terrifying. You can't imagine how awkward and daunting it is. You're led in through the flashy doors, taken to your office where your business cards are laid out. You shut the door and you think 'Oh my god, that's it, the cord is cut, I can do what I want'. So, you either cower in your room, or you take a*

deep breath, go and knock on someone's door and say, 'Hi, is there any work I can do for you?'"

steel or no deal

We'll mark your card early on this one. Training under the seat-free, non-rotational, work-where-you-like system at Jones day in London is not for everyone. Indeed, current disciples of the Jones Day Way suggest it demands "*confidence,*" "*confidence*" and "*confidence.*" To be more specific, "*you've got to be comfortable being knowledgeable and authoritative on the spot with clients who may not even know you're a trainee;*" "*you've got to thrive under pressure,*" "*take full responsibility for your own work and know when to say no.*"

"*I wouldn't swap it for any other way of training,*" said one source, speaking for many we interviewed; "*it's made me more confident, more mature and been the best education I could envisage.*" These trainees truly are masters of their own destiny, sallying forth from their own offices to seek the work they want in the areas that interest them. Where they sit within the building tends to influence what they do, simply "*because it's easiest to ask the people working near your office,*" a fact recognised in the not uncommon trend of "*making people change office space every six months.*" The benefits of the system are that "*if you like a certain area, you can focus on it from the beginning*" and since "*people see you as a fixture, there for the long term, they give you more important work.*" To Jones Day trainees, "*leaving a department after just six months would be hell. I've just seen a deal take nine months from initial instructions through starting the sale, completing it and being taken to dinner by the client.*"

It's fair to say that not everyone is cut out for this unique training and "*some people do leave because they want more supervision or the system doesn't work for them.*" Consequently, you must be very clear that you and 'the method' are a good match. The people who thrive here are "*inde-*

pendent characters;" however, as the opening anecdote illustrates, Jones Day trainees aren't afraid to admit when they're anxious or in need of help, so confidence doesn't have to mean pig-headed arrogance.

smells like keen spirit

If you think you'd enjoy this style of training you'll want to know more about the firm as a whole, so here's our summary. Four years ago, Cleveland-based Jones Day, a member of the exclusive $1 billion-a-year turnover club, sur-prised the City by merging with (read 'taking over') the big-spending, free-wheeling, maverick lawyers of Gouldens. Jones Day brought to the merger table around 2,200 lawyers spread over 29 worldwide locations, while Gouldens slapped down 40 partners and a punchy reputation in smaller-scale but top-notch work. It was a great way for Jones Day to improve its position in the capital and gave Gouldens' lawyers access to a well-established international network. Since the merger there has been some cultural adjustment in London and those partners and staff who were unhappy with the union have moved on.

This year is the first in which we've interviewed trainees whose experiences are pure Jones Day. Interestingly they are *"sick to the back teeth of any-one who carps on about Gouldens. We couldn't care less; we're Jones Day trainees and it's neither partic-ularly healthy, nor probably even true, to hark back to a mythical Gouldens era when everyone was drunk every lunchtime."* Even if we wouldn't put it quite so strongly, we couldn't agree more, but the very bullishness of the statement emphasises that the spirit of Gouldens does live on.

cleveland, we have a problem...

In the London office, just behind Fleet Street, trainees say: *"You don't feel like you are in a huge international firm."* In part this is because the *"sheer magnitude of the firm is impossible to comprehend,"* even if the minutiae of daily life constantly remind you that it is there. By way of examples, if the computer system goes down at night you call Cleveland, and *"if you need Spanish law advice you contact the lawyers in Madrid."*

The UK practice frequently works with other Jones Day offices and so trainees encounter plenty of cross-border deals. *"I'm working on an M&A transaction at the moment which is French and Spanish,"* explained one source. *"It really makes you feel you're at a global law firm."* One of the most important events of the opening months of the training contract is a trip to Wash-ington, DC to meet all the other new recruits. *"You make contacts and get to know faces,"* with the result that *"you can log on to our internal version of messenger and the banter starts flowing in from around the world."*

looking to grow

The UK operation does very well in all main-stream commercial areas: litigation, real estate, corporate and finance. Apparently, in 2006 the firm looked into the idea of merging with Lon-don firm Denton Wilde Sapte, which has key interests in the areas of energy, finance and restructuring, each of which were complemen-tary with Jones Day's interests internationally. That the talks came to nothing is not necessarily a signal that Jones Day doesn't want to expand fur-ther in the UK, but we'll have to wait and see what the next move is.

Even without a second London merger the office is doing well: following last year's advice to three defendants (including Britannia Airways and Lunn Poly) in a construction dispute con-cerning Coventry Airport, litigators have this year represented Merlin Biosciences in a Serious Fraud Office investigation and Standard Bank with respect to a $15 million alleged claim arising from the financing of an Uzbekistani cotton pur-chase contract. Other litigation clients include

Motorola, Occidental Petroleum, Dell and Inter-Continental Hotels.

Not to be outdone, real estate lawyers secured a role on the £520 million sale of the CityPoint building in Moorgate. Meanwhile, the investment funds practice got to grips with the £12 million AIM listing of a Chinese company and multiple high-value IPOs, and the energy and natural resources team continued to advise on the Kovykta project to transport natural gas from eastern Siberia to China and South Korea. Finally, the corporate department acted for Russia's Alfa Group on its English law-governed $3.3 billion joint venture investment in Turkey's Cukurova Telecom.

overpaid and over here

With new starters receiving a phenomenal £39,000 in their first year, Jones Day's trainees are among the best remunerated in the City. *"Our salaries have gone up absurdly about every two months lately,"* confirmed one source with an eye on their £60,000 qualification salary. Another particularly forthright source confidently reckoned they had *"probably made my salary back for the firm several times over with the work I've billed."*

As we emphasised above, it isn't a system that suits every personality, not least because *"it leaves you very exposed to clients"* and *"partners aren't afraid to push you once they're happy you're not a lunatic or a liability."* As such, running client meetings alone and being *"effectively an associate"* is entirely normal. All our sources admitted to *"feeling overexposed at times."* Similarly, there was agreement that *"it's possible to just stagnate in your office if things aren't going well... some people fall through the net in that way."* Reviews of personal checklists every three to six months help, as do appraisals. Initially these are with a single mentor partner but trainees find they can end up with multiple mentors after time working closely with

other partners or assistants. Those who are proactive when facing difficulties fare best, a fact illustrated by this anecdote: *"The worst time for me was on a corporate deal when the partner went away leaving me to handle things. At the same time I had longstanding commitments to litigation. It was harsh, but I spoke to the litigation partner and he helped me to prioritise my work."*

willy what?

The *"nice and spacious but a bit dull in terms of decor"* Jones Day offices sadly don't have a canteen, but there is a chef to provide food at weekly training lunches. These are well worth attending, as are monthly group meetings with the training partner and trainee manager. By and large this is a *"contented"* workplace that is described as *"a broad church where everyone has big personalities."* On the basis of our interviews, we'd add that big doesn't necessarily have to mean brash. The trip to Washington (*"I've never been as persistently and cheaply drunk in my life"*) and the legendary Christmas panto ensure that socialising is never dull and *"the partners are very generous – there's always a card behind the bar when we're out for drinks."*

Regarding that trainee-written and trainee-performed panto, our sources say that *"no punches are pulled."* The *"Willy Wonka script this year had five partners receiving golden tickets and destroying themselves one by one through personal folly."* Apparently censorship isn't an issue and partner-in-charge Russell Carmedy receives his annual pasting with good grace. *"He loves it – the character of Willy Wonka was basically him, but instead it was Willy Wanka."* Such stories do back up the feeling that *"there's less hierarchy here than elsewhere... after all, where else would the senior partner call you up in the pub to ask you to play golf?"* They also explain why it is that trainees feel *"a loyalty"* and *"sense of community"* that makes the decision to stay on an easy one. *"The real prob-*

lem is where else could you go that would be as challenging?" Fortunately, relatively few have to face the problem as the firm has excellent year-on-year retention figures. That said, in 2006 a relatively low 15 out of 20 qualifiers stayed on.

and finally...

Jones Day offers a truly distinctive training in London. Having assessed your suitability realistically, if you think you and the method could get along together it's a cracking choice.

Kendall Freeman

the facts
Location: London
Number of UK partners/solicitors: 22/31
Total number of trainees: 17
Seats: 4x6 months
Alternative seats: None

This mid-sized commercial practice emerged in 2003 from the dissolution of well-known London legal landmark DJ Freeman. Since then it has targeted the insurance market to great effect, acting for all the big guns like Direct Line, AXA and Chubb, as well as Lloyd's names. For anyone with a taste for the unforeseen, or disaster, this is an area, and a firm, that deserves closer investigation.

in case of disaster
Train here and you'll be presented with a standard four-seat programme that will take you through the mainstream commercial practice areas of litigation, and corporate, plus a few extras such as insolvency/restructuring. In terms of seat choices, "everyone does at least one seat in insurance litigation but then the firm is pretty accommodating for the other three seats." So, for example, "someone was particularly keen on IP and media and the firm arranged for a secondment to a client."

Read this next bit twice: it's crucial. There's a greater emphasis on contentious work than at a lot of firms, and a good whack of what you'll be working on will have a whiff of insurance about it. Since you're not likely to have had any contact with insurance law, the best way to understand it is as "contract law with special principles and standards, additional levels of honesty and expertise. It is a very specific area and you need to enjoy getting your head round pernickety points." Trainees describe insurance litigation as "our flagship practice, with work ranging from aviation and asbestos, to marine and reinsurance." When asked to explain the appeal, one trainee told us: "There's lots of work arising from catastrophes like the Asian tsunami, and it's interesting working in an area where you see everyday life feeding into it." One source had been exposed to complicated multinational cases involving tricky insurance points: "We had to muddle through contract after contract. It was a big deal and impossible to know what was going on! There was a hurricane involved!" With cases so big, "you'll rarely get to see something all the way through;" nevertheless, trainees do get to see all stages of the litigation process, and "if you want to go to the High Court or the House of Lords, the kinds of cases that are going to get there are insurance cases."

Another interesting point about insurance work is that while you may not get a chance to visit Bermuda, you will at least become familiar with its international dialling code. The country is "at the head of the insurance industry worldwide because the regulation is not too severe... Let's just say they're open with regulation."

the rich and infamous
Of course, not every piece of work has an insurance element; indeed, the commercial litigation department has some "real bonuses." Public international law is a very specialised area of practice

that marks a KF training contract out from the crowd. The PIL team is presently instructed by the Government of Pakistan with respect to the recovery of the proceeds of alleged corruption by former Prime Minister Benazir Bhutto and her husband, and tying up the Nigeria/Benin maritime boundary negotiations. One of our sources was thoroughly impressed by the work, not least because the group was *"friendly and fun – people who make a living out of chasing corrupt politicians have got to be interesting!"* Similarly international, we heard about a trainee working on a foreign dispute concerning *"a contentious probate matter regarding a Nigerian gentleman with an extensive family."* Closer to home there's a treat in store in the form of libel litigation, an area in which KF has risen to prominence through clients such as Harrods and Mohamed Al Fayed, as well as Saudi businessman Sheikh Khalid Bin Mahfouz, who has successfully sued a number of newspapers and authors for damages following allegations that he is Osama Bin Laden's brother-in-law and a financial supporter of terrorism.

Away from litigation, in their corporate seat one trainee had been involved in *"completing two transactions, dealing with the company administrative side – drafting minutes and EGM notices, that kind of thing. In corporate you have greater day-to-day responsibility, and you can find yourself as the key point of contact for a client."* Some trainees take client secondments. Said one: *"I really enjoyed my time in the commercial department of a big company... it was a great learning experience."*

carpe diem

When asked to explain their initial attraction to KF, one source told us: *"I was looking for a firm which wasn't going to demand your blood in return for good pay and training. At the open day the people I met and the atmosphere seemed to be happy."* Another said: *"I really liked the attitude and*

approach that the firm took. From day one here you're given responsibility, but you never feel out of your depth because there's a good support network." You needn't worry about being molly-coddled; *"you're definitely rewarded for taking the initiative."* Apparently, *"you want to make the day as productive as you can... you want a feeling of satisfaction when you leave at night, and you want constant stimulation."* Blimey!

One disadvantage about life in a smaller firm is that *"when it's quiet there are less departments to feed off each other. If there's a dip you end up twiddling your thumbs."* Of course, the beauty of a firm of this size is that *"in the first few months you quickly get to know the people from other departments. It is a sociable place and everyone is working for the greater good, including the support staff."* Be aware that hours can vary. In the early days in quiet departments you might get away with 9am to 6pm, but this could end up being 9am to 9pm when things hot up. However, these trainees are *"not the sort to shy away from responsibility"* and *"like to seize the initiative."* Said one: *"Everyone wanted a smaller firm with high-profile work. This is a firm where you won't get shoved aside."* And there's more: *"There's a lot of enthusiasm for getting involved in what the firm is doing as a whole;"* apparently, *"one senior partner literally walks round opening people's office doors."*

blackberry martini

KF moved offices in June 2006 (*"not before time!"*) and trainees happily report that it has stuck to the system that places them in a room with a partner. *"It's great sharing an office – you get a real insight into what they're doing and see the bigger picture."* One trainee applauded the HR team by saying: *"They're very good at matching up personalities."* Another praised them for *"bending over backwards to give me the seats that I wanted."* In fact trainees were upbeat to the point that we thought there might have been an HR manager with a P45 and a cattle prod in the room with them (contra our research methodology and the Human Rights Act). It is all the more impressive that trainees spoke so favourably given that in September 2006 only two of the eight qualifiers stayed on at the firm, some disappointed by lack of jobs in non-contentious areas and others choosing to leave London. It is worth mentioning that this figure is a reversal of the 2005 result when six out of eight stayed on.

Remember, KF won't offer the same facilities as the giants of the City, so "*if you want to feel like you're in a flash firm, don't apply. We're not given BlackBerrys here!*" Where it makes ground is in its ability to give a very personalised training. Once a month everyone gets to sit down with a training partner to talk about what they'd like to gain exposure to. There are mid and end-of-seat reviews, and each trainee has a mentor with whom they meet regularly. "*They give you useful advice; it's not just whether you're doing well or not, but things like needing to raise your profile by writing articles and suchlike.*"

From the moment you get your training contract you are involved in the life of the firm, and "*everyone from the managing partner to the post boy knows your name from the first day.*" On the social side, there are plenty of sports – five-a-side football, squash and tennis tournaments – and when we called them trainees were busy planning what they were going to do at the firm's charity fair. "*Our stall is going to involve stocks and custard pies... and maybe karaoke*," revealed one. The annual summer ball and the Christmas party are high points, not least because of the fact that at the last Christmas bash partners dressed as Santa and his elves. Less surreal was the recent winter party for current and future trainees, held at the Hotel Malmaison. In what could well be the most important aspect of their two years of training, a barman taught them how to make proper cocktails.

and finally...

The most important advice trainees give is this: "*Don't come here if you are not interested in litigation. You'll have to do two of your four seats there.*" Sounds pretty simple, but beyond this they also say: "*You feel like you're part of a team that's going to win!*" It goes without saying, everyone loves a winner.

Kimbells LLP

the facts

Location: Milton Keynes
Number of UK partners/solicitors: 11/21
Total number of trainees: 4
Seats: 4x6 months
Alternative seats: None

This Milton Keynes firm only handles corporate and commercial work and has more in common with a London firm than most others in Bedfordshire. It's ideal if you're looking for a commercial training without the craziness of the capital.

fancy a brew?

Kimbells arrived on the scene in 1986. "*It's very much a City firm in Milton Keynes,*" trainees explained, pointing to the fact that "*the senior partners all seemed to have trained and qualified in the City.*" Corporate finance is a key area of expertise and in 2005 Kimbells worked on more than 50 deals with a total transaction value in excess of £250 million. It was particularly proud of its involvement in the £100 million sale of a health business to global pharmaceutical company Smith & Nephew. The clients who use the firm's corporate services include various venture capital and private equity institutions, banks and other finance providers. On top of that, the firm also offers a corporate finance advisory service, involving lawyers on deals way earlier than is common, sometimes at the stage when the deals are found and priced and funding is sourced.

The drinks and hospitality sector, especially brewing, is a big one for Kimbells. It also targets clients in the automotive and logistics sectors. As one trainee acknowledged, not many firms have brewing as a specialism. The department is "*very loud and boisterous,*" but more fool you if you think a seat here is all about sampling the latest tipple from the breweries. The clientele includes Scottish & Newcastle and several other top-ten pub companies and brewers. The department offers a "*property-focused*" seat looking after brewing clients' interests, be this "*landlord and tenant issues or buying and leasing premises.*" Trainees also gain experience in drafting and reviewing commercial contracts and advising on competition law, IP and licensing. It is "*almost a given*" that a trainee will do this seat in their first year and it provides an ideal introduction to the way the firm works. An "*enjoyable seat, you can settle in and get to know the system,*" said one. You "*absorb a lot without realising it,*" added another.

catching cabs

Working for every kind of client from owner-managed businesses to major PLCs (Konica Minolta, Exel, London Luton Airport, RBS/NatWest and Enterprise Inns being among the best known), Kimbells is adept at giving general commercial advice. It advised Computer Cab (ComCab) on a 20-year licence agreement with leading black cab manufacturer Manganese Bronze Holdings for ComCab's Zingo mobile phone taxi-hailing system. Kimbells is the sole supplier of employment law advice to the large HR team within the financial services arm of DaimlerChrysler. It also acts as sole employment adviser for the London bus company Metroline. The IP team has worked on the protection and enforcement of well-known brands, including one of the UK's best-known, late-night bar oper-

ators and a national pizza delivery company. Meanwhile, the commercial property group was recently involved in a £50 million development in the Midlands. The scheme included leisure, retail and residential properties and was a far cry from the joint venture on which the team advised to develop a luxury holiday resort on an island off the coast of Thailand.

This firm may "*try to deliver a City-quality service*" but "*we don't do the same City hours.*" Officially the day runs from 9am to 5.30pm, but we heard of trainees regularly working from 8.30am until 6pm and "*later if you need to,*" perhaps 8.30pm at busy times. Sounds pretty full-on to us, yet interviewees assure us that this "*is a good place to work.*" Describing its mood as "*very relaxed, in as much as I can walk up to the senior partner and can have a joke and a laugh,*" one source explained that trainees feel "*no sense of inferiority.*" We learned that "*in the last three years there has been a determined effort to modernise*" the firm; a recent rebranding, a "*more modern*" look to the office and "*a proper IT and HR department*" are all part and parcel of this. An "*influx of younger blood*" has also "*changed the feeling of the firm.*" The junior level recruits have bonded well with the small trainee group, which is itself set to increase.

To recap, trainee seats are available in commercial litigation, employment, coco and, of course, brewing services. You pretty much "*get what you want*" and there is "*quite a lot of flexibility with the seat structure;*" for example, you could split a seat "*as long as you can show that there is a reason to do so.*" Interviewees found coco a "*slightly more sedate and heads-down*" experience compared to the brewery services department. However, despite its "*very hard-working*" reputation, this does not prevent coco being popular. Even though it is one of "*the busiest departments*" in the firm, you should expect the volume of work to fluctuate. One trainee described *"running my own files from receiving the heads of terms right up to completion."* It seems that trainees are *"let out on a leash until you make a mistake and then they reel you in."* The employment department is also popular, not least because of the team's well-defined sense of pride in its work. As one interviewee rightly pointed out, *"departments often take on the personality of the partner running them."*

power trips

Kimbells open-plan office – the impressively named Power House – is a modern building on a business park *"bang opposite"* the Milton Keynes Bowl. This location may well have been *"useful for the Robbie Williams' concert in September"* and benefit from its proximity to parkland, but there are definite downsides. *"We are slightly out of the centre of Milton Keynes"* so *"you have to drive to go anywhere"* and *"you don't have quick access to shops and eateries."* In the evening the driving can be *"a bit of a problem if you want to go to the pub."* Kimbells has an active social committee that aims to put on four to six events per year plus a Christmas party. Past events include bowling nights, tobogganing at the Xscape centre and theatre trips. For the firm's 20th anniversary there was a boat cruise on the Thames. For the *"fun"* Christmas party last year, the firm hired a bar. Invariably, people *"drank a lot and danced a lot"* and there was *"90% participation by the partners on the dance floor."*

There is no on-site canteen so fee earners make the effort to attend an informal monthly lunch off-site and, not be done outdone, the trainees *"go out for lunch as a group"* every few months at the firm's expense. Sports aren't a big thing at the firm (unless you count throwing a Frisbee around in the park at lunchtime) although some people take part in local charity events, recently dragon boat racing and a half marathon.

and finally...

Kimbells really won't work for you if you want to be part of a big trainee intake in a firm with a million different departments. However, if you want a *"more personal"* experience somewhere where you can *"make an impact"* it will definitely tick those boxes. Most trainees stay with Kimbells after qualifying, and in September 2006 the single trainee who completed their contract stayed with the firm. But what of those who move on? Apparently they *"go to the big City firms,"* recently Norton Rose and Macfarlanes. Given that the firm wants to hold on to its qualifiers, the recruiters *"try to look at people who are committed to the region"* and *"who aren't seeing the firm as a bridge to London."*

Kirkpatrick & Lockhart Nicholson Graham LLP

the facts

Location: London
Number of UK partners/solicitors: 52/65
Total number of trainees: 21
Seats: 4x6 months
Alternative seats: Secondments
Extras: Pro bono – Battersea Law Centre; language training

This firm could be a contender for the prize awarded to the law firm most likely to change. If you're wondering why, read on...

times they are a-changing

In 2005, medium-sized English firm Nicholson Graham & Jones merged with 10-office US firm Kirkpatrick & Lockhart. Casting our minds back to pre-merger NGJ, we recall a place where graduates applied because they were seeking a supportive training environment where life wouldn't be too tough and everyone would know their name. Our interviewees could still vouch for the fact that *"everyone knows who everyone else is here"* and that lawyers would still *"rather have a life than a huge pay cheque."* Nonetheless, things have changed since the Brits got into bed with the Americans.

Expanding overnight from a 135-solicitor organisation to one with almost 1,000 lawyers, the London firm became the third-largest office in a network stretching from Boston to San Francisco via New York, Washington, DC, Miami, Dallas, Los Angeles and one or two other places in between. NGJ has in effect become the first step in K&L's plans to enter Europe. The stated aim is to double the size of the London office over the next five years, and the firm has already flexed its European muscle by acting alongside a Portuguese firm to advise clients on a €320 million acquisition involving companies in the UK, Turkey, Spain and Romania. Merger talks, albeit recently abandoned, with international law firm Salans highlight the firm's commitment to expansion. To prepare itself for the changes ahead in Blighty, the London arm has recently taken over the remaining floors of its Cannon Street office block. *"Now that we have the top floor, the building has really come into its own; the views are fantastic,"* one source enthused. If *Cribs* covered law firms, we'd get them in to do a show on the new, snow-white, minimalist client suite on the tenth floor. The same design team is behind every one of KLNG's offices, hence the wall of plasma screens in the reception area transmitting footage of lush foliage. Apparently in the Boston office there is a virtual tree that changes with the seasons. Don't ask us how that works, we're not entirely sure.

the future's bright

Thanks to the merger and a ready-made portfolio of US clients there seems to have been an immediate hike in the quality of work on offer in London. In particular, growth is tipped in the transactional arena, aided by the recent arrival of two M&A

partners from other City firms. For example, the UK office recently acted for longstanding Kirkpatrick & Lockhart client Halliburton (famed for its activities in the oil and gas field) on the sale of one of its subsidiaries. The corporate team also recently advised the first Japanese company to be admitted to AIM, having secured the instruction through a referral from a US source, and acted on cross-border transactions for blue-chip US corporations listed on the New York Stock Exchange. IP litigation has been a strong suit of K&L stateside and now the UK media practice looks set to improve its work, especially in relation to digital media. Admittedly it's still early days but the US offices' focus on investment funds, insurance and construction litigation looks set to filter into London. Once viewed as a downtrodden mid-sized law firm, things are certainly looking more exciting for the former NGJ.

Trainees receive a tried-and-tested training system of four six-month seats. It is not uncommon for them to sit with a departmental head, although supervisors are usually senior assistants or partners. A *"sparky team with lovely people and lots of banter,"* interviewees told us, the corporate department now has its *"sights set on the FTSEs and ever upwards."* Trainees reckon you can expect to do a seat here. Dispute resolution is another of the largest departments with specialist teams that work on niche areas such as travel and construction litigation as well as general commercial disputes. Other seats include IP, construction, tax and real estate.

sold on the idea…

Kirkpatrick & Lockhart was founded by seven young lawyers following their return to Pittsburgh after WWII. Nowadays, new arrivals to all offices in the network are flown to Pennsylvania to see where it all started and to gain a sense of the firm's heartland for themselves. *"Pittsburgh is our flagship; that is where we came from,"* explained a first-year trainee. Shortly before starting their training contracts, the first-years *"got this fantastic e-mail saying there has been a merger; get your passport, you're going to America,"* another told us. *"They were spending money on us from day one and we were sold on it."* Upon their arrival, the new UK trainees took part in a 'first-year academy'. *"We mixed with people from across the States, and because we were the Brits everyone wanted to meet us."* The academy included seminars ranging from finance topics to networking skills. *"The speakers were excellent. If it was brainwashing, it was very effective,"* a source laughed. *"The trip was a really good way of selling Kirkpatrick & Lockhart Nicholson Graham to us as an American firm."* Most tellingly, one trainee confessed: *"By the end of the academy I definitely felt as if I had joined Kirkpatrick & Lockhart Nicholson Graham rather than NGJ."*

Admittedly, long-term optimism is slightly tempered by day-by-day frustrations. *"There is more administrative bureaucracy now, which is a pain,"* muttered one source. For example, *"conflicts* [of interest checks on clients] *have to take in all the American offices, so everything has to be checked more"* and *"the phone book has gone from 10 pages to 100."* Our sources did not perceive a shift towards *"horrific"* US working hours, although they did sense that the targets are more stringently enforced than before. We asked the firm if there were any plans to increase the 1,500 billable hours target and it said there were not. Indeed, many of those we spoke to were keen to assert that things are *"still done the way they always were,"* although some expressed concern that *"London partners don't seem to have much of a say anymore."* Perhaps knowing that, of the 15 members of the firm's management board, five are partners based in the London office will allay their fears.

One of the things trainees really admire about the American side of the firm is the level of involvement in pro bono work. *"Our American lawyers do a substantial amount of impressive advisory work,"* one interviewee told us. *"They seem to have a strong sense of civic duty and are keen to put something back."* When it comes to salaries, there has been no attempt to reposition the firm in the London market and remuneration remains at second-tier UK levels.

what's the plan?

So far so good? It certainly sounds as if K&L is having a positive influence on sleepy old NGJ. However, after speaking to a range of trainees it became clear that some had mixed views on the merger. When NQ jobs were announced there was initially only space for six of the ten qualifiers. It was *"a tough time for the second-years,"* with one telling us: *"When we were still NGJ we were given the impression that if you were good enough and you wanted to stay, there would be a job for you."* The way trainees had always understood it, *"if you did a second seat in a department it usually meant that you would be offered a job there."* Not in 2006, when unfortunately the business needs of the firm did not match up to every trainee's expectations. That said, another two jobs were announced (following the dogged intervention of London partners, trainees say), one of which went to an external and one to an internal candidate, taking the retention figure to seven out of ten. For the record, jobs were offered in the banking, real estate, IP, travel litigation, construction litigation and corporate departments. A pragmatic source concluded that *"the partners here used to get quite sentimental when it came to keeping people on. Perhaps that's why we didn't make enough money."*

What is clear is that everyone knows that this is a period of change, but many trainees are still unclear as to how the firm's overall strategy will unfold and how it will affect the London office. In previous editions we have praised the 'Ask Tony' sessions where the firm's managing partner would answers questions posed by trainees. This year our sources said: *"Although you will usually get a response, whether it is a substantive response is another matter."* In all of this we sensed that the slight discomfort felt by some of our sources stemmed from the fact that almost everyone around them was flushed with excitement for the merger and what it meant to be part of such a big organisation. In stark contrast the second-year trainees and one-year PQEs of 2006 had not been given the chance to visit the USA to experience it all for themselves.

At the time of going to press the firm's website seemed slightly out of step with the thinking in the London graduate recruitment team. We were reliably informed that there are plans afoot to develop a more Anglo-friendly web page for the London office, so if you find aspects like 'Respect and Time for Life's Other Passions' and 'Opportunities to Shine Every Day' up there with the list of benefits a little disconcerting, don't fret. Over here the firm is still looking to employ the same kind of people it always did: bright, enthusiastic types with good academic credentials and a taste for a mid-sized firm. It's likely that people with language skills will be seen as especially attractive, as will those who can show an interest in areas the firm is interested in growing this side of the pond.

When we asked trainees if they thought the culture of the London office might change now that it is upping its game, they insisted that the firm would keep hold of its reputation as *"a really nice place to work."* We're not going to say they're wrong – there are already examples of London firms that have bulked up and sharpened up after a US merger and still retained their UK culture.

and finally...

One trainee summed things up well when they said: *"What made Nicholson Graham & Jones special was that it was a lovely firm to work for... but perhaps that is also what made it unprofitable, so things had to change."* It now has a new name, a new brand and, most importantly, improved quality of work from some exciting new client relationships. Although some of those who signed up to the old firm could feel threatened by the change, we reckon those who subscribe to the new model will not be disappointed.

Knight & Sons

the facts

Location: Newcastle-Under-Lyme
Number of UK partners/solicitors: 16/32
Total number of trainees: 5
Seats: 4x6 months
Alternative seats: None

If big city life is a turn off and you fancy something more regional, say somewhere between Birmingham and Manchester, Knight & Sons could be the ideal firm.

something old, something new...

This Staffordshire firm has a lineage that can be traced back to 1767 yet it is certainly no slave to the past. Trainees call it *"established rather than traditional."* Knight & Sons (be careful not to confuse it with the huntin' shootin' fishin' folk at Knights down in Kent) has developed a rather modern outlook and has a slick purpose-built office to prove it. The firm relocated there in 1995 after some clever person decided the premises it had previously occupied since the 1700s just wouldn't do any longer. Knights (remember, not the h-s-f types) has hung onto many of the old north Midlands families who have used its lawyers' services for generations while working hard to develop new business clients such as The Tussauds Group (which incorporates Alton Towers, Thorpe Park, Warwick Castle and the London Eye), Phones 4U, Stoke City FC, Wedgwood and nearby Keele University.

Knights is no stranger to quality work, and this is particularly true of its outstanding property department. Perhaps the most convincing evidence of its achievements in this area of practice is its favoured status with City of London giant Lovells. The international law firm originally developed its 'Mexican-Wave' property outsourcing model to allow its client Prudential Property Investment Mangers (PruPIM) to save costs by sending on smaller-scale work to a handful of select and trusted regional law firms. Knights gallantly rode in and took up the challenge and now works for Lovells alongside Cripps Harries Hall in the South and Ward Hadaway in the North East. Knights has also proved it can hold its own against big regional hitters such as Addleshaw Goddard, Eversheds and Trowers & Hamlins: it was chosen, along with these other firms, to be on Stoke-on-Trent City Council's legal panel for its £30 million Housing Pathfinder regeneration project.

animal, vegetable or mineral?

As well as *"good roots in the community"* Knights is connected to the local environment through the specialist work it does with mines and minerals. A dedicated unit within the firm's property department deals with coal, clay, sand and gravel, shale, slate and recycled construction materials issues; hardly unexpected when you consider Staffordshire's traditional involvement with the pottery and coal industries. The firm also has a strong farming and agriculture practice serving some *"very good clients the firm has handled for over 100 years."* This long association with local farmers and landowners has resulted in Knights' appointment to the National Farmers' Union (NFU) legal panel for nine counties in the Midlands and Wales.

Trainee seats are available in the firm's four main departments: commercial property, litigation (employment and commercial litigation

options), tax, trusts and private client, and corporate/commercial. There isn't a compulsory seat as such, but as commercial property is so important to the firm *"no trainee will go through Knights and not do it."* There is a healthy, flexible attitude to seat allocation, and the firm seems happy to take on board trainees' suggestions. For example, to accommodate individuals' preferences the seat rotation was recently changed to two sixth-month seats in the first year and three four-month seats in the second. This particular structure didn't continue for the next batch of trainees, but the important point is that a previously rigid structure was willingly reshaped to fit changing requirements.

strictly boardroom

Our interviewees spoke about the firm's *"informal professionalism"* and *"relaxed approach."* This isn't to say people don't work hard, but the atmosphere is such that everyone is pretty happy with their lot. From a trainee's perspective this means *"really hands-on training"* from solicitors and partners who are *"supportive"* without *"mollycoddling you."* Overall they feel *"staff are treated well."* Depending on their workload, trainees' hours tend to be 8.30am to 5.30pm or 9am to 6pm with *"not many people left in the office gone half six."* This is maybe the point for us to reveal that Knights was the first law firm in the country to be granted the Investors in People Recruitment and Selection Model Award. Such investment in staff helps explain why two of the three qualifiers accepted NQ positions with the firm in September 2006.

An informal approach means *"you won't see any names on doors here,"* which, admittedly, can confuse newbies – *"you could be talking to the managing partner and not even know it."* Mixing between the ranks is further encouraged by the layout of the snazzy office building (see the website for an external shot). The glass central atrium (where *"everyone can see you"*) is right in the middle of operations and is used as a coffee bar, restaurant, informal meeting place, seminar room and occasionally as a ballroom dancing studio. Thankfully, not at all the same time.

With every silver lining, there is a cloud. And with Knights, the "*downside isn't the firm but its location.*" Newcastle-Under-Lyme (which really shouldn't be confused with party city Newcastle-Upon-Tyne) is famous for giving the world Robbie Williams (he was born in its Royal Infirmary). The town is fairly close to Stoke-on-Trent, though even this may not be everyone's cup of tea – even if there is a monkey forest (we kid you not) in Trentham. Speaking candidly, one trainee said: "*If you want to live in the big city and be part of a big legal community, you won't have it.*" On the plus side, if you have a car, the Welsh coast is an hour away, as are Manchester and Birmingham, and the Peak District is also within driving distance. In terms of the local business community there are various professional and commerce groups with which trainees can become involved, including an active local Trainee Solicitors Group.

The firm goes out of its way to put on socials and "*there is a lot going on that people organise themselves.*" Staff get together for hill walking on the weekends, go-karting and ice skating and the firm has teams for football, cricket and netball (matches against a local bank) plus an annual golf day. For post-work drinks it's usually the Old Brown Jug, The Victoria or the trainee's regular haunt The Hand & Trumpet. In the pub there's no sense of segregation or that awful scenario where partners sit on one table and trainees on another.

and finally...

Knight & Sons has developed a sterling name for itself in the region and pushed its reputation even further afield in property and environmental sectors. If you know you want to make your home and your living in Staffordshire there are rich pickings to be had at this firm.

Lawrence Graham LLP

the facts

Location: London
Number of UK partners/solicitors: 85/121
Total number of trainees: 38
Seats: 4x6 months
Alternative seats: Secondments

"*Let China sleep,*" said Napoleon to an adviser, "*for when she wakes she will shake the world.*" The partners at Lawrence Graham no doubt hope the same can be said for their firm. After years sitting pretty in the mid-market of London firms, Lawrence Graham is starting to stir. It has expanded its corporate practice, rebranded and is set to move from its dated home to a flash new office complex at Tower Bridge.

broadening your horizons

We'll come onto the thrusting corporate practice in a second; first we want to discuss property, the firm's original core strength. In this area, loyal clients include Sainsbury's, O_2 and the London Development Agency and work includes pretty much everything from the redevelopment of part of Oxford city centre to assistance on The Globe Pub Company's purchase of 364 pubs. For trainees, at least one seat in the department is guaranteed. How about working on the placement of mobile phone masts to comply with radiation regulations or updating the registration of the ancestral lands of an aristocratic family or researching the details of a disused area of land to decide a suitable bid price when the land is auctioned. Whichever property team you're assigned to you should be guaranteed a decent level of responsibility and "*a hell of a lot of your own matters.*" You might be asked to handle the lease of a unit in a shopping centre or to complete a rent review. "*They're very good at teaching you things,*" said one trainee of the supervisors in the department. *"All my drafts are checked and they'll go through things with you in detail."* You'll probably also enjoy dealing with clients direct, by telephone or e-mail. *"As you progress, you're checked less and less,"* said one trainee. *"I thought I was very thoroughly supervised but given free range as well."* Play your cards right, and you could become a valued member of a client's team. *"Even though I've left the department, I still get calls from the clients,"* one trainee noted proudly. *"I'm their specialist now."*

Looking back, 2005 was a watershed year for the firm as, for the first time, the business and finance division pulled in more revenue than did property. Trainees identify a key factor in this development to be the firm's merger with the much smaller firm Tite & Lewis in 2004. Although it was tiny by comparison with the City mega-mergers we've grown used to, trainees told us the incoming lawyers had *"really shaken things up."* They say the corporate team is *"now much more organised with much tighter teams, better structure and more direction. It's one of the best to work in because it's so well organised."* If only the other key beneficiary of the merger, the IT and outsourcing team, had felt such benefits: all three Tite & Lewis partners in that team recently announced they would leave the firm.

The business and finance division is going great guns and all trainees are exposed to it at some stage in their contract. The division is a multi-headed beast with seats ranging from competition/EU law to local government work as well as the usual mainstream corporate and finance options. Trainee work runs from the slightly mundane (*"bibling, Companies House stuff... so dull"*) to the more edifying drafting and research. *"Research broadens your horizons,"* noted one. *"I never thought I'd know so much about lift manufacturers."* Throughout the division there was a consensus that, *"because the matters are huge, you can't get any ownership of them;"* however, compensation comes in the form of lots of client contact. *"I've attended plenty of client meetings and negotiations,"* said one trainee, *"and if there's one I can't come to the partner will explain why and be apologetic."* Like most corporate departments, this one does carry the risk of some long hours. *"We had one mental joint venture where I was in from Thursday morning to Friday evening,"* said one victim. *"But we were all in and, when it was done, we all got given a bottle of champagne. They were really grateful – I really felt like part of the team."* For all Napoleon's excitement about China, India is the emerging market that LG is really focusing on, and it's carved itself a niche in relation to Indian corporate deals. In 2006 it worked on a £13.7 million acquisition of an Indian company, and earlier advised on the £105 million AIM floatation of India's Great Eastern Energy.

hard to budge

The firm's third key area is litigation. Here cases range from small debt recovery matters where trainees have files of their own, to large commercial matters where *"the responsibility level does drop."* Still, most of those we spoke to had had some court time. *"They're great at giving you responsibility when they can,"* said one, and *"you're always nipping to court with documents and things."* Client contact is also on the cards. *"I handled a negotiation meeting, one-on-one with the other side and the clients in the corner,"* said one trainee. *"It was a challenge."* Not everyone relishes client contact it seems. *"Professional negligence made me realise I didn't want to work with the public,"* one recruit recalled. *"This one guy just kept ringing up and shouting at me."*

Beyond the three big divisions, the firm has teams working in tax and private capital, reinsurance and shipping, with the last two housed in a separate office in the City. No firm decision has been made, though, on the future of the City office after the move. *"The firm wants everyone under one roof,"* said one source, *"but the partners are determined to stay in EC3."* Interestingly, the private client group is expanding and the firm recently hired a team from City rival Simmons & Simmons. In the past a few trainees have spent a seat in LG's private client-focused Monaco office. Incredibly, *"they actually had trouble getting trainees to go, despite all the yachts and glamour."* The firm now offers occasional client secondment opportunities, including some to major names like Merrill Lynch. Overall, LG offers a truly impressive range of work for a firm of its size; indeed, most trainees cited this as its key appeal: *"You don't get 95% of the trainees in corporate, like in some firms."*

mustn't grumble

You'll normally sit with a supervising partner, many of whom were described as *"very trainee-focused; if they make changes to your work, they take a lot of time to explain what they'd have done differently."* A few partners were described as *"enigmatic,"* although in such circumstances assistants are always prepared to step in. *"They're amazing,"* said one. *"They'll sit you down, talk you through things, and make sure you're busy."* Occasionally the firm's respect for partner independence can disadvantage trainees. We heard of one partner who for several years made trainee's lives unpleasant. *"The partner in question was very highly strung,"* said one recruit. Another mentioned that *"trainees and secretaries were regularly in tears."* Of course, the true measure of a firm is how they deal with such problems. What we were told by our sources is that this particular problem went unchecked for several years until, eventually, the department's assistants demanded action and the partner in question no longer has trainees. It's not clear at what point the problem came to the attention of the training partner or HR staff perhaps because of what some of our sources saw as *"a culture of 'don't complain'."* Said one recruit: *"People just put up*

with things." Another told us: *"If there's a problem, you don't want to go to HR in case you're seen as a troublemaker."* The official line is that the firm believes trainees should learn to resolve problems, where possible, at ground level without the involvement of a third party. Having said that, those trainees who told us they'd gone to HR for advice or assistance called the team *"very helpful"* and other trainees had no view as they had not encountered problems.

Trainees did express some concern over the qualification procedure. They are invited to say where they'd most like to work after qualifying but, crucially, are not told beforehand which departments are expecting to recruit so feel *"left in the dark." "People speculate and hypothesise madly about where the jobs must be."* What's more, trainees seemed unsure about whether they were supposed to name a back-up choice. Once they've made the leap, the onus is on trainees to talk to the partners in the department in question. *"It's a bit embarrassing, just going in and saying 'I want a job',"* admitted one, *"but of course that's how you get clients, so they're looking for that initiative."* The firm says they're happy with the system and in 2006, at least, things worked out well for 12 out of 16 qualifiers. This was a better result than in the previous two years, although not quite back to the previously good historic rates.

daly's news

So what sort of person would thrive here? *"Friendly, outgoing and unpretentious,"* said trainees. Apparently, *"people are ambitious, but they keep it under their hat."* Trainees also recognised that *"you do need to be strong and relatively self-sufficient,"* which fits with the firm's view that they should be proactive in seeking out work and have the confidence to follow their convictions as they approach qualification. We're pleased to say the general atmosphere at LG seems to be happy, happy, happy. *"You do actually hear people laugh-*

ing," said one trainee. *"Everyone's busy, but it's relaxed and sociable all the same,"* said another. There were suggestions that the firm's newly ambitious agenda – exemplified by the office move – might engender a slightly more serious atmosphere. But don't expect anything too pressurised: outside the corporate department, trainees say they usually work manageable hours in the 8.30am to 6.30pm bracket.

For years the social life could be summed up in one word – Daly's, a wine bar opposite the Royal Courts of Justice. *"Everyone's in there on a Friday night,"* said one trainee. Thinking ahead to the office move, *"I'm seriously worried that Daly's will go under,"* said one regular. *"Perhaps they should move with us."* Other LG traditions include a winter ball and a summer soiree. We're also pleased to report that the social committee has a *"huge budget,"* and plans all manner of things from ice skating to walking tours and wine tastings.

and finally...

A new keenly commercial focus, twinned with the move to a deluxe abode in 2007, means this firm looks more interesting than ever. If you want the full London training experience at one of the City's most characterful firms get Larry G on your shortlist.

Laytons

the facts

Location: Guildford, London, Manchester
Number of UK partners/solicitors: 29/37
Total number of trainees: 20
Seats: 4x6 months
Alternative seats: None

This medium-sized commercial firm has been around since 1875 and twice survived a direct hit during the London Blitz.

three's a crowd

Ever since waving goodbye to its Bristol office in 2005, Laytons has operated as a three-office firm based in London, Guildford and Manchester. After a number of departures from the Bristol office, the remaining personnel joined South West firm Thring Townsend, so bringing to an end Laytons' interests in that part of the country. The remaining offices look to be happy enough with each other's company under the Laytons umbrella. Each has a commercial bent and each has its own strengths and distinctive qualities.

In London corporate work is key; in Guildford, property is big; and in Manchester the family law team is impressive. Admittedly, most trainees don't seem particularly in the know about what happens outside their own offices, but thankfully those higher up the chain of command are more clued up on inter-firm relations. By organising into national practice groups, lawyers from different offices can work for clients on a cross-office basis. A good example of this was the firm's advice to a multinational construction company that employed large numbers of Polish and other Eastern European workers. In a relatively new development, even trainees can cross the inter-office divide. For instance, if a trainee in the Manchester office realises overnight that they have a hitherto undiscovered penchant for tax or IP law, they could go to London for a seat.

london: bedtime coco

Based in the Carmelite building overlooking the Thames on the Victoria Embankment, the London operation is the oldest and biggest in the group. *"All the big corporate work goes through London"* and, unsurprisingly, there is a distinct *"buzz"* to this department. Trainees say the coco lawyers work *"faster and longer hours than the rest"* and advise readers to expect to be *"rushed off your feet."* The firm handles small to medium-sized (up to £100 million or so) corporate and finance transactions for domestic and international clients in a variety of sectors. Seats are also available in dispute resolution, commercial property and private client, with *"the trainees from the year before deciding where the first-years go."* It sounds like they make sensible choices based on their combined knowledge of the demands of the work and the nature of the supervisors. Our sources considered dispute resolution to be an ideal starter seat as it provides *"good hand-holding."* One of the highest profile cases recently was that brought by Premiership football club Blackburn Rovers following its insurer's refusal to pay out on a policy covering player injuries. The case reached the Court of Appeal in 2006.

The hours in all departments are pretty decent, the only exception being when a corporate deal is approaching completion. At that stage you might do *"some horrific ones,"* maybe even *"a couple of all-nighters."* The after-work social scene is reasonably low key (*"people do their own thing"*), although the firm has been known to organise some stonkingly good socials. These include pub quizzes in the boardroom, where *"people get pretty drunk,"* and the annual Christmas party, which last year started in the Marquis of Granby pub in nearby Covent Garden and ended with dancing at The Langley.

manchester: keeping it in the family

In the Manchester office (open since 1987) you can expect family and coco seats in the first year followed by commercial property and litigation/insolvency in the second. The litigation department's work incorporates employment cases so it is possible to carve yourself an employment seat if you play your cards right. A little bird tells us that litigation partner Daniel Izza has a nice line in TV and radio appearances and is often contacted to comment on insolvency issues. Among the clients using the firm are RisingStars

Growth Fund, which invests in early-stage unquoted technology companies in the North West and Manchester-based promotional products supplier 4imprint.

This office is the only one handling family work, and it does so with style. Leading light Christine Barker has an impressive reputation in this area of law: *"She is known as the Rottweiler in Manchester,"* whispered one trainee, and is quite *"a wonder to shadow."* Sources confess that in family it is *"hard to get your hands on some of the work as much of it is so confidential,"* and yet simply observing and absorbing what goes on in the *"very lively and loud"* department is an education in itself. In family law, we're told that there is plenty of scope to develop drafting skills.

When you walk into the office, just off Deansgate, the marble floors and huge entrance hall could leave you thinking you're on the set of a costume drama. The building holds both individual offices and open-plan floor areas, with trainees and secretaries occupying the latter. With just 21 lawyers in total, the Manchester branch can provide a *"more intimate"* training environment, and trainees are convinced that because there's so few of them, they get more attention than their peers in bigger firms. The size of the office may, they think, also have an effect on recruitment. Said one: *"It's a question of whose personality fits."* After work, trainees make the most of their central Manchester location and adopt the view that whether in or out of the office, *"Manchester has all the perks of London without the costs."*

guildford: plotting the future

If you don't want to work in London but are attracted to commercial practice, there are plenty of South East firms to tempt you. So why this one? Guildford is Laytons' second-oldest operation (having been in the area since 1972) and is conveniently located right in the centre of town by the railway station. It is home to a strong residential development team that acts for big-name clients including Barratt Homes. Given the size of the Guildford property practice, which comprises plot sales and commercial property teams, it's no surprise that all the trainees do either a residential or commercial property seat. The team has been growing, recently recruiting a partner from Hammonds and a consruction law specialist from Trowers & Hamlins. Among the most interesting work is an instruction to act as project solicitors on the Cambourne New Town scheme.

The other options are employment, coco and dispute resolution, although trainees still mourn the loss of some prominent IP/IT lawyers, admitting that their departure "*left a bit of a hole.*" However, there is certainly still good IP/IT/media work being handled for impressive clients such as Samsung and QVC, and, in terms of the mood in the office, trainees say "*things are picking up*" since the hire of new lawyers in private client and construction. These developments will, they hope, mean a wider selection of seats in the future.

When they get together after work, trainees go to Old Orleans in summer "*for drinks on the terrace*" and the Ha! Ha! Bar or the Five and Lime when the weather's a bit murky. To an extent the social scene is hampered by the fact that "*the majority of people here commute to Guildford and want to get back in the evenings.*" Additionally, "*quite a few of the partners have young children.*" Everyone lets their hair down at the Christmas party, held in a local hotel, and there's an opportunity to catch up with the trainees from the other offices at the annual Laytons Trophy sailing regatta that sees lawyers and their clients compete in races on The Solent.

In September 2006, all seven of those reaching qualification stayed on at the firm. They did so in the offices where they trained, even though, technically, it is possible for vacancies to be filled by qualifiers from other offices.

and finally...

Laytons has three very different alternatives for those who find the idea of being anonymous in one of the big firms a turn off. It's worth picking an office as much for its strong suit as for its location.

LeBoeuf, Lamb, Greene & MacRae LLP

the facts

Location: London
Number of UK partners/solicitors: 26/55
Total number of trainees: 12
Seats: 4x6 months
Alternative seats: Overseas
Extras: Language training

Until recently we've found 87-year-old LeBoeuf (pronounce it LeBuff) somewhat enigmatic. Having arrived in London during the 'over here and overpaid' US invasion of the mid-90s, it was hard to distinguish it from others of the same ilk. If you feel the same way, allow us to us enlighten you...

oil in a day's work

It being headquartered in New York, you might assume that LeBoeuf is as American as it gets over here in London. Better to view it as an office within a global network because the lawyers in Mincing Lane (how appropriate for a firm with so much meat in its name) represent clients from all over the world and work in conjunction with colleagues across the globe. There's another smart way of looking at the firm and that's by reference to its flagship practices. Trainees are all too aware where LeBoeuf's expertise lies: "*Other US firms are in London for transactional work alone;*" "*we are normally at the top of the rankings for energy and insurance.*" They have it spot on: much of the work of LeBoeuf's 19-office network is in these two sectors, and the energy work in particular is the reason why it has opened up in such places as Moscow, Kazakhstan and Saudi Arabia (where it works with an affiliate law firm).

Africa, Russia and the Middle East are crucial energy markets and much of LeBoeuf's large-scale work emanates from these regions. The firm continues to win instructions from a long list of energy companies including Chinese and African state-owned enterprises. Among the top deals for the London lawyers last year was China National Petroleum's purchase of PetroKazakhstan, the largest acquisition to date by a Chinese oil company. The deal required them to work with colleagues in Beijing, Almaty and New York. Another important matter was a project in Angola, advising a consortium of major oil companies on a planned $5 billion scheme to process gas from Angolan offshore fields at a new LNG plant for transport and sale to the USA.

In the insurance sector, lawyers recently advised the first post-Hurricane Katrina insurance company to raise $1 billion of capital and list on the AIM exchange here in London. On the litigation side the cases are largely UK-based, one of the current matters relating to a law firm in the north of England that has acted for sick miners seeking compensation under a DTI scheme. The firm's insurers have instructed LeBoeuf to resist an application for a Group Litigation Order by miners who claim that the client firm (and others) acted improperly. You may have already read about the issue as the Law Society has commenced a regulatory investigation into the matter and it has also been raised in Parliament and national newspapers.

the grass is always greener

Trainees in the litigation department can expect their days to be filled with *"the usual preparation of documents and trial bundles"* as well as more exciting *"trips to court and drafting witness statements."* London litigators recently represented Avon Insurance in the Court of Appeal in a case brought by Blackburn Rovers FC. The club has been trying to require the insurer to pay out on a policy following the disablement of an international player who was forced to retire from football through injury. When assisting on multi-jurisdictional cases, trainees sometimes need to go further than the RCJ. We heard tales of trainees being sent for weeks on end to assist with cases overseas, particularly in Europe. Such trips are *"not guaranteed, but I was asked to go because of my language capability,"* one source explained.

When working with the 'corporate energy' team trainees soon learn that *"long, detailed contracts are the norm"* and drafting skills are put under the microscope. It may help to understand that in this department the work is *"a bit like project finance: there are a lot of agreements that all need to hang together and often each part relates to different markets."* At the beginning of the seat a trainee's chores will be simple, but *"once you have done a job well you may be given more interesting work the next time."* On the agenda are *"due diligence and verification notes"* plus *"drafting resolutions, minutes and even agreements."* Trainees sometimes find that more rewarding tasks can be undertaken on joint venture agreements and fund raising for small energy companies.

At the moment the seats on offer are in dispute resolution (commercial and insurance lit, international arbitration and IP/IT) and corporate (energy, securities, employment, tax, real estate, environment and competition), but this is where it gets interesting. Growth is central to the firm's business strategy here in London and this should mean greater variety in the seats on offer. At the same time there is a proposal to increase the number of training places to ten per year. A typical source told us: *"I don't know the exact mas-*

ter plan, but we are not just about energy and insurance anymore." Another added: *"We are trying to expand into telecommunications and the London employment and corporate groups seem to be getting busier too."* In the USA the firm is beefing up its banking and securities litigation expertise and this too is likely to feed into the London office. Just before we went to press the firm announced the hire of three Freshfields partners specialising in environmental and property law plus another who had previously been at the magic circle firm. Our interviewees were comfortable with the changes that lie ahead. *"There is a positive vibe about the place,"* said one. *"There is a lot more work for us to do and I sense that when we finish there is a greater chance of being offered a job here."* For the record, all three of the 2006 qualifiers stayed on with the firm, two of them in the London office and one accepting a position in the New York office. A fourth trainee, already a qualified US attorney, decided to return to US practice before completing their contract.

your passport, please

Some students get wide eyed when they discover a firm with an extensive international network, assuming that guarantees time spent living and working abroad. Here, trainee seats in Brussels, Paris and Moscow are up for grabs, but it is time spent working on international deals and cases from London that characterises the training experience. For example, one source particularly enjoyed their time with the capital markets team because *"the clients and the debt instruments used are so international."*

Perhaps you think you need some level of expertise in one or both of LeBoeuf's core practices to impress at interview. Trainees assure us that *"it is not necessary to have energy or insurance knowledge before you arrive,"* although they remind readers that, as so much of their time will be spent working on matters for clients in these sectors they should work out what exactly it is about the sectors that appeals to them.

the human cocktail

With aspirations to double in size, the firm is currently recruiting at all levels. Beyond the Freshfields quartet, headline partner hires include experienced figures from Cable & Wireless, Linklaters and Norton Rose. Each group of new trainee recruits includes individuals who have grown up outside the UK and, for those born and bred here, foreign language skills are the norm. All trainees come with a strong academic record and some of the world's most prestigious universities appear on the resumés of successful applicants. Those of you who dread laborious application forms will be relieved to hear that this firm favours a simple CV and covering letter. Our sources were keen to tell us that because they work so closely with partners *"it makes sense for them to understand you as a person in your own right from day one."* As the firm grows, HR is shaping up in the London office and there are now personnel to deal with training and graduate recruitment issues full time. Previously, much of the formal training was delivered by way of somewhat dodgy video links from New York. This has been phased out and replaced by live training.

"Although the majority of the lawyers here are English, there is definitely a cosmopolitan feel to the office," confirmed a source. Continuing this theme, trainees stressed that LeBoeuf London *"doesn't feel like an American firm,"* and it is perhaps only in their second year when they are flown out to New York *"to look at the offices, attend various social events, meet the partners out there and generally get a feel for things on a bigger scale"* that the origins of the firm hit home. Like other US firms in London, the firm pays big – trainee salaries start at £36K, NQ salaries have leapt to £75K – and in 2006 the firm topped up bank accounts with a £7K trainee bonus and a £15K

NQ bonus. High salaries at 'US firms' sometimes attract candidates who may not be entirely sure about where their training contract is leading. Not so here, we sense. *"The trainees here already know where their future lies;" "they aren't still wondering if they are going to be a solicitor; they know that they want to be a LeBoeuf lawyer and many also have a clear idea about what area of law they are interested in."*

Our sources had typically chosen LeBoeuf because they wanted *"international work without being one person in a hundred;"* they wanted *"better experience and more individual attention,"* believing that this would be easier to find in a smaller office. One pointed out that *"the people here are capable of going to the magic circle but made an active decision not to."* Another explained: *"The teams aren't that big; you work directly with a partner, you go along to meetings and they even let you run your own little projects within the bigger picture."* Not only that but *"clients remember you – you are not just a trainee to them; you are a lawyer working on their deal."* Shirking responsibility or hiding for weeks in a data room is not an option; in fact, those who thrive *"like to take responsibility – they don't need really detailed instructions for every little thing and they can quickly work out what is happening in a situation."* Perhaps being taken seriously helps create what trainees say is *"an open atmosphere in the office."* They also stress that on social occasions things are equally as good; *"we all mix freely outside work."*

and finally...

In the words of one trainee: *"This is a unique place to be. As trainees we are encouraged to be independent and there is an unusual range of work on offer."* Another summed up: *"Now is a great time to be at LeBoeuf. While other American firms seem to be resting on their laurels, we are on the way up."* We concur.

Lee & Priestley

the facts

Location: Leeds
Number of UK partners/solicitors: 13/19
Total number of trainees: 6
Seats: 4x6 month
Alternative seats: None

Lee & Priestley is an emerging force in the burgeoning Leeds legal market. A century old this year, the firm has trimmed much of its high street fat to become a sleeker, more corporate-focused outfit.

chasing leeds

Lee & Priestley used to operate out of Bradford and a series of satellite offices and had a definite high street feel. How things change. In 2004 it ditched its personal injury arm and residential conveyancing operation and moved wholesale to brand new offices in the heart of Leeds. The shift to corporate and commercial work in the owner-managed business sector has only been prevented from becoming wholesale through the retention of private client and family departments that were frankly too good to let go. What L&P now offers to student hopefuls is commercial training with some rewarding exposure to private clients.

While *"lots of people are aware the firm has changed massively in a short period of time,"* current trainees have found that *"when you work with [other lawyers and advisers] they may not have heard of us – though they are always impressed afterwards."* This low profile looks set to change if a new marketing drive is as successful as everyone at L&P hopes. As such, a particular breed of trainee is now required: people who are *"confident and able to get on well with clients."* It's all about *"knowing clients and being interested in their business."* Arguably, a higher profile and the recently revamped online application process may make L&P's hiring policy more stringent, but current trainees say those who make the grade will find themselves in a *"motivated and energetic"* firm where there's *"a youthful feel that passes down from partners to everyone else."*

dreding it

L&P's recruitment process may have been overhauled but the tried, tested and *"flexible"* training set-up looks here to stay. The system works broadly on a four-by-six-month basis, with trainees allowed to squeeze or stretch seats depending on both their inclination and how desperately a department needs an extra pair of hands. The overriding message from trainees on this point is that the firm *"does listen to you"* when it comes to seat choice and length, *"especially in the second year."* Corporate, commercial property, insolvency and debt recovery are all regular placements, as is DRED, the rather ominously named dispute resolution and employment disputes department.

L&P's commercial property department has been handling plenty of weighty deals of late, including a multimillion-pound sale of a portfolio of 56 pubs. Banks and property developers are two key client groups, and a recently launched retail unit advises high street names such as O'Briens Sandwich Bars, Republic and The Yorkshire Linen Co. It is also worth noting that this department, along with corporate and employment, boasts niche expertise in legal advice to care homes. With all these commercial matters there's no chance of trainees being up to their necks in house conveyancing during their property seat. As well as helping solicitors with their work, trainees all get their own files. Admittedly these may deal with such lowly matters as *"transferring a parking space from one flat to another,"* but they at least get to *"manage a file from start to finish"* and learn *"general principles that apply in just the same way on higher-value files."*

Corporate is the one seat that is likely to throw up long hours, but in common with the other departments *"if it's not too busy then no one will bat an eyelid if you leave on time."* The corporate team managed a deal a week in 2005, one of the top transactions being the management buyout of school-wear stalwart Trutex. Trainees pitched in on many of these deals, handling everything from due diligence down to deal admin. Even the paper shuffling was viewed as *"important because it gives a real sense of how a transaction is put together."* Don't let the words debt recovery drum up images of burly bailiffs knocking on doors, because that's not really what a seat in this department is about. It's a place where trainees can get great hands-on experience by running their own files. As one recalled, by *"sitting down with [creditor] clients and working out how to make a recovery,"* you learn *"a lot about tactics"* and gain advocacy experience at various bankruptcy and winding-up hearings. Though advocacy is not something anyone is forced to do, it sounds as if you'd be silly not to have a go as it leaves you with *"a real sense of achievement."*

Despite the commercial bent of most new recruits, all are encouraged (though not forced) to do a seat in family law because experience has shown *"you get a lot out of it."* Such as? *"A huge amount of client contact,"* plenty of court visits and the chance to run your own files. When combined these make for *"a great learning curve."* Legal aid work used to be the mainstay of L&P's family practice but the balance is tipping firmly towards privately funded matters, and now a growing number of wealthy individuals bring their divorces to the firm. There is also plenty of childcare work ranging from custody, abuse and even international child abduction, and the lawyers have been involved in cases that make headlines, such as that of a couple who gave birth to mixed-race twins following the use of unauthorised sperm during fertility treatment. All in all, family life is *"action-packed"* with regular court hearings and plenty of preparation tasks for the trainee.

it's all greek

Appraisals with the training principal and head of the insolvency group, Nigel Whitfield, occur at the end of each seat. The rest of the time it's a case of *"no news is good news,"* though trainees told us they felt able to *"speak to partners on a regular basis, if issues or problems arise."* Our impression is that Nigel is a steadying influence on the new recruits. His career has been unusual in the sense that he started as an office junior, moved into casework and never let go of his goal to become a partner. Having taken his LPC and qualified as a solicitor only relatively recently, trainees feel *"he has a good understanding of the pressures we're under."* Retention rates are generally very good (all three qualifiers in 2004, both qualifiers in 2005), although in 2006 neither of the qualifiers took jobs at the firm. Trainees appreciated that the firm *"made a conscious decision to let us know early doors about being kept on."* Those who stay say it is *"a lifestyle choice – if you're expecting top money and long hours you won't get them, but you'll have a much nicer life for it."*

L&P trainees don't stray far from the office when they go out for drinks. The firm's location at the bottom of Greek Street makes it *"the perfect place to start a pub crawl and work your way up."* Prohibition and All Bar One are typical Friday night hang-outs, and the plethora of nearby drinking establishments prevents it from ever getting samey. The city centre base is also convenient during daylight hours; with *"everything on your doorstep"* the energetic can go to the gym in their lunch hour leaving shopaholics to get on with tearing through their bank accounts. L&P's social and sports committee keeps employees entertained with theatre trips or nights out at Jongleurs Comedy Club, and there's always a big bash for the NQs at a local bar. The annual summer barbecue brings everyone together, including families and future joiners, and last time was held at Cookridge Hall Golf Club on the outskirts of the city. Tales of

"bouncy castles, party games, big Jenga and Connect 4" left us with the impression that the event was designed for kids of all ages. When speaking to trainees we agreed to make a plea for new netball players. A women's team emerged in the enthusiasm following the annual interdepartmental co-ed tournament (where rules are not strictly followed) and is now aiming for Leeds domination...

and finally...

Lee & Priestley offers a *"happy medium"* between the largest outfits in the tough Leeds market and the smallest operations that are unknown beyond their postcodes. If you want a Leeds-based career at an aspirational firm, this one is worth closer inspection.

Lester Aldridge

the facts

Location: Bournemouth, Southampton, Milton Keynes, London
Number of UK partners/solicitors: 38/60
Total number of trainees: 14
Seats: 4x6 months
Alternative seats: Occasional secondments

Lester Aldridge has steadily widened its geographical reach from its original Bournemouth home. It first opened up in Southampton to capture more South Coast business, landed in Milton Keynes in 2004 and then merged with a property law boutique in London.

solent system

In late 2005 LA's then managing partner stated that part of the overall growth strategy of the firm was to double the size of its Southampton office and push forwards in its two newest locations. Trainees had clearly been monitoring developments and confirmed that *"not only has Southampton expanded quite a lot but Milton Keynes and London have got involved really quickly.*" One spoke animatedly of LA's *"bright future."* The business plan is straightforward: opportunities in Bournemouth have already been extensively exploited; the Southampton market, while holding many untapped clients, is still limited in its commercial possibilities, so LA's future relies on the development of new markets – hence London and MK. It is now busy courting new clients – particularly national and international names – to add to an existing client roster including the likes of Fat Face, Big Yellow Self Storage (which itself is focusing on developing the London market), retailer Dixons, newspaper and magazine wholesalers Surridge Dawson and outdoor gear people Kathmandu UK.

A number of those clients are serviced by an experienced retail team run out of the Southampton office, and in Bournemouth the firm's real estate practice continues fruitful relationships with house builders such as retirement home developer McCarthy & Stone. Meanwhile LA's South Coast corporate lawyers have advised on the disposal of the Hugh Symons Group communications divisions to Carphone Warehouse, and represented the management in the MBO of Lyncolec, a Poole-based circuit board manufacturer that contributed to the Beagle mission to Mars.

buy now pay later

Finance, especially asset and consumer finance, is a big area for the firm. A dedicated office in Hurn, near Bournemouth International Airport, provides lower-end debt recovery, mortgaging and conveyancing services, and the firm has a fleet of major-league finance clients. In the motor finance area it represents Volkswagen, Toyota, Daimler-Chrysler and Ford Motor Credit; beyond the motor finance sector, clients include Hitachi Capital, ING Lease, Lloyds TSB, Xerox Finance and Abbey.

We mustn't forget the private client side of LA's business. It has a fantastic reputation regionally, with lawyers representing a broad sweep of clients from the moderately wealthy to the landed and aristocratic. The firm's family lawyers are among the best in the business and look to have benefited from a flood of new City and money market clients following the firm's arrival in London.

The *"vast spread of work"* and *"good options in terms of seats"* were commonly cited as the reasons why our sources had applied to the firm. Trainees confessed they had wanted to experiment a little before making up their minds where to qualify. The majority of the seats are to be found in Bournemouth and Southampton, though some trainees spend time in Hurn on fast-track debt recovery or residential conveyancing/remortgaging. Debt recovery provides *"hands-on responsibility"* for *"court applications and some attendances, taking witness statements and instructing barristers."* In residential conveyancing and remortgaging, trainees also get their own files which means *"clients call you all the time."* The work may not be the most demanding intellectually, but as one trainee quickly found out *"it gave me skills that I have used in the other seats – independent working and client relationships especially, keeping them updated and being proactive."*

As the two newest offices are also limited in their activities (MK is finance, London is property) it is rare for trainees to spend a seat in either. The Bournemouth and Southampton offices appear to be equally popular, though some prefer *"the set up and the bigger office"* of the former and others the *"younger feel"* of the latter. Hurn has more of an open-plan layout and a lot of non-solicitor fee earners.

funny handshakes

The breadth and number of seat options seems to ensure that *"competition for specific seats is not too hard."* One that is very likely to crop up is property, where you should expect *"drafting, research queries, form filling, leases and freeholds... and stuff* relating to mortgages. You'll be working for a lot of fee earners, whoever needs assistance." Trainees also become heavily involved in the work of the internationally minded private client department. Our sources spoke of "dealing with UK and foreign probates that included cross-border considerations" and had access to both contentious and non-contentious files. In employment, "you never get too comfortable" as "you are learning all the time," and the popular environmental and planning seat strikes us as a bit out of the ordinary if the experiences of one trainee are anything to go by. They attended a judicial review hearing to decide if a Freemasons lodge had used bias in any of its dealings. Most of a trainee's time will be spent on "a mix of contentious and non-contentious matters, with research, drafting agreements and environmental prosecutions" high on the agenda.

In addition to their seat supervisor, trainees all have "an overall mentor who is always a partner. We meet with our mentors about once a month to review our experiences and make sure we are getting the level of work we need." By all accounts it's easy for a trainee to seek guidance at any time – "people are happy to stop what they are doing and help you" and "no one minds you asking stupid questions." Quarterly group meetings with management are the time to raise broader concerns affecting the trainees as a whole. Perhaps they have less to grumble about than some, as many of the thankless tasks such as photocopying are taken out of trainee hands by legal assistants and secretarial staff.

still, not sparkling

Most of the current trainees had grown up in the south of England (though not necessarily from the immediate area). All had been to well-regarded universities and were now living in or around Bournemouth and Southampton. Without a doubt, geography plays a big part in the

decision to come to LA. Bournemouth is said to have "a more relaxed atmosphere than most cities," and it is "ideal for anyone who loves the sea." The trainees' collected views are exemplified in the following statement. "It's gorgeous countryside down here; we have an amazing beach in the summer, and we have the forest as well as shops and clubs. We've got a little bit of everything; it's a great location." The sea is actually visible from the office windows in Bournemouth, and it's no chore to go down for a dip or a donkey ride at lunchtime.

Office hours usually run from 9.30am until 5.30pm, leaving plenty of time to make something of an evening. One trainee recalled that they "may have stayed until 8pm to finish off something once, but that was my own choice – no one will bat an eyelid if you go home at 5.30pm." The firm has cricket, football, rugby and netball teams and several staff go sailing or windsurfing together. Even if "the different offices mean trainees don't always see each other," "we certainly e-mail each other a lot." They do come together for formal training sessions, and drinks after work on a Friday or dinner at someone's house at the weekend are always an option. Staff in Bournemouth frequent Downes Wine Bar; in Southampton, The Cricketers is favoured for Friday lunchtimes. "This is a fun place to work," the trainees agreed. Those with a tendency towards amateur dramatics will enjoy the traditional trainee sketch show at the AGM and summer ball. The firm "gives you time off to film stuff for it and a small budget, although most of it is performed live." Despite a certain amount of secrecy about content of the latest production, we discovered it was "based on reality TV; something like Big Brother only with the trainees taking on the characters of people within the firm." Luckily "everybody takes it in good humour." Indeed, humour is something the firm isn't short of: its marketing campaigns in recent years have frequently taken a tongue-in-cheek approach. Knowing the value of good marketing is all part and parcel of being a lawyer, and in this respect our sources were glad to be able to report that *"trainees get taken along to the local marketing events."*

Readers, we have some sad news to report concerning Sparkle, the office dog who for many years wandered the corridors and meeting rooms of the Bournemouth office. After taking as active a role in the affairs of a law firm as a canine can, even earning her own profile on the intranet, Sparkle has stolen her last sandwich and barked her last bark. She will be sorely missed by all who knew her. As one trainee recalled wistfully, *"she used to walk past my office when I was in real estate; it's very sad that she has gone."* Nevertheless, she will be remembered by the four out of the five qualifiers who accepted NQ positions at the firm in 2006.

and finally...

If your ambitious streak is tempered by a desire to live and work by the sea, then putting down anchor at Lester Aldridge is a sensible option. The firm has made great strides already and plans more for the future. For trainees this can only be a good thing.

Lewis Silkin

the facts

Location: London, Oxford
Number of UK partners/solicitors: 42/68
Total number of trainees: 12
Seats: 4x6 months
Alternative seats: None

Lewis Silkin's brand of media, advertising and technology law is well positioned, as are two other core practices – employment and social housing. Beyond this the London firm performs well in mid-market corporate, property and litigation work.

product placement

Once upon a time you were cutting edge if you had a Walkman with a pair of foam-covered headphones. Now we're ipod-ed to the hilt, watching our PVRs, picking up viral marketing messages, getting bluetoothed and being tempted by interactive brand experiences. Lewis Silkin is the darling of the advertising and marketing sector and counts many media and communications companies as clients.

How strange then that when we asked trainees to define its culture and explain its success we were showered with a fine mist of obscurity. *"Everything just works well to produce a good atmosphere and a good final product,"* said one. Another hummed and hawed and decided: *"It's a very professional firm, but it's quite relaxed about it – there doesn't seem to be much pressure exerted in order to get it all done."* The self-proclaimed "rather more human law firm" knows it's a little bit different, it knows everyone knows it's a little different, but it also knows that no one really knows why. Confused? Back to the trainees: *"It's a self-perpetuating thing. People come to the firm because they hear about the ethos and then they work towards that ethos when they get here."*

Truth be told, it's probably more useful for any prospective trainee to look at the kind of work the firm does and not to worry unduly about the nature of the firm's supposed 'silkiness'. The prodigious media, brands and technology (MBT) department holds many a trainee in its thrall. This year the trainees admitted: *"We all came here to do media"* and, consequently, competition for the seat was hot. *"It was a good seat from the start,"* reported trainees who worked on *"some quite glam sponsorship deals"* alongside advertising campaign clearances and various licences. The team won a High Court victory on behalf of mobile phone company Hutchison 3G (now 3) against O_2

over the use of bubble imagery in its advertisements. It also advises Sainsbury's on its relationship with Jamie Oliver. Here, you're never far from a household name and the client line-up includes Apple, Coca-Cola, Motorola, Esteé Lauder and Gillette as well as advertising giants Abbott Mead Vickers BBDO and McCann-Erickson.

making the headlines

Lewis Silkin's employment practice is unlike most others in the City; now anything but a niche support department, it accounts for around a third of the firm's staff and work. The department has steadily built a superb reputation as one of the best in the country and, although the majority of work is for employers, the headline cases are commonly those where the client is an individual. Lewis Silkin lawyers represented Stephanie Villalba in her multimillion-pound discrimination claim against Merrill Lynch. Intriguingly the lawyers also advise a number of major law firms when they get into sticky situations with staff. Who wouldn't want to be a fly on the wall in those meetings? Naturally, as a trainee you'll never be standing up in court on the million-pound matters, but you should think about investing in a pair of sensible shoes as trainees reported attending tribunals all over London on *"sex discrimination, race discrimination and all sorts of matters... It's really interesting stuff."* One interviewee spent a great deal of time taking notes at tribunals and generally making sure the client was taken care of. Another spoke of fending off a rabid press pack after a particularly incendiary matter: *"We read a story about the case in the evening paper on the way home, which wasn't something we really wanted. It was potentially a bit worrying but we managed to sort it out."* Unsurprisingly, trainees rate the seat as *"brilliant,"* and with three spaces available at any one time, there's no need to worry about missing out.

a slice of the action

If employment and media get *"the 'sexy seat' label,"* property and social housing are *"incredibly busy departments where you get completely stuck in with a lot of responsibility."* Social housing, in particular, provides hands-on experience. Again, the team is one of the UK's best known in this sector and advises registered social landlords on some major large-scale finance and regeneration projects. A roll call of client names reveals Horizon Housing Group, London Borough of Lewisham, Notting Hill Housing, South West of England Regional Development Agency and Peabody Trust. For trainees there is an endless supply of smaller files to tackle. Said one: *"I was able to sell about six properties at auction and saw the process through from start to finish."*

In commercial litigation be prepared to be busy right from the start. *"We aren't completely dropped in it, but we aren't wrapped up in cotton wool by any means,"* explained one interviewee. Among the department's most notable work is advice to Mohamed Al Fayed in relation to the inquest into the deaths of Dodi Al Fayed and Diana, Princess of Wales plus advice to House of Fraser concerning allegations of price-fixing in the sale of Oakley sunglasses. Over in the corporate department, trainees provide general assistance on the deals that hit the partners' desks, most of them for clients in the firm's core sectors. Lately they have advised the shareholders of Glue London, a digital advertising agency, in its £14 million sale to Aegis. Other corporate clients include PizzaExpress, Hermès and Harrods. One trainee reported that *"it hasn't been the kind of late-night-working scenario that I'd had nightmares about,"* and even when the days did drag on, *"I didn't mind because I had the experience of working for some great clients."*

sparkling or still?

Clients are frequently cross-referred by departments; "*if we do their employment work it's a good lead into media work, then onto general enquiries...*" Despite the free flow of clients around the firm, we got the impression that Lewis Silkin trainees become quite attached to their individual seats, not wanting to leave at the end of the tenure. "*By then you've built up a good relationship with everyone and a good level of responsibility, and then it's back to square one,*" explained a source who then revealed their fickleness by proclaiming: "*Employment was my favourite seat... until I did media.*"

The dress code is "*formal, but it depends on the department how formal it is;*" apparently "*in the summer you'll see employment lawyers padding around in flip flops.*" These days they have further to flip and flop as 2006 saw the firm move to a large office building in Chancery Lane. It was formerly home to the shrinking Denton Wilde Sapte which coincidentally also shares a passion for the colour orange. When we last visited the firm staff were still trying to get their heads around the size of the office, in much the same way as when you move up the property ladder and realise your belongings don't fill the your new home. The obvious conclusion to draw is that the firm intends to grow into the building. "*The new canteen is a great improvement,*" said one trainee, another telling us that because the different departments no longer all occupy separate floors there is more mixing. Our favourite feature is still the taps that dispense fizzy water in the kitchens.

This year's summer party doubled up as a house warming. "*There was the usual chocolate fountain, booze, etc, and you usually find the same faces stay till the bitter end.*" The move has prompted the investigation of new after-hours watering holes. The Blue Anchor has points in its favour: "*One girl was celebrating in there with cheap champagne, but we drank so much the bar ran out of it and they gave us Möet instead, at the same price.*" Our sources valued the ability to maintain a healthy work-life balance (the office is commonly relatively clear by 6.30pm) and integrate easily with partners and staff at all levels. "*I wanted a firm that didn't drive you like a slave, even though that's such a cliché. Some people can cope with it for a few years in training then leave their firm, but I didn't want that,*" explained one. The partners' and supervisors' openness helps considerably ("*I have no qualms about speaking to the supervisor about concerns or asking for assistance*") and this is in evidence right from the start. "*It was one of the most relaxed interviews I had. The partners were very keen on trying to find out what kind of people we were rather than trying to ask us difficult questions until we cracked.*"

The orange brick road to Lewis Silkin is trod by people from quite different backgrounds and lifestyles. Perhaps it's having this "*mix of different people who want the same thing*" that makes the culture of Lewis Silkin so hard to pin down. "*This is going to sound infuriating,*" said one, "*but it's all down to fit – you'll know if the firm is right for you.*" As to how you get on here, the best and silkiest tip we heard was this: "*You need to go with the flow of a department, get integrated and get involved.*" In 2006, four of the eight qualifiers integrated themselves further into the MBT, litigation and employment teams. Other jobs were available (five in property and social housing) but those who left had their hearts set on media jobs.

and finally...

In deciding whether Lewis Silkin is a place you'd want to work, "*the indefinable thing*" that is silkiness is not the most important consideration. The real draws should be the type of work on offer and the particular client sectors that the firm has made its own.

Linklaters

the facts
Location: London
Number of UK partners/solicitors: 200/600
Total number of trainees: 268
Seats: 4x6 months
Alternative seats: Overseas seats, secondments
Extras: Pro bono – Hackney Law Centre, Legal Connections Centre, Mary Ward Legal Advice Centre, FRU, RCJ CAB; language training

Riding the thermals of a resurgent transactions market, magic circle firm Linklaters this year reached even greater heights.

the force be with them
Magic circle firms are commonly portrayed as the superheroes of the profession, as mighty colossi with unimaginable powers, operating in a landscape far beyond the ken of everyday Peter Parker outfits. By smashing through the £1 million profit-per-equity-partner mark in 2006 – when a 29% increase in turnover saw it fall just short of £1 billion worldwide – prompted some commentators to suggest that, alongside CC and Freshfields, Linklaters had broken away from other magic circle players to form a premier trio. Even if we find it hard to accept one trainee's opinion that working at the firm is *"like being in Star Wars,"* there is no doubt that Linklaters has performed amazingly well in its mission *"to be the best law firm in the world."*

Globally – if not quite galactically – Linklaters' corporate practice has long been its powerhouse. In the past year, while contributing nearly a third of the firm's global revenue, corporate lawyers handled over 20 deals with a combined worth of £21 billion. They advised AstraZeneca on its £702 million offer for Cambridge Antibody Technology, Allied Domecq on the £7.4 billion recommended public offer made by Pernod Ricard, and Saint-Gobain on its £4.3 billion cash offer for BNP Paribas. The group seamlessly combines its overseas capabilities to work on major cross-border transactions such as Gas Natural's $23 billion hostile bid for Endesa, the largest ever tender offer in Spain. Gazprom also turned to the firm for its $13.09 billion acquisition of Sibneft, the largest M&A deal in Russian history.

Linklaters' private equity and funds practice is also formidable, advising on a welter of pan-European matters including one of the largest PE fundraisings of recent times in the form of BC Partners' €5.5 billion European Capital Fund. Some high-profile departures have given the team food for thought this year, but it managed to pull itself together to act for Barclays Capital, CSFB, Deutsche Bank, JPMorgan and RBS as mandated lead arrangers on €10.65 billion facilities in support of a tender offer for TDC by Apax Partners, Blackstone, KKR, Permira and Providence Equity. Elsewhere, restructuring and insolvency work involved some of Europe's best-known problem corporates – MG Rover, Parmalat and Eurotunnel – and the competition practice has continued to blossom, lately advising Dubai Ports World on OFT and other worldwide clearances required for its acquisition of P&O.

punch drunk: that's the spirit
While its corporate prowess goes unquestioned, Linklaters has had to bust a gut to get its banking and finance teams near the top of the tree. The hard work looks to be paying off and 2006 saw the promotion of 17 senior finance and projects associates to the worldwide partnership. The London team is the brains behind a thriving European securities, syndicated loans and acquisition finance practice that numbers almost all the major banks among its clientele. Lawyers advised RBS, Citigroup and Morgan Stanley on the financing of Punch Taverns' £2.68 billion acquisition of Spirit Group and participated in some of Europe's

jumbo deals, including the £1.6 billion recapitalisation of Gala Group and a £1.2 billion facility for Deutsche Börse's proposed takeover of the London Stock Exchange. A broad finance prowess has been the foundation for a burgeoning leveraged finance practice that shows signs of putting Links on level pegging with traditional leaders A&O and CC. Last year's multiparty consortium £1.9 billion leveraged buyout of Somerfield certainly highlights the firm's ability to handle the most complex matters. This leveraged debt financing involved a structure comprising a senior bridge facility arranged by Barclays Capital, Citigroup Global Markets and RBS, a PIK bridge facility credit agreement arranged by Citigroup Global Markets and a revolving credit facility arranged by HSBC. We'll admit to finding the intricacies of such deals hard to grasp, and we expect you do too. For now, just pay heed to one trainee's observation that *"your learning curve is vertical in most of the finance seats, but boy do you learn a lot."*

around the world

Of the firm as a whole, Linklaters trainees say their employer has *"taken the right risks and is slightly ahead of the competition right now."* They unanimously agreed that the firm's *"internationalist streak"* is its most distinctive feature and point to a *"fully integrated"* international network of offices spanning 22 countries. A sizeable presence across Europe, Asia and the Middle East (plus an office in Brazil and New York) allows the firm to pursue *"an agenda of keeping our pan-European and worldwide reputation strong."* Said one particularly astute interviewee: *"The major focus right now is to get clients seeing Linklaters as a seamless entity that is working well across departments and across countries."* What this means, day by day, for a trainee is *"exciting international elements to our work,"* whether this be the simple pleasures of *"being in touch with lots of foreign offices by e-mail and phone"* or actually *"flying out to places to assist on deals."* Those eager to spend more time in one of Links' thriving colonies can justifiably expect an overseas seat. The most popular are Singapore, Hong Kong, New York and São Paulo, but there are plenty of others (Shanghai, Beijing, Tokyo, Dubai, Amsterdam, Brussels, Paris, Frankfurt, Madrid, Rome, Milan, Prague, Warsaw, Budapest, Moscow, Bucharest) and a stack of client secondments to the likes of The Prince's Trust, the Mary Ward Law Centre and a number of investment banks and companies.

grin and bear it

Around 90% of trainees take either a secondment or an overseas placement in a no-nonsense four-seat system that plays heavily to the staffing needs of the busiest departments. Whether they'd enjoyed their training or not (and we spoke to many more of the former than the latter), our sources were clear that *"the type and sophistication of the work you get depends on the luck of the draw, both in terms of the time you're in a department and the work your supervisor has."*

This rule definitely applies in corporate. Here, rationalising that *"it is good to learn the skills of project management when you're running a data room"* was the consolation for many, and *"endless proof-reading and rare bits of drafting"* seemed not uncommon. For some, the equation of *"less responsibility plus lower-quality work"* was simply *"what you expect of transactional seats in such a big firm."* More resolute individuals took pleasure in *"the big characters in the team,"* *"the structured, deadline-driven nature of IPO work"* and the challenge of *"taking the time to make sure you're not just blindly pushing paper, but instead getting a sense of the documents you're handling."* Admittedly, this is easier at midday than it is *"at 8pm when you've been in the office for 36 hours straight,"* but despite *"long, long hours,"* sometimes for extended periods, the *"camaraderie and blitz spirit in the middle of the night"* saved aching souls. Finance seats also involve "*ferocious*" hours, not least because "*if a bank decides it wants something done for tomorrow, everyone jumps to it.*"

Even self-starters determined to seek out better work in transactional seats had often found themselves "*frustrated by the same sort of dataroom and proofing work, even when I'd discussed the problem with my supervisor and mentor.*" By virtue of perseverance, some of our interviewees found that "*putting yourself out there and specifically targeting work*" could result in more responsibility. And never forget lady luck: "*My supervisor in corporate had a client who also owned a private jet, so I got loads of random queries, research points and drafting to do with that.*" In essence, very hard work on repetitive tasks is inevitable, but "*at least the mundane work lets seniors see that you are dedicated and reliable.*" Trainees recommend frequent use of "*the midnight smile*" because "*a cheery, positive disposition really helps when you're in the office after 10pm. If you mope it's very noticeable.*"

For every trainee who complained that transactional seats "*didn't enhance my legal acumen at all,*" there were more who told us how much they had learned in the big departments. "*You realise you've learned a lot over the two years when you're allowed to e-mail clients without being checked,*" one told us. Another had enjoyed the enhanced responsibility that came from "*a memo to write on something you've never seen before and you're expected to produce a document on it to be e-mailed to a client in no time at all.*"

three out of four ain't so bad

The seat allocation system "*generally leaves people satisfied,*" with most getting "*three out of their four preferences.*" Many trainees head overseas or on secondment in the third seat, but others cling to the London office in a bid to be in the right place at the right time. "*By the third seat you've got sufficient experience not to make a tit of yourself and*

maybe get a job," explained one. As for what seats are strictly compulsory there's a fair degree of flexibility, although reflecting the firm's practice, three of four seats must now be taken from the pool of mainstream corporate, banking, project finance, derivatives and structured products, equity and debt markets, securities finance group, real estate and litigation. However, each of those areas are broad and the Law Society's requirement for contentious experience can now be fulfilled by taking a two-week litigation course and doing some pro bono work. One source remembered "*a scary rent committee review for a client who cried all the time.*" Fear not, those intent on a full seat in litigation can do one. This general pattern is a little more prescriptive than in previous years and perhaps reflects the City-wide trend of encouraging trainees towards transactional seats to bump up numbers wanting to qualify into those departments. However, the majority of our sources had followed a very similar path through training, sticking closely to Links' strengths.

Niche seats are obtainable, although competition for them is stiff. Tax is a popular destination as it combines "*pleasingly uniform hours*" with "*hard, intellectual work.*" The opportunity to give the old grey matter a workout attracts those trainees who relish "*discrete research tasks and helping on know-how sessions for clients and the rest of the firm.*" The appeal can partly be explained by the fact that "*the law is constantly being updated and work never feels stale,*" and partly the "*greater autonomy*" on offer. One lucky interviewee had "*got involved with a VAT case; I was interviewing clients, drafting witness statements and ran a client meeting myself.*" Elsewhere, EU/competition, employment, employee incentives, TMT and pensions are by nature of their size and desirability "*hard to get into,*" but reward "*careful plotters*" with "*steady hours*" and the chance to "*get more hands-on experience.*" Sources who had sat in the real estate department had enjoyed *"client contact from day one,"* while those in pensions busied themselves with *"research, drafting and client meetings."*

better than all the rest?

Our sources had for the most part chosen the firm because they perceived it to be *"simply the best,"* both in terms of its business position and the way it handles training. Displaying a relentlessly self-improving streak, Links puts a lot of thought, time and money into recruitment and training and is now going out to find graduates in places as far flung as Australia and India. And why not? When your business is global shouldn't your staff be too? At this juncture we'll tell you that Links has what must be the best record of any big City law firm for diversity among its trainees. At last count, a competition-shredding 31% had been recruited from ethnic minorities. No one we spoke to seemed to think that this *"makes any difference... I mean, I can't say I feel we're a rainbow nation, but what you do feel every day is that we're part of a global village."*

One place that may feel like a village is the new College of Law branch at Moorgate, which runs an LPC course designed specifically for and taught exclusively to Linklaters' future trainees. They don't have the building to themselves, however, as a handful of other law firms have also contracted with the college. And to allay fears that the Linklaters LPC would create a generation of weird, indoctrinated drones, the firm has agreed that some classes should be taken with students heading to other firms.

Our sources typically displayed an aura of *"confidence"* and *"authority;"* they told us that *"big personalities flourish here."* There were a few more critical voices – though all were objective and happy to praise various aspects of Linklaters life – but they seemed to be those whose individualistic disposition or specific commercial ambition simply wasn't best housed in a large institution with *"a big-company ethos."* Linklaters trainees themselves are adamant that *"we don't fit a certain mould"* and we're not about to suggest that they come from one. But we do still wonder if the trend for firm-specific LPCs runs the risk of stifling students' individuality and appreciation for difference. Time will tell. Anyway, to enter City law you make sacrifices of all sorts. And in return you get a fabulous salary. True to form, Linklaters was at the forefront of the recent salary and law school sponsorship rises from UK law firms. At £55,100, its NQ salary is UK top whack, albeit that the American firms in the capital are now paying silly money. The American firms do represent an option for magic circle qualifiers (as do smaller firms – there are people who just aren't cut out for the mega-deals of the City) but overall, Linklaters hangs onto the majority of qualifiers. In 2006, 103 of the 122 qualifiers took positions at the firm. It's worth adding that a very high percentage of those who actively wanted NQ jobs got them – 103 out of 107.

come on inn

A trainee's social life is *"focused in the first instance on your intake and then increasingly on the departments you work in."* Trainees regularly fill local bars (*"Match and Digress are especially popular"*) or take advantage of *"discounted rates on all the shows, concerts and films"* at The Barbican, which is opposite the office. Back in the office *"drinks trolleys and cakes in the kitchen"* help departments cohere, even if the décor doesn't. The *Student Guide's* rustic hovel is just a short walk from Linklaters' sleek offices, so we have seen with our own eyes the acres of polished wood, beautiful artwork and in-house restaurant. Nevertheless, we couldn't help but agree with the trainee who confessed: *"I was completely bowled over by the design until someone pointed out that the reception looks like a Holiday Inn and I can't think of anything but that.*" We'd hazard that the on-site sleeping pods may actually be more comfortable than the average hotel bed and the sum total of on-site facilities would beat the Holiday Inn hands down.

and finally...

Linklaters offers a fantastic training and could launch you into the legal stratosphere. If you want the best of everything you'd do well to shortlist the firm, but do remember that this kind of best isn't necessarily what's best for everyone.

Lovells

the facts

Location: London
Number of UK partners/solicitors: 138/379
Total number of trainees: 148
Seats: 4x6 months
Alternative seats: Overseas seats, secondments
Extras: Pro bono – Disability Living Allowance Appeal Hearings, Bow County Court Advisory Service, Criminal Injuries Compensation Appeal Tribunals, National Centre for Domestic Violence and many other schemes; language training

With 25 offices worldwide and a turnover of £396 million in 2005/06, Lovells is comfortably in the UK's top ten. Its practice profile is broad and, in addition to its core corporate and finance work, a prestigious dispute resolution practice stands alongside an impressive real estate division and various specialist departments.

new deal

For many years one of the key reasons for choosing Lovells over any other big firm was the scope for trying different types of work, possibly even sidestepping – or at least minimising time spent in – the most hardcore transactional areas. Will this all change now that a new "*rejigged*" seat allocation mechanism has been introduced? On the plus side it addresses trainee "*gripes*" about the "*lottery*" of seat allocation and will hopefully prevent nasty surprises when people "*end up getting something they never wanted and never had in mind.*" Said one trainee: "*It shows they are listening to us and addressing issues.*" The new system will ensure that trainees become aware of their full seat programme during the first six months of the contract and have the opportunity to express a first choice to "*pretty much guarantee*" a must-have seat.

We have previously reported on the view from the junior end that Lovells is becoming more of a corporate and finance-led outfit. In keeping with this, a seat in either the corporate or finance streams is compulsory for all. Last year corporate lawyers advised on 270 M&A transactions with an aggregate value of €136 billion. The current year has already seen Lovells advise ITV on a proposed private equity consortium bid and help venture capital provider Softbank on the acquisition of Vodafone's Japanese interests. On such deals trainees are "*seen as fair game,*" required to pitch in whenever needed on admin jobs of the "*less than thrilling*" variety. If you are lucky "*a really lovely supervisor will protect you from the really awful work,*" but generally it's a case of taking a bullish "*all-or-nothing*" attitude and submitting yourself to the tides and currents of the department's workflow. By all accounts the hours can at times be "*quite horrendous.*" In addition to the mainstream corporate seats there are options in private equity, financial services, tax and equity capital markets.

It's much the same story in the finance division with regard to hours and workload. There are various options: international banking, capital markets, project finance, trade finance and asset finance. This last team, for example, has had a big year in aircraft transactions, dealing with the $180 million export credit financing of two Airbus A330s for Turkish Airlines as well as a multibillion-dollar aircraft finance portfolio transfer for Natexis Banques Populaires. One of our sources had thoroughly enjoyed this seat and had been busy "*drafting security documents, checking conditions precedent and getting board resolutions together.*" The experience put them "*very much in the front line, dealing with clients on a day-to-day basis.*" Responsibility can come thick and fast in certain finance seats as, although you will "*never have to negotiate loan documents yourself,*" the deals are likely to see you "*discussing amendments to documents with the other lawyers, which means you have to defend the form of wording your client wants.*"

damages, costs, interest and world peace

An abundance of contentious sub-specialisms ensures that there are many different types of dispute resolution seats – corporate and financial disputes, product liability, IP, insurance, pensions, property and insolvency and fraud. The firm is currently acting for US pharmaceutical giant Merck in defence of threatened and actual claims related to the effects of its painkiller VIOXX. These matters allow the firm to flex its international credentials since a key issue is whether or not UK and European claimants are given permission to file proceedings in the US. Speaking of international credentials, Miss World Ltd turned to Lovells for representation on the successful defence, both at first instance and on appeal, of a claim by Angela Onyeador, a Nigerian art dealer and a financial backer of a gala dinner in London to celebrate the disastrous 2002 Miss World pageant in Nigeria. And, even if some at the firm would wish to, we mustn't forget the firm's lead role in the mammoth Equitable Life litigation which ended

poorly for its client in 2006. It is "*a mixed caseload*" indeed, and trainees get right in the thick of it, carrying out document review and disclosure exercises, helping to draft witness statements and attending conferences with counsel. Yes, you will "*occasionally*" be asked to trawl through some "*mundane things*" but as more than one source pointed out, "*sometimes it is nice to sit down and do something not too taxing.*" Even the things commonly referred to as classic trainee tasks – copying, paginating, indexing and bundling – can take on more excitement if they involve, for example, "*the nitty-gritty of evidence review and analysis involving forensic copies of hard drives.*"

The high-flying real estate department featured heavily in the seat schedules of our interviewees. Time in the department results in "*more responsibility for your own files and a steep learning curve,*" though there is a danger you might "*feel swamped when you first arrive.*" In time trainees come to view high levels of responsibility very positively and become used to "*dealing with clients on a daily basis,*" "*drafting documents and arguing with your opposite number about it.*" As well as getting to grips with their own smaller deals, trainees provide invaluable assistance on more major matters: things like the sale of Prudential's £318 million half-interest in Kent's Bluewater shopping centre. When all the hard work is done there is plenty of departmental socialising, with drinks events "*geekily*" scheduled around the traditional quarter days of the property calendar. FYI, that would be Lady Day, Midsummer Day, Michaelmas and Christmas.

off the leash

A stint with the IP team or in technology, media and telecoms (TMT), employment and pensions or competition will appeal to those with a penchant for the niche. And then there's the wealth of off-site seats. Around half the trainees will at some point take a seat abroad in one of the following locations: Brussels, Frankfurt, Milan, Hong Kong, New York, Paris, Singapore, Moscow and Tokyo. Those who don't go abroad can work for six months with a UK company – eg British American Tobacco, John Lewis, Egg, Barclays or Save The Children. This time away is invariably seen as *"exciting and rewarding,"* with trainees enjoying *"more responsibility than you would necessarily have in the firm's London office."*

Trainees tell us that across the firm *"supervision is always there"* but *"you are not really on anyone's leash."* We learned of genuine commitment on the part of the vast majority of supervisors: *"They always take time out to explain things to you, are concerned with your professional development and send interesting stuff your way."* In a big firm it's all too easy for trainees to be relegated to bottom-of-the-pile jobs, but our sources were confident that *"trainees do get the opportunity to get involved and do substantial work,"* albeit that *"it is up to you to show enthusiasm."* A full, formal training programme covers all the essential skills: contract drafting, working with others, etc, and the firm makes sure legal and market knowledge is up to date by laying on regular presentations and interactive workshops. These sessions are often scheduled at the start of the day so *"they give you breakfast, which gets everyone in the right mood."* A *"very useful"* performance review process consists of a *"fairly informal"* mid-seat appraisal coupled with a more substantial session at the end of each seat. *"Two-way feedback"* is encouraged.

take it to the 'bridge

It sounds like the training programme is hitting the right spot, but at big-picture level the firm has, through necessity, undergone a strategic rethink *"after a difficult time in 2004/05."* A new course is being steered towards a *"tightened and streamlined"* profile with *"a more aggressive approach to looking for work and clients"* and a renewed focus on *"communication with clients."* In essence this has arisen because Lovells just wasn't making headway with its plan to challenge the magic circle, at a time when some of its fellow players at just-below-magic-circle level were making ground. Profits have looked sluggish and some important partners have chosen to defect. To help nudge profits up the firm de-equitised certain partners and others were effectively shown the door. We heard a tale about a certain partner who simply never came back one day and their room remained untouched *"Miss Haversham-style"* for many weeks before its contents were eventually cleared. The general view in the City is that Lovells' management needs to work some magic and get the partners to produce better results overall. At junior end there is plenty of optimism: in September 2006, 33 of the 36 qualifiers accepted jobs with the firm.

We're told there isn't a typical Lovells lawyer. We think there is. Trainees say the firm recruits *"a fairly eclectic bunch with a range of personalities;"* that it *"wants interesting people working here."* The word *"nice"* was repeated extensively – indeed *"nobody is an absolute arsehole"* – and it *"doesn't do you to be too arrogant, overtly aggressive or a self-promotionalist."* Trainees conclude that *"bright, hard-working and confident"* yet *"unstuffy"* types should apply. They also talked of having *"involvement in initiatives to ensure the firm recruits from as wide a pool as possible."* And yet Lovells still has heavy Oxbridge leanings; more Oxford than Cambridge from what we can tell. In 2006 the firm decided to spend half a mill over the next five years on an Oxford University chair in law. For the record, in recent years the firm has recruited from around 20 UK universities and a handful of overseas ones. We checked the firm's online diversity figures (published in response to a request from government to the top 100 players): their incompleteness was disappointing, but the firm assures us that it will publish full details in time.

champagne and sawdust

Lovells' 12-storey offices at Holborn Viaduct have *"everything you need"* staff restaurant, extensive library, great admin support, giant sculpture in the atrium, that sort of thing. We're told that, socially, *"each department is good at involving trainees in things... we are not invisible;"* a comment that refers to client-targeted events as well as staff jollies. With local wine bar Bacchus right underneath the building and plenty of options nearby, popping out for a drink with team mates is no drama. The notorious and *"horrible bar, Bottlescrue,"* remains popular for some reason. *"It's great if you like sawdust on the floor and no choice of beer."* The annual firm-wide summer ball is always something to look forward to, and at the time of our research the *"photos were still circulating."* For the newest employees there are always plenty of *"trainee bonding events"* and *"a couple of heavily subsidised parties a year."* Sporting opportunities are equally as plentiful with the football, rugby and cricket fixtures just the start of things. Our interviewees were also keen to point out the extent of Lovells' charity efforts, currently coordinated under the 'Touch 2006' banner, in aid of alleviating child poverty around the world.

and finally...

"A broad church" of *"top-end"* work, high-calibre colleagues and great opportunities for travel make this an ideal firm for anyone wanting to try big-City law but also looking to keep their options open.

Lupton Fawcett LLP

the facts

Location: Leeds
Number of UK partners/solicitors: 30/14
Total number of trainees: 5
Seats: 4x6 months
Alternative seats: None

Pick Leeds firm Lupton Fawcett and you'll receive a solid training and the chance to get your mitts on work for some top-quality clients. This is a commercial firm with a real *"work-hard, play-hard attitude"* but it also has a fun personality.

monkey business

Lupton Fawcett focuses on private companies and work for high net worth individuals, although if you click on its website you'll see the names of a few giants including RAC and NatWest. Corporate is widely seen as the engine room of the firm with the department attracting a selection of quality clients. For example, the firm is on the legal panel for Serco, the FTSE 100 outsourcing giant. It also has an impressive range of banking clients – Citibank, Allied Irish and Lloyds TSB Commercial Finance to name but three. Furthermore, the firm is well regarded in the area of small and medium-sized corporate insolvency and bankruptcy and has dealt with several high-profile insolvencies. In one such matter it advised PwC in the bankruptcy of Stephen Hinchliffe, the former chairman of troubled retail group Facia, a company that got itself into all kinds of problems, not least with its landlords and the Serious Fraud Office. At Lupton Fawcett, this kind of pickle is everyday business for the corporate defence and prosecution group, which has received a substantial number of cases to prosecute from bodies such as the DTI, Leeds City Council, the RSPCA and the Health & Safety Executive.

The lawyers in the IP team are winning instructions from the likes of the UK engineering division of international giant Tyco, Hong Kong firework manufacturer Black Cat and international paper and packaging manufacturer Mondi. The litigation group has acted for tobacco company BAT and automotive engineering companies Federal Mogul and TI Automotive. A specialist group conducts litigation in the Chancery and Mercantile Courts, concentrating on partnership disputes.

big ideas

This is a modern firm, oozing with character (just check out the website if you don't believe us). Trainees tell us that there is *"a lot of eccentricity – in a good way,"* and that this makes the firm a *"fun place"* to work. But don't be fooled into thinking you can just coast along. The office has recently gone open plan following a *"rebranding and revamping,"* and this means there's nowhere to hide from your supervisor unless you're prepared to squat down behind the photocopier. The makeover is symptomatic of the firm's desire to go up in the world; it has worked out that the Leeds Big Six are looking further afield for work and that the next tier of firms can corner the market in local business. If you were to study the firm's client list in detail you'd see a preponderance of smaller but growing businesses, several of them in specialist areas of engineering and manufacturing. The firm believes that such businesses need a certain type of lawyer; one who can relate to their particular concerns and who perhaps also shares the same entrepreneurial spirit. If you'd be happier churning out the same old banking document for a large finance client that doesn't want to diverge from established procedures then try another firm.

It's not only the office layout that has changed; in 2005 the firm ditched its insurance litigation division to concentrate on grabbing a good share of the local corporate market. The recent push in private client services was not inconsistent with this, as the firm believes the way to a new client is very often through its boss. The other thing to mention about the grand plan is that no one has said out-and-out that Lupton Fawcett will never merge with another firm.

if all goes according to plan

With corporate, commercial litigation, property and insolvency providing the *"bread and butter work of the firm,"* trainees tend to gravitate towards these four core areas. As the trainee population increases more options will become available, but competition for popular IP and employment seats is likely to increase. For now, seats in the firm's family, private client and charity/social enterprises teams remain out of bounds, although the last of these has a substantial clientele of 100 charities and non-profit organisations.

Litigation and corporate are both *"fairly popular"* choices. Commercial litigation is *"very fast-paced"* and trainees can expect good work from the off, even *"attending court by yourself and making applications in front of district judges."* The insolvency team is *"loud and quite hard working"* and undertakes some *"fantastic work,"* while corporate has a *"work-hard and play-hard ethos"* even though *"the hours can be erratic."* Commercial property, although *"not overly popular,"* does allow trainees to cut their teeth negotiating leases for landlords and tenants, as well as dealing with lease surrenders and the sale of freehold properties. Save for the mad times in corporate, the hours are a *"reasonable"* 8.30am to 6pm.

Having a small trainee population means that when it comes to qualification there tends not to be a scramble for jobs. Moreover, the whole qualification process is done on quite an informal basis, helping to take some of the stress out of what can be an anxious time. In September 2006 one of the two qualifiers took jobs with the firm. As to what kind of trainee applicants the firm finds attractive, we sensed that most successful candidates have a strong connection to Leeds.

leed on, mcbeal

If you're looking to spruce up your flagging post-university social life then you'll find that Leeds is an assured pleasuredome of entertainment. Among trainees there was widespread agreement that the firm's social side is really rather good. By some great fluke, Lupton Fawcett is situated in *"one of the only office blocks in a street full of bars"* and, like a homage to surreal legal drama *Ally McBeal*, there is actually a bar below the office. Consequently, you can always *"just nip down to the bar"* whenever you fancy a drink, and quite a few people do, quite often. More than this, the firm is exceptionally good at organising post-work events – pub quizzes and departmental outings are regular and there's an annual rounders match and a big summer party. The last such event was held at the Royal Armouries on the canal front and featured a Caribbean barbecue complete with *"rum punch and the receptionists dressed up in Hawaiian shirts."* Christmas brings more parties, the full, firm-wide shindig being a black-tie affair in a grand hotel featuring a ludicrously cheap bar (just like back at uni). It's not all carousing; there are *"lots of sports events such as hockey, cricket and football."* Apparently there was a ladies' football team but it was *"disbanded through lack of interest."*

One small but unanimous gripe at this otherwise very happy ship concerns trainee salaries. Our interviewees felt that *"the salary isn't great"* compared to some of the local competition. They conceded that management had recently reviewed the situation and increased their pay after a show of trainee solidarity and one source cited this as an example of how the firm is *"open*

to ideas and suggestions from trainees and will hear you out." Of course the trainee's views must be considered in context: are they comparing their pay packets with the big firms in Leeds – the Eversheds, DLA Pipers or Addleshaws – or are they making comparisons with other smaller players like, say, Gordons or Lee & Priestley? Having checked with the firm, we can tell you that a trainee's starting salary is £19,000 – not far off some of those big players.

and finally…

This smooth commercial operator *"doesn't feel like it's a corporate machine,"* say trainees. One for Leeds-minded applicants in search of a *"personal and welcoming"* firm with good credentials and big aspirations.

Mace & Jones

the facts
Location: Liverpool, Manchester, Knutsford
Number of UK partners/solicitors: 39/50
Total number of trainees: 11
Seats: 4x6 months
Alternative seats: Secondments

By closing its small Huyton office and building up its city bases, North West player Mace & Jones has undergone a process of consolidation lately. As it eyes up the region for bigger and better business opportunities, will you share its vision?

moss side story
The legal sector in the North West has put on a spirited performance in recent years, taking advantage of the flurry of regeneration projects and development schemes that are transforming Manchester and Liverpool. Much of Manchester's city centre has been transformed and its housing and businesses given a timely injection.

Meanwhile its neighbour to the west is putting on the glitz for its role as 2008's European Capital of Culture. The M&J trainees we spoke to recognised all this and that their firm is *"definitely becoming more commercially motivated; we are always looking to expand the client base. It is an ambitious firm and there is a real chance to get involved."* We checked with our colleagues on *Chambers UK* and they told us M&J performs excellently in a number of different practice areas from family law and personal injury to commercial property, insolvency and commercial litigation.

Here's a quick run-through of some of M&J's recent highlights. The seven-partner corporate and commercial team has been busy with mergers and acquisitions, disposals and flotations, recently advising the sellers in the disposal of Bradford-based holiday company Sunmaster to Global Travel. The busy property group is active in a number of residential and commercial developments and regeneration schemes. It looked after Pochin's new 790-bedroom hall of residence to be let to Manchester Metropolitan University, and acted for the property developer Modus in the £50 million sale of Winsford Shopping Centre. It also acts for large well-known developers like Barratt Homes on *"everything from buying land to turning it into housing."* On the contentious side, major achievements include a group action in which 17 men won damages from their former employer after suffering an asbestos-related disease.

work like an egyptian

M&J's broad practice is ideal for the trainee as there are so many different types of experience on offer. The first six-month seat is chosen for them but after that they can indicate their preferences. The seats on offer are: coco, property, PI, family, employment, construction and dispute resolution. The firm seems to respond to feedback on seats. For example, trainees didn't used to spend any time in the smaller Knutsford office, but after popular demand (*"I told them just how much I enjoyed it"*) the firm has reinstated a split private client/family seat there.

Some seats are more likely to come up than others; for example, *"everyone seems to do property as it is definitely an area that needs trainees."* As the residential conveyancing department based in Knutsford is not a stop-off point, all property seats focus on commercial work. Not everyone we spoke to had enjoyed the seat; one for example found it *"a little too admin-based. There's so much work going through the department at any one time, yet some of the people higher up will just give all their post-completion stuff to you and sometimes it is repetitive."* Looking on the bright side, *"it's great for a first seat when you're finding your bearings. It was also good to find out how differently each fee earner approaches their work – some are very pedantic, some scrawl all over the files."* Despite the more routine elements of the work, the degree of first-hand involvement on deals is typically high in this seat. In between deciphering hieroglyphics, one trainee had helped to remortgage a caravan park and was pleased to be *"really involved in the process from the beginning."*

M&J has an excellent reputation for employment law and trainees entering this department stronghold will encounter a garrison of major employers like Littlewoods, the Highways Agency, Shell, Merseyside Police and the National Probation Service as well as high-earning executives. The group acted for Littlewoods Pools, with success, in a test case when a concession owner claimed he was an employee of the business. *"It was always one of my favourite areas at law school and I was worried it wouldn't be the same in practice, but I really enjoyed it,"* said one trainee. Others also found just what they were hoping for – *"being on the phone to clients all the time, and often out to external client meetings."*

The family team concentrates on divorce and ancillary relief, also undertaking private law children work from time to time. Some of the most complicated cases arise where clients' assets are distributed around the world. As family advice is dispensed in all three offices, trainees may be asked to flit between locations. "*I was a kind of floating trainee and often people didn't know where to find me,*" explained one; "*but after sitting in literally the same seat for six months it can be good to get out and about.*" Getting out and about often means hitting the courts and spending time on the hearings trail. "*You can be there all day, particularly in Liverpool where they have so much on their list. A lot of your work is babysitting the client, which I really enjoyed.*"

no spinning!

When we quizzed trainees about the competition for seats we were told: "*It's not so much that people don't get the seats they want, it's more to do with the Manchester/Liverpool issue. People think, 'I really don't want to do corporate in Liverpool when I live in Manchester and could do corporate here'.*" It's a fact of life at M&J that you will move between offices during your training contract, depending on the business needs of the firm. As such you need to consider the implications of a lengthy commute when you decide where to rent or buy a house or flat. "*To be honest, the travelling is a bit of a pain,*" reported one typical trainee. "*Obviously the firm lets you know you have to do seats wherever you are needed, but in practical terms it can be difficult.*" On the upside, trainees reported strong links between the cities and liked the feeling of belonging to "*the whole firm, not just an individual office.*"

The Manchester lawyers occupy a "*new swanky building*" at the best address on the block for "*shopping at lunchtimes and going out in the evening.*" Trainees like the open-plan layout and say the office is as sociable as ever. "*We are always doing things together and yes, we still go for drinks in All Bar One.*" In Liverpool M&J has an office behind the Liver Building – "*the outside looks very old fashioned but inside it's pretty okay.*" While speaking on the phone to one trainee we heard the distinctive cry of seagulls. "*Getting off the train and walking to the office is great; you get a glimpse of the Mersey and realise the sea is close by.*" After work, staff often unwind in the popular Newz bar or The Slaughterhouse. Knutsford, with a much smaller staff and a "*quiet, old-school style office,*" is undeniably the slowest of the three socially. Sometimes clients are drawn into post-work activities; for example an annual table football tournament is held in a bar in Manchester's Deansgate. Did it get competitive? "*Did it ever,*" said one trainee. "*We were reffing and it was pretty difficult. It was only a table football tournament for goodness sake but some of them got really heated and there were clients all shouting at each other... I was so not prepared for that... it was fun, though.*"

you're not from round here

"*I don't know if it is a deliberate policy but everyone is very down to earth; there is no competition between trainees to outdo each other,*" said one interviewee. That particular requirement may not appear on the recruitment pages of M&J's website but a commitment to the North West does. "*You definitely need roots here,*" was the overwhelming opinion, though we did hear of a few interlopers. "*I wonder how I slipped through,*" mused the stranger with two heads and a limp, who did admit to "*going on about how great the North West was throughout the entire interview. I really had to prove my loyalty.*" Wherever they are from, "*the most positive thing about the firm is the people. You can approach anyone for help; you're not left feeling like an idiot.*" You're also not a dogsbody. One trainee told us how "*a partner was having trouble with some concert tickets. I joked he should tell one of the Manchester trainees to go and get them. He was incensed and told me he didn't want to be one of those partners who behaves like an arse."* Although the firm has a reasonably conservative style, with no dress-down days and a somewhat top-heavy ratio of partners to assistants, the ethos is reportedly open and trainees spoke of it as an *"employee-centred firm."* Little wonder then that two of the three qualifiers took jobs with the firm on qualification in 2006.

and finally…

This regional law firm delivers on its promise of a broad commercial training. It has set up a new programme of work-experience placements, so if you're interested in finding out more we'd recommend getting in contact asap.

Macfarlanes

the facts

Location: London
Number of UK partners/solicitors: 68/141
Total number of trainees: 49
Seats: 4x6 months
Alternative seats: Secondments,
Extras: Pro Bono — Cambridge House Advice Centre, death row appeals; language training

Small in size, tightly focused and famed for its corporate practice, this City thoroughbred is among the best in class. As a trainee you may have to do some mucking out, but in terms of the quality of the training there's not the whiff of manure you might expect to find down at the cheaper stables.

best in class

Headed up by a senior partner who is renowned for chomping cigars during meetings, Macfarlanes is viewed as a conservative place with an idiosyncratic strategy. We heard that there was some internal debate between the old guard and

the younger partners about expanding beyond its current limits, but for the time being it seems the firm is happy to carry on doing what it does best – high-calibre domestic work.

Most of the trainees we spoke to had looked at, but decided against, the magic circle. It's not that they feared hard graft on heavyweight corporate transactions, after all *"corporate makes up 50% of Macfarlanes' work."* Trainees choose the firm because they're attracted to the Macfarlanes package: they like its size, its character, and the emphasis on quality. Apparently, *"they talk about quality all the time – it's hammered into you from the first day."* Another thing that had influenced our sources was the idea that *"you definitely get more responsibility here."* One recalled with pride: *"On my first day in my first seat I was given a property file to complete by the end of the week."* Being part of a smaller outfit puts you closer to the frontline and places you in all kinds of meetings with partners. Said one trainee: *"I have friends in the magic circle who have longer hours and less responsibility. They don't get to build up the same relationships with people."* At Macfarlanes you're more likely to be confused with an assistant solicitor than a teaboy.

A pretty standard rotation puts trainees through corporate, something contentious (either litigation or employment) and property, with a fourth seat in a more specialised corporate or private client seat. Those really keen on a particular seat are advised to be assertive. Apparently, *"the best thing to do is make informal phone calls to HR."*

taxi!

In the current busy corporate market our interviewees had been exposed to *"lots of private equity work – buying businesses for clients and then helping them to exit. It's interesting because they do imaginative things in the way they structure the deals."* By contrast, the public company deals one trainee worked on *"involved a lot more rules and regulation."* The firm recently acted on two large flotations on the main London market, acting for selling shareholders on the IPOs of Partygaming plc (initial market cap £4.6 billion) and Britvic plc (initial market cap £500 million). In both private and public spheres trainees must be prepared to take the rough with the smooth. *"I really enjoyed closing a private equity fund a few months into my seat... but having to sit in a data room was pretty tedious."* Admin work is *"a necessary evil, but it doesn't happen that often"* as most of it goes to the paralegals. Yet even with their help, trainees say *"the corporate department needs more assistants."*

When telling us about mainstream corporate, one trainee had us chuckling. *"I'm not sure what I did there – it was all a blur of early mornings, late nights, and taxi rides home in the early hours."* Another had a similar story. *"Corporate hours were hard, it was 12 hours each day."* But there is pleasure to go with the pain. One corporate junkie had enjoyed closing deals – *"you do get a rush from buying or selling a company."* For another source corporate brought an amusing, if cringe-worthy, low point: *"I said what I thought of a team on the other end of the phone when I thought they were on hold, when in fact they were on loud speaker."* Ooops!

Busy teams need good monitoring systems, and at Macfarlanes these look to be in place. *"In our group we get together to discuss anything that comes up,"* said one trainee. *"It's an opportunity for you to let people know if you're swamped or quiet."* In some quarters a weekly form-based assessment lets you tell the world how you're feeling. Remember it's *"R for Ready, B for Busy and V for Very Busy."* They didn't teach you that on Sesame Street.

a shock to the system

Property was universally felt to be a shock to the system, albeit *"a good shock... you really feel like a lawyer."* Trainees find it *"very client-facing... I was the main point of contact for some clients and had 30-odd files to run."* By comparison, private client work is less outward-facing, at least for trainees.

"The firm has established clients who expect continuity, so you just do the work behind the scenes." This translates into *"lots of research, drafting wills and trusts, and some charities and immigration work."*

One trainee who had sometimes twiddled his thumbs during a litigation seat told us: *"I had the bad luck to be there at a quiet time, but when the work's there they are good at giving you a chance to try different things."* In employment a source had been *"really thrown in at the deep end. I was drafting employment contracts and pre-action disclosure letters as well as taking documents to counsel and to court."* During a stint in financial services, trainees come up against specialist corporate law, for example *"setting up institutional retail funds and establishing fund vehicles for private equity firms."* In this small group, *"the partners are supportive."* It's the same story in competition law, where you can become *"well involved"* from early on. Recently the team worked on a big competition enquiry for Ottakar's the book retailer. Across the departments there are plenty of trainee seminars and updates, so no chance of missing new law or important practice developments.

If you're desperate to get away for a foreign seat be aware that this is not the firm for you. There are, however, regular secondments to 3i.

clever clogs

Macfarlanes lawyers are *"sharp"* and *"perfectionist."* One trainee opined: *"We have a reputation for being rigorous... but without being as fierce as, say, Slaughter and May. It's a more pleasant place to work."* Another told us: *"I was at a collegiate rather than campus university, and I was attracted to the collegiate nature of the firm."* Trainees here are *"very clever – there's a high number of Firsts. People are confident in themselves and they tend to be the types who seriously want to be lawyers, rather than just doing it because it sounds sensible."* Of course this doesn't preclude people from being *"pleas-*

ant, *friendly and well mannered,*" which is exactly how the trainees strike us each year. If you want to find out more about the types who are recruited then look at Macfarlanes' website, where the trainees are all profiled. "*We're quite a sporty bunch,*" admitted one, "*but within that there is individuality. In my year there's a ballet dancer, a Scottish country dancer and a rugby player.*"

The firm's website asserts: "We don't set out to find (or create) a Macfarlanes type." And yet the majority of trainees do seem to fit in with a certain stereotype. One trainee accepted the charge, saying: "*It's true that it's largely white, middle class, Oxbridge or Redbrick,*" and in that regard it's probably no different from many City establishments. Once through the door trainees find "*the place is like a family; they are protective of you, in a good way. It's reassuring to know that they want to keep you on and they want you to succeed here.*"

The family that bills together chills together. Macfarlanes' social scene is healthy and inclusive, with local pub The Castle always a safe bet on a Friday night. Around the time of our interviews trainees were preparing for a dinner in the Cavalier & Guards Club. When asked to divulge what went on behind closed doors one trainee confessed: "*We basically get a private room and drink as much wine as possible.*" When asked for suggestions for improvements to the firm, one trainee stuck with matters social and said: "*I would make the firm's ball every two years rather than every four.*" The last ball was "*an amazing thing at Old Billingsgate Market, with the Cirque du Soleil performing and indoor fireworks.*" The only persistent grumbles relate to Macfarlanes' offices, which are perennially described as "*slightly shabby.*" Trainees agree, "*it would be nice to have everyone under one roof rather than spread across multiple sites;*" and even the most stoical of our sources admitted "*the facilities are a bit lacking. Lots of people now cycle or run into work so it would be nice to have better showers.*" Hardly cause for an uprising...

and finally...

If you're lucky enough to win a Macfarlanes training contract you're in for a full-bore, adrenaline-rich two years. The only real danger is that you might love the place so much that the idea of leaving becomes too much to bear. Thankfully, the firm has a habit of retaining practically everyone on qualification, and 2006 was no different – all 21 qualifiers took NQ positions.

Manches LLP

the facts

Location: London, Oxford
Number of UK partners/solicitors: 58/61
Total number of trainees: 23
Seats: 4x6 months
Alternative seats: Occasional secondments

London and Oxford firm Manches is a mid-sizer with a difference. Its commercial practice groups are accompanied by a spectacularly successful family law department that is ranked number one by our parent publication *Chambers UK*. If you enjoy the diary pages as much as the City pages of your newspaper and you want the chance to work with people as well as profits, this is a must-apply-to firm.

an offer you can't refuse

In the 1930s, Manches was founded by the father of Jane Simpson and Louis Manches, respectively the firm's chairman and its London managing partner. As intriguing as this may sound, especially considering that a third-generation family member also works as a lawyer, Manches should not be viewed as a family business in any sense of the word.

The last two years have been an exceptionally busy time for the firm – already expansive, it has recruited new partners and completed a small merger. A whole team of family lawyers arrived from London rival Reynolds Porter Chamberlain, the 12-lawyer London firm Marshall Ross & Prevezer was bolted on, and a total of eight other people checked in from the likes of Lovells, Farrers and Kendall Freeman.

It is Manches' diversity that usually draws trainees in. One typical source explained: "*I wanted a commercial firm that could sponsor me through law school and could also give me the opportunity to do a seat in family law.*" If this goal sounds familiar you'll soon learn that your London options are limited, and if you score at Manches you simply don't refuse the offer. We don't mean that in a swimming-with-the-fishes sense, of course.

Yet you don't have to aspire to family law for this to be a realistic choice. Speaking from experience, one trainee insisted: "*Never assume that you will have to do family. People's perception of this place does come with a huge burden of family work, with maybe a few other things below that. It used to be true historically but not any longer... in property, for example, we are ranked very highly and have a lot of really good work for retail clients, investors and banks.*" The IP/technology and media department seems equally as popular these days, and with clients such as Oxford Gene Technology, the JRR Tolkien Estate and The National Trust, it's no wonder. We probably shouldn't even mention the Hook Norton Brewery and Compass Box Delicious Whiskies for fear of a stampede.

hot property

A typical London training will involve time in family with the remaining three seats chosen from property, corporate, employment, construction, commercial litigation and IP/tech/media. Property is arguably the core of the firm, and here an impressive list of clients includes restaurant and retail chains Pizza Hut, Jigsaw, Karen Millen, Liberty and Hugo Boss, plus various banks and British American Tobacco. This ensures an endless supply of trainee work for shops and other premises up and down the country. "*With retail clients you get a high volume of smaller deals, and trainees often find themselves finishing off partners' files, which actually teaches you a lot about the deal. It's good to be able to tie it all up at the end on your own, especially if you go to the initial meeting with the client.*" Trainees don't always work on one-off transactions: "*On the large projects and deals there are always smaller off-shoots which come up, and these little things are really good for trainees to deal with.*" The department is led by the characterful Louis Manches and includes "*several big personalities.*" It is said to be the most sociable department: "*There are always a few people in the pub on Fridays... and sometimes on Thursdays too.*"

Opportunities to focus on decent tasks and make face-to-face contact with clients are found across the firm. In commercial litigation, for example, trainees accompany supervisors at client meetings and barristers at court hearings, as well as having a go at drafting letters, claims, defences and witness statements. "*Occasionally you have to do it, but I hardly did any bundles,*" one source assured us. Manches has an interesting bag of cases and a nice line in tricky overseas disputes involving elements of fraud or the seizure of assets. In one such matter the firm has been acting against an Australian airline in a misrepresentation claim concerning a jumbo jet chartered on behalf of the president of Cameroon. The legal action saw the plane detained and an application made for its seizure while on the ground in Indonesia.

love will tear us apart

Every department has its own personality and none more so than the esteemed family department, which, over the years, has featured in various landmark cases. "*Manches is famous for family, and there's a good reason for that,"* one source summed up. Clients commonly have much at stake when they divorce and there are a lot of international, cross-jurisdictional cases. Marital finances feature large, with one trainee estimating a 60:40 split between cases concerning cash and those concerning children. *"If you made it clear you wanted more of one than the other, they will listen,"* but whichever type of case you most enjoy, the exacting standards of the department must be met and client contact remains constant. *"If you don't enjoy client contact then don't do family,"* announced one trainee. *"You go to a lot of meetings and court hearings, and as a result you do a lot of attendance notes and bundle preparation."* The human drama in family work makes the seat a fascinating experience. Yes, there are long hours, but there are also stories to amaze or depress, depending on your view of life, love and relationships. One fan told us: *"I came home from work every day saying 'Oh my God!' but rarely found it depressing. A lot of it is like watching a soap opera."* Apparently the department itself can sometimes feel that way too.

"You must have heard about Alex Carter Silk?" one trainee asked when telling us about the IP/tech/media department. Naturally we had; he is famous for his advice to Elle McPherson concerning her underwear empire and his work on all sorts of interesting IP and defamation issues. *"The department takes on Alex's flavour, just as the property department takes on Louis' flavour... they're both quite dominant and charismatic,"* thought one source. Another agreed: *"Each team or department has its own personality, which perhaps no one here apart from the trainees realises."*

essential viewing

Trainees receive regular know-how top ups and three-monthly appraisals. Halfway through a seat the appraisals are *"pretty short and informal, but there's a longer one at the end with your old supervisor and your new one. It's not too bad having the three of you together like that; you can use it to ask questions and find out how the next seat is going to differ."* Overall the trainees say Manches is a supportive firm where trainees are taken seriously. Although most reported having worked some long nights and a few weekends, *"only rarely are trainees overburdened."* People spoke of building up good relationships at all levels, which makes it *"easy to go for a beer with a partner or solicitors who are a few years qualified."* The firm's style is said to be *"straightforward,"* and the trainees themselves are not the type to need a handhold. They think they are *"quite individual... usually people have had some kind of life before the firm."* Many are non-law graduates; most had attended prestigious universities; all had avoided the big City firms. For them *"Manches is definitely an alternative to the City."* One concluded: *"It's not your typical West End property firm, but neither is it a totally progressive Eversheds-style firm where they take on new ideas all the time. It falls somewhere between the two. It definitely retains some of the old-school character, which you feel when you walk out onto the Aldwych at lunchtime and you're the lawyer in the suit, but then a lot of the partners are quite young and that creates a modern feel."*

The London office on the Aldwych is an expensive piece of real estate, and the implication is that Manches would be more profitable if it had a different address, but there's something intrinsically Manches about the grand building next to the LSE and close to Covent Garden. Tourists and students fill the streets, though apparently you can tell when term ends because there are no queues in Starbucks. Every quarter the firm hosts a subsidised drinks evening in a local pub, and each Christmas it throws a fancy bash at a grand venue. However, the biggest highlight of the social calendar is the annual Manches Cup sailing regatta at Cowes. Some 800 barristers and solicitors competed in 2006 and, for the first time, the event was televised by Sky Sports.

training with a paw-pose

Manches' Oxford office is now located on the Oxford Business Park just south of the city. It takes two or three trainees each year and offers them an excellent variety of work considering its size and location away from the capital. First years encounter corporate and litigation while second years get to choose two seats from family, IP/tech/media, property and employment. The office has some cracking clients and a strong reputation among publishing companies (Blackwell, OUP, MacMillan), schools, colleges and universities in Oxford and beyond, and housing associations. The office is pushing hard to build its name in the area of biotechnology and has advised many companies that have spun out of the University of Oxford. Last year, for example, lawyers acted for Oxford Immunotec, a T-cell diagnostic company, when it raised £7 million of funding.

From a trainee perspective there seems little crossover between the two offices; nevertheless it was clear from our conversations with the Oxford recruits that their training contained ample variety and they had access to better work than they had expected. Life in Oxford does not sound that different to life in London: trainees are given excellent responsibility, work consistently hard and occasionally late, are able to get on well with their seniors and note clear dividing lines and stylistic differences between departments, which are like *"separate little kingdoms."*

Let's end on an interesting tail. Oxford lawyers gave IP advice to Classic Media, the company that owns the rights to Lassie, the canine beloved by generations and last year resurrected in a remake of 'Lassie Come Home'. With various authors, and of course the Tolkien Estate, as clients it sounds as if there's always a good story to be told, shaggy dog or otherwise. In September 2006, six of the ten qualifiers (five in London and one in Oxford) took NQ positions with the firm.

and finally...

Manches is home to some of the best family lawyers in the UK, but also has a wealth of excellent lawyers in commercial disciplines. For a training experience with more quirks than the average contract, this is an excellent choice.

Maples Teesdale

the facts

Location: London
Number of UK partners/solicitors: 9/9
Total number of trainees: 6
Seats: 2x6 months + 3x4 months
Alternative seats: None
Extras: Pro bono – LawWorks

Did you enjoy land law at university? Are you inspired by flying freeholds and reversionary leasehold interets? Would you like to work in a small London property firm? If so, Maples Teesdale will be right up your street.

property, property, property

Founded in 1782 Maples Teesdale is now known as a property boutique specialising in investment, development and landlord and tenant management. It can't compete with the City's heavyweights for size and volume of real estate transactions; however, five out of its nine partners came to the firm from just one such giant – Norton Rose – and some impressive new client wins have attracted attention in the Square Mile. The firm recently worked on the £27 million sale of Woolworths' distribution centre in Swindon and acted for offshore private investors on the purchase of a £10 million hotel and restaurant development in Leeds. One trainee revealed: *"Our strategy is to become THE niche property firm."*

Maples Teesdale isn't the sort of firm that trainees find themselves at by accident. Those we spoke to had all done their homework very thoroughly: "*I did a lot of Internet research before applying because I wanted to find a property specialist that would suit me,*" said one. "*Everyone here is interested in property – I don't think you would get a job here if you weren't.*" As one sage advises: "*It is a mistake to apply for a niche firm like this if you haven't made up your mind about the type of law you want to practice.*"

Let's assume you know your own mind and it's screaming 'Apply!' "*If you are genuinely interested, the amount of experience you'll get here doesn't even compare to that of other firms – it's miles better.*" One interviewee told us: "*We have our own files and consistently get good-quality work. My friends in the real estate departments of other firms would have no idea how to handle the type of work I do.*" As for other practice areas, "*obviously we have other departments, like construction, but they all complement the property work somehow.*" So, for example, the corporate team assists property clients and the litigation team primarily handles contentious property matters. The idea being that "*by the end of your four seats you have a snapshot of all things property-related, all the way up to post-deal matters.*"

Trainees sit with a partner or senior lawyer so "*any issues can be aired as they arise*" and their progress can be closely monitored. In fact, in the absence of dedicated grad recruitment personnel it is a partner who takes charge of all trainee matters. Seats are currently on offer in commercial property, residential property, construction, corporate and litigation. The idea is for all trainees to experience each of the departments and the firm has shown itself to be flexible where a trainee finds an area of work that really interests them.

In commercial property, typical tasks include "*drafting small leases and licences*" and "*helping with the refinancing of big developments.*" The construction department is "*quite small*" but has plans to develop. The regular trainee diet consists of "*lots of warranties,*" until you get enough experience to appreciate the bigger picture. In their litigation seat, a trainee will handle some of the many smaller scale cases floating around the department. Disputes over leases, debt collection; it all means a good dose of court time. In the corporate seat the transactions are typically larger property-related matters, although one source did insist on telling us: "*We do a bit of normal corporate work here too.*" Trainees commonly provide general assistance to a partner on funding agreements and joint ventures.

something old, something new...

According to our interviewees, Maples Teesdale has "*a long history but a modern outlook*" and "*straddles old and new very well.*" The office is situated in Lincoln's Inn Fields, a very picturesque part of legal London. Specifically, it is "*round the top of the square where there are also lots of barristers' chambers.*" Trainees say: "*It is actually quite nice coming to work here; it makes you feel like you are really part of the legal profession.*" Another source enthused: "*We have a beautiful listed building to work in, and lunch outside in the grounds during the summer is lovely.*" Interviewees also highlighted the fact that the location is "*very handy for court visits,*" with an added bonus being its proximity to Covent Garden.

The office occupies space in two of the big town houses on the square. Apparently No 21 is "*very olde worlde*" as you enter, but "*once you come into the working parts of the firm it is much more modern.*" We heard that "*some of the clients have been with the firm for hundreds of years*" and also that one partner's father and grandfather worked for the firm. On the wall there is a chart of the firm's progression and trainees told us: "*We still have all the old books from the 1800s.*" Despite a clear sense of pride in Maples Teesdale's long establishment, the emphasis on the firm's past is pretty understated. Even though it is "*over 200 years old,"* one interviewee assured us, *"the firm's history isn't rammed down our throats."* As another pointed out: *"We all seem to be more interested in where the firm is going than what it has been."*

good sports

"The trainees get on like a house on fire; we all go for lunch together three or four times a week." There are also regular impromptu social gatherings *"after work with associates, to which everyone is invited."* A netball team has recently formed and *"one of the male partners has even got involved."* We rather like the sound of the *"old-fashioned schools sports day"* which took place shortly before our interviews. Much to the amusement of bystanders, there were egg-and-spoon and three-legged races across Lincoln's Inn Fields. These childish capers were followed by grown-up drinks and dinner. As well as an annual summer party there is also a Christmas bash organised each year by the second-year trainees.

New recruits are quickly integrated into the Maples Teesdale clan. If you take a look at the firm's website, not only will you find individual pages for each of the trainees but a family tree-style diagram showing their place within the firm. *"One of the main benefits of coming to a firm this size is that you are genuinely, genuinely part of the team,"* explained a source. *"You actually make a difference and that makes you feel good."* In September 2006, one of the two qualifiers opted to stay with the firm.

and finally…

We can't overemphasise the importance of an interest in property law – or the property world – to anyone considering an application to Maples Teesdale. If you can tick the property box, and if being a name not a number is important to you, you are unlikely to be disappointed with your choice.

Martineau Johnson

the facts

Location: Birmingham, London
Number of UK partners/solicitors: 42/80
Total number of trainees: 19
Seats: 6x4 months
Alternative seats: Occasional secondments
Extras: Pro bono – The Prince's Trust

Following a move to plush modern offices in 2005, this firm is trying to break free of its previously staid image. From what trainees say, it's not doing too badly.

brave new world

Two years ago we witnessed a minor exodus of partners from Martineau Johnson, and significantly it included some of the big names in the firm's specialist practices, namely IP, energy, education and pensions. It was as if management had opened the window to let in some fresh air, fully aware that a few people might leap (or fall) out in the process. Interestingly, the departures came at much the same time as a major office move and a shift in working patterns. This year there are signs that MJ has benefited from a period of consolidation and is now in a position to look at further growth for some of its established specialist practices. A good example is the reinvigoration of the pensions team following the recruitment of Mario Conti from Nabarro Nathanson with a remit to rebuild the group virtually from scratch.

Although *"moving offices was a bit of an upheaval at the time,"* Martineau was undoubtedly wise to make the investment; trainees say everyone has finally *"settled down well."* They imply that the firm is now ready to have a go at building on its position in the competitive Birmingham market, this time with *"room to grow."* According to trainees *"the firm is certainly expanding;"* they also say a switch to open-plan working has changed the firm's culture. For example, *"with different departments on the same floor"* lawyers are finding it *"much easier to disseminate information."* From a trainee's perspective it's certainly ideal, as *"although you might have thought twice about knocking on someone's door, it's pretty easy to just walk up to their desk."*

university challenges

On arriving at the firm, new trainees discover an embarrassment of riches in terms of seat choices. Most find it a blessed relief that there is a six-seat system as this allows them to see more of the firm than they would with a typical four-seat model. As one trainee explained: *"There are plenty of opportunities to find out where you'll be happy in the long term."* Naturally there are rules about what you can choose, the most obvious of which is the fact that *"they like you to do property."* Additionally, everybody we spoke to had spent time in corporate, so we'd suggest you regard that as nigh-on compulsory too. However, that still leaves four seats to fill with whatever takes your fancy, not forgetting that one must be contentious as per Law Society rules.

You might want to consider spending time in some of the areas that have long been regarded as MJ's strong suits. In education law, for example, it represents an impressive number of institutions in higher education. Aston University, Nottingham Trent University, Cardiff University and The College of Law are all on the books, and the firm recently won a tender to be sole legal adviser to Bournemouth University from under the noses of various national competitors. The education law department also takes care of further education colleges situated all over the country. It's not only the education team that deals with the universities; they seek counsel from lawyers in the employment department too. That group has recently dispensed advice and representation to the universities of Warwick, Plymouth and Lin-coln, with typical scenarios being the defence of claims for unfair or constructive dismissal, breach of contract, disability discrimination or victimisation. One case involved all these aspects and culminated in an 11-day Employment Tribunal. Trainees encounter education clients in yet more of the firm's specialist departments – health and safety and IT to name just two.

selling pollution

MJ has long-established relationships with landed gentry and estates in the West Midlands and beyond. For them the main draw is MJs' excellent agriculture and rural affairs department, which can advise on anything from tax and inheritance planning to leases of land. Some trainees come to the firm *"because of the reputation of the private client department,"* knowing that not every commercial firm still does this kind of work. Trainees in the private client seat get bags of drafting experience on wills and trust documents, and certainly have their minds stretched by tax calculations, intricate research and trust administration. Another interesting specialism is IP which trainees say is defined by *"loads of responsibility and challenging work."*

There are two further specialist areas to mention, not least because the firm is targeting them as part of its overall strategy for growth. In the area of banking and funds work, the firm represents clients such as Lloyds TSB, RBS, HSBC, Harrods Bank and Bank of Ireland. In the area of energy/utilities it is giving both general commercial advice and very specific advice. On the one hand it is advising British Energy on the general review of its energy contracts, and on the other it is advising one of the world's leading carbon-trading companies in relation to its emission reduction purchase agreements under the Kyoto flexibility mechanisms.

If you are in any way concerned that four months is not long enough to get your teeth into any of these specialist areas of practice, then take comfort from the fact it is possible to double up in a seat. We even heard of some trainees *"spending a year in a seat if they really liked it."*

a good deal

But what of mainstream practice areas? The *"fantastic"* corporate department provides trainees with *"a steep learning curve,"* getting them *"quite heavily involved in drafting board minutes and small agreements."* Our interviewees found that *"if you showed an interest then the supervisors would involve you in the whole matter,"* and as it's a relatively compact department it was easy to *"really feel part of the team."* Typically, trainees have *"a small part in three or four deals rather than getting 200 of your own files like in property."* The only downside is that it can be a little bit *"feast or famine"* in this seat. Then again, corporate was highlighted as one of the most sociable departments as *"here the partners drag you to the pub."* In the guaranteed property seat your own caseload of files will cover lease renewals, small planning issues and title investigation in order to register land. One of the best aspects is *"seeing a case all the way through to completion."* The other side of the job involves helping senior lawyers on big deals, one recent example being the sale of a shopping centre in the south of England for £93 million.

If four months in the capital appeals, then there's a small London office that concentrates on banking litigation, private client, property and environmental law. Although a banking litigation seat can be taken in Birmingham, we heard particularly good reports of the London posting, where trainees can be *"left to run with things,"* even appearing at the High Court and in county courts in front of masters and district judges. The firm offers accommodation and a salary uplift to those visiting London, so *"it's possible to actually be better off"* for the four months.

mucking in

As any young Birmingham lawyer will tell you, the city's Trainee Solicitors Society plays a big part in the professional and social lives of each new generation of lawyers. The *"social side is massive here,"* trainees told us, stressing that the firm encourages active participation in the group and its various sporting and social events. An annual inter-firm sports competition takes in a dozen different events including football, netball, water polo, pub games and Ultimate Frisbee. *"The firm likes us to compete and show our presence,"* remarked one source. At the time we spoke to them, trainees were still buzzing from their overall victory in 2005, though admittedly they were lying in third place in the 2006 contest.

Described as a *"dirty gem"* by one trainee, The Queens Head, just around the corner from the office, is a popular haunt that alternates its Friday-night entertainment between karaoke and a disco. The group of trainees we spoke to are apparently acknowledged as being a particularly *"close-knit bunch"* by everyone at the firm. It's a trait the trainees happily admit to and they tell us they have no issue with *"mucking in together when the need arises."*

Actually it's not only among trainees that there's a sense of good will: in 2006 MJ was once again ranked in *The Sunday Times'* '100 Best Companies to Work For' survey. Perhaps it's the free massages that are available in the office. Perhaps it's the simple fact that most of the people we spoke to left the office at some point between 5pm and 6pm, depending on which department they were sitting in (although like at so many other firms there is the risk of late nights in corporate). *"It's a big commercial firm but one that doesn't want to work you until 11pm every night,"* they explained. One source understood that the good hours and cosy atmosphere *"might make the firm look a bit soft around the edges to competitors,"* but no one would have it any other way. *"It is a relaxed place to work, we leave at a reasonable time, the senior staff are very approachable and you don't have to bite your tongue all the time like you might elsewhere."* No one's saying it's an easy ride; *"you do have to knuckle down,"* if only because you don't want to get to qualification and look like you're still wandering aimlessly around the firm. In September 2006 ten of the 12 NQs stayed with the firm.

and finally...

This mild-mannered Brum firm *"doesn't have the cut and thrust of the City,"* but not everyone wants to experience that. What is offered is exposure to broad commercial practice, expertise in several niche areas of law, great clients and a positive working environment.

Mayer Brown Rowe & Maw LLP

the facts
Location: London
Number of UK partners/solicitors: 100/162
Total number of trainees: 59
Seats: 4x6 months
Alternative seats: Overseas seats, secondments
Extras: Pro bono – RCJ CAB, Toynbee Hall Legal Advice Centre, Liberty, LawWorks; language training

Mayer Brown Rowe & Maw is one of the world's biggest legal services providers, with 16 offices in six countries. Opportunities for trainees to get involved in international work and travel are growing all the time.

brains and brawn
In 2002 London's Rowe & Maw merged with Chicago big gun Mayer Brown & Platt, which already had a compact finance law operation in our capital. At the time this raised a few eyebrows but four years down the line the vestiges of both old firms have ebbed away to reveal an altogether more impressive animal. When we asked them to help us classify the beast, trainees reminded us: *"We're supposed to call it an international law firm rather than an American one. You get the feeling it's an equal partnership rather than the US arm being heavier."* They added: *"It has the global clout of somewhere like Baker & McKenzie – it's a real heavyweight – but on the ground in London you don't feel like you're in a monster company."*

The firm does well in a multitude of disciplines, and many of its clients are household names – Reuters, Motorola, BP, EMI, Selfridges, Bank of America and Cable & Wireless to name a few. Some of its more glamorous work from the past year includes libel and privacy advice to Alastair Campbell's colleague Lance Price on his political autobiography *The Spin Doctor's Diary*, and trade mark advice to Cadbury Schweppes concerning the distinctive colour purple on its chocolate wrappers. The well-respected capital markets team advised new client ABN AMRO on the $550 million synthetic CDO programme for the restructuring of ABN's North Sea Funding arbitrage conduit (yes, we're bamboozled too), while the corporate finance team advised Danske Bank – Denmark's largest – on its £967 million agreement to buy Northern Bank and National Irish Bank from National Australia Bank. Transactions featuring seemingly endless zeroes in the price tag are increasingly the norm.

broadening your horizons
Many trainees arrive at the firm with an open mind as to what they want to achieve, and the firm is reported to be similarly open-minded in its recruitment, such that *"if you haven't come straight from university it won't count against you as long as you can demonstrate that whatever time off you had helped you in some way."* A firm with international reach will always be a magnet for people wishing to work abroad and/or use for-

eign languages, and for now a few trainees get to go to Brussels for six months or to two newly created finance seats in Chicago. As you might expect the latter are more in demand than a golden ticket to Willy Wonka's chocolate factory. Those who miss out have to wait until the newly qualifieds' group trip to the Windy City, to celebrate the end of their training and meet their US counterparts.

Now for our tour of the seats, which we'll start in the firm's corporate engine room, as it is the only compulsory stop-off point. In previous years, trainees have complained about the levels of grunt work, but maybe their comments have been taken on board. More of this year's interviewees were satisfied with their experiences, though undoubtedly the levels of responsibility in the seat do still vary according to how long a trainee has been at the firm. A first seat in corporate can be *"mind-numbingly boring – I've spent the last month indexing documents;"* however, those in corporate during their second or subsequent seat spoke of better work. *"There are the typical trainee things like managing data rooms, cataloguing documents and arranging redactions,"* but you may also get decent roles on *"share sales and joint ventures."* Trainees admit that *"in your first seat people treat you like a first-seater wherever you are; you always get the most boring tasks. But in a way you appreciate that as you're fairly nervous and don't want to mess things up."* They also readily admit that the corporate department is famous for *"good levels of banter and camaraderie,"* and that *"trainees who get stuck in"* are noticed and appreciated.

standard fare

To an extent, it's a similar story in commercial dispute resolution, where *"trainees are sometimes looked upon as a research tool, behind the scenes."* The people we spoke to had encountered *"a lot of paperwork,"* which may be down to the fact that in the past the department suffered from a lack of paralegals, hence a profusion of admin jobs. *"Sometimes I was itching to take on a bit more responsibility,"* recalled one trainee. While the firm appears to have taken steps to reduce the amount of grunt work for trainees, including hiring five more paralegals, some say there is still more it could do. *"They have to make sure the work is varied. People don't mind having a god-awful task one week, as long as they can do something interesting the next."* When it comes along, interesting work takes the form of sitting in on arbitrations, drafting amendments to claim forms and affidavits, conferences with counsel and writing client letters. The department remains a popular choice for qualification as it benefits from *"a real team atmosphere,"* and handles billions of pounds' worth of claims each year. One of the most interesting and well-publicised matters the department took on lately was for Ken Livingstone when the Standards Board for England investigated certain comments he made to a journalist for the *Evening Standard* newspaper.

Finance is a daunting but rewarding seat choice. *"I was given such a lot of responsibility that I was crying out for some photocopying in the first two months, but in hindsight I learned loads."* Trainees encounter various types of loan deals, and are charged with preparing shareholder resolutions and meeting clients to get them to sign documents. We spoke to fans of the insurance and reinsurance litigation seat, which is characterised by autonomy and independence for trainees. Said one: *"Not only did I get really good work to do, but I was left to do it by myself, which was a real high point."* The work involves a lot of document review and case preparation, and one trainee *"had a hand in preparing the terms of engagement for an arbitration and got to go to several client meetings."* The department is *"incredibly friendly, though very busy. With no culture of staying late, this means that between 9am and 7pm you're flat out."* As it works from the firm's smaller Lloyd's office in the City's insurance heartland, *"you do feel a bit separated from the rest of the firm, and you need to make an effort to go back on a Friday night."*

secondment opinions

The pensions team found favour, as did the construction team, in both cases because trainees felt very involved with the work despite its complexity. Said one: *"I've been working on major projects in the Gulf, which has been really exciting."* International arbitration, employment, real estate, IP, tax and environmental law are also on offer. In the past, some trainees were drawn to the firm because of its reputation for public law matters. Nowadays anyone hankering after this will find it under the umbrella of commercial dispute resolution, where there is one training seat that touches on public law issues. The department took on a newly qualified in 2005 and was not looking to recruit another in 2006, so don't get your hopes up too much.

A complicated but thorough appraisal system involves to-ing and fro-ing between trainees, supervisors, HR and back again, ticking boxes and providing feedback left, right and centre. Done on a monthly basis, it helps everyone see how they are progressing and allows them to raise any problems. *"If you're not meeting expectations* [or vice versa, presumably], *it's a good time to make sure these things get said so you have a chance to work on them."* Trainees are impressed with the tried and trusted training programme. In the corporate seat *"you have training sessions every week, and in litigation they have a special talk called 'Everything You Need to Know about the City', which was really useful."*

If you want to try something different you can apply for a client secondment, which the firm considers an adequate substitute for a corporate seat. Unilever, Reuters, insurance broker Marsh, AstraZeneca, Cargill, ICI and its subsidiary

National Starch, plus Lehman Brothers are all on board with the programme. Brussels-based client Cerestar is an attractive option for trainees with workable foreign language skills. Whichever they choose, trainees *"get a really good insight into how a company operates,"* although those for whom a double-shot skinny latte is a morning prerequisite may want to think twice before accepting the National Starch seat as *"it's in Slough and there's no Starbucks!"*

the mayer brown social club

As a reward for everyone's hard work, the firm makes a good effort on the social front. The Christmas party last year had a Cuban theme with dancers, music and mojitos, and a venue *"decked out in fake sand and palm trees."* It has also been known to spring impromptu drinks events on staff, a recent one being held at *"a posh house in Belgravia with lots of canapés."* Annual team-building trips to Barcelona are another highlight. Back in London, trainee events are numerous and popular. There are pool tournaments and casino nights, a book club, sports clubs and a party every three months in a local boozer on Fleet Street. *"They rent it out and throw open the bar; we all pile in there and are encouraged to socialise."* Most Fridays, a decent crowd can usually be found in the nearby Evangelist. Fridays are designated dress-down days, unless you've a meeting with clients, and the firm also allows staff to dress more casually in the hot summer months.

People considering applying to this firm will probably wonder how it compares to the largest outfits in the City. Trainees thought it worth clarifying that their working patterns are not as extreme as those in, say, the magic circle firms. One typical source said this of the hours: *"They varied from seat to seat. I have worked through the night, but that was only once when a deal was completing in corporate. I left to go for breakfast and then came back, but was given the day off... It was quite exciting as I had never done anything like that before. Weekends? Yes, I worked a couple, and my average hours in corporate were 8:30am until 7pm or 7.30pm."* Sounds like someone who was pretty happy with their lot. In September 2006, 14 of the 18 qualifiers took NQ positions with the firm.

and finally...

Mayer Brown Rowe & Maw may not be magic circle, but it's certainly got a lot to boast about. It is widely accepted that the 2002 merger has been a resounding success, and there's no reason to suggest that the firm won't carry on building on this.

McCormicks

the facts

Location: Leeds, Harrogate
Number of UK partners/solicitors: 13/30
Total number of trainees: 11
Seats: 4x6 months
Alternative seats: None

This feisty firm manages to combine good-natured office hi-jinks with big ambition, billing itself as "a fearless law firm with a fearsome reputation." Its website features chess players, boxers, and a lady with a rapier looking slightly bolshy, so after a quick protein shake, we put in our mouth guards and picked up the phone...

taking the lead

When asked to explain the symbol-rich website, trainees told us the boxer, the chess player and the fencer symbolised the firm's aggression, tactical mind and creative temperament. They also say the firm's ethos is that of *"working together to create quality products,"* and we don't doubt them for a minute. With expertise in areas from accidents, and e-commerce to family law and wills, McCormicks can handle anything that life might throw at you (and it). Its clients include The FA Premier League, the Law Society and soap stars galore. On our last inspection various celebrity names were stalking the corridors. Also spotted, Gordon Strachan and Gary McAllister dribbling past the water cooler, and various assistants doing the same over Nell McAndrew. Behind the broken noses and cauliflower ears, could McCormicks be the most glamorous firm in the north?

The Don King of the operation is the eponymous Peter McCormick, and trainees love him. One star-struck source told us: *"I spent time working with him in my commercial seat on sports and regulatory issues. He does lots of work for the Law Society – dealing with other solicitors who are about to be struck off."* Another added: *"Working with him was a real high point; he is quite inspirational – he built the firm up from nothing."* Known to all simply as Peter, *"he's outspoken in a good way, and doesn't shut himself away."* So popular is he that one of his author clients wrote him into a recent thriller based in the world of horseracing.

losing the plot

Let's walk the course and inspect the various jumps trainees will face. The seat options include private client/family, coco, crime, corporate recovery, dispute resolution/employment and commercial property. We'll start with crime, for which the firm is number-one rated in the North East, and where lawyers have dealt with everything from the usual nasties (rape, pillage, etc.) through to an assault charge arising from a player head-butting a referee during an FA game, drug smuggling and white-collar fraud. If you prefer dealing with individuals rather than corporations you might want to try another of the firm's hot-shot departments, family. McCormicks is especially used to handling the kind of divorces that require the splitting of a fortune made through a business venture. Wills, probate and tax planning advice is dispensed to a broad clientele, many individuals having been referred to the firm by Age Concern, St Gemma's Hospice, Wheatfields Hospice and local authority social services teams.

sporting behaviour

In the commercial arena, McCormicks is piling on the pounds and moving up a class. According to one trainee: "*The firm's strengths are changing and the corporate team is really taking off. We see ourselves as in the first rank behind the Big Six in Leeds.*" No one's claiming that McCormicks is running the biggest deals in the region, but what it is doing is providing local enterprise with a credible alternative to the national firms. Top work of 2005/06 has included advice to the Viking Fund, a new venture capital investment company in Yorkshire using risk capital from the DTI's Early Growth Fund. Regular clients include Winners Bingo, Designer Nails and Jemella Group, which owns and operates the ghd hair brand. According to *The Sunday Times* Jemella is the fastest-growing private company in Britain.

Where McCormicks really has an edge is in media, entertainment and sports matters. Through its relationship with The FA Premier League it works on many of the things that affect English football – merchandising, intellectual property, perimeter board advertising, etc. as well as advising the organisation on its own employment law and property interests. In one case from the past year, Peter McCormick successfully represented it in proceedings at the Court of Arbitration for Sport in Lausanne, in Switzerland, arguing that the court lacked jurisdiction in the matter which involved a conflict between the rules of the International Football Association Board and FIFA relating to compensation payments for young players. Board with footie? Perhaps you'll be more intrigued by defamation or the commercial problems of clients in broadcasting or the music industry.

When it comes to seat allocation "*you must be pushy but not too fussy.*" In terms of knowing where you stand, you'll have meetings galore: a monthly review from the supervisor and the training partner, an end-of-seat review and an annual appraisal. On the subject of grunt work, one sage source advised: "*You have to face the fact that sometimes you are the best person around to be doing the admin.*" But not because you're incapable of much else: at marketing events you are expected to get out there and "*be prepared to muck in.*" We think it's telling that trainees and paralegals have website profiles – even as a new recruit "*you are very much the face of the firm.*" Those with a real talent for schmoozing can mix it up with other young professionals in the area through MyLaw, a networking group set up by a former McCormicks trainee. The NQ retention rate was three out of four in 2006.

who ya gonna call?

Those we sparred with were sound lads and lasses with a sense of humour and decidedly nononsense manner. Prima donnas should avoid this place because what really serves people well is a good bit of Northern grit and a willingness to get stuck into things. "*We are all ambitious, driven, and eager,*" concluded one source. And from another: "*We're outgoing people who aren't afraid to stand up.*" All like McCormicks' "*inclusive feel and the fact that they'll listen to even the youngest person – you can have your say in a team.*"

The Leeds office is "*bog standard, not a glass palace – we don't want to intimidate family and criminal clients.*" A more tactful soul admitted: "*It could do with a lick of paint,*" still, an open-plan layout means "*you get to shout at each other across the desks*". The advantage of the central Leeds address is that the city's bars and clubs are on the doorstep. On Friday people are always up for a few drinks after work, and even before quitting time there's often fun to be had. Corridor cricket, for example: if you're not on the team you're advised to "*duck when the ball is coming your way.*" Last Halloween a pumpkin-carving competition drew some magnificent submissions. The winner's entry incorporated a fake axe, fake blood, and brains made of mincemeat, which understandably "*started to smell pretty bad as the evening wore on.*" The efforts that went into the pumpkins led one trainee to conclude that "*there can't have been too much work on that week.*" The social committee recently organised a Mexican night in the office, for which "*everybody had to help make a team hat,*" and we also heard about a fancy dress party to which the litigation team went dressed as Ghostbusters.

Our favourite story concerns a football match between the firm and the University of Warwick's first eleven (grateful recipients of McCormicks sponsorship). To avoid a thrashing from the students, the lawyers pitched up with Messrs Strachan and McAllister in tow.

Of course it's not all fun and games: the annual fee earners conference is a time to blend social activities with more serious issues. At the last conference staff all went to a hotel for some useful team-building exercises: "*We all had to pretend we were in a virtual law firm and learn how to drive a firm forward.*" Alright, we can't pretend it was all serious and work-related – there was a free bar and "*the last person standing was around until 6am.*"

and finally...

After three rounds with the young pugilists at McCormicks we can report plenty of fancy footwork and fair play. If you're looking for a solid and personal training where you'll be a face of the firm from your first day in the office, this is a ring worth getting into.

McDermott Will & Emery LLP

the facts
Location: London
Number of UK partners/solicitors: 31/44
Total number of trainees: 5
Seats: 4x6 months
Alternative seats: Secondments

McDermott Will & Emery started life in Chicago in 1934 and since then has evolved into an international powerhouse employing over 1,000 people across 15 offices in five countries. Since arriving in London eight years ago the firm has established a broad-based, self-standing practice with "*a definite London personality*" complete with its own breed of work, culture and trainee.

bulding up
In the 1990s a number of US law firms landed on UK shores, many of them focusing on heavyweight corporate and finance transactions. Rather than aping these compatriots, MWE chose to build employment and IP practices. It's no fluke that the firm picked these areas; they reflect its strengths across the pond. MWE has not left it at that, however; it is now pushing forward in corporate matters and last year was involved in one of the largest European transactions, EFG International's IPO on the Swiss Exchange, worth 1.6 billion Swiss francs. There has additionally been a concerted effort to grow a hedge fund practice, with the firm poaching a reputed partner from SJ Berwin, and competition/antitrust, litigation and energy teams are starting to appear on the radar in the UK. As for the leisurely pace of growth, there's a certain caution about MWE's UK expansion that contrasts with other US firms in the City. Despite what trainees say is a "*risk-averse*" approach to making lateral hires and developing business areas, there is "*a definite sense of forward movement*" and the "*positive buzz*" of a firm that has yet to reach its peak.

MWE now takes on a handful of trainees each year and the class of 2006 had developed a strong sense of identity. With *"no one straight out of university"* it follows that *"all the trainees are a little bit older with more life experience."* Perhaps it was their relative maturity that led us to conclude that they fitted well with the *"eclectic"* bunch of high-flying partners and associates who have been lured to the firm. MWE trainees state adamantly that they are *"not the type who would go to a magic circle firm where recruits are two a penny – here you'll be the only one in your department, regularly working with a capital partner on a one-to-one basis with no associates in between."* Consequently *"you have to be extremely confident,"* and *"it also helps to keep a good sense of humour as partners don't want a whinging trainee at midnight."*

red-eyes are back

Talking of late nights, what of the crazy billing culture for which US firms – including MWE – are famed? There's no doubt that *"you'll regularly cancel your plans"* during a stint in corporate, but then again what's so unusual about that in City law firms? We were told time and again how MWE in London *"is not obsessed about hours"* and *"not an intense or aggressive place to work."* Our sources put this down to two things: the office being a melting pot of lawyers who were all previously at different law firms; and its self-standing status.

In case MWE London is beginning to sound like a small breakaway republic, we should stress that the trainees certainly felt a part of the wider firm. We rang them just as they were arriving back at their desks having taken the red-eye from Washington, DC after an all-expenses-paid associate retreat. New London recruits have always been treated to an induction week Stateside (Chicago in 2006), but this year there was also a second trip for a four-day gathering of all

MWE associates and trainees worldwide. Even though *"severely jet-lagged,"* our sources enthused about their experience, telling us that as well as being *"great to see everyone out of the work context"* it was an ideal way to *"get a good feel for the firm."* Admittedly the trip included relatively serious elements such as *"a talk from the chairman,"* but the main thrust was social, culminating with dinner *"among the 'planes"* at Washington's National Air and Space Museum and a ride on a flight simulator thrown in for good measure.

using your initiative

Being included on the Washington trip was a *"big, big thing"* for our sources because they took it as an acknowledgement of their right to be *"treated as associates."* In this sense MWE's London personality has not overridden American law firm culture, in which *"they don't understand the concept of trainees."* In return for being allowed to chest puff a little, *"trainees are expected to take on responsibility and to be business-minded from the start."* This doesn't mean a free rein in the office; the firm adheres to the standard model of training contract with four six-month seats in different departments. The full list of seats on offer in 2006 was: IP/IT, employment, competition, tax, banking, pensions, litigation and corporate. No department is strictly compulsory so, for example, there is *"no requirement to do a corporate seat if you're more interested in the niche areas."* FYI, in this international law firm trainees don't currently have the opportunity to take a seat abroad, although this isn't entirely ruled out for the future. For now, trainees rely on the day-to-day work exchange between offices for interaction with colleagues abroad. This is especially the case in the corporate, energy and competition groups, where a high proportion of the matters are multi-jurisdictional.

In the IP group a *"flat structure"* means you can even *"walk into a capital partner's office without even knocking."* With so few trainees vying for a place here, getting time in the group shouldn't be a problem, though *"you may have to wait a seat to do it."* The department's work covers both contentious and non-contentious matters for a diverse clientele. In the past year, lawyers have done everything from dealing with the IP and IT aspects of the IPO of an online casino and poker game operator to advising Lincoln Cathedral in respect of various artifacts. The employment seat is another popular spot. Here the lawyers act for a monumental list of clients including Coors Brewers, British American Tobacco, Land Securities, Oracle and United Airlines. The department can be defined by its capacity to handle major pieces of work such as an £8.1 million whistle-blowing claim for an oil company and a £3.5 million sex discrimination and victimisation claim.

Spend time in corporate and you will be *"working directly with partners a lot of the time"* on mergers, private acquisitions and plenty of AIM and IPO deals. This tight working arrangement means that *"sometimes you're the only other person on a deal and the more you impress them and do things right the more they'll give you."* In a small office like this training will never be an overly structured process, but *"if you show initiative you'll get what you want."* To illustrate this point, all the 2005 intake were put in their first-choice seats and then avoided future clashes by *"discussing it right at the beginning to make sure we timed our choices right."* All this talk of responsibility and initiative could leave the wary applicant concerned about a lack of support. No need to worry; trainees are assigned one official mentor and most tend to approach another unofficially. Both mentors have a lunch budget. The role of the unofficial mentor (who will most likely be a young associate) is as *"a first port of call for stupid trainee questions."*

giving back

Another American influence on MWE's London personality is *"a genuine commitment"* to pro bono activities. Trainees sense that *"the firm would like every partner and associate to do it"* and confirm that lawyers are permitted to count time spent on pro bono activities towards their billable hours target. Each seat is likely to provide an opportunity to get involved in pro bono and our sources revealed how providing legal advice to those who can't afford to pay for it gives them more than a warm glow. *"You advise on areas of law you would otherwise not experience"* and this in turn *"allows you to take responsibility in a way that wouldn't be possible if a lot more money was at stake."*

The social scene is more grown up than in many of the big City firms because, when people do go out, it tends to be as a group drawn from across the office. To cut to the chase: *"If you want to go out drinking with trainees every Thursday and Friday it's not going to happen."* Again, because *"you are viewed as individuals within departments"* rather than 'one of the trainees', *"it makes you feel more part of the firm as a whole."* Monthly firm-wide social events range from table football tournaments and casino evenings to trips to local bars. Though popular, they *"tend to attract the usual suspects and you know which ones will be still there at midnight."* Isn't that always the way?

In 2006 the sole trainee who reached qualification took a job with the firm.

and finally...

McDermott Will & Emery will suit the mature-minded applicant, so if the idea of disappearing into a trainee crowd repels you and you're up for serious responsibility from the start, you'd do well to consider an application.

McGrigors

the facts
Location: London, Scotland
Number of UK partners/solicitors: 74/222
Total number of trainees: 27 (in London)
Seats: 4x6 months
Alternative seats: Scotland, Brussels, Belfast, secondments

Too many medium-sized law firms in London; too little time. What to do if you can't see the mid-tier wood from the trees? McGrigors stands out for its Scottish pedigree and established links with the worldwide accountancy giant KPMG.

positive thinking
"*I am one of the last KLegal trainees,*" said one of our interviewees, referring to the now defunct legal arm of global accountancy practice KPMG. After the Enron collapse, the credibility of accountancy firms working in partnership with legal firms to perform services for clients (otherwise known as multidisciplinary partnership or MDP) was seriously undermined. This in turn left KLegal's future in London uncertain. McGrigors, with a legacy in Scotland stretching back over 200 years, made its first foray onto English soil in the wake of this turmoil and scooped up KLegal from its parent. A little merger dust was kicked up, some training contracts were deferred, differences were settled.

Now two years on, whether they'd lived through the changes or come in fresh, trainees were positive about the future: "*I think we have profited from McGrigors' discipline – it's one of the top firms in Scotland and from them we gained more people, some great clients and more of a presence.*" Any us-and-them feeling has largely subsided; indeed our sources reported that "*morale is very high at the moment.*"

blue-chip and pin
"*You have to see McGrigors as a Scottish firm with a London office,*" said one interviewee when we asked about the kind of footprint it has in the UK. As a Big Four law firm in Scotland, McGrigors' name up there carries a weight of which the London office can only dream. But what it lacks in history, the English operation makes up for in ambition and enthusiasm. One trainee said: "*We have the potential in London to jump up the ranks quite quickly.*" A look at the clients in London's core areas of corporate, banking and real estate (BP, RBS, O_2, Lloyds TSB and Deutsche Bank among others) suggests they may have a point. The London corporate team assisted BETonSPORTS, one of the largest US and Asia-facing online gaming companies, when it bought two other Chinese online companies to increase its presence in Asia. London lawyers also helped RBS on the financing of NHS Shared Business Services, a scheme whereby the NHS is able to outsource accounting and payroll functions. The projects group, with particular success in energy, education and healthcare, is expanding and has advised on over 100 PFI projects that have reached financial close.

And then, of course, there is KPMG with which McGrigors has maintained a 'best friends' relationship that results in valuable work and client referrals. For trainees who signed up all those years ago because they were attracted to the MDP model, "*there are plenty of opportunities to get involved in the work that KPMG does.*" In the areas of employment and pensions, for example, the two organisations work closely much of the time.

busy, busy, busy
London trainees take four seats with the idea being that everyone tries corporate, something contentious and then two other departments. Even then, "*compulsory doesn't really mean compulsory; corporate could be done in a seat like banking.*" As for

contentious experience, this need not be taken in the main dispute resolution department, as tax and construction litigation are also offered. Further seat options include real estate, IT and commercial, projects, procurement, human rights and employment. It's *"no lucky dip – you put forward your choices and the reasons for them... most people get what they want."* Many trainees seem to find the idea of corporate a touch daunting. *"It's not half as bad as people say it is; the bark is a lot worse than the bite,"* laughed one source, though they acknowledged that *"there's a huge amount of work to be done and the hours can be tough."* This can lead to times when *"you get really stressed and wonder why you didn't become a teacher and have all those summers off."* Essentially *"it's the same as at any firm – dealing with busy people is difficult,"* though at least *"your people management skills will improve dramatically."* Whether or not they'd been hesitant about corporate, trainees reported having interesting experiences of AIM flotations and other small to mid-range deals. Some of the largest matters have involved working alongside or for KPMG, as in the £489 million recommended offer for HIT Entertainment where the McGrigors team advised KPMG Corporate Finance.

McGrigors' tax litigation department is reputedly *"just fantastic,"* both in terms of the quality of its work and the *"really good, fun people."* It advises on claims against HM Revenue & Customs and allows trainees to get stuck in *"preparing instructions for counsel, drafting initial documents and note-taking."* A stint in the popular banking group is also rewarding: *"I got involved in absolutely everything,"* said a trainee who had taken the chance to see as much as possible of the group's work for both lenders and borrowers. *"It's up to you to broaden your horizons,"* decided a second. *"Because it's open plan, if you hear someone working on something, depending on your workload, you can go over and ask to get involved."* Another agreed: *"You are allocated a supervisor but it depends on the individual if you are tied to them. In one department I took many other jobs from different people."*

falklands awe

The relationship with KPMG provides a number of secondments for trainees. It's an *"extremely popular"* means of getting in with a blue-chip client and *"seeing some of the best people in the industry interact and do their magic."* Trainees reported that the amount and type of work you do on secondment is *"very much within your hands. You need to show them you are good enough."* One said, while they took full advantage of their time with KPMG, *"I'm glad I did it for my third seat when my confidence had increased and I knew the basics, as going from a safe environment to a massive company is a little scary."* Other secondment options include time with O₂ and RAB.

And if you're hankering for a piece of the Scottish action, Highland flinging yourself into the Edinburgh or Glasgow offices is easy. Those who'd already been there had relished the *"superior work-life balance"* north of the border and the *"great contact"* with a host of top clients such as RBS and HBOS. One said: *"I was given a lot of responsibility in Scotland – in other seats I had been asked not to contact clients but there I was responsible for doing it. I would ask questions of my supervisor but I was the one who would get back to the client."* A move is not compulsory, though it is very popular; our sources clearly understood that *"as a trainee going up to Edinburgh or Glasgow you certainly won't be working on lesser matters."* Indeed, one of the September 2006 London qualifiers accepted a job practising English law in the Edinburgh office. To give you the full picture 12 out of 17 London qualifiers stayed with the firm altogether.

"Very close links" between the three locations help foster a pretty good one-firm feel, with partners in many departments splitting their week

between London and Scotland. For now no London trainees visit the firm's new Aberdeen office, which it acquired when it took on the 54-strong oil and gas team from Ledingham Chalmers. Interestingly this turned McGrigors into an international firm as the oil and gas specialists had satellite offices in Baku (that's in Azerbaijan) and Port Stanley in the Falklands. *"I'm not sure they'll be offering a seat in the Falklands though... It's a bit of a one-man band and it's probably quite cold."*

your round, your card

McGrigors marked its union with KLegal by moving the London operation out of KPMG premises into a shiny open-plan pad in Old Bailey, and staff have reaped the benefits of *"a lot more breathing space"* ever since. The offices are *"right on top of All Bar One,"* providing hassle-free socialising opportunities; *"I can walk into there any night of the week on my own and find someone to have a drink with."* The partners reportedly *"pull out the American Express"* at regular intervals but that's nothing compared to the Scots. *"In Edinburgh and Glasgow the social side is much more active."* 'Café McGrigors' is an event held on the last Friday of every month in one of the break-out areas. After plenty of beer and wine, staff have the option to continue the evening in a pub. Back down in London sport enthusiasts are catered for with football and rugby, and a team recently took part in a KPMG hockey tournament in Amsterdam. At the end of the day *"they didn't actually win anything,"* but our pundits' conclusion was that after a game of two halves *"it's not about scoring goals or winning, is it?"*

Trainees had a similarly philosophical attitude to working for McGrigors. *"We're well-rounded, down-to-earth people. We know we're not Freshfields or Clifford Chance."* What they lack in bling they make up for in enterprise and self-assurance. One told us: *"I think the firm would appeal to someone who enjoys the idea of more responsibility*

rather than the excitement of, say, Singapore on a secondment." It seems to be all about *"having the chance to work on big deals for good clients but in a less demanding way. To say it is relaxed gives the wrong impression, but everyone is open for a chat and we can discuss things."* These comments not only hit the nail on the head, they also convince us that the firm in its new incarnation is still recruiting the same kind of people who were attracted to the old KLegal and the MDP ideal. Big on talent, small on ego.

and finally...

Take the high road to McGrigors' door in London and your training contract will give you the chance to work with sterling clients both north and south of the border. There's absolutely no need to question whether you'll be any less of an English solicitor at the end of the two years, though having said that, if your heritage has already left you culturally confused McGrigors sounds like a great place to nurture each aspect.

Mills & Reeve

the facts
Location: Birmingham, Cambridge, London, Norwich
Number of UK partners/solicitors: 80/333
Total number of trainees: 42
Seats: 6x4 months
Alternative seats: None

From the Norfolk Broads to the brink of the Black Country with an excursion into London, Mills & Reeve is quietly yet rapidly stretching across the middle of the country and forcing itself to be noticed. And while it does so it obviously manages to keep its staff satisfied, evidenced by the fact that the firm has once more made it into *The Sunday Times'* '100 Best Companies to Work For' survey.

where are you?

M&R has plied its wares in the city of Norwich since 1880. In 1987 a Cambridge office was added, followed a decade or so later by operations in London and then Birmingham. Even though trainees joining the firm are encouraged to experience life in more than one office – and some do so – it would be folly not to appreciate that each office is quite distinct from the others.

If you're worried that Norfolk's reputation for *"country bumpkins"* will overshadow your plans to become a hotshot lawyer, take reassurance from the ample evidence that there is more to M&R Norwich than combine harvesters and landed estates. Its corporate team increased in size last year when it took in the whole of Eversheds' Norwich contingent. Recently the team acted for Delia Smith and Michael Wynn-Jones on the sale of New Crane Publishing, publisher of *Sainsbury's Magazine*, and advised regional newspaper group Archant on its successful buy-back of £55 million of shares. Commercial dispute resolution, banking and finance, employment, real estate, tax and professional indemnity seats are all there for the taking too, with each offering exposure to decent business clients. Many trainees are drawn to the professional indemnity litigation team in Norwich, telling us that it offers *"the same services as London but at a cheaper rate."* They also enjoy their time in corporate, *"where you feel you can really make a contribution to someone's business."* If you are more of a people person you can opt for a spell in the *"tea and biscuits"* world of family law with its *"large amount of client contact,"* and if you do hanker after traditional work in agriculture or trusts and personal finance, you'll certainly not be disappointed with the firm's wealth of landowner clients. However corporate the firm gets we reckon it will always hold on tight to the landed elite of Norwich. Witness the firm's sponsorship of the Norfolk Grey Partridge Trophy, awarded to landowners who promote the recovery of the bird's numbers in the county. The nominees included the Holkham and Sandringham Estates (both clients) and the trophy was awarded at the Norfolk County Fair and Horse Show, where M&R *"hosted a breakfast for over 300 clients."*

And what of life in Norwich? Trainees readily acknowledge *"it is not the most cosmopolitan place in the world,"* but point out that *"it's very easy to get accommodation near to work, and the city provides a great lifestyle."* Typical working hours are good, making it perfectly possible to play evening cricket matches or join a salsa class – ideal for anyone wanting to get a little Latin rhythm into their cover drive. An active TSG organises boat trips and drinks evenings; in between trainees frequent a sushi bar (surely the first step to cosmopolitan living) or one of several local pubs including the Adam and Eve, among the oldest in the land and reputedly haunted to boot.

taking a punt on cambridge

Cambridge is *"mostly commercial although there are tax and trusts and family departments that are highly thought of."* Here, as in Norwich, the range of seats is considerable; *"the only thing we don't do is criminal,"* one trainee offered. This is true to the extent that *"you can do most things but you can't do insurance or health seats here."* Around half of the firm's entire corporate department is based in Cambridge, with lawyers' work including Lincoln-based agricultural machinery manufacturer Spaldings' recent reorganisation (value £9.5 million) which required intra-group property and share transfers, re-registration of certain group companies as unlimited companies and the subsequent distribution of shareholders' funds. In this office more than others, we received reports of long hours in corporate, although those involved were *"glad to be part of it, even if it meant leaving the office at about midnight or 1am."* Such working patterns are by no means widespread throughout the office, with 9am to 5.30 or 6pm more standard.

The Cambridge office is especially known for its work on IP and technology matters, activities the other offices don't really touch on. These seats were *"loved"* by trainees, who encountered *"lots of research and marketing"* as well as picking up drafting and case management skills. One recalled *"a lot of responsibility on copyright cases... I really felt they were my cases."* The firm has lately advised the engineering IT specialist Aveva Group on complex IP licensing in the energy and utilities sector, including negotiating agreements with Shell, Hyundai and the Brazilian government.

The Cambridge office is in *"a pretty cushy location"* surrounded by bars and sandwich shops and *"close to the botanic gardens... which is nice for a bit of peace and quiet."* When hot summer weather becomes too much to bear, you can cool down in an outdoor swimming pool nearby or with a drink in the garden of The Flying Pig, which we understand has been under threat from property developers. TSG and young-professionals groups organise the standard *"drinks, barbecues, bowling and pool competitions."*

healthy growth

"Hot on the heels" of Cambridge in terms of size, the Birmingham office is *"coming into its own."* The baby of the firm has grown at an extraordinary rate; after moving into new offices last year it has *"expanded from the original three floors and now taken over the fourth and final floor."* We hear it's a running joke that if the headcount rises any more the firm will have to move again. The operation is *"going strong"* and the range of seats has multiplied such that it is now as comprehensive as anywhere in the network. Originally set up to service public sector and corporate clients, last year a private client department was added. The particular strength of this office is healthcare, and here the firm handles interesting work such as prosecutions on behalf of the GMC. It also acts for a number of NHS trusts and recently successfully tendered for reappointment to existing clients Hereford Hospitals NHS Trust and Newham University Hospital NHS Trust. Only a couple of years ago this health and public sector focus dominated the office, *"but this is certainly changing"* as the firm has started to realise the wider commercial opportunities in the Midlands. Unsurprisingly some trainees envisage a time when Birmingham *"becomes the headquarters of the firm."*

Unusually for a law firm, there is a flexitime system that centres on the core hours of 10am to 4pm, leaving the rest pretty much up to the individual. As an office *"there are no airs and graces,"* and claustrophobics can take comfort from the fact that *"no one hides in the cupboard when the boss comes around."* The Brum social scene is excellent, with drinks evenings *"advertised on an amusing e-mail every Friday"* and *"plenty of bars within staggering distance now that the firm is in the centre of the city."* Treasure hunts have become a favourite out-of-work pastime, possibly because these basically involve tramping around a few of Birmingham's watering holes following a set of clues. Inter-firm trainee sports competitions include *"rugby, football, netball and even water polo... next week there's Ultimate Frisbee."* Regular readers will already know that these activities are the brainchild of the hyperactive Birmingham Trainee Solicitors' Society.

capital gains

The London outpost of the firm is rumoured to be *"looking to expand,"* although the *Student Guide* has reported this before only for nothing to come of it. Best to assume that for the moment the focus on insurance, with public law, local government and healthcare on the side, will continue. Then again, the London contingent did recently move from 2,500 sq ft to 8,000 sq ft of space, so maybe there is a plan afoot. A seat in the Big Smoke is *"open to everyone, whichever office they are in,"* and involves *"helping solicitors to pre-*

pare disclosure, going to court to file applications, lots of research, drafting court forms and gathering witness statements." While the firm pays for accommodation and travel expenses, you may have to find that accommodation yourself, "which can be tricky for just four months."

In all offices trainee seats are just four months long, which means trainees "get to see more departments" over the two years. The firm likes trainees to sample real estate and something from the corporate services group. If a seat isn't available for some reason in the trainee's current office, it isn't a problem to go to another; however, the majority of trainees tend to commit themselves to one office. Everyone we interviewed spoke of the way in which "all the offices work together in departmental teams," and trainees from across the offices meet up for their PSC training, which is held off-site in a hotel. "They put you up for the night even if you live nearby;" after all, why would anyone want to miss out on the social side of the proceedings. Every two years the firm gets together for a "big summer jolly," in 2006 held in the grounds of Knebworth House. This came as an added bonus for our sources, most of whom had chosen M&R because they could work for a top firm and still avoid London. All had been well aware of the firm's deserved reputation for skilled lawyers and high-quality advice in a number of specialist practices as well as mainstream commercial areas. In September 2006, 16 of the 17 qualifiers stayed on with the firm; the person who left moved to Australia.

and finally...

Whether looking to stay somewhere close to home or to head for horizons new, students fresh from university or those embarking on a second career will find Mills & Reeve an ambitious yet accommodating employer. Undoubtedly each office plays its part, but if you are looking for a rising star our advice would be, like this once eastern-rooted firm, to look to the west.

Mishcon de Reya

the facts

Location: London
Number of UK partners/solicitors: 44/72
Total number of trainees: 15
Seats: 4x6 months
Alternative seats: None
Extras: Pro bono – various projects, eg LawWorks

Well-established London firm Mishcon de Reya is no stranger to newspaper headlines. It acts for an array of high-profile clients and attracts some fascinating cases. A thriving litigation practice plus a successful family department are behind much of its notoriety. If you're looking for a commercial firm with a difference, then step this way.

model behaviour

Mishcons has a huge reputation when it comes to litigation and this core practice group generates over 40% of the firm's income. Mishcons actually has four main practice groupings – litigation, coco, family and property – and within these four there are a number of sub-specialisms. One of the big ones is the media and public advocacy group whose work covers defamation and privacy issues plus reputation management advice to individuals and corporate clients. In one recent case, consultant Anthony Julius advised the University of Haifa and various academics on a proposed boycott of Israeli academic institutions. This "high-pressure, fast-paced" work can become "quite stressful" as "you need to act quickly if a story is going to break."

If you're keen to deal with high-profile disputes and rub shoulders with the rich and famous, you're in for a great time. Mishcons recently represented Claudia Schiffer in a dispute over an unauthorised endorsement of a cook book written by her former chef. The employment group, too, has generated its fair share of newspaper column inches. In August 2006, lawyers won over £800,000 in damages for company secretarial assistant Helen Green, who was bullied by fellow employees at Deutsche Bank. If you're lucky enough to get a seat in this department, you could find yourself helping out on such matters or doing case management conferences and even advocacy on smaller tribunals. Other specialist groups deal with art law, immigration and sport.

lonely hearts club

During a two-year training contract you will *"get plenty of access to good-quality work and clients."* The family department is one of the more famous areas of the firm and often conducts work with an international or media element. To give a timely example Heather Mills has turned to the firm for her divorce from Sir Paul McCartney. Away from the glitz and glamour, Mishcons is doing pretty well on mainstream corporate work. Lawyers worked alongside Wragge & Co on a £116 million acquisition of facilities from Mischcons' client McLellon Group by FTSE 250 support services company Interserve. They are also developing a good reputation for AIM deals, recently acting on the £214.2 million flotation of a Canadian software company. Another new direction for the team is Indian corporate work.

Meanwhile, the ever-expanding fraud team recently won a seven-figure sum for Microsoft against a group of counterfeiters selling fake Microsoft products. The fraud group *"has a sharp sting,"* not least because within it *"you've got certain individuals who are tactically and strategically aggressive."* Apparently, *"clients come to us as they want someone to fight hard for them. The objective is to hit the fraudsters hard at the start and get out quickly."*

stake your claim

Trainees select from the following seat options: property; corporate; banking; general commercial; private client; insolvency; media; employment; family; contentious and non-contentious private work. Although no seat is strictly compulsory and it is perfectly possible to sidestep something that really isn't up your street, most people tend to go to coco and litigation and will *"almost certainly do property."* As you'd expect, the media, fraud and employment departments are hugely popular and if you want to go to family you should expect *"a bit of a scrap."* On the odd occasion there have been client secondments, recent opportunities including time at a House of Commons inquiry and Universal Records. On the whole, trainees found the seat allocation process *"fair"* but some counselled that as well as letting HR know your preferences *"you need to go and speak to partners concerned."*

Sure, Mishcon trainees, just like any other, *"obviously do menial work such as disclosure lists and photocopying,"* yet they can also *"get involved in the juicy bits of work"* that come with sharing a room with a partner. This includes drafting witness statements and appearing before masters on small High Court applications. The hours are *"normally okay"* and, again, vary between departments. Property has *"the most routinely friendly hours"* (roughly 9am to 7pm); in media, days are often longer and they can be longer still in corporate where you must be prepared for *"a few late nights,"* but *"if things are quiet you can leave at 5pm."* A full programme of seminars means that *"in most of the departments there is some kind of training run by a partner every week."*

suits you sir

If it's character you want Mishcons has tons of it. Lord Mishcon, the firm's founder, died earlier in 2006 aged 90, but he was still coming into the office when he was well into his 80s. In a career spanning six decades he acted for the famous and the infamous and worked on the divorces of The Princess of Wales and Ruth Ellis, the last woman to be hanged in Britain. With such a founder, maybe it's no surprise that the firm still has a host of big personalities. Our interviewees acknowledged that there were *"formidable people" "all over the place,"* but regarded them more with *"awe"* than *"fear."* Not *"dragons;"* the big characters are just *"strong-minded."* Their top survival tip is this: *"Don't let their reputations stop you as you can learn a lot from them"* even if *"you first have to learn how to approach them."*

Mishcons' home is an equally characterful 1930s art deco building resplendent with bright colours, modern art and a modern interior. The dress code is a more sober smart-casual with more of an emphasis on the smart until dress-down Friday. Apart from the donation to charity, we do wonder whether there really is any point to the day as all manner of articles of clothing are banned. *"No jeans or trainers. No T-shirts. Maybe polo shirts... they have to be collared shirts."* We've no idea whether the confusing dress code has been discussed formally, but on the first Monday of the month, HR meets with the trainee group for lunch and *"to update us on what's going on and to see whether we've got any problems."* It's a nice touch, but one interviewee admitted that *"sometimes if you've got a problem it's easier to speak discreetly to HR rather than in front of everyone else."* Clearly no one had any major issues last year as six of the seven qualifiers stayed on in September 2006. Litigation was the department of choice for four of them.

mingle schmingle

The firm attracts *"a real hotch potch of people from different backgrounds"* and seems to like trainees *"who can think for themselves"* and have *"experience in other areas."* Some have back-grounds in PR and media; others have travelled. In one interviewee's opinion, their peers *"don't all live and breathe law"* and all *"have outside interests."*

In previous editions of the *Student Guide* we intimated that Mishcons doesn't have a massive post-work social life. Some interviewees say this is still the case because *"what's drummed home here is the work/life balance."* Meaning? *"You work incredibly hard whilst you're in the office and when you're out of the office you go home and enjoy yourself."* Others felt that the social offering had got better. Pub quizzes, wine tastings and various *"mingling events"* are *"a good opportunity to chat to people you don't normally see."* And on Friday nights, our sources say, the firm *"basically takes over"* the charmingly named Bountiful Cow pub. On the sports front there is inter-departmental football, cricket and *"yoga on a Monday night."*

At the big Christmas bash trainees have a starring role courtesy of *"a tradition that the first-years perform a skit."* Last year their adaptation of the *Twelve Days of Christmas* was littered with Mishcon in-jokes. The first-years are also *"encouraged"* to organise a Christmas party for employees' children. In January they are then taken out for lunch as a thank you for *"putting on the party and embarrassing ourselves in front of the firm."* If nothing else, we're sure the whole thing is character building.

and finally...

Mishcons is a place where *"you've got to be a bit gutsy"* and *"make your own luck."* As one interviewee remarked: *"They won't do the thinking for you but they will provide you with an environment to stimulate it."* You could try getting on the firm's summer placement scheme as some interviewees felt that this *"definitely goes in your favour."* Apply early, as there is a lot of competition for places.

Morgan Cole

the facts
Location: Cardiff, Swansea, Reading, Oxford, Croydon
Number of UK partners/solicitors: 55/110
Total number of trainees: 20
Seats: 4x6 months
Alternative seats: None

For Morgan Cole, images of a turbulent recent past are growing smaller in the rear-view mirror. Motoring resolutely forwards, a management shake-up, impressive client wins, a 30% profit increase and lateral hires have put fuel in the tank.

freakonomics
In 1998 there was a union between Welsh dragon Morgan Bruce and Thames Valley lion Cole & Cole. The newly delivered Morgan Cole was, however, less griffin-like than expected and turned out to have some serious genetic defects. A failure to fully graft the Welsh and English operations led to internal conflicts that hampered workable integration. A subsequent merger with niche London insurance firm Fishburn Boxer was reversed just three years into the arrangement. Partners left in their droves, profits dropped massively and AXA turfed MC off its panel, a decision that led to the closure of the firm's Croydon insurance litigation office.

Despite the firm being at such a low ebb, the trainees we spoke to during those fallow years remained resolutely happy with the training they had received and, in time, perceived improvements in the firm's health. Those we spoke to this year predicted an optimistic future, telling us: *"There's been a real change in atmosphere; there's a sense that we're refocused, ambitious and back on track."* Thus, trainees who had spent early days feeling *"the firm was crawling out of difficulty"* were now *"happy to stay, whereas maybe a year ago I'd have moved on."*

These feelings arise from several things. The firm last year gained panel places with FTSE 100 companies HSBC and Tesco, while also winning the tender to advise Severn Power on a successful £400 million power station investment project. Relighting the flames of serious business, in the past twelve months Morgan Cole scorched the competition to secure instruction from the insurance company Admiral on a £200 million redevelopment programme and a place alongside Denton Wilde Sapte and Clifford Chance on British Energy's panel. Predatory panache was also on display as local Cardiff rival Dolmans was raided for a new head of corporate and that 30% profit hike was partly achieved through ruthless cost management. An unsentimental management reshuffle has paved the way for continued improvements. All in all, things are looking up.

in the valleys
As for where the reinvigoration of Morgan Cole leaves trainees, the simple answer is either in the Welsh valleys or the Thames Valley. Students make an application for either the Welsh or English side of the operation and then stay in one half of the firm. New recruits gather at the beginning of the contract for joint training (usually in an Oxford college) and begin the two years with *"keenness to keep in touch and be best mates"* but, somewhat inevitably, geographical distance means *"we've split off unintentionally."* That said, when we conducted interviews a firm-wide trainee social weekend of *"chaos and carnage in Cardiff"* was planned, although not all the TV types were due to make it along.

A similar story of partial integration characterises the working life of the firm, with *"certain practice areas working closely across regions"* and others *"largely autonomous."* In commercial seats trainees observed *"lots of crossover, partners whizzing about by train between offices and heaps of communication,"* while the employment teams in

Oxford, Reading and Swansea co-ordinate their efforts via a "*monthly video conference.*" On the other hand "*property is very much defined by the office it is in*" and "*litigation is self-contained in each location.*" It's clearly fair to say that where integration is advantageous the firm is adept at managing it and the staff willing to make the effort, a truth underlined by the pleasure our sources took in "*the away-day in Swindon, where everyone gets together. We stay overnight, have training, a meal and catch up; it's really good for unity.*"

at the apex

Thames Valley trainees switch between Oxford and Reading, either at their own whim or for specific seats. Reading offers commercial IT, employment, corporate and insurance litigation. Head for the dreaming spires and you can tackle commercial litigation, general commercial, IP, commercial property or even health and safety regulatory, not forgetting the unusual matrimonial law option. Here, as in Wales, seat allocation is a easy-going process in which "*the training partner lets us sort it out ourselves unless there's a conflict, when we refer it back to him and accept what he decides.*"

Sources unanimously agreed that the Apex Plaza premises in Reading are "*busy, young and lively,*" with the location in the heart of the town close to "*the shopping centres and the railway station*" creating something of a buzz. "*The building itself is light and airy,*" we were told; "*there's a beautiful atrium with palm trees where you can eat lunch and you constantly see everyone in the office.*" Such pleasant environs provide welcome relief during the "*longer hours*" that the corporate or commercial seats can involve. Corporate trainees reported "*more than a few late nights on big deals*" and those who'd worked in commercial IT also relished the advisory side of work for government departments, not least because "*you're out of the office a lot.*"

Situated "*about 15 minutes from the town centre,*" Morgan Cole's Oxford office is "*quiet with a reputation for being family-oriented – people simply go home at the end of the day.*" In work terms, "*strong team identities*" define the office, with commercial IP "*very close-knit; they fall over themselves to help you*" and commercial property "*involving a seriously steep learning curve, but the supervision is very hands-on and every member of the team will make time for you.*"

welsh heavyweight

Journeying west into the land of leeks and lambs, MC assumes the mantle of one of Wales' strongest firms, alongside the likes of Eversheds and Hugh James. With MC being very "*Welsh*" in work, atmosphere and staff, our sources perceived it to be the perfect compromise between what they perceive to be an "*intimidating, cutthroat*" atmosphere in the former and the "*overly local*" work of the latter. In Cardiff, a corporate heart beats strong, with lawyers recently advising PHS Group in connection with its £600 million takeover by Charterhouse Development. IT and construction lawyers also work their socks off representing a clientele including the National Assembly for Wales, the Department of Health and Milford Haven Port Authority. Litigators represent banks (Northern Rock), educational institutions (University of Wales, Swansea), government agencies (Welsh Development Agency) and other major institutions (The Royal Mint).

If Cardiff is the major transactional centre of MC Wales, further west along the coast, Swansea is a hive of general commercial litigation with two other seats in corporate and commercial property. The "*freedom to go wherever, do whatever*" in Swansea, whether it's "*police stations doing ASBOs,*" "*going to court for housing associations*" or handling "*mortgage repos in the debt recovery team,*" explains why few trainees would care to miss out on the expected seat in the office. Livelier than Cardiff in atmosphere, the office also benefits from its location in "*the middle of the new marina development*" with "*lovely views over the sea.*" Partners have a pleasing habit of "*telling you to go home at 5pm.*"

By contrast, Bradley Court in Cardiff was described by several as possessing a "*weightier,*" "*more serious*" atmosphere with corporate, banking and commercial seats renowned for "*high expectations from very intelligent partners and lots of menial proof-reading of terms and conditions, etc...*" But if gains in such seats are measured in terms of "*increased commercial awareness,*" in the "*popular*" employment, pensions and benefits seat the gauge measures excitement. Commercial property, IP, general commercial litigation and health professional indemnity are also specific attractions of an office where the hours are generally longer "*but rarely later than 8.30pm and never that for days on end.*" When they do leave the office, Cardiff trainees are well placed to take advantage of the attractions of this busy city. "*It's a great mix of city life with the possibility of getting out to the country very easily,*" said one.

a tale of two valleys

No matter which location they call home, trainees were almost unanimous in praising a "*responsive approach to training*" that means "*if you're too busy you shout and if you're not busy enough you shout.*" Giving a bit of backbone to this supple arrangement, three-monthly reviews allow supervisor and trainee to keep tabs on progress and each trainee is appointed a mentor for the duration of their contract.

Although trainees do tend (particularly in Wales) to possess some relatively strong local connection, beyond this factor our interviewees found it difficult to pin down any shared characteristics. Our sense is that if you're Welsh and looking for a corporate training in Wales, the firm stands out as an obvious choice, but students looking for a Thames Valley training should make sure the locations and seat options will allow them to further their particular ambitions. In September 2006, ten of the 14 qualifiers clearly felt that way, accepting NQ positions with the firm, although there were more than enough jobs for all.

and finally...

Offering a solid training with plenty of choice, Morgan Cole's appeal has substantially increased as its fortunes wax once more. A no-brainer for those sporting daffodils and one for St George's stock to add to the shortlist.

Nabarro Nathanson

the facts

Location: London, Sheffield
Number of UK partners/solicitors: 116/225
Total number of trainees: 52
Seats: 6x4 months
Alternative seats: Brussels, secondments
Extras: Language training

If you're eager to get on the property ladder we'll be preaching to the converted with this firm. But what if the sum total of your property interest adds up to feeling quite pleased that the shop next door is being bought by a pub company? Could you be just as happy at this firm?

clicks and mortar

Nabarro has a fantastic reputation and acts for some of the biggest names in the property industry. Think Land Securities, Quintain, British Land and Grosvenor and you're on track. The firm has a hand in the high-profile developments of Stratford City in east London and the land surrounding the new Wembley Stadium, and currently advises on the £500 million retail development of Cardiff city centre. Most of the trainees we spoke to mentioned property in almost the first breath, but were also mindful of what else Nabarro had to offer them.

The corporate team, for example, has settled into its stride on larger mid-market deals including an impressive volume of AIM transactions. It has notably scooped a role for Quintain on its joint venture with American casino company Caesars Entertainment. The two are bidding to develop the UK's first super-casino and hope to build it in Wembley. Following the closure of its Reading office in 2005 Nabarro's IT practice has regrouped in London and continues to do interesting work for IT services and software companies, a clientele the firm has successfully introduced to other departments. For example, property lawyers have helped Apple Computer open retail outlets around the UK; corporate lawyers have worked on a variety of technology sector M&A deals and floats; and IBM and Atos Origin have sought pensions advice. The firm has been similarly successful at sharing its property industry clients around. In banking, lawyers help them with all sorts of financing, lately developing a new property-based derivative product for Quintain. Construction lawyers work hand in hand with the property colleagues all the time, recently on Land Securities' construction of a £250 million office block in London's Fetter Lane. Even the employment lawyers are in on the act, advising Quintain, Slough Estates and Wembley Estates on workplace-related issues.

Corporate, employment, finance, construction; all these departments would throw their arms up in horror if described as support groups for the property department, but it is true to say that a good part of their income comes from the property industry. Said one trainee: "*You see how it all slots together; you see how each client fits within the wider business of the firm.*" In essence what the firm has done is taken advantage of its core clients' additional service requirements, worked hard to fulfil them and then used the experience to win other business. Not so many years ago we would have described Nabarro as hungry for diversification; these days it looks more like a firm that has succeeded in building on its strengths.

place your bets

In the six-seat training scheme, corporate, litigation and property are all compulsory, but within this there is room for manoeuvre when someone has "*a burning interest*" and there's a degree of flexiblity within the compulsories (eg litigation can be property lit or employment). Overall, most people get what they want, though maybe not in the order they expect. In any reasonably large trainee group you're going to hear differing views on which seats are best, worst, easiest, dullest and so on. Take property for example; it is either "*great, fantastically busy and varied*" or "*compulsory and good to get out of the way.*" Supervisors (almost always senior assistants) give trainees their own files where possible to ensure a degree of autonomy. The nature of the job means "*a lot of small things going on all at once – you are constantly juggling,*" drafting leases, rent reviews, preparing sales packs, registering properties and so on. A lack of work is never a problem; indeed, "*you have to be careful not to take on too much.*" The same can be said of property litigation, a successful department where being a stickler for detail will go a long way in your favour.

The hours in corporate "*tend to be slightly longer but are not a nightmare by any means.*" One of the firm's flagship deals was the £512 million AIM flotation of Internet gaming business Empire Online. It's a good example both of the scale of transaction with which the firm now feels comfortable and its reputation in the gaming industry. Trainees do the usual tasks in corporate – drafting board minutes, managing documentation, preparing bibles, etc. – and in true Nabarro fashion most enjoy getting stuck in and "*working towards a common goal.*"

An employment law and internal regulation secondment to Oxford University is "*a unique experience.*" Trainees lucky enough to secure this took an active role in "*internal disciplinary hearings, harassment cases, and people appealing their exam results. Also there was quite a lot of work in relation to data protection and freedom of information.*" The seat means rubbing shoulders with staff at many of the colleges and with the students bringing claims. Perhaps attracted by a mix of large-scale transactions and specialist research tasks, one source singled out the projects team as their reason for coming to the firm. Nabarro is a leading player in this field and our source spoke of the satisfaction gained from acting for a financier on a large national project: "*I had to pull together expertise from all over – employment, banking and property – and I had real exposure to the whole firm... the projects department is a great example of Nabarro acting as an integrated law firm; some of the partners have offices in London and Sheffield.*"

peak practice

Ah yes, Sheffield. Northern readers were probably wondering when we were going to discuss it. Our first question to the Yorkshire folk at Nabarro was this: with the London heart of the firm boasting a fragrant coffee lounge and softly illuminated atrium, what would make a prospective trainee take an express train to Nabarro Nathanson North? "*I wanted to settle in the North and looked for a firm that had a London pedigree as well as a northern reputation – Nabarro fitted the bill,*" replied a source without a moment's hesitation. Add in a waterfront location ("*water shimmering and boats sailing past*"), ample parking for those commuting from Leeds or further afield and the same Nabarro feel-good factor, and choosing

Sheffield becomes a no-brainer for those inseparable from the city. There are other big firms locally – Irwin Mitchell and DLA for starters – but if you prefer the idea of working in a smaller office with fewer trainees, neither of these are going to fit the bill. Quite simply, Nabarro Sheffield offers a smaller environment with the cachet of a big London name.

The list of potential seats is comprehensive – corporate, litigation, projects and property are the mainstream choices – and those looking for a more tailor-made Yorkshire experience have some interesting options. There's a first-class personal injury department where lawyers represent the government on claims arising from the activities of British Coal, the state-owned enterprise that once ran the UK's coal industry. Respiratory diseases, knee injuries and vibration white finger damage from drill use make this particular PI experience "*quite niche and very rewarding.*" Nabarro's key environmental law team is also located in Sheffield and provides "*fascinating work.*" Last year it represented the Peak District National Park Authority in its successful defence of High Court and Court of Appeal applications by a quarrying company seeking to have the dormant Stanton Moor quarries reclassified as active. The matter was the subject of intensive press coverage and the team was also asked by the judge to represent the eco-warriors occupying the site.

tonight, I am going to be...

It follows that an integrated firm is likely to have "*a collective approach to socialising.*" Sheffield and London trainees form an initial bond during a joint induction in London. They have another opportunity to compare the price of a pint when the southerners travel north for more training at the start of their second year. "*It's really so we can get training on business skills, but it's also a social opportunity... and it's a lot more fun than work* should be." Back in London "*everyone goes out on a Friday*" to either the Perseverance or the Enterprise (for the perfect pint of Adnams Broadside). Office parties are "*your typical boozy affairs,*" and when trainees change seats "*there are always welcome drinks and drinks to thank those who are departing.*" For the energetic there's the Oxfam Trailwalker challenge, "*some ridiculously long 100 km walk*" across the South Downs. To fund-raise for this last year Nabarro put on a Stars In Their Eyes show which, depending on your point of view, was either "*serious people making complete fools of themselves*" or "*performances of a very high standard – I think they spent a lot of time rehearsing.*" The night proved so successful that it was resurrected in 2006.

If "*the whole point of training is to prepare you for qualification in the round not just the black letter law*" then Nabarro is doing it right. "*They are looking for people who are intelligent but who are able to get on with everyone else, not least with clients.*" If you fit the bill "*you get exposure to lots of different projects, to charity work, to client networking.*" The firm places an emphasis on trainees gaining marketing skills and building useful contacts. It has long run a group called Contact NN, which aims to get young professionals in related sectors together for social and educational purposes. Summing up, one source concluded: "*Nabarro is very much designed to get people talking to each other rather than acting in isolation.*"

The firm has a decent retention record, although in September 2006 a cluster of qualifiers wanted employment jobs. As none were to be had this contributed noticeably to the lower than average retention rate of eight out of 16.

A great deal of emphasis is placed on Nabarro's vacation scheme, when applicants can spend three weeks doing "*a mini seat*" in a single department. All our interviewees had completed such a placement and were full of praise for the way the firm had looked after them. "*In other firms you can feel like a spare part, but here you get a mini project and a team exercise culminating in a presentation, so you can work on that when your supervisor is busy.*" For one it was such a painless process that "*by the time it came to the final interview for a training contract it was more like a chat as we already knew each other.*" Having signed on the dotted line, future trainees get a buddy from the current group to serve as a point of contact until they're settled at the firm. It certainly helps ease first-day nerves, meaning all you need to worry about is whether you've packed your lunch money and what you're going to wear on the big day.

and finally...

If you want to get your foot in the door at Nabarro Nathanson apply for the vac scheme, as this is where the firm scouts around 85% of its trainees. Early bird readers will be even happier to learn that the firm has now decided to get 'em while they're young by offering open days for first-year law students.

Norton Rose

the facts
Location: London
Number of UK partners/solicitors: 123/277
Total number of trainees: 105
Seats: 6x4 months
Alternative seats: Overseas seats, secondments
Extras: Pro bono – Tower Hamlets, Tooting and Battersea Law Centres, RCJ CAB, FRU; language training (incl. Chinese)

A top-ten player in London, Norton Rose is on the shortlist for many students. Its impressive network of overseas offices acts as a reminder that it was once a key player in shipping law, but today the name Norton Rose is synonymous with finance.

an abundance of finance

A six-seat training system stipulates that everyone spends time in the corporate finance, banking and dispute resolution divisions. This then gives three more opportunities to explore other aspects of the firm's work: perhaps an international seat or client secondment; maybe something niche. Seat allocation follows well-established rules; however, there are two important things to remember. First, it's far easier to get your preferred seat options if they are finance and corporate-related, and second, upon qualification a high proportion of the jobs tend to come up in banking and corporate teams.

NR is particularly respected for its asset finance, project finance and Islamic finance expertise, so if the smell of money – the petrol in the world's economic engine – excites you then this is a good choice as NR finance lawyers handle some pretty juicy deals. In asset finance they acted for easyJet on lending facilities to finance the acquisition cost of 82 Airbus A319 aircraft with a list price in excess of $3.6 billion. In project finance they have been advising on the development of Bahrain Financial Harbour, which aims to become the premier business and financial centre in the Gulf. Working on such matters trainees occasionally get to accompany partners to overseas offices, typically tasked with collaborating with local counsel and collecting documents as the team works towards a deal closure. Naturally, not all the finance seats are so glamorous: much of the UK-based project finance relates to transportation. Take the multi-billion-pound refinancing of the London Underground Jubilee, Northern and Piccadilly lines PPP for example.

Given the variety of different finance seat options trainees may find themselves allocated to teams focusing on acquisition finance, project finance, Islamic finance or asset finance. Although they are exposed to a range of transactions, *"drafting and proof-reading is fairly standard."* If the thought of drafting from scratch is a little daunting don't worry: *"We have got a massive precedent system here – you can just print off whichever one you need,"* one trainee reassured us. *"The training is second to none here,"* another was keen to add. *"A few of the partners are academics and they have produced amazing practice notes that are easily accessible."*

at the coal face

The *"very, very nice"* corporate team is reputed to be *"a tight, sociable group"* with *"the work-hard, play-hard lifestyle you imagine City lawyers to have."* Trainees told us: *"The champagne flows when a deal reaches completion"* and *"there are lots of team days and boozy lunches."* Whilst the 'play-hard' activities sound like fun, the 'work-hard' bit sometimes leaves much to be desired. *"As a trainee the work is quite mundane,"* one source moaned; another agreed: *"The long hours were filled with boring tasks."* Admittedly the size of deals makes it hard to get front-line exposure: the firm recently advised the Drax Group, owner of the largest coal-fired power station in Western Europe, on its refinancing and listing on the London Stock Exchange. It also advised Northern Gas Networks on a £1.4 billion acquisition of Transco's north of England local gas distribution network. Pretty impressive stuff although *"the work that seemed to be left for me in this department was usually very menial,"* one interviewee grumbled. At least *"people in the team would take the time to explain the bigger picture to me."* Verification exercises and proof-reading seemed to be fairly typical for trainees. Some of our sources had also got drafting experience; one telling us: *"The best way to learn is when a document is given back to you heavily marked up."*

Readers will be pleased to note that this year the majority view on hours, even in corporate, was pretty upbeat. *"I have never experienced the horror stories of all-nighters,"* said one relieved source; others confirmed they had never worked a weekend. Supervisors are said to approach the subject of hours *"as reasonably as they can."*

Four-month seats are available in Athens, Munich, Paris, Prague, Frankfurt, Amsterdam, Moscow, Singapore, Hong Kong, Dubai and Bahrain. Hong Kong is a popular option. *"It was fantastic,"* one interviewee told us. *"Socially it's amazing because you mix with trainees from all the other firms; there was about 40 or 50 of us out there from London."* In contrast, trainees in the Dubai office can expect their four months abroad to be more work-dominated as plenty of firms are in competition to establish themselves in the Middle East finance markets. *"We often worked on the financial close of transactions until 2 or 3am,"* recalled a source.

loyal supporters

If the thought of working with over 200 partners, 1,000 lawyers and 2,000 staff worldwide is daunting, it needn't be. NR is rightly renowned for its team-oriented culture. *"There is a great emphasis on teamwork,"* our sources confirmed. *"It is a big place but my team is only eight to ten people – that's the size of a small firm in Newcastle – they are the people I am with every day and we all get on well together."* The smart way to approach your training is to set about finding the right team that does the right kind of work for you.

Trainees were quick to praise the grad recruitment process, highlighting *"painless"* interviews that were widely viewed as *"more like a chat than a grilling."* *"Mine wasn't intimidating at all, even though I later found out it had been a senior partner interviewing me,"* said one source. On arrival everyone is assigned a mentor for the duration of the contract, *"usually quite a senior partner, unconnected with the appraisal system."* The ideal

mentor will dispense good advice and lunch on a regular basis. Indeed, *"there is a lot of support here generally; people to whom you can go, not just with a problem but to get a view."*

NR trainees are a loyal bunch; they are people for whom the quality of work relationships are of paramount importance and they tell us that *"the ethos and the way that you are treated"* encourages them to stay at NR. Affection for the firm is a big motivator on qualification: while *"some people find an obvious niche,"* one source explained, *"I know people staying on in banking and corporate when they never wanted to do that [kind of work]."*

just be yourself

Do trainees have anything in common? Apparently *"most people have travelled"* and *"language skills are a bonus."* Fittingly, the firm offers financial support to trainees-in-waiting and most use it to travel before starting their contracts. Those who take up this offer tend to start in January, whereas the September intake includes more of the *"married or settling down"* types, many of whom have worked elsewhere before embarking on a career in law. The firm is praised for recruiting *"non-Oxbridge types"* (though we are aware of no deliberate policy on this front) and sources were also quick to highlight the *"down-to-earth"* nature of their peers. *"I have met trainees at other firms who are complete space cadets but here there are decent guys who call a spade a spade,"* said one.

Perhaps it was candour that led interviewees to reiterate that because of the strong finance focus *"the opportunities for [going into niche] qualification seats are minimal."* As such, *"you would be a bit naïve coming here and expecting to guarantee qualifying into, say, employment."* As it turns out the NQ scores for 2006 were as follows: an excellent number stayed on (33 out of 35) with nine going into banking, six into corporate, five into dispute resolution and the remainder distributing themselves across the rest of the firm.

NR trainees have long enjoyed a decent social life. Last year their Christmas party took place in a Moorgate bar, with pre-joiners also invited to *"rock up for a lemonade."* Sadly the firm-wide summer party appeared to have been put on hold when we conducted our interviews and we heard that in recent years there had been cuts to the trainee social budget too. We doubt sport will ever lose its prominence at the firm. There are all manner of things available (*"football and golf for the boys, netball for the girls"*), even a weekend hiking club and *"some sort of polo."* It's not frowned upon to turn your back on colleagues at the end of the working week though. Said one busy source: *"I have a life outside London and one of my big fears was that I would be pressured to socialise heavily after hours – I just couldn't handle that."* At work and play, apparently *"this is genuinely a firm where you can be yourself."*

sugar and spice...

If you are looking for City training in a firm with a *"nice"* atmosphere, this is a fantastic choice. Some of you may find 'nice' a bland adjective and prefer to work in an environment where 'ballsy' or 'driven' spring to mind when describing the atmosphere, staff and partners. Perhaps you are looking for a dynamic environment where commercial aggression wins the day. Yes, the firm prides itself on its reputation for friendliness; yes, there is a huge emphasis on teamwork; and yes, mutual support among its personnel is more than evident. However, the flipside of this team culture is that it could be perceived to discourage the maverick individualistic characters who turbo-charge a team. The fact that *"no one is full of themselves here, not even the partners,"* might be good for nervous trainees, but is it always the best way to forge

ahead in a competitive business environment? This is a complex subject indeed, and NR is by no means the only law firm that has to balance the increasing pressures involved in creating and maintaining a working environment that both satisfies staff and boosts profit levels.

NR clearly makes considerable effort to listen to the needs of its lawyers and, with the aim of giving senior associates an alternative to the partnership track, it has created a new 'of counsel' tier to its hierarchy. When we checked in September 2006, 11 lawyers had been awarded this new status, seven of them women and six men. In terms of the gender balance at all levels of the firm, over 60% of trainees are female, as are just over half of the associates and 17% of partners. This latter figure is at the high end of average among the big City firms, although with just two out of the 13 internal partner promotions in May 2006 being women, this percentage will not have been boosted this year. What we also know is that the managing partner is female, as are a third of the global practice heads and a third of the executive committee.

The firm has not been immune from partner departures over the past five years and, even as recently as this year, lost its former global head of disputes and an M&A heavyweight among others. It's not been one-way traffic; the firm has captured some new partners too. It was interesting that trainees seemed to know little about the overall game plan: *"We don't hear much about strategy,"* one confirmed.

NR is currently split between half a dozen small offices, but is scheduled to move all staff under one roof in 2007 when it takes occupation of its smart, new, Foster-designed home at More London. The move will undoubtedly give a boost to the firm, which may in turn help it silence those critics who have labelled its recent financial performance as lacklustre when compared to some of the other big firms.

and finally...

Team players who seek a supportive training environment will be happy here. As one trainee put it: "*I look forward to coming to work every day.*" That kind of statement is hard to argue with.

Olswang

the facts

Location: London, Reading
Number of UK partners/solicitors: 75/167
Total number of trainees: 41
Seats: 4x6 months
Alternative seats: Brussels, secondments
Extras: Pro bono – Toynbee Hall and Tower Hamlets Law Centres

Once the new media kid on the block, Olswang has shed modish excesses, grown up and got serious. A 20% increase in turnover for 2005/06, bringing per equity partner profits of half a mill, has got to be the perfect 25th birthday present.

a gamble that paid off

In common with other firms of its generation, Olswang had to battle to establish itself and developed an ambitious, hungry outlook. On the back of the late-90s dotcom boom, it expanded exponentially and adopted a sky's the limit philosophy, illustrated by the fact that staff numbers have grown from 30 to 350 lawyers in the last decade alone. But as we all know, flying high can be dangerous if you soar too close to the sun, and Olswang's Icarian episode came with the 2001 dotcom crash. Pumped up with high staff numbers, many of them working for clients in the technology sector, the firm had a long way to fall. The story turns out happily though: the true grit belied by Olswang's cool persona showed through when it picked itself up and set about a process of diversification based on sound business principles rather than opportunism.

By expanding its corporate and real estate limbs while its core TMT clientele struggled, Olswang moved closer to achieving its goal of becoming a top-30 firm. First it acquired an office in Reading and hired a legion of property lawyers from disbanded London firm DJ Freeman. Eight more lawyers then joined from niche property outfit Julian Holy in late 2005, closely followed by lawyers from another property boutique, Kanter Jules. Already respected, the property department has moved to another level and now brings in around 20% of Olswang's revenue. At the same time the corporate groups have also flourished and bring in over 40% of the firm's dosh. Here lawyers recently advised the Tchenguiz family trust on its lead role in the private equity consortium that made a £1 billion takeover bid for the Somerfield supermarket group, and HIT Entertainment, a client since 1995, which it guided through the £489 million takeover by Sunshine Acquisition. As that transaction indicates, while corporate and real estate are the engine of the firm these days, a large proportion of its business involves media and technology sector clients. Firmly at the forefront of trends, Olswang has used its online gaming expertise to win work for PartyGaming on its £144 million acquisition of Empire Online. Similarly, Independent News & Media used the firm when it acquired a 20% share in UK online gaming company Cashcade.

Yet The Swang isn't satisfied with purely domestic achievements. Clearly determined to make waves internationally, it has reached out to major US firm Greenberg Traurig to establish a strategic alliance, and is not ruling out the possibility of a merger. There are also plans to create offices or close alliances in Germany, France and China.

media rare

It is tribute to the management team that has run the firm since 1997 that it now presides over a secure, broad, mid-market outfit on the up and up, but has this wider success been at the expense of all that sexy media and technology work for which Olswang was once so famous? Well, yes and no. Sure, it lost two media litigation partners to niche firm Howard Kennedy, and a life science/tech corporate lawyer to Taylor Wessing this year, but its excellence in all things meeja continues unabated. A stellar clientele includes eBay, FilmFour, M&C Saatchi, Red Bee Media (formerly BBC Broadcast), BSkyB, ITV, MTV, Working Title Films and Guardian Newspapers. Covering all bases, the media communications and technology (MCT) department comprises: Team 1 – internet, e-commerce and data protection issues; Team 2 – broadcasting, TV, publishing and advertising; Team 3 – film; and Team 4 – IP litigation.

A crucial question for many trainees is how feasible is it to gain exposure to the work of these teams. The people we interviewed were very clear that "*the old media reputation has much less to do with what's actually going on now and where the firm's priorities lie.*" Having perhaps applied with the glamour of defamation cases and film industry clients in mind, the reality of the new-look Olswang left certain, though not all, trainees underwhelmed. Views on whether it's possible to get into a specific media seat varied from the negative ("*I clearly stated that I wanted IP litigation and didn't get it*" and "*you'd be well advised to look elsewhere if you have your heart set on a media qualification job*") to the very positive ("*You will definitely do one media seat at least and some lucky people get two*"). To test the accuracy of such statements, we asked the firm to break down the retention stat of 17 out of 19 2006 qualifiers by department. It told us that while some people did go into MCT teams, the largest proportion took jobs in the corporate practice.

still got the magic

Beyond MCT, the other seat options in the four-seat scheme ensure that the training is in no way restrictive. The corporate alternatives are mainstream corporate, private equity, tax and banking; the property department can offer a myriad of work types; and for some a litigation seat can mean employment law. To add pizzazz, many trainees go on client secondments to places such as the BBC, Film Four and HIT Entertainment. A seat in competition law at the firm's Brussels office is another one to play for.

Despite the absence of compulsories, Olswang's focus means it would be a rare trainee who didn't do at least one stint in the corporate group, which is where the work is "*undoubtedly the most hardcore.*" Although trainees can at times expect "*to still be up at 4am knowing you'll be in until 12 the next night,*" some consolation is to be found in the fact that "*there's no pretence; everyone is openly miserable – we'll have a moan and put music on....the camaraderie is great.*" Trainee work can be "*document and data-management heavy,*" but even a one-time naysayer told us: "*I thought I'd hate it, but my supervisor was great and got me involved in drafting documents and negotiating smaller points with the other lawyers.*" Another fillip on corporate deals is the presence of those trendy media clients – "*It's not rational at all, but having famous names at the top of the documents just does make the work seem more appetising,*" confessed one trainee. Interestingly, when it comes to MCT seats the trainees look at it from a different perspective: "*You've got to remember that although it's film, sports or IP work, they're just names on the papers you handle and the work is complex, often quite dry law.*"

Readers, ignore such spoilsportery! MCT seats do have a certain lustre to them, whether this be through "*trips to court and research on trade marks or patents*" in IP, "*seeing cases from conception to conclusion"* in defamation, or *"drafting sponsorship endorsement agreements and researching sports agents"* in Team 2. By contrast, property offers no glamour at all but *"lots of client contact and your own files, which really refine your all-round lawyering skills."*

putting the swan in olswang

With thousands of applications landing on its doormat Olswang is very selective about who it recruits. A few older trainees arrive with backgrounds in music, advertising or TV/film; beyond that the defining criteria have more to do with personality than where you went to university or what you studied while you were there. Apparently *"you know an Olswang trainee without a shadow of a doubt,"* so we'll hand over to our sources on the inside to help you figure out if you have what it takes.

"Everyone is slightly quirky, bohemian or offbeat, has an odd background or interest, and a strong personality," thought one. *"We don't mind standing out from the crowd,"* another observed, a third adding: *"If all the individuals in a firm are like that, en masse you end up with a place that has a certain flair."* Amongst themselves trainees are friendly, but one distinctive consequence of all these strong personalities is an air of *"covert ambition."* We hear that *"people are competitive, but not outwardly,"* with the result that *"there's an amiable atmosphere but with an undercurrent."* Maybe Olswang trainees are the swans of the legal world: a smooth surface glide hiding fervid paddling below. Part of this paddling is geared towards personal reputation-building, which if done properly means *"people will look out for you and make an effort to stretch you."*

dutch courage required

Olswang's High Holborn office was designed to resemble a sail, although the closest you actually get to a whiff of sea breeze is in subsidised staff restaurant Ozone on the seventh floor. The standard corporate furnishings and *"weird art on the walls"* is a far cry from the firm's more sober Reading office, which spans two floors of a block close to the town centre and rail station. The few trainees in Reading can usually take a seat in London if they want one, and the odd City trainee spends a short spell out in the Thames Valley. The latest financial figures show that the five-partner Reading office has been doing rather well, so if you hear rumours about big law firms leaving town – one did 18 months ago – ignore them.

Across the two offices the social scene is flourishing, particularly at trainee level. In London informal drinks usually take place in BPP law school favourite the Square Pig or *"one of Holborn's many lounge bars like Torts."* Organised parties on the office roof terrace and football and softball games are interspersed with *"all-expenses-paid"* departmental away weekends to various European cities, Barcelona being the most frequently visited. However, socially the defining aspect of 2006 was the firm's 25th anniversary celebrations and quest to raise £250,000 for charity Fairbridge. To this end, staff have busied themselves with sponsored events including the London marathon and a trainee-organised karaoke night. Full respect to the trainee who revealed: *"Some of us have risen to the challenge and we're performing to the entire firm. I think the quality of my performance may depend utterly on having a few drinks beforehand."*

and finally...

Olswang's broad corporate training is garnished with some sexy clients and tasty media work. If you're ambitious this could be a great firm for you just don't expect to swan into a training contract.

Orrick, Herrington & Sutcliffe

the facts
Location: London
Number of UK partners/solicitors: 15/26
Total number of trainees: 13
Seats: 4x6 months
Alternative seats: None
Extras: Pro bono – Special Olympics

Conceived in San Francisco in 1863, Orrick's roots lie in public finance and corporate law. Orrick lawyers famously worked on the bond issue that helped finance the construction of the city's Golden Gate Bridge. More than 140 years on, the firm has established expertise in the full gamut of commercial practice areas and its brand is recognised way beyond the California state borders. It currently has 16 offices across the USA and in six countries in Asia and Europe.

keeping it international
In September 2006, Orrick was in merger talks with New York-based firm Dewey Ballantine. Obviously you'll have to keep an eye on progress on that score, but what is beyond doubt is that the firm is in a phase of aggressive growth in Europe and Asia. The London office more than doubled in size to 50 lawyers in 2005, in no small part as a result of the *"wholesale transfer"* of the London contingent of the former international firm Coudert Brothers. This acquisition was rather succinctly described by one of our interviewees as *"the Orrick/Coudert hoo-ha,"* but we are told the transfer was all pretty painless (from Orrick's point of view at least) as *"everyone blended in smoothly."* Pushing on, the London head of operations has outlined a strategy for capitalising on this momentum by building up such areas as structured finance, private equity and arbitration. The 2005 transfer included most of Coudert's trainee population as well as future

joiners lined up for the following two years. This effectively kick-started the formal training programme at Orrick London, and the firm now plans to take around five trainees a year.

So what can students expect? The short answer is four six-month seats in a decent range of departments. It was a good job our sources raved about finance as this seat is now compulsory for all. *"I was involved in a big refinancing deal – an incredible experience,"* said one. Orrick has clear strength in this area and attracts some top-quality instructions. JPMorgan and Société Générale, for example, recently sought counsel on the $5 billion acquisition finance facilities provided to fund Pernod Ricard and Diageo's purchase of the spirits and wine division of Seagram. The relatively small size of the office (compared to the firms sitting on the other side of deals) means the teams handling this kind of transaction are correspondingly streamlined. In turn this means trainees *"really feel part of things"* and have *"that extra bit of influence."* We're talking about *"a surprising amount of client contact plus contact with lawyers on the other side."* Naturally you will also be required to roll up your sleeves to muck in with document management tasks.

Corporate work also features greatly and trainees reported getting *"a bit of a buzz"* when they realised the matters clogging up their Outlook calendar were the very same as those making the headlines of the *FT*. We're talking about things such as the recent €440 million acquisition of seven Center Parcs European holiday resorts from Pierre & Vacances and the $950 million merger of OAO Vimpel-Communications, a NYSE-listed Russian mobile operator, and OAO VimpelCom-Region, a Russian regional mobile operator. As a vital member of a tight deal team you should view liaising with clients and taking conference calls as standard. Remember too that as many of the deals are cross-border you'll always be on the phone to lawyers overseas.

The international dispute resolution team has been involved in some pretty heavyweight matters before the English courts, representing the Electricity Supply Board of Ireland against ExxonMobil in its successful challenge of a price review in a long-term gas supply contract, as well as Hyundai Engineering and Construction in a $250 million bond-trading dispute with Deutsche Bank Trustee. Trainees should be prepared to work at the sharp end, clocking up some *"invaluable experience drafting letters of claim and instructions to counsel, attending court and liaising with barristers."* Orrick's ongoing commitment to pro bono work and community involvement shines through in this area, so you might have access to such worthy matters as *"a really interesting Holocaust insurance case."*

light on your feet

An employment seat will see you sitting in a small but recently expanded team and becoming *"very involved in the whole process."* Said one trainee: *"I had client contact, was sent to court and did my own advocacy – it was really exciting."* You need to be able to *"think on your feet and stay on your toes."* Again the firm's corporate law interests show through; even in employment you will contribute to the success of transaction teams by helping to structure deals in the most efficient manner from a staffing perspective. By doing this you will *"get to learn that there are international aspects to employment law."* At other times you'll be supporting lawyers in delicate negotiations over senior-employee departures, such as in the recent case of a global consumer products manufacturer that needed to remove the chief executive and finance director of one of its largest UK business operations. Don't expect to be at the client end of things all the time as *"bundles and photocopying"* appear on the to-do list as well.

Although we've talked about seats, *"one of the big pluses is that it's not quite as rigid"* as some training contracts, so although *"you will be assigned a specific department, if the business need dictates you could be seconded to another matter in a different area."* We should add that there are also possibilities to be seconded to offices in Asia or the Paris branch if you play your cards right.

One interviewee who had been led to believe there was less emphasis on formal training at US firms in London couldn't have been more pleasantly surprised, since *"training is scheduled twice a week"* with sessions from *"both internal and external speakers."* On a day-to-day basis trainees found ample support in colleagues and felt comfortable to *"speak to partners without feeling stupid or scared."* As one put it: *"When I think, 'bugger, what's happening?' I just ask."* Even if some of the specifics of this system are likely to evolve as Orrick shapes its own training scheme, it is likely that this ethos will remain.

eyes down

The firm's choice of offices on lofty level 35 of the City's iconic Tower 42 may have backfired on the productivity front: trainees say marvelling at the *"amazing views"* of *"everything"* can be *"quite distracting."* Still, the place is kitted out with all the mod cons one would expect of such a high-rise residence, so the *"general working environment is conducive to really performing well."* Out-of-office assistance comes from across the Atlantic as the firm's global operations centre – sorry, center – in West Virginia houses the technology, finance, transcript production and HR services and provides round-the-clock administrative support to lawyers worldwide. Needless to say, London trainees feel *"pretty well hooked up."* Accessing such impressive *"global resources"* from a *"human-sized"* City office delivers the best of both worlds, according to our sources. The small size of the offices allows Orrick to maintain a relatively *"relaxed"* atmosphere, even *"in the middle of big deals when tensions can run high and the adrenaline is pumping."*

We asked our interviewees what kind of people Orrick is choosing to recruit. Words like *"driven," "responsible"* and *"mature"* cropped up. By 'mature' they meant in outlook, not necessarily age, though some kind of experience outside university may well be an advantage. They certainly stressed: *"Don't come here unless you are ambitious. You have to be the kind of person who enjoys getting involved as this is not a spoon-feeding environment."* Essentially the people who train here should *"have a real contribution to make."* In September 2006, two of the four qualifiers accepted NQ positions (all four were offered jobs).

There are no real horror stories on the hours front. *"Generally not too bad"* seems to sum things up. Of course this is all relative to expectations, as one person's 'not too bad' is another's nightmare material. Predictably, the amount of time you'll spend in the office *"depends on the deal and the department;"* at times a 7pm finish could be the norm, at others you might work until 4am or pull an all-nighter or a couple of weekends when a deal is reaching its peak.

don't mention the score

Trainees talked in some detail about widely held preconceptions regarding US firms in London being *"aggressive places to be."* In Orrick's case, they told us, these ideas should be dispelled. *"It's a very social place"* and *"we do have fun,"* they assured us, citing *"drinks for almost any occasion dotted throughout the year."* Our interviews were conducted during the 2006 FIFA World Cup and we were interested to hear about the firm's decision to *"convert one of the conference rooms into a TV room for matches, with table football, beer and pizza."* The Christmas party was by all accounts *"a brilliant event at which people stayed, and stayed, and stayed – as a bonding experience it was great for the team dynamic."* If you like mixing business with pleasure, then you will be pleased to know that *"trainees are always part of marketing and client events."*

and finally...

Looking for a firm with a global network, massive resources, top-quality work and an international outlook? Magic circle's the place to be, right? Not necessarily. With bags of early responsibility and an intimate working environment in which you can make a name for yourself, the new Orrick training programme looks set to become a hot prospect. From a trainee's perspective, Coudert's demise has been no bad thing.

Osborne Clarke

the facts

Location: Bristol, London, Reading
Number of UK partners/solicitors: 86/194
Total number of trainees: 41
Seats: 4x6 months
Alternative seats: Overseas seats, secondments

Many years ago Mr Jeremiah Osborne was legal adviser to Isambard Kingdom Brunel. OC lore has it that Osborne and Brunel rowed a boat down the Avon to survey the bank for its suitability as a site for the Great Western Railway. Osborne and his colleagues then helped guide a bill through Parliament in 1835, allowing the railway to be built and thereby opening up the whole of the West of England. Neatly in keeping with this little piece of British industrial history, today OC's three UK offices are stationed at points on the very same railway line.

OCidental?

From the age of steam to the digital age, and how things have changed. Following a recent period of international expansion OC now boasts an impressive list of offices and alliance partners in Belgium, Estonia, Finland, France, Germany, Italy, Russia, Spain, the Netherlands and California. It was the technology boom of the late 90s that fuelled much of OC's international expansion, and against the odds the firm is as healthy now as it was before the dotcom downturn. It has managed this largely by beefing up in other non-tech-based disciplines and attracting a broad sweep of active clients. There are household names galore on the firm's client list, both in the tech sector and beyond it – Microsoft, Carphone Warehouse, Amazon, Yahoo!, IKEA, Bolton Wanderers FC, Ryder Cup, Imperial Tobacco and 3i – the list is truly extensive. Last year the firm handled the e-commerce aspects of Friends Reunited's sale to ITV; advised uSwitch, owner of the UK's leading online comparison and switching website, on its £210 million sale to a US media concern; and assisted Sony on its deal with Sky in respect of the supply of HDTV.

Corporate looks to be getting a lot of attention and the firm is working hard to build its name in the private equity and AIM markets, where there are many technology-related deals. In the assessment of one trainee: *"It is taking on fewer clients but making sure the ones they hold onto are really high-profile."* It is also developing a taste for poached partners from the likes of Lovells and Linklaters, doubtless to assist with plans to become a top-20 UK law firm.

OCult

The firm believes fervently in the idea of one firm, three offices in the UK, and as such trainees join OC the firm not an individual office. Seats are spread across all three offices; Bristol offering most, followed by London then Reading. There are no compulsory seats (more on that later). Although there are many options to choose from, it seems that trainees need to be flexible and open-minded about what they get.

A corporate seat is felt by many trainees to be one that they ought not miss, even if there's a bit of trepidation beforehand. *"It wasn't as bad as I thought it was going to be, and I never felt that my work was all the mundane stuff that no one else wanted,"* concluded one source. Even as a first seat *"it's not too traumatic,"* as long as you can demonstrate *"enthusiasm and passion for the work."* The advice of one trainee was to *"read The Lawyer and the FT to find out what deals are out there."* Naturally there is *"boring stuff as well as the good stuff,"* so making recognition from partners all the sweeter. *"They will e-mail you to thank you for your participation, and you feel really well appreciated."* In London, the corporate seat can entail very long hours. One source had done *"a couple of 70-hour weeks during a very busy M&A stint... one Saturday morning we finished a deal at 6am."* You'll be pleased to learn that *"crazy hours pay off with the sense of satisfaction you get. Like when I saw the Friends Reunited deal mentioned on the ITV news. I had a real buzz and sense of achievement."* For one source a high degree of client contact and responsibility was ultimately rewarded with a personal thank you and a meal from the client. If the adrenaline of all-night deal completions is more like your idea of trainee hell than legal heaven you could try a corporate tax seat. It's research-heavy and the department is one of the quieter ones – *"they just put their heads down and get on with the job."*

Most trainees also believe they should give property a whirl as it involves *"daily contact with clients, and you get your own files."* They are given varying amounts of responsibility, according to which number seat they're in, though tasks often include *"filling in forms and registrations – quite process-driven."* In a banking seat in Bristol supervisors place a lot of trust in trainees and put a fair amount of responsibility on their shoulders. Drafting resolutions, preparing for completions and ensuring registration of security documents is *"pretty much the staple diet,"* and trainees like the seat because *"it's a good chance to get stuck in and stand on your own two feet."* A banking/corporate seat in Reading takes the overspill from Bristol, putting the occupant with *"a high-pressured but supportive team."*

As almost everywhere, employment law seats are continually oversubscribed. Because they are available in all three offices, trainees may "*have to make concessions about location*" if their heart is set on one. Most see an office move as a price worth paying for the experiences on offer. "*There's a lot of research and corporate support,*" dealing with issues of appointments and terminations, immigration, race, gender, disability and data protection. For some it was the contentious side to the work that was most exciting. One reported eagerly on their exposure to trials and hearings – "*I have been to the High Court for an important case, just to sit and watch. And I've been to a tribunal and drafted instructions to counsel.*" Commercial litigation in Bristol is another popular seat, not least because of its "*friendly and open buddy atmosphere.*" It sounds like there's an interesting range of work, with one trainee telling us: "*I'm doing an international arbitration at the moment, and have also been involved in some trials and been given my own client on a small matter.*" That said, if you come to it as a first seat it can be "*fairly mundane – you only get to play a small part in a huge case.*"

OCean drives

Seats in insolvency litigation, competition and IT/IP are also offered, and some lucky people get to spend three months in OC's sunny Californian office. The California seat is a corporate and commercial position with a substantial element of business development and marketing thrown in. The office advises West Coast clients on how to set up in business in Europe, "*persuading Americans to use Osborne Clarke*" in the process. As you might expect, the California secondees have "*a brilliant time – you get a flat and a car, and you get to live in San Francisco.*" The word on the street is that new secondments to major corporate clients may be cropping up shortly, although sadly these are in damp Ol' Blighty not sunny Californi-a. Seats are also available in the firm's German offices

for those whose language skills are up to it. We pass no judgement on the weather there.

Now for the bad news. We picked up on "*a lot of discontentment*" concerning seat allocation. With no seat compulsory, too much choice seems to have resulted in too little satisfaction. Several sources suggested there should be less choice: "*People would be happier all round if there were some compulsory ones, and it would stop the backlash when people realise they're not getting what they want.*" In some, albeit rare, cases, trainees can go through the entire four-seat training contract never having managed to try any of their first-choice seats. Another problem arises when notification of the next seat comes quite late. "*Moving offices has been a massive hassle,*" grumbled one source; "*it's a big thing to pack up your life at such short notice.*" There's a general sense that "*the firm encourages movement between offices but it doesn't make it that easy.*"

OCupational hazards

As a business, OC is clearly going to offer more seats in those areas of practice which are doing well and growing. The problem is that they're not always the same areas that trainees are most enamoured with. For example, the enduring popularity of employment and commercial litigation means they are always oversubscribed and not everyone can be catered for. This naturally impacts on qualification and whether or not trainees choose to stay on. Only 17 of the 26 qualifiers took jobs with the firm in September 2006. The vacancies were apparently there, but "*in areas in which the trainees didn't want to qualify.*" Again, our sources had a suggestion to combat the problem of oversubscription of certain seats, mooting the idea of a six-seat system "*like they have at Burges Salmon.*" Accommodating needs and managing expectations is "*a tough job*" for HR, but trainees feel too much flexibility is expected of them within the current system.

Generally, the appraisal and supervision process is a model of transparency and efficiency, though in a small minority of cases (mentioning no names) it sounds like it could have been better. The worst we heard was a supervisor described as *"unresponsive, uncaring and unable to delegate work properly – making you just look crap all the time."* Such a situation *"marred"* the entire training for one source; for a couple of others it was just simply a short-term problem to be overcome. Perhaps, as one politely put it, *"consistency between departments"* could be something for the firm to work on. We should reiterate that this problem is limited in scope and for the majority of trainees relationships with supervisors were deemed very good.

OCupational therapy

So now onto the fun stuff, of which there is plenty. In Bristol the only pub near the office is a Wetherspoons (which tells us all we need to know), so the more upmarket Severn Shed has become the destination of choice. The only problem is *"Burges Salmon now go there too, causing a bit of rivalry."* Hopefully they can sort it out over pints of expensive Eastern European beer and platters of fusion food. London socialising tends to revolve around *"drinking at the Lord Raglan, regularly on Wednesday nights,"* while the Reading office has a quieter scene. All three offices come together to compare notes at a big summer bash, which in 2006 amounted to *"a medieval-themed party in a castle with a banquet and jousting."* Well, we've heard about the firm's 'one firm, three offices' UK philosophy, but surely plunging a six-foot long pike into a colleague from another office is not the best way to integrate!

and finally...

If you are prepared to practise what OC preaches on the 'one firm, three offices' idea, this high-quality training should satisfy. It has some big ideas up its sleeve at the moment, so well worth asking about these at interview.

Palmers

the facts

Location: Basildon, South Woodham Ferrers, Thurrock
Number of UK partners/solicitors: 11/13
Total number of trainees: 4
Seats: 4x6 months
Alternative seats: None

Essex: deepest, darkest Essex. How does one go about finding the right training here? *"If you know what you're looking for, you will find it,"* said one mystic who had recently landed a job at Palmers. But what if you don't know what you're looking for, if you can't tell your Essex from your elbow?

the name's bond, basildon bond

Let's start with Basildon. Through the power of research we learnt that Basildon was designated a New Town in 1949 to attract wretched city folk away from the smog and overcrowding of London. Pastoral idyll quickly turned into housing estates, yet the town retains its ability to lure trainees. *"We don't want to half kill ourselves in London, get an ulcer then retire."*

In Basildon, and indeed in the wider environs of south Essex, Palmers stands out as one of the largest commercial/private client firms offering traineeships. *"Everyone knows each other but we are one of the biggest firms in the area, so there is room to progress,"* suggested one recruit. Palmers was founded in 1983 by four lawyers who broke away from the former firm of Steggles Palmer. It now has 11 partners, 26 solicitors and legal execs plus another 90 or so staff. Our sources were keen to distinguish their employer from its rivals, telling us that *"some of the other firms in the area are happy to plod along but Palmers is pushing to grow,"* apparently *"in all areas."* To further its goals, *"Palmers is taking on more and more of the building it occupies in Basildon,"* having already set up near Grays and then opened up in Chafford Hundred, Thurrock. Apart from the famous Lakeside Shopping Centre, Thurrock has much to offer a burgeoning firm: the Thames Gateway regeneration will inevitably bring in new business and new clients. To reflect the firm's ambitions, its website has been revamped: "*The old one didn't fit too well with our profile now we are a lot bigger.*"

Palmers' business strategy is to focus on large local companies and national companies that don't want to pay London rates, while also continuing to serve the needs of individuals. Trainees were impressed by Palmers' breadth of practice, with one stating: "*I can't see myself moving to another firm in the region, definitely not.*" Perhaps this loyalty is the result of being "*treated like a fully fledged fee earner right from the start.*" To this end, trainees are kept informed about the firm's future plans and have their photo and details displayed alongside the qualified lawyers on the website. "*I like it – I'm keeping that photo for the rest of my career,*" said one. While the partners give trainees responsibility, "*they recognise you're not a fee machine and no one compels you to stay late.*" Or as one source put it: "*There are no nasty buggers here.*"

fluid thinking

The first of a trainee's four seats is allocated before they arrive at the firm and "*voicing your opinion*" is encouraged when subsequent seats are decided. There are no compulsories and the choices are as follows: commercial litigation, commercial and residential property, IT, construction, corporate finance, corporate tax, crime, defamation, employment, family, insolvency, IP and private client. Most seats are taken in the Basildon HQ; the Chafford Hundred office (coco, IT, IP and family) and the South Woodham Ferrers office (private client, property) are occasional trainee stop-off points.

Wills, trusts and probate was a high point for one source. "*Administering probates is very differ-*

ent to drafting wills. They are keen to give you as much initial responsibility as you can handle and you quickly get to grips with all you need to know so you can be let loose on your own.*" As you might expect, this leads to "*an awful lot of client contact.*" Similar opportunities exist in the family seat, available in the Basildon and South Woodham Ferrers offices which each handle divorce, cohabitation, financial agreements, domestic violence and contact disputes. "*I was attending court, meeting and greeting the clients and sitting in on new client meetings,*" recalled one trainee. The seat was "*very different in practice than in study and the paper work involved in the legal aid side of things was pretty extensive.*"

Coco seats bring a staple diet of business acquisitions and disposals, franchise deals, joint ventures and licensing agreements. One example of the commercial team's work is the £3.85 million management buyout of Coutts Packaging, a company that prints and produces corrugated cardboard boxes. "*If you're looking for a training contract out of the City with a broad range of experience and a high level of company law, it is ideal,*" said one of the trainees. "*We're not expected to do work beyond our capability but we're not just typing letters either.*" The size of the firm means trainees benefit from close contact with partners and supervisors: "*I could ask any stupid questions I wanted, and I asked a lot of stupid questions,*" chuckled one source. A seat in commercial property often lends itself to a mixture of contentious and non-contentious files, with a little bit of residential conveyancing thrown in for good experience. If the medley approach to legal practice appeals, Palmers' broad-ranging seats should satisfy: "*We don't have a hundred seats in intricate disciplines, and if you show you are doing well in one there is the option to stay there longer.*" The seats can merge into each other, which allows trainees to develop the aspects they most enjoy or excel at. "*In my commercial property seat there's* been a fair amount of non-contentious company law as the partner is well grounded in this. It's been a good blend." The seating arrangements are correspondingly fluid. "*You either have your own office, are in with the trainees or share a room with a partner.*" Whatever the seating arrangement, "*meetings with supervisors and partners really help to solve any problems that may arise. They will always monitor your work to make sure you're not overloaded.*" As well as internal training, Palmers' trainees attend relevant external courses and undergo regular progress reviews.

essex goals

In 2006 Palmers and Barclays Bank organised the inaugural Professionals Cup five-a-side football tournament. If the pictures on the website were anything to go by there were more than a few sliding tackles during the games, but trainees assured us that, in the spirit of the firm, fair play won out. On other occasions Palmers has run competitions for local schoolchildren to design its Christmas card, held staff quiz nights in the office, organised a booze cruise to France and arranged seasonal parties. More informally, "*all the trainees are quite pally and meet up outside work.*" The Moon on the Square is their hangout at the moment; "*it's a typical Wetherspoons – excellent for us on our trainee salaries.*"

Trainees were happy to talk up the benefits, both during and out of office hours, and one was keen to stress that "*the job doesn't define me.*" When recruiting, Palmers seems to pay attention to the dynamics of the team: "*They are looking for people with a range of experiences; people they want to spend time with.*" Furthermore, "*they want someone who has thought about what they are getting into and what it means to be a solicitor.*" One source explained: "*I know it's a cliché, but you need to think outside the box; they want to know we won't just give a textbook answer. Clients don't want that, they want to know how it applies to them*

and why.*" In other words the firm recruits to ensure "*it doesn't end up with a good academic lawyer but a rubbish practical one.*" In September 2006, two of the three qualifiers took jobs with the firm.

and finally...

In keeping with its position as a firm of substance within the local legal profession, Palmers recruits two years in advance of the start of the training contract and runs a summer vacation scheme.

Pannone LLP

the facts

Location: Manchester, Hale
Number of UK partners/solicitors: 90/109
Total number of trainees: 29
Seats: 4x6 months
Alternative seats: Secondments

A happy marriage of private client and commercial work marks out Pannone as a popular destination for students. At this self-appointed "complete law firm" great work and soaring profits are the order of the day. And yet, for all its success Pannone manages to grasp the elusive prize of workplace satisfaction. Lest we forget this point, the latest *Sunday Times* '100 Best Companies To Work For' survey concludes there is no better law firm in the UK for all-round fulfilment.

too good to be true?

Call us sceptical, but when something sounds too good to be true it often is. Not here, apparently. A clean sweep of endorsements came from all the trainees we interviewed, suggesting Pannone really does possess the recipe for success. While "*good-quality work and interesting cases"* are key ingredients they do not seem to lead to heavy hours or a weighty atmosphere. As one *"happy and comfortable"* trainee explained: *"We aim to succeed in business,* [but] *everything about the working environment makes you feel good."*

Even with a client base that is split right down the middle between businesses and individuals, you can expect an *"integrated"* training contract which straddles the two spheres. The classic four by six-month rotation is flexible enough to allow for a return to the trainee's preferred practice area for their last seat. Maybe it's a simple case of satisfaction being easier to find when you are able to spend your time doing the things that interest you most. For the record, there are no seats in the Hale office, but there are occasional client secondments.

badge of quality

Let's first examine the commercial side of the firm and a seat in the expanding coco department. It brings trainees into contact with every kind of business from entrepreneurial start-ups to multinational corporations, and time spent here is seen as *"an invaluable experience in terms of improvement as a lawyer."* The representation of oil giant Texaco on the provision of £16 million debt facilities serves as an example of the meaty work of the department. It may be small fry when compared to the deals handled by full-bore corporate firms but it perfectly illustrates the fact that even big multinationals want a good deal when it comes to buying legal services. Every firm has to start somewhere and today's £16 million deal can be tomorrow's £60 million deal.

EC/competition, tax, banking, advertising and marketing, e-commerce and IP law may also feature on the trainee's time sheet. In one interesting matter Pannone is representing TOFFS, The Old Fashioned Football Shirt Company, proprietor of the registration for the traditional Brazilian Football Association emblem. The matter may well hinge on the ability of the client to lay claim to an otherwise abandoned national badge.

If you think you'll enjoy the *"nitty gritty of going to court,"* head for the commercial litigation seat. One trainee, clearly the contentious kind, described the main benefit of the seat as *"the opportunity to cut your teeth in advocacy from an early stage."* Continuing their tale, they told us: *"One time I was asked what I was doing that afternoon. When I replied, 'nothing much', I was told I would be going off to a hearing on my own."* If merely the thought of this makes your mouth dry and your hands clammy then relax, *"you are given all the training in the world to get through it."* Besides, the way things run in the department, trainees may *"know the case as well as the partner anyway, having done a lot of the work on it."*

The employment department has constructed *"a halfway house between contentious and non-contentious practice."* Those keen to dispel 'fat cat' myths about the legal profession can happily do some claimant work for the *"little guy in the street."* Those that don't can represent *"massive organisations"* such as the Bank of England and Kellogg's. Either way it's *"client-facing"* work and *"the department is lovely."*

the personal touch

Pannone's flagship personal injury and clinical negligence practices are well stocked with experienced specialists. The firm's reputation in relation to major disasters and catastrophic injuries owes much to the trailblazing efforts in the 80s and 90s of Rodger Pannone, a former President of the Law Society. We're referring here to involvement in claims relating to some of the biggest and most high-profile transportation disasters, including the Herald of Free Enterprise and Lockerbie incidents. The PI team has achieved some spectacular results, such as establishing causation in cases of mercury poisoning from the manufacture of neon signs, and the first ever award of damages to a soldier in respect of failure to diagnose and treat post-traumatic stress disorder. Even with such top-end work, Pannone is not above humble trip-and-slip litigation. It has a large number of staff processing lower-value claims, and bolstered this side of its business through a late 2005 merger with Small specialist PI firm Johnson Yates. Pannone additionally acts for defendant insurance companies in this part of the PI market, having recently strengthened its relationship with broker Marsh.

Unusually, one partner in the PI department specialises in child abuse claims. Trainees count themselves "*really lucky*" to sit in this "*incredibly interesting*" seat and be involved in "*top-level stuff.*" It is not just the "*challenging*" subject matter that makes a stint so good, it's also the access-all-areas approach. "*Generally you shadow your supervisor: I followed mine everywhere.*" In the clinical negligence wing, claimant work is handled by a team with recent experience in human rights law, the removal of life-prolonging medical treatment and right-to-die cases. In both of these seats trainees draft court documents and attend hearings and client meetings, sometimes solo. All files remain under the supervision of partners, but one trainee enthused: "*There is nothing they haven't let me do.*"

partner swapping

That the recruitment process is so refreshingly transparent is perhaps an outward sign of this firm's "*no-nonsense*" way of conducting itself generally. Applicants who impress at first interview or on a vacation scheme are invited back for a lunch engagement with the managing partner, the training partner and a selection of other partners who forgot a packed lunch that day. Partners rotate around the table meeting different candidates.

Even if "*it's almost like speed-dating,*" do resist the 'Is it hot in here, or is it just you?' type lines. "*Trying to eat, be polite and impress top partners at the same time*" is something of a challenge, but overall this set-up is "*an enjoyable, comfortable and less pressurised*" way of ensuring candidates do themselves justice. As for the vacation scheme, past participants could not have been more impressed with the experience: "*The ball is in your court, so you can make sure the firm is right for you.*"

A support network is in place to ensure trainees get the most from the contract. Regular appraisals come in the form of "*a sit-down chat*" with supervising and/or training partner to discuss development, work (load and quality) and to identify any gaps. Less formal pastoral care is always there if required, and basically "*everyone chips in to help you,*" giving the feeling that the firm "*really cares about how you are progressing.*" Although the learning curve may be steep at times, the work is pitched at a manageable level so "*as confidence grows, there will be more work sent your way.*" So far, so touchy feely, but the arm round the shoulder rather than kick up the backside attitude brings benefits all round. "*It's in the firm's best interests to make sure you get a good quality of training;*" "*they get the right people coming through at the end, whilst making sure that the work is done to the Pannone standard.*"

comfort eating

The current trainee intake had arrived at the law from a variety of angles and from "*a scattering of different places, not just the North West.*" Refreshingly, our sources shared a sense of belonging and pride for their firm. Still, no one's doing this for their health, so what about the grubby subject of money? No complaints here. There's a grant for LPC fees, and a handsome trainee salary more than stands up to scrutiny against those offered by Manchester rivals, even purely commercial ones.

An ethos whereby *"each member of staff has a role to play in the success of the firm"* has filtered from the top down. Indeed, keeping the troops motivated is an issue high on managing partner Joy Kingsley's agenda. Apparently the Pannone army marches on its stomach, so there are cakes and chocolates on offer for teams meeting their targets. Potential rewards for a job well done include meals out in Manchester, or the guilty pleasure of shooting off early on a Friday afternoon. An employee-of-the-month scheme also highlights standout individuals. In September 2006, 11 of the 13 qualifiers were welcomed into NQ positions.

There are plenty of *"unforced"* activities on the social and sporting front to tip the scales in the work/life quest. Go-karting, trips to the dogs and York races, a weekend shopping trip to Scotland and a summer barbecue all attracted healthy interest, while monthly drinks involve the firm *"sticking a few quid behind a local bar."* Once again, the firm reaps the benefit – *"It's the classic no-brainer; there is a business benefit as we're now a tightly knit group."* A long-weekend jolly to the home city of a Pannone Law Group (Pannone's alliance of independent European law firms) member for a football match is open to players and supporters. Meant to be a biennial affair, the 2005 trip to Lisbon was deemed such a success that a follow up trip to Barcelona found its way onto the calendar a year early.

and finally...

Describing Pannone simply as a Manchester heavyweight with *"a friendly feeling"* would be telling only half the story. This is an ultra-successful and ambitious business where *"the law is practised as hard as it is anywhere."* If you want a firm large enough to access *"cracking lawyers"* and a varied range of commercial and private client work we recommend you look a lot closer at this firm.

Payne Hicks Beach

the facts

Location: London
Number of UK partners/solicitors: 29/22
Total number of trainees: 6
Seats: 4x6 months
Alternative seats: None

If the skyscrapers and glass palaces of Canary Wharf and Moorgate do nothing for you then cast your eye over Payne Hicks Beach, a legal treasure that has been around since 1730 and is best known for its sizeable private client and family departments. It has an impressive client list, some quality property and commercial work and surroundings straight out of *Bleak House*; all up we think you'll be pleasantly surprised by what it has to offer.

payne sailing

PHB's clients are *"a mix of old families and their businesses which the firm has dealt with for a very long time and new start-up companies."* Long-established clients tend to be connected with the firm's esteemed private client practice, which expertly offers a discreet tax, trusts, wills and probate service to a wide range of wealthy individuals, educational institutions, estates, businesses and charities. We're talking about the likes of the London Oratory School, old-moneyed families and *The Sunday Times* Rich Listers. We wish we could name a few but we can't. For family matters, partner Fiona Shackleton has a formidable reputation in the area of divorce and matrimonial finances. Dubbed by some in the business the 'steel magnolia', she handled the Prince of Wales' divorce and is currently the solicitor to Princes William and Harry. She is also handling Paul McCartney's divorce from Heather Mills.

Clients of the real estate and real estate litigation groups include British Gas, The AA, the Salvation Army, JPMorgan, Zurich and the Fiat Group, for whom the firm handles land acquisitions and offices leases and disposals, etc. PHB is also doing some good cases in administrative law. One partner currently represents the police investigation team led by the former deputy chief constable of Norfolk, concerning the public inquiry into the murder of Rosemary Nelson. Nelson was the Northern Irish human rights solicitor who was killed by a car bomb outside her home. In the sports field, the firm represents the nation's favourite yachtswoman Ellen MacArthur and ten Olympic medallists, including Ben Ainslie and Shirley Robertson.

show willing

Due to the relatively small size of the firm, PHB limits its trainee intake to just two or three per year. Their first seat is allocated on arrival (though there is "*a bit of give*" if anyone has a burning desire to do a particular seat). The available options include litigation, family, property, company/commercial and tax and trusts, and none are compulsory. It comes as no surprise that family and private client stand out as popular departments; they are after all the twin engines of the firm and tend to be the main draws for those applying for a PHB contract.

Yet, despite there being, shall we say, a few strong personalities in certain departments, this is certainly not something to "*make you dread going there.*" There are "*always people you can go to if you don't want to ask a partner something,*" and our sources felt they were listened to. Appraisals are taken seriously, with trainees getting a mid-seat meeting with their supervisor and then a full review with two training partners at the end of every six months. Levels of responsibility do vary from department to department, although "*if you show you are willing, they will give you stuff.*" For example, you can push for advocacy experience in the family department, which means that after liaising with the outdoor clerk and the supervisor "*you can go before a district judge to do a short*

application." That said, with the value of cases as high as they are, and the clients often rather prestigious, "*you won't get your hands on as much as you would if you were in a high-street firm.*"

the inn crowd

Trainees describe a firm where "*everyone knows everyone and gets on;*" where "*people don't see you as the lowest of the low because you're a trainee;*" and where you might just be able to say: "*I love coming here every day.*" They have a heartfelt belief that the firm's base in Lincoln's Inn is "*a lovely place to work.*" Facing onto the expansive New Square (built in the 1680s and 1690s) the neighbourhood is packed with Chancery barristers, crooked passageways and little second-hand bookshops. Where else could you buy a horsehair wig while popping out to get a sandwich at lunchtime? In the summer the gardens bloom and a fountain plays as lawyers scuttle to and from the Royal Courts of Justice. We honestly don't think you'll find a more charming spot in the whole of legal London. Inside PHB's home you'll find all the trappings of the classic law office – oil paintings of early partners, fireplaces and bookshelves stuffed with leather-bound volumes. Yet, despite all this, trainees say the firm is "*more old-fashioned in appearance than it actually is.*" Perhaps fearful that portraying the place as some kind of Dickensian theme park will put off would-be young lawyers they stressed that PHB is "*not stuck in the past.*" The evidence? "*A lot of people have laptops and BlackBerrys, plus there's digital dictation.*" We're not sure what Dickens would have made of such 21st-century technology, but it certainly makes life easier for the trainees, and it is no doubt necessary to attract the all-important new-money private clients and commercial customers that will allow the firm to evolve as it moves forward.

The trainees were also keen to convince us that there isn't a PHB type. To a certain extent this is true, but by its very nature the firm does tend to attract – and be attracted to – people for whom its distinctive character is a big plus. Private client and family work is not to all tastes and neither is Lincoln's Inn. When we did our interviews, most of the trainee population had attended a private school followed by a good university. Trainees are, without exception, bright, good-mannered and respectful – the sort that could be left alone with an important, long-standing client without causing anxiety to anyone, including themselves. One of the two September 2006 qualifiers stayed on with the firm.

all that jazz

The area around Lincoln's Inn has bags of trad pubs and bars for the discerning crowd at PHB. The Seven Stars, The Knights Templar, The Cittee of York – even the names conjour up an image of olde worlde. For those of a sporting temperament, tennis, sailing (courtesy of the Manches Cup), cricket, hockey and netball are all on offer and there are firm-wide socials on a regular basis. These range from trips to the theatre, wine tastings and Trivial Pursuit nights. Every Thursday a fee earners' lunch is lovingly prepared by the delightful in-house chef Fifi and smart trainees always attend as it's a great opportunity to mingle with qualified colleagues from across the firm, make your face known and get to learn more about departments you've not yet worked in. The highlight of the social calendar is the PHB Christmas party, last year held at the Law Society in nearby Chancery Lane. As part of the night's entertainment, a jazz band comprised of staff (including some trainees) wowed the assembled partygoers.

and finally...

Those looking for a big, brash City firm and the lifestyle to match need not apply. PHB is rightly proud of its history and can provide good training in a smaller but no less impressive setting. Just be aware that if the word 'tradition' brings you out into a cold sweat, it is not the place for you.

Penningtons Solicitors LLP

the facts

Location: Basingstoke, Godalming, London, Newbury
Number of UK partners/solicitors: 70/130
Total number of trainees: 28
Seats: 4x6 months
Alternative seats: None

In practice for around 200 years, Penningtons is proud of its long history of legal service in London and the South East.

southern comfort

Flick through the archives of the legal press and you will learn that Penningtons' most recent history is far from uneventful. In 1990 it merged with a small London law firm called Gamlens; in 1993 its offices and many of its files (in those days all paper) were blown up by an IRA bomb; in 1995 it demerged from its Bournemouth office; and around the time of the Millennium it was in more merger talks. The past six years have been characterised by the usual comings and goings of legal personnel, major investment in new premises and, the way we see it, a sense that the firm is increasingly at ease with its profile as a Home Counties player with a London office.

In terms of fee earner numbers, Penningtons' London office remains the biggest in the network, yet its status in the pecking order of London firms does not match what has been achieved in Surrey, Hampshire and Berkshire. Without question there is a certain prestige in having a City address on the notepaper, yet to regard the capital as its most important location is to miss the point. Trainees couldn't fail to notice that it is *"outside London where the real growth is taking place."* In each of the three locations beyond the M25 there is a viable business that could, in a parallel universe, be the leading independent firm in town. In addition to the usual coco, litigation and property teams, each office has a private client team and specialist groups that help distinguish it from the others. Newbury is the place to go for family law, whereas if social housing is your bag then Basingstoke will suit. If you want to get involved in travel law then a couple of years in Godalming may tempt. Additionally, both Basingstoke and Godalming have excellent claimant clinical negligence practices, which doubtless work closely with the excellent professional regulation team in the London office.

It would be misleading to imply that you could dip in and out of the various offices to take advantage of these specialisms. Once in an office, there you will (most likely) stay for two years. For a good snapshot of the practice profile of each office, check Penningtons' website.

how are you?

Property *"is the biggest department"* across the firm and trainees are almost certain to sit in this seat at some point. Also one of the busiest departments, it is perfectly possible that there will be a few long days (perhaps *"finishing at 10pm"*) on occasion. Newbury-headquartered Vodafone has been using the firm for property matters including new leases for its 3G mast sites. Advice has also been given to the likes of Allied Irish Banks, banana people Fyffes/Geest, Sunglass Hut and Morley Fund Management, one of the largest property investors in the UK. As a trainee you can expect to get your hands on *"lease renewals, drafting new leases and licences to assign, and sorting out problems with titles."* The deals will span commercial and residential properties, financing and securitisation and, if in Basingstoke, social housing. The seat affords *"lots of independence,"* though as you might expect, *"on the bigger deals you're just assisting more senior lawyers."* There is *"real depth in the department"* which means there are *"plenty of people to help answer any questions you might have."*

Private client seats go down well as they offer *"interesting and varied"* work. It is common for trainees to take charge of their own probate files, *"dealing with inheritance and capital gains tax"* as well as learning how to draft wills and powers of attorney *"with hardly any input from supervisors at all."* Apparently there's a certain morbid enjoyment to be had in visiting nursing homes to get wills signed.

If corporate and commercial matters are more your thing then you'll be pleased to learn that time in coco can also be guaranteed. Penningtons has handled various deals in the healthcare sector and worked for sports clubs and clients from the Indian subcontinent. Indeed, the firm has a dedicated India unit, which recently advised Indian company Shasun Chemicals & Drugs on the acquisition of part of the UK business of French pharmaceutical company Rhodia. In terms of its sports clientele, the firm acts for Wycombe Wanderers FC, particularly in relation to the club's dealings with London Wasps RFC with which it shares its Causeway Stadium. International connections have been made through the Multilaw network, so even if trips abroad are unlikely, trainees do get to work on cross-border deals. Around half our interviewees said they had not experienced too many late nights in coco; the rest found the seat *"pretty hectic,"* one telling us about *"eating pizza with the partners at midnight."*

holidays from hell

If you want to hear endless stories about *"the dumb things people have done overseas"* then pack your bags for the Godalming travel team which, despite the departure of its key partner in 2006, continues to handle injury and other holiday claims. Trainees get to see cases and do things that *"simply aren't available in commercial litigation."* In the case of Jones v SunWorld, for example, the firm represented a woman whose new husband drowned while on their honeymoon. The

Godalming office makes the most of its location in this small but wealthy Surrey town. Staff play sports and drink together in the Rose and Crown, which is a *"pretty traditional pub with a lovely garden."* A permanent dress-down policy contributes to a *"relaxed and friendly atmosphere."*

Sit with the highly regarded clin neg team in Basingstoke and you'll help them pursue cases involving spinal cord and brain injuries resulting from road, workplace and other accidents. There's also a litigation seat with an emphasis on PI that allows trainees to get *"good hands-on experience"* of drafting letters of claim and meeting with barristers to discuss cases. A seat in property will involve issues concerning the provision of affordable housing for registered social landlords. Trainees tell us there's a *"community atmosphere"* here, with staff attending bingo evenings, a cinema club, bowling nights and quizzes. Clearly popular, *"87 out of 97 people turned up for the last quiz."* However, this is probably the office least likely to go out for drinks on a Friday, as *"people largely disappear at the end of the week."*

bizarre art

If you are drawn to the drama of divorce then Newbury is the office for you. Essentially a litigation option, family practice means *"drafting divorce petitions, giving instructions to counsel and assisting at hearings."* Key players in the department have come from London firms, bringing with them wealthy clients and important referral relationships. Socially, the King Charles Tavern is a popular venue *"at lunchtimes or on Friday evenings."* Although there were grumbles about the lack of a cinema in Newbury, there was plenty of evidence to suggest that trainees are rarely bored in this *"nice part of the world."* It's *"all rather genteel really,"* concluded one source.

The Newbury office has one of the strangest pieces of corporate art we've ever stumbled across, thanks to the partner who commissioned

a replica of Leonardo da Vinci's famous painting, The Last Supper. Featuring the partners as apostles (we don't know who gets to be Judas) the *"bizarre"* and *"quite scary"* painting *"doesn't hang proudly in reception; it is in one of the stairwells,"* trainees revealed. *"Even one of the partner's dogs made it into the painting."* The *Student Guide* suggests that readers insist on viewing the masterpiece, if at all possible.

reality bites

In the London office there are niche seats in professional regulation, private client, construction and immigration. Famously, the firm helped *Big Brother 6*'s Zimbabwean contestant Makosi appeal against a deportation order following her time on the show. The office also handles a good deal of commercial litigation, some of it truly fascinating. Last year lawyers were in the Court of Appeal in the matter of The President of the State of Equatorial Guinea v Systems Design Ltd & Others, a case which arose after the 2004 attempted coup in which Margaret Thatcher's son Mark was implicated. Admittedly, much of a trainee's time will be spent on more straightforward, domestic disputes, but at least this gives them the chance to *"do most of the work on county court files,"* drafting claims, defences and counterclaims, preparing witness statements, etc. Once every month the trainees in the provinces join the London contingent for training sessions and an evening out. Beyond this integration between the offices is, trainees say, *"an area that could be improved."* There are separate seasonal parties, although everyone gets together for a big sports day each summer.

For the most part this is a firm for someone who *"doesn't care about having the biggest pay but wants to work for good clients and doesn't want a peptic ulcer by the time they're 30."* One note of caution is that NQ jobs *"were thin on the ground"* in 2006, with only one being offered in the

London office and not a lot of variety being offered in general. This left the other four qualifiers in London, and some in the regions, either heading to another office in the network or having to look elsewhere. One trainee took this as a positive thing: *"They will take you on if there is a need but they won't create a job for you."* Others were a little more contemplative: *"I was a little surprised; there wasn't much indication that that was going to be the case until the very end."* All up, five out of 12 stayed on.

and finally...

Continuing several years of quiet but consistent growth, Penningtons recently posted a 10% rise in income. This is a firm that is slowly and surely moving into the 21st century without abandoning its *"traditional,"* and at times individualistic, slant. Trainees say that *"if you are looking for a dynamic, cutting-edge law firm, this isn't it,"* but where it does score is in the potential for staff to achieve a good balance between hard work, responsibility and home life.

Pinsent Masons

the facts

Location: Birmingham, Bristol, Leeds, London, Manchester, Scotland

Number of UK partners/solicitors: 260/500

Total number of trainees: 115

Seats: 4x6 months

Alternative seats: Overseas seats, secondments

Extras: Pro bono – various legal advice schemes; language training

December 2004 brought the world a number of surprising high-profile romances: Ellen DeGeneres got together with *Ally McBeal's* Portia DeRossi; Nicole Kidman began a dalliance with Steve Bing, better known as babyfather to Liz Hurley; and polite national firm Pinsents shacked up with gruff construction giant Masons. Two years later, Ellen and Portia are still going strong, but Nicole has moved on to pastures new. What of Pinsent Masons?

a profitable marriage

The Pinsent Masons marriage was a smart one in the sense that each firm brought essentially complementary strengths to the union and worked in many of the same locations. Pinsents had large offices in Brum, Leeds and Manchester and a couple of decent outposts in London. Masons had its key office in London plus smaller ventures in Bristol, Manchester, Leeds and Scotland. Nevertheless, it's taken time to bed down. Problems integrating the two Manchester offices were blamed for a wave of partner departures in 2005 and the office in Bristol lost its property team. In a staff survey carried out by the firm in 2006, many participants reportedly complained of feeling detached from and unaware of the firm's strategy. And yet, the marriage seems to have taken off between the sheets – the balance sheets, of course. Profit per equity partner soared by an unheard-of 70% last year. Major Masons construction and energy clients have employed the firm for corporate work, and the new outsourcing, technology and commercial (OTC) group has combined Pinsents' commercial and Masons' IT strength to great effect. The northern offices look to have stabilised and are aggressively recruiting from their local competitors. The firm is now probably best described as full-service with a client base that is heavy on the construction, energy and projects side. The nature of the training and the seats available depends on your location, so let's take the tour.

going for gold

The Leeds branch is very Pinsents-influenced, offering an impressive range of seats including corporate, commercial property, tax, employment, pensions, dispute resolution, OTC, banking, corporate recovery, construction and projects. The firm's property work is fuelled by its leading regeneration practice, which sees it working with clients such as English Partnerships and One NorthEast to redevelop run-down town centres and brownfield sites from Colchester to Blackpool. It has also been advising four London boroughs on planning applications for the new Olympic Village. Because regeneration projects are huge, long-term things, trainees acknowledged that *"you do tend to play quite a junior role."* Trainees reckoned they spent *"around a third"* of their time on bibling, versioning and other mundane document tasks. Another third was *"due diligence, planning applications and stamp duty land tax assessments."* However, there's a solid third of *"much more challenging work;"* the department usually gives each trainee a couple of smaller transactional files to handle themselves. *"It could be the assignment of a lease or the transfer of part of a property,"* one explained. *"It's weird having your own cases, but you learn on your feet... and you're under close supervision."* How close? *"A three-line e-mail you can just send; a long piece of advice or a drafted document you'll need guidance on."* In addition, trainees noted that supervisors *"take you to as many meetings as possible."*

Given its corporate focus, Leeds offers reasonable hours with most trainees calling 8.30am-6pm standard. However, it was suggested that, since the merger increased the importance of London in the firm's power structure, hours have been getting later, and perhaps longer. *"It's becoming trendy to come in mid-morning and be here until seven,"* one source opined. *"Even though you're doing the same hours, you get more credit if you do the late shift."* The office offers a *"relaxed but quite focused"* atmosphere. For those easily distracted, booths in the large open-plan office aid concentration. The trainee group is *"very tight,"* venturing out *"two or three times a week"* for drinks in the evening.

lettuce before action

Birmingham was Pinsents' original home city, so it's no wonder the classic Pinsents' ethos is still in evidence here. *"We weren't really affected by the merger,"* one explained. *"We just got on with our jobs."* The office is strong across the board in transactional, contentious and advisory areas of practice and the disputes team is very active on general commercial and prof neg cases. It's also carved out a niche in disputes involving public bodies and represents, among others, government departments and universities. *"We get a lot of cases disputing degree classifications,"* explained one source. *"You pretty much run these yourself, drafting advice notes and so on. Sometimes the student bringing the case goes into bankruptcy, so you work with the insolvency team to get the costs back."* It can be *"quite challenging"* running these claims, *"especially if they've got an expensive commercial litigator in on the other side."* And does it feel strange taking on students just a few months after being one yourself? *"Not really,"* we were assured. *"They tend to be crazy and most of the claims are just wrong. You're protecting the client."*

On the commercial side, disputes vary from pricing and supply problems to repossessing vehicles on unpaid lease hire agreements. Larger matters *"can be boring – yesterday I spent a long time going through files looking for evidence."* On the other hand, occasionally something *"fast-moving and exciting"* comes along and you're also likely to attend *"a lot of pre-trial review meetings and case management conferences,"* although mostly as an observer. *"It's pure litigation training,"* said one veteran of the seat, *"not coloured by a particular speciality."* Other departments offering contentious experience include property and OTC, where the IP team has some interesting cases. One trainee had to go out and buy 30 lettuces to show that a client's competitor had copied their packaging. When no one else in the office wanted any, the trainee got to take them all home. That was a healthy week, we imagine.

Birmingham is indeed the firm's healthiest office, having stormed to victory in last year's Birmingham Trainee Solicitors' Society sports challenge. It's also one of the more sociable, with BTSS theatre trips, charity events and a new office social committee arranging four events a year plus the summer and Christmas parties. "*Last year the Christmas party had a Disney theme. Corporate all wore Dalmatian costumes and dispute resolution came as Pirates of the Caribbean.*" And is it one of those parties where the partners sit sternly eyeing staff antics? "*No chance. The partners get the drinks in, mingle – they're usually first on the dance floor.*"

manchester and bristol

In Manchester the Pinsents lawyers have moved in to Masons' pad. The office has seats in some of the firm's key practice groups, including a private equity-focused corporate team and a construction team with a heavily contentious workload. As one of the smallest branches, it's easy to get people together for drinks in the office every Friday and the Pitcher & Piano is the usual destination afterwards. The local business association, Pro-Manchester, arranges sports competitions and cultural events, and the firm competes in local cricket, netball and football tournaments.

Bristol is the firm's tiddler with around 20 lawyers "*all at arm's reach*" on one open-plan floor. The office no longer recruits its own trainees, but those in other offices can go there to take seats in its two remaining departments: construction and projects. A construction seat offers a strong mix of contentious and non-contentious work. Disputes are often resolved through written adjudication, so you might not get the thrill of seeing your case argued in court. Nevertheless, for one trainee, "*winning my first adjudication was pretty exciting.*" Major projects matters can involve some travel, perhaps even combined with

a reminder of those all-night essay crises from university days. One trainee recalled "*staying up till midnight in a hotel room with a partner preparing for negotiations the next day.*" In Bristol, with everyone jumbled up in the office, there's no scope for departmental cliquery, but trainees did express feelings of isolation from the firm at large.

mi casa, su casa

Finding itself spread across four offices after the merger, Pinsent Masons London has now whittled down to two addresses. The first is Masons' old home, an architectural delight in Clerkenwell; the second is a new lease of space in the snazzy CityPoint building in EC3. There was some raising of eyebrows that the firm isn't bringing all London lawyers under one roof and rumours circulated of stalwart Masons partners refusing to move. "*Nonsense,*" one Masons-recruited London trainee assured us, "*it's just that the details of the lease don't allow a move yet.*" It is true that the London management has made efforts to mingle the departments, but even so "*everyone said the firms were really similar, but the partisan attachments have stuck,*" observed one trainee. All we'll say is that all mergers take time to settle down.

What matters more to readers is that the firm is integrated in terms of the training programme. The combined London branch offers seats in corporate, OTC, pensions, insurance, projects and construction, banking, corporate recovery, dispute resolution, employment, property and competition law. The corporate team has built a reputation for deals relating to AIM (the mini-me to FTSE), recently assisting everything from a copper-mining company to a care home operator on their listings. It has also developed a strong private equity practice. "*That was a real eye-opener,*" said one trainee who'd spent time in the department. "*I hadn't realised just how much influence private equity firms have on the economy.*" Even people who went into the department as born litigators said: *"It's interesting to see how companies really work."*

As to the nature of trainee tasks, *"it's due diligence and document management,"* explained one source. *"You'll distribute questions to the various departments of the company involved, collate their responses, and prepare a report."* In addition there's lots of *"Companies House admin, bundling, typical trainee tasks,"* which can get *"a bit monotonous."* On the other hand, the secretarial support was dubbed *"fantastic,"* and extra help for grunt work is provided by participants in a recently implemented gap year scheme. No photocopying then? *"Oh gosh, no!"* cried one horrified source. One inevitable complaint of corporate is that the hours are consistently long. Trainees generally thought the department *"understaffed"* and hours consequently high, even by City standards. One typical source reported being *"in until 11 o'clock every night and in four weekends in a row"* during one stage of their corporate seat. Hopefully the firm's recent assistant solicitor recruitment drive will ease the pressure.

system addicts

An extensive programme of secondments is open to trainees in all offices and around 20% of them will go on one at some stage. Also on the horizon are some new overseas opportunities – the firm is piloting a seat with an allied firm in Germany.

In each office seat supervision is good. Open-plan working *"really encourages good training; you can learn from everybody,"* our sources thought. The appraisal system is as well organised as seat allocation, with a whopping six appraisals per seat. An associate in a department completely unrelated to your interests additionally serves as mentor, able to offer confidential advice on more pastoral concerns. When it comes to qualification, the same highly organised approach applies, with all applicants being interviewed for NQ positions, even where there is only one candidate. In September 2006, 38 of the 47 qualifiers stayed with the firm.

and finally...

Highly organised training, supervision, seat allocation and appraisal allows Pinsent Masons to offers a supportive, if possibly slightly prescriptive, experience. If you're an old-school type who believes you get ahead in life by talking loudly and playing squash with the right people, you might find the Pinsents approach a little cloying. But if you're a high achiever who prefers a clear system and a solid support network, you'll fit right in.

Pitmans

the facts

Location: Reading, London
Number of UK partners/solicitors: 26/105
Total number of trainees: 6
Seats: 4x6 months
Alternative seats: None

Don't be put off by the fact that Nabarro Nathanson shut up shop in Reading in 2005. For several law firms, especially the indigenous Reading ones, the area is prosperous and bulging with potential. And Pitmans is one of them...

reading between the lines

The firm was established a whopping 180 years ago by a certain Mr Pitman, and has quietly and steadily become one of the Thames Valley's leaders in commercial law. Mr Pitman himself remains something of an enigma, but contrary to popular belief, our research has uncovered that he was not the Sir Isaac Pitman who invented shorthand after a spell of court reporting.

Pitmans has long occupied a row of quaint Victorian buildings a stone's throw from the town centre. They are *"full of character and pretty historic but a bit like a rabbit warren."* In September 2006 it took on extra space in a flashier building on Castle Street. Loaded with symbolism, the move puts them next door to the offices recently vacated by Nabarro Nathanson.

slow and steady wins the race

In the dotcom boom years of the late 90s, technology businesses opened up along the M4 corridor faster than you could say 'server'. In response, law firms sprouted up in Reading and the Thames Valley, hoping for a piece of the action, but after the dotcom crash some of them shuffled off with their cyber-tails between their virtual legs. The crash, while commonly perceived to be a cataclysm of Biblical proportions, didn't seem to rock Pitmans, whose fortunes have remained consistent thanks to a loyal following of clients in more established sectors. Now, however, in what must seem an ironic twist, companies in the hi-tech sector are a catalyst for growth at Pitmans.

As the commercial hub of the Thames Valley, Reading has also attracted attention from other kinds of business, for example the Big Four accountancy firms and US corporates capitalising on the town's proximity to Heathrow Airport and high-speed rail link to London. All of which, of course, generate ample fodder for law firms. Pitmans' website lists its major clients, including household names such as the BBC, Fujitsu Siemens, HSBC, PwC and Yell. This may be the point to mention that Pitmans' current confidence has led it to move to the next level of its business plan by opening up a small London office on Cornhill, near the heart of the capital's insurance market.

We've learned that at partner level, the firm makes a point of recruiting City lawyers. This is a win-win strategy: the firm is boosted by newcomers with top-level expertise, and the newcomers – often fed up with the strain of City law and city life – come to the leafy Thames Valley with a willingness to explore career success within the bounds of more civilised hours. Do a headcount of the partners and you find that only a minority have been at Pitmans man and boy; the majority have found their way to the firm from other well-known practices, including the magic circle. The other thing to note is that the partnership is pretty much fifty-fifty men and women. By contrast, trainees commonly arrive at the firm having made the deliberate choice *never* to live and work in London. As one put it: *"When I went to an open day at a magic circle firm and saw the beds in the basement, my decision was made for me."* Many of the trainees will have grown up locally or come to Reading from more rural areas; others are graduates of Reading University and have chosen to stick with the town.

all things being equal

Pitmans' training programme acquaints new recruits with the firm's core areas: coco, commercial property and dispute resolution are compulsory, with a fourth seat being chosen from employment, defendant insurance, pensions and planning. The trainees say *"all the departments are equally important"* and confirm that the firm doesn't appear to push any one over another. We detect that the large commercial property department is a big selling point for trainees, not least because it is deemed one of the best in the region. It handles multimillion-pound land purchases across the South, and trainees can expect to help on acquisitions and disposals for commercial and residential developers such as Barratt Homes and M4 Estates. The team recently acted for Fujitsu Siemens on the acquisition of one of Bracknell's largest buildings. There's a good deal of client contact in this seat, as the supervisors *"give you responsibility as soon as you think you're ready for it."* More than this, *"you're getting all the juicy stuff, and you're getting guided at the same time – the amount I've learned is incredible."*

The corporate seat is busy, with trainees permitted to take on drafting responsibilities at an early stage. *"This was a surprise, but a pleasant one,"* reported one source. One of the team's recent significant deals is the £35 million flotation and AIM listing of financial services company Capital Group Holdings plc. Not every deal is this big, but in truth smaller deals allow trainees to extend their wings further. They may also get involved in IP-oriented commercial advice, which also surprised some, as the firm *"doesn't market itself as an IP specialist."*

In the litigation seat, we heard tales of drafting defences, going to court and meeting clients. Insolvency issues, including winding-up petition hearings, are commonplace and one trainee was given the task of evicting some squatters. *"There's loads of variety, and if something manageable comes up then you're first in line to do it."* Even someone who'd been put off litigation at law school found the seat an eye-opener – *"in practice it really comes alive."* Domestic cases are the norm here at Pitmans, but trainees occasionally find themselves working on international claims, some of which entail relatively long hours. Actually they're not too horrendous: *"The latest I've stayed in the office is 10:30pm,"* admitted one source. If you do have to stay late, *"the firm is good about paying for pizzas and taxis home."* The litigation department prides itself on its ADR focus, choosing arbitration and mediation rather than *"doggedly pursuing litigation every time."* Trainees also commented on the department's egalitarian atmosphere, saying: *"There's a sense that anyone will go and make the tea, and it doesn't matter who you are."*

another pizza the action

Pitmans social side is not as interesting as a Friday-night tour of the vodka Red Bull-drenched streets of Reading might suggest. Outdoorsy, wholesome pursuits such as hill-walking feature alongside refined Christmas parties in upmarket eateries. For the record, last year fish restaurant Loch Fyne was the scene of quite a few departmental knees-ups. Cheese and wine evenings and book nights are common, but it's not all chin-stroking and intellectual banter: trainees are not averse to the idea of a quick post-work pint in their local, the Brewery Tap, or a pizza on a Friday lunchtime. Trainees are also invited to client events laid on by the firm. These have recently included go-karting and an evening at nearby Newbury races. Such events never dominate, however, and there's *"a strong emphasis on pursuing your interests outside the firm."* This should not surprise, bearing in mind why many of the senior lawyers came to Pitmans in the first place.

and finally...

This relatively low-key firm is a Reading stalwart for a reason. Its recent incursion into the London market is not insignificant and implies closer ties to the City than might at first be apparent. Committed Redingensians should find the opportunity to work with so many City refugees extremely rewarding. All three qualifiers stayed with the firm in September 2006.

Prettys

the facts

Location: Ipswich
Number of UK partners/solicitors: 15/29
Total number of trainees: 10
Seats: 4x6 months
Alternative seats: None

If the fountain of youth is a myth then no one's told Prettys, which is looking remarkably sprightly for a firm that turns 100 this year. Still vigorous and with a mix of the traditional and the enterprising, the commercial and the personal: what's its secret?

life begins at 100

Gazing at Prettys' *"mansion-esque"* Georgian town house in the centre of Ipswich, you'd think the last century has passed by unnoticed; that here law is practised by the be-wigged and the powdered for little old ladies and the landed gentry. Appearances prove deceptive, however, as crossing the threshold reveals a hitherto unseen tower of open plan offices, conference suites and airy boardrooms. A quick glance at the firm's website provides further clues to Prettys' identity – a City brogue balanced on top of a roller skate, a briefcase attached to rucksack straps. This is how Prettys advertises its particular blend of private client heritage and commercial focus, and trainees say it is in keeping with *"a forward-thinking firm with traditional roots."* As clichéd as this sounds, you have to give their claim credence after an examination of what's on offer here.

Our interviewees spoke of valuable experiences in both the historic private client half of the firm and in the increasingly vibrant commercial half. There are no compulsories in the four-seat scheme, and allocation takes into account the must-haves as well as the please-no's. Their options are property, corporate, employment, commercial litigation, shipping, defendant insurance and 'estates'. There are occasional opportunities to take a seat in other areas such as matrimonial or French property.

The fact that *"commercial property is really expanding"* gives ample opportunity to *"tailor the experience to the kind of work you want to do."* But remember, *"if there's something you enjoy, you need to speak up."* One trainee *"made great strides"* in residential property by making full use of the conveyancing team's proximity to bag as many files as possible. We were assured they knew he was taking them. Another keen recruit was lucky, as the property group was working with the corporate group to buy a large company

for a client. *"I did the due diligence role and drafted side-leases on that."* Others will have worked on transactions such as a dock-side development on behalf of DanceEast, the national dance agency for the East of England, or a leisure development connected with a large Norwich Hotel. Affiliated to the department is a highly rated property litigation group, in which the ability to spot bad acting may prove useful. A trainee explained: *"I was on a four-day trial and one of the participants had a pseudo-heart attack half way through to buy himself some time. It was all very Eastenders. Unsurprisingly, he is still alive today."*

Such dramatics can also feature in the work of the employment department, though whether you will see any *Trisha*-style outbursts first hand depends on the case. Employment is a buoyant area, trainees reported, where *"the partner in charge is very forward-thinking; he has such a desire to expand the team and take it forward."* As such, it is a popular seat. Recently the group assisted a healthcare company that runs secure hospitals with some of its most challenging employee issues, and one interviewee spoke of working on a *"hugely exciting"* constructive/unfair dismissal claim.

mind your own business

"It's not just farmers selling their tractors," said one trainee of the corporate group, bristling with the indignation of a seasoned East Anglian. Indeed not, although most clients are indeed drawn from the tractor heartland of Suffolk. *"There's been a lot of care home work recently... and caravan parks for some reason."* Prettys also looks after Ipswich Town FC, some well-known horse studs and a convoy of transport companies. In keeping with the transport theme, trainees are able to sit with the *"quite blokey"* shipping group that is kept busy because of its proximity to the ports of Ipswich, Felixstowe

and Harwich. The clients of this department come from all over the world.

It hasn't been easy all the way and, as with most firms, when waters get choppy trainees can be left feeling queasy. Losing its place on Allianz Cornhill's legal panel meant a shake up in the defendant insurance litigation department, and trainees sense that the firm is not pushing hard on the claimant side. Some interviewees looked back fondly on their time in PI, telling us it provides *"very good litigation experience,"* and a full dose of client contact. *"I've had people trying to show me their breasts,"* said one still-stunned source. *"If you are scared of the telephone you will soon snap out of it,"* added another, who would *"recommend it to trainees even if it is not going to be their area."*

Private client in particular proves *"fantastic for nosy people."* If you like the sound of *"delving into people's lives and finding out how much money they have"* then get yourself there asap. You can expect to work on tax planning, high-value wills and multi-jurisdictional probates, right down to powers of attorney for *"the little old lady down the road."* Contentious probate can be difficult as *"you see the bad side of the client, the greed."* To balance this, *"people really rely on you and that's so rewarding."*

a fine vintage

Trainees tend to share small offices with partners or senior fee earners, with admin staff working together open plan. *"It's scary at first,"* said one trainee. *"I kept panicking over how I was going to dictate with someone else in the room, but you soon learn to get on closely with people. I also like to be able to shut the door and concentrate."* Group training sessions are a time to mingle; as well as legal topics there have also been sessions on things like 'personal protection' and 'how to deal with your secretary'. We're assured the two weren't linked.

We're told that instead of following the fickle finger of fashion, Prettys has its own unique style, which *"remains formal"* with an unashamedly traditionalist bent. This hasn't prevented the firm from hiring a new business development manager, nor putting in place more modern systems such as an electronic debt-chasing service for clients. Trainees talked about the firm's place in the Ipswich legal market: *"Prettys and our rivals Birketts go for more commercially oriented work; the other firms, such as Ashton Graham and Kerseys, aim towards members of the public more."* We learned from our interviews that plans are afoot to strengthen the Prettys name across East Anglia: *"The partnership seems to be trying to expand and develop"* to ensure that it remains *"competitive, and on the map."*

The atmosphere is described as *"not at all stuffy."* One sweet-toothed partner has a habit of sending round ice creams when the temperature nudges above lukewarm – *"Magnums are top of the list."* This breezy attitude extends to hours, where *"there's no staying late for the sake of staying late,"* and the likelihood of trainees living within walking distance of the office means *"if you're lucky you can make it home in time for the last five minutes of Neighbours."* Living in Ipswich makes it easy to join in with after-work merrymaking and *"there's always a big crowd from Prettys out on a Friday."* Venues include Mannings, *"an old man's pub,"* and Morgans, which is pitched as *"a wine-bistro-type place with stools and candles and expensive whisky."* Prettys' social calendar looks busy enough, with plenty of parties, marketing soirées and wine-tasting evenings run by an aficionado from within the firm.

We're told Ipswich is *"no amazing social Mecca"* though *"it is getting better."* Luxury apartments, bars and restaurants are springing up on the marina. Outside the town are *"the* delights of Suffolk – the coastline, Constable Country and all that," and while some bemoaned the lack of quality shopping opportunities they acknowledged that "there's always Norwich." Not so much a city that never sleeps, then, but a town that sometimes snoozes. Despite Suffolk's lack of hills, there's an annual walking weekend that stretches the calf muscles of around 25 people from all levels of the firm. The last trip enabled the most intrepid members of the firm to climb Carrantuohill, Ireland's highest peak. To aid their recovery, "partners paid for lots of rounds of drinks and meals, so we were well looked after." The sporting life continues back home where "there is a fantastic netball team that seems to win all its matches against other businesses."

For the many trainees with local connections, choosing Prettys was easy enough: "It was a natural move to migrate home to a respected regional firm." One trainee, originally from Norwich, told us: "I get a lot of stick for moving here. I still support Norwich City Football Club though." Some trainees make it through the selection process without any local connections at all. The trainees' tips for those interested in joining is to show that you're a sociable type but also that you are "prepared to take on a lot of responsibility yourself. It's fun here but don't underestimate the hard work." Once settled at the firm, many decide they want to stay and jump on the property ladder relatively quickly. The NQ retention figure for September 2006 – one out of four – was, however, the lowest for many years.

and finally...

Prettys is a firm with an "old face" and a head full of ideas. It was quite hard to get trainees to be specific about these ideas, but we reckon they would be great topics of conversation should you get an interview with the firm.

Reed Smith Richards Butler

the facts

Location: London, Birmingham.
Number of UK partners/solicitors:
RS 40/51; RB 64/133
Total number of trainees: RS 9; RB 42
Seats: 4x6 months
Alternative seats: Overseas seats secondments
Extras: Pro bono – Aldgate Advice Centre, ICSL & College of Law Legal Advice Schemes, language training.

The first day of January 2007 will see the formal merger of Pittsburgh-based behemoth Reed Smith and internationalist jack-of-all-City-trades Richards Butler. The result will be a 1,300-lawyer operation with up to 27 offices across multiple jurisdictions and 300 lawyers in the UK. Gaze into our crystal ball for a vision of what the future may hold...

a marvel-ous merger

While we can talk with some authority about the identity of both legacy firms in the UK, because the merger was only agreed in principal in May 2006, many of the practicalities of the new joint firm and its training contract were still to be set in stone when this book was published. What we do know is that the merged London office will become the largest in the whole global operation, accounting for more than 20% of turnover. The only caveat is that at the time of going to press the autonomous and highly profitable Richards Butler Hong Kong office (which turns over £30 million) had yet to decide whether to sign on the dotted line.

If you're mooching around a university law fair this autumn, you'll find a joint recruitment stand bearing the legend 'Reed Smith Richards Butler'. Apparently "it's been decided to use the combined names in jurisdictions where there are legacy RB offices for at least two years or as long as it carries goodwill and makes business sense. Then they'll just use 'Reed Smith'." As readers of the occasional comic, we can't help thinking the firm has lost a glorious opportunity to refashion itself as 'Reed Richards'. After all, as leader of the Fantastic Four, Reed Richards (aka Mr Fantastic, capable of stretching into any shape he desires) is best friend to The Thing, husband of The Invisible Woman and mentor to The Human Torch. Come on! Reed Richards: flexible, fiery, solid, discreet. What client wouldn't be impressed by those branding associations? Nevertheless, Reed Smith Richards Butler it is.

the sum of its parts

Even if we can't say exactly how quite yet, we can ask why. As the relative sizes of the two firms indicate, the merger is in essence a Reed Smith takeover; however, with a larger London office and a more-developed international network, Richards Butler is bringing plenty to the table. Reed Smith has grown frenetically via merger and high aspiration, with the past five years' activities taking it from an unglamorous Pittsburgh-centric firm to a major US national and international player. Yet 14 of its 18 locations were still Stateside. By contrast, Richards Butler is one of the most international of the London mid-market firms, with offices in Abu Dhabi, Beijing, Brussels, Greece, Hong Kong, Paris and Sao Paulo plus an associate in Muscat. Year on year, trainees at RB have told us *"at least 90% of the work I do is international; we handle few purely domestic matters."*

Richards Butler trainees had been sold the merger on the basis that *"you have to have a presence in the USA."* Over at Reed Smith our sources looked forward to their firm having *"increased impact in London and a strong basis for international growth."* Putting their comments together, everyone agreed that *"contrasting and complementary strengths in the UK"* were a key component of the merger logic. To be specific, both firms are essentially broad in their commercial activities rather than narrowly transactional. Dispute resolution, for example, accounts for 50% of turnover worldwide in each case.

We might as well go the whole hog and tell you that Reed Smith's presence in the UK is centred around real estate, finance, coco and employment. RB works in these areas too and also does brilliantly in film/TV finance, international shipping, commercial and trade disputes litigation. It is additionally known as one of the few substantial City firms that will litigate for clients against the big banks. Time will tell precisely how much business sense the union makes, but broadly speaking the reasoning was wholly sound in the minds of our interviewees. *"We've got our eyes on Reed Smith's Century City office,"* whispered one media trainee; *"being there would definitely help secure film work for big studios."* Meanwhile, a Reed Smith contemporary was looking hungrily at *"Richards Butler's breadth of corporate specialists – the partners here tend to be generalists."*

if things ain't broke

The truth be told, Richards Butler has been touting for a US merger partner for a good seven years (*"we were told on our first day, we will merge by the time you qualify"*) yet this merger comes with assurances from management that *"culturally we're a very good match."* RB types told us *"because we're the larger office, it's more like integration rather than being conquered,"* but there were some changes they welcomed, including *"a permanent dress-down policy."* No one's likely to go entirely Yankee doodle dandy; indeed, Reed Smith trainees have long told us that *"although we're a US firm, it feels quintessentially British in the UK."*

The conclusion of one RB source harked back to Reed Smith's original incursion into the UK when in 2001 it annexed the small but perfectly formed Coventry and London-based firm called Warner Cranston. *"The fact that the existing culture survived when Reed Smith took them over makes me feel quite comfortable. Reed Smith doesn't seem to try and fix things if they aren't broken."*

With all this talk of the USA and worldwide offices, it would be easy to forget that this international giant will have a Midlands office. In 2006 Reed Smith's Coventry lawyers relocated to new premises in Solihull, just on the edge of Birmingham. They also welcomed a biotech product liability litigator from Eversheds, a move that neatly ties the office in with one of the firm's great practice strengths Stateside. Reed Smith's London office also displays a keen interest in the life sciences sector, having undertaken a number of transactions for clients in the field and hired a two-partner biotech team from Bird & Bird. This year Reed Smith advised long-term American client NAPO Pharmaceuticals in a £36 million listing, the first-ever primary listing of a US company on the London Stock Exchange. All up, the Reed Smith UK operation has a string of fantastic clients – Moss Bros, Tiffany, McDonald's, Pizza Express, Respironics, McNeil Nutritionals, Tate & Lyle, Akzo Nobel, Sara Lee, Bank of Scotland and Lloyds TSB all instruct the firm.

Reed Smith trainees have not only benefited from some pretty interesting work coming in from such clients, they have also enjoyed working within a rather positive office culture. *"It's such a welcoming place, filled with relaxed and reasonable people"* who are as *"unpretentious"* as they are *"balanced in their approach to work and life outside the office."* Then again, this is no holiday camp: *"We do work incredibly hard at times, especially in corporate."*

everything butler firm

Richards Butler trainees have always enjoyed relative freedom when it comes to seat selection and a wide variety of practice areas to sample. For them, *"the choice of seats means you have to have a clearer, self-appointed idea about where you want to go."* The firm is known for its abilities in, among other things, shipping and this year snatched a dry shipping and ship finance team from Stephenson Harwood. In the media sector it has a famed film and TV finance practice, and acts for clients like the BBC, Channel 4 and MTV. The recent hire of two media lawyers from Salans has also brought *"a lot more TV production work"* to the department. In the past year the firm has worked hard to capitalise on its substantial international trade and commodities expertise by opening up a Swiss office in partnership with a local firm specialising in energy, trade finance, shipping and arbitration. In the London litigation group, dedicated teams handle international trade and commodities disputes, banking litigation, real estate litigation, commercial disputes and shipping litigation.

Trainees admit that the firm *"can be very traditional in some senses, but the merger, the new overseas offices and the management style indicate that we're a forward-looking firm – we're not a Macfarlanes or a Slaughters."* Trainees define themselves as *"strong-minded and looking for something different; that tends to mean we're slightly different to the average City trainee."*

your place or mine?

Our interviewees at both firms had enjoyed *"an initial post-merger-agreement honeymoon period of drinks and social events across the two firms."* Naturally, *"predictable speculation and rumour"* was rife, not least because they wondered which of the two firms' London offices would become the merged firm's primary home. London Bridge aficionados at Reed Smith were reluctant to lose *"the views of the river and the quick hop to Borough Market,"* while their contemporaries at Richards Butler were happier to contemplate *"the renovation of our 1980s monstrosity"* near Liverpool Street than a move. The latter were confident that *"there's more space here so it'll either be everyone here or a new building."*

As for the practicalities of the training contract, at time of going to press it was planned that a four by six-month seat system would operate, with Reed Smith's *"two corporate seats, one litigation, one real estate"* system to be ditched in favour of Richards Butler's go-anywhere policy. The RB offices in Paris, Abu Dhabi and Piraeus will continue to offer overseas seats, while client secondments to places like MTV, the BBC or Rank look set to carry on as normal. Relatively little trainee movement between London and the Midlands in the past means it is unlikely Richards Butler trainees will be able to take six months in Birmingham, and that office will continue to recruit its own small trainee intake. All trainees will benefit from The Reed Smith University, a worldwide training programme created in conjunction with the University of Pennsylvania's Wharton Business School. This scheme allows junior associates in the UK to take the New York Bar exam. Beyond these details we won't speculate.

What almost all trainees look for, of course, are jobs at the end of their contracts. In September 2006, four out of six Reed Smith (all in London) and 18 out of 23 Richards Butler qualifiers stayed on to become a part of the new firm.

and finally...

Reed Smith Richards Butler looks set to offer London (and Midlands) trainees some of the City's (and the second city's) most varied work. The success of the merger remains to be seen, of course, but there can be no doubt that *"these are exciting times."*

Reynolds Porter Chamberlain

the facts

Location: London, Tiverton
Number of UK partners/solicitors: 64/191
Total number of trainees: 26
Seats: 4x6 months
Alternative seats: Secondments

This top-50 City firm offers clients a full range of commercial services and has a superb reputation in insurance work ranging from professional negligence to major international disputes.

because litigation happenz

The work of RPC's insurance division is extremely broad. At its core is a professional negligence department where teams defend lawyers, accountants, company directors and financial advisers. The insurers who instruct RPC to help minimise their professional policyholders' liability include such giants as QBE, Aon, Hiscox and St. Paul Travelers. There's also a department dealing with employers' and public authorities' liability for injuries sustained in the workplace, out on the streets and in public buildings. The matters addressed range from the serious to the slightly bizarre, like defending one of the companies who ran an attraction inside the Millennium Dome after a gymnast fell from a balloon. What's more, the firm acts in plenty of other areas of insurance, including product liability, property, financial and political risk, and insurance coverage disputes. This last area is slightly different in that insurer and policyholder do not get together to defend a suit by a third party; the cases arise where there is disagreement over whether a certain incident is covered by a policy. The firm works for leading household-name insurers such as Allianz, Zurich and many of the influential syndicates that make up Lloyd's of London.

With such diverse work going on, trainees' experiences of seats in the insurance division also vary. In prof neg and employers' and public liability seats trainees say they get "*a good opportunity to flex your muscles,*" handling small claims solo, often two or three at a time. "*It's a scary level of responsibility at first*" but you "*soon feel much more confident.*" Because you'll be dealing with both insurers and their clients "*you sometimes have to be a little diplomatic in keeping everyone on side.*" Working on solicitors' negligence cases has one other advantage: "*It's a good way to learn what not to do.*" Although the issues might be "*extremely interesting,*" a trainee's role on big cases can be mundane. They may even spend days on end bundling documents.

If you're keen to see the most complex insurance cases, the place for you is the reinsurance department. To oversimplify, reinsurance is insurance for insurers. Disputes are massive, international, and concern major events such as Hurricane Katrina and 9/11. Trainees concluded that "*the firm tends to spot those who are interested in reinsurance pretty early on,*" so if you're really up for this challenge, be sure to make it known. Overall, trainees enjoyed their time in the insurance division, which is just as well as everyone is likely to do at least one seat here. It's possibly the hardest working part of the firm, but also one of the most sociable. Entertaining clients is an important part of the insurance lawyer's job and at RPC it is not ignored. An annual Rock Quiz, for example, brings together competitor firms, the movers and shakers of the London insurance market and "*some mean-looking inflatable guitars.*"

policemen, princes and potters

RPC's commercial division is based around its corporate department, a core part of which is the media team. Dubbed "*the firm's best-kept secret*" by trainees, they believe its profile tends to be overshadowed by the insurance division. The team defends media companies against defamation claims and its client base runs from the *Daily Mail* all the way through to the *Guardian*. It has locked horns with a similarly diverse range of celebrities from Roman Polanski to some bloke called Prince Charles. What's more, the media team shouldered the considerable responsibility of preventing the reproduction of stolen pre-release copies of the last Harry Potter book. Working in the media team is "*fast paced and exciting,*" said one trainee. "*I've never worked three straight days on the same case.*" The work is tightly controlled by partners, but that doesn't mean you won't be "*heavily involved.*" Often a partner will "*hand you a file and ask you to take a look and recommend a course of action.*" The seat can involve "*a lot of court time,*" with one trainee "*in court before a master twice a week.*" It does have its disadvantages: "*The lawyers and clients on the other side tend to be highly strung, so you have to be tactical and make sure you don't piss them off.*" While the idea of defending free speech might be attractive, some matters can provoke fierce ethical debate; for example, the *Student Guide* team was split as to whether it would want to defend the *Daily Mail*'s right to call openly-gay Metropolitan police officer Brian Paddick 'the camp commander'.

In a mainstream coco seat you'll be working on "*pretty major deals,*" often for media or insurance clients. Trainees see themselves as "*an integral part of the team*" in a department whose workload has grown faster than its staff. As such they say: "*From day to day you're treated like an assistant; on the phone to the client all day,*" and "*they really rely on you.*" While this is undoubtedly exciting, one trainee also thought it "*stressful,*" telling us: "*Everything always has to be done now*" and "*you see a lot of panicky faces.*" That said, this is a sociable department and "*every few weeks the partners fund an event. Not only do they turn up themselves, they go around the office at 6pm making you stop working and go with them.*" Internal reorganisation has created a new IT/IP seat which is expected to prove as popular as the media seat. The commercial division also offers a general commercial litigation seat.

eight into three won't go

The popularity of three teams – corporate, media and PEP (a part of the insurance division) – can create a headache for HR staff. In September 2006 all but three of the firm's 11 second-year trainees applied for jobs in those three departments, with the result that only eight could ultimately stay on. To ensure you do get that coveted place in a popular department, some trainees recommend a quick word in the relevant partner's ear. *"By the time you speak to HR, everyone's already staked out their ground,"* said one. *"It's completely cloak and dagger."* Similar issues arise when it comes to seat allocation, and few trainees who seek to sit in all three departments will succeed. The actual allocation process, however, was thought to be *"absolutely fair."* In case you were wondering, *"the booby prize in the seat competition"* is regulatory and brokers which, trainees admitted, *"no one chooses."* RPC sometimes prioritises case continuity over rigid adherence to the seat system. One trainee had been given a case in their commercial litigation seat *"and handled it right up to trial 12 months later. The partner just said, 'come to me if you need anything'... I had real independence and, when we won, it felt like a personal victory."*

RPC trainees used to split their time between commercial seats based in the firm's *"relaxed"* Holborn office and insurance seats in the *"more buttoned-up"* City office. Now the firm occupies a single, *"plush and spacious"* new office at Tower Bridge. A switch to open-plan working has led to more mingling between departments, and one studious source was pleased that *"noise levels have gone down hugely – the loud people are quieter and photocopiers have been removed to soundproof booths."* Wondering how an open-plan office could possibly be quieter, we learned about a clever piece of technology called a white noise machine. It emits background noise, *"not unlike air conditioning,"* which *"quells any sense of hubbub."* New IT facilities are deemed *"much improved"* and there's a café in the lobby that's *"great for getting together."* There was only one negative comment from a trainee who thought that *"with 100 people on each floor, you feel a little anonymous."* It all adds up to a sense that *"this is not a place to come if you want an oak-panelled, traditional law firm; that's exactly what it's moving away from."*

leading by eggsample

The change of address seems to be part of a broader cultural shift within the firm. Traditionally, RPC was known as *"a bit warm and cuddly"* with *"a real family atmosphere"* where *"the senior partner would recognise you in the corridor and stop for a chat."* Some trainees saw the darker side of this, sensing *"an old boy's club"* where *"all the partners know each other from university."* However, with new partner hires and some departures, the firm is *"becoming more commercially minded"* and perhaps *"a little less distinct."* Other examples of a cultural shift include the abolition of dress-down Fridays and a new clear-desk policy, whereby files need to be put away at the end of the day. Although this sounds like a pain, trainees generally felt that *"it really helps you stay organised."*

The move also seems to be having an effect on the hours. In the past, trainees said they mostly enjoyed fairly relaxed working hours in Holborn, with the insurance office starting earlier and often finishing later. Early indications point to some kind of averaging out in the new office, a free breakfast in the café until 8.30am recognised by trainees as *"basically a bribe."* One conspiracy theorist even suggested the building's all-glass lobby was designed to *"force partners sneaking in after 10am to do the walk of shame in front of everyone."* However, it should be said that, like many litigation-focused firms, RPC still has decent hours by City standards, with trainees rarely in beyond 8pm except in corporate, where there were a few horror stories of early morning completions. *"There's something about opening the champagne at ten in the morning..."*

With the new office comes a new local pub, the Dickens Inn. In an attempt to get staff prepared for the new location, *"all the social events in the months prior to the move were held there."* Fortunately, it's a pretty nice place with a large beer garden and thus met with the approval of trainees.

So what kind of person is the firm trying to recruit? According to trainees, it's *"people who can work with people and are flexible."* One told us: *"Polite people come here, not pushy people."* Said another: *"They don't want anyone they couldn't take to lunch with a client."*

and finally...

Reynolds Porter Chamberlain is a firm in transition, but underneath the new, slicker image it maintains an unusually supportive atmosphere. The breadth of its insurance work means an excellent litigation training, and the non-contentious side is strong enough to satisfy those who are transactionally minded. Remember, if you want a spot in those popular departments you'll need to pipe up early.

Robert Muckle LLP

the facts
Location: Newcastle-upon-Tyne
Number of UK partners/solicitors: 17/45
Total number of trainees: 8
Seats: 4x6 months
Alternative seats: None

They say good things come in small packages, and this is certainly the case at this 17-partner Newcastle firm. Commercial to the core, it packs a powerful punch for a little 'un.

the regeneration game

Robert Muckle has been around for nearly a hundred years, but waited until the 1990s to adopt its current commercial profile. Now, its two weightiest areas of practice are corporate/business services and commercial property. *"The heartland of our work – where we've really delivered – was to owner-managed businesses,"* one trainee explained. While still dedicated to these smaller companies, these days RM advises a growing number of larger ones, even some plcs. Among its clients are Bank of Scotland, RBS, Lloyds TSB, Gazeley Properties, Greggs the bakers, ambitious Northern Irish property developer McAleer & Rushe, ASDA, The Sage Gateshead and Sunderland AFC.

Last year it restructured previously broad-ranging departments into more specialised units. For example, *"technology and innovation (T&I) has come on in leaps and bounds. From an offshoot of commercial it has firmly established itself as a distinct unit."* Property, too, has come under the spotlight: *"It's massive, the highest billing group in the firm. A year ago the figures showed a 40% year-on-year growth, and last year that growth was continued and fostered. It's also been split into different teams."* Urban regeneration is one area of expertise, and the firm has lately advised two local urban regeneration companies – Sunderland arc on Holmeside and other projects, and Tees Valley Regeneration on Central Park, Darlington. The firm is also instructed by both of Newcastle's unis, with Newcastle University seeking help with planning issues affecting its property portfolio and Northumbria University engaging it on various development proposals.

making a muckle

The firm's core work dominates the training scheme. Trainees try property, a commercial seat and then either litigation or employment, by which time if they have a sense as to where they want to qualify they can return for more experience. In practice, seat allocation is influenced heavily by business needs, so this could mean a seat cut short in one unit to provide extra back-up for another.

One of the most popular seats is called corporate finance and business advisory, and *"it's an area that informs the corporate support work of all other departments."* Call it mission control if you like. Trainees work for four partners on a wide range of corporate matters including banking deals. *"There are the usual company admin tasks, but we also work for plcs and hedge funds and on some aircraft-ownership matters."* Trainees get involved in all stages of the deal life cycle and reckon they have it made. For instance, the disclosure phase can mean a bum deal for trainees where the transaction size means there are literally rooms full of paperwork to sort through. Our sources' view was quite different. *"Yes, disclosure is a paper-chasing exercise but it is not necessarily grunt work. In a big City firm on a £100 million deal you might spend weeks photocopying things and putting them into folders. Here the deals are smaller, but still good. You might have a couple of days when you think 'Oh dear, this is a bit boring', but not often."* Overall the verdict on *"the engine room of the firm"* was extremely positive, though trainees recognise that *"in Newcastle you are never going to get the massive deals."*

Property is *"the most interactive seat,"* and here you'll work in tandem with the corporate lawyers, giving support on their deals as well as encountering property finance, planning law and development. As in corporate, *"you're very much a team resource with work coming from all sides. It can feel quite daunting when you first get your own files because sometimes they seem quite big... in the first few weeks if someone had told you what you'd be doing towards the end, you'd be overwhelmed, but you slide into it."* One option is construction law which, having weathered a few senior personnel changes, is an important unit. *"I knew nothing about this area of law when I started and surprised*

myself by really enjoying it," one trainee told us. The litigation department impressed a number of interviewees, one of whom recall: *"I was adopted into the fold, settled straight in and got cracking. When you get towards the end of the seat you become more proficient and get to do the work of an NQ."*

In the T&I unit the trick is to *"step up and take responsibility."* The work takes in *"anything interesting and innovative,"* from IP and IT to university spin-outs and start-ups. *"This region has a dwindling manufacturing base but lots of innovative new businesses... and I am really interested in the nitty gritty of commercial work,"* pronounced a source. One trainee was *"managing IP portfolios for clients, small companies who had never had IP assets before and needed their hand holding. Because I was having to start with the basics myself I was in a good position to explain things to them."* Better still, *"fee earners are interested in your ideas and it's good to feel you are taken seriously."*

service excellence

Train at RM and these two words will be drummed into you. *"They pride themselves on giving that extra level of service, giving 110% not 80%,"* we learned from one source. *"It has enthused everyone,"* another said. It all started when a couple of the partners went on a busman's holiday to America to investigate the USA's famous service-oriented business methods. On their return all manner of initiatives were put in place. *"It will take a while for all the service-excellence initiatives to filter through the firm though. Certain policies and procedures will have to change and they're probably not going to change overnight... but the will is there,"* concluded one trainee. There are sessions on how to win business, trainees are welcome at client events and they feel genuinely involved at the client-lawyer interface. *"I'm very much a part of what's going on and I feel I have a voice,"* one assured us. Sessions on black letter law haven't been sidelined in the rush for professional perfection – there are compulsory sessions of one or other variety every fortnight or so.

It's easy to see why trainees in smaller firms can access decision makers more easily, and RM is no exception. Take the trainee whose views were consulted by management: "*I had a chat with Steve* [ex magic-circle lawyer returned to Newcastle, now hot-shot managing partner and yet barely out of short trousers] *and he asked me to put together my thoughts on a particular topic.*" Such communication isn't formalised by regular meetings because "*we all sit quite close together and can speak about issues as they crop up.*"

quality not quantity

Trainees distinguished their employer from others in Newcastle. "*We are a good commercial firm that is quite strategically placed in the market and getting good-quality work as a result.*" One explained: "*We grew a lot in the 90s but we've not gone down the route of the other big five firms* [Dickinson Dees, Ward Hadaway, Eversheds and Watson Burton]. *Some of them have gone for volume business; Robert Muckle has a clear idea of where it wants to be and it's nothing to do with pure volume... It's not going for bums on seats, it wants to be a well-run business, relatively small and tight knit.*" The starkest contrast was between RM and Dickinson Dees, which one source summarised as follows: "*Dickie Dees has won lots of awards and it's a huge, very well-known firm, but because it is so large they have to work that much harder to make things gel.*" Trainees feel their firm is "*genuinely sociable.*" As well as the annual summer event and Christmas party there's a trainee-organised quiz to welcome the new intake and prove which are the smartest units in the firm.

RM spares nothing in its quest for the right recruits and runs a vac scheme to spot those with the requisite talents. "*Academics are not the whole picture: you've also got to have good communica-tion, personality and the ability to work in a team. They say they recruit for attitude and train for skill.*" Our sources considered a connection with the North East to be important and were quite clear that the firm was "*not a back-up option*" for anyone who actually wanted a London career. At least RM is doing its bit to make it easier for students to opt for Newcastle; it has recognised the importance of law school sponsorship, not only covering LPC fees but also adding a little extra to keep the wolf from the door. In the words of one trainee: "*In an up-and-coming, growing market Newcastle firms are doing well and they know that in order to get good candidates they've got to keep in line with Leeds firms. Candidates up here are looking for a firm that can give them a good package and RM can afford to do that.*" Four of the five qualifiers stayed on with the firm in September 2006.

and finally...

This is the first year we've investigated Robert Muckle and we have to say we're impressed by what we hear. If Newcastle's the city for you, this is not a firm to ignore just because it's smaller than better-known rivals.

Russell-Cooke

the facts

Location: London, Kingston-upon-Thames
Number of UK partners/solicitors: 42/71
Total number of trainees: 15
Seats: 4x6 months
Alternative seats: None

Putney, Kingston-upon-Thames and Holborn firm Russell-Cooke celebrated its 125th birthday in 2005. Now employing over 290 staff and partners, it has undergone four mergers in as many years and the resulting breadth of practice ensures a fertile training ground.

mergerfest

R-C's appetite for mergers was rediscovered in 2003 when charity law specialist Sinclair Taylor & Martin was amalgamated. In 2005 it was the turn of PI firm Evill and Coleman (no sniggering, it's pronounced ev-ill). Shortly after this, Harrison Curtis' niche media and entertainment practice was brought into the fold, although the partners have since moved on. The merger mania has continued unabated with the arrival of Surrey solicitors Caporn Campbell in April 2006, adding extra conveyancing and family lawyers and a new private client capability at R-C's Kingston office. While each new arrival *"brings its own culture"* to the mix, trainees don't seem fazed by the changes, regarding them instead as an opportunity to gain extra experience.

Still undecided about what kind of law you want to practise? This is an excellent choice of firm because it acts both for private individuals and commercial clients. Consequently, whatever preferences develop *"there is a spot for you somewhere in the firm."* The only caveat is that training seats are not necessarily always available in all areas of the firm as the seat list reflects the rise and fall of the different practice groups. For example, given the recent departure of the media and entertainment team, there is no longer a seat in this field. On the other hand, there is now ample availability in the once-rarely-visited crime and family departments. In short, seat allocation is *"as much about where the firm needs you as where you want to be."* The best approach is to be vocal about your preferences. At least the current training partner is *"pretty good at listening,"* and down the line there will be *"some trade off if at first you don't get the seat you want."*

taking coles to chelsea

At some stage the *"pretty-much-unavoidable"* commercial property seat will rear its head. On this point our sources were clear: *"If you don't want to try property then don't come to Russell-Cooke."* The department is *"notorious for throwing trainees in at the deep end,"* with new arrivals acquiring up to 40 or more of their own files. This can either be viewed as *"hard work"* or *"the best training, as you're getting on with things."* Whichever view you take, people are at hand to *"pull you out of the water if you are in trouble,"* though it's worth mentioning that the trainees' experiences and hours vary depending on which office they are in. The Bedford Row property team is on a roll and has practically doubled in size lately. It can handle multimillion-pound commercial deals for clients including London estates, retailers and developers. One client recently bought a part of Camden Lock for £7 million.

The usual mainstream options of commercial litigation and coco are there for the taking, plus there are several more specialist seats. R-C's renowned charity team was listed an impressive third in the recent *Dresdner Rcm Top 3000 Charities* list of law firms. If you secure a spot in this department you could be working for the likes of UNICEF, Barnardo's, The Stephen Lawrence Charitable Trust and various housing associations. The variety of work is pretty wide: everything from IP to employment and governance advice. The firm's sports law group draws on the skills of R-C's professional regulatory lawyers and acts for some pretty big clients. Chelsea FC and Jose Mourinho turned to the firm in relation to the Premier League tribunal dealing with the Ashley Cole 'tapping up' complaint lodged by Arsenal. Liaising with colleagues in the personal injury and clinical negligence departments, the group also works in the growing area of sports injuries.

Fancy a bit of crime? Murder, rape, people trafficking and massive VAT fraud – this is more than your average crime practice. You may already be aware that R-C lawyers defended Colin

Stagg, who was wrongly accused of Rachel Nickell's murder on Wimbledon Common. Add to this a well-regarded family law group and an excellent childcare team in Kingston and it is apparent that the firm is as adept at dealing with individuals in trouble as it is in assisting corporate clients build empires.

all change at earl's court

R-C inhabits five buildings in different areas of London: there are three in Putney, one in Kingston-upon-Thames and one in central London in the legal heartland of Bedford Row. All three centres have their own distinct character. Putney offers the broadest spread of work and is the administrative hub of the firm. The majority of staff and trainees are based here and we're told of its *"really lovely atmosphere"* and *"chilled-out pace."* Socially it's the most active of the locations, with Reds a popular choice after work. *"Some of the partners come out for a drink too,"* though they rarely make it as far as the Fez Club at the end of the night. Kingston doesn't tend to offer seats and is viewed as *"a no-man's-land"* by trainees, though we suspect attitudes might change if more of them were to spend time there. The Bedford Row office in old legal London is located in a grand terrace, which means people work *"on a staircase rather than in a corridor"* à la Oxford college/barristers' chambers. It is home to teams of commercial property and property litigation lawyers plus a team handling professional regulation and law firm interventions on behalf of the Law Society. The atmosphere is certainly pleasant, though its social side is essentially lunch-hour led. Time and again our interviewees told us: *"It's hard, and rare, to get all the trainees together,"* and one was honest enough to admit: *"It's our fault as trainees. If we asked for money from the firm we would get it; we are just too lazy."*

An annual quiz and the Christmas party do bring everyone together. The last party was at the Hurlingham Club and followed the tried and tested *"plenty of free booze... everyone had a good time"* formula. The summer party rotates around the three locations, and an annual conference for all fee earners – a mixture of work and play – is yet another opportunity for trainees to meet senior staff from around the firm. When it comes to sport, tales of the netball team's demise have now become myth, with no one knowing where the line between truth and fiction lies. The firm's cricketers have fared better and some enterprising souls have tried to set up a football team. Sailing enthusiasts get to participate in the Manches Cup, which is essentially lawyers on water en masse just off the Isle of Wight.

it's good to talk

The combination of a raft of very different practice areas and three very different office locations makes a single point of contact on the training scheme all the more important. The training partner is *"readily available"* if needed, for example *"if you have an issue with people or feel that your workload is too much."* Trainees tend to share a room with their supervisors, with just a few lucky (or unlucky) souls getting a room all to themselves. Our sources were frank about the quality of formal appraisals, believing that *"some partners take it quite seriously, others not so much."* It sounds as if a fix is on the way – *"there is a push to get the appraisals more coherent throughout the firm"* and *"now there are standard appraisal forms."* Our interviewees stressed that the firm *"pays a reasonable wage for reasonable hours and doesn't work you into the grave."* Trainees are also able to share in any bonus payouts made during the year – handy for those still feeling the squeeze of student debt. According to our sources, assistance may actually be available for LPC fees, though awards are discretionary and not something the firm goes out of its way to advertise. In September 2006, one of the three qualifiers stayed on at the firm.

R-C is far more than a large, upmarket high-street firm, yet our sources warned that you *"shouldn't be fooled into thinking that because there is a central London office this is a City firm and you will be dealing with City matters."* Let's settle on the label *"hybrid."* If you want a deeper insight into this *"no-frills, no-spills"* firm you can check out R-C's entire history on its website. Its 2005/2006 'Review for Clients' will bring you up to speed with the here and now and should also help you come up with pertinent questions to ask at interview.

and finally...

If all the above has whetted your appetite, in 2006 the firm offered a summer placement scheme for the first time in donkeys' years. Keep an eye out for the repeat in 2007.

Salans

the facts

Location: London, Bromley
Number of UK partners/solicitors: 27/30
Total number of trainees: 7
Seats: 4x6 months
Alternative seats: Secondments

Salans, with its network of offices across the globe reading like the departure board at Heathrow, is the very definition of an international law firm. The firm's international reputation centres on investment in emerging markets, particularly in Russia, the CIS and Eastern European states.

international rescues

"Part of the reason I came here was for the international focus, particularly the number of offices in the former Soviet Union," one trainee told us. *"I mean, we've got offices in, like, ten countries now."* Fourteen to be precise. Sounds like someone needs a quick history lesson.

French and American lawyers founded Salans in Paris in 1978. They swiftly planned the firm's expansion, cashing in on the changing economies in Russia, then Poland, then several former Soviet states. An office in London and another in New York gave the firm its Western interests, then five offices were added in Eastern Europe when US firm Altheimer & Gray went pear-shaped in 2003. A Chinese office was established and, most recently, Salans has pushed into the German legal market by taking the Berlin office of collapsing law firm Haarmann Hemmelrath. In short, Salans has grown quickly, often by picking up staff and business from firms in trouble. Through this process it has acquired some very good lawyers and clients, but at the same time it has not been immune from partner defections itself. Earlier in 2006, for example, a small media team left the London office after a relatively brief stay. In the last few years, the firm has been looking for other potential merger candidates.

While the firm may be as international as it comes, the training contract in London brings no guarantee of foreign travel. *"We don't do a seat abroad,"* trainees confirmed, although *"with a bit of luck, there is every chance of getting out and about. People have been to meetings in Romania, or maybe to Moscow for a brief time. One guy was recently assisting on a deal in Bulgaria."* Despite the brevity of these visits, they certainly seem to whet the appetite for far-flung destinations and many trainees look forward to international postings on qualification. Two of the three qualifiers stayed on at the firm in September 2006, taking up positions in corporate and banking.

Even if your view remains the Millennium Bridge and not the Rockefeller Center or the Palace of the Shrivanshahs in Baku, your contract will nevertheless have an international feel due to the volume of cross-border business handled in London. Take Kazakhstan: Salans represents French bank BNP Paribas on its loan to KazMunaiGaz Exploration & Production, which at $600 million was the largest oil-related deal in Kazakhstan last year. Trainees were expansive when talking about how Salans' London lawyers work in conjunction with colleagues across the network to get such deals done, particularly commending the inter-office connectivity on banking and finance deals. Illustrating this, London lawyers worked with their Ukrainian counterparts on the acquisition of Piramida shopping centre in Kiev. This nifty piece of real estate financing was the first done by a Western bank in the country for five years. In the UK there's a nice line in consumer finance as well as commercial asset finance, a pretty busy area to be in given recent changes in consumer credit and financial services regulations.

a mini misadventure

So what can you expect from your training contract? The simple answer is four seats with the first one or two chosen for you. *"For the second seat you make your preference known but it's really only on the third and fourth seats when you get a choice."* There are few complaints by the end of the two years as there are no compulsory seats and *"none that are loathed by everyone."* Reflecting the firm's practice leanings, trainees found the banking and finance department buzzing with *"all sorts of work from multimillion-dollar deals to consumer credit facilities."* It's a popular department to be in, as is employment, which has a good reputation particularly in contentious matters. Employment clients are diverse and include Nationwide Building Society, Kelly Services, Medical Research Council and Chiltern Railways.

A spell in corporate provides *"an awful lot of client contact,"* whereas in litigation *"you'll do a great deal of document management"* – meaning time spent with the dreaded photocopier. Even so, *"the good bits do outweigh copying ten sets of this and that."* One trainee elaborated: *"When you're sitting in a trial and you realise they are referring to what you've put together, it is hugely rewarding."* One

recent case saw the firm representing the freeholders of London County Hall in a dispute against the owners of The Saatchi Gallery. The dispute centred on allegations that the defendants had illegally occupied parts of the building not covered by the lease. Parking a Mini inside the building on a flight of stairs may have been the final straw. Eventually, Salans' client won in the High Court, allowing it to evict The Saatchi Gallery outright.

Spend time in the property department and you will *"see a transaction through from beginning to end and handle a lot of residential conveyancing on your own."* This is great for developing file managent skills; *"the only downside is there's a lot of admin, which can get a little repetitive."* The firm also has a strong licensing unit and has advised Betfair on regulatory issues in multiple jurisdictions. Trainees can also take a seat in the insolvency department or go on a client secondment. One source *"went to a big financial client which was great; it was good to get to know people and also get a different perspective on the work."*

do you parlez französisch?

Your supervisor will be a partner and you will most likely sit with an associate, *"so already you've got two people giving you work. You'll also get work from others and if you are keen and show ability, people are likely to give you a lot."* Salans' trainees understand the pros and cons of being part of a smaller intake: *"When you're one of 50 you can hide away, but here you definitely can't. There are huge advantages to that, but if you are not going to do the work you will struggle."* Another difference from the really big firms is that *"you can't expect to come here and find a really rigid structure to the training contract; you will be expected to help out as and when it is required."* All our sources reported *"good experiences with the partners,"* one telling us: *"They took me to meetings and gave me a lot of responsibility early on."* If it all gets too much, however, *"you can always speak up. No one is going to shout at you or* chase you down the corridor." There will be long hours in some seats ("*in my first week in banking there were three nights on the trot until midnight*") but overall trainees reported a reasonably healthy hours culture.

Do you need fluency in other languages in order to impress Salans' recruiters? "*I guess speaking a second or third language is an advantage,*" said one interviewee. "*It's polite to be able to speak a little French when calling a colleague in Paris, but there are trainees here who don't have languages.*" We checked with HR and they confirmed that while there was no specific policy regarding language skills, they are seen as a positive for applicants.

You may be surprised to learn that this international player has a second UK office in the sleepy 'burbs of Bromley, where it handles high-volume, low-value consumer credit and mortgage work. Trainees do not spend time in this office. Back in the City, the London lawyers occupy plush premises overlooking the Thames next to the wobbly bridge and opposite Tate Modern. Staff have adopted a dress code that is "*at the smarter end of smart casual*" and trainees told us that there is no noticeable sense of hierarchy in the office. One claimed that "*socially it is fantastic; maybe a bit too good. We're always out and about.*" Another, clearly with more self-restraint, said: "*It's good because it is not in your face. Socialising is mainly impromptu and if you want to opt out, you can.*" As many readers will already know, "*Thursday is the new Friday. People have their own stuff to do on a Friday, so we'll go out for drinks the day before. The partners aren't backwards in coming forwards, either.*"

and finally...

Salans will appeal to independent-minded students who are prepared to sidestep the more obvious choices in the City. We're thinking about the kind of people who might head off for a holiday of discovery in Central Asia rather than hopping on a Thomas Cook flight to the Greek Islands.

Samuel Phillips & Co

the facts

Location: Newcastle
Number of UK partners/solicitors: 5/14
Total number of trainees: 3
Seats: 4x6 months
Alternative seats: None

Samuel Phillips is a five-partner Newcastle firm with a particular flair for clinical negligence and employment law.

tyne in the blood

The majority of trainees here possess such strong North East connections that their blood is in fact closer to the chemical make up of Newkie Brown than anything else. "*A connection with the region is a must,*" sources explained. These regional roots mean a close affection for the locale and its inhabitants – call it Tynophilia if you will – with trainees enthusing: "*I can't think of anywhere else I'd rather live.*"

Founded way back in 1920 by the eponymous Mr P, Samuel Phillips conducted business on Newcastle's Pilgrim Street in the heart of Grainger Town until 1998 when it made the short hop to Gibb Chambers, a larger Georgian building on Westgate Street. The location "*close to the shops and city centre, a minute or two from the station,*" has long suited clients seeking conveyancing, probate and general family law advice, all areas of practice that characterised the firm's early years. Although elements of such work remain, in the last 20 years Samuel Phillips' caseload has evolved through the development of a strong relationship with the Newcastle Upon Tyne Hospitals NHS Trust. For this client, the firm advises on matters ranging from consent and surgery risk management to the defence of negligence claims. High-value, complex cases relate to allegedly mishandled operations and birth injuries (*"cerebral palsy claims up to £4 million"*). The firm is also well regarded for its high-profile claimant work, although it *"won't act against its clients in Newcastle."*

extra py all round

Hospital clients are also important to SP's esteemed employment team, which handles a range of applicant and respondent work, both contentious and non-contentious. As part of the firm's broader civil litigation department, its activities are *"focused on the immediate area and the broader region."* The department also conducts personal injury litigation and *"disputes between small to mid-sized owner-managed businesses or larger national businesses with a local presence."* Metnor Group, Ultimate Leisure and Alfas Group are the most prominent clients regularly instructing the firm's non-contentious department. It looks to us as if suggestions that Samuel Phillips is *"looking to expand commercially"* are well founded.

In 2005 there was a merger with a small Jesmond-based firm run by ex-Eversheds partner Edward Pybus. In particular, this has boosted business in the area of *"complex tax planning and probate."* It also highlights the firm's willingness to grow. Last but not least you should be aware of a *"strong"* family department that has added team members this year. *"High-value divorce, ancillary relief, pensions and a mixture of children's work including private and public care proceedings"* are its stock in trade. It also tackles adoption, access rights and abduction cases, taking not infrequent instructions from national organisations like Relate and Reunite, as well as various private fostering and adoption organisations.

partnering up

Training at SP is a straightforward waltz around four six-month seats; one each in civil litigation & clinical negligence, family, and non-contentious,

with the final seat being taken in an area hoped for on qualification (subject to the firm's needs). However, trainees did highlight that there was room to manoeuvre. Said one: *"I made it clear I was interested in employment and so while in an unrelated seat I was drafted in to assist on several discrimination claims."* With a population of just three or four trainees *"you're the only one in each department so you get added responsibility."* For one trainee, *"the level of exposure to good work has been better than that of my friends at Eversheds or Dickinson Dees."* Another added: *"We're really thrown in the deep end."* True, there's a different scale of work going on at those firms, but for our sources here, *"size doesn't always matter."*

A clin neg seat involves *"drafting letters of advice, letters of claim, reviewing medical chronologies, conducting client interviews"* and *"reading sometimes horrific reports of operations or drugs tests gone wrong."* Civil litigation gives the chance *"to attend tribunals and client meetings"* concerning equal pay claims in the health sector and *"boundary disputes and commercial conflicts."* In the family seat and when working on the private client side of the non-contentious department, trainees find that *"the majority of work is Yellow Pages-type enquiries or walk-ins"* and had *"handled residential conveyancing files from start to finish."* In all seats, working closely with supervising partners almost guarantees exposure to more complex cases, be it big-money divorces, licensing matters or company disputes.

The ability to have close working relationships with partners is said to be *"a major reason to choose the firm."* *"You're getting one-to-one training from partners who will sit you down, explain cases or tasks to you and really take the time to run through work with you."* There are monthly *"half-hour feedback sessions where you discuss the work you're getting and what you want to do"* plus end-of-seat appraisals in which *"you analyse what could have been done better."* Everyone knows just where they stand. Mondays mean formal training sessions featuring "*a mini presentation from an assistant solicitor on courses they've attended.*" Trainees too have the opportunity to "*book yourself on relevant external training days.*"

tyne gibber jabber

Despite being a grade 2 listed building, Gibb Chambers has recently enjoyed a basement refit to accommodate Edward Pybus and his team. The building continues to "*age very well*" and fosters a "*friendly, intimate atmosphere.*" Close proximity to Newcastle's travel links (including the Metro) means commuting is a doddle and doesn't add too much to days that "*are usually a straightforward 9am-5pm.*" When deadlines approach it can mean "*coming in at 8am and not leaving until 6.30pm or 7pm.*" On Fridays the firm's 5.01 Club (go figure) arranges drinks in a local bar. "*Ghengis has been the favourite for a while,*" but "*there's always e-mail banter about where we'll go*" and recently a break-away faction has been heading for Revolution. Having experienced something of a renaissance in recent years, Newcastle has an enormous amount to offer, not least in terms of bars ("*there's a new strip of bars in the city centre plus waterfront places*"), but also when it comes to shops, art galleries and theatres. Summer and Christmas parties ("*last year in a Chinese restaurant*") are high points on the social calendar. After considering their good fortune for a moment, one source declared that "*Newcastle combines the best aspects of city and rural living: you can be in the countryside in 20 minutes and in The Lakes in an hour and a half.*" It does sound attractive, but if you're now contemplating a move up North, you'll undoubtedly have to compete with some highly qualified natives. Newcastle has two universities packed full of law students.

Proving that there can be a downside to the size-intimacy equation, it's worth remembering that the firm offers NQ jobs based strictly on business need. Last year's merger left no room for NQs and in September 2006 both qualifiers had to move on to seek jobs in their preferred areas of practice. The final fourth seat can be an opportunity to explore an area in which jobs are available at SP, but in recent years the firm has been generous in helping those pursuing specific practice ambitions obtain excellent positions elsewhere.

and finally...

Samuel Phillips offers hands-on training with all of the benefits of working at a smaller firm. If the big corporate players of the North East don't appeal, this looks to be an excellent option.

Shadbolt & Co

the facts

Location: London, Reigate
Number of UK partners/solicitors: 29/28
Total number of trainees: 9
Seats: 4x6 months
Alternative seats: Paris, secondments
Extras: Pro bono – FRU

Celebrating its 15th birthday in 2006, this firm continues to stride away from its quiet beginnings in Reigate to become an international firm with an unrivalled reputation in construction and engineering. If you harbour any ambitions of practising in this particular area of law then read on.

the accidental law firm

As its name implies, the firm is the brainchild of Dick Shadbolt who, after a sparkling career at CMS Cameron McKenna, decided to retire to the Home Counties. Before signing off altogether, he thought he would just finish a couple of cases he'd been working on. Before long, the work took on a momentum of its own, Shadbolt was back in full-time practice and more like-minded people were found to help out. Pretty soon an office was set up in Reigate near Shadbolt's home. A mere decade and a half later, the firm has offices in London and Paris, affiliations with law firms in Tanzania's Dar es Salaam and Athens, and its lawyers are involved in projects all over the world. Such expansion has required the firm to broaden the scope of its workload to encompass corporate, real estate and employment law. Having said this, no one should be under any illusion about the true nature of Shadbolt's business, so don't make the same mistake as the trainee who told us: "*I didn't realise how construction-heavy it was here.*" Another surely put their finger on it when they said: "*It's hard to separate Shadbolt from construction, one follows the other.*" Armed with this knowledge, you shouldn't be surprised if two of your four six-month seats are spent in construction departments. Of course, this means you'll be acting for major clients: Amey, ALSTOM, Galliford Try, Sir Robert McAlpine and British Aerospace, among others.

The core of the firm's activities is contentious construction law, an area in which it excels at good old-fashioned litigation and domestic and international arbitration. Lawyers recently represented Citigroup Properties in a complicated case against a building contractor involving two separate actions, three different parties and a truckload of evidence. In another case concerning a sewage works in Liverpool, the documentary evidence ran to a million pages. These sprawling disputes are not uncommon in the construction industry where many different companies and professionals are working together on projects with huge scope for errors of one sort or another, and some extremely technical reports. If you are going to try your hand at being a construction litigator or arbitrator, you'll have to grow used to "*getting your hands on lots of documents.*" Some of the trainees we spoke to "*absolutely loved*" the contentious seat because, in addition to the "*mundane, last-minute*

bundling" duties ("*Oh my God, the paginating!*"), there is also genuine scope for "*doing the work of a real lawyer.*" One trainee fondly recalled the "*cut and thrust*" of contentious construction, telling us how they had "*run disclosure exercises, prepared evidence, instructed counsel and dealt with a guy on the other side who was four or five years' qualified.*"

Should you be more inclined towards non-contentious construction matters, you can expect to work on major PFI/PPP projects in the UK and internationally. One of several prestige projects on which the firm has advised recently is the multibillion-dollar investment in a new light rail system traversing the city of Dubai on behalf of the Dubai Municipality. As yet, a seat in the region isn't on the cards for trainees; however, qualified solicitors in this department "*definitely get to travel to Middle Eastern countries.*"

building relationships

Stemming from a desire to service its construction clients' wider needs, Shadbolt has a number of smaller departments that have grown around its "*construction heart.*" These are: commercial property, corporate, employment and commercial litigation, the majority of which are centred on the Reigate office, with a smaller presence in the capital. When trainees go into these departments, they usually do so in the Reigate office. They also have the option of going on secondment to one of Shadbolt's clients; for example, six months with engineering giant Atkins. When in-house, trainees encounter everything "*from employment to IP*" and are "*left to do* [their] *own work like a real lawyer.*" Make a real impression and, like one of our sources, you may carry on looking after the client's files following your return to Shadbolt. The relationships you make on secondment are important for both you and the firm, and can be long lasting. As an aside, one trainee mentioned: "*I'm meeting the client for drinks tonight actually.*"

Shadbolt's international practice especially benefits French speakers as there is a seat in the three-partner Paris office that specialises in company/commercial matters and arbitrations at the International Court of Arbitration. Recently, one trainee jumped at the chance of a three-month secondment to a Brussels law firm, although there is no guarantee that this will always be available in the future. We hear that a seat in the firm's associate office in Dar es Salaam could possibly be on its way.

Our interviewees spoke warmly of the partners, many of whom take time to "*speak to you socially if you are in a breakout area.*" We heard a tale about one trainee who was telling a colleague of their quandary over which department they would apply to for qualification. "*A partner overheard and insisted on spending an hour every day for a week helping them think about what they wanted. In the end, he suggested to the other partners a compromise whereby the trainee could sit in commercial property but experience a lot of projects work as well.*" That the partners take so much time to help trainees is reassuring as "*there are more partners than assistants so you work closely with them.*" In September 2006, two of the four qualifiers stayed on with the firm.

surrey seems to be the hardest word

In addition to close partner contact, trainees say the firm's size translates into "*better hours than the major City players.*" This is the case regardless of which office they work in, although in Reigate more than London "*you tend to work 9am to 5.30pm.*" At this point we can put off the inevitable no longer. If considering joining this firm, you must bear in mind the pronounced differences between the two locations. Pronounced, trainees say, to the point of it feeling like "*two completely different firms.*"

All trainees will spend at least one seat in the Reigate HQ. With its "*traditional set-up*" of individual offices for lawyers, the Surrey base appeals to "*older partners and those with families*" or those

who enjoy "*having birds singing outside the office.*" On speaking to the trainees, it was apparent that the "*ideal Reigate lawyer*" was someone who'd much rather drive to work locally than commute by train to London, and whose ideal social experiences centred on cricket matches and "a *curry on a Friday night.*" The majority of trainees we spoke to were less than enthusiastic about working in the Home Counties; as one rather dryly commented "*the office is in the middle of nowhere... although it's pretty close to Dick Shadbolt's house.*" Many of the trainees live in London, which means "*a terrible commute with only one direct train.*" Comparing it to the London experience, many saw Reigate as "*just a bit too quiet*" with "*few chances to mingle unless you go to the kitchen for biscuits.*"

The London office was seen as a "*more relaxed and flexible*" place to work: for example, "*you can go out for your dry cleaning or go for coffee.*" No one's suggesting Shadbolt London is a drop-in centre; indeed, if you are involved in a big case then it is quite possible to be in the office until midnight. What trainees like is that partners "*trust you more here and don't clock watch*" and that London has more of "*a fun atmosphere.*" Even fans of the Reigate office acknowledged that the capital was "*more of a social place to be,*" perhaps because there are "*more junior staff.*" The London Shadbolt staff "*go for drinks on a Thursday or Friday after work*" and there are enjoyable client entertainment events. Speaking of clients, it was hinted that perhaps the firm keeps clients of the two offices reasonably separate: "*I'm not sure that the likes of Citibank in London especially want to meet accountants from Penge,*" mused one source.

real law

All staff get together for summer and Christmas parties, the former being "*held in Betchworth House in Surrey for the last couple of years and most likely will be so again.*" At the time of writing, the firm was preparing to gather the three offices together to celebrate its 15th birthday with a trip on the London Eye and a slap-up meal at Chez Gerard. On a more regular basis, trainees do try and meet up for picnics or drinks in Clapham, regarded as a good mid-point between the two locations.

Among the current Shadbolt trainees we spotted someone who'd previously worked in construction-related underwriting and someone with a technical degree. The majority do not have prior experience of the industry and stressed that it is not a prerequisite as long as you have a genuine fascination for the law. If you want reassurance on this point, just consider how many significant judgments in contract and tort cases have emanated from the world of construction. As one of our sources so charmingly put it: *"There is a lot of new law being made, so it is interesting for an anorak like me."*

and finally...

Shadbolt's excellent reputation is built on construction law. While there is no need for you to know that industry inside-out before joining, you must understand the extent to which it will colour your training experience.

Shearman & Sterling LLP

the facts
Location: London
Number of UK partners/solicitors: 27/105
Total number of trainees: 17
Seats: 4x6 months
Alternative seats: Overseas seats
Extras: Pro bono – various projects; language training

This behemoth of a New York law firm has figured so strongly in US history that it can justifiably consider itself an institution equal in standing to the New York Yankees or the Empire State Building, albeit that it's less of a tourist attraction. As one of the first US firms to establish a foothold in the UK over 30 years ago, its London office is reasonably Anglicised and has developed a fine reputation as a rival to the magic circle in its core areas of M&A and project finance.

a whole lotta history

Founded in 1873, Shearman wears its history on its sleeve. Thomas Shearman defeated an insurance claim on a merchant ship sunk during the American Civil War by proving that it was indeed a civil war and not a rebellion. The firm has acted for an array of legendary capitalists, including Jay Gould in his takeover of the Union Pacific Railroad in 1875, Henry Ford and his Ford Motor Company since the production of the Model T, numerous members of the Rockefeller family and the bank that would one day become Citibank. It is hard to imagine a law firm that better suits the label 'white shoe', a term thought to originate from the white buckskin shoes that were once fashionable among elite fraternities and clubs of Ivy League universities. Members of these groups went on to take up positions in the foremost companies and law firms of the day. The links between the firm and the Ivy League are strong, with John Sterling leaving the residue of his estate to Yale University in 1918. Upon receiving this bequest the chancellors considered changing the name of the world-famous learning institution, but eventually settled for building the Sterling Memorial Library, Law School and Hall of Graduate Studies as well as establishing Sterling professorships, the most prestigious of their kind at Yale.

Yet for a US firm so patently wrapped in the Stars and Stripes Shearman has been enormously successful in branching out into first Europe, then Asia and more recently South America. Its list of offices outside the USA includes Paris, Rome, Munich, Frankfurt, Brussels, Beijing, Hong Kong, Tokyo, Singapore, Abu Dhabi, Sao Paulo and a few others besides. Not least London, of course.

cracker deals

The London office opened in 1972 and started practising with dual UK/US capability in 1996 at a time when many other US firms were chancing their arm on this side of the Atlantic. It is now *"virtually its own full-service firm"* with a complement of more than 140 legal staff. Its departments are banking, project development and finance, M&A, capital markets, financial institutions (advisory), tax, competition, IP and real estate. The *"awesome"* project finance department acts for some prestigious clients, recently representing Oman Petrochemical Industries in a project to develop and finance a $7 billion ethane cracker facility. It has scooped various awards for its energy work, including that on the Egypt LNG Train 2 project that will see the development and financing of a natural gas liquefaction facility. Unusually, on this deal all the finance and security documents were prepared by Shearman as project counsel, with the finished deal then being offered to the banking market in a 'bond-style' execution process.

Unwilling to be outdone on the prestige front, the *"especially strong"* M&A team in London advised mmO2 on a major reorganisation. Shearman designed an innovative scheme to achieve all the client's objectives and saw it approved by the High Court. The firm also represented Merrill Lynch on its role in the consortium that acquired a stake in Bank of China (China's second largest bank) for over $3 billion. Add in a third team – capital markets – and you've got Shearman's *"big three houses over here in London."* The capital markets lawyers' achievements are no less impressive; for example, they represented the hedge funds (Perry Capital, Och-Ziff and Citadel) that provided much of the capital for Malcolm Glazer's takeover of Manchester United FC.

hard slog: no eggnog

Trainees take four six-month seats and, although the number of departments at the firm continues to grow, it is perfectly understandable that *"most trainees do the main transactional seats."* M&A is popular and *"there is always a queue to sit there."* Get to the front and you'll be exposed to some of the foremost corporate deals on the planet, albeit that the bigger the deal the more minor your role is likely to be. Nonetheless, our sources had picked up everything from research and small drafting assignments to *"lots of due diligence."* In project finance, trainees are *"incredibly busy with classic, trainee-type work,"* a certain amount of it fairly administrative in nature. This seat allows trainees to *"see deals from various angles,"* working as they do with a wide variety of people and getting *"great exposure to clients every day."* Of those we interviewed many said they had been given quite a bit of responsibility in this seat, some even getting to run their own *"mini-deals;"* however, there was a suggestion that if you were unlucky you might get *"stuck making bibles of closing documents."* As the only open-plan department in the firm things *"can get a little noisy but it does mean you can learn more by osmosis and it has more of a team feel to it than some of the other departments."*

In terms of hours and the demands placed on trainees, banking finance (covering acquisition, leveraged and structured finance deals) is regarded as *"the toughest seat in the firm;"* interviewees reported regularly leaving the office between midnight and 2am. Undoubtedly a hard slog for six months, but exactly how much work intrudes into your personal life rather depends on your supervisor. One trainee explained that theirs *"was extremely competent and didn't want to work weekends, so he managed the whole deal in such a way that tore the week to shreds but kept the weekends protected."* By contrast, one unfortunate source *"managed to miss all the Christmas parties."*

Financial institutions (advisory) and asset management – a lengthy department name if we ever saw one – is an *"altogether more civilised"* place to work on account of it being more academic in nature. Sit here and you'll regularly *"work eight or nine hours and then go home."* Trainees view this department as *"less hierarchical than the others"* and believe this leads to more responsibility being offered. The contentious seat option exposes them to international arbitration and commercial litigation and provides *"a nice change from transactions."* Trainees regularly *"act as a point of contact for all the other departments in the firm"* and are introduced to *"the nightmare of trying to arrange conference calls with people all over the world."* The best bits are *"popping down to court for a change of scenery and making a submission"* and sitting in on trials, tribunals and arbitrations. Anyone who refuses to be distracted from transactional work can elect to take a two-week course in litigation at the College of Law instead of six months in a contentious seat.

Shearman trainees have the chance to spend a seat in one of the firm's overseas offices. At the present time, these are available in New York, Paris, Brussels, Singapore and Abu Dhabi.

brolly good show

There have been suggestions that a degree of tension had formed in the gold star departments of M&A and project finance. Our sources confirmed that generally *"good lateral hires"* have restored a positive atmosphere to these teams, although one or two people implied that the firm could do better at *"hanging on to a few more of its senior lawyers in M&A."* Here they felt that *"growth has stalled a little"* compared with just a couple of years ago, but understood that, across the City, law firms are finding it hard to fully staff busy corporate teams. Even if in the assessment of one source the firm would get *"perhaps a B-plus instead of an A-plus,"* generally things look to be going well for it.

Across the office the atmosphere was described as *"not especially aggressive or competitive like you might think an American firm would*

be." The London office regards itself as being *"an English firm under an American umbrella"* and, for the most part, trainees *"hadn't felt the US influence very much,"* save for the transatlantic feel to the work of certain departments. There are some other *"silly things that remind you that you are in a US firm,"* such as having to use New York for IT support after 'normal office hours'. Not so silly is the hefty salary: NQ pay packets have been hiked to £72,000 and new trainees start on £36,500. That salary awaited the five of the six qualifiers who took jobs with the firm, two in M&A, one in project finance, one in litigation and one in antitrust.

It was hard to find a consensus on the length of the average day. Some people said they frequently left for home about 7pm or 7.30pm; there was also plenty of evidence to suggest that in some seats 9pm was more common with bursts of *"any time between 10pm and not leaving at all... there are beds and showers here, just in case."* You may get tired when deals get hairy, but at least you'll be able to take pride in your achievements. Trainees indicated that they regularly work opposite their peers at magic circle firms on deals, only to find that *"where you'll be running three or four matters on it they have one trainee doing one aspect each."*

Despite this, our interviewees believed the firm to be *"more relaxed than the old-school English firms"* and although *"you are unlikely to go for a drink with a partner,"* colleagues were described as *"supportive and friendly."* In answer to our questions about trainees' social lives we heard everything from *"I don't have one"* to *"everybody goes for drinks,"* so we guess it all depends on which department you're in and who you know. Those who did venture out said they could be found in Industry, a bar right next to the office, or The Papermill. The firm pays for a trainee night out every six weeks or so and there are more formal office-wide parties in the summer and at Christmas. Departmental dinners and drinks will also crop up and trainees are welcome to participate.

and finally...

This American gentleman of a firm has a place at the very top of the world's corporate tree and the London office is an important contributor to its success. For M&A and project finance deals this is one of the most exciting places to be and, with an expected surge in the size of the trainee population, more students should be able to play a part in the future. Just remember you'll need a positive 'can-do attitude' and an appetite for responsibility (and maybe a supply of Pro Plus).

Shoosmiths

the facts

Location: Northampton, Nottingham, Birmingham, Milton Keynes, Basingstoke, Reading, Solent
Number of UK partners/solicitors: 90/88
Total number of trainees: 32
Seats: 4x6 months
Alternative seats: Secondments

If you want a challenge in the regions, prepare yourself for a treat. This rapidly expanding top-50 firm is going great guns. Thanks to a sterling client roster, Shoosmiths has shown phenomenal year-on-year profit growth – a record 72% rise in 2003/04 and 51% the year after.

find the gap

It wasn't so long ago that you'd mention the name Shoosmiths and legal people would say 'debt recovery, PI and residential conveyancing' right back at you. Though it has long been active in commercial work, it is only relatively recently that its achievements in this sphere have come to the fore. *"We started to see the firm as a whole concept rather than lots of bits and pieces,"* divined one source on the firm's rebranding and renaissance. Indeed, Shoosmiths is developing at such a rate that annual turnover at the 90-partner firm

jumped from £60.8 million to £74.7 million in a single year in 2006.

Business is divided into five divisions: commercial property, property direct (the residential stuff), corporate/commercial, employment law and dispute resolution. In terms of clients, an impressive roll call includes the London Development Agency, Volkswagen, Nissan, ING Direct, HBOS and Daimler-Chrysler. Property – both commercial and residential – is a major activity accounting for over 30% of national turnover and, here, the firm recently advised Boots Group, alongside City giant Linklaters, on a £298 million transaction. Of late, various practice areas have been earmarked for growth: for example, the Midlands corporate group, where several lateral hires have paid dividends. As the big national firms focus increasingly on international work, Shoosmiths is determined to take advantage of what it perceives as a gap in the domestic midmarket. The banking litigation practice has also really taken off and, according to our sources, is *"one of the fastest-growing departments."*

the sum of its parts

Before being let loose on the firm, trainees spend two weeks bonding on a *"fantastic"* residential induction course. At that stage they are ready to investigate what their office (or group of offices) has to offer. The firm's distinct geographic footprint is one of life's many mysteries. Traditionally based away from the biggest legal centres, Shoosmiths is spread across seven locations, taking in the Midlands, the Thames Valley and the South. The office it opened most recently – Birmingham in 2003 – is an exception to this rule, which maybe says something about the direction now being taken. Each office has *"two or three national clients and then a raft of local ones."*

Employment, property and coco departments are found in all the offices bar Basingstoke;

beyond this, "*not all the offices have the same seats.*" For example, "*IP is based in Milton Keynes*" while Reading boasts a strong "*IT contracts and media and broadcast group.*" Any trainee can move offices if "*there is a real dire business need for you to do so or you actually say you want to move*" in order to do a particular seat. Bear in mind that the firm may only cover your travel costs "*if they require you to move.*" Secondments (eg to DaimlerChrysler), until recently available only to Milton Keynes and Northampton-based trainees, are now open to all.

northampton & milton keynes

Northampton and Milton Keynes are viewed as one location for training contracts, even though they are "*20 minutes down the road*" from each other. Between them these offices hold "*the widest variety of seats.*" Northampton has always been the firm's HQ and is base for "*about 400-500 staff.*" The purpose-built office at The Lakes is "*mainly open plan*" although there are "*a couple of partners holding on to the walls.*" Despite a real selection box of seats to choose from, our interviewees did note a few hiccups in the system. In the smaller offices, the staple seats tend to be "*commercial property, employment, litigation and coco,*" so trainees know what they are likely to get. In Northampton "*the number of seats available within several different departments* [means] *you can end up doing something you're not really expecting.*" In turn this can "*cause a bit of strife*" and "*people are not always happy in their first year.*"

Finance litigation and debt recovery is a major activity in this office. This group deals with the debts owed to a host of big-name banks, building societies, motor finance companies and credit card issuers. The trainee focuses more on finance lit than debt collection and can be in court several times a week for preliminary hearings. It's a similar story in property, where trainees don't touch the volume residential work and stay firmly in the

commercial realm. Similarly, any PI work is in the "*serious PI*" category, meaning "*high-value cases, not the typical trip-and-slip stuff.*" Clinical negligence claims also feature. One of the most interesting seats covers regulatory matters – health and safety, public liability problems (including food-related) and licensing. The seat was described as "*fantastic, with the level of responsibility really good.*" Clients include Boots, Next and McDonald's plus the Health & Safety Executive.

Northampton trainees say their business-park office location "*does not promote much of a social life*" and they grumble that catering facilities are lacking ("*just a vending machine*"). Those looking for adventure during their lunch break can take a free bus into town on Mondays, Wednesdays and Fridays. Make the journey under your own steam on a Friday night and you'll see that The Cherry Tree is quite popular for drinks.

Shoosmiths Milton Keynes office was launched in 2001 with an initial focus on IP/IT, pensions and competition work. Fast forward to 2006 and this has grown to a full-service office of over 50 fee earners with more moving in from the Northampton office at the end of 2006. Sources repeatedly told us how popular the MK IP seat was and that, as a result, there are interviews to decide who gets it. The team's big clients include BP, Gala Group and The Open University. As the office is "*just five or ten minutes' walk from the town centre,*" trainees say that MK "*is better than Northampton for a social life.*"

birmingham & nottingham

Completing a triangle of Midlands offices is Birmingham. If you want to do an insolvency seat it's currently the only place to go, and here the team acts for a number of national and local insolvency practitioners including Baker Tilly and PwC. The Birmingham office also offers seats in commercial property, comlit and coco, and employment law is taking off so a seat in this team is on the cards. For after-work winding down, All Bar One is just across the road.

Commercial property and coco are the star turns in the Nottingham office, with property litigation and employment each playing a supporting role. Rumours abound of a seat opening up in private client at some stage in the future. Property is a *"good seat to start off in"* as you *"automatically get responsibility"* from the word go. Sources speak of *"a very good atmosphere throughout the office,"* ascribing it to the open-plan layout where *"teams from trainees to equity partners all sit in the same bay."* Work is *"steady"* and the hours are a *"reasonable"* 9am to 5.30pm with a few late nights in the busy coco team.

The firm is *"well-located right in the centre of town"* and *"everyone gets involved"* in a range of social events from go-karting to table football. This is an office that knows how to party and there is *"never a shortage of bars to go to."* As in all offices, trainees are also encouraged to attend *"the various networking organisations in the city,"* including Nottingham's Young Professional Group.

solent, reading & basingstoke

Way down south, the Solent office is based in the Fareham business park (or *"industrial estate"* for those who don't mince their words). This *"friendly office"* is quite small in Shoosmiths' terms (only *"20 or 30 people"*) and so the choice of seats is pretty straightforward: *"commercial property, coco, a bit of civil litigation and employment."* After-work activities are a bit muted because people drive to work, but *"if you jump into the car, Whiteley Village Outlet and a big Tesco"* are both within easy reach. The word on the street is that the Solent office has expansion plans.

In Reading there's much the same seat choice plus debt recovery and IP. The office has recently moved its 100-strong workforce to new premises

in Apex Plaza. The Oracle shopping centre is close to the new office as are *"five or six nice bars on the canal."*

Finally, PI is well and truly the name of the game in the Basingstoke office where there are *"400 people in the building"* solely dedicated to low-value legal expenses insurance claims. Basingstoke grows its own trainees through the internal promotion of case handlers. The office *"takes a large amount of work from insurers for PI and road traffic accident cases"* and boasts *"good hours, largely 9-5.30."* This means *"that you can make plans outside the office and keep them."* You *"don't have all the amenities a big town would have"* working in a business park, but *"the shops [in the town centre] are only ten minutes' walk away."* This is an office where *"people don't take themselves too seriously"* and pride themselves on their enthusiastic contributions to the annual firm-wide, five-a-side football tournament and inter-office north v south cricket match.

round the benz

If you're attracted by all that talk of impressive growth and soaring profits, bear in mind that Shoosmiths has just 41 equity partners in a firm of over 1,300 people. Not exactly *"sharing the wealth,"* mused one source. Moreover, some interviewees confided that the firm *"is growing faster than we are recruiting;"* one admitted that Shoosmiths may want to *"recruit from top City firms"* yet *"the calibre of person they are after isn't always the sort of person looking for the vacancies."* At trainee level, several interviewees mentioned past failings in the HR and training function, pointing out that for almost a year the firm was without a dedicated graduate recruitment manager. It sounds as if certain seat allocation and HR issues *"have now been resolved,"* not least because a full-time grad recruitment specialist is now on board. An internal training programme also seems to be back on track with national training days every two to three months. To keep staff sweet, the firm has some novel ideas. This year it raffled a Mercedes car four times and hit on the popular wheeze of 'birthday days' – an extra day's holiday plus *"a wadge of vouchers to spend."*

Of the 12 people who qualified in September 2006, eight stayed on with the firm, all in the offices in which they had trained.

and finally...

Shoosmiths' trainees are typically *"down-to-earth"* redbrick university types with an aversion to London life. Anyone with ties to a location where Shoosmiths operates, or anyone who wants to join an *"ambitious, modern firm that is progressing and moving forward,"* is recommended to investigate their preferred office more comprehensively than we are able to do so here.

Sidley Austin LLP

the facts

Location: London
Number of UK partners/solicitors: 37/78
Total number of trainees: 10
Seats: 4x6 months
Alternative seats: None

In London, Sidley Austin is an Anglophile US firm with a nose for all things financial. If litigation leaves you cold but you are keen on negotiation and big, big numbers, read on...

windy city, big apple, big smoke

Chicago-headquartered Sidley & Austin opened the doors of its UK office back in 1974 and set about establishing a name for itself in structured finance and securitisation deals. But this is only half the story. You also need to know about the establishment of the London office of New York firm Brown & Wood, which was known for its work in debt capital markets. When the two US firms merged in 2001, their London offices combined forces to create a dominant player in the Square Mile. Nowadays it represents some of the world's most impressive financial institutions including Morgan Stanley, Northern Rock, Merrill Lynch, Goldman Sachs and Citibank.

Recently the firm cut its name back to a simple Sidley Austin, but there's been no shrinkage in its excellent reputation for securitisation, structured finance and derivatives as well as debt, equity and high yield international capital markets. We understand you are unlikely to know anything about the finer details of these fields and that's okay so long as you have *"a willingness to learn."* Typically, trainees admitted that the extent of their knowledge prior to starting their contracts was limited but, even so, they had a hunch that high finance would suit them. Said one: *"I knew Sidley Austin had a reputation for doing good finance work – it's their signature and that really attracted me."* From another we heard: *"I really liked the fact that they were quite specialised."*

Over the years Sidley has grown in London by attracting top-flight lawyers from prestigious UK firms. The upshot of this is that trainees are exposed to high-quality work that would otherwise have gone to the likes of the magic circle; indeed they continually meet their counterparts at magic circle firms when working on deals. The difference, they tell us, is that the teams at Sidley are much smaller and, whilst this makes for an environment where *"everyone knows each other,"* it also inevitably impacts on their workload. *"When we have a huge deal to work on Sidley Austin might seem to be at a slight disadvantage in terms of manpower, but we can cover it,"* one trainee assured us. *"It's when we are working on two or three huge deals at once that it gets more difficult. Other firms in the City have bigger teams and hoards of paralegals so it is sometimes easier to share the work out to more people."*

Long hours are inevitable at any firm that assists high-calibre clients on impressive transactions; however you also have to factor in the type of work that Sidley handles. It's not always easy for a fresh recruit, as this interviewee explained: *"I have seen tears of frustration because there is so much to get through at times and it isn't always easy stuff to get your head around."* This is when good working relationships make all the difference, and by all accounts they are the norm at this firm. *"There are always plenty of people around to help you out,"* one source confirmed. In particular, *"the junior associates are really good – you don't feel stupid asking them questions; they know how daunting it can be."* Moreover, when it comes to allocating supervisors *"they try to match us up personality-wise."*

sidley austin: international firm of finance

The firm adopts a standard four-seat system with all trainees spending time in the international finance group (IFG). IFG is *"an umbrella term for work including property finance, derivatives, a small bit of straight lending and a lot of securitisation."* As the firm's engine room, it is a busy department, full of *"lots of busy people."* Typical tasks include *"drafting, bibling, proof-reading and some research,"* and certain elements of transaction management are also left to trainees, particularly on post-closure matters when *"document chasing and the like"* is required. Looking at just one area, real estate lending is an important activity for the London IFG lawyers; they recently acted for Morgan Stanley on financing for the acquisition of several shopping centres and a property located in Canary Wharf. Taking you one step further into the complex world of IFG, the firm's capital markets expertise has also enabled its real estate finance practice to enjoy a worldwide reputation in the commercial mort-

gage backed securities (CMBS) field. For example, the team recently represented Société Générale in the acquisition financing of four City of London properties with an aggregate value of £1 billion, before handling the subsequent securitisation of the loan. If all that has bamboozled you, don't worry too much. Trainees reiterate that prior experience is *"not required."* One source, who has since embraced the field, admitted: *"I certainly didn't have a clue about securitisation and capital markets when I arrived."*

A seat in the corporate department is *"busy but fun."* In the USA, Sidley Austin has a great reputation for corporate finance, even if on this side of the pond its M&A achievements are somewhat overshadowed by finance matters. Apparently here there are plans afoot to expand the department, and recent growth in the firm's Brussels corporate team bodes well for London. In a wholly English law transaction, the team acted for Morgan Stanley in relation to its £1 billion acquisition of the Goldfish credit card portfolio and associated business from Lloyds TSB.

Outside the transactional arena tax is a popular seat, perhaps because it is such a useful accompaniment to the firm's meaty finance diet. Like insolvency – another seat option – it is *"a pretty academic seat."* *"There is a lot of research and time spent looking at statutes, so it's good if you really want to use your brain."* Having swiped lawyers from elsewhere, the firm has recently set up a new insurance department and already has a trainee sitting there. Other niche departments include IP and employment. One seat you won't encounter is litigation because the office is so focused on transactional and advisory work. As such, you will most likely need to fulfil the Law Society's requirement for contentious experience by attending a course at the London branch of Nottingham Law School.

it's all gone continental

Sidley is a powerful force in the States and yet it adopts a sympathetic approach to the distinctive culture of its London office. The London management board is made up of English lawyers, with two of the UK partners sitting on the firm's global executive board. *"To me, Sidley Austin feels quite English,"* said one trainee; *"there are lots of administrative things that have to go through the States, but that doesn't really affect us on a day-to-day level."* Another explained that *"going to an American firm was very much a conscious choice for me,"* but one that had more to do with the size of the office and the nature of the work than the origins of the firm.

Recent years have marked a new era of expansion for the firm. Endeavouring to secure a place in the European CMBS market, Sidley has now established a Frankfurt office and acted for Deutsche Bank as lead manager in its first pan-European CMBS transaction. In 2005 it also opened offices in Brussels and Geneva and it has further plans to set up an outpost in Italy. Overseas secondments are not yet available for London trainees although several of our interviewees had been on international work-related trips

a head for finance

We sensed there is no typical background for a Sidley Austin trainee; indeed the only things we could say, hand on heart, that a trainee really needs is a willingness to immerse themselves in finance law and a seriously organised brain. *"I wouldn't say that you needed a First to come here but I think the firm does look for bright, balanced individuals,"* thought one source. According to another, a strong candidate will be *"an intelligent and focused individual who can be left to get on with a task. It's about applying your intellect really, although there is certainly nobody stopping you from asking questions; in fact you are encouraged to do so."* Our interviewees were keen to emphasise

that *"most trainees are happy here"* and want to stick around after qualification. Where it doesn't work out, it's generally a not-liking-the-work thing rather than a not-liking-the-people thing. In September 2006, all four qualifiers decided Sidley was definitely their thing, scooping a handsome £72,000 NQ salary in the process.

Even with all the hard work, there is a social scene, albeit not as fulsome as at some of the gargantuan London firms. The calendar includes summer barbecues on the office roof terrace, quiz nights, pool competitions and karaoke where *"the support staff are the first ones to grab the microphone."* There are also *"posh but relaxed"* summer and Christmas parties *"somewhere like Claridge's or the Four Seasons."*

and finally...

Sidley Austin isn't going to be everyone's cup of tea, so apply with your eyes open. That said, don't be put off if you don't have any prior experience of finance. As one savvy individual explained: *"All you need to do is approach things with an open mind and a commercial way of thinking. What we are doing is business after all."*

Simmons & Simmons

the facts

Location: London
Number of UK partners/solicitors: 115/248
Total number of trainees: 94
Seats: 4x6 months
Alternative seats: Overseas seats, secondments
Extras: Pro bono – Battersea Legal Advice Centre, language training

Top-20 London firm Simmons & Simmons is in a bullish mood. Its renewed focus on key areas of expertise looks set to see it through a competitive market and will deliver a challenging trainee experience to anyone with a nose for finance-related deals.

according to plan

We feel it unnecessary to dwell on Simmons' bad fortune and we only mention it here to give context to the firm's current plans. The past decade has been characterised by less-than-ideal financial results, the loss of some good lawyers and clients, and a general slackening of pace. In summary, a very good firm had holes pecked in it by others – many American – that were setting up or developing their business in London. Speaking of what must have felt like endless bad press, one trainee told us: *"Simmons-baiting seems to be a popular sport, but a lot of people haven't got a clue about the reality."* This is how they saw things: *"Due to the hard times we've really had to be proactive, we've had to become leaner and we will emerge in a better place."* The most recent financial results do indicate a comeback – a 22% hike in profits combined with a 16% rise in turnover is hardly to be sniffed at, especially when it comes on the back of the previous year's hefty 40% profit increase.

Much of Simmons' recent success can be attributed to a ramped-up international business plan and *"a drive to reappraise the values of the firm and focus on four key areas."* These are energy and infrastructure, financial institutions, life sciences and technology. Right now the finance department is doing very well and corporate continues to expand. *"We know we are punching above our weight in many areas,"* one trainee told us, pointing to the firm's representation of Telefónica, the giant Spanish telecom company, on its £18.5 billion loan to buy O$_2$. Other success stories have emerged from the highly rated hedge fund and private capital teams, and Simmons' financial services group has lately advised Barclays on the placing of a $5 billion collateralised loan obligation. The communications, outsourcing and technology group has advised Transport for London on the outsourcing of the IT infrastructure for London's congestion charging scheme to Siemens and Easynet, and it also advises Yahoo! Europe. In the corporate sphere, lawyers advised HMV on the recent controversial merger between Ottakar's bookstores and rival Waterstone's, which came to the attention of the Competition Commission.

the f word

Simmons' focus on financial and corporate transactions inevitably affects the shape of many training contracts. *"When I joined it wasn't so financially oriented, but now you should be prepared to do a finance seat,"* confirmed one source. You should also be open to the idea of qualifying into the sector at the end of your traineeship as *"Simmons is looking at future applicants' interest in these areas. It's not necessarily about reading the FT every day, but you should have an awareness of things."* We heard of trainees who, as well as offering CVs packed with good academic results, also came to the firm after careers in investment banks and corporate finance and financial services roles.

This is in stark contrast to many of the students who have traditionally been attracted to the firm because of its excellent teams in IP and employment. You can understand the appeal of these teams: the IP group has been representing GlaxoSmithKline on patent litigation relating to the antidepressant Seroxat and the employment group has a hugely successful employer practice, acting for GE, UBS, Morgan Stanley, Swiss Re and Visa among others. Be aware that in both these departments, even if you get a seat – and you may well do – the competition for a job on qualification is fierce. It is much more likely for qualifiers to find positions in the big transactional departments and, indeed, according to one final-seater: *"Five people in my intake have been recruited into banking after never having even done a banking seat."*

learning the lingo

Like trainee reactions to the firm's infamous collection of modern art, their experiences of the training contract seem to vary depending on the departments visited. So much so, we began to suspect there were several versions of Simmons inside the CityPoint tower block. *"I had loads of client contact; there were no concerns about that,"* suggested one trainee; another felt exactly the opposite was true and put this down to the fact that they had taken mostly transactional seats. Our questions about appraisals (mid-seat and end-of-seat) also elicited different responses. While *"people are generally good at giving feedback,"* it *"really varies across the firm."* One source said: *"One of my supervisors wasn't interested in giving mid-seat appraisals so we didn't do one"* but elsewhere they had received *"feedback on every single piece of work I did, which was a little too much."* In general, much was said about forging your own path as a trainee and seeking out those people most receptive to offering informal assistance and training.

Our interviewees agreed on the amount of responsibility available to trainees: *"There is a good ethos of throwing you in at the deep end, but in a nice way,"* said one. In real estate, a source commented on the likelihood of dealing with your own files. *"I have about 20 – you open them up and see them through to the end; you are a mini-solicitor here."* The communications, outsourcing and technology group is known as *"the one where, if you want drafting experience, you will get it."* Across the firm, *"you do sometimes get the grunt work. There may be periods where you are doing a lot of proof-reading or photocopying, and you see that you aren't getting exposure to interesting matters... but that's the nature of working for a City practice."*

On the subject of City hours, the only trainees who said they had *"never done an all-nighter"* and spoke of usually getting away by 7pm were the ones who had not worked in the capital markets or corporate departments. *"It's no myth,"* we were told; *"there are some horrendous hours in those two. And it's getting busier and busier."* *"You can really enjoy the buzz though,"* one trainee suggested. Capital markets offers exposure to *"some pretty advanced matters and some complicated terminology."* Indicative of the state of the market, and reflecting the firm's focus, the department is *"very busy now – it's a real pressure cooker there."* There is, however, *"full-on training so you understand the lingo; virtually every other lunchtime for the first two months. If you're stuck on something there is all the professional support you need."* Trainees seemed to either *"fall in love with it and want to stay there"* or find it *"a rather tortured department."*

time to breathe

In the corporate department the trainee's role is *"more like project management; a lot of co-ordinating, running the deal and generally being a gopher."* Trainees are likely to see a major public deal, such as an AIM float, or a variety of smaller matters. They saw how team-oriented the department is and described it as *"a really friendly group – a bit of a lads' club but not in a loutish way."* For other interviewees their banking seat was the highlight. Though life can be *"up and down in terms of levels of work,"* they learnt to *"enjoy the slower periods and not feel guilty if there's not a huge amount to do, especially when you have just had a really manic few weeks."* Working for a roster of impressive clients including income funds and major retailers adds to the satisfaction.

Though it pays magic circle salaries and law school grants, trainees stress that *"it's not the magic circle."* They believe Simmons provides *"a nice medium – it attracts good-quality work but it's not so big you get lost in the stampede."* Another plus is the firm's international dimension: not only can you work with a range of multinationals in London, some trainees also swing an international secondment. There are six postings to choose from, some, like Paris, with specific language requirements. In the UK, client secondments include Barclays, UBS, Goldman Sachs and fund manager RAB Capital. "*It's a leap from being in the office but it gave me a lot more confidence dealing with clients... although it is quite alarming at the beginning when people take what you say as the gospel truth.*"

alcopop generation

"*I guess the social life is what you make it,*" said one source. Much of the fun takes place on a departmental basis and, as we already know, some departments are very busy. Additionally, whether or not the champagne flows freely depends on how well the department is doing. "*You always want to get into a successful department for the seat that you'll be in at Christmas,*" said one canny source. A football team from Simmons' London office recently flew to Italy to take on the Rome office. "*It wouldn't be diplomatic of me to say the London office won,*" revealed a trainee who was all too familiar with the firm's aims to build an integrated global network. Every two years there is a glamorous summer ball: "*I was really impressed,*" said one partygoer, reeling off the attractions of the four-course meal, chocolate fountain and fairground. Those unwilling to wait two years to put on a nice frock can partake in Simmons' 'soirees' in the staff canteen. "*Canapés and free alcopops – it's a bit odd, but usually just the start of quite a drunken night.*"

While life ticks on quite satisfactorily for these trainees, is there anything they would change about the firm? "*We want IT that works more smoothly,*" demanded one, though they admitted that serious efforts were already being made in that direction. Anything else? Not really: "*There are no hidden skeletons; it is pretty much what it says on the tin. The firm has not misrepresented itself,*" said one. We wondered about the firm's fabled 'friendlier than the average law firm' reputation and were told "*it's definitely not 'cuddly' – my boss would be displeased to hear himself described like that – but there are good people here and not many egos.*" Trainees generally favoured the description "*ambitious*" and going-places above "*friendly.*" In September 2006, 42 of the 57 qualifiers took jobs at Simmons, 26 of them going into corporate and finance jobs, three each into employment and IP, two each into real estate, competition and tax, one into litigation and three heading off to overseas offices.

and finally...

Simmons & Simmons will provide the hardworking individual with a quality training contract shot through with international opportunities, though do think carefully about your interest in and aptitude for working on the finance matters before putting pen to paper to apply.

SJ Berwin

the facts

Location: London
Number of UK partners/solicitors: 103/285
Total number of trainees: 80
Seats: 4x6 months
Alternative seats: Overseas seats, secondments
Extras: Pro bono – Toynbee Hall law centre, death row appeals; language training

This top-20 UK firm is one of the most ambitious around. A surge of activity in corporate and banking has led to a 23% hike in turnover, bringing revenue to over £150 million for 2005/06.

a child of our time

It was founded in 1982 by a charismatic City lawyer called Stanley Berwin, whose old firm, Berwin & Co, eventually became Berwin Leighton Paisner, but that's another story. After four years working in-house for Rothschild, Stanley returned to Berwin & Co to reclaim his position as senior partner. He was in for a shock; the management said no. So Stanley went and set up a novel, fast-paced, client-focused law firm where no one was afraid of playing hardball. To give you an idea, its lawyers shocked the City establishment by making an audacious judicial review application against The Takeover Panel. While clients loved the full-bore attitude of SJB lawyers, the firm also acquired a reputation for extremes of hard work. Don't worry too much; this was all taking place in the brash, cash-driven Thatcher years. Times have changed and, to a degree, so has the firm. Yet Stanley Berwin's spirit is in the air still, because even partners who never worked with him feel as if they had. One who joined at the end of the 80s told us those he trained under constantly referred to the founder, saying: "'Stanley would have done it this way' or 'Stanley would never have done that'."

Without doubt SJB's founding principles live on today; they are part of the firm's DNA. Lawyers are still eager to prove themselves, both in the UK and continental Europe, where the firm's network of offices stretches from Madrid through Paris and Brussels to Munich, Frankfurt, Berlin, Milan and Turin. The strategy is to focus on private equity work and spread out from there. So far, so successful; the client list includes the European arm of US private equity giant Hicks Muse plus the likes of Candover, Lion Capital, Apax, CVC and Nomura, a host of secondary market funds and now hedge funds. Recent transactional triumphs include the £117.4 million sale of PE-owned retailer Jane Norman to a syndicate led by an Icelandic retail specialist and the new private equity arm of Kaupthing Bank. A higher-value deal involving complex cross-border aspects was the $535 million auction of ERM Holdings, the world's leading provider of environmental consultancy services, to Bridgepoint

Capital. SJB has also built an excellent private equity fund formation practice, where its main competitor is the giant Clifford Chance.

double dose

Unsurprisingly, SJB's training contract is corporate-heavy and two corporate seats await all trainees. The London corporate practice operates as four groups, A to D. Group A covers *"general M&A/corporate, including flotations. You get the usual trainee tasks drafting board minutes, stock transfer forms, researching at companies house and due diligence, etc. There's a lot of client contact and you're acting for interesting medium-sized companies. Although a lot of the work is admin you can see how the transactions work."*

Groups B and D handle the core private equity deals. *"We all end up there at one time or another,"* one source revealed. One trainee's private equity will involve mainly buyouts; another's will centre on *"more cerebral"* fund formation; and another's will involve start-ups and venture capital. Group B handles relatively large deals compared to, say, group D, so the trainees' roles will differ; however, all groups operate on a team basis, with the experience you gain being governed to a large extent by which team you are in. One source had *"good mates in the same team. That matters when you are there all hours because you're happy to stick around to help the other guys. When we were there we worked very very hard... very hard... but it was good."* Group C handles specialist fund formation work.

stemming the flow

Partners know they must give a favourable impression because *"they are desperate for people to qualify into corporate. It's not that no trainee wants to qualify there, but more want to go where they will work better hours."* To put it in stronger terms: *"They have been haemorrhaging trainees who won't go into corporate* [on qualification].

They've even had a partners' meeting to determine the issue of what corporate assistants want." And yet you can't deny the logic that says: *"The thing SJB does best is private equity. Why not qualify in what it does best?"* One trainee on the verge of taking the corporate shilling told us: *"I like to be at the centre of a transaction. I don't want to be in a support department just putting in a contribution to the deal when asked. I like to know where the transaction is going and what it is about. And I like the idea of walking into Wagamama or Jane Norman or Jimmy Choo – names people have heard of – and seeing the results of my work."*

To up corporate's appeal there have been all-expenses-paid trips to Madrid to see Champions League football; the recruitment of extra paralegals; a highly praised programme of weekly training sessions; and time off after long hours. One source recalled working *"a 2am, a 4am and then a 6am, and then I got told to take a day off…and then another day. They are much more aware that they will lose people if they treat them like cannon fodder… it was definitely worse a year ago when there were people who got wiped out and became ill."* But is the regime any tougher than elsewhere? The view of most trainees was that their friends at the magic circle were working similar hours. Quite simply, *"you work hard, often at inconvenient times, because if a deal is on and there's a deadline you've just got to meet it."* Trainees disagree on how much this affects them. Said one: *"I have stopped arranging things for during the week;"* from another: *"I can't remember missing an engagement and if you've a serious commitment elsewhere they will find someone else."* In the up-and-down world of corporate these comments need not be contradictory.

nice and niche

Of course, as much time is spent away from corporate as in it. The real estate client roster includes heavyweights such as British Land, Hilton Hotels, Marks & Spencer, Land Securities and Sainsbury's, and SJB lawyers have been acting for Quintain on the redevelopment of the new infrastructure around Wembley Stadium. Trainee reports on this *"comfy"* department were flawless. *"There's a different atmosphere there,"* said one. *"Real estate works real estate hours, it's less pressured and more friendly. Those qualities make it popular."* Other potential seats include a *"research heavy"* EU and competition slot, a super-popular employment seat, commerce and technology, construction, various shades of litigation, mediation and arbitration, banking, tax, reconstruction and insolvency, financial services, IP and even a three-month posting to the Houses of Parliament to assist SJB partner and Conservative MP Jonathan Djanogly.

Exceptionally lucky trainees get to work on media matters, particularly TV and film financing and production. Here they encounter well-known film projects, recent examples being 'The Constant Gardener', 'Basic Instinct 2', and that absolute classic, 'Alien Autopsy'. *"A tried-and-tested strategy to get niche seats is to attend know-how meetings for that department from the start and to put it as your top choice at every seat rotation."* This still gives no guarantee, as one final-seater explained: *"The seat I am doing now I didn't choose, and it has never been in the list of things I wanted, but I was told the powers that be wanted second years in these seats. I kicked up a fuss but it made no difference."* By contrast someone whose tastes reflected the firm's corporate leanings told us: *"I can't fault them, I can't complain about a single seat."* It is worth noting that if you want to keep your training on the transactional side, this is feasible if you attend a litigation course run by the College of Law and get involved in the firm's pro bono programme.

river of dreams

In 2006 SJB traded unappealing premises just south of Kings Cross for a superb new office at Southwark Bridge, packed with a gazillion architectural and design gems. With its massive roof garden and expansive views of the Thames, the office is *"a step forward"* for the firm, and trainees are *"no longer ashamed when clients come to visit."* The move hasn't come a moment too soon: *"You get a sense that we're getting a lot larger. When they first took on the building the plan was to sublet some of it. In the two years from the drawing board to getting here we have decided not to."* This growth is something to bear in mind if you're a student looking for an idiosyncratic mid-sized employer. A trainee nearing qualification explained the original appeal of the firm. *"I saw a young and energetic firm with a lot of opportunities. I was impressed by it being only 21 years old and by the fact that it was expanding in Europe. It was going places and I wanted to be a part of a project that I could contribute to."* Already bigger, as SJB continues its expansion the challenge ahead will be to preserve its 'Stanleyist' qualities.

Hard graft has its rewards at SJB. There isn't much trainee-only socialising, but trainees are always included in the celebrations to mark deal closures, and there are firm-wide drinks once a month. When we called, our sources were mulling over a party budget of *"a few thousand pounds,"* but the consensus is that *"this is not a hugely social firm."* Said one: *"My year made plans and then cancelled them so many times that we just stopped doing it."* On the upside, trainees view SJB as a meritocracy, and tell us they get a free lunch every day (and dinner if needed). The Wagamama-esque staff dining room is appropriately called Stanley's, a reminder of one of the founder's very first decisions – that everyone would eat lunch together every day.

The firm recruits *"a nice spread of people, certainly in terms of mature trainees."* The ideal candidate is *"bright and unstuffy," "someone consistent, who can take a task and make it their own – they will steam ahead."* Apparently it's all about having the energy and drive to push yourself forwards. You may sometimes think *"Gosh, why am I doing this?"* but chances are you'll end up like the trainee who told us: *"Now I'm getting towards the end I can see I have picked up an awful lot. The training has been excellent and I am really impressed."* In September 2006, 25 of the 29 qualifiers stayed with the firm.

and finally...

Stanley Berwin's values endure – guts and hard work, with the prime objective of impressing the client and getting ahead personally. If you want to put career at the centre of your world, this ambitious, unpretentious firm could prove to be ideal. And don't forget, it is always on the front line in inter-firm salary wars.

Skadden, Arps, Slate, Meagher & Flom (UK) LLP

the facts

Location: London
Number of UK partners/solicitors: 12/70
Total number of trainees: 6
Seats: 4x6 months
Alternative seats: Hong Kong

Set up in 1948 New York, this outfit has grown into a leviathan. It now has around 1,700 lawyers in 22 worldwide offices.

just $kadden

This firm's tale is a success story of such proportions that it even inspired its own book, the arrestingly entitled *Skadden: Power, Money, and the Rise of a Legal Empire.* Anyway, apologies to the Mr Flom, who is still beavering away over in New York (some 58 years after becoming the firm's first associate, and now its only remaining named partner), but we have word limits here at the *Student Guide*, so from now on, let's keep it pally with a simple Skadden.

The London branch, opened in 1987, has flourished as one of the most visible US corporate practices in the City and acts as a self-proclaimed hub of the impressive and ever-expanding European operation. In recent times Skadden London has cranked things up and is now consistently found among (and often above) the magic circle players in terms of deal value and volume. With such a steep upward trajectory it was only a matter of time before the office started growing its own, and in 2005 the inaugural trainee intake comprised two eager bodies. We're informed by HR that there is a huge appetite within the firm for more of the same. A secondment to Skadden's Hong Kong office is also in the pipeline.

As thorough as our research is, it is not that often that we can claim to have interviewed every single one of a firm's trainees. In Skadden's case that's exactly what we did. Of course, our usual assurances about confidentiality for our interviewees went straight out the window, so it's a good job that we heard such positive feedback, really. Being a trainee in a small outfit during the dynamic early days of a training scheme has clearly allowed a *"very personalised"* training with *"a lot of attention"* from supervisors. *"It's all very fluid, so there is not an impression of the kind of tasks that are appropriate to a trainee and those that are not."* Being *"treated more like an associate"* means *"you are able to show you can be trusted and make a name for yourself more quickly."* Another selling point is that *"a trainee has more leverage compared to someone at a magic circle firm where you are one voice in 200."* The trainee pool will increase: in

September 2006 the firm made eight training contract offers for 2008, all of which were accepted.

size does matter

In this multinational firm lawyers come from all parts of the world to form *"a very diverse group."* So no Skadden 'type' here then? Trainees say: *"They recruit individuals with individual strengths who bring very different things to the firm."* One thing they do have in common, however, is the will to *"get the job done and bring excellence to transactions."*

The compact size of the office has an impact on working life. It helps to generate a *"collegial feel"* but it means Skadden can't just throw fee earners at big transactions. As part of a small deal team you will be *"working against bigger teams on the other side,"* which in turn means that *"from the time you start here you have to have a sense of urgency and get serious."* You should also get into the habit of phrasing your questions carefully, because as much as people are *"perfectly willing to answer,"* they are busy so you should *"prepare"* and keep them *"pointed."* And what of the hours expected of trainees? One simple answer is *"it depends on what stage of a transaction you are at."* Another is that there will be busy times and there will be very busy times. It helps if you *"enjoy working hard and you are not looking for downtime between deals,"* and you must also *"be prepared to come in on the weekend"* when needed. Despite all this, our sources *"never felt overwhelmed with work"* and *"you never get more responsibility than you can handle."*

Upon arrival in a new team, trainees are assigned a mentor/supervisor – most likely a senior associate – who will dish out tasks in the first month. After that it is up to the trainee to sniff out work on anything else they fancy. Even within such a loose arrangement trainees felt well looked after and that their technical ability was being honed. "*Every day I have more business nous and better judgement,*" said one: "*you can only get that from learning on the job.*" The Law Society's PSC training is dispatched in a typically slick Skadden manner and trainees are also invited to junior and senior-level seminars and know-how sessions.

top of the league

The London office has a clear focus on corporate transactions – M&A, private equity, capital markets, venture capital, IPOs and the like. "*Skadden is all about M&As in a global sense, that's the way I got turned on to the firm,*" said one of our interviewees. What follows is a quick round up.

Advice on €189.6 billion's worth of deals in the second quarter of 2006 secured its place at the top of mergermarket's European M&A league for a second successive quarter. In the last year Skadden has seen action on German energy company E.ON's €47 billion takeover of Spain's Endesa, as well as broadband ISP Easynet Group's $374 million acquisition by BSkyB. US company Yahoo! turned to the London office for representation in its acquisition of stakes in Yahoo! UK, Yahoo! Germany and Yahoo! France from Softbank Holdings, as well as its acquisition of a stake in Yahoo! Korea and Yahoo! Japan, deals valued at about $500 million.

A growing Russian practice is evidenced by the advice given to Chelsea FC owner Roman Abramovich, the majority shareholder of Sibneft, in the group's £7.4 billion sale to Russian natural gas company Gazprom. You Blues fans out there might be interested, and surprised, to learn that the Russian connection goes much further: Skadden's London managing partner is the Chelsea chairman and the club's only other shareholder apart from Mr Abramovich – owning one share to the Russian's 84 million. Anyway, people like Mr A expect the best, so there is no room for any-one to take a back seat. Come here to train and you must roll up your sleeves in anticipation of "*a good deal of responsibility.*" You might be charged with "*liaising with local lawyers in 22 jurisdictions*" or "*let loose on drafting corporate documents like shareholder agreements and board minutes and resolutions.*" Document review, due diligence exercises and research tasks will also be flying straight for your inbox.

all to play for

By the time we spoke to them, both trainees had experienced a corporate seat along with a spell in the international arbitration and dispute resolution group. The other options available to them were international taxation, banking, insolvency and restructuring and international projects and project finance.

There is plenty going on if you want to take advantage of out-of-office events in recognition of all your hard work. "*Skadden will show its appreciation by showing a good time.*" It sounds like the firm and the clients are "*very good about treating you well if you have worked hard, closing deals with an extravagant dinner and champagne.*" We're told that "*after the recent recruitment of more junior lawyers there are now more e-mails going round about drinks after work,*" so "*you will make friends*" and there is "*fun to be had*" if you want it. You certainly shouldn't bring your own packed lunch on the Fourth of July because the firm makes a big deal of the date. Plus, trainees are sent across the pond to the new associates' retreat in the New York office in neon-lit Times Square.

and finally...

If you want to train and socialise as one of a big gang of people just like you, you'll hate it at $kadden. If the opposite appeals then definitely take a closer look. The story so far suggests that this training scheme is going to be a really challenging alternative to the magic circle.

Slaughter and May

the facts
Location: London
Number of UK partners/solicitors: 126/400
Total number of trainees: 175
Seats: 4x6 months
Alternative seats: Overseas seats
Extras: Pro bono – RCJ CAB, FRU, Islington and Battersea Law Centres; language training

If you are thinking of applying to this firm it is likely that you are also considering the rest of the magic circle. They are all pretty similar, right? Wrong. Slaughter and May does things its own way. For a start, instead of adhering rigidly to a set strategy, the firm promotes a philosophy that encourages partners to follow their own professional interests. The initials of senior partners even denote departments. As one of our sources put it: *"At other magic circle firms the high command seems to be very distant from the foot soldiers. Slaughters take more of a reasonable-man approach."* As this law firm generates the highest per equity partner profits in the land don't underestimate its unique model.

daring to be different
One major difference between this and other members of the magic circle is the absence of a vast overseas network of offices. Outside London, the only offices with 'Slaughter and May' above the door are in Paris, Hong Kong and Singapore. International work is handled in conjunction with a network of 'best friend' law firms that has evolved over many years. This elite club includes many of the world's top independent law firms and Slaughters, for one, believes the approach ensures that its clients receive a top-drawer service across the globe.

Another point of difference is the fact that Slaughters' lawyers favour a generalist approach to practice. All lawyers build up a range of experience within a given area, the upshot being that its teams are flexible and market focused. Rather than being dictated by fixed skill-sets, work goes to those people who can bring first-rate general knowledge and a fresh eye to the table. This has a knock-on effect for trainees: *"The partners are willing to take on a really broad range of work, so our work is also varied."* On the flip side, one of our sources suggested that *"if you want to build up narrow expertise and real depth of expertise in one specific area, you might be better off at another firm."*

The third – and very important – thing to note is that a powerful corporate engine drives this firm. It acts on some of the largest, most-complex deals for major companies including British Airways, Boots, Whitbread, Shell and Marconi. Slaughter and May is driven by a desire to provide high-quality advice to its clients, and with over a third of the FTSE 100 on its books, it is obviously doing something right.

no nonsense
To trainees, Slaughter and May demonstrates that it is different from day one. *"I was impressed by the way the firm handled the whole application process,"* said one successful candidate. A very simple form with an attached CV and covering letter has no-nonsense appeal: *"I just skipped applications to any firms who had annoying forms or particularly stupid questions,"* a typical source admitted. Successful applicants were similarly relieved that they didn't have to endure *"a stressful afternoon filled with silly tasks or horrid role plays."* Instead *"I was just put in a room with two partners and asked straightforward questions."* Simple as that. One interviewee *"liked the attitude I saw that day. I was struck by the competent and pretty serious way they did things. No one gave me the impression that they were trying to be particularly nice or friendly; they were just very straight about everything."*

This clear-cut, professional approach pervades day-to-day life in the firm. Its partners mean business. Literally. Although in some quarters the firm's atmosphere has been described as cold, the trainees who do well here wouldn't have it any other way. "*There aren't going to be a lot of people saying, 'hi mate, how are you doing?' all the time, but if you are comfortable with working things out for yourself that's fine,*" said one. "*I don't want my boss to be my friend; I am here to learn from these people.*" Another exasperated source disagreed: "*I constantly have to defend this place. People think we are the least laid back of all the law firms and that everybody is stuck up, but it's not like that at all. I have found it to be open and relaxed here.*" Another source hit the nail on the head when they said: "*There are a lot of brows creased in thought here; you are not always going to get a grin in the corridor, but it's a question of how important that is for you as an individual.*"

Individuality is the bedrock of Slaughter and May's culture; "*it is full of colourful characters.*" The firm prides itself on employing people who think for themselves and are happy to do things their own way. For example, during our research we heard about one idiosyncratic partner who prefers to work with the lights off and the blinds drawn. Apparently such characters range from the "*the incredibly smart and well-dressed to those that quite frankly look a mess.*" This reputation for encouraging individuality is well known in the City and filled some of our sources with pride: "*I suspect I would be bored to tears if I worked in a place where everyone was bland and friendly,*" one told us. "*There is not a lot of blandness here. Everyone has their own quirks and foibles, which I think is a bonus – it makes life interesting.*" If you are beginning to build up a strange mental image of awkward personalities, fear not. "*When I arrived here I was expecting mostly braced-up City types or awkward, ivory-tower sorts – I have been pleasantly surprised that everyone is somewhere in between,*"

said one trainee. Another awestruck source told us: "*The scariest thing about some of the partners is that they are so unbelievably clever. Talking to some of them can be quite humbling.*" Perhaps this is why "*when we have training sessions, everyone does their homework.*"

nil by mouth

The corporate practice lies at the centre of the firm with other departments revolving around it like satellites. The firm enjoys a stellar reputation for its standalone tax and competition work. It also wins praise for its expertise in finance, litigation and real estate. In short, a training contract here will set you in good stead whichever departments you end up sitting in. With corporate finance being the firm's forte, you must be willing to do at least one corporate seat. The exact rules of engagement specify that there will be two corporate, commercial and financing seats for all (with financial regulation, competition or an overseas seat capable of counting as one of these two).

The corporate division is divided into three separate groups where "*guys who have been here 30 years and know it all*" work alongside "*bright young things who shout football scores to one another down the corridor.*" In corporate you can expect a "*massive variety of work,*" but checking verification notes and accompanying lawyers to client meetings are typical. The firm recently acted for Hilton Group on the proposed £3.3 billion sale of its hotel and leisure division and advised Cadbury Schweppes on the €1.85 billion sale of its European beverages business to a private equity consortium. It's an inescapable fact that trainees are quite likely to "*end up on some very tedious and large data-input sessions or due diligence,*" although with a bit of luck some may also get to run elements of a deal themselves.

The finance group was described as "*fairly open and with a good sense of camaraderie.*" Here, lawyers recently acted for Citibank on a five-year

€650 million multi-currency loan facility for a Danish telecoms operator. Trainees find themselves drafting board minutes and reviewing amended documents, and some of our interviewees had assisted with bilateral loan agreement reviews – *"it was really interesting work, the sort of thing I touched on in my LPC."* Although the department is *"still hierarchical,"* it is deemed to be less so than others and more sociable.

Year after year when we interview trainees here we find the firm's culture has both its fans and critics, albeit that there tend to be more of the former. Typically the two camps consist of those who have good experiences with their supervisors and those who don't. What did current trainees have to say on the subject? *"There are a few supervisors who have a bit of a reputation around the place"* said one. *"There are definitely some you hope not to be put with,"* another concurred. On more than one occasion we heard that such friction was usually down to a mere *"personality clash"* and that the situation *"depends on how you deal with it."* As a case in point: *"My supervisor was extremely silent – I didn't hear from him all day long but I would always make sure I said good morning and good evening."* At the opposite end of the scale, one source told us: *"Some supervisors have extremely high expectations and a very unrealistic picture of how much work can be fitted into a day."* Consequently, we heard that *"trainees have been properly shouted at."* Another saw it this way: *"The partners are under a huge amount of pressure; some take it as a point of pride to make time for you, but if others are busy they will let you know, either by shouting or making cutting remarks or just completely ignoring you."*

out of your comfort zone

"You earn their respect," said another encouraging source. *"With some partners it is just a case of proving that you can stand up and be counted."* Interviewees were keen to point out that when faced with *"difficult characters,"* it is *"strength of character"* that sees you through – *"you just need to have confidence in yourself."* In the meantime you are not left feeling unsupported, as one interviewee recalled: *"The secretaries used to say to me 'hang in there, you will be fine,' and I was."* Such experiences were in the minority and, during our interviews, those supervisors who were *"personable, competent and communicative"* were warmly praised as *"absolutely brilliant."* Such characters left trainees feeling decidedly *"un-intimidated"* and *"comfortable asking questions."* Admittedly *"with some partners there is a bit of thinking twice before rocking up in a room or asking a question, but usually it's because if you really think about it you can work out the answer for yourself."* Slaughter and May trainees are people who like to be challenged: *"The greatest worry about being here is also the greatest asset. If they think you are up to it they will throw you in at the deep end."* In short, *"if you are the sort of person who likes going out of your comfort zone, this is a great place to be."*

As a seat where an academic approach is valued, it is no wonder that competition law appeals to many trainees. Here they are exposed to high-profile, multi-jurisdictional matters such as the EU merger law aspects of Gillette's $57 billion tie-up with Procter & Gamble. When a single transaction involves businesses in several countries, trainees will encounter many foreign lawyers, various client contacts and be thrown into extensive research projects. At each rotation, four of the competition group trainees will spend their seat in Brussels.

The network of best-friend firms also enables trainees to go even further afield and the hottest secondments right now seem to be New York, Tokyo and New Zealand. *"I read the FT on my journey overseas and when I arrived I was told we were working on the front-page deal,"* one interviewee told us. International seats are popular and the admin involved is hassle-free. *"Having decided that I wanted to go I was promptly provided* with a flat near the office, a bank account and spending money. All I had to do was complete a tick list with things like 'Is your passport up-to-date?'" For the record, around half of those who ask for a secondment at each seat rotation have their wish granted. Slaughters does not have a history of seconding trainees to clients as it regards such experiences as more appropriate for associates.

cracking cvs

So who is going to get a shot at the big time with Slaughters? By all accounts, *"everyone went to a good university and did very well there."* The firm tells us that its lawyers have come from 60 different universities, but even so there's no doubting that the Oxbridge headcount is high. Yet, *"as a trainee you need to leave all that at the door."* True, one under-whelmed interviewee told us: *"After going to university for so long, I didn't expect to spend my weekend shifting boxes in a data room."* Yet the level of responsibility given *"to those who can handle it"* surprised a number of the trainees we spoke to. *"I never expected to be one of only two people working on a transaction or taking conference calls on my own,"* commented one. Like any trainee at a firm working on huge transactions, you can expect your fair share of grunt work. This is partly because *"they are not going to be negligent by giving you something that really matters."*

An emphasis on individual growth is accompanied by a *"laissez-faire attitude"* towards work-life balance. *"This is not a corporate socialising type of a place,"* we were told, but *"it is possible to make good friends here."* Out of class, alongside the usual cricket, rugby, hockey and netball, Slaughter and May offers cultural talks to further the mind. Recent topics have ranged from 'China: The Empire' to 'The da Vinci Code'. As if to demonstrate the firm's unconventional streak, *"the people who created Wallace & Gromit came in with some of their puppets one day."* We're still not sure why exactly.

and finally...

Growing up at this firm requires adaptability and, at times, fortitude, so walk in with your eyes wide open and you may find it exceeds your expectations. As it turns out, in 2006, 72 of the 83 qualifiers stayed on at the firm. And if you're one of those who see the firm as the starting point for your career, bear this in mind: *"You get Slaughter and May chips for training here and you can cash them in later."*

Speechly Bircham

the facts

Location: London
Number of UK partners/solicitors: 57/100
Total number of trainees: 11
Seats: 4x6 months
Alternative seats: None

This mid-sized City practice enjoys a fine reputation on both private client and commercial fronts. A streamlined and straightforward training contract awaits those who wish to cut to the chase.

challenges worth rising to

Trainees are recruited off the back of the firm's three-week summer placement scheme or after a two-stage interview process. From what we gather, the vac scheme is a great way to wedge your foot in Speechlys' door and check out what life would be like in three of the firm's training seats. We're told the firm is *"looking for people who are a bit more mature in their approach,"* so applicants arriving at the law after previous careers in other sectors are very much welcomed. Consequently, trainees are *"not your run-of-the-mill candidates,"* and the batch we sampled from included a former musician and a one-time accountant.

They commended the quality of their training at Speechlys time and time again. "*We are not given dire work that no one else wants to do, we are doing work that fee earners would have been doing.*" Responsibility comes in good time, and it looks like the balance is just right – "*if you rise to the challenge they will let you loose.*" Work is dished out so as to maximise exposure to larger matters, while also allowing a degree of autonomy on smaller, self-contained issues "*to keep you going.*" Give and take seems to be a theme here. If you are "*interested and willing to learn, then the partners are keen to teach.*" What comes with this is the idea that "*you've got to take personal responsibility for how you want to go forward with your training contract.*"

All very supportive then. "*If it gets difficult and you are struggling with some work you can ask, 'Am I on the right track?' The answer may be yes or no, but you will be pointed in the right direction.*" When the trainee performs well, encouragement is always forthcoming. One trainee picked out as a highlight the time when a supervising partner passed on the gratitude of a notoriously hard-to-please client for a job well done.

silent partners

We reckon Speechlys is a fair bet for anyone as yet unwilling to take the plunge and commit to a particular practice area, because after all what's the rush? The seat allocation policy follows the same "*no-nonsense*" approach evident in the firm generally. No choice for the first seat then, but "*after that, they will put in 110% to get you into the seat you want.*" At times the trainees have pitched in themselves and made things easier on the HR team by pulling names out of a hat for oversubscribed selections like employment. However it happens, the final result is that "*a tailored training contract falls into place.*" Evidence of trainees' satisfaction came in the form of full retention in

September 2006: all five qualifiers stayed on with the firm.

A corporate seat gets trainees involved in matters connected to some of the "*hot topics*" in the City. AIM admissions represent a key thrust of this practice group, with the recent representation of fuel retail system specialists Orpak on its £14.7 million flotation on AIM being a good example. The seat is viewed as a great way to get to know the firm as a whole, as corporate's tentacles stretch to every corner and ensure "*interaction with every other department.*"

The well-regarded construction and engineering group is a destination team when it comes to trainees' preferences. Our interviewees described this as "*one of the top departments in the country,*" and it seems that our parent publication, *Chambers UK*, would agree, ranking the construction lawyers among the best London has to offer. A seat here represents "*a good opportunity to get involved in high-quality work for large and established clients,*" and it sounds like a great place to go if you want to "*prove yourself.*" Expect to be meeting and corresponding with clients directly, while assisting on "*exciting*" UK and international projects and disputes.

The property and property litigation department serves up a healthy diet of responsibility on your own files. As a result "*you really learn about time-management and developing relationships with clients.*" Although "*the partners are working with you and silently supervising, it is up to you to get on and do it.*" We are told that 'silently supervising' involves partners being "*there when you need them... coming along at exactly the right time.*" Eerie.

life, death and taxes

Employment and pensions is arguably the most sought-after seat, not least because trainees are given work "*you can really get your teeth into.*" Acting for management in disputes with employees almost guarantees some tribunal action, whilst non-contentious counselling will test research and drafting skills to the max. At times things get really exciting: a recent, and understandably hush-hush, High Court matter involved emergency applications for injunctive remedies for a FTSE100 subsidiary client. Trainees may get to see the more human side of the employment relationship, through negotiations with ex-employers on behalf of redundant clients. In an area which is ever changing, the monthly know-how sessions which address the implications and implementation of any new legislation represent a vital forum for keeping up to date.

Speechly's *"flagship"* private client practice has been bolstered by a string of recent arrivals from other City firms. Now fielding 13 lawyers, the group is seen by those in the know as an established outfit on the up. The *"old-school"* client portfolio may well include the waxed-jacket-and-wellies brigade, however you are just as likely to be rubbing shoulders with wealthy entrepreneurs, dotcom millionaires and general meeja types. In terms of the work, one trainee summarised it as *"wills, inheritance tax... tax, generally."* Perhaps this person was haunted by tax inspectors in their dreams, because the work on offer here is actually much more varied than that, including advice on the investment and protection of private capital, charities law, trusts and probate litigation, residential conveyancing and family law.

room to breathe, time to live

There's a simple rule at Speechlys: *"You respect everyone, and everyone respects you."* Trainees point to a relaxed culture as a key reason for their overall job satisfaction. *"It is easy being a trainee here."* So what type of person will get on well? *"You need to want to learn, be willing to work, and to get on with people." "Confidence"* as well as *"a*

brain and common sense" are also clearly prerequisites. Trainees claim to be able to *"enjoy the job as well as time away from the job;"* they acknowledge that *"long hours might be needed at times, but out-of-work commitments can be accommodated."* The size of the firm helps, with Speechlys' mid-sized City model offering *"more partner and client contact"* and the opportunity to be *"known as a person."*

With a trainee pool of 11, you expect to find a close-knit group, and this is certainly the case here. *"Trainees try and meet up as often as possible,"* and when it comes to firm-arranged events, there's a similarly easygoing approach. After-work drinks are always in the offing, and there are occasional outings to the races at Ascot or the theatre. A trainee who had previously worked outside the law was relieved by this low-key approach. *"Some places force the social scene onto you. You have to go, and the talk is always about work. By the end of it you end up with more work."* Here off-duty actually means off-duty. In a nice touch, the monthly fee-earners lunch operates a strict 'no partners' policy, so all can relax in the knowledge that the conversation may be as free as the food. Standing as the highlights of the calendar, the summer and Christmas parties *"are always great affairs."* These events are summed up as simply *"a night out with the whole firm involving food, drinks and games."* An opportunity to *"just have fun really."*

and finally...

Plenty of opportunities for those wishing to follow the commercial path, plus the option of some top work in the private client area suggest that a well-rounded training is on offer for a well-rounded trainee. And for what it's worth we reckon Speechlys has found the classic recipe for trainee satisfaction – it's simplicity, not rocket science.

Stephens & Scown

the facts

Location: St. Austell, Truro, Exeter
Number of UK partners/solicitors: 33/25
Total number of trainees: 11
Seats: 4x6 months
Alternative seats: None

Derelict tin mines and rugged coastline. Beautiful beaches and Atlantic swell. Surfer dudes and washed-up hippies. Cornwall and Devon may not immediately bring to mind images of thriving commercial enterprises, but Stephens & Scown's stellar performance is a reminder that the legal profession stretches way beyond Bristol.

once upon a time in the west

From its start in St Austell way back in 1936 Stephens & Scown gradually spread as far west as Truro (about 14 miles) and as far east as Exeter (75 miles), also taking in Plymouth and Liskeard along the way. Early success was based on broad high street legal services, however more recently the firm has sharpened up its act to capitalise on the investment flowing into the two counties as a result of various EU and government initiatives. Five successive year-on-year increases in turnover and profitability haven't satisfied S&S: *"It now wants to be one of the biggest firms in the South West."* The firm has a self-improving *"increasingly commercial"* itch and has not been afraid to make changes in order to scratch it. In the past few years it has left Liskeard and, as changes in the legal aid landscape have taken effect, pulled the plug on its heavily crime-based Plymouth office. Left with a leaner, possibly meaner, definitely punchier operation, S&S did the natural thing and opted for a wardrobe makeover, shedding old ill-fitting premises in Truro and Exeter for swish, new, open-plan buildings. Plans are also afoot for a new St Austell office. Beyond the *"feel-good fac-*

tor" these moves have engendered, trainees observed movement away from *"a top-heavy, lots-of-partners, more traditional structure"* to *"a team-based approach with a larger number of assistants."* And just to prove that it is definitely not afraid of innovation, when managing partner Ian Pawley retired in 2006, the firm chose to replace him with a chief executive from a non-legal background.

If these changes are symptomatic of a firm transforming itself into a more modern, commercially-minded business, that isn't to say that S&S isn't already an established player in the region. The well-regarded family law team and a volume PI department are stalwarts of the S&S cause, but it is the commercial property and corporate/commercial teams that are at the forefront of recent growth. The firm acts for a solid wedge of regional and national-but-in-the-region clients. These national clients include Securicor, Weststar Holidays and Strategic Land Partnerships; from local industry there are bigger organisations such as Trago Mills, St Austell Brewery, Aggregate Industries and Pendennis Shipyard, plus smaller operations like the Eden Project. From the world of finance the firm advises Lloyds TSB, NatWest, Finance Cornwall and Finance South West. Corporate deals such as the sale of a locally owned holiday park group to Phoenix Equity Partners for over £31.5 million typify the firm's strong regional connections; recent advice to Finance South West on the establishment of an £18.5 million special investment fund for South West businesses in Objective 2 EU funding areas highlights that it is well positioned to pitch for new business.

cornish paste

Assessing the firm's place in the local legal pecking order, trainees concluded that S&S is *"competing on a level playing field"* with regional rivals like Foot Anstey and Michelmores, adding that its Cornish offices are *"a big advantage over those firms."* As to further expansion, we understand a new branch is a strong possibility. *"There's no way we'd go to Bristol, but I can imagine an office in Taunton – it would open up some of the commercial possibilities radiating out of Bristol without moving us too far from our core."* So even if S&S enlarges its patch, there's little chance of it loosening its superglue grip on Devon and Cornwall. And if future trainees are anything like the current ones we can't imagine that being a problem. *"The firm is very keen on people having a connection to the region,"* confessed our almost exclusively locally born interviewees, who even if they had spent time away at university or work had been *"drawn back."* If you do hail from outside the region, you won't need to prove true lineage to an interview panel of Cornish separatists, but you should expect to encounter *"the reasonable desire to see hard evidence that you're likely to stay on after qualification."*

Show the firm some commitment and it reciprocates. A traditionally strong retention rate (all three in 2006) and the firm's refreshed sense of purpose led our sources to say: *"You're recruited for the long haul and there are some great opportunities at the moment."* Such mutual dedication is perhaps entrenched by a preliminary trial period of roughly three months before the formal training contract begins, *"so the firm knows you're right for them and vice versa."*

pick wisely

If you fall for the firm's charms, choose your location carefully, because despite the fact that *"part of the new focus is to increase integration across offices,"* there is a structural fault line between offices at trainee level. At S&S, the theory may be that *"some trainees are offered contracts split between the Cornish offices"* (St Austell and Truro), but in practice *"no one has moved for a while"* and there is no history of moves between

Devon and Cornwall. Consequently, we'd recommend making an informed choice about where you'd prefer to be based before you arrive for interview.

Whether they are at the western or eastern end of the A30, trainees complete four six-month seats (with some flexibility to stay slightly longer in preferred departments). They can spend time in any of the main departments: family; commerce (including coco, employment and some tax work); wills, probate and trusts; commercial property; and litigation and dispute resolution (including PI). Trainees appreciate the firm's *"flexibility over where you go"* and praise *"high levels of responsibility."* Their accounts included tales of *"drafting instructions to counsel on day one"* and *"running a small claims trial"* in litigation. In property we heard about *"easements, assignments of leases, and managing 20 files"* plus *"helping to bring a complicated transaction back from the brink of collapse."* In family they were *"going to conferences and working on high net worth divorces;"* in commerce they were *"assisting partners on the buying and selling of businesses, typically worth between one and ten million."* All our interviewees indicated that six-monthly appraisals hold little fear in prospect because *"your supervisor tends to sit you down every few weeks to discuss what's going on and iron out any problems."*

devon knows

Home to *"some of the younger, more ambitious and innovative partners,"* the Exeter office is in *"beautifully"* refurbished buildings in the thriving professional neighbourhood of Southernhay. Spread over several open-plan floors, the best thing about the building is *"the great view over the medieval cathedral and surrounding countryside."* Trainees are less sure about the artwork (*"at the moment it is frosted glass photos, but sometimes it looks like paintings by children"*), but all recognise that the move there has *"energised the atmosphere* and is great for clients." The half-dozen Exeter trainees say the city offers "a good compromise between urban and rural," with one claiming it to be "the last major outpost of commerce going west. All the major banks and accountants have offices here and it's a really up-and-coming area in business terms."

So does that mean the Cornish S&S lawyers spend all their time drafting wills for farmers? In a word, no. The Truro and St Austell branches are integral to the S&S mission to "corner the commercial market in Devon and Cornwall." Housing the firm's administrative functions and the "very busy" criminal and other mainstream departments, St Austell is feeling the same force of "expansion and investment in the future" and awaiting "the right building turning up for a move." Further west, S&S Truro has been in a modern office by the banks of the River Truro for some time ("the view is beautiful when the tide's in, but all mud when it's not"). Both Cornish branches take between one and four trainees (one in each when we conducted interviews), so with relatively few sorties over to Exeter, you shouldn't expect a whole heap of ready-made trainee buddies.

countryside, and the living is easy

With an average day of 9am to 5.30pm the phrase 'work-life balance' has rarely been so apt. Needless to say trainees do work hard for the hours they are in the office, being the sort of "ambitious, easy-to-get-along-with" people who "get the job done during the day then switch off entirely at the end of the day." Though sitting in the smog and grime of London EC1 we barely wished to countenance the clean-living delights of the west, we felt obliged to allow trainees to enthuse about the moors, the beaches, the fresh air, the sun (on the day we rang at least), the surf, the swimming and the plenitude of sporting activities to be sampled. The availability of such pastimes mean "the office doesn't have to be the centre of your socialising," and one migrant we interviewed reflected, "I was a bit worried before I moved down, but I've got so many friends outside work now." As for socialising with workmates, each office has its own rituals and excitements, be it monthly drinks in the boardroom in St Austell, a riverboat trip to celebrate the new office in Truro, or "a heavy social calendar and plenty of marketing events" in Exeter. Across the firm, trainees have been instrumental in setting up a Young Marketing Group, which has been "forging links with other young professionals" through the medium of beer tasting, gin tasting, jazz nights and murder mystery events. We'd say it's a sign, if one is needed, of the commitment of S&S trainees to the firm's empire-building plans.

and finally...

A sound, steady and expanding firm, Stephens & Scown is absolutely determined to give other regional players a run for their money in the race for top-dog status.

Stephenson Harwood

the facts

Location: London
Number of UK partners/solicitors: 62/101
Total number of trainees: 27
Seats: 4x6 months
Alternative seats: Overseas seats, secondments
Extras: Pro bono – Hoxton and Camden law centres, language training

Stephenson Harwood excels in shipping finance and litigation and has growing expertise in aviation. Add in financial markets, real estate and commercial litigation and you won't be a nautical mile away from an interesting training contract.

south veering south-westerly, occasional showers

Just a few years ago observers with an eye to the telescope may have caught sight of the good ship Stephenson Harwood foundering in heavy seas. Perhaps they watched as partners and assistants abandoned ship or fell overboard as the waves beckoned the vessel on to the rocks of legal doom. It was certainly an odd time for the firm, which had just merged with fellow shipping specialist Sinclair Roche & Temperley. Following in-depth research into maritime conditions, we can now say with a fair degree of confidence that the tide has turned. Of course tides, along with time, wait for no man, which could explain why the firm has been swift and effective in its most recent restructuring.

From a rough transition *"things have calmed down, post-merger"* and the firm is plotting its course on a more even keel. *"They have sorted out the retention rate and things are a lot more solid; people who were uncomfortable after the merger have gone and we have refocused,"* said one trainee, neatly summarising the prevailing mood at SH. With its consignment of new hires (in aviation, real estate finance, corporate and shipping) there have been fresh client wins and a clear focus on core areas of strength. The firm is slimmer, tighter and no longer tries to be all things to all people. It has posted its first rise in turnover for three years and profits look healthier than they have been in a while. On the books are some fabulous clients: Yukos Oil, Transport for London, McGraw-Hill, Christie's, Singapore Airlines, United Airlines, Woolworths, Moss Bros, Canary Wharf Group – and these are just a few from the London commercial litigation department's list. Add in the clients from the rest of the London office, and then from the offices in Paris, Singapore, Greece, Hong Kong and mainland China and you've got a great portfolio.

It hasn't been plain sailing all the way but trainees were positive about the direction SH is taking; *"I feel part of something that is going somewhere,"* said one. *"If it had continually performed well you wouldn't notice the buzz when things got going. This is the kind of firm where you feel you could make a difference."* The impression we got from our interviews was that this new streamlined operation *"knows where it is going and is getting there."*

from stem to stern

As may be evident from the string of dodgy metaphors, the firm's shipping practice is once again central to business. Also stepping up to the mark are real estate, aviation and the central banking and asset finance teams, which have seen some good results in recent months. The Asian market has been key, with the firm's offices in Guangzhou, Hong Kong, Shanghai and Singapore all helping clients make inroads into the Chinese market. All this is good news for trainees, and the reduced number going through the scheme after this year (SH honoured the training contracts offered by Sinclair Roche & Temperley) should mean better prospects for staying on after qualification.

Here are some important things to note about seat allocation: one seat must be taken in either banking and asset finance (BAF) or shipping litigation, but beyond this nothing else is compulsory. The other seat choices are: real estate, commercial litigation, corporate, employment and pensions. For those looking for adventure, overseas seats are available in Hong Kong and Singapore.

So what would trainees say to those who weren't totally convinced of their sea legs? One told us: *"You will do shipping."* Another said, *"it's not something you have to do, many trainees haven't done the shipping seats."* Whether yes, no or maybe, the point seems to be that *"it would be mad to come here without any inclination for shipping whatsoever."*

banking on it

BAF is *"renowned to be a busy seat and very demanding."* Due to the nature of the transactions trainees can find themselves on some *"pretty repetitive tasks"* but there is a great deal otherwise to keep them interested and, consequently, they do find *"you learn such a lot."* The opportunity to *"work with the high-powered people"* at banks and other lending institutions sat high on the list of trainees' good points about the seat. BAF's work is split between shipping, aviation, project finance and general banking and is often international in scope. In one sea salt-flavoured transaction the group advised the marine finance division of HBOS when the bank's client purchased the state shipping fleet of Georgia. In aviation the group advised Jazeera Airways on the long-term financing of four Airbus A320s, and in general PFI it advised EDF Energy and Thames Water on the utility and infrastructure side of the MoD Project Allenby/Connaught to extend and refurbish garrisons across Aldershot and Salisbury Plain.

Shipping litigation is *"a tough first seat unless you have done shipping before"* as it is fitted out with complex terminology that can be hard for the novice to grasp. Yet trainees agreed the merits outweighed the challenges and proclaimed it *"a good, confident department to work in, with good clients."* One relished his time in the seat because he *"liked the fact that the values involved were so high that the litigation really mattered."* In commercial litigation seats trainees are steered towards particular areas of expertise, such as insurance and reinsurance, but will also see more general commercial cases. They reported working on libel and trade mark disputes as well as general banking and finance cases. As well as acting for large banks and insurers, the group extends its involvement to more cultural matters. It represented the government of Greece in its successful reclamation of a rare silver 'Brutus' coin that had been illegally taken from its original resting place. Another rather interesting matter was the claim on behalf of Westminster City Council against disgraced former council leader Dame Shirley Porter. Many of our sources singled out the corporate department for special mention, saying: *"People are interested in joining that team because it's particularly friendly."* Indeed one trainee was positively brimming with praise, claiming: *"They have a great personality, a real team ethic and being there was great fun from start to finish."*

Naturally it largely depends on who you sit with as to what work you will find on your desk, but rest assured there will be many things to assist on in corporate, from private equity and joint venture deals to AIM listings such as Charlemagne Capital's mammoth £300 million flotation. As in all seats, *"your supervisor is not the only one who'll give you work; people will ask about your busy-ness and give you things if needed."* The hours vary depending on the weight of the deals, though none of the trainees we spoke to reported pulling any particularly gruesome all-nighters.

fitter, happier, more productive

SH's office is in a *"nice but not too flash"* building right across from St Paul's Cathedral in the smart environs of Cheapside and Paternoster Square. *"I've seen the Queen three times since I've been here,"* said one interviewee proudly, and we wondered whether it was from the vantage point of the *"really swanky"* roof terrace. *"It's fantastic up there, you can lord it over everyone else, particularly on the summer evenings."*

Apparently, *"you can tell an SH trainee; they have certain characteristics in common like good academic results, people skills and commercial know-how,"* but they come from a variety of universities and backgrounds. *"There are quite a lot *of international trainees and many who are a bit older, not necessarily law graduates who intend to qualify by the age of 22."* Generally, *"if you're interesting and you have something to offer they will look at you."* And by all accounts if you show what you're made of, this firm will show confidence in you: *"They know they may as well involve us,"* one trainee said. *"We are learning all the time and can step in if a partner isn't there because we know the process."* Trainees acknowledged that *"there are always tasks that a trainee has to do but most of my time is spent doing proper work, which is why I came here."* Another felt like shouting from the roof terrace that *"I have never spent more than 20 minutes on a photocopier."* Trainees are rewarded for their hard work with a real mix of tasks, and the firm takes an active interest in their professional development, not just factoring in the obvious but also including *"whatever we need help with, like advocacy or presentation skills."*

Sociable people are well catered for. *"We help out at client BBQs by welcoming people and showing them up to the fifth floor, and then we are encouraged to mingle."* There are so many of these events that *"if you want to, you won't get through a week without going for drinks somewhere."* Shaw's Bookseller is the favourite bar for birthdays, bar mitzvahs, weddings and other special occasions, but there are *"millions of bars and restaurants"* (we noted that the tendency for exaggeration is an SH trait) around the area for informal socialising. Sportsmen and women can take part in cricket and football with clients or simply opt for the firm-wide mixed netball competition. These days team spirit pervades the firm. We were told: *"The environment is really conducive to work because you can ask anyone for advice, and people share resources very well. As long as you are not incredibly shy there is no way you wouldn't go up to someone and ask. Stephenson Harwood excels at this team ethic and it's the reason I have chosen to stay."* This

year eight other trainees from the total qualifying group of ten stayed on, qualifying into seats as diverse as shipping litigation and employment, pensions and benefits.

and finally...

"The hours are good, the money is good, the work is good." You want more? The old Stephenson Harwood spirit is back and we'd venture to suggest that the Lutine Bell at Lloyd's of London could well be rung twice on this firm. If you don't get the reference then consider it the first part of your shipping homework.

Stevens & Bolton LLP

the facts
Location: Guildford
Number of UK partners/solicitors: 27/52
Total number of trainees: 6
Seats: 4x6 months
Alternative seats: None

Guildford firm Stevens & Bolton calls itself "a City practice without the EC postcode". The question is, some 40 minutes away from London, how close to the City experience can you actually get?

taxi!

Before consolidating into a single site in Guildford, S&B operated a clutch of smaller offices across Surrey. A number of its partners have spent their entire careers with the firm, including the last managing partner. His predecessor had also trained with S&B, just as his father had before him. Despite these dyed-in-the-wool provincial roots, trainees say: *"There's no sense when you come through the door that you're entering what was once a high street firm."* Private client, family and residential property work may have underpinned the firm for eons, but such matters no longer dominate business. The S&B of 2006 is focused on all things commercial and has become one of the most profitable firm's outside London in the South East region.

The fact that "*many commercial clients are still local or regional*" does help the firm "*preserve its original image and identity,*" but there is a real sense of it having brought a dash of the Square Mile to Guildford. The best evidence of this is an expanding clientele that includes 11 FTSE 250 companies. Now at the heart of the firm is a corporate and commercial department that has adopted a strategy of hiring lawyers from City firms. Trainees reported that in this department "*all but one of the partners have City origins.*" The best example of the strategy in action was the hiring of ex-Simmons & Simmons corporate chief Ken Woffenden, whose arrival had a major impact. Through him, S&B went on to win work from multinational tobacco giant Gallaher, and more recently it advised BSI on the £52 million sale of its inspection and testing group. Key lateral hires have strengthened other departments too, not least the employment group which lured expert Stephanie Dale away from Denton Wilde Sapte. Always known for working her magic on massive employer clients, Dale hasn't let up since relocating. Lately she's been assisting British Airways through a dispute with pilots and cabin crew over the company's mandatory retirement age of 55. In September 2006 the firm also lured in an IP partner from leading firm Bristows – a sure sign of its intentions to develop in this field of practice.

Trainees told us to watch out for more "*organic growth in core areas,*" implying that S&B is on the lookout for yet more lawyers ready to make a life-enhancing career move to Guildford. Perhaps the sponsorship of three black cabs – now sprayed green and bearing the firm's branding – will persuade weary commuters of the wisdom of the idea.

the running men

Trainees take four six-month seats from coco, dispute resolution, real estate, employment and pensions, and private client, giving them access to all aspects of the firm's work. Our thanks to the source who introduced us to the novel, and may we say extremely scientific, yardstick of "*the printer walk.*" This simple measure makes it easy to gauge how busy a department is, so for example "*in corporate they run to the printer so they must be really overworked.*" Coco trainees tend to get either a corporate posting – helping out on transactions – or a general commercial posting – where they learn how to dispense day-to-day advice to businesses. In the former they would assist on deals such as the £55 million management buyout of house builder Rydon Group; in the latter they might work for a big client such as SABMiller, which turned to S&B for advice on a suite of UK brewing and distribution agreements, or Conair (owners of the BaByliss brand) which needed help with UK product labelling issues.

Weighty matters are also available in the commercial property and litigation departments. Trainees were on hand recently to see real estate lawyers advise BOC on property aspects of its £1 billion contract to supply Marks & Spencer with goods, and observe litigators representing Compass Management Consulting in a joint action with Cable & Wireless, suing IBM for damages in excess of £160 million. The counterpoint to these major pieces of work is that in all departments "*a fair chunk of work comes from regional owner-managed businesses or even individuals.*" The private client seat adds yet another dimension, and here trainees can immerse themselves in complex tax structures for estates, tax litigation or just "*drafting a simple will for a hundred pounds.*" Further contrasting experience is available ("*if you really want it*") in the family and residential conveyancing seats.

Across the seats there seems to be a good spread of activities, from *"working with counsel for a pharmaceuticals client on a dispute at the RCJ"* in litigation, to *"two months of close client contact"* or *"co-ordinating due diligence on over 100 companies for a massive deal"* in coco, to *"running a deal from opening instruction to billing"* in real estate. All those we spoke to had been satisfied with the level of exposure to decent clients and interesting tasks.

halfway house

If you do decide to head for S&B two years from now, chances are the firm will still be in residence at its *"characterful"* converted warehouse premises, perched on the banks of the River Wey. With everyone under the one roof in the centre of Guildford, there's an *"intimate, smaller firm atmosphere."* Since moving in, S&B has gradually colonised the building and consequently the internal layout is not the easiest for new recruits to navigate. *"To begin with you can get lost; to get to different parts of the building there are very specific routes you have to take,"* said one now fully oriented source. Most of those we spoke to recognised that *"new, bigger premises would be nice"* and shortly after speaking to them we learned that the firm had taken on extra office space nearby. Thus, gazing at the Guildford skyline, shying the odd Biro top at a passing canoeist and peering into houseboats will remain quintessential work-displacement activities.

Although several of the current trainees grew up in Guildford and *"recognise everyone in the local pubs,"* the majority have either *"a connection to the wider area"* or were studying in town at the College of Law when they fell for the old S&B charm. What was really compelling for those we interviewed was the perception that the firm offers – geographically, culturally and in terms of work and responsibility – a perfect halfway house between the life-consuming rigours of the City and an overly sedate or prosaic existence in the provinces.

"I didn't want a London firm, but I did want a firm with a similar ethos, mentality and clients," remembered one trainee. Another felt their aspirations had been met because of the firm's size, telling us: *"As a trainee you're utilised more within the team, and you don't just get the rubbish tasks... You couldn't ask for a better training."*

With London just a short train ride away (so close in fact that some trainees make the reverse commute each day), it certainly sounds an attractive proposition. Add in an official lunch break of one hour and 15 minutes, and an hours culture that *"can see you work until 9pm every night for an odd week,"* but usually means an *"8.45-6.30pm existence,"* the life bit of the work-life balance has the potential to flourish.

aloha guildford

Working in an office that is *"compact enough so you can approach everyone and speak openly,"* S&B seems to have cultivated *"an inclusive atmosphere."* Trainees can chip in at regular department strategy meetings, and they have two appraisals per seat to identify any problems and ensure *"you're never overloaded with menial tasks."* In addition, separate meetings with the HR manager and training partner reinforce the idea that each trainee can be individually nurtured. Nothing if not responsive, the firm has been known to allow split seats between tax and trusts and employment or family, or even a second stint in a core commercial area so as to cater to particular wishes. In September 2006 the firm was able to cater to the wishes of two of its three qualifying trainees.

We hear the firm has been tending to the social side of things with renewed interest, introducing monthly drinks on the Thursday after payday. These evenings have sometimes taken on a theme, including 'Beers of the World', which sounds absolutely fine to us, and 'Hawaii' which we reckon has the potential for real mischief making in this age of camera phones. The White

Horse and The Weyside (predictably enough on the river bank) are popular for post-work wind-downs and the town, in all its glory, is just a few steps away. A native Guildfordian explained: *"There are a few nice bars, a few chavvy ones and two passable nightclubs."* Inevitably, with many staff driving to work each day and others heading back up the tracks to London, it's often left to the *"hard core* [to] *keep things going."* Nevertheless, events are *"always well attended"* and *"stumbling back to crash on someone's floor"* is a ready option.

and finally...

Year after year trainees tell us Stevens & Bolton is City-lite. Leaving its geographical location aside – though you should be certain Guildford is where you want to work – we reckon its main selling point is the wealth of experience senior lawyers can share with trainees.

Taylor Wessing

the facts

Location: London, Cambridge
Number of UK partners/solicitors: 102/159
Total number of trainees: 46
Seats: 4x6 months
Alternative seats: Overseas seats, secondments
Extras: Pro bono – Blackfriars Settlement legal advice clinic; The Prince's Trust; St Mungo's homeless charity; language training

Fancy getting your hands on mega-stakes IP work while undertaking a broad commercial training contract in the City? If so, this firm could be a dream come true.

take the high-profit road

Taylor Wessing has its fingers in many pies and big but realistic ambitions to improve its standing in Europe. Some of the trainees we interviewed had originally applied to a firm called Taylor Joynson Garrett, back in the days before its merger with Wessing in 2002. Their time at the firm is set against a backdrop of increasing Europeanism – the initial Wessing merger in 2002 added a German dimension, and there are now also offices in Paris, Alicante in Spain and Shanghai.

Just as the firm has grown in size, so it has also broadened out its practice in the UK. We used to debate whether TW (and its predecessor TJG) was a full-service firm with strength in IP, or an IP firm with good supporting areas. As each year passes the arguments that it is the former grow more convincing. The trainees we spoke to had already picked up on this topic and told us they now regard the corporate department as *"right at the heart of the firm."* They say a corporate seat is where they *"come across most of what the firm actually does"* and that TW *"wants more people to qualify into the corporate department."* It is fitting then that corporate is now the only compulsory seat in the training contract with IP simply listed among the various optional seats, albeit that most trainees will still crawl over each other to spend time with the IP team. Fortunately such measures are largely unnecessary as there are quite a few places available.

There is ample evidence to support the full-service firm definition. The way trainees see it, *"it is strong in IP of course but there are lots of things such as real estate, employment and corporate, so you can get a taste of everything."* When tucking in to your obligatory corporate seat you at least have a choice. As well as mainstream corporate finance, the work of the corporate group encompasses financial services, finance and projects, corporate tax and more general commercial advice. True, *"some view the corporate seat as something to get out of the way,"* but the majority see it as a *"great department"* where they *"feel valued and listened to."* Those we interviewed had managed to get *"pretty decent work"* ranging from *"a lot of drafting letters, agreements and board minutes"* through to conducting due diligence and *"drafting and arranging disclosure bundles."* The role involves *"contacting different companies around the world"* and *"quite a lot of responsibility."* The average day usually ran until 7pm with most sources experiencing *"a number of 10pm or 11pm finishes"* and the very occasional Saturday thrown in for good measure.

goggles and googles

Real estate is perceived as a department that *"really cares about your training."* The level of responsibility on offer led some trainees to conclude it was *"the most challenging of the seats but, equally, the most rewarding."* Trainees take on a portfolio of their own small files, additionally assisting on *"some big transactions – shopping centre sales and big sale-and-leaseback projects."* In recent times the ever-more-successful real estate group has represented Allied Irish Banks on a £200 million secured loan facility to finance the purchase of UK investment properties and on a £212 million senior facility made available to a subsidiary of German company Bankhaus Wölbern to purchase the Woolgate Exchange office building in the City of London. Although it's a minor part of TW's business, the private client team is highly thought of. Those trainees who had tried it told us they'd looked after simple probates themselves as well as *"getting to help out on more complex offshore trusts."* Private client has a *"different pace to some of the other departments;"* things don't necessarily have to be turned around on the same day and you *"rarely, if ever, get a late night."*

Responsibility junkies should find what they are looking for in the litigation/dispute resolution seat as it is *"much more hands-on"* than some others. Trainees liked the fact that they *"knew what was going on from start to finish rather than just*

getting a small bit of a large deal." The contentious component of the training contract can be undertaken in general commercial lit, insolvency, construction, employment, property lit and, of course, IP. The ever-popular employment and pensions seat is reputed to have *"a great atmosphere where you can build a real rapport with people."* A best-case scenario would be a trainee running *"a small employment tribunal matter with only a little money at stake."* The employment group handles work for clients such as easyJet, Specsavers and Google as well as a number of clients from across the USA that are generally unaccustomed to employment practices in this country. Construction, too, provides rewarding experiences as trainees *"draft a lot of pleadings and are present at mediations and adjudications."*

knickers in a twist

Without question the area in which TW most stands out from the crowd is IP. For any science grads out there who hope to combine their acquired knowledge and skills with law, this has got to be one of their target firms. In patent litigation the firm's recent work includes the case of Mayne Pharma v Pharmacia Italia (Pfizer), a declaration of non-infringement proceeding in relation to a ready-to-use solution of the cancer drug epirubicin hydrochloride. This was the first action to come to trial using a new streamlined procedure for UK patent cases. TW IP lawyers also acted for ev3 group in its successful patent revocation proceedings against the University of California and Boston Scientific (a leading medical equipment producer) in the London Patents Court. The size and complexity of the cases handled in the department mean that for trainees there are few occasions when they can be *"let loose"* on matters and most of their work is *"investigative research behind the scenes."* Anyone tired of London could request a spot of non-contentious IP in the firm's small Cambridge office.

Not all IP work revolves around patents: TW undertakes a good deal of 'softer' work on trade marks, copyright, passing off and general brand protection. A soft IP seat is generally acknowledged to be one of the most popular seats in the firm, in part because the department "acts for some amazing clients." Day-to-day trainee work consists of sorting out domain name problems, spells of trial bundling, gathering and compiling evidence to support a client's claim or defence and researching copyright and trade mark topics. We heard a story about one trainee who, in the course of their duties, was asked to browse the adult shops of Soho in order to ascertain whether copyright infringement had occurred on a brand of saucy underwear. Some days in the office just drag on and on don't they? Clients of this team include Bose, Kellogg, Guide Dogs for the Blind, various publishers such as Associated Newspapers, Eidos, a number of music publishers and the estates of composers such as Rodgers and Hammerstein.

The firm is committed to the idea of client secondments and trainees have lately spent time with British Airways and Toyota.

chukkas a horse

From some sources we heard rumblings of "genuine frustrations" over seat allocations, while others felt HR handled things well, so we guess it depends on how easily your exact requirements can be fulfilled. IP is especially competitive; employment is also "massively popular." In past years we also heard reports that a minority of partners did not provide as supportive an atmosphere for trainees as perhaps they could. Again this year a few interviewees indicated that there were still a minority of supervisors who were ill-suited to taking trainees under their wing, leading to uncomfortable seats. To be fair, the HR department performs far better than it used to and seems willing to remove partners from the equation if need be. For the most part things are going well and "on the whole, the supervisors are pretty nice." Mid-seat appraisals are scheduled for the end of the second month in a department, which might seem rather early in a six-month seat but "in reality it is intended to make sure that they happen before the three-month point." At the formal end-of-seat appraisals, trainees are required to grade themselves and the supervisors are asked to comment on whether or not they agree.

Gleaming offices overlooking the Thames near Blackfriars Bridge provide a slick and professional environment within which each department has its "own distinct identity." The finance and projects team "handles huge deals all the time and involves the whole team working together," whereas in real estate you "work on your own a bit more," with team effort reserved for the very biggest deals. The former is also noted for being "a little more laddish than the other departments;" by contrast, employment and private client are known to have a more intimate atmosphere, reflecting the fact that the work has "more human interest." Generally, across the board, trainees "never feel uncomfortable asking partners questions" and most were "unaware of any strong hierarchy." Most trainees found the office hours perfectly manageable, commonly leaving around 6.30pm when not in corporate or IP.

The firm has an active social committee with "a generous budget" that allows for four or five events every year. Recent excursions have included a trip to the restaurant Dans le Noir?, an establishment where you dine completely in the dark. "You can't see a thing; it was hilarious. The waiters are blind and they stand by your table so that you can shout for them whenever you want something." Departmental away-days can be enjoyable, with the commercial lit seat perhaps being the best for this – we heard of picnics served by butlers and polo training on wooden horses. There's an annual TW summer party (last time black-and-white themed at The Savoy), although each department is left to its own devices at Christmas. Informal socialising revolves around a number of local bars, though if you're more inclined to play sport than drink you can join either the boys' or girls' football team. Alas, when we rang, the boys were languishing at *"the bottom of the bottom division"* in the London Legal League.

and finally...

Top of the premier league is where Taylor Wessing sits for IP, and this alone will account for a good number of the applications it receives. Whether or not you've a desire to try IP, this is a sensible choice if you're in the market for a respected mid-sizer that can train you in a number of commercial areas. As one trainee noted, *"of the people here, there is a group committed to corporate, another equally committed to IP and then a few people who are interested in things like employment and private client."* These tastes can all be catered for during the contract and at qualification time too. In September 2006, 13 out of 17 people took jobs, the biggest-recruiting department being corporate.

Teacher Stern Selby

the facts
Location: London
Number of UK partners/solicitors: 21/28
Total number of trainees: 10
Seats: 4 x 6 months
Alternative seats: none
Extras: Pro Bono – Toynbee Hall Legal Advice Centre

London's Bedford Row is lined with aged trees and even more aged barristers. It is steeped in tradition, jurisprudence and academic rigour. It's also, oddly, the place to go if you're a film star or premiership footballer rumoured to be involved in a sex scandal. Welcome to the slightly weird and slightly wonderful world of Teacher Stern Selby.

JPUTing your money where your mouth is

On the surface, TSS is a typical, slightly sedate West End property firm. In 2005 the firm had a hand in £1.5 billion worth of real estate deals ranging from pubs through shopping centres all the way up to office towers in the City of London. Each year several deals punch through the £100 million barrier. The firm acts for financiers as well as sellers and buyers, so if you want to delve into the mysteries of JPUTs (Jersey property unit trusts) and SPVs (special purpose vehicles) you could do a lot worse.

TSS also offers the budding trainee experience of coco and commercial and real estate disputes. However, it is in two other contentious areas – medical/educational negligence and media/entertainment – that the big headlines are made. Thanks largely to star partner Jack Rabinowicz, the firm acts on the most complex, interesting and important negligence cases against medical and educational authorities. It has recently represented a 23-year-old man suffering from Aspergers syndrome, alleging that a local authority's failure to meet its education and treatment duties led to him being detained under the Mental Health Act. If you came into the law because you wanted to help unfortunate people who've been let down by the state, this is a place where you could fulfil your dream.

this heading was removed by our lawyers

It may also be the right place if you came into the law to help celebrities keep their names out of the papers. Recently, the firm worked for Ashley Cole in his successful claim against *The Sun* and the *News of the World* over stories alleging the footballer was involved in various saucy activities. We're not foolish enough to talk about the case in detail here. The media practice's star is Graham Shear, who also dispenses advice to the James Bonds of this world – Pierce Brosnan and Daniel Craig. It's not all celebrity glamour; the team is also representing the Government of Cuba's music publishing arm in defending a copyright claim by a large US music label. Dry as that sounds, it's a high-profile case with the rights to many of Cuba's best-known songs at stake.

Every time we interview a firm's trainees, we always ask, *"And how do you feel about the seat selection process?"* This is where it all spills out; where trainees admit their bitter resentment at having been landed with one solid year of construction litigation while their colleague got corporate and hadn't even asked for it, etc. Well, none of this applies at TSS. The firm has come up with a blissfully simple answer to the problem of seat selection – there isn't any! Well, hardly any. Everyone takes a turn in property, commercial and litigation, before returning to their favourite for another stint pre-qualification. The system met with the approval of the those we interviewed. *"You get a huge amount of variety within each department,"* one told us. *"And you tend to work for other partners besides your supervisor, so there's extra variety there."* It can produce headaches for the firm's small HR team; one year, three out of four second-year trainees opted for litigation, the next year the same thing happened with coco. And yet, trainees somehow couldn't remember anyone being denied their choice of final seat.

up all night

The property department illustrates well the range of matters trainees encounter in just one seat. On larger commercial deals there's plenty of research, drafting (*"It's not a place where you'll be stuck by the photocopier"*), and every trainee gets at least one small file to run from start to finish. Some trainees might actually look after as many as 30 ongoing files during their seat. *"It's a bit of a shock,"* admitted one. *"I had quite a hefty caseload. You have to show that you can get on with it."* Nervous trainees can call on the collective wisdom of the department: *"You're never told to go away, although you might get the occasional 'come back later'."* And of course, your work will be checked, so there's no risk of accidentally destroying a deal with a misplaced comma.

Having said that, once you're out of your first seat the leash is often loosened. *"If you want something checked, they're happy to look at it,"* said one second-year, *"but they're not peeking over your shoulder all the time."* One thing the department can offer the enthusiastic trainee is time working closely with partners. We started blushing when a trainee mentioned *"finding myself in the office with a partner at 4am on my hands and knees..."* They continued: *"...looking at lease documents spread out across the floor."* Phew.

The firm's determination to challenge trainees extends to the coco department. *"You don't have your own files,"* said one relieved-sounding trainee, *"but that's not surprising as there are some pretty big deals going on."* Instead, you'll be *"drafting basic documents, obtaining opinions, going to a few client meetings and lots of dealings with clients on the telephone and by e-mail."* Those fearing drudgery can take heart: *"In my first week I was told by a partner not to do my own photocopying,"* said one source. *"He said my time was too valuable."* Furthermore, *"you're encouraged to learn the background to the deals."* Certainly, you'll see enough to get a sense of whether or not corporate is for you. *"I enjoyed the logicality of it all,"* someone concluded. Strangely, the coco seat also includes a small amount of private client work, so if you've got a burning desire to draft a will you can. The one big disadvantage of the department is the hours. Although at quiet moments *"you'll be out the door at 5.30pm,"* as deals creep forward the hours lengthen. *"You get to know all the takeaway menus by heart,"* lamented one source. Another reported crawling under a desk to go to sleep after an all-night completion. *"An associate tripped over me at 8.30am,"* he recalled. Fortunately, outside the coco team hours are more in the 9.30am to 6.30pm bracket.

defenders of truth

Time in general litigation is a given; working for Rabinowicz or Shear is not. Their caseloads are *"undoubtedly really exciting,"* and in Shear's case carry the thrill of secrecy: *"You can't tell anyone anything, not even your partner or your mum,"* whispered one trainee. *"Not until Graham's been on Sky News."* Said one veteran of the seat: *"The first thing Graham does when a new accusation comes in is find out if it's true. We don't do cover-ups."*

Whatever department you're in, you'll always sit with a supervising partner, and appraisals generally seem to be carried out thoroughly. There's an additional monthly trainee meeting where progress can be discussed. Having said that, when working for certain superstar partners, by all accounts your total appraisal is likely to be *"good work, thanks."* More generally, trainees seemed happy with the level of general feedback; *"no one ever changes your work without telling you why,"* noted one.

Many firms claim to have *"a family atmosphere"* but we take it with a pinch of salt in those with 900 people or more. With around 100 staff and partners TSS is the real deal. Overall, things are pretty informal; yet we don't want to give the impression it's one long party. *"People absolutely do work hard,"* trainees assured us. *"You generally know when it's time to move into fifth gear."*

bollygood fun

The last Friday of every month involves drinks in the boardroom, while on other weeks The Old Nick provides the hospitality. In winter a fair few members of the firm head home early on Fridays to observe the Sabbath. TSS has a strong Jewish heritage and closes for Jewish New Year and Yom Kippur. Similarly, everyone benefits from the office closing between Christmas and New Year. The Christmas party is always fancy dress and last year's Bollywood theme was spectacular. Little details such as Indian drummers to greet guests, taxis to get everyone home and a democratic seating plan which jumbled everyone together are indicative of the firm's attitude towards its people. *"Everyone had a present on their table,"* reported one trainee. *"They go out and buy 100 individual presents. The trainees are invited to help wrap them. You get some lunch and some donuts and have a nice time with scissors and glue."*

To get in here *"you've got to be personable. There's a lot of client contact from day one. It's not for those who want to hide behind a computer screen."* Otherwise the trainees are a heterogeneous bunch: each year's intake of four or five typically includes law and non-law grads plus slightly older candidates. A vacation scheme has been added to the recruitment programme and prospective applicants are *"strongly encouraged"* to give it a go. The firm has in very recent years taken on all its qualifiers; however, not so long ago retention was much lower, so don't assume a TC is a golden ticket: in September 2006 just two of the four found the right jobs were on offer.

and finally...

Teacher Stern Selby is traditional in the best possible way; tight-knit and slightly eccentric, it is remarkably solid despite the apparent gulf between its signature practices.

Thomas Eggar

the facts
Location: Chichester, Crawley, Worthing, London
Number of UK partners/solicitors: 55/34
Total number of trainees: 16
Seats: 4x6 months
Alternative seats: Secondments

A geographical relocation, increased revenue (now £32 million plus) and profitability, rising staff numbers – is Kent veteran Thomas Eggar reaching for the stars or just plane spotting?

eggarheads
Here's an abridged history of Thomas Eggar for the Simon Sharmas among you. Having been kicking around since 1881, Brighton's Eggars merged with two other small law firms in 1981. Around the same time, two Worthing firms combined forces and a London practice dating back to 1746 merged with an equally ancient Reigate practice. In 1998 they all collided, eventually, wisely shortening their collective name to Thomas Eggar. While still operating from Chichester, Worthing and London, most recently the firm closed offices in Horsham and Reigate to concentrate on growing a brand new operation in Crawley, near to Gatwick Airport.

Trainees estimate the firm's activity to be 75% commercial and 25% private client, and point to important differences between its offices. Still the largest, Chichester is the King Kong of private client and also home to non-lawyer investment managers trading as Thesis Asset Management. It's a similar story in Worthing, the smallest office with one trainee, though neither Worthing nor Chichester should be viewed as limited in their activities as each has a selection of commercial departments. In London a busy commercial office is working hard to make its way in the capital. And lastly, since opening in 2004 to unite commercial teams from Horsham and Reigate, the Crawley office has grown into a largely commercial operation employing 140 staff.

creepy crawlies
The new *"hub"* in Crawley dominated our interviews with trainees. For the first time there is a single office which all trainees visit for at least one seat, and they sense it represents the future of the firm. *"Chichester has previously been the head office and still retains kudos, but with the new office developing, and growing and growing, there is now a drive for the firm to be seen as one."* Alas, they are less enthusiastic about *"Creepy Crawley"* itself. Transformed from a small village into a New Town by the post-war Labour Government, there's something about it that's destructive to the soul. At least trainees are enthusiastic about their new building, an office with *"fantastic state-of-the-art facilities."* Apparently, *"one client said it could only be improved by growing a 60-foot hedge to block out the view."* In this workplace utopia everyone sits open plan, which trainees say *"makes you feel more in touch with the partners."*

We're bemused by the new office's name in TE speak. *"We are conditioned to call it Gatwick, as Gatwick sounds better than Crawley. I remember being in a trainee meeting when we had someone in to talk to us about their area of work. They kept on calling it the Crawley office, and every time they did you could see the trainee principal getting steadily more annoyed."* Everyone jokes about the town, but they can't fault the logic for relocating there. The business-rich area from Croydon down to Brighton and stretching east-west to East Grinstead and Horsham has been dubbed the Gatwick Diamond, and TE is doing its fair share of diamond mining, listing many regional businesses as clients. Aviation and transportation, pharmaceuticals, financial services, retail, hotels and leisure companies are all important, with TE acting for several smaller airlines, the Elite Hotel Group, UniChem, Britannia Pharmaceuticals and Allergy Therapeutics among others. TE also has clients elsewhere in the UK and beyond; for example it recently advised Pirelli on its sub-sea cable operations and Rockson Engineering on multimillion-pound plant contracts for power projects in West Africa.

mappa monday to friday

So how do trainees slot into this matrix of the local, the national and the sometimes international? All are sent a complete two-year, four-seat plan before starting their contracts. Its content tends to reflect the commercial/private client balance within the firm and everyone undertakes a private client, litigation, commercial property and commercial seat. *"Having all four seats mapped out is a good thing overall, though it can be a problem if you want to change,"* we learned. *"There is scope for flexibility; it's not advertised widely... it's there if you fight for it."* A key advantage to having the plan from the outset is that *"with four different offices stretching from the South Coast to London, it helps to know where you will be and when, certainly from the point of view of accommodation."* In this respect people are placed according to where they live, so if your home is in London you're most likely to end up in the capital and Crawley. If you live further south, it'll be seats in Chichester, Worthing and Crawley.

Private client seats vary depending on the specialism of the supervisor; in 'Gatwick' it has a heavy tax element and the clientele is generally more entrepreneurial than traditional old money. Chichester has everything from will drafting and probate to work for large charities and trusts. Down in Worthing there are specialist trust and probate litigators. What a trainee will find appealing in all locations is the close contact with clients. One even attended a client's funeral and, strangely, found it *"a relaxing way to spend a Friday."* Our sources also had a variety of experiences in their commercial seats. One spoke of company secretarial duties such as registrations and board minutes. Another who

secured an employment law seat had enjoyed piggybacking their supervisor's client interviews, helping to draft contracts and learning everything there is to know about unfair dismissal. All offices except Worthing have a commercial team, and between them they act for both little-known local businesses and household-name companies.

Said one trainee of their litigation seat: *"It involved lots of responsibility as I was running my own caseload, mostly contract claims. The supervisor's idea is to put you in the foreground if he has faith in you."* Our source wholeheartedly approved of this approach, believing *"you can only learn if you are given work to do, and responsibility. You can't learn just by listening."* When we asked another trainee if they'd been able to do any advocacy, *"God, yes!"* came the reply. A third described litigation as *"the most exciting of all my seats... I went along to watch a lot of injunctions and immediately felt involved in cases."* A commercial property seat can be taken at any branch, but if you are the only trainee down in Worthing *"the first couple of weeks can be lonely."* The answer is to turn to more senior colleagues because *"the only way to get ahead is to ask questions."* One Worthing veteran told us: *"When I was there an associate took it upon herself to help with my training, and that was great because a partner can't always take the time to tell you how to become a solicitor."* Get yourself adopted by a whole team and everyone ends up giving you work. In this way you get to try everything, from simple searches and registrations to drafting leases and agreements and negotiating with other lawyers. There are masses of property companies and housebuilders in the south of England and, consequently, no shortage of interesting projects to work on.

dear john

The breadth of work at TE and the four-office set-up makes it hard to find the common threads in the training experience, and we weren't surprised to learn that *"each trainer has their own way of working."* Just as one trainee told us: *"In litigation I was thrown in at the deep end and in commercial property I was a lot more controlled,"* another offered an entirely different view, having been given their head in property. While some partners were described as *"sticklers"* and *"more interested in upholding the firm's traditions,"* others were deemed *"progressive and forward-thinking."* You can't even identify rules as to where people sit and with whom. Some trainees have their own rooms, others share with a supervisor and others still sit in open-plan offices. Perhaps the only unifiers are the smart suits and good manners found in all parts of the firm. Quarterly lunchtime meetings enable the trainee group to gather, talk about their experiences and make requests from management. Past successes include travel expenses, business cards and two extra days holiday per year. Apparently their current wish list is as short as Scrooge's Dear Santa letter, which by implication suggests their satisfaction levels are pretty high. *"The training principal, John Stapleton, is fantastic,"* gushed one source. *"You can be incredibly frank with him."* Something no one has a problem with is the length of the working day. On average 8.30 or 9am until 5.30 or 6pm, it's a rare night when trainees burn the midnight oil.

In some respects the South East can be an awkward part of the country for trainee recruitment. The capital is so commutable that the question 'why not work in London?' always lingers like a bad smell. When we asked trainees why they had plumped for TE we established four key things. Most had a prior connection with the South East; most wanted to try both commercial and private client seats; all had a desire to work somewhere with a sterling reputation; and many wanted to sample working environments in both London and the provincial South East.

Every other year the whole firm gets together for a big Christmas bash, with a summer party slotted into the calendar every year. The trainees socialise as a group only intermittently, and describe a mellow office-by-office social scene. *"Friday office drinks are not massively well attended,"* confided one honest source. With a choice of bars on their doorstep, the Londoners find it easiest to get a scene going after work, but elsewhere it's a different story as many people drive to work and recognise the inadvisability of mixing cars with bars. Instead, a far healthier pastime, squash – *"it's the new football!"* – is taking off in Crawley. Sounds ideal for settling scores with colleagues or working out your frustration should the latest trainee powwow fail to produce extra holidays. In September 2006 both of the qualifiers stayed on with the firm.

and finally...

Variety and inter-office moves have long defined this training contract, so it will be interesting to see what kind of influence the new *"unifying"* 'Gatwick' office has on the scheme. One thing that isn't going to change is the key reason why you would pick the firm. If you know you want to train in this part of the country, even the scantiest research will reveal Thomas Eggar to be one of the best-respected and longest-established options.

TLT Solicitors

the facts

Location: Bristol, London
Number of UK partners/solicitors: 54/91
Total number of trainees: 14
Seats: 4x6 months
Alternative seats: Secondments

TLT's most recent financial results showed turnover increasing by 34% and a headcount shooting in the same direction, statistics that seemingly attest to an overdose of fertiliser for this

Bristol flower. However, from its germination at the turn of the millennium TLT has remained resolute in its dismissal of growth for growth's sake.

resistance is futile

Last year's merger with small London firm Lawrence Jones is a good illustration of TLT's *"nice and steady"* method of cultivation. It has helped the firm in its mission to expand business beyond the local market, particularly in banking and financial services, where it already has RBS, Barclays and HBOS on its books. A push in other commercial areas, such as leisure, retail and technology, provides further impetus for growth. It's only natural that the bright lights of the capital have beckoned TLT: its Bristol rivals Osborne Clarke and Burges Salmon have upped the ante and describe themselves as a European law firm and a national law firm respectively. However, we sense that TLT is unlikely to sideline its collection of strong regional clients and run panting in the pursuit of world domination. *"There's no doubt that Bristol is a great location,"* trainees said, adding that the firm planned to take full advantage of all the investment coming into the city. Underlining the firm's commitment to Bristol are client relationships with the Watershed Media Centre, the chirpy characters at Aardman Animations, the more prosaic Avon Rubber and Severn Delta, and the frankly intriguing HorseWorld.

You don't need to listen hard to hear managing partner David Pester's call for profitability and growth echoing through the firm. The mantra 'Top-50 law firm by 2008' seeps into the consciousness of all; *"everybody is expected to be involved and enthusiastic."* This isn't difficult when *"everybody is keen to see the firm going places."* These platitudes seem to be borne out in the day-to-day experience of the training contract in the expanding TLT universe, with *"plenty of space and bags of choice"* for those who pitch up to acquire their legal wings. There are no compulsory seats in the four-by-six month model, though trainees say: *"It's good to be seen in the areas that are big in the firm."* This effectively means a stint in commercial, corporate finance or real estate is not to be sniffed at.

the winds of change

A seat with the commercial services team provides the opportunity to *"see for miles"* across the business world. One of the things TLT does well is franchising law, and here it acts for all sorts of franchised businesses from Proton Cars to newly formed ElecLocal, a sister organisation to PlumbLocal. TLT has also made waves in the renewable energy sector, where it acts for various green energy companies, the banks that fund green electricity generation, and also certain government bodies (DTI, DEFRA and DfT via the Energy Saving Trust and Carbon Trust) on issues concerning UK grants, state aid and competition law. It's a supersonically busy posting that can ruffle the disorganised, not least because trainees take on work from around a dozen people. *"They made sure I wasn't overloaded though,"* one source told us, a sentiment shared by those who had experienced the adrenaline rush of corporate finance. *"There's a definite buzz there,"* reported trainees, though some balked at the amount of transactional paperwork and admin they had to wade through. In the past year TLT's corporate lawyers have handled a deal for the UK's fifth biggest supermarket chain, Somerfield, which spent £18 million buying part of the petrol forecourt business of rival Safeway, and assisted British County Inns with a £10 million share issue under the government's Enterprise Investment Scheme. While those who enjoyed the buzz of corporate undoubtedly found the tax seat *"quieter,"* they nevertheless acknowledged: *"It's useful as you are always going to need a working knowledge of it."*

With developers launching themselves at Bristol with all the enthusiasm of Laurence

Llewellyn-Bowen with a can of lilac paint, real estate, construction, and planning/development prove interesting seats. You can sink your teeth into property; there are "*a lot of smaller files – the local takeaway shop and the like.*" More autonomous work on small matters is matched with general assistance on larger deals for an increasingly national clientele of property portfolio owners. Leisure and retail clients feature heavily, so you might encounter the likes of Punch Taverns and the Spirit Group, both of which appear to be on a constant merry-go-round of selling and refinancing hundreds of pubs. "*The main thing you get from property is running your own files, not merely assisting fee earners,*" enthused one source, while another amateur Poirot relished the detective work the seat provided. Other trainees spoke of the lure of the "*famously nice*" property partners. "*If you're their type of person, you will get drawn into it whether you like property or not – and you'll enjoy it!*" said one. Rather sinisterly.

a bridge too far?

The banking and lender services department brings in a good chunk of the firm's income, but trainees have not always enjoyed a seat here as much as in other parts of the firm. Though debt recovery and mortgage repossession cases allow them to have their days in court making small applications in front of district judges, some find the work rather process-driven. This part of TLT's business has been corralled into a separate venture called Ontrack geared towards lenders such as Barclays Bank, Bristol & West, HBOS and RBS.

The trainees who get to try out in the family department usually end up taking at least one unsupervised meeting with a client and invariably enjoy attending court for hearings dealing with cohabitation, divorce and children. This "*brilliant*" department has a hold over many and competition for a slot here is correspondingly

tough. For completeness, there are also seats available in employment, commercial litigation and banking and finance litigation. Since the Lawrence Jones merger London berths have been available in Sea Containers House next to Blackfriars Bridge over the Thames. Thus far the London office has offered one property and one banking and asset finance seat at each rotation, and there is a good chance of more in the future. With accommodation taken care of by the firm (in a fully serviced, centrally located apartment no less!), trainees haven't been shy of accepting the offer of a train ticket to London. Those who'd been there had found the experience bracing, with a taste of real responsibility.

podcasting

"*Everything just felt right,*" purred one trainee when asked about their choice of firm. "*It was TLT from the very first interview*" for another. But sometimes love just ain't enough, and some trainees were saddened by the tough decision to be made on qualification. Should they follow their heads in terms of practice area, or follow their hearts and accept a job in another department just to stay at the firm. In September 2006 heads won the day, with just one qualifier out of four taking a job at TLT.

"*Nobody has an office at TLT,*" pronounced one source; "*there are very strict rules about this.*" The firm has "*removed the fear of crossing a partner's threshold*" with what is described as an open-plan, pod-like layout. While we suspected that the phrase "*from open plan to open culture*" had been cut-and-pasted from brochure to mouth, trainees were certainly sincere when talking about the inclusive atmosphere at the firm. "*We really are relaxed and very friendly. It's a good place to be.*" Supervisors are always available (clearly they have nowhere to hide) and formal appraisals are scheduled at three-monthly intervals to go through "*a detailed questionnaire*" dealing with the trainee's progress. The workload seems to be just about right, with some trainees claiming "*any more would be a bit of a nightmare.*" One appreciated the "*drip-drip of everyday learning,*" assuring us they were referring less to Chinese water torture and more to the sterling efforts of supervisors. People are always happy to explain work in the wider context and give feedback as needed. "*You give feedback on the supervisors as well,*" reported one trainee, eager to jump into this particular diplomatic minefield. We must also report that partners are "*paying more than lip service*" to a new employee forum, which has representatives from all levels of the firm.

yeah but no but

TLT's modern high-rise office between Temple Meads station and the main Bristol Uni buildings provides the perfect vantage point for a little horizon gazing. Alas, while window seats are rumoured to be available, in reality they prove harder to pin down than the elusive beast of Bodmin. We hear that some of the many enterprising property developers in the city have begun taking advantage of client meetings on the upper floors to survey the progress being made on their building sites. Well that's one way of winning new clients, we suppose.

The TLT social scene involves a fair bit of sport – hockey, softball and football games plus trips to 20/20 cricket and greyhound racing. A keen social committee has arranged quiz nights, teams for the hard-fought annual dragon boat race on the River Avon and, in what we suspect may be their finest event yet, a trip to Butlins. Trainees are adept at organising their own out-of-office fun, and became quite bullish when comparing their activities to those of their peers at other Bristol firms – "*They've got nothing on us!*" Watch out for the annual Christmas party where "*trainee entertainment is mandatory.*" All assured us that while "*trainees moan about it, it really is very good fun*

and a chance to get to know everyone." The last extravaganza was entitled 'TLT's Little Bristol' and gave everyone their 15 minutes of farcical fame. We're wondering who drew the short straw to play Bristol's most infamous teenager Vicky Pollard.

and finally...

These days the joviality and smiles at TLT barely disguise its ambitions to grow, grabbing bigger work and clients along the way. Bristol training contracts are always much sought after and we suspect that this will never change. However, the chance to train in both London and Bristol should now make TLT all the more attractive to those who haven't yet made up their mind between the sound of the underground and the lapping of waves against Bristol's harbour wall.

Travers Smith

the facts

Location: London
Number of UK partners/solicitors: 58/148
Total number of trainees: 40
Seats: 4x6 months
Alternative seats: Paris
Extras: Pro bono – ICSL and Paddington law centres, death row appeals; language training

Clocking up more than 200 years in the role of adviser to the City establishment, this firm remains both modest in size and independent. It also retains a distinctive character and a superb reputation.

a room with a view

At the heart of Travers' training is a room-sharing system that matches each trainee with a partner and an assistant. It allows them to experience a personal, two-on-one tuition that stands them in good stead. "*The room system means you get to see every step of the process"* and *"you pick things up almost without realising – concepts, phrases and jargon, particularly in corporate... sometimes you can just look up and ask about it."* Travers' deals are mostly moderate to large in size, and will often be handled by the occupants of a single room with specific input from other departments. Sharing with the two key members of a small deal team is certainly more rewarding than sitting at the bottom of a huge pyramid of staff waiting for work to trickle down. The system ensures the new recruits always understand the relevance and context of the jobs they perform and allows them a glimpse of the future. *"You get a sense of what partners do in terms of work and what sort of lifestyle they lead. Plus you have the assistant as a kind of buffer – it's easy to turn to them and ask questions."* A final advantage is the effect the room system has on the hierarchy within the firm. *"The approachability of people comes from the partners down, and it's due to the fact that there's no culture of working for associates and not speaking to partners. Here you are able to hold decent conversations with everyone."*

All trainees complete four seats with mandatory time in corporate, a contentious area (either employment or commercial litigation), and property or banking. A final 'wild card' seat is chosen from a list of practice areas including IP/IT, competition or tax. None of our sources questioned the wisdom of the set-up or were aware of attempts to influence allocation. In all departments, seminars are laid on for trainees, as often as once weekly for the first couple of months: *"They're a real help and you can ask questions easily."*

play to your strengths

Corporate seats come in two varieties: private equity and corporate finance. No one minds which one they do, because those who qualify into corporate are expected to cover both types of work in the following 18 months. On the straight corporate side there is a volume of mid-market

deals plus some hefty instructions. Hitting the headlines recently was Australian client Macquarie Bank's purchase of BBC Broadcast, which now operates as a private company, Red Bee Media. This deal played to Travers' strengths in competition law and broadcasting regulatory knowledge. Another whopping deal was Peel Ports' acquisition of the Mersey Docks & Harbour Co, which operates ports such as Liverpool, Chatham and Sheerness. Here the firm exploited its strength in property law.

Underpinning much of Travers' corporate success are strong relationships with an impressive list of private equity clients – 3i, Bridgepoint Capital, Phoenix, Apax, Nomura, Cazenove, Candover and many others. The firm keeps excellent company – its main competition comes from Ashurst, Clifford Chance, Freshfields, Linklaters, Macfarlanes and Weil Gotshal. Among last year's most important deals was the mammoth £2.18 billion Coral Eurobet exit, where the firm advised management on the sale of their shares to Gala. This deal, big by any standards, is indicative of the growing capabilities of a firm that has long perched at the top of the tree for mid-market transactions.

Trainees say corporate work is interesting and the amount of time spent on grunt tasks perfectly manageable. *"Obviously it depends on when you hit a deal; there is always donkey work at the start but that also means quite a lot of client contact. When I was in corporate finance I got to do a first draft of an asset purchase agreement while helping an assistant."* Another reported on private equity experience: *"To begin with I was filling out Companies House forms and bibling and so on, but as time moved on I was amending and commenting on documents."* As an added bonus the corporate department can offer good French-speaking trainees a spell in the firm's Paris office, where they have a really decent level of responsibility and an apartment in Montmartre. Thus far, however, there is no sign of a seat in Travers' small Berlin office.

it's like piccadilly circus

Ever been to the London Trocadero at Piccadilly Circus to while away a rainy afternoon with the tourists and hoody rats? Last year Travers' property lawyers advised on the £220 million auction purchase of this temple of fun for a clever company called Golfrate which intends to turn the upper floors into a 600-bedroom Ibis hotel in time for the London Olympics. Shortly after this deal, Golfrate asked Travers to help with its £112 million purchase of another Piccadilly landmark – The Criterion. Property provides ample contact with clients such as Golfrate by e-mail, phone and in person at meetings – *"They're really conscious of the need to get trainees to meet people."* As in other departments the majority of work comes from room-mates, with external calls on the trainee's time adequately monitored from within the room. *"Contrary to what I was expecting I was horrifically busy all the way through my seat,"* one source told us. *"I helped on several huge matters, as well as having everyday management work to be getting on with."*

A trainee who had taken the banking option instead of property recalled a major transaction for key client ntl. *"I was made to feel part of the team and that I was working towards the same goal as everyone else. I even went to the ntl headquarters on my own to get various documents signed by the directors. That was a fair level of responsibility. Obviously I wasn't conducting negotiations, but I did have to talk the directors through the documents."* Is there no end to trainee satisfaction, we wonder?

Over in litigation, lawyers have worked on Enron-related issues for a large bank and represented the Mirror Group Pension Trustees in long-running Maxwell litigation. They have also been running one of the most noteworthy cases of 2006, in which NatWest sued Rabobank and then Rabobank countersued. The claims, worth hundreds of millions of pounds, rest on fraud and misrepresentation. Some of our sources had taken the decision to sidestep a litigation seat, opting instead for a short course run by the College of Law. *"Clearly it's not going to be a comprehensive replacement for a litigation seat,"* they concluded, but nonetheless they were happy to leave big financial bust-ups to one side and focus on other areas.

What about playing your wild card or experimenting away from mainstream areas of practice? Even the smaller teams at Travers have plenty of seats, so, for example, tax, employment and competition each have around four spaces at any one time. Tax goes down very well with young Traversites who enjoy a heavy research element to their work and *"the shifting sands of case law."* The seat is split into three months working corporate tax and three on share schemes and employee incentives. *"You get a pretty good variety of work: you're not just drafting minutes of meetings, you're getting involved with share option plans and liaising with foreign law firms."*

port and cigars

The original Mr Travers Smith was apparently an aficionado of Havana cigars and vintage port. Conjures up a certain image, doesn't it? Outsiders commonly have a notion that Travers is an old-fashioned, clubby kind of firm where the colour of your school tie makes a difference. Trainees are the first to refute this, some sounding positively weary of hearing the claims. *"We're not posh,"* insisted one. Certainly the West Smithfield offices are a far cry from a smoke-filled gentlemen's club. One thing that's harder to refute, however, is the impression that Travers is still limited in the range of universities from which it recruits. In 2003 we reported that 70% of trainees had come from just four universities. In April 2006 the firm's own website revealed that 50% of trainees attended Oxford, Cambridge or Bristol. Admittedly, magic circle firms show much the same leanings towards Oxbridge graduates, it's just that at this smaller firm the effect seems more concentrated. To its credit, Travers does not appear to be limiting its recruitment campaign to these universities and we know for a fact that it is present at a large number of university law fairs up and down the country.

Let's open the can of worms fully. When we checked in the summer of 2006, Travers' partnership was 12.5% female; that's at the lower end of average for City firms. Its women partners are clearly important figures – several of them head up specialist departments and the head of IT is female – but not one female partner was to be found in the core departments of corporate, property, litigation or banking. Surprising, too, is the fact that when, for at least a decade, more women than men have entered the profession, the ratio of male to female solicitors is still around 2:1 at Travers. When we asked the firm about these figures, we heard nothing to suggest any deliberate plan was in place. Then again, these stats must say something... After a lengthy dicussion with the firm on this point, the only conclusion offered was that the transaction-heavy nature of Travers' practice may appeal to men more than women. What also needs to be factored in is that the firm has, in recent years, recruited slightly more male than female trainees, and this too will have affected the gender balance at associate level. When we last checked in with the firm, its recruitment figures for 2008 bucked the trend and showed more female than male recruits.

pointing the finger

We should stress that no trainee was anything other than extremely complimentary about their employer and its culture. They described *"a close firm"* with *"a supportive and friendly atmosphere"* where *"everyone has respect for each other."* Said one: *"It's not small but you do know faces; people say 'hello' in the lift and that makes a difference."* Another thing that sheds light on the culture is the fact that a number of lawyers actually returned to the firm after sampling life elsewhere.

Fittingly for a high-calibre, corporate-led firm, trainees' hours can be long, and at times very long. Our sources had all experienced plenty of 8pm to 9pms and had burned their fair share of midnight oil. But the *"good banter"* in the office continues outside, at popular departmental quiz nights or in the local pub, The Bishop's Finger. *"Goodbye and hello"* drinks or dinners at seat rotation time are also a nice touch, and rumour has it that the managing partner has a penchant for dressing up as Father Christmas (though only once a year). Sportsfolk can join colleagues for the Paris half marathon, rugby sevens, hockey and football, and we presume matches are played with the same good grace and impeccable manners that Travers' lawyers exhibit in their work.

This is a place where the required standard of personal conduct is high and the quality of training equally so. The effective and much admired room system is complemented by a thorough appraisal regime involving supervisors and a panel of training partners. With such comprehensive support and constant access to partners it's little wonder that the vast majority of trainees want to stay on after qualifying. In September 2006, 13 out of 14 were able to do so, distributing themselves across the departments.

and finally...

An undeniably classy firm, Travers is rightly popular with students looking for early responsibility and easy interaction with their seniors. The most common advice trainees had to offer was this: *"You've got to have the academic credentials, but you mustn't be overconfident."* When you speak to a Travers trainee they always impress, usually without having to try too hard. This is worth noting because, in what is still a relatively conservative environment, you'll not win favour by being brash or too loud.

Trethowans

the facts
Location: Southampton, Salisbury
Number of UK partners/solicitors: 20/48
Total number of trainees: 6
Seats: 4x6 months
Alternative seats: None

Hampshire firm Trethowans is developing a commercial operation to match its long-held private client expertise.

1866 and all that

Way back in 1866 George Nodder qualified as a solicitor and subsequently set up his own practice in Salisbury. Some 130 years later Trethowans' management decided that there must be more to legal practice than advising the good folk of Salisbury and they took the decision to move into the Southampton market. Establishing a base there in 1996 was central to their plan to win some of the more lucrative commercial work on offer in the area. Another ten years on, and with quite a few small, local mergers under its belt, it sounds as if the firm's grand plan has been rather successful. *"The way things are going, the firm is definitely getting more commercially oriented,"* confirmed one interviewee, adding: *"If you have the ambition and the drive, and if you want the complex and challenging work, it's there."*

But what if you're unsure that commercial practice is your bag? *"You can also get non-commercial training in private client."* Indeed, as a trainee you will be exposed to both types of work.

pizza the action

After conducting a mini audit of Trethowans' clientele and practice groups we can tell readers the following. Standing out on the commercial side is a strong licensing practice, acting for casinos, hotels, pubs and restaurants. The firm advises Pizza Hut, for example, on its licensing arrangements and helped major client Ladbrokes develop its important e-gaming business. Advice to Ladbrokes also spills over into commercial property, where the group assisted on new leases for 16 of its properties. The busy property department has further advised Stannah Stairlifts on its relocation to a purpose-built factory and office unit, and it takes pride in its expertise in property investment through advice to several pension funds. Work isn't just taken from the local area but increasingly comes from national brands and clients based elsewhere in the UK. *"We're kind of going the London route,"* explained a source; *"we're looking further afield for work and a lot of the partners have experience in City firms."*

The private client side of the operation is tied to the region and covers residential property, family and personal injury as well as the full gamut of wills, tax and trusts matters. Clients come from across Wiltshire, Hampshire and the South Coast. You may have heard of the family department after it hit the headlines recently with a 'cash for hairdressers' scheme involving a fee paid to businesses when they referred customers with marital difficulties.

Many of our interviewees had started life in the PI department. Here, trainees look after a portfolio of their own straightforward cases while also assisting partners on larger cases, sometimes clinical negligence claims for some *"very vulnerable clients."* The department provides some interesting, though often harrowing, experiences for trainees. *"I was working on a case where a baby had died, which did affect me quite a bit,"* admitted one. The other human interest seats are family, where the department deals with cases relating to children and domestic violence issues plus divorces (some of them big-money) and wills, tax and trusts, which is said to be *"great, if you like that kind of thing, especially for the client exposure."*

The ever-expanding commercial property department offers *"lots of work drafting leases, and sales and acquisitions of registered and unregistered land."* If that's not enough to get your teeth into, *"partners will happily dig out old files for you to read through if there isn't a current transaction in a particular area."* Trainees first cover residential property, in order to get to grips with the basics, before moving onto the commercial side *"where you can then really concentrate on the drafting."* The commercial litigation team also deal with a large amount of property-related work. One trainee told us: *"I got plenty of advocacy experience on routine possession hearings – I was going before the judge rather than sitting behind someone."*

pimm's on the lawn

Trethowans has grown the two offices such that it can *"provide the same service from each location."* One interviewee in Wiltshire said: *"I have no qualms about calling someone up in Southampton; it doesn't feel like they are 30 miles away."* Trethowans want trainees to spend time in both offices. *"One of the trainees moves house every six months but the rest of us have decided to stay where we are and commute."* The only adjustment you'll have to make, it appears, is in your social expectations: *"If you're moving from Southampton to Salisbury you'll notice the difference"* said one source; *"Southampton people go out more and it is much easier to socialise."* If you know this part of the world then you'll already be aware that Southampton is a busy student city whereas many of Salisbury's residents are *"at the richer end of the scale and a little more old-fashioned."*

Office hours are pretty reasonable, with post-6pm finishes reserved for one-off pieces of work. The firm lays on a variety of organised social activities such as bowling, barbecues and theatre trips, and successful (or simply keen) sports teams play other local firms and businesses at cricket, rugby and football. Every three months trainees get some cash to spend on a night out when they *"catch up, have a laugh and exchange information – it encourages us."* The small intake is also spurred on by *"lots of client events to which we are invited – like the Pimm's party in the summer – there is so much to get involved in but no pressure to be involved all the time."* Exposure to clients is also a part of day-to-day working life for new recruits. *"Before I joined, the trainees all told me how much hands-on experience they had,"* said one interviewee. *"You don't just sit in the office, never seen by clients; you are on the front line, managing files yourself."* Even if at times *"you're a bit swamped,"* it gives a good view, warts and all, of *"what it's really like when you qualify."*

change is good

When we rang trainees, the Salisbury office was in the process of moving from its old red-brick offices at College Chambers to large, purpose-built premises outside the town. *"At the moment we're split over two sites on the same street that are bursting at the seams, but we're getting brand-new, purpose-built offices,"* sighed one happy trainee. There are also whispers about the Southampton operation having outgrown the rather grand-looking Director General's House, next to the law courts. The training scheme itself has been shaken up a bit: with the addition of a new training partner and a review of the appraisal process, the system for trainees is now *"very smooth, more structured and more effective."* Formal feedback is given after the second and fourth month in a seat so that at the full end-of-seat review *"nothing should come as a shock."* Trainees were happy to report that seat allocation was *"never a case of them telling us where to go and forcing the issue"* (though there may be times when trainees are not offered their first choice).

There are a number of examples of trainees who initially came to Trethowans as secretaries or paralegals. The firm is good at *"encouraging people who are already working there to progress, and getting paralegals in and bringing them on."* The firm's recruiters clearly recognise the value of previous work experience; indeed, our sources said it's a case of *"the more experienced the better."* They also told us: *"If you have connections to the local area, or are committed to settling there, so much the better."* Trainees enjoy a benefits package that sits *"above the average"* and many of the staff have reportedly *"been there for years."* The firm was disappointed, then, not to be able to offer positions to the two trainees who qualified in 2006. Reassuringly, those who were about to leave the firm on qualification harboured no ill will, telling us: *"They've been really good with helping me out. I moved back to do a last seat in the area where I am going to qualify, and they have been very supportive."*

and finally...

This *"nice and genuine"* firm is looking for trainees who are first and foremost committed to a career in the South. We'd recommend taking a look at Trethowans' recently revamped website to get more of a feel for its work and whether its style will fit with yours.

Trowers & Hamlins

the facts

Location: London, Manchester, Exeter
Number of UK partners/solicitors: 80/130
Total number of trainees: 33
Seats: 4x6 months
Alternative seats: Overseas seats
Extras: Pro bono – Toynbee Hall Legal Advice Centre

Are you looking for a City-based firm with a massive presence in the Middle East and, why not, a reputation as top dog in social housing? Surely such a firm doesn't exist.

urban legends

Even the scantiest research into Trowers reveals that property law is a major activity of the firm. Yes, trainees can try out an array of different commercial activities during the training contract, but everyone will spend six months – maybe even 12 – in property seats. On offer are seats dealing with commercial property, property litigation, construction, projects and the pièce de résistance – social housing. Indeed, so prominent is this firm in the world of affordable housing and registered social landlords (RSLs) that rarely will a deal be done in this country without Trowers having played a role. That's not to say a Trowers lawyer will be representing a client in each and every deal, but chances are the structure of, or documentation for, the deal will have been devised by someone at the firm.

As the government continues to push for regeneration of cities across the UK, Trowers continues to win business. It has been advising Yorkshire Community Housing in relation to the housing PFI on the Swarcliffe estate in Leeds, a project worth approximately £265 million, and lawyers have also represented Genesis Housing Group and Family Housing Association in relation to a £60-million, mixed-use development at the Wembley Stadium site. With the cream of the deals coming Trowers' way, *"if you want to be a social housing lawyer this is the place to be."*

But what if your interests are more mainstream? The commercial property department also takes on esteemed projects, among them the redevelopment of 40 Holborn Viaduct on behalf of the Castlemore Holborn Partnership. This deal is estimated to be valued at £100 million and threw up all manner of complications concerning rights of light, oversailing rights in respect to balconies above the viaduct, the decommissioning of an electricity sub-station and transferring underground vaults to the Corporation of London. In the construction department, as you would expect, there is quite a bit of work connected to social housing projects, and as a feather in the cap for the firm it has also been appointed to the legal panel of the Building Schools for the Future programme set up by the government to rebuild the country's schools over the next 20 years. In short, right across the real estate spectrum a trainee can expect to be exposed to elements of some of the foremost work in the UK.

antisocial behaviour...

Needless to say, the trainees start on much smaller matters. In commercial property *"you will get 30 or 40 files of your own,"* usually consisting of simple landlord-and-tenant issues and some staff conveyancing, as it's good for practice. If that sounds like a lot of files then you'll be even more impressed by the feats undertaken by the trainees in the *"lively and good fun"* social housing department, where we heard of some people having over 50 files of their own. Far from being overwhelmed, however, our sources said they *"had a great six months"* in the department and *"absolutely loved"* the work. Typically their caseload included some conveyancing, dealing with general queries from RSLs and a variety of smaller issues such as the adoption of roads by public authorities after the completion of new housing projects.

In the property litigation team, trainees again had plenty of work for RSLs (regaining possession of buildings from squatters, obtaining ASBOs against unruly tenants, that kind of thing). They enjoyed drafting statements of case and instructing barristers to appear in court; on simpler cases they were able to appear in court themselves. Anyone eager to try litigation but wanting to do so away from the property arena can go to the general commercial litigation department, which handles a range of matters from debt recovery to aircraft industry disputes. We even heard talk of some human rights issues arriving on the desk of one trainee. If, on the other hand, you are absolutely certain that you don't want to be a litigator and regard this part of the training experience as *"a hurdle you have to get over,"* there is the option of spending a mere two weeks attending a course at the College of Law.

...sociable hours

Corporate seat trainees *"rarely get their own files"* but do get the chance to *"draft simple agreements, prepare completion and post-completion documents and do filings at Companies House."* For a variation on the corporate idea you could try the highly rated finance team, *"which is all very exciting with clients all over the world."* As well as the finance aspects of, you guessed it, social housing schemes, there is also plenty of aircraft finance work, and we heard stories of trainees being responsible for delivering aircraft themselves. For the record, a pilot's licence is not necessary.

For the sake of completeness we should mention that there are a few other seats available: private client (with a niche in heritage property), employment and public sector commercial (working on PFI projects). There are also UK-based secondments to the firm's offices in Exeter and Manchester. As you might expect, niche seats are harder to get than mainstream ones so, for example, *"there are four or five seats in social housing and commercial property but only one in employment."* At least, across the departments 7pm is the definition of a long day and we didn't hear of anyone staying later than 10pm, not even in corporate. *"There's no culture of leaving the coat on your chair and leaving your computer on so that people think you are still here late at night. There are no prizes for being the saddest person in the office,"* chuckled a source.

let's build a city

Do you yearn for temperatures in the 40-50°C bracket? Then step this way, as *"everybody who comes here can go to the Middle East if they want.*" Actually, Trowers is really keen for trainees to spend six months in Abu Dhabi, Dubai, Bahrain or Oman in order to get experience of an area that "*generates a lot of fees.*" This is hardly surprising when you consider that some of the world's most ambitious projects are going on out there; for instance the $15 billion Blue City and the somewhat smaller 2.5 million sq m 'Wave' residential project, both in Oman. In particular, Trowers has developed an enviable reputation for power and water projects and has won a number of key mandates including Saudi Arabia's £1.4 billion Shoaiba project.

Though some found that their arrival overseas resulted in "*quite a culture shock,*" everyone we spoke to who had gone abroad was certain of the benefits. A car, an apartment and extra money in the pocket all help trainees acclimatise to their new surroundings, and the work itself sounds pretty interesting too. Trainees get "*a little bit of everything,*" albeit with a leaning towards corporate and litigation work. Our sources spent their time "*setting up companies,*" "*playing roles in major arbitrations,*" "*drafting submissions to court for the Arabic-speaking advocates' use*" and researching employment issues for clients looking to establish themselves in the Middle East. By all accounts, the work involves "*quite different challenges,*" so for example: "*It's sometimes hard to know when the law has become effective; there are ministerial decisions that tell you how to advise, and there can be a delay in getting these. There's a lot of work with the different ministries; lots of stuff for them to approve, lots of time in cars delivering things to people.*" Perhaps this is why the working day can be so long.

Trainees tell us that whichever Middle Eastern office you visit it's important to "*build up your reputation quickly*" as "*reputation is so much more important there than in London; it's very much a case of who you know.*" An overseas seat shouldn't lead to any sense of isolation as, in most locations, trainees share apartments and "*you get to know the person you share with really well.*" The firm also encourages the trainees in overseas offices to visit each other and, once you've got your head around taking your weekend on, say, a Thursday and Friday, you can start to enjoy membership of private clubs ("*great if you want to sunbathe on private beaches,*" something you can't do as a female on the public beaches) or 4WD adventures in the desert. If you find yourself in Muscat you'll need to purchase some glamorous clothes to wear to "*Oman's answer to the Baftas,*" an event that Trowers sponsors.

dragon-free zone

Trainees spoke warmly of the atmosphere back in the London office, and it was no surprise that the firm earned itself 53rd place in *The Sunday Times'* 2006 survey of the 100 Best Companies to Work for in the UK. As one trainee put it: "*This firm doesn't seem to have the dragons that you hear about in other firms; every one is willing to be pleasant.*" There are plenty of opportunities to play sport and an easygoing social scene that benefits from the firm's Tower Bridge location. Every two months the firm lays on food and drink to mark the fact that another billing period has been completed and to say thanks for everyone's hard work. The trainee group is still small enough for them all to know each other well and every Monday they meet for lunch and to brush up on a relevant legal topic or skill. There are also plenty of occasions when trainees can brush up on their networking skills, including a rather swish "*champagne-and-canapés client do*" at the Royal Academy.

Trowers' excellent reputation in the Middle East is undoubtedly paying dividends and the firm is thriving back in the UK too, with many a London lawyer working on matters for Middle Eastern clients. "*It is definitely growing in*

London," confirmed a source; *"all of the departments are trying to boost their profits and the firm has taken on all* [14 of] *the qualifying trainees this year plus NQs from elsewhere."*

and finally...

Combining specialisms in social housing and Middle Eastern business is not something you sit down and plan from scratch. But even if it is something *"that just happened,"* somehow it works for Trowers. Remember, you don't have to be an expert in social housing or Arabic to stand a chance of getting a training contract; indeed, the majority of trainees are neither when they first arrive.

Veale Wasbrough

the facts

Location: Bristol
Number of UK partners/solicitors: 32/73
Total number of trainees: 12
Seats: 4x6 months
Alternative seats: None
Extras: Pro bono – Bristol Law Centre, Young Enterprise

Veale Wasbrough is equipped with all you need for a successful training contract: a core commercial practice with a wide range of clients, a niche education department and a strong public sector expertise. All in the comfortable environs of the popular city of Bristol.

just one cornetto

Seagulls reel and dive in the background, water laps at the harbour wall, trainees cycle to work and partners hire ice cream vans to cool down the eager workers. Is this a Bristol idyll? Our sources at VW seemed to think so. *"Our clients like us; we are a friendly firm and there aren't too many egos around,"* said one happy camper. Lest you believe

you'll grow fat and happy on too many Magnums and coast along on VW's *"genuinely friendly"* reputation, be aware that if you come here there will be some serious graft.

Of late, VW's coco team has weighed in on five key deals for South West Ventures Fund as it keeps up its programme of investing £25 million in new regional businesses. The litigators obtained an injunction for the Joint Council of Qualifications against a Mr Quinn, who was selling fake exam certificates on the Internet. They also acted for Wiltshire Police Authority on cases including a death in custody and advised on the treatment of potentially hostile demonstrators. The firm's wide client base further includes Airbus UK, Lloyds TSB, the Highways Agency, MoD Estates and a host of local authorities. The property team acted for a foundation school on its £20 million land disposal to a residential developer. This deal is a good example of the firm's immersion in the independent schools sector.

teacher's pet

A trainee's first seat is allocated before arrival; subsequent seat allocations take account of their wishes as far as possible. *"I was a little disappointed when I found out I was doing personal injury,"* one admitted, *"but you get your own caseload and get stuck in doing client interviews very early on. It turned into an interesting experience."* Operating as Augustines Injury Law, most of the work of the claimant PI team comes via the Transport & General Workers Union, an organisation for whom the firm also handles employment claims. *"I was working on discrimination and unfair dismissal cases as well as the more mundane unlawful deduction of wages cases where you're only arguing over a couple of hundred pounds,"* said one trainee. Higher-value claims give a good grounding in how to handle yourself in negotiations, explained one source. *"The partner on the other side of the case will always try to* bully you into a position early on when they know *you are a trainee. The trick is to stand your ground.*" Such contentious applicant work is kept separate from the main employment team, where there is a diet of meatier respondent work and cases for senior executives.

Taking a seat in the schools department early on in the contract provides a good introduction to the firm as "*the education clients are a key part of our business and we do pretty much everything for them.*" Trainees enjoy the "*complete variety: you can be working on litigation, on child protection matters and on school fee debt recovery. They also do charity law in the department. You never do the same thing more than once.*" A few trainees got to play a part in the Office of Fair Trading's inquiry into alleged fee fixing at seven independent schools, and in the merger of two leading schools in Leeds, which required some delicate handling.

team building, bristol fashion
The projects department is said to be "*definitely a seat for a second year: you have to be very good at managing people as well as the workload because you will be assisting on a number of high-value projects. You have to be a bit braver as a trainee.*" Of several important projects, the regeneration of Bristol's harbourside stands out. Here the team has been advising Bristol City Council in respect to the multimillion-pound development, a scheme that fed work through to the firm's property lawyers too. Trainees were "*drafting leases, completing licences and stamp duty returns, selling unregistered land; things like that.*" One told us: "*I found it all much more interesting in practice than when studying it.*" However much the work appeals to the trainee, though, it is "*undoubtedly the people that make this department a fantastic team.*" In fact, we got the impression that the whole firm was verging on one big love-in. "*We're positive people who work well together,*" explained a source.

Helpful colleagues may make finding your feet in busy coco a little easier, but the trainees still need to tackle "*challenging work.*" The seat is "*full of peaks and troughs,*" with one trainee's highlight being the completion of a business sale that they had seen through "*from start to finish.*" Expect a lot of drafting and to be let loose on clients. Said one interviewee: "*They are more than happy for you to be the first port of call, fielding enquiries.*" Dealing with lawyers on the other side of a transaction is equally useful experience, this time for honing assertiveness.

vealy interesting
VW's courtyard office, right behind Bristol Hippodrome, may not be the plushest on the block but "*it has a great deal of character and lots of beams and features.*" When tired of 'Abba Mania', 'Oliver!' and 'The Rocky Horror Show' next door, trainees get involved in local TSG events and activities organised by the firm's social committee. These include bowling, booze cruises, summer barbecues and seasonal parties. Regular Friday night drinks take place down by the water, where bars and restaurants jostle for position on the harbourside. The laidback vibe of The Watershed is drawing in the punters at the moment. Staff don't always wait until the end of the week for refreshment; in the heat of the summer the firm "*hired an ice cream van for the courtyard and we all took turns to go and visit it.*" One opportunist joked that "*we'll be asking for a sauna in the winter.*" The firm's sports teams play other firms, clients and "*anyone a bit professional.*" "*We're not overly competitive,*" said one trainee; "*that would be unseemly.*"

The hours at the firm are conducive to a life outside work and "*the firm strongly encourages getting involved in extra-curricular activities.*" One trainee "*was caught in the PI department after 6pm and the partner laughed at me and told me to go home.*" That said, we were also informed that everyone wants to work hard and "*there is scope to push yourself and take on more responsibility*" if you want it. The firm's size – not too big, not too small – means you won't compromise on work quality, but one trainee commented that "*it's just nice that you can walk around the office and know who everyone is.*" Much of the feedback pointed to the idea that "*the firm appreciates that it is worth investing time in its trainees*" and tailors the experience to suit their individual needs. Consequently, five of the six qualifiers took jobs with the firm in September 2006, three of them going into the schools department.

and finally...

A summer work experience scheme lets interested applicants experience VW life to the full. Pay attention as there is much to learn about the work of this good-natured firm.

Walker Morris

the facts
Location: Leeds
Number of UK partners/solicitors: 45/110
Total number of trainees: 30
Seats: 6x4 months
Alternative seats: Occasional secondments

A commercial big hitter with a Yorkshire home, Walker Morris is a serious player in the national market. Independent to its core, it is a down-to-earth firm that shows no sign of being unfaithful to its Leeds roots.

big game

Touring Leeds' legal landscape is a bit like going on an African safari; while there are a lot of smaller animals to spot, most attention is paid to the Big Six. Without stretching the analogy too far, just as six beasts dominate the safari scene

(that's rhino, elephant, buffalo, lion, leopard and whale, by the way), six firms prevail in Yorkshire's main city. WM is the only true independent among them; the other five – Pinsent Masons, Eversheds, Addleshaw Goddard, Hammonds and DLA Piper – are multi-site national firms with Leeds offices.

You could argue that WM has as much in common with a small elite of independent firms across the country as its fellow Big Sixers. We're talking about firms like Burges Salmon or Dickinson Dees; those that are committed to staying within their region while commanding respect and winning work on a national scale. The fact that WM's turnover topped £45 million last year and allows the firm to be very profitable is testament to the success of the strategy. Trainees say their firm is "*committed to a single centre of excellence*" and shows no sign of opening up in London or anywhere else. They are utterly convinced of the one-city strategy, telling us: "*If someone makes a decision you know exactly where it's come from. It's not been drafted in from elsewhere.*"

WM is one of those firms that sends trainees on a six-seat tour of the firm. One rookie who'd just dropped off the conversion-course conveyor belt told us: "*I've only done two years of law in the classroom so it's good to see as many areas of law as possible.*" It looks as if HR has a knack for playing Cupid, managing to "*know who to place with whom by matching personality styles.*" Each four-month date hitches the trainee to either an associate or partner, depending on the department. Mind you, the relationship need not be entirely monogamous, and trainees are encouraged to embrace an "*interlinking*" culture of "*going into other departments and finding expertise.*" If it's not a match made in heaven by the end of your seat, "*at least you've not lost a quarter of your training contract to something you don't enjoy.*" For first-years, the seats are like blind dates in that they are picked for them; second-years get together and divide the seats between themselves and the firm will step in only where they cannot reach agreement.

supersize me

A common first-year seat is property, which brings exposure to meaty commercial deals for clients such as Starbucks, Monsoon, Polo Ralph Lauren, RBS, Taylor Woodrow and Bellway Homes, and public sector bodies such as Lancashire County Council. With national clients comes national work, so when a retailer such as Debenhams turns to the firm, the trainee will help out with matters affecting parts of its multimillion-pound UK-wide property portfolio. Once into their stride they *"have more control and get files to run,"* ultimately *"dealing with queries when clients ring."* The hours in property are reputed to be *"sociable"* and it is regarded as a good place to start your training contract. There's one possible twist: the property seat could be taken with the planning team, which strikes trainees as an *"odd first seat,"* being *"something you've never done before"* and lacking the *"basics"* of client contact and simple letter drafting.

Corporate has a *"go-get-it"* vibe and a more frenetic pace than elsewhere. If you're okay with the longer hours, the intensity of the pace and the sheer number of people in the department, you'll be just fine. *"You tend to get your face known very quickly,"* one enthusiast told us; *"corporate work is so all-encompassing, it will expose you to lots of people."* WM gets a decent slice of the pie when it comes to corporate deals. To give you a taster, it handled BUPA's acquisition of Associated Nursing Services worth over £320 million, a deal tipped as one of the largest regional deals of 2005. One corporate-minded source found their role on two AIM flotations *"really hands-on and client-facing."* Drafting ancillary transaction agreements, board minutes and resolutions, helping with due diligence and collating docu-

ments are all part and parcel of a corporate seat, getting you so involved with the deal that you can share the pleasure when it's all signed and sealed. Closely aligned to the corporate team, the commercial lawyers have been gathered into one super-sized team covering a broad sweep of activities for public and private sector clients. It sounds like you've got to *"snap up"* work when sitting in the commercial department, because *"those wanting to qualify here won't specialise when they do, so they're eager to see aspects of work as a trainee."*

who ate all the pies?

Earning your litigation wings could take you into the complex world of construction litigation, where the firm has been representing Wembley Arch steel contractor Cleveland Bridge in the claim brought by main contractor Multiplex. A sporting theme is to be found in the work of the insolvency litigation team, which trainees confirm has a *"Boy's Own"* feel to it. The firm famously advised in the administration of Bradford City FC and the restructuring of Leeds United FC. As a matter of fact, WM does loads of sports-related work, everything from broadcast and sponsorship agreements to injury claims and tribunal and disciplinary appeals. Most recently the firm was especially proud to have represented Steve McClaren in negotiations with The FA over his appointment as Sven's replacement as England manager. If you don't believe in footie without a pie, the WM litigators can provide these too, having won a recent Court of Appeal case over the famous 'Melton Mowbray' name and which pork pie producers can and can't use it.

So what if you're not sports mad? The rewards of the *"non-hierarchical"* employment department are plenty of *"early responsibility"* and *"non-intrusive management."* And if you sit with the small tax team, you can expect an *"intellectually demanding"* four months where, to put it bluntly, *"you're not much use if you can't handle lots of responsibility."* Providing corporate support on major acquisitions is one aspect of tax work, and share schemes are also guaranteed to keep you busy. When trainees are particularly drawn to a department they commonly return to it for a second four-month stint to prepare them for qualification.

chipping in

Imagine the scene. You've a problem that seems really daft but you need an answer, pronto. Trainees *"tend to help each other out,"* so *"if you've got a silly question just e-mail it around and everyone will chip in with their answers."* Feeling out of your depth shouldn't be too much of an issue as *"supervisors are good at gauging how much responsibility you can handle."* Boredom wasn't an issue for our sources either; *"I haven't been given any rubbish and definitely feel I've been stretched."* As for hours, we've been told time and again about WM's *"reasonable give and take"* when it comes to staying late. Longer hours do crop up, especially in corporate, though *"you're always out before midnight"* and the firm is likely to *"get the pizzas in"* to see you through.

The likelihood of being kept on after training is pretty high, though in September 2006, just nine of the 14 qualifiers stayed with the firm. The trainees we spoke to put the firms usually healthier statistics down to WM's *"obvious investment in people."* The fact that over 50% of the partners trained at the firm shows this talk of security isn't just hot air. That said, it has escaped neither our attention nor that of trainees that WM's partnership is currently *"a fairly closed shop,"* just one contributing factor to the firm's £600k-plus profits per equity partner figure. Admittedly the prospects of partnership may seem like the least of your worries when you haven't even secured a training contract, but it's amazing how time flies when you're having fun...

all work and no play?

WM occupies three separate premises though dreams of bringing all staff together under one roof. The HQ, an imposing brick building that it is *"bursting at the seams,"* is *"definitely not the most glamorous office"* in town, but trainees rise above such superficial matters, telling us: *"You have to decide what your priorities are."*

Trainees say they have *"no airs and graces; what you see is what you get."* Their *"straight-talking"* style matches many of the clients they encounter – *"Yorkshire businessmen who have a reputation for being direct."* As to whether they need local ties to get hired, generally *"most have a connection with Leeds, as the firm doesn't want us to run off to London at the first opportunity."* More than this *"there's a strong sense of team spirit, and you've got to want to get involved"* or you'll *"struggle to integrate"* and risk *"sliding into the background."* Trainees bond at events organised by the social committee and rub shoulders with partners at the informal end-of-month drinks, an event where it is wise to *"go and make your face known."* On Friday nights, many people end up in Bar Work, just spitting distance from the office. The Christmas party season involves *"quite a lot of feeding"* at firm-wide, departmental, team and trainee parties. Add in an annual trainee dinner and the summer party and you'll almost never need to visit a supermarket. Our interviewees were very happy about the *"general inclusion of trainees"* in departmental events – go-karting, golf days, jaunts to Prague and Amsterdam – with the banking and insolvency departments' client-wooing trips to the races meaning they are *"widely touted as the glamour seats for perks."*

If you thought lawyers had little time for art and other such nonsense then think again. WM has sponsored a slew of events, our favourite being an annual painting competition for five to eleven-year-olds. The best of the entries are compiled into a calendar that is sent out to clients and other contacts. Tragically our 2006 calendar got lost in the post.

and finally...

Walker Morris has uncompromising commitment to its one-site strategy and its independence. As proud of its sociable atmosphere as it is of its roots, the firm is worth more than a second glance if your heart is set on a commercial career in Leeds.

Ward Hadaway

the facts

Location: Newcastle-upon-Tyne
Number of UK partners/solicitors: 58/142
Total number of trainees: 20
Seats: 4x6 months
Alternative seats: None

Newcastle is on a high, and it must be infectious because the energetic Ward Hadaway has also got a case of the sky's the limits. Newcastle's resurgence manifests itself in the riverside landscape, where the Millennium Bridge, the refurbished Baltic Flour Mills and the Sage are the new monuments to economic development and civic pride. As they survey the scene from their Quayside offices, it's clear to Ward Hadaway trainees that "*the Newcastle market is really taking off.*"

want to be a part of it...

'New-Castle, New-Castle...' Okay so its not as catchy as Ol' Blue Eyes' tribute to the Big Apple, but when you, your firm and your city are all on a roll, who needs New York? Made in 1988, Geordie firm Ward Hadaway has always had close links with the local business community. Managing partner Jamie Martin chairs the North East's CBI, and, together with local national newspaper *The*

Journal, each year the firm publishes the 'Fastest Fifty' league table, which identifies the fastest-growing companies in the region.

WH's own client list is fat with regional names: The Sage Group, Northumbrian Taverns, Pride Valley Foods and a new client pub chain Ultimate Leisure. Then there's Entec UK, one of the country's largest environmental and engineering consultancies, and Able UK, a leading name in the dismantling and decommissioning of ships, oil rigs and power stations. The make-up of the firm's client list reflects the new economic activity of the region: no longer reliant on traditional mining and heavy industry, the North East is diversifying into microelectronics, biotechnology, offshore oil and gas and the service sector. Newcastle has been designated as a Science City and hopes to promote activity in areas such as stem cell research, ageing and energy. An active regional development agency, One NorthEast, is leading the way on the reclamation and regeneration of places such as the former Vane Tempest Colliery at Seaham. This 32-hectare brownfield site in County Durham saw WH involved on behalf of a consortium of house builders.

Public services, including health and education, play a key role in the region and have an important place in WH's business plans. The firm was recently selected as one of three legal advisers to English Heritage, and is one of just a dozen firms nationwide on the NHS Litigation Authority panel, a mandate that allows it to defend hundreds of clinical negligence claims. Other public sector instructions evidence the spread of WH's tentacles up and down the country, including PFI matters and the LIFT projects that are renewing and developing primary care facilities. Trainees are proud of the firm's extending reach and understand that it is fuelling lateral hires from the likes of Pinsents, Hammonds and Eversheds. Bringing in new partners and associates has resulted in bigger, better instructions from clients, thus making the firm even more attractive to new lawyers.

ghostly encounters

The WH training scheme is simple: "*The firm is very keen for you to do a seat in the three main areas: commercial, litigation and property.*" Most trainees then make a return visit to a preferred area for their final six months. The two powerhouse departments – litigation and property – are in a building called Sandgate House, where lawyers work in closed offices. The commercial department occupies the adjacent Keel Row building and works open plan. Because they work in each of the two buildings, trainees get to know almost everyone. Said one who was approaching the end of his contract: "*I know about 80 to 90% of the firm now.*"

Trainees are fully aware of the dynamics within the firm and what it really excels at. "*Its expertise in litigation and property is the most well-regarded in the region,*" acknowledged one. The first of these departments offers seats in employment, commercial litigation and healthcare, and there is no shortage of takers. The NHS-dominated healthcare seat means "*assisting on a significant number of files, quite a lot of them high-value cases of cerebral palsy and other birth injuries.*" Trainees also run personal injury files for the NHS, usually cases brought by employees who have been hurt during the course of their employment. Their work involves attending hearings, taking witness statements, preparing reports for the client, reading and summarising medical records and drafting instructions to experts and counsel. "*It's rare to go to a trial, and generally you only see bits of each file as clin neg cases can run over four or five years, but as there are so many files you do get to learn about the whole process.*"

The commercial litigators have taken on a number of interesting cases, including the judicial review of a decision not to allow 13 so-called 'ghost ships' to be towed from a US naval base in Virginia to be dismantled and recycled in Hartlepool. We quizzed trainees on how they fared in the department and whether day-to-day life was dominated by mundane tasks and photocopying. Apparently not. "*The secretarial support is significant and there are paralegals, legal execs and office juniors.*" Praise, too, for supervising partners: "*Mine was so busy but she still gave me a lot of time, and I learned all the fundamentals of letter writing and claim forms, etc.*"

slammer time!

The property division has seats in property litigation, landlord and tenant, development work and planning, and trainees gave great feedback on their experiences. "*I have done everything from corporate support, where there were 27 properties in the deal, to enquiries and searches, landlord and tenant work, drafting and reviewing leases, and plenty of reports on title.*" During a planning seat one trainee had attended a fairly lengthy inquiry where residents had been "*up in arms*" over a development proposal. "*We acted for the council and I got to see the whole process,*" they told us. An interesting fact about the planning team is that "*there are lawyers and town planners working together, which is a unique selling point. The qualified planners deal more with the appeals and the lawyers deal more with the technical issues and drafting the planning agreements.*"

Property is a popular area for qualification, perhaps as a result of the firm's growing reputation nationally and its involvement in the 'Mexican wave' property law outsourcing programme. Described by one trainee as "*a real endorsement,*" giant London law firm Lovells has selected WH as one of a small band of regional firms to which it will subcontract its clients' lower-value property deals. It's a win-win-win situation for WH, Lovells and its clients.

In Keel Row the commercial department has seats in corporate finance, banking and technology. According to the firm's own blurb the corporate team completed 60 deals with a value of £320 million in 2005. You can cut those figures any way you like, but what they add up to are small and medium-sized transactions, including several AIM flotations, a little plc work and the odd international gig. Highlights from last year include the sale of northern-based engineering company Hedley Purvis to US-based Actuant, £14 million of share placings for AIM-listed Tanfield Group and the sale of Shanks Group's hazardous waste operations to Onyx Environmental for £28 million. Trainees speak positively about their experiences working with the teams that run these and other deals. Last but not least, seats can also be taken with the private client team.

well-tuned

The Pitcher & Piano is effectively the firm's third office, with the trainees often meeting there to discuss work and share experiences. Go on a Friday and *"it will be a complete mix: people just fall out of work into the place... you could, literally, because it's just below the office."* The two main social events of the year are a summer barbecue and the Christmas party, with the intervening months filled with *"a lot of camaraderie between people, a lot of socialising and a lot of sport."* When checking a rumour that the footie team had lost its best player – a semi-pro who went off to university – we were told: *"Really? Which one? We've three semi-professionals on the team."* Clearly this source hadn't spent enough time gossiping in the Pitcher & Piano.

One man who keeps his ear to the ground is managing partner Jamie Martin; at the very least *"he knows everybody's name."* As did a WH legend, recently retired post room chap Gordon Robson. *"Everyone loved him. At his retirement do he got the best send-off."* By all accounts Gordon's shoes as most popular employee remain unfilled.

Although trainees are bored of hearing that Dickinson Dees is the grand old man in Newcastle and Ward Hadaway is the hungry new kid on the block, the comparison is still useful for students. This is how one source put it: *"Compared to Dickinson Dees, Ward Hadaway is ambitious and moving up the ladder quickly but not yet settled in its structure. We still have lots of young partners... and that's a very persuasive argument for coming here."* The only thing we'll add is that the firm is no longer the youngster it was, and there's now a strong chasing pack of local firms. Six of the eight September 2006 qualifiers felt this was the only place for them.

and finally...

Ward Hadaway has moved into a new phase, one in which it has a growing interest in work beyond the North East and, who knows, maybe applicants beyond the region too.

Warner Goodman & Streat

the facts

Location: Southampton, Fareham, Portsmouth
Number of UK partners/solicitors: 19/32
Total number of trainees: 8
Seats: 3x8 months
Alternative seats: None

Warner Goodman & Streat has been a staple on the Hampshire legal scene for over 150 years. With three main offices in Southampton, Fareham and Portsmouth, plus two satellite offices in Park Gate and Waterlooville, this firm is ideal for those looking for a sizeable general regional practice that is developing some commercial muscle.

streat life

Warner Goodman & Streat has been around since 1852 and is one of the oldest practices on the South Coast. The firm today is the product of mergers that took place in 1971 (when Warner & Son merged with Goodman & Kent) and in 1981 (when Warner Goodman & Co merged with Streat Daunt & Farmiloe). Staff numbers now total more than 200.

Traditional private client and crime practice has more recently been accompanied by an expansion in commercial business. Hence the launch of 'Warnergoodman commercial' in Southampton in 2005 and the creation of a new commercial team in the Portsmouth office in 2006. The firm has won business from a number of prominent local clients including the Hendy Group, Cadogan Holidays, Botleigh Grange Hotel and Cleansing Service Group. Away from the commercial action there is a large residential conveyancing practice (which accounts for a third of all work) and a strong crime department tackling mostly everyday crime.

Our interviewees were at pains to stress that, although Warner Goodman & Streat does retain some "*high street elements*" (it has a legal aid franchise in crime and family law), it is not a high street firm in the classic sense. Their evidence is the firm's large size, its thriving commercial practice and its complex wills, probate, tax and estate planning work for privately paying individuals. Trainees also say that this "*professional but friendly*" firm has "*invested a lot in IT*" and boasts "*a good case-management system.*" This includes a case-tracking service whereby clients can log on and check the progress of their conveyancing at the click of a mouse.

lucky number three

Train here and you'll undertake three eight-month seats chosen from seven core practice groups: commercial, residential property, civil litigation, crime, family, probate, employment and financial services. Our interviewees liked this arrangement, telling us: "*You can get more involved in what you're doing*" in a longer seat. The firm also looks to be pretty flexible when it comes to trainee's choices. We heard that one recruit was given a four-week taster in a department to see whether they'd like to do a full seat there. You may not always get your first choice when it comes to seats but "*over the course of your two years you do get to go in the area you most want.*" While "*nothing is compulsory,*" sources say that "*most people tend to do residential conveyancing as it's available in most of the offices.*" They agree that this "*busy*" practice group offers "*good training*" and enjoy working in the open-plan format that the group has adopted in all offices.

The financial services department has grown quickly over the last ten years. It is now at a point where its lawyers are not only advising the firm's clients, but also assisting local solicitors who don't have the requisite expertise to advise their own clients.

ready to ex-parte

Beyond these two areas of work, a trainee's contract will be shaped after taking their wishes into account. The different office locations offer different seats, so each trainee will have a slightly different experience. For example, private client and financial services are based in Fareham; crime and family are based at Southampton and Portsmouth; PI is predominantly offered in the Southampton office and commercial property is available in Southampton and Portsmouth. The very popular employment seat can only be done in Southampton. You can't lay claim to any one office, but "*you can tell the firm where you'd like to go.*" By virtue of their size and the number of seats offered, Portsmouth and Southampton are the key locations and we can also report that the two *"smaller and quieter"* satellite offices at Park Gate and Waterlooville which handle *"mainly residential conveyancing and family"* do not normally host trainees.

Trainees are happy with the quality of work and training they receive. *"I'm not just given dross; I'm a valued member of the team,"* exclaimed one interviewee, while another raved that *"the balance between the amount of responsibility I get and the support I get"* was just right. In a family seat, for example, trainees run their own files and conduct their own advocacy in ex parte injunctions and directions hearings. Our sources also felt that the firm invests in them, which could explain the healthy retention rate on qualification in 2006 when all three who completed their training took NQ jobs. *"Providing they can find the space, the firm wants to keep people on."*

brief details

Southampton is *"the commercial arm of the firm"* as well as *"the biggest office and biggest fee earner."* In addition to the commercial teams there are also PI and medical negligence lawyers busy here. Trainees report a *"fantastic atmosphere"* and *"spacious offices,"* with hours running from 9am until 5.15pm with an hour and a quarter for lunch. The office is strategically located opposite the law courts. Like the Portsmouth office, the Southampton site is close to the sea and *"plenty of bars and clubs."* One popular haunt, The Chambers, is *"just down the road from the office."* Ocean Village in Southampton and Gunwharf Quays in Portsmouth are also good venues for post-work fun. The Portsmouth office is *"not too hardnosed, but gets on with its work."* As a reminder, it has conveyancing, commercial property, crime, family and civil litigation. Fareham is the administrative hub and provides *"a nice atmosphere to work in."* The hours are *"generally 9am to 5pm unless you are in the middle of something."* When they go out in Fareham, trainees sometimes visit Café Tusk for a curry. Even if you visit just one or two offices during your training contract, you do *"get to know the other offices"* when seeing clients. For example, even though the private client team is centralised in Fareham, you could find yourself in Southampton to visit a client who lives closer to that office and wants some probate advice.

When it comes to trainee get-togethers, our sources say the firm leaves them to make their own arrangements. *"We often go to Southampton"* because *"there's more to do there,"* explained one. They also get involved in the Southampton Trainee Solicitors Group, *"which holds regular social events,"* and Southampton's Young Professionals Group. To organise firm-wide events there's a social club and an online monthly newsletter called *The Brief*. Its contributors work across the offices, writing about such newsworthy events as target figures and *"who's had a baby."* The firm-wide Christmas party *"is always good fun."* It alternates between Fareham, Southampton and Portsmouth and for the last one the firm *"booked a hotel – there was a three-course meal and dancing, and people let their hair down."* In 2006 it seems there won't be a firm-wide event, but individual office party preparations had already begun when we rang trainees in August. Talk about keen.

and finally...

Warner Goodman & Streat is certainly worth considering if you're looking to work in a South Coast firm that neatly combines commercial practice with services for individuals. The efforts made to make the firm feel 'as one' are commendable.

Watson, Farley & Williams LLP

the facts
Location: London
Number of UK partners/solicitors: 38/70
Total number of trainees: 24
Seats: 6x4 months
Alternative seats: Overseas seats
Extras: Pro bono – Toynbee Hall Legal Advice Centre; language training

Watson, Farley & Williams began business in London 24 years ago, and from its earliest days specialising in ship finance it has evolved into a law firm with six other offices worldwide.

around the world in 730 days
WFW's mid-tier London operation is divided into four key groups. The substantial finance group encompasses traditional shipping finance, asset finance, straightforward banking and insolvency. The corporate group takes on mid-market corporate transactions, employment/immigration, competition, IP, property and, increasingly, major projects. The litigation group has a particular emphasis on banking, maritime, energy and aviation cases, especially multi-jurisdiction ship finance enforcement proceedings. And last but not least there is a team of crack tax lawyers whose expertise in high-value leasing, international finance and litigation is widely recognised. The firm's business activities are described well on its website, as are the client sectors most important to it, namely shipping, aviation and other transportation, power and energy, banking and telecoms.

The firm has adopted the popular six-seat model for its training scheme. Litigation, finance and corporate are on the cards for all, as is an overseas posting to Paris, Piraeus, Bangkok or Singapore, or maybe even the newest office, Hamburg. For their other seats trainees try tax, employment, EC competition or property, and then commonly return to their intended qualification group for their last seat. One trainee deemed the six-seat model "*a winner*" because they wanted the training to include as many things as possible. To help trainees to identify the things that most appeal, "*people come and chat to us about their area of law for an hour and a half.*" This, we sense, is characteristic of a firm where no one is left in the dark.

WFW's international clientele ensures an international training. On the books are tanker owners Golar LNG and Brunei Gas Carriers, cruise lines Carnival and Royal Caribbean, several major airlines, Kowloon Canton Railway and a host of international banks including African Export-Import Bank, Nomura, Bank of Nova Scotia, BNP Paribas, Citibank, Close Brothers, Credit Suisse and Royal Bank of Canada. To see how the average trainee encounters such clients, let's examine the most common seats.

wind farm warriors
The finance sector, particularly asset finance, is where the firm started, and it is still important today. "*It is classic Watson Farley work,*" explained one trainee. All do a stint in shipping finance, where they encounter everything from smaller deals on which they can play a substantial role, to major projects such as the biggest ever recorded shipping deal, a $1.6 billion financing for Euronav. "*Although you can be useful from day one, you get given better tasks the more you get to grips with it. All the bits fall into place and you realise why you are doing things.*" Such as? "*Drafting smaller security documents – although not the main loan agreements – attending deal closings and registering ship mortgages at the Bermudan Registry of Shipping.*" In Bermuda? "*No, unfortunately it's in London, as is the Panamanian registry.*" Even if they can't magic far-flung trips like rabbits from hats, there is considerable praise for supervisors, who are

willing to take sufficient time out to train and explain everything.

What really struck us this year was the rise of energy and power-related work in the corporate department. Take a specific projects seat and you'll end up with an *"intellectually demanding"* role on *"pretty tricky large-scale transactions."* WFW has surged forward in the financing of energy projects, especially in the area of LNG where it already had a good name in relation to tanker financing. Renewable energy has become another major source of work – pick a wind farm anywhere in the world and there's usually a WFW office close by. Recent instructions include advice to BNP Paribas as loan arranger on a 26.2 MW wind farm in Greece, as well as advice to Falck Renewables and Fred Olsen Renewables on the leasing and financing of various wind farms in Scotland. These are just the tip of the iceberg, it seems, because the lawyers have also been working for Viridis on six German wind farms, Matrix-Securities on the acquisitions of 14 Italian wind farms, and Eclipse Energy on a £5 million pre-IPO fundraising for a UK offshore hybrid generation project involving two gas fields and a wind farm. Trainees loved being involved in all this windy work. Said one: *"You start with zero knowledge and end up knowing a fair amount about renewable energy. I spent a lot of time doing Internet research, looking for statistics. It may sound corny but you feel green, like you are doing something worthwhile. If you work for a corporate law firm there's always a sense that you have sold your soul to the devil, but at least with this work you feel like you are doing something positive. It's also very 'now', there's a lot about it on the news."*

ain't no mountain high enough

The litigation and arbitration handled by WFW is often energy, shipping or project finance-related. One of the largest and most multi-layered cases in the firm's history also happened to be the world's largest (and India's first) investment treaty arbitration. WFW's client was the Government of India, the claim was worth billions of dollars and the problems all related to the Dabhol power project in Maharashtra, built by a US consortium led by Enron, GE and Bechtel. As you might imagine, a trainee can only make a tiny contribution to such a large, long-running matter, but their contribution may be important. *"There was a lot of research,"* recalled one trainee of the Dahbol case; *"a lot of jurisdictional questions as well as contractual issues."* Trainees liked the fact that they were *"given enough time to read into cases... I got the impression that people wanted you to understand them."* In commercial litigation there will always be a mountain of paperwork to manage, and as at any firm, trainees must climb these mountains on occasion. People also told us of their work on smaller cases, some of which gave them court time, either solo performances before High Court masters (*"great to get one under your belt"*) or less nerve-wracking trips accompanying barristers.

WFW invites all trainees to sample life in another office. *"It's fantastic, one of the best things about this place,"* said a source gleefully. Rarely does anyone turn down the opportunity; indeed, it would be odd to be attracted to such an international firm and yet not want to leave the UK for a spell. Bangkok means litigation and corporate work, flash accommodation and an endless string of Thai islands to occupy your free time. The Singapore posting is for finance and shipping work, with a little corporate and litigation thrown in, a view of the harbour from your desk in the Hitachi Tower and a home just on the edge of China Town. *"Singapore has a reputation for being sterile, which it is in a way, but that makes it a really easy place to live and work in. My four months there were great,"* one source recalled. Do a stint in Paris in the firm's Champs-Elysée office and you'll live in an apartment in Le Marais. The UK trainee social scene in the French capital is generally packed, and invariably you'll have a string of mates wanting to visit. Indeed, we hear the WFW trainees are not averse to a spot of inter-office socialising, so things can get quite busy. Close to Athens, the Piraeus seat is ideal for anyone with a taste for shipping finance, and it sounds as if the new, hoped-for Hamburg seat will satisfy similar tastes.

a sweet deal

If you think the training package sounds attractive then you're not alone. The people we spoke to this year were just as enthusiastic as their predecessors have always been. A famously contented firm, WFW has an inclusive and welcoming culture. *"The size of the firm lends itself to that. As a trainee you come in as part of a small intake and you get almost a family feel. You are made very welcome by the people in the previous intake; there's a very supportive team ethic."* Even the way certain partners run deals enhances a sense of inclusion: *"Each time we have team meetings the partner listens to everyone – everyone chips in."* Trainees believe the importance of full involvement and proper responsibility can't be overemphasized. *"You'll be working with an assistant or the partner directly on a deal,"* as opposed to the set-up in the biggest firms handling the very biggest deals around. There *"the number of people working on one transaction is huge and a trainee's work has to pass down through a number of layers."*

The hours trainees work can sometimes be silly; at other times they're easy. *"Just say there's no sweatshop attitude here,"* our sources suggested. Should you need to work late you can have a word with the most important person in the firm – Philippe the chef. Mention his name to a trainee and they'll rhapsodise for hours if you let them. Even if you've little or no appetite, the canteen is the smart place to be if you want to do a spot of networking. *"You can just go in and sit down with various people in different departments and at dif-*

ferent levels." Periodically there are firm-wide social events such as a giant games and drinks party, or the annual Christmas bash at a posh hotel. More regularly, the trainees meet up in a local bar, say Sosho Match or The Prophet. There is certainly no shortage of bars and restaurants to go to in the Liverpool Street area, and plenty of places to mooch at lunchtime... should you manage to tear yourself away from Philippe's food that is. Nine of the ten September 2006 qualifiers couldn't bear to do that and accepted NQ positions with the firm.

and finally...

Watson, Farley & Williams may be spreading the net internationally, but it's still sufficiently compact in London to be able to offer training that feels personal as well as rewarding. With so much going on in relation to energy, transportation and finance, these business worlds will clearly provide the most common backdrop to your training.

Wedlake Bell

the facts

Location: London
Number of UK partners/solicitors: 40/50
Total number of trainees: 14
Seats: 4x6 seats
Alternative seats: None

When asked to sum up Wedlake Bell, one trainee told us: *"This is a full-service, medium-sized firm which does commercial property, corporate and private client work with all the trimmings."*

aiming high

Wedlake Bell claims to have *"a long history and a modern approach."* And we can see what it means. It has been a feature of the London legal community since 1780, exhibiting a classic private client and property-heavy West End profile. More recently the corporate and commercial practices have grown and work with an international dimension is also becoming more common. We don't think it's lost its traditional persona entirely, but there's plenty on offer at the firm to keep a modern-minded recruit happy.

All four of a trainee's seats are assigned at the start of the two years, when new recruits notify HR of the departments they'd most like to try. *"You are pretty much guaranteed your first choice and are likely to get your second;"* some lucky trainees get all four. Corporate and property are the largest departments and take two trainees each per rotation. Once the schedule has been fixed *"you can change with someone else should there be any mutual dissatisfaction."* Sounds simple enough.

There are two seats available in the corporate department, working either on AIM floats or small-to-medium-sized M&A transactions. The trainees' reports on AIM work were consistently positive; for example one had done *"lots of corporate restructurings, be it a football club or a mining company. I was drafting directors' appointments, option agreements and peripheral documents, as well as proofreading prospectuses and doing lots of verification."* By contrast those doing private M&A tended to be given *"more company secretarial stuff – setting up shelf companies and doing lots of drudge."* The firm's top deal of last year was a £64 million fundraising for Serica Energy, which listed on both AIM in London and TSXV in Toronto. The company's assets were located in Indonesia, the North Sea and Spain, and the transaction involved bringing a British Virgin Islands corporation to the UK. Another major deal was the sale of a lawnmower business for client Hayter, whose American parent company had gone into Chapter 11 bankruptcy. The transaction involved complex international issues concerning the jurisdiction of the US bankruptcy courts over a UK company.

trading in london landmarks

"Commercial property is the powerhouse department of the firm, all the other departments link into it." In one of the two commercial property seats trainees encounter the usual *"licenses to assign, leases and rent reviews, plus the occasional residential bits and pieces. It's fantastic because you get given up to 40 files and they're all yours to play with."* Of course it takes years to get to the stage when you can run the big deals, but for readers with a long-term view here's what the firm has achieved of late – the £25 million redevelopment of The Oval cricket ground for Surrey County Cricket Club; the £30 million purchase of the Chelsea College of Art & Design building and the Ralph West Hall student residence in Battersea, London, for a client to turn them into posh flats; and the purchase, development and subsequent sale of the former Harrods depository site in Knightsbridge, London, valued at £140 million.

"Business Recovery [that's insolvency] *is a great seat; there's lots of sexy High Court litigation and agency work for Scottish and US firms. It's mainly Chancery and Queen's Bench Division work with occasional cases making it to the Court of Appeal and House of Lords."* As you might expect from a litigation-heavy seat, there will be plenty of pagination and bundling to get through. One trainee reported that they'd *"got to attend a three-week trial... I was there to provide support and take notes, and my star turn was passing a witness bundle to the witness."* The firm's construction unit is made up of six fee earners, and a stint here is *"ideal for those with an academic bent as there's lots of good-quality work, contractual problems and research."* Intriguingly, the clientele was described as *"architects, developers and a Malaysian gold mine."* To keep them on their toes, in construction seats the trainees are required to man the National Specialist Contractors Council legal advice helpline. This involves *"giving advice on convoluted contractual arrangements, for example*

to a carpet layer who wants to get paid. You even get the odd call from someone with a parking ticket and the bailiffs coming round."

MIPCOM (media, IP and commercial litigation) has all sorts of interesting cases. The firm has been assisting Lacoste with brand protection, and recently advised on a case that led to two members of a counterfeiting ring going to prison. IP litigators also successfully defended Highbury Leisure Ltd when it was sued for breach of copyright by the magazine publisher IPC Media, who said that Highbury's *Home* magazine had unlawfully reproduced elements of design commonly found in IPC's *Ideal Home*. Last, but definitely not least, we must mention the private client department, which grew in 2005 after the arrival of extra lawyers from specialist firm Beattie & Co, and from Jones Day. Growing the department in this way is a clear indication of the value WB places on private clients, and the new joiners between them brought over 1,000 new clients to the firm. Most of the private client work is too confidential to mention, but we did note several examples of the restructuring of multimillion-pound offshore family trusts and the launch and management of various UK charities. Naturally there are straightforward wills and probate matters for trainees to get stuck into, plus the occasional probate dispute, which can make for interesting reading.

life and times

The hours trainees work are typical for a firm of this size and style – generally 9am until 7pm – *"but you can get stung in a corporate run of 10 o'clocks."* The highs and lows our sources spoke about were also reassuringly typical. The highs – *"a completion meeting in corporate in my first few weeks"* and *"getting involved in a big three-week trial."* The lows – *"photocopying and bundling,"* in one case for *"ten days solid, numbering documents in a meeting room. You just stood there numbering away, coming out blinking at the end of the day."*

Our impression is of a firm where trainees see all sides of the job, good, bad and in between, but they don't run the risk of falling through cracks as they can in bigger firms.

Which brings us nicely to the reasons trainees gave us for choosing WB in the first place. *"I was looking for quality training where they'd let me have a life,"* explained one. *"I had friends in top-20 firms with no life, and they advised me not to dismiss the firms in the bottom half of the top 100."* Another trainee agreed: *"Here I think you can get quality work without getting flogged to death."* The people you'll work with are *"those who stand on their own two feet and won't disappear into a crowd."* When you're the only trainee, or just one of two in a department, that's good news. And yet trainees say *"you don't have to have a strong personality"* to be able to fit in; it's not survival of the fittest or the loudest. More prosaically, someone told us the place attracts *"the usual people, the usual lawyers..."* Maybe they were just having a bad day.

this season's colour

Two years ago the firm settled into *"brand new offices made of glass and steel with a traditional Georgian brick façade. I suppose you could characterise the firm itself like that,"* said one trainee with an eye for a metaphor. *"It did have a reputation for being a traditional Covent Garden private client and property firm; now it is in Holborn and it's expanding very fast. Ten partners have joined since I started, and lots of fee earners."* Someone else agreed: *"It's a traditional firm but with a dynamic feel to it. It is going places."* Some admit: *"There are still plenty of old-school partners but the transformation is well under way."* The firm has even had management consultants in for a makeover. *"It was controversial but well received. They've changed the website and the corporate colours from green to silver,"* which apparently is *"a progressive colour."* Remember, you read that here first.

It seems no one wanted to depart from the traditional for the last Christmas party. The firm booked the Waldorf Hotel on the Aldwych, which was "*all palm trees and marble floors.*" Also along traditional lines, there's cricket every summer at Dulwich College. "*It's dominated by the property team, and they take on a team of property agents. We get down there for late afternoon, play 30 overs and then have a full-on barbecue.*" There are "*irregular*" organised nights out for trainees ("*we've been to Guanabara in Covent Garden for cocktails and tapas, and Bloomsbury for bowling*") but the usual meeting place after work is The Old Nick, which will be familiar to anyone who has done an LPC at BPP's London campus. "*We've yet to click with it,*" said one source ruefully, perhaps remembering the firm's close bond with a Covent Garden pub before its office move. And now we come to the sorry, and yet curious, tale about a partner-level team-building weekend, at which a professional film crew captured various efforts "*to sell the firm through the medium of stunts and superheroes.*" Cue partners dressed as Batman and Superman, and a very odd sequence with a female partner playing a nurse and a male partner playing a doctor. Gender stereotype anyone?

The most pressing improvement trainees thought the firm could make related to the replenishment of the bowls that contain free fruit for staff. "*It's the usual stuff with a bit of exotica, but the secretaries hear the trolleys and pounce, taking with them all the kiwis, lychees and stuff that I don't even know the name of.*" Naturally we will be keeping a close watch on this situation. One bit of very good news trainees were keen to share was that, after some dodgy retention figures in 2005, there were more jobs than qualifiers in 2006. In the final event, four of the six qualifiers stayed on, with those departing doing so to pursue specific work interests.

and finally...

There's something reassuringly straightforward about Wedlake Bell and the way it organises its training scheme. Traditional elements have not been entirely abandoned in the firm's quest for a shiny silver future, so if you've a fondness for a good old-fashioned pint rather than a peculiar concoction in a martini glass, this is still a safe bet.

Weil Gotshal & Manges LLP

the facts

Location: London
Number of UK partners/solicitors: 22/62
Total number of trainees: 19
Seats: 4x6 months
Alternative seats: Overseas seats
Extras: Pro bono – RCJ CAB, FRU, Bar and Solicitors pro bono units

If you are the type of person who the magic circle would offer a training contract to in a heartbeat, but are concerned that accepting the offer would be like entering the "*sausage factory of traineeship,*" Weil Gotshal could be the firm for you.

magic numbers

"*The majority of us turned down offers from the magic circle because we wanted to be here instead,*" one trainee told us. So what can this US firm offer that the UK's giants can't? Exposure to high profile transactions within a medium-sized London office for a start. "*They won't chuck you in at the deep end if you won't be able to cope, but if you are able to punch above your weight you will be given challenging work.*"

Our interviewees were undoubtedly enthused by the firm's transatlantic character, and we can see why when perks include being flown out to New York for completion dinners. They find it *"satisfying when the deal you are working on makes it to the front page of The New York Times or onto CNN"* and few could conceal excitement over the prospect of being seconded to offices in New York and California for a seat. Another key advantage is the small matter of the *"tempting"* salaries on offer to UK trainees which, at £37,500 for a new starter and £75,000 for an NQ, you'd be *"crazy to turn down."* Ask yourself: *"When there is high-quality training on offer at a several firms, why would you not earn as much money as can you while doing it?"* The only duff part of the deal is that the UK/US time difference can leave you a little bleary-eyed at times. *"The Americans often forget that we should really be asleep long before their working day is over,"* chuckled one interviewee.

So, what's the catch? We heard accounts of trainees facing *"up to five or six trainees from magic circle firms doing the equivalent workload of one Weil trainee."* Just how accurate this claim would be if fully tested is unclear, but you get the point being made. Long hours and weekends in the office are taken as read, although you may be reassured to learn that *"if you are here late you will be a proper part of the team, doing something interesting – you won't be left to do photocopying."* Interviewees also hinted at days off in lieu after especially busy periods and inclusion in social events with clients as recompense. We were also interested to hear that on occasion allowances are made if you need to leave early. For example, if, like current trainees, you have booked sought-after concert tickets or just happen to have organised *"the biggest party in the village ever"* for your mum's 50th, your supervisor may feel able to excuse you. Just make sure *"you speak up well in advance – there is no point being wishy-washy about it and then moaning afterwards."* Indeed, this is a good piece of general advice, as *"you need to be assertive if you are going to feel comfortable and make the most of being at Weil."*

muse on that

Be aware that not all US firms in London are alike. Some are geared towards high finance, some towards certain industry sectors such as energy or insurance. Weil's particular bag is that it's a worldwide leader in restructuring and it has a killer corporate practice. Corporate work defines the London office and, more specifically, our sources informed us that Weil *"wants to become the best private equity firm in the world."* One small step on the road to world domination was the London hire in 2006 of Lovells' private equity doyen Marco Compagnioni (a chap previously thought to be Lovells through and through) together with his right-hand man.

The corporate lawyers in London initially made their mark through deals for US private equity house Hicks, Muse, Tate & Furst but more latterly the client roster has lengthened, giving further weight to the argument that the office has established a successful standalone practice and become a key player on the City legal scene. For the record, nearly half the corporate team's instructions originate from Europe. Recently it advised private equity houses on the $1.85 million buyout of Cadbury Schweppes and a $625 million agreement to acquire American Safety Razor, a leading global manufacturer of razors and blades. If you are thinking about applying to this firm you must be prepared for a training contract that is dominated by such massive transactions. While there are seats on offer in IP, litigation and real estate, these tend to be viewed as ancillary departments to provide support for the corporate group, so *"if you fancy your chances as a patent specialist or property lawyer, this probably isn't the firm for you."*

taxing times

Seats in corporate and litigation are a certainty and those trainees who really take to the department say a seat there is genuinely rewarding. Just like their contemporaries in the magic circle firms they do spend time on data-room monitoring and due diligence tasks, but there is also plenty of drafting and, for those people *"who can handle it,"* the chance to develop negotiation skills. *"I drafted a confidentiality agreement at the start of a deal and a disclosure letter qualifying the warranties, so those were negotiated by me,"* one confident source recalled. Interestingly, the tax seat is *"horrendously popular,"* largely because *"everything that goes on in corporate is tax driven."* While *"six months is never going to give you enough experience to handle the intricacies of tax law yourself, you learn an awful lot through observation."* And by doing this seat, if you do end up as a finance lawyer *"at least you will recognise some of the structures floating around."*

Even though this is an international firm, trainees stressed that *"if you want to travel and collect air miles this is a good firm to train with, but if you want to travel and expect to see places, please, don't apply."* One interviewee told us: *"Friends are jealous that I have been to Copenhagen, France and the States, but they were just office visits – I was there to work."* Six-month trainee secondments to the patent litigation department in California's hi-tech region – Silicon Valley – and to the New York office do, however, provide an opportunity to see a different way of life. Seats in Paris, Munich, Prague, Warsaw and Frankfurt are also available to those who can speak the right languages sufficiently well. For those trainees who would rather stay in the UK, the client/pro bono secondments available to trainees include Oxfam and The Bar Pro Bono Unit as well as a number of commercial clients.

now we are ten

This year the firm marked the tenth anniversary of its arrival in London with a champagne reception for clients at the Tower of London. Trainees were welcomed at the event and are sometimes given the opportunity to *"take the place of a partner or associate who has been invited to a swanky dinner somewhere like the Dorchester or Claridges."* This year's tenth anniversary party was a 1930s gangster-themed affair at Vinopolis on the South Bank, and every summer there's a barbecue at the managing partner's house. Our sources were perfectly satisfied with the social side of things; however they did recognise that some of the big firms have a very different social life, involving trainee balls, regular drinks events and softball tournaments. A source confessed that while *"HR does provide money if trainees put their heads together to organise something, to be honest we are not really a 'let's all go to the pub together on a Friday night' sort of place."* A meal at Groucho Grill following a group training session is more typical. That said, there is an all-expenses-paid, overnight trip to Cambridge for the Trinity College ball.

The truth of the matter is *"we hardly see enough of our friends and families as it is, so when we have spare time it is nice to have a life outside work."* We're told that *"if you are taking part in a sports event, if you are in a play, even if your children are in a play, people here are really supportive."* If you don't have a spouse or a mortgage to head home to just yet there's no need to worry about becoming a billy no-mates. *"People are always popping off to the pub together on an ad hoc basis."* One trainee told us: *"A couple of the associates will knock on my door and tell me that some beer research needs doing,"* and for another, lunch with partners has resulted in getting home at *"an embarrassing time of the morning."* In the same way that work is not always distributed in accordance with your level of qualification, when it comes to socialising *"it doesn't matter that you are a trainee; if senior people like you they will choose to spend time with you."*

the ultimate test of loyalty

In the past couple of years the fate of those reaching qualification at Weil has left us wondering why the firm has not been more successful in converting traineeships into permanent jobs. We asked trainees for their thoughts and these turned out to be enlightening. In a small trainee group there is literally *"nowhere to hide,"* so if you want to qualify here you need to show commitment to the cause from day one. Some trainees find themselves *"rather snowed under"* with the workload at the start and so they quickly learn to develop an industrious, proactive approach in order to manage the demands placed upon them. *"If you are a lists person, the sort who finds organising projects really satisfying,"* this could be the right sort of place for you. Match this with a huge dose of enthusiasm for learning a difficult trade (*"you have to be really, really, really keen – even when asked to do something that most people would find a bit dull"*) and you'll do well. The dreaded e-mails that hit inboxes at 5pm on a Friday and request weekend volunteers appear to separate those who *"really want to do their best for the firm"* from those who are prepared to work hard but are less inclined to go the extra mile. The other vital trait is *"stamina."* Just like all firms, Weil aims for high retention, but is nevertheless unsentimental about making qualification decisions. In 2006, five of the eight qualifiers cut the mustard and were offered jobs. All five accepted.

and finally...

Weil Gotshal & Manges is not a firm to choose lightly; the demands placed on trainees are high, and for those who stay with the firm after qualification they remain high. As are the rewards, of course.

White & Case LLP

the facts
Location: London
Number of UK partners/solicitors: 57/176
Total number of trainees: 52
Seats: 4x6 months
Alternative seats: Overseas seats, secondments
Extras: Pro bono – Mary Ward Law Centre, RCJ CAB, FRU, LawWorks; language training

New York-headquartered White & Case has had an office in London for 35 years, the last five of which have been characterised by serious expansion. With a trainee intake to match some of the bigger English firms, it's safe to say that White & Case has crossed the Rubicon in London.

the billionaires club

In 2005 White & Case saw its global turnover reach $1.046 billion, giving it membership of the elite, legal, billion-dollar-a-year club. Its earning power comes from having nearly 2,000 lawyers in 36 offices in 24 countries. Take a look at the location of its worldwide offices – six in the USA, 19 in Europe, eight in Asia, four in Latin America and one each in Africa and the Middle East – and you see just how international White & Case's interests are. It is famed for its 'sovereign practice' – through which it acts for heads of state and governments around the world – and has a history of taking advantage of political developments likely to lead to economic growth, wherever these crop up around the world.

Don't assume the White & Case operation in London is full of Americans abroad: *"They've done their best to give it a local flavour,"* confirmed one source. Indeed they have: White and Case is known as a firm that allows its overseas offices to take on a local character, readily promoting domestic lawyers to the partnership. This is undoubtedly the story of the rapidly growing

London office, where numbers have shot up from 89 fee lawyers in 2001 to around 230 today. Said one trainee: "*You don't hear too many American voices in the corridors, but you do feel they come and check up on us once in a while.*" Another ventured that the office feels "*more international than most US or UK firms;*" even so, "*you're always aware that New York is the head office and that London is not the centre of the universe.*"

the scoop on finance

Once you are aware that the core work of the office is finance, particularly capital markets and project finance, it's impossible to doubt the following advice from current trainees. "*You've got to be interested in finance, banking and capital markets because, depending on what you do for your seat abroad, you may end up effectively doing three finance seats.*" Everyone we spoke to was clear that first and foremost "*this is a finance firm*" so "*don't come here if you're more interested in niche areas.*"

Like that other great American export, Baskin Robbins, at White & Case finance comes in many flavours. The finance division is split into two main groups, the recently fused banking and capital markets group (which also includes structured finance lawyers) and the EIPAS group (energy and infrastructure projects plus asset finance).

A seat in banking and capital markets could be slanted to any one of the group's component practices. Sit with a banking specialist and you'll have an introduction to the fine art of dealing with conditions precedent, the pre-completion requirements that must be checked and verified before a loan can be made. For the trainee this involves "*getting documents together and chasing information.*" Other tasks include "*research, reviewing documents and proof-reading.*" When we heard that "*people hate the structured finance and capital market seats and try to avoid them like the plague*" we were compelled to dig a little deeper. Apparently certain characters had a reputation for being hard to work with and one trainee who'd worked on capital markets deals had found the experience less than rewarding. "*It involved a lot of proof-reading and lots of grunt work, but I suppose that's the nature of transactional work and it's what trainees do. I also did some drafting and attended closings, but in terms of billable hours it's fair to say that it was mostly proof-reading. It was quite mundane and it was the low point of my training.*" The good news is that "*the seats are no longer so hellish*" since the fusion of the banking, structured finance and capital markets teams. There is certainly good work going on here, and lawyers completed an innovative deal for Credit Suisse and UBS earlier in 2006, when a Netherlands-based subsidiary of a Kazakh bank issued a $150 million, 9.375%, hybrid, tier-one offering. For White & Case's London lawyers this was the third such deal in the past year (there had only ever been four tier-one offerings from Kazakh banks).

Looking at the EIPAS group, a seat focusing on asset finance will give you a close look at how companies buy, lease or lend money for aeroplanes. "*I was sent on a three-day course on aircraft finance in Dorking,*" recalled one trainee. "*We had presentations from people at Boeing and Airbus, and someone from Rolls-Royce told us about the size of their engines.*" Be aware that back in the office there can be some drudgery – "*I had to register 92 Form 395s at Companies House.*"

The work trainees do in a project finance-oriented seat reflects the fact that "*deals go on for a long time.*" Reporting on their seat, one source told us: "*I did lots of work on a term sheet for a particular projects deal and by the end I'd had more client contact than I'd imagined I would and went to meetings galore... the LNG stuff is especially interesting. Unfortunately I wasn't there for a closing, so I didn't get to see anything from start to finish.*" Someone else had worked on "*a major infrastructure financing. The hours were very intense towards closing and once I was in until 7am. It wasn't the sexiest of work – proof-reading and processing conditions precedent – I spent lots of time pushing around the conditions precedent trolley.*" We should remind readers that international project finance is a major activity for White & Case and explains the location of many of its foreign offices. In 2006, London lawyers worked in conjunction with colleagues in New York on a $9.9 billion joint venture between the world's largest oil company, Saudi Aramco, and Sumitomo Chemical for the development of a refinery at Rabigh, Saudi Arabia into a major integrated refinery and petrochemical complex. This deal was the largest project financing to date in Saudi Arabia. "*The firm handles lots of oil and gas work and is moving into mining,*" explained a source.

contentious issues?

A number of our sources gave the corporate department a big thumbs-up. "*My work was a lot more varied. I was drafting share purchase agreements, doing due diligence and managing foreign lawyers. It was a very interesting experience and I really felt the thrill even though it was more formal than in some departments,*" reported one. Corporate hours can be tough "*but that's true everywhere I think.*" Indeed it is. At least the diet is varied, one trainee's seat having incorporated "*work in conjunction with the capital markets department, some private equity, IPOs, AIM listings and ongoing projects.*"

Though not an issue for everyone we spoke to, some of our interviewees thought the opportunities to gain contentious experience were fewer than they'd hoped. Seats are available in mainstream commercial litigation, IP, employment and construction. Reflecting the views of their predecessors last year, one trainee told us: "*My litigation seat was not hugely exciting. I was working on copies, bundles and filing. You have to really search for good contentious work.*" Someone else added that "*the firm is finding it hard to channel people through their contentious experience.*" As it turns out, the firm is now piloting the idea of allowing trainees with no interest in litigation to skip a full six-month seat and instead attend a two-week course at the College of Law, thus freeing up the opportunities in the office for those who really want them.

So what of the idea that the firm's American heritage impacts on working patterns in London. One trainee was eager to stress that "*this office does not have a US work ethic, but obviously when you're working with an international client and a foreign office you get different influences coming across and, yes, certain departments do work very long hours.*" Another who was equally keen to set the record straight told us: "*I don't work any harder than people at magic circle firms, but I get paid more than them.*" Indeed, no one denied that the "*enormous pay packet*" (combined with an "*informal dress code*") were key attractions. For the record, White & Case pays £36,000 to new starters and £67,500 to NQs. These sums are indeed higher than those offered at the magic circle, although not as high as some US firms in London.

turning up the heat

If you never quite got around to renewing your passport, do it soon or look at another firm. "*You have to be the type who would enjoy heading off to Paris at a day's notice,*" cautioned one trainee. More than this, "*it is expected that you would want to do a seat abroad and you would have to give a reason why you wouldn't.*" The firm sends trainees to many of its overseas offices, among them Hong Kong, Singapore, Tokyo, Paris, Prague, Moscow and Johannesburg. As early as their first few weeks at the firm, trainees are asked where they would like to go.

One thing that certainly distinguishes White & Case from many English firms in the City is the emphasis placed on learning through practice not theory. "*You are not given lots of classroom tuition; the emphasis here is on learning on the job. Most of the formal training is directed at the whole group – the partners, associates and trainees – although some departments have training sessions just for trainees at the start of the seat.*" In the words of another: "*It's ideal if you're sick to death of LPC-style teaching.*"

In terms of the volume and quality of the feedback trainees get, we heard mixed messages. Some people felt "*there's a tendency on the part of some supervisors to delay appraisals, or else they don't happen at all.*" Others had fared better and were happy. We sense no imminent revolt because, when asked what they'd do if they could run the place for a few days, their answers were wide ranging. More classroom training and the hiring of more proof-readers were manifesto pledges from some; others were rather creative, like the trainee who said: "*I would have more team away-days. Some departments do have ski trips, but I'm always in the wrong department at the wrong time.*" It seems their timing must have been particularly off because the trend for team ski trips looks to be taking over in the office. Another trainee gave us a particularly innovative suggestion: "*A friend of mine who'd been in the Miami office told me that everyone goes home at 7pm when they turn the air con off. I would do the opposite in London and turn up the heating to an unpleasant temperature...*"

karaokesaurus

Having been told that the firm makes "*an effort to keep people that they like to work with,*" we asked what kind of person would suit the firm. "*You must be confident and you need personality and social graces. You can have a great legal mind, but you need to be able to get on with people to get on here.*" Current trainees told us: "*A few years back it was all Oxbridge but they're much more adventurous now and a lot of people have been travelling before joining. That helps you keep perspective when you're knuckling down.*" Anyone who is easily offended might wish to note that "*there's lots of banter and people express themselves very openly.*" We were warned that "*this is a City law firm – and sometimes the atmosphere can be similar to that of a City bank*" (however you choose to interpret that). More reassuring to hear was that the firm is stuffed with "*hard-working people... but there's no Byzantine feeling and no backstabbing. People seem genuine and honest.*"

The firm is well known as a sociable kind of place. Most socialising is informal, ranging from monthly office drinks and nights in the pub to "*karaoke in a private members' club in Soho. There were partners, associates and secretaries... it was a hoot.*" To bring everyone together there is a summer party and, last year, "*a great black-tie winter ball at the Natural History Museum in the room with the big dinosaur.*"

After you've completed your training, you can look forward to a distinguished career at the firm. "*Retention is good and I'm confident that if I want to work here there's a good chance of being kept on,*" said one trainee. The final score in September 2006 was stayers 11, leavers two. Five people went into banking and capital markets, three into EIPAS and one each into litigation, employment and corporate.

and finally...

When asked to sum up why a student would plump for White & Case, trainees had no hesitation in singling out the international transactions, the overseas seats, the informal atmosphere in the office and the hefty salary. Just remember the practice focus and be sure that's what you're after.

Wiggin LLP

the facts

Location: Cheltenham, London
Number of UK partners/solicitors: 12/26
Total number of trainees: 6
Seats: 4x6 months
Alternative seats: Secondments

WIG (w⊤g) *verb* (cf. wigged; wig·ging) *intransitive senses, slang*: to lose one's composure or reason. 1. *wig out, Slang*: To make or become wildly excited, enthusiastic, or crazy. 2. *wiggin out, Cotswold slang*: To become wildly excited about premier niche media firm specialising in film, music, sport, gaming, publishing and broadcasting based in Cheltenham.

Believe us when we say, it doesn't take long to wig out about a firm that is practically the dictionary definition of media boutique. "*We're solely and principally a media firm; it's all we do*," reported trainees.

no haphazard pursuit

Let's rewind for a moment. Having originally formed in the 1980s, in 2003 the firm we now know as Wiggin separated itself from a group of private client lawyers in order to pursue a destiny as "*the UK's best niche media firm*." A complete rebranding in an ultra-trendy, achingly up-to-the-minute fashion perfectly reflects the "*vibrant,*" "*very young*" partnership which enthuses trainees with their clear focus and "*brilliant ideas*." Take a gander at the website (Think Media. Think Brighter. Think Wiggin). Better still, watch the online corporate video, a super-slick piece reminiscent of Ocean's 11, replete with cross wipes, split-screen action, a pumping soundtrack and a slightly unnerving tendency for the phrase BANG ON IT to burst onto the screen at otherwise slow moments. If you imagine this

theme reconceived as interior decoration, then it's easy to visualise the Cheltenham and London offices – all "*purple walls and lime green carpets,*" "*slogans and flat screens in reception*" and "*posters for 'Sideways' and 'Kingdom of Heaven' and other films we've worked on.*"

Trainees relish what they understand to be "*the chic trappings of the industry sector,*" "*what the clients want and expect.*" They even enjoy the contradictions of "*a grandiose Georgian building on stately Cheltenham Promenade with all that trendiness inside... it is a bit meedja darling.*" But they are adamant that "*the rebrand has penetrated past the superficial,*" telling us: "*The firm is immersed in the industry; we embody and embrace all of its elements.*" Give us the substance to match the style, we challenged our sources. So they did.

"*Film has been a big growth area for the last few years. So now it's thriving, sports law is the focus.*" Having hired two lawyers from major US film studios to turbocharge film work, this year Wiggin snatched Olswang's head of sports law Michael Brader. As London Olympics 2012 approaches, there's never been a better time to focus on matters sporting, so Wiggin has also signed up former FA Executive Director and telly commentator David Davies to offer his insights. By the looks of things the partners' business plan is precise and they have no intention of over-reaching themselves. The firm's annual turnover is now around £11 million and the goal is to achieve £16 million the year after and then cap growth.

name dropping

As a rough estimate, we've only used the word 'media' 300 times so far, and maybe you're concerned that we've not being specific enough about the work. If so, be assured that if it's in, on, through, behind or to do with the media, Wiggin do it. For the most part the clientele is London-centric and comprised of businesses rather than individual celebs. Lawyers regularly take instructions from publishers, broadcasters, industry regulatory bodies, production companies, telecommunications companies, film studios, record labels, TV channels and more. To name but a few: Al Jazeera, BBC Films, British Phonographic Industry, BT, Channel 4, Columbia Pictures, Condé Nast, Emap, Five, HBO, Macmillan, Manchester United FC, Napster, Paramount Pictures, Telewest, Time Warner Books, Trinity Mirror, 20th Century Fox Film Corp and Warner Brothers.

The firm has been advising ITV on new media issues including contractual and regulatory developments across new platforms like IPTV, mobile and interactive television as well as on contracts for outside broadcasting of sports and its Formula One production contract. Meanwhile, Flextech instructed Wiggin on new transmission and playout arrangements involved in a long-term, multimillion-pound agreement with BBC Broadcast (now Red Bee Media), and broadcast lawyers also had a hand in Telewest's bid for the Football League rights. Racing UK and Super 12 Racecourses continued to put their faith in Wiggin in 2006, the latter betting heavily on the firm to resolve its ongoing litigation with Attheraces.

A welter of publishing clients means prepublication advisory work is a huge part of the defamation team's business, and they are frequently called to defend clients in court. This year Five needed Wiggin's help to beat off libel proceedings brought by supermodel Kate Moss following allegations in one of the channel's broadcasts. If you think Miss Moss is big-name news, wait 'til you hear who the music team acts for... no lesser entertainers than Nancy Sinatra and Englebert Humperdinck! Legend though he be, the Hump does not a department's work make, and lawyers have also been busy of late with litigation for the British Phonographic Industry over peer-2-peer song downloading services. Those ex-film studio partners give Wiggin the clout necessary to enjoy the patronage of each of the four major US film studios on a variety of big box office movies. By way of example the firm has recently advised on *Omen: 666*, *Notes on a Scandal*, *V for Vendetta* and *The Da Vinci Code*. Involvement in an executive producer role (securing film financing), as well as offering traditional legal advice to the team behind 'The History Boys' also highlights the firm's unquie capabilities.

who gets the booby prize?

Trainees rotate through four six-month seats. The media options are broadcasting (*"a very technical, fast-moving, jargon-heavy area"*); technology (*"lots of new-media rights essentially, lots of mobile content agreements and sports rights"*); and media litigation (*"defamation, slander, libel and the peer-2-peer court case"*). Away from straight media there are seats in property, employment and corporate... acting for media clients. One final option comes in the form of a regular secondment to the British Phonographic Industry. Needless to say rotation time is almost always a happy occasion for all concerned.

Trainees speak highly of the firm's *"demanding"* culture of *"hard work."* It requires them to be *"outgoing and have the ability to think on your feet and handle demanding clients."* Many of the duller chores like bundling and pagination are outsourced, meaning that across all departments trainees are *"pushed to the limit – you're meeting clients all the time and the exposure to sophisticated work is great."* Whether it's *"film financing matters or mid-tier media company sales"* in corporate, *"drafting agreements for High Street Honeys or 'Win a Boob Job'"* in media tech, *"writing uplink satellite agreements and outside broadcast production contracts"* in media broadcasting, *"going to court on a big file-sharing* litigation" in media lit, or "*mixing with top legal brains in the industry*" at the BPI, Wiggin trainees definitely aren't making hollow boasts. But what really impresses the Wiggsters is "*being at the cutting-edge of law. You're not riffling through a precedent bank for a matching scenario to the one you're dealing with, you're thinking, 'this has never been done before: how do we do it, how do we get round this or that?' Work is never formulaic and you turn up every day wondering what will be on your desk.*" The heightened egos of "*no-bullshit creative clients*" also keep trainees on their toes: "*These guys know their industry so well and when they have an idea, they want a solution – they can be pretty blunt about it!*"

spa from the madding crowd

The expectations of the clientele do explain Wiggin's "*very casual*" dress code, but don't account for the firm's Gloucestershire location. This can be understood when you know that Wiggin was founded by hotshot lawyers who had tired of London living. What's more, recent hires (three ex-Olswang partners and one from Ashurst) confirm that the Cotswolds continue to exert a magnetic pull. And not just on lawyers – half of London's A-list celebs are already living there. But with so many corporate clients based in London why the continued commitment to Cotswold living? When you ask trainees this question they flash back with: "*We're a city firm in terms of work that happens to be in a beautiful countryside town.*" There's no argument there, nor with "*first-class train tickets*" or "*getting a lift in the partners' chauffeur-driven cars*" on the weekly trips to the small London office. What's more, the salary is just as City-esque, which is not bad when you reside in a provincial town in "*a Georgian house that would cost a bomb in London.*" Naturally the hours can be long, especially on London days, though you'll either get "*a swish hotel room*" or "*a ten-minute walk home*" once you're back.

The trainees we interviewed were happy about their move to Cheltenham: "*It's a really cultural town that's cheap to live in,*" "*you're always in London anyway so you can keep up with friends*" and "*mates are more than happy to come to the countryside to visit you for the weekend.*" They enjoyed the social side to the firm, telling us about "*partner-organised Cotswold pub crawls,*" a "*Friday drinks trolley*" and "*wine tasting at a local manor house.*" The Residence or the Montpellier Wine Bar remain popular haunts, although amid the plethora of night spots Thirteen Nightclub drew especial praise for "*cheesy music, Gloucestershire Rugby Club players and very beautiful Cotswold girls.*"

In the confines of the office the natural confidence and "*easy-going humour*" we observed in these trainees makes for some sound friendships too. Responding to "*partners' jibes that we're unfit,*" this year three (backed up by a fourth in the capacity of "*dietician*") took on the challenge of running the 120 miles between the Wiggin's London and Cheltenham offices for charity. "*It means doing over 30 miles a day for four days. Apparently it's called power running and you're meant to complete three marathons and train for a year before you attempt it. We've never run a marathon and we've been training for three weeks, but I'm confident,*" confessed one participant. We wished them luck and so did the firm, which agreed to match whatever money they raised. In spite of this display of madness all three second-year trainees breezed into NQ jobs with the firm in 2006, waved on by Wiggin's current expansive attitudes.

and finally...

Though it's a must-make application for any media-minded student, realistically these jobs are going to go to way-above-average candidates. If you are one, and you are prepared for the move to Gloucestershire, we say get bang on it.

Withers LLP

the facts

Location: London
Number of UK partners/solicitors: 62/77
Total number of trainees: 26
Seats: 4x6 months
Alternative seats: Milan
Extras: Language training

The name Withers is synonymous with private clients and family law, but by developing commercial areas of practice – initially to serve the needs of wealthy individuals with business interests – it has secured its place among the UK's top-50 firms. This is a clever firm with a well-considered business plan.

show me the money

Withers is unashamedly focused on *"acting for people with money."* Withers without private client work would be like Donatella Versace without her permatan or Kate Moss without a scandal. The private client department is the firm's largest, accounting for more than 35% of annual turnover. As well as will-drafting and probate for *"middle-class Londoners,"* Withers advises at least 15% of the Sunday Times' Rich List and an impressive range of landed estates. *"A lot of London's private client practices are very old school,"* commented one trainee; *"the difference here is that we are giving them more of a commercial service."*

Let's look at the international side of Withers' private client work for a moment. The clients fall into two categories: UK residents with international trusts and tax-planning issues, and non-UK domiciled individuals who may or may not have assets in the UK. Trainees quickly learn just how complicated trust law can be and appreciate that the expertise is built up gradually. *"You are dealing with some of the world's wealthiest people; those who need a particular expertise that they can't get anywhere else."* Naturally with so much money at stake disputes are always a risk. In the past year alone Withers' contentious trust and probate group has handled disputes in jurisdictions as diverse as Saudi Arabia, the Cayman Islands, Panama and Liechtenstein.

italian jobs

Withers' international private client practice has helped it develop a reputation as a more modern firm in what is still regarded by many outsiders as a very traditional part of the profession. Withers was the first major firm to enter into a US merger when in 2002 it joined forces with 18-partner tax and trust specialist Bergman Horowitz & Reynolds, which operated in New Haven. The US venture was not its first foray overseas, however; it had been up and running in Milan for some years. Then in 2005 it opened a new office in Geneva – hardly a rash decision given that Switzerland is home to approximately a third of the world's private wealth. The overseas expansion programme may not be over; apparently Withers is looking into establishing a West Coast presence in the USA.

For trainees, the USA and Switzerland do not beckon just yet. But if you speak Italian there is a chance you might be seconded to the small Milan office, which is *"very corporate driven."* The office unsurprisingly handles a lot of fashion work and there is also *"an attempt to do more Italian private client work."* The Italian Republic and Max Mara are clients and the office also sends business to Withers in London. UK property lawyers, for example, advised Benetton on the acquisition of substantial retail sites throughout the UK. It was interesting to hear from our interviewees that *"the Italian connections and the international aspects of being at Withers only become apparent once you work here."* Some people also thought that the firm may *"recruit people with the Italian practice in mind."*

As we all know, the Italians don't have a monopoly on luxury brands and to prove it Withers' UK client roster is packed full of upmarket retailers, smart hotels and fashion designers. For example, lawyers recently advised Hussein Chalayan, Clements Ribeiro and Philip Treacy in relation to their participation in the Marks & Spencer Autograph range.

suits you, sir

New money and luxury brand clients have encouraged what trainees describe as an *"entrepreneurial spirit"* within the firm. It's not that the firm has changed entirely; indeed, Withers is now reckoned to have *"a mix of old-school and new-school partners"* that fit well with the diverse client base. *"As a trainee, if you are lucky you can get the best of both worlds"* and hopefully find a department that *"you can fit into."* The feel of each department is different, so much so that interviewees felt that *"working in some departments is like working in a completely different firm."* Yet they say there is *"something for everyone"* here – as long as you know where to look.

This *"friction"* – or blend, depending on your view – between old and new is also reflected in the physical environment. The front of Withers' office building *"looks Georgian"* and is in fact listed, yet the back, with its glass extension, looks *"futuristic."* *"It's a bit like a greenhouse,"* mused one interviewee. Overall, the interior is thought to be *"very trendy with very young decor"* and a testament to what you can do with a large amount of pine, chrome and glass. Amusingly the layout is often likened to a pair of trousers (we kid you not). For example, *"property is on the first floor, both legs; employment is on the third floor, right leg and the canteen is in the middle."* The trouser analogy hints at the sense of humour and character you encounter in many at Withers. Further examples are to be found in the presence of some morris dancers and partners in rock bands (pre-

sumably, unsigned). *"People you think are old-school are in fact are more clued up in pop culture than you might think,"* chuckled a source.

Withers' family team represents the rich and famous, both domestic and foreign. The judgement in client Melissa Miller's divorce case was splashed across the front pages of the newspapers when the House of Lords allowed her to keep £5 million of her former husband's £17.5 million fortune, even though her marriage had lasted less than three years. Miller's settlement was mere pocket change compared to the £48 million awarded to Beverley Charman just a few months later. Withers is representing ex-husband John Charman, who is now taking the case to the Court of Appeal. Perhaps speaking of these cases, a source told us: *"You do get involved in the sexy stuff as a trainee; it's not just about taking notes."* It is a hugely popular seat at Withers simply because *"people often come here to do family."* This can lead to oversubscription on qualification; in September 2006 there was only one NQ job up for grabs and two people contending for it. Overall though, 12 of the 13 qualifiers found satisfactory positions within the firm.

luxury hotels, fast cars

We must mention the commercial seats on offer. The corporate department deals with *"a mix of private client referrals and standalone work."* One trainee rattled off a list of the matters they'd encountered: *"Banking, the incorporation of charities, luxury hotels stuff. We have a lot of fashion clients, and links with Italian companies, food clients and bakeries."* Be prepared for a *"steep learning curve," "quite a few late nights"* and a *"fast pace,"* not least because the firm has both Ferrari and Renault Formula 1 teams on its books. There are two types of property seat: residential/commercial and rural landed estates. The seat may be *"more laid back and intimate than corporate"* but the clients are no less impressive – Great Ormond

Street Hospital Children's Charity, Cancer Research UK and the Hauser & Wirth gallery all use the firm. A team specialising in advice to hotels acts for the Rocco Forte group as well as for Soho House private members clubs and hotels. Trainees can additionally try out property litigation, encountering anything from rent arrears and trespassing cases to licensing. There are numerous contentious seat options, namely civil and commercial litigation, IP, employment and contentious trusts and probate. Anyone drawn to the charities sector will be pleased to learn that Withers has some top names as clients and scooped second place in the most recent Dresdner Rcm Top 3000 Charities list.

Before joining the firm, recruits are asked for their seat preferences, yet not everyone was convinced of the effectiveness of the allocation system. Said one source: "*I'm not sure how much attention the firm pays* [to people's choices.]" In fairness to the firm we should stress that a few changes have been introduced in the past year; private client is no longer a compulsory seat and pure IP and a charities seat have been added to the list of choices. The idea is that trainees be given more of a say in how their training seats stack up. Each new arrival has a buddy and "*a mentor partner you can go to for anything, anytime... work issues or career guidance.*" Each department has its own programme of training sessions and these provoked a variety of comments. Some people saw it as invaluable and liked the way knowledge and skills were delivered in an "*intimate*" setting; others felt there was "*sometimes too much training.*"

one of us

Our interviewees initially insisted there was no Withers type; however, when pressed, one conceded that people were "*slightly urbane, cultured and self-starting*" and another suggested "*you need to be very entrepreneurial and interested in developing yourself rather than being simply academic.*" Eventually it came out that there is "*an Oxbridge emphasis,*" with everyone else coming from other esteemed universities.

The week-by-week social scene is nice and gentle: "*The trainees are quite good at going for drinks after work; there's a core group from different departments who go out on a Friday.*" Corney & Barrow and The Magpie & Stump are the usual haunts although "*people are branching out to places in Paternoster Square.*" One time we chanced upon some of Withers' NQs in a Student Guide local up in Smithfield. The trainees regularly make the effort to lunch together, often appropriating a table in the canteen to enjoy food prepared by in-house chef, Stefan, "*who is about 20 feet tall*" and has a sideline in catering for partners' weddings. Withers' parties are fun and sophisticated. Last year's summer do at Gibson Hall showcased a chocolate fountain "*surrounded buy a swarm of greedy women,*" endless quantities of Pimm's and a troupe of morris dancers. "*The Pimm's was flowing and there was a good attendance by partners... and then you could hear this jingling...*" The Christmas party always seems to produce a tale or two. Some poor person broke their collarbone on the dance floor two years ago so the last one "*was a bit tamer.*" "*No one ended up pregnant and carpets weren't destroyed.*" Other social events include a trip to Ascot races, departmental dinners and "*a murder-mystery party at a partner's house.*" A summer sports day is a nice way of meeting colleagues from other departments, and anyone suffering from aching muscles the next day can book time with the masseur who comes into the office once a week.

and finally...

Withers is the perfect choice for someone intent on sampling up-scale private client and family work, perhaps because they are undecided as to whether the commercial route is right for them.

Wragge & Co

the facts

Location: Birmingham, London
Number of UK partners/solicitors: 111/183
Total number of trainees: 55
Seats: 4x6 months
Alternative seats: Secondments
Extras: Pro bono – College of Law and other advice schemes, language training

A Birmingham powerhouse with its eyes set firmly on national-level work, Wragge & Co has FTSE clients coming out of its ears and a staff whose satisfaction is regularly used as a benchmark. If you're Midlands-bound you couldn't ask for a better place to train.

getting tough

Adding their voices to the chorus-line of keyed-in, clued-up, strategy-aware trainees we've encountered at the firm over the years, sources define Wragges as *"an all-singing, all-dancing affair offering City service from an HQ in Birmingham."* It's not a bad summary of the tactics behind Wragges steady march to its current place as a major player alongside the likes of Burges Salmon, Eversheds or DLA. But whilst trainees naturally love the combination of broad practice, being treated well and *"regional hours,"* there are signs that Wragges is toughening up its act. Recent lower-than-expected profitability has moved the firm to action. Although practically guaranteed a place in The Sunday Times' Best Companies to Work For survey each year, ambitious financial targets (*"driving to reach £100 million turnover"*) and a self-imposed 'Year of Technical Excellence' (*"making everyone the absolute best in their practice"*) have been a little too austere for some. Trainees told us: *"There's been more focus on getting major corporate clients and billing,"* adding that *"there have been ideas*

from management, like a 24/7 service for corporate clients, which caused disquiet and they quickly had to explain it didn't mean staff would actually be working magic circle hours." If it's true that Wragge's softer edges are being sharpened up, our sources weren't complaining too much. *"Sure, it's more focused, but they're trying not to lose the distinctive people culture... and how else can you get profits per partner and ranking positions up? You've got to expect thing to get a bit tougher,"* said one.

gym and tonic

Sounds an eminently sensible viewpoint to us, not least because whilst Wragges isn't slobbishly out of shape, it undoubtedly needs to put in some serious work down the corporate gym. A more Spartan regime has allowed the firm to bounce back from recent income travails with a 15% upsurge in fees to surpass that £100 million target aim; however, the corporate division only generated 12% of the figure – a very low proportion when compared with other major firms. The steps it has taken include a re-jig in the leadership of the 17-partner team as well as hiring a senior funds practice lawyer to broaden its private equity expertise in its London branch. Rest assured the firm is far from a crisis: excellent relationships with private equity houses like 3i ensure a stream of mid-market deals such as the £41 million equity investment in Hayley Conference Centres, the £39 million refinancing of the EAT chain and the £116 million disposal of BetterCare. Transactions such as these contributed to a 54% increase in corporate revenue in 2006. What's more, the division counts Rolls-Royce, William Hill and Alliance & Leicester among its clients.

It is clear that challenging the bigger City firms has proved difficult, but the firm has at least made some headway in London. It has received a new instruction from Estonian shipping giant Tallink Grupp on its £406 million acquisition of a Finnish rival from Sea Containers and it has advised ITNET on its £235 million acquisition by Serco, each of which proves the firm's capacity to handle big transactions. Back home in Brum, a rather moribund M&A market has seen clients 3i, Ernst & Young and Royal Bank Private Equity scaling back their activities, although the team did enjoy the tonic of scoring instruction from the Phones4U management team in its £1.46 billion buyout. All in all, we'd suggest that any trainee arriving in the next few years will likely find that beefing up corporate is high on the firm's workout agenda.

bunker mentality

In other areas of work Wragges is confident it can bench press almost any weight you care to load. The firm may have lost its place on the panels of Serco, English Heritage and BT this year, but it can still lay claim to an impressively heavyweight clientele that includes BA, National Grid, Powergen, the DTI, Honda, Ford, Toyota and Lloyds TSB. Strongest of all are Wragge's real estate, construction, planning and projects/regeneration abilities, which see it advise top-drawer clients like Vodafone, Gleeson Homes and commercial developers Saint Modwen. Among this year's work highlights was advice on the property aspects of Wolverhampton & Dudley Breweries' £805 million refinancing, when Wragge's real estate lawyers worked alongside Freshfields corporate bods. Meanwhile, their colleagues in the projects department were celebrating a plum role advising Solihull Metropolitan Borough Council on a £1.8 billion regeneration scheme for a major residential area of Birmingham, also assisting Sanctuary Housing Association on a multimillion-pound project in Sheffield. In the field of construction and PFI, the firm followed up last year's advice to the MoD on its £3 billion purchase of twin aircraft carriers by tying up a £1.2 billion PFI project on the redevelopment of Northwood headquarters in north London, a complex that includes a prime ministerial bunker

to be used in emergencies. Presumably they had to coax Tony out before refurbishment began.

Wragge's pensions group is also able to compete on even terms with the big boys. This year it fought off a string of City firms to win appointment as sole advisor to international insurance behemoth Aon on its £500 million UK pensions scheme, whilst scoring the newly created Pensions Regulator and UK newsagent chain TM Retail as first-time clients. The high-flying IP practice continues to fly... er, high. IP lawyers recently advised biotech company Astex Therapeutics on its biggest-ever licensing deal, a £298 million drug discovery agreement with Swiss pharma giant Novartis. It also continues to represent O_2 over Hutchison 3G's alleged trademark infringement of the famous bubble imagery. Of course, we expect IP to be popular with trainees, but the lawyers have just as many clients desperate for their time – Microsoft, Marks & Spencer, various car manufacturers and pharmaceutical companies, Heinz and Cadbury Schweppes all being regular customers.

red wragges to the bull ring

Underlining its status in Birmingham, Wragges fills all floors of a *"beautiful, early Georgian building in Colmore Row, the nicest square in the city opposite the cathedral"* and close to the Bull Ring. But if the external decor is all period charm, the *"entirely open-plan interior with floor-to-ceiling atria," "minimalist splashes of Wragge's red"* and *"art from local artists"* speaks of a more *"modern, open atmosphere."* Trainees pinpoint the benefits of *"sitting close to your supervisor,"* a *"relaxed attitude to dress"* and a *"positive attitude to trainees: if you've got a point to make, even if it's in a meeting, you'll be listened to."* It's hard not to agree that the firm offers *"a great environment in which to learn."* Certainly, trainees approaching qualification felt they were integral to the work of their team. Said one: *"If they were to remove me from the matter it would actually take a long time to get someone up to speed."*

A full programme of seminars is backed up with a support system featuring departmental supervisors, departmental trainee partners and *"a neutral-venue training principal who looks after you for the full two years."* In fact, *"if you express a difficulty you sometimes get almost too much help."* Trainees are confident that *"nothing bad comes up at appraisals that you're not already aware of,"* even if *"there are differences in individual styles of supervision and some are better than others."* An uncomplicated rotation scheme leaves most people happy; in essence, everyone is obliged to spend time in a corporate seat, a litigation seat and a property seat and has the opportunity to play the ace of a *"guaranteed option seat."*

The *"perceived sexy areas"* of IP litigation, employment, pensions and technology and trade are all popular for an option seat but, with Wragges keen on sending *"more trainees out on secondment,"* stints with a client are growing more desirable. Getting a Unilever secondment is *"pretty competitive,"* but many interviewees who had spent time with other client companies enthused about *"the most rewarding, responsibility-filled part of training."* Further afield, the *"scaling back"* of the Brussels office the firm shares with a German partner means a seat there is not currently available.

get your goat

Trainees are recruited into Birmingham and have the option of taking a seat in London, where they can sample IP, private equity, real estate or employment/pensions. Not all are tempted but, as with secondments, many are happy to leave the Brum mothership, even in their third or fourth seat. They do so confidently because *"retention is so consistently good that there's no back-stabbing whatsoever amongst trainees."* With many more jobs on offer than qualifiers this year, in September 2006, 17 out of 18 stayed on, three qualifying into London. Another year of very high retention for Wragges.

If they work down in London trainees won't find themselves out of the loop. They are shipped up to Brum for away days, generally *"on a Sunday night so we all go out for a meal"* before engaging in the following day's event. The away-days typically include something active *"like tank driving, archery or pinging about in 4x4s."* When not getting muddy, the Brum trainees are regular customers of the many bars, restaurants and entertainment complexes in the city centre. By all accounts, Wragges organises a mean party and there are *"regular team drinks or graduate recruitment events"* to slot in between the big diary dates. The biggest of all is the Christmas bash, strangely always held in January. *"This year it had a fairground theme, so a thousand of us descended on the ICC and there were dodgems, a wall of death, rides, a coconut shy, a meal and dancing."* What's more *"the firm also finds some way of giving away money, so this year there was a coin tossing game of chance and someone won a grand."*

The *"infectious, communal atmosphere"* of such events evidently spills over into the workplace, and one trainee amused us by listing a department's weekly social calendar: *"Cakes baked for Monday, French lesson on Wednesday, GOAT on Thursday, Friday Drinks."* Sorry, GOAT? *"Golf On A Thursday, I'm terrible, but the partner is very tolerant."* Perhaps it is unsurprising that trainees who have matured in this environment are *"loyal to the firm, with most people looking to hit associate or partnership level here."* Yet it is not an unquestioning loyalty; with some having moved to the region for the firm (although most have Midlands university or family connections) our sources were all capable of weighing up their long-term options

and finally...

Wragges offers a fantastic City-in-the-second-city training. Quite how its new steel will impact on the legendary warm Wragge's ethos remains to be seen, but even if the temperature does drop a few degrees, we'd guess it'll still be a balmy place to train.

a-z solicitors

Addleshaw Goddard

150 Aldersgate Street, London, EC1A 4EJ
Sovereign House, PO Box 8, Sovereign Street, Leeds LS1 1HQ
100 Barbirolli Square, Manchester, M2 3AB
Website: www.addleshawgoddard.com/graduates
Tel: (0161) 934 6000 / (020) 7606 8855
Fax: (0161) 934 6060 / (020) 7606 4390

firm profile

As a major force on the legal landscape, Addleshaw Goddard offers extensive and excit-ing opportunities to all its trainees across the entire spectrum of commercial law, from employment and banking to real estate, corporate finance, intellectual property, employment, PFI and litigation. Ranked 16th largest law firm in the UK with a fee income in 2005/6 of £161 million, Addleshaw Goddard was listed in both The Sunday Times and The Times as one of the 'Top 100 Best Companies to Work For' and 'Top 100 Graduate Employers' in 2006 and, as a trainee with this firm, you'll be a key member of the team from day one. Whether based in the Leeds, London or Manchester office (or out on secondment), you'll work closely with blue-chip clients within a supportive yet challenging environment, and be part of a structured training programme designed to ensure your success – now and in the future.

main areas of work

The firm has four main business divisions: finance and projects, contentious and com-mercial, corporate and real estate. Within these divisions as well as the main practice areas it also has specialist areas such as sport, intellectual property, employment and private client services such as family and trusts and tax.

trainee profile

Graduates who are capable of achieving a 2:1 and can demonstrate commercial aware-ness, motivation and enthusiasm. Applications from law and non-law graduates are welcomed, as are applications from mature students who may be considering a change of direction.

training environment

During each six-month seat, there will be regular two-way performance reviews with the supervising partner or solicitor. Trainees have the opportunity to spend a seat in one of the firm's other offices and there are a number of secondments to clients avail-able. Seated with a qualified solicitor or partner and working as part of a team, enables trainees to develop the professional skills necessary to deal with the demanding and challenging work the firm carries out for its clients. Practical training is complemented by high-quality training courses provided by both the in-house team and external training providers.

sponsorship & benefits

GDL and LPC fees are paid, plus a maintenance grant of £7,000 (London) or £4,500 (elsewhere in the UK). Benefits include corporate gym membership, season ticket loan, subsidised restaurant, pension and private healthcare.

vacation placements

Places for 2007 – 75; Duration – 1-2 weeks (over Easter and the summer); location - all offices; Apply by 31 January 2007.

Partners	**182**
Associates	**500+**
Trainees	**89**

contact
The Graduate Recruitment Team
grad@addleshawgoddard.com

selection procedure
Interview, assessment centre

closing date for 2009
31 July 2007

application
Training contracts p.a. **45-50**
Applications p.a. **1,500**
% interviewed **10%**
Required degree grade **2:1**

training
Salary
1st year
Manchester/Leeds **£21,500**
London £30,000
2nd year
Manchester/Leeds **£24,000**
London £33,000
Holiday entitlement
25 days
% of trainees with
a non-law degree p.a. **45%**

post-qualification
Salary
Manchester/Leeds **£35,000**
London £53,000
(under review)
% of trainees offered job
on qualification (2006) **80%**

other offices
Leeds, London, Manchester

Allen & Overy LLP

One Bishops Square, Brushfield Street, London E1 6AO
Tel: (020) 7330 3000 Fax: (020) 7330 9999
Email: graduate.recruitment@allenovery.com
Website: www.allenovery.com/careeruk

firm profile

Allen & Overy LLP is an international legal practice, comprising Allen & Overy LLP and its affiliated undertakings, with 4,800 people in 25 major centres worldwide. The practice's client list includes many of the world's leading businesses, financial institutions, governments and private individuals.

main areas of work

Corporate, banking, international capital markets, litigation, tax, employment pensions and incentives, real estate and private client.

trainee profile

You will need to demonstrate a genuine enthusiasm for law, and both passion and initiative. The practice looks for creative, problem-solving people who can quickly identify salient points without losing sight of detail. As an international commercial practice, business awareness and an international outlook are prerequisite, as is the ability to work closely with others.

training environment

Allen & Overy offers a training contract characterised by flexibility and choice. The practice's training programme is widely regarded as the best in the City and continues throughout a career with Allen & Overy. Given the strength of the practice's international Banking, ICM and Corporate departments, trainees spend 12 months working in these areas. They also spend time in Litigation or Employment gaining contentious experience. There are opportunities to undertake international and client secondments. By working closely with trainers and colleagues, trainees develop practical experience and enjoy a high level of early responsibility. A positive, open and co-operative culture is encouraged both professionally and socially and a wide range of sporting and social activities are available.

benefits

Private healthcare scheme, private medical insurance, season ticket loans, subsidised restaurant, gym membership, six weeks unpaid leave upon qualification.

vacation placements

Places for Christmas 2006 (final year students and graduates all disciplines): 20; Duration: ten days; Remuneration: 250p.w.; Closing date: 31st October 2006. Places for summer 2007 (penultimate year students all disciplines): 75; Duration: 3 weeks; Remuneration:£250 p.w.; Closing date: 19th January 2007. Places available in London.

sponsorship & awards

GDL and LPC fees paid. Maintenance grants: LPC – £7,000, GDL – £6,000 in London, £5,000 elswhere.

Partners 460*
Associates 1471*
London Trainees 240
*Denotes world-wide number

contact
Graduate Recruitment

method of application
Online application form

selection procedure
Interview

closing date for 2009
GDL candidates
19th Jan 2007
Law candidates **End Aug 2007**

application
Training contracts p.a. **120**
Applications p.a. **2,700**
% interviewed p.a. **12%**
Required degree grade **2:1**

training
Salary
1st year (2006) **£31,000**
2nd year (2006) **£35,000**
Holiday entitlement **25 days**
% of trainees with a
non-law degree p.a. **45%**
% of trainees with a
law degree p.a. **55%**
No. of seats available
in international offices
**36 seats twice a year and
12 client secondments**

post-qualification
Salary (2006) **£55,000**
% of trainees offered job
on qualification (as at
31/3/05) **90%**
% of partners (as at
31/1/05) who joined as
trainees **32%**

international offices
Amsterdam, Antwerp, Bangkok, Beijing, Brussels, Bratislava, Budapest, Dubai, Frankfurt, Hamburg, Hong Kong, Luxembourg, Madrid, Milan, Moscow, New York, Paris, Prague, Rome, Shanghai, Singapore, Tokyo, Turin, Warsaw

asb *law*

Innovis House, 108 High Street, Crawley, West Sussex RH10 1AS
Tel: (01293) 861218 Fax: (01293) 861250
Email: donna.flack@asb-law.com
Website: www.asb-law.com

firm profile
asb law, a top-100 law firm and one of the largest in the south east, provides legal services to a diverse range of clients including high net worth individuals, businesses, financial institutions, government and public sector bodies. The firm's prestigious clients and the range of the services provided demonstrate that it is possible to enjoy a challenging and rewarding career without the grind of a daily commute to the City. asb has offices in Brighton, Crawley, Croydon, Horsham and Maidstone.

main areas of work
Principal types of work are banking, corporate finance, commercial, commercial litigation, commercial property/planning, employment, environment, technology/e-commerce, insolvency and recovery, intellectual property, licensing, personal injury – claimant and defendant, family, residential property, tax, trust and probate.

trainee profile
The firm is looking for strong intellectual ability, drive and initiative in people who are client-focused and commercially minded with strong interpersonal skills. You should relish the prospect of early responsibility and contact with clients in a supportive environment.

training environment
The programme is divided into four six-month seats, tailored to your strengths/interests. Training is structured to empower you to learn, take responsibility and interact with clients from an early stage and includes workshops/seminars as part of the firm's professional development programme. Some flexibility is required as seats can be in any of the five offices. A structured career path from trainee to partner is in place for the right candidates. asb law is proud of its history of retaining trainees on qualification.

sponsorship & benefits
An interest-free loan is available for the LPC, repayable over the period of the training contract.

Partners	37
Vacancies	5
Total Trainees	10
Total Staff	260

contact
Donna Flack
Tel: (01293) 861218

method of application
Application form downloaded from firm's website

selection procedure
2 interviews and a written exercise

closing date for 2009
31 July 2007

application
Training contracts p.a. **5**
Applications p.a **1,000**
% interviewed **5%**
Required degree grade **2:1**

training salary
£18,500 (2006)

offices
Brighton, Crawley, Horsham, Croydon, Maidstone

Ashurst

Broadwalk House, 5 Appold St, London EC2A 2HA
Tel: (020) 7638 1111 Fax: (020) 7638 1112
Email: gradrec@ashurst.com
Website: www.ashurst.com

firm profile

Ashurst is a leading international law firm advising corporates and financial institutions, with core businesses in mergers and acquisitions, corporate and structured finance. The firm's strong and growing presence around the world is built on extensive experience in working with clients on the complex international legal and regulatory issues relating to cross-border transactions.

main areas of work

Corporate; employment, incentives and pensions; energy, transport and infrastructure; EU and competition; international finance; litigation; real estate; tax; and technology and commercial.

trainee profile

To become an Ashurst trainee you will need to show common sense and good judgement. The firm needs to know that you can handle responsibility because you will be involved in some of the highest quality international work on offer anywhere. The transactions and cases you will be involved in will be intellectually demanding, so Ashurst looks for high academic achievers who are able to think laterally. But it's not just academic results that matter. Ashurst wants people who have a range of interests outside of their studies. And they want outgoing people with a sense of humour who know how to laugh at themselves.

training environment

Your training contract will consist of four seats. For each, you will sit with a partner or senior solicitor who will be the main source of your work and your principal supervisor during that seat. Seats are generally for six months. Anything less than that will not give you sufficient depth of experience for the responsibility Ashurst expects you to take on. The firm asks trainees to spend a seat in the Corporate Department and one seat in the International Finance Department. You are free to choose your remaining two seats, subject to availability.

benefits

Private health insurance, pension, life assurance, interest-free season ticket loan, gym membership and 25 days holiday per year during training. Other benefits can be found on the 'benefits and salaries' section of the firm's website.

vacation placements

Places for 2007: A two-week Easter placement scheme primarily aimed at final-year non-law undergraduates and all graduates. Two three-week summer placement schemes primarily aimed at penultimate-year law undergraduates. Remuneration £250 p.w. Closing date 31 January 2007.

sponsorship & awards

GDL and LPC funding plus maintenance allowances of £7, 500 per annum. LPC distinction and first class degree awards of £500. Language tuition bursaries.

Partners	175
Assistant Solicitors	495
Total Trainees	96

contact
Stephen Trowbridge
Graduate Recruitment Manager

method of application
Online

selection procedure
Interview with Graduate Recruitment Manager followed by interview with 2 partners

closing date for 2009
31 July 2007

application
Training contracts p.a. **50**
Applications p.a. **2,500**
% interviewed p.a. **10%**
Required degree grade **2:1**

training
Salary (2006)
First year
£30,000
Second year
£33,500
Holiday entitlement **25 days**
% of trainees with a non-law degree **58%**
Number of seats abroad available p.a. **8**

post-qualification
Salary (2006) **£55,000**
% of trainees offered job on qualification (2005) **90%**

overseas offices
Brussels, Dubai, Frankfurt, Madrid, Milan, Munich, New Delhi, New York, Paris, Singapore, Tokyo

Baker & McKenzie LLP

100 New Bridge Street, London EC4V 6JA
Tel: (020) 7919 1000 Fax: (020) 7919 1999
Email: london.graduate.recruit@bakernet.com
Website: www.ukgraduates.bakernet.com

firm profile

Baker & McKenzie is a leading global law firm based in 70 locations across 38 countries. With a presence in virtually every important financial and commercial centre in the world, the firm's strategy is to provide the best combination of local legal and commercial knowledge, international expertise and resources.

main areas of work

Corporate; commercial; dispute resolution; banking and finance; EU, competition and trade; employment; intellectual property and information technology; pensions; tax; projects; property. In addition the firm has cross-departmental practice groups, such as media and communications, insurance and reinsurance, business recovery and environmental law.

trainee profile

The firm is looking for trainee solicitors who are stimulated by intellectual challenge and want to be 'the best' at what they do. Effective communication together with the ability to be creative and practical problem solvers, team players and a sense of humour are qualities which will help them stand out from the crowd.

training environment

Four six-month seats which include corporate and a contentious seat, usually within the firm's highly regarded dispute resolution department. There is also the possibility of a secondment abroad or to a client. At the start of your training contract you will have a meeting to discuss individual seat preferences and during each seat you will have formal and informal reviews to discuss your progress. Your training contract commences with a highly interactive and practical induction programme which focuses on key skills including practical problem solving, interviewing, presenting and the application of information technology. The firm's training programmes include important components on management and other business skills, as well as seminars and workshops on key legal topics for each practice area. There is a Trainee Solicitor Liaison Committee which acts as a forum for any new ideas or raises issues which may occur during your training contract. Trainees are actively encouraged to participate in a variety of pro bono issues and outside office hours there is a varied sporting and social life.

benefits

Permanent health insurance, life insurance, private medical insurance, group personal pension, subsidised gym membership, season ticket loan, subsidised staff restaurant.

Partners	**80**
Assistant Solicitors	**195**
Total Trainees	**60**

contact
Suzanne Dare

method of application
Online application form

selection procedure
Candidates to give a short oral presentation based on the facts of a typical client problem, interview with two partners, meeting with a trainee

closing date for 2009
Non-law **18 Feb 2007**
Law **31 July 2007**

application
Training contracts p.a. **38**
Applications p.a. **2,000**
% interviewed p.a. **10%**
Required degree grade **2:1**

training
Salary
1st year (2006) **£31,500 +**
£3,000 'joining bonus'
2nd year (2006) **£34,000**
Holiday entitlement **25 days**
% of trainees with a non-law degree p.a.
Approx 50%
No. of seats available abroad p.a. **Variable**

post-qualification
Salary (2006) **£55,000**
% of trainees offered job on qualification (2006) **83%**

Baker & McKenzie LLP continued

vacation placements

London Summer Placement - Places for 2007: 30; Duration: 3 weeks; Remuneration (2006): £270 p.w.; Closing date: 31 January 2007.

International Summer Placement - Places for 2007: 3-5; Duration: 6-12 weeks divided between London and an overseas office; Remuneration (2006): £270 p.w.; Closing date: 31 January 2007.

sponsorship & awards

CPE/GDL funding: fees paid plus £6,000 maintenance.
LPC funding: fees paid plus £8,000.

additional information

As mentioned, trainees have the opportunity to spend three months working in one of the firm's overseas offices. Trainees have already been seconded to its offices in Sydney, Hong Kong, Frankfurt, Chicago, Washington DC, Brussels and Moscow. In addition, the firm also operates an Associate Training Programme which enables lawyers with 18-24 months pqe to spend between 6-24 months working in an overseas office.

trainee comments

"The support I received from Baker & McKenzie during my CPE and LPC at BPP in London was fantastic. From social events for all future trainees to an invite to the firm Christmas party, I felt like a member of the firm long before I walked through the door on my first day. My impressions of Baker & McKenzie only improved from that first day onwards. We were welcomed as an important asset to the firm from the start. You are exposed to valuable client work from the beginning and it was made clear that if I felt confident, I had the opportunity to develop my role as a key member of the legal team." [Greg Lovell – 3rd seat trainee]

"Several things attracted me to Baker & McKenzie. Obviously the international opportunities and global size of the firm are a huge bonus. I also like the medium-sized feel of the London office, and the relatively small trainee intake compared with other City firms, which means that I actually know all of my contemporaries and I am not made to feel like just another number. The quality of work and level of responsibility given to trainees is excellent. I frequently speak directly to clients and other lawyers, and as a trainee I feel that I receive the right level of supervision and support whilst also being trusted to get things done on my own. Finally, I like the fact that there is a great sense of team spirit at the firm. I feel like a valued member of the team, and I am regularly invited to attend client meetings, deal signings and even take part in corporate entertaining." [Carmen Glatt – 3rd seat trainee]

"Undoubtedly working in corporate has been a challenge, mainly because of the amount of responsibility given to trainees to ensure that everything on a particular project runs smoothly. The support from colleagues of all levels means that you are never out on a limb, and always able to ask numerous questions of partners and associates alike. The rest of the trainees within the department are always available to help each other and to take some of the strain when matters become urgent, and each task has always been manageable as a result. There is also a strong social side to life at the firm, with both departmental and firm Christmas parties, and as part of a smaller team within the corporate department." [Simon Tovey – 3rd seat trainee]

overseas offices

Almaty, Amsterdam, Antwerp, Bahrain, Baku, Bangkok, Barcelona, Beijing, Berlin, Bogotá, Bologna, Brasilia, Brussels, Budapest, Buenos Aires, Cairo, Calgary, Cancun, Caracas, Chicago, Chihuahua, Dallas, Düsseldorf, Frankfurt, Geneva, Guadalajara, Hanoi, Ho Chi Minh City, Hong Kong, Houston, Jakarta, Juarez, Kuala Lumpur, Kyiv, Madrid, Manila, Melbourne, Mexico City, Miami, Milan, Monterrey, Moscow, Munich, New York, Palo Alto, Paris, Porto Alegre, Prague, Rio de Janeiro, Riyadh, Rome, St Petersburg, San Diego, San Francisco, Santiago, São Paulo, Shanghai, Singapore, Stockholm, Sydney, Taipei, Tijuana, Tokyo, Toronto, Valencia, Vienna, Warsaw, Washington DC, Zürich

Barlow Lyde & Gilbert

Beaufort House, 15 St Botolph Street, London EC3A 7NJ
Tel: (020) 7247 2277 Fax: (020) 7643 8500
Email: grad.recruit@blg.co.uk
Website: www.blg.co.uk

firm profile

Barlow Lyde & Gilbert is a leading international business law firm with more than 300 lawyers and 81 partners. The firm's principal office in the UK is in Aldgate in the City of London. BLG is particularly well known for its expertise in insurance law having first started to practise in this area in the 19th century. The firm has long been recognised as pre-eminent in all aspects of this field and it has formed the bedrock from which the firm has expanded into virtually all areas of business law. Today BLG is widely based with strong practices in corporate, financial and commercial law, as well as in all kinds of commercial litigation. The firm also has highly rated aerospace, marine, energy & trade, information technology and employment teams.

trainee profile

BLG recruits 16-18 trainees each year and looks for intelligent and motivated graduates with good academic qualifications and with the social skills that will enable them to communicate effectively and get along with their colleagues and clients.

training environment

During your training contract you will have six-month seats in four different areas of the firm. The firm will always try to accommodate a trainee's preference for a particular type of work and there may be opportunities to spend time in its other offices, on secondment with clients or on exchange programmes with overseas law firms. A capable trainee will be given responsibility from an early stage in his or her training, subject of course to supervision, and will have to deal regularly with clients. Social activities play an important role for BLG and successful candidates can look forward to a variety of sporting and social events which ensure that people in different parts of the firm have a chance to meet and stay in contact with each other. Trainees are also encouraged to participate in the firm's various pro bono activities.

vacation placements

An increasing number of BLG's trainees come to the firm through its vacation schemes. Whether you are a law or non-law student the firm will introduce you to a City practice. You will be given the opportunity to become really involved and you can even choose which department you want to spend time in. The closing date for applications is 31 January 2007. The firm also runs open days and drop in days throughout the year.

sponsorship & awards

Full payment of fees and a maintenance grant are provided.

Partners	81
Assistant Solicitors	195
Total Trainees	35

contact
Caroline Walsh
Head of Graduate
Recruitment & Trainee
Development

method of application
Online application form

selection procedure
Interview day

closing date for 2009
31 July 2007

application
Training contracts p.a.
16-18
Applications p.a. **2,000**
% interviewed p.a. **10%**

training
Salary
1st year £29,000
2nd year £31,000
Holiday entitlement
5 weeks

post-qualification
Salary **£50,000**
Trainees offered job
on qualification (2005)
16 out of 17

other offices
Hong Kong, Shanghai,
Singapore

Barlow Lyde & Gilbert

Beachcroft LLP

100 Fetter Lane, London EC4A 1BN
Tel: (020) 7242 1011 Fax: (020) 7831 6630
Email: trainee@beachcroft.co.uk
Website: www.bemore.beachcroft.co.uk

firm profile

Beachcroft LLP (formerly Beachcroft Wansbroughs) is one of the largest commercial law firms in the UK, with a turnover of almost £100m and an average 9% growth in revenue year on year. An enviable client base and over 1,400 people working out of eight offices means they can provide truly exceptional career opportunities, whatever your aspirations.

Their national teams allow clients to benefit from some of the best specialists in the UK with expert local knowledge and a consistent commercial view wherever they are. For their fee earners and support staff it's a chance to work alongside nationally respected lawyers as part of progressive multidisciplinary teams.

main areas of work

The firm operates through specialist practice area teams to deliver an integrated service to clients in six main industry groups: Financial Institutions (including the insurance industry), Health & Public Sector, Real Estate, Technology & Telecommunications, Industrial Manufacturing & Transportation and Consumer Goods & Services. Key clients include Guy's and St Thomas's NHS Foundation Trust, Balfour Beatty, Westfield Shoppingtowns, Zurich, Allianz Cornhill, BAE Systems, L'Oreal, Unilever, Waitrose, Freescale Semiconductor and Getronics. The firm is helping them get more from their businesses, and they can help you get more from your career.

trainee profile

The firm looks for outgoing, commercially minded people preferably with a 2:1 honours degree in any subject. You will need to be an excellent team player and possess a mind capable of analysing, interpreting and applying complex points of law.

training environment

Training takes place over a two year period in London, Bristol, Manchester or Leeds, during which time you'll pursue a demanding study programme, whilst occupying 4 x 6 months seats in some of the key areas of commercial law. Responsibility will come early and the firm provides the supervision and support to enable you to develop and grow.

benefits

The firm operates a flexible benefits package where you can personalise your rewards – 'buying' or 'selling' options such as pension entitlement, private health care and holiday time. Additional benefits include well woman/man checks, eye care vouchers, employment assistance programme, discounted insurance and many other fringe benefits.

vacation placements

Beachcroft runs a paid placement scheme for law and non law students each summer. Please visit www.bemore.beachcroft.co.uk for further details.

sponsorship & awards

Beachcroft provides payment for GDL, LPC and £3,500 bursary.

Partners	147
Assistant Solicitors	297
Total Trainees	70

contact
Carrie Daniels
Graduate Recruitment Officer
Email: trainee@beachcroft.co.uk

method of application
Apply online at
www.bemore.beachcroft.co.uk

selection procedure
Assessment centre and panel interview

closing date
1 August each year

application
Training contracts per annum
40
Required degree
2:1 preferred

training
Salary
1st year, regions
£21,000 pa
2nd year, regions
£23,000 pa
1st year, London
£29,000 pa
2nd year, London
£31,000 pa

offices
Birmingham, Bristol, Brussels, Leeds, London, Manchester, Winchester

SJ Berwin LLP

10 Queen Street Place, London, EC4R 1BE
Tel: (020) 7111 2268 Fax: (020) 7111 2000
Email: graduate.recruitment@sjberwin.com
Website: www.sjberwin.com/gradrecruit

Partners	143
Assistant Solicitors	340
Total Trainees	81

firm profile
Since its formation in 1982, SJ Berwin LLP has established a strong reputation in corporate finance. It also has a number of niche specialisms in areas such as private equity and film finance. Much work is international and clients range from major multinational business corporations and financial institutions to high net worth individuals.

main areas of work
The firm has a wide range of departments, including corporate finance, real estate, litigation, intellectual property, employment, commercial, media, EU and competition, construction, banking, tax and financial services. Of these, corporate finance is the largest, generating around 45% of the annual turnover.

trainee profile
The firm wants ambitious, commercially-minded individuals who seek a high level of involvement from day one. Candidates must be bright and determined to succeed. They should be likely to achieve a 2:1 or first.

training environment
The traineeship is split into four six-month seats in a variety of departments, including two corporate seats. There are opportunities for seats in the firm's overseas offices. The firm has a dedicated training department and weekly training schedules, coupled with training designed specifically for trainees, allow a good grounding in legal and non-legal skills and knowledge.

vacation placements
Places for 2007: 60; Duration: 2 weeks; Remuneration: £270 p.w.; Closing Date: 31 January 2007.

sponsorship & awards
GDL and LPC fees paid and between £5,000 - £7,000 maintenance.

contact
Graduate Recruitment Team

method of application
online application form

selection procedure
2 interviews (early September)

closing date for 2009
31 July 2007

application
Training contracts p.a. **45**
Applications p.a. **2,000**
% interviewed p.a. **10%**
Required degree grade **2:1**

training
Salary
1st year £31,000
2nd year £35,000
Holiday entitlement
50 days over 2 years
% of trainees with
a non-law degree p.a. **40%**
No. of seats available
abroad p.a. **8**

post-qualification
Salary **£55,000**
% of trainees offered job
on qualification (2006) **85%**
% of assistants who joined
as trainees **26%**
% of partners who joined
as trainees **12%**

overseas offices
Brussels, Frankfurt, Madrid, Berlin, Paris, Munich, Milan, Turin

Berwin Leighton Paisner

Adelaide House, London Bridge, London EC4R 9HA
Tel: (020) 7760 1000 Fax: (020) 7760 1111
Email: traineerecruit@blplaw.com
Website: www.blplaw.com

firm profile

Berwin Leighton Paisner (BLP) is a premier City law firm with expertise in many major industry and service sectors. BLP is growing, ambitious and innovative, as well as nurturing and supportive. It was Chambers and Partners' UK Law Firm of the Year 2005, as well as The Lawyer's 'Law Firm of the Year' in 2004. It has an office in Brussels, and, as well as its USA/French alliance partner and German 'best friend', it works with preferred firms around the world, including exchanging associate secondees.

main areas of work

The full range of real estate work including investment, development, planning, construction, property finance, litigation and funds. Traditional corporate finance areas of M&A, equity capital markets and investment funds, as well as outsourcing, EU, competition, IT, telecoms and employment. An active banking and capital markets team with a growing securitisation capability, a project finance team that is expanding internationally, and an asset finance team. Strong and growing corporate tax team, intellectual property, commercial litigation, and reinsurance and insurance.

lpc+

The firm runs a tailor-made LPC Course, called the LPC+. From September 2006, all trainees will study at the College of Law, where tutors will be joined by BLP lawyers and trainers who will help to deliver some of the sessions, using BLP precedents and documents, discussing how theory is applied to real cases and transactions.

trainee profile

The firm is looking for intelligent, energetic, positive and hard-working team players who have an interest in business and gain a sense of achievement from finding solutions.

training environment

The office environment is relaxed and friendly, and trainees can enjoy early responsibility secure in the knowledge they are fully supported. Trainees spend six months in four seats and progress is reviewed every three months. An induction covers the practical aspects of working in a law firm, from billing to client care. There are technical education programmes for each department, with weekly skills sessions and seminars for trainees as well as Professional Skills Courses.

benefits

Flexible benefits include permanent health insurance, private medical insurance, subsidised gym membership, 25 days holiday a year.

vacation placements

Places, 2007: Assessment centres held during February, March and April at the firm's London office, application by online application form before 31 January 2007. The assessment centres could lead to one of 50 places on two-week placements in the summer vacation.

sponsorship & awards

CPE/GDL and LPC+ fees paid and £7,200 maintenance p.a.

Partners	167
Assistant Solicitors	255
Total Trainees	72

contact
Jennie Bishop

method of application
Firm application form online

selection procedure
Assessment day & partner interview

closing date for 2009
31 July 2007

application
Training contracts p.a. **40**
Applications p.a. **2,000**
% interviewed p.a. **5%**
Required degree grade **2:1**

training
Salary
1st year (2006) **£30,000 +**
£2,500 golden hello
2nd year (2006) **£33,000**
Holiday entitlement **25 days**
% of trainees with a
non-law degree p.a. **46%**
No. of seats available
abroad p.a. **0**

post-qualification
Salary (2006) **£53,000**
% of trainees offered job
on qualification (2006) **83%**
% of assistants who joined
as trainees (2005) **47%**
% of partners who joined
as trainees (2005) **30%**

offices
London, Brussels, alliance
office in Paris & New York,
best friend networks in 50
countries

Bevan Brittan

35 Colston Avenue, Bristol BS1 4TT
Tel: (0870) 194 3050 Fax: (0870) 194 8954
Email: hr.training@bevanbrittan.com
Website: www.bevanbrittan.com

firm profile
Bevan Brittan has firmly established itself as a truly national law firm and continues to attract high profile national and international clients and challenging, groundbreaking work. The firm is nationally recognised for its expertise in providing legal advice to clients in both the public and private sectors and is notable for being one of the very few practices whose work is equally strong in both sectors.

main areas of work
The firm is structured around four primary areas of the UK economy: built environment, health, government and commerce, industry & services. The firm operates in cross-departmental teams across these markets, harnessing the full range of skills and experience needed to provide top quality legal advice in the context of a specialist knowledge of both the sector concerned and the client's business. Areas of work covered include clinical negligence; commercial; commercial litigation; employment; construction, real estate, planning, corporate, projects, banking.

trainee profile
Bevan Brittan recognises that the firm's success depends upon a team of lawyers dedicated to service excellence. Its success is maintained by attracting and keeping enthusiastic, bright people with sound common sense, plenty of energy and the ability to work and communicate well with others.

training environment
During each six-month seat, the core of your training will be practical work experience in conjunction with an extensive educational programme. Together the training is aimed at developing attitudes, skills and legal and commercial knowledge which is essential for your career success. You are encouraged to take on as much work and responsibility as you are able to handle, which will be reviewed on a regular basis with your supervising partner. The firm is friendly and supportive with an open-door policy along with a range of social, sporting and cultural activities.

vacation placements
Places available for 2007: 50 across the three offices. Closing date: 31st March 2007.

sponsorship & awards
Bursary and funding for GDL and LPC.

Partners	**67**
Total Trainees	**38**

contact
HR and Training
(0870) 194 3050

method of application
Online application

closing date for 2009
31 July 2007

post-qualification
% of trainees offered job
on qualification (2006) **90%**

other offices
Birmingham, Bristol, London

Bircham Dyson Bell

50 Broadway, London SW1H 0BL
Tel: (020) 7222 8044 Fax: (020) 7222 3480

firm profile

Bircham Dyson Bell is one of the top 10 fastest growing law firms in the UK. Employing 300 people, (with 42 partners), the firm has doubled its turnover within the last five years. At the time of writing, it has been shortlisted for The Lawyer's "Law Firm of the Year" award. The firm acts for many high-profile clients from a wide-variety of sectors, including real estate, public and private companies, charities, private clients, and public sector organisations. The firm enjoys a market-wide reputation for the quality of its people, their knowledge, and their pro-active approach to clients.

main areas of work

Located in central London, Bircham Dyson Bell is recognised as having leading departments in the charity, private client, parliamentary, planning and public law fields. The firm also has strong company commercial, real estate and litigation teams.

trainee profile

Applications are welcome from both law and non-law students who can demonstrate a consistently high academic record. The firm is looking for creative thinkers with a confident and practical outlook who will thrive in a friendly, hard-working environment. Many of BDB's current trainees have diverse interests outside law.

training environment

The firm's training is designed to produce its future partners. To achieve this they aim to provide a balance of both formal and practical training and will give early responsibility to those who show promise. The two-year training contract consists of four six-month seats during which you will work alongside partners and other senior lawyers, some of whom are leaders in their field. As the firm practises in a wide variety of legal disciplines, trainees benefit from a diverse experience. Trainees undergo specific technical training in each seat in addition to the mandatory Professional Skills Course (PSC). Great emphasis is now placed on soft skills training and development.

benefits

Group health care, life assurance, health insurance and pension schemes.

sponsorship & awards

Bircham Dyson Bell provides funding for GDL and LPC fees.

Partners	42
Fee Earners	127
Total Trainees	16

contact
Neil Emerson, Training Principal
(020) 7227 7000

method of application
Please visit the careers section of the firm's website,
www.bdb-law.co.uk and go to the graduate area

selection procedure
2 interviews with members of the Graduate Recruitment Team, comprising a number of partners, associates and HR

closing date for 2009
31 July 2007 for autumn 2009

application
Training contracts p.a. **8**
Applications p.a. **450**
% interviewed p.a. **10%**
Required degree grade:
2:1 degree preferred

training
Salary
1st year (1 October 2006)
£29,000
2nd year (2006) £31,000
Holiday entitlement
25 days

post-qualification
Salary **£46,000**
% of trainees offered job on qualification (2006) **85%**

Bird & Bird

90 Fetter Lane, London EC4A 1JP
Tel: (020) 7415 6000 Fax: (020) 7415 6111
Website: www.twobirds.com

firm profile

Bird & Bird is a sector focused, full service international law firm. The firm has 133 partners and over 750 staff across offices in Beijing, Brussels, Dusseldorf, Frankfurt, The Hague, Hong Kong, London, Lyon, Madrid, Milan, Munich, Paris, Rome and Stockholm. The firm is proud of its friendly, stimulating environment where individuals are able to develop first class legal business and interpersonal skills. The firm's international reach and focus on sectors will enable you to work across borders and for a variety of companies, many of which operate at the cutting edge of the industries in which they operate. The firm has a leading reputation for many of the sectors on which it focuses: aviation & aerospace, banking & financial services, communications, e-commerce, information technology, life sciences, media and sport. From each of its offices, the firm provides a full range of legal services to these sectors.

main areas of work

Commercial, corporate, corporate restructuring and insolvency, dispute resolution, employment, EU & competition law, finance, intellectual property, outsourcing, real estate, regulatory and administrative, tax.

trainee profile

The firm looks for high calibre recruits – confident individuals capable of developing expert legal skills and commercial sense.

training environment

Following an introduction course, you will undertake four seats of six months. The choice of final seat is yours and is normally the area into which you elect to qualify. Some seats may be spent in the firm's international offices. You will share an office with a partner or senior assistant solicitor who will guide and advise you. You will develop drafting and legal research skills and gain familiarity with legal procedures. The firm encourages you to make an early contribution to casework and participate in client meetings. External lectures are arranged to cover the Professional Skills Course. Trainees are encouraged to join the number of sports teams at the firm and to attend various social events.

benefits

BUPA, season ticket loan, subsidised sports club membership, life cover, PHI, pension, childcare and eyecare vouchers.

vacation placements

Places for 2007: 20; Duration: 2 x 3 weeks; Remuneration: £260 p.w; Closing Date: 31 January 2007.

sponsorship & awards

LPC and PgDL fees paid and a yearly maintenance grant of £5,500.

Partners 133*
Assistant Solicitors 421*
Total Trainees 25 in London
denotes worldwide figures

contact
Lynne Walters
lynne.walters@twobirds.com

method of application
Online application form via the firm website.

selection procedure
Insight and Selection Days in July and August

closing date for 2009
31 July 2007 for law and non law students.

application
Training contracts p.a. **18**
Applications p.a. **900**
% interviewed p.a. **10 %**
Required degree grade **2:1**

training
Salary
1st year (2006) **£28,000**
2nd year (2006) **£30,000**
Holiday entitlement
25 days
% of trainees with a non-law degree p.a. **Varies**

post-qualification
Salary (2006) **£50,000**
% of trainees offered job on qualification (2006) **86%**

overseas offices
Beijing, Brussels, Dusseldorf, Frankfurt, The Hague, Hong Kong, London, Lyon, Madrid, Milan, Munich, Paris, Rome and Stockholm

---

Blake Lapthorn Linnell

New Court, 1 Barnes Wallis Road, Segensworth, Fareham, Hampshire, PO15 5UA
Tel: (01489) 579990 Fax: (01489) 579126
Email: graduateinfo@bllaw.co.uk
Website: www.bllaw.co.uk

firm profile
Blake Lapthorn Linnell is one of the largest regional law firms in the UK, with six offices in the south of England. Their clients include a wide range of UK and multi-national companies, from well-known retailers, banks, local authorities and property developers to major charities. They also act for private clients offering specialist services such as French property, tax planning and clinical negligence. Although a large practice they have retained a sense of community. The firm values diversity, which adds breadth to its expertise. Their professionals have very different backgrounds and skills, many having worked in city firms and in-house. Their advice is practical, providing clients with tailored solutions. They encourage innovation and imagination in order to enhance their client services.

main areas of work
The core practice areas are corporate and commercial, real estate, litigation and dispute resolution, and private client.

trainee profile
Fitting in at Blake Lapthorn Linnell is about ability, enthusiasm and contribution. In order to maintain their standards of excellence, they need high-calibre people. To be successful you need to demonstrate significant personal achievement and strong inter-personal skills as well as an excellent academic record.

training environment
Training is carefully structured and designed to provide variety, responsibility and intellectual challenge. You will have a series of six-month placements in a range of departments. Working with a partner or senior solicitor, you will be exposed to a wide range of clients and work, in private and commercial practice areas. During each placement your supervisor will involve you directly in work so you learn from hands-on experience, as well as observation and instruction. The greater competence you demonstrate, the more responsibility you will be given.

benefits
Private healthcare, life assurance, contributory pension scheme, childcare vouchers and 'You at Work' flexible benefits.

sponsorship & awards
LPC fees and maintenance grant.

Partners	**92**
Assistant Solicitors	**208**
Total Trainees	**22**

contact
Mrs Lynn Ford

method of application
Online application form with link from website.

selection procedure
Interviews and Assessment Day

closing date for 2009
13 July 2007

application
Training contracts p.a. **8-10**
Applications p.a. **300**
% interviewed p.a. **25 %**
Required degree grade **2:1**

training
Salary
1st year (2005) £18,000
2nd year (2005) £19,500
Holiday entitlement
26 days

post-qualification
Salary (2005) **£32,000**
% of trainees offered job on qualification (2006) **86%**
% of trainees offered job on qualification (2005) **84%**

offices
Southampton, Portsmouth, Oxford, London, Fareham and Winchester

Boodle Hatfield

89 New Bond Street, London, W1S 1DA
Tel: (020) 7629 7411 Fax: (020) 7629 2621
Email: hr@boodlehatfield.com
Website: www.boodlehatfield.com

firm profile
Boodle Hatfield is a highly successful medium-sized firm who have been providing bespoke legal services for more than 275 years. They still act for some of their very first clients and are proud to do so. The firm has grown into a substantial practice, serving the full spectrum of commercial and private clients, both domestically and internationally.

main areas of work
The ethos of facilitating private capital activity and private businesses underpins the work of the whole firm. The interplay of the skills between five major areas – tax and financial planning, property, corporate, litigation and family – makes Boodle Hatfield particularly well placed to serve these individuals and businesses.

trainee profile
The qualities the firm look for in their trainees are commitment, flexibility and the ability to work as part of a team. Students with 2.1 or above and high A levels should apply.

training environment
Trainees spend six months in up to four of the firm's main areas: Property, Corporate, Private Client & Tax, and Litigation. Boodle Hatfield is well known for the high quality of its training. All trainees are involved in client work from the start and are encouraged to handle their own files personally as soon as they are able to do so, with the appropriate supervision. The firm's trainees therefore have a greater degree of client contact than in many firms with the result that they should be able to take on more responsibility at an early stage. Trainees are given formal appraisals every three months which are designed as a two-way process and give trainees the chance to discuss their progress and to indicate where more can be done to help in their ongoing training and development.

benefits
Private healthcare, life assurance, season ticket loan, pension scheme, private health insurance, conveyancing grant, permanent health insurance.

vacation placements
Two week placement between June and September, for which 10 students are accepted each year. Applicants should apply via the application form on the website at www.boodlehatfield.com from 1 January 2007.

sponsorship & awards
LPC and GDL/CPE plus maintenance grant.

Partners	29
Assistant Solicitors	49
Total Trainees	10

contact
Emma Turner
020 7079 8133

method of application
Online application

selection procedure
Interviews with the Training Principal, a Partner and the HR Director plus an ability test in verbal reasoning

closing date for 2009
31 July 2007

application
Training contracts p.a. **6-8**
Required degree grade **2:1**

training
Salary
**1st year £27,500
(Sept 2005)
2nd year £29,500**
Holiday entitlement
25 days

post-qualification
Salary **£46,000**
% of trainees offered job
on qualification (2006) **100%**

regional offices
Oxford

B P Collins

Collins House, 32-38 Station Road, Gerrards Cross SL9 8EL
Tel: (01753) 889995 Fax: (01753) 889851
Email: jacqui.symons@bpcollins.co.uk
Website: www.bpcollins.co.uk

firm profile
B P Collins was established in 1966, and has expanded significantly to become one of
the largest and best known legal practices at the London end of the M4/M40 corridors.
At its main office in Gerrards Cross, the emphasis is on commercial work, including
company/commercial work of all types, commercial conveyancing and general commercial litigation. Alongside this there is a highly respected private client department
specialising in tax planning, trusts, charities, wills and probates, and an equally successful family law team.

main areas of work
Company/commercial, employment, IT/IP, civil and commercial litigation, commercial conveyancing, property development, private client and family law.

trainee profile
Most of the partners and other fee-earners have worked in London at one time or
another but, tired of commuting, have opted to work in more congenial surroundings
and enjoy a higher quality lifestyle. Gerrards Cross is not only a very pleasant town
with a large number of high net worth private clients but it is also a convenient location
for serving the extremely active business community at the eastern end of the Thames
Valley including West London, Heathrow, Uxbridge, Slough and Windsor. The firm
therefore looks for trainees who are likely to respond to this challenging environment.

training environment
The firm aims to have six trainee solicitors at different stages of their training contracts
at all times. Trainees serve five months in four separate departments of their choice.
The final four months is spent in the department in which the trainee intends specialising. The firm has a training partner with overall responsibility for all trainees and
each department has its own training principal who is responsible for day to day
supervision. There are regular meetings between the training principal and the trainee
to monitor progress and a review meeting with the training partner midway and at the
end of each departmental seat. The firm also involves its trainees in social and marketing events including golf and cricket matches, and other sporting and non-sporting
activities.

Partners	20
Assistant Solicitors	28
Total Trainees	6

contact
Mrs Jacqui Symons

method of application
Handwritten covering letter
& CV

selection procedure
Screening interview &
selection day

closing date for 2008/9
30 June 2007

application
Required degree grade **2:1**,
A & B 'A' level grades.

training
Salary
1st year £19,000
2nd year £20,000

Brabners Chaffe Street

1 Dale St, Liverpool L2 2ET
Tel: (0151) 600 3000 Fax: (0151) 227 3185
55 King Street, Manchester M2 4LQ
Tel: (0161) 236 5800 Fax: (0161) 228 6862
7-8 Chapel Street, Preston PR1 8AN
Tel: (01772) 823921 Fax: (01772) 201918
Email: trainees@brabnerscs.com
Website: www.brabnerschaffestreet.com

firm profile

One of the top North West commercial firms, Brabners Chaffe Street, in Liverpool, Manchester and Preston, has the experience, talent and prestige of a firm that has a 200-plus-year history. Brabners Chaffe Street is a dynamic, client-led specialist in the provision of excellent legal services to clients ranging from large plcs to private individuals.

main areas of work

The firm carries out a wide range of specialist legal services and Brabners Chaffe Street's client base includes plcs, public sector bodies, banks and other commercial, corporate and professional businesses. Brabners Chaffe Street is organised into five client-focused departments: corporate (including commercial law); employment; litigation (including sports and media); property (including housing association and construction); private client.

trainee profile

Graduates and those undertaking CPE or LPC, who can demonstrate intelligence, intuition, humour, approachability and commitment.

training environment

The firm is one of the few law firms that holds Investor in People status and has a comprehensive training and development programme. Trainees are given a high degree of responsibility and are an integral part of the culture of the firm. Seats are available in the firm's five departments and each trainee will have partner-level supervision. Personal development appraisals are conducted at six-monthly intervals to ensure that trainee progress is valuable and informed. The training programme is overseen by the firm's Director of Training and Development, Dr Tony Harvey, and each centre has a designated Trainee Partner. It is not all hard work and the firm has an excellent social programme.

sponsorship & awards

Assistance with LPC funding is available.

Partners	58
Associates	24
Assistant Solicitors	39
Fee Earners	28
Total Trainees	18

contact
Liverpool office:
Dr Tony Harvey
Director of Training and
Risk Management

method of application
Application form (please request by email, fax or post only). Online from 2007

selection procedure
Interview & assessment day

closing date for 2009
Apply by 31 July 2007 for training contracts commencing in September 2009

application
Training contracts p.a. **7**
Required degree grade
2:1 or post-graduate degree

training
Salary
Not less than £20,000
Holiday entitlement **25 days**

offices
Liverpool, Manchester, Preston

Brachers

Somerfield House, 59 London Road, Maidstone ME16 8JH
Tel: (01622) 690691 Fax: (01622) 681430
Email: info@brachers.co.uk
Website: www.brachers.co.uk

firm profile

Brachers is a leading firm in the South East with an established City office. The firm is principally involved in corporate and commercial work although it has a niche private client practice. The firm has a leading healthcare team, one of 14 on the NHSLA panel.

main areas of work

Company/commercial, general litigation, medical negligence, commercial property, employment, private client and family.

trainee profile

Candidates need to have a strong academic background, common sense and be team players. Both graduates in law and non-law subjects are considered as well as more mature candidates.

training environment

Trainees have four six-month seats out of company/commercial, property, general civil litigation, defendant insurance, medical negligence, family, employment, and private client. Trainees have two appraisals in each seat. The firm has an open door policy and is committed to developing a long-term career structure. Social events are organised.

sponsorship & awards

LPC/CPE £6,000 discretionary award.

Partners	19
Assistant Solicitors	32
Total Trainees	7

contact
Michelle Perry

method of application
Online application from
www.brachers.co.uk

selection procedure
Interview day with partners

closing date for 2009
31 July 2007

application
Training contracts p.a. **2**
Applications p.a. **400**
% interviewed p.a. **7.5%**
Required degree grade **2:1**

training
Salary
1st year (2005) £17,400
2nd year (2005) £19,500
Holiday entitlement **23 days**

post-qualification
Salary **(2005)**
£31,000
% of trainees offered job
on qualification **90%**

other offices
London

Bristows

3 Lincoln's Inn Fields, London WC2A 3AA
Tel: (020) 7400 8000 Fax: (020) 7400 8050
Email: info@bristows.com
Website: www.bristows.com

firm profile
Bristows specialises in providing legal services to businesses with interests in technology or intellectual property. The firm acts for some of the largest companies in the world and helps protect some of the most famous brands. Its work reaches beyond intellectual property law to corporate and commercial law, property, tax, employment law and litigation.

main areas of work
Intellectual property, IT, bio/pharma, corporate, competition, commercial litigation, mediation, ADR, publishing & media, employmenet, real estate & tax.

trainee profile
Bristows is looking for applicants with outstanding intellects, with strong analytical skills and engaging personalities. It is also looking for people who will contribute to the ethos of the firm. Bristows is a very friendly firm and believes that you get the best from people if they are in a happy and supportive working environment.

training environment
The firm's training programme gives you the knowledge and skills to build on the extensive hands-on experience you will gain in each of its main departments. You will be working closely with partners, which will accelerate your training. Part of this training may also involve a secondment to one of a number of leading clients. With the international spread of its clients, the probability of overseas travel is high, especially upon qualification.

benefits
Excellent career prospects, a competitive package, firm pension scheme, life assurance and health insurance.

vacation placements
Schemes are run for one week during Christmas and Easter breaks, two weeks during the Summer break. Remuneration: £200 p.w.; Closing Date: Christmas –23 November; Easter/Summer – 28 February.

sponsorship & awards
CPE/LPC fees plus £7,000 maintenance grant for each.

Partners	26
Assistant Solicitors	55
Total Trainees	13

contact
Graduate Recruitment & Training Officer

method of application
Application form

selection procedure
2 individual interviews

closing date for 2009
31 January 2007 for February interviews, 31 August 2007 for September interviews

application
Training contracts p.a.
Up to 10
Applications p.a. **3,500**
% interviewed p.a. **6%**
Required degree grade
2:1 (preferred)

training
Salary
1st year (2006) £30,000
2nd year (2006) £32,000
Holiday entitlement
4 weeks
% of trainees with
a non-law degree p.a. **84%**

post-qualification
Salary (2006) **£45,000**
% of trainees offered job
on qualification (2006) **87.5%**
% of assistants (as at
5/6/06) who joined as
trainees **49%**
% of partners (as at 5/6/06)
who joined as trainees **53%**

Browne Jacobson

Nottingham, Birmingham, London
Tel: (0115) 976 6000 Fax: (0115) 947 5246
Email: traineeapplications@brownejacobson.com
Website: www.brownejacobson.com/trainees

firm profile

Browne Jacobson is one of the largest and most successful law firms in the Midlands. The firm has more than tripled its turnover since 1996 and continues to drive double-digit annual growth.

The offices in Nottingham, Birmingham and London provide the flexibility to deal with national as well as regional clients, whilst also offering its people the opportunity to work in three vibrant city centres.

Browne Jacobson's track record of attracting and retaining outstanding people has led to the firm ranking 47th in 'The Sunday Times Top 100 UK companies to work for 2006'. Both its clients and its people value the open, friendly and flexible nature of the firm's culture and with over 500 people, the firm is large enough to attract some of the best talent in the country, but small enough to foster a supportive and flexible working environment.

Recent accolades include: Law Society Trainee Solicitor of the Year 2006, President and Chair of Nottingham Trainee Solicitor group and 2nd place in Nottinghamshire Law Society Hammond Cup.

main areas of work

Browne Jacobson is a full-service law firm for commercial, insurance and public sector clients. The firm has a national reputation for its work in health, retail and environmental sectors and is recognised as regional heavyweights for corporate, property, public enquiry, litigation and professional risk work.

trainee profile

The firm is looking for talented law and non-law graduates who can bring with them enthusiasm, commitment, client focus and a flexible and friendly attitude. Browne Jacobson believe in being open, straightforward and easy to deal with, and is looking for individuals who will fit with this culture.

training environment

Trainees start with a comprehensive induction programme, a fast track professional skills course and then spend four periods of six months in some of the principle areas of the firm, gaining an overview of the practice.

Trainees get great training, a friendly and supportive working environment, and real career opportunities. Trainees are given quality work and exposure to clients from early on, but are supported in achieving results and recognised for their contribution.

sponsorship & awards

LPC/PGDL tuition fees paid, plus maintenance grant for LPC/PGDL of £5,000 per year.

Partners	59
Associates	46
Assistant Solicitors	70
Fee Earners	258
Total Trainees	21
Total Staff	518

contact
Philippa Shorthouse

method of application
Apply online at www.brownejacobson.com/trainees or by CV and covering letter

selection procedure
Telephone interview, followed by an open day and/or assessment centre

closing date
31 July, two years before the training contract is due to commence

application
Training contracts p.a. **12**
Applications p.a. **600**
% interviewed p.a. **15%**
Required degree grade **2:1**

training
Salary
1st year £22,500
2nd year £25,000
Holiday entitlement **25 days**
% of trainees with a non-law degree p.a. **36%**

post-qualification
Salary **Market Rate**
Holiday entitlement **25 days**
% of trainees offered a job on qualification **80%**

brownejacobson

Burges Salmon

Narrow Quay House, Narrow Quay, Bristol BS1 4AH
Tel: (0117) 902 2766 Fax: (0117) 902 4400
Email: katy.edge@burges-salmon.com
Website: www.burges-salmon.com

firm profile
Burges Salmon is proof that law doesn't necessarily have to mean London.
Based in Bristol, the firm's turnover has more than tripled in recent years as they continue to win prestigious clients out of the hands of City rivals. Clients such as Orange, the Ministry of Defence and Mitsubishi Motors rely on their legal expertise and in doing so have helped cement the firm's reputation as creative, lateral thinkers. Burges Salmon's primary asset is its people. Trainees benefit from supervision by some of the best minds in the industry: lawyers who are leaders in their field with a formidable depth of experience. All this against the backdrop of Bristol: a city with a quality of life you would be hard pressed to find anywhere else in the UK.

main areas of work
Burges Salmon provides national and international clients with a full commercial service through six main departments: Corporate & Financial Institutions (CFI); Commercial; Property; Tax & Trusts; Commercial Disputes & Construction (CDC); and Agriculture, Property Litigation & Environment (APLE). Specialist areas include: Banking; EU & Competition; Corporate Finance; Employment; IP & IT; Planning; and Transport. The firm is ranked top tier by Chambers and Partners for 18 of its practice areas.

trainee profile
Burges Salmon's lawyers are intelligent, ambitious individuals who work hard to achieve their goals. Successful applicants demonstrate a high degree of commercial acumen coupled with a genuine enthusiasm for the law. They must possess a strong academic background and show evidence of achievement in non-academic pursuits which demonstrate an ability to build relationships with both clients and colleagues alike.

training environment
Trainees play a vital role in shaping the future of the firm and Burges Salmon invests a great deal of time and resource into training and development. The firm is justifiably proud of its reputation for offering one of the best training programmes in the profession: the Law Society recently accredited their training programme with seven points of good practice, where in previous years the maximum awarded to any firm was two. Training is personalised to suit each individual, and the six seat structure allows the opportunity to experience a wider range of practice areas before making a decision on qualification. This dedication to trainees is demonstrated by a high retention rate, which is well above the industry average.
Trainees are given early responsibility balanced with an open door policy for advice and guidance. Supervisors are partners or senior lawyers who are highly trained to ensure trainees gain as much as possible from every seat and will tailor the workload to fit with each individual's interests and abilities. There are many opportunities for trainees to take an active role in cases involving high profile clients as well as running their own files on smaller cases. The firm also encourages secondments which offer new perspectives on the profession and enable trainees to build relationships with clients.

Partners	65
Assistant Solicitors	190
Total Trainees	37

contact
Katy Edge, Graduate Recruitment Manager

method of application
Employer's application form available on website

selection procedure
Penultimate year law students, final year non-law students, recent graduates or mature candidates are considered for open days, vacation placements and/or training contracts

closing date for 2009
31 July 2007

application
Training contracts p.a.
20-25
Applications p.a. **1,500**
% interviewed p.a. **10%**
Required degree grade **2:1**

training
Salary
1st year (2006) £24,000
2nd year (2006) £25,000
Holiday entitlement **24 days**
% of trainees with
a non-law degree p.a. **50%**

post-qualification
Salary (2006) **£37,000**
% of trainees offered job
on qualification (2005) **94%**
% of assistants who joined
as trainees (2005) **60%**
% of partners who joined
as trainees (2005) **25%**

Burges Salmon continued

benefits
Annually reviewed competitive salary, 24 days paid annual leave, bonus scheme, pension scheme, private health care membership, mobile phone, Christmas gift, corporate gym membership, sports and social club.

vacation placements
Burges Salmon offers 40 two-week Vacation Placements during the summer. Individuals visit 2 departments of their choice supervised by a partner or senior solicitor, and attend court visits and client meetings. Current trainees run skills training sessions, sports and social events. Remuneration: £250 per week.

Selection for Vacation Placements is via Open Days which take place in February 2007. Please visit the website for further details.

sponsorship and awards
The firm pays GDL and LPC fees at the institution of your choice. Maintenance grants of £6,000 are paid to LPC students, and £12,000 to students studying for both the GDL and LPC (£6,000 p.a.).

comments
"The firm has managed to win work that other national rivals would kill for, and all without sacrificing quality on the altar of ambition. With client wins such as EMI Group, Reuters, and Coca Cola HBC, Burges Salmon has quietly built the elite firm outside London." A leading awards body.

"I particularly value Burges Salmon lawyers for their approachability, their interest in our business and their enthusiasm." Amanda Doyle, Vice-President, UK Legal, Orange.

"When deciding which firm to apply to for my training contract, the six seat system at Burges Salmon made the firm stand out. The opportunity to experience so many different areas of work really appealed to me, but I had not fully appreciated how useful the system is as a trainee until the final two seats of my training contract. The benefit of having a transitional period leading up to qualification is enormous, as it allows you to take on work of an increasingly complex nature in comfortable increments, rather then being confronted with an 'overnight' change." Kath Lundy, Newly Qualified Solicitor.

"The quality of work on offer was one of the main reasons I chose Burges Salmon and I have not been disappointed. The work I am involved in ranges from large, high profile deals to smaller cases where I am able to run my own files. Trainees enjoy a high level of responsibility because supervisors and other lawyers are always willing to answer questions and provide the support necessary for each case." Lucy Gray, Trainee Solicitor.

For more profiles, please visit the firm's website.

Capsticks

77-83 Upper Richmond Road, London SW15 2TT
Tel: (020) 8780 2211 Fax: (020) 8780 4811
Email: career@capsticks.co.uk
Website: www.capsticks.com

firm profile

Independently rated as the country's leading healthcare law firm. Capsticks handles litigation, administrative law, employment, commercial and property work for a variety of healthcare bodies, including over 200 NHS Foundation Trusts, Acute Trusts, Mental Health Trusts, PCTs, Ambulance Trusts, Strategic Health Authorities, private sector health providers, health-related charities and regulatory bodies.

main areas of work

Clinical Law 52%; Commercial 16%; Commercial Property 14%; Dispute Resolution 8%; Employment Law 10%.

trainee profile

Successful candidates possess intellectual agility, good interpersonal skills and are capable of taking initiative.

training environment

Six four-month seats, which may include clinical negligence/advisory; commercial property; commercial; employment; and dispute resolution. Trainees take responsibility for their own caseload as well as assisting on larger cases and work with clients from an early stage. There are numerous in-house lectures for all fee earners. There is an open door policy, and trainees receive informal feedback and supervision as well as regular appraisals. Despite the firm's rapid expansion, it has retained a friendly atmosphere and a relaxed working environment. There are regular informal social and sporting activities.

benefits

Bonus scheme, pension, PHI, death in service cover, interest-free Season Ticket Loan.

vacation placements

Places for 2007: Yes; Duration: 2 weeks; Closing Date: 9 February 2007.

sponsorship & awards

Scholarship contributions to GDL and LPC courses.

Partners	31
Assistant Solicitors	52
Total Trainees	9
Other Fee-earners	6

contact
Sue Laundy

method of application
Application form

selection procedure
Candidates are encouraged to participate in the firm's summer placement scheme. Final selection is by interview with the Training Principal & other partners

closing date for 2009
31 July 2007

application
Training contracts p.a. **4-5**
Applications p.a. **c.150**
% interviewed p.a. **c.20%**
Required degree grade
2:1 or above

training
Salary
1st year TBA
2nd year TBA
Holiday entitlement
22 days p.a. (increased by 1 day p.a. to max 25 days)
% of trainees with a non-law degree p.a. **25%**

post-qualification
Salary (2006)
TBA
% of trainees offered job on qualification (2006) **66%**
% of assistants (as at 1/9/06) who joined as trainees **43%**
% of partners (as at 1/9/06) who joined as trainees **10%**

Charles Russell

8–10 New Fetter Lane, London EC4A 1RS
Tel: (020) 7203 5000 Fax: (020) 7203 5307
Website: www.charlesrussell.co.uk

Partners	95
Other fee-earners	218
Total trainees	30
Total staff	600

firm profile

Charles Russell LLP is a leading legal practice, providing a full range of services to UK and international businesses, governments, not-for-profit bodies, and individuals. It has five offices: London, Cheltenham, Guildford, Oxford and Geneva. The practice is known for its client care, high quality, expertise and friendly approach. The strategy is simple – to help clients achieve their goals through excellent service. Many lawyers are ranked as leaders in their field. Experienced in carrying out cross-border corporate and commercial work, the practice also provides clients with access to 150 recommended law firms across the world as part of the two major legal networks, ALFA International and the Association of European Lawyers. The practice's lawyers and staff are highly motivated and talented people. The practice's commitment to training and development and strong team spirit is a key ingredient to being known as a friendly practice to work with and work at.

main areas of work

75% of the practice's work is commercial. Principle areas of work include media and communications, employment and pensions, charities, private client/family, corporate/commercial, intellectual property, dispute resolution, real estate and insurance/reinsurance.

trainee profile

Trainees should be balanced, rounded achievers with an excellent academic background.

training environment

The practice recruits a small number of trainees for its size each year. This allows trainees to undergo the best possible training. Trainees usually spend six months in four of the following training seats – litigation and dispute resolution, corporate/commercial, real estate, private client, family and employment/pensions. Secondments to clients are also often available. Wherever possible the practice will accommodate individual preferences. You will be seated with a partner/senior solicitor. Regular appraisals are held to discuss progress and direction. Trainees are encouraged to attend extensive in-house training courses. The PSC is taught both internally and externally. Trainees are encouraged to take on as much responsibility as possible. A social committee organises a range of activities from quiz nights through to sporting events.

benefits

BUPA; PHI and Life Assurance: pension plan; season ticket loans; 25 days holiday plus additional day for house moves; dress-down Fridays; croissants and muffins are available between 8:00am and 9:00am each Friday in London.

sponsorship & awards

The practice pays for course fees whilst you are at law school and also offers a grant per academic year of £5,000 to London trainees, £4,500 to Guildford trainees and £3,500 to Cheltenham trainees.

contact
graduaterecruitment@
charlesrussell.co.uk

method of application
Online application via the website

selection procedure
Assessment days to include an interview & other exercises designed to assess identified performance criteria

closing date for 2009
31 July 2007

application
Training contracts for 2008: **17**
Applications p.a.
Approx 1,500
% interviewed p.a. **4%**
Preferred degree grade **2:1**

training
Salary
1st year (2005) £28,000
2nd year (2005) £30,500
Holiday entitlement
25 days + additional day for house moves

post-qualification
Salary (2006) **£48,000**

regional offices
Also offers training contracts in its Cheltenham (2 places) & Guildford (3 places) offices.

Clarke Willmott

1 Georges Square, Bath Street, Bristol, BS1 6BA
Tel: (0117) 941 6600 Fax: (0117) 917 5591
Email: careers@clarkewillmott.com
Website: www.futurepilots.co.uk

firm profile

Clarke Willmott is a UK law firm with a national reputation in key commercial and private client services. The firm's lawyers are, first and foremost, business advisers whose objectives are: to help clients achieve their goals and to enhance the value of their opportunities. They take a straightforward, proactive approach, and have helped enterprises of all sizes and at all stages of the business lifecycle navigate a range of complex legal issues with positive results.

main areas of work

Services include corporate, commercial, real estate and construction, business recovery, dispute resolution, employment, health and safety, intellectual property, property and private capital as well as a range of services to private clients. The firm has specialist industry expertise in real estate (development, investment, residential and urban regeneration), banking & financial services, sport and food & drink.

trainee profile

The firm recruits commercially aware trainees who can demonstrate a clear commitment to a career in law. Clarke Willmott looks for trainees who have a confident, energetic approach and who have the ability to work and communicate well with others. Applications are welcomed from both and law and non-law graduates, with at least a 2:1 degree.

training environment

Trainees complete four six-month seats, providing a wide range of practical experience and skills in contentious and non-contentious work. Individual preference is sought and will be balanced with the firm's needs. Trainees work closely with partners and solicitors in a supportive team structure, and have regular reviews to ensure they are reaching their potential. Training in both legal and non-legal areas is provided to meet the needs of the individual trainee and the PSC is undertaken in-house.

sponsorship & benefits

Life assurance, group personal pension, gym membership, bonus based on the firm's financial performance, LPC fees paid (50% on starting and 50% on succeful completion).

Partners	67
Solicitors	185
Trainees	21

contact
Graduate recruitment

method of application
Application form, available online

selection procedure
Interview

closing date for 2009
31 July 2007 (interviews September 2007)

application
Training contracts p.a.: **12**
Applications p.a. **c. 500**
% interviewed p.a. **10%**
Preferred degree grade **2:1**

training
Salary
1st year (2005) £20,000
2nd year (2005) £21,500
Holiday entitlement
22 days rising to 26 on qualification

post-qualification
Salary (2006) **£34,500**
% of trainees offered job on qualification (2005) **c. 55%**

regional offices
Bristol, Birmingham, Southampton, Taunton

Cleary Gottlieb Steen & Hamilton LLP

City Place House, 55 Basinghall Street, London, EC2V 5EH
Tel: (020) 7614 2200 Fax: (020) 7600 1698
Email: lonlegalrecruit@cgsh.com
Website: www.clearygottlieb.com

firm profile
Cleary Gottlieb is a leading international law firm with more than 800 lawyers practising in the world's major financial centres. Founded in 1946, the firm operates as a single, integrated partnership, serving a clientele comprising many of the world's largest multi-national corporations, financial institutions and sovereign governments, as well as small start-ups, private clients and charitable organisations.

main areas of work
(In London) Mergers and acquisitions, corporate, capital markets and finance, tax, regulatory, competition/antitrust and intellectual property.

trainee profile
Successful candidates must demonstrate exceptional academic ability together with evidence of extra-curricular achievement and must be enthusiastic about practising law in a challenging and dynamic international setting. Language skills are an advantage.

training environment
There are no departments at Cleary Gottlieb. Trainees sit with partners and senior solicitors and work on a mix of M&A, capital markets, finance, tax, regulatory, competition and intellectual property work. Seats change every six months. There are opportunities to travel, work in other offices and go on secondment to clients in the UK and abroad. Qualified solicitors are from time to time seconded to the New York and Hong Kong offices. Trainees may have the opportunity to take the New York Bar exam. Trainees are encouraged to take responsibility early and in most respects fulfill the same role as first year lawyers in other offices.

benefits
Pension, health insurance, long-term disability insurance and health club membership.

vacation schemes
The London office runs three vacation schemes, one at easter for two weeks, and two in summer for a period of three weeks. The closing date for the 2007 schemes is February 14, 2007.

sponsorship & awards
LPC fees and £8,000 maintenance award.

Partners	15
Solicitors	48
Total Trainees	8

contact
Legal Recruitment

method of application
Cover letter and CV

selection procedure
Usually 2 interviews

closing date for 2009
July 31 2007

application
Training contracts p.a. up to **6**
Applications p.a. **2,250**
% interviewed p.a. **1%**
Required degree grade
High 2:1 from a leading university and excellent A levels

training
Salary
1st year (2005) £35,000
2nd year (2005) £40,000

post-qualification
Salary £84,000

overseas offices
New York, Washington DC, Paris, Brussels, Moscow, Frankfurt, Cologne, Rome, Milan, Hong Kong and Beijing

CLEARY GOTTLIEB

Clifford Chance

10 Upper Bank Street, Canary Wharf, London, E14 5JJ
Tel: (020) 7006 6006 Fax: (020) 7006 5555
Email: graduate.recruitment@cliffordchance.com
Website: www.cliffordchance.com/gradsuk

firm profile
Clifford Chance is a truly global law firm, which operates as one organisation throughout the world. Its aim is to provide the highest quality professional advice by combining technical expertise with an appreciation of the commercial environment in which its clients operate.

trainee profile
Consistently strong academic profile (minimum 2:1 degree), a broad range of interpersonal skills and extra curricular activities and interests, commitment to the career, ability to communicate fluently and accurately.

training environment
The Clifford Chance training contract has been devised to provide students with the technical skills and experience needed to contribute to the firm's success on a daily basis, to achieve your professional qualification and to progress to a rewarding career. The two year training contract consists of four six month seats. Most trainees spend a seat on a secondment at an international office or with a client. In each seat trainees will be working alongside senior lawyers. Trainees are encouraged to use initiative to make the most of expertise and resources available to the firm. Three-monthly appraisals and monitoring in each seat ensure trainees gain a range of work and experience.

benefits
Prize for first class degrees and top performers on the Clifford Chance LPC, interest-free loan, private health insurance, subsidised restaurant, fitness centre, life assurance, occupational health service, and permanent health insurance.

vacation placements
Places for 2006-2007: Winter Workshops, vacation placements during spring and summer breaks. There is a strong social element to the programme; Duration: 2 days for Winter Workshops, 2-4 weeks for other schemes; Remuneration: £270 pw; Closing Date: 17 November 2006 for Winter Workshops; 31 January 2007 for other schemes. A number of international placements will also be available during the summer. Selected candidates will have the opportunity to spend two weeks in London, followed by two weeks in one of the firm's European offices.

sponsorship & awards
GDL and LPC fees are paid, and a maintenance grant of £7,000 will be paid to LPC students. GDL students will be paid £6,000 if studying in London, and £5,000 if studying elsewhere.

London office	
Partners	237
Lawyers	737
Trainees	196

contact
Graduate Resourcing Specialist

method of application
Online application, followed by online verbal reasoning test

selection procedure
Assessment day comprising an interview, a group exercise & a paper verbal reasoning test

application
Training contracts p.a. **130**
Applications p.a. **2,000**
% interviewed p.a. **25%**
Required degree grade **2:1**

training
Salary
1st year £31,000
(Aug 2006)
2nd year £34,000
Holiday entitlement **25 days**
% of trainees with
a non-law degree p.a. **45%**
No. of seats available
abroad p.a. **86**

post-qualification
Salary (Aug 2006) **£55,000**
% of trainees offered job
on qualification (2006) **95%**

overseas offices
Amsterdam, Bangkok, Barcelona, Beijing, Brussels, Bucharest, Budapest, Dubai, Düsseldorf, Frankfurt, Hong Kong, Luxembourg, Madrid, Milan, Moscow, Munich, New York, Padua, Paris, Prague, Rome, São Paulo, Shanghai, Silicon Valley, Singapore, Tokyo, Warsaw, Washington DC

Clyde & Co

51 Eastcheap, London EC3M 1JP
Tel: (020) 7623 1244 Fax: (020) 7623 5427
Email: theanswers@clydeco.com
Website: www.clydeco.com/graduate

firm profile

Clyde & Co's main aim is to be the premier law firm in Insurance, Transportation, Trade and Natural Resources, providing a full service to an international client base from key strategic locations. The firm's dispute resolution practice is one of the largest in the UK. It has unsurpassed knowledge and experience in insurance and reinsurance, marine, aviation, transportation and trade & energy, offering a full corporate and commercial service in these areas and to businesses involved in international trade. Trainees are recruited to work in London and Guildford during their two-year training contract.

main areas of work

Insurance/reinsurance, marine & transportation, aviation & areospace, dispute resolution, international trade & energy, corporate/commercial, property & construction, IT/IP and employment.

trainee profile

The firm is looking for graduates with excellent academic records, outgoing personalities and keen interests. Trainees need to have the social skills that will enable them to communicate effectively and build relationships with clients and colleagues. The ability to analyse problems, apply common sense and provide solutions to situations are all qualities the firm seeks. Ultimately Clyde & Co recruits to retain and they are seeking candidates who will remain with the firm beyond qualification.

training environment

Clyde & Co is a friendly and supportive environment and they encourage their trainees to take on responsibility from as early as possible. They offer four six-month seats in the London and Guildford offices, as well as opportunities for secondments to national and international clients. They are also able to offer trainees seats in their overseas offices. Regular appraisals are held with your supervising partner to assess your progress, skills and development needs. With such a small number of trainees, the firm is usually able to accommodate individual preferences when it comes to choosing seats.

benefits

Pension, life assurance, private medical insurance, subsidised gym membership, interest-free season ticket loan and coffee shop.

legal work experience

The firm runs two-week summer vacation schemes for 20 students. Please visit the website for the exact dates. Applications are made online and the closing date for the scheme is 31 January 2007.

sponsorship & awards

GDL and LPC fees paid plus a maintenance grant of £6,000 in London/Guildford and £5,500 elsewhere. In addition, an optional £1,000 interest free loan on joining.

Partners	139
Fee-earners	250
Total Trainees	46

contact
Kate Wild
Graduate Recruitment Manager

method of application
Online via website
www.clydeco.com/graduate

selection procedure
Assessment session with Graduate Recruitment followed by interview with 2 partners

closing date for 2009
31 July 2007

application
Training contracts p.a. **22**
Applications p.a. **1,000 +**
% interviewed p.a. **5%**
Required degree grade **2:1**

training
Salary
1st year (2006) £29,000
2nd year (2006) £32,000
Holiday entitlement **25 days**
% of trainees with
a non-law degree p.a. 60%

post-qualification
Salary (2006) **£50,000**

overseas offices
Abu Dhabi, Caracas, Cardiff, Dubai, Hong Kong, Nantes, Paris, Piraeus, Rio de Janeiro, Shanghai, Singapore, Belgrade*, Los Angeles*, Moscow*, New York*, St Petersburg*

* Associated office

CMS Cameron McKenna LLP

Mitre House, 160 Aldersgate Street, London EC1A 4DD
Tel: (0845) 300 0491 Fax: (020) 7367 2000
Email: gradrec@cms.cmck.com
Website: www.law-now.com

firm profile

CMS Cameron McKenna LLP is a leading international law firm and an integral part of CMS, the alliance of European Law firms. They've earned a reputation for outstanding client service, acute business awareness and for being passionate about client relationships. They work for some of the worlds leading companies, helping to solve their problems so they can run their businesses more efficiently. The firm believes that to give the best advice, lawyers must clearly understand the industry, marketplace and concerns of their clients. All lawyers have a specialist interest in at least one major industry sector and are committed to building long- term relationships with their clients.

main areas of work

The firm's clients benefit from an extensive range of tailored services, delivered through offices in the UK. Central Europe, North America and Asia. The firm's services include banking and international finance, corporate, real estate, commercial, energy projects and constructions, insurance and re-insurance.

trainee profile

The firm looks for high achieving team players with good communication, analytical and organisational skills. You will need to show initative and be able to accept personal responsibility, not only for your own work, but also for your career development. You will need to be resilient and focused on achieving results.

training environment

The firm is friendly and supportive and puts no limits on a trainee's progress. It offers four six months seats, three of which will be in the firm's main areas of practice. In addition, you may gain experience of a specialist area or opt for a secondment to a national or international client. In each seat you will be allocated high quality work on substantial transactions for a range of government and blue-chip clients. Regular appraisals will be held with your seat supervisor to assess your progress, skills and development needs. The three compulsory modules of the Professional Skills Course will be completed on a fast track basis during the trainee induction. This enables trainees to be effective and participate on a practical level as soon as possible. The Professional Skills Course is complimented by a comprehensive in house training programme that continues up to qualification and beyond.

vacation placements

Places for 2006/2007: 55, Easter, Christmas & summer, Duration: 2 weeks, Remuneration: £250pw. Closing date for Christmas scheme 17 November 2006; Easter & Summer 16 February 2007.

benefits

Annual bonus, gym membership/subsidy, life assurance, pensions scheme with firm contributions, private healthcare, season ticket loan, confidential care line, subsidised restaurant and 25 days holiday with options to buy a further five days

sponsorship & awards

GDL and LPC sponsorship is provided. The firm will cover the cost of all law school fees and provide you with a maintenance grant (£7,500 London, Guildford and Oxford and £5,000 elsewhere).

Partners	131
Assistant Solicitors	603
Total Trainees	120

contact
Graduate Recruitment
Team (0845) 300 0491

method of application
Online application form
www.law-now.com/gradrec

selection procedure
2 stage selection procedure. Initial interview, group exercise and verbal reasoning test followed by an assessment centre

closing date
31 July 2007

application
Training contracts p.a. **60**
Applications p.a. **1,500**
% interviewed p.a. **35%**
Required degree grade **2:1**

training
Salary
1st year (2006) £30,000
2nd year (2006) £33,500
Holiday entitlement
25 days + option of flexible holidays
% of trainees with a non-law degree p.a. **40%**
No. of seats available abroad p.a. **Currently 12**

post-qualification
Salary (2006) **£54,000**
% of trainees offered job on qualification (2005) **88%**

C/M/S/ Cameron McKenna

Cobbetts

Ship Canal House, King Street, Manchester M2 4WB
Tel: (0845) 165 5045
Email: lawtraining@cobbetts.co.uk
Website: www.cobbetts.co.uk/graduate

firm profile
Cobbetts is one of the UK's leading law firms with offices in the three key commercial centres of Birmingham, Leeds and Manchester. With a consistent reputation for innovation, quality and job satisfaction, the firm continues its tremendous growth, with clients to match. The firm's client base of regional, national and international clients includes PLCs, mid-sized corporates, financial institutions and public sector / not for profit organisations, ensuring that trainees enjoy a breadth and depth of experience.

main areas of work
Cobbetts has developed true national practice areas – property, corporate, commercial, banking, employment, litigation services, social housing and private capital – and key specialist expertise in fields including media, the public sector, planning and public markets, in particular on to AIM.

trainee profile
Applications are encouraged from both law and non-law undergraduates who anticipate attaining a high class honours degree. Mature students and those wishing to change career are also encouraged to apply. Applicants must be personable with a determination to work hard and succeed.

training environment
Four six-month seats are available.
There is an opportunity for one trainee each year to spend three months in Brussels.

benefits
Opportunity to join BUPA scheme after four months, gym membership, Social Club, pension scheme, travel loan, death in service, counselling service.

sponsorship & awards
The firm offers financial assistance for the Graduate Diploma in Law and the LPC, will meet the cost of the Professional Skills Course and provides a maintenance grant which is currently £4,000.

Partners	**136**
Assistant Solicitors	**117**
Total Trainees	**65**

contact
Janet Toombs
(0845) 165 5045

method of application
Online

selection procedure
Assessment days

closing date for 2009
13 July 2007

application
Training contracts p.a.
Approx 25
Applications p.a.
approx.1,000
% interviewed p.a. **approx 10%**
Required degree grade
2:1

training
Salary for each year of training
1st year £21,000
2nd year £22,000
(both reviewed annually)
Holiday entitlement
Starting at 23 days

post-qualification
Salary NQ **£33,000**
Reviewed annually

% of trainees offered job on qualification **90%**

other offices
Birmingham, Leeds

Coffin Mew & Clover

Fareham Point, Wickham Road, Fareham PO16 7AU
Tel: (01329) 825617 Fax: (01329) 825619
Email: sarajlloyd@coffinmew.co.uk
Website: www.coffinmew.co.uk

firm profile

Coffin Mew & Clover offer an exceptional training opportunity. The firm is rapidly expanding to become one the larger southern regional firms with major offices located in the cities of Portsmouth and Southampton and just off the M27 Motorway at Fareham. The firm is in the enviable position of operating a balanced practice offering top quality commercial and private client services in approximately equal volume and is particularly noted for a number of niche practices with national reputations.

main areas of work

The firm is structured through nine core departments. Corporate & Corporate Finance, Commercial Services, Employment, Commercial Litigation, Property Litigation, Personal Injury, Property; Family & Childcare and Trust/Probate. Niche practices (in which training is available) include Intellectual Property; Finance and Business Regulation; Social Housing; and Medical Negligence.

trainee profile

The firm encourages applications from candidates with very good academic ability who seek a broad based training contract in a highly progressive and demanding but friendly and pleasant environment.

training environment

The training contract is divided into six seats of four months each which will include a property department, a litigation department and a commercial department. The remainder of the training ccontract will be allocated after discussion with the trainee concerned. The firm aims to ensure that the trainee spends the final four months of his or her training ccontract in the department in which he or she hopes to work after qualification.

sponsorship & awards

LPC funding available by discussion with candidates.

vacation placements

Open Week in July each year; applications for the 2007 Open Week may be made to the Practice Manager with accompanying c.v. between 1 November 2006 and 31 March 2007.

Partners	19
Associates	16
Assistant solicitors	26
Total trainees	11

contact
Mrs Sara Lloyd
Practice Manager

method of application
CV & covering letter

selection procedure
Interview

closing date for July 2008/9
31 July 2007 (not before January 1, 2007)

application
Training contracts p.a. **5**
Applications p.a. **400+**
% interviewed p.a. **5%**
Required degree grade
2:1 (save in exceptional circumstances)

training
Salary
1st year
Competitive market rate
2nd year
Competitive market rate
Holiday entitlement **20 days**
% of trainees with a
non-law degree p.a. **25%**

post-qualification
Salary (2006) **Competitive market rate**
% of trainees offered job on qualification (2006) **100%**
% of assistants who joined as trainees **25%**
% of partners who joined as trainees **50%**

Covington & Burling

265 Strand, London WC2R 1BH
Tel: (020) 7067 2000 Fax: (020) 7067 2222
Email: graduate@cov.com
Website: www.cov.com

firm profile
Covington & Burling is a leading US law firm, founded in Washington, with offices in London, New York, San Francisco and Brussels. The London office was established in 1988 and has continued to grow progressively since then.

main areas of work
In London, the main areas of work are corporate & commercial, employment, insurance, tax, life sciences, litigation & arbitration, IP/IT, and competition. The firm is known worldwide for its remarkable understanding of regulatory issues as well as its depth and expertise in areas including IT, e-commerce and life sciences. In such work, the firm represents many blue-chip clients including Microsoft, Pfizer, Qualcomm, Bacardi, Krispy Kreme, Business Software Alliance and Armani.

trainee profile
The firm is looking for outstanding students who demonstrate genuine commitment to the legal profession and who have not only excellent academic ability, but also imagination, and the necessary practical and social skills required to respond to the evolving needs of its clients. In return, the firm can offer innovative and fascinating work in a stimulating and supportive environment.

training environment
The firm offers a unique and personal training programme to suit the individual needs of each trainee. Following a comprehensive introduction, trainees will spend six months in each of corporate, litigation and arbitration, and IP/IT departments. The fourth seat will be spent in one of the life sciences, employment or tax practice areas. The firm encourages trainees to take early responsibility in order to get the most out of their training period and trainees will receive regular feedback to enhance their development.

benefits
Pension, permanent health insurance, private health cover, life assurance and season ticket loan.

vacation placements
16 places during summer vacation. Closing date for applications 28 February 2007.

sponsorship & awards
GDL and LPC fees paid. Maintenance grant of £7,250 per annum.

Partners:	177*
Associate Lawyers &	
Other Fee-earners:	346*
Total Trainees:	8

denotes worldwide figures

contact
Graduate Recruitment Manager
(020) 7067 2089
graduate@cov.com

method of application
Online Application Form
See website www.cov.com

selection procedure
1st & 2nd interview

closing date for 2009
31 July 2007

application
Training contracts p.a.   4
Required degree grade   2:1

training
Salary:
1st year   £35,000
2nd year   £37,000
(subject to review)
Holiday entitlement 25 days

overseas offices
Brussels, New York, San Francisco, Washington

COVINGTON & BURLING

Cripps Harries Hall LLP

Wallside House, 12 Mount Ephraim Road, Tunbridge Wells TN1 1EG
Tel: (01892) 506006 Fax: (01892) 506360
Email: graduates@crippslaw.com
Website: www.crippslaw.com

firm profile

A leading regional law firm and one of the largest in the South East, the firm is recognised as being amongst the most progressive and innovative regional practices.

Recent re-organisation into client-focused, industry sector groups promotes a strong ethos of client service and ensures the firm's solicitors are not only excellent legal practitioners but also experts in specialist business sectors. The firm is regarded by many businesses, institutions and wealthy individuals as the natural first choice among regional law firms. Although long-established, the firm's profile is young, professional, forward-thinking, friendly and informal.

The firm achieved the Lexcel quality mark in January 1999, the first 'Top 100' firm to do so.

main areas of work

Commercial 16%, dispute resolution 19%, private client 27%, property 38%.

trainee profile

Individuals who are confident and capable, with lively but well organised minds and a genuine interest in delivering client solutions through effective and pragmatic use of the law; keen to make a meaningful contribution both during their contract and long term career with the firm.

training environment

The firm offers a comprehensive induction course, a well structured training programme, frequent one to one reviews, regular in-house courses and seminars, good levels of support and real responsibility.

The training programme is broader than most other firms and typically includes six seats in both commercial and private client areas. Trainees usually share a room with a partner or an associate and gain varied and challenging first hand experience.

sponsorship awards

Discretionary LPC funding: Fees – 50% interest free loan, 50% bursary.

Partners	39
Assistant Solicitors	50
Total Trainees	14

contact
Annabelle Lawrence
Head of Human Resources

method of application
application form available
on website

selection process
1 interview with Managing
Partner and Head of Human
Resources

closing date for 2009
31 July 2007

application
Training contracts p.a. **7**
Applications p.a. **Up to 750**
% interviewed p.a. **6%**
Required degree grade **2:1**

training
Salary
1st year (2006) £17,500
2nd year (2006) £20,000
Holiday entitlement **25 days**
% of trainees with a non-law
degree p.a. **30%**

post-qualification
Salary (2006) **£31,500**
% of trainees offered job
on qualification (2006) **100%**
% of assistants/associates
(as at 1/5/06) who joined as
trainees **30%**
% of partners (as at 1/5/05)
who joined as trainees **20%**

CRIPPS HARRIES HALL LLP

Davenport Lyons

30 Old Burlington Street, London W1S 3NL
Tel: (020) 7468 2600 Fax: (020) 7437 8216
Email: dl@davenportlyons.com
Website: www.davenportlyons.com

firm profile
Davenport Lyons is a leading corporate and rights law firm offering a full service to clients in a range of market sectors including media, entertainment, property, retail, leisure, sport and banking. With a 36 partner strong practice, over 85 fee earners and supporting operational function, they are a commercially focused law firm based in the luxurious surroundings of Mayfair. Coupled with the firm's desire to retain its warm and friendly environment, Davenport Lyons is the ideal place to start your career as a successful solicitor.

main areas of work
The firm provides a full range of services through its five departments, corporate, contentious rights and dispute resolution, property, employment and private client. Areas of expertise include: corporate, commercial, corporate tax, film and TV, music, defamation, contentious and non-contentious IP/IT, commercial dispute resolution, insolvency, liquor and entertainment licensing, property, property dispute resolution, tax and trusts, matrimonial and employment.

trainee profile
Davenport Lyons is looking for candidates with excellent academic qualifications (2.1 and above, good A level results) and an interesting background, who are practical and can demonstrate good business acumen. Candidates should have a breadth of interests and foreign language skills are an advantage. In short, the firm is looking for well-rounded individuals.

training environment
The training programme consists of four six-month seats. During each seat trainees receive mid and end of seat reviews, and each seat has a dedicated trainee supervisor. Davenport Lyons has an on-going in-house training and lectures programme. They pride themselves on offering interesting, hands-on training with trainees being encouraged to develop their own client relationships and to handle their own files under appropriate supervision, therefore being treated as junior fee earners. The firm aims to make its training contracts informative, educational, practical, supportive and, let us not forget, as enjoyable as possible.

benefits
Season ticket loan; client introduction bonus; contribution to gym membership; discretionary bonus; 23 days holiday; life assurance.

vacation placements
A limited number of places are available on the Summer Vacation Scheme which runs during July and August. Remuneration is £200 per week. Closing date for applications 31 January 2007.

sponsorship & awards
The firm does not offer financial assistance.

Partners	36
Assistant Solicitors	44
Total Staff	195
Total Trainees	13-14

contact
Marcia Mardner
Head of HR
Michael Hatchwell
Training Partner

method of application
Online

selection procedure
Interviews

closing dates
Closing date for 2009
30 July 2007

application
Training contracts p.a. **7**
Applications p.a. **2,000**
% interviewed p.a. **2%**
Required degree grade **2:1**

training
Salary
1st Year trainee
£28,000 - £28,666
2nd Year trainee
£29,332 - £30,000
Holiday entitlement **23 days**
% of trainees with a
non-law degree p.a. **70%**

post-qualification
% of trainees offered job
on qualification (2005) **70%**

Davenport Lyons

www.chambersandpartners.co.uk

Davies Arnold Cooper

6–8 Bouverie Street, London EC4Y 8DD
Tel: (020) 7936 2222 Fax: (020) 7936 2020
Email: daclon@dac.co.uk
Website: www.recruit.dac.co.uk

Partners	96
Total Fee-earners	165
Total Trainees	13
Total Staff	317

firm profile
Davies Arnold Cooper is an international law firm particularly known for its dispute resolution and real estate expertise. It advises in relation to specialist areas of law, including insurance, real estate, construction and product liability, and has a leading Hispanic practice. The firm has offices in London, Manchester, Madrid and Mexico City.

main areas of work
Commercial disputes: 70%; real estate: 30%.

trainee profile
If you secure a training contract with Davies Arnold Cooper you will most probably have a 2:1 degree, either in law or in another academic subject, as well as good A level grades. You will definitely be a self-starter with plenty of energy and common sense. What you've done with your life so far counts for much more than where you went to school/university. The firm has a number of dual-qualified lawyers whose previous professions were medicine, accountancy, public service or the armed forces. They recognise that for you, a law career is a bigger decision than someone just leaving university, especially when it means giving up a decent salary.

training programme & environment
The firm encourages you to take on responsibility as soon as you join and will give you as much as you can handle, although you will always be supervised and never left alone to struggle. You will experience both contentious and non-contentious work and because the firm only takes on a handful of trainees every year, the chances are you will be able to select your preferred seats. There are five training contract positions available for September 2009. Applications should be made using the firm's application form which is available on request or from the website.

benefits
Current first year salary is £27,000. 25 days holiday, private medical insurance and season ticket loan.

sponsorship & awards
CPE and LPC fees paid plus maintenance grants.

Dechert LLP

160 Queen Victoria Street, London EC4V 4QQ
Tel: (020) 7184 7000 Fax: (020) 7184 7001
Email: application@dechert.com
Website: www.dechert.com

firm profile
Dechert LLP is a dynamic international law firm, with 1,000 lawyers across the USA and Europe. Its largest offices are in Philadelphia, New York and London.

main areas of work – london
Dechert's largest practice areas in London are corporate and securities, financial services (advising hedge funds and other investment funds), finance and real estate, and litigation.

trainee profile
Dechert looks for enthusiasm, intelligence, an ability to find practical solutions, and for powers of expression and persuasion. Graduates from any discipline are welcome to apply.

training environment
Your training contract will start with a visit to Philadelphia, to take part in the firm-wide induction. After that you will do six seats of four months. Every new seat is discussed with you, and will reflect your interests and ambitions. No two trainees have the same training contract. Your choice of seats, and general development is guided by both the Director of Training and your own Trainee Partner, who meet with you regularly.
For those who wish to travel, the firm offers secondments to its Brussels office, and sometimes to its offices in Munich and the USA.

vacation placements
Dechert runs schemes at Easter, and in July. The firm's vacation schemes are aimed at penultimate year law students. The closing date for applications is 19 February 2007.

sponsorship & awards
Dechert pays LPC fees plus £7,000 sponsorship.

trainee comments
"I decided to join Dechert following a vacation scheme, and I haven't looked back since. The firm has a great working atmosphere, largely attributable to the real mix of people, and that development and training are a top priority. That view has definitely stuck fast through my training contract. I have really enjoyed each of my six seats and been given responsibility over and above that enjoyed by my friends at other firms." (Emma Byford, Newly Qualified, read Law at Leicester)

"What has really stood out for me during my training contract at Dechert is the encouragement to take responsibility. Whilst this is a slightly nerve-wracking experience at first, it is an excellent way to make sure you really understand the deal. The added flexibility which comes from the six seat system means trainees can get a taste of many different departments within the firm without restricting their qualification options." (Duncan Batty, Newly Qualified, read Law at Nottingham)

Partners	42*
Assistant Solicitors	82*
Total Trainees	20*
*denotes London figure	

contact
Graduate Recruitment Assistant

method of application
Online

selection procedure
Communication exercises & interviews with partners & assistant solicitors

closing date for 2009
31 July 2007

application
Training contracts p.a.
Up to 15
Applications p.a. **Approx 1,500**
% interviewed p.a. **Approx 9%**
Required degree grade **2:1**
(or capability of attaining a 2:1)

training
Salary
1st year £35,000
2nd year £40,000
Holiday entitlement **20 days**
% of trainees with a non-law degree p.a. **Varies**
No. of seats available abroad p.a. **3 or 4 (plus shorter secondments to US offices)**

post-qualification
Salary **c.£56,000 to £66,000 (depending on practice area)**
% of trainees offered job on qualification **70%**
% of partners who joined as trainees **50%**

overseas offices
Austin, Boston, Brussels, Charlotte, Harrisburg, Hartford, Luxembourg, Munich, Newport Beach, New York, Palo Alto, Paris, Philadelphia, Princeton, San Francisco, Washington

Denton Wilde Sapte

One Fleet Place, London EC4M 7WS
Tel: (020) 7242 1212 Fax: (020) 7320 6555
Email: jo.wilson@dentonwildesapte.com
Website: www.dentonwildesapte.com

firm profile
Denton Wilde Sapte is a commercial law firm based in London with offices in Europe, the Middle East and the CIS. The firm's strengths lie in its sector focus, and its practice areas are as strong and diverse as its client list.

main areas of work
Banking & finance; corporate; dispute resolution; EU & competition; employment & pensions; energy & infrastructure, real estate, tax; technology, media & telecommunications.

trainee profile
The firm looks for candidates who are team players with a strong academic and extra curricular record of achievement.

training environment
Four six month seats, including at least one transactional and one contentious seat. Trainees also spend one seat in the Banking & Finance and/or Real Estate Department. The firm aims to offer trainees as much choice as possible with their seats, one of which may be spent in one of the international offices or with one of the firm's clients. You will be given as much responsibility as you can handle, working with the law, with the team and with clients in real business situations. The firm works hard to maintain a friendly and open working environment where ideas are shared and people work together to achieve goals.

benefits
Flexible benefit scheme, joining bonus. Season ticket loan.

vacation placements
Open days during December 2006 and summer schemes during July 2007. Closing date for applications for open days is 24 November 2006 and for summer schemes 9 February 2007.

sponsorship & awards
GDL and LPC tuition fees covered plus £5,500 maintenance grant for each year of study, £6,000 if studying in London. A joining bonus of £1,000.

Partners	150
Fee-earners	530
Total Trainees	65

contact
Jo Wilson

method of application
Application form

selection procedure
First interview; selection test; second interview & case study

closing date for 2009
31 July 2007

application
Training contracts p.a. **30**
Applications p.a. **1,500**
% interviewed p.a. **10-15%**
Required degree grade **2:1**

training
Salary
1st year £30,000
2nd year £32,000
Holiday entitlement **24 days**
% of trainees with a
non-law degree p.a. **40%**
No. of seats available
abroad p.a. **Currently 8**

post-qualification
Salary (2006) **£53,000**
% of trainees offered job
on qualification (2005) **72%**

overseas offices
Abu Dhabi, Almaty, Cairo, Dubai, Istanbul, Moscow, Muscat, Paris, Tashkent

Dickinson Dees

St. Ann's Wharf, 112 Quayside, Newcastle upon Tyne NE99 1SB
Tel: (0191) 279 9046 Fax: (0191) 279 9716
Email: graduate.recruitment@dickinson-dees.com
Website: www.trainingcontract.com

firm profile

Dickinson Dees enjoys an excellent reputation as one of the country's leading commercial law firms. Based in Newcastle upon Tyne and Tees Valley, the firm prides itself on the breadth of experience and expertise within the firm which enables it to offer services of the highest standards to clients. Whilst many of the firm's clients are based in the North, Dickinson Dees works on a national basis for national and internationally based businesses and organisations.

main areas of work

The firm has over 800 employees and is organised into four key departments (Company Commercial, Commercial Property, Litigation and Private Client) with 38 cross departmental units advising on specific areas. They also handle large volumes of high-quality work for a diverse client base.

trainee profile

The firm is looking for intellectually able, motivated and enthusiastic graduates from any discipline with good communication skills. Successful applicants will understand the need to provide practical, commercial advice to clients. They will share the firm's commitment to self-development and teamwork and its desire to provide clients with services which match their highest expectations.

training environment

Trainees are relatively few for the size of the practice and the environment is supportive and friendly. You are fully integrated into the firm and involved in all aspects of firm business. The training contract consists of four seats -one in each of the Commercial Property, Company Commercial and Litigation departments. You may be able to specialise for the fourth seat. Trainees sit with their supervisors and appraisals are carried out every three months. The firm has its own Training Department as well as a supportive Graduate Recruitment team. There are induction courses on each move of department with opportunities for trainees to get involved in the firm's training programme. The firm offers a tailored in-house Professional Skills Course which is run in conjunction with the College of Law.

work placements

Places for 2007: 40; Duration: 1 week; Remuneration: £125 p.w. The firm's work placement weeks are part of the recruitment process and all applicants should apply online at www.trainingcontract.com. Apply by 28 February 2007 for Easter and Summer placements.

sponsorship & awards

GDL/LPC fees paid and financial assistance offered.

Partners	71
Total Staff	820
Total Trainees	28

contact
Sally Brewis, Graduate Recruitment Adviser

method of application
Apply online at www.trainingcontract.com

selection procedure
Aptitude and ability tests, negotiation exercise, personality questionnaire, interview

closing date for 2009
31 July 2007

application
Training contracts p.a.
up to **15 (Newcastle)**
up to **3 (Tees Valley)**
Applications p.a. **800**
% interviewed p.a. **10%**
Required degree grade **2:1**
in either law or non-law

training
Salary
1st year (2006) £19,000
2nd year (2006) £20,000
Holiday entitlement **25 days**
% of trainees with
a non-law degree p.a. **40%**
No. of seats available
abroad p.a. **2**
(3-month secondments)

post-qualification
Salary (2006) **£34,000**
% of trainees offered job
on qualification (2006) **90%**
% of partners (as at 1/9/05)
who joined as trainees
34%

other offices
Tees Valley,
Brussels (associated office)

DICKINSON DEES

DLA Piper UK LLP

Victoria Square House, Victoria Square, Birmingham B2 4DL
Tel: (020) 7796 6677 Fax: (0121) 262 5793
Email: recruitment.graduate@dlapiper.com
Website: www.dlapiper.com

firm profile
DLA Piper is one of the world's largest full service commercial law firms with UK offices in Birmingham, Edinburgh, Glasgow, Leeds, Liverpool, London, Manchester and Sheffield.

The firm now has more than 7,300 employees working from 59 offices in 22 countries across Europe, Asia and the US and its clients include some of the world's leading businesses, governments, banks and financial institutions. This impressive client base coupled with an emphasis on providing high quality service and teamwork, offers a challenging fast paced working environment.

The firm holds the 'Investors in People' accreditation, demonstrating its commitment to its employees and their ongoing development, and its award-winning Client Relationship Management programme proves commitment to clients as well. DLA Piper was awarded 'Law Firm of the Year' at the 2005 Legal Business Awards and 'Global Law Firm of the Year' at The Lawyer Awards 2006.

As well as taking care of its own people, DLA Piper has extensive Corporate Social Responsibility/Pro Bono programmes in place. The firm feels that taking part in these programmes helps to broaden the perspectives of the DLA Piper people that take part. For trainees, pro bono work (for companies like The Princes Trust) means gaining valuable experience in running their own cases and experiencing a unique level of work and responsibility.

main areas of work
DLA Piper has the following main areas of work: banking; business support and restructuring; commercial and projects; corporate; human resources; litigation; real estate; regulatory; and technology, media and communications.

trainee profile
The firm is looking for individuals from either a law or non-law background who have a minimum of 3 Bs at A Level (or equivalent) and expect, or have achieved a 2.1 degree classification – but good academics are no longer sufficient. DLA Piper looks for highly motivated and energetic team players with sound commercial awareness, outstanding communication and organisational skills, and, above all, an appetite for life!

There is no such thing as a 'standard' DLA Piper trainee, they do not want to recruit clones. Trainees are encouraged to be themselves and, in that respect, be different.

As soon as future trainees are recruited DLA Piper does as much as possible to make them feel part of the firm, for example, writing to them regularly and organising social events where future trainees can meet one another as well as current members of staff.

Partners	1200
Other lawyers	1800
Total Trainees	174

contact
Sally Carthy, Head of Graduate Recruitment

method of application
Online application form

selection procedure
First interview, second interview, assessment afternoon

closing date for 2009
31 July 2007

application
Training contracts p.a. **90+**
Applications p.a. **2,500**
% interviewed p.a. **15%**
Required degree grade **2:1**

training
Salary (2006)
1st year £31,000 (London)
£22,000 (Regions)
£18,000 (Scotland)
2nd year £34,000 (London)
£24,000 (Regions)
£20,000 (Scotland)
% of trainees with a
non-law degree p.a. **40%**

post-qualification
Salary (2006)
£53,000 (London)
£35,000 (regional offices)
£32,000 (Scotland)

uk offices
Birmingham, Edinburgh, Glasgow, Leeds, Liverpool, London, Manchester, Sheffield

overseas offices
Austria, Belgium, Bosnia-Herzegovina, China, Croatia, Czech Republic, Denmark, France, Germany, Georgia, Hong Kong, Hungary, Italy, Netherlands, Norway, Russia, Slovakia, Spain, Thailand, Ukraine, USA, Japan, UAE.

DLA Piper UK LLP cont'd

training environment

From induction to qualification and beyond, DLA Piper ensures that its employees develop the necessary skills and knowledge to survive in a busy client-driven environment. Trainees complete four six month seats during the course of their training contract. If you want responsibility, they will give you as much as you can handle and your progress will be monitored through regular reviews and feedback. The compulsory Professional Skills Course is run in-house and is tailored to meet the needs of the firm's trainees. This combined with on-the-job experience, provides trainees with an excellent grounding on which to build their professional careers.

DLA Piper trainees are able to express a preference for their seats, and as much as possible is done to ensure that during the course of the training contract these preferences can be accommodated.

vacation placements

DLA Piper runs summer vacation schemes across all of its UK offices. The scheme aims to give a thorough insight into life at the firm. Attendees shadow a fee-earner in two departments and are given a range of work to do, they are also allocated a trainee 'buddy' to help out with any queries. The scheme also includes presentations from departments and social events with the trainees.

Places for 2007: Approx 200; Duration: 2 weeks; Remuneration (2006 figures) £230 per week (London), £180 per week (regions and Scotland); Closing Date: 31 January 2007.

sponsorship & awards

Payment of LPC and GDL fees plus maintenance grant in both years, is offered to future trainees who have yet to complete these courses.

benefits

Trainees are entitled to join the firm's pension, private health cover, life assurance and permanent health insurance schemes. Holiday entitlement is 25 days per year.

trainee quotes

"I was really impressed by the way the graduate recruitment team kept in contact with me while I was still at university and law school. There's regular contact, support and you receive letters, the firm's magazine and press releases. You actually feel part of the team from the outset and reassured knowing that you can always pick up the phone if you have any queries. It's a great way to start."

DMH Stallard

100 Queens Road, Brighton BN1 3YB
Tel: (01273) 223703 Fax: (01273) 223711
Email: recruitment@dmhstalard.com
Website: www.dmhstallard.com

firm profile
DMH Stallard is an approachable and innovative firm with an open culture which encourages personal development and provides its personnel with a high level of support in order to achieve this. The firm offers expertise and service comparable to City firms to a range of commercial organisations, non-profit institutions and individual clients. By focusing on the client's needs DMH Stallard provides practical and creative solutions. DMH Stallard operates from offices in Brighton, Crawley/Gatwick and London.

main areas of work
Corporate/commercial; commercial property, construction; planning and environmental; employment, intellectual property/IT; litigation; residential conveyancing; personal injury; private client; property litigation.

trainee profile
The firm welcomes applications from motivated graduates from all backgrounds and age groups. Enthusiasm, a mature outlook and commercial awareness are as prized as academic ability, and good communication skills are a must. Ideal applicants are those with the potential to become effective managers or strong marketeers.

training environment
Usually four six month seats taken from the following areas: employment, intellectual property/IT, corporate/commercial, planning and environmental, commercial property, commercial litigation, property litigation, personal injury, residential conveyancing and private client. Trainees are closely supervised by the partner to whom they are attached but have every opportunity to work as part of a team and deal directly with clients.

vacation placements
Places for Summer 2007: Limited number of unpaid places; Duration: 1 week; Closing Date: 31 January 2007.

Partners	47
Assistant Solicitors	22
Total Trainees	14

contact
Jessica Leigh-Davis

method of application
Online application form

selection procedure
First and second stage assessment days including interviews

closing date for 2009
31 July 2007

application
Training contracts p.a. **10**
Applications p.a. **218**
% interviewed p.a. **17%**
Required degree grade **2:1**

training
Salary
1st year (2006)
£20,000 (Brighton & Crawley)
£25,000 (London)
2nd year (2006)
£22,000 (Brighton & Crawley)
£27,000 (London)
Holiday entitlement **23.5 days**

Dorsey & Whitney

21 Wilson Street, London EC2M 2TD
Tel: (020) 7588 0800 Fax: (020) 7588 0555
Website: www.dorsey.com

firm profile
Dorsey & Whitney is amongst the largest law firms in the world with more than 20 offices situated across three continents. The firm has over 650 lawyers worldwide. The London office of Dorsey & Whitney has over 50 fee earners. It continues to build on its traditional strengths in corporate law, litigation, real estate and intellectual property work through its wide range of practice groups.

main areas of work
The London office offers the full range of legal services including corporate finance, cross-border M&A, commercial litigation, tax, employment, real estate, intellectual property and private equity.

trainee profile
Dorsey & Whitney is looking for 'self-starters', capable of meeting the intellectual and business challenges of a successful multi-national practice. Candidates should be committed team players who enjoy rewarding client work. An honours degree at 2:1 level or above and some relevant work experience is also required.

training environment
The training contract is split into four individual 'seats' of six months each. Each trainee will be required to complete litigation and corporate seats. Secondments to major clients are available. All trainees are supplied with the encouragement and support necessary to maximise their potential. Through the mentoring, professional development and evaluation programmes, the firm strives to develop and retain the highest calibre lawyers.

benefits
Non-contributory pension schemes; health insurance and life insurance.

Partners	12
Total Fee Earners	50
Total Trainees	8

contact
Andrew Rimmington,
Partner (020) 7588 0800

method of application
Application by letter with a current curriculum vitae addressed to Andrew Rimmington.

closing date for 2009
31 August 2007

application
Training contracts p.a. **4** (currently under review)

training
Salary
1st year (2006) £29,000
2nd year (2006) £33,000
Holiday entitlement **25 days plus public holidays**

post-qualification
Salary (2006) **£55,000**
Dorsey & Whitney aims to offer a qualified position to all candidates who have shown the appropriate level of performance during training, subject to the needs of the firm

Dundas & Wilson LLP

Northwest Wing, Bush House, Aldwych, London, WC2B 4PA
Tel: (020) 7546 2401 Fax: (020) 240 2448
Email: jennie.newlands@dundas-wilson.com

Partners	**73**
Lawyers	**271**
Trainees	**41**

firm profile

Dundas & Wilson (D&W) is a leading UK commercial law firm with offices in London, Edinburgh and Glasgow. The firm services a wide range of prestigious clients, including major companies and public sector organisations, throughout the UK and abroad.

main areas of work

Lawyers are grouped into 14 specialist skill-based teams known as Key Practice Areas: Banking & Financial Services, Construction & Engineering, Corporate, Corporate Recovery, Dispute Resolution, Environment, Employment, EU & Competition, IP / IT, Pensions, Planning & Transportation, Projects, Property and Tax.

trainee profile

D&W wants applicants with enthusiasm, commitment, adaptability, strong written and oral communication skills, excellent interpersonal skills, commercial awareness and an aptitude for problem solving and analysis.

training environment

The two year traineeship is split into four six month seats. The firm aims to accommodate trainees' preferences when allocating seats as the firm wants to encourage trainees to take an active part in managing their career development.

During the traineeship trainees receive on-the job training, two day seat training at the beginning of each seat, training in core skills such as drafting and effective legal writing and regular seminars. Trainees receive a formal performance review every three months and are allocated a mentor for each seat.

The firm's open plan environment means that trainees sit amongst assistants, associates and partners – this provides daily opportunities to observe how lawyers communicate both with clients and each other. This type of learning is invaluable and great preparation for life as a fully fledged lawyer.

benefits

Life assurance, permanent health insurance, group personal pension, season ticket loan, holiday purchase scheme.

vacation scheme

D&W offers four-week summer placements. To apply, please visit the website and complete the online application form. The closing date is 26 January 2007.

sponsorship & awards

GDL/CPE and LPC fees paid plus maintenance grant.

contact
Jennie Newlands

method of application
Online application

selection procedure
Assessment day comprising of an interview, group exercise, occupational personality questionnaire and aptitude tests

closing date for 2009
31 July 2007

application
Training contracts p.a. **26**
Applications p.a. **200**
% interviewed p.a. **25%**
Required degree grade **2:1 preferred**

training
Salary
1st year (Scotland) £18,000 (England) £30,000
2nd year (Scotland) £21,000 (England) £33,500
Holiday entitlement **25 days with ability to purchase an addtional 5 days**

post-qualification
Salary (2006)
(Scotland) £33,000 (England) £52,000
% of trainees offered job on qualification (2006) **81%**

offices
London, Edinburgh, Glasgow,

DWF

Centurion House, 129 Deansgate, Manchester, M3 3AA
Tel: (0161) 603 5000 Fax: (0161) 603 5050
Email: trainees@dwf.co.uk
Website: www.dwf.co.uk

firm profile
DWF is one of the largest and fastest growing law firms in the North West, with a national and international reach. The firm provides a full range of legal services for both the corporate and personal markets. Their business has grown rapidly and has doubled in size in the last five years. They now employ over 600 people, including 70 partners and a total of 350 legal advisers across their offices in Liverpool and Manchester. They pride themselves on providing outstanding client service that combines excellent commercial advice with an approachable style.

main areas of work
Services include; asset finance, banking, business recovery, commercial, conveyancing, corporate, dispute resolution, employee mobility, employment law, health, safety & environment, insurance, legal training, licensing, pensions, property & construction and wealthcare.
DWF provides legal services across a range of different industries and sectors, but they have developed expertise in a number of specific areas. To enable their clients to benefit from this expertise and to ensure that they transfer knowledge effectively, they have developed a series of sector-focused teams. These teams draw expertise in from across the firm to provide collaborative solutions for their clients. Within these sectors the firm is able to bring a real understanding of business and industry issues.

trainee profile
DWF's future depends on recruiting and retaining the right people. DWF only recruit people of the highest quality whether they be lawyers or non-lawyers. DWF is always on the look out for ambitious and driven professionals who are able to add value to their developing team. DWF wants its trainee solicitors to play a part in building on its success. The firm is looking for trainees who enjoy working as part of a busy team, respond positively to a challenge and have what it takes to deliver results for clients. The firm is looking for its partners of the future and in recent years virtually all of its qualifying trainees have been offered jobs. DWF is an equal opportunities employer and is committed to diversity in all aspects

training environment
DWF provides a well structured training programme for all new trainee solicitors which combines the day to day practical experience of working with a partner, associate or senior solicitor, backed by a comprehensive in-house lecture and workshop programme and the PSC course. You will very quickly become a vital member of the team, being delegated the appropriate level of responsibility from an early stage in your training.
Full supervision is provided and it is the firm's policy for each trainee to sit with a partner or associate, whilst working for a legal team as a whole. The two year training contract is divided into "seats". These will be spent in the firms main departments (corporate, insurance litigation, commercial property, commercial litigation and HRhorizons) which gives opportunities to look at specialist areas of work within each department.

Partners	**69**
Assistant Solicitors	**135**
Total Trainees	**14**

contact
Vicky Macmillan
Trainee Recruitment Specialist
(Manchester address)

method of application
Online application

selection procedure
2 stage interview/selection process

closing date for 2008/2009
31 July 2007

application
Training contracts p.a. **10**
Applications p.a. **c.700**
% interviewed p.a. **23%**
Required degree grade **2:1**
in any discipline

training
Salary
1st year (2006) £21,000
Holiday entitlement
**25 days p.a. minimum +
option to buy & sell holidays**

post-qualification
% of trainees offered job
on qualification (2005) **100%**

benefits
Flexible benefits scheme including insurance, life assurance, pension & other benefits

vacation placements
20 places offered p.a.
Paid summer vacation placements lasting 1 week

sponsorship & awards
LPC funding for tuition fees

Eversheds

Senator House, 85 Queen Victoria Street, London EC4V 4JL
Tel: (0845) 497 1067 Fax: (0845) 497 4919
Email: gradrec@eversheds.com
Website: www.eversheds.com Application Form Online at www.eversheds.com

firm profile

Eversheds LLP is one of the largest full service international law firms in the world with over 4,000 people and over 2,100 legal advisers. With 28 offices in major cities across the UK, Europe and Asia, Eversheds LLP provides services to the private and public sector businesses and the finance community. Eversheds are ranked 3rd in relation to the number of FTSE 250 clients that they act for*. Eversheds have always challenged the trends of traditional law firms and pride itself on being the most client centred international law firm, as well as a great place to work.

* Source: Chambers Client report, November 2005.

main areas of work

Core work: corporate, commercial, litigation and dispute management, real estate, human resources (employment and pensions) and legal systems group.

Sectors: Central government, local government, education, energy, financial services, food, health, retail and telecoms.

In addition to these core & sector areas, each office provides further expertise in the following areas: corporate tax, finance, intellectual property, information technology, media, risk management, environment/health & safety, EU/competition & trade, franchising, insolvency, claims management, construction, insurance, regulatory, shipping, licensing, PFI, planning and more.

trainee profile

Eversheds people are valued for being straightforward, enterprising, effective and down to earth. They expect their trainees to be business-like. Eversheds trainees will need to display commercial acumen, creativity and drive. Above all they will need to be results-driven. The firm's trainees are given as much responsibility as they can handle and benefit from the hands on, learning-by-doing philosophy that Eversheds holds. Trainee training is taken very seriously but it is fun too!

training environment

Trainees are appointed both a supervisor and a mentor to assist them throughout their training contract. During the four six-month seats, which will cover the firm's main practice areas, they will participate from an early stage in varied, complex and high-value work. There are also many opportunities to be seconded either to another Eversheds office or to a client. During the training trainees will also complete an Eversheds-designed Professional Skills Course.

benefits

Regional variations.

vacation placements

Places for Summer 2007: 250. Duration: two weeks. Remuneration: London £225, regions £175. The following offices run a one-week Easter vacation scheme: Birmingham, Cambridge, Cardiff, Leeds, Manchester and Nottingham (London's Easter scheme is two weeks). Closing Date: 31 January 2007.

sponsorship & awards

GDL and LPC fees and maintenance grants in accordance with the terms of the firm's offer.

Partners	**400+**
Assistant Solicitors	**2,000+**
Total Trainees	**180+**

contact
gradrec@eversheds.com

method of application
Apply online at
www.eversheds.com

selection procedure
Selection days include group and individual exercises, presentations and interview

closing date for 2009
31 July 2007

application
Training contracts p.a. **80**
Applications p.a. **4,000**
% interviewed p.a. **20%**
Required degree grade **2:1**

training
Salary
1st year London (2005)
£29,000
2nd year London (2005)
£32,000
Holiday entitlement **25 days**
% of trainees with
a non-law degree p.a. **45%**
No. of seats available
abroad p.a. **Up to 12**

post-qualification
Salary London (2005)
£50,000
% of trainees offered job
on qualification (2005) **82%**

offices
Barcelona*, Birmingham,
Brussels, Budapest*,
Cambridge, Cardiff,
Copenhagen, Doha** Ipswich,
Kuala Lumpur*, Leeds,
London, Madrid*, Manchester,
Milan*, Munich*, Newcastle,
Norwich, Nottingham, Paris,
Rome*, Shanghai*,
Singapore*, Sofia*,
Stockholm*, Valladolid*,
Vienna*, Warsaw*, Wroclaw*
* Associated office
** In co-operation

Farrer & Co

66 Lincoln's Inn Fields, London WC2A 3LH
Tel: (020) 7242 2022 Fax: (020) 7242 9899
Email: graduates@farrer.co.uk
Website: www.farrer.co.uk

firm profile
Farrer & Co is a mid-sized London law firm. The firm provides specialist advice to a large number of prominent private, institutional and commercial clients. Farrer & Co has built a successful law firm based on the goodwill of close client relationships, outstanding expertise in niche sectors and a careful attention to personal service and quality.

main areas of work
The firm's breadth of expertise is reflected by the fact that it has an outstanding reputation in fields as diverse as matrimonial law, offshore tax planning, employment, heritage work, charity law, defamation and sports law.

trainee profile
Trainees are expected to be highly motivated individuals with keen intellects and interesting and engaging personalities. Those applicants who appear to break the mould – as shown by their initiative for organisation, leadership, exploration, or enterprise – are far more likely to get an interview than the erudite, but otherwise unimpressive, student.

training environment
The training programme involves each trainee in the widest range of cases, clients and issues possible in a single law firm taking full advantage of the wide range of practice areas at Farrer & Co by offering six seats, rather than the more usual four. This provides a broad foundation of knowledge and experience and the opportunity to make an informed choice about the area of law in which to specialise. A high degree of involvement is encouraged under the direct supervision of solicitors and partners. Trainees attend an induction programme and regular internal lectures. The training partner reviews trainees' progress at the end of each seat and extensive feedback is given. The firm has a very friendly atmosphere and regular sporting and social events.

benefits
Health and life insurance, subsidised gym membership, season ticket loan.

vacation placements
Places for 2007: 40; Duration: 2 weeks at Easter, two schemes for 2 weeks in summer; Remuneration: £250 p.w.; Closing Date: 31 January 2007.

sponsorship & awards
CPE Funding: Fees paid plus £5,000 maintenance. LPC Funding: Fees paid plus £5,000 maintenance.

Partners	60
Assistant Solicitors	55
Total Trainees	17

contact
Graduate Recruitment Manager

method of application
Online via the firm's website

selection procedure
Interviews with Graduate Recruitment Partner and partners

closing date for 2009
31 July 2007

application
Training contracts p.a. **8-10**
Applications p.a. **800**
% interviewed p.a. **5%**
Required degree grade **2:1**

training
Salary
1st year (2006) £28,000
2nd year (2006) £30,500
The firm operates a performance related bonus scheme based on both personal and firm performance
Holiday entitlement **25 days**
% of trainees with non-law degrees p.a. **40-60%**

post-qualification
Salary (2006) **£44,000**
trainees offered job on qualification (2005) **100%**
% of partners (as at July 05) who joined as trainees **66%**

Field Fisher Waterhouse LLP

35 Vine Street, London EC3N 2AA
Tel: (020) 7861 4000 Fax: (020) 7488 0084
Email: graduaterecruitment@ffw.com
Website: www.ffw.com/careers

firm profile
Field Fisher Waterhouse LLP (FFW) is a mid-sized City law firm that provides a broad range of legal services to an impressive list of clients that range from small unlisted UK companies to multinationals and foreign corporations. They pride themselves on offering creative solutions and practical advice for clients in an ever-changing commercial world, and as part of The European Legal Alliance have a strong presence across 20 European cities.

main areas of work
Throughout their Training Contract trainees have the opportunity to work within IP & technology, corporate and commercial, banking and finance, regulatory and real estate. They also offer trainee seats in a wide range of other areas including public sector, litigation, employment and travel and aviation.

trainee profile
The firm is looking to recruit trainees from both law and non-law backgrounds who have a strong academic background, excellent communication skills, enthusiasm and the ability to work as part of a team.

training environment
FFW offers a six seat training contract and their range of practice areas enable them to offer outstanding opportunities for training. Trainees are treated as a valued part of the team and are encouraged to assume early responsibility. Practical training is complemented by a comprehensive programme of in-house seminars, workshops and external courses, accompanied by regular feedback and a formal assessment at the end of each seat. The firm invests highly in the development and training of all its trainees and provides good quality work within a friendly, relaxed and supportive working environment. You will also have additional support from your fellow trainees, a buddy and a mentor who is a senior solicitor. FFW believes this working environment is just one of the reasons that it has retained 92% of trainees upon qualification in 2006 and 100% in 2005.

sponsorship & benefits
Sponsorship and a PgDL (£5,500) and LPC (£6,000) maintenance grant is paid. Other benefits include: 25 days' holiday, life assurance, season ticket loan, medical insurance, GP service, and pension in addition to having two squash courts in the firm's offices.

vacation placements
Increasingly, trainees have come to the firm through the summer vacation scheme, which provides a useful way of getting an insiders view of FFW. The firm runs two two-week schemes during July where you have the opportunity to spend a week in two different departments and take part in a variety of work and social activities.
Please apply online for the Summer Vacation Scheme and Training Contracts, via the website at www.ffw.com/careers.
Deadline for 2007 Summer Vacation Scheme: 31 January 2007.
Deadline for 2009 Training Contracts: 31 July 2007.

Partners	93
Assistant Solicitors	145
Vacancies	17
Total Trainees	34

contact
Graduate Recruitment

method of application
Apply online via the firm website,
www.ffw.com/careers

selection procedure
Interviews and a written assessment

closing date for 2009
31 July 2007

application
Training contracts p.a. **17**
Applications p.a. **1,200**
Required degree grade **2:1**

training
Salary
1st year **£29,000**
2nd year **£32,000**
Holiday entitlement
25 days

post-qualification
Salary (2006) **£50,000**
% of trainees offered job
on qualification (2006) **92%**

offices
London

Finers Stephens Innocent

179 Great Portland St, London W1N 6LS
Tel: (020) 7323 4000 Fax: (020) 7580 7069
Email: gradrecruitment@fsilaw.co.uk
Website: www.fsilaw.co.uk

firm profile

Finers Stephens Innocent is an expanding practice in Central London, providing a range of high quality legal services to corporate, commercial and private clients. The firm's philosophy includes close partner involvement and a cost-effective approach in all client matters. They have a working style which is unstuffy and informal, but still aspires to the highest quality of output, while offering a sensible work-life balance. The firm is a member of the Meritas international network of law firms.

main areas of work

Commercial property; company/commercial; litigation; media; defamation; private client; employment; family. See the website for further details.

trainee profile

The firm requires academic excellence in all applicants. It also looks for maturity, personality, a broad range of interests, initiative, strong communication skills, and the ability to write clear English, and to think like a lawyer. The firm has for several years given equal consideration to applicants whether applying straight from university or having followed another career previously. Trainees get early responsibility, client contact and close involvement in transactions and litigation matters.

training environment

Between offering you a training contract and the time you start, the firm aims to keep regularly in touch with you, including offering you some work experience with them. When you start they provide a careful induction programme, after which you complete four six-month seats in different departments, sharing a room with either a Partner or Senior Assistant. The firm has three Training Partners who keep a close eye on the welfare and progress of trainees. There are regular group meetings with trainees, and an appraisal process which enables you to know how you are progressing, as well as giving you a chance to provide feedback on your training. The firm runs a variety of in-house training courses for trainees

benefits

20 days holiday; pension; private medical insurance; life insurance; long-term disability insurance; season ticket loan.

sponsorship & awards

LPC and CPE course fees.

Partners	33
Assistant Solicitors	37
Total Trainees	10

contact
Personnel Department

method of application
CV & covering letter

selection procedure
2 interviews with the
Training Partners

closing date for 2009
30 July 2007

application
Training contracts p.a. **5**
Applications p.a. **800**
% interviewed p.a. **3%**
Required degree grade **2:1**

training
Salary
1st year
Highly competitive
2nd year
Highly competitive
Holiday entitlement **20 days**
% of trainees with a non-law
degree p.a. **0-50%**

post-qualification
Salary
Highly competitive
% of trainees offered job
on qualification (2006) **100%**

Foot Anstey

21 Derry's Cross, Plymouth PL1 2SW
Tel: (01752) 675000 Fax: (01752) 675500
Email: training@foot-ansteys.co.uk
Website: www.foot-ansteys.co.uk

Vacancies	12
Trainees	18
Partners	30
Total staff	300

firm profile
Foot Anstey is one of the leading full service law firms in the region, with offices in Plymouth, Exeter and Taunton. It has a growing national and international client base and is recognised for its expertise in many sectors, including specialist areas as diverse as media, marine, charities, insolvency and medical negligence. The firm offers a broad spectrum of legal services across four key sectors: business, property, private client and public funding. With a strong reputation for delivering city expertise at regional rates, and with a determined business plan, the firm is experiencing a period of significant growth which will continue throughout 2007.

main areas of work
In addition to the niche areas mentioned above, the main areas of work include: commercial property, property litigation, company & commercial, commercial litigation, banking, employment, criminal advocates, family & childcare & private client. The firm has an extensive range of clients from the commercial, public & private sectors, acting for numerous local, regional & national companies & high net worth individuals.

trainee profile
The firm welcomes applications from all law and non-law graduates who have a strong academic background, established communication skills and who are committed to achieving excellent standards of customer service. A strong team ethos is paramount to the firm. Trainees can expect to be welcomed into a friendly and supportive environment where they will find the quality and variety of work both challenging and rewarding.

training environment
The wide range of legal services provided by the firm offers trainees opportunities in many areas of law, sitting in either the Exeter, Plymouth or Taunton offices. Trainee solicitors undertake four seats of six months. Whenever possible (with the exception of the first seat) trainees are able to select their seat. All trainees attend an induction course. Individual monthly meetings are held with supervisors. Appraisals are conducted halfway through each seat. Trainees are given a second year buddy to help them find their feet. Regular communication between the trainees and supervisors ensure an open and friendly atmosphere. The Professional Skills course is taught externally. The firm has Lexcel and Investors in People accreditations and has an excellent training and development programme.

benefits
Include contributory pension, 25 days' holiday.

vacation placements
The deadline for the 2007 summer placement scheme is 31 March 2007.

sponsorship & awards
£9,600 grant towards LPC and living expenses.

contact
Richard Sutton
(01752) 675151

method of application
CV and covering letter to Richard Sutton at the Plymouth office address. Alternatively email it to: training@foot-ansteys.co.uk or apply online at www.foot-ansteys.co.uk

selection procedure
Assessment day

application
Training contracts p.a. **12**
Required degree grade **2:1 (preferred)**

closing date for 2009
31 July 2007

training
Salary
1st year (2006) £17,500
2nd year (2006) £20,000
Holiday entitlement 25 days

post-qualification
Salary (2006) £30,500
% of trainees offered job on qualification (2006) 100%
% of assistant solicitors who joined as trainees (as at 30/04/06) 28%
% of partners who joined as trainees (as at 30/04/06) 17%

other offices
Plymouth, Exeter & Taunton

Forbes

73 Northgate, Blackburn BB2 1AA
Tel: (01254) 580000 Fax: (01254) 222216
Email: graduate.recruitment@forbessolicitors.co.uk

firm profile

Forbes is one of the largest practices in the north with 27 partners and over 350 members of staff based in nine offices across the north of England. The firm has a broad based practice dealing with both commercial and private client work and can therefore provide a varied and exciting training contract. The firm is however especially noted for excellence in its company/commercial; civil litigation; defendant insurer; crime; family and employment departments. It has a number of Higher Court Advocates and the firm holds many Legal Service Commission Franchises. Underlying the practice is a strong commitment to quality, training and career development – a commitment underlined by the fact that Forbes was one of the first firms to be recognised as an Investor in People and its ISO 9001 accreditation. For applicants looking for a 'city' practice without the associated hassles of working in a city then Forbes could be it. The firm can offer the best of both worlds – a large firm with extensive resources and support combined with a commitment to quality, people and the personal touch.

main areas of work

Company/commercial, civil litigation, defendant insurer, crime, family and employment services.

trainee profile

Forbes looks for high-calibre recruits with strong Northwest connections, good academic records, who are also keen team players. Candidates should have a total commitment to client service and identify with the firm's philosophy of providing practical straightforward legal advice.

training environment

A tailored training programme involves six months in four of the following: crime, civil litigation, defendant insurer in Leeds or Blackburn, matrimonial, and non-contentious/company commercial.

Partners	27
Assistant Solicitors	53
Total Trainees	15+

contact
Graduate Recruitment Manager

method of application
Handwritten letter and CV

selection procedure
Interview with partners

closing date for 2009
31 July 2007

application
Training contracts p.a. **4**
Applications p.a. **350 plus**
% interviewed p.a. **Varies**
Required degree grade **2:1**

training
Salary
1st year At least Law Society minimum
2nd year (2005) £17,720
Holiday entitlement
20 days pa

post-qualification
Salary
Highly competitive
% of trainees offered job on qualification (2004) **100%**

Ford & Warren

Westgate Point, Westgate, Leeds, LS1 2AX
Tel: (0113) 243 6601 Fax: (0113) 242 0905
Email: clientmail@forwarn.com
Website: www.forwarn.com

Partners	**21**
Assistant Solicitors	**70**
Total Trainees	**12**

contact
Debra Hinde

method of application
Handwritten letter and CV
or email

selection procedure
Interviews and exercise

closing date for 2009
31 August 2007

application
Training contracts p.a. **6**
Applications p.a. **500**
Required degree grade **2:1**

firm profile
Ford & Warren is an independent, single office commercial law firm based in Leeds. Over the last 15 years the firm has sustained a rapid and generic growth without mergers or acquisitions so that it now occupies the whole of the prestigious Westgate Point office block in the heart of the commercial centre of Leeds. The firm has 21 partners, 70 solicitors and paralegals and a total staff of over 200. Ford & Warren has the following departments: Employment; Road and Rail; Transportation; Corporate; Commercial Litigation; Commercial Property; Insurance and PI; Tax and Inheritance; Matrimonial. The firm has a significant presence in the public sector particularly in health and education. The firm has areas of high specialisation where its lawyers have a national reputation and its client base includes the largest limited companies and PLCs. These areas include transportation and the licensed and leisure industries.

main areas of work
Employment and industrial relations; road and rail transportation; corporate; insurance and personal injury; commercial property/real estate; public sector; tax and inheritance; matrimonial. The Dispute Resolution/Commercial Litigation Department has five sections: commercial dispute resolution, property litigation, finance litigation, insolvency and debt recovery.

trainee profile
The firm is looking for hard working, self-reliant and enthusiastic individuals who will make a contribution to the firm from the outset. Applicants must have a strong academic background, a genuine enthusiasm for the law and the social abilities required to work effectively with colleagues and clients. The majority of lawyers practising at the firm joined as trainees.

training environment
The firm offers seats in employment, commercial litigtion, corporate, insurance and personal injury, commercial property and private client. Usually, trainees will undertake four seats of six months, although split seats may sometimes be available. The final six months takes place in the department into which the trainee wishes to qualify. The firm has a comprehensive in-house training programme for all lawyers and the PSC is also provided internally.

selection procedure
First interviews and exercise held with the Trainee Recruitment Manager and a Partner in September and early October. Successful candidates are invited to a second interview with the Managing Partner, including a further exercise and presentation.

Forsters LLP

31, Hill Street, London W1J 5LS
Tel: (020) 7863 8333 Fax: (020) 7863 8444
Email: vemoulds@forsters.co.uk
Website: www.forsters.co.uk

firm profile

Forsters is a successful firm committed to being the best at what it does. Based in Mayfair, in London's West End, Forsters was founded in 1998. Now with more than 100 lawyers, it is recognised as being a progressive law firm which is highly regarded for its property and private client work as well as having thriving commercial and litigation practices. The working atmosphere of the firm is friendly and informal, yet highly professional. A social committee organises a range of activities from quiz nights to sporting events.

main areas of work

The firm has a strong reputation for all aspects of commercial and residential property work. The groups handle investment funding; development; planning; construction; landlord and tenant; property taxation and residential investment and development. Forsters is also recognised as one of the leading proponents of private client work in London with a client base comprising a broad range of individuals and trusts in the UK and elsewhere. The firm's commercial practice specialises in acquisitions and financing for technology, communication and media companies whilst its litigation group conducts commercial litigation and arbitration and advises on a broad spectrum of matters.

trainee profile

Successful candidates will have a strong academic background and either have attained or be expected to achieve a good second class degree. The firm considers that factors alongside academic achievements are also important. The firm is looking for individuals who give a real indication of being interested in a career in law and who the firm feels would readily accept and work well in its team environment.

training environment

The first year of training is split into three seats of four months in three of the following departments: commercial property, private client, company commercial or litigation. In the second year the four month pattern still applies, but the firm discusses with you whether you have developed an area of particular interest and tries to accommodate this. Second year seats might include construction, employment, family or property litigation. The training is very 'hands on' as you share an office with a partner or assistant who will give you real responsibility alongside supervision. At the end of each seat your progress and performance will be reviewed by way of an appraisal with a partner from the relevant department.

sponsorship & benefits

22 days holiday p.a., season ticket loan, permanent health insurance, life insurance, subsidised gym membership. Contributory pension scheme, employee assistance programme, private healthcare (after six months), active social programme. Sponsorship for the CPE/PgDL and LPC course.

vacation placements

Summer vacation scheme opportunities available. Places: 10. Remuneration: £250 pw. Deadline: 15 March 2007.

Partners	27
Assistant Solicitors	60
Total Trainees	8

contact
Victoria Moulds

method of application
Online application form

selection procedure
First interview with 2 Graduate Recruitment Partners; second interview with HR Manager and partner

training
Salary
1st year (2006) £28,500
2nd year (2006) £30,500
Holiday entitlement **22 days**

post-qualification
Salary (2006) **£47,500**

Freeth Cartwright LLP

Cumberland Court, 80 Mount Street, Nottingham NG1 6HH
Tel: (0115) 901 5504 Fax: (0115) 859 9603
Email: vicki.simpson@freethcartwright.co.uk
Website: www.freethcartwright.co.uk

firm profile
Tracing its origins back to 1805, Freeth Cartwright LLP became Nottingham's largest firm in 1994 with successful offices now established in Derby and Leicester. Whilst Freeth Cartwright LLP is a heavyweight commercial firm, serving a wide variety of corporate and institutional clients, there is also a commitment to a range of legal services, which includes a substantial private client element. This enables it to give a breadth of experience in training which is not always available in firms of a similar size.

main areas of work
Property and construction, commercial services, private client and personal litigation.

trainee profile
Freeth Cartwright LLP looks for people to bring their own perspective and individuality to the firm. The firm needs people who can cope with the intellectual demands of life as a lawyer and who possess the wider personal skills which are needed in its diverse practice.

training environment
Freeth Cartwright LLP is committed to providing comprehensive training for all its staff. The firm's training programme is based on in-house training covering technical matters and personal skills, supplemented with external courses where appropriate. The firm endeavours to give the best possible experience during the training period, as it believes that informal training on-the-job is the most effective means of encouraging the skills required in a qualified solicitor. One of the firm's senior partners takes responsibility for all its trainees and their personal development, overseeing their progress through the firm and discussing performance based on feedback. Normally, the training contract will consist of four six month seats in different departments, most of which are available in the firm's Nottingham offices, although it is possible for trainees to spend at least one seat in another location.

Members	59
Assistant Solicitors	67
Total Trainees	14

contact
Vicki Simpson

method of application
Online application form

selection procedure
Interview & selection day

closing date for 2008
31 July 2007

training
Starting salary (2005)
£19,000

offices
Nottingham, Leicester, Derby

Freeth
Cartwright
LLP

Freshfields Bruckhaus Deringer

65 Fleet Street, London EC4Y 1HS
Tel: (020) 7936 4000 Fax: (020) 7832 7001
Email: graduates@freshfields.com
Website: www.freshfields.com/graduates

firm profile
Freshfields Bruckhaus Deringer is a leading international firm with a network of 28 offices in 18 countries. The firm provides first-rate legal services to corporations, financial institutions and governments around the world.

main areas of work
Corporate; mergers and acquisitions; banking; dispute resolution; joint ventures; employment, pensions and benefits; asset finance; real estate; tax; capital markets; intellectual property and information technology; project finance; private finance initiative; securities; antitrust, competition and trade; communications and media; construction and engineering; energy; environment, planning and regulatory; financial services; restructuring and insolvency; insurance; investment funds; public international law; arbitration.

trainee profile
The firm is looking for candidates with proven academic ability, an excellent command of spoken and written English, high levels of drive and determination, good team working skills and excellent organisational ability.

training environment
The firm's trainees receive a thorough professional training in a very broad range of practice areas, an excellent personal development programme and the chance to work in one of the firm's international offices or on secondment with a client in the UK or abroad. It provides the professional, technical and pastoral support necessary to ensure that you enjoy and make the most of the opportunities on offer.

benefits
Life assurance; permanent health insurance; group personal pension; interest-free loan; interest-free loan for a season travel ticket; free membership of the firm's private medical insurance scheme; subsidised staff restaurant; gym.

vacation placements
Places for 2007: 100; Duration: 2 weeks; Remuneration: £550 (net); Closing Date: 19 January 2007 but apply as early as possible after 1 December 2006 as there may not be places left by the deadline.

sponsorship & awards
GDL and LPC fees paid plus maintenance grant of £7,250 for those studying the LPC and £6,250 for those studying the GDL.

Partners **503**
Assistant Solicitors **1,655**
Total Trainees **205**
(London based)

contact
Deborah Dalgleish

method of application
Online application form

selection procedure
2 interviews and written test

closing date for 2009
31 July 2007

application
Training contracts p.a. **100**
Applications p.a. **c.2,000**
% interviewed p.a. **c.12%**
Required degree grade **2:1**

training
Salary
1st year £31,000
2nd year £35,000
Holiday entitlement **25 days**
% of trainees with a
non-law degree p.a. **c.45%**
No. of seats available
abroad p.a. **c.68**

post-qualification
Salary **£55,000**
% of trainees offered job
on qualification **c.94%**

overseas offices
Amsterdam, Barcelona, Beijing, Berlin, Bratislava, Brussels, Budapest, Cologne, Dubai, Düsseldorf, Frankfurt, Hamburg, Hanoi, Ho Chi Minh City, Hong Kong, Madrid, Milan, Moscow, Munich, New York, Paris, Rome, Shanghai, Singapore, Tokyo, Vienna, Washington DC

Government Legal Service

GLS Recruitment Team, Chancery House, 53-64 Chancery Lane,
London WC2A 1QS
Tel: (020) 7649 6023
Email: glstrainees.tmp.com
Website: www.gls.gov.uk

firm profile
The Government Legal Service (GLS) joins together around 1900 lawyers and trainees. They work in some 30 Government organisations, including major Departments of State and the regulatory bodies. A GLS lawyer's work is quite unique, and reflects the huge range of Government activities. GLS lawyers work in the public interest and have the rare opportunity to make a positive contribution to the well-being of the country. Many move around Government Departments as they progress, developing skills and acquiring knowledge of new areas of the law. Others choose to specialise in one area. Whatever route they take, they find the work hugely rewarding and stimulating.

main areas of work
GLS lawyers have just one client – the Government of the day – and that client requires advice and support on a host of domestic and international matters. As a GLS lawyer, you could deal with ground-breaking cases in the courts, advise Ministers, work on a public inquiry or become involved in the passage of legislation through Parliament.

trainee profile
As well as a good academic background, the GLS seeks analytical minds that can get to the root of a problem, along with good communications skills. Because GLS lawyers work as part of a team, people skills are important, as is the potential to become a good manager when you progress and take on further responsibility.

training environment
The GLS provides a unique and varied training environment for trainees and pupils. Generally, trainee solicitors work in four different areas of practice over a two-year period in the Government Department to which they are assigned. Pupil barristers divide their year's pupillage between their Department and chambers. The GLS prides itself on involving trainees and pupils in the full range of casework conducted by their Department. This frequently includes high profile matters and will be under the supervision of senior colleagues.

benefits
These include professional development opportunities, excellent pension scheme, civilised working hours, generous holiday entitlement and subsidised canteen facilities.

vacation placements
Summer 2007 vacation placement scheme; approx 60 places. Duration: 2-3 weeks. Closing date 30 March 2007. Remuneration: £200-£250 pw.

sponsorship & awards
LPC and BVC fees as well as other compulsory professional skills course fees. Funding may be available for the CPE. They provide a grant of around £5-7,000 for the vocational year.

Total Trainees around 50	
contact	glstrainees@tmp.com or visit www.gls.gov.uk
method of application	Online application form
selection procedure	Day at assessment centre to undertake a group discussion exercise, a written question and an interview
closing date for 2009	31 July 2007
application	Training contracts p.a. **22-30** Applications p.a. **1,200+** % interviewed p.a. **10%** Required degree grade **2.1**
training	Salary begins at over £20,000 in London and varies acording to Government Department. It is lower outside London. Holiday entitlement **25 days on entry**
post-qualification	Salary varies according to Government Department; the vacancies section of the GLS website will give a flavour of what to expect. % of trainees accepting job on qualification (2004) at least **98%**

Halliwells

St. James's Court, Brown St, Manchester M2 2JF
Tel: (0870) 365 8918 Fax: (0870) 365 8919
Email: ekaterina.clarke@halliwells.com

firm profile
Halliwells is one of the largest independent commercial law firms in the North West. Over the last few years the firm has increased substantially in both size and turnover and now has in excess of 150 partners and 390 fee earners. This continued growth leads to an ongoing requirement for solicitors and has given rise to more internal promotions to partnerships.

main areas of work
Real estate; dispute resolution; corporate; corporate recovery; business services and trust & estates.

trainee profile
Candidates need to show a good academic ability but do not necessarily need to have studied law at university. They should demonstrate an ability to fit into a hardworking team. In particular, Halliwells is looking for candidates who will continue to develop with the firm after their initial training.

training environment
Each trainee will have five seats in at least three separate departments. These will usually include commercial litigation, corporate and commercial property. Individual requests from trainees for experience in a particular department will be accommodated wherever possible. Requests for inter-office secondments are also encouraged.
The trainee will work within one of the department's teams and be encouraged to assist other team members to help broaden their experience. Specific training appropriate to each department will be given and trainees are strongly encouraged to attend the firm's regular in-house seminars on legal and related topics.
A supervisor will be assigned to each trainee to support their development throughout the seat. Each trainee will be assessed both mid-seat and end of seat.

benefits
A generous pension scheme plus a subsidised gym membership is available.

vacation placements
63 summer vacation placements places will be available during summer 2007. The firm operates three schemes at its Manchester, London and Liverpool offices, each lasts for two weeks. Schemes commence last week in June. Remuneration is £170 per week. Closing date for applications is 31 March 2007.

sponsorship & awards
The firm pays GDL fees and LPC fees plus a £4,500 maintenance grant for each course.

Partners	155
Assistant Solicitors	390
Total Trainees	76

contact
Ekaterina Clarke
(Graduate Recruitment Officer)
ekaterina.clarke@halliwells.com

method of application
Online application only

selection procedure
Group exercise, presentation and interview

closing date for 2009
31 July 2007

application
Training contracts p.a.
Manchester - 24
London - 6
Liverpool - 5
Sheffield - 3
Applications p.a. **1,500**
% interviewed p.a. **8%**
Required degree grade **2:1**

training
Salary
1st year (2006) £22,145
2nd year (2006) £23,175

post-qualification
Salary (2006) **£34,000**
% of trainees offered job on qualification (2006) **100%**

Hammonds

Rutland House, 148 Edmund Street, Birmingham B3 2JR
7 Devonshire Square, Cutlers Gardens, London EC2M 4YH
2 Park Lane, Leeds LS3 1ES
Trinity Court, 16 Dalton Street, Manchester M6O 8HS
Tel: (0870) 839 0000 Fax: (0870) 839 3666
Website: www.hammonds.com

firm profile

Hammonds is one of Europe's largest corporate law firms and a member of the Global 100. In the UK alone, the firm advises over 200 London Stock Exchange quoted companies and 25 FTSE 100 companies. The firm has offices in London, Birmingham, Leeds, Manchester, Brussels, Paris, Berlin, Munich, Rome, Milan, Madrid, Turin and Hong Kong. The firm has 1,300 staff, including 183 partners, 470 solicitors and 80 trainees. The firm is regarded as innovative, opportunistic and highly successful in the markets in which it operates.

main areas of work

Corporate; commercial dispute resolution; construction, engineering and projects; employment; EU and competition; finance law (including banking); intellectual property and commercial; media/IT; pensions; property; sports law; tax.

trainee profile

Hammonds seeks applications from all disciplines for vacation work and training contracts. They consider four key elements in selecting trainees: strong academic performance (2:1 degree classification), evidence of work experience in the legal sector, excellent communication skills and significant achievement in non-academic pursuits.

training environment

40 trainee solicitors are recruited each year. Trainees undertake six four-month seats during their training contract. Trainees have input in seat choices and encouraged to undertake a broad selection of seats to benefit their knowledge on qualification. Trainees benefit from two-tier supervision and challenging work. The firm provides a comprehensive induction programme including on-going departmental training, seminars and workshops throughout the training contract. Trainees undertake formal appraisal meetings with their suerpvisors during each seat. Hammonds' trainees benefit from exposure to clients, cross-border work and opportunity for seats on secondment.

benefits

Pension, life assurance, subsidised gym membership, interest free season ticket loan and a flexible benefits package.

vacation placements

Places for 2007: 64 Summer Scheme; Duration: 2 weeks; Remuneration: £230 p.w. (London), £180 p.w. (Leeds, Manchester, Birmingham); Closing Date: 31 January 2007.

sponsorship & awards

PgDL and LPC fees paid and maintenance grant provided. Maitenance grant presently £4,500 p.a.

Partners	183
Assistant Solicitors	470
Total Trainees	80

contact
The Graduate Recruitment Team

method of application
Online application form

selection procedure
Assessment and interview

closing date for 2009
31 July 2007

application
Training contracts p.a. **40**
Applications p.a. **1,300**
% interviewed p.a. **10%**
Required degree grade **2:1**

training
Salary
1st year (2006)
£20,500 regional
£27,000 London
2nd year (2005)
£23,000 regional
£30,000 London
Holiday entitlement **23 days**
% of trainees with a non-law degree p.a. **25%**
No. of seats available abroad p.a. **15**

post-qualification
Salary (2006)
London £48,000
Other £34,000
% of trainees accepting job on qualification (2006) **87%**

overseas offices
Brussels, Paris, Berlin, Munich, Rome, Milan, Turin, Hong Kong, Madrid

Harbottle & Lewis LLP

Hanover House, 14 Hanover Square, London W1S 1HP
Tel: (020) 7667 5000 Fax: (020) 7667 5100
Email: kathy.beilby@harbottle.com
Website: www.harbottle.com

Partners	24
Assistant Solicitors	40
Total Trainees	8

contact
Kathy Beilby

method of application
CV & letter by post or email

selection procedure
Interview

closing date for 2009
31 July 2007

application
Training contracts p.a. **4**
Applications p.a. **800**
% interviewed p.a. **5%**
Required degree grade **2:1**

training
Salary
1st year £27,000 (2006)
2nd year £28,000 (2006)
Holiday entitlement
in the first year **23 days**
in the second year **26 days**
% of trainees with
a non-law degree p.a. **40%**

post-qualification
Salary (2006) **£46,000**

firm profile
Harbottle & Lewis LLP is recognised for the unique breadth of its practice in the entertainment, media, travel (including aviation) and leisure industries. It undertakes significant corporate commercial and contentious work for clients within these industries including newer industries such as digital mixed media.

main areas of work
Music, film and television production, theatre, broadcasting, computer games and publishing, sport, sponsorship and advertising, aviation, property investment and leisure.

trainee profile
Trainees will have demonstrated the high academic abilities, commercial awareness, and initiative necessary to become part of a team advising clients in dynamic and demanding industries.

training environment
The two year training contract is divided into four six-month seats where trainees will be given experience in a variety of legal skills including company commercial, litigation, intellectual property and real property, working within teams focused on the firm's core industries. The firm has a policy of accepting a small number of trainees to ensure they are given relevant and challenging work and are exposed to and have responsibility for a full range of legal tasks. The firm has its own lecture and seminars programme in both legal topics and industry know-how. An open door policy and a pragmatic entrepreneurial approach to legal practice provides a stimulating working environment.

benefits
Lunch provided; season ticket loans.

sponsorship & awards
LPC fees paid and interest-free loans towards maintenance.

HBJ Gateley Wareing LLP

One Eleven, Edmund Street, Birmingham B3 2HJ
Tel: (0121) 234 0121 Fax: (0121) 234 0079
Email: wendyw@hbj-gw.com
Website: www.hbjgateleywareing.com

Partners	62
Vacancies	28
Total Trainees	20
Total Staff	407

firm profile
A 62-partner, Midlands and Scottish based practice, with an excellent reputation for general commercial work and particular expertise in corporate, plc, commercial, employment, property, construction, insolvency, commercial dispute resolution, banking and tax. The firm is expanding (407 staff) and offers a highly practical, commercial and fast-paced environment. The firm prides itself on its entrepreneurial style and its work hard, live life to the full reputation. The firm focuses on owner-led businesses, but also counts some household names and internationals amongst its clients.

trainee profile
To apply for a placement in England: Applications are invited from second year law students and final year non-law students and graduates. Applicants should have (or be heading for) a minimum 2.1 degree, and should have at least three Bs (or equivalent) at A-level. Individuals should be hardworking team players capable of using initiative and demonstrating commercial awareness.

training environment
Four six month seats with ongoing supervision and appraisals every three months. PSC taken internally. In-house courses on skills such as time management, negotiation, IT, drafting, business skills, marketing, presenting and writing in plain English.

benefits
Current trainee offered as a 'buddy' – a point of contact within the firm, library available, invitation to summer party prior to joining.

vacation placements
Two-week placement over the summer. Deadline for next year's vacation placement scheme is 11 February 2007 and the closing date for 2009 training contracts is 31 July 2007. Apply online at www.hbjgateleywareing.com.

sponsorship & awards
CPE/LPC and a LPC maintenance grant of £4,000.

contact
Mrs Wendy Warburton
HR Manager

closing date for 2009
Training contracts:
31 July 2007
Vacation placements:
11 February 2007

training
Salary
1st year £20,000
2nd year £22,000

post-qualification
Salary £34,000

offices
Birmingham, Leicester, Nottingham, Glasgow and Edinburgh.

HBJ Gateley Wareing

Henmans LLP

116 St. Aldates, Oxford OX1 1HA
Tel: (01865) 722181 Fax: (01865) 792376
Email: welcome@henmansllp.co.uk
Website: www.henmansllp.co.uk

firm profile

Henmans LLP is a long-established regional practice with a national reputation, serving both commercial and private clients, charities and insurers. The firm's philosophy is to be extremely client focused to deliver exceptional levels of service. They achieve this through an emphasis on teamwork, which ensures clients always have access to a specific partner with specialist support. They run ongoing training programmes to guarantee clients optimum advice and guidance. Their policy of bespoke services and controlled costs ensure that both corporate and private clients benefit from City level standards at competitive regional prices. The firm is also accredited as an Investor in People.

main areas of work

The firm's core service of litigation is nationally recognised for its high quality. They also have an excellent reputation for their personal injury, clinical negligence, property, private client and charity work. The breakdown of work is as follows: professional negligence and commercial litigation, 24%; personal injury, 27%; property: 17%; private client (including family)/charities/trusts, 25%; corporate/employment: 10%.

trainee profile

Commercial awareness, sound academic accomplishment, intellectual capability, IT literacy, able to work as part of a team, good communication skills.

training environment

Trainees are an important part of the firm's future. The firm is committed to providing a high standard of training throughout the contract. Trainees are introduced to the firm with a detailed induction and overview of its client base. A trainee manual is provided in each seat to familiarise the trainee with the department's procedures. Experience is likely to be within the PI, Property, Family, Professional Negligence/Commercial Litigation and Private Client Departments. The firm provides an ongoing programme of in-house education and regular appraisals within its supportive friendly environment. The firm values commitment and enthusiasm both professionally and socially as an integral part of its culture and trainees are encouraged to join in social activities and become involved with the life of the firm.

Partners	23
Other Solicitors & Fee-earners	49
Total Trainees	6

contact
Viv J Matthews (Mrs)
MA CH FCIPD
Head of HR

method of application
Application form on website

selection procedure
The interview process comprises an assessment day with Head of HR & partners, including an interview, presentation, verbal reasoning test, drafting and team exercise

closing date for 2009
31 July 2007

application
Training contracts p.a. **3**
Applications p.a. **450**

training
Salary
1st year (2005) **£18,600**
2nd year (2005) **£20,400**
Holiday entitlement **23 days + 2 firm days at Christmas.**
BUPA and pension also provided.
% of trainees with a non-law degree p.a. **20%**

post-qualification
Salary (2004) **£31,000**
% of assistants who joined as trainees **25%**
% of partners who joined as trainees **20%**

Herbert Smith LLP

Exchange House, Primrose Street, London EC2A 2HS
Tel: (020) 7374 8000 Fax: (020) 7374 0888
Email: graduate.recruitment@herbertsmith.com
Website: www.herbertsmith.com

firm profile

Herbert Smith is an international legal practice with over 1,100 lawyers and a network of offices in Europe and Asia. In addition, it works closely with two premier European firms with whom it has an alliance - the German firm Gleiss Lutz and the Dutch and Belgian firm Stibbe.

The firm has a diverse, blue-chip client base including FTSE 100 and Fortune 500 companies, major investment banks and governments. What makes Herbert Smith stand out is its culture: a collegiate working environment, a pre-eminent market reputation in key practices and industry sectors and an ambition to be consistently recognised as one of the world's leading law firms.

main areas of work

Corporate (including international mergers and acquisitions); finance and banking (including capital markets); international litigation and arbitration; energy; projects and project finance; EU and competition; real estate; tax; employment and trusts; construction and engineering; insurance; investment funds; IP; US securities, IT & communications.

trainee profile

Trainees need a strong academic record, common sense, self-confidence and intelligence to make their own way in a large firm. They are typically high-achieving and creative thinking.

training environment

Structured training and supervision are designed to allow experience of a unique range of contentious and non-contentious work. You will be encouraged to take on responsibilities as soon as you join the firm. You will work within partner-led teams and have your own role. Individual strengths will be monitored, developed and utilised. On-the-job training will be divided into four six-month seats; one seat will be in the corporate division and one in the litigation division. You can then apply for specialists seats such as IP or EU and competition, or the opportunity to go on secondment to a client, the firm's advocacy unit or an overseas office. Great emphasis is placed on professional and personal development and the firm runs its own legal development and mentoring programme.

sponsorship & benefits

CPE/GDL and LPC fees are paid plus up to £7,000 maintenance grant p.a. Benefits include profit related bonus scheme, permanent health insurance, private medical insurance, season ticket loan, life assurance, subsidised gym membership, group personal accident insurance, matched contributory pension scheme and interest free loan.

vacation placements

Places for 2006/07: 115. Winter 2006 (non-law students only), Spring and Summer 2007 (law and non-law students). Closing Dates: 15 November 2006 for Winter scheme; 31 January 2007 for Spring and Summer schemes. Opportunities in some of the firm's European offices.

Partners	217*
Fee-earners	716*
Total Trainees	152*
*denotes worldwide figures	

contact
Graduate Recruitment Team

method of application
Online application form

selection procedure
Case study and interview

closing date for
Sept 2009/Mar 2010
31 July 2007

application
Training contracts p.a. up to **100**
Applications p.a. **circa 2,000**
% interviewed p.a. **20%**
Required degree grade **2:1**

training
Salary
1st year £31,000
2nd year £35,000
Holiday entitlement
25 days, rising to 27 on qualification
ratio of law to non-law graduates is broadly equal

post-qualification
Salary (2006) **£55,000**
% of trainees offered job on qualification (Sept 2006)
97% (based on no. of jobs offered)

overseas offices
Bangkok, Beijing, Brussels, Hong Kong, Moscow, Paris, Shanghai, Singapore, Tokyo

associated offices
Amsterdam, Berlin, Frankfurt, Jakarta, Munich, New York, Prague, Stuttgart, Warsaw

Hewitsons

42 Newmarket Road, Cambridge CB5 8EP
Tel: (01604) 233233 Fax: (01223) 316511
Email: mail@hewitsons.com (for all offices)
Website: www.hewitsons.com (for all offices)

firm profile
Established in 1865, the firm handles mostly company and commercial work, but has a growing body of public sector clients. The firm has three offices: Cambridge, Northampton and Saffron Walden.

main areas of work
Three sections: corporate technology, property and private client.

trainee profile
The firm is interested in applications from candidates who have achieved a high degree of success in academic studies and who are bright, personable and able to take the initiative.

training environment
The firm offers four six-month seats.

benefits
The PSC is provided during the first year of the training contract. This is coupled with an extensive programme of Trainee Solicitor Seminars provided by specialist in-house lawyers.

vacation placements
Places for 2007: A few placements are available, application is by way of letter and CV to Caroline Lewis; Duration: 1 week.

sponsorship & awards
Funding for the CPE and/or LPC is not provided.

Partners	50
Assistant Solicitors	43
Total Trainees	15

contact
Caroline Lewis
7 Spencer Parade
Northampton NN1 5AB

method of application
Firm's application form

selection procedure
Interview

closing date for 2009
End of August 2007

application
Training contracts p.a. **10**
Applications p.a. **850**
% interviewed p.a. **10%**
Required degree grade
2:1 min

training
Salary
1st year (2006) **£18,000**
2nd year (2006) **£19,000**
Holiday entitlement **22 days**
% of trainees with a
non-law degree p.a. **50%**

post-qualification
Salary (2006) **£31,500**
% of trainees offered job
on qualification (2005) **66%**
% of assistants (as at
1/9/05) who joined as
trainees **54%**
% of partners (as at 1/9/05)
who joined as trainees **32%**

Higgs & Sons

134 High Street, Brierley Hill DY5 3BG
Tel: (01384) 342100   Fax: (01384) 342000
Email: law@higgsandsons.co.uk
Website: www.higgsandsons.co.uk

firm profile

One of the leading law firms in the West Midlands providing cutting-edge legal advice in a friendly and down-to-earth way to business and private paying clients across a wide variety of legal specialisations. Founded in 1875 the firm is committed to developing long term relationships with its clients. ISO9001 accredited.

main areas of work

For the business client: corporate and commercial, employment law, commercial litigation and commercial property work.

For the private client: wills, probate and trusts, employment law, personal injury, ULR and clinical negligence, conveyancing and civil litigation, negligence work, matrimonial/family and criminal.

trainee profile

Applications are welcome from law and non law students who can demonstrate a consistently high academic record, a broad range of interpersonal skills and extra curricular activities and interests.

training environment

A first-class structured programme, fully supervised, based on experience in at least four major disciplines with regular assessments. An open-door policy. Preferences balanced with firm's needs.

benefits

Private Medical Insurance, Life Assurance.

Partners	**27**
Fee Earners	**36**
Total Trainees	**6**

contact
Pat Evans

method of application
Online application form or letter and CV

selection procedure
Interview with trainee committee

closing date for 2009
17th August 2007

application
Training contracts p.a. **4**
Applications p.a. **250 plus**
% interviewed p.a. **varies**
Required degree grade preferably **2.1**, will consider **2.2**

training
Salary **reviewed annually**
1st year **£17,000**
2nd year **£18,500**
Holiday entitlement
24 days p.a.

post-qualification
Salary **£26,000**
% of trainees offered job on qualification **100%**

Hill Dickinson

Pearl Assurance House, 2 Derby Square, Liverpool L2 9XL
Tel: (0151) 236 5400 Fax: (0151) 236 2175
Email: recruitment@hilldickinson.com
Website: www.hilldickinson.com

firm profile

Hill Dickinson LLP is one of the UK's leading independent law firms and is a national top 40 practice with offices in Liverpool, London, Manchester, Chester and Piraeus. Following the merger with Hill Taylor Dickinson in November 2006 and an aggressive programme of lateral hiring in the last year, the firm now has 141 partners and a total staff complement of more than 900.

main areas of work

Property & real estate: Hill Dickinson is a recognised leader in commercial property and in May 2006 the firm was awarded Property Law Firm of the Year 2006 at the Insider Property Awards North West.

Construction: The construction division has extensive expertise in all contentious and non-contentious legal issues affecting the industry.

Marine: The marine division, with experts in London, Liverpool, Manchester and Greece is widely recognised as one of the top league marine firms.

Medico-legal: The firm has one of the UK's largest medico-legal practices acting on behalf of health authorities, NHS trusts and other health service bodies. The firm is a member of the National Health Service Litigation Authority's panel, which was the first licensed to provide health sector/ medical negligence elements within training contracts.

Commercial: The commercial division is well respected and provides advice on all aspects of commercial law.

Intellectual property & technology: The IP team is acknowledged to be at the forefront of the profession and has leading trademark-filing experience.

Private Client: The firm provides specialist advice on tax and estate planning, financial planning matters, family law and advising charitable trusts.

Insurance: The leading UK insurance division acts on all aspects of insurance including transport, leisure and tourism, retail, environment, fraud and negligence.

Professional services: The firm deals with all areas of professional indemnity both for claimants, defendants and insurers.

trainee profile

Commercial awareness and academic ability are the key factors, together with a desire to succeed. Trainees are viewed as the partners of the future and the firm is looking for personable individuals with whom it wants to work.

training environment

Trainees spend periods of six months in four different divisions. Trainees are encouraged to accept responsibility and are expected to act with initiative. The practice has an active social committee and a larger than usual selection of competitive sporting teams.

vacation placements

One week structured scheme with places available for 2007. Apply online by 31 March 2007.

Partners	141
Assistant Solicitors	143
Associates	36
Total Trainees	27

contact
Victoria Wolff

method of application
Online application form

selection procedure
Assessment day

closing date for 2009
13th July 2008

training
Salary
1st year (2006) £20,500
2nd year (2006) £22,000
London weighting £5,000
(where applicable)
Sponsorship: LPC
Holiday entitlement
25 days

post-qualification
% of trainees offered job
on qualification 90%

offices
Liverpool, Manchester, London, Chester, Greece

Hodge Jones & Allen

31-39 Camden Road, London, NW1 9LR
Tel: (020) 7482 1974 Fax: (020) 7267 3476
Email: hja@hodgejonesallen.co.uk
Website: www.hodgejonesallen.co.uk

firm profile
Hodge Jones & Allen was founded in Camden Town in 1977. It is now one of the largest legal firms in north London, having grown from four to over 170 staff. Although the firm has private and commercial clients, it also has contracts with the Legal Services Commission in many areas of practice and is known as one of the leading, predominantly publicly funded law practices in the country. The firm is led by one of its founding partners, Patrick Allen. It has been involved in a number of high profile cases including, the King's Cross fire, the Marchioness disaster, Broadwater Farm riots, Real IRA BBC-bombing trial, the second inquest into the New Cross fire, MMR vaccine litigation and Gulf War Syndrome. The firm is located in a single modern office next to the canal, in a lively and trendy part of Camden Town.

main areas of work
Crime, personal injury, multi party actions, public law, police actions, miscarriage of justice claims, human rights, medical negligence, family, housing, mental health, property, wills and probate, prison law.

trainee profile
Trainees will have an excellent academic record, enthusiasm and a positive approach, good communication skills and a commitment to access to justice for all, regardless of ability to pay.

training environment
Trainees have a full induction on joining HJA covering the work of the firm's main departments, procedural matters and professional conduct. Training consists of four six-month seats and trainees normally share an office with a partner who assists them and formally reviews their progress at least once during each seat. The training is well structured and trainees have the benefit of a mentoring scheme. The firm provides good secretarial and clerking support so trainees can concentrate on legal work rather than administration. The firm has an excellent IT infrastructure and continues to invest heavily in IT to keep pace with innovation.

benefits
Pension scheme, Life Assurance, disability insurance, quarterly drinks, summer outing and Christmas party.

Partners 21
Assistant Solicitors 36
Total Trainees 12

contact
HR Department

method of application
Application form (available online)

selection procedure
Interview with 2 Partners

closing date for 2008
24 August 2007 (apply one year in advance)

application
Training contracts p.a. **6-7**
Applications p.a. **500**
% interviewed p.a. **5%**
Preferred degree grade **2:1 min**

training
Salary: **£20,000**
Holiday entitlement 20 days p.a.

post-qualification
Salary: **£27,000**
% of trainees offered job on qualification: **75%**

Holman Fenwick & Willan

Marlow House, Lloyds Avenue, London EC3N 3AL
Tel: (020) 7488 2300 Fax: (020) 7481 0316
Email: grad.recruitment@hfw.co.uk

firm profile
Holman Fenwick & Willan is an international law firm and one of the world's leading specialists in maritime transportation, insurance, reinsurance, energy and trade. The firm is a leader in the field of commercial litigation and arbitration and also offers comprehensive commercial advice. Founded in 1883, the firm is one of the largest operating in its chosen fields with a team of over 200 lawyers worldwide, and a reputation for excellence and innovation.

main areas of work
The firm's range of services include marine, admiralty and crisis management, insurance and reinsurance, commercial litigation and arbitration, international trade and commodities, energy, corporate and financial.

trainee profile
Applications are invited from commercially minded undergraduates and graduates of all disciplines with good A levels and who have, or expect to receive, a 2:1 degree. Good foreign languages or a scientific or maritime background are an advantage.

training environment
During your training period the firm will ensure that you gain valuable experience in a wide range of areas. It also organises formal training supplemented by a programme of in-house seminars and ship visits in addition to the PSC. Your training development as an effective lawyer will be managed by the HR and Training Partner, Ottilie Sefton, who will ensure that your training is both successful and enjoyable.

benefits
Private medical insurance, permanent health and accident insurance, subsidised gym membership, season ticket loan.

vacation placements
Places for 2007: Dates: 26 June – 6 July/16 July – 27 July; Remuneration (2006): £250 p.w.; Closing Date: Applications accepted 1 Jan – 14 Feb 2007.

sponsorship & awards
GDL Funding: Fees paid plus £5,000 maintenance; LPC Funding: Fees paid plus £5,000 maintenance.

Partners	80+
Other Solicitors & Fee-earners	120+
Total Trainees	16

contact
Graduate Recruitment
Officer - Rachel Frowde

method of application
Online application form

selection procedure
2 interviews with partners & written exercise

closing date for 2009
31 July 2007

application
Training contracts p.a. **8**
Applications p.a. **1,000**
% interviewed p.a. **5%**
Required degree grade **2:1**

training
Salary (Sept 2006)
1st year £28,000
2nd year £30,000
Holiday entitlement **22 days**
% of trainees with
a non-law degree p.a. **50%**

post-qualification
Salary **£50,000** (Sept 2005)
% of trainees offered job
on qualification
(Sept 2005) **78%**

overseas offices
Hong Kong, Nantes, Paris, Piraeus, Rouen, Shanghai, Singapore, Dubai, Melbourne

Howes Percival

Oxford House, Cliftonville, Northampton NN1 5PN
Tel: (01604) 230400 Fax: (01604) 620956
Email: katy.pattle@howespercival.com
Website: www.howespercival.com

Partners	**33**
Solicitors	**80**
Total Trainees	**14**

firm profile

Howes Percival is a leading commercial law firm with offices in Leicester, Milton Keynes, Northampton and Norwich. This year the firm won the 2006 UK Regional Firm of the Year at the Legal Business Awards. The firm's working environment is young, progressive and highly professional and its corporate structure means that fee-earners are rewarded on merit and can progress to associate or partner status quickly. The type and high value of the work that the firm does places it in a position whereby it is recognised as being a regional firm by location only. The firm has the expertise, resources, and partner reputation that match a city firm.

main areas of work

The practice is departmentalised and the breakdown of its work is as follows: corporate 30%; commercial property 25%; commercial litigation 20%; insolvency 10%; employment 10%; private client 5%.

trainee profile

The firm is looking for eight well-educated, focused, enthusiastic, commercially aware graduates with a minimum 2:1 degree in any discipline. Howes Percival welcomes confident communicators with strong interpersonal skills who share the firm's desire to be the best.

training environment

Trainees complete four six month seats, each one in a different department. Trainees joining the Norwich office will remain at Norwich for the duration of their training contract. Within the East Midlands region, there is the opportunity to gain experience in each of the three East Midlands offices. Trainees report direct to a partner, and after three months and again towards the end of each seat they will be formally assessed by the partner training them. Trainees will be given every assistance by the fee-earners in their department to develop quickly and will be given responsibility as soon as they are ready.

benefits

Contributory pension scheme. Private health insurance. LPC/CPE funding, maintenance grant.

vacation placements

Vacation placements are available in June, July and August. Please apply in writing to Emma Kazmierczak, HR Assistant at the above address (enclosing your CV) indicating which location you would prefer. The closing date is 30 April 2007.

contact
Miss Katy Pattle
HR Officer

method of application
Online application form

selection procedure
Assessment centres

closing date for 2009
31 July 2007

application
Training contracts p.a. **8**
Applications p.a. **300**
% interviewed p.a. **10%**
Required degree grade **2:1**

training
Salary
To be confirmed (see website)
Holiday entitlement
23 days p.a.

post-qualification
% of trainees offered job on qualification (2006) **80%**
% of assistants who joined as trainees **64%**
% of partners who joined as trainees **9%**

IBB Solicitors

30 Capital Court, Windsor Street, Uxbridge, Middlesex, UB8 1AB
Tel: (08456) 381381 Fax: (01895) 272116
Email: Melanie.White@ibblaw.co.uk
Website: www.ibblaw.co.uk

firm profile

IBB is a leading law firm located on the outskirts of West London, providing a full range of services to an extensive business, institutional and private client community. Due to its recent growth, IBB has expanded into larger premises in Uxbridge, taking on two floors of Capital Court, to accommodate its growing legal teams. It also continues to house legal teams at Lovell House, Uxbridge, Chesham and Ingatestone.

The firm has been rated as one of the top tier law firms in the region for its private client, commercial property and crime services by one of the UK's leading legal services directory, The Legal 500.

main areas of work

Charities, commercial litigation, commercial property, company & commercial, construction, corporate finance, crime, employment, family, insurance/reinsurance, intellectual property, personal injury, private client.

trainee profile

Success here means having the knowledge and the skills to apply that knowledge for clients. The firm recruits on the basis of potential. Selection is based on a number of criteria including academic ability (2:1 and good A levels), clear written and oral communication skills, the ability to assimilate information and the experience of working with others to achieve a task and research into and where possible experience of working in a private practice.

training environment

You will spend two weeks in October on the firm's comprehensive induction programme. This includes the opportunity to shadow the current trainee's. Training contracts will begin on 1 November and consists of two years divided into four six month seats, giving the opportunity to gain experience of quite different areas of law. You will get hands-on experience and become an important part of the team

benefits

25 days holiday, life assurance, stakeholder pension, private medical insurance, subsidised gym membership

Partners	29
Assistant Solicitors	41
Total Trainees	12

contact
Mel White
Melanie.White@ibblaw.co.uk
(01895) 207989

method of application
Online – www.ibblaw.co.uk

selection procedure
IBB creates a long list of applications and interview about 50 people; from those, they shortlist 12 people who are invited to a full day assessment centre.

closing date for 2009
30 June 2007

application
Training contracts p.a. **6**
Applications p.a. **400**
% interviewed p.a. **15%**
Required degree grade **2:1**

training
Salary for each year of training:
1st year £20,000
2nd year £22,000
Holiday entitlement: **25 days p.a.**

Ince & Co

International House, 1 St Katharine's Way, London E1W 1UN
Email: recruitment@incelaw.com

firm profile

From its origins in maritime law, the firm's practice today encompasses all aspects of the work areas listed below. Ince & Co is frequently at the forefront of developments in contract and tort law.

main areas of work

Aviation, business and finance, commercial disputes, energy, insurance and reinsurance, shipping and trade.

trainee profile

Hardworking competitive individuals with initiative who relish challenge and responsibility within a team environment. Academic achievements, positions of responsibility, sport and travel are all taken into account.

training environment

Trainees sit with four different partners for six months at a time throughout their training. Under close supervision, they are encouraged from an early stage to meet and visit clients, interview witnesses, liaise with counsel, deal with technical experts and handle opposing lawyers. They will quickly build up a portfolio of cases from a number of partners involved in a cross-section of the firm's practice and will see their cases through from start to finish. They will also attend in-house and external lectures, conferences and seminars on practical and legal topics.

benefits

STL, corporate health cover, PHI, contributory pension scheme.

vacation placements

Places for 2007: 15; Duration: 2 weeks; Remuneration: £250 p.w.; Closing Date: 14 February 2007.

sponsorship & awards

LPC/CPE fees, £6,000 grant for study in London & Guildford, £5,500 grant for study elsewhere.

Partners	**76***
Senior Associates	**16***
Solicitors	**72***
Total Trainees	**22***
*denotes worldwide figures	

contact
Claire Kendall

method of application
Typed/handwritten letter & CV, containing full breakdown of degree results & A-level grades, with contact details of 2 academic referees

selection procedure
Interview with HR professional & interview with 2 partners from Recruitment Committee & a written test

closing date for 2009
31 July 2007

application
Training contracts p.a. **8-10**
Applications p.a. **1,500**
% interviewed p.a. **5%**
Required degree grade **2:1**

training
Salary
1st year £28,500
2nd year £31,500
Holiday entitlement **25 days**
% of trainees with a non-law degree p.a. **55%**

post-qualification
Salary **£48,500**
% of trainees offered job on qualification (2006)
75%. All accepted!
% of partners (as at 2005) who joined as trainees
Approx 66%

overseas offices
Dubai, Hamburg, Hong Kong, Le Havre, Paris, Piraeus, Shanghai, Singapore

Irwin Mitchell

Riverside East, 2 Millsands, Sheffield S3 8DT
Tel: (0114) 2744482 Fax: (0870) 197 3549
Email: graduaterecruitment@irwinmitchell.co.uk
Website: www.irwinmitchell.com

firm profile
Irwin Mitchell is a rapidly expanding international practice with 95 partners and over 1800 employees. The firm's strong reputation for dealing with novel and complex areas of law and handling developmental cases such as: Herceptin, vibration white finger and CJD means that it can offer a broad range of experience within each of its specialist departments, giving trainees a high standard of training.

main areas of work
Corporate services and private client 30%; insurance 39%; personal injury 31%.

trainee profile
The firm is looking for ambitious and well-motivated individuals who have a real commitment to the law and who can demonstrate a positive approach to work-life balance. Irwin Mitchell recruits law and non-law graduates and views social ability as important as academic achievement. Irwin Mitchell believes trainees are an investment for the future and endeavours to retain trainees upon qualification. In addition to the firm's training contract vacancies it also runs a work placement scheme giving potential training contract candidates a chance to experience what it is like to be a solicitor within the firm.

training environment
Irwin Mitchell offers a week long structured welcome programme to trainees joining the practice. In addition regular training events are held throughout the firm. The Professional Skills Course is financed by the firm and is run in-house, being tailored to meet the needs of the firm's trainees. During your training contract you will be given as much responsibility as you can handle, giving you a real opportunity to work with the law, your colleagues and to develop your client relationship skills. Your development will be encouraged through frequent reviews and feedback.

benefits
Healthcare scheme, contributory pension scheme, subsidised gym membership, away day and Christmas party.

sponsorship & awards
Payment of PGDL and LPC fees plus a £3,000 maintenance grant.

Partners	95
Assistant Solicitors	195
Total Trainees	52

contact
Alex Burgess,
Graduate Recruitment
Assistant
Tel: (0114) 274 4482

method of application
Please visit the firm's website www.irwinmitchell.com and complete the online application

selection procedure
Assessment centre & interview

closing date for 2009
31 July 2007

application
Training contracts p.a. **20-25**
Applications p.a. **1,200**
% interviewed p.a. **50%**
Required degree grade:
The firm does not require a specific degree grade

training
Salary
1st year £18,540
2nd year £20,600
(outside London)
reviewed annually in September
Holiday entitlement
24.5 days

post-qualification
% of trainees offered job on qualification **80%**

Overseas/Regional Offices
Birmingham, Leeds, London, Manchester, Newcastle, Sheffield, Marbella & Madrid

Jones Day

21 Tudor Street, London, EC4Y 0DJ
Tel: (020) 7039 5959 Fax: (020) 7039 5999
Email: recruit.london@jonesday.com
Website: www.jonesdaylondon.com/recruit

firm profile
Jones Day operates as one firm worldwide with 2,200 lawyers in 30 offices. Jones Day in London is a key part of this international partnership and has around 200 lawyers, including around 40 partners and 40 trainees. This means that the firm can offer its lawyers a perfect combination - the intimacy and atmosphere of a medium sized City firm with access to both UK and multinational clients.

main areas of work
Jones Day has five core departments: corporate; lending and structured finance; real estate; litigation and tax. There are specialist groups for competition, construction, environment, planning and insolvency, insurance, employment and pensions.

trainee profile
The firm looks for candidates with either a law or non-law degree who have strong intellectual and analytical ability and good communication skills and who can demonstrate resourcefulness, drive, dedication and the ability to engage with clients and colleagues.

training environment
The firm operates a unique, non-rotational system of training and trainees receive work simultaneously from all departments in the firm. The training is designed to provide freedom, flexibility and responsibility from the start. Trainees are encouraged to assume their own workload, which allows early responsibility, a faster development of potential and the opportunity to compare and contrast the different disciplines alongside one another. Work will vary from small cases which the trainee may handle alone (under the supervision of a senior lawyer) to larger matters where they will assist a partner or an associate solicitor. The firm runs a structured training programme with a regular schedule of seminars to support the thorough practical training and regular feedback that trainees receive from the associates and partners they work with.

vacation placements
Places for 2006/07:
Christmas (non-law): 20 places; 2 weeks; £400; closing date 31 October.
Easter 2007 (non-law): 10 places; 2 weeks; £400; closing date 31 January.
Summer 2007 (law): 40; 2 weeks; £400; closing date 31 January.
Placements last for two weeks with an allowance of £400 per week. Students get to see how the firm's non-rotational training system works in practice by taking on real work from a variety of practice areas. They also get to meet a range of lawyers at various social events.

benefits
Private healthcare, season ticket loan, subsidised sports club membership, group life cover.

sponsorship & awards
CPE/PgDL and LPC fees paid and £8,000 maintenance p.a.

Partners	40
Assistant Solicitors	80
Total Trainees	40

contact
Jacqui Megson
Graduate Recruitment Manager

method of application
CV and letter online at www.jonesdaylondon.com/recruit

selection procedure
2 interviews with partners

closing date for 2009
31 August 2007 - please apply by end of July to ensure an early interview slot

application
Training contracts p.a. **15-20**
Applications p.a. **1,500**
% interviewed p.a. **12%**
Required degree grade **2.1**

training
Salary
1st year (2006) **£39,000**
2nd year (2006) **£45,000**
Holiday entitlement
5 weeks

post-qualification
Salary (2006) **£60,000**
% of trainees offered job on qualification (2006) **75%**

overseas offices
Continental Europe, Asia, North America

Kaim Todner

5 St Bride Street, London EC4A 4AS
Tel: (020) 7353 6660 Fax: (020) 7353 6661
Email: drogers@kaimtodner.com
Website: www.kaimtodner.com

firm profile

Kaim Todner is one of the largest criminal and mental health legal aid firms in the country with four offices in London and one in Ashford, Kent. The firm delivers high quality legal services to those most desperately in need. The firm also has a thriving public law and family department. The firm deals with many high profile criminal and mental health cases and is equipped to deal with the whole criminal spectrum from volume Magistrates' Court work up to matters at the highest level including the House of Lords.

main areas of work

General crime, serious fraud, court martials, mental health review tribunals, judicial review, public law, family, actions against the police, prison law.

trainee profile

Strong academic profile, committed to a career in criminal or mental health law, preferably with previous work experience in a relevant area.

training environment

The two year training contract consists of one year in two departments working alongside their managers, working towards their own caseload under supervision in a relatively short period of time. Trainees are encouraged to have initiative and take responsibility at an early stage. The firm supports the application for accreditation to panels such as police station accreditation and mental health review tribunal panel membership.

benefits

The firm has previously been the recipient of training grants from the Legal Services Commission and has recently applied for a further training grant.

vacation placements

Christmas, Easter and summer break at both the London and Ashford offices.

Partners	6
Lawyers	44
Trainees	14

contact
Deborah Rogers
Human Resources
Manager

method of application
CV and letter or online

selection procedure
Interview with Human
Resources Manager and
Partner

application
Training contracts p.a. **7**
Applications p.a. **400**
% interviewed p.a. **5%**
Required degree grade **2.2**

training
Salary
1st year £17,150
2nd year £17,500
Holiday entitlement
23 days

post-qualification
Salary (September 2006)
£24,000
% of trainees offered job
80%

other offices
Ashford, Kent

www.chambersandpartners.co.uk

Kendall Freeman

43 Fetter Lane, London, EC4A 1JU
Tel: (020) 7583 4055 Fax: (020) 7353 7377
Email: graduaterecruitment@kendallfreeman.com
Website: www.kendallfreeman.com

firm profile
Kendall Freeman handles high value and complex matters for corporates, banks and clients in the insurance and reinsurance industry and public sectors. The firm was awarded the LCN/TSG 2004 award for Best Trainer at a Medium-Sized City Law Firm and has been nominated as the LCN/TSG best recruiter for a medium sized City firm 2006.

main areas of work
Arbitration, ADR, banking, commercial litigation, company and commercial, construction, corporate finance, employment, energy and offshore engineering, insolvency, restructuring, insurance/reinsurance, mergers and acquisitions and international law.

trainee profile
The firm is small by City standards with 21 partners, but successfully competes and acts alongside the largest international and UK firms of solicitors in its work. It can therefore offer excellent training with high quality work in a more personal environment than the larger firms. The firm seeks motivated individuals with initiative and commercial sense who do not want to be one of a crowd. Trainees need to have a very strong academic backround and excellent people skills as they will have early client interaction.

training environment
Trainees spend six months of their training contract in four of the firm's major practice areas and once a month are able to discuss their progress with a partner. Believing supervised, practical experience to be the best training, the firm soon gives trainees the chance to meet clients, be responsible for their own work and join in marketing and client development activities. Regular workshops in each seat help develop basic skills in the different practice areas. There is a trainee solicitors' committee which meets regularly and which is attended by two trainee representatives where any suggestions or concerns can be voiced. Each trainee is allocated a partner as a mentor.

vacation placements
The firm runs a vacation scheme during July and is introducing a work experience scheme for first years from 2007 onwards.

sponsorship & awards
Full CPE/GDL and LPC funding and a maintenance grant of £6,500 (London) / £6,000 (outide London).

Partners	22
Assistant Solicitors	28
Total Trainees	15

contact
Marisa Barber
(020) 7556 4414

method of application
Firm's online application form
http://graduate.kendallfreeman.com

selection procedure
Assessment morning plus one interview with two partners

closing date for 2009
31 July 2007

application
Training contracts p.a. **7**
Minimum required degree grade **2:1**

training
Salary
1st year £29,500 (Sept 06)
2nd year £33,000 (Sept 06)

post-qualification
Salary £52,000 (Sept 06)

summer placements
10 p.a.
open days
3, accommodating 75 students
closing date for summer placements
28 February 2007
closing date for open days
18 May 2007

KENDALL FREEMAN

Kirkpatrick & Lockhart Nicholson Graham LLP

110 Cannon Street, London, EC4N 6AR
Tel: (020) 7648 9000 Fax: (020) 7648 9001
Email: traineerecruitment@klng.com
Website: www.klng.com

Partners	52
Fee Earners	65
Trainees	21
Total Staff	286

firm profile

Kirkpatrick & Lockhart Nicholson Graham LLP (K&LNG) is an international law firm with approximately 1,000 lawyers practising across 12 offices, one located in London and 11 in major cities in the US. Representing leading global corporations, growth and middle market companies and entrepreneurs, both nationally and internationally, its practice is cutting-edge, complex and dynamic, with innovative thinking a core strength. The firm is committed to a strategic growth plan, with the London office at the forefront of the development initiative. The firm retains its commitment to a work-life balance, target chargeable hours for the London office remain at 1,500.

main areas of work

In London the firm offers extensive experience across its eight main practice areas, namely: corporate finance; real estate; banking; construction and engineering; corporate tax and VAT; litigation and dispute resolution; intellectual property and capital markets. They are also highly regarded in a number of niche areas including employment, financial services, insolvency, hedge funds, insurance coverage, music rights and digital media, planning and environment, private equity, sport, telecoms and travel and leisure. As a leading firm in the US for funds, insurance coverage and energy work, the mission for the UK is to further develop its practice in these areas.

trainee profile

Highly motivated, intelligent graduates of any discipline with (or expecting) a 2.1 degree or higher, who are looking for comprehensive training in a firm with a lively, informal atmosphere.

training environment

Trainees spend six months in four of the following training seats: corporate; dispute resolution and litigation; intellectual property; construction; tax and real estate. Each trainee sits with a supervisor and is allocated an individual mentor to ensure all-round supervision and training. The firm has a thorough induction scheme which includes attendance at its First Year Academy in the US and has recently won awards for its career development programme. Trainees are encouraged to participate fully in all the activities of the firm. High importance is placed on the acquisition of business and professional skills, with considerable emphasis on client contact and early responsibility.

benefits

Permanent health insurance, life assurance, season ticket loan, subsidised gym membership, pension, private health insurance, 25 days holiday and bonus scheme.

vacation placements

The London office runs two schemes held during the month of July. Applications should be made online prior to 15 February 2007.

sponsorship & awards

GDL Funding: Fees paid plus £5,000 maintenance grant.
LPC Funding: Fees paid plus £7,000 maintenance grant.

contact
Hayley Atherton

method of application
Online only

selection procedure
Assessment day including interviews

closing date for 2009
31 July 2007

application
Training contracts p.a. **up to 15**
Applications p.a. **1,000**
% interviewed p.a. **10%**
Required degree grade **2:1**

training
Salary
1st year (2006) **30,000**
2nd year (2006) **33,000**
% of trainees with a non-law degree p.a. **Varies**

post-qualification
Salary (2006) **£53,000**
% of trainees offered job on qualification (2006) **70%**

overseas offices
Boston, Dallas, Harrisburg, Los Angeles, Miami, Newark, New York, Palo Alto, Pittsburgh, San Fransisco, Washington

Knight & Sons

The Brampton, Newcastle-under-Lyme, Staffordshire, ST5 0QW
Tel: (01782) 619225 Fax: (01782) 717260
Email: info@knightandsons.co.uk
Website: www.knightandsons.co.uk

Partners	16
Assistant solicitors	37
Trainees	5

firm profile

Knight & Sons is a medium sized commercially orientated firm with a strong private client department. The firm was founded in 1767 and still acts for many of the older businesses and facilities of the north Midlands. They have 16 partners and approximately 140 members of staff. There is no such things as a "Knight & Sons clone" - they thrive on different personalities, knowing how vital it is to be able to meet the needs of a wide range of clients.

main areas of work

The firm's main areas of work are commercial property (38%), corporate and commercial (17%), commercial litigation (24%) and tax, trust and private client (21%).

trainee profile

The firm is keen to recruit trainees who will stay on once they have qualified. They like people with outstanding academic achievement, a commercial approach, drive, a "can do" attitude, and who are computer literate; but apart from these aspects, whether you are sporty, arty or intellectual you have a fair chance with them. An outgoing personality is important, as is an ability to communicate well with others, colleagues and clients alike.

training environment

Trainees generally spend six months in each of the four main departments but may also gain experience in the specialist units such as planning and environment, employment, personal injury, agriculture and charity. You will receive three-monthly reviews with your immediate training supervisor and the training principal. Your Professional Skills Course will be arranged and paid for by the firm. You will also be given the opportunity to attend Knight & Sons' internal workshops and seminars. The firm runs in-house skills-based programmes designed to enhance business and client care skills for all fee earners.

benefits

Subsidised restaurant, free on-site parking, reduced private health care premiums.

sponsorship & awards

Interest free loans may be available but are strictly subject to individual negotiation.

contact
Jane Selman, HR & Training Manager

method of application
Apply online by visiting the website or make a handwritten application

selection procedure
2 stage interview including presentation

closing date for 2009
31 July 2007

application
Training contracts p.a. **3**
Applications p.a. **200**
% interviewed p.a. **10%**

training
Salary: **Above the Law Society minimum with a six month review.**
Holiday entitlement **21 days per year**

offices
Newcastle-under-Lyme

Latham & Watkins

99 Bishopsgate, London, EC2M 3XF
Tel: (020) 7710 1000 Fax: (020) 7374 4460
Email: london.trainees@lw.com
Website: www.lw.com

firm profile
Latham & Watkins has more than 1,800 lawyers in 22 offices across Europe, America and Asia. Their London office advises on some of the most significant and ground-breaking cross-border transactions in Europe. They are proud of the culture, the work and the people at their firm and believe their non-hierarchical management style and 'one firm' culture makes them unique.

main areas of work
Corporate, finance, project finance, litigation, employment and tax.

trainee profile
Candidates with a strong academic background, excellent communication skills and a consistent record of personal and/or professional achievement will be rewarded with first class training. The firm is dedicated to diversity and equal opportunity and they value originality and creative thinking.

training environment
The firm believes that it can provide a very different experience to that offered by the rest of the elite law firms. Every one of their small group of trainees will receive bespoke supervision and outstanding support while being encouraged to recognise that they have their own part to play in the growth and success of the firm. They expect that each trainee will be given meaningful responsibility from the outset and they will have sig-nificant legal experience on qualification. Trainees will also be given the opportunity to spend one of their four six month seats in one of the firm's overseas offices.

benefits
Healthcare and dental scheme, pension scheme and life assurance.

sponsorship & awards
All GDL and LPC costs are paid and trainees receive a maintenance grant of £8,000 per year whilst studying.

vacation placements
The firm has a two-week vacation scheme in August and students are paid £300 per week. The deadline for applications is 31 January.

Partners	37
Assistant solicitors	98
Trainees	2

contact
Tracy Davidson

method of application
CV & covering letter

selection procedure
3 x 30 minutes interview with a partner and an associate

closing date for 2008
31 July 2007

application
Training contracts p.a. **10-15**
Required degree grade: **2:1**

training
Salary: **£35,000 (2006)**. This increases by £500 every 6 months during the training contract.

post-qualification
Salary: **£88,000 (2006)**

overseas/regional offices
Brussels, Chicago, Frank-furt, Hamburg, Hong Kong, London, Los Angeles, Milan, Moscow, Munich, New Jersey, New York, Northern Virginia, Orange County, Paris, San Diego, San Francisco, Shanghai, Silicon Valley, Singapore, Tokyo, Washington DC.

Lawrence Graham

190 Strand, London WC2R 1JN
Tel: (020) 7379 0000 Fax: (020) 7379 6854
Email: graduate@lawgram.com
Website: www.lawgram.com

Partners	85
Assistant Solicitors	117
Total Trainees	35

contact
Vikki Horton

method of application
Firm's application form.
For law **After 2nd-year results**
For non-law **After final results**

selection procedure
Interview

closing date for 2009
31 July 2007

application
Training contracts **20-25**
Applications p.a. **800**
Required degree grade **2:1**

training
Salary
1st year (2005) £28,000
2nd year (2005) £32,000
% of trainees with a
non-law degree p.a. **45%**

post-qualification
Salary (2006) **£53,000**
% of trainees offered job
on qualification (2006) **75%**

firm profile
Lawrence Graham is a London-based firm delivering a full range of commercial and legal solutions worldwide. Driven by its corporate and real estate practices, the key sectors in which the firm operates are financial services, real estate, insurance, hospitality & leisure, banking, IT, natural resources and the public sector. The firm has strong relationships with law firms around the world, particularly in the US and Asia, as well as a Monaco office.

main areas of work
The firm's four core departments are: business & finance (including corporate/M&A, banking & finance, IT & outsourcing, investment funds, employment, insurance, pensions, EU/competition, housing & local government); real estate (commercial property, planning, construction, environment & health & safety, real estate litigation and finance); dispute resolution (commercial litigation, corporate recovery, insurance & reinsurance disputes, shipping, contentious trusts & estates, corporate investigations); and tax & private capital. Work is often international in its scope.

trainee profile
The firm is looking for individuals from a variety of backgrounds with refined communication skills who can demonstrate a commitment to a career in the commercial application of law. A strong academic track record with a minimum 2.1 degree is a basic requirement. Also required is a good record of achievement in other areas - indicative of the ability to succeed in a demanding career - and evidence of team working skills and the ability to handle responsibility.

training environment
Under partner supervision trainees will be given early responsibility. Training is structured to facilitate the ability to **manage** one's own files and interact with clients. In addition to the Professional Skills Course, there are departmental training and induction sessions. Training consists of four six-month seats: a real estate, business & finance and a contentious seat are compulsory. The other seat can be either in tax & private capital or a second in business & finance or real estate.

benefits
Season ticket loan, on-site gym, life assurance.

vacation placements
Places for 2007: 32; Duration: 2 weeks during Easter break and 3 x 2 weeks between June and July; Remuneration: £220 p.w; Closing Date: 31 January 2007.

sponsorship & awards
GDL Funding: Course fees and maintenance grant. £4.5k outside London, £5k in London.
LPC Funding: Course fees and maintenance grant. £4.5k outside London, £5k in London.

Laytons

Carmelite, 50 Victoria Embankment, Blackfriars, London EC4Y 0LS
Tel: (020) 7842 8000 Fax: (020) 7842 8080
Email: london@laytons.com
Website: www.laytons.com

firm profile
Laytons is a commercial law firm whose primary focus is on developing dynamic business. The firm's offices in Guildford, London and Manchester provide excellent service to its commercial and private clients who are located throughout the UK. The firm's approach to legal issues is practical, creative and energetic. The firm believes in long-term relationships, they are 'client lawyers' rather than 'transaction lawyers'. The key to its client relations is having a thorough understanding of businesses, their needs and objectives. Working together as one team, the firm is supportive and plays to each others' strengths.

main areas of work
Corporate and commercial, commercial property (including land development and construction), dispute resolution, debt recovery, insolvency, employment, intellectual property, technology and media, private client and trusts.

trainee profile
Successful candidates will be well-rounded individuals, commercially aware with sound academic background and enthusiastic and committed team members.

training environment
Trainees are placed in four six-month seats, providing them with an overview of the firm's business, and identifying their particular strengths. All trainees have contact with clients from an early stage, are given challenging work, working on a variety of matters with partners and assistant solicitors. Trainees will soon be responsible for their own files and are encouraged to participate in business development and marketing activities. The firm works in an informal but professional atmosphere and its philosophy is to invest in people who will develop and become part of its long-term success.

vacation placements
Places for summer 2007: 6. Duration: 1 week. Closing Date: 31 March 2007.

sponsorship & awards
LPC and CPE funding: consideration given.

Partners	29
Assistant Solicitors	32
Total Trainees	15

contact
Neale Andrews (Guildford)
Stephen Cates &
Lisa McLean (London)
Christine Barker (Manchester)

method of application
Application form (on website)

selection procedure
Usually 2 interviews

closing date for 2009
31 August 2007 (although posts are filled as soon as suitable candidates are identified)

application
Training contracts p.a. **8**
Applications p.a. **2,000**
% interviewed p.a. **5%**
Required degree grade
1 or 2:1 preferred

training
Salary
1st year (2006) Market rate
2nd year (2006) Market rate
Holiday entitlement
23 days per year

post-qualification
Salary (2006) **Market rate**
% of trainees offered job on qualification (2006) **83%**
% of assistants (as at 1/9/06) who joined as trainees **45%**
% of partners (as at 1/9/06) who joined as trainees **40%**

regional offices
Training contracts are offered in each of Laytons' offices. Apply directly to desired office. See website for further details: www.laytons.com

LeBoeuf, Lamb, Greene & MacRae

No. 1 Minster Court, Mincing Lane, London EC3R 7YL
Tel: (020) 7459 5000 Fax: (020) 7459 5099
Email: traineelondon@llgm.com
Website: www.llgm.com

Partners	26
Counsel	4
Associates	58
Total Trainees	13

firm profile

LeBoeuf, Lamb, Greene & MacRae is an international law firm with over 670 lawyers worldwide in offices across Europe, the US, Africa, Middle East and Asia. The London office of LeBoeuf Lamb is the firm's largest international office, with 26 partners, and around 100 legal staff. The London office handles varied, interesting work and will suit people who want early responsibility. Culturally, the firm aims to combine a dynamic and energetic atmosphere with a congenial, supportive environment.

contact
Gail Sorrell

method of application
CV & covering letter

closing date for 2009
31 July 2007

main areas of work

General corporate, litigation and dispute resolution, energy, corporate finance, project finance, capital markets, private equity, insurance, insolvency, real estate, tax, intellectual property and employment.

application
Training contracts p.a. **10**
Applications p.a. **950**
% interviewed p.a. **6%**
Required degree grade 2:1,
A,A,B 'A'Level Equivalent

trainee profile

LeBoeuf, Lamb, Greene & MacRae is looking for outstanding people in the broadest possible sense. The firm welcomes applications from varied, non-traditional backgrounds. Interpersonal skills are very important: the firm likes bright, engaging people. The London office is international in outlook and language skills are highly valued. The firm wants proactive people who will contribute from day one and who will thrive in a diverse and cosmopolitan environment.

training
Salary
1st year £36,000
2nd year £39,000
Holiday entitlement **25 days**
% of trainees with a
non-law degree p.a. **50%**

training environment

Trainees spend six months in four seats. The firm encourages its trainees to see and experience as much of the practice as possible. The firm's training programme is comprehensive and, in addition to the professional skills course, covers an induction programme, participation in internal seminars and training sessions together with attendance at external courses. You will be encouraged to act on your own initiative from an early stage. Trainees sit with a partner or senior associate, who give ongoing feedback; progress is formally reviewed every six months. There are opportunities for placements in Brussels, Moscow and Paris.

post-qualification
Salary **(2006) £75,000 and
performance related bonus**

overseas offices
Albany, Almaty, Beijing,
Boston, Brussels, Chicago,
Hartford, Houston,
Jacksonville,
Johannesburg, Los
Angeles, Moscow, New
York, Paris, Pittsburgh,
Riyadh, San Francisco,
Washington, D.C.

benefits

Firm contributes to health, life and disability insurance, season ticket loan and discretionary performance-related bonus.

sponsorship & awards

Full payment of CPE/LPC fees and maintenance grant of £7,000 provided.

Lester Aldridge

Russell House, Oxford Road, Bournemouth BH8 8EX
Tel: (01202) 786161 Fax: (01202) 786110
Email: juliet.milne@LA-law.com
Website: www.lesteraldridge.com

firm profile
Lester Aldridge is a dynamic business providing both commercial and private client services across central southern England. The firm also operates in a number of niche markets nationally including asset finance, corporate finance, licensing, marine and retail. The effective corporate management structure ensures LA is focused on delivering pragmatic solutions to their clients. LA places great emphasis on a positive working environment, and the work/life balance, understanding that this will ultimately be of benefit to clients.

main areas of work
Corporate, banking and finance 32%; litigation 30%; private client 21%; commercial property 12%; investments 5%.

trainee profile
Candidates should have strong intellectual capabilities, be commercially aware, resourceful and able to relate easily to other people. IT skills and a team approach are also required.

training environment
Training consists of four six-month seats across the firm. About half way through each seat trainees discuss their preferences for the next seat and every attempt is made to match aspirations to the needs of the firm. Trainees have a training principal for the duration of the contract who will discuss progress every month. They receive a formal comprehensive appraisal from their team leader towards the end of each seat, and the managing partner meets all trainees as a group every three months.

benefits
Life assurance, pension schemes, flexible benefits.

vacation placements
Places for 2007: 8; Duration: 2 weeks; Remuneration: £75 p.w.; Closing Date: 31 March 2007.

sponsorship & awards
LPC.

Partners	37
Total Trainees	12
Total Staff	370

contact
Juliet Milne

method of application
Letter, CV & completed application form

selection procedure
Interview by a panel of partners

closing date for 2009
31 July 2007

application
Training contracts p.a. **10**
Applications p.a. **300**
% interviewed p.a. **5%**
Required degree grade **2:1**

training
Salary
Starting: **£16,500 at present, increasing by £500 after each seat**
Holiday entitlement **22 days**
% of trainees with
a non-law degree p.a. **20%**

post-qualification
Salary (2004) **£31,000**
% of trainees offered job
on qualification (2005) **100%**
% of assistants (as at 1/9/05)
who joined as trainees **36%**
% of partners (as at 1/9/05)
who joined as trainees **10%**

offices
Bournemouth (2), Southampton, Milton Keynes & London

Lewis Silkin LLP

5 Chancery Lane, Clifford's Inn, London EC4A 1BL
Tel: (020) 7074 8000 Fax: (020) 7864 1200
Email: train@lewissilkin.com

firm profile

Lewis Silkin is a commercial firm with 41 partners. What distinguishes them is a matter of personality. For lawyers, they are notably informal, unstuffy…well, human really. They are 'people people'; as committed and professional as any good law firm, but perhaps more adept at the inter-personal skills that make relationships work and go on working. They place a high priority on the excellent technical ability and commercial thinking of their lawyers and also on their relationships with clients. Clients find them refreshingly easy to deal with. The firm has a friendly, lively style with a commitment to continuous improvement.

main areas of work

The firm has a wide range of corporate clients and provides services through five departments: corporate, employment & incentives, litigation, property and media, brands & technology. The major work areas are commercial litigation and dispute resolution; corporate services, which includes company commercial and corporate finance; defamation; employment; marketing services, embracing advertising and marketing law; property, construction and project finance; technology and communications, including IT, media and telecommunications. They are UK leaders in employment law and have a strong reputation within social housing and the media and advertising sectors.

trainee profile

They are looking for trainees with keen minds and personalities, who will fit into a professional but informal team.

training environment

The firm provides a comprehensive induction and training programme, with practical hands-on experience from day one. You will sit with either a partner or senior associate giving you access to day-to-day supervision and guidance. The training contract consists of four six-month seats. At least three will be in one of the main departments, with the possibility of the fourth being in one of the firm's specialist areas.

benefits

These include individual and firm bonus schemes, life assurance, critical illness cover, health insurance, season ticket loan, group pension plan and subsidised gym membership.

vacation placements

There are four vacation scheme sessions which take place during June and July. Two two-week placements and two one-week placements, giving 16 participants the opportunity to gain first-hand experience of life at Lewis Silkin. Applications should be made via the firm's application form between October 2006 and the end of January 2007.

sponsorship & awards

Funding for LPC fees is provided plus £4,500 maintenance. Funding for GDL fees is provided.

Partners	41
Assistant Solicitors	75
Total Trainees	11

contact
Lucie Rees
Graduate Recruitment Manager

method of application
Online application form

selection procedure
Assessment day, including an interview with 2 partners & an analytical exercise

closing date for 2009
31 July 2007

application
Training contracts p.a. **5**
Applications p.a. **800**
Required degree grade **2:1**

training
Salary
1st year £30,000
2nd year £32,000
Holiday entitlement **22 days**

post-qualification
Salary (2006) **£46,000**

Linklaters

One Silk Street, London EC2Y 8HQ
Tel: (020) 7456 2000 Fax: (020) 7456 2222
Email: graduate.recruitment@linklaters.com
Website: www.linklaters.com/careers/ukgrads

firm profile

Linklaters is the global law firm that advises the world's leading companies, financial institutions and governments on their most challenging transactions and assignments. This is an ambitious and innovative firm: the drive to create something new in professional services also shapes a very special offer to graduates.

main areas of work

While many law firms have strengths in particular areas, Linklaters is strong across the full range of commercial, corporate and financial law; this makes the firm an especially stimulating place to train as a business lawyer.

trainee profile

Linklaters people come from many different backgrounds and cultures; by working together to achieve great things for clients, they are encouraged to achieve their own ambitions and potential. Training with Linklaters means working alongside some of the world's best lawyers on some of the world's most challenging deals. The firm expects a lot of its trainees, but the rewards – personal and professional as well as financial – are very high indeed.

training environment

The firm recruits graduates from both law and non-law disciplines. Non-law graduates spend a conversion year at law college taking the Graduate Diploma in Law (GDL). All trainees have to complete the Legal Practice Course (LPC) before starting their training contracts. The firm meets the costs of both the GDL and LPC. The training contract is built around four six-month seats or placements in a range of practice areas. This develops well-rounded lawyers, but it also helps trainees plan their careers after qualifying.

sponsorship & benefits

GDL and LPC fees are paid in full, plus a maintenance grant. Life assurance, private medical insurance (PPP), permanent health insurance (PHI), pensions, corporate health club membership & in-house gym, in-house dental service, medical services (including flu jabs, eye & eyesight tests), wedding cheques, subsidised staff restaurant, maternity & paternity arrangements (enhanced), interest-free season ticket loan, adoptive leave, group personal accident & holiday travel insurance, performance-related bonus, profit-related bonus scheme, concierge service.

vacation placements

Linklaters offers a two-week Christmas Vacation Scheme for 30 final year non-law students, and three Summer Vacation Schemes (choice of either two or four weeks) for 80 penultimate year law students. The four-week summer schemes offer some students the opportunity to spend two weeks in another European office.

Partners	500
Associates	1,500
Trainees	250*
*(London)	

contact
Charlotte Hart

method of application
Application form (available online)

selection procedure
Critical reasoning test, 2 interviews plus commercial case study (same day).

application
Training contracts p.a. **130**
Applications p.a. **3,500**
Required degree grade **2:1**

training
Salary
1st year (2006) **£31,300**
Holiday entitlement **25 days**
% of trainees with a non-law degree p.a. **35%**

post-qualification
Salary **£55,100 +**
discretionary performance-related bonus

offices
Amsterdam, Antwerp, Bangkok, Beijing, Berlin, Bratislava, Brussels, Bucharest, Budapest, Cologne, Dubai, Frankfurt, Hong Kong, Lisbon, London, Luxembourg, Madrid, Milan, Moscow, Munich, New York, Paris, Prague, Rome, São Paulo, Shanghai, Singapore, Stockholm, Tokyo, Warsaw

Lovells

Atlantic House, Holborn Viaduct, London EC1A 2FG
Tel: (020) 7296 2000 Fax: (020) 7296 2001
Email: recruit@lovells.com
Website: www.lovells.com/graduates

firm profile
Lovells is one of the world's leading international business law firms with offices in the major financial and commercial centres across Europe, Asia and the United States. The range of work at Lovells is very broad. It is one of the firm's strengths as a business and a long standing attraction for candidates.

main areas of work
The firm's international strength across a wide range of practice areas gives it an exceptional reputation. The firm's core areas of practice are corporate, dispute resolution, finance and commerce with specialist groups including real estate, intellectual property, employment, EU/Competition, insurance and tax.

trainee profile
The firm is looking for people whose combination of academic excellence and specialist knowledge will develop Lovells' business and take it forward. As well as demonstrating strong academic and intellectual ability, candidates should have strong communication and interpersonal skills, a professional, commercial attitude, and be happy working in a team yet capable of, and used to, independent action. Above all, candidates should have a single-minded ambition to succeed in a top law firm.

training environment
Lovells treats continuous training and development as a priority for those undertaking the LPC, trainees and qualified lawyers. Clients expect informed, effective legal and business advice from all Lovells lawyers. As a trainee solicitor at Lovells you will participate in an extensive training programme, which covers legal, business and technology skills. The firm is committed to providing you with the highest possible standard of training, throughout your training contract and beyond, so you will develop into an accomplished legal and business adviser.

Trainees spend six months in four different areas of the practice to gain as much experience as possible. All rainees must spend six months in a corporate or finance group, and six months gaining contentious experience in the firm's dispute resolution practice. In the second year of training, there is the option to spend a seat on secondment either to one of the firm's international offices or the in-house legal team of one of the firm's major clients

Throughout your training contract, the firm will work closely with you to advise and provide feedback on your progress. This involves formal and informal assessments as well as advice on practice areas, secondments and qualification. Trainees are offered as much responsibility as they can handle as well as regular reviews, six-monthly appraisals and support when they need it. Lovells' task is much more than merely recruiting – it means ensuring that your ambitions are met by the firm.

Partners	**319**
Assistant Solicitors	**1609**
Total Trainees	**142**

contact
Clare Harris, Head of Graduate Recruitment

method of application
Online application form

selection procedure
Assessment day: critical thinking test, group exercise, interview

closing date for 2009
31 July 2007

application
Training contracts p.a. **90**
Applications p.a. **2,500**
% interviewed p.a. **20%**
Required degree grade **2:1**

training
Salary
1st year (2006) £31,000
2nd year (2006) £35,000
Holiday entitlement **25 days**
% of trainees with a non-law degree p.a. **40%**
No. of seats available abroad p.a. **25**

post-qualification
Salary (2006) **£53,000**

international offices
Alicante, Amsterdam, Beijing, Brussels, Budapest, Chicago, Düsseldorf, Frankfurt, Hamburg, Ho Chi Minh City, Hong Kong, London, Madrid, Milan, Moscow, Munich, New York, Paris, Prague, Rome, Singapore, Shanghai, Tokyo, Warsaw, Zagreb

Lovells continued

future trainee solicitor benefits

All trainees receive a £1,000 bonus and £1,000 advance in salary on joining the firm. The firm also offers £500 for a First Class degree result, £500 for getting the top overall marks within the Lovells LPC cohort, an interest-free season ticket loan (for London Underground and overground services) during the LPC year, Lovells discount card offering discounts at retailers local to the firm, and access to an extranet site specifically for future trainee solicitors .

trainee solicitor benefits

PPP medical insurance, life assurance, PHI, season ticket loan, in-house gym, subsidised staff restaurant, access to dentist, doctor and physiotherapist, discounts at local retailers.

vacation placements

The firm offers 90 vacation placements each year at Christmas, Easter and during the summer. Christmas: 4-15 December 2006; Easter: 19-30 March 2007; Summer: 18 June-6 July 2007; 16 July-3 August 2007. Applications for all schemes open on 1 October 2006. The closing date for Christmas is 10 November 2006. For Easter and the summer programmes, please apply by 31 January 2007. Remuneration: £300 per week.

sponsorship & awards

GDL and LPC course fees are paid, and a maintenance grant is also provided of £7,450 for all students reading the LPC and GDL in London and £6,450 for students reading the GDL elsewhere.

additional information

All second year trainees have the opportunity to apply to spend six months abroad. This is not compulsory and if you want to remain in London you can do so. The firm currently sends trainees to Brussels, Frankfurt, Milan, Moscow, Hong Kong, New York, Paris, Singapore and Tokyo. Currently about 12 trainees will go to the international offices and about 12 will go on client secondments at each seat change.

future & current trainee comments

"When it came to choosing where to apply for a training contract, my first criterion was simple – I was only interested in applying to the very top firms. This goes well beyond the fact that Lovells is one of the largest firms in the city, though. What I was most interested in was that Lovells offers, first, an almost unrivalled breadth of practice, which means that during my first two years at the firm I will have ample opportunity to find the area into which I want to qualify. More important, though, is a client-list of the calibre that Lovells boasts which tells you that the quality of work here is amongst the highest in the city. You can't fail to be impressed – and tempted – by the prospect of working with high profile clients."
Nick Root [1st seat trainee]

"I chose Lovells for the reputation of the people as well as for the quality of work/client I knew I would experience. I have found partners to be approachable and helpful, and experienced a high level of client contact (I have enjoyed various client entertainment evenings) and a great team atmosphere. Adjusting to working life has been a bit of a challenge but I have made great new friends and am very happy with the level of training I have received. I have worked a lot of long hours but the support of the team has made it a lot easier. My knowledge and confidence has increased way beyond expectation in a very short time."
Una Ferris [4th seat trainee]

Lupton Fawcett LLP

Yorkshire House, East Parade, Leeds LS1 5BD
Tel: (0113) 280 2000 Fax: (0113) 245 6782
Email: hr@luptonfawcett.com
Website: www.luptonfawcett.com

Directors	24
Assistant Solicitors	17
Associate Solicitors	10
Total Trainees	5

firm profile

Lupton Fawcett is a well-established yet dynamic and integrated practice. The firm offers a full range of legal services to both commercial and private clients alike on a quality-driven and client-led basis with the emphasis on providing first-class cost effective and practical solutions which exceed the clients' expectations. The firm was one of the first in Leeds to hold both Investors in People and the Law Society's Lexcel quality standard.

Lupton Fawcett is the trading name of Lupton Fawcett LLP, a limited liability partnership, registered in England and Wales, with partnership number OC316270. The registered office is at the above address, where a list of Members' names is open to inspection. Regulated by the Law Society. Authorised and Regulated by the Financial Services Authority.

contact
HR Department
(0113) 280 2251

method of application
Online at
www.luptonfawcett.com

selection procedure
Interviews & assessment days

closing date for 2009
31 July 2007

main areas of work

The commercial division offers the chance to gain experience in corporate, commercial property, employment, intellectual property, insolvency and commercial and chancery litigation. On the private client side, opportunities are available in financial services, trusts and probate, family and residential conveyancing. Further specialist areas of the firm include employment, licensing and advocacy, IT and e-commerce, sports law, debt recovery, insurance litigation and specialist personal injury.

application
Training contracts p.a. **2-3**
Applications p.a. **300**
% interviewed p.a. **10**
Required degree grade **2:1** preferred

trainee profile

Although strong academic achievements are required, the firm places a high value on previous experience and interests which have developed commercial awareness, maturity and character. Trainees will also be able to demonstrate enthusiasm, confidence, good interpersonal and team skills, humour, initiative, commitment and common sense.

training
Salary
Competitive with similar size/type firms
Holiday entitlement
(under review) **23 days**

post-qualification
Salary
Competitive with similar size/type firms
% of trainees offered job on qualification (2004-05) **100%**

training environment

Training at Lupton Fawcett is normally split into four six-month seats. Trainees office share with the director or associate with whom they are working and are an integral part of the team, assuming a high degree of responsibility. Appraisals following each seat take place to ensure that progress is monitored effectively. A full in-house training programme enables continual development as well as from training gained from excellent hands-on experience. Trainees will have the chance to meet clients and be responsible for their own work, as well as being involved in and actively encouraged to join in marketing and practice development initiatives. There is a full social programme in which the trainees are encouraged to participate as well as sporting events organised by the office and an excellent informal social culture.

benefits

Health insurance, season ticket loans, assistance towards LPC funding is available by discussion with candidates.

Mace & Jones

19 Water Street, Liverpool L2 0RP
Tel: (0151) 236 8989 Fax: (0151) 227 5010
Email: duncan.mcallister@maceandjones.co.uk
Pall Mall Court, 61-67 King Street, Manchester, M2 4PD
Tel: (0161) 214 0500 Fax: (0161) 832 8610
Website: www.maceandjones.co.uk

firm profile
Mace & Jones is a leading regional practice in the North West with a national as well as a regional reputation for its commercial expertise, especially in employment, dispute resolution/insolvency, corporate and real estate. It also has one of the best private client teams in the region. The firm's clients range from national and multinational companies and public sector bodies to owner managed businesses and private individuals, reflecting the broad nature of the work undertaken. Sound practical advice is given always on a value-for-money basis.

main areas of work
Dispute resolution/insolvency 15%; real estate 25%; company/commercial 15%; employment 20%; personal injury/private client/family 25%.

trainee profile
The firm seeks to recruit highly motivated trainees with above average ability and the determination to succeed. The right calibre of trainee will assume responsibility early in their career. The firm provides a comprehensive internal and external training programme.

training environment
Trainees complete an induction course to familiarise themselves with the work carried out by the firm's main departments, administration and professional conduct. Training consists of four six-month seats in the following departments: company/commercial, employment, dispute resolution/personal injury litigation, real estate, family law. Strenuous efforts are made to ensure that trainees are able to select the training seat of their choice. A trainee will normally be required to share an office with a partner who will supervise their work and review the trainee's progress at the end of the seat. The PSC is taught externally. The firm operates an open door policy and has various social events.

Partners	39
Assistant Solicitors	37
Total Trainees	11

contact
Duncan McAllister
Liverpool Office

method of application
Online

selection procedure
Interview with partners and HR

closing date for 2008
31 July 2007

application
Training contracts p.a. **4/5**
Applications p.a. **250**
% interviewed p.a. **10%**
Required degree grade **2:1**

training
Salary
1st year (2004) £17,000
2nd year (2004) £17,500
Holiday entitlement **20 days**
% of trainees with a
non-law degree p.a. **40%**

post-qualification
Salary **Negotiable**
% of trainees offered job
on qualification (2005) **50%**
% of assistants (as at 1/7/06)
who joined as trainees **30%**
% of partners (as at 1/9/06)
who joined as trainees **25%**

Macfarlanes

10 Norwich Street, London EC4A 1BD
Tel: (020) 7831 9222 Fax: (020) 7831 9607
Email: gradrec@macfarlanes.com
Website: www.macfarlanes.com

firm profile
Macfarlanes is a leading law firm in the City of London with a strong international out-look. The firm's success is founded on first-class lawyers, hard work and excellent training at all levels. Much of their work is international, acting in complex cross-boarder transactions and international disputes. This work is driven by the firm's excellent relationships with leading independent law firms outside the UK.

main areas of work
The firm has a large corporate, property and litigation department and, unusually for a City firm, a significant private client department. They serve a broad range of clients in the UK and overseas, from multinationals, quoted companies and banks to private individuals.

trainee profile
Trainees need to be highly motivated, high-achieving graduates from any discipline with (or expecting) a strong 2:1 degree or higher, who are looking for top quality work and training in a cohesive firm where everyone's contribution counts and can be seen to count. Macfarlanes needs people who can rise to a challenge and who will relish the opportunities and responsibilities that will be given to them.

training environment
Anyone joining Macfarlanes cannot expect to lose themselves in the crowd. Because they recruit fewer trainees, each individual is expected to play their part and everyone's contribution counts. There are other benefits attached to working in a firm of this size: It helps retain an informal working atmosphere – people quickly get to know one another and are on first name terms across the board. There is the sense of community that comes from working closely together in smaller teams. Everyone at Macfarlanes has a vested interest in getting the best out of each other, including their trainees.

benefits
A comprehensive benefits package is provided.

vacation placements
Places for 2007: 54; Duration: 2 weeks; Remuneration: £250 p.w.; Closing Date: 28 February 2007.

sponsorship & awards
CPE/GDL and LPC fees paid in full and a £7,000 maintenance allowance. Prizes for those gaining distinction or commendation on the LPC.

Partners	**68**
Assistant Solicitors	**141**
Total Trainees	**48**

contact
Louisa Hatton

method of application
Online via website

selection procedure
Assessment day

closing date for 2009
31 July 2007

application
Training contracts p.a. **30**
Applications p.a. **900**
% interviewed p.a. **20%**
Required degree grade **2:1**

training
Salary
1st year **£31,000**
2nd year **£34,000**
Holiday entitlement **23 days, rising to 26 on qualification**
% of trainees with a
non-law degree p.a. **50%**

post-qualification
Salary (2006) **£55,000**
% of trainees offered job
on qualification (2006) **100%**
% of partners (as at 1/9/06)
who joined as trainees **63%**

Manches

Aldwych House, 81 Aldwych, London WC2B 4RP
Tel: (020) 7404 4433 Fax: (020) 7430 1133
Email: sheona.boldero@manches.com
Website: www.manches.com

firm profile
Manches is a full-service commercial firm based in London and the Thames Valley with strengths across a range of services and industry sectors. Their current strategy has seen a greater concentration and focus on the firm's core industry sectors of technology & media, property, retail and construction, while continuing to be market leaders in family law. The firm offers 10 trainee places each September.

main areas of work
Industry Sectors: Technology & media, property, retail and construction.
Legal Groups: Commercial property, commercial litigation, corporate finance, construction, family, trusts & estates, employment, intellectual property, information technology, biotechnology (Oxford office only), and environment & planning (Oxford office only).

trainee profile
Manches aims to recruit a broad cross-section of candidates with different ranges of experiences and backgrounds. However, all candidates should demonstrate consistently good academic records, together with cheerful enthusiasm, high levels of commitment, an appreciation of commercial issues, the ability to think for themselves and have warm and approachable social skills.

training environment
The firm gives high-quality individual training. Trainees generally sit in four different seats for six months at a time. The firm's comprehensive induction week, followed by its practically based "learning by doing" training programme enables them to take responsibility from an early stage, ensuring that they become confident and competent solicitors at the point of qualification. Trainees have the opportunity to actively participate in departmental meetings, presentations, client seminars and briefings and they receive regular appraisals on their progress.

benefits
Season ticket loan, BUPA after six months, permanent health insurance, life insurance, pension after six months.

vacation placements
Places for 2007: 24 approx.; Duration: 1 week; Closing Date: 31 January 2007; Remuneration: under review.

sponsorship & awards
CPE/PgDL and LPC fees are paid in full together with an annual maintenance allowance (currently £5,000 p.a.).

Partners	59
Assistant Solicitors	65
Total Trainees	18

contact
Sheona Boldero
sheona.boldero@manches.com

method of application
Online application form

selection procedure
1st interview with HR, 2nd Interview with 2 partners.

closing date for 2009
31 July 2007

application
Training contracts p.a. **10**
Applications p.a. **900**
% interviewed p.a. **5%**
Required degree grade **2:1 min**

training
Salary
1st year (2006)
London £28,000
2nd year (2006)
London £31,000
Holiday entitlement **24 days**

post-qualification
Salary
London £50,000
% of trainees offered job on qualification (2005) **90%**

Martineau Johnson

No 1 Colmore Square, Birmingham B4 6AA
78 Cannon Street, London, EC4N 4NQ
Tel: (0870) 763 2000 Fax: (0870) 763 2001
Email: jennifer.seymour@martjohn.co.uk
Website: www.graduates4law.co.uk and www.martineau-johnson.co.uk

Partners	42
Assistant Solicitors	80
Total Trainees	21

contact
Jennifer Seymour

method of application
Online application form
www.graduates4law.co.uk

selection procedure
Assessment centre - half day

closing date for 2009
31 July 2007

application
Training contracts p.a. **10-12**
Applications p.a. **500**
% interviewed p.a. **10%**
Required degree grade **2:1**

training
Salary
1st year (2005) c. **£20,000**
2nd year (2005) c. **£21,500**
Holiday entitlement **25 days**
% of trainees with a
non-law degree (2005) **30%**

post-qualification
Salary (2006) **£34,000**
% of trainees offered job
on qualification (2006) **100%**
% of assistants (as at 1/9/06)
who joined as trainees **49%**
% of partners (as at 1/9/06)
who joined as trainees **42%**

firm profile

Martineau Johnson is a dynamic and passionate law firm that combines a commercial and vibrant atmosphere with a personal and caring attitude.
Providing national and international advice to its clients, the firm is recognised as market leader in many of its areas of practice and is well known for providing high level expertise.
Martineau Johnson, named in the Sunday Times' Top 100 Companies to Work For, looks for enthusiastic and committed graduates with good degrees, not necessarily in law, to contribute to its successful practice.
The prestigious premises in the heart of Birmingham city centre, coupled with its expanding London office, provide trainees with an ideal base to gain experience in a variety of core and niche practice areas.
As a founder member of Multilaw, an international network of law firms, opportunities also stretch far beyond the UK.
The firm's commitment to client care and quality is endorsed by the ISO 9001 standard.

main areas of work

Commercial 20%; corporate services 23%; commercial disputes management 14%; property 18%; private client 14%.

trainee profile

Trainees are vital to Martineau Johnson's future and no effort is spared to give the best possible experience and support to them, whilst treating them as individuals. There is a very high retention rate at the end of training contracts, when trainees are generally offered roles in their preferred departments and specialisms.

training environment

Martineau Johnson's aim is to work in partnership with trainees, providing them with mentoring, supervision, support and an exposure to the key areas of the firm's practice. Trainees are actively encouraged to be an integral part of the team delivering legal solutions to its clients whilst benefiting from quality work, flexible seat rotation in a small and friendly team environment. Generally, the firm's trainees are given experience in its chosen sectors: commercial, corporate services, commercial disputes management, property and private client – they are then given the opportunity to carry out further work in areas of their choice and specialism. There are opportunities for Birmingham-based trainees to be exposed to the London scene. Trainees benefit from a structured career training programme tailored to their personal development needs – and it covers not only legal technical matters, but also a business and commercial approach which have never been more central to successful professional careers. In giving training and offering experience that matches the best city firms, Martineau Johnson offers a rare opportunity for trainees to lay great foundations for their legal career in a fast-moving, ever-changing but supportive environment.

MARTINEAU JOHNSON

Mayer, Brown, Rowe & Maw LLP

11 Pilgrim Street, London EC4V 6RW
Tel: (020) 7248 4282 Fax: (020) 7782 8790
Email: graduaterecruitment@mayerbrownrowe.com
Website: www.mayerbrownrowe.com/london/careers/gradrecruit

firm profile
Mayer, Brown, Rowe & Maw LLP is among the largest law practices in the world with over 500 partners and more than 1,400 lawyers worldwide. It has offices in Berlin, Brussels, Charlotte, Chicago, Cologne, Frankfurt, Houston, Los Angeles, New York, Palo Alto, Paris and Washington DC. The firm also has an alliance with leading Italian law firm Studio Legale Tonucci, an association with the Mexican firm Jauregui, Navarette y Nader and trade consulting offices in Shanghai and Beijing in China

main areas of work
The firm advises leading financial and commercial companies around the world. Its client base includes many of the FTSE 100 and Fortune 500 companies together with other global leaders in target industries. The major emphasis in Europe is across industry sectors including chemicals, construction & engineering, energy, insurance & reinsurance, mining, pensions, pharmaceuticals & biotechnology, real estate, TMT and securitisation.Working within this framework core practice lines include corporate and securities (including M&A and corporate finance), litigation and dispute resolution, finance and banking, financial restructuring and insolvency, tax, environment and public law, employment, pensions, intellectual property, outsourcing, advertising, music and publishing, antitrust and international trade.

trainee profile
The practice is interested in motivated students with a good academic record and a strong commitment to law. Commercial awareness gained through legal or business work experience is an advantage. Applications are welcomed from both law and non-law students.

training environment
Students looking for a leading international law practice that offers exposure to a multitude of blue-chip companies and a wide range of international work, combined with the confidence of knowing they have a place in its future, should contact Mayer, Brown, Rowe & Maw LLP. Trainees will participate in a lively, energetic and positive business culture, spending time in four six-month seats including the Corporate and Litigation Departments. The practice's culture of getting immersed in a client's business means that there are excellent secondment opportunities. In addition to the Professional Skills Course, the practice offers an individual professional development and training programme. Three-monthly appraisals assist trainees in reaching their true potential.

benefits
Benefits include 25 days holiday per annum, interest free season ticket loan, subsidised sports club membership and private health scheme.

vacation placements
Places for 2007: 32; Duration: 2 weeks during Easter and Summer vacations. Experience in two of the principle work groups plus a programme of seminars, visits and social events.

sponsorship & awards
The firm will cover the cost of the GDL and LPC fees, and provide a maintenance grant of £6,500 (£7,000 for London and Guildford).

Partners	101
Assistant Solicitors	165
Total Trainees	56

contact
Maxine Goodlet, Graduate Recruitment Manager

method of application
Online application form

selection procedure
Selection workshops including an interview, a business analysis exercise, a group exercise & an online verbal reasoning test

closing date for Sept 2009/March 2010
31 July 2007

application
Training contracts p.a.
Approx 25-30
Applications p.a. **1,000+**
% interviewed p.a. **10-15%**
Required degree grade **2:1**

training
1st year (Sept 2006) **£31,000**
2nd year **£33,500**
Holiday entitlement **25 days**
% of trainees with a non-law degree p.a. **41%**
No. of seats available abroad p.a. **3**

post-qualification
Salary (2006) **£55,000**
% of trainees offered job on qualification (2006) **85%**
% of partners who joined as trainees **35%**

overseas offices
Berlin, Brussels, Charlotte, Chicago, Cologne, Frankfurt, Houston, London, Los Angeles, New York, Palo Alto, Paris, Washington DC

McCormicks

Britannia Chambers, 4 Oxford Place, Leeds LS1 3AX
Tel: (0113) 246 0622 Fax: (0113) 246 7488
Wharfedale House, 37 East Parade, Harrogate HG1 5LQ
Tel: (01423) 530630 Fax: (01423) 530709
Email: l.jackson@mccormicks-solicitors.com
Website: www.mccormicks-solicitors.com

firm profile

McCormicks is a unique legal practice at the heart of a vibrant commercial region. With core traditional values of integrity, technical excellence and hard work, the firm is committed to deliver an unrivalled quality of service and innovation to its clients and quality of life to its people. McCormicks combines the full range and depth of skills across its entire practice with the firm's renowned fearlessness and ability to punch above its weight in order to deliver the best possible result.

main areas of work

With a diverse range of clients from private individuals to high profile international organisations its work is never dull. Trainees are exposed to all its practice areas including sports law, media and entertainment law, corporate and commercial, commercial property, commercial litigation, charity work, family, corporate crime, insolvency and intellectual property.

trainee profile

Intellectual achievement, ambition, a sense of humour and commitment to hard work are crucial qualities of a McCormicks trainee. The firm will challenge you but support you at every step of the way.

training environment

Trainees are assigned to one of six departments and supervised throughout by a mentor. The firm's training work will develop skills, knowledge and ambition within a friendly, progressive and supportive environment. Your development will be reviewed regularly by the mentor, team supervisor and the training partner. There is an open door policy and a great team spirit.

vacation placements

Places for 2007: Available in summer vacation. Closing Date: Application forms by 23 February 2007.

Partners	13
Assistant Solicitors	30
Total Trainees	9

contact
Linda Jackson

method of application
Application form

selection procedure
Assessment Day &
Interview with two partners

closing date for 2009
27 July 2007

application
Training contracts p.a. **4**
Applications p.a. **350**
% interviewed p.a. **22%**
Required degree grade **2:1**

training
Salary
highly competitive

post-qualification
Salary (2006)
Highly competitive
trainees offered job
on qualification (2006) **2 of 3**
% of partners (as at 1/1/2006)
who joined as trainees **50%**

McDermott Will & Emery UK LLP

7 Bishopsgate, London EC2N 3AR
Tel: (020) 7577 6900 Fax: (020) 7577 6950
Website: www.mwe.com/london
Email: graduate.recruitment@europe.mwe.com

firm profile

McDermott Will & Emery UK LLP is a leading international law firm with offices in Boston, Brussels, Chicago, Düsseldorf, London, Los Angeles, Miami, Munich, New York, Orange County, Rome, San Diego, Silicon Valley and Washington DC. The firm's client base includes some of the world's leading financial institutions, largest corporations, mid-cap businesses, and individuals. The firm represents more than 75 of the companies in the Fortune 100 in addition to clients in the FTSE 100 and FTSE 250. Rated as one of the leading firms in The American Lawyer's Top 100, by a number of indicators, including gross revenues and profits per Partner.

London Office: The London office was founded in 1998. It is already recognised as being in the top 10 of the 100 US law firms operating in London by the legal media. The firm has 80 lawyers at present in London, almost all of whom are English-qualified. The firm provides business oriented legal advice to multinational and national corporates, financial institutions, investment banks and private clients. Most of the firm's partners were head of practice at their former firms and are recognised as leaders in their respective fields by the most respected professional directories and market commentators.

main areas of work

Banking and finance; corporate, including international corporate finance and M&A; private equity, EU competition; employment, IP, IT and e-business; litigation and arbitration; pensions and incentives; taxation; telecoms and US securities. London is the hub for the firm's European expansions.

trainee profile

The firm is looking for the brightest, best and most entrepreneurial trainees. You will need to convince the firm that you have made a deliberate choice.

training environment

The primary focus is to provide a practical foundation for your career with the firm. You will experience between four and six seats over the two-year period and the deliberately small number of trainees means that the firm is able to provide a degree of flexibility in tailoring seats to the individual. Trainees get regular support and feedback.

benefits

Private medical and dental insurance, life assurance, permanent health insurance, season ticket loan, subsidised gym membership, employee assistance programme, 25 days holiday.

sponsorship & awards

GDL and LPC funding and mainenance grant.

Partners	585*
	29 (London)
Associate Lawyers &	
Other Fee-earners	427*
	51 (London)
Total Trainees	3 in 2005
	3 in 2006

* denotes worldwide figures

contact
Áine Wood

method of application
CV & covering letter. See website for selection criteria

selection procedure
2 interviews with partners and written exercise

closing date for 2009
31 July 2007

training
Salary
1st year (2005) £31,500
2nd year (2005) £35,000

post-qualification
Salary (2005) £60,000

McDermott
Will & Emery

www.chambersandpartners.co.uk

McGrigors LLP

5 Old Bailey, London, EC4M 7BA
Tel: (020) 7054 2500
Email: graduate.recruitment@mcgrigors.com
Website: www.mcgrigors.com

Partners 75*
Assistant Solicitors 130*
Total Trainees 69*
*denotes firm wide

firm profile
McGrigors is a law firm based across the UK with 75 partners and 350 lawyers in total. As the only law firm in the UK that practices in all three jurisdictions, McGrigors has the strength and depth to commit to multiple, large, complex and high-value transactions simultaneously, and has earned an enviable reputation for providing excellent technical legal services, whilst at the same time being small enough to retain a friendly feel. The firm has a blue-chip client list which includes KPMG, Ministry of Defence, Royal Bank of Scotland, Fairview New Homes Ltd and BP.

main areas of work
Practice areas include banking and finance, commercial litigation, competition, construction procurement, contentious construction, corporate, dispute resolution, employment, energy, health & safety, human rights, intellectual property & commercial, planning & environment, projects/PPP, project finance, public law, public policy, real estate, tax litigation, and telecoms. McGrigors has a particular focus on a number of key industry sectors including energy & utilities, house builders, regeneration, financial services, infrastructure & public sector.

trainee profile
The firm takes on people, regardless of background, who have drive, ability, and confidence. Trainees need to prove that they are interested in business, not simply black letter law, as the firm prides itself on providing commercial solutions to clients. In addition, its trainees are highly visible in the firm and are expected to get actively involved, whether in business or social events.

training environment
The firm's training is based upon a standard rotation of six-month seats in four main practice areas. To widen trainees' experience and enable them to see a broader range of legal work, the firm encourages trainees to spend a seat in one of the other offices, and there are also opportunities for a secondment to a client. The firm was recently nominated as Best Trainer amongst Large City Firms in the lawcareers.net awards and their last Law Society Monitoring Visit concluded that training of trainee solicitors at McGrigors was, "excellent and of a very high standard".

benefits
The firm offers private medical cover, income protection, life assurance, pension, a daily lunch allowance, 33.5 days holidays including bank holidays, season ticket loan, and plenty of social events throughout the year.

sponsorship & awards
CPE and LPC fees are paid plus maintenance of £4,500 (under review) for each year in England.

contact
Georgina Bond – London
Margaret-Ann Roy – Scotland/Belfast

method of application
Online application

selection procedure
Half day assessment including interview, presentation and aptitude tests

closing date
31 Jan 2007 for summer scheme
31 July 2007 for 2009 training contracts

application
No. of training contracts p.a.
10-15 in London
22-25 in Scotland
1 in Belfast
% interviewed - **15%**
Required degree grade realistic estimate of **2.1** or higher

training
Salary
London **1st year £29,000**
2nd year £33,000
Scotland **1st year £17,000**
2nd year £20,000
Holiday **33.5 days including bank holidays**

post-qualification
Salary
London **£52,000**
Scotland **£33,000**
% offered job **85%**

overseas/regional offices
London, Edinburgh, Glasgow, Aberdeen, Belfast (Baku, Azerbaijan and a satellite office in the Falkland Islands)

Mills & Reeve

112 Hills Road, Cambridge CB2 1PH
Tel: (01223) 222336 Fax: (01223) 355848
Email: graduate.recruitment@mills-reeve.com
Website: www.mills-reeve.com

firm profile

The firm acts for commercial organisations; ranging from PLCs to multinationals to start-ups, as well as more than 70 universities and colleges, more than 100 healthcare trusts and NHS bodies, and over 65 local government institutions. The firm also has a national centre of excellence in private client services.

Mills & Reeve has offices in Birmingham, Cambridge, London and Norwich.

For the third year running Mills & Reeve has been listed in the Sunday Times Top 100 Best Companies to Work For, which recognises that the firm puts people at the centre of their business.

main areas of work

A full-service law firm. Core sectors are: corporate and commercial, banking and finance, technology, insurance, real estate, healthcare, education and private client.

trainee profile

The firm welcomes applications from both law and non-law disciplines. Candidates should already have or expect a 2.1 degree or equivalent. Trainee solicitors should display energy, maturity, initiative, enthusiasm for their career, a professional approach to work and be ready to accept early responsibility.

training environment

Trainees complete six four-month seats and are recruited to the Birmingham, Cambridge and Norwich offices. Trainees can temporarily move to another office, including London, to complete a seat not practised in their base office. The firm will support the move with an accommodation allowance. Trainees work alongside a partner or senior solicitor. Regular feedback is given to aid development. Performance is assessed by a formal review at the end of each seat. The firm encourages early responsibility. Training is supported by a full induction, in-house training programme developed by a team of professional support lawyers and the professional skills course (PSC). Job opportunities on qualification are good and a high proportion of trainees remain with the firm.

benefits

Life assurance, a contributory pension scheme, 25 days holiday, bonus scheme, sports & social club, subsidised staff restaurants and catering facilities, season ticket loan, discounted rate for private medical insurance, corporate gym membership. The firm runs a flexible benefits scheme.

vacation placements

Applications for two week placements during the summer must be received by 1 March 2007.

sponsorship & awards

The firm pays the full costs of the CPE/GDL and LPC fees and offers a maintenance grant during the GDL and LPC.

Partners	**80**
Assistant Solicitors	**300**
Total Trainees	**43**

contact
Fiona Medlock

method of application
Online

selection procedure
Normally one day assessment centre

closing date for 2009
31 July 2007 for training contracts
1st March 2007 for work placements

application
Training contracts p.a.**20**
Applications p.a. **Approx 600**
% interviewed p.a. **10%**
Required degree grade **2:1**

training
Salary
1st year £22,500
2nd year £23,500
Holiday entitlement
25 days p.a.
% of trainees with a non-law degree **50%**

post-qualification
% of trainees offered job on qualification (2006) 94%

Mishcon de Reya

Summit House, 12 Red Lion Square, London WC1R 4QD
Tel: (020) 7440 7198 Fax: (020) 7430 0691
Email: graduate.recruitment@mishcon.com
Website: www.mishcon.com

Partners	45
Assistant Solicitors	59
Total Trainees	15

contact
Human Resources
Department

method of application
Online application form

closing date for 2009
31 July 2007

application
Training contracts p.a. **8**
Applications p.a. **1,000+**
% interviewed p.a. **5%**
Required degree grade **2:1**

training
Salary
1st year £29,000
2nd year £31,000
Holiday entitlement
25 days p.a.
Occasional secondments
available

post-qualification
% of trainees retained
(2005) **75%**
% of assistants who joined
as trainees **42%**
% of partners who joined
as trainees **15%**

firm profile

Mishcon de Reya is a mid-sized central London law firm offering a diverse range of legal services for businesses and individuals. Their foundation is based upon a dynamic range of corporate clients that seek effective advice through close collaboration. Through their expertise and entrepreneurial spirit they deliver legal and commercial solutions to businesses of all sizes.

main areas of work

Mishcon de Reya's expertise falls into four main areas: corporate, litigation, property and family. The firm also has a number of specialist groups including banking & debt finance, betting & gaming, brands & rights, corporate recovery & insolvency, corporate tax, employment, financial services, investigations & asset recovery, immigration, IT, media & public advocacy and personal tax, trusts and probate.

trainee profile

Applications are welcome from penultimate-year law students, final year non-law students and other graduates wishing to commence a training contract in two years' time. The firm wants people who can meet the highest intellectual and business standards, while maintaining outside interests. Candidates should therefore be enterprising, enthusiastic and committed, and see themselves as future partners.

training environment

Trainees have the opportunity to experience four different 'seats' of six months each. All trainees get exposure to at least three of the four core departments and are also able to gain experience in specialist groups during their time with the firm. Trainees share a room with a partner or assistant solicitor. Because of the relatively few training contracts offered, trainees can expect to be exposed to high quality work with early responsibility. In order to support this, the firm has a wide-ranging training programme and provides extensive internal training in addition to the Professional Skills Course. Quarterly appraisals and monitoring in each seat ensures trainees gain a range of work and experience.

benefits

Medical & travel insurance, EAP, subsidised gym membership, season ticket loan, permanent health insurance, life assurance and pension, in-house doctor.

vacation placements

Places for 2007: 15; Duration: 2 weeks; Expenses: £250 p.w.; Closing Date: 15 March 2007.

sponsorship & awards

CPE and LPC funding with annual allowance.

Morgan Cole

Buxton Court, 3 West Way, Oxford OX2 0SZ
Tel: (01865) 262699 Fax: (01865) 262670
Email: recruitment@morgan-cole.com
Website: www.morgan-cole.com

firm profile
Morgan Cole is one of the leading regional commercial law practices in the country, providing a comprehensive service to both individual and corporate clients in both the public and private sectors. The firm has a reputation for excellence and therefore attracts the highest quality of staff from all fields. The firm is a founder member of the Association of European Lawyers, one of five leading UK law firms responsible for establishing a network of English speaking lawyers throughout Europe. The firm's areas of work consists of seven practice areas: insurance; health and regulatory; dispute management; commercial; corporate; private client; employment and banking. Within these practice areas the firm's work includes: acquisitions and disposals; technology; insolvency; intellectual property; joint ventures; management buy-outs and buy-ins; partnerships; PFI; commercial property; construction; personal injury; professional indemnity; commercial litigation and alternative dispute resolution.

trainee profile
Successful candidates should be commercially aware, self motivated individuals with drive and initiative who are able to apply a logical and common-sense approach to solving client problems. The firm is seeking applications from graduates/undergraduates in both law and non-law subjects, preferably with at least a 2:1 degree.

training environment
Trainees spend six months in four different practice areas, and since each practice area handles a wide variety of work within its constituent teams, there is no danger of over specialisation.

Vacation scheme
A vacation scheme is held in the Oxford, Reading, Cardiff and Swansea offices between June and July. The application deadline date is 30 April 2007.

sponsorship & awards
The firm offers full funding of fees for attendance on the CPE/PgDL and LPC as well as making a contribution towards maintenance.

Partners	50
Lawyers	179
Total Trainees	28

Trainee Places for 2008:

Cardiff/Swansea	5
Oxford/Reading	5
Total	10

contact
Janice Okuns

method of application
Apply online at www.morgan-cole.com/careers

selection procedure
Assessment Centre & interview

closing date for 2009
31 July 2007

application
Required degree grade
Preferably 2:1

training
Salary
1st & 2nd year (2006)
Competitive for the Thames Valley and South Wales regions which are reviewed annually in line with market trends

other offices
Cardiff, Croydon, London, Oxford, Swansea

Nabarro Nathanson

Lacon House, Theobald's Road, London WC1X 8RW
Tel: (020) 7524 6000 Fax: (020) 7524 6524
Email: graduateinfo@nabarro.com
Website: www.nabarro.com

Partners	115
Assistant Solicitors	225
Total Trainees	50

contact
Jane Drew

method of application
Online only

selection procedure
Assessment Day (including interview)

closing date for 2009
31 July 2007

application
Training contracts p.a. **25**
Applications p.a. **1,500**
Required degree grade **2:1**

training
Salary
1st year (2006)
London £30,000
Sheffield £22,000
2nd year (2006)
London £33,000
Sheffield £24,000
Holiday entitlement **25 days**

post-qualification
Salary (2006)
London £53,000
Sheffield £34,000
(reviewed annually)

overseas offices
Brussels

firm profile
One of the UK's leading commercial law firms with offices in London and Sheffield. The firm is known for having an open but highly professional culture and expects its lawyers to have a life outside work.

main areas of work
Corporate and commercial law; real estate; TMT (Technology, media and telecommunications); projects; PPP; PFI; pensions and employment; commercial litigation; construction and engineering; IP/IT; planning and environmental law.

trainee profile
Nabarro Nathanson welcomes applications from undergraduates and graduates with law or non-law backgrounds. Candidates must be able to demonstrate strong intellectual ability through the achievement of at least an upper second at degree level or equivalent relevant experience. Applicants also need exceptional qualities including: enthusiasm, drive and initiative, common sense, strong interpersonal skills and team working skills.

training environment
Trainees undertake six four-month seats which ensures maximum exposure to the firm's core practice areas (company commercial, commercial property and litigation). In addition to the core seats, trainees have the opportunity to gain further experience by spending time in specialist areas (eg pensions, IP/IT, tax, employment), possibly in Brussels, or completing a further seat in a core area. In most cases trainees will return to the seat they wish to qualify into for the remaining four months of their training contract. This ensures a smooth transition from trainee to qualified solicitor. The firm aims to retain all trainees on qualification.

benefits
Trainees are given private medical insurance, pension, 25 days holiday entitlement per annum, a season ticket loan, access to a subsidised restaurant and subsidised corporate gym membership. Trainee salaries are reviewed annually.

vacation placements
Places for 2007: 60; Duration: 3 weeks between mid-June and end of August; Closing Date: 9 February 2007.

sponsorship & awards
Full fees paid for GDL and LPC and a maintenance grant (London and Guildford: LPC £7,000, GDL £6,000; elsewhere: LPC £6,000, GDL £5,000).

Norton Rose

Kempson House, Camomile Street, London EC3A 7AN
Tel: (020) 7283 6000 Fax: (020) 7283 6500
Email: grad.recruitment@nortonrose.com
Website: www.nortonrose.com/graduate

firm profile
Norton Rose is a leading city and international law firm. They provide an integrated business law service from a network of offices located across Europe, Asia and the Middle East. The firm works primarily for international corporates and financial institutions on large, complex,cross-border transactions, offering them the full range of business legal services.

main areas of work
Corporate finance; banking; dispute resolution; property, planning and environmental; taxation; competition and regulatory; employment, pensions and incentives; intellectual property and technology.

trainee profile
Successful candidates will be commercially aware, focused, ambitious and team-orientated. High intellect and international awareness are a priority,and language skills are appreciated.

training environment
Norton Rose operates an innovative six-seat system. The first four seats (16 months) include one seat in each of the firm's core departments – corporate finance, banking and dispute resolution – plus an optional seat in one ofthe firm's other, non-core departments – employment, pensions and incentives, tax, competition and EC, intellectual property and technology, or property, planning and environmental. The remaining eight months can be spent in the department in which you wish to qualify, or you can visit a different practice area for four months to help you to decide, and spend the last four months in your qualification seat. Alternatively, from your third seat onwards, you can elect to spend four months in one of the firm's international offices or apply for a client secondment. The firm's flexible seat system makes the transition from trainee to qualified solicitor as smooth as possible. The system has won the firm's trainees'approval, and from their point of view, develops associates with the adaptability and expertise the firm needs for its future.

benefits
Life assurance (21+), private health insurance (optional), season ticket loan, subsidised gym membership.

placement programmes
Places for 2006: 15 Christmas.Places for 2007:30 summer and 15 Christmas; Duration: summer: Four weeks, Christmas: Two weeks; Remuneration: £250 p.w.; Closing Date: 31 October 2006 for Christmas 2006, 31 January 2007 for summer and 31 October 2007 for Christmas 2007. Approximately six open days per year are also held.

sponsorship & awards
£1,000 travel scholarship, £800 loan on arrival, four weeks unpaid leave on qualification. GDL/LPC fees paid plus £6,000/£7,000 maintenance grant (respectively).

Partners   212*
Assistant Solicitors 568*
Total Trainees   129
*denotes worldwide figures

contact
Ruth Edwards

method of application
Online only

selection procedure
Interview and group exercise

closing date for 2009
31 July 2007

application
Training contracts p.a. 60
Applications p.a. 2,500+
% interviewed p.a. 9%
Required degree grade 2:1

training
Salary
1st year £31,000
2nd year £35,000
Holiday entitlement 25days
% of trainees with a
non-law degree p.a. 40%
No. of seats available
abroad p.a. 22 (per seat
move)

overseas offices
Amsterdam, Athens,
Bahrain, Bangkok, Beijing,
Brussels, Dubai, Frankfurt,
Greece, Hong Kong,
Jakarta,* London, Milan,
Moscow, Munich, Paris
Piraeus, Prague, Rome,
Shanghai, Singapore,
Warsaw
*Associated office

Olswang

90 High Holborn, London WC1V 6XX
Tel: (020) 7067 3000 Fax: (020) 7067 3999
Email: graduate@olswang.com
Website: www.olswang.com

firm profile

Forward thinking and progressive, Olswang's ethos has always focused on realising the potential of its clients, of all of its people and the potential within every situation. The firm's aim is simple: to be the preferred law firm of leading companies in the technology, media, telecommunications and real estate sectors. Olswang knows the players, knows the business and above all, understands the issues. Established in 1981, the firm has a total staff of 550 and has offices in London, the Thames Valley and Brussels.

main areas of work

Advertising; banking; bio-sciences; commercial litigation; corporate and commercial; media litigation; e-commerce; employment; EU and competition; film finance and production; information technology; intellectual property; music; private equity; real estate; sponsorship; sport; tax; telecommunications; TV/broadcasting.

trainee profile

Being a trainee at Olswang is both demanding and rewarding. The firm is interested in hearing from individuals with a 2:1 degree and above or equivalent, exceptional drive and relevant commercial experience. In addition, it is absolutely critical that trainees fit well into the Olswang environment which is challenging, busy, individualistic, meritocratic and fun.

training environment

Olswang wants to help trainees match their expectations and needs with those of the firm. Training consists of four six-month seats in the corporate, media, communications and technology, litigation or real estate groups. You will be assigned a mentor, usually a partner, to assist and advise you throughout your training contract. In-house lectures supplement general training and three-monthly appraisals assess development.

benefits

Immediately: life cover, medical cover, dental scheme, subsidised gym membership, subsidised staff restaurant, season ticket loan. After six months: pension contributions. After 12 months: PHI.

vacation placements

Places for 2007: June & July; Duration: 2 weeks; Remuneration: £250 p.w.; 17 students per scheme; Closing Date: 31 January 2007.

sponsorship & awards

LPC and GDL fees paid in full. Maintenance grant of £7,000 (inside London), £6,500 (outside).

Partners	**78**
Assistant Solicitors	**175**
Total Trainees	**39**

contact
Victoria Edwards
Recruitment Manager

method of application
Online

selection procedure
Business case scenario, interview, psychometric test and written exercises

closing date for 2009
31 July 2007

application
Training contracts p.a. **20**
Applications p.a. **2,000**
% interviewed p.a. **4%**
Required degree grade **2:1**

training
Salary
1st year (2006) £30,000
2nd year (2006) £34,000
Holiday entitlement **24 days**
% of trainees with a non-law degree p.a. **50%**

post-qualification
Salary **(2006) £53,000**

overseas offices
Brussels

Orrick, Herrington & Sutcliffe

Tower 42, Level 35, 25 Old Broad Street, London EC2N 1HQ
Tel: (020) 7562 5000 Fax: (020) 7628 0078
Email: recruitlondon@orrick.com
Website: www.orrick.com

firm profile

Orrick was founded in 1863 in San Francisco, California, and is now one of the world's leading international law firms with more than 850 lawyers worldwide. Orrick is known for its market-leading finance practices, as well as its corporate, restructuring, intellectual property and litigation practices.

Orrick's London core practices are acquisition finance, arbitration and litigation, banking, capital markets, trade and asset finance, competition and European Union law, corporate and corporate finance, employment, energy and project finance, global bankruptcy and debt restructuring, international dispute resolution, private investment funds, real estate, structured finance and securitisation, and tax. Much of Orrick's client work involves cross-border transactions which have increased substantially in recent years with the development of the firm's European network consisting of offices in London, Paris, Milan, Rome and Moscow.

trainee profile

If you set your standards high, have a strong work ethic and are a bright, talented graduate of any discipline, early responsibility and broad-based experience are guaranteed. Applicants should have at least three A-level passes at grades A and B and a 2.1 degree.

training environment

Orrick is not a firm for every graduate: They value team players and reward collaboration over competition. They give individuals the opportunity to flourish in a lively work environment and encourage interaction among lawyers across international offices at every level of experience within the firm. They support learning through a steadfast focus on training and a mentoring programme that will provide you with the right foundation for building your legal career and for working with clients. There are regular appraisals throughout the two year training contract. Trainees work closely with fee earners and gain practical experience in research, drafting, procedural and client-related skills. The firm offers the benefits of a major international law firm providing leading practices in a variety of sectors with the opportunity for interaction in an informal office environment.

benefits

Pension, health insurance, subsidised gym membership, season ticket loan, private medical insurance, dental care and childcare voucher scheme.

sponsorship & awards

PgDl: Funding: Fees paid plus £4,000 p.a. maintenance (discretionary).
LPC: Funding: Fees paid plus £4,000 p.a. maintenance (discretionary).

Partners 15 (London)
Assistants 24 (London)
Total Trainees 13 (maximum)

contact
Simon Cockshutt

method of application
Letter & CV (by post or email)

selection procedure
2 interviews with HR & partners

closing date for 2009
31 July 2007

application
Training contracts p.a. **6**
Required degree grade **2:1**

training
Salary (subject to review)
1st year (2006): £28,000
2nd year (2006): £32,000
Holiday entitlement 25 days

Overseas offices
Hong Kong, London, Los Angeles, Milan, Moscow, New York, Orange County, Pacific Northwest, Paris, Rome, Sacramento, San Francisco, Silicon Valley, Taipei, Tokyo and Washington DC.

Osborne Clarke

2 Temple Back East, Temple Quay, Bristol BS1 6EG
Tel: (0117) 917 4322
Email: graduate.recruitment@osborneclarke.com
Website: www.osborneclarke.com

Partners	100
Lawyers	247
Trainees	41

firm profile

Osborne Clarke is a leading business law firm that operates globally through an international network of legal businesses. Including its Alliance offices, the firm has a presence in 11 European countries and almost 1,000 people in Europe and the US. The firm has particular strength in transactions and advisory services, and areas of expertise include corporate, finance and property transactions and the full spectrum of business law services, including commercial contracts, employment, pensions, outsourcing and dispute resolution. Years of investment in gaining true insider knowledge across specific industry sectors has enabled it to adapt its legal solutions to clients' business needs and to provide them with access to the firm's envied networks.

main areas of work

Banking, corporate, employment, pensions & incentives, litigation/dispute resolution, property, commercial and tax.

trainee profile

As you might expect, the firm looks for highly driven and committed trainees who are passionate about their career in law. Candidates must be commercially minded, ready to take on responsibility, and able to show initiative. A strong academic performance is a given – candidates should have (or expect to achieve) at least a 2:1 – but the firm also values additional activities that show effective communication and teamwork skills.

training environment

The firm is committed to building a future career for its trainees and its two-year training programme offers trainees continuous support throughout the training contract. Departmental inductions are held at the beginning of each seat rotation and regular training is held throughout each seat. The firm offers four six-month seats, one of which will be spent in the corporate department. This ensures that trainees gain a broad experience and exposure to different areas of law. There are also opportunities for trainees to undertake secondments to the German or US offices. Trainees work closely with their training supervisors and fee earners in the department and can expect a high level of responsibility at an early stage in their training contract. Regular three-month reviews are held with the training supervisor to assess progress and development needs.

benefits

25 days holiday entitlement, life assurance, private medical insurance, permanent health insurance, employer's pension contributions, interest free season ticket loan, firm wide bonus scheme.

vacation schemes

Places for 2007: One-week scheme offered at Easter and during June and July in Bristol, London and Thames Valley offices. The closing date for applications is the 31 January 2007.

sponsorship & awards

GDL and LPC fees paid plus a maintenance grant.

contact
Melanie Ross, Graduate Recruitment & Development Manager

method of application
Online application form

selection procedure
Assessment day comprises of group exercises, psychometric tests, partner interview and presentation exercise

closing date for 2009
31 July 2007

application
Training contracts p.a. **20**
Applications p.a. **1,000**
% interviewed p.a. **12%**
Required degree grade: **2:1**

training
1st year £24,000/£30,500
2nd year £25,000/£31,500
Holiday entitlement **25 days**
% of trainees with a non-law degree p.a. **40%**

post-qualification
Bristol £36,000
London £51,000
Thames Valley £43,000

offices
Bristol, Cologne, London, Munich, Silicon Valley, Thames Valley

overseas offices
Osborne Clarke Alliance Locations: Barcelona, Brescia, Brussels, Copenhagen, Helsinki, Madrid, Milan, Paris, Rome, Rotterdam, St Petersburg, Tallinn.

Pannone LLP

123 Deansgate, Manchester M3 2BU
Tel: (0161) 909 3000 Fax: (0161) 909 4444
Email: julia.jessop@pannone.co.uk
Website: www.pannone.com

firm profile

A high profile Manchester firm continuing to undergo rapid growth. The firm prides itself on offering a full range of legal services to a diverse client base which is split almost equally between personal and commercial clients. The firm was the first to be awarded the quality standard ISO 9001 and is a founder member of Pannone Law Group – Europe's first integrated international law group. Pannone was voted 3rd in the 'Sunday Times' 100 Best Companies to Work For in 2006 and is the highest placed law firm in the survey.

main areas of work

Commercial litigation 13%; personal injury 30%; corporate 13%; commercial property 7%; family 7%; clinical negligence 7%; private client 18%; employment 5%.

trainee profile

Selection criteria include a high level of academic achievement, teamwork, organisation and communication skills, a wide range of interests and a connection with the North West.

training environment

An induction course helps trainees adjust to working life, and covers the firm's quality procedures and good practice. Regular trainee seminars cover the work of other departments within the firm, legal developments and practice. Additional departmental training sessions focus in more detail on legal and procedural matters in that department. Four seats of six months are spent in various departments and trainees' progress is monitored regularly. Trainees have easy access to support and guidance on any matters of concern. Work is tackled with gusto here, but so are the many social gatherings that take place.

vacation placements

Places for 2007: 50; Duration: 1 week; Remuneration: None; Closing Date: Easter 26 January 2007, Summer 27 April 2007.

sponsorship & awards

Full grant for LPC fees.

Partners	**92**
Assistant Solicitors	**99**
Total Trainees	**30**

contact
Julia Jessop

method of application
Online only

selection procedure
Individual interview, second interview comprises a tour of the firm & informal lunch

closing date for 2009
31 July 2007

application
Training contracts p.a. **14**
Applications p.a. **1,200**
% interviewed p.a. **10%**
Required degree grade **2:1**

training
Salary
1st year (2006) **£21,500**
2nd year (2006) **£23,500**
Holiday entitlement **23 days**
% of trainees with a
non-law degree p.a. **30%**

post-qualification
Salary (2006) **£33,000**
% of trainees offered job
on qualification (2005) **80%**
% of assistants who joined
as trainees **33%**
% of partners who joined
as trainees **29%**

Payne Hicks Beach

10 New Square, Lincoln's Inn, London WC2A 3QG
Tel: (020) 7465 4300 Fax: (020) 7465 4400
Email: lstoten@paynehicksbeach.co.uk
Website: www.paynehicksbeach.co.uk

firm profile
Payne Hicks Beach is a medium-sized firm based in Lincoln's Inn. The firm acts for both private clients and businesses. It is highly rated for private client and matrimonial advice and also specialises in commercial litigation, property and corporate and commercial work.

main areas of work
Private client 41%; matrimonial 22%; property 17%; commercial litigation 13%; corporate and commercial 7%.

trainee profile
The firm looks for law and non-law graduates with a good academic record, an ability to solve practical problems, enthusiasm and an ability to work hard and deal appropriately with their colleagues and the firm's clients.

training environment
Following an initial induction course, trainees usually spend six months in four of the firm's departments. Working with a partner, they are involved in the day to day activities of the department, including attending conferences with clients, counsel and other professional advisers. Assessment is continuous and trainees will be given responsibility as they demonstrate ability and aptitude. To complement the PSC, the firm runs a formal training system for trainees and requires them to attend lectures and seminars on various topics.

benefits
Season travel ticket loan, life assurance 4 x salary, permanent health insurance, contribution to personal pension plan.

sponsorship & awards
Fees for the CPE and LPC are paid.

Partners	29
Assistant Solicitors	24
Total Trainees	5

contact
Miss Louise Stoten

method of application
Letter & CV

selection procedure
Interview

closing date for 2009
1 August 2007

application
Training contracts p.a. **3**
Applications p.a. **1,000**
% interviewed p.a. **3%**
Required degree grade **2:1**

training
Salary
1st year (2006) **£28,500**
2nd year (2006) **£30,500**
Holiday entitlement
4 weeks
% of trainees with a
non-law degree p.a. **50%**

Penningtons Solicitors LLP

Bucklersbury House, 83 Cannon Street, London EC4N 8PE
Tel: (020) 7457 3000 Fax: (020) 7457 3240
Website: www.penningtons.co.uk

firm profile
Penningtons Solicitors LLP is a thriving, modern law firm with a 200-year history and a deep commitment to top quality, partner-led services. Today, the firm is based in London and the South East with offices in London, Basingstoke, Godalming and Newbury.

main areas of work
In the business sphere, Penningtons advise on matters relating to all aspects of commercial property, intellectual property, management buy-outs and buy-ins, mergers, acquisitions and joint ventures, as well as dispute resolution. Advice is also given on information technology, business recovery, commercial contracts, agricultural and environmental law, and company secretarial services are offered. The firm also helps families and individuals with advice on property, tax and estate planning, family law, general financial management, the administration of wills and trusts, charities, personal injury, clinical negligence and immigration. Clients often ask Penningtons to advise on both their private and commercial affairs.

trainee profile
Penningtons seeks high calibre candidates with enthusiasm and resilience. A high standard of academic achievement is expected: three or more good A level passes and preferably a 2:1 or better at degree level, whether you are reading law or another discipline.

training environment
You will be given a thorough grounding in the law, spending time in three or four of the firm's departments – corporate and commercial, litigation, dispute resolution, property and private client. The firm ensures a varied training is given, avoiding too specialised an approach before qualification. Nonetheless, the experience gained in each department gives you a solid foundation, equipping you to embark on your chosen specialisation at the end of your training contract with the firm. Penningtons knows its trainee solicitors are happiest and most successful when busy with good quality work. The firm believes in introducing trainees to challenging cases. The value of giving its trainees responsibility, and allowing direct contact with clients is recognised. However, experienced solicitors are always ready to give support when needed.

benefits
Life assurance, critical illness cover, pension, private medical insurance, 23 days holiday, interest free season ticket loan, sports and social events.

vacation placements
The firm offers both summer vacation placements and information days. Applications are accepted from 1 December 2006 to 31 March 2007.

sponsorship & awards
Full fees and maintenance for the LPC plus a maintenance grant of £4,000.

Partners	71*
Assistant Solicitors	130*
Total Trainees	27
*denotes worldwide figures	

contact
Tamsin Kennie

method of application
Online via firm's website

closing date for 2009
31 July 2007

application
Training contracts p.a. **14**
Applications p.a. **1,000**
% interviewed p.a. **5%**
Required degree grade **2:1**

training
Salary
1st year (2006)
£28,000 (London)
2nd year (2006)
£30,000 (London)
Holiday entitlement **23 days**

Pinsent Masons

30 Aylesbury Street, London, EC1R 0ER
Email: graduate@pinsentmasons.com
Website: www.pinsentmasons.com/graduate

Partners	**250+**
Lawyers	**900**
Total Trainees	**112**

firm profile

Pinsent Masons is a top 15 UK law firm that is committed to sector-focused growth through its core sectors approach. This approach aligns the firm to specific business sectors to achieve market-leading positions. As a result, the firm has developed a successful and innovative approach to building strong, broad and deep corporate relationships. Client service is at the core of the firm and it works with a substantial range of FTSE 100 and FTSE 250, Fortune 500 and AIM quoted organisations as well as a variety of public sector clients.

main areas of work

Banking & finance, corporate, dispute resolution & litigation, employment, insurance & reinsurance, international construction & energy, outsourcing, technology and commercial, pensions, projects, property, tax and UK construction & engineering.

trainee profile

The firm welcomes applications from both law and non-law graduates with a good honours degree. In addition to a strong academic background, the firm is looking for people who can combine a sharp mind with commercial acumen and strong people skills to work in partnership with its clients' businesses.

training environment

Trainees sit in four seats of six months across the practices, and are supervised by partners or associates. There are also opportunities for trainees to be seconded to clients. The firm offers a supportive team culture with early responsibility and contact with clients is encouraged.

In addition to the training required by the Law Societies, the firm offers a broad-ranging and custom-made training programme designed to deliver superb technical and management skills that link with the needs of the business. This is the first stage in the firm's focused development programme that supports individuals on the route to partnership.

The firm has an open-door policy and informal atmosphere with a positive focus on work-life balance.

summer vacation placements

Places for 2007: 130; Duration: 2 weeks; Closing Date: 31 January 2007.

sponsorship & awards

In England, a full sponsorship is offered for the CPE and LPC fees, as well as a maintenance grant. In Scotland, financial assistance is offered for Diploma fees, together with a maintenance grant.

contact
Kate Fergusson
Recruitment Hotline:
(0845) 300 3232

method of application
Online application form

selection procedure
Assessment day including interview

closing date for 2009
31 July 2007 (English offices) and 21 October 2007 (Scottish offices)

application
Training contracts p.a. **55**
Applications p.a. **2,000+**
Required degree grade **2:1**

training
Salary
1st year (2006) £30,000 (London)
2nd year (2006) £33,000 (London)
Holiday entitlement **25 days**

post-qualification
Salary (2006)
£53,000 (London)

UK offices
London, Birmingham, Bristol, Edinburgh, Glasgow, Leeds, Manchester

Pinsent Masons

Prettys

Elm House, 25 Elm Street, Ipswich IP1 2AD
Tel: (01473) 232121 Fax: (01473) 230002
Email: agage@prettys.co.uk
Website: www.prettys.co.uk

firm profile
Prettys is one of the largest and most successful legal practices in East Anglia. The firm is at the heart of the East Anglian business community, with the expanding hi-tech corridor between Ipswich and Cambridge to the west, Felixstowe to the east and the City of London 60 minutes away to the south. The firm's lawyers are approachable and pragmatic. It provides expert advice to national and regional businesses.

main areas of work
Prettys' broad-based practice allows it to offer a full-service to all its clients. Business law services: company, commercial, shipping, transport, construction, intellectual property, information technology, property, property litigation, employment, commercial litigation, insurance, professional indemnity, health and safety and executive immigration. Personal law services: French property, personal injury, clinical negligence, financial services, estates, agriculture, conveyancing and family.

trainee profile
Prettys' trainees are the future of the firm. Applicants should be able to demonstrate a desire to pursue a career in East Anglia. Trainees are given considerable responsibility early on and the firm is therefore looking for candidates who are well motivated, enthusiastic and have a good common sense approach. Good IT skills are essential.

training environment
A two-week induction programme will introduce you to the firm. You will receive continuous supervision and three-monthly reviews. Training is in four six-month seats. Trainees work closely with a partner, meeting clients and becoming involved in all aspects of the department's work. Frequent training seminars are provided in-house. The Law Society's Monitoring of Training Officer recently visited the firm and concluded "Prettys offers a very strong commitment to training within a supportive environment."

additional information
One day placements are available (apply to Angela Gage).

Directors	2
Partners	14
Total Trainees	10

contact
Angela Gage
Human Resources Manager

method of application
Application letter & CV

closing date for 2009
July 31 2007

application
Training contracts p.a. **5**
Required degree grade
**2:1 preferred in law or
other relevant subject.
Good A Levels**

training
Salary
**Above Law Society
guidelines**

Holiday entitlement **25 days**

post-qualification
% of trainees offered job
on qualification (2005) **75%**

PricewaterhouseCoopers Legal LLP

1 Embankment Place, London, WC2N 6DX
Tel: (020) 7212 1616 Fax: (020) 7212 1570
Website: www.pwclegal.co.uk

Vacancies	8
Trainees	10
Partners	14
Total staff	105

firm profile

PricewaterhouseCoopers Legal LLP (formerly Landwell) is a niche law firm with close working relationships with the business specialisms of PricewaterhouseCoopers LLP and also a number of network law firms across the world. This gives them access to over 2,000 legal professionals in 40 countries.

The firm delivers its services through key divisions including areas of specialisation such as corporate restructuring, M&A and private equity work, intellectual property, IT, employment, immigration, pensions, financial services, banking, real estate & litigation (commercial and VAT). Depending on the transaction type, the firm's lawyers work either on a domestic standalone basis or as part of a wider team of business lawyers from the international network. Their strong working relationship with PricewaterhouseCoopers LLP also enables their lawyers additionally to work in multi-competency teams of business advisers delivering complete solutions to a variety of complex business problems.

Clients include local, national and multinational companies; partnerships and LLPs; governments; and financial institutions. The PricewaterhouseCoopers Legal LLP approach recognises that today's lawyers must adapt to the changing needs of clients and must offer more than just legal services. By adopting a multi-disciplinary approach, solutions are not pigeon-holed under the disciplines of accountancy, tax and law, and PricewaterhouseCoopers Legal LLP (through its relationship with PricewaterhouseCoopers LLP) provides its clients with a single seamless offering of legal, tax and consultancy expertise. A diverse workforce enhances creativity and PricewaterhouseCoopers Legal LLP strives to achieve and maintain diversity throughout the firm.

method of application
Complete the online application form from the website www.pwclegal.co.uk

closing date for 2009
Trainees: July 31 2007
Summer vacation programme 2007: March 31 2007

application
Required academic grade
280 UCAS points or equivalent
2:1 degree or equivalent

training
Salary
London
1st year (2006) £28,000
2nd year (2006) £32,000

trainee profile

The firm wants to see applicants with a genuine interest in business law and the ambition to be part of a new model of legal practice. In return, PricewaterhouseCoopers Legal LLP offers you something unique. Its relationship with PricewaterhouseCoopers LLP means you will be part of an integrated multi-disciplinary team comprising specialists from a range of professional backgrounds. While the quality of its work and the excellence of its training can match those of any traditional law firm, its lawyers spend more time than most out there in the real business world, alongside their clients and other professionals, reaching out into new ground.

training environment

A formal induction programme will introduce you to the firm. You will receive continuous supervision and three-monthly reviews. Training is in four six-month seats.

vacation schemes

The firm runs a summer vacation programme for two weeks in June and July, for which it welcomes quality applications.

sponsorship & awards

Trainee lawyers joining the firm are eligible to apply for a scholarship award to assist with the costs of the Pg Diploma in Law course and the Legal Practice Course. If successful, you will receive the total cost of the tuition and examination fees (from the date of signing your contract) and also a significant contribution towards your living expenses. More details can be found on the firm's website.

PRICEWATERHOUSE(COPERS 🌑 LEGAL

Pritchard Englefield

14 New St, London EC2M 4HE
Tel: (020) 7972 9720 Fax: (020) 7972 9722
Email: po@pe-legal.com
Website: www.pe-legal.com

firm profile

A niche City firm practising a mix of general commercial and non-commercial law with many German and French clients. Despite its strong commercial departments, the firm still undertakes family and private client work and is renowned for its ever-present international flavour.

main areas of work

All main areas of commercial practice including litigation, commercial/corporate/banking (UK, German and French), IP/IT, property and employment, also estate and trusts (UK and off-shore), pensions, charities, personal injury and family.

trainee profile

High academic achievers with fluent German and/or French.

training environment

An induction course acquaints trainees with the computer network, online library and finance & administrative procedures and there is a formal in-house training programme during the first week. Four six-month seats make up most of your training. You can usually choose some departments, and you could spend two six-month periods in the same seat. Over two years, you learn advocacy, negotiating, drafting and interviewing, attend court, use your language skills every day and meet clients from day one. Occasional talks and seminars explain the work of the firm, and you can air concerns over bi-monthly lunches with the partners comprising the Trainee Panel. PSC is taken externally over two years. The Social Committee of the firm organises regular drinks parties, French film evenings, quiz nights and of course a Christmas party.

benefits

Some subsidised training, monthly luncheon vouchers, and eligibility for membership of the firm's private medical insurance scheme as well as an interest free loan for an annual season ticket.

sponsorship & awards

Full funding for LPC fees.

Partners	21
Assistant Solicitors	13
Other Fee Earners	7
Total Trainees	6

contact
Graduate Recruitment

method of application
Standard application form available from Graduate Recruitment or online

selection procedure
1 interview only in September

closing date for 2009
31 July 2007

application
Training contracts p.a. **3**
Applications p.a. **300–400**
% interviewed p.a. **10%**
Required degree grade
Generally 2:1

training
Salary
1st year (2005) £22,250
Subject to 6 month review
Holiday entitlement **25 days**
% of trainees with a non-law degree p.a. **Approx 50%**

post-qualification
Salary (2006)
Approx £42,000
% of trainees offered job on qualification (2002) **75%**
% of assistants (as at 1/9/03) who joined as trainees **50%**
% of partners (as at 1/9/03) who joined as trainees **40%**

Reed Smith Richards Butler LLP (as of 1 January 2007)

Beaufort House, 15 St. Botolph Street, London, EC3A 7EE
Tel: (020) 7247 6555 Fax: (020) 7247 5091
Email: gradrecruit@richardsbutler.com

Partners	102*
Fee-earners	136*
Total Trainees	58*

* denotes combined UK figures for Reed Smith and Richards Butler

firm profile

The respective partnerships at international law firms Reed Smith LLP and Richards Butler LLP have voted in favour of merging their practices with effect from 1 January 2007. The merger will see the formation of a global top-20 law firm comprised of 20 offices with more than 1300 lawyers working from fourteen locations in the United States, five in Europe and one in the Middle East.

main areas of work

The merged entity emerges as an acknowledged leader in counsel to industries including financial services, life sciences, shipping, international trade and media. Departments include shipping, corporate, commercial litigation, real estate, media and finance.

trainee profile

Candidates should be players rather than onlookers, work well under pressure and be happy to operate as a team member or team leader as circumstances dictate. Candidates from diverse backgrounds are welcome, including mature students with commercial experience and management skills.

training environment

Four seat rotations enable Reed Smith Richards Butler to provide practical experience across as wide a spectrum of the law as possible. Trainees can also apply for secondment to one of the firm's overseas offices, Paris, Abu Dhabi, Piraeus or to one of their client's in-house legal teams.

benefits

Performance related bonus, life insurance, BUPA, interest-free season ticket loan, subsidised staff restaurant, staff conveyancing allowance.

vacation placements

Places for 2007: 30; Duration: 2 weeks; Remuneration: £250 p.w.; Closing date: 31 January 2007.

sponsorship & awards

GDL Funding: Fees paid plus £6,000 maintenance with effect from September 2006.
LPC Funding: Fees paid plus £7,000 maintenance with effect from September 2006.

contact
Mark Matthews

method of application
Online application form

selection procedure
Selection exercise & interview

closing date for 2009/10
31 July 2007

application
Training contracts p.a. **30**
Applications p.a. **1500**
% interviewed p.a. **7%**
Required degree grade **2:1**

training
Salary
1st year (2005) £29,000
2nd year (2005) £32,000
Holiday entitlement **25 days**
% of trainees with a
non-law degree p.a. **35%**
No. of seats available
abroad p.a. **10**

post-qualification
Salary (2006
£50,000 plus bonus
% of assistants who
joined as trainees **59%**
% of partners who
joined as trainees **45%**

overseas offices
New York, London, Paris, Los Angeles, Washington DC, San Francisco, Philadelphia, Pittsburgh, Northern VA, Wilmington, Newark, Midlands UK, UAE, Century City, Richmond Greece.

Reynolds Porter Chamberlain LLP

Tower Bridge House, St Katharine's Way, London, E1W 1AA
Tel: (020) 3060 6000 Fax: (020) 3070 7000
Email: training@rpc.co.uk
Website: www.rpc.co.uk/training

firm profile
RPC is a leading London-based commercial law firm with 64 partners and around 250 lawyers in total. It is best known as one of the UK's leading insurance and litigation practices. However, it also has a highly-rated and fast growing corporate and commercial practice, as well as property, construction, employment and intellectual property expertise. Another key area for the firm is media – the firm has handled some of the most sensitive and high-profile defamation actions in recent years. In June 2006, RPC moved into stunning new offices on St Katharine Docks overlooking the Tower of London and now operates on a fully open-plan basis.

main areas of work
Litigation 60%; corporate 15%; commercial property 10%; construction 10%; media 10%.

trainee profile
The firm appoints 15 trainees each year from law and non-law backgrounds. Although proven academic ability is important (the firm requires a 2:1 or above), RPC also values flair, energy, business sense, commitment and the ability to communicate and relate well to others.

training environment
As a trainee you will receive first rate training in a supportive working environment. You will work closely with a partner and be given real responsibility as soon as you are ready to handle it. At least six months will be spent in each of the main areas of the practice and the firm encourages trainees to express a preference for their seats. This provides a thorough grounding and the chance to develop confidence as you see matters through to their conclusion. In addition to the internally provided Professional Skills Course, the firm provides a complimentary programme of in-house training.

benefits
Four weeks holiday, bonus schemes, private medical insurance, income protection benefits, pension, season ticket loan, subsidised gym membership, active social calendar.

vacation placements
Places for Summer 2007: 20; Duration: 2 weeks; Remuneration: £250 p.w.; Closing Date: 28 February 2007.

sponsorship & awards
GDL Funding: Fees paid plus £6,000 maintenance.
LPC Funding: Fees paid plus £6,000 maintenance.

Partners	64
Assistant Solicitors	250
Total Trainees	23

contact
Kate Gregg
Legal Resourcing Manager

method of application
Online application system

selection procedure
Assessment days held in September

closing date for 2009
10 August 2007

application
Training contracts p.a. **15**
Applications p.a. **900**
% interviewed p.a. **6%**
Required degree grade **2:1**

training
Salary
1st year (2006) **£29,000**
2nd year (2006) **£33,000**
Holiday entitlement **20 days**
% of trainees with a non-law degree p.a. **Approx 25%**

post-qualification
Salary (2006) **£50,000**
% of trainees offered job on qualification (2005) **90%**
% of assistants (as at 1/9/05) who joined as trainees **20%**
% of partners (as at 1/9/05) who joined as trainees **30%**

Salans

Millennium Bridge House, 2 Lambeth Hill, London EC4V 4AJ
Tel: (020) 7429 6000 Fax: (020) 7429 6001
Email: london@salans.com

firm profile

Salans has an open and friendly culture with an informal, but hardworking environment. It is a multinational law firm with full-service offices in the City of London, Paris and New York, together with further offices in Almaty, Baku, Berlin*, Bratislava, Bucharest, Istanbul, Kyiv, Moscow, Prague, Shanghai, St Petersburg and Warsaw. The firm currently has over 500 fee-earners, including 139 partners worldwide, with 30 partners residing in the London office. Its lawyers strongly believe in assisting individuals and groups unable to access legal services, through a positive commitment to pro bono work. Salans was named the Eastern Europe Law Firm of the Year at the Chambers Awards 2004, and were runners-up in the Employment Team of the Year Award at The Lawyer Awards 2005. Its Banking and Finance Team advised on the Trade Finance Deal of the Year 2004 which was announced summer 2005.

main areas of work

London Office: Banking and finance; corporate; litigation; employment; real estate; insolvency and corporate recovery; information technology and communications; and betting and gaming.

trainee profile

You will have high academic qualifications, including good A-Level (or equivalent) results, and the ability to approach complex problems in a practical and commercial way. The firm is looking for highly motivated, creative and enthusiastic team players. It looks to recruit trainees who make a difference, want early responsibility and live life in the fast lane of the ever-changing legal world. Relevant work experience demonstrating a desire to pursue a career in law will be viewed positively, and language and computer skills are also valued.

benefits

Private healthcare, pension, life assurance, critical illness cover, season ticket loan.

sponsorship & awards

LPC tuition fees paid.

Partners (Worldwide)	139
Assistant Solicitors (Worldwide)	300+
Total Trainees (London)	7

contact
Vicky Williams
HR Manager

method of application
Handwritten letter & CV

selection procedure
Interview programme and selection workshop

closing date for 2009
31 July 2007

application
Training contracts p.a. **3-4**
Applications p.a. **500+**
% interviewed p.a. **3%**
Required degree grade **2:1**

training
Salary
1st year (2005) £27,000
2nd year (2005) £29,000
Holiday entitlement **25 days**
% of trainees with a
non-law degree p.a. **Variable**
No. of seats available
abroad p.a. **None at present**

post-qualification
Salary (2005) **Variable**
% of trainees offered job
on qualification (2005) **100%**

overseas offices
Almaty, Baku, Berlin*,
Bratislava, Bucharest,
Istanbul, Kyiv, Moscow,
New York, Paris, Prague,
Shanghai, St Petersburg
and Warsaw

*Salans LLP

Shadbolt & Co LLP

Chatham Court, Lesbourne Road, Reigate RH2 7LD
Tel: (01737) 226277 Fax: (01737) 226165
Email: recruitment@shadboltlaw.com
Website: www.shadboltlaw.com

firm profile
Shadbolt & Co LLP is an award-winning, dynamic, progressive firm committed to high quality work and excellence both in the UK and internationally. The atmosphere at the firm is friendly, relaxed and informal and there are various social and sporting activities for staff. The firm comprises a lively and enterprising team with a fresh and open approach to work. The firm's qualified staff have a high level of experience and industry knowledge and some are widely regarded as leading practitioners in their field.

main areas of work
The firm is well known for its strengths in major projects, construction and engineering and dispute resolution and litigation with established expansion into corporate and commercial, employment, commercial property and IT and e-commerce. The firm provides prompt personal service and its client list includes some of the world's best known names in the construction and engineering industries.

trainee profile
Applicants must demonstrate that they are mature self-starters with a strong academic background and outside interests. Leadership, ambition, initiative, enthusiasm and good interpersonal skills are essential, as is the ability to play an active role in the future of the firm. Linguists are particularly welcome, as are those with supporting professional qualifications. The firm welcomes non-law graduates.

training
Four six month seats from construction and commercial litigation, arbitration and dispute resolution, major projects and construction, employment, corporate and commercial and commercial property. Where possible individual preference is noted. Work has an international bias. There are opportunities for secondment to major clients and work in the overseas offices. Trainees are treated as valued members of the firm, expected to take early responsibility and encouraged to participate in all the firm's activities, including practice development. The firm is accredited by the law society as a provider of training and runs frequent in-house lectures. The PSC is taught externally.

sponsorship & benefits
Optional private healthcare, permanent health insurance, group life assurance, paid study leave, season ticket loan, discretionary annual bonus of up to 5% of salary, paid professional memberships and subscriptions, full refund of LPC upon commencement of training contract.

vacation placements
Places for 2007: 6; Duration: 2 weeks; Remuneration (2006): £200 p.w.; Closing Date: 28 February 2007; Interviews: March 2007.

Partners	29
Associate/Assistant Solicitors	28
Total Trainees	10
Total Staff	119

contact
Andrea Pickett

method of application
Online application form

selection procedure
Interview (1) written assessment & group exercise

closing date for 2009
31 July 2007 (interviews September 2007)

application
Training contracts p.a. **4**
Applications p.a. **100**
% interviewed p.a. **20%**
Required degree grade **2:1 (occasional exceptions)**

training
Salary
1st year (2006) £26,000
2nd year (2006) £30,000
Holiday entitlement
20 days rising to 25 on qualification, with opportunity to 'buy' an additional 5 days holiday p.a.
% of trainees with a non-law degree p.a. **50%**
No. of seats available abroad p.a. **1**

post-qualification
Salary (2006) **£46,000**
% of trainees offered job on qualification (2006) **75%**
% of assistants (2006) who joined as trainees **43%**
% of partners (2006) who joined as trainees **0%**

other offices
Reigate, City of London, Paris, **associated offices:** Athens, Dar es Salaam

Shadbolt & Co LLP
Solicitors

Shearman & Sterling LLP

Broadgate West, 9 Appold Street, London EC2A 2AP
Tel: (020) 7655 5000 Fax: (020) 7655 5500

firm profile

Shearman & Sterling LLP is one of New York's oldest legal partnerships, which has transformed from a New York-based firm focused on banking into a diversified global institution. Recognised throughout the world, the firm's reputation, skills and expertise are second to none in its field. The London office, established in 1972, has become a leading practice covering all aspects of English and European corporate and finance law. The firm employs over 140 English and US trained legal staff in London and has more than 1,000 lawyers in 19 offices worldwide.

main areas of work

Banking, leveraged finance and structured finance. Project finance. M&A. Global capital markets. International arbitration and litigation. Tax. EU and competition. Financial Institutions Advisory & asset management (legal and regulatory advice to financial instititions and infrastructure providers, both in a retail and wholesale context, and both online and off-line). Executive compensation & employee benefits (sophisticated advice on the design and implementation of compensation and benefits arrangements). Intellectual property. Real estate.

trainee profile

The firm's successful future development calls for people who will relish the hard work and intellectual challenge of today's commercial world. You will be a self-starter, keen to assume professional responsibility early in your career and determined to become a first-class lawyer in a first-class firm. The firm's two year training programme will equip you with all the skills needed to become a successful commercial lawyer. You will spend six months in each of four practice areas, with an opportunity to spend six months in Abu Dhabi, New York or Singapore. You will be treated as an integral part of the London team from the outset. The firm will expect you to contribute creatively to all the transactions you are involved in. The firm has an informal yet professional atmosphere. Your enthusiasm, intellect and energy will be more important than what you wear to work. The firm will provide you with a mentor, arrange personal and professional development courses and give you early responsibility.

sponsorship & awards

Sponsorship for the CPE/PgDL and LPC courses, together with a maintenance grant of £7,000.

Partners	26
Assistant Solicitors	105
Total Trainees	17

contact
Kirsten Davies
Tel: (020) 7655 5082

method of application
Online at
www.shearman.com

selection procedure
Interviews

closing date for 2009
31 July 2007

application
Training contracts p.a. **15**
Required degree grade **2:1**

training
Salary
1st year (2006) £36,500
2nd year (2006) £39,500
Holiday entitlement
24 days p.a.
% of trainees with non-law
degree p.a. **40%**
No of seats available
abroad **3**

post-qualification
Salary (2006) **£72,000**
% of trainees offered job
on qualification (2006) **100%**

overseas offices
Abu Dhabi, Bejing,
Brussels, Düsseldorf,
Frankfurt, Hong Kong,
Mannheim, Menlo Park,
Munich, New York, Paris,
Rome, San Francisco, Sao
Paulo, Singapore, Tokyo,
Toronto, Washington DC

Shoosmiths

The Lakes, Bedford Road, Northampton NN4 7SH
Tel: (0870) 086 3223 Fax: (0870) 086 3001
Email: join.us@shoosmiths.co.uk
Website: www.shoosmiths.co.uk/careers

firm profile
Growing steadily, with seven offices across the country, 90 partners and 1,200 staff,
Shoosmiths is one of the big players outside London. By joining the firm you can
expect to experience a full range of interesting and challenging commercial work. In a
demanding legal market, Shoosmiths has developed exciting, even radical, services
helping it to exceed the highest expectations of its clients. The firm supports and
encourages its people to develop exhilarating, balanced careers. Shoosmiths' workplace culture offers a stimulating environment, time for family and the opportunity to
put something back into the community.

main areas of work
Corporate/commercial; commercial property; dispute resolution; employment; planning; banking; financial institutions; private client; personal injury.

trainee profile
You will be confident, motivated and articulate with natural intelligence and the drive
to succeed, thereby making a real contribution to the firm's commercial success. You
will want to be a part of a winning team and will care about the kind of service you give
to your clients, both internal and external.

training environment
You will be involved in 'real' work from day one of your training contract. Sitting with
a Partner who will oversee your training and career development, you will have direct
contact with clients and will draft your own letters and documents. Your experience
will build through your daily, practical, workload complemented by the training you
would expect from a leading national law firm. In addition to the compulsory Professional Skills Course, the firm offers a comprehensive internal training programme that
includes managerial, legal and IT training as standard. Over the course of two years,
you will complete four seats of six month duration to help you decide which area you
would like to qualify into.

benefits
Flexible holidays, pension (after 3 months service), life assurance, various staff discounts, Christmas bonus.

vacation placements
Places for 2007: 35; Duration: 2 weeks; Remuneration: £230 p.w.; Closing Date: 28 Feb
2007.

sponsorship & awards
LPC funding: £13,000 – split between fees and maintenance.

Partners	90
Assistant Solicitors	250
Total Trainees	26

contact
Sally Stagles

method of application
Application form via website

selection procedure
Selection centre - full day

closing date for 2009
31 July 2007

application
Training contracts p.a. **14**
Applications p.a. **1,000**
% interviewed p.a. **10%**
Required degree grade **2:1**

training
Salary
Market Rate
Holiday entitlement
23 days + option to flex

post-qualification
Salary **Market rate**

offices
Northampton, Nottingham,
Reading, Solent, Milton
Keynes, Basingstoke,
Birmingham

Sidley Austin

Woolgate Exchange, 25 Basinghall Street, London EC2V 5HA
Tel: (020) 7360 3600 Fax: (020) 7626 7937
Email: ukrecruitment@sidley.com
Website: www.sidley.com

firm profile
Sidley Austin is one of the world's largest full-service law firms. With more than 1,600 lawyers practising on three continents (North America, Europe and Asia), the firm provides a broad range of integrated services to meet the needs of its clients across a multitude of industries.

main areas of work
Corporate & securities; debt & equity capital markets, corporate reorganisation and bankruptcy, employment, financial services regulation, insurance, IP/IT, real estate and real estate finance, securitisation and structured finance and tax.

trainee profile
Sidley Austin look for focused, intelligent and enthusiastic individuals with personality and humour who have a real interest in practising law in the commercial world. Trainees should have a consistently strong academic record and a 2:1 degree (not necessarily in law).

training environment
The firm is not a typical City firm and it is not a 'legal factory' so there is no risk of being just a number. Everyone is encouraged to be proactive and to create their own niche when they are ready to do so. Trainees spend time in the firm's main groups. In each group trainees will sit with a partner or senior associate to ensure individual training based on 'hands on' experience. You will be encouraged to take responsibility where appropriate. Regular meetings with your supervisor ensure both the quality and quantity of your experience. In addition, there is a structured timetable of training on a cross-section of subjects and an annual training weekend.

benefits
Private health insurance, life assurance, contribution to gym membership, interest-free season ticket loan, income protection scheme, pension and subsidised restaurant.

sponsorship & awards
Tuition fees for the GDL/CPE and the LPC. Maintenance grant of £7,000 p.a.

Partners	34
Assistant Solicitors	65
Total Trainees	10

contact
Anna Niblock,
Senior HR Manager

method of application
Application form

selection procedure
Interview(s)

closing date for 2009
28 July 2007

application
Training contracts p.a. **15**
Applications p.a. **500**
% interviewed p.a. **15**
Required degree grade **2:1**

training
Salary
1st year (2005) £29,000
2nd year (2005) £33,000
Holiday entitlement **25 days**
% of trainees with a
non-law degree p.a. **50%**

overseas offices
Beijing, Brussels, Chicago, Dallas, Frankfurt, Geneva, Hong Kong, London, Los Angeles, New York, San Francisco, Shanghai, Singapore, Tokyo, Washington DC

Simmons & Simmons

CityPoint, One Ropemaker Street, London EC2Y 9SS
Tel: (020) 7628 2020 Fax: (020) 7628 2070
Email: recruitment@simmons-simmons.com
Website: www.simmons-simmons.com/traineelawyers

firm profile
Dynamic and innovative, Simmons & Simmons has a reputation for offering a superior legal service, wherever and whenever it is required. Their lawyers' high quality advice and the positive working atmosphere in their 20 international offices have won admiration and praise from both the legal community and their business clients.

main areas of work
The firm offers their clients a full range of legal services across numerous industry sectors. They have a particular focus on the world's fastest growing sectors, that is: Energy & infrastructure; financial institutions; life sciences; and technology. They provide a wide choice of service areas in which their lawyers can specialise. These include corporate & commercial; communications, outsourcing & technology; dispute resolution; employment & benefits; EU & competition; financial markets; IP; projects; real estate; taxation & pensions.

trainee profile
The firm looks for a strong track record of achievements from their candidates. They are interested to find out about your academic successes but they will also explore your ability to form excellent interpersonal relations and work within a team environment, as well as your levels of motivation, drive and ambition.

Show them evidence of a rich 'life experience' as well as examples of your intellectual capabilities and they will provide you with everything you need to become a successful member of their firm.

training environment
Their training programme is constantly evolving to build the skills you will need to be successful in the fast moving world of international business. The firm provides experience in a range of areas of law and a balanced approach to gaining the knowledge, expertise and abilities you will need to qualify in the practice area of your choice.

vacation placements
The firm's summer internship scheme is one of its primary means of selecting candidates for a career at Simmons & Simmons. It provides them with the chance to test your suitability for a training contract. It is also a unique opportunity for you to get to know the firm, decide if it is the best firm for you and for you to prove your potential during your time with them.

Undergraduates usually apply for internships in their penultimate year. However, the firm is also happy to offer internships to final year students, graduates, mature and international students and those changing career.

sponsorship & awards
The firm will cover your full tuition fees at law school and offer a maintenance allowance of up to £7,500.

Partners	218
Assistant Solicitors	581
Total Trainees	175

contact
Vickie Chamberlain
Graduate Recruitment
Manager

method of application
Online application, at www.simmons-simmons.com/traineelawyers Applications should be made from 01 November, 2006

selection procedure
Assessment day

closing date for 2009
31 July 2007

application
Training contracts p.a. **50**
Applications p.a. **2,500**
% interviewed p.a. **15%**
Required degree grade **2:1**

training
Salary
£31,000, 1st and 2nd seat
£34,000, 2nd and 3rd seat
Holiday entitlement **25 days**
% of trainees with a non-law degree p.a. **50%**
No. of seats available abroad p.a. **varies**

post-qualification
Salary (2006) **£55,000**
% of trainees offered job on qualification (2006) **84%**

overseas offices
Abu Dhabi, Brussels, Dubai, Düsseldorf, Frankfurt, Hong Kong, Lisbon, London, Madeira, Madrid, Milan, New York, Oporto, Padua, Paris, Qatar, Rome, Rotterdam, Shanghai, Tokyo.

Skadden Arps, Slate, Meagher & Flom (UK) LLP

40 Bank Street, Canary Wharf, London E14 5DS
Tel: (020) 7519 7000 Fax: (020) 7519 7070
Email: graduate@skadden.com
Website: www.skadden.com

firm profile
Skadden is one of the leading law firms in the world with approximately 1,700 lawyers in 22 offices across the globe. Clients include corporate, industrial, financial institutions and government entities. The London office is the gateway to the firm's European practice where they have some 200 lawyers dedicated to top-end, cross-border corporate transactions and international arbitration. They have handled matters in nearly every country in the greater European region, and in Africa and the Middle East. They consistently rank as a leader in all disciplines and amongst a whole host of accolades, they were recently voted Global Law Firm of the Year (Chambers and Partners) and Best US Law Firm in London (Legal Business).

main areas of work
Lawyers across the European network focus primarily on corporate transactions, including domestic and cross-border mergers and acquisitions, private equity, capital markets, leveraged finance and banking, tax, corporate restructuring and energy and projects. They also advise in international arbitration, litigation and regulatory matters.

trainee profile
The firm seeks to recruit a small number of high-calibre graduates from any discipline to join their highly successful London office as trainee solicitors. They are looking for candidates who combine intellectual ability with energy, enthusiasm, creativity and a demonstrable ability to rise to a challenge and to work with others towards a common goal.

training environment
The firm can offer you the chance to develop your career in a uniquely rewarding and professional environment. You will join a close-knit but diverse team in which you will be given ample opportunity to work on complex matters, almost all with an international aspect, while benefiting from highly personalised training and supervision in an informal and friendly environment. The first year of your training contract will be divided into two six month seats where you will gain experience in corporate transactions and international litigation and arbitration. In the second year of your training contract, you will have the opportunity to select your remaining seats in order for you to gain exposure in areas of greatest personal interest.

benefits
Life insurance, private health insurance, private medical care, travel insurance, subsidised gym membership and restaurant, employee assistance programme, pension and technology allowance.

vacation placements
Skadden offers the opportunity for penultimate year law and non-law students to experience the culture and working environment of the firm through two week vacation placements. Vacation placements are paid and take place during Easter and over the course of the summer. The deadline for applications is 12 January 2007 for placements in 2007.

sponsorship & awards
The firm pays for GDL/CPE and LPC course fees and provides a £7,500 grant for each year of these courses.

Partners	21*
Assistant Solicitors	100*
Trainees	6*

*London office

contact
Kate Harman
Graduate Recruitment
Assistant

method of application
Online application

selection procedure
A selection event comprising of an interview and a short exercise

closing date for 2009
31 July 2007

application
Training contracts p.a. **8**
Applications p.a. **700**
% interviewed p.a. **8%**
Required degree grade **2:1**

training
Salary
1st year **£35,000**
2nd year **£40,000**
Holiday entitlement **25 days**
% of trainees with a
non-law degree p.a. **50%**

overseas offices
Beijing, Boston, Brussels, Chicago, Frankfurt, Hong Kong, Houston, London, Los Angeles, Moscow, Munich, New York, Palo Alto, Paris, San Francisco, Singapore, Sydney, Tokyo, Toronto, Vienna, Washington DC, Wilmington.

Slaughter and May

One Bunhill Row, London EC1Y 8YY
Tel: (020) 7600 1200 Fax: (020) 7090 5000
Email: grad.recruit@slaughterandmay.com (enquiries only)
Website: www.slaughterandmay.com

firm profile
One of the leading law firms in the world, Slaughter and May enjoys a reputation for quality and expertise. The corporate, commercial and financing practice is particularly strong and lawyers are known for their business acumen and technical excellence. As well as its London office, in order that the firm provides the best advice and service across the world, it nurtures long-standing relationships with the leading independent law firms in other jurisdictions.

main areas of work
Corporate, commercial and financing; tax; competition; financial regulation; dispute resolution; technology, media and telecommunications; intellectual property; commercial real estate; environment; pensions and employment.

trainee profile
The work is demanding and the firm looks for intellectual agility and the ability to work with people from different countries and walks of life. Common sense, a mature outlook, the ability to communicate clearly and the willingness to accept responsibility are all essential. The firm expects to provide training in everything except the fundamental principles of law, so does not expect applicants to know much of commercial life. Trainees are expected to remain with the firm on qualification.

training environment
Four or five seats of three or six months duration. Two seats will be in the field of corporate, commercial and financing law with an option to choose a posting overseas (either to one of the firm's offices or to a "best friend" firm), or competition or financial regulation. One seat in either dispute resolution, intellectual property, tax or pensions and employment is part of the programme and a commercial real estate seat is also possible. In each seat a partner is responsible for monitoring your progress and reviewing your work. There is an extensive training programme which includes the PSC and the firm's own unique business and finance course. There are also discussion groups covering general and specialised legal topics.

benefits
BUPA, STL, pension scheme, subsidised membership of health club, 24 hour accident cover.

vacation placements – summer 2007
Places: 60; Duration: 2 weeks; Remuneration: £275 p.w.; Closing Date: 26 January 2007 for penultimate year (of first degree) students only.

sponsorship & awards
CPE and LPC fees and maintenance grants are paid.

Partners	126
Associates	413
Total Trainees	181

contact
Charlotte Houghton

method of application
Online (via website) preferred or by posting to the firm a CV and covering letter

selection procedure
Interview

application
Training contracts p.a.
Approx 85-95
Applications p.a. **2,000+**
% interviewed p.a. **25%**
Required standard
Good 2:1 ability

training
Salary (May 2006)
1st year £31,000
2nd year £34,500
Holiday entitlement
25 days p.a.
% of trainees with a
non-law degree **Approx 50%**
No. of seats available
abroad p.a. **Approx 30-40**

post-qualification
Salary (May 2006) **£54,000**
% of trainees offered job
on qualification (2006) **94%+**

overseas offices
Paris, Brussels and Hong Kong, plus "Best Friend" firms in all the major jurisdictions.

Speechly Bircham

6 St Andrew Street, London EC4A 3LX
Tel: (020) 7427 6400 Fax: (020) 7353 4368
Email: trainingcontracts@speechlys.com
Website: www.speechlys.com

firm profile

A City law firm handling a distinctive blend of advisory, transactional and disputes work in each of its principal areas of practice: corporate, private client, employment, property and construction. With over 160 lawyers, the firm acts for a high quality client base including quoted and privately owned businesses, financial institutions, international trust companies and wealthy individuals.

Speechly Bircham's strengths lie in the synergy of the relationships between its four main departments: private client, corporate and tax, litigation and property.

main areas of work

Corporate and tax 25%; property 25%; litigation 25%; private client 25%.

trainee profile

Both law and non-law graduates who are capable of achieving a 2:1. The firm seeks intellectually dynamic individuals who enjoy a collaborative working environment where they can make an impact.

training environment

Speechly Bircham divides the training contract into four six-month seats. Emphasis is given to early responsibility and supervised client contact providing trainees with a practical learning environment.

benefits

Season ticket loan, private medical insurance, life assurance.

vacation placements

Places for 2007: 16. The firm's summer placement scheme for students gives them the chance to experience a City legal practice. In a three-practice placement, students will be asked to research and present on a legal issue at the end of their placement; Duration: 3 weeks; Remuneration: £250 p.w.; Closing Date: 16 February 2007.

sponsorship & awards

CPE and LPC fees and a maintenance grant.

Partners	57
Assistant Solicitors	100
Total Trainees	10

contact
Nicola Swann
Human Resources Director

method of application
Application form (available by request or online)

selection procedure
Interview

closing date for 2009
31 July 2007

application
Training contracts p.a. **7**
Applications p.a. **500**
% interviewed p.a. **25%**
Required degree grade **2:1**

training
Salary
1st year
£28,000-£29,000
2nd year
£30,000-£31,000
Holiday entitlement **20 days**
% of trainees with a
non-law degree p.a. **50%**

post-qualification
Salary (2006) **£48,000**

Stephenson Harwood

One St Paul's Churchyard, London EC4M 8SH
Tel: (020) 7809 2812 Fax: (020) 7003 8263
Email: graduate.recruitment@shlegal.com
Website: www.shlegal.com/graduate

firm profile
Established in the City of London in 1828, Stephenson Harwood was the overall winner at the 2006 Association of Graduate Recruiters Awards, an independent national voice for all employers involved in graduate recruitment. The firm was praised for its entire campaign as well as being singled out for the prize for best literature. Stephenson Harwood has developed into a large international practice, with a commercial focus and a wide client base.

main areas of work
Corporate (including corporate finance, funds, corporate tax, business technology); employment, pensions and benefits; banking and asset finance; dry and wet shipping litigation; commercial litigation; and real estate.

trainee profile
The firm looks for high calibre graduates with excellent academic records, business awareness and excellent communication skills.

training environment
As the graduate intake is relatively small, the firm gives trainees individual attention, coaching and monitoring. Your structured and challenging programme involves four six month seats in areas of the firm covering contentious and non-contentious areas, across any department within the firm's practice groups. These seats include 'on the job' training and you will share an office with a partner or senior associate. In-house lectures complement your training and there is continuous review of your career development. You will have the opportunity to spend six months abroad and have free language tuition where appropriate. You will be given your own caseload and as much responsibility as you can shoulder. The firm plays a range of team sports, offers subsidised membership of a City health club (or a health club of your choice) and has privileged seats for concerts at the Royal Albert Hall and access to private views at the Tate Gallery.

benefits
Subsidised membership of health clubs, private health insurance, BUPA membership, season ticket loan and 25 days paid holiday per year.

vacation placements
Places for 2007: 18; Duration: 2 weeks; Remuneration: £250 p.w.; Closing Date: 16 February 2007.

sponsorship & awards
Fees paid for CPE and LPC and maintenance awards.

Partners	70*
Assistant Solicitors	219*
Total Trainees	34

* denotes world-wide figures

contact
Carly Butler (Graduate Recruitment)

method of application
Online application form only

selection procedure
assessment centre

closing date for Sept/March 2009
31 July 2007

application
Training contracts p.a. **12**
% interviewed p.a. **10%**
Required degree grade **2:1**

training
Salary
1st year (2005) £28,000
2nd year (2005) £32,000
Holiday entitlement **25 days**
% of trainees with a non-law degree p.a. **50%**
No. of seats available abroad p.a. **8**

post-qualification
Salary (2006) **£52,000**
% of trainees offered job on qualification (2006) **100%**
% of assistants (as at 1/9/06) who joined as trainees **38%**
% of partners (as at 1/9/06) who joined as trainees **43%**

overseas offices
Paris, Piraeus, Singapore, Guangzhou, Hong Kong, Shanghai

associated offices
Greece, South Africa, Kuwait, Croatia, France, Bucharest

Stevens & Bolton LLP

The Billings, Guildford, Surrey GU4 1YD
Tel: (01483) 302264 Fax: (01483) 302254
Email: gradrec@stevens-bolton.co.uk
Website: www.stevens-bolton.co.uk

Partners	26
Assistant Solicitors	45
Total Trainees	6

firm profile

Stevens & Bolton is a leading law firm based in Guildford with a national reputation. The firm provides clients with a City-calibre service and offers its trainees a supportive culture and excellent training. This was recently recognised when the firm won two awards, in 2005 Best Recruiter and in 2004 Best Trainer (medium regional law firm) both awarded by LawCareers.net and the TSG. The firm has 26 partners and over 130 staff in total. The firm has grown rapidly in the past five years and is one of the major firms in the region, described recently by The Legal 500 as a 'regional heavyweight'. In 2005 the firm was shortlisted by Legal Business for Regional Firm of the Year. The firm's work is over 80% commercial, the remainder being private client work advising medium and high net worth individuals. The firm acts for a diverse range of clients. These include FTSE 100 businesses, subsidiaries of major international groups and growing, owner-managed companies. The firm receives instructions from household names such as Gallaher Group plc, Hays plc, The BOC Group and Morse plc to name a few!

contact
Julie Bounden
(01483) 302264

method of application
Online application form available from website

selection procedure
Two interviews & other processes

closing date for 2009
30 September 2007

application
Training contracts p.a. **4**
Applications p.a. **200**
% interviewed **13%**
Required degree grade **2:1**

main areas of work

Corporate and commercial, real estate, dispute resolution, employment and pensions, tax & trust, private client and family.

trainee profile

The firm requires a good academic record and individuals with interests such as music, sport, travel and who have a genuine enthusiasm to work in the law.

training
Salary
1st year (2006) £24,000
2nd year (2006) £26,000
Holiday entitlement **25 days**

post-qualification
Salary (2006) **£41,250**
% of trainees offered job on qualification (2006) **70%**

training environment

Usually you will sit with a partner who will act as your supervisor and you will get real responsibility early on. There is a comprehensive cross-departmental training programme and regular reviews of performance, with a formal appraisal at the end of each seat.

overseas/regional offices
Guildford only

benefits

Private medical insurance, life assurance, pension, rail or car park season ticket loan, permanent health insurance and 25 days holiday.

sponsorship & awards

Providing no local authority grant is available, full fees for the GDL and LPC plus a £4,000 maintenance grant for each course.

STEVENS & BOLTON LLP

Tarlo Lyons

Watchmaker Court, 33 St John's Lane, London EC1M 4DB
Tel: (020) 7405 2000 Fax: (020) 7814 9421
Email: trainee.recruitment@tarlolyons.com
Website: www.tarlolyons.com

firm profile

Tarlo Lyons is a City law firm, based in Farringdon. The firm has a leading reputation for its technology work and its expertise provides real benefits for its clients across a range of sectors.

main areas of work

The firm is divided into six main practice areas: property; corporate; technology; dispute resolution; employment; and recruitment & resourcing. They specialise in providing legal advice to companies and individuals in the following industry sectors: banking, insurance and financial services; IT and outsourcing; hotel, leisure and gambling; and health/care. In addition, they specialise in white-collar crime, fraud and customs and excise.

trainee profile

Tarlo Lyons lawyers can be identified as smart, commercially savvy, fun and professional – they aren't defined by the school they went to or their examination results. The firm welcomes applicants who have taken a gap year or who have had work experience in business. It values the differences in skills, strengths and ideas each person brings.

training environment

Opportunities for learning are provided throughout the training contract. You will gain work experience in most departments, including at least three months in the firm's Dispute Resolution Department, with the PSC taught externally. Your work experience will be interactive and varied and you will participate in a wide range of business development and marketing activities.

benefits

Tarlo Lyons offers competitive compensation and your salary may be enhanced by a discretionary bonus payment. The firm's benefits package includes a 50% subsidy to a nearby gym, private health cover and an interest free season ticket loan.

sponsorship & awards

LPC fees paid.

Partners	19
Assistant Solicitors	10
Total Trainees	6

contact
Trainee Recruitment
Co-ordinator

method of application
Application form available
from website

selection procedure
2 interviews

closing date for 2009
3 August 2007

application
Training contracts p.a. **3**
Applications p.a. **200**
% interviewed p.a. **10%**
Required degree grade **2:1**

training
Salary
1st year (2005) £28,000
on average
2nd year (2005) £30,000
on average
Holiday entitlement **25 days**
% of trainees with a
non-law degree p.a. **50%**

post-qualification
Salary (2005) **£44,000**
(Salary levels may
increase subject to
market conditions)

Taylor Walton

28-44 Alma Street, Luton LU1 2PL
Tel: (01582) 731161 Fax: (01582) 457900
Email: luton@taylorwalton.co.uk
Website: www.taylorwalton.co.uk

firm profile

Strategically located in Luton, Harpenden and St Albans, Taylor Walton is a major regional law practice advising both businesses and private clients. Its strengths are in commercial property, corporate work and commercial litigation, whilst maintaining a strong private client side to the practice. It has a progressive outlook both in its partners and staff and in its systems, training and IT.

main areas of work

Company/commercial 15%; commercial property 20%; commercial litigation 15%; employment 10%; family 5%; private client 10%; residential property 25%.

trainee profile

Candidates need to show excellent intellectual capabilities, coupled with an engaging personality so as to show that they can engage and interact with the firm's clients as the practice of law involves the practice of the art of communication. Taylor Walton sees its partners and staff as business advisers involved in clients' businesses, not merely stand-alone legal advisers.

training environment

The training consists of four six-month seats. The trainee partner oversees the structural training alongside a supervisor who will be a partner or senior solicitor in each department. The firm does try to take trainees' own wishes in relation to seats into account. In a regional law practice like Taylor Walton you will find client contact and responsibility coupled with supervision, management and training. There is an in-house training programme for all fee-earning members of staff. Trainees are given the opportunity to discuss their progress with their supervisor at a montly appraisal meeting. In addition, at the end of each seat there is a post seat appraisal conducted by the trainee partner. The PSC is taught externally. The firm is friendly with an open door policy and there are various sporting and social events.

vacation placements

Places for 2007: 8; Duration: Up to 3 weeks; Remuneration: £183 per week; Closing Date: 30 March 2007.

sponsorship & awards

Full LPC sponsorship.

Partners	24
Assistant Solicitors	32
Total Trainees	7

contact
Jim Wrigglesworth

method of application
CV with covering letter

selection procedure
First & second interview with opportunity to meet other partners

closing date for 2009
30 July 2007

application
Required degree grade
2:1 or above

Taylor Wessing

Carmelite, 50 Victoria Embankment, Blackfriars
London EC4Y 0DX
Tel: (020) 7300 7000 Fax: (020) 7300 7100
Website: www.taylorwessing.com

firm profile

Taylor Wessing is a powerful source of legal support for commercial organisations doing business in Europe. Based in the three largest economies in Europe, Taylor Wessing provides the full range of legal services to major corporations and growing enterprises. Taylor Wessing boasts a strong reputation in the corporate, finance and real estate sectors alongside in-depth experience across the full range of legal services including property, tax, litigation & dispute resolution, employment & pensions and private client.

main areas of work

Corporate, intellectual property, finance & projects, real estate, litigation & dispute resolution, employment & pensions and private client.

trainee profile

High intellectual ability is paramount and the firm seeks a minimum of ABB grades at A Level and at least a 2.1 degree in any discipline. The firm looks for team players who have excellent communication skills, energy, ambition, an open mind and a willingness to learn. You will also need to demonstrate a commitment to a career in law and a genuine interest in business.

training environment

As part of your training, you will spend six months in four different departments, including a seat in the corporate department. There is also the possibility of a secondment to another office or a client. Trainees work closely with a number of partners and associates in the departments – so are directly involved in high-quality work from the start. At the beginning of the training and throughout you have ongoing discussions about your interests and how they fit in with the growth and needs of the departments. There is support every step of the way, with regular feedback and appraisals in the middle and at the end of each seat. Not forgetting the Professional Skills Course, which is run in-house, along with other training courses as necessary during the two years.

benefits

Private medical care, permanent health insurance, season ticket loan, subsidised staff restaurant, non-contributory pension scheme.

vacation placements

Places for 2007: 38 Duration: 2 weeks; Remuneration: £250 per week; Closing date: 31 January 2007.

sponsorship & awards

GDL and LPC fees paid in full. Maintenance grant £7,000 per annum.

Partners	260
Fee-earners	598
Trainees	43 (UK)

contact
Graduate Recruitment Department

method of application
Online application form

selection procedure
Two interviews, one with a partner, and psychometric test

closing date for 2009
31 July 2007

application
Training contracts p.a. **22**
Applications p.a. **1,195**
% interviewed p.a. **8%**
Required degree grade **2:1**

training
Salary
1st year £30,000
2nd year £34,000
Holiday entitlement **25 days**
% of trainees with a non-law degree p.a. **40%**

post-qualification
Salary **£53,0 00**
% of trainees offered job on qualification (2003-04) **93%**

overseas offices
Berlin, Brussels, Cologne Dusseldorf, Frankfurt, Hamburg, Munich, Paris and representative offices in Alicante and Shanghai. Associated office in Dubai.

Teacher Stern Selby

37-41 Bedford Row, London WC1R 4JH
Tel: (020) 7242 3191 Fax: (020) 7242 1156
Email: r.raphael@tsslaw.com
Website: www.tsslaw.com

firm profile
A central London-based general commercial firm, with clientele and caseload normally attributable to larger firms. It has a wide range of contacts overseas.

main areas of work
Commercial litigation 24%; commercial property 38%; company and commercial 22%; secured lending 12%; private client 2%; clinical negligence/education/judicial review 2%.

trainee profile
Emphasis falls equally on academic excellence and personality. The firm looks for flexible and motivated individuals, who have outside interests and who have demonstrated responsibility in the past.

training environment
Eight months in three departments (company commercial, litigation and property). Most trainees are assigned to actively assist a partner who monitors and supports them. Trainees are fully involved in departmental work and encouraged to take early responsibility. Trainees are expected to attend in-house seminars and lectures for continuing education. The atmosphere is relaxed and informal.

vacation placements
Places for 2007: Approximately 20 places to those that have applied for training contracts.

sponsorship & awards
Considered.

Partners	**21**
Assistant Solicitors	**28**
Total Trainees	**10**

contact
Russell Raphael

method of application
Online application

selection procedure
2 interviews

closing date for 2009
31 July 2007

application
Training contracts p.a. **3-6**
Applications p.a. **500**
% interviewed p.a. **5%**
Required degree grade
2:1 (not absolute)

training
Salary
1st year £29,000
Holiday entitlement
4 weeks
% of trainees with a
non-law degree p.a. **50%**

post-qualification
Salary (2006) **£41,000**
% of trainees offered job
on qualification (2006) **50%**
% of assistants (who joined
as trainees **28%**
% of partners who joined as
trainees **42%**

Thomas Eggar

The Corn Exchange, Baffins Lane, Chichester PO19 1GE
Tel: (01243) 813253
Email: mark.james@thomaseggar.com
Website: www.thomaseggar.com

firm profile

Thomas Eggar is rated as one of the top 100 law firms in the UK. Based in the South East, it is one of the country's leading regional law firms with a staff of over 400. The firm offers both private client and commercial services to a diverse range of clients, locally, nationally and internationally. It also offers financial services through Thesis, the firm's investment management arm, which is the largest solicitor-based investment unit in the UK.

main areas of work

Apart from its strength in the private client sector, the firm handles property, commercial and litigation matters; among its major clients are banks, building societies and other financial institutions, railway and track operators and construction companies.

trainee profile

The firm seeks able trainees with common sense, application and good business acumen, with a 2.1 degree in any discipline. Applications can be made up to 1 August 2007 for training contracts to commence in March/September 2009 and March 2010. Applications should be in the form of a CV and covering letter. You should give details of your attachment to the South East region in your covering letter.

training environment

Trainees would normally have four seats covering commercial property, commercial, litigation and private client. In order to give good exposure to various specialisations, some of the seats are likely to be in different offices.

vacation placements

There is a very limited summer placement scheme in July and August each year: this runs for five days, three days in the Gatwick office and two days in tone other office. Applications should be made with CV and covering letter to Mark James by 31 March 2007. Please give details of your accommodation plans in your covering letter. Travel expenses are paid.

sponsorship & awards

LPC 50% grant, 50% loan.

Vacancies	8
Partners	58
Trainees	16
Total Staff	429

contact
Mark James BEM

method of application
Letter & CV

selection procedure
CV, assessment centre & interview

closing date for 2009/2010
1 August 2007

training
The firm aims to pay the going rate for a South Eastern regional firm. A London weighting is paid to those who undertake seats in the London office. The firm also pays a taxable travel allowance to all its trainees.
Required degree grade
2:1 (any discipline)

other offices
Chichester, Gatwick, London, Worthing

Thomson Snell & Passmore

3 Lonsdale Gardens, Tunbridge Wells, Kent TN1 1NX
Tel: (01892) 510000 Fax: (01892) 549884
Email: solicitors@ts-p.co.uk
Website: www.ts-p.co.uk

firm profile

Thomson Snell & Passmore continues to be regarded as one of the premier law firms in the South East. The firm has a reputation for quality and a commitment to deliver precise and clear advice which is recognised and respected both by its clients and professional contacts. It has held the Lexcel quality mark since January 1999. The firm is vibrant and progressive and enjoys an extremely friendly atmosphere. Its offices are located in the centre of Tunbridge Wells and attract clients locally, nationally and internationally.

main areas of work

Commercial litigation 14%; corporate and employment 14%; commercial property 14%; private client 24%; personal injury/clinical negligence 12%; residential property 15%; family 7%.

trainee profile

Thomson Snell & Passmore regards its trainees from the outset as future assistants, associates and partners. The firm is looking for people not only with strong intellectual ability, but enthusiasm, drive, initiative, strong interpersonal and team-working skills.

training environment

The firm's induction course will help you to adjust to working life. As a founder member of Law South your training is provided in-house with trainees from other Law South member firms. Your two-year training contract is divided into four periods of six months each. You will receive a thorough grounding and responsibility with early client exposure. You will be monitored regularly, receive advice and assistance throughout and appraisals every three months. The Training Partner will co-ordinate your continuing education in the law, procedure, commerce, marketing, IT and presentation skills. Trainees enjoy an active social life which is encouraged and supported.

sponsorship & awards

Grant and interest free loan available for LPC.

Partners	32
Assistant Solicitors	60
Total Trainees	8

contact
Human Resources
Manager
Tel: (01892) 510000

method of application
Letter & application form
available from website

selection procedure
Assessment interview

closing date for 2009
31 July 2007

application
Training contracts p.a. **4**
Applications p.a.
Approximately 500
% interviewed p.a. **5%**
Required degree grade
2:1 (any discipline)

training
Salary for each year of
training
**Competitive regional
salary**
Holiday entitlement **25 days**

post-qualification
% of trainees offered job
on qualification **75%**

overseas/regional offices
Network of independent
law firms throughout
Europe and founding
member of Law South

TLT Solicitors

One Redcliff St, Bristol BS1 6TP
Tel: (0117) 917 7777 Fax: (0117) 917 7778
Email: graduate@TLTsolicitors.com
Website: www.TLTsolicitors.com

Partners	54
Assistant Solicitors	284
Total Trainees	13

firm profile
At the heart of TLT's strategy is a belief that great people make a great business. It is this attitude and strategy that has lead TLT to be listed in the Sunday Times 100 Best Companies to Work For in 2005 and has won the firm awards such as the Legal Business UK Regional Law Firm of the Year Award in 2004. These accolades reflect TLT's reputation which is built on an eagerness to understand its clients' businesses and a "whatever it takes" approach to client service.

main areas of work
An impressive national and international client base ensures high quality work in a broad range of specialist areas: banking, capital markets, commercial dispute resolution, construction, corporate, employment, family, insolvency and business breakdown, intellectual property, lender services, mergers and acquisitions, partnerships, pensions, planning and environmental, property, tax, technology and media.

trainee profile
Strong academic background together with commitment and drive to succeed.

training environment
TLT's commitment to excellence will ensure that trainees benefit from a well developed and challenging training programme. Training is delivered through four seats of six months duration, chosen in consultation with the trainee. In each seat the trainee will sit with a lawyer although their work will be drawn from all members of the team in order to gain the widest possible experience. Regular monitoring and development planning ensures that trainees get the most out of their training and helps them to identify their long term career path from the varied specialisms on offer.

benefits
Pension, private medical insurance, life assurance and subsidised sports/health club membership, 25 days holiday entitlement.

vacation placements
36 paid placements available, each lasting 1 week. Apply online by 31 January 2007.

sponsorship & awards
CPE and LPC fees plus maintenance payment

contact
Human Resources

method of application
Firm's application form
online

selection procedure
Assessment Centre

closing date for 2009
31 July 2007

application
Training contracts p.a. **8**
Applications p.a. **500+**
% interviewed p.a. **10%**
Required degree grade
2:1 prefered
non-law degree p.a. **17%**

training
Salary: **£22,000 (1st year)**
    £23,000 (2nd year)
Holiday entitlement **25 days**

post-qualification
Market rate

offices
Bristol, London

Travers Smith

10 Snow Hill, London EC1A 2AL
Tel: (020) 7295 3000 Fax: (020) 7295 3500
Email: graduate.recruitment@traverssmith.com
Website: www.traverssmith.com

firm profile

A leading City firm with a major corporate and commercial practice. Although less than a quarter of the size of the dozen largest firms, they handle the highest quality work, much of which has an international dimension.

main areas of work

Corporate law (including takeovers and mergers, financial services and regulatory laws), commercial law (which includes competition and intellectual property), dispute resolution, corporate recovery/insolvency, tax, employment, pensions, banking and property. The firm also offers a range of pro bono opportunities within individual departments and on a firm wide basis. Solicitors from the firm were recently awarded two separate national awards in recognition of their outstanding contributions to pro bono work.

trainee profile

The firm looks for people who combine academic excellence with common sense; who are articulate, who think on their feet, who are determined and self motivated and who take their work but not themselves seriously. Applications are welcome from law and non-law graduates.

training environment

Travers Smith has earned a phenomenal reputation in relation to its size. The work they undertake is exciting, intellectually demanding and top quality involving blue-chip clients and big numbers. This means that their trainees gain great experience right from the outset.

The firm has a comprehensive training programme which ensures that trainees experience a broad range of work. All trainee solicitors sit in rooms with partners and assistants, receive an individual and extensive training from experienced lawyers and enjoy client contact and the responsibility that goes with it from the beginning of their training contract.

benefits

Private health insurance, permanent health insurance, life assurance, corporate health club membership, subsidised bistro, season ticket loan.

vacation placements

Summer 2007: 3 schemes with 15 places on each; Duration: two weeks; Remuneration: £250; Closing Date: 31 January 2007. The firm also offers a two week Christmas scheme for 15 students.

sponsorship & awards

GDL and LPC paid in full plus maintenance of £7,000 per annum to those in London and £6,500 per annum to those outside of London.

Partners	**58**
Assistant Solicitors	**148**
Total Trainees	**40**

contact
Germaine VanGeyzel

method of application
CV and covering letter
online or by post

selection procedure
Interviews (2 stage process)

closing date for 2009
31 July 2007

application
Training contracts p.a. **Up to 25**
Applications p.a. **2,000**
% interviewed p.a. **15%**
Required degree grade **2:1**

training
Salary
1st year (2006) £31,000
2nd year (2006) £35,000
Holiday entitlement **25 days**

post-qualification
Salary (2006) **£55,000**
% of trainees offered job
on qualification (2006) **94%**
% of assistants (as at 1/9/06)
who joined as trainees **72%**
% of partners (as at 1/9/06)
who joined as trainees **78%**

Trethowans

The Director General's House, Rockstone Place, Southampton, SO15 2EP
Tel: 023 8032 1000   Fax: 023 8032 1001
Email: kate.lemont@trethowans.com
Web: www.trethowans.com

firm profile

A leading regional practice in the South of England, offering a comprehensive range of services (except criminal) for businesses and individuals throughout the UK. Commercial clients range from start-ups to larger corporates, with a particular emphasis on owner-managed businesses. The commercial services offered are comparable to those of a London practice, but a competitive price structure and direct partner involvement are key bases for differentiation. Partners and fee-earners offer genuine expertise in their respective fields, and acknowledged reputations include property, employment, commercial/corporate work and licensing for national brand names. Private client work is undertaken across all sites with the Salisbury office at its core. The firm aims to adopt an open and forward-thinking approach to work and strongly believes in gaining and maintaining a thorough understanding of clients' objectives. Where necessary, specialist teams are built to ensure the optimum level of expertise. The firm has 20 partners and achieved the Law Society's Lexcel Accreditation in 2002.

main areas of work

The breadth of the firm's practice areas provides a broad experience for trainees across a comprehensive range of areas: corporate, commercial, commercial property, commercial litigation, employment, personal injury, clinical negligence, residential property, landed estates and agriculture, family and private client work, (wills, probate, trusts and tax).

trainee profile

Trainees should possess sound academic abilities and be able to demonstrate commercial acumen. Flexibility, ambition and enthusiasm are valued. Candidates should be good communicators and adopt a problem solving approach to client work.

training environment

The firm's trainee solicitors normally undertake four separate specialist seats, each lasting six months. Trethowans offers a flexible approach in deciding trainees' seats to suit individual needs, while providing a broad training programme in accordance with the Law Society's guidelines. Trainees work closely with the supervising fee-earner/partner to whom they are responsible and are appraised every six months. This enables the trainee scheme to be continually evaluated and also ensures that the highest possible standards are maintained. Prospects for trainees are excellent – most trainees are offered a post as an assistant solicitor at the end of their training contract.

benefits

Incremental holiday entitlement up to 28 days, contributory pension scheme, death in service benefit, PHI scheme, performance-related bonus scheme, car parking, new staff recruitment bonus, company car insurance scheme, childcare voucher scheme.

sponsorship & awards

Course fees paid for LPC.

Partners	20
Assistant Solicitors	24
Total Trainees	6

contact
Kate Lemont
023 8082 0503

method of application
Applications by covering letter and application form (available online)

selection procedure
Two stage process; interview and assessment day

closing date for 2009
27 July 2007

application
Training contracts p.a. **3-4**
Applications p.a. **250+**
% interviewed p.a. **10%**
Required degree grade **2:1**

training
Salary: in excess of Law Society minimum
Holiday entitlement **23 days**

post-qualification
Market rate
% of trainees offered position on qualification
66%

Regional offices
Salisbury, Southampton

TRETHOWANS

Trowers & Hamlins

Sceptre Court, 40 Tower Hill, London EC3N 4DX
Tel: (020) 7423 8000 Fax: (020) 7423 8001
Email: hstallabrass@trowers.com
Website: www.trowers.com

Partners	92
Assistant Solicitors	168
Total Trainees	35

contact
Heather Stallabrass,
Graduate Recruitment
Officer

method of application
Online application form

selection procedure
Interviews, psychometric
tests & practical test

closing date for 2009
1 August 2007

application
Training contracts p.a. **20**
Applications p.a. **1,600**
% interviewed p.a. **4%**
Required degree grade **2:1+**

training
Salary (subject to review)
1st year £28,000
2nd year £30,000
Holiday entitlement **25 days**
% of trainees with a
non-law degree p.a. **40%**
No. of seats available
abroad p.a. **8-12**

post-qualification
Salary (2006) **£50,000**
% of trainees offered job
on qualification (2006) **100%**

offices
London, Exeter, Manchester,
Abu Dhabi, Dubai, Oman,
Bahrain and Cairo

firm profile

Being one of only nine law firms who were ranked in the 2006 "Sunday Times Best Companies to Work for" is one reason why Trowers & Hamlins is a desirable law firm to train with. Based in the City, they are a medium sized international firm with offices in the UK and the Middle East. With specialisms ranging from Housing and Urban Regeneration to Litigation, Islamic Finance and international infrastructure projects, they are one of the few firms who are able to boast a 100% trainee retention rate. Their training contracts offer the prospects of work in their London, regional or Middle Eastern offices, and have a maximum of six trainees abroad every six months. As well as excellent client focused opportunities, they also offer the chance to get involved with community projects and pro bono work. Sound good? Then read on...

main areas of work

Being the number one firm for social housing projects, it's obvious that they cover a variety of property work (housing, public sector & commercial). But that's not all they do. They also have award winning projects and construction and structured finance teams and Chambers & Partners consistently confirm their status as one of the No 1 firms in the Middle East. Their other major practice areas include corporate, banking and finance, employment, litigation, private client and commercial property.

trainee profile

Excellent academics are, of course, essential. However, the firm believes in the merits of having a diverse workforce. Their commitment to this is demonstrated by their recent 4th position in "The Lawyer's" Ethnicity League Table (for the Commission for Racial Equality/Black Solicitors Network). They encourage applications from all backgrounds and disciplines. They look for candidates who combine a passion for the law with commercial awareness but who are real individuals. If you possess excellent communication and analytical skills, are a strong and effective team player who wants to work in a fast paced, challenging but fulfilling environment then they want to hear from you.

training environment

The firm prides itself on the quality of training that they offer. You will typically rotate around four departments sitting with either a Partner or a Senior Solicitor. Client contact is something they encourage from an early stage and you will find that you are quickly given real responsibility. Their dedication to your training is further demonstrated through their bespoke trainee development programme.

benefits

25 days holiday, bonus schemes, pension and health care (after 6 months), life assurance, interest free season ticket loan, subsidised staff restaurant and wide choice of social events.

vacation placements

Places for 2007: 25-30; Duration: 2 weeks; Remuneration: £225 p.w. (London); Location: London and Manchester; Closing Date: 1 March 2007; Open Day: June 2007.

sponsorship & awards

GDL and LPC fees paid together with a maintenance grant of £5,500 (£6,000 for London) p.a..

 trowers & hamlins

Vertex Law LLP

39 Kings Hill Avenue, Kings Hill, West Malling, Kent, ME19 4SD
Tel: (0870) 084 4040 Fax: (0870) 084 4041
Email: robert.dodgson@vertexlaw.co.uk
Website: www.vertexlaw.co.uk

firm profile
Vertex Law LLP is a dynamic legal business featuring some of the South East's most experienced corporate and commercial lawyers, recognised as leaders in their field. Founded in October 2004, Vertex works on the principle that a law firm must evolve alongside its clients' commercial needs. Staff welfare and reward are a key part of the ethos.

main areas of work
Vertex was formed with the specific intention of only serving a corporate and commercial client base and covers the following areas: commercial and finance, commercial property and environmental, dispute resolution, mergers and acquisitions, private and public equity and technology, with a fully outsourced and established relationship for the provision of employment, human resources, employee benefits and pensions advice.

trainee profile
Excellent communication skills, a good academic record and a passion to work in a truly commercial environment are pre-requisites.

training environment
A fully supervised and structured programme will involve four six month seats covering areas such as Corporate, Dispute Resolution, Technology and Property which will include regular reviews by the relevant supervisors within each seat. Exposure to "real" work, clients and the chance to develop relationships with the region's other leading advisors would come at an early stage, as will responsibility.

benefits
Private medical insurance, life assurance, pension, paid professional memberships and subscriptions and 25 days holiday.

sponsorship & awards
Discretionary LPC Funding on the basis of 50% fees paid and 50% interest free loan.

Partners	9
Assistant Solicitors	11
Total Trainees	0

contact
Robert Dodgson
(0870) 084 4003

method of application
Online application form via website

selection procedure
Trainee day and interview; second interview

closing date for 2008
31 December 2008

application
Training contracts p.a. 2
Required degree grade 2:1
(occasional exceptions)

training
Salary
1st year £21,000
2nd year £23,000
Holiday entitlement 25 days

Walker Morris

Kings Court, 12 King Street, Leeds LS1 2HL
Tel: (0113) 283 2500 Fax: (0113) 245 9412
Email: hellograduates@walkermorris.co.uk
Website: www.walkermorris.co.uk

firm profile
Based in Leeds, Walker Morris is one of the largest commercial law firms in the North, with over 740 people, providing a full range of legal services to commercial and private clients both nationally and internationally.

main areas of work
Litigation 40%; property 27%; company and commercial 26%; private clients 2%; tax 2%; other 3%.

trainee profile
Bright, articulate, highly motivated individuals who will thrive on early responsibility in a demanding yet friendly environment.

training environment
Trainees commence with an induction programme, before spending four months in each main department (commercial property, corporate and commercial litigation). Trainees can choose in which departments they wish to spend their second year. Formal training will include lectures, interactive workshops, seminars, interactive video and e-learning. The PSC covers the compulsory elements and the electives consist of a variety of specially tailored skills programmes. Individual IT training is provided. Opportunities can also arise for secondments to some of the firm's major clients. Emphasis is placed on teamwork, inside and outside the office. The firm's social and sporting activities are an important part of its culture and are organised by a committee drawn from all levels of the firm. A trainee solicitors' committee represents the trainees in the firm but also organises events and liaises with the Leeds Trainee Solicitors Group.

vacation placements
Places for 2007: 45 over 3 weeks; Duration: 1 week; Remuneration: £180 p.w.; Closing Date: 28 February 2007.

sponsorship & awards
LPC & PGDL fees plus maintenance of £5,000.

Partners	45
Assistant Solicitors	110
Total Trainees	30

contact
Tom Peel

method of application
Online application form

selection procedure
Telephone & face-to-face interviews

closing date for 2009
31 July 2007

application
Training contracts p.a. **18**
Applications p.a.
Approx. 800
% interviewed p.a.
Telephone **16%**
Face to face **8%**
Required degree grade **2:1**

training
Salary
1st year (2006) £20,000
2nd year (2006) £22,000
Holiday entitlement **24 days**
% of trainees with a
non-law degree p.a.
30% on average

post-qualification
Salary (2006) **£34,000**
% of trainees offered job
on qualification (2006) **80%**
% of assistants (as at 1/7/06)
who joined as trainees **60%**
% of partners (as at 1/7/06)
who joined as trainees **50%**

Ward Hadaway

Sandgate House, 102 Quayside, Newcastle upon Tyne NE1 3DX
Tel: (0191) 204 4000 Fax: (0191) 204 4098
Email: recruitment@wardhadaway.com
Website: www.wardhadaway.com

firm profile

Ward Hadaway is one of the most progressive law firms in the North East and is firmly established as one of the region's heavyweights. The firm attracts some of the most ambitious businesses in the region and its client base includes a large number of plcs, new start-ups and well established private companies.

As a business founded and located in the North East, the firm has grown rapidly, investing heavily in developing its existing people, and recruiting further outstanding individuals from inside and outside of the region. The firm is listed in the top 100 UK law firms.

main areas of work

Corporate finance, commercial, commercial property, planning, debt recovery, dispute resolution, technology, intellectual property, healthcare, employment, construction, licensing and private client services.

trainee profile

The usual academic and professional qualifications are sought. Sound commercial and business awareness are essential as is the need to demonstrate strong communication skills, enthusiasm and flexibility. Candidates will be able to demonstrate excellent interpersonal and analytical skills.

training environment

The training contract is structured around four seats (property, company/commercial, litigation and private client) each of six months duration. At regular intervals, and each time you are due to change seat, you will have the opportunity to discuss the experience you would like to gain during your training contract. The firm will always try to give high priority to your preferences. You will work closely with a partner or associate which will enable you to learn how to deal with different situations. Your practical experience will also be complemented by an extensive programme of seminars and lectures. All trainees are allocated a 'buddy', usually a second year trainee or newly qualified solicitor, who can provide as much practical advice and guidance as possible during your training. The firm has an active Social Committee and offers a full range of sporting and social events.

benefits

23 days holiday (26 after five years service), death in service insurance, contributory pension, flexible holiday scheme.

vacation placements

Applications for summer vacation placements should be received by 28 February 2007. Duration one week.

sponsorship & awards

CPE & LPC fees paid and £2,000 interest-free loan.

| Partners | 58 |
| Total Trainees | 20 |

contact
Carol Butts
Head of HR

method of application
Application form & covering letter

selection procedure
Assessment Centre and interview

closing date for 2009
31 July 2007

application
Training contracts p.a. **10**
Applications p.a. **400+**
% interviewed p.a. **10%**
Required degree grade **2:1**

training
Salary
1st year (2005) **£18,500**
2nd year (2005) **£19,500**
Holiday entitlement **23 days**
% of trainees with a
non-law degree p.a. **Varies**

post-qualification
Salary (2006)
£33,750

Watson Burton LLP

1 St James' Gate, Newcastle upon Tyne NE99 1YQ
Tel: (0191) 244 4444 Fax: (0191) 244 4500
Email: enquiries@watsonburton.com
Website: www.watsonburton.com

Partners	39
Assistant Solicitors	60
Total Trainees	16

firm profile

Watson Burton LLP is one of the top law firms in the North of England with almost 200 years' experience and a well-earned reputation for helping its clients succeed. Over the last few years the firm has become one of the fastest-growing law firms in the country operating from offices in Newcastle and Leeds. The senior partner was recognised in The Lawyer's Hot 100. This is the definitive run down of the 'new breed' shaping the legal profession. And the firm as a whole has been recognised by The Lawyer Magazine as "Ones to Watch" and quoted as "the fastest organically growing UK practice" for the second year running.

For the firm's trainees, this represents an exciting time to join the firm, providing you with an opportunity to work across the full range of legal services for a leading law firm that is going places.

contact
Margaret Cay
(0191) 244 4301
margaret.cay@watsonburton.com

method of application
Download & complete the application form on the website, return along with a covering letter, to Margaret Cay, stating which office you wish to be considered for.

closing date for 2009
15 July 2007

main areas of work

Watson Burton LLP's business is mainly commercial and they have particular strengths in business advice, property services, employment, dispute resolution, debt recovery, professions and insurance, technology, IP and media, corporate finance, education and wealth protection. In addition to providing the full range of legal services, they have recently launched a brand-new sports law unit and they have the largest construction and engineering practice outside of London voted number one by The Legal 500.

application
Training contracts p.a. **7**
Applications p.a.
around **1,000**
% interviewed p.a. **2%**
Required degree grade **2:1**

trainee profile

The firm seeks to recruit talented and bright law graduates with a flair for communication and a common sense approach to business. They value an approachable, down to earth attitude. This way they can continue their track record in first-rate client service and can continue to put their clients first. Although law graduates are preferred, the firm's primary focus is on character and intellectual strength, and outstanding graduates of other disciplines are always considered. They have positions in both the Newcastle and Leeds offices and recruit separately to appoint trainees into these positions.

training
Salary
£16,750 plus Leeds weighting for Leeds based trainees, rising by £1,500 over the two year training period, plus an annual cost of living increase and salary review in May of each year.

training environment

The firm provides top-class training from modern office environments in both Leeds and Newcastle. They have the best technology and the right resources to provide a thorough and comprehensive introduction to the law. And they have a vast team of experienced lawyers who you can call on for assistance and guidance where needed. Watson Burton LLP's training programme includes both in-house and external seminars. Trainees are encouraged to assist in the firm's marketing from day one. Alongside careful and regular supervision, they offer trainees a high level of responsibility at an early stage.

post-qualification
Salary
Not less than £34,000
% of trainees offered job on qualification (2005)
100%

regional offices
Newcastle & Leeds

sponsorship & benefits

The firm provides ample study leave, offers paid professional memberships and subscriptions, and give full payment for LPC fees.

Watson, Farley & Williams LLP

15 Appold Street, London EC2A 2HB
Tel: (020) 7814 8000 Fax: (020) 7814 8017
Email: graduates@wfw.com
Website: www.wfw.com

firm profile
Established in 1982, Watson, Farley & Williams has its strengths in corporate, banking and asset finance, particularly ship and aircraft finance. The firm aims to provide a superior service in specialist areas and to build long-lasting relationships with its clients.

main areas of work
Shipping; ship finance; aviation; banking; asset finance; corporate; litigation; e-commerce; intellectual property; EU/Competition; taxation; property; insolvency; telecoms; project finance.

trainee profile
Outgoing graduates who exhibit enthusiasm, ambition, self-assurance, initiative and intellectual flair.

training environment
Trainees are introduced to the firm with a comprehensive induction course covering legal topics and practical instruction. Seats are available in at least four of the firm's main areas, aiming to provide trainees with a solid commercial grounding. There is also the opportunity to spend time abroad, working on cross-border transactions. Operating in an informal and friendly atmosphere, trainees will receive support whenever necessary. You will be encouraged to take on early responsibility and play an active role alongside a partner at each stage of your training. The practice encourages continuous learning for all employees and works closely with a number of law lecturers, producing a widely-read 'digest' of legal developments, to which trainees are encouraged to contribute. All modules of the PSC are held in-house. The firm has its own sports teams and organises a variety of social functions.

benefits
Life assurance, PHI, BUPA, STL, pension, subsidised gym membership.

vacation placements
Places for 2007: 30; Duration: 2 weeks; Remuneration: £250 p.w.; Closing Date: 23rd February 2007.

sponsorship & awards
CPE and LPC fees paid and £6,500 maintenance p.a. (£5,500 outside London).

Partners	62
Assistant Solicitors	150
Total Trainees	22

contact
Graduate Recruitment Manager

method of application
Online application

selection procedure
Assessment centre & Interview

closing date for 2009
31 July 2007

application
Training contracts p.a. **12**
Applications p.a. **1,000**
% interviewed p.a. **20-30%**
Required degree grade
Minimum 2:1 & 24 UCAS points or above

training
Salary
1st year (2006) £29,000
2nd year (2006) £33,500
Holiday entitlement **22 days**
% of trainees with a non-law degree p.a. **50%**
No. of seats available abroad p.a. **12**

post-qualification
Salary (2005)
Not less than £50,000 at the time of writing
% of trainees offered job on qualification (2005) **80%**
% of assistants (as at 1/9/04) who joined as trainees **60%**
% of partners (as at 1/9/04) who joined as trainees **4%**

overseas offices
New York, Paris, Piraeus, Singapore, Bangkok, Rome, Hamburg

Wedlake Bell

52 Bedford Row, London, WC1R 4LR
Tel: (020) 7395 3000 Fax: (020) 7395 3100
Email: recruitment@wedlakebell.com
Website: www.wedlakebell.com

firm profile
Wedlake Bell is a medium-sized law firm providing legal advice to businesses and high net worth individuals from around the world. The firm's services are based on a high degree of partner involvement, extensive business and commercial experience and strong technical expertise. The firm has over 80 lawyers in central London and Guernsey, and affiliations with law firms throughout Europe and in the United States.

main areas of work
For the firm's business clients: Banking & asset finance; corporate; corporate tax; business recoveries; commercial intellectual property; information technology; media; commercial property; construction; residential property.
For private individuals: Tax, trusts and wealth protection; offshore services; residential property.

trainee profile
In addition to academic excellence, Wedlake Bell looks for commercial aptitude, flexibility, enthusiasm, a personable nature, confidence, mental agility and computer literacy in its candidates. Languages are not crucial.

training environment
Trainees have four seats of six months across the following areas: corporate, business recoveries, banking, construction, media and IP/IT, employment, pensions, litigation, property and private client. As a trainee the firm encourages you to have direct contact and involvement with clients from an early stage. Trainees will work within highly specialised teams and have a high degree of responsibility. Trainees will be closely supervised by a partner or senior solicitor and become involved in high quality and varied work. The firm is committed to the training and career development of its lawyers and many of its trainees continue their careers with the firm often through to partnership. Wedlake Bell has an informal, creative and co-operative culture with a balanced approach to life.

sponsorship & benefits
LPC fees paid and £2,500 maintenance grant where local authority grant not available. During training contract: pension, travel loans, subsidised gym membership, health and life insurance.

vacation placements
Places for 2007: 8; Duration: 3 weeks in July; Remuneration: £200 p.w.; Closing Date: End of February.

Partners	42
Assistant Solicitors	43
Total Trainees	14

contact
Natalie King

method of application
Application form

selection procedure
Two interviews

closing date for 2009
End of July 2007

application
Training contracts p.a. **7**
Required degree grade **2:1**

training
Salary
1st year (2006) £27,000
2nd year (2006) £29,000
Holiday entitlement
1st year **23 days,**
2nd year **24 days**
% of trainees with a
non-law degree p.a. **50%**

overseas offices
Guernsey

Weightmans

India Buildings, Water Street, Liverpool L2 0GA
Tel: (0151) 227 2601 Fax: (0151) 227 3223
Email: hr@weightmans.com
Website: www.weightmans.com

Partners	82
Trainees p.a.	up to 12
Total staff	700

method of application
online:
www.weightmans.com

closing date for 2009
31 July 2007

other offices
Birmingham, Leicester,
London, Manchester

firm profile

Weightmans is a national firm of solicitors, with offices in Birmingham, Leicester, Liverpool, London and Manchester. There are over 700 people in the firm's dedicated teams, including over 80 partners. Weightmans are the market leader in public sector work, dominant in insurance litigation work and a major commercial law firm.

trainee profile

The firm looks to recruit up to 12 trainee solicitors each year. When considering training contract applications they look for applicants from a variety of academic backgrounds, who can demonstrate an ability to achieve results. Above all, the firm values well motivated candidates with a pragmatic approach, who can make a positive contribution to a team.

training environment

Four seats, over two years, designed to deliver breadth and depth of contentious and non-contentious work. Trainees develop their own caseload and establish client contact, within a well-structured supportive environment. During each seat trainees have two formal and four informal review meetings with their supervisor. The training programme is planned to take account of individual professional ambitions and provide opportunities to work in different locations. Training programmes are geared to developing individuals in a manner that will maximise both their own and the firm's long term potential.

application details

The application form can be found on the firm's website. After 31 July 2007 you will be contacted to let you know whether your application has been successful.

benefits

Weightmans pay a starting salary well above the minimum recommended by the Law Society and this is reviewed every year to ensure that it is competitive. They also offer an excellent benefits package, which includes a pension, health cover, life assurance, 25 days holiday and flexi time. From the moment you accept a training contract with Weightmans, the firm pledges their support to you, paying all course fees for LPC and GDL and inviting you to be part of the team.

www.chambersandpartners.co.uk

Weil, Gotshal & Manges

One South Place, London EC2M 2WG
Tel: (020) 7903 1074 Fax: (020) 7903 0990
Email: graduate.recruitment@weil.com
Website: www.weil.com

firm profile
Weil Gotshal & Manges is a leader in the marketplace for sophisticated, international legal services. With more than 1,200 lawyers across the US, Europe and Asia, the firm serves many of the most successful companies in the world in their high-stakes matters and transactions.

main areas of work
Established in 1996, the London office now has over 110 lawyers. It has grown rapidly to become the second largest of the firm's 20 offices – it is the hub of the firm's European practice. Key areas are private equity, M&A, business finance and restructuring, capital markets, securitisation, banking and finance, dispute resolution and tax. The firm's expertise covers most industries including real estate, manufacturing, financial services, energy, telecommunications, pharmaceuticals, retailing and technology. Due to the international nature of the business, the firm's lawyers are experienced in working closely with their colleagues from other offices – this ensures a co-ordinated approach to providing effective legal solutions efficiently.

vacation placements
Places for 2007 Easter & Summer: 20 places. Closing date for applications by online application form: 14 February 2007.

Partners	**23**
Assistant Solicitors	**73**
Total Trainees	**19**

contact
Jillian Singh

method of application
online application form

closing date for 2009
31 July 2007

application
Training contracts p.a. **12**
Required degree grade **2:1**

training
Salary
1st year (2006) £37,500
Holiday entitlement **23 days**

overseas offices
Austin, Boston, Brussels, Budapest, Dallas, Frankfurt, Houston, Miami, Munich, New York, Paris, Prague, Providence, Silicon Valley, Singapore, Shanghai, Warsaw, Washington DC, Wilmington

White & Case

5 Old Broad Street, London EC2N 1DW
Tel: (020) 7532 1000 Fax: (020) 7532 1001
Email: trainee@whitecase.com
Website: www.whitecase.com/trainee

firm profile
White & Case is a global law firm with more than 1,900 lawyers worldwide. The firm has a network of 36 offices, providing the full range of legal services of the highest quality in virtually every major commercial centre and emerging market. They work with international businesses, financial institutions and governments worldwide on corporate and financial transactions and dispute resolution proceedings. Their clients range from some of the world's longest established and most respected names to many start-up visionaries. The firm's lawyers work on a variety of sophisticated, high-value transactions, many of which feature in the legal press worldwide as the firm's clients achieve firsts in privatisation, cross-border business deals, or major development projects.

main areas of work
Banking & structured finance; capital markets; construction and engineering; corporate (including M&A and private equity); dispute resolution (including arbitration & mediation); employment & benefits; energy, infrastructure, project & asset finance; IP, PPP/PFI; real estate; tax; and telecommunications.

trainee profile
Trainees should be ambitious, creative and work well in teams. They should have an understanding of international commercial issues and have a desire to be involved in high profile, cross-border legal matters.

training environment
Trainees undertake four seats, each of six months in duration. The firm guarantees that one of these seats can be spent in Asia, Europe or Africa. Regardless of where they work, trainees get a high level of partner and senior associate contact from day one, ensuring they receive high quality, stimulating and rewarding work. Trainees are encouraged to take early responsibility and there is a strong emphasis on practical hands-on training, together with plenty of support and feedback. The firm recruits and develops trainee solicitors with the aim of retaining them on qualification.

benefits
The firm operates a flexible benefits scheme, through which you can select the benefits you wish to receive. Currently, the benefits include private medial insurance, dental insurance, life assurance, pension, critical illness insurance, travel insurance, retail vouchers and gym membership.

vacation placements
Places for 2007: 20 one-week Easter placements and 40 two-week Summer placements available. Remuneration: £300 per week; Closing Date: 31 January 2007.

sponsorship & awards
GDL and LPC fees paid and £7,500 maintenance p.a. Prizes for commendation and distinction for LPC.

Partners	56
Assistant Solicitors	180
Total Trainees	52

contact
Ms Emma Fernandes

method of application
Online application via firm website

selection procedure
Interview

closing date for 2009
31 July 2007

application
Training contracts p.a. **25-30**
Applications p.a. **1,600**
Required degree grade **2:1**

training
Salary
£36,000, rising by £1,000 every 6 months
Holiday entitlement **25 days**

All trainees are guaranteed to spend a seat overseas

post-qualification
Salary (2006) **£67,500**

overseas offices
Almaty, Ankara, Bangkok, Beijing, Berlin, Bombay, Bratislava, Brussels, Budapest, Dresden, Düsseldorf, Frankfurt, Hamburg, Helsinki, Hong Kong, Istanbul, Johannesburg, London, Los Angeles, Mexico City, Miami, Milan, Moscow, Munich, New York, Palo Alto, Paris, Prague, Riyadh, São Paulo, Singapore, Shanghai, Stockholm, Tokyo, Warsaw, Washington DC

Wiggin LLP

95 The Promenade, Cheltenham GL50 1WG
Tel: (01242) 224114 Fax: (01242) 224223
6 Cavendish Place, London, W1G 9NB
Tel: (020) 7612 9612 Fax: (020) 7612 9611
Email: law@wiggin.co.uk Website: www.wiggin.co.uk

Partners	12
Assistant Solicitors	18
Total Trainees	6

contact
Office Manager

firm profile
Wiggin are experts in the constantly evolving field of media law. They focus exclusively on media with particular emphasis on film, music, sport, gaming, technology, broadcast and publishing. They are recognised for the uncompromising excellence of their work and an unrelenting determination to deliver the best possible results for their media clients. In over 10 years they have earned an international reputation for their innovative approach, fresh thinking and cutting edge experience in media law; a sector that is changing with mesmerizing speed. The firm offers a highly personalised relationship, working in partnership with its clients to address the complex legal challenges that the fast evolving media industry presents. They have the knowledge and experience, as well as the commitment and confidence, to deliver straightforward and genuine advice motivated only by the need to achieve the best possible outcome for clients. Based primarily out of their Cheltenham office, and also in London, and with blue-chip clients based all over the World (primarily London and the west coast of America) the firm goes to where clients need them to be.

method of application
Online application only –
www.wiggin.co.uk

selection procedure
Two-day selection

closing date for 2009
31 July 2007

application
Training contracts p.a. **3**
Applications p.a. **500**
% interviewed p.a. **8%**
Required degree grade **2:1**

main areas of work
Commercial 42%, Corporate 12%, Litigation 42%, Property 4%.

trainee profile
If you want to experience high profile media issues in a forward thinking environment then contact Wiggin. They're looking for you if you can demonstrate a passion for media and the law, strong academic ability and a commitment to success... One word of warning though, their seats are not for the faint hearted! They need trainees that relish hard work and a challenge. As each seat is focused on media it is fiercely competitive but if you think you've got what it takes they want to hear from you. They'll be at the law fairs so come and see what they are all about.

training
Salary
1st year (2005) £26,500
2nd year (2005) £31,500
Holiday entitlement **20 days**
+ one day per annum up
to max 25 days
% of trainees with a
non-law degree p.a. **50%**

training environment
Training is split into four seats and these will be allocated from company/commercial, commercial media (2 seats), media litigation, employment, film and property. Although based at the Cheltenham office, you will be meeting clients in London and could end up on a six-month secondment there with the British Phonographic Industry (the record industries trade association).
They don't want you to do the photocopying. Their trainees are encouraged to take an active role in transactions, assume responsibility and deal directly with clients. In-house seminars are held regularly and training reviews are held every three months. You'll get an experience just like your friends in the City but within the exciting and niche area of media law and within a firm small enough to recognise the importance of a personal approach.

post-qualification
Salary (2005) **£44,000**
% of trainees offered job
on qualification (2005) **100%**
% of assistants (as at 2005)
who joined as trainees **29%**
% of partners (as at 2005)
who joined as trainees **25%**

benefits
Life assurance, private health cover, pension scheme, permanent health insurance, gym membership at corporate rates.

sponsorship & awards
PgDL and LPC fees and £3,500 maintenance p.a.

Withers LLP

16 Old Bailey, London EC4M 7EG
Tel: (020) 7597 6000 Fax: (020) 7329 2534
Email: emma.macdonald@withersworldwide.com
Website: www.withersrecruitment.com

firm profile

Withers LLP is the first international law firm dedicated to the business and personal interests of successful people, their families, their businesses and their advisers. With 95 Partners and over 550 people, Withers serves its diverse and global client base through a choice of offices in London, Milan, Geneva, New York, Greenwich (USA) and New Haven (USA).

Withers' reputation in commercial law along with its status as the largest private client team in Europe and leading Family team sets it apart from other City firms.

main areas of work

The firm has unparalleled expertise in commercial and tax law, trusts, estate planning, litigation, employment and family law and any legal issues facing high net worth individuals.

Withers provides integrated solutions to the international legal and tax needs of their clients, whether this means restructuring their own assets, buying or selling businesses or properties, coping with divorce, terminating employment or setting up charitable foundations.

clients

Withers' international client base is diverse including more than 15% of those mentioned on the Times Rich List and a significant number of those on the Forbes 400 list of the Richest Americans.

training environment

Trainees spend six months in four different departments – choosing between Private client, Family, Litigation, Charities, Corporate, IP or Property. Italian speaking trainees have the opportunity to spend six months in the Milan office. On-the-job training is supplemented by the firm's in-house and trainee-specific training programmes. Buddy and Mentor systems ensure that trainees are fully supported from the outset.

benefits

Private medical insurance, life assurance, contributory pension plan, bonus, season ticket loan, subsidised café, social events, PC purchase scheme, Denplan.

work experience placements

Two-week Easter and Summer vacation placements are available in either the London or Milan offices. The firm's scheme was nominated for 'The Best Vacation Scheme' award in the 2006 LawCareers.Net Awards. Apply online by 31 January 2007 for places in 2007.

sponsorship & awards

Fees plus £5,000 maintenance for both the GDL and LPC are paid. An award is paid to those attaining a distinction at Law School.

Partners	95
Legal Staff	253
Total Trainees	26

contact
Emma MacDonald
Senior Recruitment Officer

method of application
Application form (available online)

selection procedure
2 interviews incl. written exercise and presentation

closing dates for 2009
training scheme:
31 July 2007
2007 work experience:
31 January 2007

application
Training contracts p.a. **14**
Applications p.a. **1,000**
% interviewed p.a. **10%**
Required degree grade **2:1**

training
Salary
1st year (2006) £28,750
2nd year (2006) £30,000
Holiday entitlement **23 days**
% of trainees with a
non-law degree p.a. **50%**

post-qualification
Salary (2006) **£48,000**

overseas offices
Milan, Geneva, Greenwich (USA), New York, New Haven

Wollastons

Brierly Place, New London Road, Chelmsford, Essex CM2 0AP
Tel: (01245) 211211 Fax: (01245) 354764
Email: graduate.recruitment@wollastons.co.uk
Website: www.wollastons.co.uk

firm profile
Wollastons is a dynamic, regional law firm,widely recognised as the leading, commercial practice in Essex. Wollastons has a strong reputation as a forward-thinking and energetic organisation, offering high levels of service to both businesses and private clients. The firm's first-class resources, including sophisticated IT, and the lively atmosphere attracts high calibre lawyers, keen to work in a modern, professional environment. The Investors in People accreditation demonstrates a strong commitment to staff development and training at all levels.

main areas of work
Main practice areas include corporate and commercial; commercial property; commercial disputes; employment; planning and property disputes; private client and family.

trainee profile
Applications are welcomed from able and ambitious graduates with a 2:1 degree. Candidates should have a commercial outlook, be confident, outgoing and able to demonstrate a wide range of interests. A link with the Essex area would be desirable.

training environment
Trainees have four six-month seats. These will normally include: company and commercial; commercial disputes; commercial property and employment. Trainees sit with a partner or a senior solicitor and form an integral part of the team. Trainees are fully involved in a wide range of interesting work and, although work is closely checked, trainees are encouraged to take responsibility from an early stage. The firm is very friendly and informal and trainees receive a great deal of individual attention and support. Progress is kept under constant review with mid-seat and end of seat appraisals.

sponsorship & awards
LPC fees paid.

Partners	**13**
Fee-earners	**42**
Total Trainees	**4 (2 p.a.)**

contact
Jo Goode, Graduate Recruitment Manager
(01245) 211253

method of application
CV and application form, see website for details

selection procedure
3 stage interview process

closing date for 2009
1 November 2007

application
Training contracts p.a. **2**
Applications p.a. **Approx 500**
Interviewed p.a. **Approx 50**
Required degree grade **2:1**

training
Salary
1st year £22,000
2nd year £23,000

INVESTOR IN PEOPLE

Wragge & Co LLP

55 Colmore Row, Birmingham B3 2AS
Tel: Freephone (0800) 096 9610
Email: gradmail@wragge.com
Website: www.wragge.com/graduate

firm profile

Wragge & Co is a major UK law firm providing a full-service to some of the world's largest and most successful organisations. Working from London or Birmingham on high profile national and international instructions, you will be part of a team passionate about providing the very best client service.

Wragge & Co is a relationship firm, taking time to form lasting relationships with clients to ensure they really understand what makes a business tick.

Relationships within the firm are just as important, working together to support colleagues and clients alike. This effort has been recognised with their highest position in the Financial Times 50 Best Workplaces – ranked 13 – the only law firm to make the list. They also came 39th in the Sunday Times 100 Best Companies to Work For.

But why not hear what the trainees have to say? Their views ensured the firm were number one in the 2005 Lex 100 table of the UK's 100 top law firms.

main areas of work

The firm has a national reputation in many areas, including dispute resolution, employment, tax, IP, and transport and utilities. It also has the UK's third largest real estate group and leading practices in corporate, construction, banking and pensions. The quality of its work is reflected in the firm's client list, which includes British Airways, Marks & Spencer and McDonald's.

trainee profile

The firm is looking for graduates of 2:1 standard at degree level, with some legal or commercial work experience gained either via a holiday job or a previous career. You should be practical, with a common sense and problem solving approach to work, and be able to show adaptability, enthusiasm and ambition.

training environment

The firm aims to transform its trainees into high quality, commercially-minded lawyers. You will spend six months in four different practice areas, usually including real estate, corporate and litigation, with a chance to specialise in a seat of your choice.

benefits

The firm has a comprehensive benefits package.

sponsorship

The firm will provide your tuition fees for LPC and GDL and a maintenance grant.

vacation placements

Easter and summer vacation placements are run at Wragge & Co. Again, you can apply on-line at www.wragge.com/graduate (paper application form available on request). The closing date for applications is 31 January 2007.

Partners	111
Assistant Solicitors	419
Total Trainees	51

contact
Joanne Dowsett,
Graduate Recruitment Advisor

method of application
Applications are made
online at
www.wragge.com/graduate

selection procedure
Telephone discussion &
assessment day

closing date
Sept 2009/March 2010: 31 July
2007. If you are a non-law
student, please complete
your application form as
soon as possible, as the
firm will be running assessment days over the forth-
coming year

application
Training contracts p.a. **30**
Applications p.a. **1,000**
% interviewed p.a. **25%**
Required degree grade **2:1**

training
Salary Birmingham (Sept 2006)
1st year £22,000
2nd year £25,000
Holiday entitlement **25 days**
% of trainees with a
non-law degree p.a. **Varies**

post-qualification
Salary (2006)
Birmingham £36,000
London £51,000
% of trainees offered job
on qualification
(Sept 2006) **100%**

Wragge & co LLP is a Limited Liability Partnership

barristers

barristers timetable

law students • penultimate undergraduate year	non-law students • final year
Throughout the year	Start thinking about getting some relevant work experience. Do plenty of research into chambers/mini-pupillages
By the end of January	Apply for the GDL
By the end of April	Apply for a pupillage under the year early scheme on OLPAS
May	Apply for a GDL scholarship from an Inn of Court. If successful, join that Inn
June to September	Do pre-GDL mini-pupillages
September/October 2007	Start final year of degree / Start GDL
November	By November apply through BVC Online for the BVC. Apply to an Inn of Court for a scholarship
During final year/GDL	Apply for pupillage to non-OLPAS sets. Do mini-pupillages
April	Before 30th April apply for pupillage through OLPAS
June	Apply for Inn membership
September 2008	Start the BVC. Apply through the September tranche of OLPAS; make further pupillage applications to non-OLPAS sets
April	If unsuccessful last year, apply for pupillage before 30th April
June	Finish BVC
September	Apply for pupillage through OLPAS if you have yet to be successful
October 2009	Start pupillage
Summer	Be offered tenancy at your pupillage chambers or apply for tenancy or a 3rd six elsewhere
October 2010	Start tenancy
2040	Be appointed to the High Court Bench
2050	Get slapped on the wrist by DCA for falling asleep in court

www.chambersandpartners.co.uk

barcode

Don't let the often curious terms used at the Bar confuse or intimidate you!

barrister – a member of the Bar of England and Wales.

bench – the judiciary.

bencher – a senior member of an Inn of Court. Usually silks and judges, known as masters of the bench.

brief – the documents setting out case instructions.

bvc – the Bar Vocational Course. Currently, its successful completion entitles you to call yourself a barrister in non-legal situations (ie dinner parties), but does not of itself give you rights of audience. Moves are afoot to require part of pupillage to have been completed before the title is conferred.

bvc online – the application system through which applications to Bar school must be made.

cab-rank rule – self-employed barristers cannot refuse instructions if they have the time and experience to undertake the case. You cannot refuse to represent someone because you find their opinions or actions objectionable.

call – the ceremony whereby you become a barrister

chambers – a group of barristers in independent practice who have joined together to share the costs of practising. Chambers is also the name used for a judge's private office.

circuit – The courts of England and Wales are divided into six circuits: North Eastern, Northern, Midland & Oxford, South Eastern, Western, and Wales & Chester circuits.

clerk – administrator/manager in chambers who organises work for barristers and payment of fees, etc

counsel – a barrister.

cracked-trial – a case that is concluded without a trial. This will be because the defendant offers an acceptable plea or the prosecution offers no evidence. Cracked and ineffective trials (where there is a lack of court time or the defendant or a witness does not attend) frustrate the bench and are considered a waste of money.

devilling – (paid) work done by a junior member of chambers for a more senior member.

employed bar – some barristers do not engage in private practice at chambers, but are employed full-time by a company or public body.

first and second six – pupillages are divided into two six-month periods. Most chambers now only offer 12-month pupillages, however it is still possible to undertake the two sixes at different sets.

inns of court – ancient institutions that alone have the power to 'make' barristers. There was a time when there was a proliferation of them but now there are only four: Gray's Inn, Inner Temple, Lincoln's Inn and Middle Temple.

junior – a barrister not yet appointed silk. Note: older juniors are known as senior juniors.

junior brief – a case on which a junior is led by a senior. Such cases are too much work for one barrister alone and may involve a lot of research or run for a long time. Ordinarily, junior counsel will not conduct advocacy.

keeping term – eating the dinners in hall required to be eligible for call to the Bar.

mini-pupillage – a short period of work experience spent in chambers.

olpas – the Online Pupillage Application System.

pupillage – the year of training undertaken after Bar school and before tenancy.

pupilmaster – a senior barrister with whom a pupil sits and who teaches the pupil. The Bar Council is encouraging the term pupil supervisor.

QC – one of Her Majesty's Counsel, formerly appointed by the Lord Chancellor. The system fell into abeyance in 2004 and has now been revived with a new, more open appointments system.

set – as in a 'set of chambers'.

silk – a QC, so named because of their silk robes.

supervisor – the new name for a pupilmaster.

tenant/tenancy – permission from chambers to join their set and work with them. A 'squatter' is someone who is permitted to use chambers' premises, but is not actually a member of the set. A 'door tenant' is someone who is affiliated with the set, but does not conduct business from chambers' premises.

a shot at the bar

will you make it?

As jobs go, being a barrister is hard to beat for excitement, truly extraordinary experiences, a sense of personal fulfilment and kudos. At the same time the Bar is a highly competitive world in which the hours can be punishing and the work arduous. Equally arduous for many is the process of getting a foot in the door so prepare yourself for the most challenging game of musical chairs you've ever played. Roughly one in three people who enrol on the BVC end up with a pupillage, and one in five from the original number end up with tenancy in chambers. Look at the table below if you think this is an exaggeration.

What you really want to know is will you be one of the lucky ones? This is a hard question to answer, especially for yourself. Meet enough pupils and barristers and you can see what makes someone successful. Ask a chambers recruiter to define the qualities they look for and they will speak in fairly general terms (academic credentials, people skills, analytical skills, commitment, passion, an ability to express ideas) and then round off with a statement to the effect that 'you know a good one when you see one'. If only there was something like a height chart that you could measure your suitability against.

Just because you're really gobby/argumentative/confident and your nan/your boyfriend/the barman at your local says you'd make a great barrister doesn't mean you will. Equally, just because you got 17 A*s in your A-levels and can complete The Times crossword in three minutes doesn't mean

you will either. Those people who make it at the Bar are the ones who offer the right traits for their chosen area of practice. Crime: it's all about guts, personality and a readiness for any challenge. You need an affinity with ordinary people and the way you communicate should draw others in. You need to be to-the-point and down-to-earth more than you need to be a genius. You should be able to assimilate and recall facts easily. Commercial practice is a far more sophisticated game. This part of the Bar is stuffed with brain boxes – especially in Chancery work – and those who love nothing more than to create a masterpiece of written advice. Advocacy is certainly an important element, though it is unlike that displayed at the criminal Bar. Persuading a judge is a different proposition to persuading a jury; someone who can deliver a clever legal argument succinctly will do far better than a charming raconteur.

By reading the **Chambers Reports** and **Barristers Practice Areas** you will understand more about the skills needed in different parts of the Bar.

is the cost of training prohibitive?

Deciding to embark on a career as a barrister could be one of the most expensive life choices you make. The GDL conversion course is quite expensive, the BVC is painfully expensive, and during a poorly funded pupillage year your circumstances are likely to remain impecunious. The Bar Council requires all pupillages to be funded by chambers at a minimum level of £833.33 per month, and many criminal and

	99-00	00-01	01-02	02-03	03-04	04-05	05-06
BVC applicants	2,370	2,252	2,119	2,067	2,570	2,883	n/a
BVC enrolments	1,490	1,407	1,386	1,332	1,406	1,697	n/a
Students passing the BVC	1,201	1,110	1,182	1,121	1,251	n/a	n/a
First six pupils	681	695	812	586	518	571	n/a
Second six pupils	704	700	724	702	557	598	n/a
Pupils awarded tenancy	511	535	541	698	601	544	n/a

Certain figures were unavailable from the Bar Council at the time of going to press. Please check our website.

www.chambersandpartners.co.uk

mixed sets think that figure is just fine. It's a completely different story for pupils at commercial sets as the awards they receive are more akin to those of trainee solicitors at commercial firms, and funds can be advanced for law school. Read the Funding section on page 52 for more ideas on how to pay for law school. Of all the potential sponsors out there, the four Inns of Court have the deepest pockets.

If you thought the Bar would allow you to serve your community and earn a pile of cash, take note. The remuneration for publicly funded work has always been pretty bad and it all came to a head in autumn 2005 when talks between leaders of the Bar and the Lord Chancellor about proposed cuts collapsed. Some criminal barristers started refusing work. Promises of a complete review into the provision of advocacy services calmed passions. Then in July 2006 Lord Carter of Coles published a set of proposals as part of his overarching review/shake-up of the provision of publicly funded legal services. Civil, family and criminal services are all subject to a range of new proposals, not least affecting the way they are funded. The Bar wasn't bowled over by the changes, but there was some good news for younger practitioners in relation to the funding of one-to-ten-day Crown Court cases.

If you thought training as a barrister was a good way to become a highly paid business adviser, don't let us stop you – around 20 barristers in London are thought to be earning £2 million or more per year. For the pupils who make it to tenancy in good-quality sets, the future looks very good indeed and within just a couple of years they can expect to overtake their solicitor colleagues in the money stakes.

Do remember, though, that the Bar is like football in the sense that within any area of practice there are a few Premier League sets and many others in lower divisions. The difference in earnings at the top and the bottom is substantial.

i want to get started

If you're still at university there's plenty you can do to prepare yourself for a shot at the Bar. If there is anything a little outré about your CV – you're mature or you have poor A-levels, for instance – getting a First is a really good idea. 2:1s are two a penny and as for 2:2s, well, if you end up with one of these you'll have to be pretty remarkable in some other respect to persuade a recruiter to give you a try. In general, chambers are much more interested in your undergraduate performance than what you can muster up at Bar School, and for the record we have it on excellent authority that good pupillages can be secured with the scantiest of passes on the GDL. That said, 'Very Competent' grades proliferate on the BVC, so why be awkward and get a 'Competent'?

mini adventures

Let's look a little closer at your commitment to the Bar. The best way to demonstrate that you possess any is to carry out some mini-pupillages, which is just high-falutin' barristerspeak for work experience. They come in two flavours: assessed and unassessed. During an unassessed mini you will observe a barrister in his or her chambers and probably also in court. How much you will be involved in proceedings varies hugely. In the course of a good mini you will sit in on a pre-trial conference (with the client's permission) and will be included in discussions about the law. One person we spoke to was invited to spend nearly every moment from fry-up to nightcap with their supervising barrister, though we suspect this is not the norm. Another reported turning up at chambers on the appointed day only to be told by a clerk to go to a particular court; after finding the court and sitting in the public gallery for a while, they eventually tracked down their putative supervisor in the robing room where they were greeted with something between bemusement and indifference. It is not unheard of for mini-pupils at commercial sets to go days at a time without seeing the inside of a court. Don't become fixed on the idea of spending a whole week with chambers as you may find it easier (and more beneficial) to get a couple of days here and there. Arguably the benefits are the same and you'll be able to compare your experiences.

Some sets will only recruit those who have undertaken an assessed mini-pupillage. These minis are more formal and will keep you on your toes. The most likely scenario is that you'll be given a set of papers to analyse and then be asked to produce a piece of written work. Take notes throughout and don't be afraid to ask your supervisor questions at appropriate moments. Afterwards, write notes on what you saw and learned about the place and the work you did. Think about the quality of any advocacy you observed and what you thought about the lifestyle in general. This will be helpful when completing pupillage application forms and chatting with recruiters at interviews. In fact, approach all relevant 'experience' from now on mindfully and with a pen.

how do i get one?

Not all sets offer mini-pupillages, so start off by checking their websites and making a list of those to which you're going to apply. A set's website will tell you the format your application should take and the person to whom it should be addressed. In general, chambers will want a CV and covering letter.

As with everything else in this game, demand for mini-pupillages is high so apply as you would Calamine lotion on a rash – liberally and at the first sign of an itch for the Bar. This is when personal contacts really come in to their own. People get pupillage by means of whom they know less than some people would have you believe, but getting a mini is different. Speak to any barristers you know and make your intentions clear. If Uncle Eddie dated some woman at 17 Ramshackle Row back in the 80s, get him to contact

her again. She'll either report him to the police as a stalker or you'll get a contact. Most barristers are flattered by the idea of some youngster wanting to follow in their footsteps and are genuinely willing to help. If your little black book isn't overflowing then create your own contacts. Apply to an Inn of Court to be assigned a sponsor, and if you've started dining at your Inn then for goodness sake stop hiding in the corner and schmooze.

Do enough mini-pupillages to give you a good sense of what areas of practice interest you, but if you are close to needing your toes to count them you are in danger of looking like you've nothing else going on in your life.

prizes mean points

The Bar Council prescribes that BVC students undertake a certain amount of pro-bono work. To ensure that you do land on something that interests you and has real weight on a pupillage application form it is a good idea to start researching as soon as possible. There are plenty of ways to get involved in pro bono work and page 31 lists a non-exhaustive selection.

What else should you do? *"Everything you can,"* advises one QC. Get involved with every debating and mooting opportunity that crops up. At law school you'll have the chance to enter mock trial competitions and you might also want to keep an eye out for essay competitions. The scholarships offered by the Inns are not just a way of funding your education – don't underestimate the capacity of a prize or award to mark you out from other well-qualified candidates.

olpas: getting a foot in the door

The Online Pupillage Application System has operated since 2001. It is not compulsory for chambers to participate, but every pupillage provider is required by the Bar Council to advertise its vacancies on the OLPAS website, **www.pupillages.com**. The info is also produced in the *Pupillages and Awards Handbook*, published to coincide with the opening of the online system and the National Pupillage Fair held in March in London. OLPAS has two 'seasons': summer and autumn. The closing date for summer season applications is 30 April, allowing three months for interviews with offers made after 31 July. The autumn season opens at the end of August and closes on 30 September, with just a month for interviews and offers being made after 31 October. A set of chambers may participate in one or other season. It need not participate in either.

Students may apply through OLPAS during as many seasons as they like, but are limited to 12 sets in each. Most LLB candidates make applications during their final year at uni, although some of the top commercial sets encourage students to apply in their penultimate year in an attempt to snap up the best candidates. Twelve-month pupillages are the most convenient option, although it is not unusual for pupils to end up doing a 'first six' in one set and a 'second six' in another.

The beauty of OLPAS is that all correspondence regarding interviews, offers and rejections is sent via e-mail. This is actually likely to lead to RSI as you spend whole days impatiently pressing the 'refresh' button in the hope that a message has landed in your inbox. Some sets show a healthy disdain for the whole shebang and choose to call on that old-fashioned contraption, the mobile telephone.

perfect pitch

Think carefully when choosing where to apply. If you know you're top dollar and that's what you're after then off you go. If you're not sure of your calibre then take a look at the CVs of a chambers' latest recruits. This will give you some indication of the kind of person the set wants. If you didn't go to one of 'those two' universities, why apply exclusively to sets whose members are all dyed-in-the-wool Oxbridge types. Also, you must appear consistent. Chambers won't see which other sets you are applying to, but because of the way the OLPAS form is designed they will see the list of your preferred practice areas.

an exercise in form filling?
Here are our top five tips:

○ **Keep it personal:** Include nothing that you cannot talk about eloquently, evenly passionately. A good example of this is FRU. Who isn't commencing/about to complete their FRU training? If you haven't actually signed out a case, mentioning FRU will look desperate. Anchor your spiel in your own experiences and your application will be more persuasive.

○ **Keep it pithy:** As Shakespeare once said, brevity is the soul of wit. It should also be the spirit of an OLPAS form. For each section you can write no more than 150 words. Keep it concise and this will be plenty. Long sentences can be tedious and your chances are greatly improved if the recruiter stays conscious.

○ **Avoid being trite:** You will be asked to explain why you want to be a barrister and why you are interested in your chosen practice areas. That a career at the Bar offers an attractive combination of academia and practicality is a given. This is the section where you run most danger of getting lost in the crowd so think what the obvious answer is and then write something more meaningful.

○ **Write proper:** 'Practice' is the noun; 'practise' is the verb. If you haven't learnt this already, now is the time. As one senior QC put it: *"Given that this is a job in which a strong command of the English language is paramount, we are often amazed at some of the fundamental errors that crop up in the OLPAS applications."*

○ **Don't make silly mistakes:** Your mantra should go something like this: *"Save, print, check. Save, print, check."* With some sets getting 500 applications, they are itching for a reason to put yours in the bin. Don't give them this one.

olpas is not the only fruit

A good number of sets recruit pupils outside the OLPAS machinery because they don't like its format or timetable. A set's decision not to be part of the online scheme says nothing about its quality: it's more a reflection of their view that their interests will be better served by other means. For example, some chambers choose not to participate because their special interest in aspects of an applicant's background cannot be adequately satisfied by reading a completed OLPAS form.

The application method at each non-OLPAS set will be different; however, all must still advertise vacancies on www.pupillages.com. Research things well in advance to make sure you don't miss any deadlines. As one successful applicant counselled: *"Applying to non-OLPAS sets requires a great deal of motivation. There are a lot of them out there and many of them are very good. They should be taken very seriously."* Some sets choose to mirror the OLPAS timetable in their own application procedures, but many don't and this can bring its own problems. One pupil cautioned: *"The exploding offer phenomenon is a real difficulty. Shortly before my first OLPAS interview I was made a very attractive offer from a non-OLPAS set that I just couldn't pass up. While they were a great set, it did stop me from trying my hand elsewhere."*

expect the spanish inquisition

So you've got an interview – well done. Our first piece of advice: dress like you're going to court not the set of *Ally McBeal*. Opt for neat and discreet with hair tidy, teeth flossed, tie sober, jacket done up. Most first interviews are reasonably painless. The panel will want you to stand out and they will want to like you. Most chambers will be grading you on standard criteria that include everything from intellect to personality. Check their website to see if they publish any guidelines.

As a rough guide, you can expect your first interview to involve a discussion of the hottest topics in your prospective practice area and some gentle investigation into you and your application form. Of course, we need not tell you to read *The Times* every Tuesday, keep your subscription to *Counsel* up to date or suggest you set the Bar Council website as your homepage. Yet, preparation for your interviews should consist of more than boning-up on the law; it is important to be clued-up on current affairs too. And when we say clued-up what we really mean is develop an opinion. "Oh yes, terrorism, isn't it awful" is never going to cut it. Finally, think about what isn't on your CV and how you can account for anything that is missing or disappointing grades. It is probably best to approach these things with honesty rather than creativity but, whichever you go for, prepare your answer well.

For second interviews expect a larger panel made up of a broader cross-section of people from chambers. While the format of the interviews may vary between sets, the panel will always want to assess the depth of your legal knowledge, your advocacy potential and your mettle. Weaknesses on you CV will be sniffed out and pursued with tenacity. Don't let them push you around, if you can support your position then stick to it. Resolve is just as necessary for a career at the Bar as receptivity; they want to know that you can fight your corner.

Criminal and mixed sets will commonly give you an advocacy exercise, such as a bail application or a plea in mitigation (their basic structures will fit on a post-it, so why not note them down and keep with you at all times). Most, if not all, sets will pose a legal problem of some sort, with the amount of preparation time you are given ranging from ten minutes to a week. If you know that this is going to happen then do take an appropriate practitioner's text unless you know that one will be made available to you. That said, chambers generally aren't looking for faultless knowledge of substantive law, but are trying to get an insight into how your mind works. As one seasoned interviewer explained: *"We are more interested in seeing how a candidate approaches a problem than whether or not they get the right answer."*

A second interview is often the time when an ethics question may raise its head. You can prepare by reading the Bar's Code of Conduct, which is available on the Bar Council's website. It's a real page turner.

Of course, to all rules there are exceptions. Some sets only conduct one round of interviews. If you are invited somewhere like this expect the interview to be reasonably long and rigorous. Other chambers don't have a second round but instead host a drinks evening to which all successful first-round interviewees are invited. Sounds like the easy option, but approach with caution and don't get pissed and indiscreet.

pupillage: don't forget your flashes

If you find yourself among the one in three or so who end up with pupillage, you can expect the trials to begin again. How the year is divided varies from set to set. Yet no matter how many pupil supervisors you have, the broad division is between the first, non-practising six months and the 'second six' when pupils are permitted to be on their feet in court. During the first six, pupils are fairly tethered to their supervisor, shadowing them at court, conferences and in chambers. The days of being strategically placed next to a window to protect your master from the offensive glare of the sun are gone. That said, you can't rule out all errand running.

It goes without saying that you must understand the nature of any given task before you embark on it. One beleaguered pupil told us of the day they were loitering in the corridors of the RCJ when a sizable member of chambers asked them to perform an errand. *"He said, 'Dash back to chambers and pick up my court stuff, and don't forget my flashes.' So, off I go, confident that I am the only person this side of The Strand who doesn't know what flashes are. More fool me. No one in chambers has the foggiest, so I grab what I understand to be court dress. As it turned out flashes – which are just bands – were the least of my problems. Unfortunately for me, the man in question shares a room with a petite lady barrister. I am saved from taking him her lacy collar but not her gown. The effect could be likened to covering a giraffe with a pony blanket."*

A second six at a Chancery set is likely to be little different from the first six. Even if entitled to accept a brief to appear in court, because of the nature of the work you will probably still be far too inexperienced to take it. A second six at a busy criminal set, however, could mean court every day. *"I really didn't have a clue the first time I had to get robed up,"* said one young barrister. *"Before leaving chambers I had to get my supervisor to do my collar for me and in the robing room someone kindly told me that my bands were the wrong way round. It should have come as no surprise to me that when I tried to go to the loo my boxers were on wrong too."*

crunch time

Gaining pupillage is not the end of it; gaining tenancy is the real prize. Effectively, an offer of tenancy is an invitation from a set to take space in their chambers and share the services of the clerking and administrative team. It's not exactly a job offer as you will be self-employed, but it can feel rather like one. How many tenants a set takes on post-pupillage is usually as dependent on the amount of space and work available in chambers as on the quality of the candidates. If you are curious about a set's growth you can check to see how many new tenants have joined in recent years by checking the list of members on its website. You can then compare the number of recent additions to the number of pupillages offered in recent years.

Usually tenancies are awarded after a vote of all members of chambers after taking advice from a committee, clerks and possibly also instructing solicitors. Decisions are commonly made in the July of the pupillage year, allowing unsuccessful pupils time to cast around for other tenancy offers or a 'third six' elsewhere. There is evidence to suggest that civil and commercial sets have higher pupil-to-tenant conversion rates than criminal sets. Certainly, it is quite usual for a 12-month criminal pupillage to be followed by a third or subsequent six somewhere other than a pupil's first set. If you mentally prepare yourself for being passed around the houses, you'll be pleasantly surprised if things go more smoothly.

dust yourself off and try again

What if you still don't have pupillage by the time you have finished the BVC? Rather than seeing an enforced year out as a grim prospect, view it as a time to improve your CV and become more marketable. If you are interested in a specialist area of practice consider a master's degree. If the thought of another year in education brings you out in a cold sweat then seek out some useful practical experience. The most obvious answer is to apply for paralegaling and outdoor clerking jobs at law firms. The work you do as a paralegal may give you an enviable understanding of how a case actually works and how solicitors – your future clients – work. As an outdoor clerk you will be in court all the time taking notes. This will give you insight into the procedures and politics of trials. The year might also be spent with an organisation that works in an area related to your legal interest. We have interviewed several lawyers who secured pupillages following a period with a charity or not-for-profit organisation.

and finally…

If we're honest, we don't expect too many readers to have changed their minds about a career at the Bar after reading this section. The one thing that wannabe-barristers have in common is a belief that if anybody is going to succeed then why not them. That's fair enough because self-belief is what will sustain them through the darkest days. Those who do succeed are in for what one sage member of the profession describes as *"quite simply, the best job in the world."*

lincoln's inn
www.lincolnsinn.org.uk

The biggest of the four, beautiful Lincoln's Inn is the setting for the opening scenes in Dickens' Bleak House. Its large membership boasts some A-list celebrities, including Cherie and Tony, and the Inn is favoured by overseas barristers. Students recommended its "free-flowing wine and the great atmosphere." Its library is described as "impossibly grand with stained-glass windows, thick carpets and bad lighting." As well as the usual activities, the Inn organises an annual trip to visit the ECJ, the ECHR and the Hague Tribunal.

inner temple
www.innertemple.org.uk

From Chaucer to Charlie Falconer, this Inn has more history than we've had hot dinners. It is a place for firsts: the first female barrister was a member, as was Dame Elizabeth Butler-Sloss, who became the first female High Court judge and then the first female Lord Justice of the Court of Appeal. It gives some generous scholarships and runs an "excellent advocacy course." Its wood-panelled library has a good collection and air conditioning – "very important in the summer." The Students' Association's social diary is busy and the mooting society is a regular contender in international competitions.

the inns of court

The four ancient Inns of Court bear a striking resemblance to Oxbridge colleges (chapel, hall, library, etc) and were originally places of residence and learning for young barristers. The Inns still perform some important functions: they alone have the power to 'call' a person to the Bar and before you can be called you must 'keep term' by attending 'dinners' or other 'qualifying sessions' organised by the Inns.

Students must join one of the Inns by the June before they start their BVC, but our advice is to investigate what they have to offer much earlier than this as the Inns have millions of pounds to award in annual scholarships to GDL and BVC students as well as to pupils. Take care not to miss the deadlines for applying as these fall earlier than you'd imagine: commonly in the calendar year before the start of the course to which the award relates. You don't have to be a member of an Inn to apply for one; the trick is to make applications and then join the Inn where you've been successful. You must join an Inn if you're going to take its money and having picked one of the four, that's it – you can't then switch. There's a competitive selection process for scholarships, so expect an interview. The panel will look at the usual criteria: academics, commitment to a career at the Bar, etc. With some awards, but certainly not all, the Inn will consider your financial circumstances.

The Inns reserve funds to help students from the regional BVC institutions meet their costs when visiting the Inn, and for students of any BVC provider to help pay for qualifying sessions. There are additional funds for certain international internships. For specific details of the amounts on offer, start by checking the Inns' websites and ask them if they publish any other related material.

The Inns can be a great source of general help and advice to a prospective barrister. If you want to go and visit them just ring to arrange a tour. All have mentoring schemes that will match student members with a practitioner in their chosen field, and they also run marshalling schemes so students can spend a week sitting alongside a judge, observing court proceedings and discussing the case at the end of the day. For pupils there are advocacy workshops and seminars at Cumberland Lodge in the heart of Great Windsor Park. All four Inns offer mooting, whether it be at internal, inter-Inn or national competition level, and the Inns' various students' associations all have active social calendars.

middle temple
www.middletemple.org.uk

As former member Charles Dickens put it, the Middle Temple has "something of a clerkly monkish atmosphere which public offices of law have not disturbed and even legal firms have failed to scare away." Debating is a particular forte and the 'Christmas Revels' are notorious. Students recommend lecture nights for "copious amounts of food and wine and excellent guest speakers."

gray's inn
www.graysinn.org.uk

Here, at the smallest and most traditional Inn, toasting is the order of the day during dinners, particularly on Grand Day when a communal chalice of wine is passed down the table in "pious memory of Good Queen Bess." Students say: "You get to know other students and Benchers really quickly and there are always familiar faces at dinner." Gray's Inn library is described as "quite plain, but good, with the most helpful librarians of the four Inns."

practice areas at the bar

the chancery bar

You'll see from the diagram on page 136 that the High Court has three divisions: Family, Queen's Bench (QBD) and Chancery. Cases are allocated to and heard by the most appropriate division based on their subject matter, but what makes a case suitable for the Chancery Division? Historically it has been the venue for cases with an emphasis on legal principles, foremost among them the concept of equity. Put another way, Chancery work epitomises legal reasoning.

Cases are often categorised as either 'traditional' (trusts, probate, real property, charities and mortgages) or 'commercial' (company law, shareholder cases, partnership, banking, pensions, financial services, insolvency, professional negligence, tax, media and IP). Most Chancery sets will undertake both types of work, albeit with varying emphases.

To muddy the waters, however, the distinction between Chancery practice and commercial practice (historically the latter is dealt with in the QBD) is less apparent than it once was. Barristers at commercial sets can frequently be found on Chancery cases and vice versa, though some areas, such as tax and IP, beg specialisation.

the realities of the job

- This is an area for those who love the law and love to grapple with its most complex aspects. It's all about the application of long-standing legal principles to modern-day situations.
- Boffins beware: you need to be a master of communication and very practical in the legal solutions you offer to clients. Solicitors will come to you with complex and puzzling cases. After unravelling them you must explain legal arguments and principles in such a way that the solicitor and lay client both understand. At the same time, you also need to be able to present your argument to a judge in a persuasive and sophisticated manner.
- While advocacy will be a core element of your work, you will spend most of your time in chambers, perusing papers, considering arguments, drafting pleadings, skeletons and advices, or conducting settlement negotiations.
- Some instructions fly into chambers, need immediate attention and then disappear just as quickly. Others can rumble on for years – although not quite as long as Dickens' Jarndyce v Jarndyce.
- There's plenty of variety in Chancery practice. The traditional side appeals to those more inclined towards human interest – little old lady who signed her house over to the window cleaner, the bonkers billionaire who disinherited his children, or the errant tenants who haven't paid rent for years. Commercial Chancery practitioners get to deal with the blood-on-the-boardroom-table disputes, the Equitable Lifes and the bust-ups between co-writers of million-selling songs.
- Your schedule won't be set by last-minute briefs for next-day court appearances. Instead, you'll need self-discipline and an instinctive sense of exactly how much time and energy you need to devote to each of the instructions on your desk.
- As in any area of practice, at first you'll be instructed on low-value cases – straightforward possession proceedings in the county court, winding-up applications in the Companies Court, appearances before the bankruptcy registrars. In the more prominent sets, you'll be brought in as second or third junior on larger, more complex cases.

some tips

- An excellent academic record is essential. Most pupils in leading sets have a First-class degree, although a surprising number are non-law grads. Whatever you study at university, you should enjoy the analytical process involved in constructing arguments and evaluating the answers to problems. If you're not a natural essay writer, you're unlikely to be a natural-born Chancery practitioner.

- Don't wander into this area by accident. Are you actually interested in equity, trusts, company law, insolvency, IP or tax? If the grit and excitement of crime sounds more appealing then follow your instincts.
- Show an aptitude for public speaking. If you're studying law, get involved in mooting.
- Complete at least a couple of mini-pupillages with – or including – Chancery sets.
- Though not necessarily an accurate portrayal of modern practice, Dickens' novel Bleak House is the ultimate Chancery saga. Give it a whirl, or rent the DVD.

current issues

- The scope of the Chancery Division means that practitioners get involved in the most enormous commercial and public law matters. Chancery barristers were all over the BCCI cases in 2005, as well as Equitable Life and Spectrum. Another Chancery victory was the shaming of Stephen Byers in the Railtrack litigation (Weir & Ors v Secretary of State for Transport/Department of Transport). The Apple v Apple row involved the Beatle's former record company Apple Corps taking the US computer giant to task in what is but the latest battle in a long war. This round was won by Apple Computer, but Apple Corps vows to fight on.
- The amount of international work carried out in the Chancery Division shows no signs of falling off. Russian and Eastern European business affairs are taking up a sizeable amount of court time in the commercial arena, and massive off-shore business and private client trusts in the Cayman Islands, the British Virgin Islands, Bermuda and the Channel Islands means that more barristers than ever are clipping through airport terminals. But no one knows what they're up to and they can't say: multimillion-pound advisory work is as ever kept very quiet.
- The Chancery Bar seems immune to the shrinking work and tumbling brief fees found elsewhere in practice. At this, the Rolls-Royce end of the Bar, practitioners continue to attract not only plenty of high-value, complex domestic cases, but also an increasing number of offshore and cross-border instructions.

the commercial bar

The Commercial Bar handles a variety of business disputes. In its purest definition, a commercial case is heard by the Commercial Court or one of the county court business courts. A broader and more realistic definition includes matters dealt with by both the Queen's Bench and Chancery Divisions of the High Court, and the Technology and Construction Court (TCC). The Commercial Bar deals with disputes in all manner of industries from construction, shipping and insurance to banking, entertainment and manufacturing.

Almost all disputes are contract and/or tort claims, and the Commercial Bar remains rooted in common law. That said, domestic and European legislation is increasingly important and commercial barristers' incomes now reflect the popularity of the English courts with overseas litigants. Cross-border issues including competition law, international public and trade law and conflicts of law are all growing in prominence.

Alternative methods of dispute resolution – usually arbitration or mediation – are also popular because there is some prospect of preserving commercial relationships that would otherwise be destroyed by the litigation process.

the realities of the job

- The barrister's job is to steer the solicitor and lay client through the litigation process, selecting the most appropriate manoeuvres to put them in a better position with their opponent. Clients position themselves through witness statements, pleadings and pre-trial 'interlocutory' skirmishes. The role blends advice and paper advocacy with courtroom advocacy, and much of the barrister's time is spent in chambers, assessing the likelihood of winning, and then probably doing a deal.

- Advocacy is certainly at the centre of the job. Even so, most of it is paper-based, which means that written skills are just as important as oral skills, possibly more so. The good barrister will spot the argument that most others won't see and identify the one that is most likely to be persuasive.

- To build confidence and allow you to get used to the sound of your own voice in court, you will handle your own small cases as a new junior barrister. These will include common law matters such as personal injury, employment cases, possession proceedings and winding-up or bankruptcy applications.

- New juniors become exposed to larger commercial cases by assisting more-senior colleagues. As a 'second junior' you will carry out research and prepare first drafts of documents to assist the 'first junior' and the QC leading the case. Just as importantly, you will observe them in action in court, learning how to cross-examine witnesses and how best to present arguments.

- In time, your own cases will increase in value and complexity: claims relating to shipping, insurance and reinsurance, commodities, banking, and general contractual matters are all

standard fare. Most commercial barristers specialise by building up expertise on cases within a particular industry sector – eg shipping, insurance, entertainment or banking. It gives them the added value that solicitors look for when deciding who to instruct. This added value is usually a product of a barrister's commercial acumen. You have to develop this and be able to understand the client's business objectives. Clearly you should bear a set's specialities in mind when deciding where to accept pupillage.

- Bear in mind also that commercial cases can be very fact-heavy. The evidence for a winning argument can be buried in a room full of papers. The barrister will need to work closely with the instructing solicitor to manage the documentation.

- Are you willing to fully commit yourself to developing your practice? You'll have to work long hours, often under pressure. Furthermore, to survive, your service standards must be impeccable and your style user-friendly. A solicitor could send you something that's urgent or poorly organised, but you can't complain. Even if they ring you late in the day, you need to be obliging. Get into a good set, though, and you can make an exceedingly good living.

some tips

- Competition for pupillage at the commercial Bar is fierce. A first-class degree is commonplace, and you'll need impressive references.

- You also need to be able to show evidence of mooting and debating at university and/or law school.

- Complete at least a couple of mini-pupillages at commercial and common law sets.

- Don't underestimate the value of non-legal work experience; commercial exposure of any kind is going to help you understand the client's perspective and motivations.

current issues

- The trend for huge litigation with multiple interests was nowhere more evident than last year, with massive cases like the BCCI fallout, in which the liquidators of the bank brought a case against the Bank of England (as well as the Bank of India and others in separate cases), which was eventually dropped by Deloitte & Touche, BCCI's liquidators in November 2005, bringing an end to 14-year proceedings. Another massive case was the Equitable Life drama – a £2.6 billion negligence case against former auditor Ernst & Young – that was eventually settled. Spectrum Plus was a third monster: the House of Lords overturned a 2004 decision by the Court of Appeal to clarify the order in which creditors of insolvent companies are paid. Take a look at Taylor Thomson v Christie's (a dispute about £2 million fake Louis XV urns) and HSH Nordbank v Barclays Capital as well.

- In what is seen by some to be enduring faith in the uprightness of British law, a lot of Eastern European and Russian concerns are now brought before the courts here, coinciding with a decline in similar domestic litigation.

- Solicitor-advocates are on the march, although the increase in alternative dispute resolution (ADR) or in-house involvement means that smaller cases are unlikely to demand representation.

- Shrinking small-end work has impacted on the livelihood of junior barristers in common law sets; however the commercial Bar is faring well.

the common law bar

English common law derives from the precedents set by judicial decisions rather than from the contents of statutes. Most common law cases turn on principles of tort and contract and are dealt with in the Queen's Bench Division (QBD) of the High Court and the county courts. At the edges, common law practice blurs into both Chancery and commercial practice. Yet the work undertaken in common law sets is broader still, and one of the most appealing things about working at one of these sets is the variety of work available.

Employment and personal injury are bread and butter for juniors. They also deal with licensing matters, clinical negligence, landlord and tenant, winding-up and bankruptcy applications, and small commercial and contractual disputes. At some sets you'll even get inquests and criminal cases. Common law barristers tend to carry on practising on a full range of cases throughout their careers, but there is an opportunity to begin to specialise between five and ten years' call.

the realities of the job

- Will there be much advocacy? Yes, lots. On average you could expect to be in court three days per week. Even second-six pupils can have their own cases. Small beginnings such as 'noting briefs' (where you attend court simply in order to report back on the proceedings) and masters' and district judges' appointments lead to lower-value 'fast-track' personal injury trials then longer, higher-value, 'multi-track' trials and employment tribunals.

- In addition to minor instructions which they can run solo, newer barristers assist as a junior on more complex cases, conducting research, drafting documents and observing more-senior lawyers in court to learn how to present arguments and cross-examine.

- Interpersonal skills are important. A client

who has never been to court before will be very nervous, and it's your responsibility to put them at ease. This is especially important if they are a witness. They may be expecting someone older than you, but somehow you have to win their trust and confidence.

○ In order to deal with the volume and variety of cases that will come your way you will need a good grasp of the law and the procedural rules of the court, and must be adept at assimilating the facts of each case.

○ At the junior end, work comes in at short notice, so the night before going to court you may have to digest a file of documents. Planning ahead can be difficult; your friends may have to get used to you letting them down at short notice.

○ But it's not all about advocacy. When you're not in court you'll be in chambers, researching, assessing the merits of cases and meeting with solicitors and lay clients. There will also be plenty of statements of claim, defences and opinions to draft.

some tips

○ Though there are a lot of common law sets, pupillages and tenancies don't grow on trees. You'll have to impress to get a foot in the door and then make your mark to secure your next set of instructions.

○ If you want to specialise, thoroughly research the sets you apply to.

○ As ever, mini-pupillages are a good way to show your commitment, and you'll also want to show that you've taken part in mooting and debating.

current issues

○ The trend for mediation and arbitration of disputes has reduced the number of cases going to court, and this has resulted in less small-end work for juniors. The position is also exacerbated by a trend for solicitors to undertake more advocacy themselves, although while solicitor-advocates frequently take on directions hearings, they are still rarely seen at trial.

○ Legal aid cutbacks and conditional fee agreements – especially for PI claims – have definitely affected remuneration. The government is also planning further changes to the public funding of legal services: read **Get Carter** on page 17.

the criminal bar

Horace Rumpole, Henry Farmer in The Brief, Kavanagh QC… most people know more about the criminal Bar than any other part of the legal profession. Are the lives of these courtroom heroes anything like reality? Arguably criminal barristers do need an appreciation for theatre and an innate sense of dramatic timing. But good oratory will only take you so far. A keen tactical sense, an agile understanding of the law and good-time management will also prove invaluable.

Barristers are instructed by solicitors to represent defendants in cases brought before the UK's criminal courts. Lesser offences are increasingly dealt with by solicitors in the magistrates' courts; more serious charges go to the Crown Courts, which are essentially still the domain of barristers. Most defendants prefer this. In the year ending September 2005 there were 905,587 convictions in magistrates' courts and 71,099 in the Crown Court.

The job includes everything from theft, fraud, drugs and driving offences to assaults of varying degrees of severity and murder. Second six pupils cut their teeth on motoring offences, committals and directions hearings in the magistrates' courts, and by the end of their pupillage should expect to be instructed in their own right and not infrequently make it into the Crown Court. Within two or three years junior tenants will probably have seen it all. Their trial work will start small – smaller offences such as common assault – and then move onto ABH, robbery and possession of drugs with intent to supply. Perform well and impress the instructing solicitor and this could lead to a role as a junior on a major Crown Court trial.

A summary of the expanding opportunities at the Crown Prosecution Service is given on page 21.

the realities of the job

- Pupils and juniors rely on the relationships that their seniors and managers have built with instructing solicitors. Although it is important to market yourself in the early years, be relatively subtle. Denigrate others or acquire a reputation as a 'diary watcher' and this will come back and bite you.
- Defendants can be tricky creatures and at times you'll need the patience of a saint. You have to listen to what they have to say, and give them a realistic assessment of their case and the likely ramifications of their stance; you certainly won't be thanked for your cheery optimism when they get sent down.
- A jury is a captive audience, and the impact of a closing speech can swing the result either way. If you can't learn how to give a charismatic performance your appeal to solicitors will be as limited as your income stream.
- Criminal barristers are connecting with and persuading people at all times, whether they are defendants, witnesses, victims, judges, members of a jury or even their own clerks in chambers. Interpersonal skills are hugely important in almost all aspects of the job, not just while advocating. It goes without saying that at times you'll meet some unpleasant or scary characters. Others will have pretty

unfortunate lives, some will be addicted to alcohol or drugs, have poor home lives and little education.
- Even the most skilful advocate knows that success rests on effective case preparation, and never forgets that the law and sentencing policies evolve constantly.
- Stamina and adaptability are both vital. You'll have to manage several cases on any one day, some of them poorly prepared. If you're lucky they'll all be at the same court; otherwise you'll be haring between venues. You'll have to take additional cases without prior warning and cope with missing defendants and witnesses on a regular basis. Soon enough you'll believe you can cope with anything. Chances are you can.

some tips

- It goes without saying that both mini-pupillage experience and plenty of mooting and debating is required before you can look like a serious applicant.
- The criminal Bar tends to provide more pupillages than other areas, but these don't necessarily translate into tenancies because the market is so competitive. Third and fourth sixes are not uncommon at the criminal Bar these days so be prepared for this possibility.
- There are many ways of getting exposure to the criminal justice system and plenty of your contemporaries will be on the case. See page 31 for tips on useful voluntary activities.

current issues

- Thus far getting on 'the CPS list' has allowed barristers to prosecute as well as defend. Recent figures reveal the CPS' annual bill for external advocates prosecuting cases of between one and ten days in length is around £81 million. It has decided to bring all advocacy in-house, a move which will save an estimated £34 million by March 2008. Whereas CPS instructions gave young barristers useful trial experience on both sides of the fence, the new system will leave advocates firmly on one side or other. CPS defence jobs will provide financial certainty and job security for those who take them but the change will hit the pockets of juniors in private practice. As if all this weren't bad enough, legal aid cutbacks will make the life of junior tenants even more demanding than ever. The government is on the brink of overhauling the system of public funding for criminal cases, and we'd recommend you get up to speed on the likely changes. Our feature **Get Carter** on page 17 is a good place to start. The rise of solicitor-advocates has also impacted on the amount of work available. If you're willing to accept the likelihood of more limited financial rewards, the criminal Bar should still prove irresistible...

the employment bar

It's hardly surprising that employment lawyers are busy: the general public is more aware of employment rights than ever before and cases are widely reported in mainstream newspapers. You'll recall stories about Prince Harry's former art teacher at Eton and various banking executives in the City, some of whom have claimed millions of pounds in compensation for breach of contract, harassment or discrimination.

Accessibility is a key aim of the employment tribunal system. Legal representation is not required and only rarely will there be a costs penalty for the unsuccessful party. Such is the emphasis on user-friendliness that employment claims can even be issued online. Nonetheless, many cases are so complex, or worth so much money, that specialist legal representation is sought from solicitors and barristers.

Tribunals deal with claims relating to redundancy; unfair dismissal; discrimination on the grounds of gender, sexual orientation, race, religion or age; workplace harassment; contract claims and whistle-blowing. The people who make the claims are called 'applicants'; the employers who defend them are called 'respondents'. High-value claims and applications for injunctions to prevent the breach of restrictive covenants or use of trade secrets are usually dealt with in the county courts or the High Court.

the realities of the job

- Most advocacy takes place in employment tribunals or the Employment Appeals Tribunal, as opposed to the courts. The atmosphere and proceedings in each are deliberately less formal so, for example, hearings are conducted with everyone sitting down and barristers do not wear their wigs.

- Tribunals follow the basic pattern of examination in chief, cross-examination and closing submissions; however barristers have to modify their style, especially when appearing against someone who is unrepresented.

- A corporate respondent might consider a QC well worth the money, while the applicant's pocket may only stretch to a junior. But what a fantastic opportunity for a junior to advocate against a silk. The other type of opponent frequently encountered is the solicitor-advocate – this area of practice is full of them.

- Employment specialists tend to be good with people. Clients frequently become emotional or stressed, and it's part of the barrister's job to ensure that this doesn't prevent the satisfactory resolution of the case. If you think about it, employees can spend more time in the workplace with colleagues than with their families, and so there are an endless number of situations and conflicts that can arise.

- Few juniors limit themselves solely to employment practice; most also undertake civil or commercial cases, some criminal matters. Similarly, few juniors act only for applicants or only for respondents. At senior level this changes because respondents can generally afford to pay the higher legal fees of seniors.

- UK Employment legislation mirrors EU law and changes with great rapidity, and you'll be forever having cases stayed while others with similar points are being heard on appeal. Keeping abreast of developments in the law is crucial because you won't always have much time to prepare for trial.

some tips

- Find out about how to get involved with the work of the Free Representation Unit (see page 31). It has much to offer students and pupils by way of exposure to employment law, and realistically no application for pupillage will look complete without some involvement of this kind.
- Mini-pupillages and mooting or public speaking are as important for budding employment barristers as any other kind.
- Practically any kind of temporary or part-time job will give you first-hand experience of being an employee. Not to be underestimated, especially when you consider that as a barrister you will be self-employed.

current issues

- High-value claims by employees in the banking sector continue to make headlines. Witness Helen Green's £800,000 award in her bullying case against Deutche Bank.
- The Bar continues to feel the impact of equal pay cases, which as they largely bypass City firms are tying up a large proportion of silks and juniors. Degnan and others v Redcar and Cleveland Borough Council went to the Court of Appeal and cases spread from the North East across the country. Barristers settled Wilson v North Cumbria Acute Hospitals NHS Trust, a case involving 1,500 women employed by Cumberland Infirmary and West Cumbria Hospital that lasted eight years. Each woman is likely to receive between £35,000 and £200,000 each, leaving the NHS facing a potential £300 million payout.

- The Work and Families Bill covers new rights to maternity and paternity leave for parents, and the relationship between employer and parent during a period of childcare leave. The Bill includes a new right to request flexible working.
- Age discrimination cases are coming to the fore and various aspects of the law will be tested in the near future.

the family bar

A lot of marriages break down in the UK and divorce can be a messy business, especially when it involves children. According to the government's number-crunchers, 53% of the couples divorcing in 2004 had at least one child aged under 16, and together their divorces affected nearly 150,000 children, some 64% of them under the age of 11. The law can never fix the problems caused by marital breakdown and other family situations, but it is one of the few tools people have at their disposal. Consequently, a huge amount of court time is allotted to divorce, separation, adoption, child residence and contact orders, financial provision and domestic violence.

This is an emotionally charged and demanding practice area for a barrister, who is likely to be involved only in the most complex or combative cases. Juniors learn the ropes on simple county court matters, progressing to complex matters in the Family Division of the High Court. In the early years there will be a lot of private law children work (disputes between parents), small financial cases and injunctions in situations of domestic violence.

the realities of the job

Financial cases and public and private law children's work each offer their own unique challenges and intellectual demands.

- A certain degree of emotional resilience is required, but you also need a capacity for empathy as the work involves asking clients for intimate details of their private life and breaking devastating news to the emotionally fragile. Private law children's cases can sometimes involve serious allegations between parents and require the input of child psychologists. The public law counterpart (care proceedings between local authorities and parents) invariably includes detailed and often harrowing medical evidence.

- For most people, getting involved with the courts is just as much a once-in-a-lifetime experience as the divorce itself. They will rely on you to guide them through this unfamiliar terrain.

- The end result of a case will have a significant impact on the lives touched by it, so it is crucial to find the most appropriate course of action for each client. The best advocates are those who can differentiate between a case and client requiring a bullish approach and those crying out for settlement and concessions to be made. The job calls for communication, tact and maturity.

- Where possible, mediation is used to resolve disputes in a more efficient and less unsettling fashion. This requires a different approach to litigation.

- Teamwork is crucial. As the link between the client, the opposing barrister, the judge, solicitors and social workers, it is important that you win the trust and confidence of everyone.

- The legislation affecting this area is comprehensive, and there's a large body of case law. You must keep abreast of all new decisions because, while no two families are identical,

the basics remain the same in relation to the problems they experience. The job is, therefore, more about negotiating general principles than adhering strictly to precedents.

- Finance-oriented barristers need an understanding of pensions and shares and a good grounding in the basics of trusts and property.

some tips

- The family Bar is quite small and competition for pupillage is intense. Think about how you can evidence your interest in family law. Our **Pro Bono and Volunteering** section on page 31 should give you some tips.

- Younger pupils might find it daunting to advise on mortgages, marriages and children when they've never experienced any of these things personally. Arguably those embarking on a second career, or who have delayed a year or two and acquired other life experiences, may have an advantage.

- Check the work orientation of a set before applying for pupillage, particularly if you don't want to narrow your options too early.

- Mini-pupillages will give you that all-important taste of life as a family barrister.

current issues

- A few years ago barristers believed that mediation and an increase in solicitor-advocates threatened a downturn in work for juniors. Yet, with the exception of children's cases in which solicitors have always been encouraged to do their own advocacy, the volume of instructions appear to have continued largely unabated... as has the incidence of divorce in the UK.

- London is arguably becoming the divorce capital of Europe. In such cases the wealth and assets involved far outstrip the reasonable needs of the parties, and lawyers are looking for precedents. The House of Lords recently

obliged with decisions in two hot cases –
Miller, where the issue is how to deal with a
short marriage, and McFarlane, where the wife
had given up a career to raise a family. Neither
could have foretold the size of the £48 million
payout ordered in August 2006 to the ex-wife
of insurance magnate John Charman, who is
unsurprisingly appealing the judge's decision.

- Lawyers are interested to see how the courts
will handle the division of assets following the
breakdown of a civil partnership.
- A Bill is currently going through Parliament
regarding contact in private child law cases.
- The government's latest review of public
funding for legal services will affect family
cases and presumably the pockets of family
barristers. Read **Get Carter** on page 17 for
more information.

public law and the bar

Public bodies must operate within statutory con-
straints and their decisions may be challenged on
procedural grounds. Perhaps they haven't considered the relevant facts in reaching a decision;
perhaps the body or officer didn't have the
authority to make the decision at all; perhaps they
won't reveal how and why they made a decision;
perhaps it is deemed to undermine a person's
rights, as embodied in the European Convention
on Human Rights.

Centred on the Administrative Court, public
law cases range from pro bono or legal aid matters
for individuals to commercial judicial review for
magic circle firms and government instructions.
In particular, a barrister with a local authority
clientele will have a very wide range of work,
much of it relating to planning, housing or environmental matters, education, health and
children. Cases concerning community care issues
and the provision of social services by local

authorities are especially hot at the moment, and
judicial reviews of immigration decisions still
make up a significant chunk of the Administrative
Court's case list. At the other end of the spectrum
sit some high-profile and contentious matters,
such as the case of Ann Marie Rogers who went to
court after she was denied the breast cancer drug
Herceptin by Swindon NHS. In Ms Rogers' case
the judge ruled that the trust had not been acting
unlawfully when it denied her the treatment, but
she was given leave to appeal against the decision.
Similarly the Administrative Court was recently
asked to consider the case of baby 'MB' when his
parents and doctors failed to agree on whether he
should be kept alive.

Where an event is deemed to be of great public
importance, inquiries are commissioned by the
government and then operate independently. The
Bloody Sunday Inquiry, the Victoria Climbie
Inquiry and the Hutton Inquiry into the death of
Dr David Kelly illustrate well the different types of
issue that come under scrutiny. Another type of
inquiry is the planning inquiry, which usually
arises because of a conflict between the interests of
a local community and the proposed developer –
the much-publicised Terminal 5 Inquiry into the
extension of Heathrow Airport is a good example.
In all these inquiries, barristers will speak on
behalf of the many interested parties.

Most public law barristers also work in other
areas: some are crime specialists; others have commercial caseloads. For example, criminal
barristers will often handle issues relating to prisoners or breaches of procedure by police, and
commercial barristers might handle judicial
reviews of DTI decisions. In reality, even those
who do not profess a specialism in public law may
also undertake judicial review work.

the realities of the job
- The barrister will only spend a part of their
time in court, with the rest spent in chambers

drafting skeleton arguments and opinions. If representing public bodies, they will need to advise on the implications of their decisions and whether their structures comply with public law principles.

- Junior barristers do get to hone their advocacy skills early on. The preliminary 'permissions' stage of judicial review proceedings provides excellent opportunities in the form of short 30-minute hearings. However, in this area of law there are usually just the barristers and the judge: no jury, no witnesses or cross-examinations.

- The Administrative Court is one of the most inundated branches of the High Court, so you'll need to develop an efficient style of advocacy. Long and dramatic performances are rarely well received; you must learn how to cut to the chase and deliver the pertinent information, draw on the relevant case law or statutory regulations and present your arguments promptly.

- You'll need a genuine interest in the fundamental laws by which we live and the legislative process. If administrative and constitutional law subjects were not your favourites you might want to rethink your decision.

- Public law is a discursive area of practice where you are more likely to find interesting arguments than you are a precise answer.

- Providing real remedies for real people demands a practicality, common sense and a willingness to stand back and look at the broader implications of what you are saying. Individual applicants and public bodies both have an equally valid interest in proper decision-making processes and you have to be able to see both sides of the coin.

- Barristers who work on planning inquiries may have to spend periods of time away from home.

some tips

- Sets usually go for people with excellent academic credentials, often those with masters' degrees. Certainly you'll need to show a keen intellect. Sets with local or central government clientele are also attracted to those with prior experience of the public sector, eg a role within local government or time spent as an MP's researcher.

- Get a few mini-pupillages under your belt, do as much mooting as possible and read quality newspapers to familiarise yourself with the public law issues raised in them.

- The Human Rights Act has undoubtedly affected public law, although it is still early days in relation to various areas, for example, the issue of privacy.

- Public international law appeals to many students but there are few openings at the pupillage stage. Traditionally, PIL has been the preserve of academics – the leading names are predominantly sitting or ex-professors at top universities and Foreign Office veterans, with the occasional pure but very experienced barrister thrown in. Governments want tried-and-tested counsel and will expect those they instruct to be recognised, published authors. This is not an area of work you'll fall into by accident, nor is it one you're likely to get into until much more experienced. If the academic route is not for you, good luck in your search for pupillage at a leading public law set.

- Interesting opportunities are available within the Government Legal Service. See pages 346 and 803.

current issues

- The number of people looking for pupillage in the field far exceeds the number of available positions, so you must evidence your commitment. A CV referencing voluntary work at a law centre or specialist voluntary organisation (eg the Howard League for Penal Reform), or membership of Liberty or Justice will help, as will a healthy interest in current affairs and the latest cases in the news.

- In immigration law there have been many modifications of late, among them changes affecting people applying for leave to remain or settle in the UK. Another example is the rule that migrant applications now need to be submitted to and dealt with at diplomatic posts overseas. This is causing concern amongst lawyers who feel that a move away from a centralised system will lead to loss of efficiency and poorer supervision. There is also much criticism of the abolition of various appeal rights and the substitution of an administrative review procedure.

- It looks as if there is more change to come. In March 2006 the Home Office published a paper on proposals for the UK immigration system called 'Controlling our Borders: Making Migration Work for Britain – Five Year Strategy for Asylum and Immigration'.

- The Government's latest review of public funding for legal services will affect public law cases and, as a result, the livelihoods of barristers acting for legally aided clients. See **Get Carter** on page 17.

- Anti-terror laws have been a hot topic. In the past year the House of Lords has ruled against the Government in cases examining the legality of the detention of foreign nationals without trial and the admissibility in UK courts of evidence obtained by torture.

- Last year the Court of Appeal looked at whether the Human Rights Act applies to British forces in post-war Iraq, and whether it was violated.

- Clinical advances have also led to important decisions: in the so-called 'designer-baby case' the House of Lords allowed a couple to have fertility treatment to select an embryo whose umbilical cord could be used to save the life of an existing child.

shipping, international trade and the bar

Essentially, shipping and international trade concerns the carriage of goods or people by sea, air and land, plus all aspects of the financing, construction, use, insurance and decommissioning of the vessels, planes, trains and other vehicles that carry them. A large proportion of the world's trade goods are transported by sea, and consequently a large number of the cases dealt with by barristers concern ships – what happens when they are arrested, sunk or salvaged, and what happens when there is a problem concerning the condition or ownership of their cargo.

Shipping and trade cases mostly turn on contract and tort; indeed English case law is awash with examples from the world of shipping – everything from rotten grain cargos to a criminal case about some sailors who ate a cabin boy. Shipping cases can be complicated because of the number of parties involved or the nature of the events leading to the dispute. Imagine a Greek-owned, Pakistani-crewed, Russian-captained ship, last serviced in Singapore, carrying forestry products from Indonesia to Denmark. It might be insured in London and chartered by a French company. There might be a collision with a Liberian-registered vessel somewhere off the west coast of Africa; the salvors who deal with the stricken vessels could be Dutch. Luckily for the Bar, the English courts are very often the preferred forum for the resolution of such complex matters. Indeed, London has a very prominent position in the world of shipping and international trade, not least because of the involvement of its insurance market.

You'll encounter the terms 'wet' and 'dry' shipping. These refer to the location of the dispute, so for example: wet cases include difficulties at sea; dry cases relate to disputes in port or concerns over the manufacture and financing of vessels.

The Bar also has a number of aviation specialists and those with experience dealing with road haulage and other modes of transportation. The sets that dominate all these areas will also be able to offer experts in the realm of commodities trading. Trade disputes are often resolved through arbitration conducted in various parts of the world, Paris and London being among the most important.

the realities of the job

- Cases are fact-heavy and paper-heavy. To develop the best arguments for a case you need an organised mind and a willingness to immerse yourself in the documentary evidence. This can be time-consuming and exhausting.
- There are opportunities for international travel.
- Cases can run on for years and involve large teams of lawyers, both solicitors and barristers. The young barrister will work their way up from second or third junior to leader over a number of years.
- New juniors do get to run their own smaller cases, eg charter party and bills of lading disputes.
- It's inevitable that at first the world of shipping and trade will seem very alien. Before long you'll pick up the language and customs.
- Your solicitor clients will usually work at one of the established shipping firms. Your lay clients, however, are going to be a real mixed bag of financiers, ship owners, operators, traders and charterers, P&I clubs, salvors and underwriters.

some tips

- The leading sets are easy to identify. A mini-pupillage with one or more of them will greatly enhance your understanding of the work involved.
- Despite the prominence of English law, the work calls for an international perspective and an appreciation of international laws. This can be developed within a first or masters' degree and on the BVC.
- Advocacy, both written and oral, is at the heart of the work. Show recruiters your flair for it by getting involved in mooting.
- What the heck is commodities trading? Step one: watch the Eddie Murphy/Dan Aykroyd movie 'Trading Places.'

current issues

- There is a general downturn in cargo claims due to the increased safety of ships and the success of various conventions such as the International Safety Management Code.
- An upturn in the commodities market and the international sale of goods – not least because of economic growth in China – has caused freight and hire rates to spike.
- P&I clubs in particular continue to be increasingly watchful of costs. This has sparked the recent development of instructing barristers directly, cutting out the solicitor middleman.
- Clients are further trying to save money by embracing mediation.

chambers UK bar practice areas tables 2007

Administrative & Public Law: General
London

1 **Blackstone Chambers**
(Mill QC & Beazley QC)

2 **11 King's Bench Walk**
(Griffin QC & Goudie QC)
39 Essex Street
(Davies QC & Wilmot-Smith QC)
Brick Court
(Sumption QC & Hirst QC)
Doughty Street
(Robertson QC & Thornton QC)
Landmark Chambers
(Christopher Katkowski QC)
Matrix Chambers

3 **1 Crown Office Row**
(Robert Seabrook QC)
1 Temple Gardens
(Ian Burnett QC)
3 Hare Court
(James Guthrie QC)
4-5 Gray's Inn Square
(Appleby QC & Straker QC)
Garden Court
(Davies QC & Griffiths QC)

Banking & Finance
London

1 **3 Verulam Buildings**
(Symons QC & Jarvis QC)
Fountain Court Chambers
(Brindle QC & Lerego QC)

2 **3/4 South Square**
(Michael Crystal QC)
Brick Court Chambers
(Sumption QC & Hirst QC)
Essex Court Chambers
(Gordon Pollock QC)
One Essex Court
(Lord Grabiner QC)

3 **20 Essex Street**
(Iain Milligan QC)
Serle Court
(Lord Neill of Bladen QC)

Commercial Litigation
London

1 **Brick Court Chambers**
(Sumption QC & Hirst QC)
Essex Court Chambers
(Gordon Pollock QC)
One Essex Court
(Lord Grabiner QC)
Fountain Court Chambers
(Brindle QC & Lerego QC)

2 **Blackstone Chambers**
(Mill QC & Beazley QC)
3 Verulam Buildings
(Symons QC & Jarvis QC)

3 **20 Essex Street**
(Iain Milligan QC)
7 King's Bench Walk
(Kealey QC & Flaux QC)
Serle Court
(Lord Neill of Bladen QC)

4 **Erskine Chambers**
(John Cone QC)
Maitland Chambers
(Lyndon-Stanford/Aldous/Driscoll QCs)
XXIV Old Buildings
(Steinfeld QC & Mann QC)
3/4 South Square
(Michael Crystal QC)
4 Stone Buildings
(George Bompas QC)

Banking & Finance
Western

1 **Guildhall Chambers**
(Peter Blair QC)

Chancery: Commercial
London

1 **Maitland Chambers**
(Lyndon-Stanford/Aldous/Driscoll QCs)

2 **Serle Court**
(Lord Neill of Bladen QC)
4 Stone Buildings
(George Bompas QC)

3 **XXIV Old Buildings**
(Steinfeld QC & Mann QC)
3/4 South Square
(Michael Crystal QC)
Wilberforce Chambers
(Jules Sher QC)

4 **Enterprise Chambers**
(Bernard Weatherill QC)
New Square Chambers
(Charles Purle QC)
3 Stone Buildings
(Geoffrey Vos QC)
11 Stone Buildings
(Edward Cohen)

Chancery: Traditional
London

1 **Wilberforce Chambers**
(Jules Sher QC)

2 **5 Stone Buildings**
(Henry Harrod)

3 **Maitland Chambers**
(Lyndon-Stanford/Aldous/Driscoll QCs)
New Square Chambers
(Charles Purle QC)
XXIV Old Buildings
(Steinfeld QC & Mann QC)
Ten Old Square
(Leolin Price CBE QC)
Radcliffe Chambers
(Waters QC & Marten)
Serle Court
(Lord Neill of Bladen QC)

4 **9 Stone Buildings**
(Vivian Chapman QC)

practice areas at the bar (continued)

Clinical Negligence
London

1 **1 Crown Office Row**
(Robert Seabrook QC)
3 Serjeants' Inn
(Francis QC & Grace QC)

2 **Doughty Street Chambers**
(Robertson QC & Thornton QC)
Hailsham Chambers
(Pooles QC & Ritchie QC)
Outer Temple Chambers
(Philip Mott QC)

3 **1 Chancery Lane**
(Edward Faulks QC)
2 Temple Gardens
(Ben Browne QC)
7 Bedford Row
(David Farrer QC)
Crown Office Chambers
(Edwards-Stuart QC)

4 **22 Old Buildings**
(Benet Hytner QC)
39 Essex Street
(Davies QC & Wilmot-Smith QC)
Cloisters
(Robin Allen QC)

Company
London

1 **Erskine Chambers**
(John Cone QC)

2 **4 Stone Buildings**
(George Bompas QC)

3 **3/4 South Square**
(Michael Crystal QC)
Maitland Chambers
(Lyndon-Stanford/Aldous/Driscoll QCs)
Serle Court
(Lord Neill of Bladen QC)

4 **Enterprise Chambers**
(Bernard Weatherill QC)
One Essex Court
(Lord Grabiner QC)
XXIV Old Buildings
(Steinfeld QC & Mann QC)

Crime
London

1 **2 Bedford Row**
(William Clegg QC)
Cloth Fair Chambers
(Nicholas Purnell QC)
Hollis Whiteman Chambers
(Robinson & Whiteman)
6 King's Bench Walk
(Roy Amlot QC)
3 Raymond Buildings
(Clive Nicholls QC)

2 **Doughty Street Chambers**
(Robertson QC & Thornton QC)
2 Hare Court
(David Waters QC)

3 **25 Bedford Row**
(Rock Tansey QC)
9-12 Bell Yard
(Lord Carlile of Berriew QC)
18 Red Lion Court
(David Etherington QC)

4 **Atkinson Bevan Chambers**
(Atkinson QC)
9 Bedford Row
(Anthony Berry QC)
Carmelite Chambers
(Richard Ferguson QC)
Charter Chambers
(Stephen Solley QC)
187 Fleet Street
(Andrew Trollope QC)
23 Essex Street
(Christopher Kinch QC)
Furnival Chambers
(Andrew Mitchell QC)
Garden Court Chambers
(Davies QC & Griffiths QC)
Matrix Chambers
5 Paper Buildings
(Carey QC & Caplan QC)

5 **2 Dyers Buildings**
(Michael Gledhill QC)
Nine Lincoln's Inn Fields
(David Nathan QC)
Tooks Chambers
(Michael Mansfield QC)

Environment
Midlands

1 **No5 Chambers**
(Gareth Evans QC)

Construction
London

1 **Atkin Chambers**
(Robert Akenhead QC)
Keating Chambers
(John Marrin QC)

2 **4 Pump Court**
(Friedman QC & Moger QC)

3 **39 Essex Street**
(Davies QC & Wilmot-Smith QC)
Crown Office Chambers
(Edwards-Stuart QC)
Four New Square
(Roger Stewart QC)

Competition/European Law
London

1 **Brick Court Chambers**
(Sumption QC & Hirst QC)
Monckton Chambers
(Paul Lasok QC)

2 **11 King's Bench Walk**
(Tabachnik & Goudie)
Blackstone Chambers
(Mill QC & Beazley QC)
Matrix Chambers

Environment
London

1 **2 Harcourt Buildings**
(Robin Purchas QC)
39 Essex Street
(Davies QC & Wilmot-Smith QC)
Landmark Chambers
(Christopher Katkowski QC)

2 **Blackstone Chambers**
(Mill QC & Beazley QC)
Matrix Chambers
Old Square Chambers
(John Hendy QC)

3 **4-5 Gray's Inn Square**
(Appleby QC & Straker QC)
6 Pump Court
(Stephen Hockman QC)
Brick Court Chambers
(Sumption QC & Hirst QC)

Environment
Northern

1 **Kings Chambers**
(Frances Patterson QC)

the bar

Employment
London
1. **Blackstone Chambers**
(Mill QC & Beazley QC)
11 KBW Chambers
(Tabachnik QC & Goudie QC)
Littleton Chambers
(Freedman QC & Clarke QC)
2. **Cloisters**
(Robin Allen QC)
Devereux Chambers
(Colin Edelman QC)
Matrix Chambers
Old Square Chambers
(John Hendy QC)
3. **Essex Court Chambers**
(Gordon Pollock QC)
12 King's Bench Walk
(Andrew Hogarth QC)
Outer Temple Chambers
(Philip Mott QC)

Employment
Western
1. **Old Square Chambers**
(John Hendy QC)
Queen Square Chambers
(T Alun Jenkins QC)
2. **Albion Chambers**
(Neil Ford QC)

Employment
Midlands
1. **No5 Chambers**
(Gareth Evans QC)
St Philips Chambers
(William Davis QC)

Employment
Northern
1. **9 St John Street**
(John Hand QC)
2. **Atlantic Chambers**
(John Benson QC)
3. **8 King St**
(David Thomas Eccles)

Family/Matrimonial
London
1. **1 Hare Court**
(Bruce Blair QC)
1 King's Bench Walk
(Richard Anelay QC)
Queen Elizabeth Building (QEB)
(Andrew Moylan QC)
2. **29 Bedford Row Chambers**
(Francis QC)
One Garden Court Family Law
(Platt QC & Ball QC)
4 Paper Buildings
(Jonathan Cohen QC)
3. **Coram Chambers**
(Roger McCarthy QC)
1 Crown Office Row
(Robert Seabrook QC)
14 Gray's Inn Square
(Forster & Brasse)
22 Old Buildings
(Benet Hytner QC)
Renaissance Chambers
(Setright QC & Jubb)

Fraud: Civil
London
1. **3 Verulam Buildings**
(Symons QC & Jarvis QC)
Fountain Court Chambers
(Brindle QC & Lerego QC)
One Essex Court
(Lord Grabiner QC)
2. **4 Stone Buildings**
(George Bompas QC)
Blackstone Chambers
(Mill QC & Beazley QC)
Brick Court Chambers
(Sumption QC & Hirst QC)
Essex Court Chambers
(Gordon Pollock QC)
Serle Court
(Lord Neill of Bladen QC)
3. **11 Stone Buildings**
(Edward Cohen)
3/4 South Square
(Michael Crystal QC)
New Square Chambers
(Charles Purle QC)

Fraud: Criminal
London
1. **2 Bedford Row**
(William Clegg QC)
3 Raymond Buildings
(Clive Nicholls QC)
Cloth Fair Chambers
(Nicholas Purnell QC)
Hollis Whiteman Chambers
(Robinson QC & Whiteman QC)
2. **18 Red Lion Court**
(David Etherington QC)
7 Bedford Row
(David Farrer QC)
9-12 Bell Yard
(Lord Carlile of Berriew QC)
3. **23 Essex Street**
(Christopher Kinch QC)
6 King's Bench Walk
(Roy Amlot QC)
Furnival Chambers
(Andrew Mitchell QC)
4. **187 Fleet Street**
(Andrew Trollope QC)
2 Hare Court
(David Waters QC)
25 Bedford Row
(Rock Tansey QC)
5 Paper Buildings
(Carey QC & Caplan QC)
Charter Chambers
(Stephen Solley QC)
Doughty Street Chambers
(Robertson QC & Thornton QC)
Matrix Chambers

Human Rights
London

1. **Blackstone Chambers**
(Mill QC & Beazley QC)
Doughty Street Chambers
(Robertson QC & Thornton QC)
Matrix Chambers

2. **11 KBW Chambers**
(Tabachnik QC & Goudie QC)
39 Essex Street
(Davies QC & Wilmot-Smith QC)
Brick Court Chambers
(Sumption QC & Hirst QC)
Garden Court Chambers
(Davies QC & Griffiths QC)

3. **1 Crown Office Row**
(Robert Seabrook QC)
Tooks Chambers
(Michael Mansfield QC)

Human Rights
Northern

1. **Garden Court North**
(Ian Macdonald QC)

Immigration
London

1. **Garden Court Chambers**
(Davies QC & Griffiths QC)

2. **Blackstone Chambers**
(Mill QC & Beazley QC)
Doughty Street
(Robertson QC & Thornton QC)
Matrix Chambers
Tooks Chambers
(Michael Mansfield QC)

3. **39 Essex Street**
(Davies QC & Wilmot-Smith QC)
6 King's Bench Walk
(Sibghat Kadri QC)
Mitre House Chambers
(Francis Gilbert)
Renaissance Chambers
(Setright QC & Jubb)

Immigration
Midlands

1. **Number 8 Chambers**
(Ian Strongman)

Immigration
Northern

1. **Garden Court North**
(Ian Macdonald QC)

International Arbitration: General Commercial & Insurance
London

1. **Essex Court Chambers**
(Gordon Pollock QC)

2. **20 Essex Street**
(Iain Milligan QC)

3. **7 King's Bench Walk**
(Kealey QC & Flaux QC)
One Essex Court
(Lord Grabiner QC)

4. **Brick Court Chambers**
(Sumption QC & Hirst QC)
Fountain Court Chambers
(Brindle QC & Lerego QC)
Littleton Chambers
(Freedman QC & Clarke QC)
Matrix Chambers
Quadrant Chambers
(Persey QC & Rainey QC)

International Arbitration: Construction/Engineering
London

1. **Atkin Chambers**
(Robert Akenhead QC)
Keating Chambers
(John Marrin QC)

Information Technology
London

1. **11 South Square**
(Christopher Floyd QC)

2. **4 Pump Court**
(Friedman QC & Moger QC)
8 New Square
(Mark Platts-Mills QC)

3. **3 Verulam Buildings**
(Symons QC & Jarvis QC)
Atkin Chambers
(Robert Akenhead QC)
Henderson Chambers
(Roger Henderson QC)
Hogarth Chambers
(Wilson QC & Wyand QC)
Three New Square
(Antony Watson QC)

Intellectual Property
London

1. **11 South Square**
(Christopher Floyd QC)
8 New Square
(Mark Platts-Mills QC)
Three New Square
(Antony Watson QC)

2. **Hogarth Chambers**
(Wilson QC & Wyand QC)

3. **One Essex Court**
(Lord Grabiner QC)
Wilberforce Chambers
(Jules Sher QC)

the bar

Insolvency/ Corporate Recovery
London

1 **3/4 South Square**
(Michael Crystal QC)

2 **11 Stone Buildings**
(Edward Cohen)
4 Stone Buildings
(George Bompas QC)
Erskine Chambers
(John Cone QC)
Maitland Chambers
(Lyndon-Stanford/Aldous/Driscoll QCs)
Serle Court
(Lord Neill of Bladen QC)

3 **Enterprise Chambers**
(Bernard Weatherill QC)
XXIV Old Buildings
(Steinfeld QC & Mann QC)

Insurance
London

1 **7 King's Bench Walk**
(Kealey QC & Flaux QC)
Brick Court Chambers
(Sumption QC & Hirst QC)
Essex Court Chambers
(Gordon Pollock QC)

2 **3 Verulam Buildings**
(Symons QC & Jarvis QC)
Fountain Court
(Brindle QC & Lerego QC)

3 **20 Essex Street**
(Iain Milligan QC)
4 Pump Court
(Friedman QC & Moger QC)
Devereux Chambers
(Colin Edelman QC)

Media & Entertainment
London

1 **Blackstone Chambers**
(Mill QC & Beazley QC)

2 **8 New Square**
(Mark Platts-Mills QC)

3 **Essex Court Chambers**
(Gordon Pollock QC)

4 **11 South Square**
(Christopher Floyd QC)
5RB
(Browne QC & Page QC)
Hogarth Chambers
(Wilson QC & Wyand QC)

Personal Injury
London

1 **12 King's Bench Walk**
(Andrew Hogarth QC)
39 Essex Street
(Davies QC & Wilmot-Smith QC)

2 **2 Temple Gardens**
(Ben Browne QC)
Crown Office Chambers
(Edwards-Stuart QC)
Outer Temple Chambers
(Philip Mott QC)

3 **9 Gough Square**
(John Foy QC)
Devereux Chambers
(Colin Edelman QC)
Farrar's Building
(Patrick Harrington QC)
Old Square Chambers
(John Hendy QC)

4 **1 Chancery Lane**
(Edward Faulks QC)
1 Crown Office Row
(Robert Seabrook QC)
1 Temple Gardens
(Ian Burnett QC)
Doughty Street Chambers
(Robertson QC & Thornton QC)

Personal Injury
Western

1 **Guildhall Chambers**
(Peter Blair QC)
Old Square Chambers
(John Hendy QC)
St John's Chambers
(Christopher Sharp QC)

Personal Injury
Wales & Chester

1 **30 Park Place**
(Jane Crowley QC)
33 Park Place
(Graham Walters)
9 Park Place
(Ian Murphy QC)

Personal Injury
Midlands

1 **No5 Chambers**
(Gareth Evans QC)
Ropewalk Chambers
(R F Owen QC)

2 **St Philips Chambers**
(William Davis QC)

Personal Injury
Northern

1 **9 St John Street**
(John Hand QC)
Byrom Street Chambers
(Benet Hytner QC)
Deans Court Chambers
(Mark Turner QC)

2 **18 St John Street**
(Peter Birkett QC)
Exchange Chambers
(Turner QC & Braithwaite QC)
St Johns Buildings
(Michael Redfern QC)

Personal Injury
North Eastern

1 **Park Lane Chambers**
(Stuart Brown QC)

2 **Plowden Buildings**
(Jeremy Freedman)

practice areas at the bar (continued)

Planning
London

1. **Landmark Chambers**
   (Christopher Katkowski QC)
2. **2 Harcourt Buildings**
   (Robin Purchas QC)
3. **2-3 Gray's Inn Square**
   (Anthony Porten QC)

Planning
Midlands

1. **No5 Chambers**
   (Gareth Evans QC)

Planning
Northern

1. **Kings Chambers**
   (Frances Patterson QC)

Real Estate Litigation
London

1. **Falcon Chambers**
   (Gaunt QC & Morgan QC)
2. **Maitland Chambers**
   (Lyndon-Stanford/Aldous/Driscoll QCs)
3. **Landmark Chambers**
   (Christopher Katkowski QC)
   Wilberforce Chambers
   (Jules Sher QC)
4. **Enterprise Chambers**
   (Bernard Weatherill QC)
   Henderson Chambers
   (Roger Henderson QC)
   Selborne Chambers
   (Romie Tager QC)
   Serle Court
   (Lord Neill of Bladen QC)
   Tanfield Chambers
   (Peter Hughes QC)

Police Law: Mainly Claimant
All Circuits

1. **Doughty Street Chambers**
   (Robertson & Thornton)
2. **Garden Court Chambers**
   (Davies QC & Griffiths QC)
3. **Matrix Chambers**
   Tooks Chambers
   (Michael Mansfield QC)

Police Law: Mainly Defendant
All Circuits

1. **5 Essex Court**
   (Simon Freeland QC)
2. **3 Serjeants' Inn**
   (Francis QC & Grace QC)
3. **1 Chancery Lane**
   (Edward Faulks QC)
   Ely Place Chambers
   (Ronald Thwaites QC)
   9 Gough Square
   (John Foy QC)

Shipping & Commodities
London

1. **20 Essex Street**
   (Iain Milligan QC)
   7 King's Bench Walk
   (Kealey QC & Flaux QC)
   Essex Court Chambers
   (Gordon Pollock QC)
   Quadrant Chambers
   (Persey QC & Rainey QC)
2. **Stone Chambers**
   (Steven Gee QC)

Tax
London

1. **Gray's Inn Tax Chambers**
   (Milton Grundy)
   Monckton Chambers
   (Paul Lasok QC)
   Pump Court Tax Chambers
   (Andrew Thornhill QC)
2. **11 New Square**
   (John Gardiner QC)
3. **15 Old Square**
   (Rex Bretten QC)
   3 Temple Gardens Tax Chambers
   (Bramwell QC)
   One Essex Court
   (Lord Grabiner QC)

chambers reports

Making an informed choice about where to apply for pupillage is no easy task. Getting as far as working out the practice area in which you want to specialise is just the start; you then need to select your dozen OLPAS sets and consider how many other non-OLPAS choices to make. How do you know where you'll fit in and whether a set will be interested in you?

Chambers' websites are by and large pretty good at delivering pertinent information concerning size, nature of work, location, etc, but Internet surfing will only take you so far. The best course of action is to go and see inside a set for yourself on a mini-pupillage. There's still that same problem – which do you approach? Because it is impossible to do minis at every set that takes your fancy, the Student Guide has done some of the hard work for you. Since the summer of 2003 we have been calling in on an ever-increasing number of chambers, taking time to speak with pupils, juniors, QCs, clerks and chief execs.

The task is a big one so we took the decision to visit chambers every second year, reprinting the existing 'Chambers Report' on them in the intervening year. This year's roll call of 53 sets includes 29 new features and 24 features from our 2006 edition. Each year our collection of reports grows larger.

We have tried to visit as many different types of set as possible to give a good flavour for the range of potential areas of practice out there. Our tour took us from the grandeur of the Chancery Bar to the more modest surroundings of sets conducting mainly publicly funded work. There should be something to suit all tastes, be they commercial, common law, criminal, family, IP, tax, regional or otherwise. Given that most sets (and pupillages) are based in London, the majority of those covered are in the capital, but this year we went up to Manchester to see three sets and called in on the two giant-sized chambers in Birmingham. We have also reprinted our 2006

edition feature on Exchange Chambers in Liverpool.

The wild card in the pack is the Government Legal Service which, although not a set operating out of chambers, still offers what we regard as a cracking pupillage.

What we have deliberately avoided is poor-quality sets. We make no excuses for our decision to choose only top sets. Bear in mind, however, that our selected sets are not the only ones in the Premier League in each practice area. Given the time we would visit many others.

Whichever chambers you do choose, be reassured that the prime aim of recruiters is to find talented applicants and then to persuade them to accept an offer. They do not expect ready-formed barristers to turn up at their door for interview, and gladly make allowances for candidates' lack of knowledge or experience on specific subjects. Much has been said and written about how awful pupillage interviews can be, and how pupillage itself amounts to little more than a year of pain and humiliation. From what we can tell, this is not the norm. Sure, interviews can be challenging, but they are for the most part designed to get the best out of candidates. As for pupillage, it is in the best interests of any set that it should provide a useful and rewarding experience for pupils.

The itinerary for our visits included conversations with members of the pupillage committee, pupilmasters or supervisors, the senior clerk, junior tenants and, most crucially, current pupils. The aim was not merely to get the low-down on pupillage at each set but also to learn something about each chambers' life and to pick up tips for applicants. To this end we drank endless cups of tea, munched our way through five kilos of biscuits and took numerous guided tours, checking out artwork and libraries along the way. If we've communicated the qualities that make each set unique then we've done our job and it's over to you to make your choices.

Top Tips For Internet Research

- Check the pupillage page on a set's site to look for: info on mini-pupillages and how to apply for them; how to apply for a pupillage; application forms for non-OLPAS sets; confirmation of the OLPAS season in which a set participates; numbers of places; funding details; the structure of pupillage; the set's policy document on pupillage and the selection of pupils.

- Look at the list of members and in particular the biographies of the set's cadre of junior tenants. This can reveal much about what appeals to chambers' recruiters, particularly in relation to academic and other achievements. You will also be able to see the areas in which baby juniors gain experience.

- Gongs and rankings! Various organisations give out awards, and Chambers and Partners is no exception. Ours are handed over at an annual Bar Awards ceremony in October. The sets' websites frequently publicise the findings and editorial comment of the annually published legal directories, not least our own – *Chambers UK*. The entire contents of our directory can be read online for free.

- Knowing which recent cases a set is most proud of will help you at interview.

- If you get wind of who will be on the interview panel do your homework on them before you submit yourself to a grilling from them.

- Take note of the identity of any clients that are mentioned on a set's website.

- The weekly mainstream legal press, *The Lawyer* and *Legal Week*, are both available online and, although coverage of the Bar is sparse in comparison to the solicitors firms, big stories will usually be covered and there will be the occasional interesting article about key barristers and sets.

- Keep an eye on the Bar Council's own website (www.barcouncil.org.uk).

the chambers reports sets

No	set	Location	Head of Chambers	(QCs/Juniors)
1.	2 Bedford Row	London	William Clegg	13/48
2.	Blackstone Chambers*	London	Mill/Beazley	31/36
3.	Brick Court Chambers*	London	Sumption/Hirst	25/40
4.	Cloisters*	London	Robin Allen	4/42
5.	Crown Office Chambers*	London	Antony Edwards-Stuart	14/66
6.	Devereux Chambers*	London	Colin Edelman	9/36
7.	Doughty Street Chambers*	London	Robertson/Thornton	17/71
8.	Erskine Chambers*	London	John Cone	7/15
9.	Essex Court Chambers*	London	Gordon Pollock	32/38
10.	One Essex Court*	London	Anthony Grabiner	21/40
11.	20 Essex Street*	London	Iain Milligan	17/32
12.	39 Essex Street	London	Davies/Wilmot-Smith	23/50
13.	Falcon Chambers*	London	Gaunt/Morgan	10/26
14.	Fountain Court *	London	Brindle/Lerego	24/40
15.	Garden Court Chambers*	London	Davies/Griffiths	12/91
16.	One Garden Court	London	Platt/Ball	7/45
17.	Government Legal Service	London	n/a	n/a
18.	2-3 Gray's Inn Square	London	Mark Lowe	10/52
19.	4-5 Gray's Inn Square	London	Appleby/Straker	12/35
20.	1 Hare Court	London	Bruce Blair	9/27
21.	2 Hare Court	London	David Waters	12/37
22.	Henderson Chambers	London	Roger Henderson	7/35
23.	Hogarth Chambers*	London	Wilson/Wyand	4/22
24.	Keating Chambers	London	John Marrin	16/31
25.	7 King's Bench Walk	London	Kealey/Flaux	18/23
26.	11 King's Bench Walk*	London	Tabachnik/Goudie	13/35
27.	Landmark Chambers	London	Christopher Katkowski	19/46

the chambers reports sets *continued*

No	set	Location	Head of Chambers	(QCs/Juniors)
28.	Maitland Chambers*	London	Lyndon-Stanford/Aldous/Driscoll	15/49
29.	Matrix Chambers*	London	n/a	14/58
30.	Monckton Chambers	London	Paul Lasok	11/31
31.	Four New Square	London	Roger Stewart	12/45
32.	Old Square Chambers	London	John Hendy	11/48
33.	XXIV Old Buildings	London	Steinfeld/Mann	6/29
34.	Outer Temple	London	Philip Mott	14/51
35.	Pump Court Tax Chambers	London	Andrew Thornhill	10/16
36.	4 Pump Court	London	Friedman/Moger	15/36
37.	Quadrant Chambers	London	Persey/Rainey	11/31
38.	Queen Elizabeth Building*	London	Andrew Moylan	3/28
39.	3 Raymond Buildings	London	Clive Nicholls	15/31
40.	5RB	London	Browne/Paige	6/29
41.	3 Serjeants' Inn	London	Francis/Grace	8/44
42.	Serle Court*	London	Lord Neill of Bladen	13/33
43.	3/4 South Square*	London	Micheal	18/28
44.	4 Stone Buildings*	London	George Bompass	6/27
45.	2 Temple Gardens	London	Ben Browne	8/42
46.	3 Verulam Buildings*	London	Symons/Jarvis	19/40
47.	Wilberforce Chambers*	London	Jules Sher	18/27
48.	No5 Chambers	Birmingham/London/Bristol	Gareth Evans	16/169
49.	St Philips Chambers	Birmingham	William Davis	11/147
50.	Exchange Chambers *	Liverpool/Manchester	Turner/Braithwaite	13/81
51.	Deans Court Chambers	Manchester/Preston	Mark Turner	10/58
52.	Kings Chambers	Manchester/Leeds	Frances Patterson	9/58
53.	St Johns Buildings	Manchester	Christopher Sharp	10/100

* 2005 visits. All others visited in 2006

chambers reports

2 Bedford Row

Chambers UK rankings: Crime, fraud: criminal, health & safety

In business since 1983, 2 Bedford Row is nestled just behind High Holborn on the edge of Gray's Inn. Attached to the set and its most well-known members is a certain gravitas in the world of criminal law that most others can only dream of. Serious crime is the name of the game and a dizzying array of headline-grabbing cases has seen members defending the likes of nail bomber David Copeland, who wreaked havoc in Brixton, Brick Lane and the Admiral Duncan pub in Soho, and the accused in the murder cases of Lin and Megan Russell in Chillenden and Rachel Nickel on Wimbledon Common. Renowned founder and head of chambers William Clegg QC has certainly racked up more than his fair share of major cases, the latest being the defence of a British paratrooper charged with the murder of an Iraqi civilian. Fellow QC Jim Sturman also defended soldiers accused of the murder, while on duty, of an Iraqi teenager. In the past year, members have also appeared for the defence on the Jubilee Line fraud trial and the QPR blackmail trial. Peruse the pages of your first-year criminal law textbooks and you'll see several more cases bearing a 2 Bedford Row stamp: R v Brown (yes that one) and the Herald of Free Enterprise prosecution are two of the most famous examples.

Chambers and Partners
Crime Set of the Year 2006

In addition to defence work, barristers also undertake prosecutions and work on public inquiries (Harold Shipman, Victoria Climbie, Stephen Lawrence). Unusually for a criminal set, chambers has carved a niche in health and safety law, with members regularly instructed by the Health & Safety Executive as well as major City law firms. Recent cases have included the Hatfield rail crash and the Buncefield oil depot explosion. Nevertheless, those recruited undertake a pupillage that is focused on crime. Last year a new system was introduced and pupils are now allocated two supervisors for each six, rather than just one. This initiative *"means that if one is caught up in a long case the pupil can go with the other."* It went down a treat with current pupils, one of whom avoided getting caught up on a six-month fraud trial in Birmingham by switching to a supervisor working on a couple of cases closer to home. Also new are in-house advocacy training sessions, which are viewed as *"an opportunity to show what you can do."* When we visited there was some ambiguity as to whether these advocacy sessions 'count' in the bid for tenancy: though not officially assessed, pupils sensed *"they surely must be gauging what you're like."*

The first six will inevitably involve plenty of shadowing, either at *"three to four-day Crown Court trials"* or longer stretches where serious crimes are at issue. One pupil recounted his experience of a particularly gruesome murder trial in which, after conviction, the defence QC *"went back over my notes to analyse all the legal arguments and to draw up grounds for appeal – it was great that he used my work."* As the second six approaches, pupils are advised to *"get down to the mags"* to pick up a few tips before boarding the advocacy rollercoaster. Watching third-sixers on their feet in the magistrates' court is a great way to see how advocacy is done in that setting and gives an opportunity *"to ask silly questions without worrying."* Once the second six starts the pupil's schedule is hectic, and we heard from one in July who told us he had been on his feet *"every day bar one since March."* All pupils defend a trial during the first week of the second six to ensure they are ready for the onslaught of trials over the months that follow. All the experience will *"stand you in good stead elsewhere if you're not taken on here."* As well as dashing from court to court, pupils need to put themselves about in chambers doing work for as many members as they can. That said, supervisors *"don't want to overburden pupils,"* so the schedule should never get too out of hand.

And what of the atmosphere in chambers? *"It's not a case of don't speak until you're spoken to,"* insisted one source; *"members are always supportive and approachable"* and it's not uncommon for seniors to stop by the basement library where pupils tend to congregate. There's also *"a bit of banter at the end of the day"* with the clerks. Even the dress code is fairly informal: *"I know pupils elsewhere who are always required to wear a three-piece suit, but I can't imagine that here."*

Tenancy decisions are made in September by a committee of senior and junior members. Rather than just relying on the opinions of those in chambers, the set encourages pupils to obtain references from instructing solicitors who *"have a much better idea of whether a pupil has shone in a particular case."* The clerks will also have a good idea as to how the pupils are performing, and of their strengths and weaknesses. In their second six, all pupils work closely with the clerk who deals with magistrates' court work. If they get hold of something in the Crown Court then they'll deal with any number of other clerks. *"But the junior clerks are overseen, so the senior clerk knows what's going on...they know which pupils will rush back after court,"* and by implication which pupils won't.

Making the grade is tough; last year just one pupil was taken on and none hit the pass mark the year before. Although the official line is that third-sixers aren't in direct competition for places, in 2006 the four second-sixers were up alongside three third-sixers so the odds didn't look good for everyone. Knowing that those not taken on *"all go to good sets"* and *"aren't booted out but allowed to stay and sort something out"* does at least take the edge off the nervous wait for the decision. If you do need a drink to calm your nerves or to wind down after a harrowing day in court there's no need to stray far. The Old Nick pub across the road from chambers tends to have one or two members propping up the bar, so *"familiar faces are almost guaranteed."* It's almost as common to *"see senior members buying a round."*

Competition for pupillage at 2 Bedford Row is about as fierce as it comes. A successful first-round interview (*"large volume* [around 650 candidates], *short meet-and-greet with one or two legal questions gently thrown in"*) is followed by a more involved second-round grilling including a plea in mitigation. Take time to form a few opinions about current legal issues (eg whether it is right for a sex offender to have their sentence increased) as you'll need to *"show you are serious about crime"* to stand a chance. We hardly need to say that you must display the usual *"great academic results, motivation and judgement,"* but what really counts is *"evidence of a strong human touch"* because chambers wants people whose demeanour will convince any lay or professional client that they really care about what they are doing. Given that many people only acquire this with age or life experience, it's not surprising that 2 Bedford Row often takes on pupils with some kind of career history. One we spoke to had been an actor then worked in publishing for several years. A quick glance at the biogs of the juniors in chambers reveals a genuine diversity in recruitment and absence of Oxbridge dominance.

2 Bedford Row is one of a handful of top-notch criminal sets with the *"real stars"* who are instructed on the country's leading cases. *"There can be no better place to learn,"* one pupil insisted. We'd find it hard to disagree.

Blackstone Chambers

Chambers UK rankings: Admin & public law, commercial litigation, competition/European law, employment, environment, financial services, fraud: civil, human rights, immigration, media & entertainment, professional discipline, public international law, sports law, telecommunications

"This is the world of the Temple: the fountain, the chambers, the quad; where Brick Court speaks only to Blackstone and Blackstone speaks only to God." Normally we are resistant to such poetic praise but there is no mistaking the reverence in which the 67 members (31 of them silks) of this set are held. Leaders in pretty much every area in which the set decides to dip its toes, *"anything short of excellence is just not acceptable,"* according to one seasoned tenant.

Chambers and Partners Employment Set of the Year 2006 and Human Rights & Public Law Set of the Year 2006

It would probably take less space and time to detail the high-profile matters that members of Blackstone haven't appeared in than to provide an exhaustive list of all the set's notable cases but just as a taster, how about the recent House of Lords case confirming that officials of the Kingdom of Saudi Arabia should be protected by state immunity even when facing allegations of torture, hunting ban litigation, challenges to human fertilisation, or various sports matters such as litigation over ex-Chelsea player Adrian Mutu. As you can see, Blackstone Chambers has its fingers in a lot of pies. Apparently a few years ago, in a particularly memorable chambers meeting the clerks asked the members whether they wanted to be the best-paid members of the Bar or just well-paid but with the most interesting workload. They chose the latter.

The set moved to Blackstone House in 1998, having previously resided at 2 Hare Court. The change of location is credited with galvanising the set into a more forward-thinking entity and led the way for younger members to take the reins with a mandate to innovate. Everyone knows about the set's pre-eminence in public law, employment and human rights but in recent years members have found themselves at the forefront of new practice areas such as sport and media, as well as taking a lead role in the trend for mediation.

The road to pupillage at Blackstone is a tough one and to get there you're going to have to mark yourself out as someone who is *"capable of sustained academic brilliance."* Careful though: *"A fat Oxbridge First will not be enough on its own to get an interview."* Candidates who make it through the paper cut will have shown unquestioned commitment to the Bar. For the most part this will mean mini-pupillages and voluntary work, but given that the set prides itself on the quality of its advocacy, it is also worth accumulating significant public speaking experience through mooting or debating. At interview you're going to have to be completely on top of the legal issues of the day. Candidates are supplied with a list of topical questions half an hour beforehand and are expected to be able to discuss and defend when under extreme questioning (although we were assured that *"any attack is done in a good-natured way"*). One recent example asked whether libel laws offer too much protection to celebrities. Clarity of presentation and speed of thought are the key attributes recruiters want to see. *"We're not so bothered with the candidate's depth of knowledge on the issue. The question is whether they are able to argue elegantly and elo-*

quently." If you've impressed and haven't already completed a mini-pupillage with Blackstone, you will be invited to undertake one so members can take a longer look at you. Make the most of it as the second round of interviews will focus on your experiences within chambers. *"The people who have made it through to the second round will have passed with flying colours. What we're trying to work out is whether they really want to come to Blackstone or not."*

Pupillage is split into spells with four pupil-masters in different areas of practice. As it is rare to find a Blackstone barrister with just one core specialisation this leads to exposure to a wide range of work. The matters encountered will often receive considerable media attention: one pupil's first day involved accompanying his pupilmaster to address a nine-member panel of the House of Lords on whether the imprisonment of suspected terrorists at Belmarsh prison was unlawful.

Pupils only work for their PMs and do no paid work in their second six; the key thing is to make a good impression with every PM and score highly in the monthly videoed advocacy exercises. *"Yes, it's pressurised, but the fact that it's on videotape means that you can be sure the whole process is pretty objective."* Every pupil receives a formal letter after six months detailing how they're getting on and identifying areas for improvement. The tenancy committee collates this information and places it before a chambers meeting in July when a decision is made as to who gets taken on. Although we were told that it is possible for every pupil to get tenancy, recent history suggests that about half make it. And those that don't? *"Blackstone pupils don't get turned down when they knock on doors."*

Blackstone is very much the set that pioneered a relaxed dress code and while *"no one wanders around in their underwear"* the tenants we met did look pretty comfortable on the sweltering day that we visited them. Then again, the pupils we met were wearing suits, so perhaps it is the case that

true comfort at work can only be achieved after pupillage is over. As befits a set that is very consciously progressive, the decor is highly contemporary and a stroll around different members' rooms revealed furniture worlds apart from the dark brown mahogany we so often encounter on our visits. Readers will also be pleased to know that the goldfish stationed in the middle of the clerks' room that so struck us on our last visit to Blackstone are all alive and well and have managed to breed prolifically. With picturesque views of the Thames the pièce de résistance is chambers' roof garden, which weather allowing plays host to Friday evening drinks. It was also the setting for last year's Christmas party. Continuing the social theme, chambers has a softball team that can often be found playing against various firms of solicitors in Hyde Park.

The eighteenth-century English jurist William Blackstone once remarked on how "the public good is in nothing more essentially interested, than in the protection of every individual's private rights." Although barristers at this set work both for individuals and the state, ultimately their ideals reflect those of their namesake.

Brick Court Chambers

Chambers UK rankings: Admin & public law, aviation, banking & finance, commercial litigation, competition/European law, environment, fraud: civil, human rights, insurance, international arbitration, professional negligence, public procurement, sport, telecommunications

This 65-member set is a giant at the commercial Bar, but that's just the start of it. It also leads in the fields of European Union law and public law. Beyond the English courts, the set's EU specialists appear at the Competition Appeal Tribunal, as well as the Court of Justice and Court of First Instance in Luxembourg. Public law specialists are familiar with the European Court of Human Rights in Strasbourg and various other international fora. Sheer variety of activity could alone be regarded as Brick Court's greatest selling point. In fact, it is the quality of legal advice and the strength of its advocates that make chambers stand out.

Chambers and Partners
Competition/EU
Set of the Year 2006

Of the 26 silks in chambers, key names include the likes of Jonathan Sumption and Sir Sydney Kentridge, and their track records bear testimony to a phenomenal work ethic. No wonder a handful of the top guys earn a million or more each year. Sumption lately acted for the government in the claim brought by Railtrack shareholders, Kentridge in the case challenging the legitimacy of the hunting ban. Both had a big hand in the long-running Three Rivers litigation. Draw in other members' achievements and you have a pretty impressive portfolio of top work. Christopher Clarke QC was Counsel to the Tribunal in The Bloody Sunday Inquiry (and was recently appointed as a High Court judge) and various members have been participating in the Equitable Life litigation, EU competition wrangles on behalf of Microsoft, and an international dispute between Trans-world Metals and a Russian oligarch concerning a smelting plant in Kazakhstan. Some of chambers' other cases have things other than money at stake – members were involved in controversy concerning the Greek Olympic sprinters and various right-to-life cases. Knowing all this, you begin to get a sense of why Brick Court is such a colossus.

By the sounds of things, pupillage at Brick Court is "a steep learning curve and a real shock to the system." Fortunately, there are no hidden agendas: "It's quite simple; if your work is up to scratch then you'll make the grade." (Though, naturally, 'up to scratch' means damned good.) In 2005 two of the four pupils were given tenancy and in 2006 the set took on both pupils. "At the end of the day, it's all about ability. That's not to say that the people we don't take on aren't able, it's just that they haven't reached our absolute magical standard."

The nine gruelling months leading up to the tenancy decision in July are spent with three separate pupilmasters, and attempts are made to ensure that pupils see a good spread of the different types of work on offer. PMs do allow their charges to carry out work for others in chambers, but the pupillage committee has a definite view on pupils not needing to hawk themselves around chambers impressing all and sundry. The pupil we spoke to had spent her time working in each of the set's three major areas – public, EU and general commercial law, observing "highly cerebral matters right from the off." The option of spending a week in the set's annex in Brussels is taken up by some, and one pupil who had done so described it as "a nice change of scene and great from an EU law awareness point of view."

Besides "working prodigiously hard," the best tip for a Brick Court pupil is to "imagine every piece of work is your own. Putting your name to something has to be like a stamp of quality." Also, when doing work for your PM, "look at the bigger picture... it's about picking the right points, not all of them." This definitely isn't the place to come if you intend to pack up and head home at 6.02pm every day because the standard to which you are aiming inevitably requires late nights and weekends spent working. Another factor in the equation is the series of monthly assessed advocacy exercises that see pupils slug it out with each other in front of a panel of eminent members. "It's not a gladiatorial trial," we were assured; indeed, pupils actually seemed to find solace in having their compatriots beside them. "*It's more fun staggering through the waterfall with everyone else. We all go for a drink afterwards.*" Real-life advocacy is available in the second six, via small matters such as social security and possession hearings, which the clerks secure through relationships that are deliberately cultivated with a view to building up pupils' experience.

The tenancy decision is made in July, after the pupillage committee makes its recommendations to the entire set. By this stage the pupils should have an inkling as to how things will go, if only because they'll have had an appraisal of their prospects at the six-month stage. Almost all choose to stay for a full 12-month pupillage, appreciating what it can do for them, even if they must look elsewhere for tenancy.

How do you get onto the Brick Court pupillage shortlist? Although the set does participate in OLPAS, this really is little more than a final sifting stage. An assessed mini is a prerequisite for interview (although, confusingly, you have to interview for the mini-pupillage as well). The running theme of a successful candidate's application will be "*sustained academic excellence;*" at the interview stage this must be backed-up by evidence that they can "*articulate, process and analyse.*" The panel's questions will be demanding and intense, much like the style of advocacy in the commercial court. "*We find it exhilarating answering incisive questions in court and we expect those we take on will find it the same.*" In addition to a pre-prepared problem question, expect to discuss a topical legal matter. In 2005, interviewees were asked to discuss the decision to allow Roman Polanski to give evidence in his libel trial via video-link.

We felt duty-bound to ask about the supposedly austere atmosphere within chambers. Does it really exist? "*We've probably got that reputation because we're quite an introverted set and less concerned with outward appearances than some of our competitors,*" came the answer. "*Once people get here, the myth soon dissipates.*" There's still a sense of hierarchy. Clerks still call seniors Mister and Sir, while a pupil confessed: "*There are members that I wouldn't address because I'd have no idea what to call them.*" One of the juniors probably had it spot-on when they told us: "*Yes, there is a degree of respect and deference, but these characters have more than earned it. It's an absolute meritocracy and everyone is happy with that.*" The plush Essex Street premises have a certain majestic quality to them, with the fifth-floor roof garden offering a magnificent vista over the city. This choice spot is the setting for various marketing events with solicitors' firms, and as the senior clerk told us: "*You can sometimes see the Blackstone crew launching a book or something.*"

Brick Court attracts true high-fliers, those prepared to make sacrifices in order to succeed. The pupil we spoke to had obviously enjoyed pushing herself to her legal limits – her opinion on the year: "*It was the easiest money I've ever earned because every day was just so interesting.*" You have to ask, if it is such a demanding place, why would anyone choose pupillage at Brick Court? Again, the answer is simple. If you want to be at the best set for commercial work, or public law, or EU law, you have to put it right at the top of your shortlist. Brick Court does have equally good competition – in commercial cases it's the likes of Fountain, Essex Court and One Essex; in EU law it competes with Monckton; on the public law side it has rivals in Blackstone, Doughty Street, 11 KBW and a few others – but no other set achieves the same degree of excellence in all of them.

Cloisters

Chambers UK rankings: Clinical negligence, employment

Fifty-three years old and counting, the Cloisters juggernaut shows no signs of putting on the brakes. Its 44 practitioners continue to handle headline cases, more often than not on the winning side. Recent matters have included Harrygate (the unfair dismissal case of former Eton art teacher Sarah Forsyth); Saudi torture victims; appearances on behalf of members of the public who had made allegations of electoral fraud against three Labour councillors in Birmingham; the case of Ross v Ryanair (in which a disabled man was charged a fee for taking a wheelchair from check-in to the departure gate) and the public inquiry into the racist murder of Zahid Mubarek at Feltham Young Offender Institution. Evidently the Pump Court-based set is as committed as ever to its founding values of "fighting for the individual." Given this motto, you might think that members would appear primarily for claimants, but we learn that in the employment sphere, approximately 50% of the set's work is now respondent-based. Inevitably, justifications are advanced for this: you can only know your enemy by working for him and the social conscience work has to be financially supplemented by the respondent work.

As these cases indicate, Cloisters has its fingers in a number of pies. In all areas of practice within chambers, members have taken on landmark challenges. In employment, agreement was finally reached in Wilson v North Cumbria Acute NHS Trust, a widely reported equal pay matter that has resulted in the largest ever settlement in the UK. The case involved 1,500 women represented by UNISON and may pave the way for further equal pay cases against the NHS. Members have additionally won permission to take the UK's leading age discrimination case to the House of Lords. In

sport, a member has acted in a landmark case in the Court of Arbitration for Sport in Lausanne concerning the football transfer market. In human rights, although ultimately not successful, members tried to bring a case for unlawful exile on behalf of thousands of Chagossians removed from the island of Diego Garcia in 1965. In personal injury, clinical negligence and product liability, the set is conducting leading litigation, one recent case involving a young woman who contracted listerial meningitis as a week-old infant and hydrocephalus which remained undiagnosed for a year. Left with severe learning difficulties and physical problems, she received an out-of-court settlement of £3.9 million. In another case a leukaemia victim who was rendered paraplegic following an injection which was administered intrathetically rather than intravenously received a settlement of £1.5 million. The presence of high-profile and unusual work in so many areas ensures considerable scope for any young barrister or pupil. The set's four silks, Brian Langstaff, Simon Taylor, Arthur Davidson and Robin Allen, have each built a strong name, both in court and out. Allen is actively involved in advisory work on the drafting of employment legislation, providing Cloisters' juniors with excellent opportunities for research, and was recently appointed as a trustee of the London Bombings Relief Charitable Fund, set up to assist the victims and families affected by the 7/7 terrorist attacks.

A wide range of solicitors instruct the set, the niche operators and campaigning firms mingling with big commercial law firms. This is perhaps a testament to chambers' quality of service and a strong streak of realism as well as idealism. Regardless of who you act for, certain qualities will always stand you in good stead at Cloisters: "*You need resilience and you need to be able to pick yourself up and dust yourself down for the next big fight.*"

Pupils spend at least three months in each of chambers' two core areas – employment and personal injury. In the first six, their work will consist of drafting opinions and pleadings, attending conferences and preparing cross-examinations for their pupil supervisor. They'll have a fair idea of how well they're performing as the feedback is *"incredibly useful because they go into so much depth."* The second six is a different experience entirely. Gone are the regular 9am to 6pm days as the supervisor's shadow. They are still allocated a supervisor but a pupil's working rhythm will vary according to the size and nature of their own caseload. That's right, *their* caseload. Towards the end of pupillage, second sixers are on their feet for clients in employment tribunals and county courts. Naturally their work is initially fairly basic, simple employment claims or small civil claims, but the set has close links with various pro bono organisations which means that some quite interesting cases trickle through. Another thing to note is that the pupillage award has grown considerably in recent years, which means that pupils can focus on getting the widest possible experience without worrying too much about their finances.

Nailed to the end of the year is a series of assessed exercises to test pupils' advocacy, research and drafting skills. The results are used in conjunction with a final interview with the tenancy committee to determine whether the set will offer tenancy. If a pupil reaches a specified standard (80%), tenancy is a given. In this process there is minimal scope for subjectivity, a degree of consideration being paid to the input of the pupil supervisors. *"We're consciously trying to minimise the 'if your face fits' approach to tenancy selection,"* proclaimed one member. *"But it's certainly not a complete free-for-all,"* in recent years one or two pupils have been granted tenancy each time. We sensed that pupils are not usually overly competitive with each other. *"I feel insulated from the typical popularity contest that goes on between pupils. The objective nature of the system means we're more likely to confide than compete,"* revealed one pupil. The only fly in the ointment in this exquisitely fair system is the fact that the decision is not made until September, meaning that the unfortunates who don't get taken on can be disadvantaged when trying to locate a third six.

Getting pupillage at Cloisters is no cakewalk and if you don't show evidence of commitment to the set's core values on your OLPAS form then you're unlikely to be invited to interview. *"We want to root out the absolute mercenaries, but at the same time we're not looking to attract complete zealots."* Throw in a demonstrable aptitude for a career at the Bar plus sterling academic credentials and the chances are you'll be among the 70 or so hopefuls who are summoned for first interview. Here, you'll be given half an hour to prepare a contract or tort-based problem question and the key element the panel is looking for is an ability to order things clearly in your mind. In other words, you've got to *"get to grips with the problem and not get bogged down with the irrelevant stuff. The candidate who structures their answer well always scores highly."* The second interview is longer with much of the discussion centred on another problem question, but this time you will have had a week to prepare (and bite your fingernails to the quick).

Though Cloisters is well into middle age, there is a sense of youth and energy about the place. After our last visit we referred to the set's nickname 'Bolly Chambers', earned as a result of members' desire to crack open the champagne at every available opportunity. Nothing much has changed it would seem. *"Every time there's a birthday, engagement or anniversary, we make sure we celebrate it. We're certainly a chambers that comes together for a party."* A relaxed dress code is illustrative of the set's informal nature – *"pomp and circumstance is not the Cloisters way."* Something that is 'the Cloisters way' is an informal commitment by every member to do at least five days of pro bono work each year. This is just one part of a set of collective values that defines and binds chambers together but, we're happy to say, doesn't overwhelm it.

Crown Office Chambers

Chambers UK rankings: Clinical negligence, construction, personal injury, product liability, professional negligence, professional negligence: construction

With 80 practitioners, Crown Office Chambers comfortably holds the title of London's largest common law set. In May 2005 Anthony Edward-Stuart QC took over the reins from previous joint heads of chambers Michael Spencer QC and Christopher Purchas QC, who had steadied the ship since the merger between One Paper Buildings and 2 Crown Office Row in 2000. The point of the merger was to fuse two first-class insurance-led sets into one superset that could better ride the ups and downs of the market. A sort of if you can't beat 'em join 'em' merger, if you like. Though not quite a unified body in geographical terms just yet, there is certainly a commonality of purpose at COC. That commonality is insurance litigation, the thread that runs through even the specialist areas of practice. COC can justifiably boast expertise in six key areas: construction, insurance, health and safety, product liability, professional negligence and personal injury. It is also developing an impressive education practice. This spread of expertise has placed it in various notable cases including a number of work-related stress matters heard in the Court of Appeal following the House of Lords decision in Barber v Somerset County Council; class action litigation in relation to MMR, tobacco and oral contraceptives; and representation at public and judicial inquiries into major rail crashes and the racist murder of Zahid Mubarek at Feltham Young Offender Institution.

The list of solicitors that instruct the set is long and features leading firms from around the country including Halliwells, CMS Cameron McKenna, Pinsent Masons, Beachcroft Wansbroughs, Berrymans Lace Mawer, Lovells, Morgan Cole and Vizards Wyeth. Again, the common denominator for many is their insurance clientele. Although it varies according to each member's practice, the majority (roughly 70/30) of the work undertaken at COC is on the defendant side, typically insurance companies disputing liability and/or quantum. Is it difficult, when defending claims brought by injured individuals, to have as a principal aim the minimisation of insurance companies' financial outlay? Not a bit. "*There is no monopoly on virtue in a PI claim,*" countered one junior tenant. Indeed, the public backlash against ambulance chasers and the compensation culture lays the path open for the argument that it is the defendant barristers who actually have the moral high ground. Having said this, our sources had to concede that the client contact on offer in claimant work "*does get the old adrenaline flowing a lot more than when you're doing defendant work.*"

As with many sets, the first three-month segment of pupillage is a bedding-in period, with a little more required of you in the second three. All up, the first six is split between time in chambers learning to draft pleadings etc., and accompanying your supervisor or another practitioner to court a couple of times each week. This is an opportunity to see the nuts and bolts of common law advocacy and the other court skills that will be required of you in practice. One pupil recalled the buzz of seeing one of the most eminent silks in chambers tearing strips off an expert witness in cross-examination. "*It was a highly inspirational experience. When you see people of that quality doing their stuff and then get the chance to talk with them afterwards, you feel very privileged indeed.*" Our thanks go to the seasoned campaigner who gave us the lowdown on what it takes to be a successful common law practitioner. "*You need to be exceptionally strong at fact management. Being able to work out which facts undermine and which facts help is an integral part of what we do.*"

The second-six pupil is a busy animal. In addition to doing work for their pupil supervisor and appearing in court three or four times a week on CMCs, infant settlement approval hearings and some small claims trials worth under £5,000, after a little practice they progress to fast-track claims (worth up to £15,000). Most hearings at this level tend to be within the M25 although travelling further afield is certainly not unheard of. As well as court hearings you'll do paperwork for other members of chambers too. Fortunately supervisors are on hand to act as gatekeepers, ensuring that you don't make promises you can't keep. Certain members hold more sway than others in the tenancy decision meeting and, knowing this, supervisors will gently nudge you in their direction from time to time so you get your chance to impress. Another important tip is to make sure you're always courteous to your instructing solicitors because the feedback they give to the clerks will be factored into the tenancy decision in July. Supervisors at COC are a conscientious bunch and clearly concerned with their pupils' welfare. Said one: "*We're not a 'good morning, good night' sort of set. We like to engage with the pupil.*" We have to say, in the money-driven world of insurance, it's refreshing to find a set that is as intent on developing pupils' professionalism and ethical responsibilities as it is their commercial nous and courtroom skills. And supervisors aren't the only port of call for problems: the most junior tenants take the role of aunts and uncles to the pupils, and because they don't get a say in the tenancy decision "*you don't have to worry about what you say and how stupid you sound.*"

As a non-OLPAS set, all applicants need to complete COC's own application form. This is your opportunity to show off an excellent academic record and an extensive knowledge of what the set is all about, whilst also demonstrating outside interests. Jump through this particular hoop and you'll find yourself at a first interview. But be prepared for some off-the-wall questioning – one recent example required candidates to explain an iPod to a Martian. The recruiters are looking for a blend of "*articulacy, assertiveness and aptitude;*" the candidate who is able to "*argue unattractive positions without preparation*" will score highly.

The reality is that if you make it to pupillage, you'll never get to know everyone in chambers given its size. It got us wondering whether the presence of such a large number of barristers had a negative or positive impact on the set's self-image and social life. We learned that weekly drinks in one of the conference rooms are "*always well attended*" and that Chez Gerard and The Gaucho Grill provide the setting for spontaneous drinks when the junior end of chambers is in the mood. Pupils are invited to all of these events and the supervisor we spoke to makes a point of ending each of his pupil's sojourns with lunch in the restaurant of their choosing. Cricket matches with solicitors firms feature in the summer's entertainment programme, the idea being "*to lose competitively so that the firms continue to instruct us.*" Surely it's not that simple!

Devereux Chambers

Chambers UK rankings: Employment, insurance, personal injury, telecommunications

If it's a busy mix of cases and a convivial atmosphere you're after and you rather like the northern edge of the Temple, Devereux Chambers is absolutely your set. Okay, so it is not top dog in any one area of practice but its members do have a habit of cropping up in the rankings for an impressive number of areas. In addition to three core specialisations of employment, personal injury and commercial, members have a presence in health and safety, telecommunications, sports law, education, environment, professional negligence and even tax. Head of chambers Colin Edelman

QC has an excellent name for insurance and reinsurance. He has acted in several notable cases recently, including one dealing with 9/11 compensation. On the employment side, where there is an even balance of applicant and respondent work, chambers has been involved in cases that have attracted considerable media attention, particularly in the realm of high-value discrimination and bullying claims against big international banks. In a case where employment meets PI, one member of chambers, Oliver Hyams, acted for the employee in the recent House of Lords matter McCabe v Cornwall County Council which defined the conditions in which an employee can sue an employer for stress-related personal injury.

The story of how Devereux became a jack of many trades is quite interesting. Until the mid-seventies, it operated happily on a diet of crime and personal injury. Then, in a classic case of right place, right time, members became involved in a number of high-profile trade union matters which in turn led to the set developing a growing reputation in the employment sphere in the 1980s. Gradually the criminal work died away and was replaced by an increasingly commercial caseload. Throw in the fact that this was where Alan Moses QC (now a senior Court of Appeal judge) once plied his trade and you can see how the set has managed to upgrade the quality of its work over the years. Top-level work doesn't lead to top-level stuffiness however. "*Even though we're a bit more specialised these days we've managed to retain that common law set ethos which means that no one's up their own arse.*" This is also a set with advocates who enjoy their time in court. "*We're not court jesters but it's definitely true that well-deployed wit can produce many benefits in the courtroom.*"

The way to navigate a successful course through pupillage at Devereux is to show proficiency in each of the set's core areas by impressing a different pupil supervisor every three months. Whether this bar has been cleared will become apparent in a vote by all tenants in a July meeting. If at least two-thirds of members are on-side then you're in. A tip: put in maximum effort when doing personal injury work as this is the biggest group in chambers. In addition to the report sheets filled in by supervisors there are also a number of assessed advocacy exercises to be taken throughout the year. The constant feedback pupils receive is not only extensive, it can be critical and "*you get the feeling that they are always trying to encourage and not undermine confidence.*"

Typically pupils will research an aspect of a case and write an opinion. The temptation to try and impress your PM with all the law you can muster should be avoided as Devereux prides itself on providing clear and concise practical advice to clients – not bamboozling them with spurious exceptions to the rule. In your second six, you're on your feet from the word go with instructions including RTAs and relatively straightforward employment tribunal claims.

If you set your heart on pupillage at Devereux, be prepared to go the extra mile to get an interview. It's not just what you write on your application but the way you write it. "*Even the most mundane detail can be written in an interesting way.*" A consistently high level of academic achievement is important but most of all the recruiters are looking for "*people who are on their way up.*" The candidate's motivation for applying to Devereux is also key: "*If they can show that they would be a good fit with the set we take that into account.*" The first interview is a getting to know you session with a discussion on any interesting aspects of the candidate's CV. Fair play to them, our sources were happy to confirm that extreme examples of altruism are not the deciding factor here. "*Everyone seems to have dug a well in Namibia these days so we're on the lookout for the candidate who grabs our attention.*" Display the requisite combination of articulacy, poise and humour and you'll probably be back for a second interview when you'll be presented with a problem question half an hour before proceedings. This is your chance to demonstrate your ability to give structured answers in a fluent manner with minimal preparation time. "*The successful candidates are those who are able to organise their minds and engage the panel. Everyone who gets to the final stage is manifestly very bright, but some can't cope with pressure.*"

After the second interview candidates can have a confidential chat with a baby junior and "*ask as many stupid questions as* [they] *like.*" This is the perfect opportunity to get the low-down on chambers whilst also finding out the correct answer to the problem question they have just tackled. The new tenant we spoke to saw this gesture as pivotal in influencing her decision to choose Devereux over other sets. "*It gave the impression of an open, friendly, supportive set and I can honestly say nothing I've seen since has altered that impression.*"

As is increasingly common in the Temple, a lack of space in chambers has resulted in approximately half of the 45 members moving to Queen Elizabeth Building overlooking Middle Temple Gardens. We wondered whether this led to a slightly polarised atmosphere – not a bit, as "*everyone comes up from QEB most days to have a bit of a gossip.*" Although we are always wary of extensive claims of friendliness and camaraderie within sets, we have to say that our visits to Devereux more than substantiate the assertion. There's no formal chambers tea at Devereux, just "*ad hoc sandwich sessions in a conference room depending on who is about.*" If there is a major sporting event during the week, the set will normally reserve seats in a local pub so people can go and watch it. A netball team has been formed ("*it puts everyone on a level playing field*") and the clerks-v-barristers football match "*always proves entertaining.*" Evidently there is a thriving social scene, though our sources stressed "*there is no assessment on social interaction – we don't make judgements on who's going to be the best drinking buddy.*"

As we left Devereux, before navigating our way back down the alleyways towards the RCJ, we paused to admire the colourful geraniums and fuchsias on show in the window boxes. They seemed an apt reflection of the barristers on show at Devereux – vibrant, natural, cheerful. In 2006 the set offered tenancy to both of its pupils.

Doughty Street Chambers

Chambers UK rankings: Admin & public law, clinical negligence, crime, defamation/privacy, fraud: criminal, human rights, immigration, personal injury, police law, product liability, social housing

Many people say they want to make a difference, but few actually do so. We'd venture that Doughty Street has more than its fair share of the kind who are not only motivated to fight the good fight but actually climb into the ring eager for the sound of the bell. Ranked by *Chambers UK* in more 'worthy' areas of practice than you can shake a stick at, the set plays host to practitioners who battle to protect and develop human rights. Doughty Street's website sets out its collective values and, in short, these boil down to "defending freedom and citizens' rights" and running chambers according to principles of "equality, respect and diversity."

Imagine you're a man who has been imprisoned for 25 years following a conviction for the attempted murder of a nine-year-old boy. Imagine you were just 15 years old and living in care when you were accused of the crime and you were never told of your right to consult a solicitor. Imagine you're a gypsy unable to stay on a site you've come to regard as your home. Imagine you're one of 417 prisoners sitting on death row in Uganda, praying that your sentence will be commuted to life imprisonment. These are situations embraced by Doughty Street lawyers.

Long involvement in criminal and immigration law is complemented by high-level expertise in areas such as press freedom and personal injury cases connected with, for example, Gulf War Syndrome and forces' post-traumatic stress disorder. This is the place to go if you want to rub shoulders in the library with real big hitters such as Helena Kennedy QC, Edward Fitzgerald QC and Keir Starmer QC, whose clients include the McLibel two and MI5 whistleblower David Shayler.

Putting 85 barristers together in a relatively small Georgian terrace inevitably means space is at a premium. As pupils and junior tenants are often in court this isn't an insurmountable problem, but we do suggest you put aside any notions of having your own magnificent office complete with mahogany desk and grandiloquent bookcase stacked with law reports. Pupils tend to be based in the less glamorous confines of the set's civil and criminal libraries in the basement where they have access to chambers' extensive computer facilities.

No one pretends pupillage at Doughty Street is easy. It is in fact "a year-long interview, with a seemingly endless parade of assessments and hurdles to clear." Before kicking off, pupils are provided with a list of all the potential supervisors and invited to select the one with the practice that most appeals. Depending on the area in which they want to specialise, their first six is spent with either a civil or a criminal practitioner. Naturally enough, the criminal pupils spend the majority of their time in court while their civil counterparts are more likely to be found in the basement researching or preparing written work. Regardless of this distinction, when it comes to the second six all pupils take to their feet for their own magistrates' court criminal cases as well as occasional immigration and asylum hearings. Pupils are automatically provided with the cost of Zones 1-2 travel and additional travel costs are immediately reimbursed.

The race for tenancy is very much an open competition between four pupils. Doughty Street isn't one of those 'we'll take on everyone if they're good enough' places; the set takes on one new tenant from among its pupils each year and one only. Pupils earn their stripes through a combination of written and oral assessments and the mountainous pile of report sheets prepared by their supervisors throughout the year. No feedback is offered on these set pieces of work, meaning that until the tenancy announcement in October, it can be hard for a pupil to gauge how things are going. What did become clear from our discussions with pupils past and present is that the element of the unknown leads to esprit de corps between the pupils, which in turn makes the process a lot more bearable.

One of those we interviewed sagely commented that "someone who was determined to shaft everyone else wouldn't be here anyway; that would run totally against the ethos of the place." The pupils appear to have no complaints about the nature of the decision-making process, saying: "We went into this with our eyes wide open, everyone has been completely up front about it from day one." The objective nature of the system means "there's none of that paranoia about what work other pupils have got or who they are chatting to in the library."

The "militantly fair" rules that apply to the tenancy decision are also in play when it comes to pupillage applications. OLPAS applications are scrutinised by at least two members of chambers who apply strict criteria in assembling a list of candidates for first interview. This is not the place to apply to on a whim, and unless you can demonstrate a genuine commitment to the welfare of others in addition to strong intellect and high motivation, you'll waste the time of all concerned. Although it was stressed that attempts are made to ensure that the 21-year-old LLB student and the 41-year-old candidate with bags of life experience are competing on a level playing field, it was telling that the youngest pupil we spoke to was in their late twenties. With regard to academic qualifications, nothing suggests that any particular institution is preferred, and the focus – such that it is – rests purely on your results. Applicants with less than a 2:1 must ensure they have sufficiently impressive non-academic achievements to make a compelling case for an interview. The sort of thing that will tick this commitment box may include working in a Law Centre or for a charitable organisation. Bear in mind that Doughty Street's recruiters are looking for evidence of long-term commitment so it pays to get involved with such organisations as early as possible.

First-interview candidates are given a problem question on something topical just ten minutes before meeting a panel of two barristers. In recent years questions have concerned animal rights and the right to privacy for paedophiles. The candidate must present their case persuasively and anticipate potential stumbling blocks. The panel looks for "*someone who demonstrates potential as both a barrister and a future colleague,*" so try to find a perfect blend of authority and personality. The second interview shortens the field to 20 hopefuls and follows a similar format, just with a larger panel and questioning that is noticeably more rigorous.

Doughty Street attracts people of a certain political and philosophical persuasion and there are no prizes for guessing that the underlying emphasis is somewhat anti-establishment. Said one source: "*Of course we're all political animals – you don't do this type of work without having cultivated some sort of social conscience.*" That said, we didn't get the impression that pupils are obliged to have their Amnesty International membership badges on display at all time. "*No one in chambers is impressed with political tub-thumping. The chances are if you've got something to say you'll act on it.*"

Informality is the order of the day and if members aren't due in court, chances are they'll be dressed casually. Don't mistake this informal vibe for laziness – everyone works phenomenally hard. The work demands it. Whether it's a senior QC involved in a highly publicised international war crimes case or an anonymous immigration matter conducted by a baby junior, barristers here are conscious of "*dealing with matters of major humanitarian significance*" and, as such, must always apply "*absolute commitment to the cause.*"

Although it's a set where "*everybody does their own thing outside of work*" there is ample interaction between members during the week and pupils assured us that "*no one, whatever their seniority, is too busy to offer advice if asked to do so.*" Friday evenings always involve drinks in chambers' reception room or the garden, and those not rushing back to family commitments will inevitably be drawn to nearby pub The Duke. When we visited, plans were afoot to mark the set's 15th anniversary with a garden party at one of the silks' homes.

You won't end up at Doughty Street by accident or mere good fortune; you have to be the sort of person who has a real desire to be at the sharp end of the law and work hard to stay there. In short, this set remains the destination of choice for those who wish to stay true to the ideals that got them interested in law in the first place.

Erskine Chambers

Chambers UK rankings: Commercial litigation, company, insolvency/corporate recovery

Highly professional, highly committed and highly respected, Erskine Chambers is the natural destination for the pupil whose boat is rocked by shareholder disputes, takeovers and mergers. No other set gets near Erskine for the quality and depth of its company practice. Although it sounds like a narrow branch of law, company law actually impacts on a wide range of commercial disputes. Regulars on the pink pages, members are always in the mix on the biggest and bitterest takeover fights – think Philip Green's aggressive bid for M&S and the scrap for control of the Canary Wharf Group. Those drawn to long-running litigation can't fail to be impressed with Erskine's involvement in the Equitable Life case and the 'Spice Wars' dispute between members of the Pathak family who were battling over their shareholdings and control of the family's multimillion-pound pickle business. Insolvency also features large, and highly publicised matters have included Marconi and MyTravel.

Having resisted the urge to get involved in the merger mania among commercial sets at the beginning of the decade, Erskine cemented its independence by moving to brand new Chancery Lane premises in January 2004. It has proved a big hit with all concerned. In a previous edition we noted how the set had a very private feel to it with closed doors the norm. The increase in size means that every tenant now has a huge room and enough space to pile up huge quantities of files; as a consequence open doors are now very much par for the course. That's not to say that the set has metamorphosed into a place where everybody indulges in endless conversations in the corridor but there is certainly a more open feel than when we last visited. One thing that hasn't changed is that (as is perhaps inevitable with a top specialist set) a significant number of cases end up being conducted against other members of chambers.

Let's get one thing straight: Erskine barristers are remarkably talented but they don't boast about how great they are. The typical barrister has earned a reputation for "*meticulous measured advocacy*" and epitomises quiet authority. We doubt that it was coincidence that everyone we spoke to had a cool, calm, grounded air. "*Someone with a large ego would be at a real disadvantage here. We have a tough audience, a combination of astute business people and the best commercial solicitors in the country. These aren't the sort of people who appreciate being talked down to.*"

The set would like to be a little larger but it appears that any future expansion is to be carried out in a characteristically cautious manner. "*We're not going to compromise on quality in order to beef up the head count.*" Indeed, in recent years, any growth has been organic. By the same token, those who leave Erskine rarely do so in order to join another set; the call is either to the bench or retirement. The net result of all this is that if a pupil does gain tenancy at Erskine, it's because the set sees them as someone who will still be with chambers in 30 years' time. If you suffer from any sort of commitment phobia, maybe this isn't the place for you. Among the set's eight QCs is star name and head of chambers Robin Potts. He follows in the wake of company law oracle Richard Sykes, whose opinions were treated almost as gospel in both private sector and government circles.

An applicant's academic record is going to have to be pretty strong to snag an interview at Erskine. The ideal candidate should be able to demonstrate a high degree of self-discipline because: "*We're looking for evidence of time-management skills – someone who has managed to excel academically but also do other things at the same time. A commercial practitioner needs to be able to keep a number of projects on the go at one time and devote enough time to each of them.*" Naturally enough, a further prerequisite for a successful application is a demonstrable interest in company law. "*We don't expect anyone to have an A-Z knowledge of the subject, just a genuine interest in it.*" A final piece of advice for your application form: "*Be succinct and accurate. We like applicants who say in one sentence what others say in three.*" When it comes to interview, "*the ability to think coherently and clearly and be willing to stand up and defend your position*" is highly prized, as are "*people who can be amicable and articulate.*"

The pupillage year is split up into three-month segments spent with four different pupilmasters and mistresses whose practices can have either litigation or advisory leanings. In view of the fact that company law matters can be long-running, strenuous efforts are made to ensure that pupils are kept up to speed with the progress of cases on which they have worked earlier in the year. "*It's important a pupil gets to see the twists and turns every case can take.*" At first glance, pupillage at Erskine appears to be less stressful than at other commercial sets. For the first three months "*the pupil is not in the spotlight, it's more of a bedding-in process.*" Don't get used to the easy life though because after Christmas "*things step up a gear or two*" and over the next six months pupils must complete written work (a mixture of opinions and pleadings typically) for every member of chambers. This work can come back to haunt them at a later stage as it is largely what influences the tenancy decision in July. Nonetheless, the requirement was seen as "*a great opportunity to interact with everyone and show what you are capable of on an individual basis.*" Pupils' hours are not excessively long: the one we spoke to was always away by 6.30pm and, in view of the fact that he had no security key-tag, there was no way he could physically be in the building past 7pm.

The learning experience doesn't stop at the end of pupillage; those who do get taken on as tenants often go on six-month secondments to City firms such as Slaughter and May or US practice Skadden Arps, all of which paints a picture of a set that is supportive of its younger practitioners.

This isn't a Friday-drinks-in-the-clerks-room sort of operation: "*We're not that type of set, we work hard here but those who do play hard, tend to do it outside of chambers.*" The social scene – such as it is – tends to revolve around chambers tea, the ideal moment to bounce ideas and legal concepts off others. The pupil we spoke to was "*never made to feel afraid to chip in*" and praised the event as "*extremely enlightening.*"

We were left with the impression of a set that is supremely comfortable with itself and equally clear about where it wants to go. Anyone thinking about joining its ranks must have the ability and the will to learn to uphold high standards. What the set can promise is excellent quality work, excellent earning potential and unquestioned respect from others at the Bar and beyond.

Essex Court Chambers

Chambers UK rankings: Agricultural & rural affairs, banking & finance, commercial litigation, employment, energy & natural resources, fraud: civil, insurance, international arbitration, media & entertainment, public international law, shipping & commodities

A child of the 1960s, Essex Court Chambers was formed by a group of five ambitious young barristers eager for fame and fortune. They quickly established themselves and Essex Court is now one of the elite magic circle sets at the commercial Bar. For many years it was principally fêted for its expertise in shipping and insurance law, although recently other areas have been developed, with a number of members building respected practices in fields such as banking and finance, or media and entertainment. Epitomising this multi-tasking approach is head of chambers Gordon Pollock QC, who is ranked in an impressive six different practice areas in *Chambers UK*. If you think chambers rests on the reputation of one or two giants, forget it – Essex Court has a total of 32 silks within the 74-strong membership and there are highly respected figures at every turn. For example, VV Veeder is a king in international arbitration, Andrew Hochhauser steals the show in employment and Sir Christopher Greenwood is a bona fide big hitter for public international law. The set generates instructions from a wide range of solicitors, though it has developed especially good links with firms such as Clyde & Co, Holman Fenwick & Willan and Ince & Co. Major work of recent times has included the BCCI litigation and various shipping cases including that relating to the oil tanker

Prestige which sank off the coast of Spain and caused considerable pollution. Proving that members are certainly not restricted to shipping cases, one of them represented Michael Jackson in an action relating to the now infamous documentary Martin Bashir made for Granada Television, and another took on a VAT dispute concerning mobile phone company 3G. A third worked on a dispute relating to the Iraq Oil for Food programme.

Chambers and Partners International Arbitration Set of the Year 2006

One of the first things to note about pupillage at Essex Court is that it could all be over very quickly. Unusually for the commercial Bar, the tenancy decision is made after just six months, and although the unfortunates are not immediately booted out of the door, it normally works out best for all parties if a second six is undertaken elsewhere. Those we spoke to saw the early decision date as a real advantage. "*It means you can get on with the learning side of things in the second six without the distraction of having to impress everyone.*" As to how many pupils succeed in getting tenancy, "*the bar is set high, but if you clear it then you're in. There are no other considerations like space or work.*" In 2005 the set took on three of its five pupils; the year before it was two out of four.

Whilst "*not fast and furious,*" the first three months of pupillage are an important time as pupilmasters are "*running the rule over the pupil's character,*" if only because they are required to produce written reports on pupils' progress at the end of their period of supervision. The key period is undoubtedly the first three months after Christmas. The pupil we spoke with may have been slightly understating things when he described the experience as "*short but hard.*" Five successive

fortnights are spent with five different senior practitioners (three silks, two senior juniors) who sit on the pupillage committee, and the pupil carries out an array of exercises for each one. Some may watch over your every move and give you small tasks to complete daily; others may set you one large challenge and tell you to come back in ten days with the finished article. Admittedly, you'll pick up some useful experience during this period, but pupils are left in no doubt that this stage of pupillage is "*all about assessment. You have to excel in all areas in order to clear the barrier.*" Feedback is only given at the end of the process and not during, meaning that pupils are "*completely in the dark about how things are going*" until the tenancy decision is made just before Easter. It's only fair to say that while much is demanded of pupils, much is given in return. Attention is lavished on them at "*tremendously instructive*" tuition sessions delivered weekly by silks.

Essex Court prides itself on being a "*very caring set*" that places a high priority on pastoral care for pupils. Clerks were compared to housemasters by virtue of the way they "*look after you and make sure that you're headed in the right direction.*" From what we can tell, the clerks are in no small part responsible for the learning-based approach to the second six. In essence, the pupil is able to dictate the direction of their future practice through indicating the areas in which they would like to specialise. With this in mind they can then tailor their second six in order to augment their knowledge in their chosen field. By way of example we heard about secondments to solicitors firms, lecturing appointments and pupils accompanying eminent silks to international courts.

Contrary to what one might expect from a set bursting with silks, there is considerable interaction between members: "*We're not at all toffee-nosed,*" claimed a pupil. "*Everyone is down-to-earth and exceptionally well-grounded. Arrogance just wouldn't be tolerated here.*" The weekly Friday chambers lunch is always well attended and provides "*an ideal opportunity to get your feet under the table.*" Juniors can often be found in the nearby Seven Stars chewing the cud over the day's events, but the important dates on the social calendar are the summer party and the Christmas do, which this year was at Somerset House.

"*Academic excellence is merely the starting point*" for an application to Essex Court. If you haven't got a First or a particularly compelling reason for not having earned one you won't even get a shoelace in the door, let alone a foot. "*There is a highly intellectualised collegiate feel about the place,*" said one member. "*Academic debate is strongly encouraged*" something well illustrated by the annual student mooting competition chambers has run for several years. Recruiters are equally keen on candidates who can show a nascent commercial focus. With this in mind, vacation schemes at solicitors firms and a master's degree in something pertinent to commercial litigation are looked upon favourably. It helps to be a winner as well – the CVs of recent recruits are littered with scholarships and prizes. Throw in a bit of public speaking ("*we have cultivated a strong reputation for the quality of our oral advocacy*") and you've got every chance of being among the 40 or so invited to the single round of interviews. After navigating the obligatory problem question where the panel are looking for the candidate who "*presents the relevant arguments clearly and concisely,*" the "*probing yet good-natured*" questioning then focuses on your experiences in an attempt to avoid the "*formulaic stock responses which every candidate has in their repertoire.*"

Although they're all competing with one another for the best pupils and the top work, each of the four magic circle sets has its own individual characteristics. Essex Court has 45 years of tradition on its side yet is not afraid to be forward-thinking when needs be. Its move out of the Temple in 1994 to its swish premises at 24-28 Lincoln's Inn Fields is a clear example of that... despite the fact that none of the others followed!

One Essex Court

Chambers UK rankings: Banking & finance, commercial litigation, company, energy & natural resources, fraud: civil, intellectual property, international arbitration, professional negligence, tax

One Essex Court is 40 years old in 2006 and, as it approaches middle age, it has plenty of reasons to feel proud. Firmly established in the magic circle of commercial sets, it hosts a squad of big-name silks including Mark Barnes, Ian Glick, Nick Strauss, younger star Laurence Rabinowitz and legendary head of chambers Lord Grabiner, who gets pulled in on 'bet the company' cases.

The OEC juggernaut really got up and running in the 1970s when Sam Stamler QC, along with two pupils (Strauss and Grabiner), formed strong links with the corporate law firm Slaughter and May. Stamler's measured approach became a blueprint for high practice standards, which continue today. It's a Rolls-Royce service for which many clients are prepared to pay top whack . Also important to note is the generalist nature of OEC's practitioners: they are perfectly able to "*turn their hand with aplomb to any type of commercial dispute.*" The list of firms that now instruct the set reads like a Who's Who of major litigation, and there is a certain inevitability about the high-profile nature of the cases on which members act. The multibillion-pound Equitable Life jamboree; post-Enron claims including Mahonia Ltd v West LB; and the international banking litigation involving Sumitomo and Crédit Lyonnais are all evidence of the set's claim to be a number-one choice for commercial and banking cases. And sometimes, even if the claim doesn't run to billions, clients simply want the best advocates. Earlier in 2005, Lord Grabiner found himself arguing in court over the provenance of a £2 million Louis XV urn sold at auction by Christies.

Quality advocacy is a hallmark of this set. Those in charge of pupils believe they can hone an individual's skill and performance, provided the nuts and bolts are there in the first place. "*There's no such thing as a born advocate,*" a pupilmaster told us, "*but if you don't have that sense of self-assurance then you'll never be convincing.*" Don't interpret this as arrogance: "*The commercial barrister with a God complex will never be regularly instructed on the big cases. Who'd want to put up with that for two years?*" Which brings us on to the other attributes you'll need to thrive at OEC. First, commercial awareness – can you recognise the business needs of your client and answer the questions that are important to them? This may require more than legal knowledge. Second, you'll need to be a problem solver with real attention to detail: "*Any mistake you make has the potential to cost your client millions. You have to be prepared to go over everything with a fine-tooth comb.*"

Pupillage at OEC is apparently "*a long but enjoyable slog.*" Expect a change of pupilmaster every three months, each one having a relatively broad commercial practice. If you do have leanings towards the tax and IP spheres though, feel free to bring it up and efforts will be made to accommodate your wishes. Although most of your time is spent in chambers researching and drafting, you will get a few days in court to observe the advocates in action. You will effectively become the property of your first two pupilmasters and they will only allow you to take work from other members if they think you can handle it. Having them act as gatekeepers cuts out the otherwise unavoidable sense of awkwardness that comes when you have to turn people down. As and when first six pupils do work for other members, it will usually be limited to research. Unsurprisingly, "*accuracy is the buzzword,*" and at times it can be nerve-wracking

working for some of the big names. The second six also brings advocacy and paid work. Whatever, wherever: it's all good experience.

Working the occasional weekend or series of late nights is a hazard of the job for a commercial practitioner and OEC isn't one of those sets that shoos pupils out of the door if they're still in chambers after 6pm. The pupils we spoke to expected to be in by 9am and still working until at least 7pm on an average day. When things get hairy, reach for the Red Bull. On the plus side, after gaining tenancy, decent breaks between cases more than make up for long hours, and as one member explained: "*If you get really into an interesting case you don't feel the time flying by.*" A hard-working atmosphere inevitably leads to a quiet-to-moderate social scene, though a group of regulars can often be found lunching at the unofficial 'chambers table' in Inner Temple's dining hall. There are also drinks for an hour or so on Friday evenings and showing up won't do your tenancy prospects any harm. The dress code for tenants is relatively informal, but pupils are best advised to stick to suits to be on the safe side. Apparently when it comes to conduct, appearance and demeanour, "*the test is what would some mythical elderly member of chambers think?*"

In 2006, as in the recent past, chambers has taken on three brand-new tenants. Life as a baby junior is a mix of very small cases which can be run alone, and positions as second or third junior on larger cases. The earning potential is fantastic.

OEC practitioners tend to be measured individuals who don't waste their words. That's not to say the flamboyant or garrulous individual won't survive here, rather that the focus is on substance not bluster. To that end, your academic credentials are going to have to be highly impressive to get yourself an invitation to interview. Anything less than a First in your degree and you'll need to plump up your OLPAS form with a grand slam of extra-curricular achievements. This is also the time to show an *"intelligent appreciation of what life as a commercial barrister entails."* At interview you'll be presented with a practical legal problem and a copy of *Chitty on Contracts* 90 minutes prior to meeting the panel. Here's your opportunity to display that hallowed problem-solving ability we mentioned. The panel members will also be asking themselves how well you engage with them and *"will we have confidence in this person with our hard-earned client base?"*

OEC recruits at least four pupils each year (five are starting 2007), and every year it competes fiercely with the other magic circle sets to snag pupils from the two handfuls of crème de la crème candidates. Every year the set is convinced that it comes out a winner, but what marks it out from the competition? *"It's a serious set, but at the same time there is a refreshing lack of pomposity,"* explained one member. *"You don't sense that there's any agonising about where the set wants to be. There is no identity crisis. It's exactly where it wants to be and that's the sign of good management."*

20 Essex Street

Chambers UK rankings: Banking & finance, commercial litigation, insurance, international arbitration, public international law, shipping & commodities

20 Essex Street is a bastion of excellence in shipping and international law and has been for quite some time. Nobody we spoke to knew exactly the year of chambers' birth although we were able to trace it back as far as 1926, which still makes it an old-timer. Evidently, the set is conscious of its shipping heritage – much of the art on display around chambers has a nautical theme and the key firms that instruct members include the established big-hitters on all matters maritime: Holman Fenwick & Willan, Clyde & Co, Richards

Butler, Ince & Co – you'd be hard pressed to find a major name in shipping that hasn't come knocking on its door for advice in recent years.

**Chambers and Partners
Client Service Award 2006**

As we sat in chambers' waiting room before our interviews, we glanced over at the usual newspapers and latest editions of various legal magazines. Among the literature was a copy of the brochure recording the highlights of the *Chambers Global Awards* which took place in May 2005. At this glitzy event – the Oscars of the profession, some might say – 20 Essex Street won the prime award for UK barristers: 'Commercial Set of the Year'. And it's not hard to see why. Head of chambers Iain Milligan has been one of the key players in the monolithic Equitable Life litigation; other members have been involved in film finance litigation (HIH v Chase Manhattan) as well as the EC competition dispute over the cost of replica football kit (Allsports, JJB, Manchester United and Umbro v Office of Fair Trading). The set's reputation may be closely linked with the sea but these days general commercial cases are as much the meat and potatoes of its work. Beyond this, individual members have developed other specialist areas; for example, an Article 6 Human Rights Act argument was advanced on behalf of the defendants in the Guinness fraud trial (R v Lyons, Saunders and others), whilst one junior worked with Birnberg Peirce to ensure the leader of the Kurdish resistance avoided the death penalty (Ocelan v Government of Turkey). Throw in the set's heavyweight status in public international law (eminent figures Sir Elihu Lauterpacht and Sir Arthur Watts loom large) and a panel of 18 arbitrators (including Dr Julian Lew – a recent steal from Herbert Smith) and you can see why a pupillage should not be regarded as purely an introduction to shipping law and practice. Naturally, the set attracts a number of applications from people who are keen to get involved in public international law matters, but the reality is that this type of work is rarely accessible to anyone who hasn't already made a name for themselves in the field, usually as an academic.

Even though a junior member admitted "*the obvious intelligence of certain members can be intimidating for a pupil,*" the atmosphere in chambers is not overly academic and "*certainly not at all stuffy.*" The set is not looking for "*someone who would squirrel themselves away in the library all day,*" and pupils are "*positively discouraged from working after 6pm.*" However, we doubt the pupil we spoke to was exaggerating when she described the year as the "*steepest learning curve of* [her] *life.*"

The year is divided into four equal parts, each being spent with pupilmasters of differing seniority. The majority of the work a pupil undertakes is 'live' so there is "*the novelty of actually feeling useful from time to time.*" A pupil's role will typically require them to prepare research notes for conferences or arbitrations and draft skeleton arguments. The cases undertaken will inevitably be weighty commercial matters, but no matter how senior their pupilmaster, pupils are unlikely to get stuck on a particularly paper-heavy case, as chambers views it as "*important that the learning process continues at all times – we like our pupils to see lots of different work.*" It was also stressed that "*pupils are certainly not used as fodder for menial tasks.*"

Advocacy exercises kick in after Christmas. These normally see two pupils duking it out on a matter previously argued in court by a member of chambers. The advantage of this is that afterwards "*you find out who really won and can see if anything you argued had any practical value.*"

Six months into the year, all members of chambers meet to discuss the pupils' progress. If things are not working out for one or more of them, then it's cheerio and onto somewhere else

for a second six. Show "*potential for outstanding performance*" and the journey continues until the final tenancy decision is made in July, again by all members of the set. With four pupils recruited each year, the claim that all will be awarded tenancy if they reach the required objective standard is a bold one. Evidence shows that usually two get the nod each year. Our junior sources cried fair, not foul, saying: "*You certainly feel like you are getting a fair crack of the whip and that's all you can really ask for.*" Those who are successful are then given the opportunity to augment their advocacy exposure by carrying out road traffic cases towards the end of pupillage on the basis that any court time is good court time. Once installed as a tenant they tend to balance their workload between acting as a second or third junior on a big case and building up their own practice with small commercial cases.

Although seasoned veterans admitted that the daily chambers tea is "*not as well attended as it once was,*" it still remains a useful occasion to "*get yourself known by other members.*" Outside of working hours, the junior end of chambers is fairly sociable, and whilst there isn't one favourite venue, members are known to frequent Daly's Wine Bar and The Edgar Wallace. On a sporting note, in addition to football and cricket matches, there is a chambers golf day. One year a pupil won the event and, in spite of committing such a horrendous faux pas, still managed to get taken on as a tenant.

We visited the set around the same time as it was conducting pupillage interviews and managed to visit the designated interview room to sample the atmosphere encountered by hopefuls. Bizarrely enough, the modular table had been specially shaped into something resembling a maple leaf. Sadly not some tilt of the hat towards Canada, the reasoning behind this layout was to make the candidate "*feel more at ease*" with the assembled interview panel. Don't get too comfortable though, and don't be fooled by the fact that there is only one round of interviews. If you haven't done a mini-pupillage prior to applying then your application for pupillage will double up as one for an assessed mini to be carried out during June and July. The point to make here is that the assessment process is far more in-depth than it might first appear. The interview itself lasts 30 minutes and also requires the candidate to analyse a problem question 15 minutes beforehand. The recruiters are not "*testing knowledge of the law, or of specific authorities, but are instead looking to see how the candidate responds to a lively debate.*"

This is a highly polished, intellectually rigorous set, fully aware of the esteem in which its members are held throughout the commercial world. It follows then that once admitted as a pupil you're going to have to work very hard to develop whatever potential recruiters saw in you.

ters represented the *Daily Mirror* in its House of Lords spat with Naomi Campbell over privacy and then legal costs, but they are also lauded for giving pro bono advice. Close ties to the Environmental Law Foundation, Free Representation Unit and Liberty (director Shami Chakrabarti was a pupil here) see silks and pupils offering free advice and representation on everything from housing clearance orders in Lancashire to challenging overseas communication interceptions before the European Court of Human Rights. Chambers additionally has a high proportion of members with qualifications beyond the law, and counts former solicitors, doctors and engineers among its ranks. We reckon it's not hard to sell the services of a fully qualified mechanical engineer in a messy construction dispute or a barrister with NHS consultant experience in the defence of clinical negligence.

39 Essex Street

Chambers UK rankings: Admin & public law, clinical negligence, construction, costs litigation, environment, human rights, immigration, local government, personal injury, planning, professional discipline, professional negligence

Until 1990, our subject set was a small common and public law outfit known as 2 Hare Court. In the 16 years since moving to Essex Street it has grown substantially, developing a commercial and construction law wing in the process. An environmental and planning team from Eldon Chambers joined in 2002 and the set now has almost 70 barristers, making it one of the more substantial in London. Although its main thrust is now commercial and common law practice, chambers still wins accolades for human rights, immigration, administrative law, local government instructions and costs litigation. Indeed, the range of work covered is quite staggering: barris-

Chambers and Partners
Personal Injury
Set of the Year 2006

Pupils rotate between four supervisors every three months, typically dividing their time between chambers' cornerstones of practice in public and private law. Although the pupillage committee is adamant that their training is as wide as possible, a pupil's individual experience will be taken into account. So, for example, one pupil with a background in medical and bioethics spent an extra month with a clinical negligence practitioner. For the most part pupils follow a carefully prescribed pupillage, as detailed on the schedule presented to them on the first day. "*It's clear from the very beginning that they've really thought it through,*" said one. "*They're very focused on providing a good legal education.*" Pupils are "*forcibly evicted*" from the building at 6pm each day and are not expected to work at weekends. As one supervisor put it: "*We absolutely do not want them to be burning the midnight oil, and we are ruthless if anyone breaks the code.*" Pupils typically work only for their supervisor, and even in the second six when they take on work of their own, assignments continue to be filtered through and monitored by one person. "*It works well because you're never overloaded or committed to four people at once,*" explained a current pupil. "*We have one piece of work at a time and in the later seats you're even encouraged to prioritise your own work over other commitments.*" This doesn't mean other members of chambers have no involvement: a shadow pupillage committee sets four formal written assessments to be completed in the second six and contributes to the tenancy recommendation of the official pupillage committee in July. These assessments are useful for exposing pupils to areas of law that might not be covered in their four seats. Informally, members are likely to throw their doors and most interesting cases open to the pupils, and one had actually witnessed a tussle between a senior silk and her pupil supervisor over who had the more interesting case for her to shadow that week. Supervisors also enlist baby juniors to introduce pupils to things like small claims appearances because "*they usually haven't done a small claim themselves for years.*" Additionally juniors will assist supervisors in delivering a general introduction-to-court pep talk plus a fat folder of costs information, standard RTA preparation documents and other useful goodies. Getting pupils involved in seminars is yet another way of introducing them to chambers business: one had delivered an advice session on mental health law to social workers with her supervisor. "*So many people here are genuinely interested and want you to do well. If you've sought advice on an RTA, and you meet that person after court, they will always stop and ask how it went – and they get so excited if you win.*" To cap it

all there is confidential mentoring available from a volunteer agony aunt or uncle, who takes no part in the tenancy decision and can answer embarrassingly basic questions like how to address a judge outside court.

Chambers is adamant that pupils are properly guided through pleadings and skeleton arguments, rather than running around researching minor points for the supervisor's own cases. One pupil explained: "*We're encouraged to do complete pieces of work – a pleading or decision. The point is to let you try and create something on your own, which is far more rewarding.*" Deadlines are deemed to be realistic and feedback is provided on every piece of work. A formal report summarises the pupil's progress at the end of each seat, although there's a clear sense that the later reports carry more weight. As one supervisor put it: "*The first seat or two is the time for all of the pain and agony and making a twit of oneself.*" A new advocacy assessment was introduced for the first time in 2005 and takes place in the summer, distracting pupils nicely during the run-up to the tenancy decision. "*I now feel pretty savvy about intricate procedures, costs, expert witnesses and that kind of thing,*" said one pupil before summing up her experience in the immortal sound bite: "*You learn stuff here.*"

Although not mandatory for pupillage applicants, the best way to test suitability for 39 Essex Street is a mini pupillage. As well as shadowing barristers in and out of court, students complete a written assessment that will then accompany any subsequent application to chambers. Aspiring pupils need to display impressive CV feathers – academic excellence, mooting, outside interests, volunteer or pro bono work, etc. "*We want people with a spark; people who are high academic achievers yet capable of empathy with clients from all walks of life,*" confirmed a supervisor. "*By the end of pupillage, we hope pupils will have developed their textbook skills, honed their common sense and are capable of doing things like calming an anxious client before an infant approval hearing."* In recent years the set has given tenancy to around two-thirds of its pupils, and it has a good track record of finding third-six placements for the rest. There was good news regarding tenancy for all three pupils in 2006. Those who stay can initially expect a broad practice with secondment opportunities at the FSA, various local authorities and health sector organisations.

Intensive legal training demands brain food, and this set has no shortage of ideas for nourishment. Everyone knows exactly where the Fox's biscuit tins are stored (in the basement) and the third floor of chambers is notorious for its cake runs. Pupils are welcomed on their first day with a four-hour lunch and can look forward to a Friday lunch once a fortnight, with drinks every other Thursday evening. There is strict adherence to the rule that forbids pupils from buying lunch in the company of more senior barristers and each spring the clerks host a pupil-clerk dinner, an event that also attracts a healthy number of baby juniors.

Chambers believes that pupils and members should maintain their work/life balance; in fact supervisors must devote a paragraph of each seat report to how pupils have managed to continue their extra-curricular activities. We doubt it counted as an extra-curricular activity but we rather liked the story of how one pupil was taken whale-watching in the middle of the day by a silk. Of course this was more to do with a London-wide obsession with a stranded creature in the Thames rather than a passion for cetology on either's part. At Christmas rather than the more traditional booze-fest on offer at many sets chambers holds a children's party complete with Father Christmas and elves. Pupils can expect to participate fully in this and all other social events, although any elf duties are subject to the costume fitting.

Falcon Chambers

Chambers UK rankings: Agriculture & rural affairs, real estate litigation

Climb a spiral staircase in the quiet no man's land between Middle and Inner Temple just behind Temple Church and you will chance upon the country's leading property set. Go through its front door and you enter a waiting room more in keeping with a vodka bar than that of a barristers' chambers: frosted glass partitions lit by coloured spotlights, chairs clearly the work of a hip Swedish designer called Inge and an array of abstract art more suited to a Hoxton PR agency. This set moved to its current ab fab location in the early 90s, having previously resided at 11 King's Bench Walk. Back in those days, in addition to strength in real property matters, the set also had major specialisations in construction and engineering law. When numbers reached a point of critical mass, the decision was made to split into two specialist chambers: consequently Keating and Falcon were born. With 26 out of 36 members ranked in *Chambers UK* for property litigation, it is clear that the latter houses the majority of the leading property lawyers in the country. Members author or co-author most of the leading land law texts – *Woodfall's Law of Landlord and Tenant, Megarry & Wade,* and the landlord and tenant section of *Halsbury's Laws.* Major matters handled recently have included the landmark gay tenancy rights case of Ghaidin v Godin-Mendoza in the Court of Appeal and Bakewell v Brandwood, a case concerning the rules behind acquisition of prescriptive rights of way. Classic stuff.

So what makes a successful property barrister? Those we spoke to stressed the need for strong analytical skills. *"So much of our work involves the construction of contracts. You need to be able to analyse every word in detail in order to get the right result for the client."* Specialising in one area of law can bring its own challenges. *"It's important to be enthusiastic about your work in a niche set as there are no other areas of law to escape to."* The client base is certainly varied: practitioners might one day be acting for a farmer in a restrictive covenant case and then advising a multinational company on the interpretation of a lease the next. Barristers have ample opportunity to strut their stuff in court, and although it's not quite adrenaline advocacy it does occasionally produce suitable dinner party anecdotes. One junior tenant regaled us with an amusing tale of how he acted as a human shield between his landlord client and three irate squatters.

Chambers and Partners
Real Estate Set of the Year 2006

Every law student knows that land law is like Marmite – you either love it or hate it. But what if you forget what you learned before pupillage? Anticipating this danger, in the July prior to pupillage the set lays on a comprehensive introduction to landlord and tenant law. This is the ideal opportunity for pupils to meet their future pupilmasters over lunch and inch their feet under the table. In pupillage proper, recruits sit with a different PM every three months and the subject matter tends to be pretty much the same whoever you end up with. It tends to be the pupilmasters who have the most influence in the tenancy decision and, consequently, the majority of a pupil's work will be done for these members rather than others in chambers.

One of the great advantages of being a property barrister is that the cases never last too long and are certainly nowhere near as lengthy as some of the major fraud and pensions cases the courts have seen of late. One silk told us that the longest he'd ever spent in court on one matter was two weeks. As a result, *"pupils get to see a wide range of matters and aren't just stuck on one boring case for the duration."* In the second six, when the clerks decide pupils are ready, they may start taking their own work, typically undefended possession hearings (*"the staple diet of any pupil doing real estate work"*) and small injunction applications. This progresses on to defended possession hearings in the first years of tenancy.

The pupil we spoke to admitted to being rather surprised that his year had been *"remarkably stress-free"* compared to the experiences of contemporaries at other Chancery sets. *"Although it's been taxing from an intellectual point of view, the social side of things has been the exact opposite of all those horror stories that you often hear."* The chambers institution of tea and toast in the afternoon probably contributes to this. Why toast? *"Everyone got a bit fed up with biscuits – it's nice to mix things up with jam and marmalade."* There is also the weekly lunch every Friday where all members congregate in the library to catch up and perhaps discuss recent cases. Beyond the law, members find common ground socially: some play cricket together and a keen sailing contingent meets for weekends at the coast. Closer to home The Old Cock on Fleet Street is the local watering hole (*"by proximity not choice,"* muttered one tenant darkly), or if people are feeling a little more energetic they may visit The Seven Stars on Carey Street. Pupils are always invited along to these impromptu get-togethers and it's worth attending just so you can catch up with all the chambers gossip.

The decision-making process vis-à-vis tenancy is not as transparent as we have seen at many other sets. Pupils do get detailed feedback on the work they do for each PM, but their knowledge of their tenancy prospects tends to operate on a 'no news is good news' basis. If after five months tenancy looks unlikely, the tenancy committee will have a quiet word and suggest the pupil finds a second six elsewhere. If, however, the pupil has heard nothing, it goes to a chambers meeting in

June or July, when every member has a vote. In a further twist, at the six-month point the committee makes a decision as to whether to also advertise externally for new tenancy applications. Obviously, if it does open up the field to all comers in this way it can make the Falcon pupil feel as if their future in chambers isn't looking too rosy. In 2006 both of the Falcon second-six pupils were awarded tenancy.

The best advice we can give to prospective pupils is that displaying "*real fizz*" at interview will impress the panel, as will demonstrating a "*clear ability to marshal the facts*" and "*superior powers of analysis.*" Most of those interviewed have Firsts or a very high 2:1 from... well let's just say it is business as usual for the more prestigious universities. As one source freely admitted: "*The majority of people we take on are from Oxbridge but over the years we have been known to take on individuals from places like Durham and Bristol.*" There is no particular Falcon personality type and the best we could muster by way of descriptions were "*someone we'd be happy to go out to supper with*" and "*if you're not a gregarious type then you're going to struggle.*"

Falconry is the art of training falcons to hunt and return. The legal eagles at this set are more gatherers than hunters as their reputations are such that work comes to them. This has got to be good news for any pupil who can convince the set's recruiters to make space for them up in the eyrie.

Fountain Court Chambers

Chambers UK rankings: Aviation, banking & finance, commercial litigation, fraud: civil, insurance, international arbitration, product liability, professional negligence

In the leafy surroundings of the Temple sits a fountain that is part of both legal and literary folklore. In *Martin Chuzzlewit*, Charles Dickens described the Temple fountain as a welcome fixture in the dry and dusty channels of the law and used it as a meeting place for Ruth Pinch and her brother Tom. Rumour has it that Fountain Court Chambers' main building, which backs onto Essex Street, was occupied by prostitutes in the 18th century when Covent Garden was the hub of London's nightlife. These days it's a more serious breed of commercial practitioner that inhabits the building. Think of any major commercial case in living history and the chances are that a Fountain Court barrister will have played a part. Think landmark litigation moments like BCCI, Three Rivers and, more recently, Equitable Life and then you're starting to get the idea. Any set that numbers the Attorney General (Lord Goldsmith), the Lord Chancellor (Lord Falconer) and a past Master of the Rolls (Lord Bingham) amongst its former members is always going to be a quality outfit. And with big-hitting silks such as Bankim Thanki, Michael Brindle, Anthony Boswood and Nicholas Stadlen on board, the set shows no signs of releasing its grip on top work.

Chambers and Partners

Banking & Finance
Set of the Year 2006

Commercial Litigation
Set of the Year 2006

and

overall winner of
Set of the Year 2006

With such pre-eminent names both past and present, it is understandable that a new pupil might feel somewhat daunted. Chambers recognises this and tries to make the first three months as relaxed as possible. "*We take the view that pupils will only show what they're made of if they're comfortable in their surroundings and so the first three is a bedding-in process,*" a member of the pupillage committee told us. The pupil we spoke to certainly thought life had initially felt a little less full-on compared to her peers at other major commercial sets. But the pressure does ramp up and the work schedule can become "*intense.*" As a set, Fountain has a reasonably broad commercial practice, and among the generalists there are also some specialists, for example in the fields of insurance, aviation, employment and sports law. Pupils usually sit with generalists unless they have a particular practice area preference that can be accommodated.

After the first three months of what is essentially shadowing, pupils are given bite-sized chunks of whatever is occupying their pupilmaster's time, whether it's producing a skeleton argument, preparing for a conference, writing an opinion or drafting pleadings. The level and depth of feedback given to pupils is pleasingly high: "*They go into so much detail it can make your head hurt. You can't fail to learn from this sort of attention.*" From the second three onwards pupils can also undertake work for other members of chambers, fully conscious of the fact that their performance will influence the June tenancy decision. Although strong advocacy skills are sought through the recruitment process, don't expect to be putting them to use during pupillage. "*In truth,*" confessed one source, "*it's all about paperwork, and depending on who you're with, weeks can pass by between court appearances.*" The second six continues in much the same vein. Two more PMs give you the benefit of their expertise but you will also spend time with some of the junior practitioners just so you get a taste of what's to come.

If you want to be constantly on your feet in court in your second six look elsewhere. Pupillage is in essence a long-haul exercise. Just as commercial cases can go on for considerable periods of time, requiring the set's barristers to maintain a steady pace and consistency of performance, so pupillage is all about gradually developing the right techniques and style to appeal to the leading firms of solicitors that will provide them with instructions in years to come. There's no scrimping or corner-cutting allowed at the big-money end of the commercial Bar.

We started off our tour of chambers in the waiting room, "*a blend of the modern and the traditional,*" we were assured. Since we last visited, the wall between Fountain Court and 35 Essex Street had been knocked through with the result that you can become a bit disoriented when wandering around. The grandeur of the rooms varies according to the seniority and taste of their inhabitants, but actually the communal staircases alone are magnificent enough to underline chambers' wealth. Further evidence of success comes in the form of a gym in the basement. Continuing the sporting theme, chambers organises a series of cricket matches amongst members and staff each year and sometimes also plays against magic circle firms of solicitors. It sounds as if they're not too bad at the beautiful game either – we spotted the 2005 inter-chambers football trophy proudly on display in the clerks' room. They'll hate us for saying this but we suspect the winning of the cup had more to do with the clerks than the barristers. There is a chambers tea but it tends to be frequented by the older end of the set and it's certainly not obligatory for a pupil to attend. Lunchtimes provide the best opportunity for getting your face known. Members typically either grab a sandwich together or head off to lunch in hall.

Just one look at the CVs of the junior tenants should tell you that getting a foot in the door as a pupil will be impossible without seriously impressive academic credentials. Finding the junior tenant who hasn't got a starred First from Oxbridge in this intellectual set is a tricky business. Recruiters favour those applicants who have clearly researched career opportunities within the legal profession so, for example, they tell us: "*We're* reassured when we see that someone has done a vac scheme at a firm of solicitors, as it shows that they've actually made an informed decision on coming to the Bar." Other pieces of application advice: "Avoid bullshit! It's easy to spot people quoting the website at you. Also, avoid ridiculous phrases like 'I relish the challenge.' The simpler the language the better as far as we're concerned." The first round of pupillage interviews is relatively relaxed, with the focus being on aspects of your CV. The second outing is much more formal and involves a quasi-legal problem which comes with 15 minutes of preparation time. Having made a five-minute presentation, the eight (yes eight) members of the panel will then pepper you with questions in order to ascertain whether you've got what it takes to hold your own in the commercial courts. "We're certainly not after automatons – above all we want someone with a bit of vigour."

Fountain Court prides itself on being a member-driven set. The rationale behind this is simple: "There's little point in being self-employed if you've got someone telling you what to do all the time." This certainly fits in with the impression we formed of the place – it knows it has the pick of the yearly crop at its disposal and it will often be the first choice for the driven and intellectually astute young practitioner. Newtonian principles of gravity dictate that water shot out of a fountain will eventually come down. Fountain pupils, it seems however, can continue an upward trajectory.

One Garden Court

Chambers UK rankings: Family

One Garden Court lies deep in the heart of the Inns, Fountain Court to its left, Middle Temple hall dead ahead with its gardens to the right stretching all the way to the Thames Embankment. On the day of our visit, sunlight streamed through the windows of chambers' newly decorated waiting area. The set had had a real makeover since our previous visit two years before, the most notable change being the acquisition of a floor in neighbouring premises, effectively doubling the space available to members. This physical expansion was a significant step for the set. Members no longer shoehorn themselves into cramped corners and are, instead, eager to fill the extra space by lengthening the list of members. They plan to do this through lateral 'hires' and the recruitment of tenants from among their own pupils. In 2006 three pupils took tenancy in a year when two senior barristers took silk, bringing the total QC tally in chambers to seven.

The set has been in its current incarnation since 1989, when it was formed after a group of barristers from Lamb Building – a set that had been around since the 1950s – decided to set up a specialised family law outfit. It proved to be a smart decision as, at around 52 members strong, OGC is now the largest specialist family set in the country, offering a complete service to both privately and publicly funded clients. Its members cover ancillary relief, care and adoption, international and private child law, local authority child law, mediation, human rights and family-related crime. The importance of child and care cases should not be underestimated.

During their year in chambers pupils undertake three seats of four months in an attempt to experience the spread of work undertaken at the set. The first, non-practising six is a time for attending court with their supervisors, creating first drafts of advices and opinions and preparing case chronologies, etc. "My supervisors were very supportive," confirmed a source. "They were all very busy but insisted that I left by 6pm." Naturally there will be times in the second six when the briefs and instructions pile up and longer hours are necessary: "You just have to play it by ear – if there was work to be done then you would just *have to do it. I did very few weekends though."*

Once regularly on their feet in the second six, pupils start to get a sense of which areas of family work they prefer. Chambers doesn't rush them, however, believing that it is best for them to grow slowly into their practices. As one source said: *"When you are first in court you are just happy to be taking on cases and getting paid; being out and about everyday is great."* Second-six pupils' instructions include Family Law Act applications and injunctions, directions hearings in public law cases and writing advices on jurisdiction questions. During this time they can expect to be in court almost every day of the week and see relatively little of supervisors. That's not to say they won't be around to give guidance; pupils know that members are happy to take panicked phone calls, even late at night. Additionally, a junior tenant acts as a formal pupil liaison.

When there is something particularly unusual going on in chambers, pupils will be allowed to participate; one of our sources had been allowed to assist a silk for the duration of a major matter and *"this provided an opportunity to see a more complex case than a pupil normally would."* Getting a *"sense of what a seven-week hearing is actually like and seeing what the job is like at the top end of the profession"* is undoubtedly a fantastic experience for pupils, but it also allows *"silks to meet the pupils and make a more informed decision at tenancy time."* One other bonus is that it may enable pupils to *"earn a bit of extra dosh."* Incidentally, for a family set with a good chunk of publicly funded work, the size of the pupillage award is not bad.

Chambers prides itself on being a democratic place, operating a one-member one-vote policy for the tenancy decision. Prior to this, pupils undergo a series of interviews and exercises, including answering ethics questions, making a presentation on a case and undertaking written work on a particular aspect of family law. The tenancy committee also seeks recommendations from the senior clerk and instructing solicitors before it meets to prepare its report to the rest of the membership. Any opinions at variance with the majority are put into a minority report that is also presented to the members. At the most recent tenancy vote, the pupils were judged to be equally talented and so all three were made offers.

Chambers has opted out of the OLPAS system to discourage applications from those without a genuine focus on family practice. *"It's an absolute requisite that an application discloses an interest in or a commitment to family law. Perhaps a candidate has taken a module in it, or at least states that they have interest in it – you would be surprised to learn how many people don't appear to even know what we do."* Is there a type of character that would best fit in? Initially, our sources claimed not. After pushing them a little, we learned chambers is *"not good with very stuffy sorts – other sets have hunters and shooters who went to this or that school and university, but we don't want anybody frightfully uptight."* A five-member panel spends an evening turning a mound of over 200 applications into a shortlist list of 20. These candidates are invited to a single-stage interview on a Saturday early in September. The questioning is thorough. *"When candidates arrive they are given a test question to look over. We start the interview with a general chat about their CV to settle them down. We then move on to more specific questions such as, 'Why the Bar?' and then, most importantly, 'Why family?'"* The test question is used to establish candidates' ability to reason and justify and (whether or not candidates have law degrees) it is *"a great sifter."* Chambers recruiters told us: *"You can immediately tell if a candidate is analytical and has the right kind of approach for us,"* before adding that *"we will often throw candidates a bit of a googly at the end of the interview to see if they can hit it back."* Here's one tip: make sure you've got a few genuine questions to ask at the end of the interview because *"we are not at all impressed with candidates who ask us a question already covered in interview. What we do like is a candidate who has done their homework: someone who has researched chambers' recent work or recent developments in the field and comes up with an interesting question is really going to pique our curiosity."*

OGC is conscious of its place in the family law community, staging around 30 seminars a year in London and the regions to keep solicitors abreast of developments in the field. Pupils are encouraged to attend these whenever possible, both for their own edification and to meet the solicitors who will be their future clients. The informal social scene at chambers tends to be *"based more on where you are physically in the building than on seniority."* Several members regularly go for drinks on a Friday evening.

We'll finish with a quote from the junior who told us: *"One Garden Court is the whole package. Not only does it have an excellent reputation at the family law Bar, but the variety of work you can do here is second to none."*

Garden Court Chambers

Chambers UK rankings: Admin & public law, crime, human rights, immigration, police law, social housing

In 1974 a crack commando unit of six young barristers set up in practice with the aim of ensuring representation for those who most need it. Today, still true to their founding values, they survive as soldiers of fortune. If you have a problem, if no one else can help, and if you can find them, maybe you can hire a Garden Court barrister. You might consider our comparison of a group of 87 well-respected barristers with The A-Team to be flippant; after all, practitioners at this set deal with such crucially important societal issues as immigration, housing and crime. By comparison

Hannibal et al were more concerned with welding tanks and flamethrowers together in the three minutes before Colonel Decker burst in with the military police to arrest them for the crime they didn't commit. Look closer though and you'll see that the two teams are not so different – both came into existence to protect the vulnerable.

And just in case you're confused by the set's name, Garden Court Chambers was until recently known as Two Garden Court. It made the change following its move away from the confines of the Temple to larger, plush premises at 57-60 Lincoln's Inn Fields, incidentally a former abode of Spencer Percival, the only Prime Minister ever to be assassinated (in 1812).

The typical clients for these barristers tend to be those from the outer edges of society who would be most at risk without representation. If you want specifics then how about the successful defence of Westminster anti-war protester Brian Haw in various criminal proceedings arising out of his long vigil opposite Parliament. Members were also involved in the Mubarek Inquiry (the racist murder of an Asian prisoner at Feltham Young Offenders Institution) and the gay tenancy rights case of Ghaidan v Godin-Mendoza. Chambers has more recently been involved in a number of terrorism cases. This is the set where big-name silks such as Courtenay Griffiths, Laurie Fransman and Ian Macdonald reside and, consequently, the work is very much A-grade.

Pupillage at Garden Court is undoubtedly a demanding yet enriching year. One pupil spoke admiringly of the *"full and thorough training"* that he had received, commending the strong level of guidance that had been offered in comparison to that experienced by friends at other legal aid sets. Pupils are exposed to three distinct practice areas over the two sixes. Pupillage will definitely entail spells in crime and immigration as these are the practice areas in which the majority of GC barristers ply their trade. Beyond this you could express your interest in another practice area or a specific supervisor and the pupillage committee will take this into account before the allocation process gets underway.

In addition to working for your own pupillage supervisor, perhaps drafting advices, skeleton arguments and judicial review claim forms, you can also approach any member of chambers for additional work. In fact, pupils recommend this as "*a great way of broadening your experience.*" After a first six by your master's side, most of your second six will be spent on your feet in the magistrates' courts undertaking summary trials, or in the Crown Court for first appearances, mentions and sentencings. In addition there will also be appearances at immigration tribunals plus civil and family work. It's not all in-the-field training; pupils also attend a series of seminars covering advocacy, courtroom etiquette, substantive law and legal developments.

As for your chances of gaining tenancy, things are looking up in comparison with recent years. When we visited chambers, the PTC (pupillage and training committee) was in the process of changing its policy concerning recruitment from within. It used to be the case that any tenancy vacancies would be advertised externally and opened up to all comers, with the result that (in the interest of fairness) the Garden Court pupil's application was treated no differently from anybody else's and in effect they had to regard pupillage as more of a training than a route into tenancy. It may have been fair to outsiders, but it was not a system that particularly benefited pupils. In 2005 a new plan saw one or two pupils being taken on after 12 months in much the same way as you would expect elsewhere. Those who do not make it tend to fare well at other sets and GC has been known to allow people to squat for a further six months until they find another set.

Chambers' recruiters acknowledge that cutting the approximately 700 applications down to about 30 interviewees "*always feels quite brutal and can mean that the young fresh-faced law student is at a distinct disadvantage.*" How so? "*We want more than declarations of intent; we want proof of commitment to social justice. It's going to be hard to compete with ten years of experience in an international aid charity for example.*" The message: look at the stats and do the maths. If your CV is not screaming social conscience then it's most likely going to be a wasted application. Those who do make it to interview are still advised to take care, as one of the biggest turn-offs for the set's interviewers is a lack of general social awareness. "*We've interviewed people who are obviously extremely clever and doubtless have the potential to be successful barristers, but they haven't seemed like they really cared about the Garden Court ethos.*" If you're in any doubt as to the types of individual that have succeeded in making a home in chambers you need only look at the members' profiles on the set's website.

Make it to interview and you will undertake an advocacy exercise and then answer a number of questions designed to test your knowledge and commitment to publicly funded work. It's best to display a genuine and motivated attitude at this point because "*this isn't the set for those with a cynical, laid-back attitude. We want to see drive and passion in our pupils.*"

In view of the fact that a large number of pupils (eight when we visited) all sit together in one room in chambers, it is inevitable that a social scene quickly develops among them. Pupils are very much included in the various functions within chambers, many of these organised by the different practice groups. "*They're certainly not treated like a different breed,*" said a supervisor. "*We try to make sure that they are invited to everything.*" The set's Christmas party, held at a Soho nightclub, is famed throughout the Bar.

In many ways Garden Court has been the scruffy older brother of other 'cool' sets like Matrix and Doughty Street. It started the social conscience ball rolling and showed how it was possible for a set to be united under a shared ethos. Perversely, it is the set's strong egalitarian values which may have proven to be its undoing in recent years as many of its former pupils now ply their trade at competitor sets, frustrated that their pupillage at Garden Court did not lead to anything more substantial. It is to be hoped that the move to larger premises, coupled with the implementation of a new, more pupil-friendly policy on tenancy decisions will ensure it can grow from within. And we love it when a plan comes together...

Chambers' motto is "Do right, fear no one." If you're made of the stuff Garden Court wants to see then that probably sums you up too.

Government Legal Service

Long ago the phrase "employed barrister" was a legal oxymoron, but just because life as a GLS lawyer doesn't involve clerks, silks, afternoon tea and your own self-regulated pay cheque doesn't mean it isn't worth serious thought. The small matter of a regular salary, and even – whisper it incredulously – a pension, may convince you to read on.

In essence the GLS is a legal service provider with "one client – the Government." Its CEO, we suppose, would technically be the Queen. Some 30 departments and over 600 barristers fall under its capacious administrative umbrella, but of the 25 training places offered each year few are for pupils. Needless to say, getting in is tough, so be clear about what motivates you. Most likely it will be an ardent interest in public and administrative law, as well as policy and legislation. As GLS sources put it: "We don't just advise on what the law is, we advise on what the law should be." Just to whet your appetite, here are some matters which can fall within the GLS remit: currency and coinage issues; litigation concerning night noise at Heathrow airport; prison inquests; advice on law regarding smacking children; fraudulent trading and insider dealing; implementation of the Aarhus Convention on environmental information; judicial reviews; advising ministers and preparing drafts of bills (eg new gambling legislation). Confines of space mean we can't do justice to the full variety of work available, but even a glance at the GLS website (www.gls.gov.uk) will give a fuller flavour of just how extraordinary the work can be for GLS barristers.

Actually, we shouldn't use that word. The GLS speaks of 'lawyers' rather than solicitors or barristers, even though training for both follows the norms of private practice with the pupils defined as such for one year and trainees for two. There are significant similarities in the advisory work and advocacy opportunities available to trainees and pupils, and the GLS values "the skills of individuals as lawyers, whatever their preferred branch of the profession." This being so, we refer you to page 346 for a full picture of what's on offer for trainees. Whether trainee or pupil, paperwork is the order of the day. All pupils must complete an advisory seat and, in contrast to private practice, will interact directly with policymakers ('clients' in GLS jargon). Although most of the pupils we spoke to stressed the fundamentally advisory nature of the practice ("If you want to stand up and talk, go to a criminal set instead"), any hard-won mooting experience will be put to good use in other ways. Said one pupil: "Advocacy here isn't just about the courtroom – it is required in conference and negotiation and on paper." In other words, persuading those policymakers and government ministers requires impressive intellectual agility. In addition, "it's quite easy to move to a department like the Treasury Solicitors, which does a lot of advocacy. You just have to take the initiative."

Movement around the GLS is encouraged from the top down and qualified lawyers move throughout their careers. This promotes broad experience and expertise, but does mean it is harder to specialise in the first few years post-pupillage than in private practice. The general pattern is for pupils to spend four months in three departments or up to six months in a set of chambers. Those who had taken this latter route suggested it is better to start off with a few weeks in a GLS department before moving to a chambers, telling us: "*It would have been much more difficult to understand what it means to be a government lawyer if I'd headed straight into private practice.*" Once in chambers, however, pupils enjoy the benefits of private practice without the drawbacks: "*I was treated just the same as the other pupils but had none of the stress,*" enthused one source. Another added: "*I didn't have to do as much work for other members of chambers, so I could focus on subjects most important to my development.*" Alternatives to six months in a chambers can include a secondment to the CPS, where one pupil was up on their feet prosecuting in magistrates' courts: "*Managing my own cases and handling such varied and stimulating work was really exciting.*"

Helping knit the year together, each pupil is assigned a general pupil supervisor who meets regularly with their charge to set objectives and suggest seats. While there are additional seat-specific pupil supervisors, pupils will also answer to their line manager in each department. Encouraged to work autonomously, pupils are "*pretty much thrown in at the deep end*" and seem to operate more independently of pupil supervisors than their peers in private practice. In fact, work is allocated to pupils in the same way as it is to qualified lawyers, with pupil supervisors and line managers basically there to offer feedback. "*You're not left entirely to your own devices; it's about being supervised rather than observing,*" explained one pupil, another adding: "*It's just as easy to ask others on the team if I have a*

question – someone's always assigned to look over your work, particularly in the first month of a new seat.*"

In terms of work, advice and drafting looms large. This year's crop of pupils had assisted policymakers during the bird flu crisis, drafted for the Special Immigration Appeals Commission, attended the floor of the (Parliamentary) House of Lords to advise on live debates and prepped policymakers en route to the European courts. One pupil had even worked directly for the Lord Chancellor. A specific thrill of GLS pupillage is involvement in the "*exciting*" world of lawmaking and several sources had advised on "*very high-profile bills – you'd go home in the evening and see it on the news...*"

With pupils and trainees dispersed across many departments, they need an effective unifying tool. The Legal Training Network is behind many of the social events and there are additionally various department events, although "*it's not as if we have senior silks to buy everyone drinks with their gold credit cards.*" Money is, of course, a consideration for those weighing up work as a government lawyer and on this subject all our sources were pretty much in agreement that their remuneration was "*not as much as a commercial pupillage award, but not dreadful... and you'll never have to work an 80-hour week.*" Indeed, their civil-service hours are 10am to 6pm and it's "*almost unheard of*" to work at the weekends. Flexible working is encouraged, even for pupils.

Standard hours, regular wages and life as a barrister? If the formula appeals, get in line. Application is centralised via the GLS, but you will be admitted to the supervision of a preferred 'home' department. Decide which department(s) interest(s) you most and research thoroughly, not least to discover whether they take pupils. Our sources agreed that "*applying is more difficult for pupils. Some departments haven't taken pupils before and there are generally fewer places.*" Vacation placements offer the perfect chance to suss out a department and are encouraged throughout the GLS. Applications are made two years in advance, beginning with a paper application and online verbal reasoning test. Successful applicants are then called for an assessment day in September. Negotiate this hurdle and you're in, and eligible to have the GLS pay your BVC fees and a maintenance grant. One final boon is that the GLS hires pupils on the assumption that they will be suitable GLS lawyers within the year. "*It's not a guarantee, but unless something goes very wrong you will be offered a position.*"

All in all, it is the opportunity to experience a variety of law far beyond the scope of usual private practice that defines the GLS, and we can only conclude that this is one of the most rewarding pupillages to be found at the Bar. Our interviewees had nothing but encouragement for those considering a life less set-based. Said one: "*I think that people do get tunnel vision about chambers, but they should look at the options – I'm so glad I came here.*"

2-3 Gray's Inn Square

Chambers UK rankings: Consumer law, health and safety, licensing, local government, planning, social housing

The cosy waiting area of 2-3 Gray's Inn features an enormous fishbowl crammed with candyrock that tingled our sweet tooth upon arrival. Equally chock full of eminent advocates and groundbreaking criminal proceedings, the illustrious history of 2-3 Gray's Inn could fill a book. In fact, it has. Penned by Malcolm Spence QC, the elegantly attired, venerable planning silk (who lives in the flat above chambers), it charts the set's rise throughout the 20th century. If you peruse it, you'll discover that criminal proceedings are

among the set's highest profile cases of the last 30 years, with stars like Anthony Scrivener QC defending Private Lee Clegg before the House of Lords and representing Sion Jenkins in his recent murder retrial following the death of his foster daughter.

It may therefore come as a surprise to find that, today, planning and public law are the set's bread and butter and that the clientele is dominated by local government and social housing organisations. Immigration and asylum matters are also handled, as are employment and PI concerns. The set has been clever at future-proofing itself at a time when funding issues have dented many in the profession. The recent transfer of licensing from magistrates to local government has seen it become a go-to dock for licensing work, and it looks set to provide the same niche in gambling law over the next few years. For pupils, this range means it's possible to follow a common, public or administrative bent and enjoy a great variety of work. At this set, pupils' interests can take unpredicted turns.

The set typically hosts three pupils who tend to rotate between three pupilmasters for four months at a time. The first six sees pupils getting to grips with sets of papers, skeleton arguments and opinion writing, but the style of each seat depends very much on the pupilmaster and the work to hand. While it is common for pupils to work through a historic case as an academic exercise and then discuss it with their pupilmaster, sometimes they actually assist on a significant live case and in such circumstances "*it's a really rewarding thing to have put a point forward to your pupilmaster and to then hear it presented to the bench.*" Other members are allowed to give work to pupils, but pupilmasters will apparently not hesitate to impose limits if they perceive their charges are overburdened. Towards the end of the first six, pupils are encouraged to shadow baby juniors for a more accurate taste of the court-heavy second six and are also sent out to observe the different advocacy styles of more-senior barristers. This year pupils gazed on admiringly at the House of Lords as Anthony Scrivener QC handled an enormous civil action centring on 'economy class symptoms' (aka DVT) suffered by airline passengers.

Testament to the frequency with which they're on their feet in the second six, not one pupil was in chambers on the morning we visited and only perseverance ensured we gained interviews. From day one of the second six they begin to take on their own work, securing a healthy diet of two to three court appearances a week. Appearances in Greater London tend to be the norm and, although the first time is "*just as daunting as it sounds*," all the pupils agreed that they felt well supported by chambers. A sit-down chat with chief clerk Martin Hale before the second six begins also ensures they know exactly what the clerks require of them. One challenge faced by pupils at 2-3 Gray's Inn is the likelihood, when representing a local authority, of facing a litigant in person rather than another barrister. "*There are far more personal-conduct issues in this kind of court work*," explained one pupil. "*You learn how to handle situations that just don't arise elsewhere*." When their diaries allow, pupils continue to devil for other members of chambers and work for their pupilmaster. Inevitably, the hours do lengthen beyond an eight-hour day in the second six, although working at the weekends tends to be for pupils' own clients rather than anyone else.

While there can be no disputing the set's commitment to pupils, this wasn't the most rigidly assessed pupillage we've encountered. Other than one advocacy exercise at the end of the first six (simulating a typical second-six case), they are not required to complete any other assessments before the tenancy decision is made in July. Although agreeing that a slightly more formal programme of monitoring their progress might be useful, pupils were quick to point out that an overly systematic approach wouldn't be representative of the set culture. As one said: "*This was very much the friendliest set I'd encountered at interview and that hasn't changed throughout my time here. The culture is one of education and discussion, and open doors – I have never once felt that I was interrupting anyone or asking a stupid question. Everyone wants you to do well.*" Indeed they do. Victory in the courtroom was a personal highlight for many of our sources: "*It's so rewarding doing your own work and taking that responsibility, but even more enjoyable when you manage to persuade the judge and win the case.*" On returning to base, pupils find that everyone else is quick to shower praise, not least because a tradition decrees that a pupil's first victory be celebrated with cakes for the clerks' room. Not just any old Victoria sponge: Konditor & Cook is still the patisserie of choice for these clerks, who were treated three times in one week by this year's pupils.

We don't think there's better proof that good atmosphere and pastoral care permeates this set. Proud to be traditional, yet relaxed and friendly despite numbering 50 barristers, 2-3 Gray's Inn retains a small-chambers feel. "*Although quite a few people do a lot of work from home, or are often away at planning enquiries, there is always a core group around chambers.*" The dynamism of the juniors is especially striking, with younger members at the forefront of a recent surge in immigration instructions. "*There's a lot of initiative and creativity here,*" said one pupil; "*the junior end is just phenomenal.*"

Pupils are always invited to seminars and client events and can expect to be networking with solicitors and senior silks from the outset. Within chambers, they are welcomed with drinks on their first day and are always invited to the biannual chambers' parties, usually hosted by a member at home. The set also indulges in sporadic Saturday cricket matches, though participation in these is absolutely voluntary.

The July tenancy decision is made following input from the clerks as well as pupilmasters' reports. Normally one pupil stays on but, mindful of an erroneous decision, chambers also offers an unusual option to pupils "*who might be borderline or otherwise not quite ready: we invite them to stay on as a pupil for another 12 months.*" Happily, this deferment has confirmed the set's instinct on a number of occasions. As the senior clerk said: "*We take the time to see if people turn out well.*" In 2006 chambers gave tenancy to two of its three pupils. Nor does chambers leave visitors empty-handed: we left, pockets stuffed, with the set's own-brand chocolates and some of that candyrock.

4-5 Grays Inn Square

Chambers UK rankings: Admin & public law, education, environment, local government, planning, professional discipline

Back in the 1950s this set was a small but bustling common law outfit. It became one of the first to move out of the precincts of the Temple to Grays Inn in 1965. Come the 1980s, the set had developed an impressive commercial and banking practice, showing a flair for international work. Then, in 2000, seven members left for Matrix Chambers and a further eight public law practitioners shipped out following abandoned merger talks with Monckton Chambers. Instead of folding, the remaining 30-odd barristers rallied and the set has since grown to almost 50 members who between them cover a staggering number of local government, commercial and planning law instructions.

Acclaimed above all else for their planning expertise, over half the members are happily occupied with public law and planning inquiries and High Court applications for judicial review, as well as complex planning and environmental advice to developers, local authorities and objectors. Two members, for example, have been representing the Greater London Authority at a major public inquiry into Thames Water's proposals for a desalination plant on the Thames at Beckton. This specialist practice dovetails nicely with the set's public law work, an area in which barristers represent clients on almost anything concerning public bodies – judicial reviews (including impressive human rights work), employment tribunals, European law and much more. Over 300 local authorities across the country regularly seek advice from the set, such that its "*local government work covers everything, alphabetically, from abattoirs to zoos.*" In one particularly interesting case, members represented the returning officer for the 2006 local elections in the St Katherine and Wapping ward of Tower Hamlets. In this case (eventually decided by the Court of Appeal) three prospective Respect party candidates, whose nomination papers were invalid, failed to secure judicial intervention in the electoral proceedings.

Other strains of work include sports and media law, professional negligence and defamation. In a recent action, 4-5 Gray's Inn QC Richard Spearman helped Lance Armstrong secure a libel victory against *The Sunday Times* following their publication of an article which implied he had used performance-enhancing drugs. Despite the high profile of such cases, it is chambers' growing commercial wing that increasingly catches the eye. Commercial judicial reviews, multi-jurisdictional banking cases, international trading and insurance work are bringing in a growing proportion of chambers' revenue and occupying the time of up to 20 members.

Clearly happy to embrace change, 4-5 Gray's Inn overhauled its pupillage programme some years ago, cutting the number of pupils from six to a maximum of three and establishing a tenancy selection committee. Pupils are now allocated four seats of three months each, with either three or four different pupilmasters to ensure breadth of experience in time for the third-seat tenancy decision. As one pupil supervisor explained: "*Pupils have nine months to prove themselves. We make a report on every piece of their work, whether from the pupil supervisor or other member of chambers, and it's all filed and taken into account before we make a recommendation to our management committee. We then have a full meeting of chambers where any objections and impressions are discussed, before the vote.*" Nine months may not leave long to make a good impression, but at least the carefully structured system leaves no one in the dark about how they're doing.

The recruits we interviewed were impressed by the commitment shown to pupillage, demonstrated as early as the first interview when, as one told us, "*I felt that they genuinely wanted to know about me.*" An initial grilling sees applicants face five or six members, including the head of chambers, and those who make it through to round two face a whole-day assessment. At this stage a legal problem must be worked into a skeleton argument for presentation before another panel. "*It was incredibly daunting,*" remembered one pupil, "*but also very reassuring. They didn't press me for legal knowledge, but really tested my analytical skills with some very searching questions.*"

Once installed as a pupil, similar advocacy tests are an integral part of the ongoing assessment. After any assessment, a written report is submitted to the record and pupils get feedback, courtroom tips and a chance to "*appreciate the wider legal context*" through informal discussion with the panel. Such master classes in advocacy are important because pupils' court experience is limited throughout their training, unless they take on pro bono matters. Said one recent tenant: "*I didn't appear in court at all during my pupillage,*

and although at the time I did want to get on my feet, I'm now pleased that I didn't. The pupillage focused on preparation and paperwork, which is 99% of good court work anyway. Now I have that confidence of preparation." Other sage words came from a source who pointed out that "*too many court appearances wouldn't reflect the practice of the set – about half of the work here is advisory.*"

Rest assured that time spent at your desk in chambers doesn't equate to tedium. Pupils are given a good level of work from the off, shadowing supervisors through conferences and becoming increasingly active in devilling for other members of the set. They encounter "*a huge range of drafting – everything from small bits of larger proceedings to whole opinions, pleadings and skeleton arguments.*" Throughout, feedback is constant, with supervisors correcting and advising on each piece of work produced. Pupils are tested for flexibility, commitment and "*ruthless*" diary management. In addition, the set encourages pupils to take a short secondment outside chambers, and one of those we spoke to had spent time with a London-based American law firm. For all of the activity, the consensus was that this is a "*civilised*" rather than manic training and that, "*despite high expectations, chambers feels your life shouldn't be taken over by pupillage. It adopts a nurturing attitude that goes from senior members right down to the clerks.*"

We sense that 4-5 Gray's Inn has achieved a pleasing equilibrium between the seriousness of a heavy workload and a light modus operandi. New pupils are greeted with open doors, first names and a welcome party where even senior members trot out to meet them. "*Approachable*" is very much the colour of the wallpaper here and baby juniors can be relied upon to take pupils under their wing. The set holds a formal May dinner in addition to its annual Christmas party, and also upholds a time-honoured tradition of providing a picnic lunch spread in the gardens of Gray's Inn every Monday throughout the summer.

At least one pupil secures tenancy each year and they find that the pastoral touch characterising pupillage continues. Two clerks are assigned to each team of barristers, according to call and, as they take their first steps, baby juniors benefit from the clerks' efforts to "*persuade leaders to take them on, push them forward for jobs and generally get them known*." A decision to expand into numbers 6 and 3 Grays Inn Square has ensured enough space for everyone to have their own room, and only the newest of tenants share space.

So what is this set looking for in pupillage applicants? First, it wants people with exceptional analytical and advocacy skills, so work on your mooting form. Second, it wants to see potential with regard to the ability to relate to lay clients as well as professionals. If you're serious about this set, we recommend participation in its biannual mini-pupillage scheme which enables four would-be-applicants at a time to sample its wares. Apply early if you want to get onto a session and look lively once you're in situ. As far as 4-5 Gray's Inn is concerned, they'll start getting to know you then and there.

1 Hare Court

Chambers UK rankings: Family

On the day we visited 1 Hare Court an electrical explosion on Fleet Street had left much of the Inns without power. However, the chaos we noted on our arrival in chambers proved to be but a temporary loss of composure from a set that contemplates the legal market with perfect equanimity. Long respected for its excellent family and matrimonial law abilities, divorce continues to be the stock in trade at a set "*historically seen as more commercial than QEB*," but

competing both with that set and 29 Bedford Row for top billing. Consequently, while children's law (child abduction, residence or contact applications), inheritance, trusts of land and even medical ethics cases do feature, 1 Hare Court is increasingly concentrating on the most rarefied ancillary relief cases. In fact, such matters now constitute over 90% of chambers' caseload, with barristers continually involved in high-profile separations that lead to ground-breaking decisions.

Divorce is, of course, an issue "*affecting the whole of society from the richest to the poorest, from the famous or infamous to the completely unknown.*" Precedent-setting decisions tend to emerge from the divorces of the fabulously wealthy and, here, members of chambers have worked on the divorce of former Arsenal footballer Ray Parlour, the Miller divorce involving a disputed £30 million fortune, and the MacFarlane case, which dealt with the financial implications of divorce for a wife who had given up her career for marriage. More recently, barristers (including family bar prima barristerina Nicholas Mostyn) have been engrossed in assisting Sir Paul McCartney on his divorce from Heather Mills and Mrs Charman in her divorce of the insurance multi-millionaire John Charman, one of the richest men in the City with assets said to be approaching £150 million.

The story of how 1 Hare Court came into being is a relatively simple one. In the 1970s a merger of two sets – one expert in family cases, the other in pure divorce matters – led to the creation of 1 Mitre Court Buildings, which grew organically until the early 21st century when two events turbocharged its development. When the set lured five senior barristers from rival 29 Bedford Row shockwaves went through the matrimonial Bar and the set's reputation went from very good to stellar. Not long after this, it moved into "*newly refitted, all mod cons and technology"* premises at 1 Hare Court, finally uniting all its members under one roof for the first time. The benefits of *"appearing cohesive and modern"* are obvious and *"the move has also given a real energy boost"* to the set. Extra space has allowed it to recruit well at the junior end. Its success has not gone unrecognised: a Chambers and Partners 'Family Set of the Year' award sits proudly in the reception and members proudly told us that one of the clerking team had recently scooped the Bar Council's award for 'Junior Clerk of the Year'.

Three pupils join chambers each year and the set requires them to switch pupil supervisor every four months. First and foremost this gives them the opportunity to observe *"three different styles of approach to essentially similar work."* As one pupil commented: *"There are some aggressive courtroom performers, but you need to develop your own style for the family court and for me that's a more conversational, less formal approach... one that is attuned to the emotions in the room."* Unless they have *"a pretty convincing reason otherwise"* members become pupil supervisors as soon as they are eligible as the set is concerned to see *"a ten to 15-year age gap, not a 25-year one"* between pupil and supervisor. The result for pupils is *"good relationships"* with supervisors *"who are always there to listen"* and *"take the default position that your work is good and point out where it isn't."*

Attendance at court and tribunals *"three to four times a week"* with a supervisor is backed up by the basic tasks of *"going through five or six lever-arch files,"* *"making disclosures of assets,"* *"research,"* *"filleting bank, mortagage or tax and trusts data into spreadsheets"* and *"taking notes at conference."* Because assets are often held overseas, complex jurisdictional conflict issues arise. As well as shadowing their supervisors, pupils are encouraged to *"spend time with more junior members to experience domestic violence*

cases or children's cases." The overall result is that *"as a pupil you will get a taste of all aspects of family law."*

In the first four months of pupillage supervisors give *"a lot of leeway, because no one studies ancillary relief before arriving and you still need to get a grounding."* Subsequently, pupils find a *"marked raising of expectations in the second four months, when you're expected to put the learning into practice."* Because this second period bridges the traditional transition into the practising six, it also sees pupils acquire rights of audience. It is a time to start handling their own smaller family and matrimonial finance instructions. In the third and final four-month period, pupils are acutely aware of the required *"high standards in terms of the documents you produce and your focus on the important issues in a case."* The tenancy decision is taken towards the end of July by the six-strong Tenancy and Pupillage Committee and is based on the collated written reports of each supervisor and *"feedback from anyone who you've worked for"* plus an interview. Normally only one pupil is taken on, but all those we spoke to were confident that *"you're being judged fairly on your own abilities and merit, so you can't complain."*

Those who do stay on find that *"developing a flexible arsenal of different techniques"* is the way forward. They benefit from *"a great team of clerks"* (who may or may not call them Mr or Miss, depending on how closely they follow the plan to use first names only). Pupils and junior tenants are on occasion to be found drinking together in some local pub, although *"few people's social lives revolve around chambers."* The sense overall is that *"taking pride in work"* and *"a strong work ethic, but with a light touch"* is the common theme for members in a set that *"rightly thinks highly of itself and is confident in continuing to do well."*

Let's assume you have this set on your shortlist; what should you know about its approach to recruitment? What is clear is that chambers is taking an "*increasingly structured*" approach, reflecting the need to "*follow the spirit as well as the letter of our equal opportunities policy.*" The recruiters tell us they are determined to privilege excellent candidates of whatever background and are willing to look further than the most traditional universities, placing importance instead on "*something exceptional in extra-curricular terms*" and "*something that indicates a particular interest in family law.*" Needless to say, sound academic achievement remains as important as ever and a dissertation on a family law topic would be a plus. It is also worth pointing out that as first-hand experience of marital finance or the divorce courts is unlikely unless you shadow a barrister, a family law mini-pupillage is highly recommended and chambers offers its own week-long version.

A first-round interview is "*relatively informal and relaxed,*" but the second features a panel of six people who will ask "*a sequence of questions that test a candidate's ability to think and justify themselves.*" As to reasons why you want to be a divorce lawyer, think carefully. As one sage source observed: "*It would be a bit worrying if you said you'd wanted to divorce people since the age of 13.*" What is more likely to sway the panel is "*an understanding or interest in human nature and personality*" because "*even though the case might be a long time after an actual split, divorce still has the capacity to be a very emotional experience on many levels.*" Along with a head for figures, this need to "*enjoy working with real people, real problems and real emotions rather than faceless corporations*" is paramount. Whether it's a phenomenally rich banker with assets stashed in complex trusts, "*a husband who's run up tens of thousands on hookers,*" a "*standard middle-class divorce*" or the occasional legal aid matter, few cases are the same.

2 Hare Court

Chambers UK rankings: Crime, fraud: criminal

Who says crime doesn't pay? After 50 years as one of the Bar's leading criminal sets – handling everything from murder and terrorism to the kidnapping of pop stars, and people and drug trafficking – 2 Hare Court has made it do just that. It is one of the few sets that both prosecutes and defends in equal measure and shows no sign of abandoning its tradition of sending senior members to the bench. Taking the idea of comprehensive coverage to its logical conclusion, members recently acted on both sides of R v Milroy Sloane (a perversion-of-the-course-of-justice case brought against the woman who accused the Hamiltons of rape), while barristers have also figured prominently in the Bloody Sunday Inquiry, the Barry George trial (murder of Jill Dando), the Lee Bowyer public order charge and the Victoria Beckham kidnap plot. Strong relationships with government departments such as Defra, HSE and the Environment Agency ensure a steady stream of high-profile instructions. The set's impressive credentials also mean routine involvement on the part of the Serious Fraud Office and HM Revenue & Customs in some of the most complex and newsworthy fraud cases. Recent highlights include the R v Alibhai appeal (largest anti-piracy case in English legal history, concerning Microsoft software products). Another string to chambers' bow is a well-defined licensing and gaming practice.

The pupillage committee works hard to ensure that pupils are exposed to a wide variety of work during their 12 months. "*We don't see the point in pupils spending all their time with people who prosecute, or just those who do fraud, so we mix it up.*" Pupils added: "*It seems they try and vary the personality types too, so some supervisors are more rigorous and some more relaxed.*" The first six is spent predominantly in the company of a designated supervisor, learning the ins and outs of court procedures and the skills needed to handle clients. Where possible, the pupil will also work with other members. The emphasis is upon *"pupils being treated as members of chambers; we're proud of them and want to include them in every aspect of chambers' life from trial to lunch."* When things get busy, late nights and weekends are not uncommon. Pupils were sanguine on this point: *"When you come to a set as good as this and have faced such fierce competition for the place, the expectations are high and you don't want to disappoint. It comes down to this: are you committed to this job or not?"*

As the start of second-six looms, life becomes all about advocacy. *"The last month of first-six is mainly spent following other members around and getting as much exposure to the magistrates' court as possible."* This period is also an opportunity to engage in a mopping-up exercise and, together with their supervisors, pupils *"consider what you haven't seen yet and go see it."* Duly armed with broad experience and a helpful information pack *"that could be considered an idiot's guide to anything you would normally do during your second six,"* pupils get up on their feet. And, once up, they rarely sit down. Chambers' lofty position in the overall hierarchy of criminal sets is reflected in the quality of work second-six pupils and new tenants enjoy, but our sources had nevertheless travelled far with their early briefs. At least the set pays travel expenses. Towards the end of pupillage, things start to change: *"You spend the majority of your time in the Crown Court conducting mentions, plea and directions hearings, sentences, applications to dismiss and legal arguments."* There is even *"the possibility of a first Crown Court trial, depending on the individual and the relationships they have built with solicitors."* And if that isn't enough to fill their time, there's also the opportunity to take a two-week secondment at the CPS.

Advocacy is at the heart of a 2HC pupillage and, with in-house *"advocacy exercises for pupils every two weeks in chambers,"* you wouldn't think there'd be much call for further support. How wrong. Our sources detailed a new scheme: *"We have three resident judges at the Old Bailey and we do evening mock trials. This year we have had two."* Even though it must be every aspiring criminal barrister's dream to appear in the Old Bailey, it's fair to say that doing so – even in a mock trial – is daunting. *"I was absolutely nerve-wracked, especially looking around the courtroom at everybody's faces,"* admitted one pupil, *"but once I got going I no longer felt intimidated and at the end I got some brilliant feedback."* As in a number of other criminal sets *"it is unusual for pupils to be taken on after 12 months because it is unlikely that we would learn enough about them within the second six."* Any likely candidates for tenancy stay on at 2HC for a third six, after which a tenancy decision is reached. A committee considers feedback from instructing solicitors and judges and assesses their performance in court and written work. Pupillage is undoubtedly a long haul and current pupils advised *"pacing yourself appropriately."* On the plus side, *"we have no minimum or maximum number of tenants each year,"* confirmed a source; *"if a candidate demonstrates star quality and excellence and it is felt that they will have a flourishing career here, then they will be taken on."*

Life at 2HC is described as *"friendly but very tough." "You have to be an extrovert to come here,"* some sources thought, adding that *"shrinking violets might struggle."* Crime sets are sometimes characterised as dangerously social places and here, true to form, members *"socialise with each other at the pub regularly."* They also make an effort outside the Temple: *"Quite a few of us recently went to the christening of a member's child in Cyprus and we all went to the wedding of another."* They take *"pride in being a friendly set,"* and pupils confirmed that they had been included in the social side of chambers. "*When we're in the pub with members of the pupillage committee after advocacy exercises, they really try to make us feel like we can talk to them.*"

For students looking for pupillage, 2HC is one of the most popular on the criminal circuit. It gets hundreds of applications and, on average, invites 50 candidates for a 15-minute first interview. Analysing the quality of applicant, one member of the committee told us: "*Everyone has marshalled or done numerous mini-pupillages,*" so the selection process aims to detect evidence of "*application, intellect and aptitude*" through a consideration of candidates' broader experiences. "*Whether you play a musical instrument or climbed Everest, for instance, can be more telling,*" one recruiter told us. "*Although academic success is important, it's not the sole criteria; we have interviewed those with a 2:2.*" A dozen candidates make it through to the second-round interviews, when the questioning tends to focus more on criminal matters, normally including a practical exercise such as a plea in mitigation. Undoubtedly a tough process, the interviewers are aware that some candidates may not previously have undertaken such tasks. "*We are not looking for a polished performance but for advocacy potential.*" There are 40 mini-pupillages per year at this set so if you're serious about applying for pupillage perhaps you should also be serious about getting a mini here.

Henderson Chambers

Chambers UK rankings: Health & safety, information technology, product liability, professional discipline, real estate litigation

A set that definitely doesn't like to be pinned down by narrow legal categories or outside preconceptions, Henderson defines itself both by the scope of its practice and a working culture characterised by "strength derived from unity." Perhaps this latter trait reflects the long history of a set that has consistently evolved at its own pace over the last 60 years. To illustrate: way, way back, what was then 2 Harcourt Buildings enjoyed a reputation as a pre-eminent divorce set. Come the 1950s, criminal and civil practitioners co-existed at the set. Fast forward to the 1970s and crime was phased out, thus allowing civil matters to take centre stage. An already "*strong pedigree in tort*" made the development of product liability and health and safety practices all the easier. Other successful practices have been built in relation to IT, local government and public law, European law and real estate. As one no-nonsense source observed: "*you get* [incorrectly] *pigeonholed for your abilities – I mean, we have been involved in some of the largest sports PI cases, advise Formula One and the greyhound racing regulatory body, but we don't market ourselves as a sports law set, so we're not seen as such even though the work is there.*"

Although resistant to easy categorisation, the set fully deserves its reputation for excellence in certain areas. Members have advised on some of the largest-ever group actions involving products such as MMR/MR vaccine and tobacco, plus litigation over Sudan Red 1, benzene contamination and Lloyds Names. The set's H&S abilities see barristers involved with everything from industrial disease litigation and public inquiries to defending HSE or local authority prosecutions. Furthermore, strong relationships with the railway industry and rail regulators mean that Henderson has participated in some of the most significant rail disaster inquiries and corporate manslaughter cases of recent times. Even though members are well known for defending big pharmaceutical and tobacco companies, an increasing number of claimant insurance matters are also taken on. One current instruction relates to a group action by miners against solicitors firms and a trade union concerning their handling of industrial disease compensation claims.

Having briefly experimented with a modern practice manager, Henderson quickly returned to the more traditional steerage of head of chambers and senior clerk. An internal structure centred on 'business groups' is complemented by the "*fantastic entrepreneurial abilities*" of senior clerk John White. Any notion of merger has been eschewed in favour of "*organic and gradual expansion*" and growth in recent years means that the set is on the verge of taking on another floor of the Harcourt buildings. A slinky reception and waiting area suggest you're very much in the 21st century with Elizabeth Blackadder prints and a plasma screen TV booming out BBC News 24 updates. Once on the upper floors there are roaring fires, abundant artwork and views of Temple Gardens.

How do pupils, juniors and even more senior members fit into this matrix of work and styles? There is no straightforward answer; indeed many settled on Henderson because of the "*broad experience on offer in the early years.*" Said one source: "*You don't need to profess undying commitment to product liability to get in; everyone is free to develop their own interests and specialisms alongside chambers' traditional fortes.*" Provided with a laptop and two supervisors ("*about eight to 15 years' call to ensure a broader range of work*") over the course of the year, pupils initially work solely for their supervisor before being farmed out to other members. The first six is characterised by "*possession proceedings,*" "*small landlord and tenant cases,*" "*easements and property disputes*" on which pupils do "*lots of research, writing of advices and drafting of pleadings.*" On the day we visited, one pupil was rushing off to the V&A museum "*to research a contractual point in a potential copyright dispute.*" Uniquely, all pupils spend four weeks in Brussels working with the set's long-time associated members who are now part of the law firm McDermott Will & Emery/Stanbrook LLP. Although their accommodation over there is pot luck ("*sometimes amazing, others not*"), the quality of work and experience is uniformly "*fantastic, with close-quarters exposure to EU law.*"

The second six is all about "*being on your feet in court or at tribunal anything up to three times a week.*" Pupils cut their teeth on "*property and housing, PI and small employment matters,*" but also get to "*junior on larger cases; for example, public procurement.*" The clerks keep a watchful eye on a pupil's progress to ensure as broad an experience as possible. Breadth of experience is also likely for juniors up to five or six years' call. One young junior who had just been instructed on their first judicial review ("*a disgruntled applicant for a local authority business grant*") reflected that "*what's exciting is continually picking up something entirely new and getting to the heart of the matter. You have to be able to expand the boundaries of your knowledge and process information quickly but, more importantly, you have to have the confidence to act on it in court.*"

The feedback system at Henderson is one of the most impressive we've come across on our chambers visits. Every piece of work in pupillage is submitted together with a feedback form to be filled out by the relevant member of chambers. "*Everything is very constructively framed,*" commented sources, "*but you're told about your mistakes. You will be picked up if your legal reasoning was insufficient or just plain poor.*" This constant commentary "*takes the horror out of the process*" because "*you always know what you have to work on.*" It also makes the three-monthly appraisals and the tenancy decision a more transparent process. Early in the summer, a pupil's feedback forms are collated, together with an overview written by each supervisor and feedback via clerks from solicitors. Once this material has been submitted to the tenancy committee *"you wait for a call from the head of chambers."* With one new tenant per year being the norm, someone is usually left disappointed, but it is not absolutely unheard of for several pupils to be successful. In 2006 two pupils gained tenancy, one of them a third-sixer.

Those who take tenancy tend to be *"open people with a relaxed manner socially and a willingness to learn the hard way."* This set prides itself on *"a mutually supportive atmosphere"* with a *"cohesive, congenial"* ethos. One of the more characterful members garages a large remote-controlled battle tank in his room – *"it will sometimes trundle past your door and down the corridor if he's a bit restless."* Outside the confines of the building, pupils join junior tenants for drinks, and the fact that two juniors recently married each other gave cause for more celebrations than usual this year. Add in events like a *"Champagne-powered Christmas party at the Bucks Club"* and set-promoting moments like a recent product liability seminar that had *"solicitors queuing up to get in,"* and there are many occasions to rally round the Henderson flag.

If this set gets onto your shortlist you'll need to know what to expect from its recruiters. The *"intentionally relaxed and informal yet exacting"* interview process currently bucks the trend of setting a written problem for discussion. *"This approach winds candidates up; we prefer people to be fresh, calm and very much themselves."* Of greatest importance to the interview panel is *"roundness of personality, an interest in broad, common law work and a commitment to exploring diversity of practice."* In short, you're *"not expecting to have fixated on one area of practice before you arrive"* because chambers believes strongly that *"even though increasing specialisation is a watchword at Bar, there's still a call for broadly experienced barristers with varied ability."*

Hogarth Chambers

Chambers UK rankings: Information technology, intellectual property, media & entertainment

As all you legal historians will be aware, celebrated 18th century painter and satirist William Hogarth caused considerable upheaval when he had the nerve to suggest that artists' work should be protected from other people passing it off as their own. He felt so strongly about this that he successfully petitioned Parliament to introduce a copyright bill. And so the foundations for successive generations of intellectual property lawyers were laid down...

When One Raymond Buildings and 5 New Square merged in 2001, Hogarth was deemed an apt figurehead for their alliance. A further merger with 19 Old Buildings in 2004 brought more IP practitioners on board. High-profile cases such as Arsenal v Reed (where a man selling Arsenal merchandise outside the stadium was prosecuted for breach of copyright) and Douglas v Hello! (where a man and a woman got upset at a magazine taking pictures of them eating cake) have cemented the set's strong reputation in IP and related fields. Nonetheless, there are still enough pure Chancery practitioners knocking around in Hogarth Chambers to ensure pupils are exposed to a variety of work, if they wish.

The fact that the set takes only one pupil per year enables it to tailor the whole experience according to the pupil's needs and practice preferences. In theory, the pupillage is split into four three-month periods spent with different pupil supervisors; in practice this can vary depending on whether a pupil has particular strength in a given area such as patents or media and entertainment. It's certainly not uncommon for a pupil to be away from their supervisor for a number of weeks to assist another member on a case in an area in which they have expressed interest. The idea is that *"the pupil has the opportunity to excel."* Recent recruits were quick to salute the efficacy of the system, saying: "*It stops you feeling like a spare part when you're able to contribute in an area that you actually know something about.*" It is possible to have a pure IP pupillage, which will encompass the full range of both 'hard' and 'soft' work. The reason for offering it is simple – chambers wants to ensure that those fully intent on specialising in IP from the outset are not put off by the thought of months spent on Chancery matters. Pupils will find themselves jetting off (at chambers' expense) to Luxembourg or Munich with their pupil supervisers to sit in on European trade mark or patent cases.

A pupillage at Hogarth won't give you much advocacy experience. The majority of a pupil's time is spent in chambers researching and then producing written work, ie opinions and pleadings. Although some of the subject matter can be a little dry (corkscrew patents, anyone?), there is ample glamorous 'soft' IP work on offer. "*The sort of person who thrives here has the ability to analyse material in considerable depth and then explain it clearly and concisely.*" With a varied client list that includes drugs companies, manufacturers and elements of the artistic community, it is vitally important to be able to maintain a real handle on the facts to ensure that your advice is accessible yet comprehensive.

So how do you become the intellectual property of Hogarth, for a year at least? Chambers expects a hand-written covering letter with typed CV. It's hard to tell whether this is an attempt to thwart the copy-and-paste approach to covering letters or if they just want to see how close you sat to the front in calligraphy class; either way it undoubtedly gives candidates the chance to "*make their case for interview clearly.*" What the recruiters look for above all is "*strong academic credentials,*" and whilst the briefest glance at the CVs of junior tenants might indicate that the best place to establish these credentials is Oxbridge, it is worth noting that the two most recent pupils (and most recent tenant) studied elsewhere. "*We're after people who aren't afraid to engage with a complex subject in real depth,*" noted one member, and the more a candidate can demonstrate this the better their chance of being invited to a first interview. An assessed mini-pupillage is "*a good foot in the door.*" Do well and you've probably just doubled your chance of pupillage interview. The set also values good interpersonal skills as "*when you're dealing with a wide-ranging client base including blue-chip companies such as Nike and Microsoft you need people who are able to press the flesh and inspire clients with confidence.*"

At interview the emphasis is on a candidate's ability to think quickly and "*fight their corner well.*" With the interview panel attempting to pick holes in your argument, "*your back is against the wall and it's very much a case of sink or swim.*" If you stay afloat through to the second round, expect more of the same, but also be on the look out for increasingly bizarre questions. One of our sources was asked to describe a spiral staircase without using the words 'spiral' or 'staircase'...

At 5 New Square the fourth floor is home to many junior tenants and is the driving force behind chambers' social life. Friday evenings might see people amble down to the Seven Stars or go for drinks at someone's home. A not-to-be-missed event – especially if you see yourself as a bit of a Freddie Flintoff – is the annual cricket match against patent and trade mark attorneys Marks & Clerk which "*always leads to quality banter.*" Indeed, getting known by solicitors, patent attorneys and trade mark agents is essential in the early years; to this end junior practitioners are encouraged to get involved with seminars and write articles on new developments.

The daily ritual of chambers tea does not seem to be too much of an ordeal for pupils. Admittedly no one portayed it as the most fun you can have without laughing, but it is "*a good opportunity to *get everyone on side."* Attendance at tea is not compulsory but pupils tend to *"go with the flow of their pupil supervisor"* so removing the anxiety of the decision about whether to pop in for a cheeky digestive. Speaking of decisions, when the tenancy decision was made in 2006, the set chose not to award tenancy to its pupil.

We're not sure if we quite agree with the person who described the set as having *"a magical vibe to it"* as the dominant characteristics of those we spoke to were more connected to intelligence, hard work and ambition than hocus-pocus and abracadabra. More Hogarth than Hogwarts then, and we think that's just the way they like it.

Keating Chambers

Chambers UK rankings: Construction, energy & natural resources, international arbitration, professional negligence

If you've browsed the shelves of your university law library you may be familiar with one of this set's proudest offerings – *Keating on Building Contracts*. The so-called building contracts bible was last updated by chambers' luminaries Stephen Furst QC and the Hon Mr Justice Ramsey. Only recently appointed a judge, the latter is continuing the set's proud history of sending members to the bench, but don't imagine Keating to be hidebound by tradition...

Chambers and Partners Construction Set of the Year 2006

Purchased by its members three years ago, chambers' expansive, bright and disarmingly calm premises at 15 Essex Street are two minutes from The Royal Courts of Justice and the TCC, housing some 45 barristers. Keating's transfor-

mation into a leading construction set started in the early 1980s and today all members are specialists in construction cases. Frequently instructed on different sides of the same case, they handle big-money matters from around the world, with ongoing instructions including the myriad disputes relating to the new Wembley Stadium, power stations in several South American countries, Russia's mining industry consolidation and transport projects including the Taiwan high-speed rail link.

Admitting that their work is less attractive to students than the cases offered in more general commercial sets, Keating barristers were keen to advertise its appeal. *"Construction has been at the forefront of jurisprudence for the last 20 years. It's a very dynamic area. What we do is contract and tort,"* explained one. Many of the recent leading cases in the law of negligence have been construction-related and this *"exploration of negligence"* is inevitable when you consider that construction projects are essentially *"a contractual matrix of employers, contractors, subcontractors and sub-subcontractors, coupled with the likelihood that one or more will go bust."*

If the academic nature of the work doesn't grab you, the lure of advocacy might. *"You may need to roll your sleeves up and cross-examine a site foreman, contractor or employer. They could give conflicting factual accounts as to what they did or didn't agree on."* It's this human dimension to work that prevents cases from being purely fact-based or technical. As one barrister explained: *"Factual witnesses may also be protecting their own position, and you have to be sensitive to the reality of the politics within companies."* Fortunately *"as a pupil you pick it up because your pupilmasters chat through these dynamics with you."*

However, you should never underestimate the technical and factual aspects. Sometimes cases rest on rooms full of supporting documents, although as one old hand revealed: *"With* most there's just a handful of really important documents that could fit into one lever arch file... you do have to identify those documents and to do so you have to be able to grasp and manage the rest." As for the technical side, "first you learn the basics, then more-sophisticated concepts of engineering, sometimes chemistry, sometimes physics..." True, at least half a dozen members are technically qualified, but amazingly we met barristers at Keating who'd studied only arts subjects and law after the age of 16.

A Keating pupillage involves four spells of three months with different supervisors to ensure broad experience. Pupils also undertake work for other members of chambers, although "pupil-masters are active in making sure people are not overloaded." The view of one PM was that pupils "should be able to manage workload without being here seven days a week." Nonetheless, working evenings and weekends is normal, so unless you're prepared to place your career centre-stage consider your application carefully – "£35,000 is a big investment in someone and you have to remind yourself of that." The set thrives by "not being stuck in an ivory tower; clients come here because we understand their business..." and pupils' lives reflect that commerciality. "It's about rolling up your sleeves and realising you are part of a team with solicitors, experts and clients."

Pupils spend most of their time learning how to draft statements of case, particulars of claim, defences and replies. Opinion-writing practice might focus on the liability of an architect for incorrectly estimating future project costs, for example. Additionally, there are opportunities to see PMs and other barristers in action, be it in court or arbitration proceedings or in conference with solicitors and lay clients. Compared to ten years ago there is now significantly greater flexibility of approach in resolving construction disputes and this means a broader range of skills to acquire. "Pupils help to prepare cases day in day out, they research cross-examination ideas and witness statements; draft mediation position papers, learning that they have to have a different tone to a set of submissions to a judge." While there are no set written assessments, "effectively everything we do is assessed." By contrast, there are four formal advocacy exercises in the year and these take place in one of chambers' many arbitration rooms, with a member taking the role of the judge.

In the second six and the early months of tenancy, pupils cut their teeth on small applications and RTA trials, progressing at an early stage to second-junior work on bigger cases. Specifically an advantage of being at a specialist set, juniors can "get a lot of cross-referrals from other people's practices," meaning higher-quality work. Within two to three years after pupillage, young barristers can earn as much as in the major commercial and Chancery sets.

The all-members tenancy decision is made in July after considering a report from the eight-strong tenancy committee comprising the head of chambers, two silks and a spread of juniors. They consider reports from each PM (and any other barrister familiar with the pupil's work) as well as feedback from instructing solicitors and general comments from senior clerks on pupils' conduct and demeanour. "We try to strip politics out of the decision, but personality does count," acknowledged one committee member. In the last five years pupillage hasn't always produced an abundance of new tenants, yet there is an appetite for growth at Keating and in 2006 three of the four pupils gained tenancy. Every member has their own room, and even baby juniors enjoy plenty of space.

As to what leads to success, one PM told us: "We're looking for a real star; someone who surprises you with their ability at that age." Taking this idea a step further, it's about "demonstrating that very serious thought has gone into your work, coming up with good points after a couple of *hours."* The tip from one PM was to *"try and put on a few years and act as old as you can sensibly get away with."*

Unlike many of the top Chancery and commercial sets, Keating isn't a pure Oxbridge environment. And just in case you were thinking that this is a male-dominated part of the Bar, half the members under ten years' call are women. One young junior admitted that, even today, a few clients are initially doubtful about instructing a female barrister but can be won over really quickly.

Male or female, the barrister's best ally is the Keating brand, and don't members know it – *"Rarely do people think they are better than the brand."* By all accounts, *"everyone has time for each other"* in an atmosphere that is *"wonderfully, blissfully apolitical; probably because everyone is happy with their practice and can't work the steam up to get bothered by things."* Thursday is a day for lunching together, although pupils aren't invited. Instead they are taken to the pub after work, usually The Edgar Wallace or Daly's Wine Bar. The annual garden party is a time for people to let their hair down, and every now and then it's a time for romance. *"It's led to three weddings and countless babies,"* revealed a source. Other social distractions include cricket and football, parties at members' houses and occasional point-to-point days with *"champagne and sarnies out of the back of cars."*

As with any kind of specialist practice, a mini-pupillage is a must if you're serious about an application. Keating offers ten week-long, funded and assessed opportunities plus up to 25 that are unfunded and unassessed. Attendance should equip you with a sense of the set's work so you don't look stupid at a pupillage interview. Familiarising yourself with the basic concepts of ADR will also help, but no one expects a fully prepped construction expert at interview. That can come later.

7 King's Bench Walk

Chambers UK rankings: Commercial litigation, insurance, international arbitration, professional negligence, shipping & commodities

Described by one observer as a 'smooth classic', 7KBW is the matinee idol of a world slowly disappearing from view. Our initial impressions did little to dispel the sense that this is the Bar of which films – and dreams, perhaps – were made.

Chambers and Partners
Insurance Set of the Year 2006

Sleek but compact rooms with working fireplaces and pink tape scattered about; on one wall a portrait of an 18th century judge observing proceedings with an amused but detached air – this is genuinely the stuff of legal legend. Yet in the last ten years 7KBW has aimed to distance itself from its deeply traditional past by promoting a more user-friendly environment. Although pupils are intently aware of what they are in a position to inherit, they find that the emphasis is less about bowing to one's seniors than maintaining exacting standards. The recollection of being admonished by a senior barrister for referring to a senior barrister as *"Mr"* prompted one former pupil to point out that everyone under 15 years call is close-knit and wont to share a drink rather than *"standing to attention."* Another important shift has seen a growing number of women members – if the current headcount of seven sounds scarce, bear in mind that for many years it was just one. So, no elaborate image makeovers or drastic restructuring, but a gradual evolution befitting a set with a long history to live up to. The contribution made to chambers history in 2006 was the appointment of six new silks, the highest number for any set in this year.

Although chambers' main home is still no 7, KBW barristers also reside in Nos 4, 8, 9, and part of 10, making it the biggest set still nestled in the Inns of Court. Over the centuries 7KBW has produced some of the most prominent figures at the Bar: in 1820 Serjeant Wilde defended and saved Queen Caroline's life and honour in the face of an accusation of adultery, and in the 1850s Lord Halsbury occupied rooms here with renowned prosecutor Sir Harry Bodkin Poland. Together they defended a former Governor of Jamaica on a murder charge. The modern-day set was born in 1967 following the merger of 7KBW with 3 Pump Court (another commercial set of antiquity) and over the following four decades chambers has become synonymous with breeding masterful judges. Lords Denning, Brandon, Goff, Hobhouse and Mance as well as Messrs Justice Tomlinson and Cooke are all former members. Work-wise, shipping was the traditional mainstay until the 1990s, when the set's prominence in the massive Lloyd's insurance litigation highlighted its insurance and reinsurance groups as among the foremost in the country. Insurance now accounts for almost 70% of all work, with members taking central roles in enormous, high-profile cases. The Barings litigation was a recent highlight, as were the cases covering insurance liabilities for breast implants and asbestos-related illnesses plus some interesting marine insurance matters. General commercial cases make up the remainder of the workload with banking, professional negligence and international arbitration featuring regularly.

Instructions pour in to 7KBW from "just about everyone;" not for nothing is the set known as the place to come for rigorous, technical and often dazzling application of the law. One pupil enthused: "There are some absolute geniuses here. They're very understated – people don't boast, probably because they don't have to – but there are just so many clever, clever barristers." You may be thrilled to hear that court work is just as important as drafting here, with another pupil describing the sight of two senior 7KBW silks against each other in court as "extraordinary – the most brilliant advocacy I've seen." Breeding such stellar performers often results in departures to the Bench ("often too early, I think," moaned the senior clerk), which is why pupillage aims to train hopefuls in the same mould. So, if you don't fancy being groomed as an insurance and reinsurance expert look elsewhere, but if policies and finances are your thing expect a dazzling range of experience.

Pupils each sit with four pupilmasters, the first for three months, then for progressively shorter periods of time with each subsequent PM. Unusually, in only the first three months is the emphasis on learning the ropes and taking work exclusively from the PM; pupils are expected to be "*almost fully fledged*" by the time they move on to their second assignment. By the third switch "*the pressure can get fairly intense and I would say that the learning curve is absolutely vertical,*" reported a source. After the initial three months, pupils can expect to work for any member of chambers, all of whom will make a concerted effort to try out each of them ahead of voting in the final tenancy decision. It means pupils do "*anything and everything, from drafting pleadings for a QC with huge amounts of paperwork to following up a small research point. It's a good mix of live cases, some of which have been ongoing for one or two years, and previous judgments, where we're encouraged to give something a go ourselves.*" Current pupils had covered a massive employment class action in the USA and worked on a previous judgment for a £170 million oil drilling platform. They were quick to praise their overseers as "*very pleasant and down-to-earth, with absolutely no airs and graces,*" with one former pupil telling us: "*I'm still always popping my head around the door to ask my old pupilmaster's advice.*"

The pace and pressure of pupillage is undoubtedly strenuous with very high expectations, although the end-of-first-six review and advocacy assessment is only rarely the prompt for a departure. For the most part pupils feel "*the confidence in us is very reassuring;*" "*we're treated very humanely, often sent home at 6 or 7pm, and there's a general sense of goodwill towards pupils.*" Fulsome feedback and "*careful allocation of work and assessments*" means "*We're always given a reasonable amount of time to do our very best and we know how we're doing.*" One pupil had recently spent a week on circuit with a High Court Judge, but when it comes to advocacy they are not that lucky – second-six pupils do not appear in court alone themselves. Is this a hindrance? Apparently not: "*Too many court appearances wouldn't gel with the work that chambers does. Also, there's just so much to learn – we can't waste time with bail applications.*"

Two senior clerks are the "*driving force*" of chambers' social life; they even arrange a night out for pupils and juniors in December. Pupils are also invited along to formal chambers events, as well as the newly initiated monthly buffet lunch. Afternoon tea, however, remains off limits for pupils, the rationale being "*we don't want pupils to feel uncomfortable nor do we want to create a desperate-to-impress situation.*" Not that they'd have to try that hard to impress. Although the Oxbridge quotient is high, chambers says it wants "*the best, irrespective of university.*" Backing up this claim, recent pupils have come from South Africa, Australia, New Zealand and France. Getting through the single-stage pupillage interview is no cakewalk and includes tough questioning from a five-person panel on a skeleton argument – unsurprisingly, something like an application for leave to appeal to the House of Lords. "*We look for analytical and intellectual rigour, and we do take our pupils to task,*" confirmed a source; "*we treat them as if they know what they're doing.*"

Pupils are explicitly told not to compete with one another, though we can't help thinking that it must be hard not to.

New tenants can expect secondments to City law firms and some of the best work around. One junior cited a solo appearance before the Court of Appeal and a turn in the House of Lords with a leader in his first two years. We were suitably impressed. We'll leave the last word to one of the pupils though: "*This isn't for the faint-hearted and I feel very lucky indeed to be here.*"

11 King's Bench Walk

Chambers UK rankings: Admin & public law, competition/European law, education, employment, human rights, local government, public procurement

1981 was an important year. In the USA it heralded the appointment of the first female justice in the Supreme Court. In the UK 11 KBW was launched. Among its founder members were a future Lord Chancellor (Derry Irvine) and a future prime minister (Tony Blair).

Whilst not exactly operating on a law for law's sake manifesto, there is little doubt that this is the place for those who want to fully engage with the theoretical side of the law. "*Debate is strongly encouraged; the sort of work we're involved in means that there is no such thing as a spurious point.*" Further evidence of the academic esteem that the set generates becomes clear when you tot up the number of legal textbook authors housed within chambers; almost half the set contribute to Tolley's Employment Handbook, a practitioner's bible often cited in tribunals. But it's not all intellectualising and there is a practical significance to the work undertaken. Members have recently been involved in the challenges to the new hunting legislation and have been contributing to the ongoing debate on how to treat suspected terrorists.

Chambers has all the usual trappings and trimmings: mahogany desks, bookcases crammed with law reports and case papers strewn over busy practitioners' rooms. The set's communal space has a number of colourful Philip Sutton works (Derry's a fan of this Slade School artist apparently) adorning the pale cream walls. Until recently, quite a few members were accommodated outside chambers, but the set recently took a vote to rent further space next door at No. 10 KBW where it already has its extensive library facilities.

In general, 11 KBW has grown from within, with the exception of a few years ago when barristers from 4-5 Gray's Inn Square (Cherie Booth's old set) joined around the same time as Matrix formed. In spite of all its connections the temptation to paint the set as a bastion of New Labour should be resisted. 11 KBW is a political animal only in that it handles government instructions; one senses that this is because of the advanced and interesting legal appeal of the work and not because the set has any particular political affiliations.

For a pupil the first three months are a low-key experience; it's not until the second and third quarters that they start doing work for members of chambers other than their supervisor. This is also when the "scrupulously fair tenancy system" kicks in and each piece of work is double-marked and filed away until July when the decision is made. The required standard is that of a new tenant. Hit that consistently and the pupil will be welcomed with open arms. To give pupils an indication of the way things are going, after six months there is a formal review with the head of the tenancy committee. If things have not gone as well as hoped this may be the point where it is gently suggested that the pupil should move on somewhere else for a second six.

Typical work involves drafting opinions, skeleton arguments or cross-examinations and research notes for conferences. Pupils complete a minimum of six of these every three months,

treating every piece like an exam problem question where they have to explore all the areas, no matter how tenuous they seem, in order to get the top marks. "The stuff we work on ends up getting argued in the House of Lords or the Court of Appeal so there will always be very clever people on the opposite side going through everything with a fine tooth comb in order to find a weakness." Nothing less than perfect will do by the sounds of things.

Having endured 12 months of predominantly paper-based activity, the focus shifts dramatically for new tenants, who are instantly on their feet in employment and education tribunals. To prepare prospective tenants in the last three months of pupillage they ride shotgun with new tenants. Nonetheless, it's clear that the jump from theory to practice is quite a shock to the system. The first year of tenancy is rent-free so as to allow you to fill the coffers after years of relative hardship. In 2006 the single pupil took tenancy.

As well as exceptionally strong academic credentials applicants must have an ability to express ideas cogently because "it's no good someone having prodigious intelligence if they can't communicate it to the client." The way to jump ahead of the pack is to bag yourself an assessed mini-pupillage. One pupil felt it gave him the edge: "Having already done work for them meant that I knew what to expect and what they were looking for." The academic nature of the set is apparent in the sort of questions you're sent a week prior to the single-round interview. Typically, there will be a couple of cases to read through and comment on. The interview panel isn't just concerned with what you say, it's also the way that you analyse things that is important. "It's not enough to come out with brilliant-sounding assertions. Showing how you get to them is key."

Make no mistake, this is a seriously demanding pupillage and its paper-based nature means that it can be quite solitary at times. Most days a group of people go for lunch at Inner Temple, but don't expect to be part of a conga line wending its way to the Witness Box or Pegasus Bar every night. The chances are you'll be working late in the library and in early the next day. The flip side of this is that you are at a set that is at the vanguard of public law and you'll never be short of intellectual stimulation. In 2006 one of the set's pupils gained tenancy.

Landmark Chambers

Chambers UK rankings: Admin & public law, agriculture & rural affairs, environment, local government, planning, real estate litigation

Landmark's brand new premises on the corner of Fleet Street and Fetter Lane have a certain air of Bond-villain hideout about them. A silent lift transports you to the reception where you are greeted by an impeccably polite host who was once former head receptionist at the New Zealand Parliament building. You glance around: an army of clerks goes about its business behind plate glass windows; the conference rooms boast all manner of Q-inspired gadgetry; giant plasma screens hang from several walls; the door to the post room bears the ominous legend 'No Entrance to Barristers'. Is there is a pool filled with carnivorous fish? Are the chief exec and head of chambers hatching plots in their corner offices with views across the City? Well, no. In truth, the slick detail of the new premises reveals little more about Landmark than its confidence as a business and a defining aura of professionalism. While other chambers take baby steps away from the Inns, Landmark has powered into its second external home, confidently signing a 15-year lease of 180 Fleet Street. It has reason to be optimistic: the set's combined turnover grew by 10% to £15.9 million last year.

Formed just four years ago from a merger of leading planning and public law chambers 4

Bream Buildings and planning set Eldon Chambers. Landmark is widely acknowledged to be the Bar's pre-eminent planning law chambers. Its capacity for other types of public law and a burgeoning environmental law practice are also well known. Landmark planning barristers have worked on multiple aspects of the site proposals and associated regeneration schemes for the 2012 Olympics, as well as on inquiries into the Shard of Glass (aka London Bridge Tower) and Arsenal's new Emirates Stadium. The set's public law practitioners were involved in The Hutton Inquiry and aspects of the London Eye's landlord's attempts to either recover possession of the site or increase its rent. Their environmental law colleagues have featured on The Shell Haven Inquiry into the new Thames Gateway port and matters pertaining to the Crossrail Bill. Among chambers' best known figures is new head Christopher Katkowski QC, commonly referred to as Kit Kat.

Chambers is *"working hard to stay at number one"* and is doing so in a number of ways. Working on the basic premise that *"specialisation is the way forward: it's what clients want,"* there is a mandate to engage more directly with specific sectors; for example, *"the water industry, which is facing massive reservoir and water shortage issues."* At the same time, in the area of public law, recruitment at senior level is helping the set towards its target of *"being on a par with Blackstone."* In property law, the aim is to *"add quality people"* and *"develop the areas of overlap, say, between property and human rights."* This desire for increased specialisation does not narrow a pupil or junior tenant's prospects; indeed those we interviewed saw Landmark as offering both *"an enormous amount of varied, junior-level work"* and *"a real opportunity to shape your own career."*

Pupils sit with a total of four supervisors, the first three covering the set's main practice areas in no particular order. Being exposed to the full extent of chambers' work helps develop "*an understanding of the complex intersection between disciplines; for example, focusing on right-to-property matters crosses over public and property law.*" Within the 'seat' structure there is some room for manoeuvre. One pupil had "*secured more time for public law-oriented work in my three months in property because it was my forte.*" The exact nature of work does vary between disciplines; for example, property law is "*more chambers-based drafting and research*" than public law, which can involve more "*site visits, conferences and heavy opinion writing.*" Whatever the practice area, supervisors "*give virtually constant feedback, both positive and negative,*" on the pupils attempts at skeleton arguments, research notes and draft pleadings. As well as occasional work for other members, each three-month period involves a short time shadowing a QC ("*so that you see high-profile cases and the top-end stuff*"). It doesn't sound as if pupils are stretched to breaking point at this stage. One told us: "*You're sometimes almost physically thrown out of the office if you're still there after 6pm.*" Chambers' recruiters were clear in their views on pupillage, telling us of their "*determination that it should not be a horrible experience*" and their belief that "*pupillage is a coaching and mentoring exercise to help pupils achieve their potential.*" Whatever happened to having a rugby ball thrown at you at interview or a year of character-building slavery for a lunatic pupilmaster?

In the second six, being on your feet in court once or twice a week is "*an essential part of the process.*" At this stage pupils are still carefully protected by their supervisors and the clerks, and none of them go out without completing an advocacy exercise. "*To be honest it was more scary getting up in front of senior people in chambers to practise than on the first day in court,*" one source confessed. After their practice run, Leasehold Valuation Tribunals and small possession hearings await the second sixer.

Landmark pupils were relatively sanguine about the tenancy decision, confident that "*if there is the capacity for three pupils to stay, and three are good enough, three will be kept on.*" Such composure is perhaps a product of an assessment system that sees pupils complete the same three QC-set written tasks (one per practice area). Each assessment is "*contemporary and based on what the QC is working on.*" Pupils told us that their most recent assessment had been "*to write a speech for the European Court of Human Rights.*" These tests – together with supervisor reports and external feedback – influence the tenancy decision. In 2006 two of the three pupils were offered tenancy. Those who aren't offered tenancy are helped with their search for a third six elsewhere; those who are enter "*a bubble of constant work*" where regular "*practice meetings with clerks*" enable them to "*define and develop* [a] *career depending on interest and ambition.*" Based on our interviews this is no hollow claim: describing their caseloads, young juniors listed educational tribunal work, public inquiries and claimant immigration cases, worked on planning matters for housing associations and local authorities, been involved with environmental cases, freedom of information matters and judicial reviews.

At Landmark, the social life is "*balanced and not all-encompassing.*" A group of junior tenants meets for drinks at the Wine Cellar "*just downstairs*" or, "*now we're a little better off, cocktails at One Aldwych.*" This group forms a welcoming committee for incoming pupils, organising "*dinners and drinks*" as well as providing "*heads around the door and advice on where to turn if you need help with work.*" Supervisors are said to make time to get to know their charges, and one pupil told us they had come to enjoy "*daily tea, cake and chat breaks at 4.30pm with my supervisor.*"

We observed a high calibre of pupil at Landmark. While there were no common denominators in terms of university background, degree subject or personality, all possessed post-graduate qualifications and had practical experience in a field related to the set's interests. Whether it was working for immigration and housing charities, being an election observer in Eastern Europe or taking a post at the EU or UN, these pupils were able to demonstrate close involvement with public, environment and/or planning law. Perhaps in an attempt not to scare off applicants, one chambers recruiter explained that "*any evidence of interest in the set's work is enough; perhaps there was a local planning case that caught the candidate's eye and they went to the inquiry.*" The interview process was undergoing review when we visited and the plan was to add a second stage or some form of assessment exercise. Suffice to say that if you are one of the 150 who apply, or one of the roughly 20 who are called to interview, you can expect "*straightforward questions that aren't intimidating but focus on competencies*" and "*give you the chance to shine.*" Landmark has just added to its calendar a pupillage open day complete with Q&A session because "*student feedback told us they weren't involved enough.*" It sounds like the perfect precursor to a mini-pupillage.

Maitland Chambers

Chambers UK rankings: Agriculture and rural affairs, Chancery: commercial, Chancery: traditional, charities, commercial litigation, company, insolvency/corporate recovery, partnership, professional negligence, real estate litigation

Created in 2001 out of the merger of 13 Old Square and 7 Stone Buildings, in 2004 Maitland also incorporated 9 Old Square and now has 64 barristers – the "*perfect number*" for a commercial Chancery set apparently. Among the 14 QCs are many leading names including Catherine New-

man, Charles Aldous, Michael Lyndon-Stanford and Christopher McCall. It excels in both traditional and commercial Chancery, and the 9 Old Square arrivals brought with them an extremely strong property practice. Maitland is the doyen of the contentious Chancery world: members were involved in the House of Lords case of National Westminster Bank Plc v Spectrum Plus Ltd & Ors, which rewrote many of the rules on insolvency and naturally enough they are also involved in the huge Equitable Life dispute that was lumbering through the courts. Other matters of interest and intrigue have included advice to the Beckhams in the privacy dispute with their former nanny, and the Barings and BCCI cases. When not in court, members are busy contributing to or editing legal texts, among them *Snell on Equity*, Hill & Redman's *Law of Landlord & Tenant* and *Halsbury's Laws*.

Chambers and Partners
Chancery Set of the Year 2006

The first three months of pupillage are a time for "*bedding in*" and, as such, supervisors are more lenient with mistakes. After Christmas "*the honeymoon is over*" and the pupillage transforms into a "*highly intense environment*" where "*you are aware that every error is harmful to your tenancy prospects.*" If you think this sounds overly harsh, remember, clients pay top whack for the best advice possible and in this undoubtedly tough world, a "*huge amount of industry and diligence*" is required at all stages of one's career. Chancery practice attracts "*intellectually disciplined*" individuals with accurate judgement: those who are adept at legal reasoning and readily come up with coherent justifications for their conclusions. As one junior put it: "*You can't wing it in the Chancery courts.*" It is because the necessary skill and knowledge doesn't come about overnight that "*you need to be prepared to put in the hours in order to get to the required standard.*"

In an effort to put pupils on a level playing field, they all sit with the same group of pupil supervisors. This additionally ensures exposure to several of the areas of specialisation on offer within chambers, including company, insolvency and professional negligence. Supervisors are keen to fully utilise their pupils' talents, reasoning that "*an able pupil is a real asset to your practice.*" The payback is that there's no skimping on feedback; "*when they go through your work they really go to town, the red pen is well and truly out in force!*" During the year, there are five advocacy exercises judged by eminent members. Besides being quite nerve-wracking, "*they improve your case management skills*" and they stand as a substitute for actually getting on your feet in court during the second six.

Due to the merger with 9 Old Square, Maitland had five pupils when we visited in 2005, which may have exacerbated the somewhat competitive atmosphere we encountered. Nevertheless, any set which lets its pupils know how far up the pecking order they sit after six months is hardly discouraging competition. We weren't entirely surprised to hear stories of pupils working at weekends in order to create a good impression. The crunch comes at the tenancy decision in June when all members meet. When we visited, four out of the five pupils had made it past the six-month stage and two had just been taken on as tenants. In 2006, a further two joined the ranks.

Chambers tea at Maitland is one of those occasions when it's best to be seen but not heard. One pupil didn't feel deprived of the opportunity to take centre stage, telling us: "*To be honest, it's a relief to be able to veg out and not worry about trying to say anything too intelligent!*" If pushed we'd have to say one gets the impression that at Maitland you're best advised to mind your ps and qs

during pupillage and "*there is the feeling that senior members of chambers are keeping an eye on things.*" That said, Thursday nights in a local pub are an opportunity to unwind with juniors. The venue is dependant on the whims of one of the set's most important committees – Pubco – which convenes to make a decision on a Thursday afternoon. Usually they plump for somewhere like the White Horse or The Seven Stars.

When a set becomes as large as Maitland, especially if it has grown through mergers, attempts to promote cohesion are important. Chambers sprawls across four separate premises in Stone Buildings and Old Square, with its main hub at 7 Stone Buildings. The calmness of the traditional waiting room belies the intensity of labour and firepower within chambers. Make no mistake, this is a seriously talented, extremely polished and remarkably well-managed collection of lawyers. It's a style and standard that is sought out by the pupillage committee each year. To impress them on paper you must show "*a first-class academic record*" (look at the CVs of members on the website). Make the paper cut and there are two rounds of interviews. The first is a "*challenging chat*" during which it will become clear to the panel whether you've got "*the 'it' factor.*" This will be ascertained via a question on something fairly topical, such as that asked in 2004 – whether the English cricket team were right to visit Zimbabwe. Make it through to the second interview and there's another problem question, this time with 30 minutes of preparation beforehand. The question will involve some sort of legal problem, and this is your chance to show an ability to spot issues and come up with practical solutions; in other words, to display the shoots of the legal, analytical skills and "*commercial pragmatism*" that is so sought after in the top sets. Make it through these two stages and we reckon you deserve that pupillage!

As befits a set that is named after a legal historian, Maitland wants to make legal history itself by not only securing a king of the hill position on mainstream Chancery work, but also going toe-to-toe with a number of niche and commercial practices. The ambition and drive of members and managers makes this an exciting place to be right now.

Matrix

Chambers UK rankings: Admin & public law, competition/European law, crime, defamation/privacy, education, employment, environment, fraud: criminal, human rights, immigration, international arbitration, police law, public international law

Hatched in the innocence and optimism of the new millennium, it is no exaggeration to say that Matrix has tried to revolutionise the ways of the Bar. The idea is to "*change attitudes by changing terminology*" so the old terms 'pupil', 'tenant' and 'clerk' have been consigned to the waste paper bin and replaced by 'trainee', 'member' and 'practice manager.' Although not alone in professing to live by core values, Matrix prides itself on ensuring that these beliefs are actually upheld in day-to-day practice. Those core values in full then: independence; client care and quality of service; teamwork and co-operation; practice diversity; public service ethos; innovation; a democratic structure; efficiency in administration and management; promotion of equality of opportunity; and closer links between practising and academic lawyers. Every angle is covered by the looks of things. Active links with the community also mean that more and more people are being exposed to the progressive end of the Bar, and just in case there were any doubt as to Matrix's intentions, it has deliberately taken on premises that look more like an ad agency than barristers' chambers.

So, aside from the vocabulary and mission statements, what's different about Matrix? Let's start with the absence of any noticeable hierarchy. There is no head of chambers (instead a perpetually changing management committee) and the names of the 58 members are displayed alphabetically on the board outside, meaning that the most respected silks like Clare Montgomery, Philippe Sands and Rabinder Singh are afforded no more acclaim than their lesser known junior counterparts. The thing that really catches the eye, however, is the range and calibre of the work undertaken. Matrix has been highly successful in balancing considerable amounts of 'worthy' work with a thriving civil caseload. "*Not everyone is hankering after the sexy cases,*" we heard. "*As a set we're aware of the need to maintain a broad practice.*" Rankings in ten practice areas in *Chambers UK* add weight to this contention, but you can only really appreciate the magnitude of chambers' achievement when you look at some of the big cases on which members have worked. If you like your cases 'sexy' then, try these on for size: R v Dunlop (the first 'double jeopardy' case). The Deepcut Review, Siôn Jenkins murder trial and a collection of Iraq/terrorism cases. On a more commercial note, members acted for the National Association of Health Food Stores in challenging a European Directive on food supplements in the ECJ, whilst Cherie Booth QC acted for the trade union Amicus in its challenge to the government's implementation of European Directives on discrimination on the grounds of sexual orientation. Many Matrix practitioners are active on the academic side of the law, highlighting the fact that the set has an academic approach rather than simply a moral approach to human rights.

We say forget the terminology entirely and accept that a Matrix traineeship works much like pupillage elsewhere. There are three three-month stints with practitioners in different fields, and then the decision as to whether you get taken on as a member in June. One seat will inevitably be spent with someone with public law/human rights leanings "*as that, deep down, is at the core of the set's work,*" though trainees are allowed input as to the nature of their other seats. Naturally, if you're with a criminal practitioner, much of your time will be spent in court, preparing cross-examinations and observing first hand the extent of your supervisor's advocacy powers. Time spent with a civil practitioner will involve considerably more paperwork – pleadings, opinions, skeleton arguments or judicial review applications. The trainee we spoke to recounted how she had observed and been copied into everything: "*I heard every telephone call and saw every piece of written work that my trainee supervisor produced. It's the only way to learn the right habits.*"

Regardless of the practice area you work in, certain attributes will stand you in good stead when the membership decision is made. "*There's no soft landing here. You need to be intellectually astute from the word go.*" Equally, the ability to produce written work of a "*consistently high standard*" will always stand you in good stead. In addition to work for other members, a trainee's capabilities are assessed by written and oral exercises throughout the year. One area of traineeship that Matrix is conscious it needs to increase is the amount of advocacy available to trainees in the second half of the year. At the moment it can feel like "*a big leap into the unknown*" when a trainee becomes a full member. The sort of matters undertaken by trainees during this period vary according to which practice area they've steered themselves towards; eg those interested in employment undertake any low-level tribunal claims that come into chambers.

Although it was admitted that the raft of well-known members can be "*quite intimidating*" before the traineeship begins, one young barrister we spoke to recalled how "*any feeling I had of walking on eggshells disappeared very quickly.*" As one would expect from such a self-consciously forward-thinking organisation, everyone is on first-name terms and there is "*certainly no defer-*

ence to seniority.*" A trainee is encouraged to work a 9am to 6pm day, although must accept that weekends may be impinged upon "*whenever you need to finish off a piece of important work.*" On the social side, "*things have picked up in the past 12 months and we're definitely coming together as a set,*" hence (or perhaps because of) the introduction of Thursday lunches and fortnightly chambers drinks. The Christmas party is apparently a good one, if only because "*watching the silks strutting their stuff on the dance floor is always entertaining!*" And speaking of showy moves, a group of members popped to the local cinema to see the screening of 'The Matrix 3: Revolutions' when it came out. It was unavoidable, we suppose.

The application process for traineeships is typically transparent. Points are awarded to applicants for academic ability, advocacy experience, voluntary work and demonstration of 'Matrix values'. Reach the required number of points and you'll be invited to a first-round interview. This lasts for 15 minutes with discussion tending to focus on a current issue, though you do also have the opportunity to make a good impression by "*steering things in the direction of your interests.*" The second-round interview is longer and confronts you with a tricky legal question designed to "*stretch your problem-solving capabilities to the hilt.*" Remember, the recruiters are looking for the sort of candidate who is able to take a knock in their stride and won't despair if things don't appear to be going well. With almost 500 applications per year for traineeship, it's clear that the set is not attracting any one particular breed of applicant. The single characteristic that is bound to unite all successful candidates will be an "*absolute drive and commitment to becoming an accomplished barrister.*" In 2006 two of the three trainees became full members of chambers.

The Matrix brand has undoubtedly become an important and successful one in a short space of time but we'd venture to suggest that it means different things to different people. Some prefer the way that *"independence and autonomy are respected within the set,"* whilst others cite the lack of tradition as *"enormously liberating."* One junior member did confess that he had started to refer to chambers as 'the office'. We're not convinced it will catch on. Matrix will always be at the forefront of developments in the law but we imagine that as it gets older it may become a little less self-aware and the work alone will be able to speak for the set.

Monckton Chambers

Chambers UK rankings: Competition/European law, public procurement, tax, telecommunications

As everyone knows, exteriors can be misleading. The sunny gardens of Gray's Inn look like a welcoming oasis in the heart of Holborn, but the weary public can only rest there for two hours in the middle of the day. Similarly, if you walk into the gardens from Theobald's Road and cast your eye to the right you'll see an immaculate 17th century brick terrace with period sash windows. But if you were to press your nose to the glass of Monckton Chambers you'd find much more than aged wigs and dusty legal tomes. Ten years ago the set *"took the view that for everyone to work to their fullest capacity we needed a full-time marketing and administration team."* It adopted a sleek corporate face to go with the administrative changes, and a slick refurbishment of its premises – including the addition of Nos 1 and 2 Raymond Buildings – shows the set has the steel to follow through on what it starts.

The history of this set goes right back to the 1930s when renowned constitutional lawyer Walter Monckton was head of chambers. Following a distinguished career as a barrister Monckton twice became a cabinet minister, then chairman of Midland Bank and eventually earned the title of viscount. A trusted adviser to Edward VIII, he is widely credited as the author of the King's 1936 abdication speech.

After moving to Gray's Inn in the 1960s the set began to develop its competition law practice, gaining a stranglehold on work before the Monopolies and Mergers Commission (now the Competition Commission), initially for the regulators then increasingly for private sector clients. In recent times members have represented the OFT in the MasterCard litigation in the Competition Appeals Tribunal (CAT), several parties in the replica football kits case and the British Horseracing Board in its private competition litigation with At The Races in the Court of Appeal. A number of members of chambers are especially well regarded for their expertise at the intersection of competition, state aid and procurement advice. Competition and EU law now amounts to roughly a third of chambers' workload, with tax and VAT cases making up another significant tranche. In tax matters, Monckton barristers have recently taken key roles in Marks & Spencer v HMRC and Hutchison 3G and Others v CCE, which is potentially the biggest VAT case ever in terms of the amount of money at stake. The third of Monckton's main areas is public law, where it handles commercial and regulatory judicial reviews as well as human rights matters. The subject matter of some of the cases may surprise you – how about the claim brought by someone who lived close to the site of a proposed bird fair and feared the spread of bird flu. In January 2006 the Lord Chancellor appointed former joint head of chambers Kenneth Parker QC as the new Public Law Commissioner, also authorising him to sit as a Deputy High Court Judge. Aside from the three core strands there is plenty of other expertise within chambers; for example, public procurement, environmental, construction and general commercial cases are all handled with aplomb.

Another important influence on Monckton came in the 1980s when good relations were cemented with various government departments, not least through the appointment of (now Justice) Stephen Richards as Treasury Devil. All Monckton juniors now aim to get on at least one list of government-approved counsel and this source of work has a major influence on the set. In the simplest terms, Monckton is one of the premier sets for European, competition and tax law, rivalled by only a small handful of other elite outfits.

With numbers capped to two per intake and every single pupil in the last four years offered tenancy, there's a real sense that if you can make it through the pupillage recruitment stage there's an excellent chance your name will be added to the roll call of Monckton barristers within a year. First-round interviewees are invited for a getting-to-know-you chat with five panellists and are sometimes asked to endure, sorry enjoy, a mini-pupillage before the second interview some weeks later. At this stage applicants receive a mock brief and, just 30 short minutes later, are grilled by the rigorous pupillage committee which "*tests for outstanding analytical skill and for sharp, intellectual prowess.*"

Of course, winning tenancy should never be taken for granted. Pupils sit with four supervisors for three months each, with the all-important decision coming in July at the end of the third stint. They become very familiar with the individual practices of their supervisors, so if the person you sit with has a very niche practice, then chances are you'll "*know more of the area by the end of your seat than all but about six or seven practitioners at the entire Bar.*" One pupil explained: "*Some of the work is extremely specialist... I had done no public procurement work, and for a few weeks I was flying by the seat of my pants.*" The pupils of 05/06 hadn't been restricted to such specialist work; they had also discovered the delights of VAT law and been able to indulge long-held passions for EU law.

The first three months is all about getting to grips with life as a Monckton barrister and pupils will work almost exclusively for their supervisor. In a reflection of the nature of practice in chambers, pupils will spend a considerable amount of time researching points of law and having a go at writing opinions. There's more of the same in the second three months, by which time they'll have visited court a few times to see how their supervisor handles advocacy. At this stage other members of chambers are also encouraged to find work for the pupils to ensure that they are exposed to a range of legal issues. In the final three-month period before the tenancy decision the pace quickens – one pupil had recently assisted on an "*extremely high-profile case, which was quite something to see on the Ten O'Clock News when I got home.*" Another had used fluent German to translate a piece of legislation for a matter being heard by the European Court of Human Rights. Our sources agreed that pupillage is "*intellectual and challenging.*" "*There's a lot of background research on very intricate points of law, or bespoke drafting for the area's experts.*" And they have to be able to adapt to different styles of working as "*some of the pupil supervisors are very collaborative and others are more inclined to let you get on with it. Either way, the expectations are very high.*"

Compared to most other sets, this is not a court-heavy environment. Chambers will pay for additional advocacy courses, but within pupillage itself there is little formal advocacy assessment. Our sources were sanguine on this point, one recognising that "*if I'd gone elsewhere after pupillage the advocacy might have been more of an issue, but the amount I'd done as a pupil – and beforehand – was appropriate for my practice at Monckton.*" In some sets, second-six pupils are prevented from taking their own paid work but here at Monckton, if the clerks can find something, they are free to take it. Usually it will be something like a small VAT tribunal application; nothing too demanding. With tenancy decided in July after nine months in chambers, it's not uncommon for successful pupils to take on a fair bit of their own work before tenancy begins. Fondly reflecting on the closing stages of the year, a new tenant remarked: "*I found that there really isn't much that separates the pupils from the baby juniors – apart from managing your own practice, of course.*" Clerks and more senior colleagues will do their utmost to put baby juniors forward for work: "*I've been busy since the first week and have no worries about where the work is coming from,*" confirmed one. What they can expect is a string of VAT tribunals, various smaller government instructions and roles as second or third junior on cases at the Competition Appeal Tribunal.

Monckton Chambers may portray a slick, almost corporate, image to the outside world but within chambers there is a good-natured, informal atmosphere. On the day we visited, this mood was summed up by a group of senior and junior barristers dressed in jeans and bright shirts sitting having coffee in a bright, glass-panelled conference room. New faces are warmly welcomed by chambers and from the outset pupils can participate in all social events, perhaps even taking a position in the newly formed football team. If our visits to Monckton are anything to go by we reckon a new recruit could feel comfortable here pretty quickly.

Four New Square

Chambers UK rankings: Construction, financial services, product liability, professional negligence

Elegant, sleek and industrious, Four New Square in Lincoln's Inn bears worthy comparison with the racehorse that runs in its colours. But while chambers' current nag, Burnham Hill, is proving

rather more successful than its predecessor, Wasted Costs, this set has long been known as a true professional liability law thoroughbred. All members of chambers practise in this field, with instructions galloping in from almost every major (and minor) litigation firm or insurer in the country. Recent cases have included Cable & Wireless's claim against law firm Collyer-Bristow and others, and the Football League's claim against law firm Hammonds. Additionally, chambers' business extends to construction (members are involved in Wembley Stadium claims), insurance and reinsurance, product liability and other group actions (eg vCJD and tobacco), financial matters and general commercial litigation, with a recent and developing line in commercial Chancery work. Given the set's reputation for hard graft, don't be surprised to see it moving up the field in many of these practice areas.

Chambers and Partners Professional Negligence Set of the Year 2006

Proving it's not averse to change, Four New Square's interview process involves a standard first-round interview (albeit with no less than ten members of chambers) and advocacy exercise, followed by a less conventional few days spent in chambers, when would-be pupils shadow members and submit a piece of written work. The prize at stake is pupillage for up to four people who are happy with the idea of getting up to their eyeballs in professional indemnity, building disputes and contract claims.

With confidence being bolstered by the set's ambitious outlook and the space available in its main building and Chancery Lane annexes, pupils told us: "*It is made clear from the start that we're not pitted against each other... if we were all to* meet the objective criteria, we'd all get tenancy." In 2005, none of their own pupils were taken on – chambers instead recruited from its third six intake. However, in 2006 two out of three did so. Objective assessment is aided by the fact that pupils rotate around the same four supervisors for three seats each. The first two seats last three months, the third stretches from the start of the second six until after the tenancy decision at the end of June. Pupil supervisors are selected with the aim of offering pupils the broadest experience within professional indemnity. Their charges start off by shadowing them and learning how to get to grips with paperwork. Court attendances naturally afford greater thrills, even if you are only observing. "It can be really exciting and you do very much feel like one of the team," confirmed one pupil.

Our sources observed continuity of experience across the opening six months: "The first seat is of course about learning the ropes and then building on that, but otherwise there wasn't much difference between my first and second seats," said one, with another noting that "I was writing skeleton arguments and cross-examinations right from the start – the type of work itself doesn't really change." Though ideally the pupil's performance does. In addition to regular informal feedback, chats with pupillage head Ben Hubble at the end of each seat give the pupil a more formal report on their progress. At the beginning of the second six everyone gets five written tasks (usually advice or a skeleton argument) set by a five-member panel. Feedback on these help ensure "you always know where you're going and what you need to work on."

In the first six months pupils only work for their supervisor, but the main feature of the second six is time in court. "We believe that barristers should be advocates and we place a huge amount of emphasis on this throughout the pupillage," said one supervisor. First-six outings accompanying

baby juniors to a variety of hearings will have given them an idea of what they'll face, but no amount of preparation can disguise the "significant" change of pace when pupils finally go it alone. "It's challenging but good to be more independent. Your pupilmaster will set you slightly less work throughout the second six, just to make sure that you have adequate time to prepare. And they'll always go through your court work and cross-examination questions with you." Second-sixers are instructed on everything from small commercial debt claims and possession hearings to RTAs, simple fast-track trials and employment tribunals. "Very supportive" clerks carefully cultivate relationships with solicitors to ensure a steady supply of such work. Add in ready support from baby juniors and more senior members and it's no wonder "you really start to feel as if you're finally able to do what you set out to do in law school."

But there's more... Pupils must also square up to each other before an audience from chambers for three moots, the first of which takes place before Christmas. The largest audience is to be found at the final engagement, which usually takes place in an RCJ courtroom before Mr Justice Rupert Jackson, a former silk at the set. According to one sanguine source: "The first moot is the most nerve-wracking but after that you get into the swing of it and it's very enjoyable." Even performing in front of a High Court judge isn't as scary as you might expect; three of the pupils of 2006 had spent a week marshalling for Justice Jackson. Apparently "you can hold forth in front of any district judge after that moot."

Not to mince words, there's lot of work to get through in this pupillage and expectations are high. Chambers doesn't actively encourage pupils to slave until midnight but should occasion and your supervisor's workload demand, you will be expected to get stuck in. Right from the early years of tenancy barristers put a lot into their careers and must be prepared to devote whatever time is necessary to get the job done. Our impression is of a set committed to recruiting at junior level and prepared to reward those who work hard. "*The culture is very much a meritocracy... If you're good enough you will go through. We have a lot of work at the junior end and we're prepared to take four out of four if they make the grade.*" If they don't, pupils know about it come the end of June, leaving plenty of time to look elsewhere. Those who do stay on start tenancy under the watchful and supportive eye of their former pupil supervisor, as well as being allocated a clerk who will help establish and develop practice preferences. "*It's a bespoke clerking system,*" concluded one new junior, "*your interests are taken into account and members as well as clerks will recommend you for work.*" Like pupils, juniors are brought into the "*big, ritzy cases*" so they can gain vital experience as a second or third junior while also managing their own caseload of smaller matters.

Socially, there's perhaps nothing better than the communal thrill of Burnham Hill's race day performances. When they aren't watching the wonder horse in action there's always the odd Saturday playing cricket. "*We're a sporty team,*" said one member (although they didn't suggest that having a good square cut would assist a bid for tenancy). Indeed pupils praised an "*inclusive and relaxed atmosphere*" which allowed them to participate in other non-legal pursuits with members. Monthly drinks in chambers, the Christmas party, a summer party attended by members' children; it all sounded rather pleasant. Almost as fresh-faced as the teeny tots, the recent appointment of (young silk) Roger Stewart as head of chambers is a good indicator of where this relatively young, focused and modern set is at.

Be aware that Four New Square prefers applicants to do a week-long assessed mini-pupillage before their application for pupillage proper will be considered.

XXIV Old Buildings

Chambers UK rankings: Chancery: commercial, Chancery: traditional, company, insolvency/corporate recovery, partnership, pensions, professional negligence

Some 30 years ago a well-established traditional Chancery set and a newish civil set merged to create XXIV Old Buildings, tucked away in a quiet corner of Lincoln's Inn. This brief thumbnail sketch is all you need to know of what has passed because you get the sense history isn't weighing heavily on this "*genuinely unpretentious*" set. Chambers is performing excellently and in 2006 it posted a 16% increase in turnover.

Handling a broad mixture of traditional and commercial Chancery work, insolvency matters, commercial litigation and pensions, not to forget expertise in partnerships and professional negligence, XXIV Old Buildings is in part defined by the multidisciplinary abilities of its barristers. "*Most people have specialist experience in anything up to five areas of practice,*" we were told, a statement backed up by our colleagues at *Chambers UK*, who rank joint head of chambers Alan Steinfield in a whopping eight fields. Carefully planned strategic development has produced a relatively compact 29-strong membership, with recent recruitment designed to "*strengthen core areas*" and develop the set's ability to "*support a wider commercial business approach.*" Recent arrivals have brought aviation and travel expertise plus offshore trusts know-how and commercial experience.

XXIV can offer clients a broad service, but perhaps the most distinctive and attractive feature of chambers is its overseas capabilities. Here, it has a unique calling card in the guise of a Geneva annexe. International and offshore instructions, whether in traditional Chancery, tax and trusts or large-scale commercial litigation, account for more than a third of chambers' business. Consequently, silks, juniors and sometimes even pupils are just as likely to be working in BVI or the Cayman Islands as in London. They must be equally at home offering advice to the president of an African republic after an attempted coup d'etat as assisting a moneyed UK national on a landlord and tenant dispute. Recent cases have included a multi-jurisdictional matter that is taking place in BVI, Switzerland, Sweden, Russia, the Netherlands, the Bahamas and London. This highly complex dispute concerns the ownership of a very valuable shareholding in a Russian mobile telecommunications company. In another case a £120 million UK claim was brought by AWG (Anglia Water Group) over fraudulent misrepresentation in the run up to its purchase of water services construction company Morrison in 2000. Away from commercial matters, the much-publicised case of Sherrington v Sherrington centred on a £10 million disputed will.

A multidisciplinary approach and strong international caseload mean XXIV Old Buildings is well placed to ride out any potential decline in domestic claims. It also demands that pupils possess and develop a varied skill set. Current pupils told us, first and foremost, that "*if you're not interested in Chancery then you'd be a fool to apply here,*" but also highlighted the very specific capabilities required to flourish here. "*It's academically very challenging because there's a lot of highly technical black letter law; more so than in commercial work,*" stated one source. Chambers' recruiters confirmed that they look for "*commercial awareness, intelligence and imagination; if you don't understand the business scenario you don't understand the problem so you can't apply the law. And yet if you don't understand the law you can't help the business client by proposing a solution.*"

In short, you have to ask yourself whether you could be comfortable engrossing yourself in seriously detailed research one minute, then applying the results of your research "*often in entirely new ways or transplanted to a parallel jurisdiction*" the next. Moreover, you have to be able to explain both the legal research and the subsequent ideas to clients and solicitors in plain English. Despite the fact that it isn't a prerequisite for a successful application, we observed that many current pupils and juniors had previous experience in industry or commercial law. Chambers' recruiters additionally observed that "*barristers in this field deal with sophisticated, high-achieving and demanding clients in fluid commercial situations, so a degree of maturity of personality is an important attribute.*"

Full details of what you might expect at a pupillage interview appear on the 'Recruitment and Pupillage' page of the XXIV Old Buildings website. In itself this is reflective of the set's commitment to transparency and good practice. In brief, the first round involves a 30-minute panel interview during which you'll discuss a pre-set legal problem. Successful candidates move onto a longer, second-round interview when there will be another legal problem, set the day before the interview. Don't expect to get too far unless you can display "*articulacy, flexibility, good reasoning skills and the ability to respond to another line of argument.*"

Roughly 40 candidates attend the first interview and two at most are rewarded with pupillage. Once in situ, pupils benefit from a highly structured year that places the emphasis firmly on learning. They switch pupilmaster four times "*to ensure exposure to all our main areas of work.*" Pupils spend their time on "*first drafts of pleadings, witness statements and research,*" not forgetting "*going along to court and conferences*" and even "*being a sounding board and sometimes coming up with an idea that gets used.*" By all accounts, it's impossible to forget that "*you're under constant scrutiny,*" even if "*it is all done with a light touch.*" Our sources had received a healthy level of informal feedback, coupled with the opportunity to repeat similar tasks "*so you can work on your faults.*"

It's important to be on the ball from day one because, at the end of the first six, a pupil who is judged not to have a serious chance of gaining tenancy may be asked to move on. Assuming they are still there for the second six, life continues in much the same vein, with pupils only likely to be up on their feet in court once the tenancy decision has been made. In common with many Chancery sets, the view is that pupillage is for learning not earning, but the size of XXIV Old Buildings' pupillage award compensates for this. If chambers decides to recruit from current pupils, it is common for two contenders to be looking at a single place, although "*if you're good enough, and there's capacity, the set may keep on two.*" Again the policy document on the website contains full details, but to summarise, they face a written test and an advocacy exercise. One thing we'll add is that overly competitive behaviour between pupils is not recommended as "*it's quietly known that stupidity like that doesn't do you any favours.*" In 2006 one of the two pupils gained tenancy.

Overall, chambers benefits from an "*informal*" and (that word again) "*unpretentious*" atmosphere and a "*cohesive identity and feel.*" As one pupil pointed out: "*It's not like the stereotype of the solitary criminal barrister – you're often working on larger cases with a QC and several juniors.*" Again, in contrast to criminal practice, "*we're not in court five days a week and we're rarely in front of a jury.*" The out-of-hours social scene is pleasant rather than riotous and pupils tell us that "*a group of juniors looks after you especially well when you start.*" A recent dinner and theatre trip to see 'A Man for All Seasons' offered more of a busman's holiday than a break. "*It starred Martin Shaw, so in effect we spent our evening off watching Judge John Deed.*"

Old Square Chambers

Chambers UK rankings: Employment, environment, health & safety, personal injury

Numbering some 60 barristers, Old Square is first and foremost an employment and PI specialist set with environmental, clinical negligence, product liability and health and safety law making up most of the remainder of its work. The nature of the employment practice has changed from the applicant-heavy days of the 1970s such that chambers now offers a "*good balance between applicant and respondent work.*" Beyond advice to a wide range of employers, the set has formidable trade union links – head of chambers John Hendy QC is standing counsel to no less than 12 unions – and regularly advises on high-profile problems like the 2006 Gate Gourmet/TGWU stand-off at Heathrow, and the thousands of equal pay disputes in the health sector and beyond. Public inquiries figure prominently, with barristers recently representing the Prison Service in the Zahid Mubarek Inquiry, and involvement in almost all the major rail crash inquiries of the last few years. John Hendy QC was instructed on behalf of a number of those injured or bereaved in the Potters Bar rail crash and sought a judicial review of the Secretary of State's for Transport's refusal to hold a public inquiry into the tragedy. While the application did not succeed, the matter has not been put to bed. If the inquest (to be presided over by a High Court judge) does not satisfy the families' questions, the subject of an inquiry may still be revisited.

Several seniors have forged a name for themselves in the area of major environmental litigation and the instructions they receive can be a boon for the set's juniors. Some of them have been led in the House of Lords on cases such as Sutradhar v Natural Environment Research Council (the Bangladesh water poisoning litigation). The set has had a hand in a number of well-known product liability litigations of recent times, among them the multiparty action over the drug Larium. Other work has dealt with the safety of consumer goods including cars, cosmetics and toys.

Old Square Chambers-branded water and pencils in the meeting rooms are not quite what you'd expect of a set where barristers maintain "*we're a collective of very different individuals rather than a team.*" Laughing off the idea of a "*house style,*" one source said: "*We don't even have a dress code.*" In a sense there is a house style: Old Square has clear ideas about what barristers should not be. It is proud to have been one of the first places to relax conventional clerk/barrister formalities – "*We broke the mould there and it's very much first-name terms for everyone now.*" Old Square says it continues to "*try to do away with redundant traditions.*" While we certainly detected an easy atmosphere at the place there's no doubting the hard graft expected from barristers. Briefly donning his Sgt Major cap, the senior clerk barked: "*It's not a holiday camp here, but everyone is in it together.*" Another source concurred: "*People work very hard but aren't competitive; we take pride in others' successes.*"

Pupils sit with four supervisors over the course of 12 months, although the tenancy decision is made in the last week of June before the fourth changeover. The pupils we interviewed were most interested in the set's employment and PI specialisms, but it is possible for recruits to request particular supervisors or to ask to work in particular areas. "*Chambers are always aware of what you're interested in even if they try to expose you to all areas of practice.*" A review at the end of each seat gives pupils the opportunity to assess personal strengths and weaknesses with their supervisor, so that "*although it can sometimes be a bit of a guessing game during the seat, when the review comes around you get a very thorough idea*

of where you are and what they think of you." There are no formal written assessment exercises for pupils to undertake and they seemed quite happy about this. "*We'd have been really overworked if they'd been added in; formalising things like that would have added to the stress.*"

The work given to pupils and the expectations of them varies from supervisor to supervisor, but all the pupils we spoke to had enjoyed "*a good mix of court and paperwork, with plenty of exposure to supervisors of different styles and years of call.*" In addition to research assignments and notes for clients or conferences, skeleton arguments and other drafting tasks are standard from day one. When not assisting their supervisor, first-six pupils devil for other members of chambers who are supposed to approach them via the supervisor. In practice our sources had been perfectly comfortable sourcing devilling work themselves. By the second six this is construed as "*a good sign that pupils are getting much better at managing their own workload.*"

The nature of chambers' work means that pupils are in court for themselves throughout the second six. They are assigned a particular clerk and limited to three days of court appearances per week until the tenancy decision. "*The second six really marks this pupillage out from the others,*" commented one new tenant. "*The work is really good quality, but it is managed very well. Being limited to three days in court allows more time to give the cases the preparation they need.*" Everyone seems to understand that being "*brand new on your feet makes everything scary and you take twice as long as you should to prepare.*" The clerks are careful about where they send pupils; "*you're covering your own expenses so they try to keep the instructions close to London.*" The furthest our pupil sources had been was Birmingham and Bournemouth, although one supervisor felt that "*it's not a bad idea to get used to travelling for six hours to attend a ten-minute hearing. It's the reality of practice."* Pupils' solo appearances are primarily RTA and infant approval hearings, with smaller employment matters featuring increasingly. One pupil told us how they had assisted on a five-day High Court stress-at-work trial with another member of chambers. *"In the first six, it was rare to be in chambers after 6.30pm,"* said one pupil, *"but as you start juggling your own work you will work long hours."* From an early stage, new tenants notice a drop-off in smaller instructions and their diaries begin to fill up with fast-track PI trials and employment tribunals. One baby junior told us he had already been led three times by the head of chambers.

Chambers had a 14-member strong – and growing – Bristol base to which all pupils are despatched for at least a week, the main purpose being to allow them to meet all members of chambers. Until recently, some would spend a six-month stint there but an increase in work at the Bristol site now makes it likely that it will recruit its own pupils. If the prospect appeals, be sure to check out the set's website for details.

Chambers' single-interview recruitment process was praised by our junior sources. One declared it to be *"by far my friendliest pupillage interview; my most enjoyable even."* Perhaps less enjoyable for pupils, the tenancy decision is reached after a formal interview, and pupils are asked to clear a week in their diaries at the end of June to undertake a written assessment and prepare for an oral argument to be made to a panel. By all accounts, *"you're given plenty of opportunities to fight your corner and there's no regimental-style questioning."* Having enlisted most of the two to three pupils each year, there's weight to the claim that *"you're made to feel like a member of the set right from the start of your pupillage."* Furthermore, pupils are involved in the social scene including the recently instigated monthly drinks. *"Everyone here had become so busy so we thought it a good idea to try and organise some social events. This week we have a Champagne-tasting session,"* a baby junior explained.

We got a strong sense that the pupils feel supported here at Old Square Chambers. The senior source who told us: *"We want to see excellent barristers at the end of pupillage and we will go very far to help someone develop those skills"* didn't need to try hard to convince us of this fact.

In September 2006, Old Square Chambers moved to new premises on Bedford Row. We're looking forward to our invitation to visit members and pupils in their new home.

Outer Temple Chambers

Chambers UK rankings: Clinical negligence, employment, health & safety, pensions, personal injury, professional discipline

In a neat metaphor for the way Outer Temple Chambers straddles the different elements of the Bar, its building can be accessed via both the hustle and bustle of the Strand and the hallowed environs of the Temple. Back in 2001, the 32 former incumbents of 35 Essex Street held a strategy meeting at which, rumour has it, a phenomenal quantity of beer was downed. Even so, they hatched a five-year plan to buy a new building and a strategy to create standalone work groups in each of the set's key practice areas. Five years on, how's it all going?

The move to 222 Strand has united all members under one roof and the work group template has paid dividends. The set has swelled in size, in breadth of coverage and in reputation. Today some 70 barristers call Outer Temple Chambers home, a majority practising across PI, clinical negligence and healthcare, crime with a regulatory bent and employment and pensions. Others handle public and family law, professional negligence and commercial cases, and disciplinary and regulatory matters. Diversification has not come at the cost of excellence; our colleagues on *Chambers UK* rank chambers highly in several areas.

Growth has been facilitated through judicious lateral recruitment, the most recent additions being a group of five PI barristers from 199 Strand. "*We took the view that we needed to augment our groups to make them viable. A barrister can't be an expert in five or more areas of law, so we went hunting and got some very good people in,*" explained a source. Members old and new have acted in prominent cases, one of these being a recent landmark High Court victory for the parents of a severely disabled child who were resisting efforts to have his ventilator turned off. In PI, members secured a settlement of £6.8 million for a client who was severely brain damaged in a road traffic accident. Turning to crime, the set takes on both prosecution and defence instructions and has a nice line in fraud. Recently, barristers successfully persuaded the Court of Appeal to uphold the conviction of an employee involved in a £12 million password fraud at HSBC bank. As well as regular instructions from the Serious Fraud Office, there have been numerous manslaughter instructions from the CPS following major rail crashes (Hatfield, Potters Bar, Ladbroke Grove) and work-related and other deaths caused by negligence. Following the manslaughter conviction of two brothers in the Damilola Taylor case, senior silk Alan Rawley QC has been appointed to the panel carrying out the independent review of the forensic work conducted during the police investigation. In truth there's so much interesting, high-value work that we simply can't summarise it here.

Step into chambers and you are immediately struck by a sense of diverse and abundant activity. With three floors and multiple staircases, it's quite possible that a pupil could spend an entire year here and never meet everyone. Our sources admitted that "*the size of chambers is good or bad depending on your view of what you want from chambers life. If you want to know and be friends with all members then the recent expansion means it can't provide that.*" However, if a pupil does happen upon an unknown pocket, chances are they'll be warmly received because the set prides itself on "*not being stuffy*" and claims that "*none of us take ourselves too seriously – we're sharp and quick-witted but very relaxed.*"

Chambers does not recruit through OLPAS, preferring instead to see 14 or so applicants sometime around Easter for a 30-45 minute first-round interview. It sounds fairly gruelling: "*In addition to a general chat and maybe a hypothetical legal question, we ask interviewees to prepare a five-minute talk from a list of ten topics that we give them 15 minutes before the interview. People should also expect some surprises...*" The seven best candidates are invited back for a second time the following day to endure "*a legal question, an ethical question and a more in-depth talk about their application form.*" We say endure, but chambers assures us that "*we just want candidates to flourish when faced with fairly demanding questions.*" Chambers offers a generous pupillage award (£35,000 at the time of going to press) and has considered the sum carefully. "*We want to pitch one peg below the big commercial sets. We want to attract the very best candidates, but we don't want people coming here because we were giving loads of money.*"

Pupillage is divided into four sets of three months and the average pupil will sit with pupilmasters whose specialisms ensure broad coverage of chambers' work. By way of example, one source told us they had spent three months with an employment barrister, three with one specialising in PI and clin neg and three with one of chambers' more commercially oriented members. Life for pupils sounds reasonably straightforward. Said one: "*On my first day I was told quite explicitly that – barring exceptional cir-*

cumstances – I was only expected to be here from 9am till 6pm and that I would never be judged on the amount of time my jacket spent on the back of my chair." All written work is commented upon and, at the end of each quarter, pupils sit down with their PM and the head of the pupillage committee to discuss a formal, written report on their progress.

In the second six, pupils are on their feet pretty swiftly. They undertake a wide range of work including infant settlement approval hearings, employment tribunals, winding-up petitions and possession hearings. There's also criminal work to be sampled. "It came as a bit of a surprise to find myself in a magistrates' court doing everything you could think of other than full-blown trials," confessed one source, quickly adding: "I'm very pleased to have done it as the experience was great." The pace undoubtedly changes in the practising six and pupils reflected on the fact that "the most immediate difference is the hours; you go from knowing you're not expected to stay late to suddenly finding yourself working until 3am and getting up at 6am to go to a tribunal." The fact that second-sixers are also encouraged to do work for other people requires them to acquire the all-important skills of prioritisation and time management.

All pupils are formally assessed through four pieces of written work and, until recently, four advocacy assessments, the last two of which are open to all members of chambers. The pupillage committee has now decided that the first two advocacy exercises will be more about education and less about assessment, on the basis that they can then be more effective at helping pupils get on their feet in court. After the assessments are completed the committee discusses the pupils' quarterly reviews, their assessment results and any other general feedback before making a recommendation which is put to the chambers vote. "Seventy-five percent is the magic number that gets you tenancy." A good record in awarding tenancy explained why our pupil sources were sanguine about this process. "The sense that if you do well you will get taken on has meant that there's never been any sense of competition between us. We're told we'll all be taken on if we meet the standard." The absence of any third-sixers also helps.

Outer Temple Chambers has a "warm" atmosphere. Afternoon tea is a feature of daily life, but our sources assured us that "it is quite typical of chambers that tea is a wholly informal affair conducted in a pokey kitchen. It was initiated by a junior tenant to instil a community feeling in chambers after the recent expansion." A pupil told us: "I am as free to speak at afternoon tea as I am in any other part of my life." The overall picture is of an appealing set with an appealing pupillage scheme. But with another of those famous strategy weekends taking place in autumn 2006, we can only guess at how we might describe chambers in five years time...

Pump Court Tax Chambers

Chambers UK Rankings: Tax

Taxes are a fact of life for us all but they are more a way of life for the members of Pump Court Tax Chambers. This is a QC-heavy, tight-knit community of 26 barristers, all dedicated wholeheartedly to tax law. It is also a self-declared traditional set that doesn't come with the marketing and sharp-edged interiors that now characterise many commercial chambers.

In the last 50 years Pump Court has evolved into one of the leading specialist sets in the field and there isn't a facet of tax law that at least one member can't tackle. It competes with mainstream Chancery sets in the trusts realm and has a couple of rivals on the VAT front, but when it comes to pure tax there's no substitute for dedicated expertise: "*Commercial sets would like to see tax as a bolt-on* [to their main business] *but it's impossible just to dabble.*"

It's a source of frustration for chambers that students think tax law is about "*crunching numbers and wading through accounts.*" The sheer range of issues and activities that fall under the tax umbrella may come as a pleasant surprise to some – personal tax planning for individuals, trusts or estates; employee remuneration cases on share options or pension schemes; the UK and international tax aspects of corporate M&A, demergers, transfer pricing and structured finance. In the realm of indirect taxes there is VAT, Landfill Tax and stamp taxes relating to property transactions. And then to round off the list there's a raft of professional negligence cases involving tax advice. As our sources stressed the subject is "*not at all narrow;*" in fact "*much of it borders on public and European law with human rights points and proportionality issues often arising.*" Those looking to get tight to the top of this field should note that "*there is a disproportionate number of tax cases in the House of Lords; tax always passes the public interest test.*" The intersection of tax law with several other legal disciplines leads to "*considerable interaction with other sets,*" and there is "*a good referral system when there are non-tax elements to instructions such as insolvency, company-commercial or insurance.*" Pump Court "*drafts in juniors*" to work on non-tax points, with such collaboration resulting in "*plenty of teamwork.*"

Instructions are equally as likely to come from accountants as from solicitors, and the UK and foreign governments also send a steady stream of work. "*I expect our client list is the wish list of most chambers,*" one source postulated, and considering "*most City firms and the Big Four accountants*" use the set, this is quite likely. It was also pointed out that direct relationships with accountants allow "*more commercial, less formal relationships*

than when there is an instructing solicitor*" as an intermediary. The other really important point to make here is that such clients are tax experts themselves and so they expect their barristers to have an exceptionally high level of knowledge and expertise.

Chambers and Partners Tax Set of the Year 2006

Tax cases are normally "*light on facts, heavy on law,*" making this type of practice a "*very pure, intellectual and conceptual*" area where barristers concentrate on "*solving knotty legal problems,*" not unravelling what happened when, where and with whom. Instructions are sometimes so "*short and pithy*" that they fit onto one sheet of paper. The relevance of this for a pupil is that they do not encounter the fact-heavy cases that can lead to "*sitting in a dark room sifting through 40 boxes of files from Freshfields, hoping to find the crucial contract.*" It follows that the set looks for "*rigorous analytical skills*" in its potential pupils. "*Being prepared to read legislation carefully and take analysis through to its conclusion*" is key. "*But we're not looking for geeky people who want to bury their heads in paperwork,*" a source added hastily; "*we want all-rounders who enjoy the academic side of the law.*" Reassuringly, chambers' recruiters "*don't expect any tax knowledge*" from pupillage appicants: "*we just want to see how you think.*"

With there being so many misconceptions about tax law, Pump Court Tax has had to find ways to reach out and convert students. As well as unassessed mini-pupillages, assessed (and paid) minis have been introduced to give would-be applicants insight into life at the tax Bar. Student visitors are shown a range of work and are asked to write an opinion. The week is intended to be mutually beneficial and "*the aim is that by the end we have a good idea whether or not someone is pupillage material."* An assessed mini is not a prerequisite to making an application and if you do decide to throw your hat into the ring, do remember that this set has now opted out of OLPAS after finding the shackles of the online system too *"restrictive."*

Pump Court Tax is *"not wedded to any particular type of pupillage."* First sixes, second sixes and occasionally 12-month stints are offered, depending on the applicant. A first six may be extendable to a year and those doing a second six usually have a Chancery or commercial first six behind them. Even pupils in chambers for only six months can expect to sit with *"four or five pupilmasters all doing completely different areas of practice."* Pupils have their own room but sometimes sit with their PM to *"hear how to interact with accountants and solicitors."* Chambers likes to *"start pupils off with a relatively young pupilmaster... rather than chucking them in with a senior."* Despite the brevity of the programme pupils see *"a fair amount of litigation"* and get *"a good grounding in private client, corporate work and VAT."* There may even be exposure to high-level work; the current pupil told us about finishing off *"written observations for the European Court of Justice."*

As pupilmasters are *"realistic about the fact tax is difficult, a couple of glaring mistakes won't be held against you."* The baby junior we spoke to told us he *"didn't feel the pressure of being examined or assessed until the very end."* Potential tenants complete one or two assessments which are then copied to every member of chambers and have an influence in the tenancy decision. Those who are awarded tenancy must learn the virtue of patience. Such is the complexity and value of cases that *"the bulk of work comes from devilling for the first couple of years."* As a more senior source stressed: *"We can't let them loose on* [their own] *client work right away."* In 2006 one of the two pupils was awarded tenancy.

Though the barristers spend less time in front of judges than those at crime, common law or commercial sets, there are advocacy opportunities before the Special Commissioners and the High Court in London, plus at VAT tribunals across the country. Those with established VAT practices can be in court *"non stop,"* and the growing European dimension of tax law means that members are appearing with increasing regularity at the ECJ in Luxembourg. For pupils and baby juniors a *"cautious"* approach means that advocacy will be thin on the ground; with a foot in the door you *"might get very small cases at the General Commissioners or VAT tribunal"* but there will be no advocacy as a pupil.

When the clock strikes eleven each morning chambers' business halts for coffee, a ritual that is *"like the afternoon tea you have in Chancery sets but more worthwhile."* This is no social gathering; the main idea is to talk about the law and current cases. The prospect of sitting with your cup of Kenco while silks argue complex points is *"quite daunting at first though soon enough you begin to understand what they're talking about."* The trick is to listen and not contribute, not only to *"hear the rhythm of arguments"* to but enjoy the *"stimulating sensation that you are close to the action."* The morning coffee tradition endures for the simple reason that *"large sums of money are at stake and clients like to know they are getting broad input on their problem."* After all, 26 heads are better than one.

Of all the misconceptions around, the one about *"the tax Bar being full of old men in the library"* is perhaps the most inaccurate. *"This set is a great advert for the Bar,"* we were told. Indeed there is a growing female contingent moving up the ranks to redress the male dominance at the top end. Chambers regards itself as *"genuinely friendly"* without the *"them-and-us mentality of some chambers."* Invitations to formal drinks and dinners are always extended to pupils, the recent

Revenue Bar annual dinner being *"a surprisingly enjoyable evening,"* apparently. What's important is that pupils *"don't feel like second-class citizens"* in this particular tax haven.

You may have never studied tax and you may not think it's sexy, but don't knock it if you haven't tried it. Those at Pump Court Tax Chambers certainly know they're onto something, so if you're a real brain box we'd recommend an assessed mini-pupillage if you're curious to find out what that something is.

4 Pump Court

Chambers UK rankings: Construction, information technology, insurance, professional negligence

Although elegant courtyards with graceful doorways are hardly a rarity around the Inns, we think Pump Court, nestled between the Temple Church and the thoroughfare of Middle Temple Lane, is one of the loveliest. Tucked into the corner of this enclosure is number 4, which for all of the detached period charm of its architecture is decidedly *"not an ivory tower set."* An early history of criminal and family practice (still principal areas of activity as recently as 15 years ago) may explain the *"unpretentious"* and *"non-traditional"* atmosphere at a chambers which these days focuses on construction, insurance, technology and professional negligence. The set enjoys a significant presence in the Technology and Construction Court, where a number of members sit on the bench in some capacity.

At the end of 2005, with the help of one of the set's QCs, HM Revenue & Customs achieved a £71.25 million settlement (possibly the largest ever paid by a supplier for failure on a government IT contract) from computer services giant EDS following serious IT system problems with the government's tax credit scheme. Star performer Sean Brannigan took four cases to the Court of Appeal last year, among them the widely reported matter of Great Eastern Hotel v John Laing Construction, in which Sir Terence Conran's hotel claimed significant losses as a consequence of professional negligence by the construction managers. Ultimately, the hotel secured judgments worth in excess of £20 million. Not all cases are dealt with by way of court litigation; mediation and arbitration feature large in the set's work. It should also be noted that an increasing amount of work is dealt with overseas in jurisdictions such as the Cayman Islands and Bermuda.

While a healthy number of pupils arrive at the set with a keen interest in construction or IT law, most undertake a general training in which they gain exposure to all four of the set's key areas. Normally three pupils rotate around the same three supervisors in three-month stints, although chambers discourages members who are working on long-running or especially large cases from taking pupils. With the tenancy decision made in June, they have just nine months in which to prove themselves – not long, even if *"ample space and plenty of work at the junior end"* mean all three pupils have a good chance of being taken on if they make the grade.

Chambers doesn't believe in throwing pupils in at the deep end. *"We don't have huge first-seat expectations,"* said one pupilmaster. *"We expect people to pick things up quickly and be effective legal researchers from day one, but if things go wrong, they go wrong – we're very forgiving."* Early on, pupils are presented with a folder of *"the basics"* and encouraged to interact with clerks by signing in each morning. Shadowing barristers at court appearances, fulfilling discrete research points and first attempts at drafting and advisory work are all on the cards. Clearly careful of their charges, supervisors were at pains to stress that pupils finish at 6pm each day and never work weekends. "*We're not slave drivers,*" declared one. As they enter their second seat, just after Christmas, pupils start to take on work for other members of chambers, albeit that this is strictly filtered through senior clerk Carolyn McCombe. Feedback is collected on each piece of work undertaken and a vigilant pupillage committee keeps an eye on pupils' breadth of exposure to ensure there are no practice area "*black holes.*" Whatever the subject matter (whether honing an eye for legal detail on the diagrams and expert reports of construction cases or getting to grips with the make-up and traditions of the insurance world) the first six is emphatically about learning the all-important skills of drafting.

In addition to their work for supervisors and other members, pupils also complete two written and two advocacy-based assessment exercises during the first six. The written assessments are submitted anonymously, while the advocacy exercise usually pits pupils against each other. We're told that any sense of inter-pupil competition is contained within the exercise as "*assessment here is so transparent that there really isn't any one-upmanship among pupils.*" A mid-December informal chat with the pupillage director and a formal end-of-first-six review help keep pupils apprised of their progress.

Having shadowed juniors in court during the last few weeks of the first six, second sixers head out under their own steam to cover smaller hearings. "*Although there's definitely a lot more work to handle in the second six, I did feel prepared,*" confirmed one source. Although their hours lengthen, an average week with three court appearances means "*you're never too overloaded.*" That said, grace under pressure is definitely required as pupils juggle work for supervisors, other members of chambers and their own clients... all while contending with heightened levels of expectation. "*We usually see a steep improvement in the last seat in terms of thorough*

and rigorous analytical skills. We try to make it as pleasant as possible, but there's no escaping the very high standards that are required in order to be kept on," commented one supervisor.

"*Everyone here makes the time to help; I was never made to feel gormless for asking,*" breathed one pupil with audible relief. The paperwork involved in construction cases can be challenging as it takes a little time to pick up the terminology of, say, gravel laying; the intricacies of insurance policies are also mind-boggling at times. Yet members assured us that "*no one should be put off by these specialisms*" and "*all of these areas of law have a lot more in common with each other than not.*" We have it on good authority that "*you can learn a lot in a few days with a dictionary of mechanical terms.*"

Not all of a second-six pupil's work will be particularly technical in its subject matter. Many of their instructions related to RTAs, infant settlements and small insurance claims. Those we spoke to were excited by their new independence, one telling us: "*The first case is a real highlight. Not only do you have sole responsibility, but you're putting everything you've observed into practice and it all starts coming together.*" Cross-examining elderly drivers, for example, teaches "*a lot about posing questions and when to bite your lip.*"

As the tenancy decision looms, a committee considers the pupils' performance in the written and oral assessments, together with supervisors' reports and feedback from other members. The committee's recommendations are generally accepted by the rest of the membership. Successful pupils are likely to display "*common sense and good judgement*" as well as a demonstrably "*sustained and a steady improvement in oral advocacy and confidence.*" In 2006 all three pupils gained tenancy.

Once pupils are newly minted as 4 Pump Court tenants, it's a little easier for them to enjoy the camaraderie of the set. Inhabited mainly by practitioners under seven years' call, the top floor of the building is a hive of activity as members drop into each others' rooms with queries or coffee. Weekly drinks and regular buffet lunches are open to all and the juniors get together for pub and curry trips. These occasions are not closed to pupils, but our sources confessed that "*while you can drop your guard a little, you're always aware of the assessment process simmering away in the background.*" Lest this sound too ominous, our sources were quick to praise "*a really well-regulated pupillage with fantastic pastoral support.*" In recent years the majority have been offered tenancy.

This set interviews a year earlier than most so apply in good time. Candidates are grilled in a single interview that incorporates a legal problem and some ethical or moral questions on topical subjects. Evidence of sound advocacy skills are likely to hold more sway than a dubious profession of a lifelong love of construction law, but do think carefully about the set's strengths in its chosen areas of practice. A short mini-pupillage – these are offered throughout the year – would be highly beneficial to your understanding of 4 Pump Court's work.

Quadrant Chambers

Chambers UK rankings: Aviation, international arbitration, shipping & commodities, travel

When we last visited Quadrant, the dust had barely settled on the magnificent Fleet Street conversion housing the chambers formerly known as 4 Essex Court. Two years later and we remain impressed by the set's accommodation: a large glass atrium links four grade II-listed buildings, which in their time housed a branch of Lloyds Bank and the renowned 17th-century Rainbow coffee house. With just under 50 barristers currently in chambers, the set has ample space for modern facilities – in a neat combination of modern commercial savvy and decorous tradition, a former ladies' dining room now features cutting-edge video conferencing equipment as well as a delicately decorated ceiling. A suite of meeting rooms for mediations and a location just a few steps away from the Royal Courts of Justice allow Quadrant to offer a perfect base for foot-weary, out-of-town solicitors.

Much used by ancient mariners, the humble quadrant, which lends the set its title, is an apt namesake. Shipping work has steered the set ever since founder Barry Sheen QC developed a wet shipping practice after quitting the navy post WWII. Appointed as judge in the Admiralty Court in 1978, Cap'n Sheen started a tradition of senior Quadrant QCs being appointed to the Admiralty Bench. Those following in his wake included Sir Anthony Clarke QC (now Master of the Rolls) and Sir David Steel QC, who helped chambers break into the insurance world via Lloyd's of London. Then, in the late 90s the acquisition of new members from niche aviation law set 5 Bell Yard added an airborne twist. Traditionally known for its work on liability arising from air crashes or phenomena such as Deep Vein Thrombosis, the aviation specialists also do well on general carriage issues and tour operator disputes. In addition to hulls, wings, international trade and goods carriage, chambers also enjoys a wide range of general commercial instructions, including some sports and media matters. The other key thing to know about Quadrant's work is the amount of disputes, particularly international, that are resolved through arbitration. Chambers has long been top of the tree in shipping-related arbitration, but more recently members have popped up in a string of important insurance, reinsurance and aviation arbitrations.

The existence of the core specialisms shouldn't put off pupils hoping to gain broad commercial experience. Once in situ they can expect a general commercial training that allows exposure to each of the four main areas of practice. To reiterate, that's: commercial litigation, shipping, aviation plus insurance and reinsurance. "*You can't be too picky at this stage,*" explained a source, "*it's about learning how to think like a commercial barrister and taking it from there.*"

Pupils sit with four pupilmasters for three months each, being assigned a shadow supervisor who "*keeps an eye on you and does things like involve you in his workload when your main pupilmaster is busy.*" Both mentors complete a written report on the pupil, which is discussed in an end-of-three-month review. A wide pool of pupilmasters ensures exposure to different types of practice, and the first period especially is a whirl of "*whatever the individual supervisor is doing at the time.*" Paperwork fills a pupil's day, whether it be finding your feet with research points or progressing onto full sets of papers with a view to presenting advice or drafting claims or defences. "*The idea is to get the pupils thinking commercially,*" said one pupilmaster who shared the set's tolerant perspective on early-day errors: "*We all make mistakes.*"

"*There's a huge emphasis on developing pupils here,*" sources told us. Whether it's "*getting a second set of papers sent through from solicitors*" so pupils can have their own copies to work on or "*encouraging us to work for other members of chambers,*" everyone agreed that "*we're pushed to succeed.*" Devilling opportunities (effectively having a member of chambers subcontract work to you) are plentiful and could see the pupil contributing to a merchant shipping case in the Court of Appeal for example. One pupil who had "*seen some wigs in my time here...*" had devilled for his shadow pupilmaster in a three-week High Court trial as well as assisting a silk in preparation for the House of Lords. Definitely "*not an everyday experience.*" Yet pupils stressed it is the range of work not just the high-profile nature of cases that characterises their training. As the year progresses an increasing number of members will enlist their services, although pupilmasters carefully regulate such additional work. "*They don't let you get swamped and they're always aware of what you're doing.*"

Pupils do not undertake paid work before the tenancy decision in July, which means that getting on their feet is an exercise restricted to chambers – albeit one attended by most of the Pupillage Committee. There are usually two or three of these advocacy exercises throughout the first nine months and chambers seeks to make them as realistic as possible, with senior silks sitting on the 'bench' to watch pupils battle it out. "*After months of paperwork it's quite exciting to prepare a mock brief for a Court of Appeal appearance or a three-day trial,*" confirmed one pupil. Ample support and "*plenty of time to prepare*" mean the experience is not too traumatic. Following the tenancy decision, tenants-to-be can expect to be in court for smaller carriage of goods matters and debt recovery hearings for banks, as well as advising on small contractual or banking disputes. There can also be some surprises: one pupil had assisted a silk in a case lost at the first instance but referred for appeal. Following the pupil's successful tenancy bid, "*the same silk called me back as a junior in the Court of Appeal.*" For those who do not make the grade in July, chambers has been known to suggest a deferral of the decision until October in some cases. In 2006 the set's sole pupil took tenancy.

All new tenants are allowed to select a 'godfather' to act as a long-term mentor and additionally share a room with another more senior member who casts a friendly eye over their work. The net result is that there is never any risk of isolation in the crucial early years of tenancy. Even those working at far-flung ends of the vast building are quite likely to encounter one another in Daly's Wine Bar just down the street. "*We have no time for institutionalised jollity,*" said one member, "*but that doesn't mean that people here don't get along and socialise outside working hours.*"

Commercial and straightforward are the watchwords here and applicants should be prepared to display these traits in the rigorous interview process. Those selected at the paper stage are sent a written assessment to be completed and returned. Around 20 of those who impress are then called for interview, where they will be grilled on their assessment in what one member unashamedly referred to as "*an intense, tough interview.*" Incidentally, "*it's also when we find out if someone's tutor wrote the test brief...*" (Surely not.) Although non-law graduates are handed the same brief as those with an LLB, the focus is not so much on legal knowledge as on analysis and argument, and we were assured that the top candidates "*distinguish themselves irrespective of the conditions.*" Quadrant pupils reflected on the "*gruelling but fair interview,*" telling us: "*They don't ask silly questions.*"

The clean, modern lines of Quadrant's converted historic home leave no doubt that this is a pragmatic commercial operation that takes only what it needs from tradition. "*We're straightforward,*" opined one member; "*all about being decent and upfront.*" Eager pupillage applicants are advised to demonstrate a commercial bent as the set seeks "*sensible, coherent and confident future tenants who are focused on the commercial Bar.*" If you are detail-oriented and contract law is one of your favourite areas, these are good signs that Quadrant's work will suit you.

Queen Elizabeth Building

Chambers UK rankings: Family

Within sight of Queen Elizabeth Building the Thames runs seawards and traffic inches along the Embankment to Blackfriars Bridge. Inside the Middle Temple chambers of this century-old, top-drawer family set, walls hung heavy with oil paintings of robed judges and a pervading decorous air combine to suggest a strong current of conservatism. Though the building was constructed less than 50 years ago, QEB has made a home that feels considerably older. But perhaps this is only fitting for a set defined by "*a sense of pride in the institution,*" whose people place "*value on loyalty*" and where people are "*very aware of a long-standing reputation for excellence.*" Whilst it may not be moving at a million miles an hour, we heard: "*It has changed incredibly in the last 14 years, losing the Eton-Harrow-Oxbridge feel.*"

QEB possesses a keen sense of a heritage of excellence, reflecting its long-held status as one of the – if not *the* – best family sets. Top-ranked by *Chambers UK* for family law, QEB has for many years represented the well-off, the powerful, the famous and even the notorious as their marriages unravel. Beyond this it has continually acted on law-making matters. Earlier highlights include the divorces of Charles and Diana, Bob Geldof and Paula Yates, Mick Jagger and Jerry Hall. In the law-making category are cases like White v White and Cowan v Cowan.

Equally important in the QEB psyche is a tradition of senior members moving on to judicial appointments. The roll call includes Sir Harry Philimore (Nuremberg War Trials/Lord Justice of Appeal), Sir Roger Ormerod (CA) and latterly Dame Florence Baron, who now sits in the High Court. Whilst the prestige of such a record is undoubted, it tends to leave QEB a little short of QCs with just three currently in situ. That said, chambers is happy to be "*small and self-contained*" and has "*no plans to increase beyond the 31 of us here at the moment.*" This comment puts the tenancy decision in context – up to four pupils per year chase one or two tenancies. In 2006 two pupils stayed with the set.

"*Becoming a judge isn't necessarily a burning career ambition at the forefront of pupils' minds but it's definitely a good career progression.*" The upshot of excellence past and present is that QEB is a no-brainer for those seeking a family law pupillage. "*There just wasn't any contest, I wanted family and it's top of the tree*," confirmed juniors and pupils alike. Lest you worry that your lack of detailed family law knowledge will see you fail to score even an interview, rest assured that chambers considers the likely inexperience of some applicants. "*Some people do have a feel for the discipline, others not and whilst we look for evidence of interest in the form of work experience at family law sets or solicitors, it's not a requirement*," recruiters told us. Nevertheless, at interview you could be asked to discuss recent reported cases so do some homework.

But homework can only prepare you so much for life in chambers and pupils tell us "*no Bar course really gives a feel for ancillary relief. The first six months involve a massive learning curve.*" The first six is "*the time to ask stupid questions and get all the help you can, because it's harder to get help when you're up and running.*" Pupils train under three supervisors for four months each, observing them on what can only be described as top-grade work. They are in the enviable position of seeing high-value and often high-profile cases, frequently possessing an international aspect. The specific approach of a supervisor will dictate the pupil's experience but all were reported to be good at "*checking your work and giving feedback*," whilst one even "*insists that you do all his work before he does it to help you understand.*" It should be emphasised that the core work is "*rich people's divorce,*" with cases involving children much less frequent than financial matters. Inevitably this means carving up large country estates rather than care proceedings on council estates. Although some members have practices that include PI and clinical or professional negligence, such work is a sideline. All pupils are assigned a buddy from among the juniors and in the first six will accompany them to court to get a feel for what will follow.

Second six pupils and juniors find that "*at the bottom end you get non-family-related possessions and bankruptcies,*" and delusions of glamour are dispelled by being sent out "*to crappy cases at god-knows-where court.*" Typical instructions for a junior range from "*small money cases for council tenants on legal aid to ancillary relief for those in the middle-income bracket.*" It is essential that "*you are able to deal well with a wide variety of clients who are all likely to be going through a period of upheaval in their lives.*" And this is a very important point – as members were keen to point out to us, chambers possesses a good balance of "*aggressive advocates and sensitive types.*"

A key attraction of family law is "*the all-round challenge.*" Said one source: "*I didn't want to work for a faceless company; here you have the dual responsibility of dealing firmly and sensitively with emotional clients, whilst keeping your eye on the legal ball.*" The benefit of pursuing these challenges at a top set like QEB is that "*the family law articulates with almost every aspect of business life, includes pensions and trusts and also embraces social issues like civil marriage and human rights.*" In other words, commercial acumen and "*high intellectual standards*" are just as important tools of the trade as social skills.

QEB has the highest of expectations and its July tenancy decision means that pupils "*enter what is effectively a nine-month assessment process.*" Younger sources were keen to stress that "*you have to pace yourself,*" while those further up the ladder pointed to the importance of being "*exact and precise.*" In addition to formal advocacy and written tests, clerks and supervisors "*do their best to ensure that you have worked for everybody in chambers,*" so that when members meet to take the tenancy decision all are well informed. While no one pretends that getting tenancy isn't a competitive business, those with whom we spoke were adamant that "*although there is an expectation of excellence, mistakes aren't held against you.*" One junior we interviewed recalled when, as a pupil, she slept in and in so doing missed a court appearance with the head of chambers by several hours. *"But when I called in apologising profusely, everyone acted as though my alarm clock had betrayed me!"* Lucky.

Senior clerk Ivor Treherne has held the post for over 25 years and is described as *"paternal but with authority"* or, more baldly, *"God for pupils."* Though he has neither a beard nor apparently a sense of Old Testament justice, he is seemingly omniscient when it comes to scheduling. *"Ivor always seems to know just what you can handle in your timetable, whether you can take on extra work or if you're making trouble for yourself."* This oversight can be valuable at a time when pupils are trying to impress as many members of chambers as possible.

However full the days become – they seem to average 8.30am-6pm for pupils and anything from two to four days a week in court – there is always time for afternoon tea. Tea lady Tina is at the heart of this set-defining event, providing biscuits and chocolate that prove the downfall of many a vow of abstinence. *"If I go I end up eating 25 biscuits,"* said one source, *"...so many calories in one room."* Tea offers *"a break in the day when you can bounce ideas off people, ask for advice or just have a chat."* Otherwise, the social life in chambers is relatively quiet, though *"juniors do invite pupils out for drinks and lunches,"* giving them opportunity to *"ask the silly questions."* There is also a party to welcome new pupils and chambers meals or drinks events *"to mark the big occasions."* At such events old members might pop in for a chinwag.

Overall, QEB genuinely seemed to us to be a *"good-humoured"* place defined by *"a cohesive sense of identity"* that still leaves some room for the individual touch. Recent pupils hailed from backgrounds as diverse as performance, journalism and higher study, though in all those we met we noted a certain single-minded determination to succeed... or as one source put it: *"Ambition and a hard-working attitude."* This is not a set for those with crusading tendencies or a habit of rocking the boat. QEB knows what it is and sees no need to change. And who can blame it when the formula is a winning one?

3 Raymond Buildings

Chambers UK rankings: Crime, fraud: criminal, licensing.

Blue blooded, patrician, living in an ivory tower – these are all accusations that have been levelled at 3 Raymond Buildings. As one member readily admitted when we visited them, *"there is no doubt that we are different. We have a character and reputation that marks us out from the general criminal fold."* So what's the truth about this, one of the country's finest criminal sets?

Even a cursory glance at the long list of top cases in which members have been involved will convince you of its credentials. Of late, they have secured the first two dismissals in the Hatfield rail crash prosecutions, prosecuted Siôn Jenkins and the defendants in the Chohan family murders, and secured the conviction of Afghan warlord Zardad. As the leading set for extradition cases, chambers has members working on the matters that make the biggest headlines – cases such as the NatWest Three (one member represented the directors facing extradition to America, another represented the US Government and a third acted for the Attorney General) and Muslim cleric Abu Hamza (where two members are representing the US Governement). As one member explained: *"In extradition work there is no trial; there are no witnesses to handle – it is pure law. You are at Bow Street Magistrates' Court and the High Court very quickly. The first line of appeal without leave is at the High Court and this exposure forces you to be disciplined about time limits, etc. You need a much sharper appreciation of the law because Lord Justice So-and-So will eat you for breakfast if you don't."* Our source went on to say that experience on extradition cases means that *"when you are conducting a regular criminal trial, you are so much fitter."*

The expression 'regular criminal trials' sounds like something of an understatement when you consider some of the complex and academic matters that are sent to the set. Take, for example, the question of whether undertaking an act in order to prevent the commission of war crimes can be used as a defence to criminal charges, or whether the customary international law 'crime of aggression' is in fact a crime under English law. Both of these issues have taken the set's barristers to the House of Lords in the past year. Chambers is known for its academic approach to practice. *"We are a three-dimensional set,"* said one source. *"It is no longer enough to have your standard crime approach when you are undertaking international work, fraud and so on. What we try to do is always look at the potential civil aspects of a criminal case and the other way round."* Continuing this theme, we were told: *"We are better at the law and we aren't scared of delving into the more esoteric aspects of the law. We think this makes us much better criminal practitioners than your usual."*

Already, you'll have a fair idea about the calibre of pupil the set wants to recruit. Chambers offers three pupillages per year and last year received over 400 applications through OLPAS. How many applicants are invited to a first interview depends entirely on the quality that year. *"If we got 400 brilliant applications then we would interview all of them. This year we interviewed between 70 and 80; last year it was 100."* That's a remarkable number. *"Part of the criteria is obvi-*ously good academics – it is impossible to ignore that."* The recruiters were clear in telling us that *"an Oxbridge degree is not a prerequisite here"* and indeed the further down the member board you go, the less it is Oxbridge-dominated.

All first-round interviewees must tackle a structured problem on a recent legal issue or improvised scenario. *"We give them this to see their reaction. It is not about whether someone is right or wrong – let's face it they are invariably wrong – it is more to see their judgement, how they handle it and what that says about their intellectual ability. Their knowledge base is somewhat taken as read."*

Again, the number of candidates who come back for a second interview depends on the quality that year. More than 20 were invited back in 2006. The second interview is very much like the first, just longer and more detailed with an advocacy exercise. *"We are really trying to see the person... this means we have to take a lot of different factors into consideration. For instance, the people we interview can differ quite widely in terms of age: we have to allow for lack of confidence when interviewing somebody very young compared to somebody who is older; someone who may have already had a career."* As to whether there's a personality type, again, we're told not. *"No matter what people think, we are not just workaholic spods,"* said a source. *"Of course the people here work hard and are academic... but we are still rounded people."*

Make it through to pupillage and you'll experience a year that is divided into four-month blocks, each spent with a different supervisor. Chambers tries to consider pupils' preferences when assigning their second and third supervisors. *"I told them that I wanted to do extradition work and was given James Hines and Hugo Keith."* A pupil's request might have more to do with getting their face better known around chambers: *"If you say you don't know people on other floors, then they'll put you there."*

One pupil spoke particularly positively about the fact that they'd witnessed a good many of chambers' top cases from the past year. "*I have had such wonderful exposure from the mags to the High Court, to the Court of Appeal, to the Lords. I have worked on skeleton arguments for headline cases. I have been able to go to the Bailey and watch things like the latest Siôn Jenkins trial. There are such massive resources to tap here.*" In terms of what second-six pupils can expect by way of their own instructions, it's very much what you would expect from a regular criminal set – mags, mags and more mags. "*I went to the Crown Court once during pupillage and my client pleaded,*" revealed a baby junior. Another hot area for chambers following recent regulatory changes is liquor licensing, so pupils and baby juniors can expect a fair amount of work in this field.

Pupils undergo no formal assessments until just before the tenancy decision. Pupils submit two pieces of their work and are interviewed by a panel that also asks them to conduct a piece of advocacy. Their pupil supervisors are asked to supply a letter of reference and further feedback is sought from other members of chambers plus judges and solicitors. One junior tenant suggested that "*if you have done very well over the course of the year but let yourself down in interview, you can still get an offer. It works the other way round too; tenancy can be won during interview.*"

More pupils are recruited than could possibly be taken on but the beauty of a pupillage here is that not being offered tenancy isn't going to mean the death of your career. "*We've a great track record of ensuring that those who don't get taken on aren't booted out straight away; they will be found a place at another chambers. We have excellent contacts and really want our ex-pupils to end up at the right place for them.*"

5RB

Chambers UK rankings: Defamation/privacy, media & entertainment

Residing in freshly outfitted rooms at 5 Raymond Buildings, next to the expansive flower beds and shady paths of Grey's Inn Gardens, you'd never suspect that 5RB has been closely involved with matters of intrigue and outraged decency since the year dot. Founded by the legendary Sir Valentine Holmes, who enjoyed successes in a plethora of famous libel cases in the 1940s and 50s, the set continues to be at the very forefront of pioneering defamation and privacy work for the rich, famous and infamous. Basically if you're loaded and have tangled with the media, be it newspapers, magazines, book publishers or TV channels, chances are you'll turn to 5RB to clear your name. Kate Moss did just that when Channel Five broadcast a programme that claimed she consumed so much cocaine that she'd entered a coma. A certain Wayne Rooney was helped to an out-of-court settlement with *The Sun* and *News of the World* publishers News Group over allegations that he slapped fiancée Coleen in a nightclub. Strong relationships with newspaper groups also see 5RB represent publishers – Associated Newspapers, for example, when HRH Prince Charles brought a claim following The *Mail on Sunday's* publication of extracts from his diary. Such is the set's renown that its barristers frequently represent both sides in the same case. Good examples are the Douglas/*Hello!* privacy scrap following publication of photos from the Hollywood couple's wedding, and the dispute between the Beckhams and News Group over the *News of the World's* allegations that the Beckhams' marriage was a sham.

On merit and specialised excellence, this purposeful chambers certainly deserves its orbit in the rarefied atmosphere of movers and shakers, so it is no surprise that, "*going forward, we're staying focused on our core areas.*" Admittedly, there has been an element of diversification: 5RB is developing an IP capacity and a number of sports personality defamation/privacy cases and strong relationships with The Jockey Club have seen the set decide to "*market our sports law abilities hard.*" Nonetheless, instructions remain "*practically 90% defamation.*"

The process of evolution has instead found an outlet in marketing, the most visible tools of which are an über-cool, monochrome website and the set's trendy name. "*You have no idea how long it took to come up with it, considering all the alternatives and getting approval from everyone,*" revealed a source. 'Raymonds', 'Arbies', maybe even 'High Five' – the possibilities must have been endless...

If you're struck by how attractive chambers' work appears, you're not alone. As one pupil commented: "*When you say you're in media law everyone is immediately interested, even other barristers and solicitors.*" So, be under no illusions that the competitive process of gaining a pupillage has an extra edge at 5RB. Becoming one of the lucky few (up to three per year) means negotiating a "*relaxed, three-person panel interview*" in which "*the last thing we want to do is inhibit or intimidate people*" as well as a written test "*on a hypothetical question centred around some area of media law.*" You'll also need to demonstrate "*genuine interest in our specialist areas,*" whether through a media law dissertation, "*being familiar with prominent current cases,*" a media mini-pupillage or wider experience in-house at newspapers, broadcasters or publishers. Going a step further to show "*a real thirst for and interest in news and the media, and also an understanding of the media, its economics and priorities*" is undoubtedly an advantage that "*gives the interviewers a sense of who is really committed to the area, rather than simply thinking it sounds interesting.*"

Looking further down the line, the "*ever-developing nature of the area*" requires a skill set incorporating "*interest in tactical lawyering and nuanced technicalities,*" as well as "*an ability to adapt arguments innovatively and flexibly.*" Because the career path at 5RB leads "*towards a great deal of high-profile, High Court jury advocacy,*" the potential to become an impressive advocate matters too.

Pupils divide their year equally between four different pupilmasters, of which one will likely be an IP specialist and the remaining three defamation specialists. Don't worry, three of the same doesn't equate to dull times because "*within privacy/media/defamation law there is a phenomenal amount of procedure to learn and variety to experience.*" It might be "*claimant Jockey Club tribunals or sports law defamation*" with one pupilmaster, "*big, defendant newspaper cases*" with another and "*high-profile defamation for big names*" with a third. However, just because you're representing celebs doesn't actually mean you'll be dropping into A-list parties yourself. "*I did meet Carol Caplin once, but that was it,*" confessed a pupil. The work does mean regularly interacting with "*heads of legal at news companies, and as a young lawyer in media work that's actually pretty exciting.*"

In both the first and second six, a pupil's work comes direct from pupilmasters, either in the form of "*academic tasks – basically 'dead issues' where you complete them and then go through them together*" or "*simultaneously doing a pupilmaster's work and maybe even supplying the first draft if it's good enough.*" While the former method ensures "*great feedback,*" the latter offers "*a more interesting experience*" and "*the occasional thrill of working on household name cases.*" Unless they bring their own laptop to chambers, pupils share a PC for frequent "*research and opinion-writing tasks.*" They can expect written appraisals of their performance on tasks during each three-month stint, all of which are collated after six months. *"If you're not flourishing, people will explain why,"* we were told.

Because there is *"next to no pupil-level advocacy beyond the very rare application for an extension of time,"* the second six involves almost no court time. For this reason, pupils are encouraged (if they haven't being doing it already) to sign up with FRU or the Islington Law Centre. Although they admitted to envying contemporaries elsewhere when they headed off to court alone, few felt that the short-term loss was significant. *"All the time you're watching, talking with and listening to colleagues, observing courtroom style, picking up tips from silks and gaining experience."* In fact, this pattern continues post-pupillage because *"there is just not a lot of entry-level civil work."*

Most pupils spend a short time on secondment to one of the media organisations with links to 5RB – eg the BBC or Channel Four – and there is an opportunity to earn much-needed ready cash through *"pre-publication advisory work"* or *"taking witness statements on larger cases for your pupilmasters."* This advisory work or 'night lawyering' for newspaper publishers is a key component of a junior's working life and is described as *"vital to learning about practice in this area of law."* It may not sound much, but sitting in the newspaper's offices scanning copy for potentially contentious or libellous material is a perfect introduction to the pitfalls and scrapes of the publishing world. In the meantime, you could do far worse than read Piers Morgan's diaries, *The Insider*, for an in-depth exposé of the national media.

In between pupillage and junior tenancy is of course the small matter of the tenancy decision. This process involves the pupillage committee considering feedback from each pupilmaster and any other member for whom the pupil has worked. It is not unheard of for two pupils to be kept on in the same year. This was the case in 2006, but those who are less fortunate can rely on *"a full explanation and help to achieve tenancy or a third six elsewhere."*

5RB tells us it is a *"liberal set"* and, *"unlike many chambers, not factional at all."* It sounds like it is similarly cohesive in social situations, as *"you could find the head of chambers at a pub quiz with the junior tenants."* Normally there are drinks in the clerks' room at the end of the week, to which *"pupils are invited, but there's no sense that you have to schmooze everyone."* Pupils also appreciate *"being invited along when your supervisor goes out with clients – you're not made to feel invisible."* Perhaps best of all, aspiring 5RB tenants told us they felt privileged to have *"got the holy grail of pupillages."*

3 Serjeants' Inn

Chambers UK rankings: Clinical negligence, police law, professional discipline

Situated in an old bank on Fleet Street, flanking the Temple, no. 3 Serjeants' Inn is somewhere between a boutique hotel and a movie set. Yet the grandeur of the premises belies the set's history, ethos and personality. Established as recently as 1974, this is a young set with a somewhat pioneering spirit. Chambers is best known for its medical law practice, an area where it has a wealth of quality advocates covering both claimant and defendant work, the latter for NHS trusts, private hospitals and their insurers, as well as medical defence bodies. Members have been instructed in almost every headline-grabbing case of recent times: Bland (the separation of conjoined twins), Sidaway (extent of a doctor's duty to inform patients prior to gaining consent) as well as the public inquiries into Harold Shipman and the Bristol Royal Infirmary.

Despite the obvious "*dedication and passion*" barristers have for their work, we reckon 3SI has an opportunistic streak. Its dominance of the medical field was borne out of a determination to exploit the emerging clinical negligence market in the 1980s. The work has unsurprisingly broadened in scope and now incorporates all manner of advice on clinical issues and the healthcare profession generally. Disciplinary proceedings brought by the General Medical Council (GMC) and other professional bodies are a key source of work. For example, one of the set's QCs recently helped Professor Sir Roy Meadow successfully appeal a GMC ruling that he should be struck off the medical register. You may recall that Meadow's evidence was instrumental in the wrongful murder conviction of three innocent mothers, including solicitor Sally Clarke who served three years of a life sentence.

According to one junior source: "*It takes a while to get going on medical stuff and it's likely you'll get experience in other things first, such as PI, which is related in terms of the damages.*" This hadn't alarmed our source: "*Chambers know what they're doing; the clerks have lots of experience in nurturing people's practices. I have had a gradual introduction but I am entirely happy with the way things are developing.*"

At the moment we would suggest paying serious attention to chambers' police law group, which is one of the best around. Acting mainly for police authorities, barristers defend civil actions brought against the police, work on judicial reviews and disciplinary proceedings, and assist the police in obtaining ASBOs or orders for the closure of crack dens. The headcount of experts in this area continues to grow and it is now a major source of revenue. 2006 has also been a good year for the set's employment practitioners with the establishment of a formal practice group. The other string to chambers' bow is construction law.

It is almost an understatement to say that pupillage is taken seriously here. The year is divided into three periods of four months so that pupils can try their hand at each of the main practice areas. Particular interests can be accommodated and there is dialogue between pupils and the pupillage committee before a new supervisor is chosen. The sales pitch is that chambers offers "*a combination of interesting, paper-based work that can be technically challenging, balanced with a good amount of court work. This place is perfect for anybody who wants to work with human clients but doesn't want to dirty their fingers with crime.*"

Drafting skills are a cornerstone of civil practice and a great deal of attention is paid to developing the quality and style of pupils' opinion writing and pleadings. All paperwork undertaken during pupillage is assessed in the sense that "*everything is formally written down and fed back to the pupils. It is also used to help make the final tenancy decision.*" Pupils are additionally reminded that being self-critical will better prepare them for when they are out on their own. "*You are encouraged to think about better, more efficient ways of working,*" perhaps utilising chronologies and spreadsheets more or "*being more creative in how you approach things.*" A formal in-house programme of advocacy assessment has been running for the past two years and is split into two parts. "*For each session we have three members of chambers including a junior and a senior who are involved and give us feedback.*" A typical assessment might involve a basic trip-and-slip case.

Long hours are discouraged in the early stages by applying a strict 9am to 6pm policy. As soon as pupils get on their feet in the second six this changes and 12-hour days and weekend work are not unusual. As you may be aware, it is increasingly difficult for civil pupils to gain good advocacy experience due to a diminution in the amount of small-end work available. To remedy this, chambers ensures that pupils undertake a good amount of magistrates' court appearances. This work is available because of the special efforts made by senior clerk Nick Salt, who maintains contact with criminal sets willing to pass on small instructions. Recalling the start of the second six, one source told us: *"It really is a baptism of fire but once over the initial shock it is fantastic training; it really toughens you up."* As may the travel – don't always expect to be able to work in or near the capital.

This is a straightforward kind of set with a commitment to keeping pupils apprised of their performance every step of the way. Younger tenants assured us that, as a result, when the tenancy decision is made there are no real surprises. Supporting the idea that the pupillage year is taken seriously, tenancy decisions are left until the autumn. On the one hand this gives pupils the maximum amount of time in which to flourish and prove their credentials; on the other, those pupils who do not get taken on will miss the start of the cycle for applying for third sixes elsewhere. We're led to believe this is less of a problem than you might think, as chambers is large and busy enough that neither a paucity of work nor space need have an adverse effect on decisions. Those who simply don't make the grade are usually allowed to squat until they can find another home. In 2006 both pupils were offered tenancy.

Chambers was remarkably candid in telling us that the calibre of the pupils and tenants on paper has improved greatly since the set was first established. *"It is possible that our current silks wouldn't make it to the first round,"* they half-joked. Certainly all the junior members have impressive CVs, many of them educated at Oxbridge, LSE, UCL and the like. Academics alone will not impress the pupillage committee, and candidates must display other desirable qualities to succeed. Members see themselves as having a down-to-earth style that comes from both academic strength and practical mindedness. In truth there are no hard-and-fast rules as to what makes a candidate ideal for this set, so the only advice we can offer is that it is pointless trying to appear a certain way at interview. What you can work on is how you demonstrate your interest in their specific areas of expertise. Unsurprisingly, undertaking a 3SI mini-pupillage is a good idea. Though not formally assessed, a mini pupil's performance will be taken into account in their application for full pupillage. It may have been a coincidence but all of those we interviewed in chambers had done minis with the set.

They say the chambers that drinks together, stays together (or something along those lines). Pupils appreciate members' efforts to include them socially, whenever possible, and also appreciate being allocated an 'aunt' or 'uncle' to act as informal mentor. *"It's nice to have someone you can chat to; they have a different perspective on things. Having someone to turn to who has been through pupillage relatively recently is just another part of the jigsaw."* It is clear that in the junior ranks people genuinely do get on famously and enjoy spending time together outside the work environment. There's even a group ski trip each winter. The knock-on effect is a self-sustaining support network within chambers for those just starting out on their careers. They way we see it, as good as things are here, all the policies and procedures in the world are no substitute for healthy work relationships.

Serle Court

Chambers UK rankings: Banking & finance, Chancery: commercial, Chancery: traditional, commercial litigation, company, fraud: civil, insolvency/corporate recovery, partnership, professional negligence, real estate litigation, telecommunications

The Serle Court story is one of élan, innovation and no little foresight. In 2000, the Chancery set at 13 Old Square merged with the commercial set at 1 Hare Court, leading to the creation of an entity with genuine expertise in both the Queen's Bench and Chancery divisions of the High Court. This has enabled the set's 47 practitioners (12 silks among them) to attain recognition in an impressive spread of practice areas. The most notable exponent of this jack-of-all-trades approach is *Chambers UK's* leading Star at the Bar, Michael Briggs QC, who is ranked in the guide in a staggering 12 areas of practice. Serle Court members have acted in much of the biggest commercial Chancery litigation in recent years: Sumitomo, Spectrum, BCCI, actions against drug manfactuerers by the NHS and many more.

Chambers and Partners
Insolvency/Corporate Restructuring
Set of the Year 2006

Pupillage is split into four three-month periods spent with different pupilmasters. Attempts are made to ensure that both pupils share the same PM to ensure some degree of uniformity of assessment. The sort of work they encounter can vary from highly specialised Chancery areas such as partnership law to general "*knockabout commercial*" work. According to those we spoke to, pupillage at Serle Court is "*all about learning not earning.*" Pupils don't undertake their own work during the year, but this shouldn't put anyone off applying as the size of the pupillage award ensures no one is forced to live off the minimum wage. Chambers' thinking is simply that it makes more sense for a pupil to fully benefit from the experience and guidance of those at the top of their profession than to "*flounder around on your own for a couple of months taking on low-grade work.*" The commitment to providing top-level training is exemplified by the assessed advocacy exercise that takes place halfway through pupillage. In recent years, the judging panel has been headed by Michael Briggs QC and featured other big hitters from within chambers. As one pupil reasoned: "*These people's time is extremely valuable. If chambers is prepared to free them up for a couple of hours for our benefit then it shows they mean business.*"

So, if it's not the place to aim for if you want to be on your feet straight away in pupillage, what about the period straight after? "*The key thing in the first few years of practice is producing a consistently high standard of paperwork.*" Interestingly, most of the work you secure during the first couple of years of tenancy will stem from the contacts you made during pupillage. A very junior tenant described his pupillage year as "*a bit of a marketing exercise; it's not just about impressing people so that they take you on, you want to get passed work in the future as well.*" Initially the advocacy a junior might experience will be small-scale (eg bankruptcy petitions and consent orders), but it does grow in time. Another thing to note is that Serle's excellent reputation for offshore work can also mean that juniors are sometimes needed in exotic locations such as the Cayman Islands. Talk about hardship!

We certainly got the feeling that we were in the company of some highly intelligent individuals though it's less a case of off-the-cuff brilliance and more to do with measured excellence. Perhaps this is borne out by the type of work encountered by commercial Chancery barristers. As one seasoned tenant put it: "*Jury advocacy is not the key skill for practitioners here. When we do actually get into court we're concerned with placing reasoned arguments in front of judges and anticipating questions. It's never about winging it.*" Our visit leads us to conclude that those who apply here should have "*an enquiring mind.*" That is to say, apply if you're someone who is consistently "*thinking outside the box.*" As with the other leading sets in commercial and Chancery work, the emphasis is on intellectual ability, and the member of the pupillage committee we spoke to was fairly candid when discussing how to demonstrate this. "*The vast majority of people we interview have Firsts, and a significant number of them have been to Oxbridge. It just happens that way.*" Once at interview, you need to present yourself as someone who is able to "*fully engage with and then answer the questions we ask.*" Seasoned debaters beware: "*Having an answer for everything will only impress if the answer has substance. The candidate who takes a deep breath and actually thinks about the question before answering will score more highly than the one who plays for time with obviously pre-prepared spiel.*"

The tenancy decision is made in July, and the factors taken into consideration include the work you've done for other members, how much you've impressed your PMs and your performance in an assessed advocacy exercise that takes place after six months. Your chances of being taken on are good. As one tenant explained it: "*The presumption is that you'll be a tenant here. We just need to see if you've been able to get from A to B in the learning curve quick enough.*" Unfortunately neither of 2000's pupils achieved tenancy.

Recognising the need to cast aside the crusty old image of the Chancery Bar, Serle Court is not alone in wanting to portray itself as a modern and progressive set. A couple of years ago it went to the trouble of commissioning a respected architect in order to attain a contemporary feel in its New Square premises. Gone are the wooden name boards that sit proudly outside other Lincoln's Inn sets; gone are the landscape paintings hanging in the waiting room. Walk in to Serle Court and you have to agree that designer chap did a pretty good job. Readers of our last report may remember reading about three yellow plastic ducks that had been launched by some enterprising prankster into the pigeon netting above the courtyard behind chambers. We're pleased to report that the ducks are alive and well and showing no signs of waddling off. Not even to the set's annexe nearby on Chancery Lane, where 14 members ply their trade. Serle Court practitioners can justifiably claim to be a sporty bunch; its football and cricket teams lead the way in igniting inter-chambers competition. On a marginally less energetic note, the social life at Serle Court is also thriving. Thursday drinks at the Gaucho Grill are always well attended, and the chambers tradition of never letting pupils put their hands in their pockets for anything ensures that each year's batch is well looked after. Sometimes clerks will address pupils in formal terms "*but that's only to impress solicitors*" confided one source.

We have to concur with the individual who described pupillage at Serle Court as "*very civilised – nowhere near as barbaric as elsewhere.*" If it's modernity and meritocracy that you're after, then you'll find it here.

3/4 South Square

Chambers UK rankings: Banking & finance, Chancery: commercial, commercial litigation, company, fraud: civil, insolvency/corporate recovery

Ever thought about why some people are so fascinated by other people's misfortune? Witness the gawping crowd that gathers around a traffic accident or the glee of the tabloids when lurid tales emerge and bring down a celebrity. We're not accusing 3/4 South Square of this ugly addiction, but by their own admission, "*wherever something collapses we're there.*" A self-styled "*broad and modern set*" that "*prides itself on its commercial and business knowledge,*" this chambers is widely regarded as *the* insolvency practice in the UK. As such, it loves a good corporate collapse. When the mighty fall, odds are that one of the set's 15 silks or 29 other tenants are helping to pick through the rubble. They had prominent involvement in the biggest cases of the last ten years – BCCI, Maxwell, Lloyd's of London, Barings, Enron, Railtrack, Marconi, ntl, TXU and Spectrum Plus.

While chambers has a not unreasonable desire to be seen as "*a rounded commercial set,*" it is also wholly justified in its claim that "*no one else in the world has such a collection of insolvency experts.*" Giving proof to the claim is a well-developed network of "*loose associations with overseas law firms*" from Paris to Hong Kong, South Africa to Singapore. This means chambers "*often functions like an international call centre, referring work to our contacts.*" And, yes, the process is two-way, so that "*around 45% of work litigates here but is driven by overseas clients.*" To illustrate this point, members of the set have been involved in the UK end of the Italian Parmalat bankruptcy, as well as matters in the Cayman Islands and at the ECJ. Emphasising chambers' diversity, we also learned that some hard-core overseas shipping arbitration has recently been handled.

With work pouring in from across the world, and not forgetting that time and insolvency wait for no man, 3/4 South Square "*is practically a 24-hour practice.*" Whether it is (head of chambers) Michael Crystal or a junior tenant, "*someone is always working through the night.*"

Run strategically by a "*steering committee, which meets regularly with barristers,*" 3/4 has developed a sense of purpose and identity that it is impossible to ignore. The people we spoke to were well aware that chambers is frequently compared to a small law firm. Certainly, the set "*doesn't like to sit around and wait for the ball.*" Instead, practice managers, silks and juniors will "*go out, to the Caymans say, to meet prospective clients.*" Discreetly branded and with a website packed with helpful Big Smoke advice for international or non-London visitors, a lot of thought has gone into positioning 3/4 in its marketplace. On our previous visit to the set's home in Gray's Inn, one of its buildings was receiving a makeover; two years later and the adjoining premises were getting the same "*light and open,*" "*clean and commercial*" touch.

If you're attracted to the set's style but have no idea what insolvency practice entails, then apply for a mini-pupillage. You'll get to see the barristers work and all parties get to "*look each other up and down.*" There are a limited number available and they "*by no means guarantee a better chance of pupillage.*" What they will do is allow you to fast-track to the second round of interviews, should you decide to go further. Given that, of the 200 who apply each year, 50 make it to the first round and only 20 to the second, this sounds like some advantage.

No matter how you get there, by round two you'd better have some clear ideas about insolvency. "*Of course we'd be suspicious of anyone claiming a passionate interest in it,*" said one member of the pupillage committee, "*but we're nevertheless keen for people to show an interest in developing a career in our core areas of work.*" "*Sound commercial sense*" and "*good reasoning and analytical skills*" are sought beyond the obvious good academic grades. And "*if you've had the opportunity to take insolvency topics on the BVC but haven't, we'd want to know why.*" Combined with "*rigorous standards,*" the fact that chambers ideally "*takes pupils on with a view to them becoming tenants*" means "*we sometimes don't fill all the pupillage places.*"

The quality that defines successful applicants is "*the ability to take a commercial view on theoretical matters.*" It is also described as "*the key*" to continuing good performance in an area that "*demands a practical approach*" to the problems of clients who "*expect you to fight tooth and nail for them.*" It's not the same as family or crime practice where clients may lose their liberty or access to their children, nonetheless company insolvencies – and certainly personal bankruptcies – involve the collapse of livelihoods. As such, "*black letter expertise alone isn't enough.*" As one pupil supervisor put it: "*It's all about a sound grasp of the business law environment. You're grappling with the technical, legal issues and you're also almost guaranteed a dust-up in court.*" Accordingly, pupils must quickly grasp the essentials of several modes of working.

At the end of the first six, "*feedback is gathered from every pupil supervisor and the pupillage committee grades the pupil.*" Grade A means "*super talented,*" B means "*a good chance of tenancy,*" and C signifies "*slim prospects.*" The C-grade pupil will be recommended to pursue a second six elsewhere. No one is forced to leave before the year is up, but "*we find it's fairest all round... no one is labouring under illusions.*" Accordingly, "*the pressure is on from day one*" and pupils do their level best to impress. However, a system of rotating between supervisors every six weeks ensures "*pupils have lots of chances to make a good impression*" as well as exposing them to a broad range of work and people. The dominance of insolvency work leads to a certain continuity of experience. Said one junior tenant: "*We all basically do about 60% insolvency and 40% spin-offs from insolvency.*"

Researching and composing written advices, "*drafting letters to clients and preparing for conferences*" are all standard tasks, as is getting used to "*the principles of real court work; the need to absorb relevant facts and research the law.*" Variety emerges from the differing characteristics, seniority and training methodology of supervisors. "*Some are superb advocates,*" while "*others have an incredible eye for detail,*" observed one pupil. A junior recalled "*different training styles – some give you daily training, you do their work and go over it. Others give you a broader area to study, which you then discuss. Several give you mock applications to prepare and present.*" The system involves practically every eligible member. Chambers additionally defines its training by way of "*heavy involvement for pupils*" and "*constant feedback, not just letting people sit in the dark.*" The year is undoubtedly hard, but those who "*shine and impress*" are received well, especially if they possess "*a talent for inquiry, the ability to ask the right questions.*"

"*The incredibly complex nature*" of insolvency work means those who stay for a second six are "*rarely on their feet in court.*" They continue to watch and learn, "*observing mediations and advocacy*" and "*assisting in the drafting of skeleton arguments.*" The wait is worthwhile for those who make the grade, and a July tenancy decision is made in much the same way as the end-of-first-six cut. "*By late July, August and September, pupils start to take their own briefs;*" once in the swing of junior tenancy they are "*continuously in and out of court*" with Companies' Court applications and winding-up petitions. Said one source: "*I see our junior tenants and they've got smiles on their faces. Their brains are being pushed and they're advising everyone from small clients to the senior partners of law firms.*"

Members enjoy "*friendly working relationships,*" although "*we're not constantly in each other's pockets.*" Despite the cohesion of the set's external identity, a characteristic self-sufficiency leads individuals to "*work hard, but each in our own way.*" There is no afternoon tea, but "*there are regular Friday night drinks*" and an "*array of dinners*" as well as "*a convivial summer party in*" *the Gray's Inn Walks.*" Pupils don't find it too hard to get involved, especially as "*supervisors take them along to everything with a professional angle, even if it is meals out with clients.*" All in all, we took away an impression of a modern, confident and self-assured set that is comfortable with its reputation. If you've a penchant for business or a nose for corporate disaster, this is the place for you.

4 Stone Buildings

Chambers UK rankings: Chancery: commercial, commercial litigation, company, financial services, fraud: civil, insolvency/corporate recovery

Size isn't everything and here is the set that proves it. With just 24 members, 4 Stone Buildings is a relative pygmy, yet that hasn't stopped it achieving the distinction of second place in the latest edition of *Chambers UK* table that measures the ratio of individual rankings to size of set.

Originally a Chancery specialist, chambers' focus on company and commercial law kicked off in the 1970s with the arrival of eminent silk Peter Curry from leading commercial law firm Freshfields. His arrival also signalled the development of supplementary expertise, notably in insolvency, but also financial services and civil fraud. As any of you with half an eye on the commercial world will know, these strands have each proved to be rich seams of quality work. Today's crop of stellar QCs includes the likes of Robert Miles and head of chambers George Bompas, and the pedigree of the cases on which they worked is unquestioned. Their activities additionally demonstrate how the set's unofficial maxim of 'quality not quantity' continues to pay off. Members have been working on the BCCI litigation and, as in keeping with other top commercial sets, Equitable Life. Chambers also receives a considerable amount of overseas work, with the Bahamas and Hong Kong proving to be particularly common destinations for barristers looking to build up their Air Miles.

With insolvency matters at the core of chambers' business, the set's client base is typically composed of liquidators, administrators, bankers, company directors and accountants. For all these 'professional' clients, the ability to comprehend extremely technical concepts and then present reasoned conclusions in a clear and concise manner is crucial in the barristers they instruct. It's a similar story with those receiving specialist company law instructions, who work in the realm of mergers and acquisitions, reorganisations of share capital, and company shareholder disputes including petitions under section 459 of the Companies Act. "*The days of clients coming humbly to barristers in their ivory towers are long gone,*" stressed one member. "*More than anything, you need commercial awareness to thrive in today's market.*"

Pupillage at 4 Stone Buildings is paper-heavy and you should expect far less face-to-face interaction with clients than your peers at common law sets. "*You have to be the sort of person who is happy to sit and read papers for hours at a time,*" confided a baby junior, so it is clearly not suitable for someone with a short attention span. The first six months are split between two pupilmasters, and the work involves the usual skeleton arguments and research projects. During this time other members of chambers may borrow you for assistance on cases, the idea being that "*you're exposed to as many differing viewpoints and styles as possible.*" It seems that pupils do have their uses – one very junior tenant recalled the sense of pride he felt when his skeleton argument was quoted verbatim by a judge. One of the undoubted highlights of pupillage until 2006, when he took silk, was the time spent with Treasury Devil Jonathan Crow, who only took instructions from government sources. "*The work was so interesting and of such monumental importance, it was like you were a secret agent,*" recalled one source.

Pupils say their working hours are not unduly onerous, with 9am until 6.30pm the norm. We also noted that the assessment regime is considerably lighter than at some other top sets, the raison d'être being that the pupil is there to learn, not jump through hoops. As they are only guaranteed a first six, pupils are advised to arrange a second six elsewhere, although ideally they will acquit themselves well and be invited to extend their stay for a full twelve months. Should this be the case, the second six continues in much the same vein as the first because the work undertaken is relatively specialised and pupils will rarely be able or permitted to take their own instructions. This being the case, advocacy must wait until after pupillage when baby juniors are introduced to winding-up applications and other minor matters via the set's relationships with smaller and regional firms. Although there are no hard and fast rules, the set tends to offer just one tenancy per year after a meeting of all members in July. In 2006 it actually offered two, making both pupils very happy indeed.

The recruitment of pupils operates with the same deadlines as, but outside of, the OLPAS system. Having looked at the set's own application form we can tell you that it is quite minimalist in its approach. We are also able to advise that you should take care to convey a sense of "*clarity and articulacy*" when writing about your interests and motivations. On the academic front, there is no stated preference for a First over a 2:1 and equally it seems that the institution you attended is not the be-all and end-all. It is equally admirable that chambers telephones the referees of every single applicant for pupillage. An unassessed mini pupillage with chambers is advised but not mandatory.

If you are among the lucky 30 selected for the single round of interviews you will be presented with a problem question and given an hour's worth of preparation time before facing a panel that includes the influential senior clerk David Goddard (or 'God' as he is occasionally referred to by established members). The question is company law-based – in recent years it has included the analysis of a balance sheet – although the recruiters are not looking for a candidate who merely parrots the law; they want someone who is able to "*digest the relevant facts quickly and then formulate an appropriately structured response that holds up under intense questioning.*" Make no mistake, the questioning will be intense, though a member of the pupillage committee emphasised that "*it's not an exercise in humiliation, we will only push you if we think you're on track. The harder the questions, the better you are probably doing.*" As well as showing grace under fire, it is "*mental agility and fluency*" that will tip the balance for the successful candidate. Do well in interview and you will be invited to spend a couple of days in chambers if you have not already undertaken a mini-pupillage with the set.

In spite of all the typical barristerial trappings of huge desks, carriage clocks and copies of *Country Life* in the waiting room, we left 4 Stone Buildings and its elegant setting within Lincoln's Inn with an underlying impression of informality. We believed the person who told us that "*anyone who takes themselves too seriously won't fit in here – we are the antidote to the pompous and stuffy Chancery sets that one tends to associate with Lincoln's Inn.*" This could be because of the size of the set – "*everybody knows everybody else and there aren't any of those imposing factions that you find in the big sets.*" It could equally stem from the thriving social scene within chambers. Afternoon tea is well attended (even though the tea itself continues to be "*treacle-like*"), and once a week it is held in the set's annexe at No. 6, just so everyone feels included. Outside working hours, members seem to enjoy each other's company and have been known to go ice skating together at Somerset House. Everyone congregates at the head of chambers' house for summer parties, although we suspect those who still need the Air Miles look forward most to the annual day trip to Paris for lunch.

Chambers prides itself on being "*a user-friendly set that punches above its weight*" and it is hard to disagree. The pupil who manages to display that hallowed combination of intelligence, business sense and amiability will fit in nicely at 4 Stone Buildings. In 2006 both pupils made the grade. Make it to tenancy and the future looks very bright indeed.

2 Temple Gardens

Chambers UK rankings: Clinical negligence, personal injury, professional discipline, professional negligence

One of the stalwarts of Inner Temple, 2tg's small doorway opens onto a warren of rooms with – we were assured – the very best views of Inner Temple gardens and the Thames. Founded by Walter Frampton (who acted on the divorce of that Mrs Simpson) and BLA Malley after WWII, the set has occupied the same premises ever since. Initially a criminal and civil set with a strong insurance bent, in 1960 barristers elected to focus solely on civil instructions, gradually building up a highly regarded personal injury, clinical negligence, employment and general commercial practice. The membership has swelled, such that now over 50 barristers practise across an extraordinary palate of areas. True, personal injury remains the bedrock of the set, but public law, media and entertainment and property practices have also been putting up shoots of late. As the senior clerk puts it: "*We're a multi-specialist rather than a generalist set – our practice groups are very close-knit and work to help each other out.*"

Pupillage here is similarly varied but, with pupils encouraged to nominate supervisors, it does consider personal tastes. Saying this, chambers is keen that pupils "*turn their hand to everything – we want to see pupils manage situations irrespective of practice area.*" To that end, recruits divide their time between three pupil supervisors, two in the first six months and then a third from Easter through the tenancy decision to the end of pupillage in October. The first three months are a settling-in period: "*I assume that pupils know nothing to begin with,*" said one supervisor, "*but try to develop their factual analysis and paperwork ability, building up to more complex instructions.*" Thus, our sources had experienced "*research points or being asked to complete a set of papers for later comparison and review.*" At this stage, the set is also careful "*not to place pupils under huge time pressure that can really destroy confidence.*"

In general, first-six pupils also accompany supervisors in conferences and attend many of the five to ten seminars held per year by each of the eight practice groups. Offering wine and nibbles may give pupils the appearance of being unpaid waiters, but in fact it helps networking: "*It's much easier to approach a group of solicitors if you have a full bottle of wine in your hand...*" At the other end of the scale, members of chambers are happy to whisk pupils off to court to observe particularly interesting cases, and one of this year's pupils had even donned wig and robe for a Court of Appeal matter.

During the second three months, other barristers can approach pupils with work, and "*working for a lot of people*" is common. This ensures that, by the end of pupillage, plenty of people can provide a view on the performance and potential of each pupil. This is particularly crucial given the absence of other written assessments. A review at the end of each 'seat' incorporates these reports as well as comments from the supervisor (and clerks where relevant). "*We're kept informed,*" pupils told us; "*feedback is continuous.*" Chambers also puts pupils through two advocacy exercises, one in the first six and the second two weeks before the tenancy decision. Sources stressed the "*educational rather than assessment nature of the exercise – the point is to make an impression rather than gain a grade.*" The second exercise is the more spectacular, with pupils pitted against one another in a full-blown mock trial, usually presided over by either a silk or a former member of chambers on the bench. This year's full personal injury trial, complete with staff 'witnesses', lasted "*about three hours but was good fun.*" Having already experienced real-world advocacy in the second six, pupils say you are "*not likely to make a fool of yourself.*"

Chambers has pupils out on their feet from day one of the second six. Indeed, it is "*so committed to advocacy that we will guarantee pupils' earnings in the second six. They will do everything from small claims and fast-track cases to interlocutory hearings.*" RTAs and defective property claims are common and trips to courts as far away as Cardiff are not unusual. Clerks try to limit court appearances to three a week at this stage. The change of pace is "*a real baptism of fire,*" but pupils emphasised that their workload is managed carefully to ensure "*you never get snowed under.*" Pupils are also encouraged not to "*spend hours suffering in silence.*"

The tenancy decision is made by the end of June and, having taken on 93% of pupils as tenants over the preceding five years, chambers has an impressive record. With both pupils granted tenancy in 2006 its excellent record continues. Those not approved for tenancy in June benefit from a second-chance policy and will be reviewed throughout a third six, with the possibility of tenancy the following year. All new tenants appoint a mentor who offers an ear and friendly advice throughout the first year. The set also tries to prevent a "*juniors ghetto*" from developing, so it's not uncommon for new juniors to share corridors, or even rooms, with silks.

If you're already planning an application, you might want to sample the set's short mini-pupillage, which is universally praised as "*a perfect indicator of what to expect.*" Certainly, chambers seems to put as much thought into the three-day scheme as it does pupillage proper. Recent attendees had watched court appearances (including one in the House of Lords), been invited to the weekly Friday drinks and undertaken a short assessment that "*makes a good impression if you then apply for pupillage.*" Chambers receives a lot of applications and it sounds as if the initial cut at the paper stage is a deep one. With current tenants having worked at the European Court of Human Rights, as management consultants and even as a keyboard player for Morcheeba, we'd suggest that a mixed diet of extra-curricular activities would be the best complement to excellent academics. Once at interview, demonstrating the qualities of "*clear thinking, self-reliance, resilience and individuality*" becomes important. It would be a lot to fit into a short interview, so the set hosts a day-long assessment for around 40 first-round applicants. The assessment day includes group exercises such as mini-debates and quick-fire conferring tasks, while members of chambers drop in to give short talks on their practices and the practicalities of life at the Bar. Between 10 and 15 candidates progress to a full-blown interview. We were interested to note that the vast majority of recent recruits had non-law degrees, with more than a few of them being second-careerers.

With our sources in agreement that "*it is to everyone's advantage to promote the 2tg name,*" the senior clerk felt that solicitors and insurance companies were instructing the set rather than individuals. Chambers is "*not characterised by political games,*" one member told us, with others mentioning "*a strong team ethos.*" The pupils we met defined the set by its convivial atmosphere, saying: "*It's easy to approach people, whether with a coffee in your hand or about a point of law."* The weekly Friday drinks event is a good time for *"off-duty interaction and the chance to be human."* The big date in the social calendar is chambers' Christmas party, the last of these having taken place aboard a Thames riverboat.

The highest praise from pupils came in relation to their assessment of chambers' *"terribly straightforward"* character. *"You can take people at their word,"* said one; *"if they give a compliment it's because they do mean it."* Combine this with breadth of practice, an advocacy-heavy year and a good pupil-to-tenant conversion rate, and 2tg looks like a good bet.

3 Verulam Buildings

Chambers UK rankings: Banking & finance, commercial litigation, financial services, fraud: civil, information technology, insurance, professional negligence, telecommunications

After our last visit to 3VB we noted that the set appeared to have designs on entering the elite 'magic circle' of commercial sets. Judging by what we've heard it's almost there and although it hasn't quite joined the club yet, the application form has pretty much been filled in, put in an addressed envelope and is on the verge of being posted. If the membership decision was determined on the numbers of runners and riders each set had in the Equitable Life litigation then 3VB would be a shoo-in – various members are acting for both Ernst & Young and the executive directors. Members also played a big part in the film finance litigation that has been kicking around the courts. In addition to finance disputes – an area in which it is one of the two leading sets – chambers is historically strong on insurance and civil fraud, having been involved in cases of such magnitude as Polly Peck, Maxwell and Grupo Torras.

A respected stable of 56 barristers (of which 19 are silks) reside in the spacious premises on the eastern perimeter of Gray's Inn. In some ways, it would probably be more accurate to name the set 2-5 Verulam Buildings given that chambers occupies the lion's share of the short terrace, but we must concede that '3VB' does have a certain edge to it. The interior design now reflects this, as does the super-efficient team of practice managers ensure the smooth running of day-to-day affairs.

Chambers has tried out a number of addresses and activities in its time. The modern-day banking and commercial focus can be traced back to former head of chambers Andrew Leggatt QC who got this side of things going in the 1970s. Since then chambers has had more than its fair share of prominent players. The silks that loom large in chambers today include the current head of chambers Christopher Symons and two Blairs, Bill and Michael (who are not related to each other but Bill is the PM's brother). Coming up through the ranks are a clutch of good names (among them Ali Malek, Andrew Sutcliffe, Adrian Beltrami and Sonia Tolaney), and it is a widely held view that the presence of real talent at all levels will stand the set in good stead in years to come.

A broad range of experiences are on offer to the 3VB pupil. Although the set is best known for its work in banking and insurance, individual practitioners are increasingly recognised for their expertise in areas such as media and entertainment and professional negligence. Abandon ideas of spending much time in court, especially in the early years of practice, because the 3VB barrister is *"not primarily an oral advocate."* The job is more about *"getting to grips with vast amounts of paper"* – in other words a lot of pleadings, skeleton arguments and opinions for the pupil to draft. It is for this reason that people who are able to be *"precise, meticulous and methodical"* flourish at the commercial Bar.

Pupils develop these attributes under the tutelage of four pupilmasters, who each guide them for three months. As an extra measure designed to maximise exposure to the entire range of work on offer in chambers, pupils are additionally allocated 'shadow' PMs, who provide a taster of the work more typical at the junior end. The second six does bring opportunities for pupils to undertake their own work, usually small-end matters such as masters' appointments and small claims. *"It's a real buzz finally appearing in front of a real judge after all the training,"* revealed a pupil.

This is clearly a set that tries to look after its pupils. Said one recruiter: *"We don't believe in the school of hard knocks. Everyone remembers how tough pupillage is so we have no intention of adding to the stress."* PMs and shadows acknowledge a duty to create an environment in which pupils perform to the best of their ability. *"We want to be able to sit back at the end of the year and feel that each pupil has had a fair crack of the whip."* Tenancy is decided in July, the membership basing its decision on reports produced on each pupil by their pupilmasters and anyone else who has seen their work during the year. The set prefers to make its judgement on the basis of how you get on with 'live' work as opposed to a series of contrived assessments. The evidence of recent years shows that pupils have taken their chances well, with a decent number being taken on as tenants – in 2006 one out of two.

The set's recruiters were frank about the sort of applicants they're looking for. *"We're battling with the other commercial heavyweights for the same top characters,"* one admitted. 3VB currently offers the highest pupillage award at the Bar, no doubt in an attempt to let the brightest applicants know how seriously it wants them. Yet still, chambers finds itself making some shrewd calculations when offers are about to be made in August – *"there's no point making offers to people who you know are not going to accept."* The way of ensuring that you don't suffer the fate of being overlooked by virtue of your seemingly super candidate status is to ensure that you develop a personal rapport with the recruiters through a mini-pupillage. This three-day experience is not assessed as such but will result in the production of a slim report that is pushed in the direction of the pupillage committee should you decide to apply. You will be invited to discuss your mini-pupillage experiences at first interview, so it's probably a good idea to keep your eyes open and make detailed notes on what you've seen and learned about chambers. The second interview is more formal, and discussion will centre on a pre-prepared problem that you are sent three days prior to proceedings. The candidate who is able to display evidence of *"structured thought and clarity of expression"* will edge ahead as this is most definitely a set that values logic and articulacy above most other characteristics.

Pupils are encouraged to attend the vast majority of chambers' social functions throughout the year, although when we enquired as to the reason for not inviting pupils to the Christmas dinner, the answers were uncharacteristically hazy. A desire to ensure that the pupil *"doesn't feel on edge"* was the stock response when we really pressed the point, but we can't help suspecting that it's more to do with the events of a couple of years ago when a pupil is alleged to have overdone it on the wine and in one fell swoop managed to administer a near-fatal blow to their tenancy chances. A more established venue for indulging in a few drinks is the Yorkshire Grey on Gray's Inn Road where the junior tenants take the pupils once a month.

3VB is recognised throughout the profession as a highly successful commercial outfit, and one that is particularly renowned for its standards of client service. We're of the opinion that pupillage here represents a tremendous opportunity for a young barrister to learn the commercial ropes, yet not be exposed to the stuffiness and pomp more readily associated with some of its competitors.

Wilberforce Chambers

Chambers UK rankings: Chancery: commercial, Chancery: traditional, charities, intellectual property, pensions, professional negligence, real estate litigation

We suppose it had to happen at some point but it still doesn't make it any less of a surprise. The Chancery Bar has shed its crusty image, in favour of a sleeker, more modern approach to business. Presumably designed to wow the big commercial firms that bring the most valuable cases through the door, the change in style was a necessary response to the fact that the boundary between commercial cases and commercial Chancery cases was no longer as clear and the strict demarcation as to which sets handle each has been crumbling. To take some examples, barristers of both Chancery and non-Chancery persuasions have been involved in many of the major cases of recent times such as Barings, BCCI and Gruppo Torras. Similarly, Wilberforce barristers have encroached on the territory of the commercial sets, bringing (according to *Chambers UK*) an "intellectually rigorous," "formidable" and "incisive" style of advocacy to a variety of commercial cases. Although the set's image might be evolving, there is no mistaking the old-school pedigree of silks such as Edward Nugee, Jules Sher, David Lowe, Michael Barnes, Terence Mowschenson and Michael Bloch. Though members do stray into the QBD, it should be noted that the set's workload is still predominantly Chancery-based, with a considerable number of cases in the property, professional negligence and banking spheres. Members were extensively involved with the landmark undue influence case of Etridge that went all the way to the House of Lords and acted for one of the defendant directors in the ongoing Equitable Life litigation. They were joined in 2006 by a QC and senior junior from 199 Strand.

The fact that Wilberforce retains its status as the leading set for traditional Chancery work (good old-fashioned trusts, probate, real property and that kind of thing) might excuse it for being set in its ways, yet Wilberforce seems happy to change many things. In a move that would have been unheard of in the old days, it has breached the traditional solicitor-barrister divide by adding a couple of partners from magic circle law firms to its list of members. One such is Anna Carboni, former IP chief at Linklaters. Her arrival has boosted the set's reputation in the IP field, where it was already involved in many of the leading cases. In trade marks and passing off, there was Mars v Nestlé (scraps over the shape of the POLO mint and the registrability of the slogan 'Have a Break') and on the patent side, the ICC arbitration Oxford Gene Technology v Affymetrix.

Most members of chambers are housed at No.8 New Square in the leafy surrounds of Lincoln's Inn, that bastion of Chancery practice. Its neighbours include several other Chancery sets and what can probably be described as a cluster of fairly traditional solicitors firms. Inside No.8 huge rooms with imposing desks and even more imposing bookcases are the norm on the lower floors where more senior members sit. As you climb the broad wooden staircase the rooms get smaller and smaller until only suitable for the humblest new tenant. From time to time a couple of the QCs bring their dogs into work – last time we visited, Terence Mowschenson's two King Charles Spaniels sprawled by the fireplace in his room. So far, so quaint. Cross over New Square to the modern building at No.16 and things are entirely different. Built on the site of 'The Boghouse' – toilets that dated back to 1693 – it is generously equipped with state-of-the-art conference facilities. The new clerks' room, complete with CCTV screens depicting all the comings and goings at number 8, is also up to the minute.

At Wilberforce the tenancy decision is made after six months. "*We don't believe in mucking people around or raising false hopes. We think six months gives a pupil enough time to make their mark.*" Jump through the hoop at this stage and then you can relax for a while. "*The emphasis is on learning in the second six, you've proved yourself by then, so it's not all about end product.*" If you're not successful at this point then you need to find a second six elsewhere sharpish, but chambers will do what it can to make the process easier. As for the set's track record for taking on pupils: in 2006 one out of two made the grade, in 2004 all three made the grade, in 2003 no one did and the year before that one person came up with the goods.

Although it's undeniably a bonus to know where you stand early on, the flipside of the coin is that you have to hit the ground running in order to impress. The crucial period is split into three two-month spells with different supervisors. The tenancy decision will be largely based on their opinion of your performance, as they will be the providers of the vast majority of your work. Typically this will include writing opinions, drafting statements of case, producing skeleton arguments or preparing cross-examinations. The road to success at a top Chancery set is not always easy. As one practitioner put it: "*Chancery work is more intellectually challenging than the other branches of the law. You need to love the law in order to get the most out of it.*" This fondness must also extend to research-based activity in the library, as, unfortunately, the brilliant points made by your pupil supervisor in court will not just be plucked out of thin air. Although most of your time will be spent in chambers, the second six will provide the occasional county court hearing in which to hone your advocacy skills and thus ease the transition into tenancy.

If you're hoping to be recruited as a Wilberforce pupil you can choose one of two routes. Option one involves filling in chambers' own pupillage application form and trying to get on the list for a first interview. Option two bypasses the first interview stage, replacing it with a week-long assessed mini-pupillage. Whichever avenue you pursue, certain qualities will serve you well. "*The search is always for someone who is unflappable, self-assured and confident.*" In addition to impeccable academic credentials – incidentally chambers readily admits to liking GDL applicants and the pupil without a First is very much in the minority – a further judgement is made as to how well the candidate will get on with solicitors and clients. "*They may well have buckets of intelligence but do they have the ability to be articulate and forthcoming with everyone?*"

Members of similar vintage tend to stick together. More often than not, it is the set's numerous marketing events that bring all members together after work. The regular time for gathering is the "*universally popular*" fortnightly chambers lunch. "*Everyone makes an effort to attend and we try and ensure that the conversation doesn't just centre on the latest Chancery developments.*"

With its sleek brochures and solicitor hires, Wilberforce makes a convincing argument that it has blown away the cobwebs associated with Chancery practice. The process of modernisation is what has kept Wilberforce at the forefront of its traditional areas of strength and it is what will enable it to develop a name in other chosen fields such as IP.

No5 Chambers, Birmingham

Chambers UK rankings: Chancery, clinical negligence, commercial litigation, crime, employment, energy & natural resources, environment, family, personal injury, planning

For the best part of a century, the beating heart of the Birmingham Bar was brick-built Fountain Court, home to some nine sets. But one by one, sets folded or moved elsewhere, leaving just two. One of these is the largest set in the country with seven practice groups, two further offices springing up in London and Bristol and a self-confessed "*Fantasy Football League*" approach to choosing "*the very best barristers around the country. We don't merge – we select.*" Rather than leave its Midlands home in search of bigger and better work, it has created a national hub from Steelhouse Lane, Birmingham, complete with Japanese-style decor and bright modern art. Welcome to No 5.

The rate of chambers expansion has been remarkable. Only 30 barristers strong in the early 1980s, an ambitious but measured 'hiring' strategy of "*quality rather than quantity*" has seen that figure rise to around 180 today. PI is "*the backbone*" of chambers, and clinical negligence and criminal practice occupy many other members. A planning team is going great guns. Three other practice groups focus on family, employment and Chancery/commercial, and there is a growing profile in white-collar crime and regulatory and business law. Chambers director Tony McDaid describes the melange as "*groups of specialists under one common law umbrella.*" Each practice group has its own head, deputy head, marketing and recruitment teams as well as a dedicated group of clerks (officially referred to as "*practice managers*").

A membership measured in triple digits doesn't equate to tens of pupils. In fact, the average intake each year is just two, and they are restricted to the set's Birmingham HQ. "*We make a market-driven decision on pupils,*" said recruiters. "*We're very aware of things like decreasing criminal work at the junior end; we want to continue to promise quality work.*" It is pleasing to hear that No 5 aims "*to look beyond academic qualifications to find the raw talent. If we insist on only the most prestigious academic candidates, we might well miss out on a better barrister.*" The main challenge for a pupillage candidate is to "*catch the selection committee's*

eye," but with this year's pupils including a former paediatric neurosurgeon and an archaeology graduate, there's clearly no hard-and-fast rule for achieving that. Applicants who make it to the first-round interview face a series of general and legal questions from a small panel of three, with a second, "*more-gruelling*" interview awaiting those who impress. The second stage involves squaring up to eight members. Chambers does not set a problem but expects candidates to "*think on your feet about any number of issues.*" Those who had successfully negotiated the process advise pupillage hopefuls to "*rise to the challenge... if they play devil's advocate, don't be afraid to stand up for yourself.*"

All recruits must commit to as broad a pupillage as possible. Assigned one pupilmaster in an "*appropriate practice group*" for the duration of the year, the first three months see them "*gaining a grounding in that practice area and the profession.*" In other words, drafting, pleading and shadowing at court. Thereafter, they take one-month stints in two other practice areas. To illustrate, one source had started out in the PI group and then hopped to family and criminal for their one-month stints. The latter was "*with a grade-four prosecutor, largely busy with CPS instructions, but also defence work.*" Throughout these short periods, pupils keep in close contact with their original supervisor. "*Mine liked to see me every day, at the very least once or twice a week,*" confirmed a source. "*You can tailor your pupillage here,*" a current pupil told us; "*they do listen to what you'd like to do.*" Indeed, a review at the end of the first three months – usually with the head of the pupillage committee – is an opportunity to voice preferred interests as much as it is an appraisal of work. Whilst pupils will shadow or assist other members of chambers on "*particularly interesting cases,*" devilling is kept to a minimum and there are no written assessments or formal advocacy exercises.

Pupils spend the final month of the first six acquiring a taste for *"grubbier junior work"* before getting on their feet in the second six. By trailing junior barristers it offers the chance *"to see the kind of work you'll soon be doing yourself – pupilmasters here are much more senior juniors, and their caseloads are high-level."* The second six begins a tornado of *"just about anything and everything."* One source got off to a flying start with *"a coroner's inquest in which I was for the driver of the car... that was quite a plunge."* Meanwhile, a breathless list from another included *"interim applications on larger cases, Chancery injunctions, breach-of-contract trials for smaller companies, employment discrimination cases, pre-hearing work..."* Close communication between the clerking teams is vital to ensure a full and varied diary. By this time they operate out of the communal areas scattered throughout chambers and are in court at least four or five times a week, *"often in two different courtrooms on the same day."* Extensive travel is a fact of life for a No5 pupil: *"Four days a week I will be anywhere between Birmingham, Coventry, Wolverhampton and Stafford, and at least once a week in Manchester or even Cardiff."* In the second six, the three-monthly reviews continue and are sometimes scheduled more often. Everyone we interviewed felt *"very well supported,"* taking comfort in the possession of *"plenty of mobile phone numbers, all ready to be dialled when I'm in a panic at 9pm the night before a hearing."*

The tenancy decision is officially taken by the management board towards the end of the second six, following a recommendation made by the head of the pupillage committee. It considers pupilmasters' reports plus feedback from clerks and other members. Chambers are keen to keep pupils informed and it isn't unheard of for them to be given a sense of their chances as early as six months in. The pupillage committee is adamant that *"we're not taking on pupils for the sake of pupillage"* and a 100% recruitment record in the last seven years supports this claim. The early phase of tenancy is *"not that much different"* to the second six, as movement across practice groups is encouraged. Even a committed clin neg junior was aware that *"I'll have to do the smaller stuff in a number of areas before grappling with complex clinical negligence cases."*

This breadth of practice at No5 is a big draw for new tenants and pupils. They seem to find the prospect of being just one of 180 members relatively unconcerning. *"It doesn't feel as if there are more than 60 people here,"* opined one source. Pupils added that they felt there was *"a real sense of community – you'll know everyone on your floor and, because there's a large junior-junior population, you get to know people right across all seven practice areas."* Accordingly, social interaction at the set is well developed, but not overtly institutional. *"We don't have weekly drinks, but there are football teams, a cricket team and a fairly big group of people who'll go for a drink together,"* explained one new junior. Another told us: *"I've felt nothing but welcome here; there's a fantastic atmosphere with lots of small, tight-knit groups."* Brum's renaissance means there are plenty of bars and restaurants for socialising, but it also helps explain why none of the people we spoke to had any regrets about their choice of city. *"I live ten minutes from chambers,"* announced one. *"I'm not sitting in a tube for 40 minutes and I have the most fantastic workload."* An application could be in order if this equation appeals.

St Philips Chambers, Birmingham

Chambers UK rankings: Chancery, commercial litigation, crime, consumer law, employment, family, insolvency/corporate recovery, personal injury

The Birmingham skyline looks rather jazzy these days. From the Smartie-covered cloud of Selfridges to The Rotunda and the almost-completed-at-time-of-print Holloway Circus Tower, this is a city with some serious crane action and some bizarre architecture. A little closer to the ground on Temple Row, facing the cathedral for which it is named, is St Philips, a seriously merged and remarketed superset that is just as big and shiny as the Bull Ring itself.

Born five years ago following the mergers of Nos 1, 2 and 7 Fountain Court, the set chose to embrace a bold new future by incorporating itself. A chief executive and extensive administrative team joined the ranks of barristers and clerks in an arrangement that chambers readily admits has a lot in common with a law firm. That wasn't enough though. Planning a huge recruitment drive, chambers has begun work on a five-storey extension at the back of the Temple Row premises which it purchased when it incorporated. The new extension will bring everyone under one roof; however, for the time being (depending on how much they wish to contribute financially) barristers choose between occupying a shared room, a desk in an open-plan office or using a hot-desking facility in an annexe.

Integral to this process of reinvention, crisp direct management and marketing drives have replaced tradition and ceremony, something that is obvious from the moment you encounter a minimalist, state-of-the-art reception area and gleaming conference suite. Putting the seal on the impression, chief executive Jonathan Fox told us: "*We're a business and we operate like a law firm, with my role here being that of an on-site management consultant. The barristers here are self-employed but they are now free to get on with the law rather than administration and accounts – we hire others to provide that kind of support. We offer the ultimate self-employed environment.*"

One consequence of relinquishing management to experts is that barristers "*have to be ambitious and focused; they can't just put their feet up.*" By signing a service-level agreement all barristers are committed to certain performance requirements, and they are kept apprised of St Philips' growing turnover by monthly bulletins. But for all of its corporate trappings, this is still a set of barristers of chambers... just. The perks of self-employment (like the flexibility to work a three-day week or take sabbaticals) are all readily available, albeit with the added proviso that "*barristers must appreciate that they're working within a larger entity.*"

Larger is certainly the word. "*There are no London sets like this,*" said one pupil. "*It's not only the strongest commercial set in Birmingham but also absolutely prepared for the future of the Bar.*" A current headcount reveals 158 barristers working across the main practice areas – commercial, civil, crime and family. There are plans afoot to beef up the employment and PI groups. Commercial Chancery, banking and professional negligence cases are also handled, as well as niche areas like courts martial and tax law. Neither is there any prospect of publicly funded work being dropped. In short, there's little that this multidisciplinary set can't or won't do. In their own words: "*We cover almost every other area of practice apart from very specialised work like human rights law that demand a presence in London.*" Instructions arrive primarily from the Midlands and Black Country, but chambers' management is also chipping away at the traditional exodus of local work to London.

The set takes a maximum of four pupils per year, each of whom are assigned a principle pupil supervisor in the practice area which most interests them. "*It's a generalist pupillage but weighted to your preference,*" explained one; "*chambers are always aware of where you'd like to be.*" The first four months are spent with the main supervisor, then pupils take a month in each of two other areas of law to ensure breadth of exposure. This period is all about "*living and breathing your pupil supervisor's workload,"* drafting defences or counter claims for court appearances and eventually devilling for other members of chambers. *"I was never left standing by the photocopier or, alternatively, dogsbodied out to other barristers,"* assured a source, adding that fairly civil hours, *"continuous feedback"* and quarterly performance reviews ahead of the October tenancy decision amount to good treatment. As a nice touch, new recruits are now each given a clerking contact *"so that they have someone to smile at and a place to go if they lose papers or can't remember where files go."*

Come the second six, surprises arrive thick and fast in the form of court instructions. Some of our sources were in court up to twice a day on everything from criminal proceedings in the magistrates' courts and small interim applications on personal injury claims to family court directions hearings. One pupil had appeared in an extended employment tribunal while another was still relishing the commendation received from a judge in a criminal case that *"made all the nights of preparation worthwhile."* Indeed, so busy are second-sixers that chambers enforces a one-day-per-week reprieve when they meet their supervisor *"to check in and stay connected."* It's nice to hear that supervisors go to observe pupils in court on occasion, but even if they're not there, the chances are another member of chambers will be in the robing room at least. Far from checking up on pupils they are great for answering any *"last-minute concerns about cases."*

Amusingly, any pupil making an appearance in Walsall County Court will be under instruction from the clerks to visit a famous local sweet shop. Which got us wondering: can you share even a bottomless bag of sweets with so many barristers? In theory, the fact that there is overlap between the different practice areas means everyone knows everyone else. The reality is not far off: *"Although things like dinners and nights out tend to be organised by practice groups, there are still all kinds of cross-chambers events."* Group activities include a regular billiards play-off in chambers' bright social area, which is also the converging point for monthly drinks. Cricket is another favourite, with the set recently trouncing old rivals No.5 Chambers and local solicitors Wragge & Co. Pupils are included in everything. *"Everyone is just so friendly – if I ever had the slightest concern on my face someone would stop and ask me if I was alright,"* said one pupil. Another agreed: *"I don't have one negative memory of my pupillage. I'd be delighted to work here."*

Ah yes, tenancy. The decision in October is reached following careful consideration of the feedback from supervisors, members and clerks. Chambers is looking for *"moral principles, flexibility, analytical ability, advocacy skills and the potential to be high-achieving barristers."* The senior clerk estimates that in his 25 years at the set just one pupil has been turned away. This is fairly typical of pupillages outside London where, once you're in, you tend to stay. At time of going to press in 2006 one pupil had been offered tenancy and the remaining two were awaiting a decision. Pupillage recruitment is an intense one-day affair, with first interviews taking place in the morning and only ten applicants staying on for lunch and a go at a legal problem. Daunting stuff but if you do make it to that stage current pupils will be on hand to give a tour of the building and soothe frayed nerves. As for whether you should make an application, St Philips isn't in London, but it does offer a London-sized pupillage award and the scope to suit every taste for practice.

Exchange Chambers, Liverpool

Chambers UK rankings: Chancery, commercial litigation, crime, insolvency/corporate recovery, local government, partnership, personal injury, police law

With a ticket to ride in one pocket and a host of out-dated stereotypes in the other we boarded the 9.18 from Euston to Liverpool's Lime Street and wondered what to expect from our visit to Exchange Chambers. What we found was a regional superset with a wide practice and some high-profile cases.

Exchange takes its name from its previous location at Exchange Flags outside Liverpool Town Hall. The set moved to Derby Square about 14 years ago and is now right on the doorstep of Liverpool Crown Court. There are a whopping 85 members, the majority in Liverpool and 25 or so in Manchester, where Exchange set up an annexe a few years back. Among the members are 11 silks, an impressive tally for a set outside London.

It is probably overstating things to describe the happenings of the past few years as a revolution, but there's little doubt that the make-up of the set's practice has changed considerably. Due in part to the excellence of former head of chambers John Kay QC (later Lord Justice) it was once the case that criminal work dominated. Now work is roughly split into three different areas: criminal, personal injury and commercial /Chancery. It is this last area that has grown the most of late, with the set now taking instructions on matters that might previously have been sent down to one of the London sets. This increased prominence is exemplified by instructions to act for opera singer Russell Watson in his management dispute, and instructions in relation to follow-on litigation arising out of the Enron insolvency.

The criminal team, meanwhile, hosts big name players such as Tim Holroyde QC and David Turner QC, the latter heavily involved in defending one of the directors of the company that employed the Chinese cockle pickers who died in the Morecambe Bay tragedy. In the personal injury group at Exchange, the presence of spinal injury specialist Bill Braithwaite QC is enough to ensure a valuable and varied caseload. As one would expect of a set with a long list of specialist barristers, the list of instructing solicitors is equally long – Exchange barristers work for Addleshaw Goddard, Halliwells, Burton Copeland and Pannone & Partners to name but a few. The set is also active prosecuting cases for HM Revenue & Customs, the Health and Safety Executive and the DTI.

Our magical mystery tour of chambers enabled us to cover every inch of the large single floor that accommodates the set's Liverpool-based practitioners. Step through from the hotel-like exterior and you're in the hub of chambers – in the main reception area with its potted plants and photos of members of the judiciary adorning the walls, barristers, clerks and admin staff bustle around. Separate waiting rooms prevent "*that embarrassing situation where company directors and alleged child molesters are sat next to each other; each thinking that the other is in the same situation.*" Along the striking red corridors, barristers occupy rooms painted in various bold shades. Whether it's because of space limitations or simply that they're a sociable bunch, each room is shared by as many as six of them, often from differing practice groups.

The long and winding road to pupillage at Exchange Chambers starts with the OLPAS form. When we visited, plans were in the air to outsource the paper-sifting stage, and given that the set attracted nearly 600 applications last year you can see why. No matter who ends up looking at the form, a strong academic record will be the first consideration for the recruiter. Next, the question is whether the applicant has clearly researched the set or not. "*We want people who know what we're all about, a generic reason for choosing us will not impress.*" It's a two-stage interview process here: showing that you possess "*leadership, presence and poise*" in the first 30-minute interview will improve your chances of being invited back to the second test of endurance. This lasts for two days and provides the opportunity to meet most members of chambers whilst also undertaking a series of different advocacy exercises. At the end of day one, you get the chance to 'unwind' by going out for a meal with some members. Go easy on the wine though, your social skills are being assessed.

A day in the life of an Exchange pupil is undoubtedly a demanding one. "*Beneath all of the banter and all the fun, we work really hard and expect the same from our pupils,*" confided one source. Whilst you're not quite working eight days a week, you evidently have to be prepared to adopt the "*ferocious work ethic*" shared by members if you want to be a success. A common law pupil has one pupil supervisor and two deputies who specialise in differing practice areas. The pupil drafts claims and writes opinions for his or her supervisor and is expected to be up to scratch within about six months. During this period, work will also be undertaken for other members of chambers in order to ensure every section on the Bar Council checklist is ticked off. In the second six, pupils can take on their own work and end up travelling a fair amount. By all accounts it is "*a terrifyingly pure adrenaline rush*" when you're on your feet for the first time. Let's hope it's addictive because you'll be doing a lot of it as the years go by. On the criminal side, work tends to be a mixture of bail applications, mentions and summary trials. There is also the chance to practise pure commercial law if that's the route that appeals to you. This route requires a six-month stay in Manchester as this is where a number of the commercial practitioners are based. If you want to go down this route, you should flag it up in your OLPAS form.

Regular review meetings are held with the pupil's supervisor and the chambers director and this is the opportunity to "*highlight any problems and underline all the positives.*" At Exchange, it seems nobody is afraid to ask for a little help from their friends when the need arises. "*We're always sharing problems with each other.*" Nonetheless, the ability to think for yourself is highly prized: "*If a pupil shows initiative, then we're very happy.*" Tenancy prospects are remarkably healthy for pupils at this set. To not get taken on "*you're going to have to do something pretty awful*" and this might well explain the degree of rigour when recruiting pupils. The supervisor we spoke to summed it up as "*equality of effort,*" saying: "*We've obviously seen some potential in the pupil and we feel that we've failed if we don't allow it to be fulfilled.*"

It seems that the legendary Scouse wit is alive and well at Exchange Chambers. Members of all levels of seniority eat lunch together in one of the larger rooms, and joint head of chambers David Turner QC, who has a reputation for being "*a bit of a wag,*" is especially adept at bringing pupils out of their shells with his "*wicked sense of humour.*" Friday night drinks at a local bar are always "*a bit of a laugh*" and have been known to end up as "*a bit of a session.*" Chambers' Christmas party involves a group lunch and then "*it descends from there.*" Speaking of descents, it has been known for a group of members to jump on an Easyjet flight for a weekend of Alpine skiing.

Everyone we spoke to loved Liverpool and its way of life. Exchange Chambers is very much the big noise in town right now and it has ambitions to be *the* set in the North West. In order to thrive here, your commitment to the city and to the work must go further than being able to whistle 'A Hard Day's Night.'

Deans Court Chambers, Manchester

Chambers UK rankings: Clinical negligence, crime, family, health & safety, personal injury

A hundred years and more on the Northern Circuit has left Deans Court Chambers with a darned fine reputation for high-quality work and admirable service standards. In recent criminal matters members have prosecuted Harold Shipman and defended clients as diverse as footballers Roy Keane and Jonathan Woodgate, and Lin Liang Ren, the Chinese gangmaster found guilty of the manslaughter of 21 cocklepickers at Morecambe Bay. In the field of personal injury members have worked on such issues as Gulf War Syndrome, while family lawyers have been responsible for the welfare of countless children in the region and protected the financial interests of those going through divorce. In health and safety matters one member is making a name for himself in relation to local authorities' liability for outbreaks of legionnaires' disease. There is even a growing commercial and Chancery practice. Put together, it adds up to excellent-quality work across several disciplines.

Located on St John's Street – legal enclave and Manchester's version of Harley Street – Deans Court's premises exhibit the locale's usual Georgian trappings. Downstairs, a large and airy reception lies just beyond a broad sweep of stairs. Above, the barristers' accommodation points to industry and legal brainstorming. Of particular note is the 'rogues gallery' of past and current members who have ascended to the bench. Deans Court is certainly proud of its reputation as a silk-heavy Manchester set with a history of judicial appointments, and the senior clerk is not above standing new pupils in front of the portraits to impress on them the need to work hard and dream big. Already 62 members strong, chambers has an appetite for further growth, both via pupils and more-senior lateral hires.

Deans Court is structured into a series of practice groups: civil litigation (where personal injury is dominant), family, crime, health and safety and regulatory, and now also professional and business risks. The pupillage committee encourages the busiest of these groups to screen some 350 OLPAS applications, with a view to members of these groups conducting first interviews with some 30 candidates. Those candidates who impress move to a second interview with the pupillage committee, when they must tackle a legal problem requiring them to use first principles to analyse a scenario. "*They wanted to see if you could take on board a different viewpoint,*" recalled one junior tenant, "*and if you knew when to defend your point and when to concede to a better point.*"

Having been recruited with a specific practice group in mind, new pupils are allocated a supervisor from within that group. After two months they sit with two more supervisors for a month each to gain exposure to other types of practice. The family pupil we spoke to had also spent time with a criminal practitioner and a civil practitioner specialising in personal injury. One recent pupil had chosen to focus on two areas – crime and Chancery. An unusual combination, but one that was accommodated nonetheless.

In their sixth month, pupils work with younger tenants to pick up tips for the second, very busy, practising half of the year. A source took us through her recent weeks' work: "*A family injunction, a criminal pre-trial review in the magistrates' court, a plea in mitigation, a pre-hearing review in a public law family case, an ancillary relief final hearing... quite a lot of contact disputes and injunctions, small claims trials – either RTAs or contract disputes – pleas in mitigation... I've had to hit the ground running and I see now that the first six was designed to build me up and support me.*"

For any reader who hasn't yet got the message, there's more than enough work at the Manchester Bar to keep a new barrister fully employed. And there's no need to jostle with peers to get it, nor any need to take on cases where the train fare costs more than the brief fee.

Ample support is available in the second six and beyond. "*The barristers have all said to me 'just ring at any time of day or night',*" our pupil source confirmed. A new junior concurred, speaking of "*a pupil supervisor who made it clear the relationship was one for life,*" but also warned that the early years are demanding. "*The ethos here is extremely hard working and the clerks are always looking for a lot of work to be covered... At the junior end you continue to turn your hand to all sorts, although you do have some ability to direct things.*" New juniors can be in court seven or eight times each week, commonly up to three times on any given day. However, a new pilot scheme could change all that. Ten minutes after meeting us, one of the juniors was due to speak in a case management conference miles away in Bedford – via the telephone. The courts want to see if shorter civil CMCs and interim applications can be conducted less expensively if done remotely. The impact of the pilot scheme on the junior Bar remains to be seen; for example, solicitors might decide to conduct telephone hearings themselves. All the more reason to join a set with plenty of work coming in, we say.

Chambers is busy and needs to recruit new tenants every year. It's been 15 years since a pupil was last denied tenancy so, unless something really bad happens, the three individuals starting each year can be confident of a career at the set. At the time of going to press in 2006 two pupils had been offered tenancy and one was awaiting a decision. "*This means you have a far greater sense of security,*" a source told us. "*I know the performance of the other pupils is not impacting on me; if I mess it up then it's entirely down to me.*"

A key challenge for any pupil is to develop relationships with instructing solicitors (insurance companies and local authorities too, if working in personal injury). Deans Court holds seminars and social events to keep its members at the forefront of clients' minds, and the barristers on the Northern Circuit certainly don't ignore social engagements. There's a strong sense of belonging on the Northern Circuit, and there are "*lots of well-attended messes – dinners at the Midland and Lowry Hotels, informal drinks at Heathcotes on Deansgate.*" These events attract not only pupils but also more-senior barristers and even the odd judge. "*Up here you get to know all your contemporaries; in fact it's difficult to walk more than a hundred yards without seeing someone you know.*"

The appeal of life in Manchester as a barrister is easy to see – lower house prices, an easier commute to work, a vibrant, characterful city, a strong sense of belonging and plenty of decent work. The majority of Deans Court members have some kind of pre-existing connection to the region, and you should bear this in mind if considering applying here. Illustrative of a genuinely broad-minded approach to recruitment, a recent tenant achieved a First from a lesser-known university through real dedication at a time in her life when she had other significant demands placed upon her. She impressed the recruiters in a way that someone who sailed through A-levels and Oxbridge never could. Amusingly, we found out what irks the pupillage committee – people they refer to as "*BarStars.*" Essentially, these are legal equivalents of those delusional contestants on the X-Factor who spout platitudes about how they were destined for a singing career. You've been warned: don't plan to describe how you've dreamed of being a barrister since the age of seven; do think carefully about how to prove your commitment to a legal career.

Even if your academic credentials are impressive, you'll still need to clock up some mini-pupillage time (naturally Deans Court offers minis) and you'll need to shine at interview. In short, it is no easier to win a pupillage at Deans Court than it is at any leading London set. That said two out of three pupils were offered tenancy in September 2006 with a third anticipating a decision at time of going to press. So, get your foot in the door and there's a heck of a lot on offer.

Kings Chambers, Manchester

Chambers UK rankings: Chancery, clinical negligence, commercial litigation, costs litigation, environment, insolvency/corporate recovery, local government, partnership planning, social housing

If you think Manchester is a dour, rain-sodden, independent state about three and a half weeks by stopping train from Chancery Lane, then think again. A mere two hours after hopping on a Pendolino at Euston, we were hopping off at a sun-kissed Manchester Piccadilly station and seeking out the 50-year-old set that is the Northern challenger to London's commercial and planning giants.

Back in 1946, businessman-turned-barrister Charles Norman Glidewell saw the opportunity to capitalise on the arrival of town and country planning legislation by creating a specialist planning operation. You've got to hand it to him; half a century on and the chambers he founded is one of the UK's leading sets for all aspects of town planning and highway regulation. In the intervening period the practice has expanded to include environmental and public law (think pollution assessments and diverse local government instructions), which now accounts for a third of the set's workload. The housing boom in the 1970s added a new string to the bow and in 1980

Peter Smith (now Justice Smith of da Vinci Code judgement fame) established the set's Chancery and commercial team, which generates some 40% of revenue. The third major practice team deals with common law and has, for a decade, focused exclusively on employment, costs and litigation funding, licensing, disciplinary law and personal injury law. All publicly funded work (essentially family and criminal law) was cut in the 1990s to "*give credibility to our increasing commercial profile.*"

In autumn 2006, Kings Chambers relocated to Spinningfields – Manchester's Canary Wharf – where "*glass and space*" replaced the set's former "*rabbit warren*" accommodation in King Street. The new Manchester premises features state-of-the-art IT and HotOffice facilities. Across the Pennines, Kings Chambers' Leeds base is also poised for expansion. Currently home to ten of the set's 70-odd barristers, this is no mere Manchester annexe. All the Leeds barristers are members of both the Northern and North Eastern Circuits and can call upon full clerking and admin facilities in each city.

While tenants can move between cities easily and explore the set's breadth of practice, exclusively Manchester-based pupils must select a pupillage within one of the three main practice areas. "*Chambers is very clear about the specialisation,*" one pupil told us, adding that "*there is considerable flexibility within each team.*" Depending on the potential for – but not the guarantee of – tenancy following training, pupillages are offered according to the needs of each practice group. That said, no one has been refused tenancy in the last eight years and chambers is proud to "*train people entirely with an eye to their remaining at the set.*" When we visited, the two Chancery and commercial pupils reflected on a set-up that minimises inter-pupil conflict. "*It's not at all a dog-eat-dog situation and you are well supported by your peers,*" said one. Pupils are invited to various client networking and social events from day one. "*You're introduced to solicitors and strongly encouraged to develop relationships both in and outside of the set – the entire set treats pupils as potential tenants.*" Never underestimate the importance of networking and filling up your little black book, as our sources said: "*It's often the smaller, less obvious firms that will give you really good-quality experience.*"

Pupils are assigned two pupilmasters, each for a six-month stint. In the first six, pupils shadow their PM in court and at conferences, gaining exposure to a variety of work. Our sources agreed the first six was a "*very well-managed and civilised introduction,*" with one admitting that "*it was hard work, but not as intense as I thought it would be. Typical hours for me were about 9am to 6pm.*" In addition to working with their own PMs, towards the end of the first six, pupils accompany junior barristers to court in order to see what lies ahead in the second, practising six. Assessment is continuous, with three-monthly informal reviews, as well as a "*good chat*" with the senior clerk before the start of the second six to assess pupil's strengths and preferences. Said the man himself: "*We're involved from the very start. When they get into their second six we're very good at picking out appropriate cases, giving people a little push when needed... as well as sneaking into courtrooms to watch them in action.*"

It's not unusual for a pupil to appear in court four or five times a week in their second six, working 12-hour days and often preparing for court the night before. Although still supervised and supported during this time, pupils are expected to become increasingly self-sufficient but can expect any problems to be addressed long before the tenancy interview in September. Instructions do come primarily from Manchester, Liverpool and Leeds, but it is not unusual for pupils to handle cases in London and further afield, nor to be dealing with solicitors from national firms throughout the country. If we tell you that one source had visited Stoke-on-Trent, Gateshead and Leeds in one week you'll see why we were told that "*you'll need a car.*"

Socially the achievements of the Christmas and summer party committees deserve special mention. Younger tenants do find time to enjoy "*some Friday boozing,*" but generally speaking it's true to say that Kings' barristers are busy people. Other sets regard them as a breed apart, given their high-end commercial focus. We doubt our sources would have agreed that this makes them less sociable or pleasant to work alongside, but don't expect them to be the ringleaders of robing-room hi-jinks.

Many members congregate in the large lunch room at midday. Pupils are "*strongly encouraged*" to be present to make tea for all and can expect "*to stick to first names*" in conversation. Once fully-fledged tenants, they will participate thoroughly in chambers' life, whether representing junior members on the executive committee, investing in the building or signing up to the five-a-side football team and debating club. Much to our disappointment, the usual mettle required for the set's Christmas lunch – when pupils are left to man the phones for an afternoon as members eat, drink, and make merry with prank phone calls back to chambers – went untested this year. Pupils waited in vain for suspicious phone calls requesting 'urgent' injunctions or similar emergencies, in what was an uncharacteristically muted show of festive devilment. We wouldn't be surprised if the powers that be weren't hatching a darker plan for next year's shindig.

Of course, you'll need to secure a place before you can appreciate the social scenery, and attending the annual mini-pupillage fair is the best first step. This three-day event includes advocacy workshops, court visits and guest speakers from the Northern Circuit. A "*fantastic*" taste of what to expect, it is testament to the set's interest in new pupils that most members schedule time to participate. If you manage to make a good first impression here, the *"mild grilling"* of the pupillage interview proper (CV-probing plus questions geared towards an area of interest) should seem less formidable. Bear in mind that you'll be asked which specialisation you are interested in, so turn up with reasonably firm ideas rather than just a general desire for *"something businessy."* Despite chambers' self-professedly *"bookish"* reputation, fitting the egghead mould isn't anywhere near as important as demonstrating *"backbone and a real passion for the law."*

St Johns Buildings, Manchester

Chambers UK rankings: Clinical negligence, crime, employment, family, personal injury

Early in 2006 the BBC launched *New Street Law*, a legal drama following the fortunes of two opposing common law sets at the Manchester Bar. It was the classic formula of impassioned courtroom scenes, secret crushes on opposing counsel, and wigs and robes galore. Many of the external shots were filmed in St John's Street, which you'd assume would add authenticity, but for those we spoke to at St John's Buildings this is the point at which art and reality parted. Said one junior tenant: *"The flamboyant courtroom scenes are fairly unrealistic, but the thing that cracks me up is how they've tried to make St John's Street look like a bustling thoroughfare – it emphatically is not."*

Quiet as the street may appear in reality, it is home to no less than four sets of barristers, of which our subject set, with over 100 common law practitioners, is by far the largest. It was founded in the 1940s when a small group of Jewish barristers came together at number 28 St John Street. Over the next 40 years chambers acquired a reputation for diversity and a sense of inclusion that

was unprecedented for the era. At the same time its profile increased steadily, and it was to send the first female High Court judge, Dame Joyanne Bracewell, to the bench. In 2002 the set merged with its next-door neighbour at 24a, a crime-focused heavyweight around since the 1970s. Just two years later the combined set, by now renamed St John's Buildings, was further bolstered by the addition of the members of Merchant Chambers, whose commercial law expertise plugged an acknowledged gap in St John's service. Finally, in 2005, ten more practitioners joined from Queens Chambers, a smaller common law and commercial outfit. This brings the current headcount to 105 barristers, right up there as one of the largest sets in the UK. St John's critics predicted the mergers wouldn't work, and yet it has continued to be financially successful while retaining the essentials of its tight-knit culture. Said one source: *"It really doesn't feel as if over a hundred people work here."*

St John's barristers belong to one or more of the five practice groups – personal injury, crime, commercial, employment and family law – and a full administrative team is assigned to each group. The largest are crime, personal injury and family, with around 30 barristers each; a further 20 members of chambers divide themselves between the commercial and employment groups. Although interdisciplinary working is typical, barristers are encouraged to develop specialisms. At the helm of the set, alongside head of chambers, Michael Redfern, is chief clerk Chris Ronan, for whom the phrase 'running a tight ship' is a mild understatement. Applicants be warned: this same meticulous approach is applied to pupils, whose progress is monitored closely from day one.

A pupil's first six is spent shadowing a supervisor. The pupil can choose to specialise in a practice area from the outset or, alternatively, try to get as much experience as possible in a number of areas. "*I wouldn't recommend ruling anything out,*" said one pupil; "*sometimes a particular area of law doesn't sound all that interesting, but you won't know until you've tried it.*" Day-to-day experiences include court attendance with the supervisor, preliminary research and drafting plus assistance on case preparation. Whichever direction their pupillage takes, all first sixers also complete a two-week stint in a different practice group to make sure they haven't pigeon-holed themselves too early. The consensus is that the first six provides "*a good grounding and paves the way for what's ahead.*"

There is a shift of emphasis in the second six when pupils take on paid work. "*No matter how much preparation you have, it's still daunting, but you never feel as if you're standing by yourself in the courtroom. Everyone makes themselves available to the pupils, and it's not at all uncommon to ring other members of chambers at rather anti-social hours in a panic about a point to be delivered in the morning.*" The pupil learns to be flexible and available at all times. "*Your diary will be completely unpredictable; you must expect it to change from day to day and at the last minute. I find I have to move very quickly from one thing to the next without getting a chance to really think about it until the end of the week... only to start all over again on Monday.*" The second-six pupil's work is monitored by their original supervisor and chief clerk Ronan, who meets with them once a month for what he describes as "*a progress review – we look at reports and billing, and discuss any difficulties.*" Towards the end of the year the pupil spends time shadowing baby juniors to gain a clearer understanding of what the immediate future will hold for them. Overall, chambers' approach is simple: "*We expect people to learn from experience*" and "*we want them to get used to working hard from the beginning of the second six.*" By the end of pupillage the idea is to have produced "*analytical, competent practitioners who know the law and who*

can present a succinct and coherent case. They won't be the finished article but they'll hopefully be well on their way.*"

The claim that pupillage is only offered with a view to a tenancy at the end is supported by the fact that no pupil has been disappointed in the last few years. Former pupils told us that "*chambers make a big investment in your legal training and don't keep you hanging on for a decision.*" The tenancy decision is made by the widest possible panel, usually including the head of chambers, the head of the pupillage committee, the supervisors and members of the clerking team.

The Northern circuit has plenty of work for young barristers – the consensus from the clerks' room at St John's is that "*no one under five years' call is looking for work*" – but what of its quality? Again, they tell us that unless you're looking to develop a specialist practice in, say, tax or media law the circuit can more than sustain an ambitious advocate. The circuit, and the wider professional community in Manchester, is also said to have a sense of community unmatched by London. The strong social aspect to membership of the circuit ensures that pupils at different sets have forged relationships before they ever face each other in court. And from an early stage they become acquainted with "*pretty much everyone in the robing room – as well as the judges.*" On the idea of training in London, one baby junior told us: "*I imagine you'd be a very small fish in that pond, and it's just not the case in Manchester. There's such good camaraderie and support for young barristers here.*" Another member of chambers agreed: "*It's large enough not to be cliquey but small enough to have permanent contact and communication.*"

St John's has its own lively social scene. Book club meetings, for example, throw up very divergent opinions, and at the time of our visit no less than 50 tenants were flushed with their success in the Great Manchester Run, which apparently provoked some healthy competition for both training times and the race proper. But at the heart of everything, however, is a lunchroom, deep in the bowels of the building. Rather like a revolving door, this room, with its large red table, caters for over 100 barristers by never emptying completely. A new tenant explained the drill: "*People drop in on their way to and from court for a cup of tea before rushing off... there's always a good exchange of stories from court, which is all the more interesting when it's something outside your own practice area. I was welcomed there on the first day of my mini-pupillage and now I'm sitting across the table from prospective pupils, asking them about their interests and career plans...*" The two pupils who accepted tenancy in 2006 are now able to do the same.

If you've a mind to sit at that red table yourself, here are some tips from the inside. Be adaptable, flexible and prepared for anything. Make yourself available to members and solicitors, and make a point of getting to know your clerks. Don't plan too far in advance. On a more practical note, make sure that your mobile phone is always charged and try to get some driving lessons in before your second six. Oh, and enjoy yourself! As this year's latest baby junior put it: "*This can be such a satisfying and enjoyable job, and your pupillage is only the beginning.*"

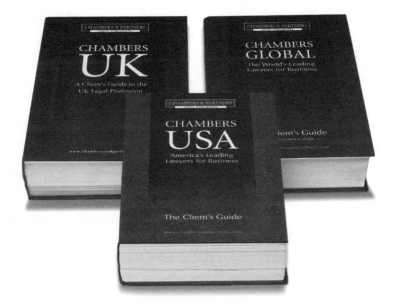

Chambers and Partners publishes a suite of legal guides that you should find helpful in your search for a training contract or pupillage.

- **Chambers UK** is the product of over 12,000 interviews with solicitors, barristers and their clients. It identifies the leading firms, sets and players across the full sweep of legal practice in the UK.

- **Chambers Global** sets out the results of our research into legal jurisdictions worldwide from Australia to Zambia. If you are considering a training contract with an international law firm, it's a must-read book.

- **Chambers USA** provides a more detailed analysis of the performance of the best firms across all US states.

These guides can all be read online:
www.chambersandpartners.com.

a-z barristers

Blackstone Chambers (I Mill QC and T Beazley QC)

Blackstone House, Temple, London EC4Y 9BW   DX: 281
Tel: (020) 7583 1770 Fax: (020) 7822 7350
Email: pupillage@blackstonechambers.com
Website: www.blackstonechambers.com

No of Silks	27
No of Juniors	40
No of Pupils	4 (current)

contact
Miss Julia Hornor
Practice Manager

method of application
OLPAS

pupillages (p.a.)
12 months **4-5**
Required degree grade
Minimum 2:1
(law or non-law)

income
Award **£38,000**
Earnings not included

tenancies
Junior tenancies offered
in last 3 years **46%**
No of tenants of 5 years
call or under **10**

chambers profile
Blackstone Chambers occupies modern, fully networked premises in the Temple.

type of work undertaken
Chambers' formidable strengths lie in its principal areas of practice: commercial, employment and EU, public law and public international law. Commercial law includes financial/business law, international trade, conflicts, sport, media and entertainment, intellectual property and professional negligence. All aspects of employment law, including discrimination, are covered by Chambers' extensive employment law practice. Public law incorporates judicial review, acting both for and against central and local government agencies and other regulatory authorities, all areas affected by the impact of human rights and other aspects of administrative law. EU permeates practices across the board. Chambers recognises the increasingly important role which mediation has to play in dispute resolution. Seven members are CEDR accredited mediators.

pupil profile
Chambers looks for articulate and intelligent applicants who are able to work well under pressure and demonstrate high intellectual ability. Successful candidates usually have at least a 2:1 honours degree, although not necessarily in law.

pupillage
Chambers offers four (or exceptionally five) 12 month pupillages to those wishing to practise full-time at the Bar, normally commencing in October each year. Pupillage is divided into four sections and every effort is made to ensure that pupils receive a broad training. The environment is a friendly one; pupils attend an induction week introducing them to the Chambers working environment. Chambers prefers to recruit new tenants from pupils wherever possible. Chambers subscribes to OLPAS; applications should be made for the summer season.

mini pupillages
Assessed mini pupillages are available and are an important part of the application procedure. Applications for mini pupillages must be made by 30 April; earlier applications are strongly advised and are preferred in the year before pupillage commences.

funding
Awards of £38,000 per annum are available. The pupillage committee has a discretion to consider applications for up to £10,000 of the pupillage award to be advanced during the BVC year. Since Chambers insists on an accessed mini pupillage as part of the overall application procedure, financial assistance is offered either in respect of out of pocket travelling or accommodation expenses incurred in attending the mini pupillage, up to a maximum of £200 per pupil.

Cloisters

Cloisters, 1 Pump Court, Temple, London, EC4Y 7AA
Tel: (020) 7827 4000 Fax: (020) 7827 4100
Email: clerks@cloisters.com
Website: www.cloisters.com

No of Silks	4
No of Juniors	40
No of Pupils	3

contact
pupillage@cloisters.com

method of application
via OLPAS

pupillages (p.a.)
2 for 12 month

chambers profile

Cloisters is a leading set with particular expertise in employment, equality, discrimination and human rights, personal injury and clinical negligence, media and sport, and public and regulatory law. Cloisters is known for its legal excellence, approachability, superb customer service and cost-effectiveness. It recruits only barristers who can offer these qualities.

type of work undertaken

Cloisters acts for both applicants and respondents in all its specialist areas. Cloisters in 2003 was the first barristers chambers to ever win the The Lawyer 'Employment Team of the Year' award. In 2005, Cloisters appears in 19 of the 50 cases to watch chosen by the respected employment commentator Michael Rubenstein. The Cloisters Personal Injury Team had a very strong 2004, appearing in many landmark cases. One of their specialisms is in cases involving occupational stress or bullying at work, which contains elements of both personal injury and employment law. Members of the clinical negligence team secured more than £60m for claimants last year. They handle a full range of cases, including cases worth more than £5m. The Cloisters sport practitioners handle disciplinary regulations, consultative work, litigation, non-professional sporting activity cases and matters arising from sports cases such as employment or contractual issues.

pupil profile

Chambers welcomes applications from outstanding candidates from all backgrounds and academic disciplines, including lawyers coming late to the bar.

pupillage

Chambers offers two twelve month pupillages to those wishing to practise full-time at the bar, normally commencing in October each year. Each pupil is supervised and the supervisor changes every three months to show the pupil different areas of practice. Second six pupils will be allocated work by clerks subject to availability of work and pupil ability.

mini-pupillage

Applications should be made in writing to Rachel Chambers with accompanying CV.

funding

Cloisters offers two funded pupillages each year. Each pupil will receive an award (currently £30,000 per year). Pupils can also ask for an advance.

Furnival Chambers

Chambers of Andrew Mitchell QC
32 Furnival Street, London EC4A 1JQ
Tel: (020) 7405 3232 Fax: (020) 7405 3322
Website: www.furnivallaw.co.uk

chambers profile
Furnival Chambers was established 1985. It is an energetic and progressive leading criminal set and the leading set in the field of asset forfeiture and confiscation.

type of work undertaken
Chambers undertakes serious criminal cases across the board but enjoys particular expertise in:
Asset Forfeiture & Confiscation: The asset forfeiture team specialises in money laundering prosecutions, mutual assistance and confiscation proceedings in the criminal courts, and injunctive and receivership work in the civil courts. Members of the team include the authors of the leading practitioners' textbook and regularly conduct cases in Commonwealth and Caribbean jurisdictions.
Extradition: Representing both individuals and foreign states. Members have advised and appeared in proceedings relating to Enron and the Madrid train bombings.
Serious & Complex Fraud: Members have advised and appeared in Guinness, Blue Arrow, BCCI, Goldman Sachs and many other significant SFO trials.
Terrorism: Members appeared in the trial of the Gloucester shoe bomber, the first Al Qa'eda funding prosecution post 9/11, the Afghan Stansted hijacking, the "Ricin" conspiracy and significant IRA trials.
Sexual Offences: Members appeared in the Deep Cut trial and R v Mohammed Dica.

pupil profile
Pupils will spend two months during their first six months with the asset forfeiture team. Applicants are expected to have excellent academic qualifications and an ability to absorb complex documentary material.

pupillage
Further information regarding Chambers' pupillage policy is available on the Chambers website. Chambers operate a compulsory in-house advocacy course which pupils must pass before being permitted to practise in their second six months. Pupils can, therefore, expect to be well prepared for an exceptionally busy second six.

mini pupillages
Assessed mini-pupillages are available. Applications should be made in writing to Clara Milligan (Chambers Administrator) with accompanying CV.

contact
Clara Milligan
(Chambers Administrator)
pupillage@furnivallaw.co.uk

method of application
OLPAS summer season 2006 for 2007

income
1st 6 months
£7,500
2nd 6 months
£7,500

tenancies
6

2 Hare Court

2 Hare Court, Temple, London EC4Y 7BH
Tel: (020) 7353 5324 Fax: (020) 7353 0667
Email: clerks@2harecourt.com
Website: www.2harecourt.com

chambers profile
2 Hare Court has long been recognised as one of the UK's leading chambers specialising in criminal law and other related fields. It is described by Chambers and Partners Guide as being in "the top band for crime on the back of widespread approval for the way in which its practitioners conduct themselves in the big trials" and by the Legal 500 as "a set of choice for many solicitors for a range of general as well as high profile and complex crime". Its first rate reputation is based on a proven track record of high quality client care together with excellence in advocacy and trial management.

type of work undertaken
The strength and depth of experience amongst its members enables this chambers to undertake all types of criminal work, particularly the more serious and complex matters such as murder, terrorism, serious fraud, corporate and financial crime, international drug trafficking, corruption and organised crime. The cases in which members of chambers have appeared read like a who's who of recent criminal litigation. Members are also regularly instructed in other related areas particularly in regulatory work before bodies as diverse as the General Medical Council and the Football Association, licensing and gaming, health and safety, environmental health, food and drugs and public inquiries.

pupil profile
Chambers select as pupils articulate and well motivated individuals of high intellectual ability who can demonstrate sound judgement and a practical approach to problem solving. Candidates should have at least a 2.1 honours degree.

pupillage
Chambers offers up to three 12 month pupillages starting in September. The year is divided into two six month periods although pupils are assigned to a different pupil master for each of the four months to ensure experience in different areas of crime. Chambers pays for the "Advice to Counsel" course and runs their own in-house advocacy training.

mini pupillages
The programme runs throughout the year with one mini pupil taken each week and two each week in the summer except between mid-December and mid-January and throughout August. Applicants must be at least 18 years old and either be studying for a higher education qualification or on or about to start either the CPE or BVC course. Please see the website for further details of the scheme, the application process and to download an application form.

funding
12 month pupils will be sponsored through a combination of an award scheme, guaranteed earnings and additional earnings. No clerks' fees or deductions are taken from earnings.

No of Silks	10
No of Juniors	39
No of Pupils	2

contact
Orlando Pownall QC

method of application
OLPAS (summer)

pupillages (p.a.)
Up to 3 12 month pupillages
Minimum degree **2:1**

tenancies
According to ability

annexes
None

2 HARE
COURT

Community
Legal Service

Quality Mark - Legal Services
Accredited Chambers

Maitland Chambers (incorporating 9 Old Square)

7 Stone Buildings, Lincoln's Inn, London WC2A 3SZ
Tel: (020) 7406 1200 Fax: (020) 7406 1300
Email: clerks@maitlandchambers.com
Website: www.maitlandchambers.com

No of Silks	**12**
No of Juniors	**51**
No of Pupils	**up to 3**

contact
Valerie Piper
(Pupillage Secretary)
pupillage
@maitlandchambers.com

method of application
See Chambers website
from January 2007.
Application deadline for
pupillage in 2008-09 is 12
February 2007

pupillages (p.a.)
Up to 3 funded

income
£40,000 p.a.

tenancies
6 in last 3 years

chambers profile
Chambers UK has rated Maitland as the pre-eminent commercial Chancery litigation set every year since 2001.

type of work undertaken
Chambers is instructed on a very wide range of cases – from major international litigation to county court disputes. Much of the work is done in London, though the set frequently advises and appears for clients in other parts of the United Kingdom and abroad. Members are recommended as leaders in their field in commercial Chancery, company, charities, insolvency, media and entertainment, traditional Chancery, property litigation, partnership, pensions, banking, energy, tax, agriculture and professional negligence.

pupil profile
Academically, Maitland Chambers looks for a first or upper second. Pupils must have a sense of commercial practicality, be stimulated by the challenge of advocacy and have an aptitude for and general enjoyment of complex legal argument.

pupillage
Pupils sit with at least three different barristers but spend their first few months with one supervisor in order that the pupil can find his or her feet and establish a point of contact which will endure throughout the pupil's time in chambers. Pupils also undertake a structured advocacy training course which consists of advocacy exercises conducted in front of other members of chambers.

mini pupillages
Applications are considered twice a year with a deadline of 30 April for the period June to November, and 31 October for December to May. Applications should be made with a covering letter and cv (listing university grades) to the Pupillage Secretary.

funding
Chambers offers up to three, 12-month pupillages, all of which are funded (£40,000 for pupils starting in October 2007). Up to £10,000 of the award may be drawn down in advance during BVC year.

Quadrant Chambers (Nigel Teare QC)

Quadrant House, 10 Fleet Street, London EC4Y 1AU
Tel: (020) 7583 4444 Fax: (020) 7583 4455
Email: pupillage@quadrantchambers.com
Website: www.quadrantchambers.com

chambers profile

Quadrant Chambers is one of the leading commercial chambers. Chambers offers a wide range of services to its clients within the commercial sphere specialising particularly in maritime and aviation law. Quadrant Chambers is placed in the first rank in both specialisms by Chambers Guide to the Legal Profession. In shipping law, seven silks and nine juniors were selected by Chambers, and Chambers concluded that 'these highly commercial barristers are at the forefront of the aviation field'. In both these areas the set had more 'leaders in their field' selected than any other set of chambers. Quadrant Chambers advises on domestic and international commercial litigation and acts as advocates in court, arbitration and inquiries in England and abroad.

type of work undertaken

The challenging and rewarding work of chambers encompasses the broad range of commercial disputes embracing arbitration, aviation, banking, shipping, international trade, insurance and reinsurance, professional negligence, entertainment and media, environmental and construction law. Over 70% of chambers work involves international clients.

pupil profile

Quadrant Chambers seeks high calibre pupils with good academic qualifications (at least a 2.1 degree) who exhibit good written and oral skills.

pupillage

Chambers offer a maximum of four funded pupillages of 12 months duration (reviewable at six months). Pupils are moved amongst several members of Chambers and will experience a wide range of high quality commercial work. Outstanding pupils are likely to be offered a tenancy at the end of their pupillage. Further information can be found on the website.

mini pupillages

Mini pupillages are encouraged in order that potential pupils may experience the work of Chambers before committing themselves to an application for full pupillage.

funding

Awards of £35,000 p.a. are available for each funded pupillage – part of which may be forwarded during the BVC, at the Pupillage Committee's discretion.

No of Silks	**10**
No of Juniors	**33**

contact
Secretary to Pupillage Committee

method of application
Chambers' application form

pupillages (p.a.)
1st 6 months **4**
2nd 6 months **4**
12 months
(Reviewed at 6 months)
Required degree
Good 2:1+

income
1st 6 months
£17,500
2nd 6 months
£17,500
Earnings not included

tenancies
Current tenants who served pupillage in Chambers **19**
Junior tenancies offered in last 3 years **6**
No of tenants of 5 years call or under **7**
Income (1st year)
c. £50,000

Serle Court

Serle Court, 6 New Square, Lincoln's Inn, London WC2A 3QS
Tel: (020) 7242 6105 Fax: (020) 7405 4004
Email: pupillage@serlecourt.co.uk
Website: www.serlecourt.co.uk

chambers profile

'...Commercial powerhouse of the Chancery Bar...' Chambers & Partners Guide to the UK Legal Profession 2006. Serle Court is one of the leading commercial chancery sets with 47 barristers including 12 silks. Widely recognised as a leading set, Chambers is recommended in 19 different areas of practice by the legal directories. Chambers has a stimulating and inclusive work environment and a forward looking approach.

type of work undertaken

Litigation, arbitration, mediation and advisory services across the full range of chancery and commercial practice areas including: administrative and public law, banking, civil fraud, commercial litigation, company, financial services, human rights, insolvency, insurance and reinsurance, partnership, professional negligence, property, regulatory and disciplinary, trusts and probate.

pupil profile

Candidates are well-rounded people, from any background. Chambers looks for highly motivated individuals with first class intellectual ability, combined with a practical approach, sound sensibility and the potential to become excellent advocates. Serle Court has a reputation for 'consistent high quality' and for having 'responsive and able team members' and seeks the same qualities in pupils.

pupillage

Pupils sit with different pupil supervisors in order to experience a broad a range of work. Two pupils are recruited each year and Chambers offers: an excellent preparation for successful practice; a genuinely friendly and supportive environment; the opportunity to learn from some of the leading barristers in their field; a real prospect of tenancy.

mini-pupillages

About 30 available each year. Apply online at www.serlecourt.co.uk.

funding

Serle Court offers awards of £40,000 for 12 months, of which up to £12,500 can be drawn down during the BVC year. It also provides an income guarantee worth up to £100,000 over the first two years of practice.

No of Silks	12
No of Juniors	35
No of Pupils	2

contact
Hugh Norbury
Tel (020) 7242 6105

method of application
Chambers application form, available from website or Chambers. Not a member of OLPAS

pupillages
Two 12 month pupillages

tenancies
Up to 2 per annum

serle court

3-4 South Square

3-4 South Square, Gray's Inn, London WC1R 5HP
Tel: (020) 7696 9900   Fax: (020) 7696 9911
Email: pupillage@southsquare.com
Website: www.southsquare.com

No of Silks	18
No of Juniors	26
No of Pupils	3

contact
Pupillage Secretary
Tel (020) 7696 9900

method of application
CV with covering letter

pupillages (p.a.)
Up to four, 12 month
pupillages offered each
year

chambers profile

Chambers is an established successful commercial set, involved in high-profile international and domestic commercial litigation and advice. Members of Chambers have been centrally involved in some of the most important commercial cases of the last decade including Barings, BCCI, Lloyds, Maxwell, Railtrack, TXU, Enron, Marconi, NTL and Global Crossing.

type of work undertaken

3-4 South Square has a pre-eminent reputation in insolvency and restructuring law and specialist expertise in banking, financial services, company law, professional negligence, domestic and international arbitration, mediation, European Union Law, insurance/reinsurance law and general commercial litigation.

pupil profile

Chambers seek to recruit the highest calibre of candidates who must be prepared to commit themselves to establishing a successful practice and maintaining Chambers' position at the forefront of the modern Commercial Bar. The minimum academic qualification is a 2:1 degree.

pupillage

Pupils are welcomed into all areas of Chambers' life and are provided with an organised programme designed to train and equip them for practice in a dynamic and challenging environment. Pupils sit with a number of pupil supervisors for periods of six to eight weeks and the set looks to recruit at least one tenant every year from its pupils.

mini pupillages

Chambers also offers funded and unfunded mini-pupillages – please see the set's website for further details.

sponsorship & awards

Currently £37,500 per annum (reviewable annually).

4 Stone Buildings

4 Stone Buildings, Lincoln's Inn, London WC2A 3XT
Tel: (020) 7242 5524 Fax: (020) 7831 7907
Email: d.goddard@4stonebuildings.com

No of Silks	**5**
No of Juniors	**21**
No of Pupils	**2**

contact
David Goddard
(020) 7242 5524

chambers profile
An established friendly company/commercial set involved in high profile litigation and advice.

method of application
On Chambers own application form

type of work undertaken
4, Stone Buildings specialise in the fields of company law, commercial law, financial services and regulation and corporate insolvency.

pupillages (p.a.)
2 x six months

pupil profile
Candidates are expected to have first class, or good second class degrees. But mere intellectual ability is only part of it: a successful candidate must have the confidence and ambition to succeed, the common sense to recognise the practical advice a client really needs, and an ability to get on well with clients, solicitors and other members of Chambers - and the clerks.

tenancies
At least 1 per year

annexes
None

pupillage
The set aim to give all pupils the knowledge, skills and practical experience they need for a successful career at the Bar. They believe that it is important for all pupils to see as much as possible of the different kinds of work in Chambers. This enables pupils to judge whether their work suits them, and enables different members of Chambers to assess the pupils. Each pupil therefore normally spends time with two or more pupil-masters within any six month period. If other members of Chambers have particularly interesting cases in Court, pupils will be encouraged to work and attend Court with them. All pupils work in their pupil masters' rooms, read their papers, attend their conferences, draft pleadings and documents, write draft opinions and accompany their pupil supervisors to Court. Pupils are treated as part of Chambers, and are fully involved in the activities of Chambers while they are with 4 Stone Buildings.

mini pupillages
Up to 20 mini-pupillages offered per year of up to a weeks duration. Application by letter and CV.

sponsorship & awards
£17,500 per six months.

funding
As above.

3 Verulam Buildings (Christopher Symons QC/John Jarvis QC)

3 Verulam Buildings, Gray's Inn, London WC1R 5NT DX: LDE 331
Tel: (020) 7831 8441 Fax: (020) 7831 8479
Email: chambers@3vb.com
Website: www.3vb.com

chambers profile

3 Verulam Buildings is a large commercial set with a history of expansion by recruitment of tenants from amongst pupils. Over the past 10 years, on average, two of its pupils have become tenants every year. Chambers occupies recently refurbished, spacious offices overlooking Gray's Inn Walks with all modern IT and library facilities. Chambers prides itself on a pleasant, friendly and relaxed atmosphere.

type of work undertaken

A wide range of commercial work, in particular banking and financial services, insurance and reinsurance, commercial fraud, professional negligence, company law, entertainment, arbitration/ADR, as well as other general commercial work. Members of Chambers regularly appear in high profile cases and a substantial amount of Chambers' work is international.

pupil profile

Chambers looks for intelligent and ambitious candidates with strong powers of analysis and reasoning, who are self confident and get on well with others. Candidates must have at least a 2:1 grade in an honours subject which need not be law.

pupillage

Chambers seeks to recruit three or four funded 12 months pupils every year through OLPAS. Each pupil spends three months with four different members of Chambers to gain experience of different types of work. Chambers also offers unfunded pupillages to pupils who do not intend to practise at the Bar of England and Wales.

mini pupillages

Mini pupillages are available for university, CPE or Bar students who are interested in finding out more about Chambers' work. Chambers considers mini pupillage to be an important part of its recruitment process. Candidates should have, or expect to obtain, the minimum requirements for a funded 12 month pupillage. Applications are accepted throughout the year and should be addressed to George McPherson.

funding

In the year 2007-08 the annual award will be at least £42,000, up to £15,000 of which may be drawn during the BVC year.

No of Silks	19
No of Juniors	40
No of Pupils	4

contact
Mr George McPherson
(Pupillage)
Mr Christopher Harris
(Mini Pupillage)

method of application
OLPAS & mini pupillage CV & covering letter stating dates of availability

pupillages (p.a.)
12 months **4**
Required degree grade **2:1**

income
In excess of **£42,000** (which was the award for 2007-08)
Earnings not included

tenancies
Current tenants who served pupillage in Chambers **Approx 41**
Junior tenancies offered in last 3 years **8**
No of tenants of 5 years call or under **9**

Wilberforce Chambers

8 New Square, Lincoln's Inn, London WC2A 3QP
Tel: (020) 7306 0102   Fax: (020) 7306 0095
Email: pupillage@wilberforce.co.uk
Website: www.wilberforce.co.uk

chambers profile

Wilberforce Chambers is a leading commercial chancery Chambers and is involved in some of the most commercially important and cutting edge advice and advocacy undertaken by the Bar today. Most members are recognised as leaders in their field by the key legal directories. Instructions come from top UK and international law firms with a complex and rewarding range of work for international companies, financial institutions, sports and media organisations, private individuals and well-known names. While clients demand high intellectual performance and client care standards the rewards are a successful career at the Bar. The atmosphere in Chambers, which is guarded with great care, is one of a united and friendly 'family'.

type of work undertaken

Practices include commercial litigation, company, financial services and banking, insolvency, intellectual property and information technology, pensions, private clients, trusts and taxation, property litigation, planning, professional negligence, sports and media and charities.

pupil profile

Wilberforce Chambers offer two 12-month pupillages. You should possess high intellectual ability, strong motivation and excellent communication skills. You need to have maturity and confidence and have the ability to work with others and analyse legal problems clearly, demonstrating commercial and practical good sense. The set looks for people who possess real potential to join Chambers as a tenant at the end of their pupillage and a 2:1 degree (in law or another subject) is a minimum requirement. The set has a track record of taking CPE students.

pupillage

Wilberforce Chambers operate a structured pupillage programme with continual assessment aimed at giving you a broad experience of commercial chancery practice under several pupil supervisors with whom you are able to develop your skills.

mini-pupillages

The set encourages prospective pupils to have a mini-pupillage with them, though this is not a prerequisite for pupillage. The mini-pupillage programme is for one week and is an opportunity to learn how the set operates, to meet members of Chambers and to see the sort of work that it does. Wilberforce Chambers runs three separate mini-pupillage weeks (two in December and one in July). Please visit the website for further information.

funding

Chambers offers a generous pupillage award which is in line with the highest awards available and is reviewed annually. The award is currently £40,000 for 12 months, of which up to £13,500 can be drawn down during the BVC year.

| No of Silks | 16 |
| No of Juniors | 30 |

method of application
Online via website

pupillages (p.a.)
2 x 12 months

mini-pupillages
Total of 21 places

income
£40,000 (2008/2009)

minimum qualification
2:1 degree

tenancies in last 3 years
4

WILBERFORCE W
CHAMBERS